CHILDREN
TODAY

CHILDREN TODAY

An Applied Approach to Child Development through Adolescence

KARIN STERNBERG
CORNELL UNIVERSITY

OXFORD
UNIVERSITY PRESS

OXFORD
UNIVERSITY PRESS

Oxford University Press is a department of the University of Oxford.
It furthers the University's objective of excellence in research, scholarship,
and education by publishing worldwide. Oxford is a registered trade mark
of Oxford University Press in the UK and in certain other countries.

Published in the United States of America by Oxford University Press
198 Madison Avenue, New York, NY 10016, United States of America.

For titles covered by Section 112 of the US Higher Education Opportunity
Act, please visit www.oup.com/us/he for the latest information about
pricing and alternate formats.

Library of Congress Cataloging-in-Publication Data

Names: Sternberg, Karin, 1976- author.
Title: Child development in the 21st century : from infancy through
adolescence / Karin Sternberg, Cornell University.
Description: New York, NY : Oxford University Press, [2024] | Includes
bibliographical references and index. | Summary: "Children today are
growing up in a world shaped by factors that seemed far less important
two or more generations ago. Climate change, immigration policy, gender
diversity, access to healthcare, youth-directed social media, and the
presence of media generally are just some of the realities shaping the
world of the child today. At the same time, many developmental processes
are common to children across generations and throughout the world.
Designed to present classic theories of child development in the context
of today's world, this new text combines comprehensive coverage of
research with abundant examples and stories that highlight contemporary
issues facing children and the people who help them grow up into
adulthood. Thoughtfully designed activities encourage students to take
the perspective of parents, caregivers, and pediatric health
professionals to help them imagine what it's like to raise a child in
our modern world. In this way, the text artfully weaves theory and
application together to make the study of child development meaningful
for students who will go on to work with children in various roles"—
Provided by publisher.
Identifiers: LCCN 2022032499 (print) | LCCN 2022032500 (ebook) | ISBN
9781605356815 (paperback) | ISBN 9780197656716 (ebook)
Subjects: LCSH: Child development. | Child psychology.
Classification: LCC HQ767.9 .S7434 2023 (print) | LCC HQ767.9 (ebook) |
DDC 305.231—dc23/eng/20220816
LC record available at https://lccn.loc.gov/2022032499
LC ebook record available at https://lccn.loc.gov/2022032500

Printed by Sheridan Books, Inc., United States of America

Dedication

Sammy, who enriches my life with his amazing "tidbits" of knowledge,

Brittany, who makes me laugh every day, and

Melody, who delights me with her creativity and passion for the arts and beauty in the world.

Brief Contents

Contents

CHAPTER 3   Genetics, Conception, and Prenatal Development   67

CHAPTER **4** **Birth and the Newborn** 105

CHAPTER **5** **Physical Development in Infancy and Toddlerhood** 137

CHAPTER 6 Cognitive Development in Infancy and Toddlerhood 171

CHAPTER 7 Social and Emotional Development in Infancy and Toddlerhood 203

CHAPTER **8**   Physical Development in Early Childhood   237

CHAPTER **9**   Cognitive Development in Early Childhood   273

CHAPTER 10   Social and Emotional Development in Early Childhood   313

CHAPTER **11** **Physical Development in Middle Childhood** 347

CHAPTER **12** **Cognitive Development in Middle Childhood** 385

CHAPTER 13 Emotional and Social Development in Middle Childhood 421

CHAPTER 14 Physical Development in Adolescence 455

CHAPTER 15 Cognitive Development in Adolescence 489

 CHAPTER 16 Social and Emotional Development in Adolescence 523

About the Author

Karin Sternberg received her undergraduate degree as well as her PhD in psychology from the University of Heidelberg in Germany. She as well has a bachelor's degree in business administration with a specialization in banking from Baden-Württemberg Cooperative State University in Karlsruhe, Germany. She completed part of her doctoral research at Yale University and her postdoctoral work at the University of Connecticut. Afterward, she worked as a research associate at Harvard University's Kennedy School of Government and School of Public Health.

Karin held a grant from the National Institutes of Health for the development of a cognitive training program for seniors. She currently teaches Child Development and Cognitive Development at Cornell University.

Sternberg's interest focuses on the application of psychological/behavioral research with the purpose of improving people's relationships and lives. This passion led her to develop the concept for this textbook, which she uses in her own Child Development course at Cornell.

In line with the effort of putting research into practice, Sternberg, together with her husband Robert J. Sternberg, has developed the concept of *True Compatibility* in relationships and is using his theory of love as well as relationship research in general to help people find their true love and create happy, life-long relationships (https://lovemultiverse.com).

Sternberg is the author of a textbook on the psychology of love, *Love 101*, and coauthor of *The Psychologist's Companion, Cognitive Psychology, The Nature of Hate,* and *The New Psychology of Love*, among other books.

Sternberg considers herself very lucky to be the wife of Robert J. Sternberg, the most devoted and loving husband she can imagine. She is also the happy (and tired!) mother of triplets—Samuel and identical twins Brittany and Melody. Sternberg loves spending time with her family, enjoys reading and playing the piano, and pursues her lifelong passion for the traditional martial arts by practicing Seido karate and Shaolin kung fu.

Preface

In the best of circumstances, we leave high school with a chosen profession we wish to pursue. That assumes, of course, that we make the right choice. My choice turned out to be a flop.

After finishing high school, I found myself in a dual-career program that combined practical work experience in a bank with studies of business administration in college. I remember sitting in the bank learning how to mechanically process payments, my mind numb with boredom. I wondered how in the world I had ended up in what, however interesting it might be to others, turned out to be such a boring field for me. I gave it my best try, but it was just a bad fit. I am sure there are others who love this kind of work; I just was not one of them.

So, after finishing my degree, I started studying psychology. Here was what I *really* wanted to do; I just hadn't known it before.

How did I end up on the wrong path to begin with? Quite simply, I had not reflected adequately on many important things: my interests and values as a person, my identity, my strengths, and what I wanted to do in life. I lacked a vision of myself as a person.

I am not the only student, of course, who has ever developed a vision of their future that missed the mark. As I look at friends and acquaintances as well as at my own students, I know that creating one's best future is a formidable task, and one that not all people achieve. I was lucky because I ultimately found my love of psychology. Had I realized at an earlier age the value and benefits psychology had to offer, I believe that I would have understood myself well enough to find the proper path out of high school and to move forward with my life.

This story from my own life distills in a few lines what, at its core, child development is about. It is about supporting children to grow and reach their full potential as the best possible version of who they want to be. Successful development involves many facets—nutrition and health, cognitive growth, the acquisition of language and memory, the ability to make friends and navigate the social world—but among the most important is gaining the self-identity and purpose in life to forge one's own path.

This book is intended as a guide to successful development for anyone engaged in helping growing children reach their potential—as educators, healthcare professionals, therapists, social workers, and parents. This book presents the field's theories, its research findings, and its tools. But it is also sprinkled with stories of children to make these theories as relatable and practical as possible. Equipped with these resources, you can go out into the world and make the greatest possible difference. **You can transform the lives of children, helping them overcome the difficulties and challenges that come with growing up.**

Approach

Theories are most useful when we can see their value in real life. The theories of Piaget and Vygotsky, for example, can be difficult to understand when they are detached from their practical applications. But put into practice, they can make a world of difference to children growing up.

In preparing this resource, I set out to show how theories connect to the lives of real children. Every discussion of theory is followed by a *Theory in Action* feature demonstrating how teachers of all disciplines—from English to swimming—can make practical use of theoretical concepts. We will consider, for example, how teachers can use information-processing theories to help students pay attention in class, or how parents can use Piaget's theory to offer children appropriate toys and help them interpret significant life events.

While writing this book, I was very conscious of the fact that children today are growing up in a digital world. I just have to look at the role of technology in the lives of my own three children, who were 5 when I started writing this book and are now 12 years old. The COVID-19 pandemic moved their learning online. Today, most of their schoolwork is done on laptops. They're equipped with tablets and phones to stay in touch with their friends, and their school bus is filled, for better or worse, with kids looking intently at their devices.

To capture this reality for children today, I have included **in every chapter a section that discusses issues children encounter in our digital society**. I consider the growing body of research on topics such as the physical and cognitive impact of screen time, the impact of social media on children's self-esteem, and the seeming omnipresence of online dares and bullying.

These two factors—**the way theory connects to practice and the way technology impacts the lives of children today**—are central to the way I approached this resource, but I followed other principles as well. Here are a few of them:

1. Put theories into action—teaching theories is just the first step; the theories are always followed by explanations of why the theories are useful and how students can apply them immediately with children.

2. Humans learn best through stories, and for this reason, I have interwoven many stories and case studies throughout each chapter. Many of the children I describe will be revisited throughout the book, showing them at different stages of development.

3. Integrate new research on the influence of digital devices, social media, and the online environment into every chapter.

4. Remind students of the big picture: Child development takes place within a vast environment that has many facets and is influenced by parents' socioeconomic status, families' culture, values, race/ethnicity, and many more factors. Countless numbers of people interact with children over the course of childhood, and all can contribute to a child's development.

5. Teach milestones in context. Children develop at their own individual pace. The order in which skills are learned is often more important than the exact time at which a skill is acquired. The milestone table in this book has a separate list of possible signs of delay as well as suggestions to help children develop appropriate skills for each age. I seek thereby to empower parents and professionals to make productive use of milestones.

Organization

Children Today takes a chronological approach, following child development from prenatal times through adolescence.

The first four chapters lay the foundation for understanding child development. They are:

- Introduction to Child Development,
- Theories of Child Development,
- Genetics, Conception, and Prenatal Development, and
- Birth and the Newborn.

The remainder of the book is divided by stages of development:

- Infancy and Toddlerhood (0–2 years),
- Early Childhood (3–5 years),
- Middle Childhood (6–11 years), and
- Adolescence (12–18 years).

Each stage contains three chapters covering, respectively, physical development, cognitive development, and socio-emotional development.

Oxford Insight

Children Today is offered with Oxford Insight. Oxford Insight pairs best-in-class OUP content with curated media resources, activities, and gradable assessment in a guided learning environment that delivers performance analytics, drives student engagement, and improves student outcomes.

Features

The following features, appearing in every chapter, make theories of child development relatable by highlighting their practical applications. Together, in this way, the text artfully weaves theory and application together to make the study of child development meaningful for students who will go on to work with children in various roles.

Introductory and Chapter Closing Scenarios

Topics central to each chapter are introduced in an opening scenario focusing on the real-life experience of one or more children. The children return throughout the chapter and sometimes in later chapters as well. The closing scenario shows how their situation has changed over time and offers the reader a glimpse into the future. Every chapter picks up a thread from these scenarios and offers a comprehensive interactive assignment for students called **Interactive Case Studies**.

Interactive Case Studies

The children featured in the opening and closing scenarios are also the stars of a comprehensive concept review that can be assigned within Oxford Insight. Students connect theory to practice by making decisions about hypothetical scenarios and learning about the consequences of their decisions on the children involved. Within these assignable exercises, students will be asked to connect theories to practice through drag-and-drop, matching, and multiple-choice questions, as well as to reflect upon their choices and the impact they might have on children via short writing assignments.

What's It Like

What makes child development so interesting to students is the variety of experiences and challenges that children encounter throughout their lives. In this feature, children and their caregivers or the professionals involved in their lives describe their experiences with a variety of circumstances, challenges, and medical conditions. Examples include growing up with dyslexia or with blindness, or dealing with the stress of timed tests. Other circumstances include being homeschooled and, sometimes, experiencing teen pregnancy. The discussion positions the child's perspective alongside that of at least one involved adult. Students learn to acknowledge, and put themselves in, the position of others. They find that challenges are often an opportunity for growth and development.

Videos

A selection of videos supports the learning path for students. These include author-narrated Section Opening Videos, an overview of each developmental stage as outlined in the text. In Research Applied videos, leading researchers highlight their work, expanding upon discussions in text. These videos are assignable in Oxford Insight and offer video quizzes to ensure students viewed and understood the content.

Theory in Action

A core feature of this book, Theory in Action sections illustrate how theories can be used practically when adults interact with children. These sections illuminate a variety of concepts, for example, how a child's zone of proximal development can be assessed or how adults can help children remember information in more effective ways.

Culture Counts

Culture, socioeconomic status, nationality, socially defined race, and ethnicity have profound effects on the way children grow up and develop. The Culture Counts feature highlights surprising and interesting research that demonstrates ways in which cultural differences show up in children's lives and development. While introducing students to techniques of data analysis, the feature examines the meanings of cultural differences and how adults can effectively support children in different circumstances.

Group and Individual Activities

Every section ends with thoughtfully designed activities that encourage students—individually and in small groups—to take the perspective of parents, caregivers, and pediatric health professionals. These activities help students imagine what it's like to raise a child in our world.

- **Act It Out!** consists of prompts featuring real-life situations in which students can choose roles and act out scenarios.

- **Show What You've Learned!** activities present students with scenarios drawn from real life and ask them to write letters, make action choices, or give advice to protagonists in a story, based on the information they have learned in the section.

- **What Would You Do?** activities highlight that helping children and making appropriate decisions is rarely easy. Every choice has its own pros and cons and must be carefully weighed against the alternatives. In What Would You Do? activities, students get to make their own choices and afterward are presented with a fictional scenario to see how their choice played out.

- **What's Your Position?** encourages students to think critically about important topics, using the material in the book and additional recommended resources to construct their own opinion and to justify that opinion in a clear way, based on facts. This activity can be used as a basis for writing assignments or in-class discussions.

Instructor Resources

(Available at oup.com/he/sternberg1e)
Instructors will discover a wealth of resources designed to support their teaching. The resources begin with **Oxford Insight**, which pairs best-in-class OUP content with curated media resources, activities, and gradable assessment in a guided learning environment that delivers performance analytics, drives student engagement, and improves student outcomes. **Lecture slides, image slides, additional videos**, and **an Instructor's Manual** enhance weekly lectures, and a **Test Bank** provides abundant questions for use in tests and exams.

A Note on Language and Research

Children in America today do not experience outcomes and resources equally. For example, children living in households below the poverty line experience higher rates of malnutrition, obesity, and school underperformance and are less likely than peers living above the poverty line to complete high school. Socioeconomic status is, in turn, correlated with other social factors, such as socially defined race and ethnicity, county, and level of education achieved by parents and caregivers in the household. Throughout this text, I present research showing correlations between children's outcomes and social factors such as these, which we know lie beyond the control of those who experience them. This is not an indictment of any social or cultural group; it is a challenge to you, particularly if you aspire to work with children, to fight for changes that will produce more equitable outcomes for all children.

How To Share Your Feedback

I wrote this book for you—students and teachers—because you have the power to make the world a better place with your study and knowledge of child development. Of course, it is much more than "a book": it is a panoply of digital resources designed to support the learning and teaching of child development in the most helpful way possible.

Do you have questions or comments? Are there things that are not clear or that could be improved in the presentation? Or is there anything you have to say that would be helpful to future students and teachers? Please get in touch if you have feedback of any kind—good or bad—or if you simply want to connect and share a story. I would love to hear from you. You can reach me anytime at SternbergChildDevelopment@gmail.com.

All my best wishes,
Karin Sternberg

Acknowledgments

This book has been in the making for a long time, and the end result you hold in your hands now is the result of the collaboration and support of many people who have been invested in a wide variety of ways.

The journey to writing this book began with Sydney Carroll (Acquisitions Editor at Sinauer Associates), who showed much enthusiasm for the concept of this book and who helped shape the overall outline and features of the book. It was a pleasure working with Jessica Fiorillo (Acquisitions Editor at OUP) in the further development of this book. I am especially grateful to Lizzy Bell (Senior Portfolio Manager, STEM), who took on this book as her own when she came to Oxford University Press and did so with a level of excitement, energy, and enthusiasm that's been wonderful. Lizzy's dedication has added greatly to the production, marketing, and development of supplements for this book.

This book would not be what it is without the steady, guiding hand of Eric Sinkins (Head of Upper-Level Content), who was the best content editor an author could hope for and was a continual and reliable source of valuable feedback as well as creative ideas for improving and developing the content.

For some people on my team, the work only started once the draft was written and revised. I would like to thank Peter Lacey (Senior Content Development Editor), Tracy Marton (Assistant Production Editor), and Ashli MacKenzie (Senior Production Editor) for their diligent and patient work as this book moved through the production process. Thank you also to Joan Kalkut (Content Development Manager) and Julia Wray (Assistant Content Editor) for their assistance with the content of the book. Caroline Kasterine (Digital Course Designer) was instrumental in developing the digital exercises for this book, and I am particularly grateful for her excitement and creativity in the development of the digital resources.

My intention in writing this book was to make a difference to teachers, their students, and—indirectly through those dedicated teachers and students— children all over the country and the world as well as their families. A book can only have an impact if it sells, and books do not sell themselves. For this reason, I would much like to thank the marketing team at Oxford—Kathaleen McCormick (Marketing Manager, STEM) and Liz Mauro (Marketing Assistant, STEM).

There are also some people who accompanied this book behind the curtains. Without my parents, this book would have never come to be—I would not have been able to change careers and become a psychologist. My parents have always backed all of my ideas, no matter how crazy they might have seemed to them.

My husband, Robert J. Sternberg, supported me from the very moment that I conceived the idea of writing this book, just as he has always supported me in all of my endeavors. He has read and commented on all of my chapters and contributed many ideas. Most of all, he was always available to help create time to write the book, taking care of our children whenever necessary. Any of my accomplishments I owe in part to him and his unwavering support.

Part of this textbook was written during the 1½ years that I homeschooled our children due to the COVID-19 pandemic, and I only could do so with the support not only of my husband but also of our three children. My deepest gratitude goes to Samuel, Brittany, and Melody, who have grown up with this book and thus have influenced my writing in their own personal ways. They were in early childhood as I wrote the early childhood chapters, lived through middle childhood as I worked on those chapters, and are now entering adolescence.

Finally, I would like to thank the colleagues who reviewed my chapters in various stages of their development and contributed many thoughtful ideas as well as helpful feedback.

Allison Butler, *Bryant University*
Amanda McPherson, *Pima Community College*
Amy Flavin, *Nyack College*
Amy Stimling, *Sacramento City College*
Andrew Franks, *Lake Superior State University*
Angela Miller-Hargis, *University of Cincinnati, Blue Ash College*
Beverly Okereke, *Riverside City College*
Brian Smith, *University of North Carolina, Pembroke*
Caroline LaBella, *University of Massachusetts, Boston*
Carol Ann Schumann, *Delaware Technical Community College*
Catherine Phillips, *Northwest Vista College*
Chris Alas, *Houston Community College*
Dana Donohue, *Northern Arizona*
David Rudek, *Aurora University*
Deanna P. Upchurch, *Bristol Community College*
Deborah Laible, *Lehigh University*
Drew Curtis, *Angelo State*
Elaine Carratello-Healy, *Montclair State University*
Elizabeth McCarroll, *Texas Woman's University*
Elmida Baghdaserians, *Los Angeles Valley College*
Ericka Hamilton, *Moraine Valley Community College*
Gaye Hughes, *Austin Community College*
Gina Brelsford, *Penn State, Harrisburg*
Gwendolyn Parsons, *Hillsborough Community College*
Hsing-chen Tung, *San Diego State University*
Ingrid M. Tiegel, *Carthage College*
Jane Moir Whitaker, *University of the Cumberlands*
Joan Steidl, *Kent State University*
Joe Anistranski, *University of California, Davis*
Judy Newman, *Penn State, Abbington*

Katerina Karaivanova, *University of New Hampshire*
Kelly Warmuth, *Providence College*
Kimberly Corson, *Penn State University, Erie*
Kristina Schaefer Courter, *Moorpark College*
Kristin Wesner, *Clarke University*
LaDonna Atkins, *University of Central Oklahoma*
Lisa Hess, *York College of Pennsylvania*
Madhavi Menon, *Nova Southeastern University*
Marla Sturm, *Montgomery County Community College*
Matt Grimes, *Radford University*
Meeta Banerjee, *California State University, Northridge*
Moira Martin, *St Edward's University in Austin, Texas*
Mollie Carter, *Union University*
Nanci Monaco, *SUNY Buffalo State*
Nathalie Franco, *Broward College*
Renee Funke, *SUNY Jamestown Community College*
Richard Langford, *University of Hawaii, West O'ahu*
Roberta McDermid, *Missouri Southern State University*
Robert Butler, *Eastern Oregon University*
Rola Al-Omar, *Riverside City College*
Ross Flom, *Southern Utah University*
Rufaro Chitiyo, *Tennessee Technological University*
Shannon Burghart, *Guilford Technical Community College*
Sheila Smith, *Solano Community College*
Sonya Kitsko, *Penn State University*
Susan Supino, *Bergen Community College*
Suzanne Cox, *Beliot College*
Teresa Segelken, *Coastal Carolina Community College*
Tim Rarick, *Brigham Young University Idaho*
Tracey E. Ryan, *University of Bridgeport*
William Aronson, *Florida International University*

Digital Resources for Children Today

Children Today: An Applied Approach to Child Development through Adolescence is available in Oxford Insight. Oxford Insight delivers best in class content within a powerful, data-driven learning experience designed to increase student success. A guided and curated learning environment—delivered either via learning management system/virtual learning environment (LMS/VLE) integration or standalone—**Oxford Insight** provides access to the e-book, digital resources, assignable/gradable activities and exercises, and analytics on student achievement and progress. As students work through the course material, **Oxford Insight** automatically sets personalized learning paths for them, based on their specific performance.

Developed with applied social, motivational, and personalized learning research, **Oxford Insight** enables instructors to deliver an immersive experience that empowers students by actively engaging them with assigned reading. This approach, paired with real-time actionable data about student performance, helps instructors ensure that all students are best supported along their unique learning paths.

With Oxford Insight, instructors can:

- Assign auto-scored multiple-choice, fill-in, and other machine-gradable questions
- Score specific items (including open-ended questions) with feedback
- Export grades and change grading points
- Establish a course roster and add/drop students
- Share courses and resources with students and faculty
- Sync real-time assignments with LMS/VLE gradebooks
- Author new content and/or customize the publisher provided content.

Contents include

For the Student

- **Self-Assessment Quizzes** reinforce understanding of chapter material through end-of-section questions.
- **Interactive Case Studies** Students connect theory to practice by making decisions about hypothetical scenarios and learning about the consequences of their decisions on the children involved. These assignable activities include drag and drop, matching and multiple-choice questions as well as short writing assignments
- **Section Opening Videos**: provide an author-narrated overview of each developmental stage.

- **Research Applied Videos**: Author Karin Sternberg speaks with leading researchers about their work and how students can apply this research to their interactions with children to support growth and development.
- **Culture Counts**: Writing assignments offer students the opportunity to analyze data and respond to prompts encouraging critical thinking.
- **What Would You Do**: Writing assignments allow students to discuss what they would do when encountering important decisions regarding children and allow them to think through the potential outcomes.

For the Instructor

- **Figure and Lecture Note PPTs** are presentations for course instruction with high-resolution images from the text, enabling instructors and/or lecturers to spend less time preparing class materials and more time with students.

- **Video Clips**: short videos for use in the classroom

- **Instructors Manual**: includes Chapter Outlines with Learning Objectives, Answers to In-Text Activities, and a Video Clip Inventory.

- **Test Banks** include over 700 questions covering key facts and concepts in each chapter with multiple-choice and short-answer questions included. Questions are categorized by Bloom's level and are also aligned with the textbook's Learning Objectives.

- For more information on how **Children Today: An Applied Approach to Child Development through Adolescence** powered by **Oxford Insight**, can enrich the teaching and learning experience in your course, please visit oxfordinsight.oup.com or contact your Oxford University Press representative.

CHILDREN TODAY

Overview

Introduction

A career in child development can be exciting and rewarding

Eight-year-old Lucia sits with her grandmother in the office of an educational psychologist. She doesn't know it, but this moment is a pivotal one in her young life. Currently in third grade, Lucia is having trouble at school. Though she's always been a bright child, she has trouble with her reading and cannot keep pace with her peers in the classroom. When the teacher calls on her to read something aloud, she tries and tries but cannot seem to make out the words on the page. It's such an excruciating, terrifying experience for her that she has sometimes feigned illness to avoid having to go to school. People frequently tell her that she is dumb or lazy. The psychologist, Dr. Mukherjee, has just administered a series of tests and concluded that Lucia has dyslexia. Both Lucia and her grandmother feel a bit dizzy and confused. They do not understand what exactly "dyslexia" is, but what they do understand is that Lucia has a diagnosis now. And to Lucia and her grandmother, a diagnosis means that there is finally hope—hope for a possible treatment and for Lucia's life to turn around for the better.

Welcome to this book and your studies in child development! Lucia's story illustrates why child development is one of the most exciting and rewarding fields to work in. All children have a remarkable potential to thrive and succeed, without regard to the circumstances into which they were born. Some children, like Lucia, need help to realize that potential. As a student of child development, you are acquiring the power to make a tremendous difference in the future of the children whose lives you touch. It is my hope that after reading this book, you will see beyond what children do, to what they are *capable* of doing with the help of those who have committed themselves to this field, as educators and childcare professionals, as social service providers and therapists, as pediatricians and clinical psychologists, as parents, or in some other role.

In this book we will consider many aspects of children's development: the growth of children's bodies, how their thinking develops, and how their interactions with others change as they get older. We will consider how public policies impact the lives of children and which challenges children face as they grow up. We will also discuss how cultural and socioeconomic factors influence children's lives. We will review the latest research and explore debates and hot topics in the field that should give you plenty of ideas and, hopefully, inspiration. Most of all, you should come to see that your interactions with children truly matter, whatever it is you choose to do with your education in child development.

1.1 How This Book Is Organized

- Outline the aspects of child development scientists study.
- List the time periods into which the study of child development is often divided.

Child development is a vast field of study that encompasses an extensive array of topics occurring within a period of about two decades. To make things more manageable, we divide child development into different topical areas, or *domains*, as well as different time periods.

Domains of Development

Throughout this book, we discuss child development in three key domains:

- physical development
- cognitive development
- social and emotional development (see **FIGURE 1.1**).

Physical development involves changes to a child's body, like gains in weight and height as well as brain growth and hormonal changes. In looking at physical development we also consider nutrition and health issues as well as the development of motor skills. We will see, for example, when infants should be introduced to solid foods and which diseases are a threat to children at preschool age.

Cognitive development encompasses any changes in children's thinking, problem-solving skills, and language abilities. We will investigate how young children start to speak and learn new words, for example, and how watching TV may affect children's thinking.

Finally, *social and emotional development* focuses on children's growing and changing relationships with others and their ability to connect with the people around them. In this section, we look at how family, friends, and the culture in which children grow up influence development. We also discuss children's growing skills in regulating their emotions as well as the development of their personality—all the characteristics that make a child a unique person. We will discuss, for example, how children make friends and what their friends mean to them.

As you read, you will quickly notice that although we separate development into these three different domains, the three domains are closely connected to

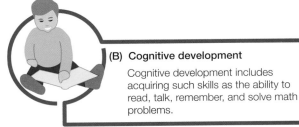

(A) Physical development

Physical development can include learning how to jump, run, and play physical games, how to tie shoes, and how to hold and draw with crayons.

(B) Cognitive development

Cognitive development includes acquiring such skills as the ability to read, talk, remember, and solve math problems.

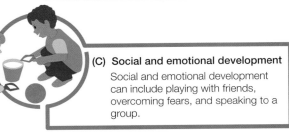

(C) Social and emotional development

Social and emotional development can include playing with friends, overcoming fears, and speaking to a group.

FIGURE 1.1 The study of child development encompasses the growth and maturation of (A) children's bodies and physical abilities, (B) children's thinking capabilities, and (C) children's emotions and their interactions with each other.

each other. For example, as the brain matures (physical development), children learn to communicate more effectively (cognitive development), which in turn changes their relationships with their parents and friends (social development).

What's It Like...

Living with Dyslexia

Lucia, 11 years old

When I was in kindergarten and first grade, reading didn't seem so bad at first. But at some point, I think it was in second grade, I noticed that I wasn't getting any better at reading. All the other kids seemed to get better, but not me. And I often felt angry because I tried really hard but I just didn't make any progress. A lot of times I felt scared to go to school because I was worried there might be a test—and I hated tests.

Finally, when I was in third grade, my grandma took me to a doctor and got me tested. I was scared of finding out there was something wrong with me, but the doctor explained that finding out I had dyslexia was a good thing because I would be able to get special help with my reading. And she was right! Now, because my teachers know I have dyslexia, I can have extra time on tests, and I'm not graded for my spelling anymore. I feel like I can be a good student again. Once a week we have a therapy dog, Ollie, visit our school, and I am allowed to read to him. When I am with Ollie, I actually almost like reading. He never tells me I'm being slow or making mistakes.

Since I've started getting extra help for reading I have gotten much better. In the beginning, letters and words seemed to jump around in front of my eyes, and I don't really experience that anymore. But I still have to reread sentences to make sure I get the meaning right. I also know I have to keep reading. If I don't, reading starts to get harder again.

Although I've been working at it a lot, I am still not a very good speller. That sometimes makes me feel bad. Other kids know I'm not a good speller, and obviously nobody wants to be known as the bad speller. I've started joking about it at school and that helps a little, especially when my friends go along with it. Still, from time to time I am worried that people will make fun of me for my bad spelling.

Even though I'm doing a lot better, I also have to say that it's really hard being dyslexic. I have to work so hard on my reading and spelling, and it's frustrating to see that these things come so easily to everyone else. I wonder if it will always be harder for me. I try to remember that other kids have things they struggle with, too. But it still makes me frustrated. Sometimes when I get really upset, I play with my cat. That helps me a lot. And I'm happy, too, for the extra help I get from my teachers, because I know that if I work hard, I can succeed. Then I don't feel like my dyslexia is something I will have to worry about for the rest of my life.

Lucia's mom, Felicity

Lucia was diagnosed with dyslexia at age 8. We were in shock when we received the diagnosis. We didn't even really know what dyslexia was, so the diagnosis marked the beginning of a very steep learning curve. But even though we were shocked, we were also relieved because it had been clear for a while that Lucia had trouble reading and keeping up with her classmates in school, and we were not sure why or what to do.

In hindsight, there were some warning signs that I shrugged off but now wish I hadn't. For example, a preschool teacher told me that Lucia didn't participate in any word games and had a hard time rhyming. So when I asked her what rhymed with "red," she said "blue." When we brought this up with her pediatrician, he said not to worry and give her some more time. I didn't think about this incident any more and did not connect it with Lucia's reading issues until we got her diagnosed with dyslexia. Now I very much regret that I wasn't more insistent on getting to the root of those issues that we saw in preschool.

That said, being able to put a name to her difficulties has made a world of difference to our family. We even found out that some of our relatives have dyslexia as well—it was just something that was never talked about until we openly discussed our struggles. After the diagnosis, we had a series of meetings with teachers at the school, and they started to implement additional services for Lucia right away. They also provided her with special accommodations.

For example, she gets more time for testing because reading and understanding written text is still a slow and cumbersome process for her. She also does not get graded on spelling, which really helps her confidence. She is not a bad student and she has a thorough grasp of the material, but her learning is affected by her reading difficulties. People often have trouble seeing what she can really accomplish when they get distracted by her poor spelling. Since her diagnosis, Lucia has made such progress.

It seems to me we are lucky that our school has been so responsive to our needs. I have connected online with other parents whose experience was quite different. How effectively teachers can help depends on the reading curriculum a school uses and how (if at all!) they are trained to teach struggling readers, for example. Some families found their school to be an excellent resource, but others in the same city eventually ended up switching schools or resorting to homeschooling. Connecting to these other families and finding professional help has changed our entire outlook, and we are now confident that Lucia will be able to do well in school and that she'll be able to overcome the difficulties she is facing.

Periods of Development

Just as we can divide our study of child development into the three domains just described, we can also break the discipline down into periods of development. The chapters of this book are grouped into parts defined by the age ranges they cover:

- beginnings (conception, the prenatal period, and the moments immediately following birth)
- infancy and toddlerhood (ages 0–2)
- early childhood (ages 3–5)
- middle childhood (ages 6–11)
- adolescence (ages 12–18).

In addition to these stages, researcher Jeffrey Arnett has proposed an additional stage he named *emerging adulthood*, which stretches from the late teenage years into the mid-twenties (Arnett & Tanner, 2016). He found that many young people at some point feel they are no longer adolescents and begin to be responsible for themselves, but they still have very close ties to their family and are exploring different identities.

All of the periods mentioned above are fluid and may overlap. For example, a two-and-a-half-year-old may show cognitive function typical of early childhood but remain very much a toddler in terms of physical and social abilities. And not every child instantly becomes an adolescent on their twelfth birthday. Nevertheless, these divisions help us to stay oriented on the path that leads from birth to adulthood.

Review!

Which aspects of child development do scientists study?

- Scientists study the three domains of physical, cognitive, and social and emotional development.
    1. *Physical development* is concerned with topics like the growth of children's bodies and brains, as well as their health and nutrition.
    2. *Cognitive development* is about children's thinking and language skills.
    3. *Social and emotional development* focuses on children's abilities to relate to other people and regulate their emotions, all while developing their own unique personalities.
- All three domains are interrelated, and progress in one domain facilitates development in the others.

Into which time periods is the study of child development often divided?

- Child development researchers often specialize in a certain period of childhood, defined by a specified age range.
- The age ranges that are commonly used to divide childhood into periods are conception to birth (beginnings or the prenatal period), birth to age 2 (infancy and toddlerhood), age 3 to age 5 (early childhood), ages 6 to 11 (middle childhood), and ages 12 to 18 (adolescence).
- Often, emerging adulthood (comprising the late teen years to mid-twenties) is added to these periods.
- The periods commonly overlap, and children often achieve the benchmarks of a given period a little ahead of or a little behind schedule.

1.2 Contexts That Influence Children's Development

- Define the role the family structure plays in a child's development.
- Explain how culture and ethnicity influence child development.
- Relate how social class and economic factors affect a child's development.
- Explain how the concepts of cohort and generation shape our understanding of child development.
- Examine how today's children use media and how this use affects them.

Even though we can divide the subject into distinct domains and time periods, child development is not as straightforward as it may seem. Children are born with different genetic makeups, talents, and challenges. Some children reach milestones earlier, some later, and a few never. Children grow up in different families, neighborhoods, and cultures, all of which influence their development. In this section, we consider some of the most important factors that influence development. Keep these factors in mind as you read through the book so that you may recognize the influence they have on the way children develop.

Family

Children spend a significant amount of their time with their families. They depend on their families to provide them with housing, food, healthcare, and education, not to mention guidance and emotional care. Over the past few decades, the makeup of the average American family has changed considerably. The "nuclear" family of the mid-twentieth century, consisting of a mother and father with one or more children, has given way to much more diverse forms. This change is a result of several trends (see **FIGURE 1.2**).

Throughout this book, we will periodically return to the influence of the family on children's development and answer important questions including the following:

- Does the way parents discipline their children make a difference in how those children grow up?
- Are children with no siblings different from children with siblings?
- Does being raised in a lone-parent household have particular implications for children?

Culture and Race/Ethnicity

Culture refers to the ideas, customs, and social behavior of a society or group of people. It essentially describes the way of life of a social group and is learned, not inherited. A culture can be national or regional, or it can be based on other characteristics, such as religion, ethnicity, or language. American culture is different from Mexican culture, but within the United States you will find that the prevailing culture of the Deep South is quite different from much of the culture you find in California. Christian culture is different from Jewish or Muslim culture, and within Christianity, Judaism, or Islam, there are many distinct subcultures. When we talk about Western culture, we usually broadly refer to the culture we find in European countries as well as in the United States and Canada.

culture the beliefs, customs, arts, and values of a society or group of people.

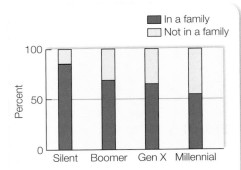

More adults live alone. Adults are increasingly less likely to live with a spouse, child, or both.

More same-sex couples raise children. From 1990 to 2006, the percentage of same-sex unmarried couples with children rose from 12% to 19% (Gates, 2011). In 2020, 292,000 children were raised by same-sex parents.

There are fewer two-parent households. In 1960, 87% of children lived with two parents; that number declined to 68% in 2014.

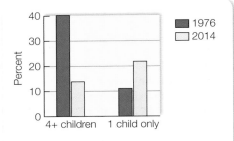

Mothers are having fewer children. From 1976 to 2014, the number of women aged 40–44 who had given birth to four or more children fell from 40% to 14%. The percentage of women who had only one child doubled from 11% to 22%.

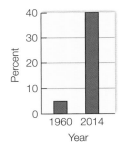

More children are born to unmarried mothers. In 1960, only 5% of children were born to unmarried women; in 2014, 40% of children had unmarried mothers.

Parents are older and more educated. In 1960, a woman giving birth to her first child was on average 21 years old. Today, the average age of a first-time mother is 26. In 1960, just 18% of mothers had attended college; today 67% of mothers have done some college.

FIGURE 1.2   The average American family from the mid-1900s differs in many ways from the average American family we find today. Two-parent households are decreasing, and families are getting smaller; more unmarried women and same-sex couples are raising children; and parents overall are older and more educated.

Data from Pew Research Center, www.pewresearch.org: "Breadwinner Moms" (2013); "Childlessness Falls, Family Size Grows Among Highly Educated Women" (2015); "As Millennials Near 40, They're Approaching Family Life Differently Than Previous Generations" (2020); U.S. Census Bureau. 2020. "Same-Sex Couples Are More Likely to Adopt or Foster Children." www.census.gov

Culture affects the way people behave and interact with each other, which values they hold, and how they raise their children. For example, do we want children to be fluent in the knowledge of religious texts, or do we place more emphasis on science, or do we want to balance the two kinds of instruction in some way? Do we aim to raise children who put forward their opinions and stand up for themselves, or do we want children to be obedient and submissive toward their parents and other adults?

Much of the United States belongs to a group of societies anthropologist David Lancy calls WEIRD, for *Western, educated, industrialized, rich,* and *democratic* (Lancy, 2015). In WEIRD societies, parents assume a proactive role and direct their children's lives from an early age, believing that children need guidance and structure. Parents teach their children intellectual and social skills almost as soon as they are born—or even before, by playing music or reading to the unborn child in utero. A drawback of shuttling children through a regimen of extracurricular activities—gymnastics and soccer, robotics competitions and spelling bees—is that they may become passive recipients and may not develop responsibility and independence.

■ Expectations of children differ dramatically depending on the culture in which they are raised.

In many other cultures around the world, children are expected to contribute to the running of the household from an early age. Children are given domestic chores or have to tend to livestock. In these cultures, children are overseen by older children or elders while their parents are engaged in their own work. The children learn by observation rather than through direct instruction and usually do not play with adults as is common in the West. People in these societies often believe that children learn what is dangerous through their own experiences (Marlowe, 2010). For example, Hadza parents in Tanzania encourage their children to throw stones at poisonous snakes and take other risks to explore their environment (Jones et al., 1996). One researcher in Mexico observed a Zinacanteco toddler almost running barefoot through a fire. The adults witnessing the incident did not try to stop or comfort the child but rather felt that the child should have paid better attention to where she was going (de Leon, 2012). In some indigenous societies in Africa and Papua New Guinea, young children and babies are allowed to play with knives and other sharp objects because parents do not want to limit their children's freedom to explore (Hewlett, 2013; Hewlett et al., 2011; Howard, 1970; Whiting, 1941).

There is a good reason why a child in Seattle is not expected to herd cattle and a child in Igbo-Ora, Nigeria, is not expected to practice piano. What is considered normal practice in child-rearing is highly dependent on culture. Western experience and science have dominated our opinion of what is normal and adequate, but not all findings and theories in this book can be applied without constraint to other cultures—even within our borders.

An **ethnic group** is defined as a group of people who share a common cultural tradition, typically based on nationality or ancestry. Different ethnic groups may coexist within one culture (**FIGURE 1.3**). Ethnicity is often regarded as something you are born into: You do not choose to be Hispanic or Irish American.

People belonging to an ethnic minority (**FIGURE 1.4**) may experience prejudice and discrimination, which can have a profound impact on their lives. Ethnicity influences child development in many ways. In the United States, ethnic groups differ in their income, education, life expectancy, family size, and academic achievements. They also differ in their beliefs and practices around parenting children.

ethnic group a group of people who share a common culture, nationality, ancestry, language, or religion.

Another term that is often used when discussing population groups is *race*. Scientists once believed—and tried to prove—that the human population comprised several races that were biologically distinct. Some people still believe that race is biologically determined, but most social science researchers today argue that race is actually socially constructed. When we say that race is "socially

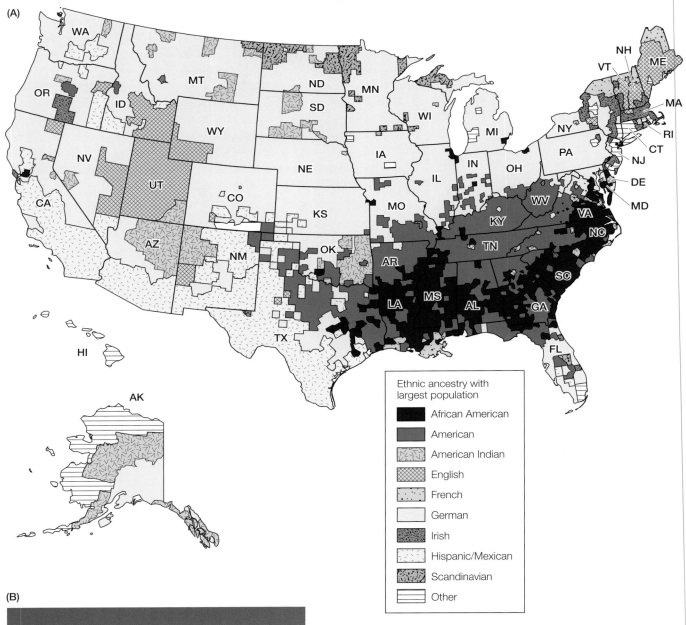

Ethnic ancestry with largest population

- African American
- American
- American Indian
- English
- French
- German
- Irish
- Hispanic/Mexican
- Scandinavian
- Other

FIGURE 1.3 (A) Ethnic ancestry with the largest population, by county, 2000. (B) People of different races and ancestries are not dispersed evenly throughout the United States but are often concentrated in particular areas. Alrye and Leandra both belong to the Hopi tribe in Arizona. Today, the states of Arizona, New Mexico, and Oklahoma are home to a particularly high number of Native Americans.

A after A. Brittingham and G. P. de la Cruz. 2004. "Ancestry: 2000. Census 2000 Brief." U.S. Department of Commerce Economics and Statistics Administration, U.S. Census Bureau, Washington, DC

© Adam Sylvester/Science Source

Shanice, Pedro, Moira, and Jennifer all attend the same preschool. In 2015, more than half of all newborn babies were racial or ethnic minorities.

FIGURE 1.4   By 2065, the majority of people living in the United States will belong to racial/ethnic minorities. Between 2014 and 2060, the share of the population made up of non-Hispanic Whites is projected to decline from 62% to 44%. The proportions of Asians and Hispanics are expected to rise significantly, from 5% to 9% (Asians) and from 17% to 29% (Hispanics).

After D. Cohn and A. Caumont. 2016. "10 Demographic Trends Shaping the U.S. and the World in 2016." www.pewresearch.org; data from Pew Research Center. 2015. "Modern Immigration Wave Brings 59 Million to U.S., Driving Population Growth and Change Through 2065: Views of Immigration's Impact on U.S. Society Mixed." Washington, DC: September

constructed," we mean that people view and judge one another in terms of the racial categories they perceive, rather than based on true biological differences (Onwuachi-Willig, 2016; Sternberg et al., 2005).

Why do people think in terms of race at all? To some degree, we can't help it. Race, unlike ethnicity, is based on visible physical features, notably (but not exclusively) skin color (Sternberg et al., 2005; Tishkoff & Kidd, 2004). In everyday life, categorization helps people process the vast amounts of information they encounter (Pauker et al., 2018). Classifying things—and people—into groups makes reasoning easier and quicker. We tend to form our initial impressions of others using categories our minds can process quickly: *men* and *women, infants* and *adults, Black people* and *White people* and *Asian people.* Then we use the information we already have about these groups to make judgments about individuals we encounter. Upon entering a room full of strangers, we do not have time to assess each person individually, and so we use the data immediately available to our senses. Race becomes problematic when we use it to form judgments about people based on stereotypes associated with racial categories. This is the basis of prejudice (Pauker et al., 2018).

Because race/ethnicity and culture can impact children and their development in many ways, we revisit these concepts from time to time, asking such questions as:

socioeconomic status an indicator of the social standing and financial resources of a person, based on income, education, and occupation.

- Is there a reason that Asian children tend to do better in math (Gibbs et al., 2016)?
- Are parenting styles similarly effective across cultures, or are there parenting styles that are more effective in some cultures than others?
- Are there any effects on children of being born to immigrant parents, and if so, what are they?

Socioeconomic Status

Socioeconomic status is a combination of someone's income, education, and occupation (Baker, 2014). It is an indicator of a person's social standing and financial means. Consider these two children: Marla and Myriam both

■ These two siblings are fraternal twins and share 50% of their genes. Are they of the same race or different races?

have single mothers. Marla's mother is a lawyer with a graduate degree and an annual six-figure income. Myriam's mother dropped out of high school and earns around $20,000 a year by working in the checkout line at the local supermarket. What do you think the lives and experiences of Marla and Myriam are like?

Think about these things:

- What kind of neighborhood and home are Marla and Myriam each likely to live in?
- What kind of school is each of the two girls likely to attend?
- What kinds of foods may the parents offer to each of them?
- What is the likelihood that Marla and Myriam each receive satisfactory healthcare?

The situation that Myriam's mother is in does not make her a bad parent, any more than Marla's mother's salary makes her a good parent. But as you can imagine, the socioeconomic status of a family impacts children at many different levels. Children who grow up in poverty are more likely to be born prematurely and at a low birthweight. They are at higher risk for developing illnesses and mental health problems. They also have a higher risk of low school attendance, poor academic performance, and dropping out of school (Bradley & Corwyn, 2002; Child Trends Databank, 2016; Dahl & Lochner, 2005; Ratcliffe & McKernan, 2012).

The United States has one of the highest rates of child poverty among developed countries even though in 2019 (that is, prior to COVID-19) child poverty in the country had reached record lows (Thomas & Fry, 2020). Every fifth child lives in poverty (Chen & Thomson, 2021), and since 2000, child poverty rates have increased across much of the United States (**FIGURE 1.5**). Across the developed world, the United States' soaring child poverty rate is only topped by Romania (Child Trends Databank, 2016; UNICEF Innocenti Research Centre,

(A)

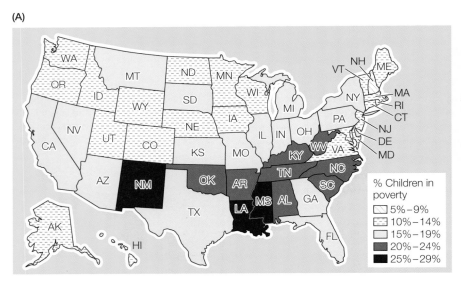

% Children in poverty
- 5%–9%
- 10%–14%
- 15%–19%
- 20%–24%
- 25%–29%

(B)

© LindaYolanda/Getty Images

FIGURE 1.5 (A) Child poverty in the United States by state, 2019. Child poverty is noticeably high in the Southern states. (B) Henry's father worked as a shift manager at a local fast food restaurant. Nine months ago he was laid off when the restaurant had to close during the COVID-19 pandemic. Henry's mother stays home to care for him and his two younger siblings. Within a few months, whatever little in savings the family had was used up. It is unclear whether Henry's father will be able to secure a new job anytime soon and the family struggles to provide for basic needs like food, clothing, and school supplies.

Data from The Annie E. Casey Foundation. 2019. Children in poverty (100 percent poverty) in the United States. https://datacenter.kidscount.org

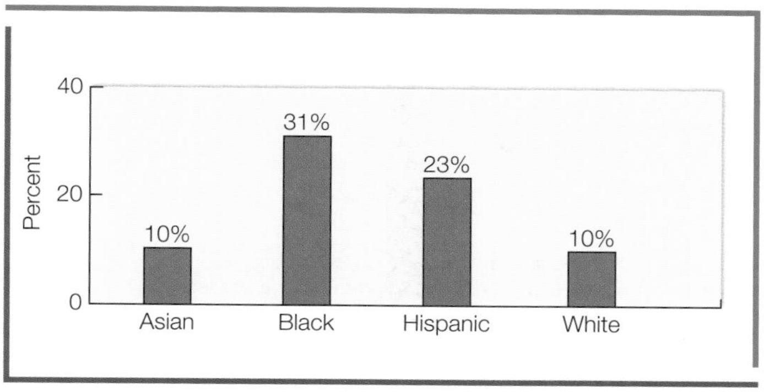

FIGURE 1.6 Percentage of U.S. children experiencing poverty, by race/ethnicity. Poverty is not equally distributed across all races/ethnicities in the United States. Children of Black or Hispanic origin have a higher risk of being affected by poverty than their White or Asian peers.

Data from The Annie E. Casey Foundation. 2019. Children in poverty by race and ethnicity in the United States. https://datacenter.kidscount.org

2012). Finland and Denmark have some of the lowest child poverty rates, around 5% (UNICEF Innocenti Research Centre, 2012).

In 2020, the poverty threshold in the United States was $26,246 for a family of four (U.S. Census Bureau, 2021). A number of factors increase or decrease the likelihood of whether children live in poverty, among them children's race/ethnicity, the place where they live, whether they have siblings, and whether their family consists of one or two parents (see **FIGURE 1.6**).

Can you imagine living on just $1.90 per day? This is what every fifth child in the developing world has to survive on (Edin & Shaefer, 2015)! Poor children are more than twice as likely as wealthier children to die before they reach age 5 and more than three times as likely not to go to school (care.org, 2017).

Throughout this book, we will revisit the impact of poverty and socioeconomic status on children's lives and ask important questions, such as:

- What impact does malnourishment have on the cognitive development of a child?

- Can early intervention increase the chances that a child will be successful at school later on?

- How can we support healthy development in children from low-income households?

Historical Context

Kyle was born in 1928 and grew up in a rural part of Oklahoma. In the 1930s, as a result of droughts and agricultural overuse of the land, dust storms swept the state and turned parts of it into what was soon to be called the "Dust Bowl." The fine dust penetrated homes. Crops and cattle died. Kyle's father was a farmer, but the family lost most of its income for years because of the dust storms. Often, Kyle went to bed hungry. Since there were no toys, Kyle learned to make his own toys out of any materials he could find.

Micah was born in 2011 in the same town as Kyle. These days, grassy green hills sweep the countryside. Micah's parents both work outside the house. Micah is particularly proud of his new smartphone, which he uses to stay in touch with his friends using social media and text messages. He loves to play role-playing games with others he meets online.

Kyle and Micah were raised in the same town, but because they were born at different times, their life experiences were vastly different. Kyle and Micah belong to different cohorts. A **cohort** is a group of people who were born around the same time and share some significant experiences. Researchers like to study cohorts because they represent a fixed population undergoing similar experiences as they age together. Researchers will also look for differences between the people from different cohorts, and call these differences *cohort effects*. People who grew up during the Dust Bowl are likely to have different attitudes and experiences compared to people who grew up at a later time.

cohort a group of people who were born around the same time and share some significant experiences.

■ Table 1.1 Overview of Frequently Used Generation Names

Name	Time period	Significant events
GI Generation (also labeled Greatest Generation by Tom Brokaw)	1901–1927	Experienced the Great Depression as teenagers; may have fought in World War II.
Silent Generation	1928–1945	Too young to participate in World War II and too old to participate in the hippie movement.
Baby Boomers	1946–1964	Grew up in times of economic upswing and postwar baby boom. May have participated in the civil rights movement and protested against the Vietnam War.
Generation X	1965–1980	Experienced as teenagers the rise of AIDS and the fall of the Berlin Wall. The "X" indicates that the generation does not like to be labeled.
Millennials (also labeled Generation Y)	1981–1996	Experienced as teenagers the invention and spread of the internet as well as 9/11.
Generation Z (also labeled iGeneration)	1997–2012	The first generation born into the digital age.
Generation Alpha	2013–present	The current generation.

Note: Depending on the source, the designated time periods for each generation can vary by a few years.
Source: M. Dimock. 2019. *Pew Res Cent* 17(1): 1–7.

generation a group of people of roughly the same age, with shared historical experiences; a generation often spans a time range of more than a decade.

A **generation**, like a cohort, is a group of people of about the same age, living at the same time and experiencing significant events together. However, a generation usually encompasses a wider span of years, typically exceeding a decade. In popular culture, generations may be given nicknames, like *Baby Boomers* and *Millennials*. These labels are created by marketing experts, journalists, academics, and others. In many cases, there is no consensus on when one generation ends and another one begins (see also **TABLE 1.1**).

Generations differ from each other in many respects, like the chances they had to pursue an education and their attitudes and values. Consider the generation of children raised in the twenty-first century. Unlike the generations that preceded it, they have enjoyed, from birth, widespread access to high-speed internet along with social media platforms that launched in the early 2000s. Their lives have been shaped by the presence of digital media. Their development has also been affected by COVID-19 and the changes it brought to education and socialization. And they have grown up with parenting practices and cultural attitudes very different from those that characterized previous generations. As you read this book, you will frequently revisit influences that affect today's generation of children and their development. In the next section, we discuss in more detail the impact of digital media on children.

■ Mara enjoys looking through her grandfather's coin collection. They enjoy spending time together and feel very close even though their life experiences differ vastly: Mara's grandfather grew up during the Cold War, when there was a palpable fear of a nuclear strike, but when most people felt that their future success lay in their hands and had hopes their children would be more prosperous than themselves. Mara's generation grows up in an era of diffuse terrorist threats and a shrinking middle class, when many parents worry about their family's financial stability and are afraid their children will be worse off financially than they themselves.

© Stephen Parker/Alamy Stock Photo

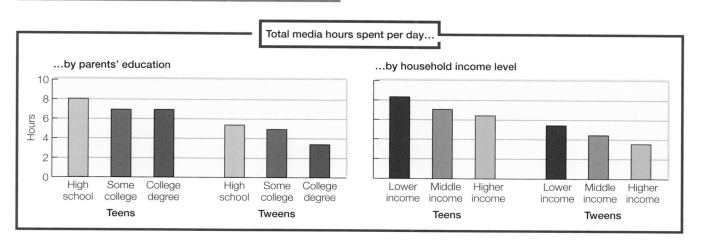

FIGURE 1.7 Some statistics on media use among U.S. teens and tweens.

Data from V. Rideout. 2015. "The Common Sense Census: Media Use by Tweens and Teens, 2015." Common Sense Media, San Francisco, CA; V. Rideout and M. B. Robb. 2019. "The Common Sense Census: Media Use by Tweens and Teens, 2019." Common Sense Media, San Francisco, CA

Digital Media

You probably grasped the significance of the nickname "iGeneration" when we discussed different generations in Table 1.1. Millennials may have experienced the birth of the internet, but the generation of children growing up today has arrived on the scene of an advanced digital age, a wireless world that operates with technological devices and capabilities that Gen Xers and their parents could hardly have dreamed of when they were growing up. Children interact with touch screens and watch videos on smartphones and tablets before they can even walk or speak. Preschoolers spend their time on games and apps, and teenagers spend much of their time consuming media in one way or another. Throughout this book, we will return to children's media use and discuss its impact on their development many times. Our discussions will focus on different media like books in paper or electronic form, screen media, or particular applications of media like social media or online gaming. When we speak of digital media, we refer to all devices that use computer technology (*Oxford English Dictionary*, 2018).

Depending on their age, children use media quite differently (**FIGURE 1.7**). The youngest ones like television the best. Even children less than a year old spend about 44 minutes a day watching TV, and children up to age 8 watch about 1.5 hours a day. Every third child under age 8 has a TV in their bedroom or lives in a household where the TV is constantly running (Common Sense Media, 2013; Rideout & Robb, 2019). Around age 8 mobile devices take over as the medium of choice, giving children a chance to communicate with their friends and access videos, games, or social media at all times of the day. Teenagers send an average of 30 text messages per day to their friends (Lenhart, 2015), and on average they use entertainment media for almost ten hours a day (Rideout, 2015; Rideout & Robb, 2019). Parents generally seem to be concerned about the

Culture Counts

The Digital Divide

For children in the twenty-first century, having access to computers and the internet is important for social and—increasingly—educational opportunities. The COVID-19 pandemic highlighted this importance, as schools closed and children's education moved wholly or partly online.

However, with respect to their education, the pandemic struck some children harder than others.

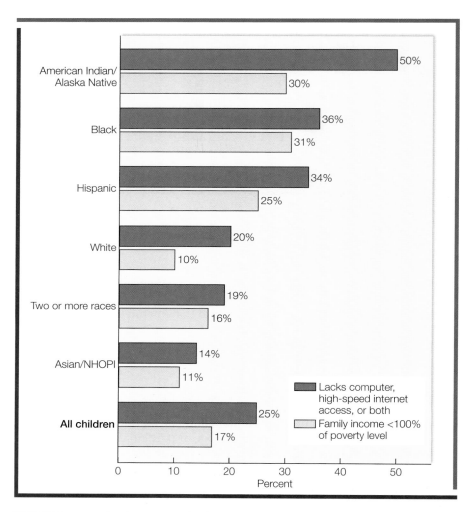

FIGURE A Digital and economic divides of U.S. children 5–17 by race/ethnicity, 2018. Note: NHOPI refers to Native Hawaiian and Other Pacific Islander.

After L. A. Jacobsen. August 18, 2020. "Digital and Economic Divides Put U. S. Children at Greater Educational Risk During the COVID-19 Pandemic." www.prb.org; data from U.S. Census Bureau. 2018. American Community Survey. U.S. Census Bureau, Washington, DC

A digital divide is splitting the United States: Half of Native American children lack access to computers, high-speed internet, or both, as do 36% of Black and 34% of Hispanic children. Among White children, in contrast, only 20% do not have that crucial access.

■ Question

Why do you think the digital divide is also an ethnic/racial divide, and what are the implications for children whose families are not digitally connected?

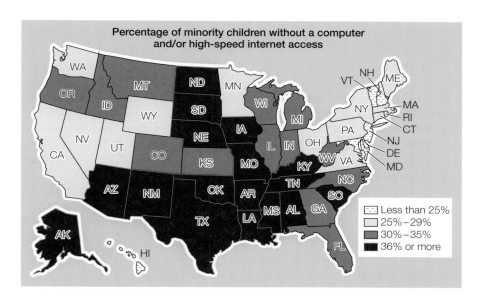

FIGURE B Percentage of minority children (top) and all children (bottom) without a computer, high-speed internet access, or both, by state, 2018.

Data from Population Reference Bureau. "Digital Divide Dashboard: U.S. School-Age Children at Educational Risk Due to COVID-19 Pandemic." https://assets.prb.org/; U.S. Census Bureau. 2018. American Community Survey. U.S. Census Bureau, Washington, DC

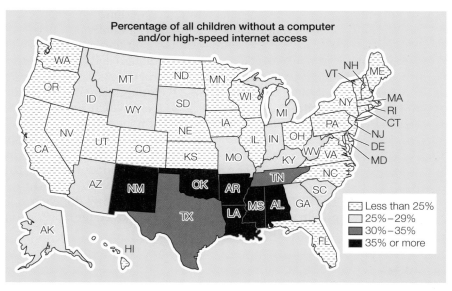

■ Overall, would you say that social media affect your life in a positive or in a negative way?

time their children spend with media and how they use their time. Almost three-quarters of tweens and more than half of teens said their parents had talked to them about the amount of time they spend with media and which content they view (Rideout, 2015).

Of course, these numbers are averages and can vary widely from person to person. Nevertheless, given that young people also spend at least 6 hours a day at school, the time they spend consuming media is dazzling. This content is bound to shape the ways they think and communicate in ways that child development researchers are only beginning to understand.

Access to such a large variety of media and content offers children immense opportunities while at the same time also exposing them to adverse effects. Digital media allow children to pursue interests and study topics they could not pursue on their own or in their classrooms by giving them access to art or other collections, as well as games, apps, and shows that help them develop reading, math, or other skills. Social media often give children a sense of belonging and can connect them to friends as well as family members who live far away. In online interactions, children and youth can hone their social skills and learn to interact with others.

But media also can cause tension within the family. About a third of all teens and parents say they argue about the use of electronic devices daily, and more than three-quarters of parents believe their teens are distracted by the devices when the family is together. However, most families feel that using mobile devices has not changed their relationship with each other or has even made it better (Felt & Robb, 2016).

Researchers and parents are also concerned that the new media are somehow involved in the decrease of empathy they have observed. Over a 30-year period from 1979 to 2009, American college students' empathy for others declined strongly, and particularly did so starting in the year 2000 (Konrath et al., 2011). The use of social media can also possibly lead to feelings of envy or even to what is now widely called "Facebook depression" (Blease, 2015; Yoon et al., 2019) or even to **cyberbullying,** where others purposely spread information that is false or meant to embarrass and humiliate some users in front of others. Around 37% of students today experience cyberbullying at some point in their lives (Hinduja & Patchin, 2019). Parents and educators express concerns that children and young adults sometimes do not understand how their online behavior affects their future reputation and digital footprint.

cyberbullying purposely spreading information on the internet that is false or meant to embarrass and humiliate some users in front of others.

multitask to perform more than one task at the same time.

With so much content to process on so many devices, children (and adults) are developing a greater tendency to **multitask**. Around half of all teens watch TV or use social media at times when doing their homework, and more than half text or listen to music while doing so. But most of them believe engaging in this kind of multitasking does not have a negative effect on their homework (Rideout & Robb, 2019). Teens do a lot of multitasking: In a 2015 study, 76% of 18- to 24-year-olds said they could only get things done when they multitask—twice as many as adults over age 64 (Consumer Insights Microsoft Canada, 2015).

■ Jeremy and his friends frequently communicate via text messages and social media. At least some of the time, face-to-face communication is replaced with onscreen communication. Do you think this has an impact on their friendships and their well-being?

■ Like Anahita, Mireille, and Jane, a large number of young people engage in multitasking when they do their homework. Do you, as well? What do you think is the impact of multitasking on children's learning?

But are younger people really better at multitasking? Many researchers question this conclusion (Rideout, 2015). They believe that switching back and forth between different tasks causes cognitive fatigue, which reduces work speed and efficiency. At this point, researchers are not certain whether multitasking just slows down people's work speed or whether it also results in a deterioration of their performance.

Throughout this book, we discuss questions that bring up many of the topics mentioned here. For example:

- What is the impact on children when the TV is constantly on in their home?
- How do social media affect children's lives?
- Does children's thinking change when they spend a significant amount of time in front of a screen?
- Where do children get their news from? Can they spot fake news, and how do they feel about the news they read?

Review!

What role does the family structure play in a child's development?

■ Children spend lots of time with their *family,* who provides a support network and resources like housing, food, and healthcare.

How do culture and ethnicity influence child development?

■ The *culture and ethnicity* of a child's family influence the family's values, customs, and beliefs as well as many other things that can have a profound impact on children and their well-being.

How do social class and economic factors affect a child's development?

■ The *socioeconomic status* of a family affects the family's ability to afford good-quality housing, food, and everyday items as well as healthcare and good schools. Poverty puts children at higher risk for chronic illnesses, low academic achievement, and teen pregnancy, among other things.

How do the concepts of cohort and generation shape our understanding of child development?

■ The *historical context* in which a child grows up shapes events that happen during childhood. It can leave a lasting impression, influencing attitudes and beliefs as well as health and education.

How do children today use media, and how are they affected by their media use?

■ Today's children have access to and use a multitude of *media* like no generation before them.

■ Media allow them to communicate with friends and family, access information, and develop social as well as leadership skills through online exchange. However, media use can also lead to tension within the family, unproductive *multitasking* habits, *cyberbullying*, and privacy concerns.

Practice!

1. In recent decades, the size of the typical American family has _____ .
   a. become smaller
   b. become larger
   c. stayed the same

2. Based on the way the demographic makeup of the American population is changing today, we can predict that within the next decades _____ .
   a. most people will belong to ethnic minority groups
   b. most people will be of African American descent
   c. most people will be of Asian descent
   d. most people will be of European descent

3. Children born within the same cohort _____ .
   a. were born in roughly the same location
   b. were born at roughly the same time
   c. belong to a single racial group
   d. belong to a single cultural group

4. Use of social media tends to have _____ on empathy for others.
   a. a positive effect
   b. a negative effect
   c. no discernible effect

5. When children multitask, their ability to perform any single task generally _____ .
   a. improves
   b. worsens
   c. stays about the same

What's Your Position?

Does multitasking make people more efficient or less efficient in what they do? These days, teens especially engage routinely in multitasking in a variety of situations: when they do their homework, when they spend time at home with their families, or when they are out with their friends. Professional opinions differ on whether multitasking makes teens more efficient.

Draft a response to this question, using information provided in the chapter and found on some of the websites below. Share and defend your viewpoint in a conversation with two or three of your classmates.

Additional Resources Online

■ "Efficient, Helpful, or Distracting? A Literature Review of Media Multitasking in Relation to Academic Performance," from the *International Journal of Educational Technology in Higher Education*

■ "Media Multitasking and Cognitive, Psychological, Neural, and Learning Differences," from *Pediatrics*

■ "More Tasks, More Ideas: The Positive Spillover Effects of Multitasking on Subsequent Creativity," from the *Journal of Applied Psychology*

■ "The Relationship Between Media Multitasking and Executive Function in Early Adolescents," from the *Journal of Early Adolescence*

■ "Does Media Multitasking Always Hurt? A Positive Correlation Between Multitasking and Multisensory Integration," from *Psychonomic Bulletin & Review*

What's Your Position?

Baby Boomers or Millennials: Who's had it easier? Every generation seems to think they grew up in more challenging circumstances than those faced by other generations. Which generation do you think had/has an easier childhood: Baby Boomers, Millennials, or Gen Z?

Draft a response to this question, using information provided in the chapter and found on some of the websites below. Share and defend your viewpoint in a conversation with two or three of your classmates.

Additional Resources Online

■ "The Unluckiest Generation in U.S. History," from *The Washington Post*

■ "Millennial Life: How Young Adulthood Today Compares with Prior Generations," from Pew Research Center

■ "Did Timing Matter? Life Cycle Differences in Effects of Exposure to the Great Recession," from the U.S. Census Bureau Center for Economic Studies

■ "7 Ways Life Is Harder for Millennials Than It Was for Their Parents," from *Business Insider*

1.3 Key Issues in Child Development

- Tell how children's genes and their environment interact to influence development.
- Explain how a child's development is continuous and how it is discontinuous.
- Compare how early experiences and later experiences are important to child development.

Earlier in the chapter we encountered some questions about the contexts that shape child development—questions about the role of family, culture, and socioeconomic status, for example. These are just a few of the many questions that thread their way through the various theories of development. In addition to these, child development researchers wrestle with a number of overarching questions that shape our thinking about the discipline as a whole. We will consider three of them here, and you will recognize the questions again as you read through the book and become familiar with different researchers, theories, and approaches that attempt to answer these questions.

Question 1: How Do the Environment and Genes Interact to Influence Children's Development?

For millennia, people have questioned whether children's development is influenced more by their fundamental biological makeup (nature) or by their experiences and environment (nurture). Today, this is not a question we ask anymore. We know that both genes and environment influence all living beings. In fact, our experiences and the environment we live in have such a strong impact that they can turn genes on and off in our bodies (O'Donnell & Meany, 2020). For example, Stefano carries a gene that predisposes him to develop diabetes, but he does not actually have diabetes—his gene for diabetes has not been expressed and is thus inactive. It may potentially stay inactive all his life unless some circumstances in Stefano's life cause it to get "switched on." Our home environment and the way family members interact with each other, work environment, stress, diet, lifestyle, and many more factors can influence the activation or deactivation of genes.

So the relationship between genes and the environment is a bidirectional one—our experiences and our environment influence the expression of some of our genes (that is, whether they are "turned on or off"), and our genes and their expression in turn affect our development and thus our life experiences. The field of **epigenetics** investigates the bidirectional relationship between the environment and expression of our genes.

But people's experiences can have far-reaching effects beyond themselves. When genes are flipped on or off in people's eggs or sperm, or in an unborn fetus, our experiences can even affect children who have not yet been born or even conceived. For example, there is some evidence that smoking during pregnancy may activate genes that are responsible for obesity and heart disease (FIGURE 1.8) (Reichetzeder, 2021; Rzehak et al., 2016; Smith & Ryckman, 2015).

The field of epigenetics is a relatively new field, and there is a lot we do not yet know. What we do know is that the interplay between an organism, its genetic

epigenetics the study of the bidirectional relationship between the environment and the expression of genes (that is, the phenotype).

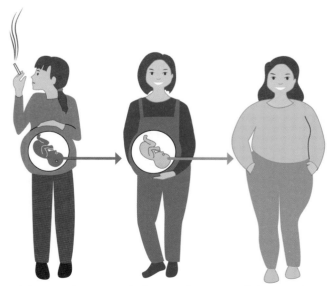

FIGURE 1.8 The diet or lifestyle of a pregnant mother may affect the expression of genes not only in herself, but also in her children and grandchildren.

1st generation   2nd generation   3rd generation

makeup, and its environment is a lot more complex than we thought even a few decades ago. Throughout this book, we will periodically return to the question of how genes and the environment influence children's development and what we can do to enhance the odds that every child has the best chances for optimal development.

Question 2: Is Development Continuous or Discontinuous?

Development can potentially happen in two different ways: It can happen gradually (i.e., continuously) or it can happen discontinuously (in stages) (see FIGURE 1.9).

In **continuous development**, changes are gradual and build on each other. This kind of development can be likened to the growth of a tree that gets larger every day but does not change in character—it is always a tree, though at first a somewhat smaller tree than in later years. Children grow and develop every day at a steady pace, learning new skills and maturing physically. For example, a child acquires more and more words and a deeper understanding of grammar rules and gradually refines her speech.

In **discontinuous** (or stage-like development) **development**, growth and development do not proceed at an even speed but go through stages. The development of a fly goes through different stages, for example: At first, a larva hatches from an egg. During pupation, the larva transforms into a fly, which is a different being from a larva. In child development, each stage is characterized by particular abilities and behaviors that are qualitatively different from the abilities and behaviors a child exhibited before. For example, a young child may not be able to understand that his view of the world differs from that of other people. When a young baby covers his eyes and cannot see anymore, he assumes that he has disappeared to the world, as well. As he gets older, he understands that other people have different viewpoints and perspectives and that he does not disappear just because he himself cannot see anymore. This change is of a qualitative nature.

Development happens both continuously and discontinuously, depending on the processes and skills considered. As we get to know various theories of development in this book, you will see that some of them (like Piaget's and Freud's theories) suggest that children develop in stages. Others, like learning theory, suggest that development is a continuous process.

continuous development
development in which changes are gradual and build on each other.

discontinuous development
development that happens in stages, with each stage bringing about behavior and abilities that differ qualitatively from the behavior and abilities in other stages.

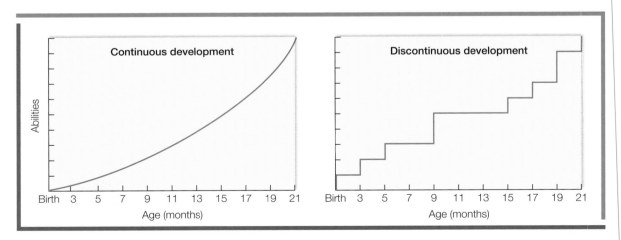

FIGURE 1.9 In continuous development, changes are gradual and build upon each other over time. In discontinuous development, changes are stage-like, and behaviors and abilities differ qualitatively from each other in each stage.

After R. S. Feldman. 2016. *Child Development*, 7th ed. Pearson, New York

Question 3: Are Early or Late Experiences More Important?

In Western countries, people often believe that a child's early years influence development significantly (Lamb & Sternberg, 1992). If the child is subjected to harmful experiences or conditions during the first few years of life, she will be affected by these experiences for life. This perspective has major policy implications, leading to the belief that the state should intervene as early as possible in children's lives to identify children (and their families) in need of additional support. For example, after a review of the research literature the White House under Barack Obama suggested that the "early years in a child's life—when the human brain is forming—represent a critically important window of opportunity to develop a child's full potential and shape key academic, social, and cognitive skills that determine a child's success in school and in life" (White House, 2013). The statement further suggested the importance of improving preschool and childcare quality and explained a new home visitation program for vulnerable children and families.

■ Many cultures of the world believe that young children cannot be taught before the age of 5.

Freud stressed the importance of early experiences in his theory and believed that the personality of a child is mostly developed by age 5. Likewise, Mary Ainsworth, who conducted research on attachment in infants (see also Chapter 7), believed that early experiences have a lasting impact on children.

Many of the world's cultures have a view that is in stark contrast to the Western emphasis on early childhood experiences. In their view, a child only reaches an "age of reason" between ages 5 and 7. Before that age, a child is not even considered teachable and consequently no occurrences before that age will make a lasting impression on the child (Lancy, 2015; Rogoff et al., 1975). In cultures like that of the Chewong in Malaysia or the Kpelle in West Africa, adults do not make efforts to teach young children for that reason. In Yemen, workers do not bother to warn children of the dangers of playing at a construction site because they believe the children have no "aql" (reason) and won't understand anyway (Marchand, 2013). Likewise, some researchers believe that later experiences deserve more attention than they have been given. While they do not disagree that early experiences are important, they feel that later experiences may be just as important (Schaie, 2012). Many of us know people who had a less than ideal start in life and were able to transform their lives later on to live happy, successful, and fulfilled lives.

Ultimately, of course, it is a combination of early and later experiences that shape development. Early experiences, particularly when they are very traumatic or involve severe deprivation (say, growing up during a famine or in an orphanage where children do not receive adequate interpersonal or cognitive stimulation), may well leave lasting effects on children. However, children are also resilient, and in many cases it is possible for them to overcome negative experiences and thrive later on.

Review!

How do children's genes and their environment interact to influence development?

- Our environment and our genes continuously influence each other.
- The field of *epigenetics* investigates how genes and the environment interact and how we can improve health and development of children (and adults) by taking these interactions into account.

In what ways is a child's development continuous, and in what ways is it discontinuous?

- Some of children's abilities and skills develop in a gradual way (*continuous development*) while others develop rather suddenly in discrete stages (*discontinuous development*).
- Child development theories usually represent one of those views on how development proceeds.

In what ways are early experiences important, and in what ways are later experiences important?

- There is an ongoing discussion on whether early or late experiences have the most serious impact on children's development.
- Few people doubt that experiences very early in childhood can have a lasting impact on children.

- We know that children can overcome adverse early life circumstances, which indicates that later experiences are very important as well, and unfortunate events in early childhood do not lead to children being "doomed" for the rest of their lives.

Practice!

1. When we talk about the impact of people's genes on their environment, we are ascribing the effects to _____ .
   a. nature
   b. the nature–nurture debate
   c. nurture
   d. prenatal development

2. A politician who pledges to invest heavily in early childhood education clearly believes in the impact of _____ on children's development.
   a. nature
   b. nurture
   c. intelligence
   d. genes

3. Discontinuous development _____ .
   a. proceeds smoothly
   b. proceeds in stages
   c. proceeds at an even speed
   d. proceeds by changes building on each other

1.4 Milestones: Why We Need Them and What They Mean

milestone significant accomplishments in terms of physical, cognitive and socio-emotional skills that most children can do by a certain age.

When working with or raising children you will frequently come across the concept of **milestones**. The term may be familiar to you from other areas of your life. Generally, milestones represent key steps in completing a project; they may be used to keep people focused and on task and to help them see when they are falling behind schedule.

The same principle applies to child development. In a way, you can see the development of a child as a big project, one that should involve steady progress that can be measured through a series of clearly defined goals. The milestones that define the development of a child are significant accomplishments in physical, cognitive, and socio-emotional growth. These milestones are normally defined by the age at which they can be expected to occur. For example, by 4 months of age, an average child can be expected to roll over from stomach to back.

Pediatricians routinely assess children using established milestones. Parents, too, may be acutely, and anxiously, aware of the milestones their children are expected to reach by certain ages. But it is important to keep in mind that children develop at very different rates. One may begin to walk at 9 months, whereas another may only begin at 17 months. Eight months separate the first steps of these two children, and yet they are both within the normal range of development.

Young children have a lot to learn, and as they work on one skill, the development of another skill may lag somewhat behind. Often, minor delays are not a cause for worry, and parents, educators, and childcare workers can rest assured that children will catch up and develop normally.

At the same time, there are many skills that parents cannot teach their young children easily: How do you teach an infant to smile or make eye contact? How do you teach them to walk if they are not interested and love crawling?

A caregiver's task is not always to teach but to motivate and to provide children with opportunities to develop by learning skills on their own.

Because there is such variability in development, it is important to watch not just for milestones but for signs of delays. Certain delays can be cause for concern: For example, a 2-month-old should react to sudden loud noises. If young children show signs of delay, it is particularly important for parents to talk with a pediatrician or nurse about these observations.

TABLE 1.2 presents significant milestones for children aged 2 months to 5 years, along with possible signs of delay and suggestions for how to help children develop crucial skills at each age.

■ Table 1.2 Developmental Milestones for Children Aged 2 Months to 5 Years

Here are some milestones for various ages. Remember there are many skills children need to learn and countless ways to help young children in their development, so this table just provides a selection. Likewise, there are many more possible signs of delays, but children's development varies tremendously so failure to reach a milestone on time does not necessarily mean the child faces serious developmental issues.

Age 2 months

	Milestones	How you can help	Possible signs of delay
Cognitive	Attends to faces Can recognize people Tries to follow moving objects with eyes Gets fussy when bored	Talk, cuddle, and play with baby	Does not watch moving objects Does not react to loud noises
Language	Turns head toward sounds Makes squealing and gurgling sounds, coos	Smile and praise infant for making sounds Pay attention to when infant tries to communicate through crying and sounds Talk and sing Read books to infant	
Social and emotional	Can calm herself for a short time by sucking on hand Looks at people Smiles at people	Find out what calms your infant and help infant to calm herself Play games like peekaboo	Does not smile at people
Physical	Lifts head Pushes up when lying on stomach	Frequently lay infant on tummy and put toy in front of him to encourage lifting his head Hold interesting toy in front of infant to encourage reaching	Cannot touch mouth with hands In tummy position, cannot hold up head when pushing up with hands

Age 4 months

	Milestones	How you can help	Possible signs of delay
Cognitive	Can reach for toy Can coordinate eyes and hands when reaching for toy Responds to other people	Provide age-appropriate toys like rattles Look at pictures together	Does not watch moving objects
Language	Copies sounds Produces sounds with expression Has different cries for different needs (pain, hunger, etc.)	Talk to baby Copy infant's sounds Praise infant for making sounds	Does not make sounds

■ Table 1.2 (*continued*)

Age 4 months (*continued*)

	Milestones	How you can help	Possible signs of delay
Social and emotional	Imitates facial expressions like smile and frown Enjoys playing with others	Play games like peekaboo Be aware of infant's likes and dislikes	Does not smile at people
Physical	Can independently hold head up steady Can roll from stomach to back Reaches for toys Holds toys and rattles them On stomach, can push up to elbows	Provide toys or objects to reach out for—hold them in front of infant or place them near infant Place rattle in hand and help hold/shake it Stand baby upright with feet on floor	Does not bring objects to mouth Feet do not push down when placed on flat surface

Age 6 months

	Milestones	How you can help	Possible signs of delay
Cognitive	Looks around in environment Shows interest in things that are out of reach and tries to get them Puts objects to mouth	Read picture books together When infant is interested in object in environment, explore it or talk about it together	Does not attempt to reach for objects close by Cannot place objects in mouth
Language	When hearing sounds, reacts by vocalizing Has "conversations" with caregivers in a back-and-forth of sounds Reacts when called by name Practices consonant sounds like "m" and "b"	Have "conversations" by responding to infant's vocalizations Repeat baby's sounds Clearly say simple words when showing objects ("bottle")	Does not react to sounds Cannot produce vowel sounds (like "aaah" or "ooooh")
Social and emotional	Recognizes familiar faces Likes to interact with others Enjoys looking in mirror Reacts when others show emotions	Play with baby often and respond to his actions Be responsive to baby's mood	Does not show interest in caregiver Does not laugh
Physical	Rolls over from back to stomach Starts to sit without support Can support weight on legs when standing	Help baby sit up by holding her or supporting her with pillows Encourage rolling over from front and back by putting toys close by	Can't roll over Tight, stiff muscles Floppy body, no muscle tone Can't bring objects to mouth Does not reach for objects

Age 9 months

	Milestones	How you can help	Possible signs of delay
Cognitive	Puts objects in mouth Can pick up small objects with pincer grasp Plays peekaboo Searches for objects that were hidden while infant watched	Demonstrate cause and effect by dropping items or building a block tower and knocking it over Play peekaboo Read together	Does not engage in back-and-forth games Does not look when others point at objects
Language	Points at objects Imitates sounds Frequently vocalizes ("dadadada" etc.)	Use words to describe objects infant is interested in ("blue bird") Have back-and-forth conversations Imitate infant's sounds	Does not babble

■ Table 1.2 (*continued*)

	Milestones	How you can help	Possible signs of delay
Social and emotional	Prefers some toys over others May show stranger anxiety or cling to known adults	Stay close by while infant explores Have daily routines Express infant's feelings in words	Does not react to own name Does not recognize familiar people
Physical	Can sit without support Crawls Pulls up to stand Can stand holding on to something	Provide safe area to move around Place infant close to objects that can be used for pulling up	Does not sit with help Does not sit with support Cannot bear weight on legs Does not put objects from one hand in the other

Age 1 year

	Milestones	How you can help	Possible signs of delay
Cognitive	Imitates gestures Bangs things together Begins to understand what things are for and uses them correctly: a cup is for drinking Finds things that were hidden while infant was watching	Read aloud often Ask child to turn pages Ask child to label objects in book	Does not search for things hidden while infant was looking Does not point
Language	Responds to simple requests Tries to imitate words Uses gestures like waving good bye Says a few words like "mama"	Clearly say no when child behaves in unwanted way Talk about what you're doing, e.g., while shopping	Does not use gestures Does not use single words Loses skills
Social and emotional	Shy around strangers Shows distress when parents leave Tries to get attention of others by making noises or performing actions Helps get dressed by holding out arm/leg	Give infant time to get used to new caregivers Give infant hugs and kisses to reinforce good behavior Provide objects like plush toy or blankie for comfort when in new environment	
Physical	Can sit up without support Walks holding on to furniture ("cruising") Beginning to take a few steps without holding on to anything Can stand alone	Provide toys that child can manipulate with hands Provide safe space for moving around Provide push toys Provide objects to play "music" with	Cannot crawl Cannot stand with support

Age 1.5 years

	Milestones	How you can help	Possible signs of delay
Cognitive	Understands the purpose of everyday objects Scribbles Follows 1-step verbal commands ("Come here")	Discipline by praising rather than punishing Provide dolls and plush animals for pretend play Hide objects and ask child to find them Provide blocks, balls, and puzzles to teach cause and effect	Does not point to objects Does not know purpose of familiar objects Does not imitate others
Language	Says several words Points to communicate wants and needs Says no and shakes head for "no"	Repeat your child's words Use simple sentences and questions Name objects in environment and in books	Does not learn new words Speaks less than six words

(Continued)

■ **Table 1.2** (*continued*)

Age 1.5 years (*continued*)

	Milestones	How you can help	Possible signs of delay
Social and emotional	Hands objects to others as play Affectionate with familiar people Simple pretend play (like comforting a doll) Explores independently but with adult close by	Describe and explain emotions ("You are sad because Tim took your ball") Show appropriate behaviors like hugging a sad person	Does not care or notice when caregiver leaves room or comes back
Physical	Can walk alone Starting to walk up steps and run Eats with spoon and drinks from cup	Encourage independent eating Provide toys to roll, kick, and push	Does not walk

Age 2 years

	Milestones	How you can help	Possible signs of delay
Cognitive	Can point to objects when asked Speaks sentences of 2–4 words Can follow simple instructions	Give child small chores Ask child to speak rather than point Provide puzzles with different shapes and colors	Does not use everyday items like brushes correctly Cannot follow simple instructions Loses skills
Language	Repeats words overheard in conversations Can name body parts Knows names of household members	Teach names of objects, animals, body parts, etc. If child makes mistakes, repeat word or sentence correctly	Does not imitate words (or actions) No 2-word sentences
Social and emotional	Imitates others Is excited when with other children Gets more independent At times defiant Begins to include others in play	Provide toys for playdates—children mostly play alongside and not with each other Praise when child follows directions or behaves well	
Physical	Can stand on tiptoes Can kick a ball Walks up and down stairs with help Climbs on furniture without help Can draw straight lines and circles	Provide blocks and art materials like paint and crayons Ask child to carry small things, turn pages in book, etc. Kick ball back and forth with child	Cannot walk steadily

Age 3 years

	Milestones	How you can help	Possible signs of delay
Cognitive	Can use buttons and levers on toys Solves puzzles with 4 pieces Can copy a circle Can build a block tower with at least 7 blocks Can turn door handles	Read every day Give 2-step instructions ("Take the brush and give it to Anna")	Does not understand simple instructions Does not make eye contact Does not engage in pretend play
Language	Follows 2- or 3-step instructions Can name a friend as well as own name, age, and sex Speaks clearly enough that strangers can understand Speaks 2–3 sentences in conversations	Play counting games Identify feelings in books and everyday life situations	Drooling Very hard to understand Does not use sentences

■ **Table 1.2** *(continued)*

	Milestones	How you can help	Possible signs of delay
Social and emotional	Shows affection for others Can take turns during play Reacts to other people's emotions Displays wide range of emotions	Let child play with agemates Help child solve problems when upset Talk about emotions and their meaning Set limits	Loses skills
Physical	Can dress/undress self Can climb and run Uses stairs with one foot on each step	Provide craft materials Teach child to hold on to railing when using stairs Play outside	Finds using stairs difficult

Age 4 years

	Milestones	How you can help	Possible signs of delay
Cognitive	Correctly names some colors Engages in pretend play Understands "same" and "different" Can follow 3-part commands ("Get up, put your shoes on, and get your jacket") Can remember parts of a story	Engage in pretend and fantasy games with child Give child simple choices Count things together Provide puzzles	Loses skills she once had No pretend or fantasy play Cannot follow 3-part commands
Language	Sentences are five to six words long Strangers can understand child Can tell stories Can say first and last name	Encourage child to use words Refrain from using parentese ("I want you to..." instead of "Mommy wants you to...") Read books together	Errors using "me" and "you" Cannot retell stories Speaks unclearly so strangers cannot understand her
Social and emotional	Likes to play with other children Tries to negotiate in conflict Likes doing new things Often not sure what is real and what is "pretend"	Encourage child to share and take turns Let child solve conflicts with friends	Does not want to sleep or use the toilet No interest in other children
Physical	**Gross motor skills:** Hops and stands on one foot for several seconds Catches a bounced ball most of the time Goes up and down stairs without assistance **Fine motor skills:** Uses scissors Draws people with 2–4 body parts Begins to copy some letters Draws circles and squares	Provide toys like balls, tricycles, etc. Give opportunity to play outside Do things like somersaults, skipping, and hopping Provide crayons and markers Provide child-size tweezers and objects to pick up Do crafts Provide blocks	Cannot jump in place Cannot ride tricycle Cannot throw ball overhand Cannot hold crayon between thumb and fingers Has trouble scribbling Cannot copy a circle Cannot stack four blocks

Age 5 years

	Milestones	How you can help	Possible signs of delay
Cognitive	Counts to at least 10 Draws people with at least 6 body parts Able to copy shapes like a triangle Can write some numbers/letters	When reading, ask child for prediction of what will happen next Let child look at pictures in book and tell story Help child solve own problems Introduce days of the week Teach concepts	Easily distracted Cannot concentrate more than 5 minutes Loses skills

(Continued)

■ **Table 1.2** (*continued*)

Age 5 years (*continued*)			
	Milestones	**How you can help**	**Possible signs of delay**
Language	Speaks clearly Can tell stories using full sentences Knows name and address Able to use future tense ("We will go swimming")	Teach child name and address Praise child for doing things right; do not pay much attention to swear words	Doesn't know own first and last name Does not talk about experiences Uses plurals or past tense incorrectly
Social and emotional	Likes to please others Aware of gender Can distinguish between reality and pretending Increasingly likely to agree with rules	Arrange playdates Give child choices: what to wear, what to play, etc.	Shows only limited emotions Behaves in extreme ways (sad, aggressive, anxious) Very withdrawn Does not respond (or hardly responds) to people
Physical	**Gross motor skills:** Can stand on one foot for more than 10 seconds Hops and does somersaults Uses toilet independently **Fine motor skills:** Uses fork and spoon	Give ample opportunities to play outside and at playgrounds Teach child how to use swings Practice bike riding Provide craft materials	Cannot wash hands or brush teeth without assistance Does not draw pictures

Source: Centers for Disease Control and Prevention. 2009. "Milestone Moments." www.cdc.gov

1.5 Summing It Up: Facts That Will Guide You through This Book

Before we delve into the science of child development in the next chapters, let us review some of the main points we discussed in this chapter. These are points that you will encounter over and over again as you read this book, and they will help you place the information you learn into a big picture.

- Physical, cognitive, and socio-emotional development are all intricately intertwined with each other. We separate these domains in this book to give your learning some structure. However, children develop as a whole, and progress they make in any domain will influence their development in other domains.

- Our health and development are, to some extent, determined by our genetic makeup. However, children are influenced significantly by their surroundings. Their family, their culture, the time and historical circumstances, their wealth or poverty, and how they spend their free time are just some factors that influence how children will grow and prosper. We can actively influence these factors and make a difference in the lives of children.

- Children are extraordinarily resilient. Harsh circumstances, experiences, disabilities, or diseases in childhood do not doom a child. They may well take a toll or leave lasting marks, but many children have grown to be well-adjusted adults despite the challenges they faced.

- Children vary widely in their development. Some walk early, some walk very late. Some are very curious and outgoing, others are very reserved and shy. The development of a child always has to be seen within the context of that child—for example, was she born prematurely, is she healthy, does she grow up in a healthy family that interacts much with her? A child lagging behind in some skills may well catch up sometime later, especially if given appropriate assistance. Table 1.2 gives you an overview of some milestones of development as well as "red flags" to watch out for. There also are suggestions on how to develop skills in children.

- Today, almost all countries, including the United States, as a nation of immigrants, are becoming more and more diverse. Culture and ethnicity influence the development and lives of children in many ways. It is important to be aware of these effects when working with children and their families.

18 months later: What happened to Lucia

It's been a year and a half since Lucia was diagnosed with dyslexia. In the past months, Lucia's life has changed significantly, and much for the better. Once her family and doctors were able to pinpoint why she was struggling at school, they arranged for a special kind of tutoring program for children with dyslexia. Within a few weeks, Lucia started to make progress and her reading abilities improved, though she still lags behind her classmates in reading ability. Moreover, once informed about her diagnosis, her teachers were able to provide much better support for her as well. They made sure she did not have to read out loud in class—a situation that always had been particularly stressful for her. She is now also provided with extra time for testing and is not graded on spelling, which has helped her deal with her test anxiety and improve her grades. But perhaps most importantly, she is much happier because she doesn't feel anymore that something is wrong with her as a person. She is neither stupid nor lazy, and she's well on her way to becoming the best student she can possibly be. ■ ■ ■ ■

© iStock/Wavebreakmedia

Overview

Theories of Child Development

The life of a child across generations

It's bedtime at the Morasi–Fletcher household. Four-year-old Luisa is in bed, and her mother, Jennifer, is getting set to read her a story. Luisa makes a request, but tonight Jennifer has something special in mind. She pulls out a book she has kept from her own childhood—her favorite book growing up. It's about a country "postman" and his encounters with various fairy tale characters he meets as he delivers the mail. Jennifer has been waiting for just the right moment to introduce Luisa to the book she cherished as a child.

But Luisa is restless. She doesn't understand what a "postman" is. She wants to read *her* favorite book—the one featuring characters from a TV show she watches. After a few frustrating pages, Jennifer sadly sets the postman book aside in favor of the book Luisa picked out.

Downstairs, Jennifer's partner, Felicia, is watching TV with their son, Marco. Marco is 11—quite a bit older than Luisa—and he is obsessed with movies and shows from or about the 1980s. He marvels at the idea of a world without cell phones and other digital technology and frequently asks Felicia questions about what they're watching—"Was it *really* like that? Was there no internet *at all?*" Jennifer herself has no great nostalgia for the 1980s, the decade when she was born, but Marco's fascination makes her thoughtful about how different the lives of children are from one generation to the next.

2.1 The Long Way toward Child Development as a Science

■ Recall how views of childhood changed over the centuries and paved the way for the scientific study of child development.

Early Views of Childhood

The nature of childhood has probably never changed faster or more dramatically than it has over recent decades. Yet if we take a step back to get an even broader view, we can see that over the past centuries there have been enormous changes not only in how children spend their everyday lives but also in how children are viewed by society. For example, a society that perceives children as little adults will treat children much differently than a society that views children as immature persons who need to be protected and given space and opportunity to develop. Here are some accounts of children's lives in Britain during the Industrial Revolution, which began around the 1780s. During this time, many children as young as 5 years old worked very long hours:

> When I was seven years old I went to work at Mr. Marshall's factory at Shrewsbury. If a child became sleepy, the overlooker touched the child on the shoulder and said "come here." In the corner of the room there was an iron cistern filled with water. He took the boy by the legs and dipped him in the cistern, and then sent him back to work. (Jonathan Downe, interviewed in 1832; quoted in Trueman, 2016)

> We went to the mill at five in the morning. We worked until dinner time and then to nine or ten at night; on Saturday it could be till eleven and often till twelve at night. We were sent to clean the machinery on the Sunday. (Unnamed man who had worked in a mill as a child, interviewed in 1849; quoted in Trueman, 2016)

> The smallest children in the factories were scavengers. . . . they go under the machine, while it is going. . . . it is very dangerous when they first come, but they become used to it. (Charles Aberdeen, who worked in a Manchester cotton factory, writing in 1832; quoted in Trueman, 2016)

Compare these accounts to the memories of a girl who grew up in the early 1980s:

> Shortly after my 6th birthday, I started going to school. In first grade particularly, school hours were quite short. We went to school between 8 and 9 in the morning and never came back home later than 12:30 p.m. The rest of the day we spent playing. There were lots of kids on my block, and we were outside playing and riding bikes. We would ride all around town and explore the fields and woods that surrounded town. Once a week, I had a group lesson to learn the recorder, which I liked quite a bit. I also liked going to the kids' gymnastics program, which took place once a week as well. My dad would always come back home from work in the city with the 4:38 p.m. train. I loved biking to the train station to pick him up.

Comparing these accounts, it is not hard to see how much has changed in the way children live and grow up in Western countries. In fact, even the later account from the 1980s depicts a childhood that is very different from childhood today, where our "digital natives" spend much less

■ During the Industrial Revolution, many young children were expected to work long hours to help support their families.

time outside and routinely use digital devices for their entertainment. Children's lives reflect the expectations of the society they grow up in: How should they grow up? How should they be treated? What should they learn?

How adults view children has changed over time, with dramatic consequences for the lives of children. These changing attitudes are reflected in the progress of child development as a science. In this chapter, we will look at the factors that have shaped the modern science of child development, from the philosophers who first reflected on what it means to be a child to the beginnings of scientific observation and study. Subsequently, we will get to know prominent theories of child development that have shaped thinking in the field and which we will encounter many times throughout this book.

■ Child's play in the 1980s. How does this differ from the lives of North American children a century earlier? Does it differ markedly from the lives of children today?

The Emergence of Child Development as a Science

How adults in a society think about children and childhood influences how their society as a whole treats children. Which legal status and which protections should children be given? What social policies should be adopted to support and educate children? What approaches should families take to raising their children? The same is true for researchers in the field of child development: The questions they ask very much depend on how they view childhood.

When people in Western cultures think about children and childhood today, they often say that childhood is a special time that is marked by children's immaturity and adults' responsibility to tend to and support them. However, this has not always been the case, nor is this view shared by all cultures around the world. Before exploring prevailing approaches to the study of child development today, let us consider how people viewed childhood in earlier centuries.

In the Europe of the late Middle Ages, little ones were tended to until the age of around 7, which was considered to be the "age of reason." Afterward, they were treated as adults and were often expected to work and earn their subsistence (Ariès, 1962; Tuchman, 1979). In sixteenth-century England, for example, parents of all classes used to send their 8-year-olds to serve in another household or to work in an apprenticeship for a number of years. Without the ability to read or write, children had no means to communicate with their families at home, even if they were just a few towns away (Kremer, 2014). Until the eighteenth century, children were often viewed as little adults, and people did not think of "childhood" as a distinct period in life.

In Europe, views of childhood began to change with the emergence of modern philosophy. *John Locke* (1632–1704) suggested that anything could become of young children—it was their experiences that made them into the persons they were. This idea will come up again later in the chapter, when we discuss behaviorism. In contrast, *Jean-Jacques Rousseau* (1712–1778) believed that children are basically good and will develop into persons of good character and morals as long as they are not exposed to corrupting circumstances in their environment. Ultimately, neither Locke nor Rousseau were correct. Today, many people believe that human nature is neither all good nor all bad, and what becomes of children is influenced not only by their experiences but also by their genes.

In the nineteenth century, *Charles Darwin* (1809–1882) published a biographical sketch of his infant son (also called a "baby biography"). At that point,

■ The Austrian Royal Family, circa 1764. During this time, children were dressed just like adults, and few concessions were made to give them what we consider today a childhood.

© World History Archive/Alamy Stock Photo

people began to recognize the scientific value of writing down details of infant development. It was American psychologist *G. Stanley Hall* (1844–1924) who first systematically used questionnaires to explore children's development ("Child psychology," 2017; "G. Stanley Hall," 2017). Around the same time, laws were gradually introduced to protect child factory workers, and compulsory schooling was introduced in many European countries and the United States. Childhood was increasingly seen as a special phase in life. Researchers started studying childhood and child development more scientifically. Their ideas and research led to the development of exhaustive theories on child development, some of which have significantly influenced the field. In the next section, we will explore some of the most important theories in more detail.

Review!

How did views of childhood change over the course of centuries and pave the way for the scientific study of child development?

■ Views of childhood and children have changed throughout human history. Even today, different cultures have different views of childhood.

■ Throughout the Middle Ages and up to the eighteenth century, children were often viewed as little adults. Consequently, they dressed and worked like adults as well.

■ Philosophers such as John Locke and Jean-Jacques Rousseau started changing the prevalent view of childhood, with Locke suggesting that children were shaped by their environment and Rousseau proposing that children are intrinsically good. Increasingly methodological work eventually led to the development of the first exhaustive theories of child development.

Practice!

1. In the nineteenth century, _____ became a popular way of chronicling the development of young children.
   a. baby books
   b. baby biographies
   c. baby stories
   d. repeated testing

2. In the view of philosopher _____ , children are basically good human beings and turn to immoral behavior only if degrading life circumstances lead them to act this way.
   a. Jean-Jacques Rousseau
   b. John Locke
   c. Aristotle
   d. Immanuel Kant

What's Your Position?

What age do you think is too young to work? Fourteen is generally the minimum age of employment in the United States, but younger people can work in certain jobs—such as delivering newspapers, or on a farm or in a store owned by their family. Is it good for children as young as 14 to work—to gain employment experience, to make money, to develop maturity—or should childhood be protected from these "adult" responsibilities?

Draft a quick response to this question, drawing on information presented in this chapter and in the articles below. Then share and defend your viewpoint in a conversation with two or three of your classmates. How did your viewpoint change after your conversation?

Additional Resources Online

■ "Beneficial 'child labor': The impact of adolescent work on future professional outcomes," from *Research in the Sociology of Work*

■ "Adolescent work, vocational development, and education," from *Review of Educational Research*

■ "The impact of adolescent work in family business on child–parent relationships and psychological well-being," from *Family Business Review*

2.2 Theories in Child Development

■ Identify why it might be helpful to consider more than one theory when explaining child development.

Why We Need Theories

Six-year-old Archer is midway through his kindergarten year. While he has fun going to school, he does not do so well academically. The children get a list of sight words they have to learn each month, but Archer has trouble recognizing them. He also gets distracted easily and works fast and superficially, so when the children do math and count objects on their worksheets, he usually doesn't arrive at the right solution.

At this point, Archer's teacher is not concerned. She suggests he may simply need more time to mature. Archer's mom, Isadora, feels that Archer may have learning issues and should get help to work things out early before he encounters more serious issues later on. Archer's grandmother Daisy disagrees. She keeps reminding Isadora that Archer's father never did well at school. She doesn't think there's anything to be done; after all, some people just aren't made for school, and "the apple doesn't fall far from the tree." Who is right?

Both Isadora and Daisy have strong beliefs about Archer's academic achievement. They have theories about why Archer isn't doing well in kindergarten. And they have views on whether his academic career is already doomed or whether he possibly can become, with some help, a better student. In our everyday lives, we all have lots of theories about why things happen or how they happen. These theories help us explain and understand what we see. Even people with no background in child development have expectations about when a child should start to speak, which skills are important for a child to learn and which are not, and how a child should interact with friends. These theories are called *lay theories*, and they often guide people's thinking and behavior. They help people understand their world, predict future events, and feel in control of their lives.

© Suzanne Tucker/Shutterstock.com

■ Six-year-old Archer gets distracted at school easily. He may sit and daydream while other children complete their worksheets. Once he gets himself to complete the sheets, he often works so fast that his work is dotted with mistakes. Do you think he'll mature and grow out of these habits, or will he be able to conquer them with some intervention? Or are some children just not made for school?

Scientific theories share many of the goals of lay theories. They are sets of principles that describe phenomena, explain them, and make predictions. But unlike lay theories, a scientific theory needs to be testable. That is, you need to be able to make a prediction on the basis of the theory about the relationships between different variables you intend to study. These predictions are also called **hypotheses**. Research is then carried out to verify whether the hypothesis can be confirmed. The research results can help confirm, disconfirm, or modify the theory. For example, researchers might hypothesize that encouragement and rewards help children learn new behaviors. This hypothesis can be tested in experiments to see if it holds up in real life. If the experiments generate unexpected results, the researchers may change or even abandon their theory. Ultimately, researchers aim to use theories to derive new knowledge that can be applied to practical problems we face in our lives.

Among the many theories in child development, certain ones have played a greater role in shaping the evolution of the field as a whole. Throughout this book, we will encounter these theories again and again as we discuss various aspects of child development. In the sections that follow, I will introduce you to these theories. We will consider these theories in chronological order, starting with the earliest ones. By looking at the theories in the order in which they were developed, we can see how they reflect an increasingly refined understanding of child development and how some of them even build on each other.

No theory presents a final view on child development; rather, each one is a reflection of how childhood and development are viewed at a particular time. You will also see that theories do not cover all aspects of development, but rather place an emphasis on particular questions. The theories we will discuss can be grouped into five different approaches to development (approaches can be represented by one or more theories):

- psychoanalytic approaches,
- learning approaches,
- cognitive approaches,
- contextual approaches, and
- evolutionary approaches.

scientific theory a set of ideas designed to explain a phenomenon and make predictions about it.

■■

hypothesis a testable prediction about the relationship between at least two variables.

■■

Evaluating Theories and Research

There are many valid approaches to studying child development

As you can tell, there are many different approaches used to investigate child development. You may wonder whether there is an approach that stands out from or is better than all of the others. The answer is no: There is no one theory or approach that is accepted by all and that has no responsible critics.

It can be difficult to compare different approaches because they focus on different aspects of development (see also Table 2.5):

- Psychodynamic approaches focus on unconscious factors and emphasize early childhood experiences.
- Learning approaches emphasize the influence of the environment on observable behavior.

- Cognitive approaches center on mental representations and processes.
- Contextual approaches assign much importance to our surroundings, like culture and our interactions with other people.
- Evolutionary approaches consider the effects of events in prehistoric times and the struggle to survive.

How, then, should we evaluate different approaches? One thing to keep in mind is that theories and approaches often go through cycles of popularity, just like clothing styles or music. A traditional theory may be displaced by a new approach that comes into vogue because it is new and exciting. After a time, the newer theory may give way to something else, or researchers may find new ways to apply the more traditional theory. Early in the twentieth century, psychodynamic approaches were at the forefront of psychology, but by the middle of the century they had been displaced by an emphasis on observable behavior, which led to the flourishing of behaviorism. Through the criticism of behaviorism's mechanistic view of a person, learning theories and cognitive theories came to rise. Today, neuroscience and evolutionary approaches are gaining in popularity.

Ultimately, we may conclude that while no one approach is best, each has something of benefit to contribute to our understanding of child development: They all ask different questions and use different methodologies to answer those questions. After all, when you ask a question, it makes sense to consider the answers from multiple viewpoints to gain a more nearly complete picture of the situation. Children are embedded in their environment, but they also have feelings and thoughts as well as genetic predispositions. Considering children from only one perspective does not do them justice in their complexity as human beings. So before you accept any answer, carefully consider whether it makes sense and holds up to critical examination.

The ability to evaluate research articles is an important skill to learn

Writing and publishing research papers is an important way for researchers to share their ideas with others. It gives other researchers an opportunity to critically assess the work and to point out weaknesses or identify needed revisions. Articles also may inspire new studies. Through this exchange of ideas and opinions, theories can be refined or, if necessary, rejected. However, being able to read and evaluate research articles is also important if you are a professional working in applied fields. You might wonder whether a particular treatment approach is appropriate for a certain disorder, what the impact of physical punishment on the well-being of children is, or how bilingualism influences the language development of preschoolers. Research also informs decision-makers in companies or the government.

Some of the main journals in the field of child development are *Child Development*, *Developmental Psychology*, *Infant Behavior and Development*, *Human Development*, and the *International Journal of Behavioral Development*. Other journals that may not focus exclusively on children but that may still contain valuable articles include *Sex Roles*, the *Journal of Consulting and Clinical Psychology*, and the *Journal of Marriage and Family*. If you are interested in literature reviews, you may want to consult the *Psychological Bulletin*, *Developmental Review*, or *Perspectives on Psychological Science*.

You will be able to obtain many articles through your campus library. If you cannot get the articles through your library, you can try to retrieve them through other resources like Google Scholar, PsycINFO, or academia .edu, where academics share their research papers. However, keep in mind that not everything you read can be taken at face value. Evaluating the credibility of a paper is thus an important skill you will need over and over again. Here are a few points that will help you evaluate research papers (Hulme, 2004).

CONSIDER THE AUTHOR   Is the author an expert in the field, or is it someone with few credentials or a lack of experience in the topic? If you do not know whether the author is an expert, you can conduct research online to see what work the author has done, whether others have cited the author's work, and which institutions the author is affiliated with.

What is the motivation of the author? For example, is the author paid by a drug company to report on a study that tests one of the company's drugs? Or has the study been funded by an organization that might have a particular agenda? Sometimes, the opinions people state may be influenced by other (and not necessarily obvious) factors like political or religious convictions or financial interests.

LOOK AT THE PUBLICATION DATE AND VENUE   When was the paper written? Some fields may have fewer practicing researchers, so the pace at which new findings are made is rather slow. In that case, a paper 15 years old may still contain lots of valuable information and be considered recent in relative terms. Other fields move very quickly, and papers written 15 or even 10 years ago are hopelessly outdated.

Where was the paper published? Many academic journals ask researchers from the author's field to read and comment on the article before it is published. This is a process known as *peer review*. Peer review acts as quality control: If enough reviewers raise serious concerns about the author's research, the article may not be published. Articles in newspapers or magazines may not have been subjected to such crucial review and thus may be more likely to contain errors. Because newspaper and magazine articles are usually written for a non-academic audience, they may oversimplify findings so that the conclusions one draws from them may be inaccurate.

EXAMINE THE STUDY IN DETAIL   Start with the theoretical basis: On what theory is the study based? Do the research question and the hypothesis follow logically from the theory? Can you draw a conclusion about the theory when you read whether the hypotheses have been supported or not supported?

Next, look at the *sample* (that is, the pool of participants for the study): Is it representative or at least adequate? For example, research results from studies conducted on adults cannot necessarily be applied to children, just as results from Western cultures cannot necessarily be generalized without reservation to non-Western cultures. Is the sample large enough to be considered representative of the larger population? (This can be determined by using a statistical technique called *power analysis*.) Keep in mind that the composition of a sample can be biased by factors like how the data were collected (online, by phone, in person) and whether participants were paid for participating.

Was the research design chosen to answer the question the paper set out to answer? Correlational studies, for example, generally cannot make any firm conclusions about the causes of a particular phenomenon. Likewise, it is hard to draw general conclusions from case studies that evaluate data from only one person.

Look for measurement issues. For instance, did the author carefully define (or *operationalize*) the variables that were studied, and were these variables measured in a reliable (consistent) and valid way? The *reliability* of a result depends on whether key concepts have been clearly defined and then measured in a consistent way, so that a test that is administered twice will give comparable results. *Validity* means that a test really measures what it is supposed to measure. For example, how does a study investigating empathy in preschoolers define empathy, and was empathy measured in a reliable way?

Finally, assess the results and conclusion. Can the results be generalized (applied universally) to the population from which the sample in the study was drawn? You can only generalize results to a group of people that is similar to the participants in the study. Does the author discuss the results that were unexpected as well as those that were in line with the author's expectations? Authors may focus on the results that confirm their hypotheses and neglect unexpected results.

Review!

Why might it be helpful to consider more than one theory when explaining development?

■ Each approach highlights specific elements and mechanisms in human development.

■ The approaches complement each other and explain different aspects of development. Which approach is best thus depends on the question we seek to answer.

What's Your Position?

Do children benefit from structured activities? Felicia is on her way to pick up her son Marco. It's Wednesday, so he has an after-school session with the math tutor. After Felicia picks him up, they'll just have time for a quick bite to eat before she takes him to his tae kwon do class. As she drives to the tutor, Felicia marvels at how different her son's childhood is from her own. She and her friends used to engage for hours after school in unstructured

play; she can't help but wonder if all of these structured, adult-supervised activities—Spanish club, soccer, drum lessons—are too much for an 11-year-old boy like Marco. What do you think: Do structured activities make young people better prepared for their lives as adults, or do they rob them of the experiences that make childhood so special? Draft a response and then consult some of the sources below to see if your opinion changes.

Additional Resources Online

■ "Less-structured time in children's daily lives predicts self-directed executive functioning," from *Frontiers in Psychology*

■ "The 3 travel goals that will boost your child's brain," from *The Guardian*

■ "Benefits of structured play for young children," from VeryWellChildren

■ "How was the weekend? How the social context underlies weekend effects in happiness and other emotions for US workers," from the *Public Library of Science*

■ "Ode to positive constructive daydreaming," from *Frontiers in Psychology*

2.3 Psychodynamic Approaches

■ Explain psychodynamic approaches to child development and name the leading theorists.

Psychodynamic theories stress the importance of unconscious factors that influence our behavior and well-being as well as relationships with others. They emphasize how early childhood experiences contribute to the way our personalities develop.

psychoanalytic theory Freud's theory that human behavior and personality are rooted in unconscious thoughts, drives, and desires.

Freud's Psychoanalytic Theory

Sigmund Freud (1856–1939) trained as a physician in Vienna, Austria. Observing his adult patients convinced him that their personality as well as the problems they experienced could be traced to experiences in their early childhood. In his **psychoanalytic theory**, he suggested that all behavior is rooted in unconscious thoughts and drives. According to Freud (1917), our personality consists of three parts: the *id*, the *ego*, and the *superego*. The *id* represents our instincts, which are present from the day we are born. It channels our drives for aggression, hunger and thirst, sex, and so on. Its main goal is to satisfy our desires. The *superego* develops from the values we learn from parents, teachers, and society. It acts as our conscience. The *ego* strives to fulfill our desires, but wants to do so in a realistic way. It mediates between the infantile desires of the id and the moral constraints set by the superego (our conscience).

Freud believed that each person goes through a series of five psychosexual stages in their development. Each stage is characterized

■ Sigmund Freud with two of his grandsons. Freud developed his theory of childhood psychosexual stages as a way to explain adult behavior.

■ **Table 2.1** Stages in Freud's and Erikson's Theories

	Freud's Psychoanalytic Theory			Erikson's Psychosocial Theory	
Age	**Stage**	**Characteristics**		**Stage (Conflict)**	**Goal**
Birth–1.5 years	Oral	The child derives pleasure from the mouth, including lips and tongue, engaging in such activities as licking, sucking, and feeding.		Trust vs. mistrust	By experiencing predictable and reliable care from parents and immediate caregivers, the infant will develop trust in others.
1.5–3 years	Anal	The child derives pleasure from the anus and the activities associated with toilet training, like controlling eliminations.		Autonomy vs. shame	By accepting parental limits around issues such as napping and toilet training, the child will learn self-control and will become more independent and confident.
3–6 years	Phallic	The child derives pleasure from genital stimulation, becomes aware of sex and gender roles, and identifies with the same-sex parent as a role model.		Initiative vs. guilt	Through play and the imitation of adults, children will learn to assert themselves and make their own decisions.
6 years–puberty	Latency	Sexuality plays a minor role in development, giving way to growth of social and intellectual skills.		Industry vs. inferiority	Through a period of instruction, children will acquire skills and knowledge while learning the value of productivity.
Puberty onward (Freud) 12–18 years (Erikson)	Genital	Interest in sexuality resumes, now focused on other people, with the ultimate goal of establishing a partnership.		Identity vs. role confusion	During adolescence, the individual will develop a sense of self by learning and making decisions about the roles the individual will take on as an adult.
18-40 years (Young adulthood)				Intimacy vs. isolation	The individual will establish intimate relationships with others.
40-65 years (Adulthood)				Generativity vs. stagnation	The individual will give back to society by raising children, working, and becoming involved in the community.
65 years and up (Mature adulthood)				Ego integrity vs. despair	The individual will feel content in reflecting on accomplishments and contributions made earlier in life and will develop wisdom.

by a focus on a particular body area that is a source of frustration and pleasure (see **TABLE 2.1**). If a person's needs either are not met or are overindulged at any stage, the person may not be able to move on successfully to the next stage. This can have lasting consequences for that person's personality.

Critics of Freud have argued that he overemphasized the role of sexual instincts in development and that many parts of his theory cannot be scientifically tested. Many psychologists dismiss his theory, partly because there is no proof of the existence of the id, ego, and superego or that children indeed go through the psychosexual stages he suggested. That said, Freud was the one to first bring to our attention the importance of unconscious processes in our mind. Modern research has shown that unconscious processes play an important role in our everyday lives, whether we unconsciously process information or use our procedural memory to carry out tasks like tying our shoes or driving without thinking (Pesciarelli et al., 2021; Wyer, 2014).

Erikson's Psychosocial Theory

Freud's ideas influenced the thinking of Erik Erikson (1902–1994), who practiced as a child analyst in Boston after immigrating to the United States from Germany. However, Erikson's theory differs from Freud's in two main aspects:

1. Erikson believed that behavior is driven by our relationships and the need to interact with others, rather than sexual drives.

2. Erikson's stages continue into adulthood, rather than being limited to youth.

According to Erikson's **psychosocial theory** (Erikson & Erikson, 1998; Mooney, 2013), development goes through eight stages. In each stage, an identity crisis has to be resolved before a person can continue to the next stage (see Table 2.1). By successfully resolving these crises, a person is able to accomplish the goals of each stage (which include such things as establishing trusting relationships with others and building confidence to navigate a way through life). The first stage (trust vs. mistrust) is the most important of all stages, because infants' experiences during this stage will shape their worldview as well as their personalities. Appropriate responses to children's needs (for food, safety, affection, etc.) ensure that children come to trust their caregivers. If infants' needs are not consistently met during this phase, they will develop a mistrust of others.

Erikson's work has had great influence on the thinking of other researchers. Nevertheless, it has been criticized for not giving enough attention to the influence of emotional and cognitive factors in shaping development. There are many details he does not specify, such as which experiences are important for a person to develop optimally and move on to the next stage, or why a child needs to develop feelings of trust before they can move on to the next stage to develop autonomy. Like Freud's theory, Erikson's psychosocial theory is hard to test scientifically.

psychosocial theory Erikson's theory of development through eight stages, each one marked by an identity crisis that must be resolved before the person can continue to the next stage.

Review!

What are psychodynamic approaches to child development, and who are the leading theorists?

- *Psychodynamic approaches* suggest that our behavior and development are driven by unconscious drives and desires.
- *Sigmund Freud* posited that children go through a series of five stages that are each characterized by a focus on a particular body area (psychosexual theory).

- *Erik Erikson* placed more emphasis on social interaction and suggested a series of eight stages that encompass not only childhood but the entire life span (*psychosocial theory*).

Show What You've Learned!

Throughout his adult life, Kevin has not been able to hold a steady job. His wife recently left him because he often became violent when they had arguments. Kevin has never had a stable home life. His father was mostly absent, and his mother frequently seemed overwhelmed, having to provide additional income for the family and take care of her four children.

Three weeks ago Kevin contacted a psychotherapist to help him cope with his circumstances and the depressive feelings he increasingly feels over his life situation. Kevin isn't really sure that psychotherapy can help him, but at the urging of his

brother, he's giving it a try. In an email to the psychotherapist, Kevin explained his reasons for considering psychotherapy but expressed his skepticism that anything going on in his life now is related to his upbringing.

Drawing on the information presented in this chapter, draft an email reply from the psychotherapist to Kevin. What would you say to reassure him that problems experienced in adulthood can indeed be traced to childhood experiences so that he might give psychotherapy a try?

2.4 Learning Approaches

- Explain learning approaches to child development and name the leading theorists.

Psychodynamic theories emphasize the inner conflicts and drives that direct and influence our development. In contrast, learning approaches look not inward but rather at our experiences and interactions with the world. They suggest that it is our environment that dramatically shapes us. John B. Watson, a learning theorist and founder of behaviorist psychology, famously claimed in 1925 that, given 12 healthy infants and his "own specified world to bring them up in," he could "take any one at random and train him to become any type of specialist I might select—doctor, lawyer, artist, merchant-chief, and yes, even beggar-man and thief, regardless of his talents, penchants, tendencies, abilities . . ." (Watson, 1925, p. 14). In other words, Watson believed that as long as he could control the learning environment, he could teach children to excel in whatever he chose to teach them. He believed this to be true regardless of their genetic disposition.

Learning approaches also suggest that development is continuous, rather than occurring in stages (like the psychoanalytic theories we discussed above). That is, children's development happens bit by bit, and every day children, learning in many different ways, add something to their repertoires of behavior and skills. In the next two sections, we will consider two different explanations of how learning occurs: behaviorism and social cognitive theory.

Behaviorism: Pavlov, Watson, and Skinner

Partly as a reaction to psychoanalytic theories' focus on unobservable and unconscious inner states, behaviorism places emphasis on observable behavior. It posits that humans are passive learners that react to their environment and that thoughts and feelings do not play a crucial role in learning. Behavior is changed through two processes: classical conditioning and operant conditioning.

In classical conditioning, subjects respond to a neutral stimulus

classical conditioning the learning process that occurs when a neutral stimulus (which originally did not provoke a response) comes to elicit a response as a result of being paired repeatedly with an unconditioned stimulus.

In **classical conditioning**, a neutral stimulus (called the *conditioned stimulus*) is paired with another stimulus (the *unconditioned stimulus*) to elicit a reaction. As a result of the pairing, the individual learns to respond to the neutral stimulus alone (see **FIGURE 2.1**). Classical conditioning was first studied by Russian psychologist Ivan Pavlov (1849–1936) in experiments with dogs. Pavlov developed a routine in which he would ring a bell before feeding his dogs. He discovered that soon the dogs started salivating not only at the presentation of their food but also before the food was presented, at the ringing of the bell.

The first researcher who systematically applied the principles of classical conditioning to children was John B. Watson (1878–1958). He presented an infant now known as "Little Albert" with a white rat. At first, Albert did not show any fear of the rat. But when Watson started pairing appearances of the rat with a scary, loud banging noise, Albert soon started to cry at the first sight of the rat. Unfortunately for Albert, his fear even generalized to other white furry animals such as rabbits and cats (Watson & Rayner, 1920).

We can see the effects of classical conditioning in many domains of our life. Often, fears develop through

1. **Before conditioning**

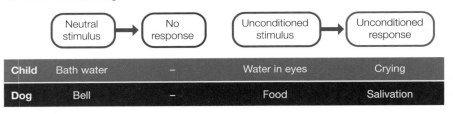

2. **During conditioning**

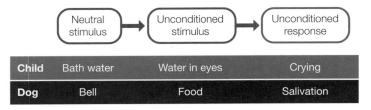

3. **After conditioning**

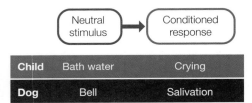

FIGURE 2.1 In classical conditioning, a person learns to react to a neutral stimulus that previously did not evoke any reaction. The learning takes place because the neutral stimulus is presented with another (unconditioned) stimulus that evokes a reaction in the person. At some point, the unconditioned stimulus is not needed anymore and the person reacts to the neutral stimulus alone.

When Anna was 6 years old, she was bitten by a dog in her neighborhood. She instantly developed a fear of all dogs, including dogs she saw on television. A child therapist later used classical conditioning to help Anna overcome the fear. How did classical conditioning work to create her fear of dogs, and what kinds of strategies might her therapist have used to help her overcome her fear?

classical conditioning. Think of a baby who hates taking a bath because water gets in her eyes. She may soon react with desperate crying to hearing the flow of bathwater in the tub because she has been conditioned to react to the sound of the bathwater (see Figure 2.1). Food preferences can be shaped through classical conditioning as well: I once knew a butcher who made the most delicious German sausages. I once had a sudden onset of flu right after eating one of his sausages. To this day, I have never been able to eat his sausages again.

Operant conditioning shapes behavior by attaching consequences to actions

As children grow up, they display many different kinds of behaviors, some desirable and others annoying or even downright destructive. Eventually, children have to learn how to behave in a positive and constructive way. They have to learn to fall asleep on their own, say "please" and "thank you" when interacting with other people, and to brush their teeth on a regular basis. Operant conditioning is one way to help us shape human behavior.

American psychologist B. F. Skinner (1904–1990) worked mostly with animals such as rats and pigeons to investigate the principles of operant conditioning, but these principles work just as well in humans. In **operant conditioning**, the effects of an action influence the likelihood of whether that action or behavior will be repeated.

Reinforcement increases the likelihood that a behavior will be repeated. There are two kinds of reinforcement: **positive reinforcement** and **negative reinforcement** (TABLE 2.2). **Punishment** decreases the likelihood that a behavior will be repeated. When a behavior is punished or does not get reinforced, it is likely that at some point it will be *extinguished* (that is, not performed anymore).

Because operant conditioning is so effective in shaping behavior, its principles are often used in behavior modification. *Behavior modification* is a form of behavior therapy with the goal to increase positive behaviors

operant conditioning a form of learning in which the consequences of an activity—positive or negative—determine the likelihood that the individual will continue to engage in the activity.

reinforcement an event that increases the probability that a behavior will be repeated.

positive reinforcement an event that strengthens behavior by providing a positive consequence when a particular behavior is performed.

negative reinforcement an event that strengthens behavior by removing an unpleasant stimulus from a situation following a positive behavior.

punishment an unpleasant consequence of a behavior that diminishes the chance that the behavior will occur again.

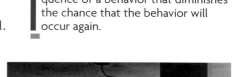

Shortly before the birth of his second child, Skinner created the "baby tender," an enclosed structure designed to give infants some freedom of movement within a safe, climate-controlled environment. The glass could be lifted to remove the child, and sheeting across the floor of the enclosure could be rolled out when soiled. Why do you suppose the idea did not catch on?

■ **Table 2.2** Two Kinds of Reinforcement

An action that . . .	. . . is called	Example
. . . *increases* the likelihood that behavior will be repeated	reinforcement	
	Positive reinforcement (positive consequence)	Darius gets a sticker after doing chores
	Negative reinforcement (removal of a negative stimulus)	Jasmine can leave the dinner table (a negative stimulus for her) to play after she eats her vegetables
. . . *decreases* the likelihood that behavior will be repeated	punishment	When Mischa whines, her mother gives her extra chores to do

and decrease negative behaviors. It can be used to teach children with special needs and can help manage temper tantrums or behavioral issues at school. For example, children throwing temper tantrums elicit a reaction from their parents—even if the reaction is negative in the form of scolding. The attention a child gets serves as a positive reinforcement, which may lead to more tantrums. If, however, the parents ignore the tantrum or interact only when the child has calmed down, they take away much of the incentive for the child to throw tantrums. The principles of behavior modification are also used to help people who are attempting to lose weight or stop smoking (Foreyt & Johnston, 2016; Graziano & Hart, 2016; Martin & Pear, 2019). Most discipline methods that are used with children also are based on operant conditioning. We will discuss these methods and their relationship to operant conditioning in more detail in Chapter 10.

Theories of classical and operant conditioning have been criticized because they portray individuals as passively reacting to the environment without processing or thinking about what is happening in any significant way. As we will see in the next section, these are shortcomings that are addressed by social cognitive theory.

Despite these criticisms, theories of classical and operant conditioning have contributed a great deal to scientists' ability to explain and predict behavior. The principles of operant and classical conditioning play out in our everyday lives, such as when a child stung by a bumblebee develops a fear of flying insects, and the techniques are widely used to modify behavior in both children and adults. The work of Watson and Skinner also significantly contributed to psychology's becoming a scientific discipline, because the theories were formulated such that they concerned observable behavior and thus are testable.

Social Cognitive Theory: Bandura

Albert Bandura (1925–2021) based his social cognitive theory on the idea that children learn through experiences, much as in operant conditioning. However, in contrast to the theory of operant conditioning, he believed that

- thinking plays an important role in learning,
- learning is not always observable, and
- we learn through interaction with others.

■ What serves as a reinforcement or punishment is highly dependent on the individual person. I once worked at a clinic for disabled and sick children. A child at this clinic loved coleslaw so much that we were able to use it effectively as a positive reinforcement. The child in the photo here receives a green token for each completed task; for every ten tokens he collects, he receives a sticker.

Bandura's early work emphasized **modeling** (also called *observational learning*), which is a form of learning that occurs through observation of others. According to Bandura, children actively choose the models they observe and imitate—usually people with status or power (like adults or older children) or people whose behavior is rewarded. Children decide which behavior to imitate by observing the consequences of the model's behavior. In contrast to the process described in classical conditioning, they do not need to experience the consequences themselves before adopting (or deciding not to adopt) the behavior (Bandura, 2011, 2016, 2019).

Observation and imitation influence our learning of gender roles, aggressive behavior, socially desired behavior like saying "thank you" and "please," and many other behaviors as well, such as how to do chores or comfort an injured sibling. For this reason, modeling has been used to accomplish a wide variety of goals, such as enhancing literacy levels, reducing unplanned pregnancies, and promoting practices that help conserve the environment (Bandura, 2016, 2019).

There is an impressive amount of research on social cognitive theory, with many of the studies confirming the basic assumptions of the theory. But social cognitive theory has also been criticized because some people believe it does not take changes in children's biology or personality into account as they get older. Biologists believe that some of our reactions to events are not learned but are instead determined by biological processes in our body, such as an increase in heart rate or blood pressure, or by hormonal changes.

■ Social learning at work: Six-year-old Jimmy despises water and refused to take swim lessons for the longest time. Then his parents had the idea of letting him watch the swim lessons of his sister Kayla, who loves to swim. After several weeks of observing his sister Kayla having fun during her swim lessons, Jimmy consented to take lessons. He will never be a passionate swimmer, but is now learning skills that at some point may save his life.

modeling (or **observational learning**) a form of learning that occurs through observation of others.

Review!

What are learning approaches to child development, and who are the leading theorists?

■ *Learning approaches* suggest that children learn through interactions with their environment. Behaviorist traditions like those of *classical* and *operant conditioning* view the learning process as a passive response to stimuli.

■ *Albert Bandura* acknowledged the importance of a person's thinking, motivations, and values in learning. He believed learning takes place when we observe others (models) and witness the effects of their actions (social learning theory).

Show What You've Learned!

Earlier in the chapter we met 6-year-old Archer, who is attending kindergarten but does not do well academically. His parents are also increasingly having trouble with him at home. Archer tends not to listen when they request any number of things, from putting his dirty clothes in the laundry basket to staying at the dinner table for the duration of the meal.

Archer's father, Joey, is scheduled to meet with the kindergarten teacher and plans to bring up the behavioral difficulties they're experiencing at home. Based on the learning approaches you have studied in this section, what could you as a kindergarten teacher tell Joey about behavior modification in young children? Do you have any specific recommendations to make? Act or write out what you would tell Joey.

See for Yourself!

Albert Bandura suggested that children learn through interaction with others. The next time you're somewhere where there are many children playing with each other or interacting with adults—a playground, a museum, a department store or supermarket, or a restaurant—look for examples of sociocultural learning around you: Are children imitating others or helping each other? Do parents give their children assistance when eating, putting on their coat, or playing? Do you find that the assistance given is adequate, or are people helping too much or too little?

2.5 Cognitive Approaches

■ Explain cognitive approaches to child development and name the leading theorists.

Behaviorism places emphasis on observable behavior and how stimuli in the environment shape that behavior. But obviously people do not only passively react to the world; they also actively think and try to shape their world. At some point, psychologists started looking for explanations that took thinking processes into account and did not depict people as machines that just reacted mindlessly to their environment. **Cognitive approaches** explain human behavior in terms of mental processes like thinking, reasoning, and perception. In this section, we will discuss Jean Piaget's cognitive-developmental theory, information-processing approaches, and cognitive neuroscience.

cognitive approaches theories that explain human behavior in terms of a combination of mental processes like thinking, reasoning, and perception.

Piaget's Cognitive-Developmental Theory

Jean Piaget (1896–1980) was a Swiss psychologist who became interested in child development when he began conducting research on intelligence in children at the Binet Institute in Paris. He became particularly interested in children's wrong answers as a result of his discovering that children of the same age tended to make the same kinds of mistakes.

Piaget developed a theory of cognitive development according to which children progress through four different stages:

1. *Sensorimotor stage (birth–2 years)*: Infants learn about and explore their environment mostly by means of their senses and motor activities.

2. *Preoperational stage (2–7 years)*: Children cannot think logically and have trouble seeing the world from other people's perspective.

3. *Concrete operational stage (7–11 years)*: Logical thinking begins, but is limited to direct experiences.

4. *Formal operational stage (11 years and up)*: Children are capable of abstract reasoning and logical thinking.

equilibrium mental balance in which children can explain new experiences and ideas with their existing knowledge; achieved through the processes of assimilation and accommodation.

adaptation In Piaget's theory, a reaction to new experiences and information. It consists of two alternative processes: assimilation and accommodation.

Each stage is qualitatively different from the one that comes before or after. So when children enter a new phase, the entire nature of their thinking actually changes compared to the previous stage and also relative to the next stage. **TABLE 2.3** gives an overview of the different stages in Piaget's theory. We will return to Piaget's theory many times throughout this book to learn more details about his thinking and the applications of his theory.

According to Piaget, what drives children's (and adults') learning is that they are constantly striving for a mental state he called equilibrium. **Equilibrium** is a mental balance between current knowledge and new ideas or experiences. Children experience equilibrium when they can explain their experiences by what they already know: Infants can grab a rattle in much the same way they were able to grab their mother's finger, and toddlers learn that a Collie is yet another kind of dog. However, new experiences often do not fit what children know and thus create an unpleasant *disequilibrium*: A ball cannot be grabbed with the same grasp as a rattle, and the four-legged creature in the backyard turns out to be a cat, not a dog.

In an effort to get back to a state of equilibrium, children react to the new information by means of **adaptation**. Adaptation plays a key role in cognitive development and consists of two different processes: *assimilation* and *accommodation* (see also **FIGURE 2.2**):

© Bill Anderson/Science Photo Library

■ Piaget loved to observe children at play and in interaction with others. He and his wife systematically observed their own children, and their observations of their own and other children inspired the development of his theory.

- In **assimilation**, children discover new information that fits into their current thinking and schemata. **Schemata** are action patterns or mental patterns that organize our knowledge about the world and influence the way we think and behave. They get increasingly complex as a child matures. For example, a toddler baking with his mother realizes that he can make dough balls much the same way as he does with clay.

- In **accommodation**, the information a child encounters does not fit what she knows about the world. For example, a toddler cries out "doggie" with delight at the sight of a big cat. When the toddler learns that the "dog" is actually a cat, they need to create a separate mental category for cats that is different from dogs (Brubaker, 2016; Kholiq, 2020; Lourenço, 2015). Obviously, accommodation is a more complex and difficult process than assimilation. However, this clash of ideas is also what leads to growth in our thinking and learning.

assimilation the process by which new information is incorporated into existing thinking and schemata.

schemata (singular **schema**) patterns of action or thought that organize our knowledge about the world and influence the way we think and behave.

accommodation modification of existing schemata because new information or experiences do not fit those schemata.

Our interactions with the world lead us to assimilate and accommodate information many times every day, constantly revising our thinking.

Piaget has been unsurpassed in his rich and detailed observations of children and their thinking processes. His work has stimulated a large number of research studies, and his notion of the child as an active learner has inspired academies throughout the world to develop curricula that encourage children to explore their environment and learn through their experience. Yet these studies have led many contemporary researchers to draw conclusions that differ from Piaget's, particularly with respect to two aspects of his work:

- Piaget may have underestimated the abilities of young children, and

- cognitive development is more continuous and less stage-like than Piaget suggested. Piaget believed that once a child has acquired a skill, the child will from then on be able to use it in virtually any situation. As recent researchers have discovered, children often appear to acquire thinking skills over time, gradually learning to apply them in more and more situations (Lourenço, 2016).

Information-Processing Approaches

Piaget did much of his work in the first half of the twentieth century. As time went on, science and technology progressed. The field of computer science emerged as computers were developed and programs were written for the computers to execute. Cognitive researchers found inspiration in those new developments and created what is known as information-processing approaches to development. They likened the human mind to a computer: Both receive input, store information, carry out operations, and generate output. We receive input when we see, hear, touch, or feel something. We store important information in our human memory banks and then use that information to solve problems or create new things. We process information when we think, and our thinking ultimately generates an output in terms of behavior, new insights or ideas,

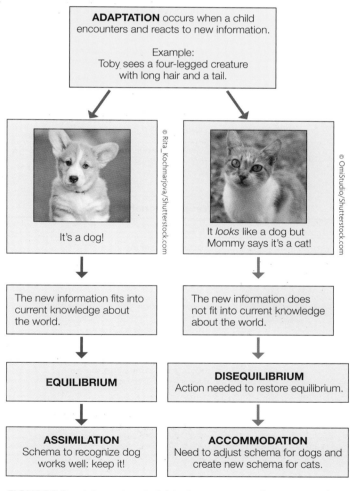

FIGURE 2.2 Adaptation: A child adapts to new information and experiences by assimilation or accommodation. When a toddler encounters a neighbor's dog for the first time and correctly identifies it as a dog, this is a case of assimilation, or fitting new information into an existing schema. When the toddler incorrectly identifies a neighbor's cat as a dog, the toddler creates a new mental schema for cats, and this is a case of accommodation.

■ Table 2.3 Piaget's Cognitive-Developmental Theory

Sensorimotor Stage: birth–2 years

	DESCRIPTION	EXAMPLE	APPLICATIONS
 © Chubykin Arkady/ Shutterstock.com	Infants learn by exploring the world with their senses and motor activities. Learning builds on reflexes (**schemata**). **Object permanence** (objects continue to exist even when out of sight) **Deferred imitation** (time lag between observation and reproduction of behavior) Beginning of symbolic thinking **The sensorimotor stage has six substages:** 1. **inborn reflexes** (birth–1 month) 2. **primary circular reactions** → adjust reflexes and repeat them (1–4 months) 3. **secondary circular reactions** → actions involve objects (4–8 months) 4. goal-directed behavior combining schemata (8–12 months) 5. **tertiary circular reactions** → change combinations of schemata to explore environment (12–18 months) 6. symbolic thought → mentally represent objects (18–24 months)	Children explore by touching and putting objects in mouth. Children will search for an item hidden while they watch. Children will observe a sibling make a block tower and try to stack blocks themselves the next day. Children begin to think about objects even when the objects are absent. Children will suck when a nipple is placed in their mouth. Children placing a finger in the mouth by accident will start sucking and then try to repeat finger sucking. Children can shake a rattle. Children can push a pillow away to reach a rattle. Children will bang different objects together and on floor to explore sounds. Children can anticipate the noise banged objects will make and chooses the object that makes the loudest sound.	Provide safe space and safe objects for children to explore by touching, mouthing, and moving around. Give children opportunities to explore different senses and object properties: cold and warm water, rough and smooth fabric, differently colored or sized objects, different sounds. Play with children and let them safely explore cause and effect even when they repeatedly throw or push objects. Give children opportunities to develop their motor skills and learn how to move and coordinate their bodies; this is also a way for them to learn about the world.

Preoperational Stage: 2–7 years

	DESCRIPTION	EXAMPLE	APPLICATIONS
 © iStock.com/wsphotos	**Egocentric thinking** (no ability to take the perspective of others) Pretend play No **conservation** (understanding that changing the appearance of something does not change its quantity) No **class inclusion** (ability to classify objects by taking more than one feature into account) No **reversibility** (ability to remember steps of reasoning or mentally reverse actions)	Children assume others know what they know. Children cook food for their dolls. Children believe they have more money when coins are spread out as opposed to close together. Children can consider apples and pears as two different groups but do not understand that at the same time they're both fruit. Children are confused by the idea that if you can count forward you can also count backward.	Children personalize events that have nothing to do with them. When critical life events happen, make sure they don't blame themselves for occurrences. Provide children with opportunities to practice real-world procedures like shopping, cooking, etc. Give children opportunities to play with materials like clay or water to understand and practice concepts like conservation and reversibility.

or an action. Essentially, information-processing approaches break down our thinking into distinct steps that may be executed step by step (*serially*) or all at once (*in parallel*).

There is not only one information-processing theory. Rather, information-processing approaches represent a framework. Researchers using this framework develop different theories based on their work on diverse topics

■ **Table 2.3** *(continued)*

Concrete Operational Stage: 7–11 years

	DESCRIPTION	EXAMPLE	APPLICATIONS
©Chekyravaa/ Shutterstock.com	Beginning of **logical thinking** helps children understand concepts like reversibility, but this understanding is limited to "concrete" real-world situations.	Abstract concepts like fractions are hard to understand unless presented with pictures or manipulatives because $\frac{1}{4}$ is more than $\frac{1}{8}$, although 8 is a larger number than 4.	Use hands-on learning whenever possible: Discover fractions by slicing pizza, create timelines of events, or conduct experiments.
	Children begin to take the perspective of others.	Children understand that a grandparent on the phone cannot see the toy they're holding.	Ask open-ended questions to stimulate creative thinking and explore topics in more depth. Reassure child that mistakes are part of learning rather than something to be ashamed of.
	Children understand **class inclusion** (objects belong to more than one group at once).	Children understand that brown and white teddy bears all belong to the group of *teddy bears*.	
	Children understand **transitivity** (infer relationship between two objects by knowing their relationships with a third object).	Children can solve riddles like this: If Ahmed is taller than Lily, and Lily is taller than Zane, who is the tallest?	
	Children can understand more complex math by using **reversibility**, **seriation**, and **classification**.	Children understand that, since $8 + 7 = 15$, $15 - 7$ must be 8 (**reversibility**).	
		Children also understand that 8 is more than 7 (**seriation**) and that all numbers from 400 to 499 are in the 400s (**classification**).	

Formal-Operational Stage: 11 years and up

	DESCRIPTION	EXAMPLE	APPLICATIONS
© iStock.com/fstop123	**Abstract thought**	Teens can think about the future and imagine themselves in different professions.	Provide teenagers the space to try out different interests and consider different future life scenarios, including postsecondary schools, places to live, and professions.
	Hypothetical-deductive reasoning (develop and test hypotheses to solve problems)	When presented with a calculation spreadsheet that does not work, teens can systematically try out different options to find the mistake.	Remember that children develop at very different rates, so teenagers' abilities for formal-operational thought may differ significantly. They may also not be able to use their new thinking skills when stressed or emotionally aroused.
	Mental trial and error	Teens who have broken a dish can consider and evaluate different ways of presenting the news.	
	Symbolic thinking	Teens will understand proverbs, puns, and sarcasm and solve algebraic equations with letters standing in for unknown numbers.	

including, for example, attention, memory, and decision-making. We will touch upon a number of these theories in later chapters of this book.

Information-processing theorists see development as continuous rather than progressing through a sequence of stages. As children mature, their processes become more efficient and they have a wider variety of strategies to process information at their disposal. For example, only around the age of 7 do children start to rehearse information they want to keep in memory by repeating it to themselves (a practice called *subvocal rehearsal*). Younger children are able to use this strategy as well but usually fail to do so unless someone specifically instructs them to do so (Gathercole, 1998; Mahy et al., 2016). Children's attention spans become longer, so that preschoolers can sit through listening to a book that they weren't able to sit through as 2-year-olds.

Ten-year-old Parker is studying hard for his upcoming tests at school. Do you think he processes and memorizes information the same way a computer does? How might humans and machines be different in their information processing?

Older children have already acquired more knowledge, which makes it easier for them to connect new information with what they know. Connecting new information with old information increases the chances they will be able to retain and apply the information.

Information-processing approaches are used in a variety of settings in child development. For example, children can be taught strategies to memorize information more effectively. Teaching materials can be designed in ways that make it easier for children to integrate the new information with knowledge they already have, thus increasing the chances that they will remember the material.

Information-processing approaches have contributed significantly to our understanding of young children's development. They break down human thinking into smaller mechanisms that can be studied in detail. However, this very advantage also makes it more difficult to develop a theory that describes the development of children as a whole. Information-processing approaches also sometimes neglect human aspects like motivation, interests, feelings, and imagination as well as the role of social interaction in learning.

Cognitive Neuroscience

In recent decades, cognitive neuroscience has become vitally important to many fields in psychology. Cognitive neuroscience studies the brain and the neural mechanisms that form the basis of human cognition. Cognitive neuroscientists often have a background in psychology, physics, mathematics, or biology. To measure activity in the brain, researchers use methods like *electroencephalography* (EEG), *magnetic resonance imaging* (MRI), or *positron emission tomography* (PET). Using these methods, researchers will sometimes ask participants to engage in different activities while their brain activity is recorded. Recordings from the different activities are then compared so that the researchers can draw conclusions about what functions different parts of the brain are responsible for. For example, researchers might examine images of the brain of a person first staring at a blank screen and then shown a pattern of dots. The parts of the brain that become active when the person looks at the pattern are the parts that are involved in visual processing. Many insights are also gained by examining patients with cognitive deficits.

Neuroscientists investigate questions like whether children's brains show abnormalities when a child has autism or a developmental disorder, or how a child's brain is affected when the mother has taken drugs during pregnancy (Cauda et al., 2017; Radhakrishan et al., 2021; Willford et al., 2016). They investigate which parts of the brain are involved when we read, pay (or fail to pay) attention, solve mental math problems, or look at photos of our loved ones (Pereira et al., 2016; Riccitelli et al., 2020; Willford et al., 2016).

Cognitive neuroscience enables us to take a peek into the working brain. Researchers can identify the functions of different parts of the brain and investigate the way the brain can reassign functions to different brain parts in people with brain injuries (a phenomenon called *plasticity*). A deeper understanding of the way the brain works may enable us to develop treatments for people with diseases and abnormalities.

Neuroscientific approaches are sometimes criticized because they tend to describe rather than explain brain functions. For example, researchers have found that the brains of children with developmental delays are less myelinated (that is, their brain cells lack insulation made up of fatty cells). Consequently, those cells cannot conduct signals as well as the brains of children without

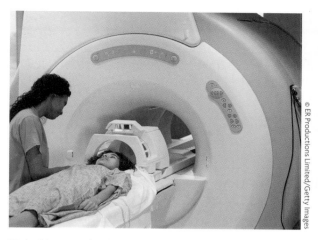 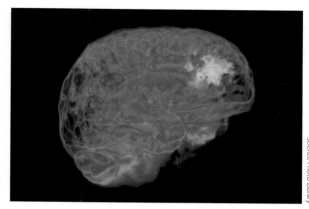

■ (Left) MRI technology is used to take detailed three-dimensional images of the body's soft tissues, including muscles, ligaments, nerves, and the brain. (Right) A colored MRI scan can show brain activity. This image shows the brain of a child who is looking at herself in a mirror. The area of the frontal cortex associated with sense of self is highlighted.

delays (Rajvanshi et al., 2021; Tang et al., 2020). At this point, this insight does not provide us with any clues as to why there is less myelination in children with developmental delays or how we can increase myelination in children's brain cells.

Review!

What are cognitive approaches to child development, and who are the leading theorists?

■ *Cognitive approaches* emphasize mental processes that help children learn and understand the world.

■ *Information-processing approaches* liken the human mind to a computer that receives data as an input, stores them, executes operations with the data, and delivers an output.

■ *Jean Piaget* suggested that children develop through a series of four distinct stages, each of them qualitatively different from the others.

Show What You've Learned!

Drawing on information presented in this section, describe an ideal environment for children going through the four stages of cognitive development according to Piaget. Consider factors such as parental variables, living situation, culture, and any other factors that seem important to you.

2.6 Contextual Approaches

■ Explain contextual approaches to child development and name the leading theorists.

Contextual approaches provide us with yet another perspective for looking at children's development. Contextual approaches emphasize the importance of the environment in which children grow up. The environment, or context, may include, for example, the people children interact with and the culture that surrounds them. Past or current events that influence children's behavior, thinking, and personality are also environmental influences. In this section, we will consider two different approaches to context: Vygotsky's sociocultural theory and Bronfenbrenner's ecological systems theory.

■ **Table 2.4** Differences between Piaget's and Vygotsky's Views of Development

	Piaget	Vygotsky
How do children learn?	Children act like scientists and learn on their own.	Children are social beings and learn from interaction with others.
What do they learn?	All over the world, children learn many of the same things, such as how to take the perspective of others and how to think logically.	What children learn is highly dependent on their culture.
What is the learning process?	Learning occurs in a series of stages that all children go through.	Learning is largely continuous.

Vygotsky's Sociocultural Theory

Lev Vygotsky (1896–1934) was a Russian psychologist who developed his theory of development around the same time as Jean Piaget. Unfortunately, his work was cut short by an early death from tuberculosis.

Vygotsky believed that interactions with others play a fundamental role in learning. Unlike Piaget, who considered his periods of cognitive development to apply universally to all children, regardless of where they lived, Vygotsky firmly believed that interactions are always dependent on culture (Vygotsky, 1986). For example, the things people talk about and what they consider important, how people work, and how they teach their children all depend on where they live. Yupik living in central Alaska will spend their days in a much different way from people living in urban California or in a rural part of Vietnam. For this reason, Piaget's and Vygotsky's views differ from one another in several aspects (TABLE 2.4).

Vygotsky introduced the concept of the zone of proximal development. The **zone of proximal development** describes anything the child *cannot* yet do alone, but *can* do with assistance (Kostogriz & Veresov, 2021). As children grow up and learn new skills, they build upon the skills they already have and try to extend them by learning something new that is just beyond their grasp. For example, 5-year-old Victoria is learning to write and is practicing drawing long straight, wavy, and zigzag lines on a sheet of paper. She does not yet have enough control to form complex patterns and letters and obviously cannot yet write any complete words or sentences. To help her form letters, her father gives her sheets that have the letters prewritten so she can trace them. Victoria's father helps her learn to write by challenging Victoria to trace the complex patterns of the prewritten letters, which are in her zone of proximal development.

These worksheets that Victoria's father has created for her serve as scaffolds. **Scaffolds** are temporary cognitive or physical aids given to a child to assist in the acquisition of new skills (Kostogriz & Veresov, 2021). Scaffolding can take many forms: Parents and teachers can use worksheets, or they may provide support through verbal coaching or physically helping a child to perform an activity, for example. As soon as the child can perform an action independently, the scaffold is not needed anymore. Scaffolding is used by teachers in the classroom, by parents and relatives, and by others. For example, mothers in both India and Germany use scaffolding to teach their children to thank others when receiving gifts. However, the scaffolds are not identical: German mothers teach their children to express positive feelings and praise the gift, whereas Indian mothers emphasize thanking and praising the gift-giver (Kärtner et al., 2016). This is another example of how, in Vygotsky's view, children's learning varies from culture to culture.

For quite some time after his death, Vygotsky's ideas were not widely known among developmental psychologists. This is largely because Vygotsky was a citizen of the Soviet Union. His writings were banned there and became widely accessible only after the federation was dissolved in 1991. Since that time, and with translations of his work into other languages, Vygotsky's ideas have been growing in influence.

zone of proximal development the range of tasks a child *cannot* yet do alone but *can* do with assistance.

scaffold a temporary aid used to assist children in the acquisition of new skills.

■ Lev Vygotsky believed that learning occurs through social interactions and is therefore greatly dependent on culture.

Culture Counts

How Well Do Theories of Child Development Apply across Cultures?

The majority of the studies that are featured in this book and that have informed prevailing theories of child development were conducted with children in industrialized countries. Can we use the results of these studies to understand child development around the world, or is there a problem when we generalize data from one group to another group living in a very different cultural context? Could it be that even the meanings of some concepts differ depending on where you live?

Take the concept of intelligence, for example. Many children in rural Kenya have an enormous amount of *tacit* (i.e. informal) knowledge that allows them to survive, and even thrive, in often adverse circumstances. They know how to use plants in their environment to make natural herbal medicines. They use those medicines regularly to treat parasitic illnesses in themselves and others. Western schoolchildren (or even adults) might get severely ill or even die within a short time in these circumstances. It seems clear that the ability to identify plants for medicines, harvest those plants, create the medicine from them, and dose the medicine appropriately in order to secure one's and one's family's survival is an intelligent behavior.

Robert J. Sternberg and his colleagues (2001) conducted a study with rural Kenyan schoolchildren and assessed their tacit knowledge—that is, the knowledge they need to survive in an environment (and that is usually not taught). He also used tests of intelligence more commonly used in Western society, including a vocabulary assessment and the Raven Matrices test (a "culture-fair" intelligence test that avoids cultural or language biases, placing its focus on logical thinking). He found that Kenyan children's tacit knowledge was negatively correlated with Western measures of intelligence: In other words, the more tacit knowledge they possessed and used to survive in their home environment, the lower they scored on the vocabulary and Raven Matrices tests.

■ Children from the Kenyan village of Malindi attending open-air primary school.

The table presented here shows correlations from Sternberg's study in Kenya (2001). As you look at the data, remember that a negative correlation means that as one variable increases, the other one decreases; a positive correlation means that when one variable increases, the other one increases as well. The table shows a strong negative correlation between tacit knowledge and success on the two Western measures of intelligence (the vocabulary and Raven tests): In other words, children with lower test scores had more of the knowledge that helped them survive at home (tacit knowledge). There was a strong positive correlation between the vocabulary and matrices tests, meaning that children were likely to perform about the same on both.

	Tacit knowledge	Total vocabulary test
Raven Matrices test	-.16	.33
Total vocabulary test	-.31	

Source: Data from R. J. Sternberg. 2004. *Am Psychol* 59: 325–338.

■ **Question**

What might explain the finding that Kenyan children who perform less well on Western intelligence tests have more knowledge that helps them survive and succeed in their home environment than those who score better on those tests?

Some aspects of Vygotsky's theory are light on details, making them difficult to test in experiments. For example, how do you accurately assess a child's zone of proximal development? Vygotsky also did not say much about other aspects of children's development, such as the role of emotions in development in general or, specifically, in how memory develops.

These facts have not stopped child development researchers from pursuing his ideas (e.g., Chang, 2021; Sternberg & Grigorenko, 2002). The notion that children learn from interaction with adults and other, more experienced children resonates with practitioners all over the world. It is appealing to many people that Vygotsky takes the influence of culture into account. Additionally, his ideas can be effectively translated for use in the classroom. We will discuss this in more detail in later chapters.

Bronfenbrenner's Ecological Systems Theory

Like Vygotsky, Urie Bronfenbrenner (1917–2005) believed that development is influenced by the interactions between children and their environment. In his **ecological systems theory**, Bronfenbrenner suggests that there are five different kinds of ecosystems that shape development (see **FIGURE 2.3**). Each of these systems interacts with the others and influences the child (Bronfenbrenner, 1995, 2005):

1. *Microsystem.* A child's immediate environment consists of multiple microsystems like children's families, teachers, friends, and neighborhoods. Children actively interact with all these people, and they help shape the microsystems they are a part of. Most studies in child development are conducted at the level of the microsystem.

2. *Mesosystem.* The mesosystem includes the interactions of all the different microsystems. Parents can influence the school setting, for example, by meeting and collaborating with teachers.

ecological systems theory theory by Urie Bronfenbrenner, through which he suggests that development is shaped by the interactions of a child with five different environmental systems.

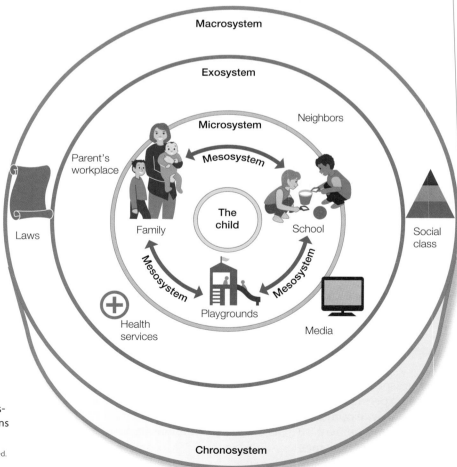

FIGURE 2.3 Bronfenbrenner's ecological systems theory proposes five different ecosystems that influence children's development.

After J. W. Santrock. 1992. *Child Development: An Introduction*, 5th ed. Wm. C. Brown, Dubuque, IA

3. *Exosystem*. The exosystem contains influences that do not directly interact with children but still have an impact on the children's lives (for example, the healthcare system, the media, the workplace of the parents, or the child's home town). For example, if the child's home town lacks playgrounds, the child's options for playing outside the home and meeting with friends are reduced.

4. *Macrosystem*. The macrosystem reflects the cultural values and beliefs as well as economic and political systems that influence children's lives. Children growing up in areas of civil unrest or war experience circumstances different from those of children growing up in a peaceful environment.

5. *Chronosystem*. The chronosystem represents significant events happening before or during a person's lifetime that influence that person's development. It includes personal events like the death of a parent and events at a larger societal level like the attacks of September 11.

Keep in mind that the different ecosystems do not exist in isolation but influence and interact with each other. If the federal government cuts welfare payments (exosystem), families may need to relocate to a more affordable part of town, leaving the child's school and friends behind (microsystem). Likewise, parents' attempts to raise a non-aggressive child (microsystem) may be thwarted if the child watches lots of movies that promote violence (exosystem).

Cultural values (macrosystem) influence not only children's development but also how we evaluate children's development and how we perceive children's skills and abilities. Let's look at an example from Alaska.

Luava and Ila live in a little village in northeastern Alaska. The winters there are long and dark. Distances are vast, and it is about 40 miles to the neighboring town. After heavy snows, the roads are often closed, and the only way to get to town is by snowmobile or dogsled. On the Arctic landscape, there are very few distinctive landmarks, so navigation can be difficult. Luava is just 8 years old, but she can easily find her way to town or back home from outings. If necessary, she is able to find shelter and food to spend a night outdoors. Ila is significantly older than Luava, but she has never learned to navigate the landscape. If she found herself alone on the tundra in winter, even in good weather conditions, she would almost certainly starve or freeze to death because she is not able to find her way back to the little village that is her home. If you had to judge the intelligence of the two individuals described above, who would you say is more intelligent?

You most likely chose Luava, who is able to navigate her surroundings and survive even in adverse conditions. But here's the catch: Luava is a young Inupiaq girl who does not do well in reading and writing and tests poorly in standardized tests. Ila is a 27-year-old teacher from the city of Anchorage, Alaska, who is the only teacher at the school in Luava's town. Ila does not think much of Luava's abilities because Luava does not fare well on the school tests and shows little interest in the academic topics Ila teaches. Ila thinks in terms of our Western notion of intelligence. This notion takes into account mostly the abstract reasoning skills that intelligence tests measure. And yet, Ila would not be able to survive a single day in bad weather out on the vast open tundra.

As you can see, what it means to be intelligent can differ quite a bit depending on the context (Sternberg, 2004). Many Brazilian street children, for example, have

■ Five-year-old Marla is having fun playing with her friends at the playground of her hometown in Switzerland. What she does not realize is how deeply integrated she is in a web of relationships that affect her life profoundly. Marla interacts almost daily with her friends and teachers, as do her parents at times. The town collects taxes to keep the playground safe and clean. And Marla is very lucky to live in a country where she can play outside with few concerns for her safety.

trouble solving abstract mathematical problems but are more than able to do the mathematical computations needed to run their street businesses (Carraher, Carraher, & Schliemann, 1985; Sternberg, 2004).

Even the timing of basic motor skills such as sitting and walking is not universal and depends on the culture in which a child grows up. People in parts of Africa and India massage their infants, do daily stretching routines, and regularly prop the children into sitting and standing positions (Bril, 1988; Weber et al., 2021). These children learn to sit and walk earlier than children growing up in cultures that restrict their movements by keeping them lying down for most of the day. The recent practice in Western cultures of putting children to sleep on their backs in order to prevent SIDS (sudden infant death syndrome) affects their motor development and actually delays the age at which they start to crawl (Boonzaaijer et al., 2021). Moreover, in cultures that do not encourage crawling, children may skip this step entirely and learn to walk right away (Fox et al., 2002; Karasik et al., 2010).

Comparing the development of children all over the world helps us identify which processes in development are universal and which ones are shaped by culture. This is particularly important in our increasingly interconnected and multicultural world. Your neighbor who immigrated from Iran 13 years ago may have very different expectations of his children and use different strategies to discipline them than you do. Many of the theories and research results in child development are based on Western cultural norms and do not appropriately reflect cultural differences, which can lead to misunderstandings and biases. For this reason, throughout this book we will frequently return to the impact of culture on child development in order to gain a better understanding of how diverse human development is and how environmental factors influence children's lives.

Bronfenbrenner's theory has helped highlight the different systems within which a child grows up and with which the child interacts. The theory has been applied to many different aspects of children's lives, for example, how the different ecosystems can affect successful parenting of children with disabilities and how these families can be supported (Algood et al., 2013), or how survivors of child sexual abuse can best be supported (Azzopardi et al., 2021).

The theory is sometimes criticized because it does not specify detailed mechanisms of how children develop. Although Bronfenbrenner (2005) added biological influences to his theory, the theory still heavily emphasizes the external contexts in which children grow up.

Review!

What are contextual approaches to child development, and who are the leading theorists?

- *Contextual approaches* highlight the effects that different contexts (for example, the neighborhood in which children grow up, the school they go to, or their culture) have on children's behavior and development.

- *Lev Vygotsky* stressed the importance of culture, believing children learn primarily through social transactions with others, and that what they are taught is dependent on their culture (sociocultural theory).

- *Urie Bronfenbrenner* hypothesized that a child's world is made up of five ecosystems that interact with each other and influence development (*ecological systems theory*).

See For Yourself!

The next time you're in a neighborhood that is very different from the one you grew up in—more rural, urban, or suburban; wealthier or poorer; more or less multicultural—think about how the lives and development of children in this community differ from your own upbringing. What role does environment play in those differences?

What's It Like...

Growing Up in a Bicultural Household

Alicia, 14 years old

My parents immigrated to the United States from Argentina before I was born. We do not have any other family in the United States; the rest of the family still live in Argentina. We visit them every 2 years. From the beginning, my mom and dad have only spoken Spanish with me and my little sister, whether we're at home or out in public. My friends know that my parents are from another country, but it's not really an issue. When I was in elementary school, they were interested in my language and sometimes asked me to say something in Spanish or teach them to say a few things in Spanish. They also asked about Argentina from time to time and found it cool that I traveled to a country in a whole other continent. But now that I am in eighth grade, we talk about other topics like music and our hobbies. Culture doesn't really play a role in what we talk about.

I am glad that I speak another language because I like being able to talk to different people who come from different places. Also, I wouldn't be able to speak to my own relatives in Argentina if I did not speak Spanish. That would be weird. When I was smaller, my mom made us do worksheets in Spanish every morning so we learned how to read and write in Spanish. I didn't like sitting down to do those worksheets but I did like learning Spanish better. So it was a mixed deal. These days, I have so much to do for school we're not doing those sheets anymore. Overall, it makes me happy when I hear people speak of my being from Argentina.

Isabella, Alicia's mother

My husband and I are both from Argentina though we are now U.S. citizens and intend to stay in this country. We speak Spanish at home and it was always clear to us that when we have children we would speak Spanish with them. We never gave them a choice. We always speak Spanish, and when they were younger and tried to speak English to us we just ignored them so they rephrased in Spanish. There are a number of reasons it is very important for us that our children speak Spanish fluently. We want them to be able to communicate with their relatives in Argentina and read poetry and other literature from our home country. But because you express yourself differently in your native language, speaking a certain language is also an expression of power. Our relationship with each other is different when we are speaking in our own language than when we are speaking English with each other. Alicia has always loved languages, so maybe that is part of the reason why she has never objected to our speaking Spanish with her.

Argentinian food differs from American. In elementary school that was not an issue and Alicia always ate whatever I packed for her. In the early middle school years she became more self-conscious when people asked her about her food and we went through a couple of years when she only wanted me to pack more generic foods like pasta and rice dishes. But recently, she has become very confident and self-assured and we're now back to packing her the food we usually eat in our household.

Overall, I feel that our lives are enriched by our two different cultures and I am glad we are able to pass on our heritage to our daughters.

2.7 Evolutionary Approaches

■ Recall how evolutionary approaches explain development.

Evolutionary approaches to child development originated from Charles Darwin's theory of *natural selection*, brought forth in *On the Origin of Species* (1859). This theory suggests that those individuals who survive and reproduce most successfully are the ones who are best adapted to their environment. Evolutionary approaches recognize that two basic drives—survival and reproduction—influence the physical as well as psychological traits we find in humans today (Giudice et al., 2015; Luoto & Varella, 2021). When researchers investigate questions from an evolutionary viewpoint, you will often find them asking how a particular trait helped people survive or reproduce. Look for the issues of survival and reproduction as we discuss evolutionary approaches below.

The Influence of Natural Selection on Physical and Psychological Traits

We can find examples of natural selection in many different domains of human life. Think about people's skin color: In the tropics, dark skin helps keep people healthy by protecting them from the ultraviolet (UV) radiation of the sun. It plays a role in preventing sunburns as well as preventing the breakdown of folate (which can lead to anemia as well as loss of fertility and a higher rate of birth defects). Over the course of evolution, in tropical areas people with dark skin have had a consistent advantage over people with light skin. They tended to be healthier and had a greater chance of giving birth to healthy infants. Thus, over time, an increasingly large number of people inherited the disposition for dark skin, simply because people with dark skin had a better chance of growing up healthy, reproduced more successfully, and were more likely to live a long life so they could take care of their offspring (Jablonski & Chaplin, 2010, 2017).

In more northerly latitudes, people had different needs to survive. In order to stay healthy, the human body needs to produce vitamin D, which can only be accomplished if some of the UV rays penetrate the skin. There was much less sunshine, so people had to be more efficient in their production of vitamin D. But there was also less of a need to protect the body against UV rays. So for people living in northern climates, it was a distinct advantage to have lighter skin because they could produce vitamin D more efficiently than their darker-skinned peers. Vitamin D deficiencies can negatively affect healthy bone and tooth growth in children. They can also cause birth defects and contribute to osteoporosis in adults. So in northern locations, people with lighter skin had a better chance of growing up and staying healthy as well as giving birth to healthy children. Over time more and more people inherited the disposition for light skin (Kotlarczyk et al., 2017; Lucock et al., 2021).

Natural selection works the same way with other traits. For example, originally humans could only digest lactose as infants and slowly became lactose intolerant as they grew up. However, around 15,000 years ago humans in some parts of the world abandoned their nomadic lifestyle and started to domesticate cows and other dairy animals. Those who could digest lactose as adults had an additional source of hydration and nutrition when water or other foods were scarce, aiding their survival and ultimately making them more likely to

© Ilike/Shutterstock.com

■ Twins Melody and Carter love playing with blocks. Carter builds castles and designates certain blocks monsters and guards; Melody builds a classroom, using blocks to represent students and the teacher. Do you think that the root of the sex differences we see here can be found in human evolutionary history, or do you believe that society and caregivers are the main cause of these differences?

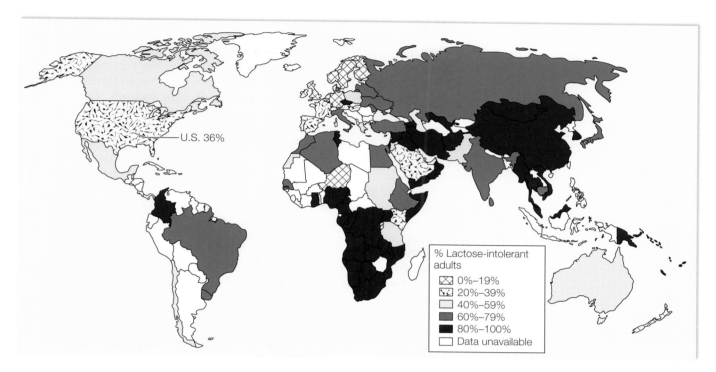

FIGURE 2.4 This map shows variations in the global prevalence of lactose intolerance.

Data from C. L. Storhaugh et al. 2017. *Lancet Gastroenterol Hepatol* 2: 738–746. Map created with Datawrapper

live longer, have children, and pass on the genetic disposition that enabled them to digest lactose. Today, we can see differences in lactose tolerance across regions of the world (**FIGURE 2.4**): In areas where the climate allowed for dairy farming, many adults are lactose tolerant, whereas in areas that did not lend themselves to dairy farming a high percentage of the population is lactose intolerant (Amato et al., 2021; Van de Vliert et al., 2018).

The traits that help individuals survive and reproduce can be physical ones, like skin pigmentation. But natural selection also applies to favorable personality traits and behaviors that increase the chance of survival and reproduction. For example, bonding behaviors in infants like gazing, smiling, vocalizing, and imitation of facial expressions increase the likelihood that the mother will satisfy the infant's needs for comfort, nourishment, and protection. At the same time, adults are very receptive to the crying of infants. They feel attracted to the looks of infants with their large eyes and bald heads (Tomasello & Gonzalez-Cabrera, 2017; Trevathan & Rosenberg, 2016). In fact, the more infants' facial features are perceived as "cute" and convey health, happiness, and a likeness with their parents, the more likely are adults to show caregiving behaviors (Franklin et al., 2018; Rosenberg, 2021).

Some researchers also suggest that the sex differences we see today between men and women in terms of size, strength, risk-taking, competitiveness, mate preferences, and many other traits can be explained by our evolutionary past (Conroy-Beam & Buss, 2018; Larsen et al., 2021; Puts, 2016). The evolutionary perspective suggests that a lot of behaviors and traits we see in humans today developed because they provided a survival advantage to our ancestors. Evolutionary psychologists study such topics as attachment, aggression, interpersonal attraction, gender development, and parenting strategies.

How the Study of Animals and Genes Helps Develop Evolutionary Theories

Evolutionary approaches also draw on a field called **ethology**, which studies animal behavior and infers how human behavior could be influenced by genetics and evolution. One of ethology's pioneers was Austrian zoologist Konrad

ethology the study of animal (including human) behavior and how it is influenced by genetics and evolution.

Lorenz (1903–1989). He studied how patterns of behavior in animals can be traced back to their evolutionary past (Lorenz, 2002). For example, he famously observed that newly hatched goslings "attach" to the first moving object they see, demonstrating a behavior called *imprinting*. In one experiment, he was present when goslings hatched. From that moment, acting in the place of their mother, he proceeded to teach them to swim, fly, and perform other activities that young geese require for survival. Other animals and human babies also display behaviors that serve to keep the youngsters close to the mother, and thus provide protection.

British psychologist John Bowlby (1907–1990) applied ethological findings about proximity-seeking behavior to humans when he developed his theory of attachment. He suggested that human babies attach to their caregivers as a survival mechanism: Staying close to their parents is a way of protecting themselves from predators. Bowlby believed that the attachment infants form early in life influences their development throughout the rest of their lives (Ainsworth & Bowlby, 1991).

Related to ethology is the field of *behavioral genetics*, which attempts to identify the impact of genetics and environmental factors on behavior. For example, some people have a genetic predisposition to certain types of cancer. However, not everyone with that predisposition will develop the disease. This is partly due to environmental factors that diminish the risk, such as regular exercise and a healthy diet (Ahern et al., 2021; U.S. National Library of Medicine, 2017).

Evolutionary approaches are frequently criticized for hypotheses that are difficult to test. They make assumptions about life and life circumstances that occurred in the distant past. And unlike for paleontology, which also studies evolutionary processes, there are no physical fossils to determine whether the evolutionary–psychological claims are true. Some scholars also believe that the evolutionary perspective places too much emphasis on the biological bases of behavior. For that reason, some evolutionary explanations like the one about sex differences are subject to considerable debate (Burke, 2014). However, evolutionary approaches have stimulated a significant amount of research and have provided valuable insight into what may have led to behaviors like aggression that otherwise might not seem adaptive.

We have now discussed five different approaches to child development that emphasize different aspects of development. **TABLE 2.5** summarizes each of these approaches to give you a concise overview.

■ Konrad Lorenz demonstrated that goslings will attach to the first moving object they see. How can this and other findings from ethology help us understand the way human children develop?

© Nina Leen/The LIFE Picture Collection/Getty Images

■ Table 2.5 Overview of Approaches and Theories in Child Development

Theory	Core ideas	Examples for application	Emphasis: environment or interaction between genes & environment	Continuous development or stages?
PSYCHODYNAMIC APPROACHES				
Psychoanalytic theory (Freud)	Unconscious thoughts and drives regulate development	Provide infants with pacifier to satisfy oral sucking need. Provide preschoolers with safe place (and appropriate explanations) to explore sexuality; teach parents that masturbation in young children is normal.	Interaction	5 Stages
Psychosocial theory (Erikson)	Identity crises that reflect our connectedness with others and society at large drive development	Use stages to guide interactions with children. For example: *Preschool phase (initiative vs. guilt):* Find out children's interests and create projects in that area. Praise and offer feedback. *Middle childhood (industry vs. inferiority):* Emphasize learning from mistakes rather than perfection. Encourage children to focus on and acknowledge their strengths.	Interaction	8 Stages
LEARNING APPROACHES				
Classical conditioning (Pavlov, Watson)	Learning occurs through the pairing of a neutral stimulus with an unconditioned stimulus.	Behavior therapy for phobias (irrational fear of something): teach relaxation while exposing to progressively more stressful stimuli (e.g., relaxation while bringing a spider closer and closer to patient). Commercials: present product with attractive model.	Environment	Continuous
Operant conditioning (Skinner)	The consequences of our actions determine the likelihood that behavior will be repeated again.	Use rewards (reinforcement) in toilet training. Adapt rewards to age and preferences of child.	Environment	Continuous
Social cognitive theory (Bandura)	Learning through observation and imitation of others	Model tooth brushing and have child imitate actions. Model conflict resolution when siblings argue.	Interaction	Continuous
COGNITIVE APPROACHES				
Cognitive-developmental theory (Piaget)	Learning occurs through adaptation: (a) integration of new information in current knowledge (assimilation) or (b) adjustment of current knowledge to new information (accommodation).	Adapt teaching to child's cognitive stage. Provide hands-on experiences to explore. Teach at child's level, using examples that reflect child's experiences.	Interaction	4 Stages
Information-processing approaches	Development occurs as children become more efficient at information processing.	Provide children with strategies that help memorize facts. Help young children focus by minimizing distractions and providing frequent breaks. Teach problem-solving strategies.	Interaction	Continuous

(Continued)

■ **Table 2.5** (*continued*)

Theory	Core ideas	Examples for application	Emphasis: environment or interaction between genes & environment	Continuous development or stages?
CONTEXTUAL APPROACHES				
Sociocultural theory (Vygotsky)	Learning occurs through social interaction.	Challenge children within their zone of proximal development. Let children of different ages cooperate so they can help each other. Provide appropriate scaffolds (e.g., when teaching how to ride a bike first use training wheels, then take them off and run alongside child).	Environment	Continuous
Ecological systems theory (Bronfenbrenner)	Learning is influenced by the interaction of five ecosystems in which the child grows up.	When working with child and parents, assess their contextual systems (community, state resources available, extended family, etc.) and tailor intervention to optimize support from all levels.	Interaction	Not specified
EVOLUTIONARY APPROACHES				
Ethology and evolutionary psychology	Behavior is rooted in genes. The behaviors and traits that are transmitted are those that facilitate survival. Humans adapt behavior to demands of their environment.	Integrate teaching into play to satisfy children's natural tendency to play. See children's abilities and limitations as adaptations to their environment: Infants have poor eyesight in order to limit incoming visual stimuli that need to be processed. Children overestimate their abilities because that helps them take on challenging tasks and persist in the face of repeated failure.	Interaction	No stages specified, but existence of critical periods

Review!

How do evolutionary approaches explain development?

■ *Evolutionary approaches* hypothesize that much of the behavior we see in children today can be traced back to the struggle for survival of our prehistoric ancestors.

■ Through the process of natural selection, those behaviors and traits that provided the most advantages to survival were passed on to the next generation.

Practice!

1. According to Freud, the _____ is the part of our personality that attempts to compromise between our desire to follow our unconscious drives and the moral values we have learned.
   a. ego
   b. id
   c. superego
   d. infraego

2. In _____ , a person learns to react to a stimulus, like a smell or the honking of a car horn, that the person did not react to before.

   a. operant conditioning
   b. positive reinforcement
   c. classical conditioning
   d. observational learning

3. In _____ , a child learns behavior by watching others.
   a. operant conditioning
   b. classical conditioning
   c. observational learning
   d. behaviorism

4. According to Piaget, accommodation and _____ are two ways in which we incorporate new knowledge and experiences into our existing knowledge.
   a. cognitive processing
   b. equilibration
   c. schemata
   d. assimilation

5. The _____ describes the difference between what a child can do without help and what a child can do with assistance.
   a. zone of proximal development
   b. scaffold
   c. culture
   d. schema

What's Your Position?

Melody and Carter may be twins, but their hobbies and styles of play are as different as can be. Carter loves soccer; in fact, he loves all team sports. He's also passionate about airplanes: He'll read books and watch videos about planes, he'll build planes with Lego, and he'll fold scraps of paper into airplanes for flying. Melody isn't interested in soccer or planes. She does enjoy figure skating—that's her favorite sport—and she loves to make jewelry for her family and friends with her beading kit.

The twins' parents have tried to raise them without gender prejudice, making sure to give each child the same access to toys and activities. They are dismayed to see their children settle into these gender stereotypes. What do you think is the cause of the twins' differences in interests? Are the parents inadvertently reinforcing gender stereotypes? Are the children's genes responsible for their behavior? Or might society be at fault with movies, ads, and stories depicting a certain "ideal" way in which girls and boys are expected to behave?

A few weeks later at the Morasi–Fletcher household: A mother ponders her childhood

It's been several weeks since Jennifer tried, unsuccessfully, to introduce her four-year-old daughter, Luisa, to her favorite book from her own childhood three decades earlier. Luisa could not relate to the story at all. Jennifer has thought back on that night often, and each time, she is flooded with a wave of disappointment. That book meant so much to her, and she's been waiting to read it to Luisa for years. She considers Luisa to be so similar to her in so many ways. Why was she not interested in the book? Aren't books timeless, after all?

Jennifer is left to conclude that there is a disconnect between her childhood interests and experiences and those of her daughter. As for her son, Marco, he seems bewildered—but also fascinated—by the differences between his childhood and his mother's. He simply cannot comprehend how anyone ever lived without the internet, streaming movies, mobile phones, and video games you didn't have to go to an arcade to play. What did children back then do all day? He bombards Jennifer with questions and eventually walks away from her stories shaking his head.

Though she has never thought about it before, Jennifer now starts to recognize how much the environment influences children—what they're interested in, what they're reading and thinking about, and how they spend their time. Luisa and Marco certainly have a much busier schedule than Jennifer's was when she was their age. Jennifer has already started thinking about her children's education and how she can prepare them to compete on the college admissions market—that certainly was not on people's minds for their toddlers when Jennifer was growing up. Jennifer is left wondering if she would even like to grow up in the time she is raising her children. ▪ ▪ ▪ ▪

Overview

Genetics, Conception, and Prenatal Development

Genetic disorders may be passed from parents to their children

Evan and Nancy are registering at the Clinical Genetics Clinic at the children's hospital in Cincinnati. They've come with their two daughters, aged 3 and 1. The older of the two children, Ava, has been here before. After experiencing repeated respiratory infections, she was diagnosed with cystic fibrosis, an inherited disease that progressively damages the lungs and digestive system. People with cystic fibrosis tend to die prematurely, usually in their forties or fifties. As a precaution, Evan and Nancy decided to get their youngest daughter, Sophia, tested as well, and were shocked to learn that she also has cystic fibrosis.

As they register Sophia for her first appointment at the clinic, Evan and Nancy tell the booking nurse about the series of events that has brought them here. They recount how shocked they were, first by Ava's diagnosis and then by Sophia's: Neither parent knew they carried the gene for cystic fibrosis, and now they are confronted with the fact they will need to change their lives in order to accommodate the serious and ongoing medical needs of their two children. Nancy expresses their angst about their plan to try for a third child: She and Evan wonder if it is reasonable to try, given that they might produce a third child with this frightening, incurable genetic disease.

In this chapter, we will look at how people pass characteristics from one generation to the next through genes. We will discuss conception and prenatal development and which factors influence prenatal development. Lastly, we will consider the importance of prenatal care as well as some common pregnancy problems.

3.1 The Construction Plan for a Human Being: Chromosomes, Genes, and Heredity

- Explain what genes are and how inheritance works.
- Conclude whether or not we are wholly products of our genes or if the environment also plays a role in our development.
- Tell what happens if there are errors in our genome.

Each one of us has about 37 trillion cells in our body. Every single cell contains the entire construction plan for the human body, set out in our genes (Bianconi et al., 2013). And yet, although the number of cells in our body is so unbelievably large, we all started with just one cell, made up of the genetic material passed down to us from our father and our mother. In this section, we will explore chromosomes and genes, how they influence what we become, and how abnormalities in chromosomes and genes can disrupt a person's normal mental or physical development.

The Basics of Heredity

The importance of genetics to life is undeniable. Small defects or errors in our genetic code help to account for substantial variation in the human population. While many of these errors in our genes contribute to inconsequential differences, others bear crucial consequences for the well-being of a person. We will start this section by defining chromosomes and genes. Then we will look at how they are copied when our cells divide and how traits are passed on to the next generation.

Chromosomes are made of DNA segments called genes

All living things are made of cells. Each cell in the human body has a nucleus that contains 23 pairs of chromosomes (or in other words, 46 chromosomes in total). **Chromosomes** are threadlike structures that contain genetic information and determine all sorts of physical characteristics, such as a person's height and hair color (**FIGURE 3.1**). Of the 23 chromosome pairs, 22 are **autosomes**, containing genetic information that does *not* determine the sex of a person. These 22 pairs are identical in males and females. The twenty-third pair consists of two **sex chromosomes** that determine whether a person is biologically male or female. Females have two chromosomes that are shaped like an X and hence are called *X chromosomes*. Males have one X chromosome and one shorter chromosome, called the *Y chromosome*. A complete set of 46 chromosomes is called a **karyotype**.

chromosome a threadlike structure found in the nucleus of most living cells, containing the genetic information of an organism.

autosome any of the 44 chromosomes that do not determine a person's sex.

sex chromosome each of a pair of chromosomes that determine a person's sex. Females have two X chromosomes; males have one X chromosome and one Y chromosome.

karyotype a complete set of 46 chromosomes.

FIGURE 3.1 Computer illustration of male (*left*) and female (*right*) karyotypes. A karyotype is the complete set of 46 chromosomes, including 23 inherited from the mother and 23 inherited from the father. The chromosomes labeled XY and XX determine the sex (male and female, respectively) of the individual.

Chromosomes in the cell nuclei for males and females

Male

Female

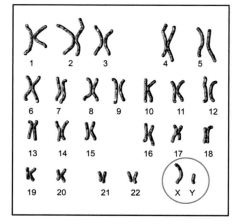
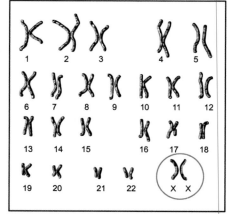

© Kateryna Kon/Shutterstock.com

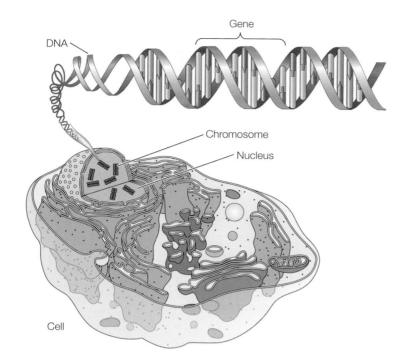

Gene

DNA

Chromosome

Nucleus

Cell

FIGURE 3.2   Chromosomes are made of long strands of DNA (deoxyribonucleic acid). Each strand is shaped like a spiral staircase.

Chromosomes are made of long strands of **DNA** (deoxyribonucleic acid), each strand shaped like a spiral staircase (**FIGURE 3.2**). Each "step" of the staircase is made of a pair of biochemical bases. The DNA strings in each chromosome are very long: If you stretched out a person's DNA, it would be around 6 feet long (National Human Genome Research Institute, 2015)! DNA strands can be divided into segments called **genes** that contain information for creating proteins needed for many body functions. Humans have about 21,000 genes (Abascal et al., 2018; Ezkurdia et al., 2014).

The entire set of an organism's genes is called the **genome**. From person to person, those genes differ just a little bit in how the base pairs are arranged. Different variants of a single gene are called **alleles**. A typical gene has between several thousand and two million base pairs, and only about one to three of those base pairs differ from person to person (Genetic Science Learning Center, 2017). These tiny variations in our genes are the reason for individual differences between people.

Children receive half their chromosomes from their father and half from their mother

Most cells in our bodies have 46 chromosomes. However, sperm cells and egg cells (together called **gametes**) differ from other cells: Each gamete has only 23 chromosomes in total, instead of 46. When an egg and sperm combine at fertilization, each contributes its set of chromosomes to form a **zygote**, which then has 46 chromosomes (**FIGURE 3.3**). That way, children receive half of their genes from their father and half of their genes from their mother.

As we discussed above, the twenty-third pair of chromosomes, the sex chromosomes, determines the sex of the child. In earlier times when traditional societies had no knowledge of genetics, people often suspected that the food eaten during pregnancy influenced the gender of the unborn child. In Turkey, for example, people believed that eating bitter foods would lead to the birth of a girl and eating sweet foods would lead to the birth of a boy. Today, we know the sex depends on whether a sperm with an X chromosome or a Y chromosome penetrates the egg (Peck et al., 2017; Zarulli et al., 2018).

DNA deoxyribonucleic acid, a molecule that carries hereditary material in humans and most other organisms.

gene a segment of a DNA strand in a chromosome, which carries genetic information.

genome the entirety of an organism's genes.

allele one of several alternative forms of a gene.

gamete sex cells or an organism's reproductive cells; female gametes are called ova or egg cells and male gametes are called sperm; gametes have only 23 chromosomes each.

zygote the cell that is created when gamete cells (ovum and sperm) are joined; the zygote has 46 chromosomes in 23 pairs.

FIGURE 3.3   Hereditary composition of the zygote.

After D. E. Papalia. 2003. *Child Development: A Topical Approach.* McGraw-Hill, New York

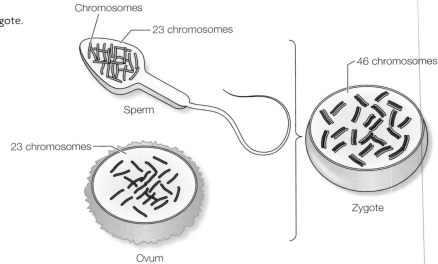

dominant trait   a heritable trait that is expressed in offspring even when the gene for that trait is inherited from only one parent.

recessive trait   a heritable trait that is expressed in offspring only when the gene for the trait has been inherited from both parents.

heterozygous   having two different alleles of a gene for a particular trait.

homozygous   having identical alleles of a gene for a particular trait on both chromosomes.

polygenic trait   a trait that is controlled by two or more genes.

The expression of a gene depends on whether it is dominant or recessive

Half of our chromosomes come from our father, and half come from our mother. But if mother and father pass on different genes for a particular trait—say, hair color—which trait do we end up with? The answer actually depends on whether the trait is *dominant* or *recessive*. **Dominant traits** are expressed even if there is only one gene for that trait and the paired second gene is for a competing trait. **Recessive traits** are expressed only if they are paired with a second gene for the recessive trait; if they are paired with a gene for a dominant trait, the dominant trait will be expressed.

Take as an example the disorder phenylketonuria (PKU) and how it is inherited (**FIGURE 3.4**). Individuals with PKU have an allele (a variation) of a gene that undermines the body's ability to process phenylalanine. Left untreated, it leads to brain damage as well as to behavioral and emotional problems (Jahja et al., 2017; van Spronsen et al., 2021). PKU is recessive, so only those people who inherit the altered gene from both parents will have the disorder.

People who have only one allele for PKU are called *carriers*. They do not have symptoms of PKU but can pass the gene on to the next generation. They are said to be **heterozygous** for PKU, because their alleles are different across the two chromosomes for the trait. People who have the same allele on both chromosomes are said to be **homozygous** for that particular trait. A recessive trait, such as PKU, shows only in homozygous people.

Most of our traits actually are not determined by a single gene. Research finds that even traits that were once thought to be determined by a single gene, like eye color, are instead polygenic. **Polygenic traits** are determined by two or more genes (White & Rabago-Smith, 2011). So for many traits, it is very difficult, if not impossible, to predict the outcome in future offspring.

Genes and the Environment

People have always been fascinated by identical twins and their astonishing similarities even when they are raised apart. But although many accounts of identical twins emphasize their "identicalness" due to their shared genes, there are plenty of differences between identical twins once you get to know them: Of my own identical twin girls, one has stage fright and the other one does not. One is very assertive and the other one just goes with the flow. One likes to sleep in and the other one is the first to rise.

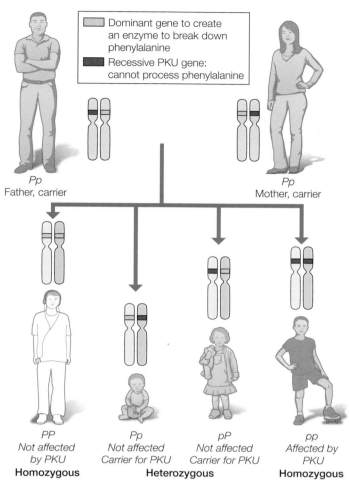

After S. M. Breedlove. 2015. *Principles of Psychology.* Sinauer/Oxford University Press, Sunderland, MA

FIGURE 3.4 When both the mother and father are carriers of the gene that causes PKU, there is a 25% chance that a child will inherit both recessive genes for PKU (*p*) and will be affected by the disorder. If a child inherits from both mother and father the healthy version of the gene (*P*) that allows the body to break down phenylalanine, the child is not affected by the disorder (25% chance). A child carrying one dominant gene (*P*) and one recessive gene (*p*) will not suffer from PKU, but is a carrier and may transmit the recessive gene to future offspring (50% chance).

Obviously our traits are influenced by more than just our genes; as we will see in this section, the environment plays a significant role in shaping human traits, in twins and non-twins alike.

Environmental factors influence the expression of genes (and vice versa): The role of epigenetics

Before we discuss how the environment influences our genes, we need to differentiate between a person's *genotype* and the person's *phenotype*. When we talk about someone's **genotype**, we are referring to the person's genetic makeup. In contrast, the term **phenotype** refers to a person's actual characteristics, resulting from the interaction of the person's genes with the environment. For example, Nicolai may carry a genotype that predisposes him to develop diabetes. However, he does not have diabetes, so the disease is not part of his phenotype. In other words, although our bodies have genetic "instructions" for all kinds of possible characteristics, not all of these characteristics will actually be expressed. In a process called **epigenetic modification**, our environment influences our genes in such a way that they are "turned on" or "turned off." When DNA is tightly wound up, it cannot be decoded, and thus the genes in that part of the DNA are "turned off." Loosely wound-up DNA activates the genes by making them "readable."

Over the course of our lives some genes get turned on or off depending on factors like stress, sleep, nutrition, exercise, drug use, and so on (**FIGURE 3.5**). For example, a number of nutrients are associated with a decreased risk of cancer. The nutrients in soybeans, grapes, and peanuts can lower a person's risk of breast cancer

genotype the genetic makeup of a person.

phenotype the actual characteristics of a person that are the result of the interaction between genes and environment.

epigenetic modification a process that activates or deactivates genes by tightly or loosely winding up DNA.

FIGURE 3.5 These two images show a pair of chromosome 3 of monozygotic twins Robert and Richard. The chromosomes have been digitally overlaid. Robert's epigenetic tags (that turn genes on and off) are dyed red and Richard's epigenetic tags are dyed green. The epigenetic tags that both twins share are marked yellow. Note that early in life the twins shared many more epigenetic tags than later in life because they are increasingly faced with different environments that leave their marks in the form of epigenetic tags.

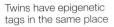

3-year-old twins   50-year-old twins

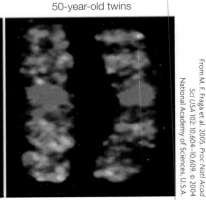

Twins have epigenetic   Twins have epigenetic
tags in the same place   tags in different places

From M. F. Fraga et al. 2005. *Proc Natl Acad Sci USA* 102: 10,604–10,609 © 2004 National Academy of Sciences, U.S.A.

monozygotic (MZ) twins twins who develop from one zygote and who have the same genome.

dizygotic twins (DZ) twins who develop from two zygotes and share 50% of their genome, like regular siblings who are born at different times.

ovum (plural **ova**) a mature female reproductive cell (egg) that can develop into an embryo after fertilization by a male sperm cell.

heritability extent to which genetic differences contribute to individual differences in traits; expressed as a numerical value ranging from 0 (genes do not contribute to individual differences in traits) to 1.0 (genes account for the entirety of individual differences in a trait)

through their epigenetic effects; flaxseed can lower the risk of ovarian cancer and improve brain development; and green tea can inhibit the growth of metastases in pancreatic cancer (Bishop & Ferguson, 2015; Nepali & Liou, 2021). To investigate the interaction of environment and genes, researchers often examine pairs of twins. In the next section, we will take a look at what twins can teach us about heredity.

Twins help us understand heredity

Twins can be either *monozygotic* (identical) or *dizygotic* (fraternal). As we saw earlier this chapter, the cell that forms at conception when sperm and egg fuse is called a *zygote*. **Monozygotic (MZ) twins** have their origin in the same zygote (*mono* = "one"). At some point within the first few days of pregnancy, the fertilized egg splits into two halves, which then develop into two individual children. Only about 3 to 5 in every 1,000 births result in identical twins, a rate that is fairly consistent across the world (Bricker, 2016; Sellers et al., 2021). MZ twins have roughly the same genome, though because cell division introduces new genetic mutations, their genes are not, strictly speaking, identical. However, their genes are similar enough that differences between monozygotic twins can be attributed to influences from their environment.

Dizygotic (DZ) twins, commonly known as fraternal twins, develop when a woman releases two **ova** (eggs) during ovulation and both are fertilized. About 70% of all twin pregnancies are dizygotic (Bricker, 2016; Tomkins et al., 2020). Dizygotic twinning rates are very low in Asia (about 6 dizygotic twin births per 1,000 births) and particularly high in parts of Africa (about 40 dizygotic twin births per 1,000 births); in the United States, about 12 out of 1,000 births are dizygotic twins (Mbarek et al., 2016). Dizygotic twins share 50% of their genes, just like any siblings born at different times.

When monozygotic twins resemble each other more closely than dizygotic twins, researchers conclude that their differences can be attributed to heredity, that is, their genes. We can also draw conclusions about the importance of genes by comparing adopted children with their biological and adopted parents. Researchers use the concept of **heritability** to describe the extent to which

■ Identical twins James Springer and James Lewis (sitting) were adopted by different families when they were one month old. At age 39, they were reunited and found they shared many striking similarities. They had both married (and subsequently divorced) women named Linda, then married women named Betty. They both smoked and drank alcohol, and both experienced headaches around the same time of day (Allen, 1998; Baggini, 2015). Are these uncanny circumstances mere coincidence?

genetics contributes to individual differences in traits. Heritability is expressed as a numerical value ranging from 0 to 1.0. A value of 0 indicates that the differences between people in one trait are due solely to differences in their environment—genes do not play a role. To the contrary, a value of 1.0 indicates that differences in a trait between people are due completely to genetics. However, heritability statistics refer to an entire population and not any one individual. That is, for any specific individual you cannot say how much of a trait can be attributed to genetics or the environment. We will have a closer look at the heritability of some traits in the next section.

Some traits have a stronger genetic basis

Most of our characteristics are produced by a combination of genetic and environmental factors. It is difficult to say how exactly genetics and environment interact. We know from research that personality differences in traits like agreeableness or extraversion have a strong genetic basis, particularly in the period before early adulthood (**TABLE 3.1**). Intelligence is partly heritable as well (Krapohl et al., 2014; Pesta et al., 2020).

■ Triplets may consist of monozygotic twins and a dizygotic sibling. Monozygotic siblings developed from the same fertilized egg; they are genetically identical and look very similar to each other. Dizygotic siblings developed from two different ova and are genetically as related to each other as any other siblings born at different times. Can you tell which of these triplets is the dizygotic brother?

■ **Table 3.1** Heritability: The Influence of Genes on Traits and Disorders

Intelligence

Highly polygenic (Benyamin et al., 2014)

Influence of genes increases significantly as a person gets older (Plomin & Deary, 2015).

Stimulating activities like reading and athletics as well as diet and other factors play a role (Sternberg & Grigorenko, 2014).

Personality

Strong genetic basis in childhood

With increasing age, environment becomes more important (Bleidorn et al., 2014; Pesta et al., 2020).

On average, 40% of individual differences in traits can be attributed to genetic factors and 60% to environmental influences (Vukasović & Bratko, 2015).

Physical and psychological disorders

Individuals inherit a predisposition for a number of disorders like autism, attention-deficit/hyperactivity disorder, or reading disorder (e.g., Cheroni et al., 2020).

A predisposition increases the probability that a disorder will be displayed; it does not indicate that a person will indeed get the disorder or how serious the disorder will be.

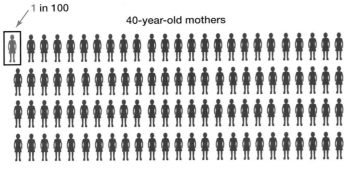

1 in 2,000
20-year-old mothers

1 in 100
40-year-old mothers

1 in 10
50-year-old mothers

FIGURE 3.6 Number of babies born with Down syndrome, by age of mother.

Data from National Down Syndrome Society. 2017. What Is Down Syndrome? www.ndss.org

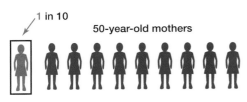

| **Down syndrome** a congenital chromosomal disorder arising from an additional (third) copy of chromosome 21.

Abnormalities in Chromosomes and Genes

Variations at gene level are often just the basis for the variations we observe between people: differences in hair, skin, and eye color, in blood type, or in whether someone has freckles or dimples. But they can also cause abnormalities that are more serious.

Chromosomal disorders are caused by structural abnormalities or incorrect numbers of chromosomes

In chromosomal abnormalities, a person has either an incorrect number of chromosomes or chromosomes that are altered from what they should be. Most chromosomal disorders are not passed on from one generation to the next but are random events. **Down syndrome** is the chromosomal disorder that occurs most often: About 1 in 700 babies is born with Down syndrome. In Down syndrome, people have an extra copy of chromosome 21. The condition is also called *trisomy 21* because there are three copies (*tri–*) rather than two of chromosome 21. Trisomy 21 is the only trisomy with which any kind of extended life is possible at all. Most other trisomies lead to miscarriages. Children with trisomy 13 or 18 rarely survive beyond their first year of life (Neubauer & Boss, 2020). Older women have a higher risk of conceiving an infant with Down syndrome (**FIGURE 3.6**).

Down syndrome can be diagnosed before birth through prenatal tests. Roughly 30 to 40% of people with Down syndrome are born with heart defects and congenital abnormalities, but advances in the use of antibiotics and heart surgeries have helped increase the lifespan of children with Down syndrome. Today, about 80% of adults with Down syndrome live to age 60 (Neubauer & Boss, 2020).

Sex-linked chromosomal disorders involve an altered, extra, or missing sex chromosome

As you know, a person's sex is determined by two sex chromosomes: one from the father and one from the mother. An extra sex chromosome, the lack of a sex chromosome, or an abnormality in one of the sex chromosomes will result in a sex-linked chromosomal disorder (see also **TABLE 3.2**).

◼ Abigail is a happy and outgoing 11-year-old girl who was born with Down syndrome. Like many other people with Down syndrome, she has a broad facial profile, an enlarged tongue, and an extra skin fold at the corner of the eyelid. Abigail's physical and intellectual development is delayed, and she experiences cardiovascular and digestive issues. Adults with Down syndrome show a wide variation in cognitive ability, physical development, and behavior. Many of them enjoy active participation in community life.

Females who lack an entire X chromosome or part of it are affected by **Turner syndrome** (also called X0 syndrome). They are usually shorter than other girls and may be infertile as adults because their ovaries have not developed adequately (Gravholt et al., 2019).

Turner syndrome a chromosomal disorder in females resulting from the lack of part or all of an X chromosome.

■ Table 3.2 Chromosomal and Genetic Disorders

Disorder	Incidence	Description	Treatment	Dominant/ recessive	Autosomal/ X-linked
Cystic fibrosis	1 in 2,000 births	Mucus buildup in lungs and pancreas leads to breathing difficulty and lung damage as well as impaired digestion. Life expectancy is approx. 40 years.	Physical therapy to clear airways of mucus; medication to treat infections and loosen mucus; enzymes to aid digestion	Recessive	Autosomal
Duchenne muscular dystrophy	1 in 3,500 male births	Progressive weakening of the muscles leads to wheelchair dependence in early adolescence.	None	Recessive	X-linked
Hemophilia	1 in 4,000 male births[a]	Abnormal blood clotting leads to excessive bleeding from both external and internal injuries.	Infusions of hormones or clotting factors (proteins involved in blood clotting)	Recessive	X-linked
Huntington's disease	3–7 in 100,000 births	Deterioration of nerve cells in the brain leads to loss of muscle coordination and cognitive function. Symptoms first appear after age 30 (approx.).	None. Condition is usually fatal within 10–20 years of the onset of symptoms.	Dominant	Autosomal
Phenylketonuria (PKU)	1 in 10,000 births[b]	Metabolic disorder in which the body cannot produce the enzyme needed to break down the amino acid phenylalanine. Subsequent buildups lead to intellectual disability.	Can be diagnosed at birth; intellectual disability can be prevented with a diet that limits foods containing phenylalanine.	Recessive	Autosomal
Sickle-cell anemia	1 in 365 African American births	Blood disorder in which misshapen red blood cells inhibit blood flow and oxygen supply throughout the body, resulting in joint swelling and pain, delayed growth, and frequent infections	Blood transfusions to increase number of healthy red blood cells; bone marrow transplants; antibiotics for infections; pain relievers	Recessive	Autosomal
Tay-Sachs disease	1 in 3,600 Jewish (of European descent) births	Neurological disorder that destroys nerve cells in brain and spinal cord	None; usually fatal in early childhood	Recessive	Autosomal
Neural tube defects: Anencephaly and spina bifida	Anencephaly: 1 in 1,000 pregnancies and 1 in 10,000 live births Spina bifida: 1 in 2,500 live births	Anencephaly: Absence of a major portion of the brain and skull Spina bifida: Exposure of parts of the spinal cord	Anencephaly: None; most children die before birth Spina bifida: Surgery to close the spinal canal	Multiple genes involved	
Turner syndrome	1 in 800 female births	Incomplete or lack of one X chromosome leads to short height, heart defects, and infertility	Hormonal treatment to stimulate growth and puberty[c]		X-linked
Triple X syndrome	1 in 1,000 female births	A third X chromosome typically leads to developmental delays	Interventions and services for cognitive and motor delays		X-linked
Fragile X syndrome	1 in 4,000 males 1 in 6,000 females	One X chromosome has a deactivated gene that leads to intellectual disabilities and behavior problems	Symptom-led treatment; often special education and speech therapy		X-linked
Klinefelter syndrome	1 in 500 males	An extra X chromosome leads to a more female appearance and intellectual disabilities	Hormone therapy to stimulate puberty; special education		X-linked

[a]U.S. National Library of Medicine. 2017. Hemophilia. https://ghr.nlm.nih.gov
[b]R. A. Williams et al. 2008. *Clin Biochem Rev* 29: 31–41.
[c]K. O. Klein et al. 2018. *J Clin Endocrinol Metab* 103: 1790–1803.

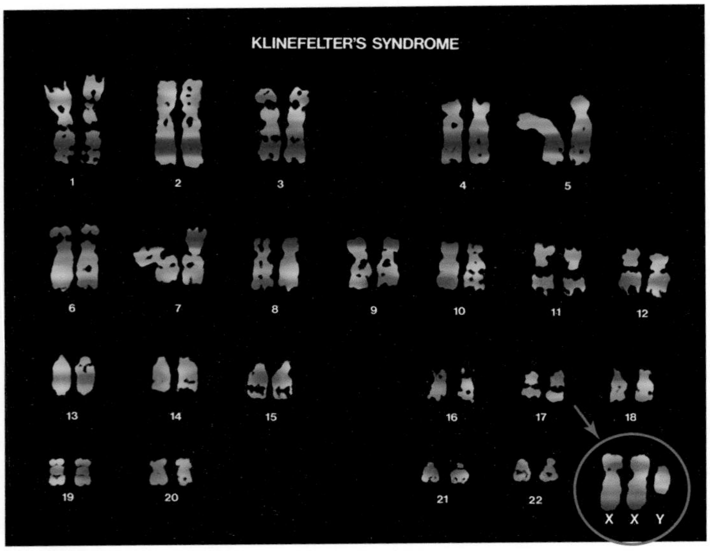

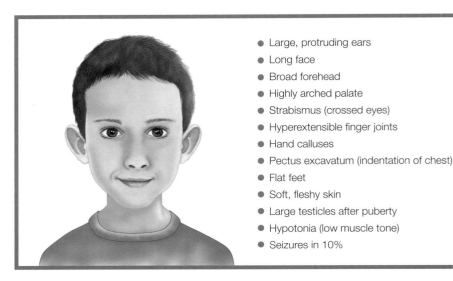

KLINEFELTER'S SYNDROME

© Biophoto Associates/Science Photo Library

FIGURE 3.7 Color-enhanced micrograph of a karyotype showing Klinefelter's syndrome, in which an extra X chromosome is present in a male.

triple X syndrome a chromosomal disorder in females resulting from an extra copy of the X chromosome.

Klinefelter syndrome a chromosomal disorder in which a male has an extra copy of the X chromosome.

fragile X syndrome a chromosomal disorder affecting males and females in which a gene located on the X chromosome and responsible for producing a particular protein is turned off.

Huntington's disease a fatal dominant genetic disorder in which nerve cells in the brain die; onset is most often in middle age.

Other females may have one X chromosome too many (**triple X syndrome** or XXX syndrome), which typically leads to developmental delays. Males can have an extra X chromosome as well, in which case their condition is called **Klinefelter syndrome** (**FIGURE 3.7**). They often experience developmental delays and have a more female appearance. Both boys and girls can have **fragile X syndrome**, in which a gene that is located on the X chromosome gets turned off because of a mutation (**FIGURE 3.8**).

Genetic disorders are caused by errors in one or more genes

While chromosomal disorders are caused by missing, malformed, or additional chromosomes, genetic disorders are caused by abnormalities on the gene level. More than 10,000 disorders are *monogenic*, which means they are caused by an error in a single gene. Although each of these disorders may be rare, together they account for a substantial number of affected newborns. Worldwide, around 1 out of 100 children are born with a single-gene disease (World Health Organization, 2017). Between 20% and 50% of infant deaths are caused by genetic disorders (Berry et al., 1987; Wojcik et al., 2019). Genetics also plays a role in diseases that strike in adulthood: About 10% of chronic diseases like heart disease and diabetes have genetic bases, as do about 15% of cancers (American Cancer Society, 2017; Schneider, 1994). Like other heritable traits, genetic disorders can be either dominant or recessive.

DOMINANT GENETIC DISORDERS A dominant disorder affects children even if only one parent carries the gene for the disorder. One of the most well-known dominant genetic disorders is **Huntington's disease**, in which nerve cells in the brain die. Symptoms include personality changes and mood swings, walking difficulties, and impaired cognitive functioning (Huntington's Disease Society of America, 2021). Huntington's disease, like other serious dominant genetic disorders, persists over generations because its symptoms occur later in life, so that its carriers may have children before they have experienced any symptoms of the disorder.

FIGURE 3.8 Children with fragile X syndrome typically have long and narrow faces, large ears, and extraordinarily flexible fingers.

- Large, protruding ears
- Long face
- Broad forehead
- Highly arched palate
- Strabismus (crossed eyes)
- Hyperextensible finger joints
- Hand calluses
- Pectus excavatum (indentation of chest)
- Flat feet
- Soft, fleshy skin
- Large testicles after puberty
- Hypotonia (low muscle tone)
- Seizures in 10%

Normal red blood cells

Sickled (abnormal) red blood cells

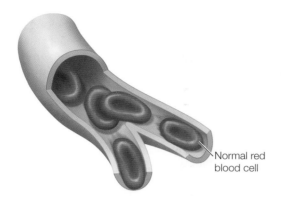
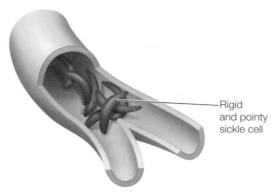

Normal red
blood cell

Rigid
and pointy
sickle cell

FIGURE 3.9   In people affected with sickle-cell anemia, misshapen red blood cells clog blood vessels and carry insufficient amounts of oxygen.

From D. M. Bozzone and D. S. Green. 2014. *Biology for the Informed Citizen*. Oxford University Press, New York

RECESSIVE GENETIC DISORDERS   A recessive disorder affects children only when they have inherited the gene for the disorder from both parents. People who carry only one gene for a recessive disorder do not exhibit any symptoms. For that reason, they often do not even know they are carriers of that particular gene. Evan and Nancy, whom we met at the beginning of this chapter, did not know they both carried the gene for cystic fibrosis until they had children. **Cystic fibrosis** is a progressive disorder affecting 30,000 Americans, in which thick mucus builds up in the lungs and pancreas, making breathing difficult and hindering food digestion (Cystic Fibrosis Foundation, 2021).

cystic fibrosis a recessive genetic disorder in which lungs and pancreas are clogged by mucus.

Sickle-cell anemia is a blood disorder found mainly in people of African descent or from the Middle East, India, and the Caribbean. It causes red blood cells to be crescent-shaped (**FIGURE 3.9**), which leads to clogged blood vessels, infections, and joint pain (Centers for Disease Control and Prevention, 2020b). People who are carriers of the gene for sickle-cell anemia actually benefit from having the gene: It protects them from malaria to some extent (Eleonore et al., 2020).

sickle-cell anemia a blood disorder in which red blood cells are misshapen, which leads to clogged blood vessels and impaired oxygen transport throughout the body.

Other recessive genetic disorders include Tay-Sachs disease and phenylketonuria (PKU), which we discussed earlier in this chapter (Figure 3.4)

X-LINKED GENETIC DISORDERS   The genetic disorders we have considered so far are all autosomal, meaning that they affect one of the 22 chromosome pairs unrelated to sex. In some dominant and recessive genetic disorders, the affected gene is located on the X chromosome of the 23rd pair—hence the name X-linked disorders. These disorders affect men more often than women because women have a second X chromosome that can in some cases compensate for the damaged genes.

Duchenne muscular dystrophy is a recessive X-linked disorder in which the body's muscles grow progressively weaker. Its onset is usually between ages 3 and 5, and children usually need to use a wheelchair by age 13 (Muscular Dystrophy Association, 2021).

Duchenne muscular dystrophy a recessive X-linked genetic disorder in which muscles grow progressively weaker, usually affecting boys.

Hemophilia is a recessive X-linked disorder in which blood does not clot properly, so that even small injuries can lead to excessive bleeding (U.S. National Library of Medicine, 2022).

hemophilia a recessive X-linked disorder in which blood does not clot properly.

Couples can get tested for genetic disorders

Let's return to Evan and Nancy. Should we be surprised that neither knew they were carrying the gene for cystic fibrosis? If no one in their immediate family has the recessive disease, they would have had no hint that they carried the gene. But sometimes people do know, or at least, suspect. Maybe there is a family history of a hereditary disease. Or perhaps an individual belongs to an ethnic group with a high incidence of a particular hereditary disease; many Jewish prospective parents are concerned about Tay-Sachs disease, for example.

Genetic counselors educate families regarding inheritance, help them understand their family medical histories and the chance that they might conceive a child with a genetic condition, and offer advice on how to deal with elevated risk situations. They also assist families who have found out they expect a baby with a birth defect or genetic condition. Genetic tests help assess the risk of future children inheriting a disorder, and counselors can advise couples on the options they have based on their particular situation (FIGURE 3.10).

Genetic testing is not without risks, however. There are many implications that have to be considered before as well as after testing is done. For that reason, involvement of a professional counselor is very important. Some of the risks are (U.S. National Library of Medicine, 2021a):

- The results may lead to emotional turmoil, anxiety, and depression.
- The results can reveal health information about family members who have not been tested.
- The tests can lead to "genetic discrimination" in which an employer or health insurance provider treats a person differently because they have been diagnosed as a carrier of a particular genetic disorder. There are state

FIGURE 3.10 Genetic testing can be done at a variety of times. Carrier testing occurs before conception. Preimplantation testing occurs after in vitro fertilization and involves testing an embryo before it is tranferred to the mother's uterus. Prenatal testing occurs during pregnancy, and newborn screening takes place after birth.

After Genetic Alliance. 2009. *Understanding Genetics: A New York, Mid-Atlantic Guide for Patients and Health Professionals*. Genetic Alliance, Washington, DC

© Syda Productions/Shutterstock.com

Carrier testing
Before conception, the parents are tested to see whether they carry the gene for a particular genetic disorder.

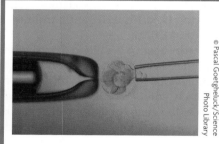
© Pascal Goetgheluck/Science Photo Library

Preimplantation testing
A couple might choose to conceive a child via in vitro fertilization, in which egg and sperm are brought together in a lab dish. Before the transfer to the mother's uterus, embryos can be tested for genetic disorders.

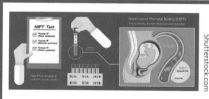
© runruay/Shutterstock.com

Prenatal testing
The fetus is tested for genetic disorders during the pregnancy. This can help parents and their medical team make special preparations for after the infant is born. It may also lead to a decision to abort the fetus.

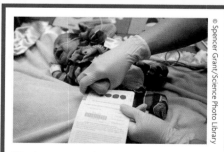
© Spencer Grant/Science Photo Library

Newborn screening
Newborns are routinely screened for a variety of genetic disorders (see also Chapter 4).

and federal laws that aim to protect people from discrimination. But laws are imperfect and cannot protect every individual in every circumstance (U.S. National Library of Medicine, 2021b).

- The test cannot predict whether a person will actually develop the disorder, whether the symptoms will be severe, and what the progression of the disease will be.
- Treatment for the revealed disorders may not be available.

Additionally, there are a number of test kits available commercially that offer to test the customer's DNA for ancestry, traits, and health information. A test kit that delivers results to the home without the involvement of a genetic counselor also may present customers with sensitive and, possibly, threatening news about their genetic information that leaves them confused and worried.

In 2013, Angelina Jolie underwent a preventive double mastectomy. Previously, genetic testing had shown that she was the carrier of a mutation of the *BRCA1* gene which, according to her doctors, resulted in an 87% risk of breast cancer (Choi et al., 2021).

What's It Like...

Having a Genetic Disorder in the Family

Mariam, age 41

When I was 14 years old, my little brother died of a rare genetic disease in which the body cannot break down sugar molecules adequately. He was fine at birth and at first developed normally, but around school age he started to regress physically and mentally and at age 8 his heart stopped beating. Even today, the disease cannot be treated successfully.

When I got married years later, my brother's disease came to the foreground again. Although my partner and I were still very young, we wanted to have a family at some point. But there was no way I'd want to see my own child suffer like my brother had. I talked with my gynecologist who suggested we see a genetic counselor. In our case, the disease was a recessive one, meaning that a future child would need to have one gene from each parent in order to have the disease. We saw a counselor and got tested, and it turned out that I am indeed a carrier of the disease. However, my husband is not. That means our babies could not possibly develop the disease, but they might be carriers.

Today we have two healthy daughters who are 8 and 11 years old. When they get older, I plan to suggest they get tested for the gene so they know what their situation is before they have a family. I think it's always better to know than not to know, and I want them to be able to make informed decisions.

Review!

What are genes, and how does inheritance work?

- Genes are segments of DNA (deoxyribonucleic acid), the molecules that make up chromosomes and carry genetic information.
- Chromosomes are made of long strands of DNA, which is made up of combinations of base pairs.
- The nucleus in each cell of our body contains our genome in the form of 23 pairs of chromosomes. One pair consists of sex chromosomes that determine whether a person is biologically male or female.
- Tiny variations in the base pairs of the genes are responsible for the differences we see between people. For dominant traits to

be expressed, a gene for that trait needs to be present on only one chromosome of a pair.

- Recessive traits need one gene on each chromosome of a pair to be expressed. However, most traits (polygenic traits) are determined not by one single gene but by a number of genes.

Are we wholly products of our genes, or does the environment play a role in what we become?

- Scientists study identical and fraternal twins as well as adopted children to find out what impact our genes have on the traits we display. Although some traits are highly heritable, not even identical twins are exactly alike, indicating that the environment influences the expression of traits as well.

- Personality and intelligence are highly heritable, but the importance of the environment grows as a person gets older.
- Likewise, a genetic disposition for a disease does not necessarily mean the carrier will eventually get the disease. Lifestyle factors like exercise and nutrition play an important role in whether a gene eventually is expressed.
- Throughout a person's lifetime, genes can be turned on and off through the process of epigenetic modification.

What happens if there are errors in our genome?

- When cells divide and copy their DNA, mistakes can happen. A chromosomal abnormality exists when a chromosome is mis-shaped, missing, or present with an additional copy.

- A trisomy occurs when there are three chromosomes instead of two; the most common example is Down syndrome.
- Abnormalities of the sex chromosomes lead to sex-linked chromosomal disorders like Turner syndrome or triple X syndrome. Many of these disorders are associated with learning disabilities.
- Abnormalities in genes lead to genetic disorders, many of them caused by an error in a single gene (in which case they are recessive or dominant, and autosomal or X-linked). A dominant autosomal genetic disorder is Huntington's disease. Recessive disorders include cystic fibrosis, sickle-cell anemia, and phenylketonuria (PKU).

Practice!

1. Huntington's disease is a _____ disease.
   a. dominant-gene
   b. recessive-gene
   c. chromosomal
   d. contagious

2. Autosomal genetic disorders are related to _____ .
   a. defects on the X chromosome
   b. defects on the Y chromosome
   c. defects on one of the chromosome pairs unrelated to sex
   d. defects on any of the 46 chromosomes

3. Susceptibility to Tay-Sachs disease is particularly common in _____ people.
   a. Jewish
   b. Catholic

   c. Buddhist
   d. Muslim

4. A disease linked to a recessive gene is most likely to display itself if it is carried by _____ .
   a. neither parent
   b. one parent
   c. both parents
   d. maternal grandparents

5. X-linked genetic disorders affect _____ .
   a. a gene on the 23rd chromosome pair
   b. a gene on any chromosome pair
   c. only women
   d. only men

Show What You've Learned!

In January 2020, researchers solved a mystery surrounding an Amish community in the Northeastern United States. Over a course of years, several children in two unrelated families had died suddenly while playing. The researchers found that the deaths were due to a mutated recessive gene the children

had inherited from both parents (see Kaur, 2020, for more information).

Imagine you work for a community health agency that serves this community. Prepare a short bulletin with advice for Amish families thinking of having children.

3.2 The Beginnings of Life

- List the stages that occur after the sperm and ovum unite at conception.
- Outline the various prenatal development stages and what happens during each stage.

Myths about conception abound. See if you agree with the following statements:

- You can't get pregnant while you have your period. (Actually, you can, but it is unlikely!)
- You can't conceive a second child while already pregnant. (Oh yes, you can—again, unlikely, but the result would be twins conceived at different times.)
- Some sexual positions are better than others for conceiving children. (Not really.)
- Older women are more likely to conceive twins. (True, actually!)

But what really happens at conception, and how does the unborn child develop while in the womb? We will find out in this section.

Conception

All human life has its beginnings at *conception* (or fertilization), when a sperm cell and an egg cell (or ovum) unite.

During sexual intercourse, the male partner ejaculates and his sperm enter the vagina. The sperm then make their way through the cervix into the uterus and onward into the Fallopian tubes. Only a small fraction of all sperm make it to the ovum; most of them either flow out of the vagina before making it into the uterus, die as a result of the acidic conditions in the vagina, or they enter the wrong Fallopian tube. For fertilization to occur, however, just one sperm is needed to unite with the ovum.

The egg and sperm cells both contain half a set of chromosomes. At fertilization, the two gametes fuse to create one cell called a *zygote,* which contains a complete set of 46 chromosomes in 23 pairs. From this zygote a new human being can develop.

Prenatal Development

Fertilization creates the basis for the development of a new baby: a full set of chromosomes in one cell. Prenatal development has begun and will end at birth. Prenatal development can be divided into three stages of varying length:

- the germinal stage, which lasts for 2 weeks;
- the embryonic stage, which lasts for 6 weeks; and
- the fetal stage, which lasts for approximately 31–33 weeks and ends with birth.

It is also common to divide prenatal development and pregnancy into three equal *trimesters*, each lasting three months. In this section, however, we will look at prenatal development in terms of the stages outlined above (and summarized in **TABLE 3.3**).

A full-term pregnancy lasts between 39 and 41 weeks (American College of Obstetricians and Gynecologists, 2017). Babies born before 37 weeks of pregnancy are considered preterm. In 2020, about 1 in 10 babies in the United States was born preterm (Centers for Disease Control and Prevention, 2021b).

Germinal stage: The first 2 weeks

The **germinal stage** is the shortest stage in prenatal development, lasting only about 2 weeks. Within about 24 hours of conception, the zygote starts to divide into two identical cells. Through *mitosis*, these cells continue to divide and duplicate, producing four cells, then eight cells, then sixteen cells, and so on (**FIGURE 3.11**).

While the cells are dividing, they move through the Fallopian tubes toward the uterus, propelled by the hairlike structures in the Fallopian tubes. After 3–4 days, the cell cluster arrives in the uterus. It is now called a *blastocyst* and has

germinal stage the first stage of prenatal development (lasting for 2 weeks from conception), in which the zygote starts to divide and attaches to the uterine wall.

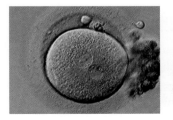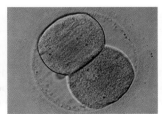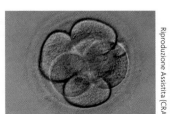

FIGURE 3.11 After conception, the zygote starts to divide in a process called mitosis.

■ Table 3.3 Prenatal Development Can Be Divided into Three Stages of Varying Length

Stage			Development	Size/Weight
FIRST TRIMESTER	1–2 weeks	© Omikron/Science Source	**Germinal stage: Conception–2 weeks** Ovum and sperm form a zygote, which has a complete set of 46 chromosomes Zygote starts to divide and implants in the wall of the uterus	¹⁄₁₀₀th of an inch long (≈ a poppyseed) © Anton Starikov/Shutterstock.com
	3–8 weeks	© Dr. M.A. Ansary/Science Photo Library	**Embryonic stage: 3 weeks–8 weeks** Cells begin to differentiate and assume different functions Neural tube forms from which brain and spinal cord will develop Major organs form Heart starts to beat First blood cells are produced Brain starts to develop First movements	By 8 weeks: half an inch long (≈ a raspberry) © EM Arts/Shutterstock.com
	9–12 weeks	© DOPAMINE/Science Photo Library	**Fetal stage: beginning at 9 weeks** Development of ovaries or testes Can suck thumb, swallow, and urinate	By 12 weeks: 3 inches long, less than one ounce (≈ a plum) © Tim UR/Shutterstock.com
SECOND TRIMESTER	13–26 weeks	© Neil Bromhall/Science Photo Library	Rapid neuron production Neurons migrate to their final destination in brain Toenails and fingernails develop Bones harden Hormone production begins Can have hiccups Mother can first feel fetal movement Responds to sound May be able to survive if born around 24 weeks	By 16 weeks: 7 inches long, 4 ounces (≈ an avocado) © Nataliya Schmidt/Shutterstock.com By 24 weeks: 12 inches long, more than a pound (≈ an eggplant) © Nataliya Schmidt/Shutterstock.com
THIRD TRIMESTER	27–40 weeks	© MEDI-MATION/Science Photo Library	Develops sense of smell Practices breathing movements Myelination of brain cells Produces fat layers for insulation Reacts to sounds Turns head down in uterus Organ systems mature and prepare for independent functioning after birth Activity level decreases as birth nears due to space restrictions in uterus	By 30 weeks: 16 inches, over 3 pounds (≈ a cabbage) © Chattaphan Sakulthong/Shutterstock.com By birth: 18–21 inches, 6–9 pounds

changed its shape to contain not only the dividing cells but also a fluid-filled cavity in the center. Once in the uterus, the blastocyst implants itself in the wall of the uterus (**FIGURE 3.12**). It is now about the size of a poppyseed.

Implantation is usually complete by the second week of the pregnancy. By then, the embryo consists of several hundred cells, which are starting to specialize

FIGURE 3.12 Once in the uterus, the blastocyst implants itself in the wall of the uterus.

After D. M. Hillis et al. 2019. *Principles of Life*, 3rd ed. Oxford University Press/ Sinauer, Sunderland, MA

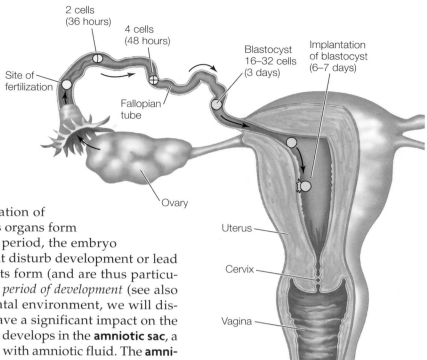

in their functions, undergoing the process known as *differentiation*. For example, some of the cells will form the placenta and the umbilical cord, while others will produce blood cells or form the amniotic sac.

Embryonic stage: Week 3 through week 8

The **embryonic stage** begins with the implantation of the embryo in the uterus. Most of the embryo's organs form during this stage. During this roughly 6-week period, the embryo is particularly sensitive to influences that might disturb development or lead to malformations. This period when body parts form (and are thus particularly susceptible to damage) is called a *critical period of development* (see also Figure 3.15). In the section below on the prenatal environment, we will discuss a number of factors that can potentially have a significant impact on the embryo's development. The vulnerable embryo develops in the **amniotic sac**, a protective pouch made of membranes and filled with amniotic fluid. The **amniotic fluid** regulates the temperature of the environment in which the embryo grows and buffers shocks.

The development of the embryo generally follows two trends. First, it develops from head to toe, giving priority to the development of the head and brain (*cephalocaudal trend*). Second, it develops from the inside out, so that organs in the center of the body are developed before body parts in the extremities (*proximodistal trend*; see **FIGURE 3.13**). In the chapters that follow, you will see that development after birth follows these trends as well: Infants first develop motor skills that involve body parts closer to the trunk (for example, they wave an arm before they can tie knots or draw fine lines with a pen), and they gain control of their arms before their legs.

Within 3 weeks of conception, the neural tube has formed. The neural tube is a hollow structure from which the spinal cord and brain will develop. At about this time, the developing heart begins to beat, reaching a rate of close to 110 beats per minute (Carlson, 2012; van Heeswijk et al., 1990). Pregnancy hormones are now present in the mother's body in such a high concentration that a home pregnancy test can detect the pregnancy.

By the end of the fourth week, buds representing the beginnings of future arms and legs have appeared (Moore et al., 2000). One week later, the liver has begun to produce blood cells and the eyes have started to develop. The cerebral cortex starts to develop at around 6 weeks, and the embryo begins to move reflexively (Visser et al., 1992). That movement is very important for healthy development of the bones and joints.

By the start of the eighth week, fingers and toes as well as facial features begin to develop. The brain now has two hemispheres and accounts for about 40% of the embryo's weight (Endowment for Human Development, 2017a; Jordaan, 1979).

| **embryonic stage** the second stage of prenatal development (lasting from the third through the eighth week), during which all major organs are formed.

| **amniotic sac** fluid-filled pouch made of membranes that protects the fetus as it grows in the womb.

| **amniotic fluid** protective fluid that surrounds the fetus in the amniotic sac.

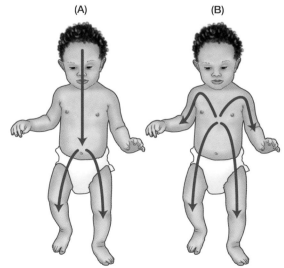

FIGURE 3.13 Children's bodies develop (A) from the head toward the toes (cephalocaudal trend) as well as (B) from the trunk outward (proximodistal trend).

From C. S. Tamis-LeMonda. 2022. *Child Development: Context, Culture, and Cascades*. Oxford University Press/Sinauer, Sunderland, MA; after E. Polan and D. Taylor. 2003. *Journey Across the Life Span: Human Development and Health Promotion*. F. A. Davis, Philadelphia

© Dr M.A. Ansary/Science Photo Library

■ Eight-week-old fetus. This fetus is seen during the first trimester. It is attached to the placenta and the mother's blood circulation by an umbilical cord (far left). The sac surrounding the fetus is known as an amniotic sac, which is filled with amniotic fluid. At the upper right are the remnants of the yolk sac. The embryo's eye and limbs are visible, as is its male sex. During the first trimester, embryos develop a distinct human appearance. In this early period, organ differentiation overshadows growth and all the major organs have been formed. At this age the embryo is about 4 centimeters in length and less than 10 grams in weight.

fetus an unborn human from the start of the ninth week of pregnancy until birth.

Fetal stage: Week 9 until birth

MONTH THREE OF THE FIRST TRIMESTER   The fetal stage lasts from the start of the ninth week until the birth of the child. During this time, the developing organism is referred to as a **fetus**.

In the months prior to birth the fetus not only grows and develops biologically but also gradually exhibits behaviors that are characteristic of humans after birth, like yawning, urinating, being startled at noises, and sucking its thumb. At the same time, fetuses increasingly show individual differences: For example, some fetuses are more active than others, and all fetuses develop at slightly different rates.

The *SRY* gene on the Y chromosome triggers the development of testes and prevents the development of female sex organs. The testes begin to produce the male hormone testosterone that subsequently is responsible for the development of male sexual organs. Neuron production begins and continues at a particularly rapid rate throughout the second trimester, by the end of which billions of neurons have formed (Stiles & Jernigan, 2010). The neurons in the brain become coated with a fatty substance called myelin, which insulates the neurons and increases the transmission speed of neuronal signals. This process will continue throughout childhood.

THE SECOND TRIMESTER   As the fetus grows rapidly and gains weight it becomes increasingly active and can move its arms, hands, and feet as well as its head. It can even get the hiccups. By just the tenth week of pregnancy, the fetus already has about 90% of the body parts an adult has. Between 10 and 12 weeks, the fetus starts to suck its thumb and swallow amniotic fluid. Over the following weeks, fingernails and toenails begin to grow, bones harden, and the fetus starts to produce hormones.

Around the 16th week, the fetus weighs roughly 4 ounces and is about 7 inches long. A pregnant woman can begin to feel the movements of the fetus. In the beginning, these movements may feel as soft as the touch of a butterfly, but as the fetus grows and gains weight and strength, movements will begin to feel more and more like kicks. Gender differences start to appear—for instance, female fetuses move their jaws more often than male fetuses (Hepper et al., 1997)—and by the 19th week of pregnancy, an ultrasound now can potentially reveal the sex of the fetus, if it is positioned in the womb in such a way to allow a view of its genitals.

During the sixth month of pregnancy—the final month of the second trimester—the fetus starts to be able to hear and respond to sounds. It also starts to experience rapid eye movements like the ones that can be observed when people dream during sleep.

THE THIRD TRIMESTER   Once it reaches the third trimester a fetus is considered *viable*, which means that it has a chance at survival if it is born. However, a fetus has low odds of surviving if it is born in the second trimester or very early in the third. Between 30% and 50% of fetuses delivered between weeks 24 and 27 do not survive. Of those very premature children that do survive, 20–50% suffer long-term physical disabilities or adverse learning, behavioral, or social issues as a result of their preterm birth (Glass et al., 2015; Kaempf et al., 2021).

The fetus performs breathing-like movements about 40% of the time. It has even developed a sense of smell. The fetus becomes increasingly aware of the mother, noticing the quickening of her heartbeat when she gets upset, listening and getting used to her voice, and being calmed down by her singing.

Because vital organs are still maturing in the third trimester, children born before the 37th week of pregnancy often need help breathing—their lungs are not yet developed enough. They may also need help feeding because they are often too weak to suck and drink enough on their own. They may be placed in an *isolette*, which is a transparent plastic incubator in which temperature, humidity, and oxygen can be carefully controlled. Many hospitals today practice *kangaroo care*, in which mothers of preterm babies (born before 37 weeks gestation) are encouraged to hold their babies with skin-to-skin contact. Kangaroo care has been shown to improve the physiological functions of the infant and helps establish a bond between mother and baby (Cho et al., 2016; Cunningham et al., 2021).

Overall, only about 1 in 10 babies is born early (Centers for Disease Control and Prevention, 2021b). Birth typically takes place between 38 and 40 weeks after conception (Endowment for Human Development, 2017b), by which point the fetus weighs about 7 pounds.

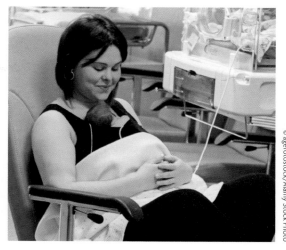

■ Although Katya's pregnancy was fairly uneventful, her son Matthew was born 7 weeks early. She was very distressed over his precarious health and felt anxious watching her tiny son struggle to gain weight and learn how to drink milk on his own. Having her infant placed on her chest for extended periods made her feel more connected to Matthew during his protracted stay in the hospital. Matthew benefitted as well and likely matured and grew better because of the physical contact with his mother.

Review!

What happens at conception?

■ When a mature ovum is released from a woman's ovary, it travels through the Fallopian tubes toward the uterus. During the first 12 hours, it may be fertilized by a man's sperm.

■ From these two gametes—the male and female reproductive cells—a new cell called a zygote is created.

■ The zygote contains 46 chromosomes arranged in 23 pairs: 23 chromosomes from the father and 23 chromosomes from the mother.

What happens during prenatal development?

■ We distinguish three different phases in prenatal development: germinal, embryonic, and fetal.

■ During the *germinal stage* (first 2 weeks), the zygote starts to divide, moves into the uterus, and then implants there.

■ Once implantation takes place, the *embryonic stage* (weeks 3–8) starts, during which most major organs develop. This puts the critical periods of development for many organs into the embryonic phase, because any organ is most susceptible to disturbances from outside factors during the time it initially forms. It is in the embryonic stage that the heart begins to beat, the liver begins to produce blood cells, and fingers and toes develop.

■ In the fetal stage (week 9 to birth), the *fetus* continues to develop and the brain changes drastically by developing folds and producing neurons. The fetus also starts to exhibit human-like behavior like thumb-sucking, yawning, or startling. A sense of smell develops, and the fetus starts to perform breathing movements and store energy in the form of fat.

■ Throughout this time, the fetus continues to mature and grow.

Practice!

1. The unborn child starts to be called a fetus _____ .
   a. during the first trimester
   b. during the second trimester
   c. during the third trimester
   d. at birth

2. A zygote consists of _____ cell(s).
   a. one
   b. two
   c. three
   d. up to five

3. A child born at the 19th week of pregnancy is _____ to survive.
   a. extremely unlikely
   b. somewhat unlikely
   c. somewhat likely
   d. very likely

4. A zygote has _____ chromosomes.
   a. 42
   b. 44
   c. 46
   d. 48

5. Myelination of brain cells occurs _____ .
   a. during the first trimester
   b. during the second trimester
   c. during the third trimester
   d. during all trimesters

Act It Out!

Aaliyah, now in her 12th week of pregnancy, has just had an ultrasound performed. To her delight, she has learned that she is carrying twins. Even better, both of them seem to be doing well. When she next meets with the doctor, she learns that there are some risks associated with twin pregnancies. With a classmate, and drawing on information presented in this chapter as well as the information below, act out a conversation between Aaliyah and her doctor. As Aaliyah, what questions would you have? As Aaliyah's doctor, what information would you need to provide?

Additional Resources Online

- "Pregnancy week by week," from the Mayo Clinic
- "Expecting twins or triplets," from the Cleveland Clinic
- "Complications of multiple pregnancy," from Johns Hopkins Medicine

Show What You've Learned!

You're teaching a sex ed class to a local youth group of teenagers. When you're discussing the topic of birth control, one boy asks you to explain how exactly children are conceived. Drawing on material presented in this chapter, write a script showing how you would explain the process of conception and prenatal development to the youth group.

---

placenta a temporary organ that sustains the life of the fetus during pregnancy by delivering nutrients and oxygen from the mother while eliminating waste products.

teratogen a substance that can interfere with the healthy development of the fetus.

■ In the 1960s, many children of mothers who took the drug thalidomide during their pregnancy were born with disfigured arms.

3.3 The Prenatal Environment: Factors Influencing Development

- Identify the maternal factors that influence prenatal development.
- Identify the paternal factors that influence prenatal development.

In 1958, Caroline was in Germany, pregnant with her first child. Her pregnancy was going well, but she was increasingly exhausted because she was not sleeping well at night. Her doctor prescribed a new medication, thalidomide, that would safely relieve anxiety and insomnia, as well as suppressing morning sickness. At the time, thalidomide was widely available in Europe as well as in countries like Canada and Brazil, but not in the United States.

When the time came for Caroline to give birth, happiness quickly gave way to shock: Her son was born with unusually short arms and twisted hands that had no thumbs. Caroline and her family as well as her doctors were as bewildered as they were dismayed: Why was the otherwise healthy newborn disfigured? In 1961, a West German newspaper first reported that there might be a link between the birth defects and the use of thalidomide during pregnancy, which eventually led to the withdrawal of the drug from the market (Dove, 2011; Vargesson & Stephens, 2021).

Caroline's story shows just one of many factors that can influence the course of a pregnancy and the health of the developing child. The **placenta** and umbilical cord that allow for the exchange of blood, oxygen, and valuable nutrients between mother and fetus can also harbor harmful substances that put the fetus's healthy development at risk. We refer to these harmful substances as **teratogens**. In this section we will consider a variety of factors that influence the health and development of a child prior to birth.

Maternal Factors Influencing Prenatal Development

Let's start by considering how an expectant mother influences her developing child. We need to consider factors the mother both can and cannot control. These include her health and diet during and before pregnancy, her use of and exposure to various substances, her life circumstances, and her psychological well-being.

The mother's dietary needs change during pregnancy

In order to accommodate the pregnancy and support healthy development of the infant, the mother's body needs about 300 additional calories per day in the second and third trimesters of the pregnancy (American Pregnancy Association, 2021b). Optimal weight gain during a pregnancy depends on the mother's prepregnancy weight. Women with a normal prepregnancy weight should gain between 25 and 35 pounds, whereas women who were obese before getting pregnant should gain only between 11 and 20 pounds (American Pregnancy Association, 2015). Because the mother's nutrition directly affects her unborn child as well (**FIGURE 3.14**), healthy and balanced nutrition is particularly important during pregnancy. Raw, undercooked, and processed meats as well as fish, raw eggs, certain fruit, and milk should be avoided because they can harbor dangerous bacteria. A daily dose of folic acid can prevent more than 70% of cases of spina bifida (Centers for Disease Control and Prevention, 1991; Kancherla et al., 2021).

From R. L Jirtle, 2009. *Epigenomics* 1: 13–16

FIGURE 3.14 Experiments with humans are limited for ethical reasons: It would be unethical to expose a pregnant mother to toxins or limit her daily diet for the sake of an experiment. Therefore, researchers often use rodents to study variables they could not possibly experimentally manipulate in humans. The mice in this photo are the same age, have the same genes, and while in the womb were exposed to the toxic substance BPA (bisphenol A), which is found in plastics used to make some food and beverage containers (Pinney et al., 2017). The key difference? The mother of the mouse on the right was fed a diet supplemented with nutrients like folic acid and vitamin B12, which helped counteract the effects of BPA exposure. The study illustrates how nutrients can counteract the toxins we encounter in the environment.

The mother's age is a risk factor

When mothers are particularly young or old, their pregnancies carry more risks. Compared with mothers aged 20–24, adolescent mothers (aged 10–19) are at higher risk of contracting infections, delivering premature babies, having babies with low birthweight, and giving birth to babies that die in infancy (Ganchimeg et al., 2014).

Being of advanced age during pregnancy carries risks as well. Women aged 40 and older have an increased risk of stillbirth and preterm delivery and of having babies who are significantly larger than the average newborn or who have chromosomal abnormalities (Kenny et al., 2013; National Down Syndrome Society, 2017).

Diseases in the mother can affect the health of the fetus

While most diseases like the common cold pose little risk to the developing fetus, some diseases can significantly affect the fetus's health. Generally, the effect of teratogens depends on the time at which the mother and developing child are exposed to them. While organs develop, they are more sensitive to influences than when they are already fully developed (**FIGURE 3.15**). We will examine some of the most common and dangerous ones in this section (see also Table 3.4, which gives you an overview of the teratogens discussed).

Some sexually transmitted infections (STIs), like *syphilis*, can cause infertility and, if transmitted to an unborn child, can put the developing fetus at risk for a variety of issues like intellectual disabilities, organ defects, and low birth

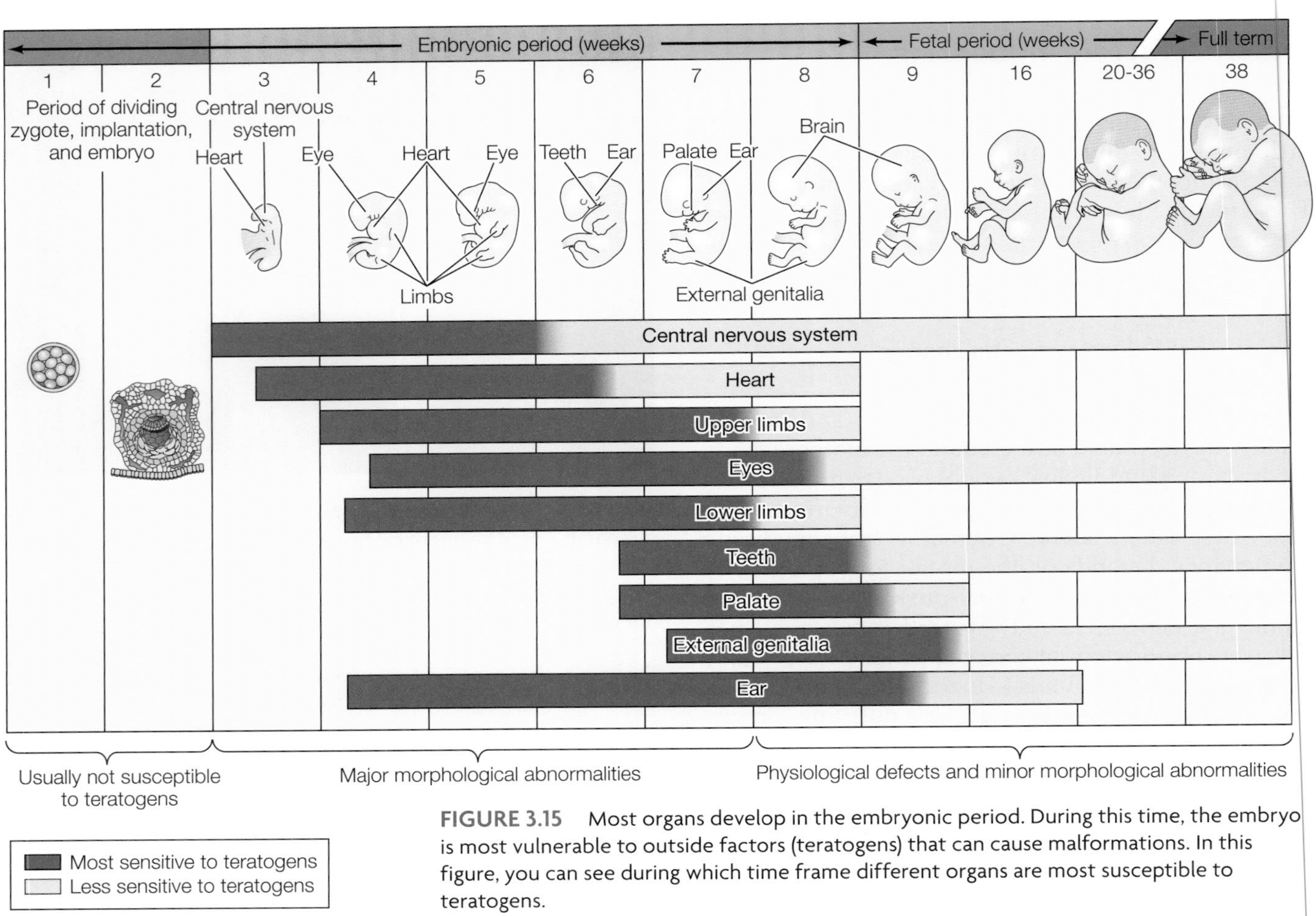

FIGURE 3.15 Most organs develop in the embryonic period. During this time, the embryo is most vulnerable to outside factors (teratogens) that can cause malformations. In this figure, you can see during which time frame different organs are most susceptible to teratogens.

After K. L. Moore. 1974. *Before We Are Born: Basic Embryology and Birth Defects.* Saunders, Philadelphia

HIV (human immunodeficiency virus) incurable but treatable infection that weakens the human immune system.

weight. In the case of **HIV (human immunodeficiency virus)**, the biggest risk is that the infant gets infected. To reduce the risk of infection, mothers with HIV often give birth via c-section, and their infants are treated with drugs during their first weeks of life.

Among non-sexually transmitted diseases, *rubella (German measles)* causes serious complications to the developing fetus. For these reasons, before a pregnancy women should be tested to see if they are immune to the disease. If they are not, they should get vaccinated against it. Before or during their pregnancy, women should also get vaccinated against influenza. Unlike the rubella vaccination, a vaccination for influenza is needed every year.

Many drugs taken during pregnancy can harm the fetus

Any drugs a person takes can affect their health in the short term as well as the long term. But as Caroline's case of thalidomide use shows, drug use in pregnant women can pose a risk to the developing infant as well. There are a number of drugs that pose danger to the developing child in particular because mothers may use them habitually or may not even consider them to be drugs that may have harmful effects on their fetus. These drugs include caffeine (which can even be found in some kinds of chocolate!), alcohol, nicotine, and recreational drugs like marijuana, heroin, and methamphetamine (see **TABLE 3.4**).

Stress produces significant biological changes

Pregnancy can greatly increase a person's usual experience of stress or depression. Stress caused by conflict with a partner, financial implications of the

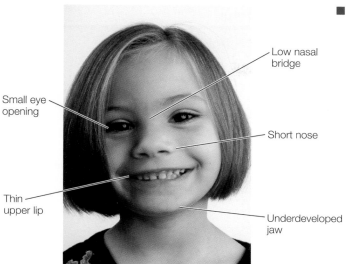

Small eye opening

Low nasal bridge

Short nose

Thin upper lip

Underdeveloped jaw

© Rick's Photography/Shutterstock.com

■ Children born with fetal alcohol spectrum disorder often display a number of physical characteristics like a smooth ridge between nose and upper lip, a small head, and wide-set eyes. They also often experience intellectual disabilities and learning difficulties.

pregnancy, or the prospect of single motherhood can lead to biological changes in the mother's body that can affect the developing fetus. Additionally, when pregnant mothers are stressed, they may cope with their stress by means of other unhealthy behaviors like smoking, drinking alcohol, or using drugs that may affect the unborn child.

Harmful environmental factors can be difficult to detect

Environmental influences that can impact a fetus's development are often hard to identify and can hide in the most innocuous places. Take biologist Patricia Hunt, for example, who was facing a mystery not too long ago. She was doing research on mice and found that about 40% of the ova of her lab mice had abnormalities in their chromosomes. But she had expected only 1.5% of the ova to be abnormal. How could such a large percentage of the mouse ova be genetically abnormal? For months, Hunt searched for an answer until she found the culprit: the janitor. He had cleaned cages and water bottles with a harsh cleaner that contained the chemical bisphenol A (commonly labeled BPA). The BPA leached out from the plastic cage surfaces and water bottles into food and water and led to the genetic abnormalities in the mice ova (Hinterthuer, 2008).

BPA belongs to a group of chemicals that act as *endocrine disruptors*, interfering with the body's hormone production (Environmental Protection Agency, 2021). BPA is contained in many objects of daily life, like plastic water bottles and food containers, CDs, and store cash register receipts. It has been linked to many issues, from increased cancer risk to early onset of puberty, obesity, and heart disease (Bao et al., 2020; Paulose et al., 2015; Prins et al., 2017; Stafford et al., 2014).

Other endocrine disruptors include *phthalates* (commonly found in toys, PVC plastics, and plastic food containers) as well as fire retardants, which can be found in products containing foam, like carpet padding, upholstery, car seats, and nursing pillows.

There are a large number of environmental hazards that put human health in general, and developing fetuses in particular, at risk. Other substances that have proven to be toxic for humans include heavy metals like lead, arsenic, and mercury (see Table 3.4). Expectant mothers (just as anybody else) would do best to avoid these substances as much as possible. However, this proves to be very difficult to do. Consider this: As of 2013, the European Union had banned the use of 1,328 chemicals in cosmetic products because they were known or suspected to cause cancer, genetic mutations, or birth defects. In the United States, only 11 chemicals are banned or restricted for the same purposes (Campaign for Safe Cosmetics, 2021).

■ Table 3.4 Effects of Teratogens on Pregnancy and Health of the Fetus

INFECTION

Agent	Effect	What you can do
STIs—gonorrhea, chlamydia	Miscarriage Premature birth Severe eye infection	Treatment of mother If necessary, treatment of infant C-section to avoid infection during birth
HPV (human papillomavirus)	Does not usually cause complications during pregnancy and childbirth	
HIV (human immunodeficiency virus)	10–20% of infants get infected	C-section to prevent transmission of virus Drugs given to infant during first weeks of life lower risk of infection (American Pregnancy Association, 2017)
Syphilis	Damage to organs, ears, eyes, and skin	
Rubella	Organ defects Deafness Blindness Intellectual disabilities Low birthweight (Centers for Disease Control and Prevention, 2016)	Vaccination before pregnancy
Influenza (flu)	Preterm birth Autism Schizophrenia (Antonson et al., 2017)	Vaccination before or during pregnancy Antiviral drugs Medication to lower fever

© Bochkarev Photography/Shutterstock.com

DRUGS

Agent	Effect	What you can do
Caffeine	Low birthweight Childhood obesity (Greenwood et al., 2014; Li et al., 2015)	Limit caffeine intake (coffee, tea, cola, energy drinks, chocolate)
Alcohol	Fetal alcohol spectrum disorder Miscarriage, stillbirth	Abstain from alcohol consumption
Nicotine	Premature birth Low birthweight Attention-deficit/hyperactivity disorder (Zhu et al., 2014) Respiratory disorders (England et al., 2015; Holbrook, 2016)	Stop smoking before or at least during pregnancy The nicotine in nicotine patches and e-cigarettes can be harmful as well About 10% of pregnant women participating in a 2011 survey reported that they smoked during the last trimester of their pregnancy (England et al., 2015; Holbrook, 2016)
Cocaine	Miscarriage Lower birthweight Smaller heads Behavior problems Cognitive deficits (Behnke et al., 2013; Buckingham-Howes et al., 2013; Smith et al., 2015)	Stop drug use before/during pregnancy Treatment of medical symptoms Special education Roughly 750,000 expectant mothers in the United States use cocaine during their pregnancy
Heroin	Infant is born addicted to heroin Withdrawal symptoms: fever, irritability, slow weight gain, seizures, vomiting Short attention span Slow language development (Buckingham-Howes et al., 2013)	Hospitalization Treatment of withdrawal symptoms Infants may get addicted to methadone if used as substitute for heroin
Methamphetamine	Premature birth Low birthweight Cognitive problems (Derauf et al., 2007)	Up to 5% of pregnant women use the drug during their pregnancy (Derauf et al., 2007)

© Daniel Heighton/Shutterstock.com

■ **Table 3.4** *(continued)*

Marijuana	Low birthweight	Stop using marijuana months before a planned pregnancy because the active ingredient is stored in the mother's fat
	Higher likelihood of hospitalization after birth	Do not use during pregnancy
	Problems with attention, impulse control, and visual memory (Gunn et al., 2016; Smith et al., 2016; Volkow et al., 2017)	From 2002 to 2014, marijuana use among pregnant women rose significantly from 2.4% to 3.9% (Brown et al., 2017)
Accutane (isotretinoin, acne drug)	Brain and heart defects	Use birth control while taking the drug
	Intellectual disabilities	Between 3 and 6 per 1,000 female users of isotretinoin become pregnant while taking the drug (Henry et al., 2016)

ENVIRONMENTAL HAZARDS

Agent	Effect	What you can do
BPA (bisphenol A)	Increased cancer risk	Can be found in plastic food containers and water bottles, store receipts, CDs and DVDs, as well as other consumer products and electronics. Avoid these products, if possible
	Obesity	
	Heart disease	
	Early onset of puberty	
	Reproductive problems (Paulose et al., 2015; Prins et al., 2017; Stafford et al., 2014)	
Flame retardants	Low birthweight	Avoid foam products that contain flame retardants, like carpet padding, upholstery, car seats, nursing pillows
	Increased risk of premature delivery and stillbirth	
	Reduced ability to pay attention	
	Lowered IQ (Bohannon, 2014; Shaw et al., 2014)	
Heavy metals (lead, arsenic, mercury)	Miscarriage, increased risk of premature birth	Lead: in drinking water and old paint; use water filter and get rid of old paint safely
	Lowered IQ	Arsenic: in drinking water; use water filter
	Permanent brain damage	Mercury: in seafood; avoid species that are particularly high in mercury
	Nervous system damage	
	Kidney damage	

© Voronin76/Shutterstock.com

MATERNAL FACTORS

Agent	Effect	What you can do
Maternal stress	Suboptimal brain development	Treatment of underlying causes like depression
	Increased risk of obesity	Relaxation methods and meditation
	Increased risk of asthma and autoimmune disorders (Entringer et al., 2015)	Counseling
	Increased risk of disorders like schizophrenia, attention-deficit/hyperactivity disorder, and autism spectrum disorders (Bronson & Bale, 2016; MacKinnon et al., 2017)	

© George Rudy/Shutterstock.com

■ In the 1990s, reports surfaced that the children of workers in a nuclear plant in Sellafield, England, had a significantly higher rate of leukemia than did other children whose fathers did not work in the plant.

Paternal Factors Influencing Prenatal Development

The influence of the mother's health and behaviors on her infant's health is quite obvious. However, risk factors associated with the father also can influence the outcome of a pregnancy. The children of fathers aged 45 and older have an increased risk of autism, attention-deficit/hyperactivity disorder, and psychiatric diagnoses like bipolar disorder or psychosis. They are also more likely to have to repeat a grade and to have lower educational outcomes than their peers with younger fathers (D'Onofrio et al., 2014). Paternal smoking seems to increase the risk of low birthweight (Banderali et al., 2015).

Fathers' exposure to other teratogens may have an effect on their future children's health as well. In the early 1990s, reports emerged showing that the children of workers from the nuclear plant in Sellafield, England, had a risk of leukemia 36 times higher than that of other children (Anderson et al., 2014). Likewise, researchers suspect that fathers who were exposed to radiation through the 1986 Chernobyl nuclear disaster experienced gene mutations that led to offspring with disabilities (Dubrova et al., 1996).

Review!

What is the mother's influence on prenatal development?

■ Although the womb seems like a safe and isolated place, many factors can influence prenatal development.

■ Overweight and obese mothers have a higher risk of adverse outcomes like gestational diabetes and birth defects as well as heart disease and hypertension in their children. A balanced diet is important to provide the fetus with needed nutrients.

■ Particularly young or old mothers also tend to have riskier pregnancies.

■ While many diseases like the common cold do not affect a pregnancy, sexually transmitted diseases like HIV and syphilis as well as rubella and the flu can put the health of the fetus at risk.

■ The use of drugs and substances like alcohol and nicotine can have negative consequences as well.

■ Additionally, exposure to substances found in our environment like lead, radiation, or bisphenol A can impair development.

What is the father's influence on prenatal development?

■ Not much is known about the impact of paternal factors on prenatal development. This is partly due to the difficulty of teasing apart the different factors that can possibly affect the developing child before as well as after birth.

■ However, there is some evidence that fathers' exposure to teratogens like radiation and advanced paternal age may affect the health of their children.

Practice!

1. The maternal disease most likely to have a profound negative effect on a developing fetus is _____ .
   a. measles
   b. rubella
   c. cold
   d. flu

2. Pregnant mothers need not avoid _____ .
   a. alcohol
   b. nicotine
   c. methamphetamine
   d. flu shots

3. A drug linked to serious birth defects in the 1950s and 1960s was _____ .
   a. thalidomide
   b. terramycin
   c. penicillin
   d. sulfamide

4. Increased birth defects are associated with older age of _____ .
   a. the mother
   b. the father
   c. both the mother and the father
   d. neither the father nor the mother

5. A commonly used drug that is a serious teratogen
   is _____ .
   a. aspirin
   b. acetaminophen

   c. isotretinoin
   d. tetracycline

See for Yourself!

Choose any place in your environment like your home, a restaurant, or a store. Look around: Can you find sources of teratogens that pregnant women (and all of us!) are exposed to? What can you do to avoid these toxins?

Show What You've Learned!

Over coffee, your co-worker Julieta shares some exciting news: She's 3 months pregnant with what will be her first child. "I think we should go to the bar on Friday to celebrate," she says. "Work has been driving me out of my mind lately, and I could really use a night out. I haven't had a cocktail in ages!" What advice would you give to Julieta?

What's Your Position?

Is prenatal education effective? Many companies try to capitalize on parents' desire to give their children an early advantage with prenatal educational aids. For example, audio lessons can be broadcast to a child in utero via maternity belts that feature built-in speakers and headphones that can be attached to the belly. Designed to promote early cognitive development, the lessons are meant to be played daily to the infant as part of a regimen not unlike taking prenatal vitamins (Baby Plus, 2017). Infants who complete the program will—according to the company—be more relaxed and alert at birth, will self-soothe better, and in the long term will achieve developmental milestones earlier and have longer attention spans and stronger learning skills (Baby Plus, 2017). Manufacturers of similar products promise regular sleep rhythms and improved mother–child bonding (Baby Plus, 2017; Lullabelly, 2017). Do you think these products keep their promise and are worth the investment in time and money that parents make? Look online for studies of the effects of sound on the fetus to see if your position is supported by research.

3.4 Prenatal Care and Prenatal Tests

- Demonstrate with examples why prenatal care is important.
- Relate the various types of prenatal testing.

When Iryna was 21 weeks pregnant with her daughter Mila, a routine ultrasound discovered that Mila had a large mass in her lung that was pressing her heart against the rib cage on the right side of her body. She was at risk for heart failure, and due to the size of the growth, her lungs could not grow properly. Within a few weeks Iryna underwent a successful prenatal surgery in a children's hospital to have her daughter's lung mass removed while still in the womb. When Mila was born at 38 weeks, Iryna and her partner welcomed a healthy baby girl in which just her scar from the prenatal surgery reminded them of the frightening times they had gone through prior to her birth.

Iryna's story illustrates the importance of prenatal care: While most babies do not have birth defects, the timely diagnosis of conditions in the mother or the child that can affect the pregnancy will increase the chances that a healthy baby will be born. Prenatal care also serves the purpose of educating the expectant mother and her family about how they can help to have a healthy child. In the following section, we will learn more about prenatal care and the tests that can be performed before a child is born.

Prenatal Care

Although many pregnancies take their course without any adverse events, the expectant mother and/or her child may experience complications of some sort during pregnancy. Expectant mothers can develop high blood pressure or diabetes, which will need to be managed medically. Medical problems in unborn children may be diagnosed before birth as well. For this reason, it is important for pregnant women to seek out prenatal care as early as possible.

Who provides prenatal care?

There are a number of options available for prenatal care: Healthy women are usually seen by

- obstetricians, who are doctors who specialize in the care of pregnant women and their unborn children;
- OB/GYNs (obstetricians/gynecologists), who additionally specialize in women's healthcare;
- family practitioners, who care for patients of all ages; or
- certified nurses and midwives, who work together with a doctor in case a c-section is needed.

Before choosing a prenatal care provider, families may wish to speak to one or even several providers to collect information. Some of the following questions can help expectant parents decide if they have any special requirements that will help them determine the most appropriate prenatal care provider:

- Does either parent have a pre-existing medical condition that might affect the infant, or has a prior pregnancy had complications? If yes, then the parents may wish to consider seeing an obstetrician or a doctor who specializes in high-risk pregnancies.
- Are the parents interested in natural childbirth and minimizing medications during the birth process? Births led by midwives tend to use less pain medication and instruments like a vacuum where a suction cup is applied to the head of the infant (Sandall et al., 2016; Sutcliffe et al., 2012).
- Do the parents feel they have a good relationship with the prenatal care provider? Do they feel they have been properly included in decisions about their care?
- Is the provider responsive to the parents' questions? Parents should bring a list of questions to their first visit. They need to feel comfortable with the answers they receive.

Up until the 32nd week of pregnancy, prenatal visits for births expected to be unproblematic are usually scheduled about every 4–6 weeks. Then, visits become more frequent (about every 2 weeks) from the 32nd to the 37th week. After the 37th week, visits are usually weekly. Women with health conditions or a high-risk pregnancy (expecting multiples or a child with a birth defect, for example) may be seen more often or by additional specialists.

■ Luciana and James met with a number of prenatal care providers to discuss questions and wishes regarding their pregnancy. Those meetings helped them choose a doctor for the prenatal care Luciana was to receive over the next months.

What happens during prenatal care visits?

A lot of people think about prenatal visits solely in terms of physical examinations. The prenatal care provider will indeed ask about the parents' health history and assess both the expectant mother's health as well as the fetus's health and development. However, expecting parents are also educated on a wide range of issues like nutrition during pregnancy, the importance of exercise during pregnancy, and the impact of teratogens on the unborn child. If needed, women can be connected with social service providers who can assist them after the birth of the infant.

Prenatal education is only effective, of course, when expecting parents truly take the messages to heart and make any prescribed changes in their behavior. Achieving lasting behavior change through any intervention, however, is difficult.

Racial and regional differences in access to prenatal care

Not all groups in the United States use or have equal access to prenatal care. In 2017, 5% of expectant White mothers received prenatal care that began only in the third trimester or no prenatal care at all, whereas 8% of Hispanic and 10% of African American mothers did (Child Trends Databank, 2021). Worldwide, only 58% of women actually have at least four prenatal care visits. Generally, women in richer countries have better access to prenatal care than women in poorer countries or poorly developed regions (UNICEF Data, 2021).

Efforts to improve prenatal care in the United States, as well as in less-developed countries such as Bangladesh, have included group prenatal care programs, where physical assessments are made by a trained clinician. Educational programs as well as discussions are held with a group of women with pregnancies of the same gestational age. Studies have shown that group prenatal programs can lead to fewer preterm births and higher birthweights. In addition, group programs can lower the cost of providing care and thus allow more women access to critical prenatal care (Ickovics et al., 2016; Sultana et al., 2017).

Prenatal Testing

Prenatal visits often include one or a number of medical tests that can help monitor the development of the fetus and potentially diagnose health issues and other complications. Physicians routinely use ultrasound to monitor the growth of the fetus and detect structural abnormalities like heart defects or

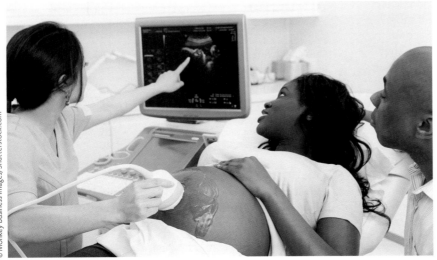

© Monkey Business Images/Shutterstock.com

■ Ultrasounds are routinely performed during prenatal visits to assess fetal health and development and to detect possible organ malformations. Additionally, seeing images of the fetus helps parents connect to it, preparing them psychologically for parenthood and making it easier for them to choose a lifestyle that maximizes the chances that the fetus will develop in the best possible way.

neural tube defects. A blood test commonly recommended is the Triple Screen Test. Screening tests do not diagnose problems, but rather indicate that more tests should be performed. The Triple Screen Test is often used to screen for genetic disorders like neural tube defects as well as trisomy 21 and trisomy 18 (Gündüz et al., 2016). One problem with prenatal testing is that tests sometimes result in a false positive, indicating there may be a problem when there is none.

Culture Counts

Prenatal Care in Minority Cultures in the United States and Canada

Even in industrialized nations like the United States and Canada, not all pregnant women receive prenatal care. A lack of prenatal care as well as follow-up care after birth leads to higher maternal and infant mortality. But not all women are equally affected. Women belonging to ethnic minorities often receive less prenatal care or receive that care later than White women, and thus they experience a higher infant as well as maternal mortality rate (Boghossian et al., 2019; Centers for Disease Control and Prevention, 2019). Black and Indigenous women are also two to three times more likely to die from pregnancy complications than White women (Centers for Disease Control and Prevention, 2019).

To understand the situation, let's consider the case of Wetaskiwin, a county in the Canadian province of Alberta. Wetaskiwin is home to four Cree Indigenous communities. Women in Wetaskiwin have a much higher fertility rate than is common in the rest of Alberta; they are also more likely to consume alcohol and smoke during pregnancy, and so their pregnancies tend to be higher-risk (TABLE).

To understand why these differences between Wetaskiwin and other places in Alberta exist, we need to look at the reasons why women from minority communities may be less likely to access healthcare resources during pregnancy. First, they are more likely to live in isolated locations, which can make it more difficult for them to access health centers. Second, they may be reluctant to visit health centers because they have experienced lack of support or understanding of their Indigenous culture by the largely non-Indigenous healthcare providers. For example, in some Indigenous cultures, it is customary not to buy any items for an unborn baby. As a result, an Indigenous woman may arrive at a hospital in labor without any baby supplies or clothes. Hospital staff who misunderstand this cultural difference may criticize Indigenous women, causing embarrassment and making it less likely the women will return for needed follow-up visits. Finally, Indigenous people have a deep distrust of state institutions owing

to their history of colonization and mistreatment. In Canada, many Indigenous children were removed from their families and forced to attend state- and church-run residential schools, which were designed to acculturate them into mainstream Canadian culture. Physical and sexual abuse was common, and the last residential school did not close until 1996. Indigenous people in North America, like many African Americans, have at times been subjected to unethical experiments by Western researchers (Pacheco et al., 2013; the same is true for African Americans). These experiences have led to many Native Americans avoiding institutional environments, including healthcare settings.

■ Health Indicators in Wetaskiwin versus Rest of Alberta, Canada

Health Indicators	Wetaskiwin	Rest of Alberta
Fertility rate (%)	74.8	53.1
Infant mortality rate (%)	6.6	6.2
Teen birth rate (% in women aged 15–19)	65.6	18.9
Smoking during pregnancy (%)	50.5	18.0
Drinking during pregnancy (%)	8.0	4.0

Source: S. Di Lallo. 2014. *NWH* 18: 38-46, with permission from Elsevier. Data from various sources.

Question

What can healthcare providers do to encourage women from minority cultures to seek adequate prenatal care and to instill trust in the care they provide?

Whether the test is correct or not, a positive result inevitably leads to more testing and significant anxiety in the parents. Amniocentesis and chorionic villus sampling are commonly used to definitively detect genetic abnormalities in the fetus. TABLE 3.5 summarizes these techniques.

■ **Table 3.5** Prenatal Testing Techniques

Method	How does it work?	What is it used for?	What are the risks?
Ultrasound sonogram © Monkey Business Images/Shutterstock.com	High-frequency sound waves create a picture of the fetus in the womb	Monitor fetal growth Detect structural abnormalities Detect multiple pregnancies Determine gestational age Determine sex of fetus (not always conclusive!)	Non-invasive; no risk Detection rate of abnormalities of up to 80% (American Academy of Pediatrics, 2017)
Triple Screen Test © Elnur/Shutterstock.com	Blood test Performed between 15th and 20th pregnancy week Recommended for women who are age 35 or older with a family history of birth defects with medical problems Screens for AFP (alpha-fetoprotein; protein produced by fetus) hCG (human chorionic gonadotropin; hormone produced in placenta) estriol (hormone produced in placenta and by fetus)	Screen for neural tube defects, trisomy 18, and trisomy 21	No risks except discomfort from blood drawing Relatively high percentage of false positive results (American Pregnancy Association, 2016c)
Amniocentesis © iStock.com/zilli	Insert needle through stomach into amniotic sac to withdraw fluid The amniotic fluid contains stem cells from the fetus that can be analyzed Usually performed between 15th and 20th week of pregnancy Often performed in women older than age 35, or when genetic abnormalities are suspected	Genetic and chromosomal disorders like Down syndrome, cystic fibrosis, and spina bifida Determination of sex of the fetus Paternity testing	Risk of miscarriage ranges around 1 in 300 (American Pregnancy Association, 2016a).
Chorionic villus sampling (CVS) © Saturn Stills/Science Photo Library	Hairlike structures from placenta are removed vaginally or through stomach wall and analyzed Usually performed between 10th and 13th week of pregnancy	Genetic and chromosomal disorders like Down syndrome, cystic fibrosis (no testing for neural tube defects possible) Determination of sex of the fetus Paternity testing	Miscarriage risk about 1 in 100 procedures (American Pregnancy Association, 2016b)

Review!

Why is prenatal care important?

- Prenatal care helps ensure the most positive outcome possible for both expectant mother and child.

- In prenatal care, the growth of the fetus as well as health of the mother are monitored. These findings may lead to further testing, monitoring of the situation, or medical interventions. Furthermore, the mother and her family are educated on factors that help ensure a safe and healthy pregnancy like nutrition, exercise during pregnancy, and how to prepare for birth and life with the newborn.

- Not all mothers have access to the level of prenatal care that is recommended—in the United States, about one-fourth of Hispanic and African American mothers do not receive prenatal care in their first trimester, and less than 60% of women worldwide have at least four prenatal visits per pregnancy.

What is prenatal testing?

- There are many different techniques of prenatal testing.

- Ultrasound is used routinely to monitor fetal growth and to scan for structural abnormalities.

- If the parents have any additional risk factors (like advanced maternal age or a family history of birth defects or hereditary diseases), further testing may be done. This can include a screening blood test like the Triple Screen Test, which screens for genetic disorders, or more invasive tests like amniocentesis and chorionic villus sampling, which examine the genetic material of the fetus and can provide definite information on whether a fetus has a certain genetic abnormality.

Practice!

1. _____ is a test that involves a nontrivial risk of miscarriage.
   a. ultrasound sonogram
   b. triple screen test
   c. amniocentesis
   d. all of the above

2. _____ is a prenatal test that involves removing hairlike structures from the placenta.
   a. amniocentesis
   b. chorionic villus sampling
   c. ultrasound

3. A midwife cannot _____ .
   a. provide prenatal care
   b. provide educational programs about birth
   c. help a woman give birth
   d. perform a cesarean section

4. Trisomy 21 is also known as _____ .
   a. mental retardation
   b. Down syndrome
   c. Tourette syndrome
   d. XYY syndrome

What's Your Position?

Is prenatal testing always the right choice for expecting parents? Nowadays, there is a whole range of prenatal tests available to couples expecting a baby. However, many of those tests are only screening tests and cannot give a definitive answer. Do you think prenatal testing makes sense in any case, or are there some cases where it is reasonable for people to opt out of it?

Additional Resources Online

- "What moms-to-be should know about prenatal testing," from Michigan Health

- "More women skip some prenatal tests after learning about risks," from National Public Radio (NPR)

- "Effect of enhanced information, values clarification, and removal of financial barriers on use of prenatal genetic testing: A randomized clinical trial," from the *Journal of the American Medical Association*

- "Pros and cons of prenatal testing," from Medical Republic

3.5 Special Pregnancy Issues: Infertility and the Premature End of a Pregnancy

- Explain the ways in which couples experiencing infertility can become parents.
- List ways in which pregnancies can end prematurely.?

Pregnancy is a topic that can bring tremendous joy and excitement, but also fear and even despair. Some couples wish for nothing more than to have a family but are not able to conceive. Other couples do not wish to have any (or any more) children and end up with an unwanted pregnancy. And yet others lose a pregnancy they wish they could have kept. In this section, we explore what constitutes infertility and what options couples experiencing infertility have to create a family. We will also discuss miscarriage and abortion as ways for a pregnancy to end before term.

Infertility

About 10% of American couples have trouble conceiving a child (American Pregnancy Association, 2021a). Generally, a couple is considered infertile if they have not conceived within 12 months of unprotected sexual intercourse. However, many providers evaluate and treat couples already after 6 months of unprotected intercourse when the woman is 35 years of age or older (Centers for Disease Control and Prevention, 2021a). With increasing age, time is of the essence: The quality of women's ova declines, the chances to conceive decrease, and the potential for complications in pregnancy increase.

Infertility may be caused by one factor or a combination of factors

Infertility can derive from many sources, and in about one-fourth of all cases, several causes simultaneously contribute to a couple's infertility (Centers for Disease Control and Prevention, 2021a). One of the most common causes of infertility in men is low sperm count. Sometimes men produce no sperm at all, or their sperm cells are malformed. Diseases also can affect a man's ability to produce healthy sperm. In about 40% of cases, male factors are the only or at least one of the factors contributing to the infertility (American Society for Reproductive Medicine, 2021). Over the past 40 years the average sperm count of men in industrialized nations has dropped by more than half for unknown reasons (Levine et al., 2017).

In females, the most common cause of infertility is irregular ovulation or absence of ovulation. Other causes include blocked Fallopian tubes, which prevent the egg from traveling to the uterus, diseases (often STIs) that prevent implantation of the fertilized egg in the uterus, or ova of suboptimal quality (American Society for Reproductive Medicine, 2017a).

There are many options for couples who cannot conceive

Nowadays, there are many different ways to build a family for couples struggling with infertility. Many couples seek medical treatment to resolve their fertility issues. In around 90% of cases, surgery is used to correct anatomical problems or hormonal medications are prescribed. Around 3% of couples use assisted reproductive technologies (American Society for Reproductive Medicine, 2021) like artificial insemination or in vitro fertilization.

ARTIFICIAL INSEMINATION In **artificial insemination** (also called intra-uterine insemination), sperm are transferred to the women's uterus during ovulation. This procedure significantly shortens the distance sperm have to travel to reach a mature egg, thus increasing the chance that the egg will get fertilized. In some cases, the woman is given hormone-based drugs before the insemination, which stimulate the ovaries and result in the maturation of more than one egg. Hormonal treatments that result in the maturation of more than one ovum as well as the placement of multiple embryos in the uterus during IVF treatment have resulted in a significant increase in multiple births in the United States: The number of twin deliveries rose from 19 per 1,000 births in 1980 to 34 per 1,000 births in 2014 and then declined to 33 per 1,000 births in 2018 (Martin et al., 2019).

IN VITRO FERTILIZATION In **in vitro fertilization (IVF)**, mature ova are removed from the ovaries and combined with sperm in the lab (FIGURE 3.16).

artificial insemination sperm are transferred to the women's uterus during ovulation.

in vitro fertilization (IVF) the process in which ova and sperm are combined in a laboratory; 3–5 days later, one or several embryos are transferred to the woman's uterus.

(A)

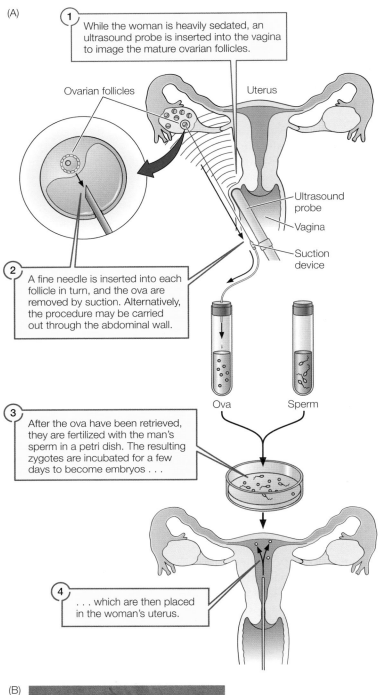

1 While the woman is heavily sedated, an ultrasound probe is inserted into the vagina to image the mature ovarian follicles.

Ovarian follicles

Uterus

Ultrasound probe

Vagina

Suction device

2 A fine needle is inserted into each follicle in turn, and the ova are removed by suction. Alternatively, the procedure may be carried out through the abdominal wall.

Ova

Sperm

3 After the ova have been retrieved, they are fertilized with the man's sperm in a petri dish. The resulting zygotes are incubated for a few days to become embryos . . .

4 . . . which are then placed in the woman's uterus.

(B)

© david gregs/Alamy Stock Photo

FIGURE 3.16 Standard in vitro fertilization. (A) The steps in the procedure. (B) An ovum is fertilized by sperm in vitro.

From S. LeVay et al. 2021. *Discovering Human Sexuality*, 5th ed. Oxford University Press/Sinauer, Sunderland, MA

After 3–5 days, a number of fertilized eggs are placed into the woman's uterus in the hope one or more of them will implant (American Society for Reproductive Medicine, 2017b). The success rate of IVF depends greatly on a woman's age (**FIGURE 3.17**).

With IVF, embryos also can be tested for whether they show genetic abnormalities before the embryos are transferred into the uterus.

The short-term health outcomes for children born through IVF are good: Although they tend to be of lower birthweight than naturally conceived children, studies indicate that they are not at a higher risk for medical conditions or developmental problems (Reigstad et al., 2016; Sicignano et al., 2010).

DONOR IN VITRO FERTILIZATION Same-sex couples or couples who have a problem with their sperm or eggs can decide to use donor sperm or donor eggs.

SURROGATE MOTHERS If a woman is not able to carry a pregnancy to term or has medical problems so that a pregnancy would put her health at risk, another option is to transfer embryos to a *surrogate mother,* who "lends" her uterus to carry the child of another couple. Surrogates can be friends or relatives of the couple, or they can be strangers who are paid to carry the child to term.

ADOPTION Many childless couples who cannot or do not want to turn to reproductive technologies decide to adopt children instead. There are other reasons for adoption as well, like wanting to give a child a better chance at life or wanting to include several ethnicities in a family. In adoption, prospective parents go through a legal process in order to take on parental responsibilities and provide a permanent home to a child that is not biologically their own.

From 2014 through 2019, the number of children adopted increased from 51,000 to 66,000 (U.S. Department of Health and Human Services, 2021). In recent years, there have been a number of high-profile cases that put adoption in the spotlight of the public as a way of building a family. Celebrities like Angelina Jolie and Brad Pitt,

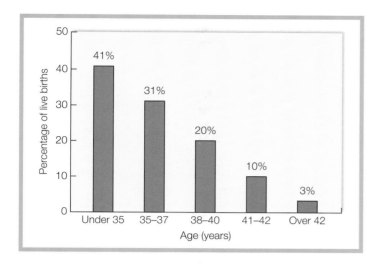

FIGURE 3.17 Live births per egg retrieval cycle. The success rate of IVF cycles depends on the age of the woman treated.

After SART. 2015. Final National Summary Report for 2015. www.sartcorsonline.com

Sandra Bullock, and Charlize Theron have adopted children, often from foreign countries and of different ethnic backgrounds than their own.

Miscarriage and Abortion

Between 11% and 22% of pregnancies end in a **spontaneous abortion** (also called *miscarriage*), which is a pregnancy loss within the first 20 weeks (Ammon Avalos et al., 2012). Most spontaneous abortions occur in the first trimester. Spontaneous abortions occurring within the first few weeks are often just experienced as a delayed period. They are often caused by genetic problems in the embryo or health conditions of the mother like diabetes or hormonal problems. A woman's risk of miscarriage increases with age: While women under age 35 have a risk of about 15%, women over age 45 have a miscarriage risk of 50% (Villines, 2018).

When the fetus dies in the womb after 20 weeks gestation, it is called a *stillbirth*. About 1% of pregnancies end in stillbirth, which amounts to about the same number of infants that die within their first year of life (MacDorman & Gregory, 2015). Studies around the world have found that stillbirths increased dramatically throughout the COVID-19 pandemic (Watson, 2020). A large London hospital, for example, found that stillbirths more than tripled in the first half of 2020 when compared to pre-pandemic numbers. The researchers suspect that this increase is due to a lack of prenatal care during lockdowns so that pregnancy complications could not be diagnosed in time (Khalil et al., 2020). Women who suffer a stillbirth or miscarriage are at risk for post-traumatic stress disorder as well as depression and anxiety (Farren et al., 2016). Losing an unborn child often makes it harder for couples to grieve because many people in their surroundings may not understand what it means to grieve for a child that never lived outside the womb.

A pregnancy also can end in an **abortion**, which is a medical intervention that terminates the pregnancy. In 2018, around 620,000 abortions were reported in the United States to the Centers for Disease Control and Prevention (Centers for Disease Control and Prevention, 2020a). Unsafe abortions that are performed by a person lacking the necessary medical skills can put the woman's life and health at a considerable risk. Between 1995 and 2008, almost all unsafe abortions (98%) were performed in developing countries (Sedgh et al., 2012). Most women who have received abortions do not experience any negative psychological consequences (Steinberg et al., 2014). However, a number of women feel the abortion is traumatic and have trouble coping with the stress (Major et al., 2009).

spontaneous abortion a pregnancy loss within the first 20 weeks (also called miscarriage).

abortion an intervention that terminates pregnancy.

Review!

How can couples experiencing infertility become parents?

- Infertility is generally defined as the inability to conceive within 12 months of unprotected sexual intercourse.

- About 10% of American couples have trouble conceiving. The most common reasons are low sperm count and irregular or absent ovulation.

- In many instances, hormone-based medications or surgery can help a couple conceive. Around 3% of couples use assisted reproductive technologies like artificial insemination (placement of sperm in the woman's uterus) or in vitro fertilization (combination of sperm and eggs in lab and transfer of embryos into uterus) to become pregnant. The success rates of these techniques depend on the reasons for the infertility as well as the age of the mother.

- Couples can also choose to use donor sperm or donor eggs, or they can have a surrogate mother carry out the pregnancy. Many couples choose to adopt a child in order to create the family they long for.

What are some ways in which pregnancies can end prematurely?

- About 15 in 100 pregnancies end in a miscarriage (defined as pregnancy loss within the first 20 weeks of pregnancy), most often within the first trimester. Miscarriages are often due to genetic abnormalities in the embryo, but they may also be influenced by the health of the mother and her age.

- Abortions are elective medical procedures to end a pregnancy. They are most often performed within the first trimester. Women may choose to abort a pregnancy when a medical problem is found in either mother or fetus or when they are faced with an unplanned pregnancy.

Practice!

1. Approximately _____ of American couples have trouble conceiving a child.
   a. 2%
   b. 5%
   c. 7%
   d. 10%

2. The short-term health outcomes for children born through IVF today are considered to be _____ .
   a. generally good
   b. generally poor
   c. good if performed on women under 30
   d. poor if performed on women over 35

3. About _____ of pregnancies end in miscarriage.
   a. 3–5%
   b. 11–22%
   c. 19–27%
   d. 32–35%

4. A woman's risk of miscarriage _____ .
   a. increases after the first pregnancy
   b. increases in winter
   c. increases with age
   d. decreases with age

5. After 20 weeks of pregnancy, the birth of a deceased child is referred to as _____ .
   a. stillbirth
   b. abortion
   c. miscarriage
   d. sudden infant death syndrome

Act It Out!

Evan and Nancy, who are the parents of two delightful young girls with cystic fibrosis, are interested in having another child. However, now that they know they are both carrying the gene for cystic fibrosis they are wondering what options they have besides in vitro fertilization. Drawing on information presented in this chapter, role-play an interaction between the two parents and a counselor advising them on other options they can consider.

Two years later in Evan and Nancy's household

Evan and Nancy, who have two children with cystic fibrosis, eventually decided that they wanted to expand their family, but did not want to risk having another child with a debilitating disease. They went to see a counselor to find out more about their options for having another child. The counselor suggested they conceive their next child via in vitro fertilization.

Evan and Nancy followed up on the counselor's suggestion and underwent in vitro fertilization. The embryos were tested for the gene that causes cystic fibrosis, and only embryos without that gene were transferred to Nancy's uterus. She became pregnant on their second attempt with a boy not carrying the gene for cystic fibrosis. Their baby is now 4 months old and thriving. Ava and Sophia are receiving treatment for their symptoms of cystic fibrosis while enjoying being big sisters to their new brother. Over the past months, as much as possible, the family has found a new routine integrating the new baby as well as medical treatments that allows for them to focus on other things than just the chronic disease that Ava and Sophia have developed. ■ ▪ ■ ▪

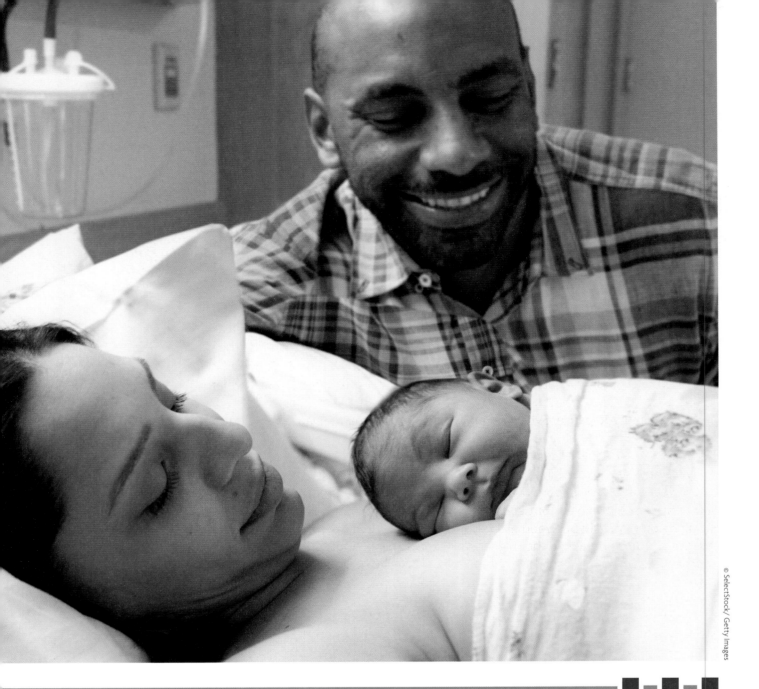

SelectStock/ Getty Images

Overview

Birth and the Newborn

Pregnancy can be a time of conflicting emotions

Sylvia is sitting in a coffee shop with two of her closest work friends, Damian and Sheryl. "So," asks Damian, "What's this big news that's too important to share in the office?"

After a dramatic pause, Sylvia replies: "I think I'm pregnant." Damian and Sheryl leap from their chairs to give her a hug, but no sooner have they congratulated her than Sylvia begins to tear up.

Sylvia and her husband had been trying for over a year to get pregnant. Then, just 3 weeks ago, a drugstore pregnancy test gave Sylvia the happy news that she was, in fact, pregnant. But ever since that moment, her moods have been swinging dramatically between elation and anxiety—about how her pregnancy will go, about the chances she might have a miscarriage, about what life as a mother will be like. Will she be able to manage? And what should she be doing now?

Sheryl reassures Sylvia by telling her these questions are natural. She had them, too, when she was pregnant with Lewis, now 2 years old. She decides not to tell Sylvia that she recently had a miscarriage, 10 weeks into her second pregnancy.

Damian is the father of a 3-year-old girl, Mathilda, that he and his husband, Davis, had through a surrogate mother artificially inseminated with Damian's sperm. He can relate to all of Sylvia's doubts about her ability to bond with and look after a newborn.

Pregnancy is a time of conflicting emotions for many expecting parents. Like Sylvia, they often feel excitement tempered by worries about the birth process and its aftermath. Over the course of this chapter, we will meet Sylvia again from time to time to accompany her on her journey into motherhood and find out more about the choices she made and how pregnancy and the idea of being a mother affected her.

4.1 From Pregnancy to Childbirth: How the Birth Process Unfolds

- Recall the occurrences during the birth process and immediately after birth.
- Explain the ways in which pain can be managed in childbirth.
- Relate the reasons for performing c-sections during childbirth.
- List and describe the professionals who may be present when someone gives birth.
- Identify the alternative approaches to childbirth parents can choose and why these options are attractive to them.

Braxton Hicks contractions intermittent weak contractions of the uterus during pregnancy; also called "practice contractions."

gestation time period between conception and birth in which a fetus develops in the mother's womb.

For 6 months Sylvia's pregnancy progressed without any problems. Then one day, during her seventh month of pregnancy, Sylvia suddenly started to feel contractions. She was alarmed and called her midwife in a panic. However, after describing her symptoms, her midwife was able to calm her fears. Sylvia was experiencing "practice contractions" (also named **Braxton Hicks contractions**, after the physician who first described them). They likely increase the blood flow to the placenta and help tone the uterine muscle, thereby preparing it for the exertion that will be required during childbirth. After an hour, the contractions stopped. They occasionally returned throughout Sylvia's pregnancy but did not have an impact on the birth of a healthy baby girl. Baby Elena was born at 39 weeks of **gestation**—that is, after 39 weeks of developing inside the womb.

The Birth Process

The birth process is generally divided into three stages (**FIGURE 4.1**). In the following sections, we will see what happens during each of the three stages, as well as what happens in the minutes right after birth.

In stage 1, contractions help to open the birth canal

The first stage (early labor) is the longest and usually lasts anywhere from 8 to 22 hours in women who are giving birth for the first time (Østborg et al., 2017;

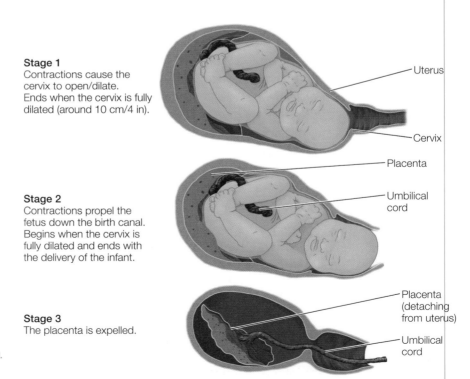

Stage 1
Contractions cause the cervix to open/dilate. Ends when the cervix is fully dilated (around 10 cm/4 in).

Uterus

Cervix

Placenta

Umbilical cord

Stage 2
Contractions propel the fetus down the birth canal. Begins when the cervix is fully dilated and ends with the delivery of the infant.

Placenta (detaching from uterus)

Umbilical cord

Stage 3
The placenta is expelled.

FIGURE 4.1 The three stages of childbirth.

From C. S. Tamis-LeMonda. 2022. *Child Development: Context, Culture, and Cascades.* Oxford University Press/Sinauer, Sunderland, MA; after D. M. Bozzone and D. S. Green. 2014. *Biology for the Informed Citizen.* Oxford University Press, New York

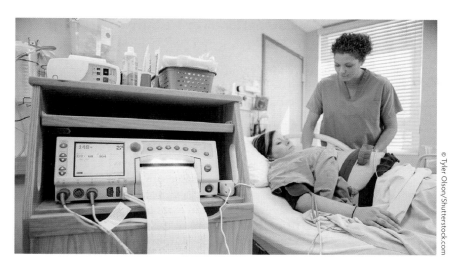

■ Electronic fetal heart rate monitors can be used to monitor the heart rate of the fetus. The heart rate gives an indication of how well the fetus is doing and of whether an emergency cesarean section or other medical measures may be necessary.

Penfield et al., 2016). In subsequent pregnancies, stage 1 can be much shorter. Frequently, it is during this first stage that the amniotic sac ruptures (or, as we sometimes say, the water breaks); this can also occur before labor begins. Contractions occur every 5 to 30 minutes and last up to around 30 seconds. Eventually, they occur every 1 to 2 minutes and last about 1 minute or more. They help to thin and **dilate**, or enlarge, the opening of the cervix (which is the lower part of the uterus) so that the head of the fetus can pass through. The end of stage 1, when the cervix widens to its maximum opening (about 4 inches), is also known as *transition*.

dilation an increase in size of the cervical opening during the birth process.

Women who intend to have a hospital birth are generally advised to go to the hospital when their contractions are 5 minutes (for their firstborn) to 7 minutes (for subsequent births) apart. The labor process for first births is usually longer than for subsequent births, which is why women giving birth to their first child should head for the hospital later in the first stage.

During stage 1, the medical team or midwife may track the baby's well-being using electronic fetal heart rate monitoring. If the heart rate is consistently too fast or very slow, the attending physician may intervene to speed up the delivery by using instruments to help guide the baby out of the birth canal or by performing a **cesarean section** (or **c-section**) to remove the baby from the mother's uterus surgically.

cesarean section (or **c-section**) a surgical intervention in which an incision is made in the mother's abdominal wall and uterus in order to remove the baby.

In stage 2, the infant is delivered

Stage 2 usually lasts between 20 minutes and 2 hours and ends when the baby is delivered. The pregnant woman tries to find a comfortable position to give birth—lying on her side, standing, kneeling, or squatting, for example. Then, the woman will feel an urge to push the baby out. After delivery, the baby is still attached to the placenta through the umbilical cord, which is usually cut and clamped right away or within a few minutes.

In a hospital birth, an **episiotomy** may be performed to enlarge the vaginal opening and prevent tearing of the vaginal tissue. Routine episiotomies benefit neither mother nor infant and have steadily declined over the past decades due to the trauma they cause to the tissue. But when medically necessary they have positive health consequences for the mother (Jiang et al., 2017).

episiotomy incision in the muscular tissue between the vagina and anus.

In stage 3, the placenta is delivered

In stage 3, small contractions help separate the placenta from the wall of the uterus and expel it through the birth canal. This process usually takes between 5 and 30 minutes. If an episiotomy was performed, the incision will be stitched.

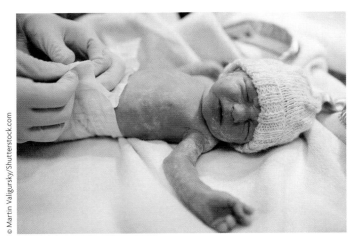

■ Newborns are often covered by vernix, which is a substance that protects them in the womb. They are often cleaned before the mother gets to hold the infant.

vernix a white, greasy substance that protects the fetus's skin in the womb.

Apgar scale a measure of a newborn's physical condition based on its appearance, pulse, grimace, activity, and respiration.

The minutes after birth are busy with many activities

The newborn rapidly adjusts to life outside the womb. Within 10 seconds of birth, the baby usually takes its first breath and expels the liquid that filled the lungs before birth. The lungs then begin to work on their own. If neither child nor mother experiences serious complications, the mother can hold the infant right after birth. Often, however, the baby is cleaned first to remove blood and **vernix**, a greasy substance that protects the fetus in the womb.

Newborns may also be covered in fine, downy hair that is called *lanugo*. They may have puffy faces or smooshed heads from the tightness of the birth canal and are not yet able to coo or smile. But, even in those early days, they can gaze at their parents' faces and grab fingers held out to them. Most of all, however, they communicate by crying (and stopping crying!) to let their parents know whether they are hungry, tired, wet, or cold.

At birth, infants weigh on average around 7 pounds and are about 19 inches tall (Villar et al., 2014). Over the next year, infants will triple their weight! Since newborns tend to be very alert after birth, this is also a good time to start breastfeeding. In the beginning, the mother produces a special, thick kind of milk called *colostrum*, which helps build the infant's immune and digestive systems. Soon, the infant (and mother) will be very tired. The birthing process requires an enormous amount of energy for both mother and child, and with any luck, they will settle down for a much-needed nap.

Right after birth, doctors or nurses assess the newborn's health for the first time to see whether any medical interventions are needed. The assessment that is used is called the **Apgar scale**. It was developed in 1952 by physician Virginia Apgar and has since saved countless lives. Before Apgar developed her scale, small newborns with bluish skin color or those who had trouble breathing were often just left to die, assuming they had no chance of survival. The Apgar scale gave physicians a protocol to follow, placing a particular emphasis on newborns' well-being and spelling out guidelines for how to respond to newborns in distress.

The Apgar scale evaluates five aspects of infant well-being: (1) **A**ppearance (or skin color), (2) **p**ulse (or heart rate), (3) **g**rimace (reflexes), (4) **a**ctivity (muscle tone), and (5) **r**espiration (breathing) (see also **TABLE 4.1**). In each area, the baby gets a score assigned between 0 and 2. The highest score is therefore 10 points.

The Apgar test is usually performed twice. Right after birth, the 1-minute Apgar score indicates how well the baby has tolerated the birth process. A score of 7 or higher indicates that the baby is in good condition. Scores between 4 and 6 are considered moderately abnormal: The baby may need some assistance to start breathing on its own. A score of 3 or lower suggests that the infant needs immediate medical care (American College of Obstetricians and Gynecologists, 2021). Most newborns have an Apgar score of 7 or above. Once infants with lower scores get some assistance (like suctioning the airways), their condition usually improves.

After 5 minutes (and possibly again, another 10 minutes later), the baby is reassessed and given a new Apgar score that indicates how well the baby is adjusting to life outside the mother's womb. Unless Apgar scores stay consistently low, however, they do not predict whether an infant is unhealthy or will be in the future. Parents do not need to worry if their infant does not score a perfect 10 on the Apgar scale. The birthing process can be stressful and lead to lower scores, and lower Apgar scores are commonly seen in premature infants as well as after a c-section or after prolonged and complicated labor and delivery (American College of Obstetricians and Gynecologists, 2021).

■ Table 4.1 The Apgar Scale

A newborn's Apgar scores help doctors and nurses judge whether medical assistance is needed.

Apgar sign	2	1	0
Appearance (skin color)	Normal color all over (hands and feet are pink)	Normal color (but hands and feet are bluish)	Bluish-gray or pale all over
Pulse (heart rate)	Normal (above 100 beats per minute)	Below 100 beats per minute	Absent (no pulse)
Grimace (response to stimulation like a mild pinch)	Pulls away, sneezes, coughs, or cries with stimulation	Facial movement only (grimace) with stimulation	Absent (no response to stimulation)
Activity (muscle tone)	Active, spontaneous movement	Arms and legs flexed with little movement	No movement, "floppy" tone
Respiration (breathing rate and effort)	Normal rate and effort, good cry	Slow or irregular breathing, weak cry	Absent (no breathing)

The Apgar test is just one of many medical tests to be done after birth. Most infants born in a hospital will undergo screening for a number of diseases and genetic conditions before they leave the hospital. Screenings may also be performed by a midwife or family physician if the baby is not born in a hospital. Screening tests do not diagnose any medical conditions, but rather identify infants who may have certain conditions requiring more in-depth testing. The newborn screening consists of three parts:

1. A sensor placed on the infant's skin measures the amount of oxygen in the blood. Low oxygen levels in the blood may point to congenital heart disease.

2. A hearing screen is performed. About 12,500 newborns are diagnosed with hearing problems through the newborn screening each year (Eunice Kennedy Shriver National Institute of Child Health and Human Development, 2017).

3. A small amount of blood is drawn from the infant's heel with a prick to test for genetic diseases. In the United States, each state has its own newborn screening panel that determines which disorders infants are tested for. However, states do not differ considerably in the number of tests that are performed and most test for about 30 to 34 disorders.

Pain Management during Delivery

Giving birth can be a very painful experience. Here is what two women have to say about labor pain:

> People told me labor would feel like very bad menstrual cramps but I did not feel that way. It was so much more intense. With every contraction, the pain became almost unbearable, and then it would slowly subside. It was so much more painful than I expected. But once I got the epidural, it got a lot easier. (Pamela, New Jersey)

> Giving birth was by far the hardest thing physically I have ever done. But when you get to the pushing stage, the worst is over. You are getting a feeling similar to having a bowel movement and you're almost done. I've had an epidural, local anesthesia, and no medication at all. I actually preferred nothing. (Melany, Arizona)

■ Giving birth tends to be very painful. Some women choose to take anesthetic medications to alleviate the pain, whereas others prefer to deal with the pain using methods like relaxation techniques or hypnosis.

| **anesthetics** medications administered to produce insensitivity to pain.

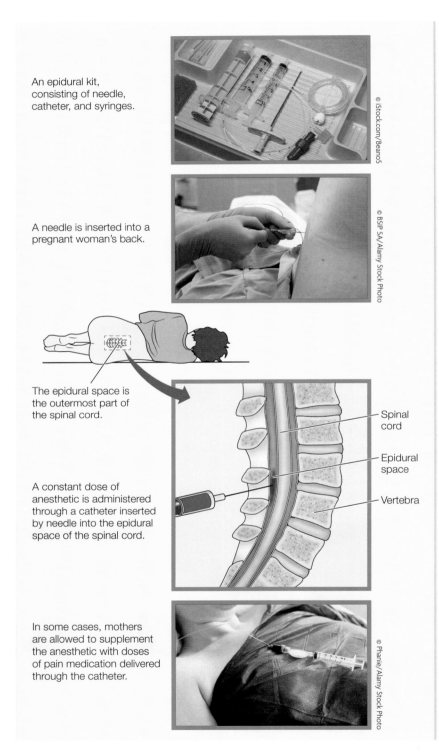

An epidural kit, consisting of needle, catheter, and syringes.

© iStock.com/Beano5

A needle is inserted into a pregnant woman's back.

© BSIP SA/Alamy Stock Photo

The epidural space is the outermost part of the spinal cord.

Spinal cord

Epidural space

Vertebra

A constant dose of anesthetic is administered through a catheter inserted by needle into the epidural space of the spinal cord.

In some cases, mothers are allowed to supplement the anesthetic with doses of pain medication delivered through the catheter.

© Phanie/Alamy Stock Photo

FIGURE 4.2 An epidural consists of continuous infusions of anesthetic medication delivered via a catheter into the spinal canal. Pain is blocked from body parts below the place of injection, but the mother stays alert during the entire birthing process.

How women manage their pain during labor depends on their individual preferences as well as on where they give birth. Women giving birth in a hospital or medical center have the option of using **anesthetics** to control pain during labor. While pain relief can help the mother focus on the birth process and give her some rest, there are also some disadvantages and risks, just like with any medical intervention. Also, pain medication given to the mother may affect the baby if the medication is transferred through the placenta.

Different kinds of anesthetics are available to relieve labor pain. Most frequently, women choose *epidural anesthesia*, in which a continuous infusion of medication is delivered to the spinal canal through a narrow plastic tube, or catheter (**FIGURE 4.2**). An epidural blocks nerve signals from the lower spine and allows the mother to stay alert and be an active participant in the birthing process. If at some point a c-section must be performed and an epidural is already in place, the dosage of the medication can be increased so that surgery can take place with minimal delay (U.S. National Library of Medicine, 2021b). Generally, the health of babies born with or without the use of epidurals does not differ (Agrawal et al., 2014; Kearns et al., 2021).

Instead of an epidural, the mother may choose to receive a local injection to numb the area around the vagina. Known as a *pudendal block*, the injection is used to relieve pain during the second labor stage or when forceps are used. A third, rarely employed option is the use of general anesthesia. With this method, mothers are put to sleep and thus cannot participate in the birth. It is also risky: Mothers who receive general anesthesia experience more severe side effects, and between 1997 and 2002, around 17 in 1 million mothers died while under a general anesthetic compared with about 4 in 1 million mothers who received regional anesthesia (Baghirzada et al., 2021; Hawkins et al., 2011). There are a number of other methods to manage pain in childbirth, like relaxation techniques or hypnosis. We will discuss these in the section below on approaches to childbirth.

Cesarean Sections

A cesarean section (or c-section) is a surgical intervention in which an incision is made in the mother's abdominal wall and uterus in order to remove the baby. Tales of such procedures date back thousands of years to ancient Greece, Egypt, India, and China. In these earliest times, the procedure would have been performed on a dead or dying woman in an attempt to save her offspring (U.S. National Library of Medicine, 2013).

A c-section should be performed when a vaginal birth seems to carry considerable risks to the baby or the mother. For example, the baby may not be positioned head down in the uterus, but rather bottom first or feet first (this is called a **breech position**). C-sections may be planned in some cases if the mother is carrying twins, if the mother has had a c-section previously, or if the mother carries an infection such as HIV that doctors may fear will be passed to the baby. Emergency c-sections are performed when complications arise during the birth process, such as when labor does not progress sufficiently or when the baby's heart rate increases or decreases for too long in atypical ways.

Sometimes, c-sections are performed for reasons of convenience rather than medical necessity—they last only 1–2 hours and can be planned according to the mother's or doctor's schedule. But in low-risk pregnancies, c-sections carry higher risks than vaginal births. The mother may develop an infection, experience increased blood loss or injury to internal organs, and have a longer recovery time. Babies delivered through a c-section are at increased risk for breathing problems and injury during the surgery (Liszewski et al., 2017; Prefumo et al., 2016). Despite these risks, c-sections are still considered generally safe and can significantly improve the outcomes for mothers and babies who experience complications during the birth process.

About 32% of births in the United States involve c-sections (Centers for Disease Control and Prevention, 2021b)—too high a number if you consider that the World Health Organization estimates that only in about 10–15% of births is a c-section medically necessary (World Health Organization, 2015). While in developed countries like the United States too many c-sections are performed for convenience reasons, an increase in c-sections is needed in some developing countries to improve birth outcomes (**FIGURE 4.3**).

When a woman has given birth by c-section once, physicians often recommend that a *vaginal birth after cesarean* (VBAC) be approached with caution. The scar in the uterus from the c-section can tear during a subsequent vaginal birth, causing serious complications. About 1 woman in 238 will experience a uterine rupture when giving birth vaginally after a c-section. In 2018, only about 13% of women who had a previous c-section gave birth vaginally to their next child (Osterman, 2020).

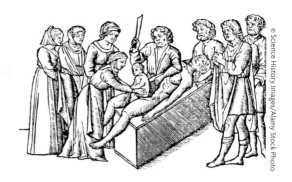

■ A woodcut shows a live (and smiling!) infant—possibly Julius Caesar—being removed surgically from the body of the dead mother. The woodcut was included in a sixteenth-century edition of *De Vita Caesarum* (*The Lives of the Twelve Caesars*), by the second-century Roman historian Suetonius.

breech position the position a baby is in when it enters the birth canal feet-first or buttocks-first rather than head-first.

FIGURE 4.3 Worldwide trends in the use of c-sections. The rates at which c-sections are performed around the world differ dramatically. C-sections can save the life of mother and child when complications arise. However, in developed countries they are at times performed when not medically necessary; in contrast, not all mothers in less developed countries who need a c-section have the option to receive one.

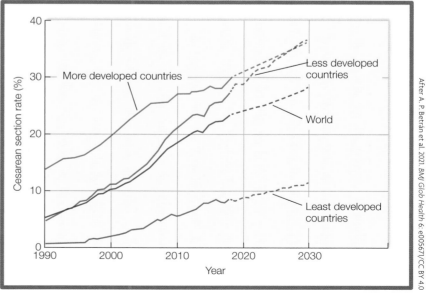

◼ What's It Like...

Giving Birth by C-section

Mandy, mother of twins Maura and Matthew

Ten months ago, my twins Maura and Matthew were born by c-section. I had known pretty much from the beginning that with twins I had a higher chance of needing a c-section, but I was still hoping they'd be born vaginally. My husband, Conrad, and I took a hypnobirthing class that explained different techniques to help deal with the pain and how my husband could support me during childbirth. We figured we'll just take things as they come, and until the end we really thought we could go through with the vaginal birth. During the prenatal exam in my 37th week of pregnancy the doctor said that Maura's umbilical cord was wrapped around her neck and that her heartbeat was irregular. They decided right then and there to deliver the twins by c-section.

I got an epidural block where they injected some medication into my spine. Soon, I could not feel any pain in my lower body, but I was fully awake. Conrad was with me and stood by where my head was. Below my chest there was a kind of curtain so that I couldn't see anything the doctors did. And then everything went really fast. They pulled the babies out within 2 minutes of each other. We could hear them cry, and the medical team showed them to us before whisking them off to be cleaned. It took a bit for them to stitch up my wound, and then I was brought to my hospital room.

I underestimated the recovery of a birth with c-section, however. I had never had major surgery before, and that's what a c-section is. For the first 2–3 days just sitting up and walking to the bathroom was so excruciatingly painful that I waited as long as I could before I went. And for several more weeks I walked more like an old person, slow and very deliberately. By now, of course, I am completely back to normal. And it was so worth it to get my two sweet babies.

Dr. Holmstrom, Mandy's surgeon

We do c-sections on a regular basis at our hospital, and there are many reasons why an expectant mother might need one. Sometimes, the fetus is in a breech position, or it may be too large to travel through the birth canal. At other times, the baby or mother are in physical distress, and doing a c-section allows us to get the baby out as quickly as possible. In Mandy's case, Maura's umbilical cord was wrapped around her neck multiple times and her heartbeat was very irregular. We were very concerned that blood flow to the baby was disrupted, and so we decided to perform a c-section at that point.

I've performed many c-sections in my life, but they never cease to amaze me. It begins with a horizontal cut across the abdomen. Then you need to cut through muscle and then through a membrane called peritoneum to reveal the uterus. It's significant surgery, not unlike the kind of procedure doctors perform to remove a tumor or fix some abnormality. But then, instead of that, you find this beautiful, fully formed human life.

The baby isn't always easy to remove: they can be so tightly wedged in the birth canal that it takes considerable force to pull them out. Then you cut the umbilical cord to fully release the baby from the mother. Once the baby is out, you still need to remove the placenta. Then, you close the wound, and the surgery is complete.

Professionals Attending Births

A number of professionals can be involved in the childbirth process. Particularly in low-risk births, who is present during childbirth depends to some extent on the wishes of the mother. In 2019, more than 98% of births in the United States took place in hospitals; 91% of them were attended by an obstetrician (National Academies of Sciences & Medicine, 2020). An **obstetrician** is a physician who specializes in pregnancy, labor, and birth. Obstetricians are a particularly good choice for a woman whose pregnancy is considered high-risk, for instance, because she is carrying a baby with a birth defect or expecting more than one baby.

obstetrician a physician trained in the branch of medicine and surgery concerned with pregnancy, labor, and childbirth.

A midwife measures the blood pressure of a woman during a postpartum visit at the Sahrawi refugee camps in Tindouf, Algeria. Why do you think the role of midwives is so important in developing countries?

In only 8% of hospital births was a midwife present, whereas a century ago and more, midwives were involved in a majority of births in the United States (Martin et al., 2017). A **midwife** is a health worker trained and certified to assist a woman during pregnancy and childbirth. Midwives believe that childbirth is a natural process and, for this reason, are a particularly good choice for a woman who wishes to have a **natural childbirth** without pain medication or other medical interventions. In European countries like Sweden and Germany most women choose midwife care for pregnancy and birth. Additionally, an increase in midwife care in developing countries without sufficient healthcare could significantly improve health outcomes for mothers (United Nations Population Fund, 2012). If complications arise, the midwife will either consult with a physician or refer the mother to a physician. Most midwives work within a hospital setting, but some also attend births at home.

Mothers can also choose to have a **doula** present during the birth. A *doula* is a professional who specializes in providing physical and emotional support during pregnancy, labor, and birth, as well as after delivery. Doula support can lower the probability that a woman will need a c-section or experience other birth complications (Font & Testani, 2020; Kozhimannil et al., 2014). Doulas can also enhance women's satisfaction with the birth experience (Simon et al., 2016) and increase the likelihood that the mother successfully initiates breastfeeding after the birth (Font & Testani, 2020; Gruber et al., 2013). Doulas are not required to be trained and licensed, so it is important to find one that has undergone a rigorous training and certification program. Many cities like New York City offer doula assistance for free to women with lower income.

midwife a healthcare worker, usually a registered nurse, with specialized training to assist a woman during pregnancy and natural childbirth.

natural childbirth a birth process with minimal medical intervention, usually emphasizing breathing strategies and relaxation techniques to manage pain and discomfort.

doula a professional without formal medical training who provides physical and emotional support during pregnancy, labor, and birth.

Birthing Options beyond Standard Hospital-Based Care

After learning that she was pregnant, Sylvia researched different options for giving birth. Her instincts told her that a hospital was the safest place for a first-time mother to give birth, and yet she found the idea of a home birth compelling for a number of reasons: She did not own a car for the 30-minute drive to the hospital, and she was concerned about how much of a hospital birth her health insurance would cover—she knew that home births cost less than hospital births. She also wanted more control over

Doulas assist mothers during pregnancy and delivery, as well as after the baby is born. They provide information as well as emotional and physical support, but they do not provide medical services.

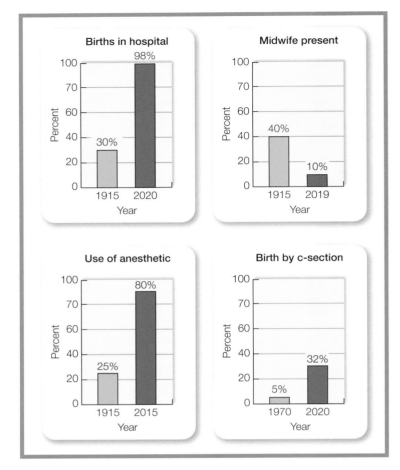

FIGURE 4.4 Changes in childbirth practices over time. Between 1915 and 2020, the percentage of hospital births grew dramatically while the percentage of births attended by a midwife fell to just 10%. Recent decades have also seen increases in the use of anesthetic and c-sections.

Data from A. Manning. 2017. What it was like being pregnant in 1915. http://publichealthlegacy .americashealthrankings.org; National Academies of Sciences & Medicine. 2020. *Birth Settings in America: Outcomes, Quality, Access, and Choice.* The National Academies Press, Washington, DC; U.S. National Library of Medicine. 2021. Pregnancy and birth: Epidurals and painkillers for labor pain relief. www.ncbi.nlm .nih.gov; Centers for Disease Control and Prevention. 2021. Preterm birth. www.cdc.gov; J. A. Martin et al. 2021. *National Vital Statistics Reports; Vol. 70. No 2.* National Center for Health Statistics, Hyattsville, MD

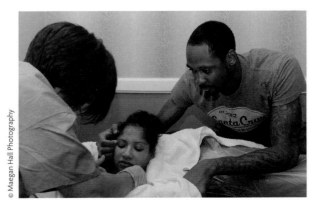

■ The Bradley method places particular emphasis on a woman's partner to help coach and support her throughout labor and delivery.

her birth experience. After consulting with a midwife who assured her that, provided there were no complications, a home birth would be just as safe as a hospital birth, Sylvia made up her mind: She would have a home birth, in a birthing pool. At the midwife's suggestion, Sylvia chose to be assisted as well by a doula, who would help her use relaxation techniques to manage discomfort in the absence of pain medication.

Sylvia's plan for a home birth attended by a midwife, while hardly the norm today, was far more common a century ago (**FIGURE 4.4**). In 2019, less than 2% of births occurred outside a hospital—about two-thirds of them took place in a home, and one-third occurred in a birthing center (National Academies of Sciences & Medicine, 2020). The American College of Obstetricians and Gynecologists recommends hospitals and accredited birthing centers as the safest places for births, but acknowledges that every mother should be free to make her own decision after consultation with health professionals (American College of Obstetricians and Gynecologists, 2017).

Perhaps it is no surprise that an increasing number of women with low-risk pregnancies are looking for a return to more "natural" ways to give birth. Natural childbirth includes nonmedical ways of managing the associated pain and creating a more wholesome birth experience. There are many approaches to childbirth beyond a traditional hospital birth, including the following:

LAMAZE METHOD The Lamaze method views childbirth as a natural process that can take place anywhere the parents wish—in a hospital, at a birthing center, or in the home. Lamaze classes teach prospective parents breathing and relaxation techniques to reduce pain in childbirth (Lamaze International, 2021), but they also educate future parents about possible complications, c-sections, anesthesia, and the care of the mother and baby after the birth (Budin, 2018; Lothian, 1999).

BRADLEY METHOD The Bradley method also views birth as a natural process and places particular emphasis on involving partners as "coaches" in the birthing process. The "coach" (usually, but not always, the future father) learns to support the mother during the birth and help her with relaxation and birth positions (American Academy of Husband-Coached Childbirth, 2021).

HYPNOBIRTHING Hypnobirthing consists of a set of muscle relaxation and breathing strategies used by the mother to achieve a heightened state of relaxation to reduce pain and fear. Many women report experiencing a sense of relaxation and calmness when using the technique in home or hospital-based births (Beevi et al., 2017; Downe et al., 2015; Finlayson et al., 2015).

■ Centering Pregnancy brings women with similar due dates together in a group setting.

© Monkey Business Images/Shutterstock.com

CENTERING PREGNANCY   This approach brings together about 8–10 women with similar due dates to have their prenatal exams in a group setting. After individual health assessments, they meet in a circle to discuss health topics and questions. Members support each other, form friendships, and feel more actively involved in their care (Centering Healthcare Institute, 2021). Participating women tend to have a lower risk of preterm births (Liu et al., 2021). Centering Pregnancy has also been shown to reduce the inequalities between different racial and ethnic groups in terms of prenatal care and birth outcomes (Crockett et al., 2017).

WATERBIRTHING   Many birthing centers and hospitals have pools for mothers in labor, but smaller tubs can also be obtained for mothers who wish to give birth at home. The warm water may provide pain relief and relaxation as well as more freedom to move around during labor. Water births are generally considered safe (Jacoby et al., 2019; Mallen-Perez et al., 2017; Peacock et al., 2018), although there are some concerns that a baby experiencing distress might take its first breath under water, that the umbilical cord might snap, or that the baby might catch an infection from the water if it is contaminated (Harper, 2014; Taylor et al., 2016).

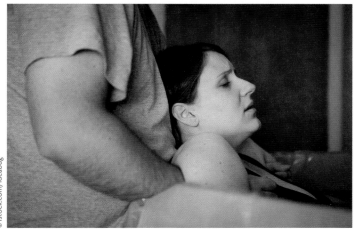

© istock.com/ideabug

■ Experiencing labor (and perhaps birth) in a pool of warm water, like Sylvia chose to do, may help the mother relax and reduce pain.

Review!

What happens during the birth process and right after the infant is born?

- In the first (and longest) stage of childbirth, contractions occur at increasingly shorter intervals, starting off 10–20 minutes apart but eventually occurring once every 1–2 minutes. Contractions help thin the cervix and enlarge (dilate) its opening so the baby can pass through.
- Once the cervix is maximally dilated, the second stage begins. It can last anywhere between 20 minutes and 2 hours. During this stage, the baby will move from the uterus through the cervix and birth canal to be delivered.
- The placenta remains in the mother's uterus and is delivered in the third stage, which lasts up to 30 minutes.
- Immediately after birth and in the days and weeks following, physicians assess the health of the newborn. The *Apgar test* is used to get a rough impression of an infant's well-being right after birth and, 5 minutes later, to see how the newborn is adjusting to life outside the womb. Sometime later, other newborn screenings are performed routinely as well, including hearing tests and genetic screenings for a number of heritable diseases.

How can pain be managed in childbirth?

- In hospital births, mothers are offered different *anesthetics* to ease the pain of childbirth.
- Epidural anesthesia, in which medication is injected into the spinal canal, is most frequently chosen and can be used for vaginal births and c-sections.
- Other options are local anesthesia, general anesthesia, relaxation techniques, or hypnosis.

Why are c-sections needed?

- *C-sections* are performed when a vaginal birth carries a substantial risk for either mother or infant, for example when the mother is carrying twins or when the infant is in distress.
- In a c-section, the infant is removed from the womb through an incision in the mother's abdominal wall and uterus.

- In the United States, about 32% of infants are delivered by c-section. Due to the inherent risks of surgery, healthcare specialists are aiming to lower the rate of c-sections.

Which professionals are present when someone gives birth?

- Most births in the United States take place in a hospital and are attended by an *obstetrician*, a physician who specializes in pregnancy and childbirth.
- *Midwives* attend about 8% of hospital births. They are trained health workers and collaborate with physicians should complications arise.
- Doulas provide physical and emotional support during pregnancy and labor as well as after delivery.

Besides a hospital birth, which approaches to childbirth can parents choose?

- North American parents are increasingly opting to approach childbirth in a more natural way that minimizes medical intervention as much as possible.
- Both the Lamaze method and the Bradley method put parents in control by promoting relaxation techniques over medical anesthesia and by educating parents about pregnancy and birth complications, c-sections, nutrition, breastfeeding, and so on. This enables parents to make informed decisions should the need arise during birth.
- Hypnobirthing is an alternative approach that emphasizes self-hypnosis and relaxation techniques as ways to cope with pain during childbirth.
- Waterbirthing involves labor and sometimes birth in a tub of warm water, which helps women move around and assume a more comfortable position.
- Centering Pregnancy is a group-based approach that actively involves women in their prenatal care and uses group meetings to provide information and support.

Practice!

1. In the second stage of childbirth, _____ .
   a. contractions occur increasingly frequently and the cervix starts to dilate
   b. the baby travels through the birth canal and is eventually delivered
   c. the placenta is expelled from the mother's uterus
   d. the baby enters the Fallopian tubes

2. An episiotomy is considered necessary _____ .
   a. in all births
   b. in the large majority of births
   c. in a small minority of births
   d. never—this procedure is not performed anymore

3. Compared with today, c-sections in 1950 were _____ .
   a. far less common
   b. about as common

   c. far more common
   d. not measured, so comparisons are impossible

4. The Bradley method of giving birth always involves _____ .
   a. use of general anesthesia
   b. use of epidural anesthesia
   c. water birth
   d. a coach

5. The main purpose of a doula is to _____ .
   a. deliver the baby
   b. check the health of a newborn baby
   c. check the health of the mother after a child's birth
   d. provide physical and emotional support to the mother

Act It Out!

During her pregnancy, Sylvia has so many questions about what to expect during childbirth. She initially plans to give birth in a hospital, just as her friend Sheryl did. With a classmate, role-play a conversation between Sylvia and Sheryl in which Sylvia asks her friend questions about what to expect. After about 5 minutes, reverse the roles and repeat the scenario.

Show What You've Learned!

When Tino in the mailroom heard that Sylvia was pregnant, he told her, "You should get a c-section. My cousin had a c-section, and she said it was the easiest of her three births!" Sylvia suspects that Tino may be kidding her, but she decides to ask her gynecologist about it at her next appointment. "Should I consider planning a c-section?" she asks. How do you think Sylvia's doctor would respond? Drawing on information presented in this chapter, write out a response to Sylvia, and then compare notes with a classmate.

What's Your Position?

Is a natural birth better? After she started telling people she was pregnant, Sylvia was asked one question more than any other: Are you going to have a "natural birth"? It's something she hadn't given much thought to at first, and now she's suddenly receiving lots of conflicting information—from friends, family, even strangers—about the pros and cons of managing the pain of childbirth with and without anesthetics. What's your position? Do you think a natural birth is safer, healthier, and better for mother and baby? Have a look at the information presented on the websites below before debating the topic with a classmate.

Additional Resources Online

- "Natural Childbirth," from Nemours KidsHealth
- "What You Need to Know about Natural Birth," from Healthline
- "Why Natural Childbirth?," from the *Journal of Perinatal Education*
- "An Infant's Death Has Sparked a Heated Debate Around the 'Free Birth' Movement," from BuzzFeed
- "I Kind of Wish I'd Gotten the Epidural—Both Times I Gave Birth," from Today's Parent

4.2 Problems in Childbirth

- Explain the symptoms and potential outcomes when a newborn is deprived of oxygen.
- Outline the causes of low birthweight and preterm births and explain the consequences and treatments.

Sylvia chose to give birth at home. She had the pool set up, and when contractions started, her husband, midwife, and doula were all with her. Sylvia was in high spirits, looking forward to the things to come. Hour after hour passed, however, and delivery did not progress as planned. After 28 hours, she was exhausted beyond belief and in worse pain than she ever thought possible. In a rush, her husband packed up a few things and called a taxi to take them to the nearest hospital. Sylvia eventually gave birth to her daughter by c-section.

While most deliveries in the United States take place without any notable problems, not all do. Prolonged labor like Sylvia's can indicate that the baby is too large for the mother's birth canal or that the baby is in the wrong position for a vaginal delivery. Other problems that can complicate the birth process include preterm birth and low birthweight. We will consider each of these issues in the sections that follow.

Oxygen Deprivation

As soon as Sylvia arrived at the hospital, she was outfitted with a fetal heart monitor to check on the condition of her baby. The monitor revealed that her baby's heart rate was too slow, and consistently so. Concerned that the fetus was not receiving enough oxygen, the attending physicians decided that the baby needed to be delivered as soon as possible. They opted for an emergency c-section, which was performed successfully.

Babies with birth asphyxia receive breathing support to ensure an adequate oxygen supply until they can breathe by themselves.

When a baby's body or brain does not receive enough oxygen during the birth process, we speak of **birth asphyxia**. An infant born with birth asphyxia may have a bluish skin color, low heart rate, weak or no breathing, and possibly seizures. Without sufficient oxygen supply, the body's cells cannot work properly and waste builds up inside the cells, causing temporary or permanent damage (Pappas & Korzeniewski, 2016). Birth asphyxia is not uncommon—it occurs in about 2 in every 100 births and is the cause of around 30% of newborn deaths (Ahearne et al., 2016; Mosiro et al., 2019)—but babies affected by mild or moderate asphyxia often recover completely. More serious cases may result in developmental disabilities or eyesight problems. In the worst case, organs may become damaged, possibly leading to death.

Particularly in premature babies, asphyxia can also cause **cerebral palsy** (cerebral = of the brain; palsy = paralysis or body tremors), a neurological disorder that adversely affects body movements and muscle coordination.

birth asphyxia a condition characterized by a lack of oxygen supply to the body and brain.

cerebral palsy a neurological disorder that affects body movements and muscle coordination.

preterm birth birth that occurs before the completion of the 37th week of pregnancy.

Preterm Birth and Low Birthweight

For children and their parents, low birthweight and preterm birth can have serious and lifelong consequences. Although low birthweight and preterm birth are often associated with each other, they do not always occur together.

In preterm births, a child is born before the end of the 37th week of pregnancy

Preterm births are births that occur before the end of the 37th week of pregnancy (Centers for Disease Control and Prevention, 2021b). However, not all preterm births are the same: Because crucial development occurs in every week, right up until the very last week of pregnancy, the consequences of a preterm birth are vastly different depending on how early a child was born. For this reason, we further subdivide preterm birth into three categories (World Health Organization, 2021):

- extremely preterm (birth before 28 weeks of gestation)
- very preterm (birth between 28 and 31 weeks of gestation)
- moderate to late preterm (birth between 32 and 36 weeks of gestation).

According to estimates of the World Health Organization, every year about 15 million babies are born preterm—that is more than 10% of all babies born. Almost 1 million of these infants will die as a result of having been born preterm. In fact, prematurity is, worldwide, the leading cause of death in children younger than age 5 (World Health Organization, 2021). The countries with the highest rates of preterm births are all located in Asia and Africa; they include Malawi, Congo, Zimbabwe, Pakistan, and Indonesia. These countries see between 15 and 18 preterm births for every 100 live births (Blencowe et al., 2012). In the United States, about 10 in 100 infants are born preterm (Martin et al., 2021) (see also **FIGURE 4.5**).

Infants with low birthweight weigh less than 5.5 pounds at birth

Preterm births are often associated with low birthweight. An average infant weighs between 5.5 and 9.0 pounds at birth. Babies born weighing much less are at increased risk for health problems, even if they are born at term. As with preterm births, we distinguish between three categories of low birthweight:

Layla is unemployed and lives in a room in her mother's house with her newborn daughter Kaylee. She has not had health insurance in many years. Insufficient access to healthcare puts both mothers and infants at risk when complications arise before, during, or after the birth.

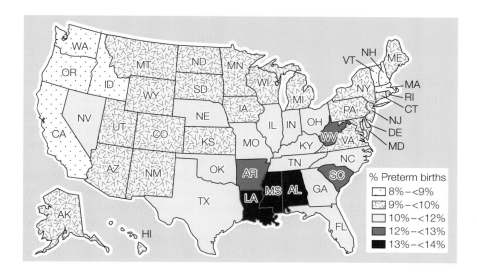

FIGURE 4.5 Percentage of preterm births by state, 2019.

After Centers for Disease Control and Prevention. 2020. Percentage of births born preterm by state. www.cdc.gov

- very low birthweight: less than 1,500 grams (3.25 pounds)
- low birthweight: less than 2,500 grams (5.5 pounds)
- small for gestational age: smaller than 90% of babies born at the same gestational age.

Very low– and low-birthweight infants are typically products of preterm births. Small-for-gestational-age children are often, but not always, preterm babies.

About 15% of babies worldwide are born with low birthweight. This number may be an underestimate, however, because only about half of all babies born worldwide are weighed at birth (UNICEF, 2021). The region of South Asia (Afghanistan, Bangladesh, Bhutan, India, Maldives, Nepal, Pakistan, and Sri Lanka) has the highest rate of low-birthweight babies: 27% of South Asian babies are born with low birthweight (UNICEF, 2021). In the United States, low birthweight is less of a problem than in other parts of the world: About 8% of infants are born with low birthweight, and just 1.4% are born with very low birthweight (Martin et al., 2021).

Preterm labor may be extended to give the fetus more time to develop

Preterm labor is very serious, but it can possibly be extended by a few days or even stopped if it is recognized in time. Signs of preterm labor include frequent contractions, abdominal cramps, and a low, dull backache (Iams, 2003). Unlike the Braxton Hicks contractions Sylvia experienced, true labor contractions will be regular in duration and interval and will steadily become longer and more frequent.

Once it has been established that a woman is in preterm labor, medications can be administered in an attempt to delay the birth by a few days. These few days can greatly improve the survival chances of the baby and improve its pre-birth development. If the cause of the preterm labor can be discovered, physicians may be able to treat it and bring the labor to a halt. During my own pregnancy, I experienced preterm contractions at 30 weeks due to a urinary tract infection. A course of antibiotics successfully stopped the contractions and gave the developing fetuses 6 more weeks to mature.

The earlier infants are born and the less they weigh, the higher their risk for developmental problems

Survival chances vary greatly depending on where a baby is born. In high-income countries, almost all babies born prematurely at week 32 or later survive. In low-income countries, half of such babies die as a result of insufficient care. In

viability the gestational age at which half of all infants born will survive.

developed countries, **viability**—the gestational age at which preterm newborns have at least a 50% chance of surviving—is around 24 weeks (Glass et al., 2015; Myrhaug et al., 2019). Girls have a higher survival rate than boys.

Physicians track fetal growth with ultrasound throughout the entire pregnancy in the hope of being able to spot any potential problems as early as possible. However, these assessments are not always accurate, particularly in the later stages of pregnancy. When my children were born by scheduled c-section at 35 weeks, it was a surprise that one of the girls was very small for her gestational age. She soon caught up with her siblings and did not suffer any apparent negative effects from her low birthweight, but not all children are so lucky.

Generally, the earlier infants are born and the less they weigh at birth, the more they are at risk for premature death or health issues like cerebral palsy as well as hearing and vision impairment (Child Trends Databank, 2016). They tend to perform less well in school and are at higher risk for developing social and behavioral problems (Dombrowski et al., 2021; Hughes et al., 2016; Kajantie & Hovi, 2014). As adults, they may be more likely to develop cardiac disease and diabetes (Soleimani et al., 2014).

Social, medical, and behavioral factors influence the risk of having a premature or low-birthweight child

A number of factors, summarized in **TABLE 4.2**, can have an impact on whether a baby may be born too early or with a low birthweight.

The high rate of preterm and low-birthweight births among African American mothers (**FIGURE 4.6**) is a cause for great concern because it is a major reason for infant mortality. Researchers believe that the following factors may play a role: (a) genetic variants within the African American population (Frey et al., 2016), (b) experiences of racial discrimination (Collins et al., 2004), (c) greater susceptibility to sleep disturbances and stress (Blair et al., 2015), and (d) socioeconomic factors resulting in suboptimal access to prenatal care and healthcare (Braveman et al., 2015). The Centering Pregnancy program we discussed above has aimed at reducing racial disparities in prenatal care, with women being actively involved in their prenatal care and receiving social support from other pregnant women. However, at this point it is not clear whether the approach is really able to significantly lower preterm birth rates (Carter et al., 2016).

Preterm infants need special care

Preterm infants have had less time to develop than full-term infants, and their organs may not be mature enough to take over their various bodily functions (in

FIGURE 4.6 Low-birthweight and preterm births in the United States in 2019. Low-birthweight and preterm births are somewhat more prevalent among Black families than among Hispanic and White families. Nearly 100% of triplets are born preterm, compared with roughly 60% of twins and 8% of singletons.

Data from J. A. Martin et al. 2021. *National Vital Statistics Reports; Vol. 70. No 2.* National Center for Health Statistics, Hyattsville, MD

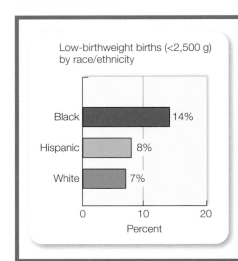
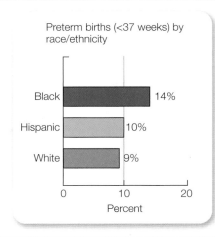
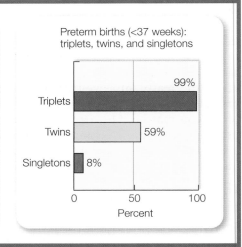

■ Table 4.2 Factors That Can Affect the Risk of Preterm Births

Social, personal, and economic characteristics

Age of mother (younger than 17, older than 35) (Haldre et al., 2007; Waldenström et al., 2017)

Ethnicity: African American mothers have particularly high rates of both preterm and low-birthweight babies (Martin et al., 2021) (Figure 4.6).

Socioeconomic status: Women with lower levels of education or financial security may have less access to medical insurance or may not be able to afford prenatal care (Centers for Disease Control and Prevention, 2021b).

Medical and pregnancy conditions

Pre-existing medical conditions or medical conditions developed during the pregnancy like high blood pressure or gestational diabetes (Romero et al., 2014)

Multiple pregnancy: Twin or triplet (as well as higher-order) pregnancies account for a large percentage of premature births (Martin et al., 2021) (Figure 4.6).

Prior preterm birth

Infection

Behavioral conditions

Drug use: smoking, alcohol use, and use of other drugs

Substance abuse

Late prenatal care

Stress

Source: Centers for Disease Control and Prevention. 2021. Preterm birth. www.cdc.gov

---

other words, they are *pre-mature*). Premature infants may have shallow or irregular breathing. They may have trouble digesting food, may be more prone to infections, or may have trouble feeding (Demers-Mathieu et al., 2018; Zimmerman & Rosner, 2018). Therefore, preterm infants may spend their first days, weeks, or even months of life in the neonatal intensive care unit (NICU), which is equipped with medical instruments specially designed for the care of frail babies.

Infants may be placed in an **incubator** that encloses the crib in a clear plastic shield to control temperature and oxygen while insulating the infant against harmful germs. If needed, oxygen may be supplied through nasal prongs or tubes placed in the windpipe. Infants may also be fed through intravenous (IV) lines or flexible tubes in their nose or mouth.

Infants with no medical issues may be "feeders-and-growers," needing to remain in the NICU just for a short length of time to gain some weight and establish proper feeding and breathing mechanisms before they are sent home.

Parents can do a number of things to help their babies thrive in the NICU. In "kangaroo care," infants are placed on the parent's bare chest for skin-to-skin contact. The baby's head is

incubator an apparatus consisting of a bed enclosed in a clear plastic shield, in which air temperature and oxygen content can be controlled.

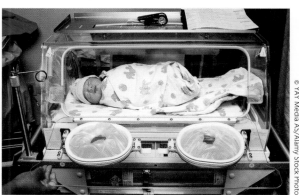

■ Ethan was delivered by c-section 6 weeks early due to the gestational diabetes his mother developed. He spent the first 2 weeks of his life in an incubator that kept him warm and protected him from the germs that visitors or medical personnel may bring in.

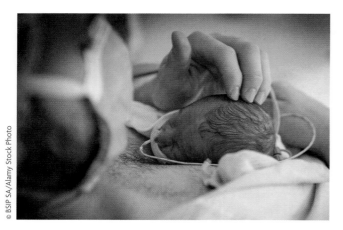

■ In kangaroo care, an infant is placed on the parent's bare chest for skin-to-skin contact, with the baby's head turned sideways so that it can hear the heart of the parent.

turned sideways, allowing it to hear the heart of the parent. Kangaroo care has been shown to ease the pain of medical procedures (Avcin & Kucukoglu, 2021; Murmu et al., 2017; Pagni et al., 2017), facilitate breastfeeding (Tully et al., 2016), and increase weight gain (Evereklian & Posmontier, 2017). Mothers' breast milk can be fed to the child through a feeding tube. Breast milk can be frozen easily, so if the baby is fed through an IV, the breast milk can be used later on. Between 35 and 37 weeks of gestation, most babies are ready to breastfeed (Horgan, 2015).

As you can imagine, most parents feel a significant amount of stress and anxiety when their child is born preterm and needs to spend some time in the NICU. The high-tech environment with its regular sound of beeps and alarms, many of them routine, may add to their stress. Women may experience feelings of failure because they could not carry their baby to term (Baum et al., 2012), and preterm infants may not look as plump, rosy, and healthy as their full-term peers (Holditch-Davis & Shandor Miles, 2000; Spinelli et al., 2016). Parents may be scared and feel alienated from their infants because they seem so frail and require medical care (Meijssen et al., 2011). Infant massage has been shown to alleviate the anxiety new parents feel and also has a positive impact on the child (Afand et al., 2017; Campbell & Jacobs, 2021).

Parents expecting multiples often have a very different expectation for the birth of their children than parents expecting singletons because they know there is a much higher likelihood of the babies being born preterm. They are often better informed about the risks associated with preterm births and less likely to be surprised by the appearance of their infants after birth. When our triplets were born at 35 weeks, they were considered "feeders-and-growers," who mostly needed to gain some weight. Because we were well informed about the kind of care preterm infants would require and were not faced with any surprising medical issues, we were spared the emotional rollercoaster ride experienced by parents of infants born unexpectedly early.

Review!

What happens when a newborn is deprived of oxygen?

■ *Birth asphyxia* occurs when an infant does not receive enough oxygen during birth.

■ Most infants with mild or moderate asphyxia recover completely. More severe cases, however, can result in *cerebral palsy*, vision or developmental problems, or, in the worst case, death.

■ Causes include high or low blood pressure in the mother, restricted blood flow to the fetus resulting from pressure on the umbilical cord, or obstructed airways in the fetus.

What causes low birthweight and preterm births? What are the consequences, and how are they treated?

■ Most *preterm births* are caused by preterm labor, although some infants are born early because of a c-section or because labor was induced.

■ Generally, very young and old mothers have a higher risk of giving birth to preterm or low-birthweight children. Medical issues in either mother or fetus also can lead to a preterm birth, and the

number of fetuses a mother is carrying plays a role as well: Twins and other multiples are often born early.

■ Rates of preterm and low-birthweight infants are higher among Black mothers than among White or Hispanic mothers.

■ A mother in preterm labor can be given drugs to delay contractions for hours or days, so that medications can be given to speed up the fetus's lung development and increase its survival chances.

■ Preterm infants may require immediate medical care if they are very low weight or premature. Premature infants whose organs are insufficiently developed are fed intravenously and placed in an *incubator*, which controls temperature and oxygen supply. More mature preterm infants may need only additional nutrition through a nasal tube until they can feed on their own.

■ Many preterm infants fare quite well, though there are risks, including chronic health problems as well as behavioral and learning problems.

Practice!

1. Preterm infants are those born before _____ weeks.
   a. 40
   b. 37
   c. 34
   d. 30

2. A child suffering birth asphyxia lacks _____ .
   a. oxygen
   b. water
   c. human emotion
   d. sufficient body temperature

3. Today, infants generally have to be born after _____ weeks to have a 50% chance of surviving.
   a. 22
   b. 24
   c. 26
   d. 28

Show What You've Learned!

Damian and his partner, Davis, have a 3-year-old daughter, Mathilda. She is a very artistically inclined whirlwind who loves to draw (on anything and everything) and keeps her parents on their feet. Although she is doing well now, there was a time when her parents were very worried about her health. She was carried by a surrogate mother who lived a few hours away from Damian and Davis. In her 32nd week of pregnancy, the surrogate went into preterm labor. Damian and Davis left town that night and drove to the hospital. Two days later, Mathilda was born, weighing just 4 pounds.

What might the doctor have told Damian and Davis about the health of baby Mathilda at the time? What else might the doctor have told them about caring for a preterm infant and any complications that might arise?

4.3 The Newborn Baby

- List and describe newborn reflexes.
- Recall the ways newborns perceive the world and list the senses developed prior to birth.
- Assess whether or not newborns are able to learn.

Healthy newborn infants are perfectly outfitted for life outside the womb. Over the *neonatal period* (which lasts 4 weeks), the newborn continues to adjust to life outside the womb. In the following section, we will learn about newborn reflexes, how newborns perceive the environment with their senses, and how newborns learn.

Newborn Reflexes

Although infants seem quite helpless when they are born, they show a number of reflexes that have evolved to help them survive (TABLE 4.3). **Reflexes** are automatic and unlearned responses to a stimulus. If you're riding your bike and a fly hits your eye, you automatically close your eye. You do not have to think about closing your eye; blinking is one of a number of reflex responses your body uses to protect itself. While many of the newborn reflexes disappear within a few months, others remain into adulthood (among them the cough reflex, the gag reflex, and the sneeze reflex).

Infant reflexes tell us whether the infant's brain and nervous system are functioning as they should. If adequate reflexes are not present in a newborn, it is cause for concern. Likewise, if the reflexes disappear and then return, or if they do not disappear around the expected age, it is a reason to suspect that the baby's brain and nervous system are not developing appropriately (U.S. National Library of Medicine, 2021a).

The reflexes of an infant as well as other abilities are assessed by the **Brazelton Neonatal Behavioral Assessment Scale** (**NBAS**), which is often just called "the

reflexes automatic und unlearned responses to a stimulus.

Brazelton Neonatal Behavioral Assessment Scale (NBAS) a neurobehavioral test that assesses newborns' behaviors and neurological status.

■ Table 4.3 Newborn Reflexes

Reflex	Stimulus	Response	Age at which reflex disappears	Function
Root reflex © violetblue/ Shutterstock.com	Area around an infant's mouth is touched	Head turns into the direction of the touch, and the mouth opens	About 4 months of age	Helps find breast or bottle
Suck reflex © wavebreakmedia/ Shutterstock.com	Roof of the mouth is touched	Infant begins sucking		Not fully developed until 36 weeks of gestation; premature infants may have weak sucking reflex
Moro reflex © Alex SG/ Shutterstock.com	Loud sound or sudden movement	Infant throws head back and extends arms and legs, then pulls them in	About 4–6 months of age	May help clinging and holding on to mother
Tonic neck reflex © Artur Bogacki/ Shutterstock.com	Infant's head is turned to one side	Infant extends one arm on side of face; other arm bends at elbow (fencing position)	About 6–7 months of age	May help prepare baby for later voluntary reaching
Grasp reflex © iStock.com/ RuslanDashinsky	Object touches palm of hand	Infant closes fingers to grasp	About 5–6 months of age	May prepare baby for later voluntary grasping
Babinski reflex © Pavel_Kostenko/ Shutterstock.com	Stroking of the feet	Infant spreads toes	12–24 months of age	May prepare infant for curling toes in order to grasp and hold on to caregiver
Step reflex © Prasit Rodphan/ Alamy Stock Photo	Infant is held upright with feet touching a flat surface	Infant lifts feet after one another in motion that looks like walking	About 2 months of age	May prepare infant for later walking

■ The creator of the Brazelton Neonatal Behavioral Assessment Scale (NBAS), T. Berry Brazelton, believed that his biggest contribution to the science of child development was the NBAS, which helps people see individual differences even in newborn babies and allows them to adjust their caregiving to the needs of the infant (Hellmich, 2013).

Brazelton." It was developed in 1973 by pediatrician T. Berry Brazelton (1918–2018) and his colleagues. The NBAS examines the ability of infants to:

- breathe and regulate their temperature
- control their motor movements
- respond to stimuli from their environment
- interact with others (Brazelton Institute, 2013).

Seeing what their infant is capable of over the course of the NBAS assessment often amazes parents and encourages interaction between parents and their children. The results can also be used to identify what can be done to support the development of an infant.

Experiencing the World as a Newborn: Senses

In 1906, a clinical professor of children's diseases at the University of Pennsylvania, J.P. Crozer Griffith, published an article about babies' growth in the magazine *American Motherhood*. He stated that "when the baby is just born, and during the first few days of life, it is very little more intelligent than a vegetable. Its soul and its intellect are there, but they are dormant, waiting to be awakened" (Crozer Griffith, 1906, p. 10). Over the past century, researchers have revised their assessments of babies' competencies dramatically, changing emphasis from what babies cannot do to the things that babies can actually do. And considering that the infant spent the past 9 months in a dark environment with muffled sounds and a constant temperature, many of a newborn's senses are surprisingly well developed.

Newborns need to learn how to see

In the dim environment of the womb, there is not much to see. So when they are born, infants need to learn how to use their eyes—how to focus, how to move their eyes, and how to use the information their eyes send to the brain. Newborns are nearsighted and can see best at a distance of 6 to 10 inches (Mayer & Dobson, 1982), which is just about the distance between the newborn's and their parent's face when the parent is cradling the baby. Seeing parents' faces clearly may help promote bonding between parents and children. Additionally, newborns' eyes are quite sensitive to bright light. They are most likely to open their eyes in less bright environments (Harris & MacFarlane, 1974). Babies also like to view objects that have high contrast, like patterns of black and white, which is why parents often choose images with strong contrasts to decorate the nursery.

■ The retinas of infants are not as highly developed as those of adults. For that reason, infants can best perceive strong contrasts like that between black and white. Providing babies with objects in contrasting colors helps develop their vision.

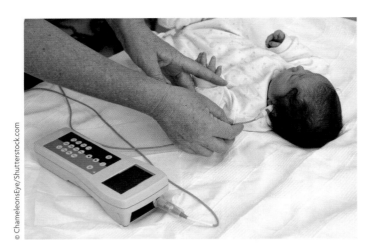

■ Hearing screenings are routinely performed before newborns leave the hospital. Here, sounds are played into the child's ears through headphones. A sensor on the forehead measures the response of the brain to the sounds. If the response pattern is close enough to the expected pattern, the baby passes the test.

Hearing is well developed in newborns

Hearing begins to develop in fetuses by the third trimester of pregnancy. Newborns are startled by loud sounds and may turn their heads toward the sound. Not only can they recognize their mother's voice (and prefer it over other people's voices), but it also has a calming effect on them (DeCasper & Fifer, 1980).

Almost 2 in 1,000 newborns suffer from hearing loss, with many having no risk factors for such loss (Centers for Disease Control and Prevention, 2021a). Many parents believe they are able to detect hearing loss by observing their baby, but this is often not the case if the baby still has some degree of hearing. For that reason, a newborn hearing screening should be performed, either in the hospital or within 3 weeks of leaving the hospital. The tests used are quick and painless and can even be done while the infant is sleeping.

Sense of smell develops very early in pregnancy

By 10 weeks of gestation, a fetus's smell receptors, which are responsible for detecting smells, are already formed. As a result, infants are born with a very good sense of smell (Rotstein et al., 2015). They have a preference for their mother's smell and can recognize her by the smell of her breasts or armpits (Coulthard, 2019; MacFarlane, 1975; Marin et al., 2015). Preferring the smell of their mother makes sense from an evolutionary perspective: The newborn's survival is dependent on the mother, and so an infant's ability to recognize the mother is of crucial value.

Taste buds develop by the start of the second trimester

Taste buds develop early and are functional already by the beginning of the second trimester (Bradley, 1972). An infant at birth has about as many taste buds as an adult (Eckstein, 1927). The taste preferences of newborns are similar to those of fetuses. Premature and full-term infants suck more frequently and in a stronger way when provided with a sugar solution as compared with water (Desor et al., 1973; Forestell, 2017; Tatzer et al., 1985). Newborns show their taste preference not only through sucking, but also through their facial expressions (FIGURE 4.7).

Infants are sensitive to touch and pain

Perhaps not surprisingly, newborn infants are sensitive to touch. They can be calmed down by physical contact. Many of their reflexes, like the rooting reflex, are triggered by touch.

Today, we know that newborns can feel pain just as adults and older children can (Goksan et al., 2018; Maxwell et al., 2019). But until the late 1980s, infant surgery was conducted with little or no anesthesia (Unruh, 1992), and even in 2017 a study in 18 European countries found that fewer than one-third of newborns in neonatal intensive care units were assessed for chronic pain (Anand et al., 2017).

But research has also revealed some rather unconventional means of soothing pain in newborns: Exposing infants to the smell of lavender, breast milk, or amniotic fluid before a heel stick resulted in less pain compared with infants who were exposed to the smell of water (Akcan & Polat, 2016). Additionally, sugar solution is a good way to ease pain for minor procedures and possibly even more efficient than the pain reliever paracetamol (Eker et al., 2017; Hoarau et al., 2021; Ohlsson & Shah, 2016).

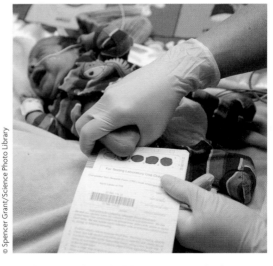

■ The pain infants feel from minor medical procedures like a heel stick can be reduced by giving them sugar solution prior to the procedure.

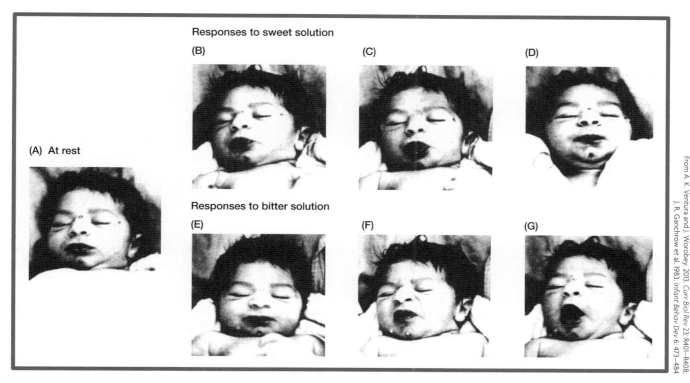

FIGURE 4.7 Characteristic responses of newborns to sweet and bitter tastes: Sweet tastes are met with smiles, lip sucking and smacking, as well as a faster sucking rate. Bitter solutions evoke frowning, nose wrinkling, and head shaking (Desor et al., 1975; Steiner et al., 2001).

From A. K. Ventura and J. Worobey. 2013. *Curr Biol Rev* 23: R401–R408; J. R. Ganchrow et al. 1983. *Infant Behav Dev* 6: 473–484

Learning in Newborns

As we have seen in the preceding sections, most of the sensory capabilities of newborns still need to mature; their level of functioning does not compare to that of older children and adults. And yet, even newborns have some capability to learn. There are at least three ways in which newborns learn: by classical conditioning, by operant conditioning, and by habituation. Contrary to what researchers traditionally believed, more and more research indicates that there is one way in which newborns do *not* learn: by imitating others (Anisfeld, 1996; Leys, 2020; Oostenbroek et al., 2016). Imitation skills are likely learned during the first few months of life, and we will discuss them in more detail in Chapter 6.

Through classical conditioning, newborns learn to connect stimuli with each other

Before we discuss classical conditioning in newborns, let us quickly rehash what we learned in Chapter 2 about classical conditioning. Remember Russian psychologist Ivan Pavlov and his dogs? Whenever he fed his dogs, he rang a bell. Soon, his dogs started salivating just when the bell was rung. Pavlov paired an unconditioned stimulus (the bell) with a conditioned stimulus (the food). The dogs learned to associate the bell with the food and started reacting to the unconditioned stimulus. It turned out that what works in dogs works in humans as well: John B. Watson taught the infant Albert to fear white rats and other white furry objects by producing a loud noise whenever Albert saw the rat.

Newborns are exposed to a continuous onslaught of stimuli from their environment. There are noises all around them, conversations, people touching them, changes in temperature, different things to see, and much more. They take that information in as much as they can. Soon, they learn to associate some of those stimuli with things that happen to them: When the lights are switched on it is time to wake up, and when the faucet sounds to fill up the bathtub, it is time for a bath.

■ From the time they are born, infants take in the sights, sounds, and smells of their environment and try to make sense of them. Baby Mateo has learned that the jingling of the keys outside the door indicates that his father is coming home and will soon be there to greet him.

Many studies have confirmed the ability of newborns to learn by way of classical conditioning. In one study, infants who were presented with a citrus scent just before being stroked soon turned their heads just when they smelled the citrus odor (Sullivan et al., 1991). Likewise, infants who were stroked on the forehead just before receiving a sugar solution soon began to start sucking when they were stroked (Blass et al., 1984). So the infants in these studies quickly learned that one stimulus was followed by another event.

If that doesn't sound impressive enough, would you believe that newborns can even learn in their sleep? In one study, sleeping infants were played a tone that was paired with an air puff on the eyelid. They responded to the air puff with eye movements. Very soon, they had learned to move their eyes just at the sound of the tone, even when no air puff was blown on their eye anymore (Fifer et al., 2010; Tarullo et al., 2016).

Infants react to and learn from stimuli in their environment

habituation a form of learning in which the response to a stimulus decreases when that stimulus is presented repeatedly.

In operant conditioning (which we also discussed in Chapter 2), the kind of response a newborn gets to an action influences the likelihood that the behavior will be repeated. An infant is more likely to repeat behaviors that are met with a positive response and less likely to repeat behaviors that are followed by an unpleasant response. Through operant conditioning, children learn to provoke responses from their environment through the actions they take—for example, if you want some attention from the adults around you, crying is a good way to get it!

Newborns become accustomed to stimuli through habituation

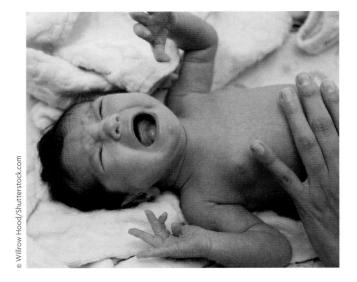

■ Through operant conditioning, newborns quickly learn that their actions have an impact on what others do. When infants start to cry and are then approached by an adult who tries to soothe them, they quickly learn that crying gets them the attention of the adults around them.

Colten is happily lying in his crib after a feeding. Suddenly, he hears the neighbor's new dog barking outside. He startles and turns his head in the direction of the window from which the sound came. The dog barks a few more times that afternoon. In the beginning, Colten still reacts to the sound of the barking and turns his head, but at some point he begins to ignore the barking and doesn't react to it at all anymore. Colten has habituated to the sound of the barking.

Habituation is a basic form of learning in which the response to a stimulus decreases when the stimulus is presented repeatedly. When Colten first heard the dog barking, it was a new stimulus that prompted him to look around and listen. After the dog had been barking for a while, Colten became habituated to the sound and did not react anymore.

■ Kai does not need ear plugs to take a nap when his older sister is playing at home. He has gotten habituated to the sounds of her playing and happily sleeps through her playtime unless some unexpected loud noises wake him up.

© MIA Studio/Shutterstock.com

Habituation can be observed in infants in different ways. When they are presented with something interesting (a new stimulus!), their heart rate, breathing rate, brain activity, and sucking rate change. They may become quiet and look into the direction of the stimulus. Humans can habituate to stimuli no matter which senses the stimuli arouse. Colten got used to a noise when the dog barked, but he also has the ability to get used to visual sights, smells, tastes, or tactile sensations.

Researchers measure the time it takes infants to habituate to a new stimulus to draw inferences about the infants' information-processing capabilities. The faster an infant habituates, the better the infant is at information processing and learning. Physicians and other professionals are quite interested in indicators of early learning because they can help identify infants for participation in early intervention programs. The sooner early intervention programs are started in a child's life, the more effective they are. At this time, no such tests are used routinely to assess infants' learning capability. However, researchers are exploring the possibility of assessing how preterm and low-birthweight infants habituate to new stimuli. Children who habituate at a lower rate are at higher risk for intellectual disability and may be suitable candidates for early intervention (Marino & Gervain, 2019; Weber et al., 2016).

Review!

What are newborn reflexes?

■ *Reflexes* are unlearned, automatic responses to stimuli from the environment.

■ Examining newborns' reflexes at birth and throughout infancy allows professionals to find out whether the nervous system and brain are appropriately developed.

■ Among newborn reflexes are the sucking reflex, the grasp reflex, and the Moro reflex.

How do newborns perceive the world?

■ Newborns' vision is not yet well developed. Newborns can best see objects within 6–10 inches of their eyes in dim lighting. Babies like to look at faces as well as objects with high contrast.

■ Newborns' hearing, taste, and smell are much better developed than their vision. They can recognize their mothers' voice and

smell and show a preference for sweet tastes, which can even act as a pain reliever.

Are newborns able to learn?

■ Newborns learn primarily in three different ways: classical conditioning, operant conditioning, and habituation.

■ In classical conditioning, infants learn to react to stimuli in their environment. Being placed on the diaper table may be enough to provoke crying in an infant who has learned that this exercise means a cold wet wipe will soon be coming her way.

■ In operant conditioning, infants learn to act in ways that increase or decrease the likelihood of an event. For example, they learn that crying is a good way to get mother's attention.

■ In *habituation*, infants get used to a stimulus (e.g., a dog barking outside or a sibling's loud play) so that what was once new is soon not anymore.

Practice!

1. The highest Apgar score is _____ .
   a. 5
   b. 7
   c. 10
   d. 100

2. Reflexes present at birth _____ .
   a. all disappear within 6 months
   b. never disappear

   c. may or may not disappear, depending on which one
   d. vary greatly from one child to another

3. Habituation is associated with a(n) _____ reaction to a stimulus.
   a. increased
   b. decreased
   c. increased or decreased (depending on the stimulus)
   d. startle

4.4 Adjusting to Life with a Newborn

- Explain how parents and infants become attached.
- Define postpartum depression.

The arrival of a new baby is an exciting—and exhausting—time in the life of parents. Parents start establishing a bond with their infant, and the baby bonds with its caregivers. The adjustment to life with a baby does not always go smoothly for the parents, however. In this section, we will first explore how infant and caregivers bond. Then we will consider the problems parents can encounter when they start life with their new family member.

Bonding

bonding the development of a close attachment between an infant and its parents.

Bonding is the development of a close relationship between parents and their children. This relationship is the basis for parent–child attachment and influences the child's development. A lack of attachment can have a negative effect on children's development, resulting in issues like aggressive behavior, tantrums, or a lack of problem-solving skills (Newman, 2017). Bonding ensures that parent and child stay in close contact and thus increases the offspring's survival chances.

Bonding can also be observed in many animal species. Unlike the imprinting process in Konrad Lorenz's goslings (see Chapter 2), human bonding is a process that takes considerable time and certainly does not happen within minutes of giving birth. Early research suggested that the minutes after delivery are crucial for mothers and their infants to bond and that a lack of immediate bonding opportunities (for example, when preterm infants need to stay in the NICU for a period of time) leads to differences in maternal behavior even 2 years later (Klaus & Kennell, 1976; Ringler et al., 1978). However, more recent studies raise doubts about whether such a critical period for bonding after birth truly exists. Bonding may be delayed when mothers are separated from their infants or suffer from postpartum depression, but research suggests that these essential bonds can be formed later (Bigelow & Power, 2012; Miles et al., 2006; Raby & Dozier, 2019).

Parents may not feel a bond with their infant right away; such lack of bonding is normal and is no cause for concern. What can be a big burden on parents, however, are the expectations society places on them to deeply and completely fall in love with their newborn immediately. Here is what Jessica says about her experience giving birth to a preterm infant who she wasn't sure would survive her first weeks:

© Dragon Images/Shutterstock.com

■ Everyday caregiving helps children and their parents bond.

Slowly coming to feel the love I've always had for Sera was inevitable—I don't believe our relationship could have grown any other way. What was preventable, though, was the guilt. There was no reason for me to be so cruel to myself, beating myself up daily for being a terrible mother and awful person who couldn't love the tiny human being who needed me the most. But in a world that tells women that immediate and all-encompassing love for their children is the only "natural" response to birth, I didn't stand a chance.

This expectation is incredibly damaging, not only to mothers like me—whose babies come into the world without congratulations, but hushed tones—but to all women who are made to feel like monsters if they don't love their children at once and with everything they have. (Valenti, 2011)

Engaging in everyday caregiving activities like feeding and diapering the infant will help create a bond. Fathers can improve bonding with their children by creating their own activities and having one-on-one time with their infants. There is no need for fathers to act like replacement mothers; rather, they can build up their own routines with games or songs, give the child a bath, or use a baby carrier to go on outings together.

Sometimes, mothers discourage or prevent fathers from interacting with their infants or take over caregiving activities because they insist on fathers' "getting it right." This phenomenon is called "**gatekeeping**" and can lead to fathers feeling left out and decreasing their involvement with the infant (Altenburger et al., 2018). However, the father's involvement with the newborn and its family is very important and positively impacts his children's social, cognitive, and physical development (Jeong et al., 2016; Kim et al., 2016; Miller et al., 2020).

Parents whose infant is in the neonatal intensive care unit (NICU) can still start the bonding process with their baby even if interactions are limited by medical equipment. They may be able to touch their baby through the opening in an incubator, sing to their baby, or talk to it. They may also be able to spend some skin-on-skin time with their baby and help with the feeding or start to breastfeed.

Adoptive parents and children can form bonds with each other at a later time as well. Adoptive children are usually able to attach to their new parents within a few months even if they come from orphanages that did not meet their social needs (Carlson et al., 2014; Raby & Dozier, 2019). This is good news for all the parents and children for whom the start into life did not work out quite as picture-perfect as one would ideally hope.

gatekeeping the tendency for parents (most often mothers) to engage in activities that control others' access to or interaction with the child.

Baby Blues and Depression in Parents

For days following the birth of her baby girl, Sylvia felt very depressed. She was sleep-deprived and worried she was not taking good enough care of the baby. She also felt guilt-ridden over the way the birth had taken place, despite her best intentions. With the encouragement of her husband and doula, however, she soon felt more secure in taking care of her baby, and caretaking began to seem more routine and not as scary as in the beginning. She still sometimes feels a loss over the birth experience she did not have, but she has learned to move on.

Having a baby is a life-changing event that turns parents' lives upside down. About 80% of new mothers experience what is commonly called the "baby blues"

© Elnur/Shutterstock.com

■ In her effort to provide the very best care for their fragile newborn, Maggie expects her husband Dave to change the baby's diapers and feed her in a very particular way, instead of letting Dave handle the infant in his own way. Maggie's maternal gatekeeping discourages Dave from wanting to participate in daily caregiving activities, feeling whatever he does is not good enough.

© R. Born/Getty Images

postpartum depression
depression that affects women after they have given birth; it is characterized by feelings of sadness, exhaustion, anxiety, and guilt.

■ Over the past years, a number of celebrities like Brooke Shields have spoken publicly about the postpartum depression they experienced. Their testimony has helped reduce the stigma and educate the public about postpartum depression.

(National Institute of Mental Health, 2017). A new mother suddenly finds herself exhausted, sleep-deprived, and anxious about the development of her baby. Fortunately, for most people, these feelings last for a week or two and then disappear. However, about 1 in 7 women develops a more serious disorder called **postpartum depression** (PPD) (Mughal et al., 2021), which is a kind of depression that affects women after they have given birth. Postpartum depression is most likely caused by a combination of physical and emotional factors. After birth, women experience a hormonal drop in estrogen and progesterone levels that potentially can cause depression. In addition to hormonal changes, new mothers do not get enough sleep and understandably may have feelings of doubt or anxiety. Women who have experienced depressive episodes earlier in life or who have experienced stressful life events during or after their pregnancy are at higher risk of developing PPD (National Institute of Mental Health, 2017).

Postpartum depression may begin anywhere from a week to 1 month after delivery and can last weeks or months. Symptoms include:

- unusually strong feelings of inadequacy, guilt, anger, anxiety, sadness, and exhaustion
- sleep problems
- overeating or not eating enough
- withdrawal from family and friends, and/or
- thoughts about harming oneself or the baby (and, in the worst case, acting on those thoughts) (Mughal et al., 2021).

Unlike the baby blues, postpartum depression usually needs to be treated. Treatment may consist of counseling or psychotherapy. Alternatively, or additionally, antidepressive medication may be prescribed. Untreated depression can last for many months and impair a mother's ability to take care of herself and her baby. Depressed mothers interact less with their infants than do mothers who do not feel depressed.

PPD is a disorder that occurs throughout the world, though rates can be as low as 4% in Malaysia or as high as 63% in Pakistan (Abdollahi et al., 2011; Wang et al., 2021; see also FIGURE 4.8). Researchers suspect that in countries with particularly high PPD rates, social factors play a major role: Women may experience distress when they have to participate in rituals they want no part of. Or tensions may arise when they are caught in rigid and inflexible relationships with caregivers and other family members (PostpartumDepression.org, 2022).

It is worth noting that adoptive mothers can experience PPD as well and do so with about the same frequency as biological mothers (Mott et al., 2011). Additionally, between 4% and 25% of new fathers are estimated to experience PPD within the first 6 months of birth (Anding et al., 2016; Biebel & Alikhan, 2016). What complicates men's situation is that, unlike women, they are not screened for depression after the birth of their child, and assessments for postnatal depression may miss their symptoms because men often experience different symptoms from those of women. They feel irritated and restless and may have trouble controlling themselves. A study of fathers in Sweden showed that one-third of depressed fathers had thought about hurting themselves, and more than three-fourths had not even talked to anyone about their depression (Psouni et al., 2017). For that reason, screening for depression should be implemented routinely not only for women but also for men.

Data from Z. Wang et al. 2021. *Transl Psychiatry* 11(543). https://doi.org/10.1038/s41398-021-01663-6; map created with Datawrapper

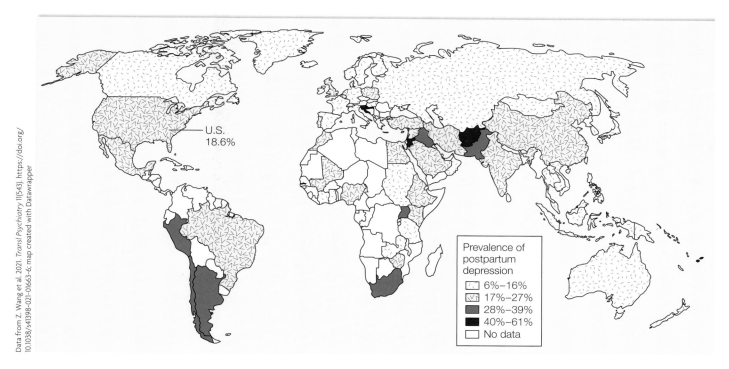

Prevalence of postpartum depression
- 6%–16%
- 17%–27%
- 28%–39%
- 40%–61%
- No data

FIGURE 4.8 The prevalence of postpartum depression worldwide varies widely from country to country, from 6% in Denmark to 61% in Afghanistan. Which factors could be responsible for these significant differences?

Review!

How do parents and infants get attached to each other?

- From the moment they are born, infants are ready to bond with and attach to others. *Bonding* happens through the interactions of parents and children and helps them to stay in close contact, which improves children's survival chances.

- Bonding can sometimes get delayed, such as when a child needs to stay in the neonatal intensive care unit after birth or when children are adopted. However, bonds between children and caregivers can be formed later as well, and in many cases delays do not seem to have any lasting consequences.

What is postpartum depression?

- Postpartum depression is a form of depression that can occur in both men and women after the birth of a child. Affected parents feel hopeless, anxious, worried, sad, and desperate and often have sleep problems.

- Compared with the "baby blues," these feelings are more intense and last for weeks or months rather than a few days. Correct diagnosis and treatment is important to improve the well-being of the parent as well as the child—depressed parents have a hard time giving adequate care to the newborn and tend to interact less with their children, which can ultimately lead to developmental delays.

Practice!

1. Delayed bonding _____ results in disturbed development.
   a. always
   b. almost always
   c. sometimes
   d. never

2. Rates of postpartum depression _____ across countries.
   a. are consistent
   b. vary slightly

   c. vary greatly
   d. have never been studied

3. Use of an incubator is most common for _____ babies.
   a. very small
   b. very large
   c. misbehaving
   d. apathetic

Act It Out!

After Elena's birth, Sylvia felt very depressed for a number of days. Her husband, Danny, started worrying about her and her ability to take care of their newborn, but when he tried to talk to her, Sylvia would just say she was fine. Still worried and knowing that Sheryl had been a big support to Sylvia throughout the pregnancy, Danny contacted Sheryl to ask her to speak with Sylvia about her depression.

Role-play a conversation between Sylvia and her friend Sheryl. How might Sylvia feel? And what advice might Sheryl give her? Is there a clear line between a clinical postpartum depression that is in need of professional treatment and a case of baby blues that goes away on its own again?

A play date 4 months later

Sylvia has invited her co-workers Damian and Sheryl over for a visit with their children. Mathilda and Lewis are happily playing alongside each other while Elena is peacefully sleeping. This gives the young parents a rare opportunity to chat in the presence of their children. Despite the complications Sylvia experienced during the birth and her subsequent feelings of depression, she has now settled nicely into the role of a mother. She is not yet back at work, and caring for Elena has become a happy, fulfilling (though tiring) routine.

Damian is busy explaining to his two friends why he and Davis made the decision not to stay in touch with Mathilda's surrogate mother. He is hoping they understand—his sister had recently criticized his decision, and he still feels troubled over the conversation they had.

Sheryl listens quietly to her co-workers discuss the recent changes in their lives. She is happy for them both, but she is still upset about her miscarriage and hasn't spoken to anyone about it. She wonders if today will be the day she finally musters the courage to talk about what happened to her. However, she doesn't want to overshadow the otherwise happy occasion and is secretly worried that the others might belittle her feelings.

There are many paths to parenthood, and the journey is rarely straightforward. As often happens with children, carefully made plans are upended by unexpected events. It is what makes parenthood an adventure, one the three friends are all happy to be on. ■ ■ ■ ■

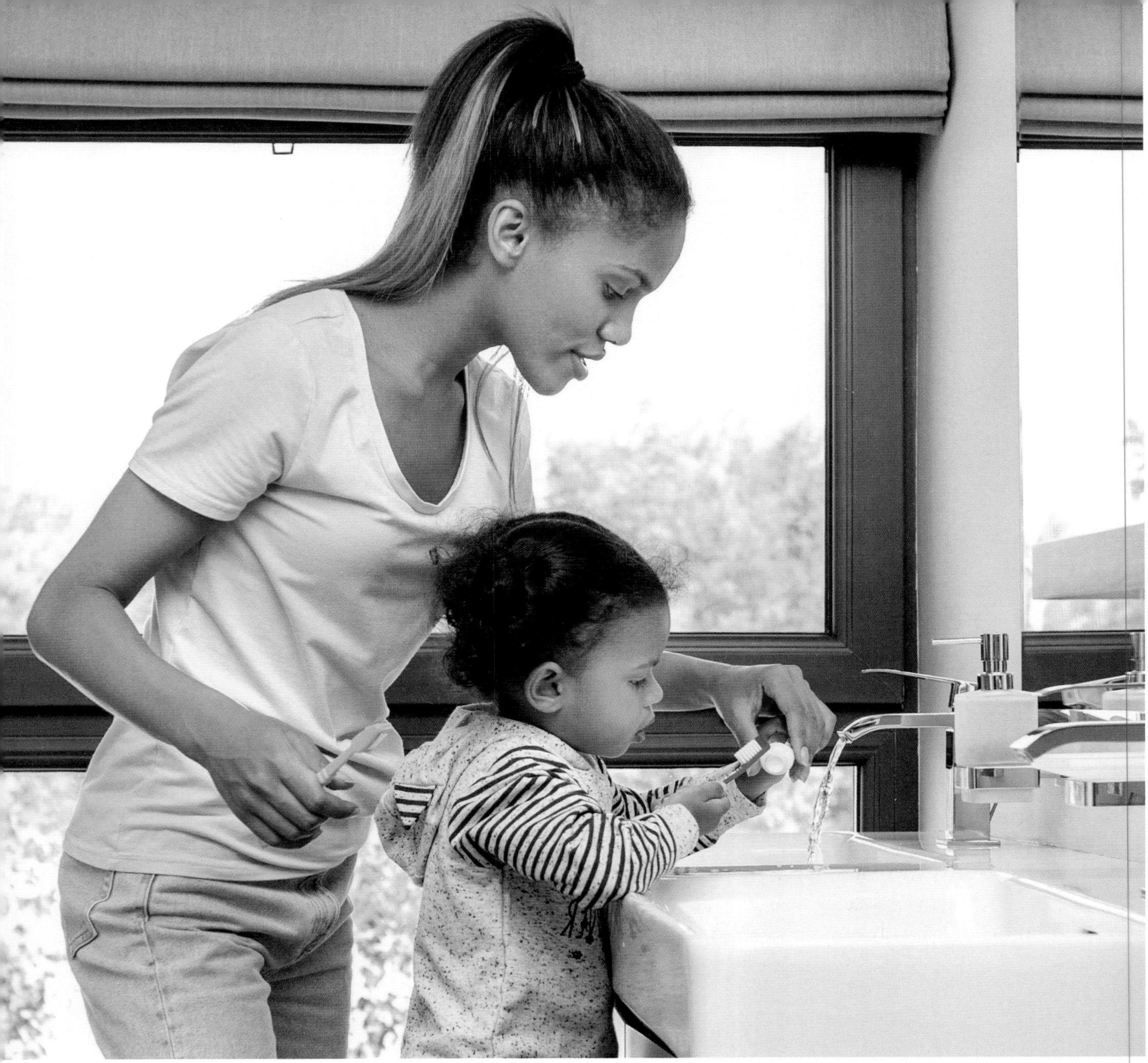

© iStock.com/Viktoriia Hnatiuk

Overview

Physical Development in Infancy and Toddlerhood

Children at play

Jeff and his 18-month-old son, Ricardo, are at the local toy store attending a parent–child play group. Ricardo is Jeff's first child, and his development has held some major surprises for Jeff. Ricardo was an easygoing baby, but ever since he learned to walk, he is always on the move and getting into mischief. At the toy store, Ricardo tries to run away whenever possible, and Jeff can hardly keep him from climbing the shelves. It seems to Jeff that Ricardo is always just a split-second away from disaster, and he can't help but wonder if he is raising a troublemaker. Watching Ricardo's every move is 20-month-old Rona, who is sitting with her mother, Lisa. They both look tired, but they usually do. Two-year-old Lana is too busy fishing crackers out of a plastic cup to watch the other children. She is with her nanny, Maria, and both are taking a break from play to refuel with a little snack. Sitting off in a corner, far removed from the fray, are 10-month old Ludy and his Grandpa Leo, who take turns improvising on a colorful electronic keyboard and seem equally delighted with the toy.

Infants and toddlers develop at an astonishing rate. Within months they transform from virtually helpless beings into children who are agile, aware of their surroundings, and able to get themselves into trouble in no time. Not only do their little bodies grow rapidly, but so do their motor skills: They learn to sit and stand up and, not much later, to walk. They learn to use their hands and grasp items. Soon thereafter, they will try to open cupboard doors, containers, or anything that challenges their curiosity.

In this chapter, we will learn more about infants' and toddlers' physical growth and brain development. We will discover how infants learn to move and use their bodies to accomplish their goals and how they perceive the world. Then we will discuss the nutritional needs of infants and toddlers. Finally, we will consider health in infants and toddlers and how best to keep children at this age safe and healthy.

■ Toy stores and book stores are places where you will observe children acting on their natural curiosity. If you find yourself in one of these places, take a casual survey of the children there. Notice how they interact with the environment, and see if you can estimate ages based on the body control, fine motor skills, and speech they display.

5.1 Brain and Body Growth in Infancy and Toddlerhood

- List the ways children's bodies grow in infancy and toddlerhood.
- Explain the stages of brain growth during infancy and toddlerhood.
- Identify factors that influence both infant and toddler brain development positively and negatively.

Children's bodies and their physical abilities do not develop randomly. Young children follow the same growth patterns we see in embryos (see Figure 3.13). The body develops from head to toes, so that children learn to hold their heads up before they begin to use their arms and legs. Motor skills develop from the trunk out, starting with arms and legs and then moving to hands and feet, fingers and toes.

Height and Weight Changes

Infants grow rapidly during their first year of life, as any young parent who finds their baby outgrowing their clothes about every 3 months can confirm! The average infant weighs around 7 pounds at birth and triples her weight within the first year of life (Vilar et al., 2014) (TABLE 5.1). Height-gain patterns resemble those of weight gain (Centers for Disease Control and Prevention, 2010a, 2010b). A typical 2-year-old may be about half the height of an average adult and about one-fifth the weight. The differences between boys and girls are relatively small in children of this age, but boys tend to be somewhat heavier and taller than girls.

But children do not only grow heavier and taller: Their overall proportions change dramatically as well, as the body grows at a faster rate than the head. A newborn's head is about one-fourth the size of the body, measured in terms of height; as an adult, the head accounts for only one-eighth of total body height (FIGURE 5.1).

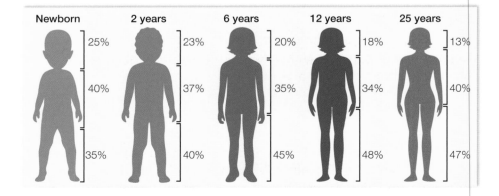

FIGURE 5.1 Body proportions from birth to 25 years. At birth, the head makes up about one-fourth of the body length of a newborn. In adulthood, the head accounts for only one-eighth of body length.

■ Table 5.1 Average Height and Weight of a Child at Birth, Age 1, and Age 2 (in the United States)

	Age	Average weight	Average height
© Christophe Testi/Shutterstock.com	Birth	7 pounds	19 inches
© Susan Northcutt/Alamy Stock Photo	Age 1	20 pounds	29 inches
© Phanie/Alamy Stock Photo	Age 2	26 pounds	34 inches

Pediatricians track height and weight gains in every well-child visit. They use growth charts to compare a child's height and weight with those of other children of the same age and sex (**FIGURE 5.2**). If a child's weight is in the 90th percentile for their age group, it means the child weighs more than 90% of children and less than 10% of children. Growth charts enable professionals to monitor the overall pattern of growth over time and detect developmental problems. For instance, a child who fails to gain length or weight over successive well-child visits may be experiencing a condition called **failure to thrive**, in which weight and height do not increase enough compared with the expectations for a certain age. Failure to thrive typically is caused by poor nutritional intake, which in turn can be caused by many different problems, such as repeated vomiting, inadequate food offerings, or health conditions that cause a child to need more calories than expected (Stanford Children's Health, 2021a).

failure to thrive a condition in which children's weight and height gain is slowed abnormally.

Brain Growth

Let's have a look at how the brain develops in children. Understanding brain growth and the factors that affect this process can help us identify children who are at risk for developmental delays and create interventions to help them.

FIGURE 5.2 A pediatric growth chart. Pediatricians use growth charts to track children's growth and weight gain. Growth charts are helpful because they compare a child's development with that of peers, using percentiles.

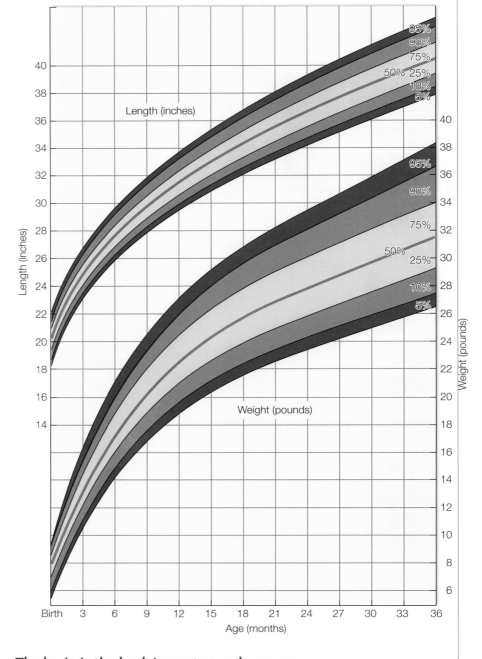

cerebrum the largest part of the brain, divided into two hemispheres and responsible for complex cognitive processes.

cerebral cortex the furrowed outer surface of the cerebrum, composed mostly of gray matter, and involved in complex brain functions like thinking and reasoning.

corpus callosum a thick bundle of neuronal fibers connecting the right and the left hemispheres.

cerebellum part of the brain involved in the coordination of movements, balance, and posture.

The brain is the body's most complex organ

The brain is the most complex organ of the human body. Without it, we cannot see the faces of those around us, listen to our favorite music, enjoy the sight of a beautiful sunset, or fall in love. In the following chapters, we will discover what it is that makes the human brain so special and allows for humans' complex thinking capabilities. Our focus in this chapter is on how the brain grows.

Before we delve into the development of the brain, let's review some basics. Entire volumes are devoted to describing human brain anatomy and function; the purpose here is to provide you with just enough information to understand more detailed discussions of brain development in this chapter and throughout the book.

PARTS OF THE BRAIN The **cerebrum** is the largest part of the human brain and, in our evolutionary history, the last part of the brain to develop. The outer surface of the cerebrum is called the **cerebral cortex**. Responsible for complex cognitive processes like thinking and reasoning, it is divided into left and right halves, or *hemispheres*, each of which can be subdivided into four lobes: frontal, parietal, occipital, and temporal.

The hemispheres connect and communicate through a bundle of nerve fibers called the **corpus callosum**. The **cerebellum** (or "little brain"), located at the bottom back of the brain, is involved in the coordination of movements, balance, and posture. The **limbic system** contains several structures that are involved in regulating emotions, forming memories, and learning; these include the **hippocampus**. Below the limbic system is the **brain stem**, also made up of several structures, which regulates basic but vital body functions like breathing, heart rate, and blood pressure (**FIGURE 5.3**).

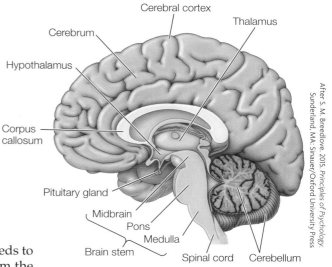

After S. M. Breedlove, 2015, *Principles of Psychology*, Sunderland, MA: Sinauer/Oxford University Press

FIGURE 5.3 Anatomy of the brain.

COMMUNICATION WITHIN THE CENTRAL NERVOUS SYSTEM

In order for the human body to work effectively, information needs to be carried from different parts of the body to the brain and from the brain to the rest of the body. This messenger task falls to the central nervous system. It carries information throughout the entire body and coordinates body activities.

The central nervous system comprises two main structures—the brain and the spinal cord—and is made up largely of specialized nerve cells called **neurons**. Neurons are nerve cells that can receive and send nerve impulses in the form of electrical signals. There are about 100 billion neurons in the human brain. Communication between neurons is the basis of our thinking, learning, and memory.

A neuron consists of three basic parts: a cell body, dendrites, and an axon (**FIGURE 5.4**). **Dendrites** are branchlike structures that receive information from other neurons and transmit the information to the cell body. Axons send information from the cell body out to other neurons through the dendrites of those other neurons. This process occurs even though the ends of the axon, also called the synaptic terminals, do not directly touch the dendrites of the other neurons. There is a gap, called a **synapse**, that the electrical signal coming from the neuron needs to cross. In order for this to happen, the electrical signal must be converted into chemical signals, called **neurotransmitters**. These chemical signals cross the gap and transmit the neural signal to the receiving dendrites of the other neuron.

limbic system set of structures that are involved in emotion regulation as well as forming memories.

hippocampus each of two structures of the limbic system (there is one in each hemisphere) that are central to emotion regulation, memory formation, and learning.

brain stem set of structures that regulate basic but vital body functions like breathing, heart rate, and blood pressure.

neuron a cell of the nervous system that can receive and send nerve impulses in the form of electrical signals.

dendrites branchlike structures that receive information from other neurons and transmit it to the cell body.

synapse gap through which neurotransmitters transmit a signal from the axon terminal of one neuron to the dendrite of another neuron.

neurotransmitters chemical substances that transmit neural impulses from one neuron to another.

Pre-synaptic (sending) cell

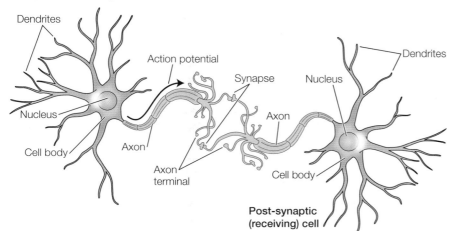

Post-synaptic (receiving) cell

FIGURE 5.4 A neuron consists of a cell body, an axon, and dendrites. Information received by the dendrites is sent out to other cells through the axon. At the end of the axon, electrical impulses are translated into chemical impulses in the form of neurotransmitters, which cross the gap (synapse) to the dendrites of another neuron, where they are again converted into electric signals.

myelin a fatty substance that covers axons and allows for faster signal transmission.

A neuron's dendrites may receive thousands of impulses. The sum of all these impulses determines whether the neuron will create an electric charge and pass on the signal to other neurons. The networks of neurons throughout the brain and nervous system allow different body parts to communicate with each other.

Many axons are covered with a fatty white substance called **myelin**. These myelinated (myelin-coated) axons transmit electrical impulses much faster, helping to make information processing more efficient. The human spinal cord is about half an inch in diameter. If it were not myelinated, it would need to have a diameter of about 3 feet to transmit information as effectively as it does with myelination (Kagan & Herschkowitz, 2006).

The brain continues to grow well into adulthood

The human brain grows and matures over an extended period of time that is not shared by any other living species. Brain development begins about 2 weeks after conception, but the brain's structure and function are not fully developed until the third decade of life (Bick & Nelson, 2016). In fact, there is some evidence that brain development continues throughout our life span (Beck et al., 2021; Götz et al., 2016; Wallis, 2013).

During the first years of life, a child's brain grows particularly fast. It doubles in size within the first 12 months, and by around age 3 the brain has reached roughly three-fourths of its adult volume (Gilmore et al., 2007). Brain development happens faster in more basic systems, such as the brain stem and the areas that process sensory stimuli. Areas such as the prefrontal cortex that are involved with more complex processes are the last ones to mature (Bick & Nelson, 2016; Uytun, 2018). Most of the increase in brain size and weight can be attributed to two factors: (1) an increase in myelination and (2) the formation of new neural connections.

INCREASE IN MYELINATION Although myelination starts during the second trimester of pregnancy, it is not even close to complete at birth. It occurs rapidly in very young children and continues into adulthood. Different parts of the brain become myelinated at different rates. When an infant is born, the brain pathways that process touch are already well myelinated. Pathways in the auditory cortex, the part of the brain related to hearing, start developing in the second trimester of pregnancy and continue to myelinate until about age 4. Vision pathways start to myelinate after birth and develop rapidly during the first months; for that reason, children's vision improves significantly during this period. Myelination of areas involved in sensory processing is generally complete by age 4 or 5 (Bick & Nelson, 2016; de Faria et al., 2021).

Myelination also aids in the performance of more complex cognitive processes: Children become gradually more aware of their own and others' emotions. They start to speak and become more physically active and capable. In fact, myelination is not only important for young children. Even the adult brain needs to myelinate new pathways that form when an adult is learning a new practical skill, like playing the trumpet or doing yoga (de Faria, 2021; McKenzie et al., 2014).

FORMATION OF NEW NEURAL CONNECTIONS The second factor involved in rapid brain growth during the first years of life is an increase in the number of dendrites and the formation of new synaptic connections with neighboring cells. Remember that synapses help information flow from one neuron to another. In the first years of life, more than one million new neural connections form every second in a child's brain (Center on the Developing Child, 2021).

Although new synaptic connections form rapidly during the first 2 years of life, over time, only some of these connections will survive. As connections

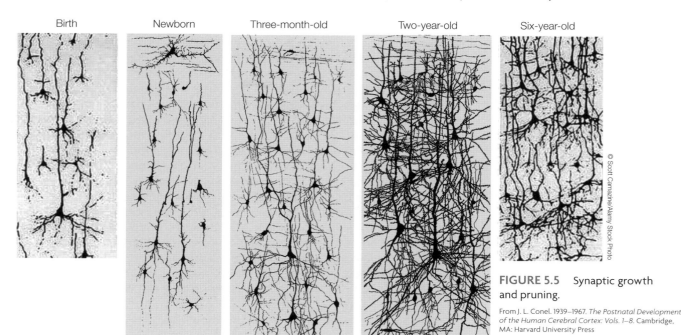

Birth   Newborn   Three-month-old   Two-year-old   Six-year-old

© Scott Camazine/Alamy Stock Photo

FIGURE 5.5 Synaptic growth and pruning.

From J. L. Conel. 1939–1967. *The Postnatal Development of the Human Cerebral Cortex: Vols. 1–8.* Cambridge, MA: Harvard University Press

that are frequently stimulated grow stronger, those that are not used grow weaker and eventually disappear in a process called **synaptic pruning**. As certain connections disappear with pruning, the neurons themselves remain in a neutral state, where they can connect with other neurons again in order to take over other functions.

To provide space for the new synaptic connections, some neurons in the surrounding areas die off. The number of neurons left depends on the brain area. Up to 80% of surrounding neurons can die (Stiles, 2008). Most neurons are not replaced when they die, although adults can produce new neurons in a process called neurogenesis (Babcock et al., 2021; Götz et al., 2016). Up until old age, the human hippocampus produces around 700 new neurons per day (Spalding et al., 2013). **FIGURE 5.5** shows how neural connections grow and get pruned from infancy to age 6.

synaptic pruning process during which the brain eliminates extra synapses in childhood.

Influences on Brain Development in Infants and Toddlers
Genes and experiences interact to promote brain growth

During prenatal development, genes have a strong effect on how the brain develops, although factors such as a mother's stress, nutrition, and drug use can also play a role. Genes determine the growth of neurons as well as their location and how they interact with each other (National Institute of Neurological Disorders and Stroke, 2021; Skaliora, 2002).

After birth, genes continue to play an important role in brain growth, but now the environment also exerts an effect, especially in the early years, when a child's skills and dispositions are shaped. The brain responds to experiences and stimulation from the environment and reorganizes itself accordingly. At the same time, genes influence how the brain reacts to environmental influences. Thus, brain development in the infant involves a complicated interplay between genetics and experiences.

Children need adequate sensory stimulation to develop their full potential. They interact with others through babbling, touching, or facial expressions. When other people respond to these actions, they stimulate the child's brain activity. This is why singing, reading, and talking to young children is so important: Not only do these activities give children a sense of connectedness with the caregiver, they also activate different areas of the brain and spark synaptic connections. The more certain pathways are used, the stronger they become. As noted earlier, weak pathways will ultimately be pruned and disappear.

Keep in mind that early childhood experiences help determine both which information the child's brain processes and how the brain processes that information (Urban Child Institute, 2017). No fancy apps, videos, or high-tech toys are needed to provide children with the kind of stimulating environment that supports their development. Knowing about brain development helps caregivers match activities to children's developmental stage (TABLE 5.2).

While parents and caregivers can influence the kind of stimulation a young child receives, other factors that influence the developing brain are more difficult to control. Research has shown that the more education a child's parents have attained, the smaller the child's amygdala (the brain area that processes stress) will be. Children who are abused, neglected, or deprived of social interaction tend to have larger amygdalae than those of peers growing up in happier circumstances (Bick & Nelson, 2016; Herzog et al., 2020). As parents' income increases, so, too, on average, does the volume of their children's hippocampus, which plays an important role in learning (Noble et al., 2012). These results show that both lack of stimulation and stressful experiences can significantly shape the development of a child.

The brain is both fragile and resilient

It takes only an instant to disrupt the development of an infant's brain, with devastating consequences. Young children are known to try their caregivers' nerves with demanding and sometimes inconsolable crying and fussing. A desperate (and perhaps overtired) adult may react to the crying by shaking the child; this kind of abuse is called **shaken baby syndrome** (or *abusive head trauma*). It occurs when caregivers shake a baby so violently that the infant's brain moves back and forth within the skull so that blood vessels and nerves break. Afterward, the injured brain may swell, increasing pressure within the skull and aggravating injuries to the head. Damage to the retina may occur if the eyeballs move back and forth in their sockets (Barr, 2012). About one-fourth of babies who are violently shaken die and around 80% suffer lifelong disabilities, such as learning disabilities, vision or hearing impairments, seizures, cerebral palsy, or behavior problems. About 1,300 cases of shaken baby syndrome are reported in the United States each year (De Paula et al., 2020; National Center on Shaken Baby Syndrome, 2017).

The good news is that many cases of shaken baby syndrome are potentially preventable. In a study in upstate New York, for example, videos and print materials on the dangers of shaking babies reduced the incidence of shaken baby syndrome by almost half (Dias et al., 2005; Hunchak, 2020).

At the same time, the brain has a remarkable ability to change and reorganize itself, in response to both everyday stimulation and major isolated events. This ability is called **plasticity**. A striking example of brain plasticity is evident in children who have undergone a hemispherectomy to have one-half of their brains surgically removed. Hemispherectomies are used to treat epileptic seizures that originate in one side of the brain and are difficult to control. Following such a procedure, children need to undergo intensive physical, occupational, and speech therapy. They may need to relearn how to walk, speak, and perform many actions they were able to perform

shaken baby syndrome syndrome that is the result of shaking an infant with force. Can result in a variety of injuries and disabilities.

plasticity the ability of the brain to change and reorganize itself.

■ At the age of 2 months, Emma was shaken violently by a relative, which ultimately led to the loss of one-half of her brain function. Today, she has a sunny personality and her own interests, but she also requires around-the-clock care and will never be able to live independently.

© Goldsithney/Shutterstock.com

■ Table 5.2 Supporting Brain Development in Infants and Toddlers

Brain area	Brain area functions	Activities to stimulate development
Birth to 1 year of age		
Cerebellum	Coordinates motor activities: rolling over, sitting up, crawling, etc.; triples in size during this period	Use moving toys or place interesting toys close to infant to encourage head lifting, rolling over, and crawling. Make pillow obstacle course. Dance with infant.
Visual pathways	Vision becomes clearer, sharper	Ensure there are interesting things for the infant to look at: faces, photos, pictures, or slowly moving objects like mobiles. Make eye contact, smile, and make different facial expressions.
Language areas	Perceive speech sounds	Talk, sing, read books, or tell stories to the child. Point out names of objects and explain what is happening in surroundings. Engage in "conversation" and react to infant's cooing and babbling.
Frontal cortex	Reasoning, learning	Provide objects to touch, taste, smell, and play with. Provide little cups that can be filled with water or other materials and dumped.
1–2 years of age		
Motor pathways (cerebral cortex, basal ganglia, cerebellum)	Movement	Provide push and pull toys to practice walking. Provide riding toys. Keep space safe for movements. Ask child to bring objects. Provide enough opportunity to move around. Provide opportunity for fine motor development: puzzles, pencils and crayons, play dough, etc. Allow children to feed themselves.
Language areas	Language; brain can process words more quickly; language areas develop more synapses and become more connected → language explosion	Get down to child's eye level to talk. Point out object names and explain activities. Sing and do nursery rhymes with repetition. Elaborate on what child says. Listen to child.
Prefrontal cortex	Reasoning, learning	Encourage exploration and provide a safe retreat the child can return to during and after exploring the environment. Provide pretend play toys, puzzles, blocks, etc. Allow mistakes.
2–3 years of age		
Motor pathways	Movement; motor pathways myelinate	Provide opportunities to practice fine motor skills with puzzles, zippers, blocks, crayons, play dough, etc. Provide playtime outside for development of gross motor skills.
Language areas	Language	Speak with child during everyday activities.
Prefrontal cortex	Reasoning, learning; synaptic density peaks (about 200% of adult level)	Remember that toddlers learn best by playing. Provide toys and plenty of playing opportunities. Talk, sing, play, and give children chance to become more independent. Be patient: let toddlers figure things out on their own.

Source: Urban Child Institute. 2017. Baby's brain begins now: Conception to Age 3. www.urbanchildinstitute.org; Zero to Three. 2016. Baby brain map. www.zerotothree.org

before the surgery. However, the prospects for recovery are generally excellent, as the remaining side of the brain learns to take over the functions once performed by the part of the brain that has been removed (Shurtleff et al., 2021; van Schooneveld et al., 2016). Even adults tolerate the procedure surprisingly well: only about 10% have speech problems afterward, though 20% of adult patients experienced a muscular weakening on one side of the body (Gross, 2020; Schusse et al., 2017; van Schooneveld et al., 2016).

Review!

How do children's bodies grow in infancy and toddlerhood?

- Height and weight increases are particularly rapid during the first year of life. Children almost triple their birthweight by the time of their first birthday. Their length increases about 50% over their first year of life. After the first year, length and weight increases slow down somewhat.

- Children's body proportions change as well. Over the course of childhood, the head will grow proportionally smaller compared to the rest of the body.

How does the brain grow during infancy and toddlerhood?

- The part of the brain that distinguishes humans from other animals is the *cerebral cortex*, which allows for complex processes like thinking and reasoning. The prefrontal cortex is involved with planning complex cognitive behavior, personality characteristics, and decision-making. It does not fully mature until around age 25, which explains why young children do not excel in rational thinking.

- Much of the brain's growth can be attributed to increases in my-elination and the formation of new neural connections. *Myelin* is a fatty substance that surrounds the axons of most *neurons* and allows for rapid signal transmission within the nervous system and brain. Different parts of the brain myelinate at different rates. In infancy and toddlerhood, sensory pathways (like those responsible for our vision and hearing) myelinate quickly. Within the first years of life (but particularly over the first 2 years), children's brains generate a vast number of connections between neurons. Eventually, however, *synaptic pruning* sets in, and only those connections will survive which are used frequently.

Which factors influence brain development in infants and toddlers?

- During prenatal development, genes have a particularly strong effect on brain development. After birth, experiences become a very important factor in shaping brain growth because the brain reacts to stimulation from the environment, though genes continue to influence exactly how the brain reacts to the stimulation.

- For optimal brain development, children need stimulation in many different forms that caregivers can provide through dis-plays of affection, singing, talking, and playing as well as providing a balanced nutrition. Negative experiences like social deprivation (that is, not enough interaction with others) or abuse affect the developing brain as well. Children's brains show extraordinary *plasticity*, which means that the brain can change and reorganize itself to a certain extent.

Practice!

1. Synaptic pruning results in _____ of synapses in the brain of a growing young child.
   a. an increase in the number
   b. a decrease in the number
   c. an increase in the size
   d. a decrease in the size

2. The brain's ability to change and reorganize itself is called

   _____ .

   a. transformation
   b. generalizability
   c. plasticity
   d. changeability

3. Hemispherectomies are used to treat _____ .
   a. epileptic seizures
   b. brain cancer
   c. tears in the corpus callosum
   d. symptoms of cerebral palsy

Act It Out!

You've been babysitting 1-year-old Liam on a regular basis for about 7 months now. During the time you have spent with him and his family you have noticed that his parents do not interact much with him. They comfort him when he cries, they feed him well and attend to all his physical needs, but you have never seen them play with him, read a book to him, or engage in a back-and-forth conversation. You tried to bring this up once, but his mother replied that it doesn't make sense to interact much with him while he is so young because he does not react to what they do, doesn't speak or understand language, and doesn't quite get what is going on around him yet. Do you agree with her? With a classmate, role-play a conversation with Liam's mother or father. What could you tell Liam's parents about brain development in young children that might help them change their mind?

Show What You've Learned!

Lisa is concerned about the weight of her daughter Rona, who is almost 2 years old. Rona is very slender—like her mother—and her weight is consistently at about the 10th percentile of the weight chart whenever they see the pediatrician. As a nurse, what can you tell Lisa about Rona's weight? Does Lisa have a rea-son to be concerned, and what can she do?

5.2 Sleep in Infants and Toddlers

■ Outline how children's sleep patterns change over the first three years.

Few things have greater impact on the life and well-being of new parents than their babies' sleep habits. Rona and her mother, Lisa, whom we met briefly at the start of the chapter, are going through a difficult time because Rona has trouble falling asleep at night when her mother is not holding her. Ricardo, who is just 8 weeks younger than Rona, has no trouble falling asleep at night, according to his father, Jeff. Lisa, concerned for her daughter's well-being and overtired herself, wonders if two children can really be so different when it comes to their sleeping and whether there is something she can do to help Rona sleep without so much soothing.

The sleep behavior of infants changes frequently as they age, but there is no pattern that applies universally to all children. It is not unusual for two children of the same age, like Ricardo and Rona, to have very different sleeping experiences. But as we will see in the following section, there are things that parents can do to increase the chances for a good night's sleep.

■ Parents of twins often find they spend most of their daytime and nighttime feeding their infants. Putting the infants on a schedule—that is, feeding them at the same time and putting them to sleep at the same time—gives overtired parents a chance to get some rest.

Sleep Requirements for Infants

Newborn babies sleep a lot—around 16 hours a day. Short periods of wakefulness are interspersed with naps spread throughout day and night because newborns have to eat every 2–3 hours, around the clock. In addition to the frequent feedings, newborns do not have a sense of day and night. It usually takes between 2 weeks and 2 months for a newborn to develop an appropriate day–night rhythm.

Even at young ages, however, infants vary tremendously in their sleep habits. Some already sleep for 6 hours at night at 3 months of age; others may take a year to get to that point (Paruthi et al., 2016). By the time they are 6 months old, many children do not need to be fed during the night anymore, and by 9 months most infants sleep through the night. Toddlers need between 11 and 14 hours of sleep.

The frequency and length of naps decreases as well as children get older. In their first year of life, many infants take around three naps a day, each

■ Depriving babies of sleep during the day will not help them sleep better at night. I learned this lesson after a week of trying to put our newborn children down for their night's sleep around 7:30 p.m. During that time, they managed to ruin every single dinner my husband and I had (or tried to have)! Over a period of a few days, I moved the bedtime up to 5:30 p.m., which did wonders for their sleep and our dinners.

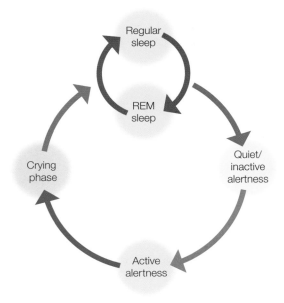

FIGURE 5.6 The sleep–wake cycle in infants. Sleeping infants alternate between regular and REM sleep phases. Once awake, infants go through a sequence of alertness phases including quiet alertness, active alertness, and crying.

REM sleep phase of sleep that is associated with rapid eye movements, body movements, and dreaming (in adults).

■ Newborns show they are tired by rubbing their eyes, fussing, or yawning.

lasting between one-half an hour and 2 hours. At 18 months, most young children will take only one nap a day, lasting between 1 and 3 hours.

During their sleep, infants alternate between regular and REM (rapid eye movement) sleep phases. Adults dream during **REM sleep** phases, but it is generally believed that newborns and toddlers do not dream (Givrad, 2016), even though their eyes, like those of adults, move rapidly during the REM phases. Half of newborns' sleep is REM sleep. By the time they are 3 years old, children's REM sleep will have decreased to about one-third of their total sleep time (Hoban, 2004).

Once an infant wakes up, they will go through several phases of alertness in sequence (**FIGURE 5.6**):

- *Quiet alertness*: Upon awakening, infants are usually quiet and quite alert. They may lie in their crib and curiously look around.
- *Active alertness*: Infants not only respond to the environment but also move actively.
- *Crying phase*: Infants are easily overstimulated, move randomly, and may cry. Crying is also a sign of hunger in infants, so it is best to feed the infant before the crying phase (Stanford Children's Health, 2021b).

After the crying phase, infants are getting ready to take another nap again. The sleep cycle begins once more with a period of drowsiness (which is part of the regular sleep phase).

Supporting Infants' Sleep

Infants show they are ready to go to sleep when they start to rub their eyes, yawn, or fuss. Generally, routines that include soft music, bedtime stories, or rocking help infants (as well as older children) fall asleep. However, if infants routinely fall asleep in their parents' arms, they may not learn to fall asleep by themselves. For that reason, pediatricians often recommend holding babies only until they are very sleepy and then putting them into their cribs so they can fall asleep by themselves (Stanford Children's Health, 2021b).

Sleeping in the same room, or possibly even sharing a bed, makes it easier for parents to monitor young children and take care of them overnight. In many parts of the world, such as Japan and Guatemala, co-sleeping with infants is the most common sleeping arrangement. In 2015, about 24% of American parents shared a bed with their children (Bombard et al., 2018). But this practice goes against advice from the American Academy of Pediatrics, which recommends that while parents should sleep in the same room with their infants, they should not sleep in the same bed (Task Force on Sudden Infant Death Syndrome, 2016). The reason is that bed-sharing increases the risk of sleep-related deaths (Carpenter et al., 2013).

According to the Centers for Disease Control and Prevention, around 3,400 infants in the United States die each year in their sleep owing to sudden infant death syndrome, suffocation, or strangulation (Centers for Disease Control and Prevention, 2021d). However, it is worth noting that many studies on sleep-related deaths do not tease out situations that were influenced by other factors, like parental alcohol or drug use. The bed-sharing risk may not be as high when other risk factors are excluded. Some experts are now rethinking the traditional advice against bed-sharing in favor of a more personalized approach that takes into account individual risk factors. For instance, parents of healthy infants wishing to co-sleep could be advised to abstain from alcohol and drug use and create a safe sleep environment by using attachments to their bed so that the infant has a

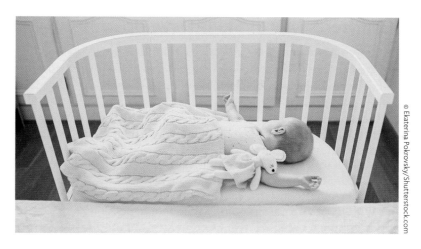

■ Parents who wish to co-sleep with their infants can use a crib that attaches to the bed, providing a safe, separated sleep surface while keeping the baby close.

separate, harder sleep surface. This way, rollovers can be prevented (Moon, 2021). Ultimately, a conversation about risks and benefits and a tailored approach may be more helpful than strong directives that go against some parents' instincts. We will discuss sleep-related infant deaths in Section 5.6 of this chapter.

Review!

How do children's sleep patterns change over the first 3 years?

- Children's need for sleep decreases significantly over their first 3 years of life.
- Newborns sleep around 16 hours per day in short intervals between feedings and periods of activity. During their first year, the length of their sleep periods increases, and by the time they are 1 year old, most children sleep through the night. Toddlers

need between 11 and 14 hours of sleep. They may still sleep during the day, but they take fewer and shorter naps than infants.
- Infants' sleep alternates between regular sleep and *REM sleep*, in roughly equal amounts.
- When they are awake, infants go through three phases of alertness: quiet alertness, active alertness, and a crying phase. The third phase signals that they are getting ready for another nap.
- Routines help small children fall asleep.

Practice!

1. Newborns sleep on average about _____ .
   a. 12 hours per day
   b. 14 hours per day
   c. 16 hours per day
   d. 18 hours per day

2. During the first year of life, napping by infants is _____ .
   a. common and recommended
   b. common but not recommended
   c. uncommon but recommended
   d. uncommon and not recommended

3. Children's need for sleep during the first 3 years _____ .
   a. increases
   b. decreases
   c. remains constant
   d. increases at first and then decreases

Show What You've Learned!

After Sylvia's daughter Elena was born, Sylvia was very tired. Most parents of newborns are tired, and in Sylvia's case, she was also recovering from a c-section. Although Sylvia's husband helped with their daughter during the day when he was not at work, feedings fell exclusively to Sylvia during the night. Since she was breastfeeding, Sylvia felt it would help her if their daughter slept in their bed with them. Her husband vehemently disagreed, stating it wouldn't be good for their marriage and potentially harmful to the infant if they shared a bed. Imagine you are Sylvia's friend Sheryl. What advice would you give to Sylvia?

5.3 How Children's Motor Skills Develop

- Recall the stages of gross motor skill development in infancy and toddlerhood.
- Recall the stages of fine motor skill development in infancy and toddlerhood.
- Assess whether or not the development of motor skills depends on the child's cultural environment.

Motor skills are the actions we perform voluntarily by using and controlling our muscles. Developing motor skills enables children to move their bodies, but it has an impact on other aspects of children's development as well. Infants who can lift their heads long enough to scan their surroundings can find out more about their environment: Where did that noise come from? Who else is in the room? Motor skills help children develop their cognitive and social skills by making actions and interactions with their surroundings and other people possible.

We generally distinguish between two different kinds of motor skills. **Gross motor skills** are involved when we move large body parts like arms and legs. They are important for activities like walking, jumping, or throwing balls. In contrast, **fine motor skills** involve movements of smaller muscles and small movements like those of hands and fingers. Fine motor skills are used to tie shoes, write a letter, or zip up a jacket. Hand–eye coordination plays an important role in fine motor activities because our eyes help us coordinate our movements. In the following sections, we will consider how gross and fine motor skills develop in infants and toddlers and how we can support their development.

gross motor skills skills that are involved when we move large body parts like arms and legs.

fine motor skills skills that involve movements of smaller muscles and small movements like those of hands and fingers.

Gross Motor Skills

If you have ever held a newborn, you will know that you have to use one hand to support his head. This is because a newborn's head is very large in proportion to the rest of his body. By 4 or 5 months of age, most infants have developed the gross motor skills to keep their heads up without support when someone holds them (FIGURE 5.7).

At around 4 months of age, infants are able to roll from stomach to back, and soon thereafter the other way around. By 6 months, many infants can sit without support, and within another couple months they will practice sitting up all by themselves.

Being able to move around and explore the world independently is a great motivation for infants. At around 8 months of age, infants usually begin to crawl, but some adopt other means of movement prior to or instead of crawling. Some infants use their hands to pull themselves forward on their bellies in a slithering motion or on their bottoms in a scooch. Others may move from point to point by rolling.

At around 9 months, babies can use furniture to pull themselves up to stand, and soon after they will practice walking by holding onto furniture or the hand of a caregiver. Between 12 and 15 months, most children start to walk independently. Stairs are often a particularly exciting place for children, who may attempt climbing stairs even before they can walk. Going upstairs safely is much easier than going downstairs, but this will not deter children from trying, which is one of the reasons why they must be monitored so closely whenever they are on the move.

Learning to walk with a secure and steady gait takes extensive practice. Researchers observing children aged 12–19 months found that the toddlers took more than 2,300 steps per hour and fell about 17 times in the process (Adolph et al., 2012). By the time they are 2 years old, most children can kick a ball, walk backward, and jump in place.

Fine Motor Skills

Newborns are born with a number of reflexes (see Chapter 4 for more details). One of them is the grasping reflex, which allows them to close their hand around an object that is placed in their palm. This reflex disappears as the infant gradually

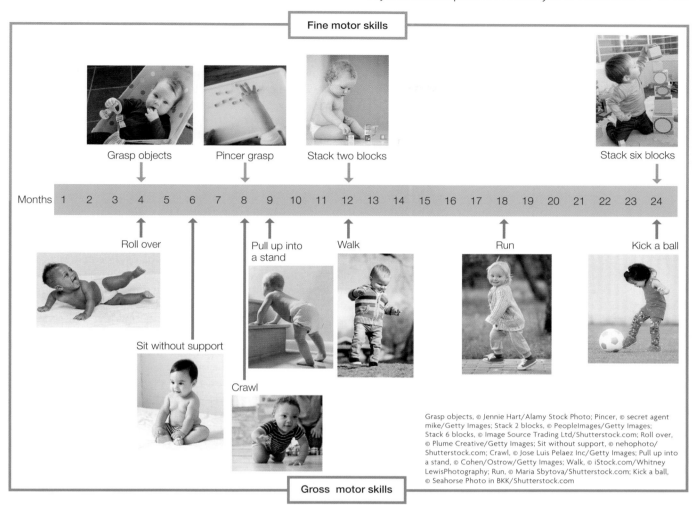

FIGURE 5.7 Milestones of motor development. The timeline shows the average ages at which 50% of children can perform various skills, from grasping objects and rolling over (4 months) to stacking six blocks and kicking a ball (24 months).

becomes more adept at grasping and holding objects. Around 4 months, infants reach out for objects and grasp them. Once infants can hold an object, they start to practice transferring objects from one hand to the other. Picking up small objects is more difficult and requires the **pincer grasp**, in which a piece of cereal or another small object is grasped with thumb and index or middle finger. Infants usually master the pincer grasp between 8 and 12 months of age.

Grasping for and picking up objects requires more than motor skills, however. To pick up an object, children need to coordinate their movements with what they see. Their hand–eye coordination will develop even further over the next months during play: 1-year-olds build towers up to two blocks high, and 2-year-olds can stack around six blocks. By the age of 2, children are learning to coordinate the movements of their hands, wrists, and palms so that they are better able to turn doorknobs or open jars. They also are likely to very much enjoy drawing. Toward their third birthday, they may show a preference for their right or left hand. Children should be encouraged to use their dominant hand so they can strengthen its muscles and skills. Some children take significantly longer to find a hand preference, however.

pincer grasp a grasp using the thumb and index or middle finger of the same hand to pick up small objects.

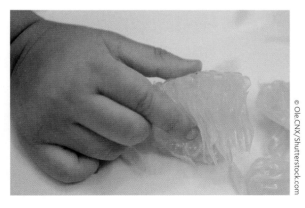

■ Infants from around 8 months of age can use the pincer grasp to pick up small objects.

Intercultural Differences in Motor Skill Development

There are many factors that influence whether and how infants crawl. People used to think that motor development was something that was "written" in our genes and always happened in a certain order that was biologically determined (Gesell et al., 1934). However, more current thinking suggests that motor development is influenced by a larger number of factors. In her **dynamic systems theory**, Esther Thelen (2005) proposed that motor development is influenced by:

- a child's body (the developmental state of brain, muscles, etc.), as well as
- the child's motivation to accomplish a goal (for example, to get over to that new ball) and
- the help that is available to the child in the environment (the caregiver who is there to lend a hand for walking over to the ball).

Thelen suggests that motor development can, within some limits, play out differently in different children and different cultures. For instance, some infants may be very active and may have to learn to keep those flailing limbs under control to learn walking, whereas others may be more quiet and calm and have to work on moving more in order to learn how to walk. Likewise, culture can influence development as well (Keller, 2017; Smith, 2006; Thelen, 2005). In some parts of Africa, India, and the Caribbean, mothers daily massage their infants and stretch their limbs. They also prop them into a sitting position rather than laying them down. Their infants tend to sit and walk earlier than infants in Western cultures (Karasik et al., 2015; Super, 1976). In areas of Northern China, in contrast, infants are placed on their backs in bags filled with fine sand for a considerable part of their day. The sand replaces the child's diaper and is only exchanged once a day. Spending so much time in a horizontal position delays independent sitting and walking (Mei, 1994).

Mothers in societies like that of the Au hunter–gatherers of Papua New Guinea either carry their babies in slings or prop them in a sitting position on the ground. As a result, Au infants never crawl. Before they walk, they scoot on their bottoms while propelling themselves with their hands. Keeping children off the ground reduces their risk of developing parasites or diarrhea and of encountering any dangers on the ground, such as snakes or glowing embers (Johnson, 2014; National Library of Medicine, 1986; Wong, 2009).

dynamic systems theory
a theory by Esther Thelen that proposes that motor development is the result of interaction between different systems and the environment.

■ The gahvora cradle, used in Tajikistan and other parts of Central Asia, restricts the movement of an infant's arms, legs, and torso (Karasik et al., 2018). Why might mothers place their infants in such a cradle?

But motor development of infants is also changing in the United States. In 1992, after the American Academy of Pediatrics started to recommend that infants sleep on their back to decrease the risk of sudden infant death syndrome, researchers noticed that infants began to roll over, sit, and crawl somewhat later than their stomach-sleeping peers. The sleep position did not have an effect on when the infants start to walk, however (Boonzaaijer et al., 2021; Davis et al., 1998; Eunice Kennedy Shriver National Institute of Child Health and Human Development, 2017).

Supporting Motor Skill Development

Children do not need instruction to learn how to roll over, sit up, or walk. All they need is space to explore, to practice, and to extend their physical skills. Caregivers can encourage this exploration by placing toys close to but just out of reach of infants, which can motivate them to turn, roll over, reach out, or crawl toward the object. Children learning to walk like push toys that give them more stability and help them balance. As they become older, they also enjoy balancing on different kinds of objects—tree trunks, playground equipment, a low garden wall—though they may need the help of a caregiver in the beginning. Playing with balls can help develop the coordination of arms and legs.

There are many toys designed to help children develop fine motor skills, from blocks for stacking to puzzles, shape sorters, and peg toys where pegs have to be fitted in holes, but young children enjoy play dough, crayons, and just about anything they can manipulate with their hands. They also like sensory boxes, containers filled with rice or uncooked pasta, where they can dig, explore different textures, and experiment with little shovels and buckets. See Table 1.2 for more suggestions.

Review!

How do gross motor skills develop in infancy and toddlerhood?

- *Gross motor skills* involve the movements of large body parts like arms and legs.
- One of the first things newborns have to learn is how to lift and hold up their head. By 5 months of age, most infants can hold their head up without support when they are picked up. By 6 months, many infants can sit independently when they are propped in a sitting position, and by 8 months they typically can sit up by themselves. Around this time, they also begin to crawl, though some infants may skip this step or move in other ways like rolling or scooting.
- Most children walk between 12 and 15 months of age. Around 18 months, many toddlers can run and walk up stairs. By 2 years of age, most children can kick a ball and jump in place. However, they continue to refine their motor skills through play for many more years.

How do fine motor skills develop in infancy and toddlerhood?

- *Fine motor skills* involve the movements of smaller muscles and body parts like hands and fingers.
- Infants start grasping objects around 4 months of age. Once they can hold an object, they need to learn how to transfer objects from one hand to another. Small objects need to be picked up with a *pincer grasp* (held by thumb and middle or index finger), which most children have mastered by 12 months of age.
- Many fine motor skills require visual motor coordination that needs to be practiced over the next several years. Two-year-olds practice coordination of hand and wrist movements to open doors and jars. They also learn how to hold and use crayons.
- Three-year-olds may already show a hand preference and continue to refine their fine motor skills so they can increasingly build higher block towers and add more intricate details to their drawings.

Does the development of motor skills depend on the culture a child grows up in?

- Although motor skills tend to develop in a similar sequence across all cultures, culture can have an impact on motor development.
- In some cultures of Africa and the South Pacific, children spend most of their time held by caregivers or propped in a sitting position. Many never crawl but will start walking at around the same time as children in Western cultures.
- Infant massage and stretching, common in some cultures of Africa and the Caribbean, may cause children to sit and walk earlier than children in Western cultures.

Practice!

1. Tying your shoes is a _____ .
   a. gross motor skill
   b. fine motor skill
   c. gross perceptual skill
   d. fine perceptual skill

2. Newborns' heads are _____ in proportion to the rest of their body.
   a. very large
   b. slightly large
   c. slightly small
   d. very small

3. _____ is not a variable that influences motor development in Thelen's dynamic systems theory of motor development.
   a. The developmental state of the brain
   b. The child's motivation to accomplish a goal
   c. The help that is available to the child in the environment
   d. The difference between the number of afferent neurons and the number of motor neurons

Act It Out!

At the start of this chapter we met Jeff and his 18-month-old son, Ricardo. Ricardo has become very active lately and gets himself into trouble by running away from his parents, climbing on things that aren't meant to be climbed on, and taking apart everything he can get his hands on. Jeff is worried that Ricardo is growing into a troublemaker. At the toy store, Ricardo has discovered a wooden train set, and he's pulling the magnetized cars apart and throwing them on the floor, to Jeff's grave embarrassment. It's such a scene that 2-year-old Lana takes a break from her snack to watch. Lana's nanny, Maria, is a retired pediatric nurse. Team up with another student and role-play a conversation between Jeff and Maria. What other concerns might Jeff have? What advice could Maria give?

5.4 How Infants and Toddlers Experience the World: Senses

■ Explain how children's senses of sight and hearing develop in infancy and childhood.

Lana, the 2-year-old toddler we met at the start of the chapter, is happily sitting in a corner of the toy store with her nanny, snacking on a banana. She loves bananas. She loves to touch them, squish them, smell them, and eat them. As Lana is playing with the banana, she comes to a better understanding of the essence of a banana by using all of her senses together.

The ability of newborns to sense and process the world around them develops rapidly and involves two processes. In **sensation**, the sensory organs of the infant sense a stimulus from the environment. Light might meet the infant's eyes, her ears may pick up on the soothing words of a parent, or the infant may feel a reassuring rub on her back. The sensory organs encode information of the stimulus and send it to the brain through neural impulses. When the brain processes and interprets these signals, making sense of the world, **perception** occurs.

In this section, we discuss how the senses of seeing and hearing develop in young children and how children learn to use their senses together to interact with their environment.

sensation an experience that is the direct result of the stimulation of a sense organ.

perception the processes by which we recognize, organize, and make sense of the sensations we receive from environmental stimuli.

Vision

The visual system of newborns is relatively immature (**FIGURE 5.8**). Newborns are very nearsighted and can best see objects that are 6–10 inches from their face. Children's visual acuity—that is, the "sharpness" of their vision—will increase steadily until it is similar to that of adults, which typically happens when children are between 4 and 6 years of age (Leat et al., 2009).

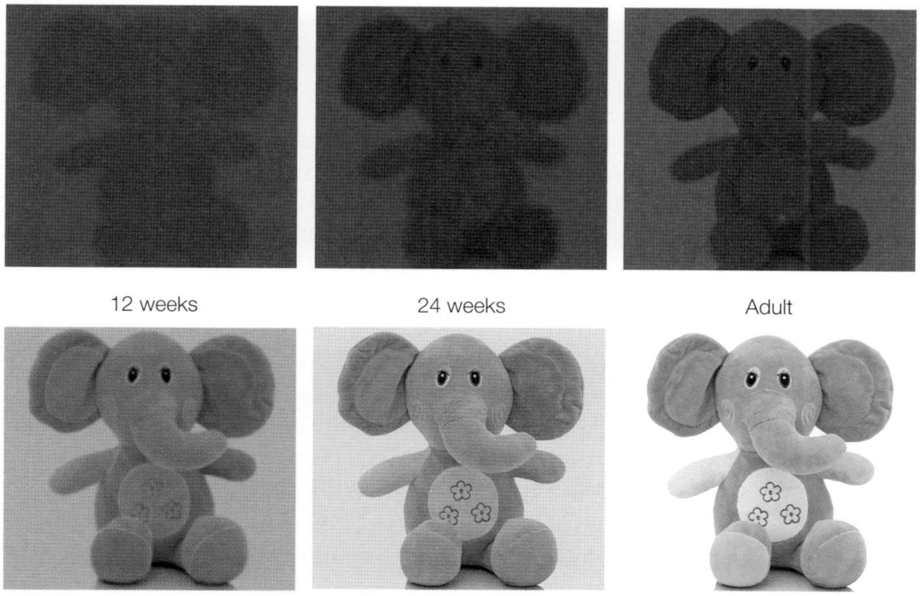

Newborn 4 weeks 8 weeks

12 weeks 24 weeks Adult

© boitano/Shutterstock.com

FIGURE 5.8 Changing visual acuity from birth to adulthood.

For the first 2 months, infants lack the muscle control to coordinate their eyes. From time to time, it may seem like their eyes are crossed: this is normal unless one eye is constantly turned in or out. By 3 months, infants start to follow moving objects with their eyes. Starting around 5 months, infants may be able to coordinate their eyes and fuse the two images to a single one that allows them to perceive depth (**FIGURE 5.9**). Around 1 year of age, babies are already quite skilled at judging distances (American Optometric Association, 2021).

From birth on, children like looking at faces (Fantz, 1961; Johnson et al., 1991). Perhaps this inclination should not be a surprise: Looking at adults' faces is a way of communicating and bonding with them. Interestingly, infants share adults' notions of attractiveness. Even newborns spend significantly more time looking at attractive faces than at unattractive faces (Kuraguchi et al., 2020; Langlois et al., 1987; Slater et al., 1998). But how do newborns judge attractiveness when they have seen so few faces in their lives? As adults, we consider faces that are most symmetrical to be particularly attractive, and young infants share our liking for symmetry (**FIGURE 5.10**) (Bornstein et al., 1981; Griffey & Little, 2014; Huang et al., 2018).

But infants also lose some skills in their first year of life. Within their first months only, infants can recognize faces of all races (as well as monkey faces!) equally well. At 9 months, they recognize faces of their own race significantly better than those of other races; this has been called the **other-race effect** (Clerc et al., 2021; Ge et al., 2009; Kelly et al., 2009; Quinn et al., 2016). These results are not an indication of early racism. Rather, they illustrate a process called **perceptual narrowing**, in which infants become particularly attuned to information that is available to them and

other-race effect the phenomenon that people are better at recognizing faces of their own race than faces of other races.

perceptual narrowing process by which infants become increasingly attuned to the sensory stimuli of their environment, at the cost of becoming less efficient at processing stimuli that are foreign to their environment (see, for example, the other-race effect).

FIGURE 5.9 Visual cliff. In a well-known study, Gibson and Walk (1960) constructed a "virtual cliff" to judge visual acuity in infants aged 6–14 months. The virtual cliff consists of a sheet of glass that is raised above the floor. On the "flat" side, patterned paper covers the glass; on the "deep" side, the paper covers the floor but is visible through the glass. Across the middle of the glass runs a centerboard, where children were placed for the test. Across the uncovered part of the glass stood the mother, who would call her child. Most children did not venture off the "cliff" but stayed on the centerboard on the flat side.

© Science History Images/Alamy Stock Photo

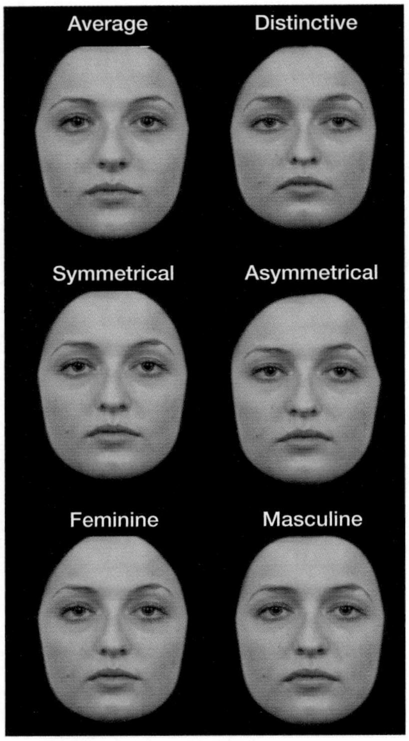

Average Distinctive

Symmetrical Asymmetrical

Feminine Masculine

FIGURE 5.10   When two versions of the same face were presented to infants between 12 and 24 months of age, infants showed a significant preference for the symmetrical version as well as the female version of the faces (Griffey & Little, 2014).

specialize in processing that kind of information (Krasotkina et al., 2021; Maurer & Werker, 2014). When infants are born, they have to be open to all experiences and sensory stimuli because they do not know what to expect and what their environment is like. However, in order to become more efficient information processors, infants soon start to specialize in processing the information that is available (and therefore relevant) to them.

So how can we support infants' visual development?

- Infants up to 4 months of age should not be exposed to bright lights, so it is better to use a dim light in their nursery. They can best see toys that are held between 8 and 12 inches in front of them. Talking to the infant while you walk around the room gives the child a chance to track you visually as you move and to locate your voice from different locations.

- Infants between 5 and 10 months love to look at and explore all different kinds of objects: blocks, any toys they can manipulate, and mobiles that can be suspended above the crib.

- Starting around 10 months of age, roll a ball back and forth with the infant or use moving toys to practice tracking of moving objects. Building toys like blocks also help children coordinate what they see with the movements of their hands (American Optometric Association, 2021).

■ What's It Like...

Growing Up Blind

Ramona, who has been blind since birth and is the mother of two sighted children
A child who is born blind does not know what it is like to see. Until he is old enough to begin to understand how other people do things, blindness seems normal. Therefore, a small child will not feel bad about blindness until someone teaches him or her (directly or indirectly) to feel bad. . . .

Blindness is something we explain little by little as a child progresses toward school. Because nobody knows when a blind child really understands what blindness is, it should be discussed in a positive manner. Anything associated with blindness should also be approached positively. Learning to use a white cane or being able to read Braille can be an opportunity and a privilege, not a last resort. Braille is a special way to read with your fingers. These positive approaches convey the attitude, "It's okay to be blind."

We must not lament the fact that a child cannot see. It isn't helpful to make comments such as: "I wish you could see the birds out the window," Or "I wish you could see the pictures in this book." But we can say, "Do you hear the birds singing? They sound nice. They have pretty colored feathers that look nice, too." Or "This is a funny picture. It shows an elephant in a dress! Isn't that silly? Do you remember the elephant you rode on at the zoo? Can you imagine it in a dress?"

In other words we must share what we see with a blind child as a pleasant and normal part of communicating, not as a constant sad reminder of something a child is lacking. It is impossible to guard blind children from all excessive admiring, crying, and gushing about blindness, but parents can begin by setting an example. This means getting your own grief and frustration about blindness out of your system as early as possible. . . .

You have heard statistics about how much learning is visual. These are often used to indicate that blind children don't learn as much or as fast as other children. This is not necessarily so, unless we don't use the alternative techniques that are available to the blind.

If a blind infant drops a set of keys on the floor, and you lean down to pick them up, that can be a fun game. If you lower the baby down and put her hand on the keys, it might be even more fun. If you encourage the little one to move her hand back and forth on the floor to find the keys, that's another kind of game, and that's learning. As the baby becomes a toddler, a little talk about where things go when they get thrown and dropped increases learning gradually. Sometimes the child will cooperate and enjoy the games, and sometimes not. But you keep playing them and making them more challenging and complex as she learns. . . .

And what about using the word, "blind?" Does it make you uncomfortable? It might be hard for you, but it could be a relief for your child to be able to name the difference he senses, but no one will talk about. I can remember feeling that something was wrong with me before anyone used the word blind. When I was in kindergarten in public school, the teacher guided my hand to teach me to print. I couldn't see the large letters she put on the paper. I learned to print, but the whole thing was embarrassing and confusing to me. Some explanation about what was happening might have been helpful, although I know that the adults involved were as unsure about what to do as I was. . . .

Your child needs reassurance that blindness is okay even before she really understands what blindness is. This is true because of what others say about it, and because a blind youngster may have fears (as I did) that are associated with their lack of vision. If you have created an atmosphere where it's okay to talk about blindness, your child will have the language, and the "permission" she needs to express some of the things she is thinking or experiencing about it. . . .

Sight is convenient and blind people rely on sighted people for certain things. This is not bad, but good and proper. Blind children need to learn how eyesight works and how to interact with sighted people. It's a part of learning about blindness. But too much reliance upon someone else's sight deprives the child of skill and confidence. Thus, a blind child must learn how to balance trusting his blind techniques and understanding the uses of vision. It is part of growing up for a blind child. . . .

Source: R. Walhof. 1996. *Future Reflections* 15(2), www.nfb.org

Hearing

Infants' sense of hearing at birth is much better than their vision, although they do not hear quite as well as adults do. In fact, it is not until their tenth year of life that children have adult-like hearing (Saffran et al., 2006). At birth, infants can roughly determine the direction from which a sound is coming. By approximately 2 years of age, they can locate sound sources almost as well as adults can (Burnham & Mattock, 2010).

Newborns prefer women's voices to those of men (Jusczyk, 1997). Even newborns can recognize their mother's voice and prefer it over other voices. And there is evidence that they can recognize sounds they heard while still in utero: Newborns prefer to hear stories their mothers read to them during pregnancy. In an experiment, they activated the recording of the familiar story more often by adjustment of their sucking rate (DeCasper & Spence, 1986).

Perceptual narrowing also affects infants' sense of hearing. At the very beginning of their life, infants are able to distinguish sounds from any language. As they get older, they become more and more attuned to the speech properties of languages spoken around them while losing the ability to distinguish sounds from foreign languages (Krasotkina et al., 2021; Maurer & Werker, 2014; Saffran et al., 2006; Singh et al., 2017).

A common reason for impaired hearing in young children is chronic ear infection, in which fluid accumulates behind the ear drum. For treatment, a tube may be placed in the inner ear to drain the fluid. The tube stays in the ear for several months until it falls out on its own (National Institute on Deafness and Other Communication Disorders, 2017).

If ear infections are not to blame, a hearing aid that makes sounds louder may help children hear. However, if hearing loss is so profound that a hearing aid does not help, a cochlear implant may help. The **cochlea** is a part of the inner ear that receives sound vibrations and converts these vibrations into nerve impulses that are sent to the brain. It usually takes weeks or months

cochlea part of the inner ear that receives sound vibrations and converts these into nerve impulses that are sent to the brain.

© Peakstock/Shutterstock.com

■ Cochlear implants can help children whose hearing is impaired to develop (almost) normal speech and to communicate better with others.

for children to fully benefit from a cochlear implant. But the sooner they receive one, the better the chances they will learn how to speak and be able to understand others (David et al., 2016; Robertson et al., 2021). However, a cochlear implant is not a cure-all, and many experts recommend that children with cochlear implants receive instruction in sign language as well as other services (Canadian Association of the Deaf, 2015).

Review!

How do children's senses develop in infancy and toddlerhood?

■ Newborns cannot see well, but their visual system develops rapidly over the first year of life. By 3 months, they start following moving objects with their eyes, and by 5 months they can coordinate their eyes well enough so that the two images they see can be fused into one, thus allowing them to perceive depth.

■ Young children enjoy looking at faces and, like adults, demonstrate a preference for facial symmetry.

■ Infants' hearing is much better than their vision. A newborn can recognize his mother's voice. By age 2, children can determine the source of sounds just about as well as adults.

■ Within the first months of life, *perceptual narrowing* causes children to specialize in the perception of some stimuli at the expense of others. They may become less adept at recognizing faces of people belonging to ethnic groups they do not see frequently and may lose the ability to distinguish different speech sounds from foreign languages.

Practice!

1. The cochlea is found in _____ .
   a. the outer ear
   b. the inner ear
   c. the nasal septum
   d. the retina of the eye

2. In the other-race effect, members of other races are _____ to recognize than are members of one's own race.
   a. generally harder
   b. generally easier

   c. harder but only for one's own sex
   d. easier but only for one's own sex

3. At the beginning of life, infants are _____ .
   a. unable to recognize sounds of any language
   b. able to recognize sounds of their own language
   c. able to recognize only vowel sounds of languages
   d. able to recognize the sounds of any language

What's Your Position?

Should young children with hearing loss be given cochlear implants? Your infant has recently been diagnosed with hearing loss. Tests have shown that she has almost no hearing and that both ears are affected. Your physician has brought up the

possibility of getting her cochlear implants. Is that something you would consider? Write a response to this question, and then debate the issue with a classmate. Did your opinion change?

Additional Resources Online

■ "Paediatric cochlear implantation: The views of parents," from T. H. Sach & D. K. Whynes, *International Journal of Audiology*

■ "Benefits and risks of cochlear implants," from the U.S. Food & Drug Administration

■ "Pros and cons of cochlear implants," from BabyHearing.org

5.5 Nutrition in Infants and Toddlers

- Outline the ways in which optimal nutrition can be ensured in infants and toddlers.
- Identify the types of suboptimal nutrition and discuss both causes and effects.

Infants and toddlers grow very rapidly, and they require certain nutrients for healthy and adequate growth. Nutritional deficiencies can result in health problems and developmental delays and, in the worst case, death. In the following subsections, we will discuss feeding practices with breast milk and formula as well as the introduction of solid foods. We also consider different forms of malnutrition that can cause children to be either overweight or undernourished.

Breast Milk and Formula

For most of humans' evolutionary past, infants were breastfed. In 2017, around 84% of U.S. mothers breastfed their children, though by the time they are 6 months old, only 58% of infants are exclusively breastfed (Centers for Disease Control and Prevention, 2020) (FIGURE 5.11).

(A)

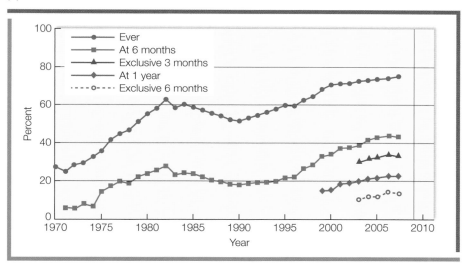

(B)

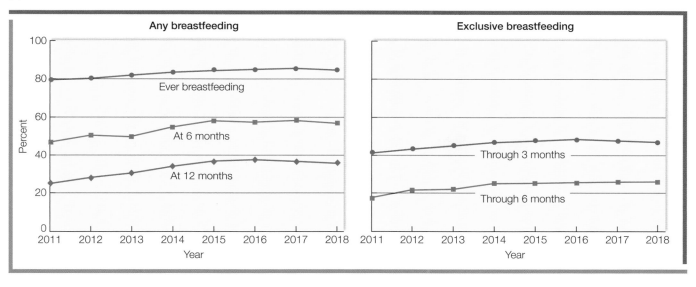

FIGURE 5.11   Breastfeeding rates in the United States (A) from 1970 to 2009 and (B) from 2011 to 2018. Breastfeeding rates reached a historic low in 1972, when only 22% of women breastfed their babies. Around 1975, breastfeeding rates began to increase again and reached 85% in 2018.

A after Office of the Surgeon General (U.S.). 2011. The Surgeon General's Call to Action to Support Breastfeeding: Rates of Breastfeeding. www.ncbi.nlm.nih.gov, based on various sources; B after Centers for Disease Control and Prevention. 2017. Breastfeeding: Results: Breastfeeding rates. www.cdc.gov

Socioeconomic status and ethnicity influence how likely a mother is to breastfeed. Generally, the more educated and wealthy a woman is, the more likely she is to breastfeed. In the United States, around 75% of Black and Native American mothers breastfeed their children, compared with 86% of White, Hispanic, and Asian American mothers (Chiang et al., 2021). Mothers often stop (or do not even begin) breastfeeding when they do not receive information about the benefits of breastfeeding or when they return to work soon after giving birth—a situation that some mothers cannot avoid (Centers for Disease Control and Prevention, 2017).

For about three days after birth, the breasts produce colostrum. Colostrum is a thick milk that is low in fat but high in carbohydrates, protein, and antibodies. After 3 days, the breasts start producing milk, which provides nutrients but also disease-protecting antibodies. Breast milk is also more easily digestible for infants than formula.

Infants who were breastfed have a lower risk of sudden infant death syndrome and may have a lower risk of getting diseases like hypertension, type II diabetes, cardiovascular disease, and obesity (Kelishadi & Farajian, 2014; Pattison et al., 2019; Thompson et al., 2017). Breastfeeding also lowers the mother's risk of breast and ovarian cancer and provides an opportunity for mother and child to bond (Babic et al., 2020; ElShmay, 2016; Holmes et al., 2017).

Breast milk provides the best nutrition for most infants, but not for all. Premature babies weighing less than 1,500 grams need fortified milk because they cannot drink as much as older infants (Underwood, 2013). Mothers infected with HIV (human immunodeficiency virus, which causes AIDS) can potentially transmit the virus to their infant via breastfeeding. The infection risk can be significantly lowered if both mother and child take antiviral drugs during the time the child is breastfed.

While research shows that breast milk is the best source of nutrition for infants, contemporary infant formulas from major manufacturers are based on extensive research and provide a satisfactory alternative to breast milk if a mother cannot breastfeed or chooses not to breastfeed for lifestyle reasons. In this case the American Academy of Pediatrics recommends the use of cow's milk–based formula with added iron. Most infant formulas also have fatty acids like DHA added, which are important for brain and eye development (American Academy of Pediatrics, 2020). Few children have an allergy to cow's milk, but for those who do, soy formulas are recommended as an alternative.

Introducing Solid Food

Infants should not be introduced to solid food before about 6 months of age, since the digestive tracts of younger infants cannot readily digest solid foods. As well, introducing solid food too early may put infants at risk for developing chronic diseases like diabetes, obesity, and eczema (Clayton et al., 2013; Huh et al., 2011; Waidyatillake et al., 2018).

The most common solid foods to start an infant on are cereals made from a single grain, pureed vegetables, and fruit. The order in which foods are introduced does not really make a difference. After a few months, an infant's diet should consist of a variety of solid foods like fruit, vegetables, cereals, meat, fish, and eggs in addition to milk. There is no need to hold back foods believed to

■ It is important to serve young children food that is soft and cut into little pieces to prevent them from choking. By picking up food with their thumb and index finger, children also practice their pincer grasp.

■ The rise of obesity in North America can be attributed in part to the ready availability of inexpensive processed foods with low nutritional value. (Left) A food truck serves a fast-food meal to a family in Florida. (Right) A mobile food pantry in Toronto offers up fresh foods rich in calcium, vitamin C, and iron.

cause food allergies, such as eggs: Delaying their introduction does not prevent food allergies (American Academy of Pediatrics, 2021). In order to prevent choking, food should be soft and cut into small pieces. Not only do the smaller pieces of food, like cereal, prevent choking; they also help children practice their fine motor skills and learn to feed themselves. Often, it will take many tries before children accept a new food. It is important that parents eat a healthy and balanced diet because their children observe and imitate them (American Academy of Pediatrics, 2017).

Water can be introduced at the same time as solid food. Juice contains lots of sugar and should not be given to infants younger than 1 year. Afterward, children should only get pure juice (with no added sugar) and in small quantities (American Academy of Pediatrics, 2021).

Malnutrition

There are two kinds of malnutrition: undernutrition and obesity. Undernutrition is a serious problem in many parts of Africa and Southern Asia. Almost half of deaths among children younger than age 5 are related to undernutrition (World Health Organization, 2021a). But consider that in the United States in 2020, 15% of children lived in households with food insecurity, which means that they have limited access to adequate food (U.S. Department of Agriculture, 2021). A variety of programs like the Supplemental Nutrition Assistance Program (SNAP) help parents provide food for their children; as a result, about 15 million children receive benefits through SNAP each month (King & Giefer, 2021). Still, many children are susceptible to deficiencies in their diet because their diet is not well balanced.

Conversely, children who are too heavy for their height are overweight. In the United States, about 8% of children aged 5 and under are overweight. Particularly among children in low-income families, obesity rates are rising each year (World Health Organization, 2021b). The rise in obesity can be explained at least partly by the increased availability of processed foods, the marketing of junk food to children, and lower levels of physical activity. Overweight children are at higher risk of developing chronic diseases like diabetes, kidney disease, or cardiovascular disease later in life. We will discuss obesity in children in the United States in more detail in Chapter 11.

Culture Counts

Undernutrition

Many children throughout the world are not growing well. But it is not only too little food that keeps children from growing—too much food (or too much of the wrong foods) can impair children's growth as well.

Undernutrition can take different forms. Children who are too small for their age suffer from *stunting*. They may never grow to full height and often have cognitive deficits and learning difficulties. Children whose weight is too low for their height (that is, they are too thin) suffer from *wasting*. Wasting is a life-threatening condition that requires treatment. Wasted children are more susceptible to diseases as well as death and are at risk for developmental delays.

The WHO estimates that in 2020, 149 million children around the world were stunted in their growth, and that 45 million were so malnourished that they were wasted. Almost half of deaths among children younger than 5 are related to undernutrition (World Health Organization, 2021a). Wasting and stunting rates are particularly high across countries in Africa as well as the southern and southeastern regions of Asia. Undernutrition can lead to complications like marasmus and kwashiorkor. **Marasmus** is caused by undernutrition and a lack of protein in the diet. Infants and very young children are particularly often affected. Affected children have ribs that can clearly be seen through the skin, have loose skin that may hang in folds, are often active but easily irritated, and have diarrhea.

Kwashiorkor results from insufficient protein intake. It most often affects children older than age 1 and delays growth and development. The hair becomes fine and of yellow/orange color. The skin may develop dark or light blotches as well as skin lesions. The body retains large amounts of fluids so that lower legs, arms, hands, abdomen, or face swell. For that reason, a child with kwashiorkor may not look undernourished.

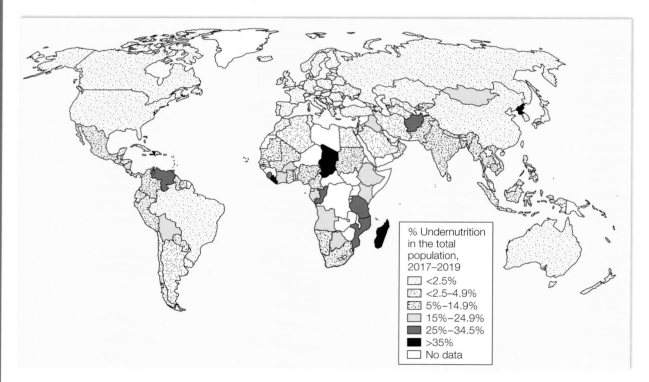

◼ Undernutrition around the world. Undernutrition is a problem in many countries of the world. This map shows the percentages of children that are affected by undernutrition in different countries.

Data from FAO, IFAD, UNICEF, WFP, and WHO. 2020. The State of Food Security and Nutrition in the World 2020. Transforming food systems for affordable healthy diets. Rome, FAO. https://doi.org/10.4060/ca9692en

◼ Question

Can you guess in which countries undernutrition is a more likely problem and in which countries obesity is the greater problem? What characteristics does a country need to have to make you guess it's more likely to have high rates of obesity or undernutrition?

Review!

How can optimal nutrition be ensured in infants and toddlers?

■ The best source of nutrition for infants is breast milk, except in some circumstances where the mother takes illegal drugs or suffers from a disease that may be passed on to the child through the breast milk. Infants lighter than 1,500 grams will need to have their breast milk fortified with additional nutrients to ensure adequate growth and weight gain.

■ Some mothers may choose not to breastfeed or may be unable to breastfeed for various reasons, such as needing to return to work shortly after childbirth.

■ At 6 months of age, children should be introduced to solid food; the order in which such foods are introduced does not make a difference. After a few months, children should eat a balanced diet that consists of fruit, vegetables, meat, fish, and eggs in addition to milk.

What are the effects of suboptimal nutrition?

■ We distinguish two different kinds of malnutrition:
1. When children are too heavy for their height, they are overweight. Obesity is a growing problem in industrialized nations as well as some lower-middle-income countries like Ukraine and Kenya. Families who cannot afford fresh fruit and vegetables often turn to processed foods that are rich in calories and low in nutrients.
2. Undernutrition is particularly common in parts of Africa as well as in Southern and Southeastern Asia. However, many children in the United States live in households that do not have permanent access to adequate food (food insecurity), which puts them at particular risk for nutritional deficiencies.

Practice!

1. Generally speaking, _____.
   a. sensation and perception occur at the same time
   b. perception comes before sensation
   c. sensation comes before perception
   d. sensation and perception amount to the same thing psychologically

2. An infant's sense of hearing at birth is _____.
   a. better than their sense of vision
   b. worse than their sense of vision
   c. equal to their sense of vision
   d. equal to their sense of vision for middle-pitched tones but worse for high-pitched tones

See for Yourself!

The next time you are at a family restaurant, observe what parents are feeding their toddlers. Are most children drinking water, juice, or soda? Are they eating fruit or vegetables? What foods are the parents eating? Can you observe some trends?

Show What You've Learned!

Sonyia is having trouble getting her 2-week-old baby, Andre, to breastfeed. Andre won't "latch," or take the breast, and when he does, it's causing Sonyia a lot of pain. She wants to give up breastfeeding and put Andre on formula right away. Sonyia explains all of this to her friend Gina, who volunteers once a week at a shelter for mothers with young children. Gina has helped many mothers going through the same frustrating situation. What kind of advice do you think Gina might give to Sonyia?

5.6 Health and Safety in Infants and Toddlers

■ Assess whether or not infant mortality rates in the United States vary from state to state or by income level.
■ Explain the role injuries play in the health of infants and toddlers.
■ Define sudden death syndrome and explain how it can be prevented.
■ Examine the impact electronic media has on children's health in infancy and toddlerhood.

marasmus syndrome resulting from chronic undernutrition and lack of protein that results in diarrhea, dizziness, and rapid weight loss.

kwashiorkor syndrome resulting from insufficient protein intake that results in developmental delays and changes in hair and skin color and texture as well as fluid retention.

The health of young children depends on many variables. Some of these are biological or genetic, but there are many factors that caregivers can influence in order to maximize their child's health. In this section, we will consider infant mortality and injuries, sudden infant death syndrome, and the impact of media on the health of infants and toddlers.

FIGURE 5.12 Infant mortality rates by state, 2020. Infant mortality rates vary greatly across the United States.

After Centers for Disease Control and Prevention. 2021. Infant Mortality Rates by State. www.cdc.gov

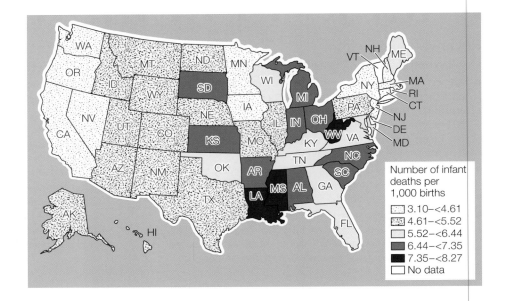

Number of infant deaths per 1,000 births

- 3.10–<4.61
- 4.61–<5.52
- 5.52–<6.44
- 6.44–<7.35
- 7.35–<8.27
- No data

Infant Mortality

Until not too long ago, infant deaths were a common reality. Over the past 3 decades, however, infant mortality has declined steeply. From 1990 to 2019, the worldwide infant mortality rate declined from 5 million to 2.4 million (World Health Organization, 2020). Whereas in poorer countries, birthplace conditions and lack of equipment are leading contributors to infant deaths, in the United States the main causes of infant death are birth defects and complications due to preterm birth (Centers for Disease Control and Prevention, 2021b).

Compared with other developed nations, the United States does not fare particularly well, however. While the United States is the seventh richest country in the world, its infant mortality rate is about the same as that of countries like Serbia, which produces about one-tenth of the income per person of the United States (International Monetary Fund, 2018). Within the United States, infant mortality varies significantly, from 3.1 deaths per 1,000 live births in New Hampshire to 9.1 in Mississippi (Centers for Disease Control and Prevention, 2021c) (see also **FIGURE 5.12**).

While there is only a slight difference in infant deaths at birth between the United States and European nations, a gap starts to show over the first year of infants' lives. In the United States, children in families with low incomes have a higher risk of dying than those in families with higher incomes. No such income-related difference can be found in Austria or Finland, for example (Chen et al., 2016). But American mothers who have lower income or less education or who are single often have difficulties securing high-quality healthcare. Helping families gain better access to healthcare and arranging for in-home nurse visits would make advice and support more available to parents (Chen et al., 2016).

Injuries in Infants and Toddlers

Do you remember our rambunctious toddler Ricardo from the beginning of this chapter? His father, who worried almost constantly about accidents that might happen to his son, is actually in good company. Many parents worry for the safety of their young children, and for good reason. Children of Ricardo's age not only lack the ability to recognize dangerous situations but

© Halfpoint/Shutterstock.com

■ Toddlers become increasingly mobile and fast, but they are not able to recognize dangerous situations. For that reason, accidents and unintentional injuries are the leading cause of death in young children.

also are often unable to help themselves once they are in a treacherous situation. Perhaps not surprisingly, the leading causes of death vary depending on the age of the child (see **FIGURE 5.13**).

After the first year of life, an infant's risk of dying decreases significantly (Murphy et al., 2017; World Health Organization, 2020). However, the risk of dying from unintentional injuries increases as children get older, mostly because children are much more active and involved in a variety of activities (Centers for Disease Control and Prevention, 2021a).

More than three-quarters of American children who died of suffocation were under 1 year old. Most of those suffocation incidents occur in the child's home. But there are some things parents can do to decrease suffocation risk. Sheets should fit the crib mattress tightly so infants cannot get trapped. Items like pillows, stuffed animals, and other soft objects should not be placed in the crib with an infant. Some infants suffocate when a parent or sibling sleeping with them rolls onto them. To prevent this, infants should sleep in their own crib or in a separate bed attachment (see the photo in Section 5.2 earlier in this chapter).

Nonfatal injuries in American children under 5 were mostly due to falls, followed by injuries in which the children were struck by objects (not including cars), bitten by an animal, or stung. These injuries from non-intentional causes are often, though not always, preventable (Dellinger & Gilchrist, 2019). It is very important for parents and caregivers of young children to childproof their homes and all areas where children move freely. We will discuss childproofing in more detail in Chapter 8.

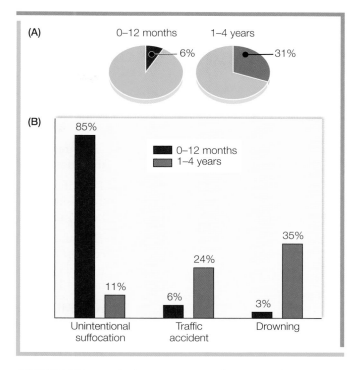

FIGURE 5.13 Deaths from unintentional injury in infants aged 0–12 months and children aged 1–4 years. (A) Unintentional injuries as a cause of death. (B) Leading causes of death in unintentional injuries.

A after M. Heron. 2017. Deaths: Leading causes for 2015. https://stacks.cdc.gov; B data from B. A. West et al. 2021. *J Safety Res* 78: 322–330

Sudden Infant Death Syndrome

A particular scene plays out in about 1,300 American households each a year (Centers for Disease Control and Prevention, 2021d): Parents put their healthy infant down for the night or for a nap and return to find the child unresponsive and not breathing. Nothing has changed in the regular bedtime routine except for the tragic outcome.

The sudden and unexpected death of an infant under 1 year of age is called **sudden infant death syndrome** (SIDS). Infants are more likely to suffer sleep-related death when:

- they are between 2 and 4 months of age
- they are boys
- they have been born prematurely or at low birthweight
- their mother is younger than 20 years of age
- their mother used drugs during pregnancy
- there is a family history of SIDS
- the weather is colder (KidsHealth.org, 2017).

But SIDS correlates with other social factors as well. Within the United States, SIDS rates are more than twice as high among Black and Native American children as they are among White children. For unknown reasons, Asian infants have the lowest SIDS rate (Centers for Disease Control and Prevention, 2021d). Researchers suspect that people in Asian cultures may engage in more

sudden infant death syndrome the sudden and unexpected death during sleep of an infant younger than 1 year.

behaviors that protect their children from factors associated with SIDS: Asian mothers tend to smoke less and drink less alcohol, and they are more likely to sleep in the same room as their children (Ball et al., 2012).

SIDS is particularly frightening to parents because it appears to be so unpredictable. Yet although we do not know the exact cause of SIDS, researchers have developed a model they believe can help identify risk factors for SIDS. The model is called the Triple-Risk Model because it is based on three risk factors (Spinelli et al., 2017):

1. The infant has some kind of vulnerability that is undiagnosed, like a genetic mutation or defect in brain parts that regulate breathing and heart rate.

2. The infant is in a critical developmental period in which rapid growth destabilizes internal systems that regulate breathing, blood pressure, heart rate, etc.

3. The infant is exposed to stressors like tobacco smoke, overheating, breathing congestion (i.e., from a cold), or a stomach sleeping position. These environmental stressors alone do not usually lead to death, but infants at risk from factors 1 and 2 may not be able to deal with these stressors adequately.

According to the Triple-Risk Model, SIDS can occur when all three risk factors are present. Caregivers only can control the external stressors in point 3. However, by removing these stressors, they can possibly remove the third factor that could cause SIDS and thus reduce the risk that their infant will die suddenly.

In 1994, the U.S. government started a national "Back to Sleep" campaign that recommended parents put their children to sleep on their back. Within the following 5 years, the SIDS rate in the United States dropped by more than one-half, while the number of infants sleeping on their back more than doubled (Safe to Sleep, 2017) (**FIGURE 5.14**).

Why would back-sleeping reduce the rates of SIDS? Researchers believe that stomach-sleeping may block infants' airways and increase the risk that infants "rebreathe" the air they exhaled, which is rich in carbon dioxide (KidsHealth.org, 2017).

In 2016, the American Academy of Pediatrics updated its recommendations to prevent SIDS (American Academy of Pediatrics, 2016b). Here are some of

FIGURE 5.14 U.S. deaths per 1,000 live births and percentage of infants sleeping on back, 1988–2019. The decline in the SIDS rate coincides with campaigns promoting back-sleeping for infants.

After Centers for Disease Control and Prevention. 2021. Sudden unexpected infant death and sudden infant death syndrome. www.cdc.gov; U.S. Department of Health and Human Services. 2021. Progress in reducing SIDS. https://safetosleep.nichd.nih.gov

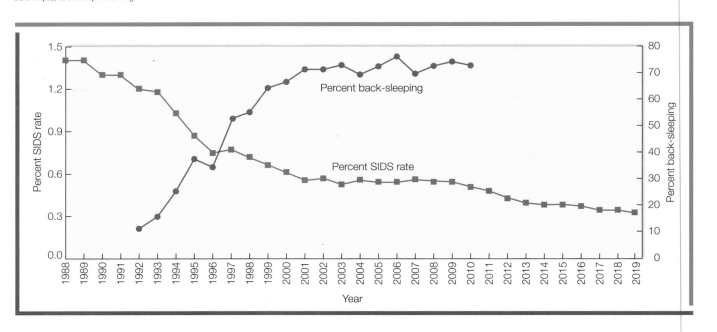

the recommendations to caregivers in order to decrease the chance of SIDS (Moon, 2021):

- Create a safe sleep environment:
  - Place the infant on his back for sleeping.
  - To prevent suffocation, use a firm mattress and no pillows, bumper pads, or stuffed toys.
  - Share a room with the infant, but do not sleep in the same bed.
- Breastfeed as long as possible.
- Do not let the infant get too hot (that is, use at most one layer more than you would use yourself while sleeping).
- Do not expose the infant to cigarette smoke.
- Attend all well-child visits and have your child immunized.

Media and Children's Health

How much screen time would you give your infant if you were a parent? Not even the experts are quite sure what to recommend. The American Academy of Pediatrics (AAP) publishes guidelines that were last revised in 2016 and lowered the recommended age at which children can start using screens from 2 years to 18 months. Children up to 18 months should have no screen time at all, except perhaps an occasional video chat with their grandparents. Once they are over 18 months, according to the guidelines, parents can introduce high-quality programming if they watch with their children to help them understand the content of the show. For children aged 2 to 5 years, the recommendation is not to exceed 1 hour of screen time a day (American Academy of Pediatrics, 2016a). The AAP also offers an online tool that allows families to custom-tailor media use plans for children of different ages. These plans spell out when and where children are allowed to use their digital devices and the activities which are allowed and not allowed, as well as media manners (American Academy of Pediatrics, 2021).

But, as so often in life, not everybody agrees. One study investigating screen time and children's psychological well-being did not find that screen time by itself took a negative toll on children. The researchers conducted 20,000 phone interviews with parents and found that children between 2 and 5 whose parents limited screen time were somewhat more resilient than others, which means they were able to recover more quickly from difficulties they experienced. However, they also had lower levels of positive affect than their peers who spent more time in front of a screen (Przybylski & Weinstein, 2017).

It seems most Americans are not following the AAP's recommendations anyway. In 2020, children under age 2 spent an average of 49 minutes per day watching TV or videos (Common Sense Media, 2020). Other researchers come to different conclusions and estimate the daily TV consumption of infants to be as high as 3–4 hours a day (Christakis, 2009; Thompson et al., 2013).

Does the use of screen media have an impact on children's health? It is possible. One study found, for example, that the more children aged 6–36 months use touch screens, the less they sleep and the more their sleep pattern changes (in particular, they sleep less at night and more during the day). For every hour of tablet use, they sleep about 15 minutes less. But why is it that children are sleeping less when they use tablets? For one, they might have less time to sleep. Additionally, falling asleep may be harder due to arousing content and the blue light emitted by the screen that may suppress children's melatonin production (Cheung et al., 2017; Janssen et al., 2020). (Melatonin is a hormone that regulates our sleep–wake cycle.)

The TV-watching habits of toddlers also influence their eating habits and weight in later years (Duch et al., 2013). The more young children watch TV, the poorer their diets tend to be when they are teens and the less effort they tend to show

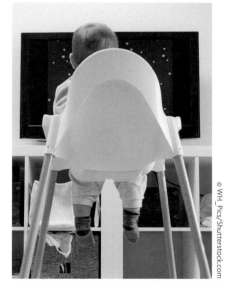

© WH_Pics/Shutterstock.com

■ Many Americans do not follow the guidelines of the American Academy of Pediatrics, letting their infants watch TV on a daily basis. Parents often let their children watch TV so they can complete chores and other activities that might be hard to accomplish with a young child that needs to be entertained or distracted. Do you think it is acceptable for parents to use the TV as a "babysitter"?

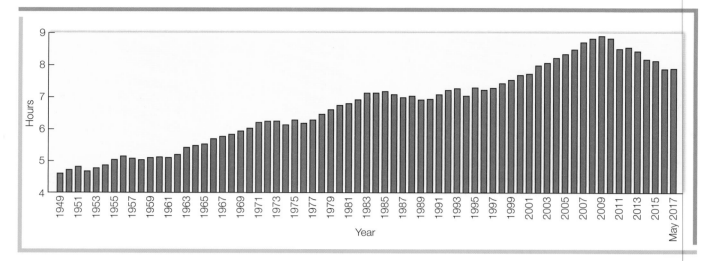

FIGURE 5.15 Hours of TV viewing per day in American households, 1949–2017. Over the past decades, both the weight of American children and the time that TVs are on in American households have increased.

Data from Nielsen. 2009. Historical daily viewing activity among households & persons 2+. www.nielsen.com; A. C. Madrigal. 2018, May. When did TV watching peak? *The Atlantic*. www.theatlantic.com

in middle school (Bang et al., 2020; Myszkowska-Ryciak et al., 2020; Simonato et al., 2018). More TV watching also predicts higher weight. In fact, over the past 50 years, not only has the time that TVs are on in U.S. households increased, but so has the weight of American children (Christakis, 2009; Sanyaolu et al., 2019) (**FIGURE 5.15**). Researchers suspect that increased screen time is also a culprit for the increase in obesity during the COVID-19 pandemic during which overweight and obesity increased from 36% to 46% in 5- to 11-year-olds (Woolford et al., 2021).

The use of TV and entertainment media increases significantly as children get older. Perhaps, what may be more important than the time spent in front of the screen is how that time is spent. We will return to this topic throughout the book to consider the effects of media on older children and to explore the features of apps and other digital media that make them suitable for children.

Review!

Does infant mortality vary across the United States or across different ethnic groups?

■ Globally, the leading causes of infant mortality are related to a lack of oxygen during birth and infections. Within the United States, birth defects and preterm birth are leading death causes.

■ Compared with other wealthy countries, the United States has a high rate of infant deaths. This difference may be partly attributed to variances in reporting. However, infant mortality within the United States also varies dramatically by state. In the United States, children in families with low incomes have a higher risk of dying than those in families with higher incomes. Provision of high-quality healthcare and in-home visits by nurses could potentially reduce high infant mortality.

What is the role of injuries in infants' and toddlers' health?

■ Injury causes vary depending on children's age.

■ About 72% of infant deaths (<1 year) due to an unintentional injury were caused by suffocation, whereas the leading death causes in children ages 1–4 were drowning and traffic accidents. Nonfatal injuries are most often due to falls as well as accidents in which children are struck by an object.

■ It is obviously hard for parents to foresee every kind of accident that might happen, but childproofing the areas of the house young children have access to as well as infants' cribs can help reduce the likelihood of unintentional injuries or deaths.

What is sudden infant death syndrome, and can it be prevented?

■ About 1,300 infants die each year due to *sudden infant death syndrome* (SIDS), in which apparently healthy children are put to sleep and do not wake up anymore. Most children affected by SIDS are between 2 and 4 months of age. It is not entirely clear why SIDS happens, but the Triple-Risk Model suggests that three factors play a role:

1. The infant suffers from an undiagnosed medical problem that affects his heart or breathing rate.
2. The infant is going through a period of rapid growth that can destabilize vital body systems.
3. The infant is exposed to external stressors like tobacco smoke, heat, or stomach-sleeping.

■ SIDS is most likely when all three factors are present. Caregivers can only control the external stressors listed in point 3, but this may be enough to prevent SIDS. For that reason, parents should
   1. Be careful not to overdress their infant to avoid overheating.
   2. Reduce exposure to tobacco smoke.
   3. Put their infant to sleep on her back.

4. Keep any soft objects like stuffed toys or pillows out of the crib.

What impact do electronic media have on children's health in infancy and toddlerhood?

■ The American Academy of Pediatrics recommends that children start using screen media at the earliest at the age of 18 months. About one-third of children under age 2 watch TV every day.

■ Screen media can negatively impact children's sleep patterns. The more time children spend in front of a screen, the higher their weight tends to be and the worse their eating habits. Children who spend a lower amount of time in front of screen media tend to be more resilient, but they also may have lower levels of positive affect than their peers who are allowed to watch more.

Practice!

1. Which of these is **not** associated with increased risk of sleep-related death?
   a. a family history of SIDS
   b. an infant who is female
   c. an infant who is 2–4 months of age
   d. a colder climate

2. The American Academy of Pediatrics recommends _____ screen time per day for children under 18 months.
   a. no more than 2 hours
   b. no more than 1 hour
   c. no more than 30 minutes
   d. no

Six months later: How Rona and Ricardo are developing

Six months after we first met Rona and Ricardo with their parents at the toy store, they still attend the parent–child play group every week. Not only is it fun for the toddlers, it is also a great opportunity for parents to share their experiences and discuss the many issues that come up when raising young children. Ricardo is still very lively and active. His father has come to realize that this is just a reflection of his son's personality and not necessarily a sign of troubles that are yet to come. But still, he has also learned to keep a close eye on Ricardo, who recently darted out into the street chasing after his favorite soccer ball. Jeff and his wife are in the process of childproofing their apartment to make Ricardo's environment as safe as possible for him.

Rona is consistently gaining weight, though she still hovers around the 10th percentile when compared to her age-mates' weight. The nurse has assured Lisa that there is no reason to worry as long as Rona keeps gaining weight consistently and eats a healthy diet. There is nothing inherently wrong with being slender. Rona still has a hard time falling asleep, but she is now used to sleeping in her own room. When she cannot fall asleep, Lisa or her husband sits beside her bed to keep her company until she drifts off. While this is not a perfect solution, both parents are happy about the improvements they have seen over the past few months. ■■■■

© Zoia Kostina/Shutterstock.com

Overview

Cognitive Development in Infancy and Toddlerhood

Children in the community

Cassie is in the waiting room at her local community health center. She is terribly nervous. She recently had her first child, Alessandro, who is now 3 months old and making his first well-child visit. Cassie's brother has a child who was recently diagnosed with a severe case of autism spectrum disorder (ASD). Now Cassie is afraid that something might be wrong with Alessandro as well. She has never spent much time with children—she didn't even babysit when she was younger—and now she feels she does not know what to expect in terms of Alessandro's development. Why does he put everything in his mouth? And why doesn't he pay more attention when she takes him to the zoo or reads to him?

Along with Cassie are two other mothers with children waiting to be seen. Valeria is sitting with her 16-month-old daughter, Jimena, who is looking intently at a picture book she selected from a table in the corner of the waiting room. They're here for a regular well-child checkup, but Valeria is also worried that Jimena hasn't really started speaking yet. It is something she plans to discuss with the doctor.

Across the room is 21-month-old Ava, who sits on her mother's lap, contentedly watching YouTube videos on her mother's phone. Alyssa has brought Ava to see the doctor about a cough that just won't go away.

In this chapter, we will touch on some of the issues that bring worried parents to the pediatric waiting room. We will look at how children's thinking develops over their first 3 years of life, and we will consider how young children go from not speaking or understanding spoken language to expressing themselves in full sentences within a few years. We finish the chapter with a look at how media technology available to children today impacts the cognitive development of a growing child.

6.1 Learning to Think

■ Recall and describe how infants' thinking develops in Piaget's sensorimotor substages.
■ Outline the memory changes children experience from birth to their first three years.

Infancy is an exciting age for newborns and their parents. Within 3 years, children develop from virtually helpless beings to toddlers who boldly strive for independence, actively explore the world, and quite fluently speak in their native language or languages. Children's ability to think and process the world around them progresses enormously. Alessandro, who at 3 months of age immediately forgets his favorite neon-colored ball when his grandfather takes it out of sight, will soon set out to search the entire apartment when his beloved ball is missing. In the following section, we will learn more about how young children's thinking develops during the first 3 years of their life.

Scientific Theories and the Real World: A Word on Limitations

Throughout this book, we discuss theories of cognitive development. It is important for both researchers and practitioners to have theories they can base their work on because theories help us understand how and why children develop as they do. Most of the theories we discuss have been developed by researchers in Western countries. They are based on observations of children who have grown up immersed in Western culture, spending their childhood in good, or at least acceptable, life circumstances.

Most of the world's children, however, are raised outside of Western culture, and in circumstances more varied than those accounted for in some leading theories of child development. As a result, the cognitive development of these children may not proceed quite the way the theories describe. Consider some of the variables that can affect the cognitive development of young children:

• *Culture.* Culture influences how children think about themselves and how they remember events that happened to them. When recalling events, for example, American children tend to focus more on detailed descriptions, their feelings, and their opinions. In contrast, Chinese children focus more on people and their relationships (Wang, 2016; Wang et al., 2015).

• *Environment.* Children growing up in low-income neighborhoods and inner cities tend to exhibit more behavioral problems, have lower math and reading scores, and repeat grades more often than children from middle- and upper-income neighborhoods (Kim et al., 2014). Negative effects of a family's socioeconomic status are more pronounced when the family lives in a poorer neighborhood (Lippman et al., 1996).

• *Resources.* Malnutrition can inhibit cognitive development in children. Iron deficiencies and iodine deficiencies, which affect about 45% of children in developing countries and 7% of children under age 5 in the United States (Gupta et al., 2016; Jáuregui-Lobera, 2014), have contributed to intellectual disabilities in over 6 million people worldwide (De & Chattopadhyay, 2019; Hetzel, 1993).

These are just a few examples of how children's lives and their development are ultimately a lot more complex and influenced by many more factors than theories can describe. The point to bear in mind as you read through this book is that the theories we will consider assume a cultural background or a favorable set of circumstances that are not the norm for many children around the world, including some here in the United States.

■ After Hurricane Maria hit Puerto Rico in September 2017, about 7% of children experienced symptoms of post-traumatic stress disorder (PTSD) (Orengo-Aguayo et al., 2019). Some researchers believe that islanders' prevalent Hispanic culture, which places an emphasis on strong family ties, may have contributed to the relatively low rate of PTSD (Elkins et al., 2019; La Greca et al., 2013).

© Mario Tama/Getty Images

What's It Like...

Supporting Children's Cognitive Development: Early Intervention Services

Colleen, mother of 18-month-old twins Rudy and Kara

My husband and I found out we were going to have twins when I was about 9 weeks pregnant and had an ultrasound done at my first checkup. We learned that twins are at a higher risk for being born prematurely, but we did not expect that to be an issue. What a mistake that was! When our children were born at 32 weeks, they were tiny and weighed under 4 pounds.

Obviously, we've been worried about their development because they were born early and with low birthweight. I was particularly anxious because they are our first children, and I do not even know what to expect in terms of their development.

At the suggestion of our pediatrician, we had a couple of specialists come to our house to see if the children qualify for early intervention services. It turned out that both children had more trouble turning over and holding their head up than was expected for their age—they were at risk for a possibly substantial developmental delay. Kara was also babbling significantly less than Rudy. We now have both early intervention specialists and a speech therapist come to our house several times a month to work with the children.

All those services are free, which is important because we could not afford such professional care on a long-term basis. It is wonderful to have someone watch over the babies' progress together with us and help us navigate any difficulties we may encounter. The therapists show us exercises we can do with the children and answer any questions we might have. Physically, the twins are developing wonderfully, and I am hopeful that together we eventually may be able to overcome Kara's speech difficulties.

Muna, early intervention specialist

I am one of several early intervention specialists in our area and work primarily with children aged 0–3 years. I work with about 15–20 families on a regular basis and typically see them in their homes about once or twice a week. The cases I work on vary widely.

In the case of Rudy and Kara, we mostly have practiced physical skills and coordination. An example would be grasping small pieces of food like Cheerios, holding crayons, or sitting up for longer periods of time. We mostly work with materials that can be found in a young child's environment like toys, books, swings, or spoons. Depending on the skills we need to practice, we may eat snacks together, play, try to take a bath, or go to the grocery store together.

An important part of my work is collaborating with the parents and other family members who are often present during my work with their children. This observation enables them to continue to practice these skills during the week and voice any concerns. I also observe family interactions and come up with ideas to help make families' lives easier. My tasks also include doing assessments with newly referred children as well as attending staff meetings and writing reports. I love what I am doing because I get to help families on a daily basis and I see the direct impact my work is having on their lives.

Piaget's Sensorimotor Stage

You will recall Jean Piaget from Chapter 2, where we first met the Swiss cognitive theorist whose work with children began with his study of intelligence testing. Piaget's theory of cognitive development was based on a series of four stages that children go through (see Table 2.3):

- sensorimotor (lasting from birth to around age 2),
- preoperational (lasting from ages 2 to 7),
- concrete operational (ages 7 to 11), and
- formal operational (ages 11 and up).

schemata (singular **schema**) patterns of action or thought that organize our knowledge about the world and influence the way we think and behave.

sensorimotor stage the first stage in Piaget's theory of cognitive development, in which children learn primarily through their senses and motor activity.

Piaget asked one of developmental science's hardest questions: How do children start to think? He theorized that infants' first thinking comes from **schemata**, patterns of thought or action that organize our understanding of the world and influence the way we think and behave. In infants, schematic action patterns are the reflexes healthy children are born with (see Chapter 4). They play an important role in the first stage of Piaget's theory of cognitive development, the **sensorimotor stage**, where children use schematic action patterns to learn about and explore their environment by means of their senses and motor activities. For example, Alessandro may develop a schema to categorize the world into things he can put in his mouth and things he can reach out for. As he learns through experience, he adjusts his schemata, and they become more complex. Later, he will develop schemata that help him tell cats apart from other animals or understand the way we shop for food in a supermarket (Brubaker, 2016).

The sensorimotor stage has six substages

Throughout the six substages of the sensorimotor stage, infants modify their schematic reflexes and become more flexible and creative in using those schemata (**TABLE 6.1**). By the end of the sensorimotor stage, children have become capable of **symbolic thought**: They can create mental representations of objects, people, or events in order to think about them without their having to be present.

symbolic thought a type of thinking that uses symbols (words, numbers, or internal images) to represent objects, events, or people who are not present.

FIRST SUBSTAGE: SIMPLE REFLEXES (BIRTH TO 1 MONTH) Healthy infants are born with a number of simple reflexes—unlearned, automatic responses to stimuli in the environment. Examples include rooting, sucking, and grasping (see Table 4.3).

SECOND SUBSTAGE: PRIMARY CIRCULAR REACTIONS (1–4 MONTHS) Within a few weeks of birth, infants begin to adjust their reflexes and behaviors. They may adjust the movements of their mouth and tongue slightly depending on whether they are sucking on a nipple, a finger, or a doll. They also learn to repeat actions because they enjoy the activity in itself. Repetitive actions such as finger sucking are called **primary circular reactions** because they are repeated in a circular fashion (**FIGURE 6.1**) and center on the infant's own body.

primary circular reaction an action that first occurred by chance and now is repeated by the infant to reproduce a pleasant sensation; it centers on the child's body.

secondary circular reaction a repetitive action that produces an effect involving other people or objects.

THIRD SUBSTAGE: SECONDARY CIRCULAR REACTIONS (4–8 MONTHS) In the third substage, infants try to produce pleasurable experiences like those they produced in the second substage, but now their actions involve not only their own body but also objects or people from their environment. These repetitive actions that involve other objects or people are called **secondary circular reactions** (Figure 6.1).

■ Table 6.1 The Six Substages of Piaget's Sensorimotor Stage of Cognitive Development

Substage	Description	Example	
1. **Simple reflexes** (birth–1 month)	Infants react to their environment by using their inborn reflexes (sucking reflex, grasping reflex, etc.) as well as senses.	© violetblue/ Shutterstock.com	An infant turns her head when she hears her mother's voice and sucks when the nipple is in her mouth.
2. **Primary circular reactions** (1–4 months)	Infants adjust their reflexes and repeat behaviors that occurred by chance and were pleasurable.	© wavebreakmedia/ Shutterstock.com	An infant sucks happily on his own toes.
3. **Secondary circular reactions** (4–8 months)	Infants become interested in their environment and perform actions that include people or objects.	© Rohappy/Shutterstock.com	An infant enjoys shaking a rattle to hear the sounds it makes.
4. **Combination of schemata** (8–12 months)	Infants begin to act purposefully to achieve goals. They combine several actions.	© iStock.com/dlinca	A child can now look for and crawl toward a toy in order to retrieve it.
5. **Tertiary circular reactions** (12–18 months)	Infants can change their schemata in order to manipulate objects and actively explore their environment.	© iStock.com/Daniela Jovanovska-Hristovska	A child drops a toy from the crib to see what happens.
6. **Mental representations** (18–24 months)	Infants can use mental images of people and events (called mental representations), which allow them to think before or instead of acting.	© iStock.com/wsphotos	A child understands that each piece of a puzzle has its own place.

FOURTH SUBSTAGE: COMBINATION OF SCHEMATA (8–12 MONTHS) In this substage, infants begin to combine several schemata to accomplish their purposes. They can also draw on past experiences to solve new problems.

FIFTH SUBSTAGE: TERTIARY CIRCULAR REACTIONS (12–18 MONTHS) In the fifth substage, infants start experimenting with different behaviors to see their effects. Now they not only combine their schemata but can also change them slightly so they can better accomplish their goals. These explorative actions

FIGURE 6.1 Primary, secondary, and tertiary circular reactions.

After D. E. Papalia. 1998. *Human Development*, 7th ed. McGraw-Hill, New York

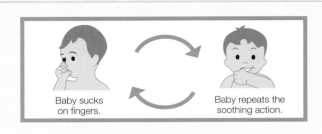

Primary (1 to 4 months)

Action and response center on the infant's own body.

Baby sucks on fingers.

Baby repeats the soothing action.

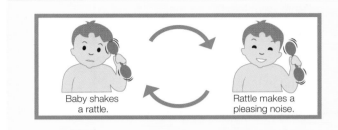

Secondary (4 to 8 months)

Action receives a response from another person or object, causing the infant to repeat the original action.

Baby shakes a rattle.

Rattle makes a pleasing noise.

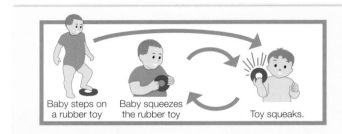

Tertiary (12 to 18 months)

Action results in pleasure, leading infant to perform similar actions to get similar results.

Baby steps on a rubber toy

Baby squeezes the rubber toy

Toy squeaks.

tertiary circular reaction
Actions that are aimed at exploration of the environment and involve changes of schemata to fit new situations.

■ In the fifth substage, children are able to change their schemata and engage in a trial-and-error process to explore the world and accomplish their goals—in this case, to make as much noise as possible!

in which children change their schemata are called **tertiary circular reactions**. For example, a rattle makes noise not only when shaken but also when it is banged against another toy.

Infants also start to solve problems by trial and error. Their thinking is still limited to physical actions on objects, however. That is, they cannot anticipate what will happen if they drop a spoon, since they do not yet possess symbolic thought; instead, they will have to drop the spoon to see what happens.

SIXTH SUBSTAGE: MENTAL REPRESENTATIONS (18–24 MONTHS) At this substage, children are able for the first time to think about objects without needing to handle them. They can imagine, for instance, what might happen if they pull their sibling's hair. Mental representations of people and objects become the basis of the more advanced thought processes involved in what Piaget called symbolic thought. As they age, children will use their symbolic thinking to engage in pretend play, to acquire language (where words are symbols for objects they stand in for), and to solve problems just by thinking about them.

During the six substages of the sensorimotor period, children come to understand important concepts that form the basis of more complex thinking processes. We will now consider two of these processes: object permanence and deferred imitation.

Object permanence means things exist even when they are out of sight

To an infant, the world can seem a very confusing place. People come and go, and as they leave the infant's field of view, it is not clear to the

FIGURE 6.2   An examiner hides a toy at location A while Alessandro watches. Alessandro retrieves the toy from location A. After repeating this game a few times, the examiner then hides the toy in location B. Alessandro, however, continues to search for the toy in location A. This mistake, called the *A-not-B error*, may indicate a lack of object permanence, although it is also possible that an infant who has forgotten where the toy was placed will automatically search in the first location (Diamond, 1991; Johansson et al., 2014; Mulder et al., 2020).

infant if they continue to exist or have literally vanished, never again to return. **Object permanence** is the understanding that objects and people continue to exist even when they are out of sight. Children show their understanding of object permanence when they search for hidden objects—you can look for a missing toy only if you know it exists even though you cannot see it.

Children show an understanding of object permanence early on:

- Before 7 months of age, children do not search for hidden objects.

- Starting at 8 months, infants will pull away a cloth used to cover a toy if allowed to do so immediately after the toy is covered. They will not remove the cloth after a few seconds.

- As infants get older, they remove the cloth even if there is a short delay between covering the toy and their search (Diamond, 1985).

- Around 2 years of age, children display full understanding of object permanence; they no longer commit the A-not-B error (**FIGURE 6.2**).

Disagreements among researchers about when children achieve object permanence illustrate just how difficult it is to do research with infants and young children. Regardless of when precisely children develop knowledge of object permanence, we know that object permanence develops gradually over a period of months and may well show in one context earlier than in another. The timing has some very practical implications for caregivers: If a fussy infant wants to play with an object they are not allowed to have, the fuss can easily be stopped by putting the object out of sight. Once the child has achieved object permanence, around 2 years of age, removing an object will no longer help—it will just trigger a search.

This is when caregivers must begin placing things out of reach or locking them away, particularly if the objects of interest are potentially dangerous, such as cleaning solutions or knives.

Researchers have learned that certain life circumstances can make it harder for young children to understand object permanence (Cook et al., 2017). For example, **child abuse**, which includes all intentional actions to harm a child psychologically or physically (see Chapter 8), has been shown to delay the development of object permanence. Experiences of abandonment and abuse can make it harder for children to construct mental representations of people or objects when they are absent, which can cause these children to experience anxiety when they are separated from a favorite object or toy (Arntz, 2020; Green, 1983).

Deferred imitation is a milestone of the sixth substage

Piaget identified deferred imitation as another milestone of the sixth substage. In **deferred imitation**, a child observes an action and some

object permanence the understanding that objects and people continue to exist when they are out of sight.

child abuse any actions that harm a child physically or psychologically.

deferred imitation the performance of an observed action after a significant delay.

■ Games like peek-a-boo help children develop object permanence.

time later mimics that action. For example, Ava, whom we met at the start of the chapter, once observed her older sister banging on pots with a spoon. A few days afterward, when she was alone with her father in the kitchen, Ava picked up a cooking utensil and started banging on the pots as well.

Piaget reasoned that deferred imitation only appears in the sixth substage because children first have to be able to mentally represent events before they can memorize and reproduce them at a later time. But as with object permanence, later researchers found that even infants under 12 months of age may be capable of deferred imitation. In fact, infants as young as 9 months old were shown to imitate actions they had witnessed up to about a month earlier (Rovee-Collier & Giles, 2010). How did researchers discover this? In one experiment, they presented children with a train set. They showed the children how to make the train move by pressing a lever. After a few weeks, the children were invited back to the lab. The older the children were, the longer they remembered and imitated the action required to make the train move. Nine-month-olds pressed the lever to see the train move for up to 6 weeks after they had first been in the lab. In contrast, 18-month-olds remembered for as long as 13 weeks (Hartshorn & Rovee-Collier, 1997; Rovee-Collier & Giles, 2010).

Children with autism spectrum disorder (ASD) tend to engage less in deferred imitation than other children do. Language appears to play a role, since speaking children with ASD engage in deferred imitation more than nonspeaking ASD children do (Heimann et al., 2016; Pittet et al., 2021; Taverna et al., 2021).

Contemporary research supports Piaget's ideas of cognitive development—with some important adjustments

Piaget was a masterful observer of children's cognitive development. He was a pioneer in child development studies, and his work provided the foundation for a large body of subsequent research. Forty years after his death, child development researchers recognize that cognitive development happens basically in the order he described.

But as we have seen above, subsequent research suggests that Piaget may have underestimated just how quickly infants develop. Piaget believed that both deferred imitation and object permanence develop only in the sixth substage of the sensorimotor stage. But studies have shown that infants may have some sense of object permanence at the beginning of the fourth substage (around 8 months of age) (Baillargeon & DeVos, 1991). Likewise, infants as young as 9 months may be capable of deferred imitation.

We can identify some of the reasons that might have led Piaget to underestimate children's rate of cognitive development. First, Piaget mostly observed his own three children, yet as we know, children differ considerably in their development. Incorporating many more children into his study would have bolstered Piaget's findings. Second, the tasks that Piaget used may not have been ideally suited to younger infants. Piaget may have underestimated infants' abilities partly because they lacked the language and motor skills to solve the problems he presented them with. For example, when a baby does not reach for a toy that is concealed beneath a cloth, is it because the child does not yet have object permanence or because the child lacks the motor skills required to reach out and pull away the cloth?

Some researchers dispute Piaget's notion that development takes place in discrete stages. Robert Siegler has suggested that children's abilities grow in waves—that they have different ways of thinking that overlap and compete with each other over longer periods of time (Chen & Siegler, 2000; Davis & Evans, 2021; Forestier & Oudeyer, 2016). More advanced ways of thinking take over slowly. For example, during a transition period children developing object permanence may be able to understand object permanence in one situation but not in another.

■ Little Alex observes his parents cooking in the kitchen every day. When he is playing in his kitchen, he imitates his parents' actions while cooking his own pretend food.

Yet despite having somewhat underestimated the abilities of young children, Piaget remains one of the researchers who most potently influenced the field of child development.

Piaget's Theory in Action

Admittedly, Piaget's theory of cognitive development is complex, and it may be hard at first to see its implications for practical interactions with children. But there is a range of takeaways that we can put into practice quite easily.

Remember that the sensorimotor stage is all about perceiving the environment with the senses and developing motor skills. The best thing parents and caregivers can do to help children's development in this stage is to provide them with a variety of opportunities to play and learn and to explore objects freely as they please. Here are some detailed suggestions.

Prepare activities that encourage sensory experiences

Provide lots of sensory experiences so children can learn about the world. For example, you can provide a box filled with sand or rice, a hot and a cold washcloth, or "touch and feel" books that integrate different materials like felt and sandpaper.

■ When the nurse met with Cassie and Alessandro, she made several suggestions for how Cassie could support Alessandro's development. Playing with different materials gives children a chance to explore the world and learn.

Teach cause and effect through play

Let children explore cause and effect to see the effect of their actions on other people and objects. Ball play, for example, lets children practice motor abilities, interact with other children or adults, and explore object permanence (such as when the ball rolls under the bed and disappears from sight).

Explore differences

Use different objects to explore differences together. You can compare the sizes, shapes, or colors of objects and explain how they are the same or different.

Provide opportunities to develop motor skills

Children in the sensorimotor stage experience the world through their movement and senses, so they need safe places to move and play. Gated play areas in the home, toddler playgrounds, or safe areas in the backyard allow children to explore freely without being exposed to dangers like staircases, poisonous plants, or sharp objects.

Information-Processing Approaches: Memory and Early Thinking

Information-processing approaches comprise an assortment of theories that share a similar perspective on cognitive development. A common feature is their use of computers as an analogy for the human mind. For example, proponents of information-processing approaches might suggest that we

- *receive input* when we hear, see, or otherwise sense something;
- *store information* in our memory;
- *retrieve information* from our memory when we need it; and
- *process information* when we think.

Information-processing approaches investigate a variety of topics that we will explore in detail throughout this book. Here, we will take a closer look at how infants' memory develops and how information processing relates to intelligence.

To some extent, even very young children have a good memory

Although infants' memory cannot be compared with the memory of adults, we know that even young infants have a memory for different kinds of perceptions. For example, they can recognize their mother by her smell, voice, and physical appearance—an ability that is important for bonding (Bushnell, 2001; DeCasper & Fifer, 1980; Leo et al., 2018; Macfarlane, 1975; Roberts & Eryaman, 2017).

As infants get older, their memory improves. One kind of memory that is evident as early as 3 months of age is motor memory. This was demonstrated in an experiment in which infants were placed in a crib with a mobile suspended above them (**FIGURE 6.3**). The infants could make the mobile move by kicking, thanks to a ribbon running from the mobile to their legs. When the same infants were brought back to the lab, those who remembered how to move the mobile started to kick again right away, even though their legs were not connected to the mobile. The study showed that 3-month-old children could remember how to move the mobile for up to 1 week. Compare these results with the results of the train experiment described earlier in the chapter: That study showed that 18-month-old children could remember for up to 13 weeks (Rovee-Collier, 1999)!

Reminders help infants just as they help adults. In the mobile experiment, returning infants who were allowed to watch the mobile typically remembered to move their legs when they were connected to the mobile the next day. But other factors made remembering harder: If the liner of the crib was changed from a striped pattern to a checkered pattern, the infants could *not* transfer their memory to the new environment. Interestingly, color changes did not have the same negative effect on memory that pattern change did (Shields & Rovee-Collier, 1992).

You might argue that these memories are relatively meaningless. But these findings show that even young infants have the ability to remember. What about children's memories of their experiences as they grow up? Can children recollect episodes from when they were very young? We will discuss this question next.

Infantile amnesia: Why it's so hard to remember events from our earliest childhood

Take a moment to think back to your own childhood. What is the earliest memory you have?

Chances are you do not remember anything that happened before your third birthday. Even for the period between your third and seventh year of life, recollections of events may be

From J. C. Heathcock et al. 2005. *Phys Ther* 85: 8–18

FIGURE 6.3 To test infant memory, Carolyn Rovee-Collier attached a ribbon from infants' ankles to a mobile suspended above the crib. When they returned to the lab later, infants as young as 3 months could remember the setup (Rovee-Collier, 1999).

fuzzy and much more sparse than from later periods (Madsen & Kim, 2016; Peterson, 2020). This is curious, given that many studies have demonstrated that experiences in early life—whether we remember them or not—affect our health, personality, and social behavior into adulthood (Afifi, 2012; Goff et al., 2013; Strüber et al., 2014).

Very young children do form memories. At a certain age, however, they lose the ability to recall their earliest life events, experiencing a phenomenon that researchers call **infantile amnesia**. For example, when my family was moving to our current hometown, we stayed in a hotel for a few days with our then 3-year-old triplets. For some years afterward, the children called out "Hotel, hotel!" when we passed the hotel. At around age 7, they no longer remembered ever having stayed in that hotel. Why did they not remember anymore? Researchers have proposed two hypotheses to explain infantile amnesia (Travaglia et al., 2016).

1. *Memories are lost.* We know that the hippocampus is very important in the creation of long-term memories. It develops continually throughout early childhood and continues to generate new neurons for some time. Some researchers believe that when those new neurons are integrated into the existing neuronal networks, those networks can get destabilized. The researchers believe that it is this destabilization of the neuronal networks that leads to the disappearance of early memories (Akers et al., 2014; Sahay et al., 2011; Stone et al., 2011).

2. *Memories cannot be retrieved anymore.* Other researchers believe that supposedly lost memories are merely "latent." This means they are still present, but they are out of reach. In other words, memories from early childhood are stored in a way that makes them inaccessible. It has been shown that memories create physical traces (that is, long-lasting physical changes) in the brain that are still there, even if a particular event cannot be recalled (Alberini & Travaglia, 2017; Ramsaran et al., 2019). The existence of traces could explain why later in life, under the right circumstances, some of these "lost" memories will suddenly come to mind, or how early experiences that cannot be remembered can still have an effect on a person's well-being and health.

The inability to retrieve memories may also have to do with children's language abilities. Adults and older children mostly use words to encode and recall memories. However, infants lack the language skills to encode memories using words, so instead they encode memories in terms of action patterns. Possibly, because these early motor memories are not connected to words, they cannot be recalled by older children and adults, who (unsuccessfully) try to use verbal clues to recall preverbal memories (Hayne & Simcock, 2009).

The notion that early-life memories are not lost but latent makes sense when we consider the intensity of certain early-life experiences. Think, for instance, of children who grow up in areas of civil unrest or war, or who witness devastating natural disasters. To them, infantile amnesia must be a blessing. But could they really lose all memory of such events? Research shows that in many ways memories of traumatic and nontraumatic events are very similar. Children who were traumatized before age 2 will likely not be able to recall their experiences verbally. However, stress hormones released during traumatic events may damage the hippocampus and thus negatively affect children's memory performance. And even events that cannot be remembered may still affect children's future health, predisposing them to depression, anxiety, learning difficulties, or personality disorders (Alberini & Travaglia, 2017; Cordon et al., 2004; Peterson, 2020).

infantile amnesia inability to recall events from early in a person's life, generally before age 2–4 years.

■ Emily went on a winter vacation with her parents when she was 2 years old. She loved playing on the beach and talked about her "special vacation" for months. When she looked through photo albums with her mother a couple years later, she had no recollection of the vacation anymore.

■ Even though Aram may not remember the war in his native Syria and his family's dramatic escape to nearby Europe, the traumatic experiences in his early childhood still make it more likely that he will experience learning difficulties at school or suffer from anxiety or depression.

Petros Giannakouris/ASSOCIATED PRESS

Ultimately, it is improbable that infantile amnesia can be explained by just one mechanism. Rather, it is likely that a number of factors, such as brain development, neurotransmitters, and retrieval cues, are involved (Madsen & Kim, 2016; Tsai et al., 2019).

An evaluation of information-processing approaches

Information-processing approaches compare human cognitive functioning with the information processing that computers do. Using such an analogy has several advantages. For example, it allows researchers to study complex cognitive functions as a set of individual activities that can be measured and tested more easily when viewed separately. Studies often are conducted in a lab, which makes it possible to control variables that may influence the research findings.

However, the information-processing approach does not always accurately reflect how humans process information. Humans often perform several cognitive processes at a time, unlike computers, which process information in a number of steps. More importantly, human thinking does not occur in a perfectly controlled environment but is influenced by factors like emotions, motivations, language, and culture. And while breaking down human thinking into an array of different skills can be helpful, it makes it harder to gain an overall picture of cognitive development.

If we strive for a true understanding of human thinking and its development, it is imperative to look toward all the different approaches that investigate human development. Each one of them offers a perspective that can help explain a part of the complexity in life that we observe. As of now, we do not have a theory that can adequately explain all psychological phenomena; indeed, we may never have such a theory.

■ Information-Processing Approaches in Action

An important prerequisite to learning is the ability to pay attention for an extended period. However, young children have a notoriously hard time paying attention to any one thing for very long. A wide-eyed infant's keen focus may shift from a toy to their own toes to the face of the person closest to them, all in a matter of seconds. Until recently, researchers had mostly assumed that paying attention was an activity solely within the control of the child, and therefore not something that others could influence. However, recent research has shown that caregivers can improve children's attention span in a number of ways (Yu & Smith, 2016), for example,

- through shared attention—i.e., by engaging with children while they play instead of simply observing; or
- by following their children's lead and engaging in activities in which their children show an interest. Children will frequently pay more attention to objects they find interesting than to an object an adult wants them to pay attention to (Nierenberg, 2016; Yu & Smith, 2016).

Caregivers can also play a role in helping children develop event memory, by asking questions and prompting their answers. A father may ask his child: "Do you remember Uncle Max? We met him at the party yesterday. He's daddy's brother. He is the one who gave you the toy bear." Through conversations such as this, children learn that remembered stories have a certain structure that specifies details like time, location, people, and what happened. They also learn which events are important to remember and which are not. Generally, the more questions parents ask about an event, the more details their children will remember (Leyva et al., 2020; Ratner, 1984). Photos are a good aid to this kind of conversation.

■ Remembering together teaches children how to remember events and which information is particularly important to remember.

Culture Counts

How Culture Affects What We Notice

Culture not only influences the language we speak and the traditions we grow up with but also has a bearing on what we pay attention to. Experiments with adults from Asian countries like Japan and China as well as from the United States have shown that those from the U.S. pay more attention to *objects* they see, whereas those from Asian countries pay attention to the *context*. If they are presented with an aquarium scene, for example, people from America are most likely to describe a big fish at the center of the scene; people from Asian countries tend to describe the fish in terms of what it is doing (swimming) and take the context into account (it's swimming around some plants) (Chua et al., 2005; Nisbett et al., 2001). But how far back into childhood do these tendencies go?

One experiment (Waxman et al., 2016) tried to find out by outfitting Chinese and American 24-month-olds with eye trackers. Eye trackers help researchers pinpoint what infants pay attention to: They tend to look longer at scenes that are new (Kateleros et al., 2011). The children were then presented with dynamic scenes on video. For example, in one scene, a woman petted a plush dog. Later on, they were presented with two scenes at the same time (on the left and on the right of the screen). One scene featured a new object that was petted (for

example, a pillow), and the other video featured a new action that was performed on the object (for example, the plush dog was kissed).

American and Chinese children differed in what interested them the most—that is, in what they looked at the longest. Chinese children preferred to look at the scenes that showed a new action, whereas American children liked better those scenes where the object had been changed. This is an indication that by the time children are 2 years old, culture has begun to influence the way they perceive the world.

■ Question

Do you think it makes a difference to people in their everyday lives what they pay most attention to? How so?

Review!

How does infants' thinking develop in Piaget's sensorimotor substages?

- During Piaget's *sensorimotor stage,* children learn by means of their senses and motor activities. They build on reflexes (schemata) they have had since birth. The sensorimotor stage ends around age 2 with the development of symbolic thought.

- The sensorimotor stage is divided into 6 substages (see Table 6.1):
  1. birth–1 month: Infants have inborn reflexes.
  2. 1–4 months: Infants start to adjust their reflexes and often repeat them → *primary circular reactions.*
  3. 4–8 months: Infants' actions start to involve other people or objects → *secondary circular reactions.*
  4. 8–12 months: Infants act to achieve goals and combine schemata.
  5. 12–18 months: Children change their combinations of schemata (trial and error) to better accomplish their goals → *tertiary circular reactions.*
  6. 18–24 months: Children can mentally represent objects → *symbolic thought.*

- Children develop *object permanence* and understand that objects continue to exist even when they are out of sight.

- Children become capable of *deferred imitation*: They observe behavior, remember it, and reproduce it at a later time.

How does young children's memory change over the first 3 years of life?

- Information-processing approaches use computers as an analogy to the human mind.

- From birth, infants can remember their mother by her smell, voice, and looks → they have a memory.

- Starting around 3 months, infants can remember how to make a mobile move. Their memory persists longer as they get older: 3-month-old children can remember for 1 week; 18-month-olds can remember for more than 3 months!

- Reminders or a change in environment can affect memory.

- Although even very young children have memories, they tend to forget, or those memories become irretrievable → *infantile amnesia.*

- The hippocampus is likely involved in infantile amnesia.

- People usually cannot remember much from their lives before age 3 and have few detailed memories from before age 7.

Practice!

1. Piaget's sensorimotor stage has _____ substages.
   a. four
   b. five
   c. six
   d. seven

2. At the end of the sensorimotor stage, children are capable of _____ .
   a. reflexive thought
   b. symbolic thought
   c. elaborative thought
   d. sensorimotor thought

3. Object permanence is an understanding that objects _____ .
   a. cannot be easily destroyed
   b. are not usually translucent
   c. can be used as tools
   d. exist even when they are out of sight

4. Information-processing approaches compare human thinking with _____ .
   a. cars
   b. computers
   c. birds
   d. supernatural phenomena

5. Young infants can recognize their mother by her _____ .
   a. smell
   b. voice
   c. face
   d. all of the above

6. Infantile amnesia leads children to _____ .
   a. remember only bad events from their early childhood
   b. remember only good events from their early childhood
   c. not remember events that happened in early childhood
   d. remember events from their early childhood particularly well

Act It Out!

Cassie and Alessandro are back at the community health center for Alessandro's 1-year checkup. But Cassie is worried about her baby: He doesn't appear to pay much attention to anything. At their most recent trip to the zoo he was more interested in the pigeons and a set of stairs by the gift shop than he was in the tigers or the exotic birds. With a classmate, role-play a conversation between Cassie and a nurse at Alessandro's 12-month well-child visit. Why is Cassie worried, and how could the nurse react based on what you have read so far?

Show What You've Learned!

Cassie could hardly believe how Alessandro, at 3 months of age, was putting everything in his mouth. Nine months later, his behavior hasn't changed: He is still determined to take a bite out of everything he can get a hold of! Why does he do this, Cassie wonders?

Drawing on information presented in this chapter, write an explanation for Alessandro's behavior in terms of Piaget's developmental stages.

6.2 Learning to Speak

- Explain how very young children's language skills advance from their first weeks to their second year.
- Identify the various language development theories and list their main characteristics.

We work to make sense of the world almost every waking moment of our everyday lives. Most of the time we organize our thoughts using words to describe objects and the meaning of experiences. Young infants are not born with this luxury. For them, speech sounds blur together in such a way that it isn't clear where one word ends and the next one begins. (You may experience the same thing when overhearing a conversation in a language you don't know.) And when someone points to an object and says a word, are they naming the object, a part of it, or possibly its color?

Nevertheless, young children, though cognitively immature and in many ways less capable of thinking than adults, are well equipped to take on the challenge of learning a new language. In the following sections, we will explore the steps in which children learn to understand and speak their native language(s). We will learn which factors influence children's language learning and how researchers, in their theories, try to make sense of children's impressive achievements. Lastly, we will consider some things caregivers and parents can do to help children learn to speak.

The Universal Sequence of Learning Language

All over the world, children learning language go through the same phases (TABLE 6.2). It doesn't matter what their native language is or which culture they belong to. Even children born deaf and learning American Sign Language go through the same phases!

From J. M. Wolfe et al. 2021. *Sensation and Perception*, 6th ed. Oxford University Press/Sinauer, Sunderland, MA

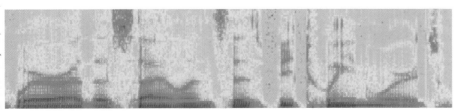

Wherearethe s i l en c e s be t w een wo r d s ?

■ When we speak, there are no audible breaks in between words; instead, the words flow into each other. In the example shown here, you can see that short breaks within words are more frequent than breaks between words. How do infants learn which sounds belong together and make up a word?

■ Table 6.2 Milestones in Infant Language Development

Age (months)	Language milestone
0	Crying, noises related to body functions like sneezing and coughing
2	Begins cooing, fussing, laughing
5	Understands first word
6–8	Begins babbling (consonant–vowel combinations, like da, di, or ba)
8–12	Loses ability to discriminate sounds of foreign languages
9–12	Starts using gestures like pointing and nodding
10	Intonates clearly Imitates speech sounds
12	Understands many words and short requests ("look at me")
13	Speaks first word Vocabulary grows slowly
18	Start of vocabulary spurt Speaks about 50 words
18–24	First 2-word sentence
24	Speaks about 200 words Tries to communicate Many 2-word sentences (telegraphic speech)
36	Speaks up to 1,000 words Communicates needs and wants reasonably well Longer, more complex sentences Some grammatical mistakes

sensitive period the period when a child is particularly receptive to particular kinds of stimuli in the environment, aiding in the acquisition of new skills like language.

■ Grace and Bao are cousins who do not get to see each other often—Grace's family lives in San Francisco and Bao's family lives in Beijing. Bao is only learning Mandarin Chinese, whereas Grace is growing up bilingual: Her mother speaks English with her, and her father speaks Chinese. Yet, despite these differences, both girls go through the same phases as they learn to speak.

Some researchers believe there is what they call a **sensitive period** for language learning during which humans learn language with particular ease. This period likely ends somewhere between 5 and 10 years of age, but the duration of the sensitive period is difficult to determine precisely because children are usually exposed to language early on (Hartshorne et al., 2018). But cases like that of Genie, a girl who was discovered in 1970 by Californian welfare authorities and who had been isolated in a locked room until she was 13, help researchers refine their theories. Genie spent her childhood restrained by a straightjacket, caged at night, and confined in a small room by her father from the time she was just short of 2 years old. When she was found, she could not talk or extend her arms and legs. She also had trouble chewing and swallowing. Genie was able to learn new words, but she never fully learned to build grammatical sentences with those words. The failure to build grammatical sentences suggests that her sensitive period for language learning had passed, although we do not know the effect that years of abuse and malnutrition had on her development (Carroll, 2016; Fromkin et al., 1974).

Even among typically developing children, there is wide variability in the speed with which they learn how to speak. As we consider the different phases of language acquisition in the following sections, keep in mind that the language learning of normally developing children may be somewhat faster or slower than the time ranges indicate.

Young infants communicate well without language

Infants are born into a world whose language they do not understand. For their first year of life, and sometimes longer, they are not able to speak even single words. This does not mean they aren't listening, however: Children understand words long before they are able to speak them. Even before they speak, they are able to communicate reasonably well with others around them. In this section, we will find out how infants communicate without words and pave the way toward learning to speak.

CRYING IS COMMUNICATING   Spend a day with a newborn and you will quickly discover an infant's most important means of communication: crying. Infants cry when they are hungry, uncomfortable, tired, or in pain. They cannot help but cry: Their undeveloped vocal tracts are not capable of producing speech-like sounds (Lieberman, 2012). But infants' crying is effective: Adults find their crying aversive, and upon hearing it, they are typically quick to soothe a crying baby.

Language learning at this point is already in process. Within a few days of birth, infants imitate with their cries the "melody," or intonation, of their native language (Mampe et al., 2009).

■ Sophie cries, and does so often; sometimes much to the despair of her tired parents. For newborns and young infants, crying is one of the main ways to communicate with their caregivers.

LANGUAGE LEARNING IN THE FIRST FEW MONTHS   In the first few months of their lives, infants are prepared to learn any of the world's 7,000 or so languages and can tell apart the various speech sounds from any language (Lewis et al., 2009). But through the process of *perceptual narrowing* (see Chapter 5), they soon start specializing in the sounds of their native language (or languages, if they are multilingual) and lose much of their ability to distinguish sounds in foreign languages (Krasotkina et al., 2018, 2021; Kuhl et al., 2006; Singh et al., 2017). Infants prefer to listen to their native language over other languages (Kinzler et al., 2007) and favor songs that have been introduced by speakers of their own language as opposed to speakers of a foreign language (Soley & Sebastián-Gallés, 2015). Research has shown that they expect to get more information from a native speaker than from a speaker of a different language. A study with 11-month-old infants found that their brain waves changed when they expected to receive information—just as in adults. However, their brain waves changed much more when they interacted with a native speaker than a nonnative speaker (Begus et al., 2016; Fell et al., 2011). All of this specialization ensures that language learning is as efficient as possible.

"CONVERSATIONS" WITH ADULTS   At around 2 months of age, infants start to coo, squeal, gurgle, growl, and make noises that somewhat resemble vowels like "ahh" and "ohhh" (Lee et al., 2018). They start to have their first "conversations" with adults—a back-and-forth of listening and vocalizing. In return, most adults raise their voice when they speak to infants and draw out the vowels, cooing "Ooooohhh, looook at what a cuuuutieeee you aaare!" This is called **child-directed speech** (or *parentese*). Infants prefer to listen to child-directed speech because it makes speech sounds more understandable (Fernald & Kuhl, 1987; Golinkoff et al., 2015; Meltzoff & Kuhl, 2016; Nencheva et al., 2021). Children of parents who use a lot of parentese tend to babble more and are better at discriminating speech sounds (Liu et al., 2003, 2007).

Children's language development depends on not just *how* parents speak to their children but also *how much* they speak to their children. Hart and Risley (1995) assessed 42 families for 2.5 years, observing parent–child interactions once a week for 1 hour. They estimated that by their fourth birthday, children living in families with a high socioeconomic status (SES), with well-educated, well-earning parents, had heard about 30 million words more than children in families of the poorest socioeconomic status. This estimate is known as the *30-million word gap.* Differences in the number of conversations at home are also reflected in children's brains: When listening to audio recordings, Broca's area (an area in the brain that

child-directed speech high-pitched style of speech in which adults speak with infants, drawing out vowels to highlight differences between speech sounds.

■ Izzy and her father love to engage in energetic conversations. Speaking a lot with children, imitating them, and using child-directed speech helps young children learn their native language.

© TommL/Getty Images

is involved with speech production) is more active in those children whose parents have frequent conversations with them (Romeo et al., 2018).

Why would socioeconomic status make such a difference? Parents who have to work several jobs may have less one-on-one time with their infants. Interactions between parents and children in lower-SES families also tend to be shorter and more pragmatic. Responsiveness is key: Children of low-income parents who respond readily and fully to their child's communication efforts will develop larger vocabularies than those of children in less-responsive families (Tamis-LeMonda et al., 2004).

Recent research suggests that the gap may only be about 4 million words, but the point is that quantity matters: Infants learn to speak faster and develop a richer vocabulary if their parents speak more with them (Brushe et al., 2021; Goldstein et al., 2003; Hoff, 2003; Schmitt et al., 2011).

babbling a child's repetitious production of speech-like syllables, first appearing between 6 and 8 months of age.

BABBLING   Between 6 and 8 months of age, infants begin babbling. In **babbling**, infants repeat consonant–vowel combinations like *da-da-da* or *gu-gu* (Lee et al., 2018). These vocalizations become more elaborate with time. Around 1 year of age, infants combine whole series of speech-like syllables. Babbling infants may sound like they are having entire conversations with themselves. Their intonation resembles that of their native language, lowering and raising the pitch in which they speak. However, the speech sounds have no meaning.

Babbling is an important precursor to speaking, and children generally babble for about 5 to 8 months before they attain a vocabulary of five words they can say (McGillion et al., 2017; Oller et al., 1998). Although children's babbling does not have any meaning, parents often treat their infants' babbling as potential words (Papoušek, 1994). Deaf infants babble as well, but at some point, they stop and increasingly use gestures to communicate. Lack or late onset of babbling can predict a range of developmental disorders, such as autism (Patten et al., 2014), Down syndrome (Locatelli et al., 2021), or fragile X syndrome (Belardi et al., 2017).

GESTURES   Imagine you're traveling in a country whose native language you do not speak. How do you communicate with the people who live there? You will likely use some gestures. Infants do the same thing, beginning between 9 and 12 months of age. Most often, the first gesture children produce is pointing to an object. Pointing requires an understanding of another person's perspective: You need to understand that you are seeing something someone else does not see and that you can make that person aware of what you're seeing.

Children produce other gestures as well, waving goodbye to visitors leaving, nodding their head to indicate "yes," or shaking their head for "no." If by 12 months of age a child does not point or use other gestures, such as reaching out the arms in order to be picked up, this may be a sign of a communication disorder or ASD (Lowry, 2018).

Once children start speaking, they continue to use gestures alone or with words to express things they cannot yet say or get an adult's attention. Gestures like pointing can help children learn new words because adults usually respond verbally to a gesture (Iverson & Goldin-Meadow, 2005). When Alessandro points to a pigeon at the zoo, Cassie responds, "Yes, that *is* a bird."

Once children speak their first words, their vocabulary grows rapidly

As Alessandro grows, so does his ability to communicate with others. At 13 months of age—10 months after his mother anxiously spoke with the nurse at the pediatrician's office—Alessandro said his first word, to the delight of his family: "Mama." Over the following weeks, he continued to add words, like "ki'ee" for their cat and "amma," his term for his beloved milk. In speaking his first words at 13 months, he was on par with other infants: Most children say their first word around their first birthday, and some may not speak their first word until 17 months of age. After speaking their first words, most children's spoken vocabulary will grow quite rapidly until around age 2, when word learning begins to slow down (Huttenlocher et al., 1991). The rapid growth of spoken vocabulary in young children is called **naming explosion**, or *vocabulary spurt*. Most children experience a naming explosion at around 18 months of age (Bloom et al., 1985; Gopnik & Meltzoff, 2021).

Generally, the number of words children understand (their *receptive vocabulary*) is much greater than the number of words they can say. At 18 months, a child can speak on average about 50 words but can understand about 150 words (Bloom et al., 1985; Kuhl, 2004). However, even with a vocabulary of just a few words, children can communicate regarding a whole range of issues. When Alessandro cries out "Mama!", he expresses excitement that mummy has come home from work. He says "Mama" when he sees his mother in a photo and anxiously asks "Mama?" when he is searching for his mother at home. Entire statements and sentences can be expressed in one word. We call these one-word sentences **holophrases**.

Children may not use their new words correctly. Alessandro calls any furry animal with four legs "kitty." When children use words in a wider context than appropriate, they *overextend* that word. Sometimes children use words in a way that is too narrow. If Alessandro only labeled his family cat but no other cat "kitty," this would be *underextension*.

First sentences contain only the most important words

Between 18 and 24 months, children start forming two-word sentences to express a variety of issues. They can ask a question ("Mommy milk?"), indicate what is theirs ("Lisa car"), point out what they see ("big bird"), or describe something that is going on ("sissy walk"). In two-word sentences, children use only the most important words to convey meaning, which is why this kind of speech is called **telegraphic speech**. The word order in

■ Marilisa is pointing at the swings in the park, communicating her preferences to her caretaker. Learning to point is an important milestone for infants. It indicates that infants know they see something someone else is not aware of and that they can show that person what they see.

naming explosion rapid word learning, starting on average at about 18 months of age. Also called *vocabulary spurt*.

holophrase a word that expresses an entire sentence or thought.

telegraphic speech an early, efficient form of speech that uses only the most important words to convey meaning.

■ In baby sign language, parents use gestures together with spoken words to help their infants communicate. Research on the benefits of the practice is mixed, but it is likely that baby sign language neither gives infants a significant edge nor hurts them (Johnston et al., 2005; Kirk et al., 2013).

FIGURE 6.4 Percentage of children speaking a language other than English, by state (2019). Spanish is by far the most frequent foreign language spoken in homes in the United States.

After Kids Count Data Center. 2020. Children who speak a language other than English at home in the United States. https://datacenter.kidscount.org

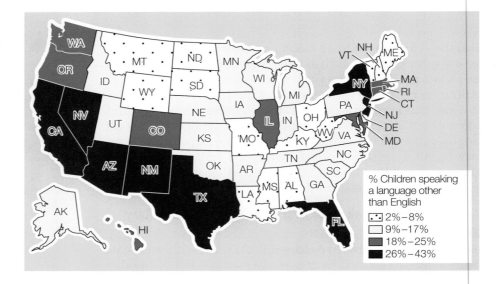

telegraphic speech is usually grammatical, reflecting the fact that children of this age already understand the structure of their native language. For example, a young child might say "Keisha drink," but not "drink Keisha."

Infants are capable of learning more than one language at the same time

In many parts of the world children routinely learn more than one language as they grow up. In fact, more than half of the world's population is multilingual (Grosjean, 2010). In the United States, a growing number of people are bilingual due to immigration (**FIGURE 6.4**), and around 22% of American children speak a language other than English at home (Statista, 2021).

People who have not grown up speaking multiple languages often have questions and concerns around bilingualism. Here are a few of the more common ones:

- *Can children effectively learn two languages at the same time?* Yes, children can acquire more than one language at the same time. Bilingual children may acquire language at a slower rate, but will usually catch up with their monolingual peers if they are exposed to a language often enough. Children may not become fully fluent in a language they do not use often (Grosjean, 2010).

- *Don't bilingual children mix up their languages?* Bilingual children may occasionally use words from both languages, as do bilingual adults. However, when bilingual speakers speak to monolingual speakers, they tend to be very aware of their languages and use only words from the language that their conversation partner understands (Grosjean, 2010; Yow et al., 2018).

- *Should I wait until my toddler is more or less fluent in one language before introducing a second language?* Research suggests it is best to start immersing children in both languages right away (Thordardottir, 2017). But ultimately, what determines a child's proficiency in a language most significantly is the extent to which the child is exposed to the language.

- *Do children benefit from speaking two or more languages?* Research has shown that bilingual children tend to be less egocentric than monolingual children and better able to take others' perspectives (Fan et al., 2015). Bilingualism also enhances executive control, which helps people distinguish between relevant and irrelevant information in their environment and which is involved with working memory (Bialystok, 2015; Thomas-Sunesson et al., 2018).

Language delays are one of the most common kinds of developmental delay

Learning a language from scratch is a formidable task for anyone, so it may be no wonder that about 20% of young children start to talk later than their peers do (American Academy of Pediatrics, 2021). Often, language problems come with some behavioral problems, because children feel frustrated when they try to communicate their needs and are not understood.

Scientists distinguish between:

- *speech delays*, in which children are unable to produce speech sounds accurately and are thus difficult to understand; and

- *language delays*, in which children may not be able to string words together into sentences as well as their peers do (Othman, 2021).

Speech and language delays can signify a number of underlying issues, including anatomical problems in the mouth, hearing issues (see Chapter 5), or ASD (see Chapter 7) (American Academy of Pediatrics, 2021). Around three-fourths of late-speaking children eventually catch up with their peers (Dale et al., 2003; Ellis & Thal, 2008).

When parents notice that their child's language development may be delayed, their first recourse should be an appointment with their pediatrician, who may recommend speech therapy or further evaluation to rule out more general developmental disorders or ASD (American Academy of Pediatrics, 2018). Untreated language delays can have many negative consequences for a child, such as difficulty in following instructions at home or in school, difficulty in communicating needs, an inability to understand jokes, and social isolation and low self-esteem (Law et al., 2015).

Explaining Language Development

We have seen, so far, what an impressive feat it is for young children to learn language from scratch. What we have not yet discussed is *how* they do so well. What is it that enables infants and young children to pick up language skills with such ease? We will now consider some of the theories that attempt to explain how children learn language.

Learning approaches: Adults teach children how to speak

Thinking back to Chapter 2, you will remember that learning approaches suggest that learning is driven primarily by our environment, rather than by our genes or inner drives. Essentially, these theories posit that children learn to speak largely through the influence of their parents and caregivers. Two aspects of these learning approaches are particularly relevant for language acquisition: operant conditioning and imitation.

In his theory of **operant conditioning**, B. F. Skinner argued that positive reinforcement (essentially, a reward) increases the likelihood that a behavior will be repeated. As Alessandro begins to babble and happily repeat syllables, his mother encourages his talking by showing her delight. She smiles at him, imitates what he just said, and carries on a pretend dialogue with him as though he were an equal conversational partner. Her affections and interactions positively reinforce Alessandro's attempts at speaking. Alessandro enjoys his mother's attention and realizes she is reacting to his babbling. This makes him more likely to babble and imitate her in the future.

But then his mother changes the game. She no longer praises him when he says "ma." However, when he says "mama," she fawns over him happily once again, providing plenty of positive reinforcement for his attempts to speak. Later her excitement will fade at the mere uttering of "mama" until the moment he uses the word in the correct context, when his mother appears in view.

operant conditioning a form of learning in which the consequences of an activity—positive or negative—determine the likelihood that the individual will continue to engage in the activity.

◼ By reacting to their children's babbling and utterances—smiling, showing excitement, and responding—parents shape their children's language by providing reinforcement. After a while, parents stop getting excited about syllables and only appear delighted when their children produce two-syllable words. Parental reactions thus influence and regulate children's speech.

© iStock.com/jbryson

shaping in operant conditioning, the process of reinforcing successively closer approximations of a target behavior.

Through her praise and affections, Alessandro's mother guides his learning. By reinforcing each step he makes toward "proper" adult speech, she plays an active role in **shaping** Alessandro's vocabulary, pronunciation, and usage.

Learning approaches essentially suggest that children are taught how to speak by their parents and other caregivers and will learn faster the better and more frequently they are taught in interaction. Critics of this view argue there must be more to language learning than operant conditioning. They point out that very early on, children produce novel utterances and sentences they cannot possibly have heard before, and therefore cannot have learned through principles of reinforcement. Note, however, that the novel sounds and sentences children make are often just a little different from things they *have* heard before, suggesting they may be generalizing what they have learned (Sturdy & Nicoladis, 2017).

Two other criticisms of operant conditioning are worth noting. First, adult speech is notoriously messy. When we speak, we often correct ourselves in mid-sentence, have slips of the tongue, and leave sentences unfinished. Yet these errors in adult speech tend to be absent in children's earliest language. Second, when children do make errors—very different from the ones that adults make—they are often praised for incorrect speech. Alessandro's grandparents can't help but laugh when they hear him say "Doggie eated all his food," and Alessandro is clearly pleased when he makes his grandparents laugh. But if caregivers reinforce incorrect speech, how do their reinforcements teach children to speak in a grammatically correct way?

One of the most outspoken critics of learning theories applied to language acquisition is Noam Chomsky, whose theory we will consider next.

Proponents of nativism believe humans are "programmed" to learn language

Noam Chomsky was highly skeptical of the suggestion that children learn language through operant conditioning (Chomsky, 1959). How could parents possibly shape each individual utterance and teach grammar with their notoriously ungrammatical speech?

Chomsky noticed that worldwide, all typically developing children learn language at around the same time and following the same sequence. Based on this finding, he argued that there must be some kind of innate mechanism that helps humans acquire language. He called this mechanism **language acquisition device (LAD)** and characterized it as a "mental organ," though it is not an actual part of the brain. With some input from the environment in order to become

language acquisition device (LAD) a hypothetical brain mechanism that helps humans to speak and understand language.

activated, the LAD analyzes language, lets children understand the rules of language, and helps them learn to speak.

Chomsky has also argued that all human languages share an underlying structure, which he calls **universal grammar**. For example, all languages comprise large vocabularies, consist of different types of words (verbs, nouns, and so on), and combine words into sentences. From birth, children have some knowledge of this universal grammar, which they apply to their native language. Then, they make modifications so that the rules they know from their universal grammar fit their particular language (Chomsky, 2014; Renxiu, 2020; Yang et al., 2017).

> **universal grammar** in Chomsky's theory of language acquisition, the structure that all human languages share.

There is some support for Chomsky's position, which proposes an explanation for why children around the world learn to speak at roughly the same time and without explicit instruction. It also explains, in a way that learning approaches cannot, how deaf infants learning to sign from their deaf parents go through the same stages of language acquisition as hearing infants (Moreno et al., 2018; Petitto et al., 2004). Moreover, the fact that infants can at first distinguish the sounds of any language and only later begin to specialize in the sounds of their native language supports Chomsky's concept of universal grammar and the LAD (Maurer & Werker, 2014).

Chomsky's theory cannot, however, explain why some children acquire language more easily than others. Even siblings who share the same linguistic environment at home show differences in the ease with which they acquire and use language. And we know that the environment has an impact on language skills: The more parents speak with and read to their children, the better are their children's language skills (Brushe et al., 2021; Tamis-LeMonda & Song, 2013). Could it be that Chomsky and the learning theorist are both partly right?

According to interactionist approaches, language is learned in interaction with others

We have seen that learning approaches emphasize the role of the environment in language acquisition, while nativist approaches hold that our capability to learn language is mostly inborn. Some researchers believe the key to understanding language development lies not in one or the other of these approaches but in the way inborn genetic capabilities and environmental factors interact with each other.

At around 4 months of age, infants show a preference for adults who react to their actions, behaviors, and sounds and interact with them. Responsive, back-and-forth interaction helps infants learn new words at a faster pace and also increases prosocial behavior, like sharing and helping others (Goldstein et al., 2003; Meltzoff & Kuhl, 2016; Thompson & Newton, 2013). One experiment exposed three groups of 9-month-old children to Mandarin Chinese over a 1-month period. Each group received a different presentation of the language: video recordings, audio recordings, or "live" by means of a playdate with a native Mandarin speaker who read to and interacted with the infants. At the end of the month, the children who had interacted with live Mandarin speakers still remembered Mandarin syllables, but the children who had watched videos or listened to audio recordings performed no better than a control group of infants who had participated in English-language play groups (Kuhl

■ Alessandro's grandparents live a day's drive away from his home. Using Skype, Alessandro can build a relationship with them even though he does not get to see them often. Interacting with his grandparents via video chat also helps him refine his language skills.

& Rivera-Gaxiola, 2008; Kuhl et al., 2003). But interactions do not need to be in person to be effective: More recent studies show that young children learn words even when they interact with others through video chat programs like Skype (Gaudreau et al., 2020; Roseberry et al., 2014).

Ultimately, there is no approach that has been able to fully explain language development. We know that children are active learners whose genetic dispositions and innate abilities influence language learning just as much as their environment.

Language Development in Action

It is an exciting time when children learn to speak, and there are many milestones to celebrate: a child's first word, the first time they call a parent or sibling by name, the first time they string words together into a sentence, and so on. Parents, caregivers, and professionals working with children can all play an active role in helping children learn to speak and understand their language. Here are some things that can help when spending time with a young child:

Talk a lot
Describe what the two of you are seeing, describe what is happening, and name the objects around you: *"That is a car. The car goes vroom vroom."* Remember that even before children are making speech sounds, they are listening to everything you say.

Be responsive and attentive
React to gestures, sounds, or other attempts the child makes to communicate with you. Be an active conversation partner. Put in words what the child is trying to say: *"Yes, mummy is coming home. Do you want to go say hi?"* Additionally, use an expressive voice: The tone of voice you use can be as important as your words in conveying a message.

Use child-directed speech
Draw out vowels and speak slowly and succinctly. It will help children understand what you are saying.

Use gestures
Show infants how to nod to say "yes," shake their head to indicate "no," point to objects of interest, or wave goodbye. Place a finger on your mouth to indicate they have to be quiet (Talbott et al., 2015).

Model good listening behaviors
Adults not only provide interaction but also serve as models for how to communicate. Show how to listen attentively without interrupting and how to respond, providing relevant information in response to questions (Hoff, 2006).

Sing nursery rhymes and read aloud
Books and nursery rhymes help children distinguish sounds and introduce new words. They help children to pay attention and practice comprehension skills. They also provide opportunities for interaction between adult and child (Concannon-Gibney, 2021; Harper, 2011).

Do not compare siblings
Siblings develop at different rates. Be aware of milestones and signs of language delays (see Table 6.2), but allow for individual differences between children.

It can be challenging for some families to find opportunities for the kind of parent–child interactions shown to promote language acquisition. Recognizing this fact, a group of researchers, companies, and community members devised projects to inspire communication between parents and children about what they see outside the home (Ridge et al., 2015).

■ Syrah loves reading with her father. Reading together gives her some one-on-one time with her dad. It also exposes her to new words and gives her a chance to practice her attention and interaction skills with an adult.

They developed four posters to be displayed in the milk and vegetable sections of supermarkets (**FIGURE 6.5**). The signs prompted parents to chat with their children, using such questions as "Where does milk come from?" or "What's your favorite vegetable?" Observers found that in one supermarket setting, adults and children were almost four times as likely to have a conversation when the signs were posted as they were when the signs were not posted. Thus, posting these signs was an easy and cost-effective way to stimulate conversation between children and their caregivers and highlights for all families that there are many opportunities to promote language development outside the home. The project resembles the Urban Thinkscape initiative designed to inspire parents to engage with their children in public spaces like bus stops (**FIGURE 6.6**).

FIGURE 6.5 The study by Ridge et al. (2015) was replicated in Tulsa, Oklahoma. As part of the city's Healthy Language campaign, signs were posted in four grocery stores, prompting parents—in English and Spanish—to turn the everyday experience of shopping into a communication and learning opportunity with their children.

FIGURE 6.6 Urban Thinkscape promotes "playful learning" with architectural installations in shared public spaces, like this playground in the Belmont neighborhood of West Phila-delphia, which features a puzzle wall, a canopy with "hidden figures" to find, and this "guided play" structure with connected images that encourage children to create stories.

Review!

How do very young children's language skills advance?

■ During their first weeks of life, infants communicate mostly through crying. Yet even at this age, they can already distinguish different speech sounds and show preference for their native language.

■ At around 2 months of age, infants start to make sounds that resemble vowels, coos, and gurgles.

■ Between 6 and 8 months, infants begin to *babble,* producing consonant–vowel combinations that do not have any meaning.

■ Between 9 and 12 months, infants start gesturing. Some parents use baby sign language to jump-start their children's language development, but it is unclear whether this benefits language development.

■ At around 13 months, children say their first words.

■ At around 18 months there may be a *naming explosion,* in which children acquire roughly 200 spoken words. Word learning slows somewhat around the age of 2.

■ Young children communicate in *holophrases,* in which a single word expresses one entire thought.

■ Children often overextend or underextend word meanings, applying the new words to contexts that are too wide or too narrow.

■ Around 1½ to 2 years, children begin to put two words together to create sentences. Sentences contain only the most important words and resemble *telegraphic speech.*

What are some theoretical explanations for language development?

■ Learning approaches (B. F. Skinner) suggest that caregivers shape children's language skills by providing positive reinforcement for their attempts at communication. The environment is especially important.

■ Nativist approaches (Noam Chomsky) propose the existence of a *universal grammar* among world languages and suggest that children have an innate *language acquisition device* (LAD) that helps them learn language. Innate abilities are especially impor-tant to this approach.

■ Interactionist approaches suggest that innate abilities as well as the environment are important factors in language acquisition.

■ Ultimately, each theory explains part of language acquisition but not the entire process.

Practice!

1. The sequence in which children learn to speak is roughly _____ .
   a. dependent on the child's culture
   b. the same all over the world
   c. the same for hearing but not for deaf infants
   d. dependent on the child's language

2. The phase of rapid word learning that often starts around 18 months of age is called a _____ .
   a. word spurt
   b. word burst
   c. naming race
   d. naming explosion

3. A word that expresses an entire thought is
   called a _____ .
   a. wordphrase
   b. uniphrase

   c. holophrase
   d. hologram

Show What You've Learned!

At the beginning of the chapter we met Valeria and her daughter, Jimena. Valeria immigrated to the United States from Venezuela with her family when she was 6 years old. Now 26 and fluent in English, she often speaks Spanish with Jimena. Her husband, Mark, is non-Hispanic and speaks only English with their daughter. Recently, Mark's mother, who lives with them, has started to forcefully complain about Valeria's speaking Spanish with Jimena. She has even demanded that Valeria stop speaking Spanish completely. She is convinced that Jimena has a language delay and that teaching her two languages at once confuses her and makes things worse. Ultimately, she claims, Jimena will not be able to speak any language with sufficient fluency. As a doctor, what advice would you give Valeria?

6.3 Media and Cognitive Development

- Evaluate the various media and interpret their impact on very young children's cognitive development.

The increasing availability of mobile media has dramatically changed the way many children spend their free time. However, for children under the age of 2, mobile media do not play as big a role as some may believe: In 1997 as well as in 2014, young children spent more time in front of a television than with a tablet or cell phone. What has changed the most is the amount of time children spend with screen media: Children under 2 in 2014 spent over twice as much time in front of screens per day as their counterparts did in 1997 (Chen & Adler, 2019) (FIGURE 6.7). This may have to do with the fact that entertainment devices today are so portable and are a convenient way to keep children occupied. Ava had no trouble waiting for her turn at the pediatrician's office, probably because she was watching YouTube videos on her mother's phone.

But even though TV is still a favorite among young children, parents are now faced with a much wider choice of apps, learning games, educational shows, and electronic toys. In the following section, we will take a closer look at how toys and media should ideally be designed to maximize learning in young children.

Influences on Learning

How much screen time young children should have and whether digital media are more likely to improve or hinder cognitive development are hotly debated topics among parents and child development experts alike. There is evidence that certain digital apps can aid children's learning if they are chosen carefully and used with restraint. TABLE 6.3 outlines some characteristics of apps that successfully help children learn. However, another recent study shows a correlation between long hours in front of a screen and developmental delays. The findings are difficult to interpret, though: Is the excess of screen time the *cause* of developmental delays, or are parents of children at risk for developmental delays more likely to use media to help manage their children's challenging behavior (Madigan et al., 2019)? Some experts also believe that factors like sufficient sleep and reading to children are much more important for children's cognitive development than screen time (Leung, 2019).

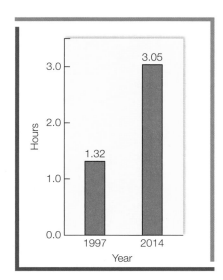

FIGURE 6.7 Total daily screen time among children aged 0–2 years, 1997 and 2014.

After W. Chen and J. L. Adler. 2019. *JAMA Pediatr* 173: 391–393

■ Table 6.3 How Children Learn Best from Digital Apps

Children learn best if they . . .	In an app designed to teach the properties of geometric figures, that means . . .
are actively thinking	they need to identify what different squares have in common.
are engaged	there are no distracting sound effects.
can connect information to life	they are asked to identify square-shaped objects in their house.
get responsive feedback	they get feedback in case of mistakes.

Source: K. Hirsh-Pasek et al. 2015. *Psychol Sci Public Interest* 16: 3–34.

We do know that media use by parents can disrupt learning. If you spend some time around families—on a bus, at a playground, or in the waiting room of a doctor's office—you will probably see a young child with a parent who is deeply involved with their cell phone. A lack of interaction or frequent interruptions can have a negative effect on learning (Reed et al., 2017). Children whose mothers often check their cell phones also tend to whine and get frustrated more often (McDaniel & Radesky, 2018).

Different Kinds of Media and Their Effect on Learning

When we speak of media more generally, we are considering not just electronic devices—tablets, video games, and electronic toys—but also traditional media, including books. In the following sections, we will explore the effects of digital as well as print media on developing children.

Screen media are effective when children can interact

As noted earlier, the screen of choice for children 3 and under is the television (Common Sense Media, 2018). In fact, in about one-third of homes with children under 2, a TV is on most of the time (Kirkorian et al., 2009; Vandewater et al., 2007).

There is little evidence that even educational TV shows have a positive effect on young children's language development: Children are shown to learn best from interactions with live people (see, for example, Clemens & Kegel, 2021; Richert et al., 2010; Zimmerman et al., 2007). Realistically, though, children will watch some television; when they do, they learn best when watching shows with familiar characters. One study showed that American children learned to sort cups from a show with a familiar character, Elmo, but not from a show with a Taiwanese character, DoDo (Lauricella et al., 2011).

Video chats are interactive enough that real learning can occur when adults talk to children or play peek-a-boo with them. FaceTiming also helps children stay connected with relatives who live far away (Dore et al., 2018; McClure et al., 2015; Roseberry et al., 2014).

Bells and whistles only help learning if they are related to the content

Parents today face many choices. Should they choose e-books over print books? Among print books, are those with interactive features better? Some studies have found that children understand and remember stories better when using a print book

■ When parents interrupt activities with their children to take calls or check messages, their children's learning process gets interrupted as well.

Every day, Marcus watches Brainy Baby episodes designed to teach him colors, numbers, and words for everyday objects. While he watches TV, his parents typically do laundry or other chores. Do you think Marcus benefits from his TV viewing?

instead of an e-book. But as long as adults interact with their children and ask questions, it probably does not matter that much which kind of book they use (Clemens & Kegel, 2021; Dore et al., 2018; Lauricella et al., 2014; Parish-Morris et al., 2013).

Interactive features benefit learning only when they relate to important aspects of the story. For instance, an animated picture of a person riding a horse or the sound of a lawn mower may well help word learning. But unrelated sounds, animations, or even lift-the-flap features in books hinder learning more than they help (Parish-Morris et al., 2013; Shinskey, 2016). The same principle applies to electronic toys. The features of an electronic shape sorter, for example, tend to dominate interactions of adults and children ("Press that button!"), whereas traditional versions of toys encourage more communication and eye contact, which are beneficial to learning (Wooldridge & Shapka, 2012; Zosh et al., 2015).

Making the Most of Media

So what can parents do to help their children make the most of new toys and apps? The most important thing is not to fear that children are missing out when they play with traditional toys. Children learn just as well—and perhaps better—with homemade and nonelectronic toys. Parents and caregivers who do plan to integrate electronics into their children's lives can follow a few pieces of advice:

1. *Do not overdo it.* Children are resilient, and electronic media consumption, within reasonable limits, is unlikely to be harmful. Limited use of an app, e-book, or educational TV show may both entertain and educate a child when no adult is available to interact

Jessica is using an app that teaches her how to count to 30. Her parents are impressed by how quickly she learned to count to 30. When her mother prepares dinner, she asks her to give her five tomatoes, but Jessica fails to count out the tomatoes. Would you recommend the app to other parents? Why or why not?

Children can learn most from watching TV when adults are watching with them. The adult can help the children understand what they watched and how to apply new concepts to their environment.

with them. Overexposure and diminished interaction with the parent or caregiver may harm a child's development. The American Academy of Pediatrics recommends that children under 18 months not be allowed the use of any screen media at all (except video chatting) and children between 2 and 5 years have their screen time limited to 1 hour per day (American Academy of Pediatrics, 2016).

2. *Evaluate media and toys, keeping in mind how children learn.* Using the criteria presented in Table 6.3, assess media options to identify the ones most likely to promote learning (Zosh et al., 2017).

3. *Talk to children about what they see on-screen.* Apply the learned information to the child's world: Statements like, "Look, our salt shaker looks like a cylinder, just as you saw on *Sesame Street*" and questions like, "Can you find a letter A here in the supermarket?" connect learned concepts to the environment. Use children's failures in app games to teach the children about persistence.

The study of the effects on young children of digital media exposure is still a new field that changes rapidly to keep up with evolving child-centered technology. There is no consensus on whether digital media improve or hinder young children's learning. Where the research is clear is that children learn best when they are interacting with parents, grandparents, early childhood educators, and other caregivers. Digital media exposure is likely safe as long as its use is limited and supplements rather than replaces the human interaction that young children unquestionably need for their cognitive development.

Review!

What impact do media have on very young children's cognitive development?

■ Children spend a lot of time with screen media—just a bit over 3 hours per day for children ages 0–2 years.

■ Carefully chosen media can benefit learning when children

■ actively think about the task,

■ concentrate and are engaged,

■ are taught information that relates to their life, and

■ learn in an interactive way.

■ Television, because it is not interactive and uses pictures children may be unable to interpret, is not an effective aid to learning.

■ E-books can support learning if they do not have too many "bells and whistles" and the animations clearly illustrate concepts and words.

■ Likewise, electronic toys that have too many distracting features can inhibit learning.

■ Interruptions caused by cell phones can have a negative impact on children's learning and behavior.

Practice!

1. Children have an easier time learning new information with media that are _____ .
   a. boring
   b. funny
   c. interactive
   d. in color, rather than black-and-white

2. A large number of diverse electronic features on a toy for infants can be _____ .
   a. ideal for intellectual development
   b. distracting

   c. helpful in training selective attention
   d. useful, but only for infants with early signs of attention disorder

3. The problem with TV shows as a means of developing learning is that, for the child, the learning tends to be too _____ .
   a. active
   b. passive
   c. visual in its presentation
   d. auditory in its presentation

What's Your Position?

Is it okay for parents to use TV shows or videos to occupy their children? In the waiting room, Alyssa was keeping 21-month-old Ava calm by letting her watch a video on her cell phone. A TV show or video can keep children still while caregivers attend to other things, like making an important call or preparing dinner. But screen time can easily add up with small children.

See for Yourself!

Go to a toy store or the toy section of a department store and look at the selection of toys. Identify the ones best suited to enhance children's learning. How did you make your selection? Compare notes with a classmate to see where your choices overlapped and where they differed.

See for Yourself!

In a public space like a family restaurant, a playground, or a grocery store, observe how many young children use mobile devices. How are they using the devices? What are their parents doing? Then see how many parents are using mobile devices. What do your findings suggest about parents' attitudes around the use of mobile devices?

After you have formulated an answer to the question, have a look online at the American Academy of Pediatrics' recommendations for children's media use (American Academy of Pediatrics, 2016). What do you think of the recommendations?

© alexmak7/Shutterstock.com

Nine months later: What Cassie and Alessandro have learned

Nine months after their first visit with the nurse at the community health center, Cassie and Alessandro have returned for Alessandro's 1-year well-child visit. They visited only once in between, when Alessandro was 7 months old—not as often as the American Academy of Pediatrics recommends, but the nurse is happy that Cassie is trying to get Alessandro examined on a regular basis.

A lot has happened since that first visit. Alessandro has started to show an understanding of object permanence and loves to play hide-and-seek games with his mother, where Cassie hides his toys and Alessandro must find them. Cassie delightedly tells the nurse about how Alessandro tries to imitate her when she cooks their meals. He increasingly uses gestures to communicate with her, but he has not yet said his first word. When asked by the nurse, Cassie explains that Alessandro loves to watch children's shows on TV and does so on a regular basis for about 1–2 hours a day. The nurse and Cassie have a conversation about limiting his screen time, but the nurse understands that Cassie lives alone with her son and uses Alessandro's TV time to catch up on other tasks she needs to complete. Cassie has grown much more confident in her parenting skills and makes an appointment for Alessandro's 15-month visit as they leave the clinic. ■■■■

Overview

Social and Emotional Development in Infancy and Toddlerhood

Shopping with Seneca

Carla and Frederic are shopping with their 2½-year-old son, Seneca. They are walking together through the aisles of the supermarket, adding items to their cart. All goes well until Seneca discovers a Superman figurine that he would like to have. He grabs it and hugs it tight. However, his parents make it very clear that they are not willing to buy the figurine for him. Within a few seconds, a very happy Seneca turns into a very unhappy Seneca. He falls down to the floor and rolls around, screeching and screaming in a high-pitched voice that is most uncomfortable for all who happen to be anywhere close by. His parents try to calm him down in any way they can think of, all to no avail. Then, in his utter desperation, Seneca's father starts hopping up and down, flapping his arms like wings and loudly clucking like a chicken. Seneca stops whining, looks at his father, first in confusion and then in wonder, and starts laughing. The tantrum is over, and Seneca's world is whole again.

Carla thinks of her friend Erin's daughter, Marie, who will soon be turning 3. Marie seems so much calmer than Seneca. Seneca reacts to any little thing in his environment with such passion, whereas Marie is such an easygoing child. Carla wonders whether she might somehow be causing Seneca's violent outbursts of temper.

The toddler years are fully packed with intense emotions that can infuse the everyday life of a young child with bursts of joy, wonder, and amusement, but also panic, fear, and desperate unhappiness. These moments may pass quickly, but when they occur they are intense. In this chapter, we will learn how children's emotions develop from the basic ones we can observe in young infants to the very complex spectrum of emotions that older toddlers can show. We will also consider how children build relationships with others and how their social development may be influenced by caregivers other than their parents and by screen media.

7.1 Differentiating Emotions: The Development of Emotions over the First Years

- Explain infants' emotional development stages and give examples of expressed emotions.
- List the signs of autism spectrum disorder and explain how it is treated.
- Relate how social referencing helps children regulate their emotions.

emotion a subjective reaction that usually arises from interaction with people or objects and that leads to physiological and behavioral changes.

primary emotions emotions that develop early in life and that can be observed in both humans and animals.

self-conscious emotions emotions that depend on a sense of self and include jealousy, empathy, embarrassment, shame, and guilt.

The first years in children's lives come with many changes—physical, cognitive, and emotional. An **emotion** is a subjective reaction that usually arises from interaction with people, animals, or objects and that leads to physiological and behavioral changes. In this section, we will see how infants go from showing pleasure and displeasure to feeling and expressing an array of emotions that resembles the range of emotions adults feel.

In the beginning of their lives, infants show mostly what we call **primary emotions**. Primary emotions can be observed in both humans and animals. They develop within the first 6 months and include joy, surprise, sadness, and fear (Lewis, 2012; TenHouten, 2017). In their second year of life, children develop a sense of self. The awareness of being a separate being gives rise to other, more complex emotions, also called **self-conscious emotions**. Self-conscious emotions, which include jealousy, empathy, embarrassment, shame, and guilt, can be felt only by children who have a sense of self and who see themselves in a network of relationships with others (Lewis, 2011; TenHouten, 2017). If you are not aware of others and the expectations they have, then you can't feel shame or embarrassment, for example. There is, however, some discussion among researchers about the age at which children start displaying emotions and in which order, with some researchers arguing that these emotions appear earlier than Lewis suggests (Hart, 2016).

■ You can often read an infant's emotional state by their facial expression and behavior. Clockwise from top left: joy, sadness, fear, surprise.

First Emotions

When you spend time with an infant, you will quickly see that their lives are dominated by two states: contentment and crying. Unhappy infants may stiffen their bodies, flail their arms and legs, and cry. Infants show their contentment by being calm or calming down when someone strokes or interacts with them. Let's take a closer look at these primary emotions.

Crying is infants' way of communicating

When children cannot yet speak, one of their main ways of communicating with others is crying. Infants cry when they are hungry, when they are in pain, when they feel uncomfortable in their wet or dirty diapers, when they are tired, and in many other situations.

Caregivers who are familiar with the infant can usually tell from the cries whether the infant is in pain, angry, tired, or just fussy. For example, *pain cries* are often piercing, with a sudden onset and a brief period of breath-holding, whereas *anger cries* tend to be rhythmic with short breaks (Fuller, 1991). Researchers are using the differences between cries to develop devices that can help physicians make diagnoses based on the characteristics of the cries. It may be possible to distinguish between ailment cries due to a cold and pain cries that are caused by internal pain (Mittal, 2016). Parents can also often tell the crying of their child from the crying of other children. I can usually tell which one of my three children is crying when they're out of sight, and on a crowded playground I can often distinguish whether cries are those of my children or those of other children.

Much to the chagrin of parents, infants tend to cry a lot. Their crying increases until around 6 weeks of age, when they cry for about 3 hours each day (Freedman et al., 2009). But 10% of infants cry much more: They are affected by *infant colic*, which means they cry excessively and persistently for no apparent reason (de Kruijff et al., 2021; Zeevenhooven et al., 2018). Colic is commonly caused by discomfort from indigestion or gas, over- or underfeeding, or sensitivity to the milk they're receiving. There is no one remedy that works for all babies, but parents occasionally find success in reducing colic by switching to a different formula or changing the diet of the breastfeeding mother. Caregivers can also try holding the baby upright or across their arm, or singing to or walking with the infant. Over-the-counter remedies for colic may or may not work, depending on the infant.

Across all nations, mothers react very quickly to their crying infants by holding and talking to them. When parents hear their infants cry, their brains show increased activity in regions that are connected with caregiving behaviors,

© BaLL LunLa/Shutterstock.com

▪ From their earliest days on, infants show signs of distress when they hear another infant cry. Researchers believe their distress shows the very early beginnings of empathy (Geangu et al., 2010).

FIGURE 7.1 Techniques to soothe a crying or fussy infant range from swaddling, rocking, and singing to the baby to managing the sleep environment by shutting off lights and creating white noise.

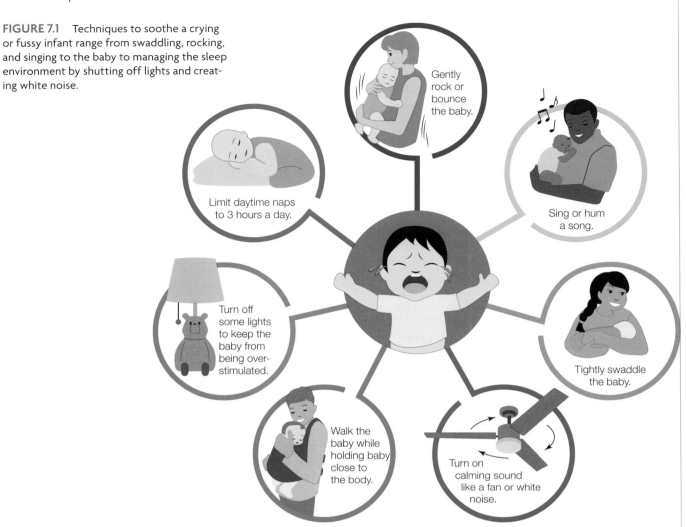

movement, and speech (Bornstein et al., 2017; Li et al., 2018; Rilling et al., 2021). The hormone oxytocin can be found in elevated levels in parents, and it likely plays a role in the brain's response to children's cries. For example, women with postpartum depression consider their infant's cries to be more urgent after taking a nasal spray with oxytocin (Mah et al., 2017).

The many methods caregivers can use to soothe a crying infant include swaddling, holding the baby close to the body, rocking or bouncing the baby, singing or humming, using calming sounds, limiting daytime naps, and turning off lights to keep the baby from being overstimulated (**FIGURE 7.1**). Ultimately, parents need to try out what works for their baby.

Newborns do not smile in response to others

Few things make new parents happier than to see their infant smile at them. However, infant smiles in the very beginning have little to do with the sight of a parent's face: They are reflexive and occur mostly during sleep (Emde et al., 1971). After about 6 weeks, however, infants start to show a **social smile** in reaction to seeing the face of a caregiver (Anisfeld, 1982; Harker et al., 2016). Around 4 months of age, infants start timing their smiles to make their mothers smile (Ruvolo et al., 2015). The frequency of social smiles increases significantly up until 6 months of age (Bell, 2020; Messinger et al., 2008).

social smile smile elicited by the sight of another human; appears around 6 weeks of age.

From M. Venezia et al. 2004. *Infancy* 6: 397–406. © International Congress of Infant Studies (ICIS)

■ Smiling helps infants communicate with others when they cannot yet speak. This infant smiles at an object and then turns to an adult with the smile in attempt to communicate excitement about the toy (called anticipatory smiling).

Around 4 months of age, infants can also be observed laughing (Kret et al., 2021; Sroufe & Waters, 1976). The ability to laugh evolves together with the joy of playing with others. You can see infants laugh mostly in interactions with others—when they are lifted high in the air, when someone makes silly faces at them, or when playing a game of peek-a-boo. Both laughing and smiling have an evolutionary function: They help infants survive by making parents happy and thus increasing the caregiving behaviors as well as playful interactions (Kret et al., 2021; Mendes et al., 2009). Just as with infant cries, oxytocin seems to play a role in parents' receptivity to infant laughter. Administering oxytocin to participants in a study changed the way their brains reacted to the sounds of infant laughter. Perhaps this is why the laughing of a baby is so uniquely rewarding to parents (Riem et al., 2016).

Smiling is not only an expression of happiness but a way for infants to communicate with others and express interest in an object. In *anticipatory smiling*, which appears around 9 months of age, infants first smile at an object and then turn toward an adult, still smiling (Chohan & Jones, 2019; Venezia et al., 2004).

Very young infants do not show signs of fear

It takes about 6 months for infants to show the first signs of fear. By that time, their memory is getting better and they recognize the people they know. More importantly, they realize there are a lot of people whom they do *not* know. This is why at around 9 months, many infants start to develop **stranger anxiety**: They are scared of and start to cry in the presence of strangers. Stranger anxiety increases throughout a child's first year of life and slowly decreases toward the end of the second year (Brand et al., 2020; Brooker et al., 2013; Sroufe, 1977) (**FIGURE 7.2**). Seneca, for example, reacted with such aversion to strangers that, for several months, Carla and Frederic did their best to make sure that one of them was always at home with him. They did not want to go through the ordeal of leaving Seneca with a babysitter.

stranger anxiety fear or wariness evoked by the presence of strangers, typically appearing around 9 months of age.

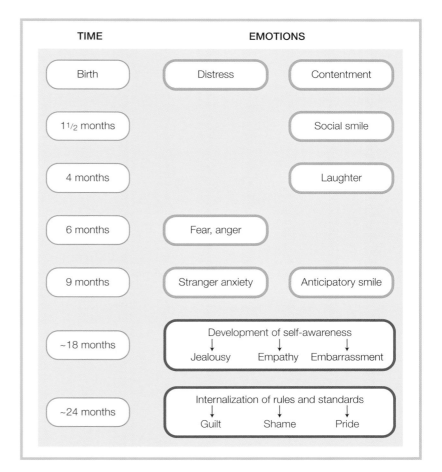

FIGURE 7.2 Milestones in infant emotion regulation. At birth, infants experience distress and contentment. By 18 months, they have developed the self-awareness to experience jealousy, empathy, and embarrassment. By 24 months, they have internalized rules and can experience guilt, shame, and pride.

■ When Mika was about 13 months old, she developed intense separation anxiety. Her mother soon dreaded having to leave the house and leaving Mika in the care of her babysitter. Nothing helped to make Mika feel better when her mother had to leave, but eventually she grew out of her separation anxiety when she was about 4 years old.

separation anxiety an infant's expression of distress when being separated from a caregiver.

Not all children display stranger anxiety, but whether or not they do is largely a matter of temperament and not secure attachment to their parents (Brooker et al., 2013; Davidson & Fox, 1989). Parents can certainly influence their children's anxiety, and anxious parents may pass their anxiety on to their children (De Rosnay et al., 2006). If stranger anxiety is extreme, children are at higher risk for developing social anxiety.

Along with stranger anxiety often goes **separation anxiety**, the tendency to protest and cry when infants are separated from their caregivers. Separation anxiety is strongest around 15 months of age (Kagan, 2008) and usually does not last past the preschool years. When young children need to be left in the care of babysitters or childcare workers, often heartbreaking scenes ensue. The children cry and cling to their parents. Children usually stop crying after a few minutes. Keeping good-byes quick and consistent, perhaps with a short ritual like a nose kiss at the door, helps. It is also helpful to practice being apart, by scheduling playdates or short stays over at a family member's house. Children also appreciate specific information about when the parent will be back, for example, after naptime.

Infants can get scared by anything that is not familiar or unexpected, be it a woman passing in a puffy white fur coat or the sound of a flushing toilet. Often, these fears can be quite persistent (though also strange to adults), so that parents have to find a way to deal with those fears. Young children may be afraid of taking a bath for fear they may be sucked down into the drain, or they may be scared of the sight of balloons because one happened to pop beside them unexpectedly at some point.

As they get older, children also become aware of things they just did not notice before. Toddlers are notorious for having trouble distinguishing between reality and fantasy, which makes many objects and occurrences in everyday life scary. My children were literally terrified of their own shadows for more than a year. No explanations or shadow plays could alleviate the fear that made going out on sunny days a bit of a challenge. At some point they just grew out of it, and today they cannot believe they were ever scared of their own shadows.

Young children across all cultures have a fear of imaginary predators like monsters. They are also scared of some threats based in reality, like darkness or being left alone. From an evolutionary perspective this makes sense: Children may be prone to fearing threats they are particularly vulnerable to at a certain age (Boyer & Bergstrom, 2011). Although such fears are universal, the environment in which children grow up influences their fears.

One cross-cultural study asked children to explain why a child featured in a story felt scared. American and Palestinian children had different explanations of why the child in the story was scared. American children more often suggested an imaginary cause of the fear, whereas Palestinian children believed the fear was rooted in reality. The researchers believe that the Palestinian children came up with more realistic sources of fear because they may have been exposed to more realistic fears than their American peers (Kayyal & Widen, 2015).

Later Emotions

Self-conscious emotions develop once children understand that others evaluate them

Around 18 months of age, children slowly become aware of themselves: They start to understand they are separate from their parents and that people look at and evaluate them. This insight enables the development of *self-conscious emotions* like jealousy, embarrassment, and empathy. These emotions depend on our understanding that we're connected with others. For example, Seneca was toilet-trained at 14 months. There were occasions in the months that followed when he didn't make it to the bathroom in time, but he only became embarrassed about these accidents at around 20 months of age (Lewis, 2011; TenHouten, 2017).

One study on jealousy had mothers, in the presence of their infants, interact with a doll as though it were their real child. The infants reacted with distress and tried to get closer to their mother (Mize et al., 2014). The children in this study were less than 1 year old, reminding us of the fact that there is still debate over when emotions like jealousy first appear.

Around their second birthday, children accomplish another important milestone in their emotional life: Once they start to internalize the rules set by others, it isn't long before they evaluate themselves in terms of these rules. This gives rise to new emotions like guilt, shame, and pride (Lewis, 2011; TenHouten, 2017). Two-year-old Timmy feels guilt when he hits his baby sister and makes her cry, because he understands that he is not allowed to hurt her.

The culture in which a child grows up also influences the emotions felt: In the United States, parents encourage children to feel proud of their achievements, whereas Asian parents tend to expect modest behavior of their children (Genyue et al., 2011). A possible consequence is that children in the United States who expect less of themselves may accomplish less because they are satisfied with a more modest level of accomplishment.

■ Children can only feel guilt once they have developed an understanding of the rules they are expected to follow.

Children with autism spectrum disorder have trouble interpreting and expressing emotions

Understanding one's own emotions and those displayed by others isn't easy and does not come naturally to some children. Children who have been diagnosed with autism spectrum disorder (ASD) often display an inability to interpret and therefore empathize with others' emotions. ASD includes a wide range of subtypes. The condition varies in severity from person to person. In addition, each child has their own particular strengths and challenges. ASD therefore looks very different from child to child. Here is what Simon's mother, Lynn, has to say about her son and his ASD diagnosis (see also the What's It Like feature in Chapter 11):

> A few months after Simon's birth I noticed that some things were off. He never looked at us or smiled when we came to pick him up. In a way, it almost was like he didn't much care if we were there or not. He seemed content just to be by himself most of the time. But then again, he was my first child and I thought, maybe it's just too early to expect him to socialize a bit more with his parents. Maybe it's my expectations that are off here, and not his behavior. But honestly, I had a gut feeling that things were off early on.
>
> My husband and my parents all thought it was just Simon's personality, so I let it go for a while. I felt so bad about myself, thinking that I was a bad parent and that he behaved that way because of me. When he was about one-and-a-half years old, he still did not say a single word, and it was like we did not exist for him. That is when my husband started worrying, I think. At some point, Simon started flapping his arms like he wanted to fly, and he did this for hours at a time. We made an appointment with our pediatrician, who arranged for further testing. In a way, it was a terrible shock when Simon was diagnosed with autism, but in a way it was also a relief because we finally could get started getting Simon the help he needed.

The number of children diagnosed with ASD has steadily risen in recent decades. In 2016, about 1 in 54 children were diagnosed with ASD. The number of boys diagnosed with ASD is roughly four times higher than the number of girls (Maenner et al., 2020). Worldwide, the WHO estimates that 1 in 160 children are affected by ASD (World Health Organization, 2021). In the United States, more white children are identified with ASD than children of other races. However, scientists are concerned that this number does not actually mean that fewer children of other ethnicities are affected by ASD, but rather that ASD in children of other ethnicities is not identified, so these children do not get access to the interventions they may need (Centers for Disease Control and Prevention, 2019). Similar reasons may account for higher autism rates in the United States than in other countries. In the United States, growing awareness of ASD as well as an increasing number of routine screens for ASD lead to a higher number of diagnoses (Wright, 2017).

An early diagnosis is crucial. Children as young as 2 years old can be screened for ASD, but many children are not diagnosed until after age 4, once signs of the condition are more apparent (Autism Speaks, 2021). Because an early diagnosis is crucial to the teaching and development of important skills, the American Academy of Pediatrics recommends that all children be screened for ASD at 1½ and 2 years of age in addition to the regular developmental checkup they receive (American Academy of Pediatrics, 2020).

AUTISM SPECTRUM DISORDER AFFECTS CHILDREN'S SOCIAL AND EMOTIONAL DEVELOPMENT   Children with ASD often display a lack of empathy when seeing another person's emotions (Dyck et al., 2001; Trimmer et al., 2017). Around 18 months of age, typically developing children show concern for others when they see them in distress and are able to help the person in distress by comforting them with words or physical affection, or by trying to distract them (Zahn-Waxler et al., 1992). Children with ASD typically do not show such an interest. However, this may not necessarily mean that they cannot feel empathy for others. Some researchers suggest that a lack of empathy in individuals with ASD may be due to their problems in identifying emotions in themselves and others as well as a lack of social skills (Komeda et al., 2019).

One study found that toddlers who would later be diagnosed with ASD showed less empathy for their distressed parents than toddlers who were not diagnosed with ASD. That is, even before their diagnosis these toddlers showed lower levels of empathy (McDonald & Messinger, 2012). The more severely

■ Children with ASD may take comfort in toys with spinning wheels or other parts that offer predictability and regularity.

affected toddlers are by autism, the higher the likelihood that they are insecurely attached to their caregivers (Martin et al., 2020; Naber et al., 2007).

Autism comes with other symptoms as well. Around 40% of people with ASD are nonverbal, which means that they cannot speak (Autism Speaks, 2022). However, many of them can communicate at least to some extent by other means. For example, they can use visual supports to communicate their needs (e.g., by using pictures illustrating different emotions or objects).

About one-third of children with autism have an intellectual disability with an IQ that is below 70. Almost two-thirds of children with autism have been bullied at school (Zablotsky et al., 2014). Almost half of children with ASD wander away from time to time, which can make things very challenging (and at times, scary) for their caregivers (Law & Anderson, 2011; Wiggins et al., 2020). Parents indicated in one study that the main reasons their children wander is to escape an unpleasant situation, to head to a favorite place of theirs, or simply because they enjoy exploring (Anderson et al., 2012).

Some habits that children with ASD demonstrate can cause self-injury. They may engage in head-banging, scratching the skin, or biting their own arm (Martínez-González et al., 2021; Soke et al., 2016). Many children diagnosed with ASD also are affected by ADHD (attention-deficit/hyperactivity disorder), anxiety disorders, epilepsy, and gastrointestinal problems (Autism Speaks, 2022; Holmes et al., 2021).

The economic costs of autism to individuals and society are great; they include medical and therapeutic costs, informal care costs, and the cost of lost productivity for caregivers. Therapeutic costs mostly arise through services for adults: It is estimated that each year, services for children are around $66 billion a year, whereas for autistic adults it is $196 billion dollars a year (Buescher et al., 2014).

THERE ARE SIGNS THAT MAY INDICATE ASD IN A CHILD EARLY ON Autism is a condition children are born with, though not all children start experiencing symptoms at the same time. Some children exhibit symptoms of ASD within their first months. Others seem to first develop normally before starting to lose skills they once had. Mostly, signs of autism are indicative when a number of them occur together. For example, children with autism may:

- lose speaking skills they once had;
- have delayed language development;
- avoid eye contact with others;
- keep repeating words or phrases (echolalia);
- show repetitive behaviors like arm flapping or rocking;
- have trouble understanding other people's feelings and actions, which makes the world an unpredictable place for them; and
- be very sensitive to particular sounds, smells, flavors, sights, or textures (Autism Speaks, 2021).

But before affected children even exhibit some of these signs, there may be indicators early in infancy that lead parents to seek an evaluation of their child. These signs include:

- little or no eye contact and no smiles by 6 months of age;
- no smiles, facial expressions, and back-and-forth conversations with adults by 9 months;
- little babbling, pointing, and response to the child's name by 12 months;
- few words by 16 months; and
- few two-word phrases by 24 months (Autism Speaks, 2021).

WE DON'T FULLY KNOW THE CAUSES OF AUTISM We know that genetic factors play a role in most cases of ASD, although there is no single gene that causes ASD. Studies with identical twins have shown that if one twin is diagnosed with autism, the other one is affected between 36 and 95% of the time (Colvert et al., 2015; Hallmayer et al., 2011; Taniai et al., 2008). The wide range of numbers reflects the fact that we still need a lot of research in this area. Nevertheless, the relationship between genetic factors and ASD is clear, even if we do not yet know the extent of that relationship.

There are, in addition, some factors that can increase a person's risk of developing autism:

- parental age: Children with older parents, and particularly with older fathers, have a higher risk of developing autism (Durkin et al., 2009; Krug et al., 2020; Lyall et al., 2020).

- diagnosis of siblings: When parents already have one child who has been diagnosed with autism, they have a higher chance (around 2 to 18%) of having another child with autism (Hallmayer et al., 2011; Hansen et al., 2019; Jain et al., 2015; Taniai et al., 2008).

Contrary to the fears of some parents, however, vaccines do not cause children to develop autism (American Academy of Pediatrics, 2021; Jain et al., 2015; Zerbo et al., 2017).

Most of the genetic and environmental factors causing autism work by effecting changes in the way the brain grows and works. For this reason, ASD is considered a neurodevelopmental disorder. For example, children with autism tend to have a greater brain volume than other children. By observing the brain growth of high-risk children, it may be possible to predict the development of autism as early as 6–12 months of age (Hazlett et al., 2017; Samian et al., 2021). Researchers are also investigating the connection between the microorganisms living in children's guts and the development of autism (Vuong & Hsiao, 2017; Yu & Zhao, 2021)—remember that many children with autism also have gastrointestinal problems. It has been shown that there is an interaction between the microbiome, gut, and brain, and some researchers believe they might one day be able to cure autism by treating the gut microbiome (Fiorentino & Fasano, 2019; Yang et al., 2018).

AUTISM INTERVENTIONS VARY DEPENDING ON THE SYMPTOMS Interventions always have to be tailored to the need of a child because ASD is a spectrum, and symptoms range from mild to severe and differ in each child. Children with more severe symptoms may get speech therapy to improve communication on

social referencing using adults' reactions and facial expressions to understand and evaluate situations or objects.

■ Early diagnosis and intervention are important for children with autism spectrum disorders and have been shown to improve long-term outcomes of symptoms and children's skills.

© Africa Studio/Shutterstock.com

all levels—verbal, nonverbal, and social. Occupational therapy helps children become more independent by helping them develop skills they need in their daily lives. There are also a number of programs like TEACCH and the Early Start Denver Model (ESDM) that aim to help children improve a whole range of everyday skills: build better relationships and social connections, improve communication and interaction, increase attention and academic performance, and decrease behavioral problems.

Additionally, children with ASD may need treatment for related medical conditions they have, such as epilepsy, anxiety, depression, sleep problems, or gastrointestinal problems.

Emotion Regulation

The life of a child is full of events that elicit strong emotional reactions. Children need to learn to control their emotions, and the path to emotion regulation in humans is a long one that lasts into adulthood.

As they mature, children depend less on adults for emotion regulation

In the beginning of their life, infants are almost completely dependent on their caregivers to help them regulate their emotions. Parents soothe their children by holding them, singing to them, distracting them, or taking them out of an upsetting situation (Brazelton, 2018; Gianino & Tronick, 1988) (FIGURE 7.3). Infant response to distressing stimuli is unplanned and reflexive. For example, when they hear a loud sound, babies may turn away, cry, or start sucking their thumb.

As children get older, their threshold for emotional arousal gets higher, and they do not get upset as quickly anymore (Thompson, 1991). Around the time they are 5 months old, infants react differently to an adult who displays positive or negative emotions (Fernald, 1993). Between 6 and 12 months, infants also become more active in requesting the help of an adult when they are upset by adding gazes and gestures to their crying (Gustafson & Green, 1991).

By the time they are 1 year old, infants use social referencing to guide their emotions. In **social referencing**, children look to caregivers' reactions to a situation or object in order to evaluate and understand it (Eggleston et al., 2021; Walle et al., 2017). At a playdate, 15-month-old Theo sees a toy on the floor he's never seen before. He looks at his mother, who smiles and nods encouragingly at him. It doesn't take long before he crawls to the new toy and starts playing with it. If his mother had shown negative

0–3 months

Reflexive, unplanned

Parents do a lot of the soothing

5 months

Reacts to adult emotions

6–12 months

More active in requesting help

12 months

Self-distraction

Social referencing

2 years

Verbal expression of feelings

FIGURE 7.3 Timeline of the development of emotion regulation. Newborns depend on caregivers to help them regulate their emotions, and their response to stimuli is unplanned and reflexive. As they get older, they begin to react to the emotions displayed by adults. By 12 months, they use social referencing to guide their emotions.

■ Lissy is 2½ months old and doesn't have many ways to soothe herself when something upsets her. However, when she is in a new situation or meets new people, she starts sucking her thumb to calm herself down. Soon, she will become more proactive in managing her emotions.

emotions, Theo would have been much less likely to approach the toy (Hornik et al., 1987; Moses et al., 2001). In one study, an experimenter showed one-and-a-half-year-old infants a toy and what to do with it while another adult watched. If the watching adult reacted angrily to the experimenter's toy play, the infants were very hesitant to try out the toy themselves (Repacholi et al., 2016).

Curiously, it seems that the location where children are raised also plays a role in the emotions they display. Infants from rural areas tend to show anger and frustration more often and tend to be more fussy than babies living in cities (Neumann et al., 2020).

At around 1 year of age, children start to distract themselves when they feel distress. After they have turned 2, children's executive attention—the ability to tune out distractions and focus attention—becomes much more effective. This allows children to more easily switch their focus from an upsetting thought or situation—an important strategy in emotion regulation (Nigg, 2017; Posner & Rothbart, 1998; Tajik-Parvinchi et al., 2021).

Between 2 and 2½ years of age, children's evolving language skills come to help with emotion regulation as well: They are now able to express their feelings and to talk about them with others (Bretherton et al., 1986). This way they get direct feedback and advice on how to regulate their emotions. Children using infant sign language may be able to regulate their emotions even earlier because they are better able to communicate their wishes or distress (Karsten et al., 2017).

Although children's ability to regulate their emotions develops most dramatically in the first years of life, learning to deal with feelings is a process that continues throughout childhood and adolescence into adulthood (Eisenberg & Morris, 2002).

■ By 12 months of age, most infants engage in social referencing, looking to others for clues about how to understand and react to a situation.

Child Development in Action

Adults can help children regulate their emotions

As anyone who has spent time with young children can attest, it is of great interest to both caregivers and children that children learn to regulate their emotions. Even a small reduction in the frequency of temper tantrums, angry outbursts, or crying spells can make life for everyone involved a lot easier.

What can parents and caregivers do to help children learn to regulate their emotions? In infants, it is important to watch for cues that signal babies' needs or feelings: A head turned away may signal no more kisses, and an arching back may indicate that a child dislikes something. Older children can be helped in different ways:

Do not minimize children's feelings

When Pedro's baby brother spills his milk over Pedro's latest crayon masterpiece, Pedro has a right to be upset. Talking his anger down by saying "Don't be upset. Tomorrow you can draw an even nicer picture" won't help him feel better. Instead, acknowledge that Pedro is angry: "I see you're angry because your drawing is ruined. Juan didn't mean to spill his milk on it. Next time, let's put your picture in a safe place out of Juan's reach."

Help children label their emotions

When children experience intense feelings, they are often not sure exactly what they are feeling and do not have a word for their emotion. By saying "You are sad because Grandma is leaving and won't be back until Christmas," you can help children identify emotions, show that you understand how they feel, and affirm that their feelings are normal.

Teach children how to cope with their feelings

There are many ways to cope with intense emotions, and offering those tools to young children gives them ways to learn how to calm down even when no adult is there to help. Upset or sad children can count to ten, take deep breaths, go to a calm-down place, ask someone for a hug or for help, or jump up and down. Rather than trying to fix the situation that may be causing a child distress, teach them how to identify, label, express, and cope with their feelings. This will help them be better prepared to independently manage future situations when a parent may not be around to help (Lerner, 2018).

Review!

How do infants develop emotions?

- We distinguish two kinds of emotions: primary emotions (which develop early on) and self-conscious emotions (which develop after 18 months of age and for which the child has to see himself as a part of a network of relationships).

- At first, infants show *primary emotions*. Those can be observed in both humans and animals. They develop within the first 6 months of life and include emotions like joy, surprise, sadness, and fear. Later, *self-conscious emotions* like jealousy and embarrassment develop that can only be felt once a child has an understanding of being part of a network of relationships.

- Crying is one of the main ways young infants communicate. It leads adults to tend to their children and their needs.

- Around 4 months of age, infants smile to evoke reactions in others and communicate with them. Around 6 months, children start to show fear, and 3 months later we can see signs of stranger anxiety and separation anxiety, which usually start to diminish around 15 months.

- As children become aware of themselves, they develop self-conscious emotions like empathy and embarrassment.

What are signs of autism spectrum disorder, and how is it treated?

- Signs of autism include little or no eye contact with others, as well as little babbling/speaking and other interactions like smiling or facial expressions. Many children with ASD also show repetitive behaviors like arm flapping or rocking and are sensitive to particular sounds, sights, or smells. There is no medical treatment for ASD, but there are a number of interventions, depending on the symptoms a particular child shows. For example, children may get speech or occupational therapy, treatment of any medical conditions they may have, as well as therapy that is aimed at improving their relationships with other people.

How does social referencing help children regulate their emotions?

- When children are born, they are completely dependent on adults to help them regulate their emotions. As they get older, they learn to regulate their emotions themselves. One way they do this is by looking at their caregiver's reaction to a toy or situation. The infant's emotions are likely to reflect the emotions the caregiver displays. Adults can help children deal with their emotions by labeling and explaining them and showing them ways to cope with their feelings.

Practice!

1. Two-month-old infants _____ .
   a. protest when separated from their parents
   b. display stranger anxiety
   c. show no signs of fear
   d. tend to cling to their parents when they fear being separated

2. _____ is a self-conscious emotion.
   a. Joy
   b. Jealousy
   c. Fear
   d. Anger

3. _____ is frequently an early sign of autism.
   a. Frequent laughing
   b. Avoiding eye contact with others
   c. Sleepiness
   d. Voracious appetite

See for Yourself!

Young children experience a wide range of intense emotions like anger and fear. They are dependent on caregivers to help them regulate those emotions. The next time you are eating at a restaurant, shopping at a store, or passing through a park with a playground, observe the ways that adults and children interact. Can you see a young child display emotions? How do the adult caregivers handle those emotions? Do adults differ in the way they react to the same emotion?

Show What You've Learned!

Your older brother and his partner have left you in charge of their 2-year-old son, Danilo. When he was younger, Danilo was a somewhat fussy child. Now when he gets upset, he starts crying and doesn't calm down. He cries for what seems like hours; even his parents don't know what to do!

What can you do to help Danilo when he's having one of his crying spells? Based on the information you've read in this chapter, outline some strategies you could adopt to calm Danilo. Describe the benefits of each one so that you can provide the information to your brother when he comes to pick Danilo up.

Additional Resources Online
- ▪ "Crying: Babies" from the Raising Children Network
- ▪ "Crying: Children 1–8 years," from the Raising Children Network

Act It Out!

Izak is 2½ years old and has just been diagnosed by a specialist with autism spectrum disorder. Today his mother, Tracy, has brought him to their family doctor, Dr. Shastry, to discuss the diagnosis. With a classmate, act out a conversation between Tracy and Dr. Shastry, drawing on the information presented in this chapter and on the websites mentioned below. As Tracy, what are some of the most pressing questions you have for the doctor? As Dr. Shastry, how would you respond to Tracy's questions and provide reassurance?

Additional Resources Online
- ▪ "Autism Spectrum Disorder," from the National Institute of Mental Health
- ▪ "Data and Statistics on Autism Spectrum Disorder," from the Centers for Disease Control and Prevention

7.2 Temperament

- ▪ Examine key findings from studies of temperaments and conclude why they are important.

Are you a happy and exuberant person or more pensive and introverted? Do you jump at every opportunity for a new adventure, or is your idea of a good time to be in a familiar place with familiar people? Your answers give clues to your temperament. **Temperament** is the characteristic way people respond to different situations. It is reflected in their behavior and display of emotions.

temperament the characteristic way people respond to different situations, reflected in behavior and display of emotions.

One of my friends, Sally, recently asked me a few weeks after the birth of her first son how long it would take for his temperament to show. You can actually see indications of infants' temperament as soon as they are born. My friend had a very calm and happy baby, which she thought was normal in infants—she had no other babies to compare her son with. When our triplets were born, the difference in personalities and temperament were obvious because we could compare them with one another. Infants differ in many ways, for example how much they cry, how easily they can be calmed, how happy they are, or how intensely they react to noises or objects they see.

Learning about temperament and how it influences behavior can help parents, clinicians, and educators understand differences in how children act, interact, and respond emotionally to different stimuli. They can then develop strategies to improve the **goodness of fit** between the child and their environment.

goodness of fit the degree of match between a child's temperament and the environmental constraints.

There Are a Number of Ways to Describe Temperament

There are various ways in which researchers attempt to assess children's temperament. They range from observations in research labs to physiological measures (for example, the analysis of heart rate variability or cortisol level in response to stress) and parent reports. Researchers debate which method, if any, is the best to measure children's temperament. Physiological measures are relatively objective, but it is not clear whether the measurements are actually a cause or consequence of the behavior and emotions the children display. Parent reports are often detailed, but most parents only know the behavior of their own children, so it may be hard for them to judge reactions adequately. Lab observations tend to be more objective than parent reports, but children can only be observed in a limited environment in the lab, and their behavior may not be representative of how they usually behave in everyday life.

Researchers also do not agree on how to classify different types of temperament. One classic longitudinal study conducted by Alexander Chess and Stella Thomas (Chess & Thomas, 1977) followed 135 children from birth into adulthood. The researchers found that 65% of children fit neatly into one of three categories:

1. *Easy child*: smiles at strangers and warms up to others quickly; generally in a good mood; adapts easily to new routines and situations

2. *Difficult child*: suspicious of strangers; often in a negative mood; has a hard time adapting to new routines and situations

3. *Slow-to-warm-up child*: somewhat suspicious of strangers; emotional reactions are mild (both positive and negative); needs time to adapt to new routines and situations (but has an easier time than the difficult child).

© TierneyMJ/Shutterstock.com

■ Children with a difficult temperament tend to react strongly to changes in their routine.

However, 35% of the children did not fit easily into one category; for example, they might be happy to interact with strangers but also have intense crying bouts.

More recently, other classifications of temperament have been developed. One of them is the classification of Rothbart and Bates (Putnam et al., 2019; Rothbart, 1989; Rothbart & Bates, 2007), which has found three broad factors in children's temperament:

1. *Extraversion*: activity and impulsiveness, interest in new things and experiences

2. *Negative affectivity*: negative emotions like anger, sadness, and fear, as well as shyness

3. *Effortful control*: how easily children get agitated, how much they are able to focus.

It is important for caregivers and educators to understand that there are no "good" or "bad" temperament traits. Rather, temperament is an expression of the unique ways in which we behave or respond to the world. However, the temperament of children may be a better or worse fit for the environment in which they grow up—an issue that we will consider shortly.

Temperament Is Genetically Influenced

It probably does not surprise you that children's genes influence their temperament. Some children appear to be naturally easygoing and happy, whereas others are anxious and seem withdrawn. Researchers have found that there are biological differences between children who are *inhibited*—shy and timid—and those who are not. In particular, inhibited children tend to have a stable higher heart rate. They startle more easily, and they have a higher cortisol level in their saliva (Fox et al., 2008; Poole et al., 2017). Remember that cortisol is a hormone the body produces when a person feels stressed. All these symptoms may be caused by an overly aroused limbic system. One study even found a correlation between the cortisol in mothers' milk and the affect of the child: The more cortisol the milk contained, the more negative was the affect of the child (Grey et al., 2013).

At the same time, the environment has an impact on temperament as well. In one cross-cultural comparison that used parent reports, for example, Chilean toddlers showed significantly more negative affect than children from the United States, Poland, and South Korea. South Korean toddlers scored significantly higher on measures of effortful control than children from the other three countries. It is not entirely clear why there are cultural differences in temperament, but theorists believe those differences may be due in part to whether a culture is collectivist or individualist and the way children are taught when and how to display their emotions (Krassner et al., 2017).

Temperament Is Relatively Stable

Children's temperament is relatively stable over time. A child who displays a certain temperament in infancy is likely to show similar traits in early childhood and even beyond. The temperament of 3-year-olds can roughly predict their personality as teenagers, how well they can deal with uncertainty, and whether they have an increased risk for mental illness (Bohlin & Hagekull, 2009; Caspi et al., 2005; Hawes et al., 2021; Morales et al., 2021). One study that followed children from early childhood through young adulthood found

■ Temperament is relatively stable. The temperament that children exhibit early in their childhood is often remarkably similar to their temperament many years later.

that children who had an easy temperament around age 3 tended to be more well-adjusted as young adults than their peers who had had a more difficult temperament when they were young (Chess & Thomas, 1977).

Ideally, Children's Temperament Is a Good Match to Their Environment

As noted earlier, there are no good and bad temperament traits; however, a child's individual temperament can be a good or bad fit with her environment and the people she most interacts with. Children who are anxious and easily distressed need a different kind of parenting and environment than children who are natural explorers and happily wave to and interact with strangers. For example, subdued children will do better than active children in tight spaces or when they have to sit for a long time. We call this match between a child's temperament and his environmental constraints *goodness of fit*.

Children with more difficult temperaments are the most sensitive to the quality of parenting they receive. Think about it: Children with an easy temperament are not as easily distressed and can adjust to changes in their environment or other people's behavior more easily. Anxious children, to the contrary, need someone who is patient with their roller coaster of emotions, and they react much more intensely when a caregiver acts in an inconsiderate way (Stright et al., 2008).

It is important for parents to remember that children who are more easily distressed and have a negative affect are not purposely acting that way to give their parents a hard time. Rather, their behavior and emotions reflect their temperament. When parents recognize the temperament of their child and adjust their behavior accordingly, they may be able to avoid distress. For example, if a child tends to take her time when switching activities and a teacher quickly changes from reading to math centers at school, the child may not want to engage in the new activity. A caregiver familiar with the child's temperament may just give the child more time to transition to the new activity and find that eventually, the child comes to like the activity quite a bit.

Review!

Why is it important to study temperament, and what are some key findings?

- Temperament is the characteristic way a person responds to different situations.

- Temperament is shaped by genetic and environmental factors. It is relatively stable through childhood and adolescence and into adulthood, although it can change somewhat as children get older.

- One way to classify different temperaments is by using the categories established by Chess & Thomas (1977): They group children into "easy children," "difficult children," and "slow-to-warm-up children." A more recent classification by Rothbart & Bates (1989, 2007) focuses on extraversion, negative affectivity, and effortful control as broad factors in children's temperament.

- Temperaments are neither good nor bad. Understanding a child's temperament enables parents and caregivers to place the child in an environment that is the best fit for their temperament.

Practice!

1. Chess and Thomas's classification of childhood temperament proposes _____ different categories.
   a. 2
   b. 3
   c. 4
   d. 5

2. Goodness of fit indicates _____ .
   a. the degree of match between a child's emotions and the parents' emotions
   b. the degree of match between a child's character and the siblings' character
   c. the degree of match between a child's temperament and the environment
   d. the degree of match between a child's health and the ability of the parents to secure adequate health care

7.3 Building Relationships with Others: Attachment

- Outline how attachment develops and explain the types of attachments children may form with their caregivers.
- Recall the factors that influence the development of attachment patterns in children.

Few things have such a significant impact on our well-being as our relationships with others. Soon after infants are born, they begin to establish relationships with the people around them. First, they just react to those who interact with them. Later, they also initiate interactions themselves. In this section, we will learn in more detail how infants form relationships with others.

Forming Bonds with Others

Three-year-old Marie is settled in comfortably on the sofa with her father, reading a book, when they hear the sound of a key as it is inserted in the lock of their front door: Marie's mother is home from work. Although Marie has enjoyed reading the book, she jumps up immediately and runs to the door to greet her mother with a big hug.

What looks on the surface like nothing more than a regular family scene is indicative of something much more significant: Marie is attached to her mother and shows her attachment by excitedly greeting her when she comes home. **Attachment** is an affectional bond between two people that is expressed in behaviors like seeking the other's closeness or showing distress when that person is not nearby.

Some of the research that informs our understanding of attachment in humans was actually conducted with animals. Konrad Lorenz (1903–1989) studied imprinting in newly hatched goslings and found that they automatically follow

attachment an affectional bond between two people that is expressed in behaviors like proximity seeking or distress upon separation.

FIGURE 7.4 Harlow's monkeys. Baby rhesus monkeys preferred to spend time with their terry cloth "mother" that provided comfort and warmth rather than the wire mesh "mother" that provided food.

the first moving object they see after they hatch—usually their mother but, in his experiments, Lorenz himself (see Chapter 2; Lorenz, 2002). Lorenz's findings disproved the commonly held assumption that goslings imprint on their mother because she provides food for them. Then, Harry Harlow (1905–1981) and his colleagues (Harlow & Zimmerman, 1959) conducted experiments with newborn rhesus monkeys that were separated from their mother and raised in cages with different "surrogate mothers." One was a cylinder of wire mesh through which food was provided, the other a model of wire mesh covered with terry cloth to provide warmth (see **FIGURE 7.4**). The monkeys spent much more time with the cloth "mother" than with the wire "mother." Harlow recognized that the cloth mother provided physical comfort and concluded that comfort is more important for the establishment of bonds than food. It is worth noting that due to ethical considerations, Harlow could not conduct his experiments nowadays the way he did several decades ago.

John Bowlby, inspired by Harlow and his own work with children in a psychoanalytic clinic, reasoned that attachment is essential to infants' survival (Ainsworth & Bowlby, 1991; Bowlby, 1979), particularly because the mother provides safety.

Strange Situation experimental technique that is used to assess attachment patterns in infants.

secure attachment attachment pattern where infants use the mother as a safe base for exploration, show some distress when the caregiver leaves, and seek the caregiver's comfort upon return.

The Four Patterns of Attachment

Not all children attach to their caregivers in the same way. Bowlby's student Mary Ainsworth went a step further and developed a method to assess children's attachment. The method she developed is called **Strange Situation** (Ainsworth, 1979). Children, usually between 10 and 24 months old, come to the lab with their mother (or caregiver) and are situated in a room that has some toys. A third person participating in the experiment is a collaborator who is a stranger to the infant. Throughout the assessment, both mother and stranger enter and leave the room at different times. Thus, the baby may be left alone in the room at some point and also spends some time in the room with the stranger but without the mother. Ainsworth was interested in observing how the infant reacts when the mother leaves the room and when she enters the room again.

Based on their observations, four different attachment patterns can be identified:

1. **Secure attachment**. Infants cry or fuss when the mother leaves the room and react positively when she returns by smiling at her, getting close to her, or letting her provide comfort. Infants use the mother as a safe base from which to explore the room. About 60 to 75% of American low-risk children show secure attachment patterns (Barnett & Vondra, 1999; Moullin et al., 2014). Securely attached children tend to be happier and more optimistic (Cruz-Vargas & Sanchez-Aragon, 2021; Hashemi & Akbari, 2017; Moghadam et al., 2016); they also get along better with others and tend to fare better at school (Borelli et al., 2010). Secure attachment even seems to serve as a protective factor from cognitive decline in aging adults (Ma et al., 2021; Walsh et al., 2019).

■ Mary Ainsworth (left) tested young children's attachment through an experiment she called Strange Situation.

avoidant attachment attachment pattern in which infants do not interact much with the caregiver and show little reaction to the caregiver's leaving or return.

ambivalent/resistant attachment attachment pattern in which infants protest loudly when the caregiver leaves but show a mix of approach and avoidance behaviors at the caregiver's return.

disorganized/disoriented attachment attachment pattern in which infants seem confused and show contradictory behaviors when the caregiver returns.

2. **Avoidant attachment.** Infants do not show much of a reaction when the mother leaves or reenters the room. They show little preference for the mother over the stranger. Between 15 and 25% of American infants show avoidant attachment patterns (Barnett & Vondra, 1999; Moullin et al., 2014). Avoidant attachment is significantly correlated with feelings of anxiety and depression in teenagers (Joeng et al., 2017), which in turn may lead to an increased risk of having a smartphone addiction (Kim & Koh, 2018). Avoidant attachment in foster children also decreases the likelihood that they complete their college degree (Okpych & Courtney, 2018).

3. **Ambivalent/resistant attachment.** Infants tend to cling to their mother and do not explore the room. When the mother leaves the room, they get extremely upset and cry loudly but refuse to interact with her or push her away when she returns. Around 10 to 15% of American infants show ambivalent attachment patterns (Barnett & Vondra, 1999).

4. **Disorganized/disoriented attachment.** Infants seem confused and fearful. They do not have a clear strategy for how to deal with their mother's leaving and return and might approach the stranger for comfort or approach the mother while looking away from her. Around 10% of American infants show disorganized attachment patterns, although the percentage is likely higher among infants of mothers who are addicted to drugs or who behave in a way that might frighten their babies, or infants who are maltreated (Barnett & Vondra, 1999; Granqvist et al., 2017; Moullin et al., 2014). Children with disorganized attachment often display behavioral problems as they get older (Bernier & Meins, 2008; Kohlhoff et al., 2020).

Of those four attachment styles, secure attachment is considered the most functional and adaptive; the others are often called *insecure attachment*. Although Ainsworth identified these patterns several decades ago, they are still used today by researchers and clinicians. In the next sections, we will learn more about the way attachment develops and the impact it has on children's lives.

Development of Attachment

Children are not born with particular attachment patterns. Rather, attachment develops over time as children interact with their caregivers. Let's go back to Seneca and his mother, Carla. Ever since Seneca was born, he and his mother interacted many times throughout the day. When Seneca cried, his mother came up to him to find out why he was crying and changed his diapers or fed him. As Seneca grew older, their interactions became more complex, but Seneca's mother always reacted when he needed assistance or gave him a supportive nod when he tried something new. Over time, Seneca came to expect certain behaviors from his mother. It is through interactions like these that attachment patterns form.

The attachment patterns that Mary Ainsworth identified develop in four phases (Ainsworth et al., 2015):

1. *Preattachment phase* (birth to about 3 months): Infants do not differentiate between one person and another. They respond to their mother the same way they respond to other people.

2. *Attachment-in-the-making phase* (around 3 months): Infants are able to discriminate between different people and start to show more elaborate attachment behaviors, like reaching out for someone.

3. *Clear-cut attachment phase* (between 6 and 12 months): Infants are now much more active in seeking closeness to their caregivers. When they seek closeness and comfort, they are now actively working toward that goal by embracing their caregiver or moving closer to them.

■ Stranger anxiety develops around 9 months of age, coinciding with the third phase of attachment formation: Only once children have started to feel attached to a caregiver do they start making distinctions and realize that not all people around them are people they trust and that provide safety.

4. *Goal-corrected partnership phase*: After about 3 years of age, mother and child create a more complex relationship that resembles more of a partnership, because children begin to see things not only from their own viewpoint, but also from that of others.

Attachment patterns tend to be relatively stable, particularly when the relationship between children and their caregivers is stable as well. As we will see in the next section, attachment patterns are strongly influenced by the personality and temperament of both caregiver and child, which are factors that do not easily change.

However, when caregivers or the situation at home change, or when a child gets adopted, attachment patterns can change as well. Securely attached children can become less securely attached, but the reverse is also true: Changes in the situation at home—such as when a parent receives treatment for a drug addiction and is, as a result, able to more consistently care for the child—may help insecurely attached children develop a more secure attachment pattern (Levendosky et al., 2011; van Londen et al., 2007).

Intervention programs involving home visits that help young at-risk mothers to react in a more sensitive and responsive way to their babies' needs have been quite successful: Infants whose mothers participate in these interventions are significantly more likely to be securely attached (Berlin et al., 2018; Slade et al., 2020; Suess et al., 2016).

Influences on the Development of Attachment

The factors that most directly influence a child's attachment patterns have to do with the quality of caregiving and the temperament of the child. Parents who are responsive to their child's needs and efforts to communicate are more likely to have a securely attached child. In fact, responsiveness appears to have a greater role than parental warmth in the development of a particular attachment style. Curiously, mothers' and fathers' responsiveness seems to have different effects: Less responsiveness in mothers leads to ambivalent attachment; in fathers, it leads to avoidant attachment (George et al., 2010). Securely attached children tend to have parents who are consistently responsive to their needs and show their love for their children in many ways (Bigelow et al., 2010). Mothers with mental illness or abusive tendencies are less likely to have children who are securely attached (Hoffman et al., 2017).

Children's temperament can have an indirect influence on attachment patterns by affecting the responsiveness of their caregivers. If a baby is fussy and irritable and generally cries a lot, his mother may feel helpless and incompetent, and as a result may be less responsive to the baby's needs. This in turn can lead to insecure attachment (Braungart-Rieker et al., 2019; Solmeyer & Feinberg, 2011). It is another reason why caregivers and healthcare workers should be particularly attuned to the temperament of children in their care.

Another crucial factor plays a role in children's attachment patterns: Children must be given the ability to closely interact with someone else in order to form an attachment. As basic as this sounds, not all children are given that chance. Children growing up in orphanages or frequently changing foster homes, for example, do not have a constant caregiver in their lives. We will consider children growing up in institutions next.

Orphanages and Attachment

During the Cold War that lasted from the end of World War II (1945) until 1991, Western access to the Soviet Union and its allies was severely limited. After the fall of the "Iron Curtain" in 1991, a British journalist named Bob Graham was able to travel to Romania, a former Soviet Bloc state, where he visited an orphanage in the capital city of Bucharest. He was horrified by what he saw there:

> There were two things I remember most vividly of all, they will stay with me forever: the smell of urine and the silence of so many children. Usually when you enter a room packed with cots filled with children, the expectation is of noise, chatter or crying, sometimes even a whimper. There was none, even though the children were awake. They lay in their cots, sometimes two to each cot, sometime three, their eyes staring. Silently. It was eerie, almost sinister. The smell, with which I became familiar in the months and years visiting the institutions throughout Romania, was rank. (Odobescu, 2015)

The situation in many of the Romanian orphanages was dire and rife with abuse. Workers at the orphanages did not talk much to the children, much less encourage them to be active, so many 3-year-olds could neither walk nor talk. They did not get enough food and suffered from the cold in their unheated, overcrowded rooms. As they got older, they were asked to hit each other as a punishment, and were beaten by the staff as well. Perhaps worst of all, no one loved them, and no one showed them any affection (Odobescu, 2015).

Many childless couples from Western countries proceeded to adopt children from Romanian orphanages. Children whose stay in those orphanages was 6 months or less tended to recover relatively well by the age of 6. They gained weight quickly and developed intimate relationships with their adoptive parents. Today, most of them do not seem to suffer any long-term effects from their time spent in the orphanage (Rutter et al., 2010).

Children who had spent longer periods in the orphanage, however, have not fared so well. They grew up experiencing cognitive, emotional, and social problems, many of which have persisted into adulthood. One study showed that at age 11, children who had spent more than 6 months in one of the Romanian orphanages had an average IQ of only 85—they had not caught up with the general population, whose average IQ is 100 (Rutter et al., 2010). Many of the children also actively approached strangers and interacted with them, which is a sign of insecure attachment (Rutter et al., 2007). Even today, they

■ Children at an orphanage in Vulturesti, Romania, 1990.

© Cynthia Johnson/Getty Images

have trouble building relationships with other people or have difficulties concentrating on tasks in school or at work (BBC, 2017).

You might think that orphanages like the ones in Romania are a thing of the past, but they are not. About 8 million children around the world live in orphanages (Batha, 2018). The patterns we see in Romanian orphans who are adults now are similar to the ones we see today in children growing up neglected in other parts of the world. For example, many Indigenous children in Canada were forced to attend residential schools. Those schools were in operation from around 1870 through 1996. Many of the teachers were underqualified, and abuse was common (Canadian Encyclopedia, 2020). Researchers also recently studied children in an orphanage in India. Those children (ages 1–6) spent 80% of their time in isolation, not interacting with caregivers or peers. They exhibited a severe delay in cognitive development that did not improve 12 months after some of them were taken out of the orphanage and placed in foster families (Juffer et al., 2017).

Theory in Action: Attachment Theory

Attachment is ultimately about danger or perceived danger and how we react to that danger. Securely attached children know their caregiver will reliably provide protection. This gives them a feeling of security as well as a safe base from which to venture out and explore the world. Children who do not have a caregiver who consistently provides safety will likely feel anxious or confused.

Some mothers who suffer from postpartum depression worry that their inability to take adequate care of themselves and their infant will harm their infant's development. However, in the first months of life the infant is in the preattachment phase and not attached to any person in particular. Thus, mothers can be assured that as long as there is someone to reliably care for their child, the needs of the infant will likely be met.

Interventions can successfully help high-risk parents (like teen parents, parents with substance addictions, and parents who themselves have a pattern of insecure attachment) respond sensitively and consistently to their infants' needs. These interventions improve the odds that their children will develop a secure attachment (Berlin et al., 2018; Slade et al., 2020; Suess et al., 2016).

Insecurely attached children tend to have more trouble at school than securely attached children. Instead of simply trying to change children's behavior, it is important to acknowledge their feelings and take their attachment style into account when teaching (Golding et al., 2012). Ideally, teachers will communicate to their classes that all children are accepted and safe. Being attentive and responsive to children's needs and helping them manage their emotions is useful as well.

Students with an avoidant attachment style tend to be indifferent and withdrawn at school. Often, they do not have many friendships or their friendships are rather superficial. They do not like to have the teacher close by and reject help even if they need it. They prefer to focus on their work rather than on relationships, because engaging with others feels risky to them. Students should be encouraged to ask adults for help and get involved in team or small group work. You can show them that you are thinking of them by saying things like "I was thinking of you when…". The goal is to help the children develop trust in adults.

Students with an *ambivalent attachment style* are often anxious and need a lot of attention. They have trouble concentrating and need lots of support from their teacher. They easily get hostile when they are frustrated and may act as the "class clown" in

■ Attachment patterns in children can be used to help tailor instruction to their needs.

© Kiselev Andrey Valerevich/Shutterstock.com

order to call attention to themselves. They have trouble focusing on their work because they put so much emphasis on keeping other people's (and particularly the teacher's) attention. Since children with ambivalent attachment often have concentration problems, it is helpful to break up their work into smaller steps and hold them responsible for whatever they're working on. Timers can also help those children stay on task. Children should be taught how to manage their emotions. It is helpful for them to have an assigned adult whom they can approach at school when they need assistance.

Students with a *disorganized attachment style* often seem controlling and have a distrust of authorities like teachers. They suffer from anxiety and may react strongly to triggers that are not apparent to others at first glance. They refuse to participate in work because they are afraid to fail. They often have trouble in unstructured times like breaks and lunch time. For these students, it is helpful to have a contact person like a teacher or teacher's assistant with whom they can check in daily. They need lots of positive feedback, and it's important to avoid threatening their feeling of safety or their self-image. Additionally, they need help controlling their emotions and strict boundaries and routines.

Review!

■ Attachment is an affectional bond between two people. Children form attachments with their primary caregivers in four phases (see below).

■ Attachment can be measured in the lab with a procedure called "Strange Situation," in which the children go through a series of separations and reunions with their caregiver. Depending on their reaction to the caregiver's leaving and returning, four attachment patterns are distinguished: secure attachment, avoidant attachment, ambivalent/resistant attachment, and disorganized/disoriented attachment.

■ The formation of secure attachment is impaired when parents are not responsive to their children's needs and actions, or when (as happens in institutional care at times) caregivers do not even interact regularly with the children.

■ Intervention programs that teach parents how to best interact with their infants have been successful in increasing the likelihood that children will develop secure attachment to their parents.

How does attachment develop, and what kinds of attachment are there?

■ Attachment develops in four phases; a preattachment phase (birth–3 months), an attachment-in-the-making phase (around 3 months), a clear-cut attachment phase (6–12 months), and a goal-corrected partnership phase. Throughout these phases, children move from not distinguishing any caregiver to being able

to tell caregivers apart, and from forming a preference for their main caregivers to creating complex relationships with one or more caregivers.

■ Children can be securely or insecurely attached to their caregivers. We distinguish three different kinds of insecure attachment: avoidant attachment, ambivalent/resistant attachment, and disorganized/disoriented attachment. Whereas children who are securely attached use their relationship with the caregiver as a safe haven from which to explore the world and feel comfortable turning to the caregiver when they are distressed, insecurely attached children do not consider their primary caregiver a reliable source of security and comfort. The more responsive a caregiver is to the actions and needs of a young child, the more likely it is the child will develop a secure attachment.

Which factors influence the development of attachment patterns?

■ There are two main factors that influence the attachment patterns of children: parental responsiveness and the child's temperament. The more responsive parents are to a child's needs, the more likely it is the child will be securely attached to them. Additionally, children with a difficult temperament are more likely to be insecurely attached. This may be because overtired mothers may become less responsive to an infant's need if the infant is very irritable and cries a lot.

Practice!

1. The attachment pattern that is NOT considered insecure attachment is _____ .
   a. avoidant attachment
   b. disorganized/disoriented attachment
   c. secure attachment
   d. ambivalent/resistant attachment

2. Attachment develops in _____ phases.
   a. 2
   b. 4
   c. 3
   d. 5

3. Children who spent a year or longer neglected in Romanian orphanages _____ .
   a. recovered fairly quickly when adopted into loving families
   b. often experienced problems that lasted into adulthood
   c. caught up quickly in school after adoption
   d. avoided strangers at all costs

Show What You've Learned!

You have just spent a week with your friend Alex and his 1-year-old daughter, Ellie, who were visiting from out of town. Alex moved away for work just after Ellie was born, and you're thrilled to see them again. As you observe Alex and Ellie over the course of the week, however, you can't help but notice that Ellie doesn't react much when your friend leaves the room or returns. She also does not approach her parent to be picked up or comforted when crying. When Alex calls Ellie, it is more of the same: The baby doesn't really react, and sometimes turns away. You'd like to write Alex an email with some tips on how to better interact with Ellie. How do you explain to him what you see and what actions he can take? Use the information presented in this section to identify and describe the attachment pattern, along with some solutions that you can provide to your friend.

7.4 Working Parents and Daycare

■ Assess whether or not relegating an infant's care to someone other than the parents significantly impacts their development.

In 2020, around 3.6 million children were born in the United States (Hamilton et al., 2021). In that same year, 92% of all fathers and 69% of married mothers of children under age 3 worked. The rate of working mothers with no spouse was somewhat higher—around 76% (Department of Labor, 2021). If offered a chance, many of the new parents would likely have chosen to stay at home with their newborn. However, eligibility for paid parental leave depends on the country in which the family resides.

Among 41 developed countries, the United States is the only country that does not grant newly minted parents or adoptive parents any paid parental leave at all (FIGURE 7.5). Estonia, for example, allows parents up to 85 weeks of paid leave, and a number of countries—Bulgaria, Hungary, Lithuania, and Slovakia—offer more than a year of paid leave. In 34 of those countries, paid parental leave is also available to fathers (though in most cases not to the same extent as it is to mothers). However, while there is no paid parental leave available to new parents on a national basis in the United States, a number of states, such as New Jersey, New York, and California, require companies to offer paid parental leave (Livingston & Thomas, 2019).

Given that the United States does not universally offer paid leave for parents, and given that many parents may not be able to forgo their income, a large percentage of young children are routinely cared for by someone other than their parents typically from a very early age. About 61% of American children under the age of 5 are in some kind of regular childcare arrangement, which may include more than one nonparent caregiver (as when a grandparent looks after the child at the end of the day, having picked them up from daycare). Forty-two percent are in the care of relatives of the mother, most often grandparents, or fathers. Thirty-three percent are cared for in an arrangement with no relatives, such as a daycare center or home daycare. Children living below the poverty line are more likely to be cared for by a sibling than children living at or above the poverty line (21% vs. 9%) (Laughlin, 2013). There are some ethnic group differences as well. Most notably, Asian Americans are less likely than other groups to have their children in the care of their grandparents. African Americans are more likely to have their children cared for by a sibling or in a daycare center.

FIGURE 7.5 Total weeks of paid maternity leave mandated by select national governments to new parents, 2020. Note that of 41 developed countries that participated in the study, the United States is the only country that does not offer paid leave to new parents. What do you think are the implications for parents raising children in the United States?

Data from OECD. 2021. Family leave database. www.oecd.org

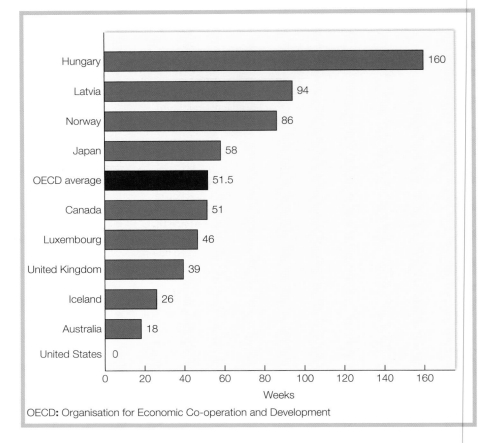

OECD: Organisation for Economic Co-operation and Development

More than one in four children below age 3 have more than one regular childcare arrangement, meaning they have to get used to more than one adult who takes care of them on a regular basis. When their mother is employed, children spend on average 36 hours per week in the care of other people (**FIGURE 7.6**); but even when the mother is not employed, children still spend around 21 hours per week with someone else (Laughlin, 2013).

What is the impact on attachment when children spend so much time with other people? An experiment involving the Strange Situation described earlier in this chapter found there was no difference in reaction between children who were in childcare and children who were cared for by their mother when their mother left the room during the experiment (NICHD Early Child Care Research Network, 1997). As you know, the responsiveness of the mother plays a significant role in the development of secure attachment: More responsive mothers tend to have children who are securely attached. So being in childcare on its own does not seem to affect attachment patterns one way or the other.

However, children in childcare *were* found to be more prone to developing insecure attachment when certain risk factors were involved. These include a less responsive mother coupled with more than minimal childcare hours, low-quality childcare, or multiple childcare settings (NICHD Early Child Care Research Network, 1997).

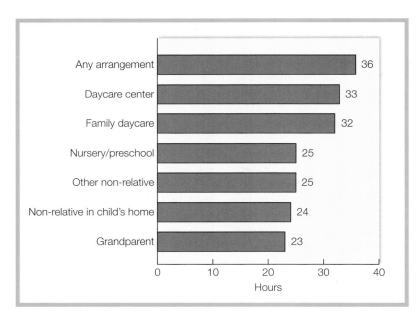

FIGURE 7.6 Average hours per week preschoolers of employed mothers spent in select childcare arrangements, in hours (2011).

Data from L. Laughlin. 2013. Current Population Reports, P70-135. U.S. Census Bureau, Washington, DC

Culture Counts

Racial Differences in Access to Paid Parental Leave

In the United States, there is no national policy guaranteeing paid leave for parents of newborns or sick children. While some employers provide paid leave to their workers, data from the 2017 National Compensation Survey shows that low-paid workers are less likely than better-paid workers to have access to paid leave (Bureau of Labor Statistics, 2021).

A 2019 report by the U.S. Bureau of Labor Statistics adds to our understanding of paid leave for parents by revealing that when it comes to paid family leave, there are racial and ethnic disparities in addition to socioeconomic ones. The researchers produced three different statistical models. The first one represents the data in their data set by ethnicity/ race. The researchers then created Model 2 to see whether racial and ethnic differences persist if they control for individual differences (for example, differences in the number of children, age, gender, or marital status). Since the racial and ethnic differences were still present, they created Model 3, which additionally controls for employment variables (for example, whether someone works full time or part time, or whether they belong to a union). As you can see, the disparities are consistent across all three models. More parents had access to paid leave to care for a sick child (or other family member), but the same disparities appear.

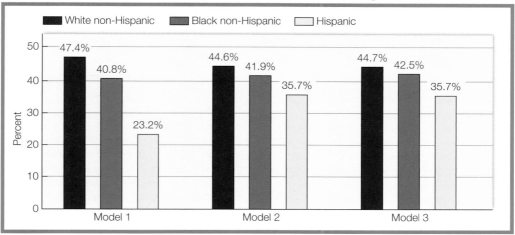

(A) Percentage of families with access to paid leave to care for a newborn by racial and ethnic status

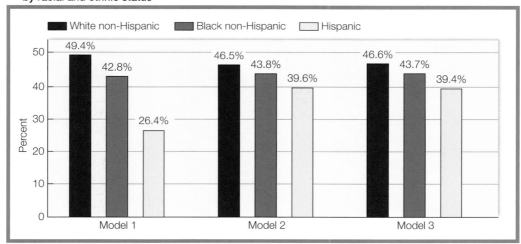

(B) Percentage of families with access to paid leave to care for a sick family member by racial and ethnic status

A. B after A. P. Bartel et al. 2019. Monthly Labor Review, U.S. Bureau of Labor Statistics, January 2019. www.bls.gov; data from American Time Use Survey, 2011. American Time Use Survey Leave Module. www.atusdata.org

■ Question

What alternatives exist for parents of newborns or sick children if they do not have access to paid leave?
What are the effects of these alternatives on the healthy development of young children?

In terms of cognitive development, research shows that children who spend more time in (high-quality) daycare display greater cognitive abilities as well as better language abilities than do children without such advantages (Drange & Havnes, 2019; Sylva et al., 2011). Family-based daycare at age 3 is also associated with greater sociability later in a child's life (Oksman et al., 2019). However, it is important not to forget other factors that play a significant role in children's cognitive development, which may correlate with—and be difficult to separate from—high-quality childcare. For example, 3-year-old Miguel attends a private daycare in a wealthy neighborhood in Glendale, Arizona. His mother, Angela, works as a dental hygienist. Her socioeconomic status means she can afford to keep Miguel in a well-run daycare facility with lots of new toys and other resources. Because Angela has a job with regular work hours, she is able to spend quality time with her son every day, reading books to him or taking him on excursions in the area—activities that mothers who have to work several jobs to earn enough money may not be able to offer their children on a regular basis. Maternal education and socioeconomic status have an impact on development regardless of whether or not a child is in daycare (Barnes & Melhuish, 2017; Lurie et al., 2021).

Review!

Does it have a significant impact on infants' development if parents relegate their care to others?

■ Around 61% of American children under the age of 5 are being cared for regularly by someone other than their parents, and more than one-quarter of them have more than one regular arrangement. Negative effects of extended childcare mostly arise when several factors are paired together (like a mother who is less responsive, low-quality childcare, and a high number of hours spent in that childcare). In terms of cognitive development, children who are in high-quality daycare tend to have cognitive skills that are more developed than those who spend their time exclusively at home. The effects of childcare on aggression are not quite clear; early research showed that children in childcare tend to be more aggressive, but there are also a number of studies that suggest that children cared for by their mother are more aggressive.

Practice!

1. Compared with other developed nations, the United States _____ .

   a. offers very generous paid parental leave
   b. offers the least paid parental leave
   c. offers generous parental leave for mothers but not for fathers
   d. offers generous parental leave for fathers but not for mothers

2. The majority of American children under age 5 are _____ .

   a. cared for by their fathers
   b. cared for by their grandparents
   c. cared for by their mothers
   d. cared for with some kind of childcare arrangement

3. Children who spend significant amounts of time in childcare tend to have _____ .

   a. the same attachment patterns as children cared for exclusively by their parents
   b. more secure attachment patterns
   c. more ambivalent/resistant attachment patterns
   d. more avoidant attachment patterns

What's Your Position?

Should the government ensure American families have job-protected paid leave to look after infants? Other developed countries have much more generous paid leave policies than we have in the United States. Do you think there should be a federal policy guaranteeing parents paid leave to take care of their children? Why or why not? How long should that leave be? And should it be extended to fathers as well as mothers? Draft a response to this question, using information provided in the chapter and found on some of the following websites. Share and defend your viewpoint in a conversation with two or three of your classmates.

Additional Resources Online

- "Parental leave: Is there a case for government action?" from the Cato Institute
- "The case against government-mandated parental leave," from the Reason Foundation
- "The economic consequences of family policies: Lessons from a century of legislation in high-income countries," from the American Economic Association
- "Why America doesn't have paid leave," from *Business Insider*
- "Millions of Americans could finally get paid family leave—if lawmakers can agree on who pays," from *Time*
- "The conservative argument over paid family leave," from *The Atlantic*

7.5 Digital Media and Socio-emotional Development

- Conclude whether the use of screen media influences children's socioemotional development.

Marie, Seneca's young friend, is happily lying on the floor watching *Dora the Explorer*. Marie loves that series. It features a girl, Dora, and a monkey named Boots as they experience adventures in animated worlds inside a computer. The bilingual Dora takes particular pride in being able to speak both English and Spanish.

Erin, Marie's mother, lets her watch the show every day. Often, Marie is allowed to watch more than one episode. It has become her quiet time, since Marie has stopped napping in the afternoons. Erin uses her daughter's TV time to do sorely needed housework. She also works from home and finds she can cut into the backlog of emails and other tasks in the time it takes Marie to watch two or three episodes. Erin also feels the time in front of the TV is well spent because Marie is learning some Spanish and seeing how a strong female character overcomes a variety of obstacles.

Marie and Erin's situation is not uncommon. As we have seen in Chapter 6, very young children are being exposed more than ever to digital media, via laptops, tablets, smartphones, and especially television (Christakis, 2009; Common Sense Media, 2020; Sigman, 2012). Does it affect their social and emotional development? That is what we will explore in this section.

TV Watching Means Less Time for Interaction

Why be concerned about media use in children at all? In Chapter 5, we learned that the brain is rapidly developing over the first 3 years of life (Balbernie, 2013; Keenan et al., 2019). Young infants and children mostly learn through interactions with others. Those interactions provide a basis for the development of attachment with children's caregivers. They also foster the development of self-control and influence how children react to threat and anxiety (Lincoln et al., 2017; Napier, 2014; Zeedyk, 2013). When children spend long periods of time watching television, this is time they spend typically alone, not interacting with anyone (Christakis, 2009; Fidler et al., 2010).

Much more research is needed before we can draw definite conclusions, but studies have raised a number of concerns over the use of televisions with young children with respect to their social and emotional development (Gunter & Gunter, 2019; Liu et al., 2021; Napier, 2014). When a television is running—and even if it is just on in the background—interactions between child and adult are impaired. Children may interact less frequently or not at all with a caregiver. The quality of those interactions is also likely to be diminished when a TV is running. If the television is on in the background, parents and children may be

■ Studies have shown that many Americans are unaware of the recommendations for screen usage in young children and may need more information about activities that could help them develop the potential of their children (Christakis, 2009; Vandewater et al., 2007).

distracted by the pictures and frequently look at the screen (Kirkorian et al., 2009; O'Toole & Kannass, 2021). Impaired interactions and distractions lead mothers to be less responsive to their children's needs, which, as we have seen, impairs the development of secure attachment (Schmidt et al., 2008), as well as emotional development (Napier, 2014).

Parents let infants watch television for a variety of reasons. Turning on the TV can give parents a much-needed break, it can reduce conflicts between siblings, and for many parents it is considerably safer than some other activities. Although the research is still evolving, some studies have found that children in households of lower socioeconomic status, with single mothers or less educated mothers, spend more time in front of the TV (Calvert & Wilson, 2010; Dore & Dynia, 2021). The attachment style of the parents may also influence how much they let their children watch TV. Avoidant parents tend to rely more on TV as a regulator of their children's behavior than securely attached parents (Nathanson & Manohar, 2012).

With respect to the social and emotional development of young children, it is likely better for parents to err on the side of caution and limit TV exposure of their children. One advantage for later in life is that children establish healthy TV viewing habits early on. After age 2, educational TV programs can also teach children to have empathy with others, act prosocially, and develop respect toward other people (Canadian Paediatric Society, 2017; Greitermeyer, 2021; Kirkorian et al., 2008; Thakkar et al., 2006).

Recommendations for Parents

There is consensus among child development researchers that there is no educational benefit to exposing very young children to screen media (Napier, 2014; Supanitayanon et al., 2020). But as we have seen, parents do not always let their children watch TV with the belief that their children are becoming better educated. Television can encourage active children to stop for some quiet time, while giving parents an opportunity to do some chores or just take a break. So while the general recommendation from the American Academy of Pediatrics is for children under age 2 not to watch any TV at all, this is not always realistic.

It is important to give parents suggestions for how to best make use of screen media when they use them. Parents should understand that the use of media shortens the time they have for real-life interactions with their children and may also worsen the quality of their interactions. To reduce negative implications, parents should:

- try to watch TV together with their children, if possible;
- avoid long shows or shows that, because they are very fast-paced, can unsettle young children;
- turn off all TVs and digital devices when they are not in use;
- have no devices on during mealtimes or in the background when children are playing; and
- not, or at least not exclusively, use screens to calm their children down when they are distressed (Hill et al., 2016).

Abiding by these recommendations helps parents make the most of their time with their young children. Parents and children should have plenty of time during which they do not get disrupted or distracted by devices so they can have the quality interactions that promote healthy patterns of attachment. When parents do not use screens to calm or distract children, children inevitably learn other ways of self-soothing.

In the twenty-first century, media play a role in the lives of very young children, and the best course of action is to help parents understand the impact media can have and give them options for how to best integrate those media in their daily lives.

Review!

Does the use of screen media influence children's socio-emotional development?

■ At a very young age, if children spend time with screen media they usually watch TV. Researchers mostly agree that children under the age of 2 learn very little, if anything, from watching TV shows. However, consumed in moderation, TV shows are also not likely to cause lasting harm to a child.

■ Most concerns around TV watching and socio-emotional development center on the fact that children learn most from interacting with others. Any time spent watching TV alone, or having interactions disrupted by background media, is time that could potentially have been spent in interaction with the child.

Practice!

1. In infancy and toddlerhood, the entertainment medium that children mostly use is _____ .
   a. tablet
   b. television
   c. cell phone
   d. computer

2. Most American parents _____ .
   a. do not care about recommendations for the use of screen media in young children
   b. are aware of recommendations for the use of screen media in young children
   c. are unaware of recommendations for the use of screen media in young children

   d. follow recommendations for the use of screen media in young children very strictly

3. Concerns around the use of screen media in infants emphasize that _____ .
   a. the use of screen media is harmful for young children's vision
   b. siblings are at elevated risk for extended arguments over the shows they watch
   c. the use of screen media is harmful for young children's hearing
   d. children who sit in front of the TV a lot do not have enough time to interact with their caregivers

Show What You've Learned!

Imagine you are a co-worker of Erin's. In an email to you, Erin mentions that she's getting some work done while her daughter Marie is watching *Dora the Explorer*. "She's on her third episode now," Erin writes, "but she seems happy and I'm grateful for the time to get caught up." As a parent of two older children, you have already been through the family debates around screen time. Drawing on the information presented in this chapter, write a reply to Erin in which you sympathize with her need for a break while advising her of the guidelines your family adopted to limit screen time. Be sure to mention attachment patterns when explaining your own family's decision to limit TV viewing.

Additional Resources Online

■ "Cyber babies: The impact of emerging technology on the developing infant" in *Psychology Research*

■ "American Academy of Pediatrics announces new recommendations for children's media use," from the American Academy of Pediatrics

A few months later: Seneca in the supermarket

It is Saturday again—shopping day for Seneca's family. Seneca is now 3 years old and about to start preschool, much to his excitement. He and his mother, Carla, are doing the shopping, as always—though things have improved. It was clear to both Carla and her husband, Frederic, that although they had to go shopping and Seneca had to tag along because he had no other caregiver at home, something needed to change—but it wasn't going to be Seneca. At least not anytime soon. . . .

Carla suspected that Seneca might be acting out because he didn't like finding himself in a situation where he did not have her undivided attention. So she began turning their shopping expeditions into a game. As she drew up her weekly list ahead of time, she noted the items in each aisle that she could ask Seneca to retrieve—nothing on high shelves, nothing in jars that might break. "Can you find a can with a green label and tomatoes on it?" she asks—and he goes off to find it, pleased with himself as he does. Seneca feels like he's helping, and their expeditions are more interactive. The game doesn't always hold his attention, but when Seneca tires of the game, Carla puts him in the child seat of the cart and gives him his favorite stuffed animal, which she now brings whenever they go to the store. Carla knows Seneca won't be able to ride in the child seat for much longer, but she also knows he will outgrow his tantrums. ■■

© Pavel Kobysh/Shutterstock.com

Overview

Physical Development in Early Childhood

Children at play may be prone to mishaps

It's the Labor Day long weekend, and the botanical garden is hosting its annual end-of-summer town fair. Local farmers are selling goods from white tents in the parking lot, and the visitor center has craft tables and educational activities set up for children of all ages. Four-year-old Carrie is having the time of her life. She has always enjoyed trips to the garden, with its lush trees and colorful flowers and the little pond full of fish. Today, she's tried her hand at braiding a basket, colored pumpkins, and listened intently to a Native American elder talking about the medicinal properties of plants. As Carrie leaves the visitor center, the familiar pond comes into sight, and she starts running toward the water along the uneven walkway, broken up by tree roots. Suddenly Carrie falls forward, landing face-first on the path. She starts bleeding profusely from her nose and mouth. Her parents are just a step behind but are unable to prevent the accident; they take Carrie home to care for her injuries.

Georgia and Jamal are walking the same path with their 3-year-old son, Eli. Though Eli loves to walk, his parents keep him strapped into his stroller so that he can't get into trouble. He strains to get closer to the ferns, the butter churn on display at one of the tents, the craft table. But he has a habit of putting things in his mouth, and his parents don't want to take any chances with so many nonedible temptations—glue, sparkles, crayons. And what if he breaks something! Georgia and Jamal are relieved they have managed to prevent anything like Carrie's fall.

As you can imagine, falls and injuries are quite common in early childhood. Children's physical skills develop rapidly, but children nevertheless often have a hard time recognizing danger and controlling their bodies in effective ways to prevent accidents. In this chapter, we explore how children's bodies change between the ages of 3 and 6. These changes have an enormous impact on their motor skills as well as on their cognitive abilities (which we will discuss in the next chapter). We also consider the nutritional needs of young children as well as their eating and sleeping habits. Lastly, we consider injuries and illnesses that are common among young children and how these problems can be minimized.

8.1 How Do Children's Brains and Bodies Grow?

- Recall how children's bodies grow in early childhood.
- Explain brain growth in early childhood and how it influences preschoolers' skills and behaviors.

Height and Weight Changes

During the first 2 years of life, children grow very rapidly. Their growth slows down as they enter early childhood. They grow about 3 inches and gain around 5 pounds per year (National Library of Medicine, 2021). A typical North American 3-year-old is 39 inches tall and weighs about 35 pounds. A typical 6-year-old is 47 inches tall and weighs about 52 pounds (Fryar et al., 2012). However, there are wide variations in how tall children are and in how much they weigh. Height and weight are influenced by sex, ethnicity, nutrition and diet, and family history, among other factors. Pediatricians and healthcare providers use growth charts to track a child's growth compared with other children of the same age and sex. They also permit professionals to see the overall pattern of growth over time.

In early childhood, individual differences in height and weight are much greater than the differences between groups. While boys may be slightly taller and heavier than girls, and children of Western European descent are taller than those of Latin American or South Asian children (Blum & Baten, 2012), the greatest factor determining a child's height and weight is their individual genetic makeup. As children grow taller, their body stature changes as well and takes on a more adult appearance.

Brain Growth

In early childhood, the brain grows much more rapidly than the rest of the body. As we learned in Chapter 5, most of the increase in brain size and weight can be attributed to two factors:

1. an increase in myelination and
2. the formation of new neural connections.

© Waridsara_HappyChildren/Shutterstock.com
© Anur Yossundara/Shutterstock.com

■ Children's body proportions and physical development set natural limits on what they can do. Because there is tremendous variation in growth and, consequently, physical ability in children, it is important to consider their growth stage in addition to their age. In sports, for example, you may consider grouping children according to physical development rather than according to their age. Children who are developing at a slower rate than some of their peers can nevertheless be very successful later on when they receive instruction that takes their level of development into consideration.

While the brain grows as a whole in early childhood, certain structures develop particularly rapidly. This development is important because it forms the basis of a child's growth in all areas: emotional, cognitive, social, and motor. Here we will take a closer look at the growth of the cerebral cortex, corpus callosum, cerebellum, reticular formation, and hippocampus, while considering what that growth means for a child's development.

THE CEREBRAL CORTEX   The **cerebral cortex** is the brain's outer layer, covering the cerebrum (see Figure 5.3). It makes up roughly three-quarters of the entire brain volume (Hofman, 2014; Swanson, 1995) and consists of four lobes. The maturation of the frontal lobes, which grow fastest in early childhood, allows young children to develop in many areas. They learn to control their emotions better and to have fewer tantrums. They also learn to understand their own and other people's emotions (Dum et al., 2016; He et al., 2021; Schore, 2015). Cognitively, they learn to plan their actions, develop strategies for problem-solving, pay better attention, and remember information. Their reasoning skills improve drastically (Menon & D'Esposito, 2021; Stuss & Knight, 2013).

THE CORPUS CALLOSUM   The **corpus callosum** is a bundle of nerve fibers that connects the two hemispheres of the cerebral cortex. The myelination of the corpus callosum progresses rapidly in early childhood, enabling the left and right hemispheres to communicate more effectively with each other. This is important because the brain is lateralized, meaning that the hemispheres are not exactly alike: Each specializes in particular functions. In most people, the left hemisphere is involved with language tasks such as speaking, reading, and thinking. The right hemisphere specializes in tasks that involve spatial relationships, music, and emotional and facial expression (Bryden, 2012; Dundas et al., 2013; Zickert et al., 2021). **Lateralization** helps us carry out several tasks at once (Rogers et al., 2004; Zickert et al., 2021).

© Rawpixel.com/Adobe Stock

■ Pujol and colleagues (2004) used functional magnetic resonance imaging (fMRI) to investigate brain differences in children aged 4½ years with and without developmental delays. The researchers found that myelination in the group of non-delayed children was on average more than 3 years ahead of the myelination of the children who were developmentally delayed!

cerebral cortex the furrowed outer surface of the cerebrum, composed mostly of gray matter and involved in complex brain functions like thinking and reasoning.

corpus callosum a band of nerve fibers that connects the left and right hemispheres of the brain.

lateralization functional specialization of the brain; some functions and activities tend to be located in the left or right hemisphere of the brain.

© nadisja/Shutterstock.com

■ In some societies, left-handed children are forced to write with their right hand. Why do you think that is?

In children with autism spectrum disorder (ASD), the corpus callosum develops differently and has less myelination than in children without ASD. Researchers suspect that abnormalities in the corpus callosum play a role not only in ASD but also in many other cognitive-developmental delays (Al-Hashim et al., 2015; Loomba et al., 2021; Paul et al., 2014; Travers et al., 2015).

cerebellum the part of the brain that coordinates movements and balance.

THE CEREBELLUM   Located in the lower back of the brain, the **cerebellum** coordinates movements and helps us keep our balance. As children grow older, the connection between the cerebellum and the cortex grows stronger. As a result, children's abilities to jump and climb, as well as to throw and catch balls, improve significantly. Toddlers typically do not have the ability to catch a ball, but by the time they are 5 years old, they may have developed the coordination to make throwing and catching a favorite game. In recent years, researchers have also found that the cerebellum plays a role in emotion processing and thinking processes that require precise timing (Hans et al., 2014; Pierce & Peron, 2020; Tiemeier et al., 2010).

reticular formation the part of the brain that regulates consciousness and attention.

THE RETICULAR FORMATION   The **reticular formation** is located in the brain stem and regulates consciousness and attention. During early childhood, the reticular formation myelinates rapidly, helping children pay attention for longer periods of time. Although it is often hard to keep a 3-year-old's attention on a single task in preschool, by 5 years of age, kindergarteners can be expected to sit still for 10 to 15 minutes at a time while listening to a story or working on tasks like writing and drawing (Jones, 2003; Yeo et al., 2013).

hippocampus part of the limbic system that plays a crucial role in our ability to create and retrieve memories.

THE HIPPOCAMPUS   The **hippocampus** is part of the limbic system and plays a crucial role in our ability to create and retrieve memories. In order to remember anything over a longer stretch of time, information must be transferred from short-term memory to long-term memory. The hippocampus is involved in this information transfer. The older children get, the more they are able to retain information. This improvement in retention is important not only for the formal schooling that begins around age 5 but also for retention of childhood memories (autobiographic memories). Because of the immaturity of the hippocampus, our memories usually do not go back much before our third or fourth year of life (Aly, 2020; Gogtay et al., 2006; Uematsu et al., 2012).

■ As the reticular formation matures and gets myelinated, children are able to sit still and pay attention for increasing amounts of time.

© Rawpixel Ltd/Alamy Stock Photo

■ This is Jonathan Keleher. When you first meet him, you may not notice how he differs from other people. He works a regular job and loves to talk and relate to his co-workers. But he is missing an important part of the brain: He has no cerebellum. This was discovered when Jonathan, at the age of 5, had a brain scan. Now an adult, Jonathan walks awkwardly, and his speaking style is unusual. He cannot ride a bike, and he lacks the introspection that characterizes deep, thoughtful conversation; he is sometimes unsure how to behave in social situations. But he can live his own life and hold a regular job (Hamilton, 2015).

Review!

How do children's bodies grow in early childhood?

■ In early childhood, children's growth slows down compared with that in their first 2 years of life. They gain about 3 inches and 5 pounds each year.

■ The variations in children's height and weight are considerable and depend on many factors like heritability, ethnicity, gender, and nutrition.

■ During the preschool period, children's body stature changes as well. They lose some of their baby fat and start looking more adult-like.

How does the brain grow in early childhood? How does brain growth influence preschoolers' skills and behavior?

■ The brain grows more rapidly than does any other organ during the preschool period.

■ Most of the brain growth can be attributed to increasing myelination of the axons in the brain as well as a growing number of synaptic connections between brain cells.

■ The brain parts that develop particularly rapidly are the cerebral cortex, corpus callosum, cerebellum, reticular formation, and hippocampus.

▪ Development of the frontal lobes of the *cerebral cortex* enables children to reason better and to solve problems, plan their actions, and remember information.

▪ The hemispheres are specialized (*lateralization*) and thus may take over different subtasks when a person works on a complex task.

▪ The *corpus callosum* connects the two brain hemispheres, which makes brain functioning and communication between the hemispheres more effective.

▪ The *cerebellum* aids in balance and execution of movements. Children also gradually learn to pay attention for longer amounts of time and can remember information more easily because of progress in the development of the *reticular formation* and *hippocampus*.

Practice!

1. True or false: In early childhood, we first start to see marked gender differences in height and weight between boys and girls.
   a. true
   b. false

2. Why is myelination of the brain so important?

3. The cerebral cortex constitutes roughly _____ of the brain's volume.
   a. ¾
   b. ⅔
   c. ½
   d. ⅓

4. What is lateralization?

5. The brain structure that aids the two brain hemispheres in communicating with each other is the _____ .
   a. corpus callosum
   b. cerebellum
   c. reticular formation
   d. amygdala

8.2 Sleep in Early Childhood

- Relate how you would characterize preschoolers' sleep.
- List preschoolers' common sleep problems.
- Identify how the use of electronic devices can influence sleep either positively or negatively.

Some Facts on Sleep

Preschoolers should get around 10–13 hours of sleep per night (see also **FIGURE 8.1**). However, the average amount of sleep they get is only 9.6 hours. The majority of preschoolers go to bed between 8 and 10 p.m., with an average bedtime of 9 p.m. It usually takes a child around one-quarter of an hour to fall asleep. In the mornings, the majority of children wake up between 6 and 8 a.m. (National Sleep Foundation, 2021). About half of preschoolers stall when bedtime comes around—more than in any other age group. The upshot is that many preschool children get too little sleep.

Fortunately for parents, children tend to wake up less during the night as they get older. But there is still a substantial number of preschoolers who wake up and need assistance from their parents at night. In fact, one-third of all preschoolers wake up in need of attention roughly twice per week (National Sleep Foundation, 2021). While younger children often still take a nap during the day, most children do not take naps anymore by age 5.

Sleep plays a significant role in the development of children. For some domains like visual development, the brain is much more plastic and thus more changeable at night than it is during the day (Frank, 2019; Kurth et al., 2013). But sleep at any time of day helps children develop: Naps support memory and language learning in children as young as infants (Horváth et al., 2015; Morrow & Duff, 2020). Children who sleep less also tend to go to sleep later and consume more calories per day (Fisher et al., 2014; Skjåkødegård et al., 2021).

nighttime fears fears that appear at night.

nightmares vivid and realistic dreams that are disturbing and anxiety-provoking.

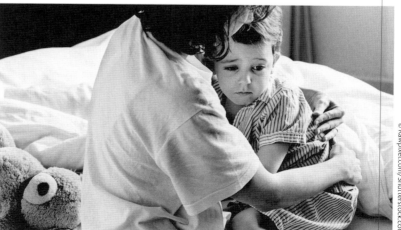

■ Nightmares and nighttime fears can be so disturbing that young children develop a fear of going to bed.

FIGURE 8.1 Sleep duration recommendations from the National Sleep Foundation. Children should sleep 14–17 hours per day until the age of 1 and at least 10 hours per day through their fifth year. Sleep requirements decrease until the age of 18, when 7 hours becomes the minimum standard for adults.

After E. Suni and A. Singh. 2021. How much sleep do we really need? www.sleepfoundation.org

In the long run, this consumption can lead to obesity. When children do not sleep enough, they also have a harder time concentrating at school and tend to have more physical accidents and weaker immune systems (Liu et al., 2021; Taheri, 2006; Zimmerman, 2008).

How can you help young children fall asleep more easily? There are several things parents and caregivers can do (National Sleep Foundation, 2021):

1. Keep children on a regular schedule so they go to bed around the same time every day.

2. Develop bedtime routines that can help children relax and fall asleep. Indeed, more than 90% of preschoolers have some kind of a bedtime routine. Many families include a bath, nighttime story reading, or songs in their daily bedtime routine. About 20% of families use media like television to calm their children down before bedtime (National Sleep Foundation, 2004). Television is not the best way to help children fall asleep. If one uses television, one has to ensure it is helping the child go to sleep rather than keeping the child awake (Helm & Spencer, 2019).

3. Let children sleep in the same room each night so they are used to their environment. Keep the room dark and cool, and don't have any electronic devices or TV sets in the bedroom.

Sleep Problems

Early childhood is a time during which children's imaginations develop significantly. Their vivid imagination can have an impact on sleep. Children of preschool age frequently experience nighttime fears and nightmares.

Nighttime fears are fears that appear at night. They come in many variations, like a fear of the dark, fear of a ghost or a particular monster, or fear of being kidnapped. Fears vary from child to child, but when they are strong enough, affected children fear going to bed and have trouble falling asleep and sleeping through the night. Around 7% of preschoolers experience nighttime fears. The fears usually resolve on their own after some time. Children with severe nighttime fears tend to have more fears than other children in general and often have more behavioral problems (Kushnir & Sadeh, 2011; Lewis et al., 2021).

Nightmares are vivid and realistic dreams that are disturbing and anxiety-provoking. For young children, it is often difficult to distinguish between dream and reality, which makes nightmares all the more frightening. Between 10% and 50% of children have such realistic

Newborns (0–3 months)

✗ <11 hours
✓ **14–17 hours**
✗ >19 hours

Infants (4–11 months)

✗ <10 hours
✓ **14–17 hours**
✗ >18 hours

Toddlers (1–2 years)

✗ <9 hours
✓ **11–14 hours**
✗ >16 hours

Preschoolers (3–5 years)

✗ <8 hours
✓ **10–13 hours**
✗ >14 hours

School-aged children (6–13 years)

✗ <7 hours
✓ **9–11 hours**
✗ >12 hours

Teenagers (14–17 years)

✗ <7 hours
✓ **8–10 hours**
✗ >11 hours

Young adults (18–25 years)

✗ <6 hours
✓ **7–9 hours**
✗ >11 hours

■ **Table 8.1** Strategies to Cope with Nighttime Fears and Nightmares

How You Can Help

Nighttime fears	Nightmares
Give the child the opportunity to talk about her fears or dreams. Are there stressors in the child's life that may be influencing the dreams? Is there a recurring theme?	
Ensure that bedtime routine is upbeat and fun.	
Install a night-light and offer to leave the bedroom door open.	
Do not reinforce beliefs in fantasy creatures.	Make sure the child gets enough sleep. Well-rested children often have fewer nightmares.
Reassure the child that he is safe.	Calm down and reassure the child. Stay with the child for a short time but let him sleep in his own bed.
Praise the child when she is able to stay in bed.	Be creative: For instance, let the child draw a picture of the dream and then tear it up and throw it away.

When to consult a doctor

Nighttime fears	Nightmares
If fears continue over a long time or get worse	If nightmares occur more frequently or get worse
If fears start occurring after a traumatic event	If daily life is affected by nightmares
	If nightmares are very upsetting or real-life issues are causing nightmares

Source: Cleveland Clinic Children's. 2021. Nightmares. http://my.clevelandclinic.org

nightmares that they need the help of a caregiver to calm down. Nightmares are often related to the child's developmental stage. Very young children may be afraid to become separated from their mother, preschoolers may be afraid of the monsters they read about in books or of diseases they have heard about, and school-aged children may be afraid of dangers and monsters they saw in scary TV shows (Cleveland Clinic Children's, 2021; Lewis et al., 2021).

TABLE 8.1 shows some strategies that can be used to help a child experiencing nightmares or nighttime fears to fall asleep.

Media and Their Impact on Sleep

In 2011, 75% of children had at least one electronic device in their bedroom (National Sleep Foundation, 2015). Unfortunately, being surrounded by electronics changes children's (and adults') sleep in an unfavorable way (Radesky & Christakis, 2016; Uebergang et al., 2017). These devices affect sleep by

- delaying bedtime;
- stimulating rather than relaxing children; and
- producing light that communicates to children's bodies that it is daytime: It suppresses the production of melatonin, which is a hormone that regulates sleep.

A meta-analysis of 20 studies investigating the relationship between use of media devices and sleep quality in children found strong and consistent relationships between use of media devices at bedtime and insufficient sleep duration, poor quality of sleep, and daytime sleepiness. Children were more likely to have these problems even if they did not use their devices at bedtime but plainly had access to them (Carter et al., 2016). In fact, up to 40% of children report being woken up at least once a month by incoming text messages on their phones, which obviously has a negative effect on their sleep quality (Foerster et al., 2019; Zimmerman, 2008).

There are some media that can promote sleep, however. Some television shows are purposefully designed to relax and calm down children in order to

■ The blue light emitted from digital screens reduces melatonin production in the body. Melatonin is a hormone that is produced in increasing amounts at nighttime to help us go to sleep.

help them transition to sleep. In Germany, for example, many children watch a show called *The Sandman*, which is broadcast around 7 p.m. It is about 5 minutes long and has repetitive features with no surprise elements that help children wind down: In the series, children always see the Sandman arrive at a child's home and bring a calm, non-exciting bedtime story.

When watching TV, children typically are too far removed from the light source for it to decrease their melatonin production (Christakis & Zimmerman, 2006). However, studies have found that the amount of TV that children currently watch decreases sleep time (Helm & Spencer, 2019; Thompson & Christakis, 2005). TV shows or electronic games also can cause nightmares if they feature frightening content (Christakis & Zimmerman, 2006; Götz et al., 2019).

Review!

How would you characterize preschoolers' sleep?

■ Preschoolers need between 11 and 13 hours of sleep per night. Many children do not get enough sleep, however.

■ Sleep is crucial for children's development because memories are consolidated during sleep and new connections in the brain are forged.

■ Sleep also becomes more regular as children get older. They do not wake up at night as often anymore, but there are still a significant number of children who need assistance from their parents during the night from time to time.

■ To help children fall asleep and sleep well, it is best to keep them on a regular schedule.

What sleep problems are common in preschoolers?

■ Preschoolers frequently experience *nightmares* or *nighttime fears*. These events may reflect real-life experiences of the children, anxieties they harbor, or things they saw on TV or in video games, for example.

Does the use of electronic devices influence sleep?

■ The majority of children have at least one electronic device in their bedroom. These devices can disturb sleep in several ways:
  ▮ They can keep children up late.
  ▮ They can disrupt sleep when they make noises during the night.
  ▮ They may excite children before bedtime or provide anxiety-provoking content.
  ▮ They emit blue light, which suppresses melatonin production.

■ However, media can also be used to relax and calm children down before bedtime, for example, with specifically designed TV shows or meditation programs.

Practice!

1. The average preschooler gets _____ .
   a. enough sleep
   b. less sleep than needed
   c. more sleep than necessary

2. In early childhood, _____ .
   a. most children wake up on a regular basis and need their caregivers' attention several times a night
   b. children are old enough that they do not need the attention of their caregivers anymore when they wake up
   c. children sometimes need their caregivers' attention at night

3. During sleep, _____ .
   a. children make finger movements to practice fine motor skills acquired during the day
   b. the brain continues to develop and change, even more so than during the day
   c. dreams can help slow down or accelerate progress in the development of gross motor skills

4. Around _____ of preschoolers have a regular bedtime routine.
   a. 7%
   b. 32%
   c. 60%
   d. 90%

5. Nighttime fears are _____ .
   a. quite common in early childhood
   b. a strong indicator that a child experiences abuse
   c. an early indicator of academic problems at school
   d. caused by an abnormally high level of melatonin

6. Electronic media _____ .
   a. help children go to sleep because they don't move much while watching movies or playing games
   b. emit light that can disrupt the production of the hormone melatonin
   c. should be placed in children's bedrooms so they can go right to sleep after using the media
   d. are one of the best ways to help children fall asleep fast

Act It Out!

Five-year-old Fumiko recently got a tablet for her birthday. She has a reading app on the tablet that allows her to choose from a wide variety of books. Fumiko has started reading under the covers at night, and her parents don't discourage her; after all, it's good that she's reading! Lately, though, her kindergarten teacher has noticed that Fumiko looks very tired in the afternoon, and so she calls Fumiko's parents in for a chat. Role-play a conversation between Fumiko's parents and teacher in which they discuss her sleeping habits.

Show What You've Learned!

For a few weeks now, 4-year-old Adrianna has been waking up frequently at night from nightmares. Once awake, she is so scared that she has trouble falling asleep again, although her mother spends considerable time trying to calm her down. Adrianna is beginning to fear bedtime itself because she is afraid the "monsters" will return to her at night once again. Imagine you are a nurse discussing Adrianna's nightmares and bedtime problems with her parents. What advice can you give them?

8.3 How Do Children's Motor Skills Develop?

- Outline the gross motor skills children develop in their preschool years and explain their importance.
- Recall which fine motor skills children develop in their preschool years.
- Explain how children's ability to create art progresses.
- Tell at what stage of development most children complete their potty training.

Motor development refers to children's changing ability to control their body movements as their bones and muscles grow. In this section, we will look at the difference between gross motor skills and fine motor skills and consider how these skills relate to children's ability to produce art. Finally, we will consider a very important part of toddlerhood or early childhood: toilet training.

Gross Motor Skills

gross motor skills skills that are involved when we move large body parts like arms and legs.

Gross motor skills are involved when we move large body parts like arms and legs. They are important for activities like running, jumping, throwing balls, and swimming. They are also a result of enormous amounts of practice—young children are always on the move!

Gross motor skills develop quickly

Gross motor skills develop rapidly during early childhood. Whereas a 2-year-old is still toddling around with a somewhat robot-like gait, 3-year-olds can walk pretty much automatically, and a 4-year-old is walking like an adult. Three-year-olds already can run, but only around the age of 4 or 5

■ Within a few years, children progress from the early stages of walking to being secure runners who can stop or turn abruptly.

can children suddenly stop or turn when running. Children also gradually become better at catching and throwing balls. Around age 5, children can catch a ball thrown to them and throw a ball so that it can be caught by another person. Many other skills like hopping, galloping, skipping, and the like develop as well. TABLE 8.2 shows some of the gross motor skills pre-schoolers are developing.

■ Table 8.2 Development of Gross and Fine Motor Skills in Early Childhood

GROSS MOTOR SKILLS

3 years	4 years	5 years
Walks fluidly	Can stop and turn suddenly when running	Descends stairs with alternating feet
When climbing stairs, places both feet on one step before moving on	Climbs stairs like an adult, alternating feet on steps	Can throw a ball so that others can catch it
Stands on one foot for about 5 seconds	Throws a ball overarm	Catches a small ball with hands only
Pedals a tricycle	Catches a ball that was bounced	Rides bicycle
Climbs jungle gyms	Jumps a short distance from standing	Good balance
		Jumps a distance of up to 3 feet
Indicators of difficulties with gross motor skills	Late in reaching milestones (but remember there is some variation in when children reach the milestones) Avoids physical activities Body movements look stiff or awkward Loses a skill she had mastered before Tires easily when physically active Has difficulties in using skills in different settings (for example, cannot switch easily from throwing a light ball to throwing a heavy one)	

FINE MOTOR SKILLS

3 years	4 years	5 years
Cuts paper	Always uses the same hand for fine motor tasks	Uses crayons effectively
Builds tower with 10 blocks	Starts cutting curved lines	Draws geometric forms like triangles and circles
Completes puzzle with large pieces	Can string beads	Ties shoes
Can copy a cross	Prints name	Colors within lines
Holds crayons with fingers		Cuts and pastes simple shapes
Indicators of difficulties with fine motor skills	Late in reaching milestones Tires easily when performing fine motor activities Has difficulties dressing self in a way expected for age Draws or writes in a way that is atypically messy and labored Dislikes tasks that require hand–eye coordination (e.g., playing with Legos)	

The development of gross motor skills can be affected by a number of factors. Children with muscular dystrophy (a disease that causes progressive loss of muscle mass), cerebral palsy (a disorder that affects movement and motor skills and is caused by damage to the developing brain), or some other neurological conditions may not develop in a typical way. Injuries and illnesses obviously also affect children's ability to move.

Certain factors can cause individual differences in gross motor skills

In early childhood, differences in gross motor skills are relatively small. Where they exist, they are often due to the following factors:

- *sex differences*: Boys tend to have more muscle mass than girls and may engage in different activities.
- *genetic factors*: A child may be more coordinated, flexible, or athletic based on those traits in their parents and grandparents.
- *environmental factors*: Parents may encourage boys and girls to engage in different physical activities.

Although differences due to sex in early childhood are small, boys at this age tend to have more muscle mass and strength than girls at this age, and boys may be more physically active than girls. Girls tend to have better gross motor control and coordination, as seen in the ability to hop on one foot (Moser & Reikerås, 2016; Rodriguez-Negro et al., 2021).

In preschoolers, individual differences generally play a greater role than gender differences. Genetic differences lead some children (and adults!) to be more coordinated and stronger than others. Children who like to move also practice their motor skills a lot more than sedentary children. Because parents often tend to encourage different activities in girls versus boys, you will typically not find as many boys in dance or gymnastic classes, for example, as in soccer or hockey classes (Spessato et al., 2013).

Adults can support children's gross motor development

Parents and caregivers today tend to emphasize the development of cognitive skills in their children. You may wonder, then, how important it is to support children in the development of their motor skills. Having good motor skills is beneficial for a number of reasons. Children moving easily and in a coordinated way enjoy their movements and will continue to engage in physical activities. Less physically oriented children will likely avoid playing physical games or participating in sports because participation requires much effort and they may lack confidence. These children are at more risk for obesity. As they get older, their risk for other diseases related to inactivity (like diabetes or heart disease) increases as well. Additionally, children whose gross and fine motor skills are well-developed exhibit better social behavior and are better able to pay attention at school and follow directions they may be given (Cornejo et al., 2021; MacDonald et al., 2016; Pica, 2008).

There are many ways you can support young children's gross motor development. As is often the case with children, play is one of the best ways to support their development: Play catch, hop on one leg, play ball, or do some dancing. Children develop motor skills by playing with others, so giving them the opportunity to play with friends is often more important than is instruction by an adult.

Fine Motor Skills

fine motor skills skills that involve movements of smaller muscles and small movements like those of hands and fingers.

Fine motor skills involve movements of smaller muscles and small movements like those of hands and fingers. In the following sections, we will discuss which fine motor skills develop in preschoolers and how we can support their development.

The development of fine motor skills helps children develop more independence

Between ages 2 and 3, children eagerly scribble on paper with crayons and form play dough into large sculptures (see also Table 8.2). They like to do puzzles with large pieces that have to be placed into matching holes.

Around age 3, children also start developing their skills in zipping and buttoning their jackets, closing the Velcros on their shoes, and trying to dress and undress themselves. They start cutting paper and holding a crayon between thumb and forefinger. They also get better at the twisting motions used for opening doorknobs and cans. Children continue to practice using a spoon and fork at meal times.

By age 4 or 5, most children have become relatively adept at buttoning and unbuttoning their clothes. Their grasp of crayons between thumb and forefinger becomes more stable and enables them to have more control over their writing and drawing. A lot of children can already print their names. As children grow older and approach school age, their fine motor skills mature even more. This maturation enables the children to learn how to write letters and numbers at school. Usually, either no or little adult assistance is needed at mealtimes anymore.

Adults can support children's fine motor skill development

Fine motor skills are important in many ways. Children need to have command of a pencil by the time they start kindergarten. This is of particular significance because, in recent years, kindergartens teach more and more reading and writing skills than what used to be taught. Children with better fine motor skills perform better in math when they enter kindergarten and achieve greater gains over the school year (Luo et al., 2007; Son & Meisels, 2006). In fact, good motor skills in preschool predict reading achievement even in third grade (Cameron et al., 2012; McPhillips & Jordan-Black, 2007; Mohamed & O'Brien, 2021)!

■ Learning to zip jackets and button shirts is no easy task for small children.

You can help children develop their fine motor skills by providing objects for play that need to be handled and explored with hands and fingers. These objects can be art materials like finger paints, brushes and crayons, and play dough. Building materials like blocks and Legos also work well, as do pretend play toys like dolls and stuffed animals. You can also provide books, instruments like xylophones, and many other things children can manipulate with their hands. Ideally, challenge children by giving them tools they have not used before or asking them to draw things or perform movements they have not made before.

Creating art helps children develop fine motor skills

Most small children love drawing and creating art in various ways. There is little room for self-criticism. Children enthusiastically share their artwork with all around. Their ability to handle pencils, brushes, crayons, scissors, and clay is associated with their fine motor skills.

Children's ability to draw progresses through four stages (Kellogg, 1969):

1. *Scribbling*: In this earliest stage, children are just starting to draw. You may think of the scribbles as random products, but Kellogg actually categorized children's scribbles into 20 distinct types, like dots, single loops, or vertical lines.

2. *Shape*: Around age 3, children start using single shapes in their artwork. These shapes include circles to represent the sun or balls, squares to represent buildings, and the like.

Courtesy of Karin Sternberg

FIGURE 8.2 Drawings of a 3- and a 5-year-old child. The drawing of the 3-year-old (left) is rather abstract, containing lots of lines and loops. The drawing of the 5-year-old (right) shows careful planning of different objects that viewers can recognize without help from the artist.

3. *Design*: Once children are able to draw shapes, they start combining shapes.

4. *Pictorial*: Between ages 4 and 5, children enter the pictorial stage, where their artwork resembles real-life objects, and people can recognize what was drawn even if they are not told by the young artist. When drawing people, children at first draw "head people," attaching arms and legs to the head and ignoring the torso. Around age 5, most children draw people realistically, including the torso. At this age, they also start planning their drawings instead of just starting to draw and then see what comes out of it.

In the beginning, children just start drawing and then decide when they are done what their picture depicts. Around the age of 4 or 5, children start planning and decide what to draw before they start drawing (Rübeling et al., 2011) (see **FIGURE 8.2**).

Toilet Training

Marcella turns 3 today, and her parents, Robyn and Toni, have invited some families from the neighborhood for a backyard birthday party. The parents chat while the children play but are interrupted momentarily by one of the children, Dino, who pulls on his mother's hand and tells her he needs to pee. Robyn and Toni are surprised and a little embarrassed: Dino is only a few weeks older than Marcella, who is still in diapers and has shown no interest in potty training. Are they doing something wrong?

Toilet training is an area of strong interest and much discussion among parents. Everyone seems to have ideas about the best way to approach this delicate topic, and new parents may receive a lot of (sometimes unsolicited) advice from well-meaning family and friends, including those who don't have children! This often serves only to increase parents' uncertainty about when and how to potty train. In fact, a 2014 study found that around one-third of parents are unsure when to begin the process of toilet training (Kaerts et al., 2014; see also Sundnes, 2018). Parents are naturally anxious to begin toilet training as soon as possible, since diapers are expensive, and changing a child's diaper outside of the home is not always convenient.

It is important to know that successful toilet training depends on a child's physical development. In order to control elimination, a child needs to be able to control the muscles that open and close the bladder and bowels (sphincter muscles). In this sense, it is no different from learning to run or hop: Toilet training cannot succeed until the child is ready in terms of motor development, and that age will vary from child to child.

Most children are physically ready to toilet train between the ages of 18 months and 3 years. Sufficient control over their bladder and bowel movements develops only around the age of 18 months. But many children in the United States do not train until significantly later. Toilet training is no easy task for a young child. At the very minimum, children have to:

- realize they have to empty their bladder or bowel,
- remember they no longer wear diapers and so have to use the potty,
- communicate to a caregiver that they have to go,
- interrupt their play, and
- control their bladder or bowel until they are on the toilet.

■ There is no general consensus as to when children are ready for toilet training and what the readiness signs are.

Eventually, other skills are needed as well: Children need to be able to pull down their pants, wipe themselves, and wash their hands (Pantley, 2010).

There are a number of signs that indicate that a child is ready to toilet train. These signs include a child's interest in potty training, the child staying dry in diapers for 2 hours or more, bowel movements having become predictable, and an ability to pull clothes up and down independently. A child also needs to be able to follow simple directions (American Academy of Pediatrics, 2016; Baird et al., 2019). However, there is no general consensus as to which readiness signs to use. Depending on the indicator used, the time at which toilet training is started varies a lot (Kaerts et al., 2012).

When the time for potty training comes, there are a lot of different approaches that caregivers can try. These approaches are often hotly debated, but ultimately it is important to find the approach that works best for the individual child. If it is summer or if a house does not have carpet, children sometimes just can run around without clothes. When they eliminate without a diaper it makes them quickly aware of the fact they need to use a toilet—an effect that cannot be achieved with the comfort of wearing a diaper.

Another approach is to put a child on the potty at frequent intervals, like every 15 minutes. Some people just watch their children's facial and bodily expressions closely and rush with them to the bathroom when they see that the child has to go. You can try to entice children with potty stickers or by letting them choose nice underwear or a potty seat. It usually takes around 3 months for a child to be toilet-trained.

However, experiences very much depend on the child: My own children toilet trained after age 3. We tried several approaches with them earlier but neither were they interested nor did we have any success! At long last, their preschool

■ Cultures around the world approach toilet training in a wide variety of ways and at vastly different ages. In China, for example, parents often use open-crotch pants called kaidangku. When little children feel an urge to empty their bladder or bowels, they can relieve themselves much faster than when they do not have to undress first and are less dependent on adults. There are many places they may do so: under trees and bushes, on sidewalks, or held by their parents over a trash can. In urban areas, Chinese parents increasingly make use of disposable diapers or use a combination of diapers in public and open-crotch pants at home. But in rural areas, open-crotch pants still prevail (Bruno, 2012).

announced that they had to be potty-trained by the end of the coming summer. So we had to do something! Months ahead of time, I started telling the children that we were going to visit their grandparents in Germany in the summer and that unfortunately there were no diapers at their grandparents' house. I made this point quite often before our travels. Once we got to Germany, we took off their diapers and, like a miracle, they were all potty-trained from day 1. This procedure would not have worked with children much younger, but the older children are at the time of potty training, the faster it usually goes.

Most important is to keep the pressure low. There is little chance for success if the child feels pressured too much. Try to keep it low-key and fun, and if the child is not ready, wait a little longer. It is also important to remember that toilet training often comes with setbacks. The younger children are, the more time they may need to learn the process. Sometimes they may just be too busy playing to go to the bathroom. Often, children who are toilet-trained during the day still need a diaper at night. By age 5, most girls and around 75% of boys do not need a diaper at night anymore.

Review!

Which gross motor skills do children develop in their preschool years?

- Due to brain development and much practice through active play, children's *gross motor skills* develop rapidly in early childhood. They become secure and versatile when running and throwing or catching balls. They learn to stand and hop on one foot as well as to ride bikes.
- There are large differences in gross motor skills as well as the rate of development of motor skills between children.
- Gross motor skills are important not only for anything movement-related but also because they contribute to children's confidence, physical fitness, social behavior, and ability to pay attention at school. Additionally, many children toilet train between 2 and 3 years of age.

Which fine motor skills do children develop in their preschool years?

- *Fine motor skills* are practiced through activities like writing and drawing, or playing with clay or play dough. In early childhood, children learn to zip or button their jackets, hold a pencil correctly between thumb and forefinger, and start writing their first letters.
- Fine motor skills are a predictor of math achievements.

How does children's ability to create art progress?

- Artwork changes from unplanned, unrecognizable "scribbles" to planned works that observers can recognize without explanation from the artist.

When do most children complete their potty training?

- In most developed countries, many children complete potty training during the preschool years.

Practice!

1. Gross motor skills help with _____ .
   a. the execution of complex movements
   b. the execution of simple movements
   c. the execution of movements involving large body parts like legs and arms
   d. the execution of movements involving small body parts like fingers and wrists

2. Motor skill development can be effectively supported by _____ .
   a. watching educational movies that explain how to play sports
   b. giving kids the opportunity to take a nap on a regular basis
   c. playing outside and doing crafts
   d. teaching reading skills as early as possible

3. An activity that does not involve fine motor skills is _____ .
   a. opening a tube of toothpaste
   b. tying a shoe
   c. using knife and fork
   d. jumping on one leg

4. American children are toilet-trained usually _____ .
   a. in infancy
   b. between 1 and 2 years of age
   c. between 2 and 4 years of age
   d. around age 5

Show What You've Learned!

When his son Marco was born, John could not wait to teach him to play soccer, John's own favorite sport. When Marco turned 3, John gave him a colorful soccer ball and immediately took him to the park to start playing. But it has been frustrating for John: Marco will run after the ball, but even after many months, he isn't able to kick the ball in a way that it ends up anywhere close to where it should go. He seems to have no talent at all, especially compared with other 3-year-olds. And now, on their daily trips to the park, Marco is showing more interest in the swings and the big slide than in soccer. John worries that, at this rate, his son will never be a great player. Imagine you are a parent at the park, listening to John express his despair about his son. What would you say to him?

Act It Out!

Marcella's birthday party has ended, and most of the neighbors have gone home. Dino's mother, Andrea, has stayed to help Marcella's parents, Robyn and Toni, tidy up. That's when they ask Andrea her advice on toilet training. They have lots of questions for Andrea, who is a kindergarten teacher. Why is Marcella still in diapers when other children her age are already potty-trained? Are they doing something wrong? Will she be able to go to preschool in the fall if she is still in diapers? With two of your classmates, role-play a conversation between Marcella's parents and Andrea. As Robyn and Toni, what are your concerns around toilet training? As Andrea, what advice and reassurance would you give?

8.4 Nutrition in Early Childhood

- Identify ways caregivers can balance eating behavior with proper nutritional needs in preschoolers.
- List some of preschoolers' feeding problems.

Children can develop to their full potential only if they eat a wholesome and well-balanced diet. In the next two sections, we will consider the nutritional needs of young children, their (sometimes strange) eating habits, and some feeding problems that can develop.

Eating Behavior and Nutritional Needs

As children enter preschool age, their appetite tends to decline. Parents often view small appetites and erratic eating behavior with alarm. In most cases, however, there is nothing to worry about. Children in early childhood don't grow as fast as babies do. For this reason, they don't need to keep up the calorie intake they used to have when they were younger. Children are generally quite good at regulating their food consumption. On some days they seem to be eating hardly anything, on other days they are eating a lot. As long as a child is growing adequately and is healthy, parents do not need to be concerned about the child's eating.

Generally, preschool children need between 1,200 and 1,400 calories a day. Children learn to eat the foods their caregivers prepare for them, so it is of crucial importance to begin healthy nutritional habits as early as possible. Oftentimes, parents assume that children will only eat sugary and unhealthy foods like white pasta, French fries, and sweet cereals. However, children's behavior is influenced by the behavior of those around them. When adults eat and enjoy healthy foods on a regular basis, their children will learn to do the same (Mitchell et al., 2013; Vaughn et al., 2018).

Enjoying family meals is another crucial factor for a healthy lifestyle. Research has shown that children who frequently eat meals together with their family eat better and are generally healthier than children for whom family meals are a rare occurrence. Well-nourished children have better social interactions with others and have a better basis to develop their cognitive and motor skills as well

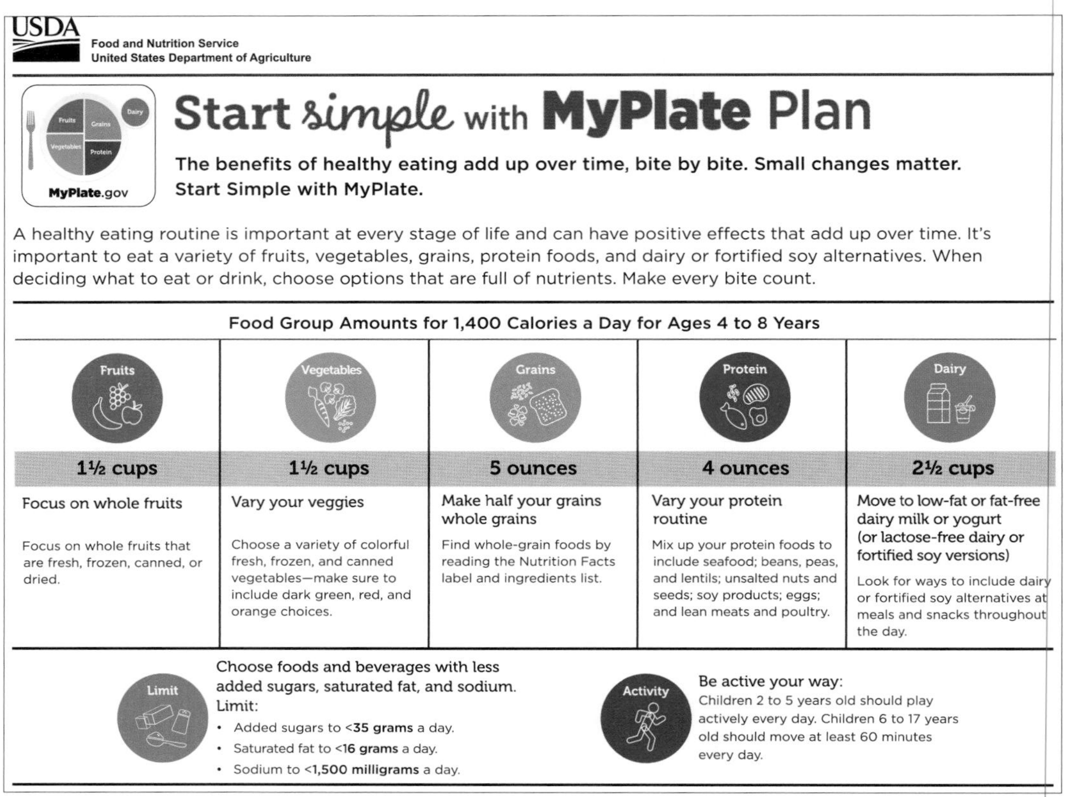

USDA
Food and Nutrition Service
United States Department of Agriculture

Start *simple* with **MyPlate** Plan

The benefits of healthy eating add up over time, bite by bite. Small changes matter. Start Simple with MyPlate.

MyPlate.gov

A healthy eating routine is important at every stage of life and can have positive effects that add up over time. It's important to eat a variety of fruits, vegetables, grains, protein foods, and dairy or fortified soy alternatives. When deciding what to eat or drink, choose options that are full of nutrients. Make every bite count.

Food Group Amounts for 1,400 Calories a Day for Ages 4 to 8 Years

Fruits	Vegetables	Grains	Protein	Dairy
1½ cups	1½ cups	5 ounces	4 ounces	2½ cups
Focus on whole fruits	Vary your veggies	Make half your grains whole grains	Vary your protein routine	Move to low-fat or fat-free dairy milk or yogurt (or lactose-free dairy or fortified soy versions)
Focus on whole fruits that are fresh, frozen, canned, or dried.	Choose a variety of colorful fresh, frozen, and canned vegetables—make sure to include dark green, red, and orange choices.	Find whole-grain foods by reading the Nutrition Facts label and ingredients list.	Mix up your protein foods to include seafood; beans, peas, and lentils; unsalted nuts and seeds; soy products; eggs; and lean meats and poultry.	Look for ways to include dairy or fortified soy alternatives at meals and snacks throughout the day.

Limit Choose foods and beverages with less added sugars, saturated fat, and sodium. Limit:
- Added sugars to <**35 grams** a day.
- Saturated fat to <**16 grams** a day.
- Sodium to <**1,500 milligrams** a day.

Activity Be active your way: Children 2 to 5 years old should play actively every day. Children 6 to 17 years old should move at least 60 minutes every day.

FIGURE 8.3 Recommended daily food portions.

From United States Department of Agriculture. 2021. Back to Basics: All About MyPlate Food Groups. www.usda.gov

(Faith & Hittner, 2016; Hong & Henly, 2020; Prado & Dewey, 2014). Parents who as children had frequent family meals with their family also tend to have more frequent family meals as adults (Friend et al., 2014). During mealtimes, a family ideally should turn off the TV and put digital devices and cell phones aside.

Parents should ensure their child eats a well-balanced diet consisting of fruit, vegetables, grains, proteins (like beans or meat), as well as dairy. FIGURE 8.3 shows what a well-balanced diet looks like for a preschooler.

Young children often have idiosyncratic food preferences. They are notoriously difficult to feed. Some don't like food of a particular color or have a preference for white food, others give their parents trouble with any vegetables, and yet others don't like soft or hard food. There is no limit to the food aversions they may have. This pattern of behavior is normal as long as it does not impair a child's growth and does not become a chronic eating behavior. Here are some strategies to encourage picky eaters to eat (Mayo Clinic, 2020):

- Be patient when serving new foods: You may have to serve them several times before a child warms up to them.
- Make eating fun: Serve brightly colored foods, offer dips, or cut food out with cookie cutters.
- Let your child help make the week's meal plan.
- Let your child assist you in food preparation.
- Be a good example and eat healthily as well.
- Don't offer dessert as a reward, because your child may learn that dessert is the best and most desirable part of dinner.

Feeding Problems

Mild, temporary feeding problems occur in about 25%–45% of children in the United States, but only 1% of children develop chronic problems (Satter, 1990; Sdravou et al., 2021). Here are some of the problems children may develop (Liu & Stein, 2013; Sdravou et al., 2021).

INSUFFICIENT WEIGHT GAIN When a child's weight falls below the third percentile on the relevant growth chart (that is, only three percent of children are lighter than him), this level is considered a "failure to thrive" and can put a child at risk for impaired growth and developmental delays.

RESTRICTED FOOD PREFERENCES It is normal for children to be picky eaters and to have restricted food preferences. Their preferences change with time. If the limited food preferences impair feeding significantly and do not improve over time, it can develop into a behavioral disorder.

STRANGE FOOD CHOICES Some children eat things like hair or soap. If children over the age of 2 regularly eat items that are commonly considered nonedible, they may be diagnosed with a disorder called pica.

NUTRITIONAL DEFICIENCIES When children consume enough calories but do not have a well-balanced diet, they may chronically lack nutrients like iron, zinc, or calcium. Children are particularly partial to foods high in sugar. These foods often lack nutrients and lead to excessive sugar consumption.

EXCESSIVE WEIGHT GAIN Increasingly, children in developed nations tend to be overweight as a result of poor eating habits. Whereas between 1971 and 1974 around 5% of American children aged 2–19 were obese, the comparable figure was 19% in 2018 (Centers for Disease Control and Prevention, 2021a; Fryar et al., 2016). Obesity also varies by age and ethnicity: In 2018, around 13% of children aged 2–5 were obese. In 12- to 19-year-old children, the obesity rate was already 21%. African American (24%) and Hispanic American children (26%) tend to be more likely to be obese than White (16%) and particularly Asian American children (9%) (Centers for Disease Control and Prevention, 2021a).

FOOD ALLERGIES Six million children are affected by food allergies. Even small amounts of a food allergen can cause a reaction (Food Allergy Research & Education, 2021). Food allergy symptoms range from itchy skin to stomach pain, vomiting, sneezing, coughing and wheezing to fainting. A serious allergic reaction is called anaphylaxis and can be deadly if left untreated. Ninety percent of food allergies in children are caused by six foods: cow's milk, eggs, peanuts, tree nuts (like walnuts or cashews), soy, and wheat (Food Allergy Research & Education, 2021).

© ChameleonsEye/Shutterstock.com

■ In developed nations, obesity in children is more and more common. What do you think are some of the underlying causes?

What's It Like...

Managing Food Allergies

Tamika, School Nutrition Coordinator

I've been working for our local school district for 21 years now. I love my job—it's certainly never boring! I do a lot of menu planning, and I help teach kids about healthy nutrition, and assist the ones with special dietary needs. I train new employees, and I even do some public speaking from time to time.

In the 13 years since I started working for the school district, there's been an 18% increase in food allergies in children at our schools, and no one really knows why.

Children are allergic to lots of different foods, but a few foods like milk, eggs, peanuts, tree nuts, wheat, soy, and fish account for the majority of allergic reactions.

Children with food allergies face a lot of challenges at school. They may get teased or bullied. Sometimes, other students will threaten them with the food they're allergic to. In a lot of cases, it starts as a joke because kids without allergies don't understand how serious it is—that's where education comes in. Severe food allergies are actually considered a disability, and so our schools have to accommodate children with food allergies in a reasonable way.

As a nutrition coordinator, my job is to help parents and children feel confident that they can manage food allergies safely in our school environment. There are a lot of steps that go into accommodating food allergies, but it is a doable task with some planning. Here are just some of the things we have to do:

- Create teams for managing food allergies, including families, administrators, nurses, teachers, and food service professionals.
- Always use separate utensils for every dish and item.
- Label allergens where items are served as well as where they are stored.
- If possible, prepare foods containing allergens only when other items have already been prepared.
- If possible, prepare foods containing allergens in a specific area away from other foods.
- Educate staff about the risks of cross-contamination.
- Give families access to recipes and ingredient lists.

We've found that with careful planning, we're able to provide a safe environment for all our students, which ultimately benefits not only the affected students but their classmates and our staff as well.

Bruce, father of Abby (14 years old)

We first noticed Abby's food allergies when she had an allergic reaction to the soy formula we fed her as a baby. She suddenly had a swollen face and eyes; her back, arms, and legs turned red; and she had trouble breathing—that first episode was really scary.

What followed was an odyssey of reading books and ingredient lists, trying out different foods, and always being on edge. We obsessed over what we fed her, and we had to be super-vigilant whenever she was around other kids with food. Whenever she went to a birthday party or playdate, we had to make sure other parents were aware of her allergies. Then it was friends, relatives, teachers—we've had to educate just about anyone who is in contact with her. Now we see an allergist on a regular basis, but we've still ended up in the emergency room a handful of times.

The things Abby is allergic to today include ground nuts and tree nuts, shellfish, and different kinds of fruit, like apples and strawberries. When she started school, we had several meetings with teachers, the nurse, and other staff. Fortunately, the school was used to having children with food allergies, so the path had already been forged for us. The school placed all the children with food allergies (there were actually two more in Abby's grade) in one class that was made nut-free. We were really grateful she was in a safe environment there, or at least, as safe as any place could be for her. The school has been great ever since, and when Abby moved to middle school, it was still in the same school district, so the transition was very smooth.

As Abby gets older, things have become harder in some ways and easier in others. She understands her allergies and the threat they pose to her, and she takes responsibility for her actions and what she eats. She also knows which situations to avoid. Her friends know about her allergies as well. At the same time, she is only 14. And she is becoming more independent and goes out more, which exposes her to more risks. A trip to the ballpark, for example, can be dangerous because people tend to eat lots of peanuts there. If we go to a restaurant, the first thing I do is wipe the table and chairs. I often think that if more people were educated about food allergies, the world would be a much safer place for our children than it is now.

Source: Collins, 2012; Heideman & Poronsky, 2021

Review!

How can caregivers ensure proper nutrition in preschoolers?

- Due to erratic eating habits and slowing growth, parents often worry about adequate food intake, but children rarely starve themselves.
- To grow and develop optimally, children need a balanced diet of fruit, vegetables, grains, protein, and dairy.
- Their appetite decreases compared with their baby and toddler years because their growth rate slows down.
- It can be a hard and frustrating experience to feed preschoolers, because their appetites vary a lot from day to day and they may have peculiar food preferences or dislikes. But as long as they are thriving and get offered a healthy diet, there is usually no need to worry, because they are adept at regulating their food intake.

What are some feeding problems in preschoolers?

- The large majority of children only have temporary feeding problems that come and go. If children refuse entire food groups for a long time or fail to gain (or even lose) sufficient weight, some intervention may be needed.
- Children in developed countries are rarely malnourished but can have nutritional deficiencies because their diet does not provide them with the necessary nutrients. An increasingly worrisome problem is obesity.

Practice!

1. Children in early childhood need around _____ .
   a. 800–1,000 calories a day
   b. 1,000–1,200 calories a day
   c. 1,200–1,400 calories a day
   d. 1,400–1,600 calories a day

2. A healthy diet consists of _____ .
   a. fruit, vegetables, grains, proteins, and dairy
   b. fruit, vegetables, grains, saturated fat, and sugar
   c. fruit, vegetables, grains, lactose, and dextrose
   d. fruit, vegetables, grains, high-fructose corn syrup, and trans fats

3. Among children age 2–5, around _____ .
   a. 37% are obese
   b. 22% are obese
   c. 13% are obese
   d. 7% are obese

4. Failure to thrive indicates that _____ .
   a. a child's motor skills are not developed age-appropriately
   b. a child's sleep patterns are not developed age-appropriately
   c. a child refuses to eat a healthy diet
   d. a child's weight and height have fallen below the third percentile

What Would You Do?

You are a pediatrician in Decatur, a suburb of Atlanta. A young immigrant mother from South America presents you with her 4-year-old son, Pedro. One month ago, they immigrated to the United States from Chile. The move came with an almost complete switch in diets. Many foods Pedro used to eat in Chile are not readily available in the United States. Pedro's mother does not have the time or ingredients to prepare authentic Chilean meals. Since their arrival, Pedro has refused most foods and is eating very little. He also shows little willingness to try new foods. His mother is worried about his health and development. As the pediatrician, what advice do you give her?

8.5 Health and Safety in Preschoolers

- Outline the diseases affecting children in early childhood and explain their impact.
- Explain the role of injuries in preschoolers' health.
- Identify child maltreatment and its contributing factors and describe the intervention programs created to prevent it.
- Examine whether electronic media has an impact on children's health.

In the following sections, we discuss childhood diseases as well as accidents and what can be done to prevent them. We also discuss child maltreatment and the effects of media on children's health.

Childhood Diseases

Parents, teachers, and childcare workers all know that kids in early childhood pick up many minor illnesses, particularly in colder climates during cold and flu season. However, a significant number of children experience serious chronic diseases that need to be managed on a daily basis. In this section, we discuss minor and major illnesses a child can contract and what can be done to help prevent them.

Minor illnesses help children develop immunity

Any parent of young children will tell you their children get sick a lot. Some winters it seems they are catching another sickness just as they are recovering from their prior one. Fortunately, most of the illnesses affecting young children in the United States are minor and nothing to be overly concerned about.

Preschoolers most often get sick from respiratory viruses that cause the common cold or flu. The common cold can be caused by more than 100 viruses. It infects the nose and throat areas. Young children tend to catch colds a lot because they have not yet built up immunity to the large variety of cold viruses. Once children have had a cold, they become immune to that particular virus so that as they get older, they get sick less often. Parents usually do not need to be concerned if a child gets many colds. This mostly means that the child is exposed to many viruses, probably because of time spent in daycare or around many children or older siblings (American Academy of Pediatrics, 2018).

Some viruses cause more serious symptoms. The influenza (flu) virus and SARS-CoV-2 (COVID-19), for example, can cause fever, body aches, and breathing problems serious enough to require medical treatment. Virus infections are spread by air when children cough and sneeze, or by touch when they touch their mouths and noses and afterward touch other objects or children. A large number of children are also afflicted by ear infections. Although few children in the Western world die of respiratory diseases, about 5 million children die of them each year in less developed countries (Caballero et al., 2019; Kesson, 2007).

Another group of minor illnesses involves gastrointestinal diseases, which include nausea, vomiting, and diarrhea. In the United States, children often contract diarrhea in childcare centers or through food poisoning caused by bacteria in food. This group of diseases is also highly contagious and is passed on through dirty hands, direct contact with the fecal matter, or of course by eating the contaminated food. Not only bacteria but also viruses can also cause diarrhea. One of the most common viruses is the rotavirus, which causes explosive diarrhea. People with severe diarrhea and vomiting lose a lot of fluids and salts, so it is important that they receive lots of adequate hydration. In some cases, children need to receive IV fluids at a hospital to receive enough hydration.

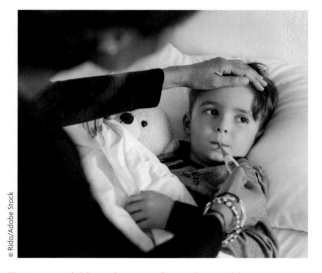

■ A young child gets between five and ten colds per year.

Tragically, although diarrhea is preventable and treatable, worldwide, around 370,000 children under age 5 die of diarrhea each year. Worldwide, diarrhea is one of the leading causes of death in children under 5 as well as one of the leading causes of malnutrition (World Health Organization, 2021a).

There are some benefits to children getting sick. For example, through exposure to infections, children build up immunity so they get sick less often as they get older. Children also learn to identify symptoms and communicate them to their caregivers, and they gradually learn how to cope with diseases, how it feels to be sick (so they can empathize with and support others when they are sick), and how to prevent the spread of diseases.

Cancer is the major disease that most affects American children

As we have seen above in our discussion of diarrhea, what is considered a serious disease depends on where you live. In the United States, the disease that kills most children is cancer (8% of deaths of children age 1–4 and 19% of deaths in children 5–9 years old). Around 10,500 children are diagnosed with cancer each year. Because of major advances in cancer treatment, more than 84% of these children will survive for 5 years or more. About 28% of all childhood cancers are cancers of the bone marrow and blood (leukemias). Brain tumors constitute around 26% of cancers in children. In most cases, childhood cancer cannot be prevented. Just like in adults, childhood cancer is treated with established therapies like surgery, radiation therapy, and chemotherapy, but also with newer therapies like immunotherapy (American Cancer Society, 2021).

Many other diseases that used to kill children in the United States and other developed nations have now been virtually eliminated due to the widespread availability of vaccines. However, in many developing countries where people do not have routine access to health care, vaccines, and a healthy diet, and where the people live in unsanitary circumstances, these diseases still sicken and kill many children. Among these diseases are pneumonia, malaria, diarrhea, polio, and measles. Malnutrition and crowded conditions, such as in refugee camps, make children even more susceptible to disease.

Children with chronic diseases have to manage their condition on a daily basis

Around 15% of children in the United States have a chronic condition. This means that any given day they may feel sick or feel well, but they live with their condition and have to manage it on a daily basis. The most common chronic disease is asthma, but there are many others like diabetes, cerebral palsy, sickle cell anemia, cystic fibrosis, and AIDS. Children with chronic conditions typically need to go to the doctor or the hospital more often than do healthy children.

Managing a chronic condition is challenging for the child and her caregivers. The symptoms of the disease may be scary and painful, and the treatments may be as well. Preschoolers do not understand the nature and causes of diseases, and it is hard for them to wait in doctors' offices, stay in hospitals for extended amounts of time, or sit still for treatments. They may not comply with the limits and directions their

■ Ten-year-old Sebastian is running around outside. Suddenly, he stops and bends over: He wheezes and struggles to breathe. His older sister immediately recognizes the signs of an asthma attack and runs to get his inhaler. Sebastian inhales deeply and within a few minutes is able to breathe without difficulty. The treatment is not always effective: Sometimes, he has needed to go to a hospital emergency room for treatment. Over the past decades, the number of children with asthma has steadily risen, so that around 10% of children ages 5–11 have asthma.

parents give them. Their family is affected as well: Parents may feel stressed and struggle with their child's disease, and siblings may feel left out or neglected. Families often find it helpful to plan in advance for procedures that are scheduled and routinely plan for some fun in everyday life as a family. Coordination of the child's needs with his daycare center, school, or caregiver is very important. Parents also should take into account their own need for a break or for some time together by using childcare services or respite care. And it is important to integrate the other siblings to keep negative feelings and jealousy at bay (Boyse et al., 2012).

Preventing infectious diseases: Vaccines

The recent COVID-19 pandemic has made us aware of how vulnerable we are to infectious diseases. But while many of us had never experienced anything like the coronavirus, older Americans may recall major flu pandemics that occurred in 1968 and, before that, in 1957. (The most serious pandemic of the twentieth century was the outbreak of the Spanish flu that occurred in 1918.) They might also recall the 1964–65 epidemic of rubella (or German measles), which infected more than 12 million people; 2,000 babies died during the outbreak, and more than 20,000 were born with serious birth defects. Today, the rubella virus has been all but eliminated in the United States, except for people who bring it to the United States from other countries (Centers for Disease Control and Prevention, 2017b, 2017c). And whereas hundreds of Americans died every year from measles in the early part of the twentieth century, there were just 13 cases of measles in 2020, and deaths are extremely rare (Centers for Disease Control and Prevention, 2017a, 2017c).

The cause of these tremendous changes will not surprise you. As with COVID-19, we can attribute the reduction in cases to the development of vaccines. One disease—smallpox—has even been completely eradicated from our planet thanks to the development and use of an effective vaccine (Centers for Disease Control and Prevention, 2021f). **Vaccines** are substances prepared from weakened or dead germs that help the immune system to fight a disease more effectively. They often (but not always) lead to **immunization** against a disease, which means that a person is protected against that disease.

Young children are particularly susceptible to infectious diseases. It is therefore important that they get vaccinated according to an immunization schedule that has been developed by the Centers for Disease Control and Prevention. The 2021 immunization schedule recommends vaccinations against 21 diseases, to be given in several doses across childhood (Centers for Disease Control and Prevention, 2021c).

Vaccinations are not only important for the person being immunized. They contribute to greater protection for the entire community in a phenomenon called **herd immunity** (FIGURE 8.4). The more people get vaccinated, the harder it is for the disease to spread among the few who do not get vaccinated, either for personal reasons or because they are unable for medical or practical reasons. In this way, vaccinations protect even the unvaccinated. However, if vaccination levels on a national basis drop to too low a level, the herd immunity is diminished, and diseases that had become rare over the past decades could become common again. The United States has seen mumps outbreaks in 2016 and 2017, where more than 6,000 individuals were affected, compared with 122 cases in 2021 (Centers for Disease Control and Prevention, 2021e). Likewise, in 2022 New York State saw a rise in cases of mumps. In the winter of 2014–15, a measles outbreak started at California Disneyland theme parks, resulting in 125 confirmed cases of measles among U.S. residents. Researchers suspect that an infected visitor from overseas passed the infection on to other park visitors (Centers for Disease Control and Prevention, 2021d).

In some parts of the world, vaccines are not easily and widely available to children. In 2020, the percentage of the world's children who received needed

vaccines substances prepared from weakened or dead germs (or their parts) that help the immune system to fight a disease more effectively.

immunization the process of becoming protected against a disease.

herd immunity indirect protection from infectious diseases for non-immunized individuals, resulting from vaccinations of a large part of the population.

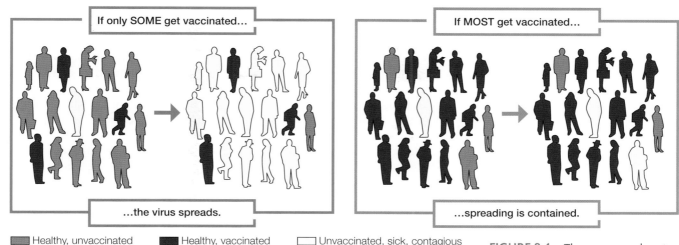

FIGURE 8.4 The more people get vaccinated, the less likely it is that a disease will spread.

After Centers for Disease Control and Prevention. 2017. What would happen if we stopped vaccinations? www.cdc.gov

vaccines dropped by 3% to 83%. This left about 23 million children unvaccinated—a number which has never been higher since 2009. Vaccination efforts have been slowed down by the global COVID-19 pandemic (World Health Organization, 2021b). About one-third of deaths of children age 5 and under could be prevented by vaccines (UNICEF, 2016).

In the United States, the availability of vaccines is generally not an issue. However, some American children do not get vaccinated because of their parents' religious or personal beliefs or concerns over safety, a concern that now also extends to COVID-19 vaccines (Bagateli et al., 2021; Khattak et al., 2021). Some of these beliefs are not supported by scientific findings. Here are some examples:

- **Autism may be caused by the MMR (measles, mumps, rubella) vaccine.** In a 1998 paper, British physician Andrew Wakefield and twelve coauthors (Wakefield et al., 1998) published a study that suggested that the use of the MMR vaccine might lead to bowel disease, which in turn might lead to autism. The paper was covered widely by the press (Boseley, 2010).

  In the aftermath of his paper, immunization rates for measles, mumps, and rubella started to plummet around the world (Gallagher, 2015). In the following years, many concerns were voiced that the research was flawed in a number of ways. Numerous studies performed in later years showed that there was no association between the MMR vaccine and autism (see, for example, Farrington et al., 2001; Honda et al., 2005). In 2010, *The Lancet* (Murch et al., 2004; *Nature Medicine*, 2010) retracted the paper, which was judged to be invalid.

- **Multiple vaccinations may overwhelm a young child's immune system; it is better to space out vaccinations.** Some parents fear that the CDC's current vaccination schedule overloads children's immune systems and may put them at risk of developing a number of disorders, including diabetes and developmental delays. However, health experts disagree. Each day, children are exposed to thousands of foreign substances and germs their body needs to fight off. By the age of 2, a child vaccinated in accordance with the CDC's vaccination schedule has only been exposed to around 300 antigens through the vaccinations (Wessel, 2017), which is a small fraction of the antigens her body is exposed to every day. Spacing out vaccinations also delays protection against serious diseases and requires additional office visits.

- **Some ingredients in vaccines are toxic.** Vaccines contain a number of ingredients besides the actual antigens. Some of these ingredients have come under suspicion. One of them is aluminum, which is used in vaccines as an additive to improve the immune response. However, aluminum is found not only in vaccines but also in our food, drink, and air. Most of the aluminum is processed by the body within a few days. Whereas the vaccines an infant receives over the first 6 months of life contain 4 milligrams (mg) of aluminum, in the same time frame that infant will ingest about 10 mg of aluminum through breast milk or even 120 mg of aluminum through soy-based formula. There is no reason to believe that the amount of aluminum found in vaccines causes harm to humans (Children's Hospital of Philadelphia, 2014).

    Another ingredient that worries some parents is formaldehyde, which is used to kill or weaken the viruses and bacteria in a vaccine. Formaldehyde can damage a person's DNA and possibly cause cancer. But formaldehyde is also found naturally in the human body. The small doses of formaldehyde that are contained in vaccines have not been shown to be harmful to humans (Children's Hospital of Philadelphia, 2016).

- **A child may get the disease from the vaccine.** When a vaccine contains dead viruses or bacteria, an infection is not possible. However, some vaccines contain weakened antigens and may cause what appears to be a mild case of the disease. For example, a child getting a flu shot may develop a fever, muscle aches, and a headache that may last for 1–2 days. Children receiving the MMR vaccine may get a rash and fever for about 2–3 days. However, these side effects merely show that the vaccine works; they are not harmful (Centers for Disease Control and Prevention, 2016).

Myths such as these lead too many parents to deny or delay their children's vaccination, exposing their children to great risk (**FIGURE 8.5**).

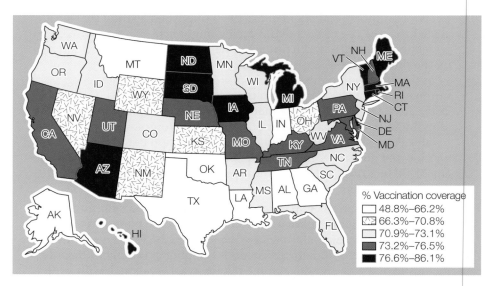

FIGURE 8.5 Percentage of children getting recommended doses of vaccines. In the United States, there are still too many children who do not get the recommended vaccinations at the recommended times or who do not get sufficient doses of the vaccines needed (often, more than one dose is necessary to provide sufficient immunization). This map shows what percentage of children receives the vaccines for diphtheria, pertussis, tetanus, poliovirus, measles, mumps, rubella, hepatitis B, *Haemophilus influenzae* type b, varicella, and pneumococcal infections. What are some reasons people do not immunize their children or themselves?

After Centers for Disease Control and Prevention. 2021. Vaccination Coverage among Young Children (0–35 Months). www.cdc.gov

© Rich Pedroncelli/ASSOCIATED PRESS

■ In September 2019, amid fierce protests, California passed legislation limiting medical exemptions for vaccines among schoolchildren. Why do you think the issue of vaccinations arouses such strong emotion on both sides of the debate?

Vaccines can, in fact, cause some side effects. Most of these are mild. After a shot, children may be fussy, run a low-grade fever, or experience discomfort at the injection site. These symptoms usually go away within 2 days.

Injuries in Young Children

Accidents are the leading cause of death in young children

Young children are very active, playing and running around for a good part of the day. Their high activity level, coupled with ever-increasing abilities and limited knowledge about dangers, puts them at high risk for accidents. A 3-year-old happily climbs up shelves, not knowing that the shelves may topple on him if they are not fastened to the wall. Electrical outlets look like they are just there to be explored with things like sticks or wires. And even a 5-year-old may run after a ball into a busy street, despite having been warned by parents many times not to enter the street. So it does not come as a surprise that accidents are the major cause of death in children. This is true even for older children and young adults. In children ages 1–4, accidents cause about 31% of all deaths (Xu et al., 2021).

In all age groups, boys are injured more often and die more often of their injuries than do girls: They tend to be more active than girls and take more risks (Xu et al., 2021). Children from lower-income households are at greater risk of accidental injury and death than children from higher-income households; they are more than twice as likely to be hospitalized due to injury and are up to 3.5 times as likely to die in an accident involving a motor vehicle (Birken & MacArthur, 2004; Seah et al., 2018).

The leading cause of death in 1- to 4-year-olds is drowning, whereas in older children, most deaths are due to car accidents. Drowning is a silent killer. Movies often depict drowning with lots of splashing and screaming noises. However, drowning usually occurs not only silently, but also very quickly. Caregivers may not hear a child fall into the water even if they are close by (Centers for Disease Control and Prevention, 2021b). Children can drown in just 1 minute, and in a few inches of water—when their face is underwater, they may not remember that they can just get on their feet and stand up!

In order to reduce risk of drowning, pools should always be fenced off, and children should wear life vests around water. Additionally, children must always be closely supervised around water, whether they are in a bathtub or

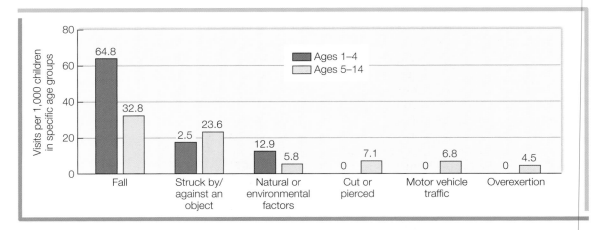

FIGURE 8.6 Emergency room visits for children aged 1–4 and 5–14 by leading causes of injury, 2017–18 (rates per 1,000).

After Forum on Child and Family Statistics. 2021. Child Injury and Mortality. www.childstats.gov

playing around in another water source. Small children should never be left out of sight when they are in or near water. Everyone should know the basics of CPR (cardiopulmonary resuscitation).

Let us now have a look at nonfatal injuries. More than 9 million children visit an emergency room each year for injuries. For all children younger than 15 years of age, the majority of injuries was due to falls (see **FIGURE 8.6**). For preschool children, the next two causes of injury are being struck by or against an object and animal bites or stings. Poisoning, fires, and suffocation are also significant sources of injury (Borse et al., 2008; Forum on Child and Family Statistics, 2021).

Another common danger for children is the poisonous substances that can be found everywhere in our environment. Children can be poisoned by medications like pain relievers, colorful dishwasher or washer pods, alcohol, cleaning products, button batteries, or pesticides used to kill bugs and rodents. Many children are also at risk for lead poisoning. All homes built before 1978 are likely to have been painted with paints that contain lead. When the paint peels off, children may touch it and then put their fingers in their mouth, or even eat the paint flakes. Lead may also be present in older water pipes, toys, jewelry, art supplies, and ceramics. Lead levels build up in the body over weeks and months and can lead to severe mental and physical impairment. Lead damage cannot be reversed. There are many signs of lead poisoning, including stomach pain, sleep problems, headaches, irritability, loss of appetite, behavior problems, and learning difficulties. Lead poisoning is diagnosed with a blood test.

Children from low-income families are particularly at risk for lead poisoning because the housing available to them tends to be older and may have peeling paint on windows or walls. Their parents may not have access to information about the dangers of lead, and they may not see their pediatrician as often as children from more affluent households (Kennedy et al., 2016).

ronstik/Shutterstock.com

■ Childproofing a home with young children can help prevent unintentional injuries.

Many injuries can be prevented

Studies show that around 90% of childhood injuries can be prevented (Rimsza et al., 2002), and from 2010 to 2014 both fatal and nonfatal injuries among children declined by 14% (Dellinger & Gilchrist, 2019). The question is what needs to be done in order to prevent the injuries that continue to occur.

An interesting study showed that young boys and girls need different interventions from their parents in order to reduce their accident risk. Mothers were given an attractive, colorful object they placed in their home. They were instructed to tell their children that the object was dangerous and should not be touched. The mothers then frequently left the room and observed if the children approached the object. Girls responded best to disciplinary measures, like being threatened with punishment if they touched the object or being prohibited to touch it. Boys did not respond well to disciplinary measures—it probably just enhanced their interest in the curious object. Instead, boys reacted best when parents engaged in frequent teaching about the dangers of the object (Morrongiello et al., 2016c). This finding is of particular importance because parents tend to discipline boys rather than engage in teaching behavior when their sons display risky behaviors (Morrongiello et al., 2010).

There are programs that teach young children and their parents about the everyday dangers they encounter and how injuries can be prevented. It has been shown that both parents and children learn a lot if they participate in these group programs (Morrongiello et al., 2016b, 2016c; Peck & Terry, 2021).

In order to prevent a wide array of accidents in the home, parents generally should childproof their house to ensure that poisonous or dangerous objects are out of reach or secured. TABLE 8.3 lists a number of things that can be done to prevent injuries to young children.

■ **Table 8.3** Injury Prevention in Young Children

Injury in the home

© SolStock/Getty Images

Lock up or store out of reach all potentially poisonous substances like household cleaners, medicines, and washer and dishwasher detergents.

Cover all electrical outlets.

Install gates at the bottom and top of stairs.

Ensure cords of shades are out of reach.

Mount TVs to the wall.

Affix shelves to the wall.

Put knives and other dangerous kitchen appliances out of reach.

Buckle up children in the car.

Lead poisoning

© Donald Bowers Photography/ Shutterstock.com

State or local health departments can help to get one's house tested for lead.

If a home has lead pipes, let cold water run for a minute before using it.

If a home has lead-based paint, check regularly for peeling paint. Do not sand, because the dust will contain lead.

Wash hands and toys on a regular basis.

Wet-mop floors and window parts on a regular basis.

Do not let children play in soil if a lead problem is suspected.

(Continued)

■ **Table 8.3** (*continued*)

Drowning

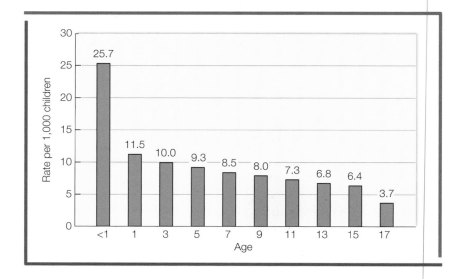

Never leave children unattended in, or close to, water.

Use a lock for toilet lids.

Install fencing around pools.

Dump water from inflatable pools, buckets, etc. when not in use anymore.

Teach child to swim, but remember that being able to swim does not necessarily prevent drowning.

Keep children away from drains that can suck in body parts and hair.

© ChromaCome/Getty Images

Child Maltreatment

child maltreatment includes physical abuse, sexual abuse, psychological maltreatment, and neglect.

child abuse refers to intentional actions that harm a child physically or psychologically.

child neglect describes a failure to provide a child with essentials like food, housing, medical care, and education to such an extent that the child's health and well-being are endangered.

Child maltreatment includes physical abuse, sexual abuse, psychological maltreatment, and neglect. It is an umbrella term for any intentional harm done to a child or harm that could have been prevented. You may have often heard people speak about child abuse and child neglect. **Child abuse** refers to intentional actions that harm a child physically or psychologically. **Child neglect** describes a failure to provide for a child's basic physical (e.g., housing and food), medical, educational (e.g., schooling), and emotional needs.

In 2019, around 8 million children were the subject of at least one report of child maltreatment in the United States. Around 1,900 children died in 2019 as a result of the maltreatment they experienced; 70% of them were younger than 3 years old (Child Welfare Information Gateway, 2021).

Babies in their first year of life had the highest rate of abuse, with 26 out of 1,000 children having been abused. From age 1 onward, the rate of abused children decreases (see also **FIGURE 8.7**). Between ages 1 and 5, 11 children per 1,000 children are abused. Three-fourths of the victims were neglected, whereas 18% experienced physical abuse and 9% experienced sexual abuse (Child Welfare Information Gateway, 2021).

FIGURE 8.7 Child maltreatment: rates of victimization (per 1,000), 2019. Babies in their first year of life are at the highest risk of being abused. Victimization rates were roughly the same for both boys and girls.

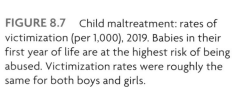

After U.S. Department of Health & Human Services, Administration for Children and Families, Administration on Children, Youth and Families, Children's Bureau. 2021. Child Maltreatment 2019. www.acf.hhs.gov

Both physical and psychological abuse can have devastating consequences for a child. In fact, children who are emotionally abused or neglected sometimes develop worse mental health problems than children who were sexually or physically abused. However, few prevention programs or treatments address psychological abuse extensively (Spinazzola et al., 2014). Maltreatment affects cognitive functioning even as children start a life on their own as adults. Many victims show reduced executive functioning, so they may have trouble planning actions, keeping information in working memory, or controlling their emotions (Gould et al., 2012). Abuse also affects victims' social behavior by making them more hostile toward others. Victims are more likely to become involved in criminal activities, become alcoholics, or die at a young age (McCord, 1983; Petrenko et al., 2012; Strathearn et al., 2020). It has even been suggested that many diseases that we usually regard as adult diseases should be considered developmental disorders, for example, heart disease, autoimmune diseases, and depression. This is because stressors during childhood like poverty and maltreatment set the foundation for these diseases (Shonkoff et al., 2012).

■ **Table 8.4** Signs of Child Maltreatment

	Signs in children	Signs in adults
Neglect	Often absent from school Steals food or money Is often dirty Does not have adequate clothing Seems to lack medical or dental care Is often alone at home	Seems indifferent to child Behaves in irrational ways Abuses alcohol or drugs Seems apathetic or depressed
Abuse	Unexplained injuries Frightened of parents and/or adults in general Abuses animals Experiences nightmares or bed-wetting Refuses to change clothes for gym or wears long clothes in hot weather to conceal injuries Displays atypical behavior like extreme aggressiveness or compliant behavior Not attached to caregiver Physical and/or emotional development are delayed	Unconvincing explanation for child's injuries Describes child in very negative way or constantly belittles/berates child Uses harsh physical discipline Is secretive or isolated Limits child's contact with other children Seems unconcerned about child

There is a wide range of warning signs that may signal that a child is being abused. Signs can be observed in the child, but also in his caregiver. TABLE 8.4 gives an overview of some of them.

Many warning signs can indicate possible child maltreatment. If you suspect a child may be a victim of maltreatment, you can call the Childhelp National Child Abuse Hotline (800-4-A-CHILD) to receive more information and guidance on what to do. Remember that reporting suspicions does not mean an accusation is made; it is a request for an investigation (Department of Health and Human Services, 2019).

Knowing the factors contributing to child maltreatment helps us prevent it

Before we discuss how to help prevent child maltreatment, we need to consider why child maltreatment happens at all. As we saw above, about 80% of all maltreatment cases involve the parents. Therefore, programs targeted at parents are one of the most promising avenues to prevent child maltreatment. Several factors increase the risk of maltreatment, including:

- Lack of parenting skills and stress: When caregivers do not know how to handle a situation or feel overwhelmed, their own behaviors can escalate.

- Excessive stress (caused by things like medical or financial problems, unemployment, or the demands of raising children)

- History of abuse: People who were themselves abused as children are at higher risk of becoming abusers later on.

- Lack of support through family, friends, or communities in tackling the challenges of parenting
- Unrealistic expectations with respect to a child's development (Department of Communities, 2019; Koçtürk & Yüksel, 2019)

Effective intervention programs need to address these factors. There are several kinds of intervention programs. *Home visitation programs* are geared toward new parents. Professionals visit parents and their children in their own home so challenges in parent–child interaction can be identified and addressed early on. Additionally, the safety of a child's environment can be assessed, and the interactions can be observed in the environment in which they usually occur.

Group-based programs bring parents together so they can share their challenges and concerns with others and build up a support network. It can be very reaffirming for a caregiver to hear that others are facing similar challenges. Growing friendships and support also tend to prevent caregivers from dropping out of these groups (Daro & Cohn-Donnelly, 2002; Kim, 2021).

Programs offered through schools and pediatric offices have the advantage that parents are already in contact with these institutions. Officials or volunteers can easily reach out to caregivers when they see them, provide information, and identify families who may be in need of support. For example, a program called Healthy Steps for Young Children offers conversations with Healthy Steps specialists during pediatric well visits. These specialists can screen for parenting challenges and offer guidance, referrals, and home visits. The program is offered in 15 states and serves more than 26,000 children each year (Healthy Steps, 2021).

Sexual abuse prevention programs differ from other prevention programs because they are not targeted at the perpetrators of abuse but rather at the victims. These programs instruct children how to protect themselves or how to respond when someone tries to sexually abuse them. These programs are often offered by schools or youth organizations. There is some concern that these programs shift the responsibility of preventing abuse to children who often do not even have the physical strength to resist abuse, but studies have shown that children gain useful knowledge through these programs (Daro & Cohn-Donnelly, 2002; Davis & Gidycz, 2000; Letourneau et al., 2017).

Public education programs have the advantage that they can reach a large number of people and spread awareness about child maltreatment. They also can inform the public how to act if someone suspects child abuse (Daro & Cohn-Donnelly, 2002; Vlahovicova et al., 2017).

A meta-analysis that analyzed the effects of 30 parenting programs targeted at the prevention of child maltreatment found that these programs were effective in reducing child maltreatment as well as in reducing risk factors for child maltreatment (Chen & Chan, 2014). Given that child maltreatment can be at least partially prevented through programs and that the average lifetime cost per victim is around $830,000, prevention efforts should be ramped up in high-risk areas (Fang et al., 2012; Peterson et al., 2018).

Media and Children's Health

Media, if used responsibly, generally neither impede nor support physical development of preschoolers (Gold, 2014). Preschoolers need to move a lot in order to develop their motor skills, so it is important for parents to ensure that their children have enough time to be physically active. There are apps like GoNoodle and entire game systems like Nintendo Wii Fit that are specifically designed to get kids moving with videos and games that animate dance or exercise. But there is no need for these systems as long as children are given an opportunity for free active play.

Too much screen time can contribute to obesity. Many studies point in the same direction, indicating that the more time children spend in front of the TV, the higher their risk for being overweight as children but also as they enter adulthood (Fang et al., 2019; Reilly et al., 2005; Viner & Cole, 2005). TV watching increases especially if a TV is present in the bedroom, so parents should consider carefully whether they want to place a TV in their child's bedroom (almost 40% of 2- to 5-year-olds have a TV in their bedroom!) (see Common Sense Media, 2017). Of course, sitting down for hours with a digital device or in front of the TV also leads to more sedentary behavior as well as an increased consumption of sweetened beverages, which also contribute to obesity (Shqair et al., 2019; Shukla & Jabarkheel, 2019; Strasburger, 2011).

Review!

Which diseases affect children in early childhood?

- Preschoolers get sick frequently with minor diseases like the common cold or stomach issues. In developed countries, these diseases are minor and typically do not pose a threat to children's health. In developing countries, diarrhea and respiratory diseases can prove to be deadly.
- Serious diseases are rare in young children, also due to *vaccinations* available nowadays.
- The disease that kills most children is cancer. A substantial number of children have chronic conditions like asthma that need to be managed on a daily basis.

What is the role of injuries in preschoolers' health?

- Accidents and unintentional injuries constitute the main cause of death in children and young adults.
- Children ages 1–4 most often die of drowning, and in older children, most injury-related deaths involve motor vehicles. Falls are another frequent cause of injuries, as is poisoning.
- Around 90% of accidents can be prevented, so monitoring children and childproofing the house and environment can make a crucial difference.

What are the different forms of maltreatment, and how can they be prevented?

- There are four different kinds of *maltreatment*:
  1. physical *abuse*
  2. sexual abuse
  3. psychological maltreatment
  4. *neglect*.
- The younger a child, the higher the child's risk for maltreatment. Maltreatment puts children at a high risk for long-term consequences because it often happens over long periods of time.
- There are different kinds of programs aimed at reducing child maltreatment. Most of them target adults, either in in-home sessions, group sessions, or through public education. Another kind of program targets children and teaches them how to protect themselves from and react to sexual abuse.

Do electronic media have an impact on children's health?

- Children's physical development is generally neither supported nor impeded through electronic media.
- Overuse of media and resulting inactivity, however, can lead to obesity and lack of practice in motor skills. There are also media programs and apps specifically designed to get children moving.

Practice!

1. By the time children reach early childhood, _____ .
   a. they are no more susceptible to colds than adults
   b. they catch around five to ten colds a year
   c. they catch around 15 colds a year
   d. they usually do not get many colds because they routinely get vaccinated with the flu vaccine

2. Around _____ % of children in the United States have a chronic condition that needs to be managed on a daily basis.
   a. 8
   b. 15
   c. 22
   d. 29

3. Many diseases have been virtually eliminated in the developed world because of _____ .
   a. vaccines
   b. access to safe drinking water
   c. access to clean toilets, soap, and water
   d. all of the above

4. Most deaths in early childhood are due to _____ .
   a. accidents
   b. cancer
   c. lead poisoning
   d. fires and burns

5. In the United States, around _____ children were the subject of a maltreatment report.
   a. 4 million
   b. 3.2 million
   c. 8 million
   d. 560,000

What's Your Position?

***When it comes to caring for toddlers, is it possible to be too pro-
tective?*** Consider the hazards a young child may encounter every
day: traffic, pets, playground equipment, poisonous substances,
stairs, electrical outlets, peanuts, to name just a few. Should you do
everything you can to protect a child from risks? Or should children
be exposed to some risks so that they can learn to exercise caution?

Draft a brief initial response to this question, and then consult
the websites below to get more information. How did your position
change after you looked at the online sources?

© Alexandr Grant/Shutterstock.com

Additional Resources Online

- ▌ "Refusing to baby proof is a parenting trend that's catching on,"
  from SheKnows

- ▌ "Yes, you absolutely need to baby proof," from the *New York Times*

- ▌ "How far is too far when childproofing?," from the *Chicago Tribune*

See for Yourself!

The next time you're in a grocery store, try to imagine what it
would take to make the premises safer for children. Then go
to an environment designed for children, such as a park or a
public library, and look at the measures designed to reduce
the risk of child accidents. What are the differences between
the two locations in terms of child safety? Is there more that
could be done in either of them to make the environment
safer?

One year later at the town fair

It is the year after Carrie's fall at the town fair, and her family is back with their
now 5-year-old daughter. While Carrie remembers her fall when asked about
it, she certainly does not show any signs that the previous year's incident has
made her more cautious or tentative. As excited as always at the fair, she runs
back and forth between the different tents and activities, hardly able to contain
her excitement. Young children are generally very resilient and heal quickly.
Their resilience helps them develop new skills at a rapid pace rather than getting
discouraged and giving up on the many skills they still need to practice.

Georgia and Jamal are also back at the fair with 4-year-old Eli. This past
summer, they had the scare of their lives. As they were on vacation, Georgia was
sitting by a pool with Eli playing right by her side. They were expecting Jamal to
join them momentarily, and Georgia craned her neck to look out for him. A
moment later she found that Eli was not by her side anymore. He had silently
slipped into the pool and was gasping for air as he came up struggling to stay
above the surface. Georgia had not heard anything. Just in time, she pulled him
out of the water. Had she looked a few moments later, who knows what might
have happened! She felt they were always so careful in trying to keep Eli safe
and was shocked that this happened to her. But particularly with small children,
accidents can happen quickly and unexpectedly despite the best measures
parents take. ■ ■ ■ ■

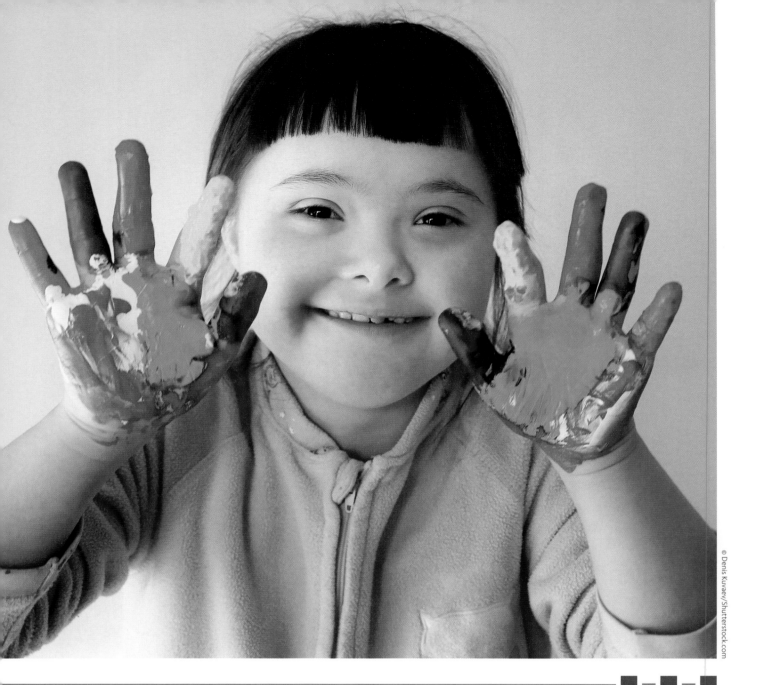

© Denis Kuvaev/Shutterstock.com

Overview

Cognitive Development in Early Childhood

Iris's third birthday party

Iris is celebrating her third birthday, and her parents have invited some of her classmates from preschool. Max is sporting a superhero cape. He repeatedly comes to his mother and tells her, "Mommy, you're the monster, okay?" Then he rushes off for a brief adventure before returning again.

Twin siblings Sienna and Oliver are playing with a doctor's set that Iris received for her birthday. Using two stuffies as patients, they imitate various procedures involving the plastic stethoscope and a syringe. Iris herself is sitting contentedly beneath the dining room table chatting with Mayme, her imaginary friend.

The dining room is decorated with items from Iris's favorite television show, a cartoon about a young explorer who must repeatedly outsmart her antagonist, a masked fox. When Max catches sight of a balloon displaying the masked fox, he immediately rushes in fear to his parents. "It's that fox," says his mother to Iris's dad. Then, by way of explanation to the other parents, she says, "Max is convinced the fox is after him. The show is so popular that we see that character everywhere, and every time, Max's reaction is the same."

The children's emotions and behavior provide some insight into how young children think and perceive the world. They live in a world they cannot understand and explain, where miraculous things happen and lifeless objects can come alive. They are quite unlike adults in their thinking and reasoning.

In this chapter, we focus on the cognitive development that occurs during the preschool years. We start by discussing advances in children's thinking, before taking a closer look at the development of language. Finally, we discuss the impacts of early childhood education and TV on preschoolers.

9.1 Changes in Children's Thinking

- Explain how Piaget characterizes the thinking of preschoolers.
- Outline how Vygotsky explains young children's learning.
- Identify how attention and memory change in early childhood.
- Assess whether preschoolers can think about their own and other people's thinking.

Human thinking is complex. Researchers look at different aspects of thinking and take different approaches to studying thinking. Here, we'll examine four prominent theories that explore children's thinking: the theories of Jean Piaget and Lev Vygotsky, information-processing theory, and theory of mind.

Piaget: The Preoperational Child

You may remember from our discussion in Chapter 2 that Piaget believed children's development occurs in four stages. By the time they are preschoolers, children are in the second stage, which Piaget called the preoperational stage. In the **preoperational stage**, children cannot yet use logic in their thinking and have trouble combining or separating ideas.

"Preoperational" means the children are in a stage where they cannot yet use operations. **Operations** are organized and logical thinking processes that help us imagine the outcome of something that happens in the future. They allow us to sort things, find relationships among things, and draw logical conclusions. In the sections that follow, we will explore the features that characterize preoperational thinking.

Preoperational children are egocentric

Egocentrism refers to young children's inability to view things from a viewpoint other than their own. They cannot take someone else's perspective. They believe that others see, believe, and feel the same things they themselves do (**FIGURE 9.1**).

Consider 4-year-old Henry. During a long car trip with his family, he was watching a cartoon about ponies on a tablet. During the show, he would repeatedly call out with excitement: "Mommy, Mommy, look at that pony—it looks just like the one I have at home!" He did not realize that his mother, sitting in the front seat, was not able to see what he was seeing.

Children's inability to take other people's perspectives can be seen in many other situations, including games. Hide-and-seek was always a hilarious game to play with our preschool-age triplets. They would be standing or sitting in different parts of the room, in plain sight but with their hands or a pillow in front of their eyes. They thought that because they could not see us, we could not possibly see them.

preoperational stage the second stage in Piaget's theory of cognitive development. Children cannot yet use logic and reasoning skills.

operations organized, flexible, and reversible mental thinking processes like sorting objects according to size or recognizing relations between objects and drawing conclusions.

egocentrism young children's inability to view things from a viewpoint other than their own.

FIGURE 9.1 Piaget demonstrated egocentric thinking in his famous Three-Mountain Experiment (Piaget & Inhelder, 1956, 1969). Child participants were seated at a table with a model of three different mountains. A doll was placed on a seat at the opposite side of the table. When presented with illustrations showing the model from different perspectives, children could not pick out which illustration showed the landscape from the doll's perspective. Instead, they chose a picture that showed how they themselves saw the scene.

From C. S. Tamis-LeMonda. 2022. *Child Development: Context, Culture, and Cascades.* Oxford University Press/Sinauer, Sunderland, MA; based on J. Piaget and B. Inhelder. 1967. *A Child's Conception of Space.* Norton, New York

■ Hannah loves "reading" to her doll. Although Hannah cannot yet read, in her pretend play she practices valuable skills like how to place a book right side up, how to turn pages, and that reading happens from the front to the back of a book. She also practices her language skills by telling her doll about what's happening in the story.

Preoperational thinking is characterized by animism, the belief that things are alive

Closely related to egocentrism is **animism**, which is the tendency to believe that inanimate things have a consciousness and are, in one way or another, alive. Children's fear of curtains that turn into monsters at night is a good example. Likewise, a child running into a table and then scolding it may genuinely believe that the table intended to cause harm (Merewether, 2019).

animism tendency to believe that inanimate things have a consciousness and are alive.

Preoperational children engage in elaborate pretend play

As children enter their preschool years, the way they play changes dramatically. Their pretend play becomes more complex. They assign roles to all participating children like the "monster" and the "princess" or may cook elaborate meals for their dolls. Children who engage in particularly elaborate pretend play tend to do better in school later on and may be more creative (Hoffmann & Russ, 2012; Whitebread & O'Sullivan, 2020).

Pretend play is influenced by the stories children encounter, especially in movies and books (Leung, 2015). One of our daughters fell in love with the movie *Frozen* at age 4 and imagined that Princess Anna comforted her when she was in distress. Having imaginary friends is relatively common in young children and usually of no concern—in fact, children with imaginary "friends" are often more able to take another person's perspective and are more cooperative than children without such friends (Taylor et al., 2009).

Preschoolers who engage in pretend play alone, even when other children like siblings or classmates are around, may have trouble relating to their peers or may have social adjustment issues. However, you always have to take a child's temperament into account. There is nothing inherently wrong with children's being quiet and preferring to play by themselves, as long as they are able to communicate and successfully get along with their peers when they need to.

Preoperational children take time to learn conservation

A change in a thing's appearance does not necessarily change its other characteristics. This is the essence of **conservation**, and it presents a challenge for young children. The twins Sienna and Oliver usually drink milk from identical kid-sized glasses, but one night Oliver is served his milk in an adult glass that is shorter and wider than his usual glass. He cries out in protest because it looks to him as though he has received less milk than his sister has. Of course, as adults we understand that when you change the appearance of something—like pouring the same amount of milk into glasses of different dimensions—its quantity, weight, volume, and so on do not necessarily change as well. This is the principle of conservation.

conservation knowledge that when you change the physical appearance of something, its properties like mass, number, or weight do not necessarily change as well.

■ Why do you think Oliver was upset when he was served his milk in the glass on the right?

centration focusing on only one aspect of a situation while ignoring other aspects.

irreversibility lack of understanding that actions can be reversed.

Psychologists test children's understanding of conservation in different ways (**FIGURE 9.2**). To understand conservation, a child needs to be able to consider more than one aspect at once (in our milk example, height and width of the glass). When a child focuses on only one aspect of an object, the child is exhibiting **centration**. Oliver thought that Sienna had more milk because her glass was filled almost to the brim.

Young children often believe in the **irreversibility** of actions, which hurts their conservation abilities. If you cannot imagine pouring milk from one glass into another and then back into the original glass, you cannot fully understand that the act of pouring does not change the amount of liquid.

Taken together, young children are unable to understand the law of conservation because of:

- *Centration*: The tendency of preschoolers to concentrate on one aspect of a situation
- *Irreversibility*: The tendency to believe that when you transform objects into other states/forms, you cannot bring them back to their original state.

Type of conservation	Original presentation	New presentation	Age when conservation is learned
Number	Number of objects in a set	Rearrange or separate the objects	6–7 years
Substance (mass)	Amount of pliable material, like a lump of clay	Change the shape	7–8 years
Length	Extent of a line or object	Change its shape or arrangement	7–8 years
Area	Amount of surface area covered by a set of squares	Reconfigure the squares	8–9 years
Weight	Weight of an item	Change the shape	9–10 years
Volume	Volume of liquid by displacement	Change the shape of the container	14–15 years

FIGURE 9.2 Young children tend not to understand conservation—that when you change the appearance of something, its quantity (or other characteristics like its weight or volume) does not necessarily change as well.

After R. S. Feldman. 2016. *Child Development*, 7th ed. Pearson, Boston

FIGURE 9.3 Asked if there are more brown teddy bears or more teddy bears, young Iris will likely reply that there are more brown teddy bears than teddy bears, even though she can count correctly. She is not yet able to consider a subgroup (brown teddy bears) and the larger group it belongs to (teddy bears as a whole) at once (see also Borst et al., 2013).

Grouping things together is classification

Young children's tendency to concentrate on just one aspect of a situation (centration) leads them to make other errors in thinking as well. One of them is the failure to understand that objects can belong to more than one group at once, an understanding called **class inclusion**: A brown teddy bear belongs to the group of brown teddy bears as well as to the group of teddy bears in general (**FIGURE 9.3**). **TABLE 9.1** provides an overview of concepts related to Piaget's preoperational stage.

class inclusion ability to understand that objects can belong to more than one group at once.

Piaget's ideas have been further developed

Piaget has been unsurpassed in his rich and detailed observations of children and their thinking processes. Some studies show that most of the principles Piaget found are still valid today (see, for example, Asokan et al., 2014). Yet many contemporary researchers have drawn conclusions from those observations that are different from the ones Piaget drew. Current researchers generally criticize two aspects of his work: They believe that (1) he underestimated the abilities of young children and that (2) cognitive development is more nearly continuous and less stage-like than he suggested.

Piaget focused a lot on what young children cannot yet do. Researchers today believe that children are actually capable of more than Piaget thought. They think that it was partly because of the nature of Piaget's tasks that Piaget underestimated the abilities of children (**FIGURE 9.4**).

The way Piaget asked questions also may have influenced his results. He tended to ask lots of open-ended questions, like "Where is the rain coming from?" Researchers have found that they could get more correct answers when they asked more specific questions, such as "Do people make the rain?" (see, for example, Meltzoff, 2011).

Additionally, children often appear to acquire thinking skills not in stages but rather over time, gradually learning to apply them in more and more situations.

■ Table 9.1 Overview of Basic Concepts of Piaget's Preoperational Stage

Concept	What is it?	Example
 **Egocentrism**	Inability to take others' perspective	Belief that parents know what the child saw even if they were not there Children cover their eyes and hide in plain sight.
 **Animism**	Belief that inanimate objects live and have some kind of consciousness	Thunder rumbles because it wants to scare children. Teddy bears are sad when you leave them alone.
 **Conservation**	Understanding that changing the physical appearance of an object does not necessarily change its features like mass, volume, or number	The same amount of juice looks different in glasses of different width. A row of pennies looks different depending on how closely together you place the pennies.
Centration	Tendency to concentrate on only one aspect of a situation	When looking at juice glasses with the same amount of juice, the child disregards that a different level of juice might reflect the glasses having different widths.
 **Irreversibility**	Belief that when you change the shape/ form or arrangement of an object or objects, you cannot go back to the original state	Thinking about pouring juice into a differently shaped glass renders the child unable to think back to the original state of the juice.
 **Class Inclusion**	Consider two different groups of objects that belong to a subclass and larger class at the same time	If there are red and green apples, the overall number of apples is greater than the number of either red or green apples.

© Zarubina_Yuliya/Shutterstock.com

© Pavel L Photo and Video/Shutterstock.com

© Karaevgen/Dreamstime.com

© Lightfieldstudiosprod/Dreamstime.com

© Nadeshda Goettmann/Dreamstime.com

FIGURE 9.4 In one variation of the Three-Mountain task, children were asked to hide the doll so that the policeman figures would not be able to see it. Most children between 3 ½ and 5 years of age were able to place the doll correctly (Hughes, 1975). The Three-Mountain task is also used in experiments with adults of different ages—the results suggest that around middle adulthood people's ability to take someone else's per-spective starts to decline again (Inagaki et al., 2002).

After M. Hughes. 1975. Egocentrism in pre-school. children. https://era.ed.ac.uk/handle/1842/22329

▪ Piaget's Theory in Action

To students, Piaget's ideas often seem quite abstract. But we still can use them in our daily interactions with children. Here's how.

Keep in mind that thinking skills can alternate

Children's abilities may regress when they are stressed or anxious. For example, a preschooler who has already learned to take others' perspective may not be able to use this skill well when he is scared or stressed. This alternation between more mature and immature thinking is normal and should not be cause for concern (see also **FIGURE 9.5**)

Help children interpret events

Sometimes preoperational children experience significant life events like disease or the divorce of their parents. At this egocentric stage and with their lack of reasoning capabilities, they believe many things are related to, or even caused by, them and their actions. One child around the age of 3 explained her parents' divorce this way: "Daddy went away because we threw food at dinner." So when children experience major events in their life, it is important to discuss with them their

Courtesy of Karin Sternberg

FIGURE 9.5 It is normal for skills to alternate somewhat as children develop. Melody's drawings of people were more realistic at age 4 years, 10 months, than a few months later when she reverted back to drawing "head people" for a short time.

feelings and beliefs about the event. This ensures that they do not fear for their personal safety or falsely blame themselves for events that are out of their control.

Prepare adequate activities

Different children will reach a developmental level at different times. Facilitate learning on an individual basis and tailor teaching and activities to where the children are in their development (see also Slavin, 2005), rather than using a one-size-fits-all approach.

Toys and games will aid the cognitive development of young children

Thinking processes play a major role in Piaget's theory. Rather than only teaching children facts and correcting them when they are wrong, they should be shown and taught what the underlying processes are so they understand how things work.

Which activities are particularly useful to help children learn in the preoperational stage?

- Build lessons around topics and use materials that are familiar to the child (such as blocks, crayons, etc.).
- Use materials that can change shape, like water, clay, sand, or play dough, to help children understand conservation.
- Encourage children to understand the perspective of others by reenacting stories and playing dress-up.
- Provide children with hands-on experience that relates to what you are teaching (for example, if you teach about the ocean, provide shells, sand, water, and the like to play with).
- Keep instructions short and include active demonstrations whenever possible: Young children have trouble understanding abstract explanations and have trouble remembering instructions that include many steps.

Vygotsky: Learning through Interaction

According to Lev Vygotsky, interacting with family, friends, and peers is an important way for children to learn about their world and develop socially and cognitively.

Consider how Austin and his mother are interacting in the situation below. Austin is 4 years and 6 months old. He loves clocks, and he and his mother are assembling a plastic clock with detailed step-by-step instructions:

Cindy: "We just put in the blue gear. What do we have to do next? Can you tell from the picture?"

Austin: "It's the green gear. We have to put it right there." Austin puts the gear into the body of the clock, placing it upside down.

Cindy: "Take a closer look. Do the green and the blue gear connect? When you turn one gear, does it make the other one turn as well?"

Austin: "Oh! They don't turn! What's wrong?"

As Austin and his mother work to assemble the clock, his mother helps him to read the instructions and place the parts. Austin is learning from the *guided interactions* with his mother.

Of course, personal interactions and their meaning will be very different depending on where the child grows up. Children growing up in South America or Africa will experience a very different environment than American children, but even within the United States children's environments can differ significantly (see **FIGURE 9.6**).

◼ Through guided interactions, Austin's mother helps him assemble a toy clock.

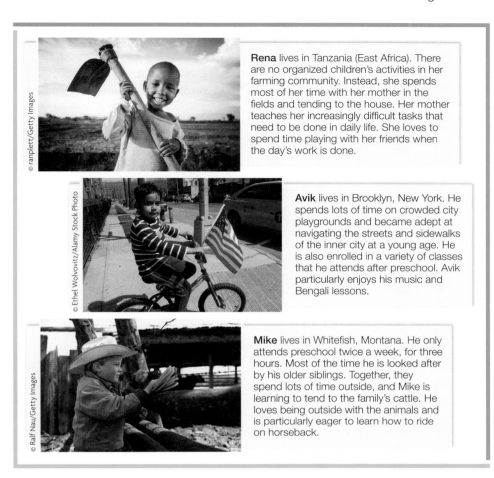

Rena lives in Tanzania (East Africa). There are no organized children's activities in her farming community. Instead, she spends most of her time with her mother in the fields and tending to the house. Her mother teaches her increasingly difficult tasks that need to be done in daily life. She loves to spend time playing with her friends when the day's work is done.

Avik lives in Brooklyn, New York. He spends lots of time on crowded city playgrounds and became adept at navigating the streets and sidewalks of the inner city at a young age. He is also enrolled in a variety of classes that he attends after preschool. Avik particularly enjoys his music and Bengali lessons.

Mike lives in Whitefish, Montana. He only attends preschool twice a week, for three hours. Most of the time he is looked after by his older siblings. Together, they spend lots of time outside, and Mike is learning to tend to the family's cattle. He loves being outside with the animals and is particularly eager to learn how to ride on horseback.

FIGURE 9.6   Children's skills, knowledge, and values differ depending on the cultures within which they grow up.

Vygotsky suggested that three different concepts play an important role in children's learning: the zone of proximal development, scaffolding, and private speech. We'll have a look at these three concepts next.

Help children accomplish goals within the zone of proximal development

Look at **FIGURE 9.7**. In the center of the figure you can see the activities that children can do on their own, without any help. The outer circle shows the things that are completely beyond a child's reach.

In addition, there are things children cannot do alone but can do with the assistance of an adult or older child. Austin, for example, would not have been able to put together the toy clock by himself, but he did so successfully with the help of his mother. The **zone of proximal development** contains all of those things a child *cannot* yet do alone but *can* do with assistance. When teaching, you should aim toward the zone's higher end and give the child instruction and assistance to accomplish her goals (Eun, 2019; Roth, 2020).

Use scaffolding to help children learn new skills

You are likely quite familiar with scaffolds used in daily life: They are temporary structures that help workers construct or repair buildings, bridges, or other built structures.

zone of proximal development the level at which a child can perform activities *with* assistance.

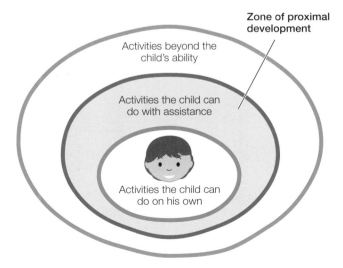

FIGURE 9.7   Activities that a child cannot yet do alone but can accomplish with assistance take place in the child's zone of proximal development.

Scaffolding can also help children accomplish a task that is in their zone of proximal development, that is, a task they can do only with help from someone else. That can be as simple as asking a child "How can I help you?", providing explanations, or giving some physical assistance (Vinson & Parker, 2019).

As children make progress and get better at the task at hand, they will need less and less scaffolding, until eventually they can do the task without any assistance. At that point, the task is no longer in the zone of proximal development because the child can independently master it (Castagno-Dysart et al., 2019).

Private speech is normal, especially in children aged 4–6

private speech speech directed to oneself in order to understand something or guide one's behavior.

As Austin is busy assembling his clock, you can hear him talk to himself: "Green gear. We need the green gear. It goes over the blue gear. . .". When children talk to themselves in order to understand something or guide their behavior, it is called **private speech**. Private speech can be seen most often in children between the ages of 4 and 6. The more complex a task is, the more likely it is that children talk to themselves while they work on it. And they are generally more successful when they use private speech than when they do not (Aro et al., 2015). As they get older, children increasingly think silently by themselves, but private speech can occasionally also be seen in adolescents and adults (Duncan & Cheyne, 2001; Sawyer, 2016).

Evaluating Vygotsky's ideas

For quite some time after Vygotsky's death in 1934, his ideas were not widely known among developmental psychologists because Vygotsky was a citizen of the Soviet Union (USSR). His writings were banned in the USSR and became widely accessible only after its dissolution. Also, there were not enough translations of his work into other languages. Thus, Vygotsky's ideas are still growing in influence.

Because Vygotsky did not specify in detail many of the concepts he used (for example, how do you accurately assess a child's zone of proximal development?), there has not been a large number of experiments conducted to test his theory, although researchers certainly have pursued his ideas (e.g., Hong & del Busto, 2019; Sternberg & Grigorenko, 2002; Vinson & Parker, 2019). Experiments, however, are necessary to test whether assumptions made in a theory are true. Vygotsky also did not say much about other aspects of children's development, for example, the role of emotions in development in general or, specifically, in how memory develops.

The notion that children learn from interaction with adults and other, more experienced children resonates with practitioners all over the world. It is appealing to many people that Vygotsky takes the influence of culture into account. As you will see, his ideas can be effectively translated for use in the classroom.

■ Vygotsky's Theory in Action

All of Vygotsky's key ideas discussed above can be used in the classroom. Here are some suggestions for how you can apply these ideas.

Know what children can and cannot do yet

When planning what to teach the children in a classroom, it is important to know their zone of proximal development (that is, what they are able to achieve with assistance). Identify what the children are already able to do and then find key concepts and abilities that are a step above that.

How do you identify a student's zone of proximal development? This task can be difficult, particularly when you have an entire group of children to work with. One strategy is to work backward from the learning objectives you set for the children to any individual student's achievement.

■ **Identifying the Zone of Proximal Development in a Swimming Class for 4-Year-Olds**

Steps	Application
Write down what skills and knowledge your students need to have to reach their learning goal.	Learning goal: Holding on to pool edge, lie horizontally in water and do frog kicks. Skills: Get into pool safely, hold on to edge, keep face up and move body horizontally, execute frog kicks.
Plan activities that help you find out students' current state of knowledge.	Practice getting in and out of the water. Practice holding on to edge for a longer period of time. Practice getting body horizontal.
Observe and listen to each student to see where he is at and where he might need more help.	Are students comfortable in the water or are they scared? Can students get into the water safely? Can they hold on to the edge safely?
Adjust your instruction for each student.	Help timid students get used to deep water. Show more advanced students how to hold on to the edge of the pool or how to execute frog kicks.

Give adequate assistance

Which activities you plan and the scaffolds you provide depend on the children's knowledge and skill level. For example, when a child is uncomfortable in the water, an adult may first hold her in his arms to get her more comfortable. Children that are more comfortable in the water can be given pool noodles as scaffolds to practice leg movements.

Don't forget that older and more experienced children can provide assistance as well. In learning groups with children of different ages and experience levels, children can help each other learn.

Encourage children to use private speech as they learn new things

Actively encourage preschoolers to use private speech while solving a problem. As children get older, the focus will then switch at some point to internalizing their speech and doing their thinking silently.

Attention and Memory: Information-Processing Approaches

Information-processing approaches are useful for exploring topics such as how we pay attention or remember things. The development of computers in the 1950s inspired psychologists to consider human thinking in terms of information processing of the kind computers do.

In the information-processing view, the outside world provides us with information. Humans then store some of this information ("We went to a playground and I fell down the hill"), use the information in one way or another ("I wonder what I can do next time so I don't fall anymore"), and ultimately also produce an output ("That hill was too steep for me. I'll stay away from it next time").

Today the information-processing approach is one of the most important approaches to studying cognitive development. In this section, we will learn more about what influences young children's ability to pay attention and how young children's memory develops.

Paying attention is an acquired skill

It is not easy for young children to concentrate and pay attention for a long period of time to just one thing. As children become older, their attention span grows. Two factors help them pay better attention: processing speed and automaticity.

The quicker you can think, the faster your *processing speed*. Young children's processing speed is relatively slow (Heim et al., 2015; Kail & Ferrer, 2007). Thus, they often get confused or quit activities because their thinking just cannot quite keep up with what they are doing.

Automaticity refers to processes that are so well practiced that you do not need to devote much attention to them anymore. Riding a bike and tying your shoelaces are things you can do automatically as an adult while concentrating on other things. As children learn how to stack blocks better, they can start to focus on other things like building a city with their blocks.

Children vary widely in their ability to pay attention. This variation is partly due to genetic factors, but it also depends on their home environment (Posner et al., 2007). Children have more trouble concentrating when their parents are stressed or very critical of their child, or tend to give them lots of commands without explaining the background of their requests (Dilworth-Bart et al., 2007; Mathis & Bierman, 2015).

Memory is crucial to building knowledge

The ability to remember is very important for anything we do. Moreover, remembering helps us shape our identity and makes us who we are. The older children get, the more they will be able to form memories of events and facts, store them, and use strategies to retrieve facts and knowledge. However, any memories of early childhood will get blurred or seem to disappear. Children also often remember different things than adults do. When our son was 4 years old we spent a week in Vienna. We visited the local aquarium, which was being renovated at that time and smelled so awful we had to leave. His main memory from the trip was that "Austria stunk."

In this section, we discuss the components of memory and how we store and retrieve memories. We also examine the special memories we have of our life and about child witness testimonies.

long-term memory store that holds information over long periods of time with nearly unlimited capacity.

working memory store that holds information we are currently processing. Very limited in its storage capacity.

central executive controls information processing and attention within working memory.

THE COMPONENTS OF MEMORY   One popular theory of memory suggests that there are two main memory stores: long-term memory and working memory (Gathercole & Baddeley, 2014). Our **long-term memory** has an almost unlimited capacity and holds information over long periods of time. **Working memory** contains the information we are currently processing. This could be information that you just heard or saw, like someone's phone number. But it also could be information from long-term memory that just got activated, like your parents' address when you are sending them a package.

Working memory is limited both in its capacity (how many pieces of information we can hold in working memory) and in the time it can hold the information. An average adult can hold about seven pieces of information at once in working memory for around 5–10 seconds (Miller, 1956; Saaty & Ozdemir, 2003). Young children do not have the same working memory capacities as adults (Cabbage et al., 2017; Gilchrist et al., 2009). Gradually, children begin to chunk information into larger pieces—a strategy that will help them keep more information in working memory. For example, instead of remembering a phone number as "3743682055", they learn to create groups of numbers like "374 368 2055" that can be remembered more easily (Jones, 2012; Li et al., 2017; Miller, 1956).

An important element of working memory is the **central executive,** which is like a central steering instrument: Executive functioning (EF) helps us to decide which information is important and should go into long-term memory, to divide our attention between two tasks, or to switch back and forth between different tasks. A child might be drawing a picture, for example, while her mother is engaging her in a conversation. She is thus dividing her attention between drawing and speaking to her mother.

© Michelle Siu/The Globe and Mail

■ Organized physical activities—especially those like tae kwon do that emphasize self-discipline—help to improve brain function and executive control.

The development of EF stretches into early adulthood. However, during the preschool years, children's skills develop so rapidly that, for the first time, differences between different children's thinking skills become obvious.

Preschoolers may have issues with EF if:

- their answers to questions are often off-topic,
- they get frustrated easily when things don't go their way, or
- they forget what comes next when they are doing something (Morin, 2014).

Executive functioning is so important for learning and attention that it can predict many events later in their life, such as academic achievement, enrollment in college, and income (McClelland & Cameron, 2012; Moffitt et al., 2011). Fortunately, there are quite a few ways to develop these skills. Engaging in sports generally improves brain function and executive control in particular. Particularly helpful are martial arts like karate or tae kwon do that place an emphasis on self-control and discipline (or impulse control) (Diamond & Lee, 2011).

STORING AND RETRIEVING MEMORIES   There are three steps to storing and retrieving memories: encoding, storage, and retrieval (see **FIGURE 9.8**). But how do these processes work?

1. We **encode** information in a way that our memory can store it. You can encode information in many different ways, connecting it to what you already know or possibly to sounds or pictures. Facts about the goldfish, for example, will get connected with your knowledge about animals and fish.

2. Once we have encoded the information, it is ready to be **stored**. Once information gets stored in long-term memory, we may be able to remember it for a lifetime.

3. When we need to remember something, we **retrieve** it from memory again. There are two main ways we can retrieve information in our memory: by recognition and by recall. **Recognition** is the identification of something you have seen before. **Recall** is the production of information from memory.

By the time children go to preschool, their recognition abilities are almost as good as those of an adult (Brown & Campione, 1972). But their recall abilities are not yet strongly developed. They make significant progress in developing

encoding preparing information so it can be stored in and retrieved from long-term memory.

storage placing new information into memory for later retrieval.

retrieval accessing information from memory storage.

recognition ability to identify something seen before.

recall ability to produce information from memory.

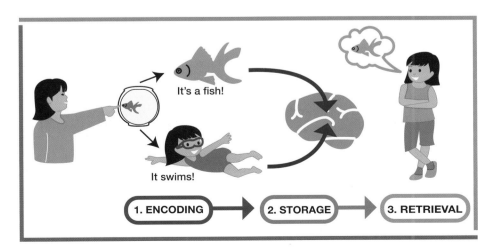

FIGURE 9.8   The three steps to storing and retrieving memories.

■ When Iris, who has long wished to get a Rapunzel costume, sees another child wearing the costume at a Halloween party, she recognizes the costume. When she keeps nagging her parents at home to buy the overpriced costume, she recalls it.

autobiographical memories ·
the memories you have of your own life.

memory skills during preschool years. This progress stems in part from their language development—it is far easier to remember things when you have a name for them or when you understand what happened at a certain event.

AUTOBIOGRAPHICAL (LIFE) MEMORIES Autobiographical memories are the memories you have of your own life. Even children younger than 3 years of age have a pretty good memory for things they did and for things that happened to them. They do not remember everything, however, but rather the things that impressed them or that were unique or unusual, like a birthday party or hospital visit.

One reason we forget things that happened to us when we were very young is that it takes time to develop a sense of self. Something can only happen to you if *you* know you are an independent person and if you have established some kind of sense of who you are (Howe et al., 2009). Children around age 3 recount what happened to them in very simple terms, like "I went camping." Older children tend to include a lot more details when they reminisce and share what they did ("In summer, I went camping in Yosemite with my sister and her friend").

Preschoolers still have trouble distinguishing between fantasy and reality. A preschooler might report that she recently visited Boston, for example, when in fact all she did was visit the city in her pretend play.

The way parents talk with their children influences how much children remember of past events. When parents use an *elaborative style* in conversations with their children, the children generally remember more details. In an elaborative style, parents:

- ask about details ("What did we do when we visited grandma?"),
- add details when the child does not remember anymore ("We baked that beautiful cake you liked so much, remember?"), and
- interpret events ("Grandpa had that big smile because your cake was so delicious") (McDonnell et al., 2016).

■ ## What's It Like...

Autobiographical Memories: Losing a Parent to COVID-19

Maura, widowed mother to Lilly (5)

My husband, Karl, caught COVID-19 in May 2020 when it was going around at the meat factory where he worked. At first we thought he was going to be fine, but after a few days he started to have serious difficulties breathing.

One night, after Lilly had gone to sleep, Karl went to the hospital because it just kept getting worse. He never came back home and died about 3 weeks later. His death has been hard on all of us, and Lilly is trying to cope with it in her own way. Ever since that morning when she woke up and her dad was not there anymore, Lilly has been terrified to go to sleep at night. She is afraid that when she wakes up, I will be gone, too. She's sleep-deprived most of the time now, which makes everyday life much harder. She also clings to me during the day, making it almost impossible to get things done.

She is old enough to have some understanding of death, but I am not sure she truly understands the finality of death. She brings up her dad routinely, like when we are in town and she says, "I used to go there with Dad." I am often not sure what to say.

It's been several months now since Karl's death, but I still often find her just sitting there, staring into outer space. I wish I could help her, but I really don't know what to do. I recently enrolled her in therapy, and I hope the therapy sessions will help. I've been in therapy ever since my husband's death, and I feel it's been good for me to have someone to talk to.

Vivian, psychotherapist specializing in children

It's been estimated that for every 13 adults who die due to COVID-19, a child loses their parent. In roughly 1 year since the beginning of the COVID-19 pandemic in the United States, around

40,000 children have lost one of their parents (Kidman et al., 2021). And they're losing more than just a parent: They need to deal with the loss of future opportunities and possibilities—the ability to spend time with their parent and make memories, go on trips, or have the parent attend their graduation ceremony. Or they may have lost the person who was their main caregiver.

Children suffer in a variety of ways. Some have trouble sleeping, some can't concentrate at school anymore, and we've now got children as young as 2 years old attending therapy sessions. Children who lose a parent also have a higher chance of suffering from depression.

It's important for bereaved children and their families to try to keep some kind of a routine: Shower every day, leave the house at least once a day, and be in touch with people outside the family on a regular basis, for example.

Of course, many of the families who lose a parent are also losing income, which puts them at increased risk for slipping into poverty. Some parents may have trouble providing enough food for their family, or they may have to move, which involves changing schools for their children. Children whose families cannot afford to hold a proper funeral may never even get a chance to really say goodbye to their deceased parent.

What made the situation for grieving children during the pandemic even harder is that they were not able to see relatives, friends, and teachers as much as they potentially could have in a normal situation. The support system children usually have just wasn't there.

These children will need help for many years to come, and I am afraid that many children do not even have anyone who can connect them to services that can assist them. It would be helpful to have a central organization collect the names of all the affected children so that they can receive the assistance they need.

CHILD WITNESS TESTIMONY Helping young children recall past events is a way to help them build knowledge, which is crucial to their cognitive development. But the way children recall events in the presence of adults can have some weighty consequences to others as well. Consider the matter of child witness testimony. In 2019, almost 8 million children in the United States were named in reports related to maltreatment (Children's Bureau, Department of Health and Human Services, 2021). Insufficient or wrong evidence from investigations can lead to innocent persons being wrongfully convicted or child abusers going free. However, finding out what really happened in cases involving children is often difficult because there may be insufficient physical evidence and few or no witnesses other than the child (Ceci et al., 2002; Klemfuss & Olaguez, 2020; Pichler et al., 2019). Such cases need to be handled with care and sensitivity to encourage an accurate recollection of events by the child or children involved.

Here is an example of a conversation between a boy, a social worker, and a detective (Appellate Court Brief as cited in Bruck & Ceci, 2013, pp. 422–423):

> Social Worker: Don't be so unfriendly. I thought we were buddies last time.
>
> Boy: Nope, not any more.
>
> Social Worker: We have gotten a lot of other kids to help us since I last saw you. . . . We talked to a few more of your buddies. And everyone told me about the nap room, and the bathroom stuff, and the music room stuff, and the choir stuff, and the peanut butter stuff, and everything. . . . All your buddies [talked]. . . . Come on, do you want to help us out? Do you want to keep her in jail? I'll let you hear your voice and play with the tape recorder; I just need your help again. Come on. . . . Real quick, will you just tell me what happened with the wooden spoon? Let's go.
>
> Boy: I forgot.
>
> Detective: Now listen, you have to behave.

Social Worker: [To the detective] Do you want me to tell him to behave? [To the boy] Are you going to be a good boy, huh? While you are here, did he [the detective] show you his badge and his handcuffs? Back to what happened to you with the wooden spoon. If you don't remember words, maybe you can show me [with anatomical dolls present].

The interview above is an example of many things gone wrong in the examination of a child. First, the social worker puts peer pressure on the interviewed boy, stating that a lot of other kids have helped the police already. Second, he tries to bribe the boy by promising he may use the tape recorder when they are done. Third, when he refers to the handcuffs of the detective, the child may feel threatened. Fourth, he is asking a number of leading questions when he refers to the wooden spoon and the rooms in which things are supposed to have happened. Finally, the tone is anything but objective. He sounds like he wants a certain result and plans to get it.

Even preschoolers' reports can be very accurate, but a biased interviewer can easily contribute to the child's testimony becoming unreliable (Bruck & Ceci, 2013). There are guidelines regarding how best to interview child witnesses. But in many cases, even well-trained interviewers do not follow these guidelines (Warren et al., 1999).

Here are some strategies that interviewers should use when interviewing children (Bruck & Ceci, 2013; Klein et al., 2020; Lamb et al., 2007):

- Interview the child as soon as possible after the alleged offense. The child's early testimony is the most reliable.
- Explain to the child the roles of the interviewer and other people involved. Say why the interview is being done. Ask that the child report only what really happened.
- Introduce as little additional information as possible. Instead, attempt to encourage the child to provide as much information as he can.
- Use open-ended prompts: "Explain to me what happened."
- Use recall questions ("Did he use this object?") as late as possible in the process and only if needed.
- Avoid yes/no questions ("Did he do this every day?") because small children often believe adults want to hear an affirmative answer and thus say yes to please the adult.
- Avoid suggestive questions ("He wanted to touch your parts, didn't he?").

Evaluating information-processing approaches

Information-processing approaches have contributed significantly to our understanding of young children's development. Their strength comes from their technical approach of breaking down human thinking into smaller parts and mechanisms. These elements can then be studied in detail in the lab or elsewhere. We now understand much better how people create memories and store facts, how they categorize information, how attentional processes work, and how people solve problems.

That said, researchers tend to break down thinking into smaller and smaller processes. This practice has made it more difficult for the researchers to develop a theory that describes the development of children as a whole. It has proven rather difficult to put all those pieces together to form a theory like Piaget's.

Furthermore, when you compare the human mind to a computer, you may miss out on the "humanness" of people. We do not just compute information; we also have interests, motivations, and feelings. A child working on a puzzle in a preschool classroom may not be able to concentrate because she is hungry or because her attention gets caught by the big snowflakes that have begun to fall outside. The information-processing approach also may not fully take into account that we are social beings. We learn through interaction with family, friends, and teachers (as Vygotsky pointed out). Creativity and imagination play a vital role in children's learning.

script a sequence of expected behaviors in a particular situation.

Information-Processing Approaches in Action

Information-processing approaches explore how we pay attention to the world around us, how we think and learn, and how we remember what we learn and experience.

Guided by information-processing approaches, teaching strategies can be formulated to:

- gain and keep students' attention,
- help them understand the new material they learn,
- integrate the material into the knowledge they already have, and
- facilitate the memorization of material so it can be used later on.

TABLE 9.2 shows you a number of key ways to facilitate children's learning using what we have learned from information-processing approaches. These strategies apply not only to preschoolers, but also to older children. Of course, as the previous section has shown, you can use information-processing approaches in almost any area of your daily life.

In unfamiliar situations such as in a restaurant or when seeing a doctor, children often do not know what is expected of them and feel anxious. By exploring these situations in play, we can help them build **scripts**—sequences of expected behaviors—that can reduce their anxiety and help them understand the situation. For example, you can anticipate what a doctor will do with a child during an examination and play the doctor visit through with the child beforehand. In this way, the child knows what to expect and how to behave.

■ Table 9.2 Application of Information-Processing Approaches in the Classroom

Concept	What?	How?
Attention  © Sergey Novikov/Dreamstime.com	Learning can only take place if we pay attention.	Present new material in ways that excite children. Help students focus on important information through the use of gestures, pauses, emphasis, etc. Eliminate unnecessary distractions (for example, the sun shining through the windows in students' eyes, loud noises, uncomfortable temperature in the classroom, etc.).
Active learning © antoniodiaz/Shutterstock.com	Children learn best when they are actively involved and are thinking about the material.	Ask questions. Have discussions. Give assignments.

(Continued)

■ **Table 9.2** (*continued*)

Concept	What?	How?
Meaningfulness 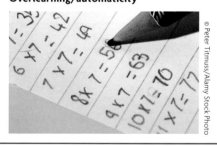 © Mcimage/Shutterstock.com	Children learn best when they can relate personally to the material.	Give many concrete examples. Relate the information to the children's lives. Connect the material to other areas children already know about.
Organization © Marjorie Kamys Cotera/ Bob Daemmrich Photography/ Alamy Stock Photo	Organized material helps students integrate material into their already-existing knowledge and increases retention (the chances that they will remember the material).	Present the material in an organized way. Use outlines. Teach children to create outlines themselves.
Memory aids © FamVeld/Shutterstock.com	Help students remember the material.	Link the material to things students already know. Give students aids to remember, such as visual images, creating a sentence with the beginning letters of a series of important concepts (acronym), etc. Teach students to develop their own memory strategies, such as organizing items into different categories, repeating material multiple times, etc.
Overlearning/automaticity © Peter Titmuss/Alamy Stock Photo	Material is remembered best when it is overlearned (past the point of initial mastery) or automatic (requiring little or no conscious thought, like reading or use of mental multiplication tables).	Repeat material or do daily drills. Ask questions. Use Trivial Pursuit quizzes. Give meaningful practice opportunities.

Source: J. R. Slate and J. R. Charlesworth, Jr. 1988. Information processing theory: classroom applications. https://eric.ed.gov/?id=ED293792

Understanding Our Own and Other People's Thoughts: Theory of Mind

Theory of mind is our ability to understand our own and others' thought processes—that they, as well as we, can dream, think, have wishes, believe things, and even trick others. A theory of mind enables us to understand things not just from our own point of view, but from others' as well. Knowing that other people think helps us understand those people and predict their actions.

Understanding what others know and how they think is not easy. Consider Iris in a phone conversation with her mother, Miriam, who is on a business trip. Iris is sitting on the floor playing with a yellow truck.

> Miriam: "Hi, Iris—it's Mommy. I am so glad to hear you! How are you doing?"
>
> Iris: "Fine."
>
> Miriam: "What are you and Daddy doing tonight?"
>
> Iris: "I'm playing with this!"
>
> Miriam: "What is this, Iris? What are you playing with?"
>
> Iris: "Mommy, you know. It's my favorite."

When Miriam asked her what she was doing, Iris did not say she was playing with a truck—she assumed her mother knew that she was playing with her yellow truck.

The more we know about others and how their motivations and thoughts influence their behavior, the less confusing are our interactions with them because we already expect they may behave in a certain way. Until recently, the study of theory of mind was mostly concerned with people's thoughts and knowledge. However, researchers are now also including other people's feelings in their studies: Are we aware of what we and others are feeling, and can we understand what these feelings are (Westby & Robinson, 2014)?

Young children make frequent mistakes in their assumptions about other people's knowledge. This is quite apparent in the false beliefs they often have.

False beliefs reflect a lack of understanding of other people's perspective

Children need to learn that other people's knowledge about a situation may differ from their own. Between ages 3 and 4, children increasingly start to take into account their own as well as other people's thoughts and beliefs (Wellman, 2020). Consider a situation like the one in **FIGURE 9.9**. After having been shown that crayons are in the candy box, 3-year-olds likely will believe that their friend knows the candy box contains crayons even though the friend hasn't seen the contents. They may even change their mind and say that they knew from the beginning that the candy box contained crayons.

Five-year-olds, however, are more likely to suggest that their friend will believe the candy box is filled with candy. They are able to separate their knowledge from the false beliefs others may have about a situation. It is also only around the age of 4 or 5 that children come to understand that assumptions about a situation cannot always be made with certainty and that there are different degrees of certainty (Bartsch & Wellman, 1995; Gopnik & Astington, 1988). They also develop an understanding of a person's feelings and motivation based on that person's traits and can infer that shy people do not like to be with others they do not know well (Heyman & Gelman, 1999).

Studying theory of mind in children

When researchers conduct experiments with young children, one issue they face is that children cannot always articulate their thoughts and feelings. For this reason, Henrike Moll and her colleagues (Moll et al., 2017) studied facial expressions of young children to see if they possessed a more elaborate theory of mind than researchers had previously believed. They devised a series of puppet shows about a character with a box of valuable—but fragile—objects. In the opening scene, the character shows the audience the precious contents of the box and then leaves the stage.

© Aflo Co., Ltd./Alamy Stock Photo

FIGURE 9.9 A young child is shown a candy box and asked what is inside. The child likely suggests that there is candy in the box, but the adult then proceeds to show that there are actually crayons inside. When the child is asked what a friend will think is in the box, what will she say? (Gopnik & Astington, 1988).

From H. Moll et al. 2017. *Child Dev* 88: 114–122. © The Society for Research in Child Development

■ The puppets and materials used in the story with the puppet show study.

Another puppet enters the stage and accidentally destroys the contents of the box. Subsequently, the first character returns to fetch the box. There are three variations of the play, each premised on a different condition:

1. In the false-belief condition, the character does not know that the contents of the box have been destroyed because he was out of sight when it happened.

2. In the true-belief condition, the character knows the contents were destroyed because—visible to the audience—he was watching from the edge of the stage.

3. In the ignorance condition, the character has never seen the contents of the box, having received it as a present without opening it.

Moll and her colleagues filmed the facial expressions of 2- and 3-year-old children as they watched different variations of the play. They rated the children based on the amount of suspense they showed as the events unfolded. (When children felt suspense, they most often smirked, bit their lips, or bit or stuck out their tongue.) They found that the children showed more suspense in the false-belief condition than in the true-belief or ignorance conditions, indicating that they possessed at least some knowledge—a gut instinct—about the unpleasant discovery the main character was soon to make. Children who were not quite 3 years old showed through their affective reaction that they understood the consequences of the character's false expectations—about 2 years before they would pass the standard false-belief test with a candy box discussed above!

From H. Moll et al. 2017. *Child Dev* 88: 114–122. © The Society for Research in Child Development

■ A child watching a false-belief play (left) and a true-belief play (right).

Culture Counts

Theory of Mind in Non-Western Cultures

A majority of research in psychology and child development is conducted in Western countries, even though the majority of the world's population lives in non-Western countries. Theories that were developed and validated in Western countries may not adequately reflect the development of children in other parts of the world. For example, researchers generally agree that children develop a theory of mind and learn to correctly respond to false-belief tasks around ages 4 and 5 (Mayer & Traeuble, 2013).

But consider this study with children in Vanuatu, a country in the South Pacific: The children were presented with a false-belief task in which a boy placed a ball in one box and then left. In his absence, the ball was placed in a second box. The children had to predict in which box the boy would search for his ball upon his return. Whereas 5-year-old Australian children are able to correctly predict the location where the boy will search, only slightly more than half of 13-year-olds from Vanuatu are able to predict the location correctly (Dixson et al., 2018).

This study shows that we cannot always generalize the results of studies conducted in Western countries to non-Western countries. It illustrates that children do not develop a theory of mind at the same time all around the world. In this case, the authors of the study suggested that previously neglected factors like urbanization, formal schooling, and differences in children's learning environment (rather than cultural differences) play a role in the development of theory of mind as well.

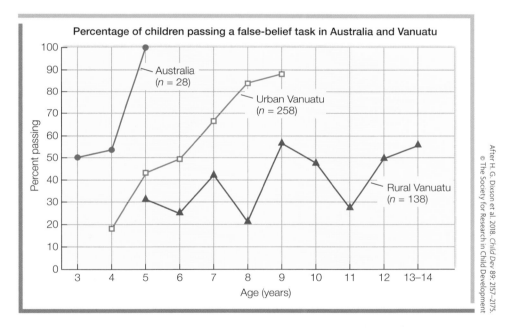

Percentage of children passing a false-belief task in Australia and Vanuatu

Australia (n = 28)

Urban Vanuatu (n = 258)

Rural Vanuatu (n = 138)

After H. G. Dixson et al. 2018. *Child Dev* 89: 2157–2175. © The Society for Research in Child Development

■ Question

Were these results ones you would have expected? Why or why not?

At the age of 5 or 6, children can distinguish between appearance and reality

Shortly before Easter, 3-year-old Jacob went to visit his grandmother. She had decorated the house with brown wax bunnies and warned him that they were decorations and not to eat. When no one was looking, Jacob nevertheless took a hearty bite out of one of the wax bunnies. It just looked too much like one of the delicious chocolate bunnies Jacob knew and loved.

Jacob thought that the bunnies must be made of chocolate because they looked like they were made of chocolate. He was not able to understand the difference between reality and appearance. Although children start learning around age 2 that imagined things are not the same as real things, it takes a long time for them to fully internalize this insight. Even children as old as 6 years (or older!) still may get scared when they wake up and see shadows in their room that take the appearance of a monster.

In one experiment, young children were shown a glass of milk, which was obviously white. Then the children put on special glasses that were tinted green and therefore made the milk look green. When asked what color the milk was, 3-year-olds replied that the milk was green, even though they had seen before that it was really white (Flavell et al., 1986). Only around the age of 5 or 6 can children make a difference between what is and what seems to be.

Many factors influence the development of a theory of mind

Theory of mind is about being aware of other people's thoughts and emotions. The less egocentric children are and the more they can take the perspective of others, the more they will be able to understand that others think independently and that their thoughts and feelings lead them to act in certain ways.

The extent of interactions with others also influences a child's theory of mind. Children who have siblings may have a more mature theory of mind than do children who do not have siblings (McAlister & Peterson, 2007). However, not all siblings are made equal: Kids with older siblings are best off in terms of the theory of mind, whereas twins do not have an advantage over only children. This difference is probably due to the fact that siblings of varying ages can more easily take on different teacher/student roles (Leblanc et al., 2017).

Advanced language also facilitates the development of a theory of mind. Around age 3, children start to use words like "think," "remember," and "know" when they speak. Bilingual children typically show more advanced theory of mind than do monolingual children. They know from experience that there is more than one word to describe an idea or an object, and they adjust their language depending on the specific person to whom they are speaking.

Children with autism spectrum disorders (ASD) have particular problems understanding other people's thinking. They also often experience communication difficulties and display repetitive behaviors such as rocking. Children affected by ASD do not interact with their environment as much as their peers do and hence may not develop such understandings. As a result, they have much less experience and practice than other children when it comes to understanding the people around them.

Evaluating theory of mind

Theory of mind is a valuable theory that has stimulated a large amount of research. There appears to be a relationship between theory of mind and ASD, though it is not clear whether one causes the other or whether even a third variable is involved (Baron-Cohen et al., 1985; Stone et al., 2013).

Another question that has not been answered yet is whether understanding one's own mental processes and other people's thinking are the same "thing" or whether they are different things. Gardner (2011), for example, distinguishes between intrapersonal (understanding oneself) and interpersonal (understanding others) intelligences, suggesting that theory of mind may involve two distinct parts.

It is clear, however, that the theory of mind has many implications for our everyday life and the development of children. For example, children need theory of mind to understand what kinds of behavior are expected of them by their friends, parents, and teachers.

■ Children who have siblings may have a more mature theory of mind than do children who do not have siblings.

Theory of Mind in Action

There are quite a few things you can do to help children develop a more elaborated theory of mind.

Encourage pretend play and role-playing

Children playfully take the perspective of others and develop their capacities to understand how others think. There are many roles children can play. For example, you can pretend to be a patient and the child to be a doctor, or you can be a customer at a supermarket and the child can be the person at the checkout.

Explain situations

Explain things that have happened so children can gain a better understanding as to why things happened as they did. Martin is smiling because he received a gift; Pauline is frustrated because she just can't seem to finish a puzzle by herself. Any time you spend time with a child, you have the opportunity to put thoughts into words and to explain how the people around her think and act.

Read and discuss books

Read and discuss what happens in books. How do various events make people feel? Why do the people in the book choose to act one way or another? People generally have a reason when they act a certain way, but it can be very difficult for children (and sometimes also for adults) to figure out why they behave the ways they do.

Keep in mind that there are some groups of children who have particular problems developing a theory of mind. These groups include not only children with ASD, but also children who experience attention-deficit/hyperactivity disorder (ADHD). Children affected by ADHD show persistent inattention (for example, they cannot concentrate), impulsivity (for example, they have trouble waiting for their turn), and/or hyperactivity (for example, they may be very fidgety). If you encounter children who seem to have a particularly hard time understanding other people's thinking and emotions, it is worth investigating where these troubles might come from, so that the children can be given extra help to develop their theory of mind.

Review!

How does Piaget characterize the thinking of preschoolers?

- Between the ages of 2 and 7, children are in the preoperational stage. In this stage, children cannot yet apply logic to their thinking like adults can. Rather, their thinking is guided by intuition.
- Children see the world mostly from their own perspective (egocentrism). They have trouble anticipating other people's viewpoints and assume those viewpoints are the same as their own.
- Pretend play becomes increasingly more common and complex, with intricate stories that are enacted.
- Children do not yet understand that when the appearance of objects changes, other qualities like their weight do not necessarily change as well (conservation). Their lack of understanding is due to an inability to consider more than one aspect of a situation at once (centration).
- Children are often unable to mentally reverse actions (irreversibility). Not being able to think about how things were before a change or considering the consequences of what they do before they act hurts their ability to think logically.
- Helping children understand why things happen and how things work assists them in their cognitive development.

How does Vygotsky explain young children's learning?

- Vygotsky believed that children learn through interaction with other people. For this reason, the culture in which they grow up significantly influences their learning.
- Teaching is most effective when it takes place in the zone of proximal development, doing things they cannot yet do alone but are able to do with help from others.
- The assistance of others when children learn new skills is called scaffolding.
- Young children often talk themselves through difficult tasks in order to guide their behavior (private speech).

How do attention and memory change in early childhood?

- Children's ability to pay attention increases significantly during early childhood. Children vary greatly in their ability to pay attention.
- Three important components of our memory are:
  - long-term memory (which stores information over long periods of time),
  - working memory (which holds the information we currently process), and

■ the *central executive* (which is a part of working memory and helps us divide our attention or switch back and forth between tasks).

■ Young children often remember things differently than adults, and their memories can be unreliable. Facts can get skewed or blurred, or they may remember only aspects of a situation. They also may have trouble distinguishing between reality and fantasy.

■ When children's testimony is used as evidence, unbiased questioning is therefore of the utmost importance.

Can preschoolers think about their own and other people's thinking?

■ Preschoolers are only starting to develop a theory of mind. They have trouble anticipating other people's thoughts, feelings, and actions.

■ By age 5, children come to understand that others do not necessarily know what they themselves know and that there are different degrees of certainty when judging situations.

■ Around age 5, children tend to understand that things are sometimes different than they appear—for example, a crying person may be very happy and cry tears of happiness.

Practice!

1. The inability of young children to view things from any other perspective but their own is called _____ .
   a. animism
   b. egotism
   c. egocentrism
   d. centration

2. Vygotsky believed that children learn best _____ .
   a. by working with others
   b. by working alone
   c. by reading children's books
   d. by drawing pictures about what they experience

3. When you provide a scaffold to a child, you may be _____ .
   a. feeding her a snack
   b. giving an explanation for something

   c. helping her go to sleep
   d. telling her to stop an obnoxious behavior

4. Private speech helps children _____ .
   a. keep secrets
   b. keep their voice low
   c. work on complex tasks
   d. exchange information with others

5. Working memory holds information _____ .
   a. for a limited amount of time
   b. for long periods of time
   c. we processed a long time ago
   d. that is of particular personal importance to us

Show What You've Learned!

After bringing out the birthday cake, Iris's father, Eli, is chatting with the twins' mother, Kay (or, as she is known at school, Principal Rosen). Iris is back under the table, serving cake to "Mayme"—much to Eli's dismay. "We invited Iris's friends hoping she'd be a little more social, but clearly she'd rather spend the time with an imaginary friend than with real people. She's 3 now, isn't she too old for this kind of make-believe?" How do you think Kay might respond? Write out a response based on the information on preoperational play presented in Section 9.1.

Act It Out!

Three-and-a-half-year-old Max has just come back from a trip to the zoo with his Uncle Eddie. "How was it?" Max's mother, Josie, asks her son when Eddie drops him off. Act out a short dialogue between Max, Eddie, and Josie. As Eddie or Josie, use an elaborative style to help Max recall the events of the day.

See for Yourself!

Go to a toy store and pick out three toys for young children that you think would be effective in stimulating cognitive development. For each one, explain why you think it would be effective and what skills it would promote.

9.2 Changes in Children's Language

■ List the ways children's language skills advance in early childhood.

Here is what Ivy tells people about herself at age 4 years, 8 months:

> I like being a princess. Princesses always wear dresses. You cannot be a princess without a dress and a tiara. Yesterday Mommy made me wear pants. I was so mad at her. Princesses need tights. But Mommy buyed [sic] me new tights. Then I wasn't upset anymore.

Obviously little Ivy really likes princesses. But her speech tells us a lot more than that. Over the past years, she has learned hundreds of words and progressed from speaking not at all, to speaking individual words and short, two- or three-word sentences, to being able to produce complex sentences. She is able to stay on topic while she talks and is addressing another person to tell them something about her life. Of course, she still has a way to go until she can speak like an adult, but the ability of Ivy and her peers in preschool to express themselves is nevertheless impressive. How do they acquire these skills?

Learning New Words

Children learn new words at an astonishing rate. By age 3, they can use around 900 words. At age 6, they can already use around 2,600 words and understand more than 20,000 words (Owens, 2015).

Have a look at **FIGURE 9.10**. You can see a mother speaking to her child. How can the child possibly figure out what the different words mean? If the child points to a bird and the mother then says something, does the word refer to the bird itself, or is she maybe talking about the bird's feathers or its beak or wings? Children have a remarkable capacity to figure out what the people around them are talking about, even though they don't know the meanings of most of the words.

The process by which children learn a large number of words so quickly is called fast mapping (Brady & Goodman, 2014). In **fast mapping**, children quickly make a connection between a word and its meaning. They form a hypothesis about the meaning of the word and then refine and revise its meaning whenever they encounter the word again. Imagine, for example, that a family is driving in bad winter weather when they encounter a car that is stuck in the snow. The father calls out, "Look at the maroon car!" His 3-year-old daughter may never have heard the term *maroon* but she starts looking around at the cars in view. Because there is only one car that warrants the call-out, she may infer that *maroon* has something to do with that car. And from what she already knows about the way sentences are constructed and how words are formed, she infers further that *maroon* is likely some kind of adjective that describes the car. She decides it is probably the color because no other car has that particular color. It is generally easier for children to fast map words describing objects than verbs or adjectives because objects are more concrete.

There are a number of steps adults can take to help children learn new words:

- Point to the object and repeatedly say the name of the object, thus increasing the chances that the child will understand what thing you are referring to and can remember its name;
- Stress new or important words in a sentence;

fast mapping process in which children learn the meaning of new words after having heard them just once or twice in a conversation.

Lat piraak doy ma lisum!

FIGURE 9.10 Young children have a remarkable capacity to understand the speech of adults.

- Use different games like nursery rhymes that use gestures, question games that ask children to point to their nose, mouth, and the like, up to more advanced games in which children have to find as many words as possible starting with a particular letter or in which they have to name all the activities you can do in a gym.

When children learn new words or rules to build sentences, they tend to *overextend*—that, is, to apply words too broadly. For example, my son used to exclaim "yummy, yummy" when he saw stairs because he loved stairs so much and knew that yummy was a word that described things he got excited about.

Creating Correct Sentences: Grammar

Of course, children do not only need to know words, but also have to put them together into sentences. In order to create grammatically correct sentences, words need to be adjusted in many ways. For example, people can adjust words to indicate singular or plural (*man* vs. *men*) or to indicate that something happened in the present or in the past (*go* vs. *went*).

Around age 3, children usually produce short and simple sentences ("Teddy is cold"). They also use plurals (add an -s to a noun: "There are two *boys*") and past tense (add -ed to a verb: "I *played* with Lisa"). In addition, they can use possessives ("The *boy's* ball") to indicate to whom something belongs. They can ask and answer questions that begin with "what" and "where." See **TABLE 9.3** for some examples of how the speech of Iris progressed over the course of a year.

Between ages 4 and 5 they begin to use more complex question words like "*why*." Their sentences become longer and more complicated. Children can even apply the grammatical rules they learn to words they have never encountered before (**FIGURE 9.11**) (Berko, 1958).

Applying grammatical rules is not easy, and at first, children extend general rules to irregular verbs, a phenomenon called **overregularization**. A child that has learned to add "-ed" to the end of a verb to indicate past tense, for example, might say "We buyed bananas at the store" because he applies the "-ed" rule to regular as well as irregular verbs. The less a verb is used in conversations with parents at home, the more a child is prone to overregularize it. Overregularization errors will persist for quite a few years until children have learned the fine details of their language (Marcus et al., 1992; Montrul & Mason, 2020).

overregularization application of regular grammatical patterns to irregular words.

Communicating with Others: Social Speech

Most often, speech is used to communicate something to a listener (also called **social speech**). Young children use their language for communication all the time, for example to call the attention of their caregivers to a new animal they have seen, or they may use their words to get a cookie they can't reach.

The amount of social speech increases significantly around the age of 3. Children start talking more to each other, and it is important to them to be listened to and to be understood. They repeat themselves when others do not understand and despair when they still do not succeed: When Austin (age 3 years,

social speech speech that is used to communicate with another person.

FIGURE 9.11 Preschool and elementary school children were shown a picture of a bird-like creature called a "wug." Then they were shown a second picture showing two creatures. The experimenter said, "Now there is another one. There are two of them. There are two _____ ." Three-quarters of the preschoolers and almost all of the first-graders could form the word "wugs" (that is, the plural of "wug") correctly.

From C. S. Tamis-LeMonda. 2022. *Child Development: Context, Culture, and Cascades.* Oxford University Press/Sinauer, Sunderland, MA; based on J. Berko. 1958. *Word* 14: 150–177

One wug.　　　Two _____.

■ Table 9.3 Some of Iris's Expressions at Various Ages

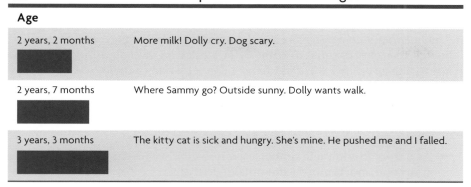

Age	
2 years, 2 months	More milk! Dolly cry. Dog scary.
2 years, 7 months	Where Sammy go? Outside sunny. Dolly wants walk.
3 years, 3 months	The kitty cat is sick and hungry. She's mine. He pushed me and I falled.

2 months) was taking the train one day, he looked out the window and saw an interesting trash can in a train station. He tried to point it out to his mother, but she did not understand, no matter how many times he repeated the word. He ended up rolling around screaming on the floor of the train, furious that his mother would not understand him.

Children also learn fast that in order to get something, the way they request it matters. Saying "May I please get a glass of milk?" is more likely to result in their getting what they want than their just belting out "Milk!" They learn *how* to speak by paying attention to the effect their words have on others.

There are lots of rules for children to learn in order to have conversations and communicate with others. The knowledge needed to use language effectively for communication with others is called **pragmatics**. For example, children learn to:

- use the word "please" when they make a request;
- take turns in a conversation;
- give answers when someone asks a question;
- stay with the topic someone else is talking about; and
- speak differently, perhaps more politely, when they speak with their teachers as opposed to their siblings, for example.

pragmatics knowledge needed to use language effectively for communication with others.

Preparing to Read

There are many ways adults can support children in their quest to learn to read. Obviously, it is very important for adults to read books to children. Children who are being read to on a regular basis, in comparison with other children, know more words, recognize more letters of the alphabet, and are more aware of the different sounds in their language. They further practice other prereading skills like holding books the right way, turning pages, and reading by themselves.

In the United States, only about 43% of children between the ages of 3 and 5 are being read to frequently. In general, the less education parents have, the less they read to their children. Socially defined race also plays a role: On average, White parents read books the most to their children, Hispanic parents read to their children the least, and Asian and Black families fall somewhere in between (Child Trends Databank, 2015). This difference can be explained, at least partly, by considering that Hispanic families in the United States are more than twice as likely to live in poverty as are White families (17% versus 8%). Parents with low income frequently work more than one job to provide for their family; as a result, they may not have the chance to spend as much time with their children as those with a higher income, and when they do spend time with their children, they may be too exhausted from having more than one job to spend that time reading (Koball, Moore, & Hernandez, 2021; Shrider et al., 2022). As you would expect, children who live in poverty do not get the chance to listen to as many books as do their peers from higher-income families (see section below).

The more interactive the reading process is, the more children benefit from it. One technique that you can use when reading with young children is called "dialogic reading" (Arnold & Whitehurst, 1994; Coogle et al., 2020). In dialogic reading, the adult and the child have a conversation (a dialogue) while they are reading a book. The conversation should be a thoughtful one and not just repeat what has happened in the book.

Here are some suggestions for how to strike up a conversation when reading to a child:

- Ask them to complete sentences you read: The sun came out late that afternoon and Tommy went outside to _____ .
- Ask "wh-" questions: Who, what, where, when, and why, as well as how? Why did Mia act a certain way? What happened? When did it happen and where did it happen? How should Sally react?
- Ask them to remember: Why did Michael go out? When are his parents returning?
- Ask them to describe: What is happening in this picture?
- Apply to the child's own life: Connie lost her mom in the department store. Have you ever lost your parents in a store? How did you find them again? What can you do if you lose your family when you are out?

Remember to adjust your questions to the child's level of development: The questions should not be too easy but they also should not be so hard that the child does not have a chance of answering correctly. Put another way, the questions should target the child's zone of proximal development.

The Impact of Poverty on Children's Learning

In 2019, 17% of children lived in poverty in the United States. The poverty threshold for that year was an annual income of around $25,926 for a family consisting of two adults and two children. However, when discussing the impact of poverty, many researchers and advocates actually double the poverty threshold to identify low-income families. That is, any family of four with an income

■ Children can learn much from reading with adults: They get to know new words and familiarize themselves with letters. The more adult and child talk about the book and its content, the more learning opportunities are created.

of around $52,000 was considered a low-income family in 2014. And almost 38% of children lived in a low-income family that year (Koball et al., 2021)!

Children from Black and Hispanic families are more likely than children from White and Asian families to live below the poverty line: In 2019, 30% of Black children and 23% of Hispanic children lived below the poverty line, compared with roughly 10% of White and Asian children (Koball et al., 2021). Children in families living below the poverty line are at a disadvantage for learning.

Perhaps not surprisingly, children from lone-parent families were much more likely to live in poverty than children from families with two parents. Families living in poverty often do not have enough money for food, clothes, or even their rent. But the impact on their children is much greater.

In 2016, the average annual cost for preschool for one child was $8,933, with the best preschools being much more expensive than that. With costs that high and many families having more than one child, preschool is financially out of reach for many families. As we discuss preschools and daycare in the next section, keep this in mind.

When living in poverty, parents have to devote a significant amount of their time to securing the survival of their family. Their economic situation leads to additional social and emotional stress, which can make it even more difficult to find time for active play with their young children. Children from low-income families are at risk for many things: They tend to do worse at school and have a higher likelihood of dropping out of school than do their peers from higher socioeconomic backgrounds. They experience more abuse and are more at risk for developmental delays as well as behavioral problems (like being disruptive or aggressive) and emotional problems (like being depressed or feeling anxious) (American Psychological Association, 2016). By age 3, children from higher-income homes have a vocabulary of about 1,000 words, whereas their peers from low-income families produce only about half as many words (Hart & Risley, 1995). This is important because language and literacy skills significantly influence how well children do at school. And perhaps most drastically, brain volumes were smaller in children who had experienced poverty (Luby et al., 2013). The effects of growing up in poverty are devastating and, one could say, all-encompassing.

However, there is some good news as well. As we will discuss in the section on Head Start, preschool interventions can help young children get school-ready and may even influence the life of the child well beyond the first school years. Parents in disadvantaged situations can be reminded that any time they can spend actively involved with their children can have a great impact on their children's development. For example, they can:

- use supportive parenting practices like praising their children instead of threatening them with negative consequences. A supportive parenting style can support brain development and lead to a higher volume of the hippocampus in the brain (the hippocampus helps us form long-term memories) (Luby et al., 2013).

- read and speak more with their children. By age 2, children's vocabulary may already differ by 300 words depending on the number of words their parents use to talk to them (Huttenlocher et al., 1991; Kotaman, 2020).

- try to find time to play with their children. Play does not need to involve expensive toys. What is important is the one-on-one time spent with the child that creates an emotional bond between parents and children. Play also contributes to brain development and supports the physical health of the child (Milteer et al., 2012).

Review!

How do children's language skills advance in early childhood?

■ Young children learn new words at a rapid rate, from around 900 words they can actively use at age 3 to around 2,600 words they can use at age 6.

■ Word learning is fast through a process called *fast mapping*, in which children make hypotheses about the meaning of a word and revise their assumptions when necessary.

■ Around age 3, children can produce short sentences. As they get older, their sentences become longer and more complex.

■ Children intuitively apply grammatical rules to new words, which can lead to *overregularization* errors.

■ As children increasingly use *social speech* to communicate with others, they also have to learn rules about how to use their speech most effectively (*pragmatics*): They learn to let others finish their sentences or say "please" when they request something.

■ Reading to young children is an important way to help them learn new words, become aware of letter and word sounds, and recognize letters.

Practice!

1. In _____ , children quickly make a connection between a word and its meaning.
   a. fast mapping
   b. overextension
   c. overregularization
   d. pragmatics

2. Learning how to communicate efficiently with others involves learning communication rules, also called _____ .
   a. rule mapping
   b. fast mapping
   c. pragmatics
   d. social speech

3. In the United States, _____% of children are being read to on a regular basis.
   a. 63
   b. 4
   c. 33
   d. 23

4. In dialogic reading, children _____ .
   a. read about characters having dialogues with each other
   b. talk with others while reading a book
   c. talk to themselves while reading a book
   d. read aloud

5. When Timmy says "My mommy swimmed across the whole lake!", he makes the mistake of _____ .
   a. underregularization
   b. overextension
   c. overregularization
   d. underextension

Show What You've Learned!

Max's mother and father feel that 3 ½-year-old Max is behind in his language development. They're worried that he seems to use a smaller vocabulary than many of his friends. They have asked Max's grandmother, who often watches Max during the day, to read him lots of books so that he can learn more words. However, Max's grandmother says that Max is too young to understand books. She thinks there is nothing much that can be done to help children learn to speak—just be patient and he will get there eventually. What could Max's parents say in response? Act or write out a reply that explains the value of reading to children as young as Max. Draw on the concepts of fast mapping, dialogic reading, and literacy rates in young children.

9.3 The Impact of Education on Cognitive Development

■ Explain how early education programs influence young children's development.

In 2019, 74% of American children ages 3 to 6 (not yet in kindergarten) attended early childhood care and education programs (National Center for Education Statistics, 2021a). These programs are offered in a variety of settings like day-care centers, preschools, nursery schools, pre-K programs, or Head Start programs. The more educated a child's mother is, the more likely it is that the child will attend an early childhood education program. There are also significant regional differences in enrollment, with enrollments of 88% of all children in the District of Columbia but only 46% of children in Idaho (National Center for Education Statistics, 2021b).

High-quality early childhood education can have a significant impact on children's cognitive and social development as well as on their language. However, there is a tremendous variety in preschool approaches and philosophies as well as quality of care. In this section, we explore different kinds of programs and their impact on children. We also will discuss why the quality of a program is so important and how to find high-quality care.

Preschool Programs

Preschools differ tremendously in their goals and in the ways they approach teaching young children. All of these philosophies have merit. Which approach parents choose for their children depends on their own values as well as the character and needs of their child. Three of the most well-known programs are the Montessori, Reggio Emilia, and Waldorf approaches.

The Montessori method offers children a prepared learning environment

The Montessori method was developed early in the twentieth century by Maria Montessori (1870–1952). She was one of Italy's first female physicians. She soon became particularly interested in teaching methods for children with disabilities. In 1907, she opened a childcare center in a poor inner-city area of Rome, the Casa Dei Bambini. Montessori developed her teaching methods by careful observation of children's learning and experimentation with different ways to teach.

She believed that children are eager learners who readily learn on their own if given a chance. All aspects of the child contribute to learning—cognitive, social, physical, and emotional. Children learn through all five senses, not just through listening and watching. Montessori developed a "prepared learning environment" in which children can freely choose from a number of activities that are appropriate for their level of development. Different work centers scattered throughout the classroom focus on subject areas like language, math, or geography. Children are placed in multiage groups where older children spontaneously assist younger ones. Strict Montessori classrooms do not offer the opportunity for pretend play, arguing that children should be given the

© Children's House Montessori School of Reston, VA

■ A Montessori classroom has a number of centers that focus on the development of subjects like language or math. Often, you can find several children working and playing together.

opportunity to do the "real thing" (for example, cooking a meal or doing laundry) rather than engaging in pretend play (Lillard & Taggart, 2019).

Research that followed children over the course of 1 year shows that children attending Montessori schools had significantly higher gains in areas like executive function, reading, math, and social problem-solving than did their peers who attended conventional programs (Ackerman, 2019; Lillard, 2012). Children in Montessori preschools also tend to spend more time moving around than children in other preschools (Byun et al., 2013).

Parents often are interested in a Montessori education because they hope it will foster leadership skills and independence in their children. Although Montessori preschools are most widely known, there are some schools that provide Montessori education up to high school.

The Reggio Emilia approach teaches children to express themselves in different ways

The Reggio Emilia approach has its roots in Italy as well. It was developed in the city of Reggio Emilia after World War II when educators and parents collaborated to create a new system of preschools. Their goal was for families to participate in their children's education and to strengthen relationships between the child, family, society, and environment.

The Reggio Emilia approach is not a method like Montessori in that it does not have defined methods or accreditation processes. Founding director Loris Malaguzzi's thinking was influenced by Piaget, Vygotsky, and others (Dodd-Nufrio, 2011). However, he felt that the picture Piaget drew of children's abilities was too narrow and limited. Children are seen as curious and intelligent social beings who early on establish relationships with the people surrounding them as well as with their environment. Children have many "languages," like words, painting, sculpting, or music that they explore in the classroom. The results of the children's work are not viewed as "art" per se but rather as an expression of the learning that is taking place. Teachers follow the children's interests by observing and listening to them. Based on their observations, they then plan activities and projects. Projects are the most important part of the learning experience. The daily schedule allocates time for individual, small-group, and large-group activities (Emerson & Linder, 2019).

Reggio Emilia–inspired preschools are of interest particularly to parents who place great value on their children becoming "good citizens" and being involved in a whole community network. Because emphasis is placed on artistic expression, this kind of preschool may also be a particularly good fit for children who are learning English as a second language at school.

The Waldorf approach emphasizes practical and artistic activities

The Waldorf approach is based on the research of Austrian scientist Rudolf Steiner (1861–1925). He founded the first Waldorf school in Stuttgart (Germany) in the year 1919. Waldorf schools generally have a set routine so that children find predictability and comfort in their daily schedule. One day of the week may be focused on gardening, for example, while another one may be devoted to baking or handicrafts. Rather than placing emphasis only on academics, Waldorf schools allow domestic, practical, and artistic activities to take center stage (Stehlik, 2019). Additionally, the schools develop children's imagination by storytelling and free play. The goal is to develop the "head, heart, and hands" of the children (Haleakala Waldorf School, 2016). Waldorf schools can be attended up to high school. A distinguishing characteristic is the absence of regular transcripts of grades. Instead, students receive written narrative evaluations for each course.

Children in Waldorf schools get to spend lots of time outdoors. The school strives to be a place that has a home-like feel. Preschool classrooms have children of multiple ages, and the children usually stay with their teacher for several years. There are no electronic media in the classrooms, and toys are usually made out of wood or other natural materials. The goal of the school is to create enthusiasm for learning in the children.

Parents who want to foster their child's individualism often choose Waldorf schools because the schools' focus is not on what to think, but rather on teaching children how to think and how to express themselves in many different ways.

The Head Start program is aimed at children from lower-income families

Many families living in poverty are not able to afford high-quality childcare for their children. The Head Start program was founded in 1965 to support the development of young children from low-income families. It focuses on preschoolers, and 80% of the children served by Head Start are 3 or 4 years old. The Head Start program is comprehensive and includes many different services that are delivered at centers, schools, family childcare homes, or directly in the home of the children.

Head Start focuses on three areas (Office of Head Start, 2019):

- Cognition, language, and learning: Teachers support children's cognitive development to increase school readiness. Social and emotional development is promoted as well.
- Health: Children are provided meals and receive health screenings. The program can also connect families with health services of various kinds.
- Family well-being: Families are assisted in setting and achieving goals like finding a stable housing situation and having stable finances. They are also provided with social services. Parents are supported in raising their children with the goal of strengthening parent–child relationships.

In 1995, Early Head Start was founded in order to serve the needs of children younger than 3 years of age, as well as of pregnant women. Early Head Start assists parents in raising their young children. Once the children turn 3 years old, they transfer to the Head Start program. Both Head Start and Early Head Start programs vary in how their services are offered and what is offered, depending on the needs of the community they serve.

In 2019, the Head Start and Early Head Start programs served around 1 million children and their families (Head Start ECLKC, 2021).

So, does the Head Start program actually work? The results of the research on the outcomes of Head Start are mixed. Some studies show that the benefits do not last long. Attending a Head Start program for 1 or 2 years improved children's cognitive skills, but by first grade these gains had mostly faded away. The more children were at risk (through factors like speaking English as a second language, having poorly educated parents, or having a lone parent), the more they benefited from the program (Cooper & Lanza, 2014; Puma et al., 2010). However, children who have graduated from Head Start are also less likely to be placed in special education or to repeat a grade (Deming, 2009). Children generally benefit more from the program when their parents are actively involved (Marcon, 1999).

Why the Quality of Childcare Is Important

There are several benefits of attending preschool. The social effects are quite obvious: Children get to play and interact with their peers when they are at preschool, so they learn how to get along with others, solve conflicts, and gain confidence when they are around classmates. When children attend preschool, their independence increases as well. However, preschoolers also tend to be more aggressive and less compliant than their peers who do not attend preschool. Once they enter school, children who attended preschool tend to be more disruptive; this effect appears to last into the sixth grade (Belsky, 2006).

Of course, there are also cognitive benefits. Children who attend preschool score better on tests of verbal skills, memory, and listening comprehension

■ **Table 9.4** Choosing a High-Quality Preschool or Daycare Program

FAMILY–SCHOOL FIT

Key considerations	Questions to ask
What kind of a preschool am I looking for?	Small school or a school with lots of other children? Which educational philosophy? Lots of time for free play or a structured environment?
Is the school a good fit for my child? And for our family?	Can the school cater to the child's need in terms of napping, toileting, special needs, etc.? Is the tuition affordable? Do hours fit the family's schedule? What is the distance from home? Can you imagine dealing with the director and teachers, particularly if problems with your child may arise?
Visit the school: Plan in advance, and see more schools than you think you need.	Watch and observe: Can you imagine your child thriving there? Do you like the school, ambience, toys, and ways children and teachers interact with each other? What do other parents have to say about their experience with the school?

QUESTIONS ABOUT CAREGIVERS

Key considerations	Questions to ask
Teaching style	Are the teachers actively involved with the children, and do they interact with the children in a positive way? Do the teachers respond to the children's interests and needs and support them accordingly in a warm, supportive way? Are teachers aware of children's strengths, weaknesses, and interests?
Group size for teaching	Do teachers take the time to teach children in smaller groups or individually? Are children's individual interests accommodated?
Teachers' credentials	Are the teachers trained in child development? What are their credentials?
Teacher turnover rate	Are staff members being treated well and staying with the school, or are they turning over because of dissatisfaction in how they are treated?
Communication between parents and caregivers	Is it easy for parents to get in touch with the school? Are teachers available for meetings if requested? How often do parents and teachers meet? Do parents learn about what their child did on a given day? Is there a newsletter?

QUESTIONS ABOUT THE SCHOOL AND PROGRAM

Key considerations	Questions to ask
Child–caregiver ratio	Does the school meet the guidelines set by my state for child–caregiver ratios? Generally, the ratio should be: 7:1 for 3-year-olds 8:1 for 4- and 5-year-olds
Class size	What is the average class size? Generally, the maximum group size should be no more than: 14 for 3-year-olds 16 for 4- and 5-year-olds
Is the program licensed by the state?	Does the school meet the licensing standards for health, safety, and curriculum? Note that standards differ from state to state.
Is there enough time and space to play?	Are children given enough time to learn and explore their interests through pretend play and play with toys like blocks? Are children given time for physical activities and exercise?
Daily schedule	Is there a schedule to give children the structure they need? The schedule should include time for supervised activities and teaching as well as free play.
Cleanliness and safety	Is the school facility up to code, free of dangers to the child, and clean?
Closely examine the school rules and parent handbook	Does the school have a handbook? Note that schools are free to set their own rules, and the rules can be quirky, especially for private schools (for example, the school may be closed all day if the school district calls a 1-hour delay). Make sure you can live with those rules.
Look and feel of the school	Is the setup of the school messy, or is it organized and clutter-free? Is the atmosphere cold or warm?

(Clark-Stewart & Allhusen, 2002). The positive effects of high-quality child-care can be long lasting: Children who attended a high-quality preschool even showed effects as much as 10 years later in terms of higher academic achievement at school (Vandell et al., 2010). Disadvantaged children from low-income households benefit even more from quality childcare. They receive extra cognitive and social stimulation that they would not get in their family home. Higher-income parents, in contrast, often ensure presentation to their youngsters of a multitude of stimuli.

Most important for children to reap the benefits of a preschool education is that they receive high-quality care. Several organizations have published recommendations about minimum standards that should be met by childcare centers. These organizations include the National Association for the Education of Young Children (NAEYC), the American Academy of Pediatrics, and the National Institute of Child Health and Development (NICHD). However, most childcare centers in the United States do not meet even these minimum requirements. Research has shown that the more standards a program meets, the better the children perform in terms of school readiness and behavior issues (Francis & Barnett, 2019; NICHD Early Child Care Research Network, 1998).

But how do you actually determine the quality of a childcare facility? Many factors play a role, like the curriculum, caregivers, and caregivers' interactions with the children (see **TABLE 9.4**).

Review!

How do early education programs influence young children's development?

- More than half of American children attend early childhood care and education programs.
- Children attending a good preschool or daycare program learn how to interact with others and solve conflicts. They become more independent and tend to have better verbal skills and listening comprehension than their peers who stay at home.
- However, preschoolers also tend to be more aggressive and disruptive than children who do not attend preschool.
- Early childhood education is particularly important for children who grow up in poverty and thus are particularly at risk for having

problems at school later on. The Head Start program was developed for low-income families and focuses not only on the child but also on the well-being of his family. Head Start graduates are less likely to be placed in special education or repeat a grade.

- The quality of a program does not depend on the approach or method of education it uses. Rather, it is dependent on factors like whether the school is a good fit for the child and his family, whether the teachers are well trained, and whether there are enough teachers for the number of children attending the program.

Practice!

1. The _____ approach aims to give children many different ways to express themselves through art.
   a. Waldorf
   b. Montessori
   c. Reggio Emilia
   d. Head Start

2. Children from _____ families tend to perform worse when their language and cognitive abilities are measured.
   a. well-to-do
   b. low-income
   c. large
   d. one-parent

3. Head Start is a program that was created for children who are _____ .
   a. orphaned
   b. from families living in poverty
   c. not well developed for their age
   d. struggling with disabilities

4. When choosing an early childhood education program, it is especially important to focus on its _____ .
   a. number of teachers
   b. location
   c. ability to provide healthful snacks and meals
   d. quality

What Would You Do?

Iris, who has just turned 3, is normally cared for by her stay-at-home dad, Eli. Eli has a degree in computer science and is thinking of returning to work. He is in a very favorable position, however, in that his wife, Sara, earns enough to support the family if he chose to stay home to care for Iris. Eli's decision comes down to what is best for Iris: to start preschool in September or to stay at home with her father. If you were Eli, would you stay at home to continue to care for Iris, or would you enroll her in preschool? Explain how you think your decision would affect Iris's development over the next year.

Additional Resources Online

▪ "Weighing the pros and cons of nannies vs. daycares," from Very Well Family

▪ "Preschool, nanny, parental care, daycare? What's best?" from *Psychology Today*

9.4 Media and Cognitive Development

■ Evaluate how the use of media like TV and apps affect children's thinking skills.

According to a 2017 study, children between the ages of 2 and 8 spend around 2 hours in a typical day watching TV or videos while spending only about half an hour reading a book, either alone or with an adult reading with them. In fact, 29% actually have a TV in their bedroom, and 42% of children live in a household where the TV is on most or all of the time (Common Sense Media, 2017). While the use of mobile devices and apps is on the rise, television still dominates young children's media use. Most parents are not concerned about the amount of time their young children spend watching (He et al., 2005). Should they be?

Understanding the Content of TV Shows

Young children's understanding of TV programs is limited. Many of the programs targeted at preschoolers are around 25 minutes long. The longer the plot of a story, the more children have trouble following and understanding it. The educational benefits of watching a program are limited when children do not understand the story or fail to remember significant details.

Preschoolers also tend to have problems distinguishing between reality and television. They may believe that places like Sesame Street really exist or want to invite TV characters like Dora the Explorer or Bianca from *Wishenpoof* into their house for a playdate.

Additionally, TV shows often involve commercials, and young children do not understand that the purpose of commercials is to sell products. They often are unable to tell the difference between commercials and the TV program itself (Kundanis & Massaro, 2004; Palmer, 2003). When our children were young, they sometimes complained about annoying commercials when in fact those "commercials" were the show themselves.

Are TV Programs Educational?

Before age 2, the educational effects of TV seem to be extremely limited, if there are any. Take Baby Einstein videos, for example, which are developed specifically to improve cognitive development. Multiple studies have found that babies between 9 and 18 months watching those programs on a regular basis did not learn any more words than babies who did not watch the programs. One study even found that the TV-watching babies had smaller vocabularies than their non-watching counterparts. Parents who liked the DVDs tended to overestimate how much their children learned from them (DeLoache et al., 2010; Zimmerman et al., 2007).

Over age 2, TV watching can have positive educational effects if children watch the right programs. Research on *Sesame Street*, for example, has shown that children watching the program experience increased pre-academic skills (Wright et al., 2001). Watching TV also can help children develop skills they need to learn how to read and write, for example the ability to identify sounds or syllables in words (Uchikoshi, 2006).

As opposed to *educational* TV, *entertainment* TV has mostly negative effects on children. The more entertainment television children watch, the poorer their executive functioning (EF) skills like shifting or dividing attention between tasks and the higher their risk for ADHD (attention-deficit/hyperactivity disorder; Zimmerman & Christakis, 2007). The younger children are when they start watching, the weaker their EF tends to be (Kostyrka-Allchorne et al., 2017;

■ Young children may believe that animated characters they see on TV actually exist.

Nathanson et al., 2014). Even a running TV in the background leads to shorter play episodes than when the TV is off (Schmidt et al., 2008).

About 60% of TV shows feature violent behavior that children tend to imitate (Common Sense Media, 2013). Not surprisingly, TV watching contributes to aggressive behavior that may even last into adolescence (Comstock & Scharrer, 2006; Graber et al., 2006; Seger & Potts, 2017).

Watching TV Wisely

Because TV is an inherent part in most families' lives and can have positive effects on children's development, it is not always realistic to try to eliminate TV from children's everyday lives. When selecting TV shows for children, choose programs that:

- are educational,
- are adequate for the child's age,
- have short episodes,
- are calm and quiet (if the child is watching before bedtime),
- do not contain advertisements, and
- deal with topics and teach lessons that are important to you and to them.

By choosing children's TV shows carefully and limiting their screen time, parents can maximize the positive effects of television while minimizing the negative effects at the same time.

■ Videos designed to increase learning in infants tend to not deliver on their promises. Studies have shown that video-watching infants do not learn more than infants who do not watch. Additionally, interaction is very important for infants, and watching TV deprives them of that interaction.

Apps: A New Way to Learn

In 2021, around 3.8 million apps were available in Apple's App Store (Statista, 2021), many of them geared toward children as educational apps and games. There are also entire companies that have devoted themselves to digital learning systems, like LeapFrog. Half of all children under the age of 8 have used apps on a mobile phone or tablet.

■ Table 9.5 Choosing High-Quality Apps

Do's	Don'ts
App should require mental effort and keep child active.	App contains lots of passive activities like repetitive swiping.
App should keep child engaged and focused.	App has lots of distracting "bells and whistles" like sounds or hotspots (areas of the screen that can be touched and respond with a sound, a visual effect, etc.).
App teaches information that is relevant to the child's life and connects new knowledge with knowledge the child already has.	App teaches knowledge in a vacuum.
App encourages social interaction, for example, through discussion or conversation with caregivers.	App does not involve social interaction.
App assists child in exploration of new knowledge she can discover on her own terms, either digitally or in the real world.	App tells the child what to know.

Source: K. Hirsh-Pasek et al. 2015. *Psychol Sci* 16: 3–34.

Apps help children become tech-savvy, are available for play whenever a child is interested (independent of an adult's presence), and potentially present information in a fun and interactive way. They often offer a variety of learning modes—text-based learning, videos, multiple choice, games, audio-narration, and more. One study found that, after 4 months, American 4-year-olds knew six times as many letter sounds than they had known before. And in South Africa, second graders could read four times as many words as those who did not have a tablet with the apps (Hardesty, 2016).

Of course, like any other media, apps must be used in a responsible way. The American Academy of Pediatrics suggests that children over the age of 2 have no more than 1 hour of screen time a day (American Academy of Pediatrics, 2018).

There are a number of reasons for this recommendation. Excessive use of digital media puts children at risk for attention problems, sleep disorders, and obesity. Screens also offer a limited sensory environment: You cannot really smell and feel an app or manipulate things with your hands. If apps are used to keep young children quiet or calm them down, it is also questionable whether the children can appropriately develop the skills to calm themselves down.

Given the multitude of apps on the market, how can parents and educators choose apps that are high quality and deliver the results they promise? TABLE 9.5 provides some guidelines.

Review!

How does the use of media like TV and apps affect children's thinking skills?

- Watching educational TV shows can help children acquire prereading skills like identifying sounds or syllables in words.
- Educational apps use a variety of modes like video, games, and narration to teach prereading and reading skills as well as math skills or scientific thinking.
- Media can help support children's learning if they are carefully chosen by caregivers and teachers and children do not spend excessive amounts of time in front of a screen each day.
- Risks of media consumption include increased aggression, obesity, and sleep as well as attention problems.

Practice!

1. Children between the ages of 2 and 8 spend around
_____ watching TV shows or movies per day.
   a. 1 hour
   b. ½ hour
   c. 2 hours
   d. 3 hours

2. What percentage of TV shows feature violent behavior?
   a. About 90%
   b. About 60%
   c. About 50%
   d. About 30%

3. In children younger than age 2, the effects of educational TV
are _____ .
   a. stronger than in older children
   b. weaker than in older children
   c. about the same as in older children
   d. extremely limited

4. Preschool children should not spend more than _____
hour(s) in front of a screen each day.
   a. 1
   b. 3
   c. 4
   d. ½

See For Yourself!

Visit a few websites that name the best apps for preschoolers
and choose three apps to evaluate. Based on your own research
and the information in Section 9.4, are the apps truly as educational as they are made out to be? What can children learn from
these apps, and are there any downsides? Compare your notes
with your classmates to see if they agree.

Additional Resources Online

■ "Best educational apps for preschoolers," from Very Well
Family
■ "The best learning apps for kids," from Parents.com
■ "Best Preschool Apps," from Commonsense Media

One year later: Iris's fourth birthday party

One year later, Iris and her friends are assembled again to celebrate her fourth
birthday. Much has happened in the past year. Max's vocabulary has exploded
over the past months, and his parents are thrilled to hear him chat eagerly with
his friends. He is still scared of the masked fox, but fortunately Iris's birthday
theme this year is unicorns, so there are no foxes anywhere around. Though Iris
is still a shy child, she tends to spend less time with her imaginary friend Mayme
and has started to interact more with other children. Her parents credit this
development at least in part to their decision to enroll Iris in a preschool that
offers a curriculum based on the Waldorf approach. Iris has quickly started to
bond with other children over the hands-on activities she loves at her school
like cooking and gardening. At this moment, she is happily showing Oliver and
Sienna the iPad she got for her birthday and how to play her favorite game. The
adults are standing around chatting and catching up whenever the children give
them a break and do not need their assistance. ■▪■▪

© iStock.com/PeopleImages

Overview

Social and Emotional Development in Early Childhood

Children at play

It's a warm and sunny fall afternoon in Lansingville, Ohio. On this particular Sunday, everybody appears to be out enjoying the last days of warm weather. The playground in the park is bustling with children playing—children swinging, children playing in the sandbox, children climbing the monkey bars. Many of the toddlers are playing by themselves, and some of the preschoolers are playing in groups, all under the watchful eye of parents, grandparents, and other caregivers positioned along the perimeters of the playground.

Four-year-old Raymo slides down a big slide and falls to the ground as he reaches the bottom. He starts crying. His father observes him from the sidelines and calls out: "Come on, Raymo, toughen up! You don't have to cry like a girl just because you fell down."

Meanwhile, 5-year-old Aldo and 4-year-old Sarina are getting into an argument while building their sandcastles. The playground has a few plastic shovels of varying size, and both children want to use the big one for their projects. Aldo pulls the shovel away from Sarina, who starts screaming and hitting him in return.

The playground scenario highlights a lot of topics that we'll discuss in this chapter. We will explore how children's play changes as they grow older and how adults can help children learn to play together and interact with each other. We will also take a look at how children learn which behaviors are desired and which are undesired and what influences how aggressive they become.

We will discover that parents interact with their children in different ways (called parenting styles), and we will discover how parents' ways of interacting influence their children. And we will examine how children learn to act in ways that reflect societal norms around gender.

■ Children's self-concept becomes increasingly more complex over the preschool years.

10.1 Developing a Sense of Self

- Relate how children develop their self-concept in stages and explain how it refines as they age.
- Explain how children establish a gender identity.

In early childhood, every child gradually comes to understand that they are different from other people. People differ from one another in how they look, how they act, and how they feel about things. People can be boys or girls, for example, and they can be older or younger. When children understand what is different and special about them, they start forming a sense of their own identity.

Here is what 3-year-old Jason has to say about himself:

> I'm 3 years old, I'm a boy, and my name is Jason. I live with my mommy and daddy, who really love me. . . . I have blue eyes and a kitty that is orange and a television in my own room; it's all *mine*! I have a nice teacher at preschool; she thinks I am great at everything! (Harter, 2015, p. 29)

This is how 6-year-old Martin describes himself:

> I have made a lot of friends, in my neighborhood and at school. One is my very best friend. When I was littler, I could climb to the top of the jungle gym, but now I can climb to the top of the diving board. That's a lot higher! . . . If my parents know I did something bad, they might be ashamed of me. But mostly, my parents are real proud of me. . . . (Harter, 2015, p. 50)

Did you notice a difference between the two self-descriptions? Three-year-olds think about themselves in a very different way than do 6-year-olds. As children mature, relationships with others become more important. Older children also start comparing themselves to their peers and to their younger selves. In the next section, we will explore how children's thinking about themselves changes in early childhood and what impact that has on their life.

Developing a Self-Concept

How would you describe yourself in a few words? You probably think about many different characteristics and traits you have: where you are from, how old you are, what your goals and aspirations are, and what you like to do, for example. Your self-concept is quite complex and has developed over many years.

Children start to create their self-concept early on. The **self-concept** is people's belief about themselves and includes characteristics, abilities, attitudes, personality traits, and values. As children mature, they become increasingly more aware of who they are and what distinguishes them from others. When they are still very young, children's views of themselves are rather flawed and optimistic.

self-concept people's belief about themselves; it includes characteristics, abilities, attitudes, personality traits, and values.

■ Young children tend to overestimate their abilities and have trouble distinguishing between what they would like to do and what they can do.

What did you notice when you read Jason's description of himself? For one thing, it is unrealistically positive and optimistic (e.g., he believes that his teacher thinks he is good at everything) (Trzesniewski et al., 2011). He has trouble distinguishing his real self from the person he would like to be (Harter & Pike, 1984). He describes himself in terms of the possessions he has (a kitten and a TV!) and in terms of his abilities (e.g., others think he's great at everything he does). Young children also often talk about activities they like when they describe themselves.

As they get older, children refine their self-concept. They concentrate more on specific competencies they have and compare themselves to their younger selves and to their peers (Harter, 2015). They also see themselves more realistically: Parents of a 5-year-old are more likely to agree with their child's self-description than are the parents of a 3-year-old.

The positivity of young children's self-reports does serve a purpose though. Remember that young children are generally quite helpless and lack most abilities they need to get through their day, or even just to survive. A positive self-image helps children to stay motivated and keep trying as they attempt to acquire many new skills. It gives them the confidence to keep going. Otherwise, they might want to just give up, for example, when they have failed for the twenty-third time to do up the buttons on their jacket (Shin et al., 2007).

An important aspect of the self-concept is self-esteem. **Self-esteem** is a person's evaluation of their personal value. Self-esteem is associated with positive or negative feelings: People with low self-esteem may feel badly about themselves. Children start evaluating themselves early in life. Two-year-olds are proud when they accomplish a task like building a little block tower and proudly show their accomplishment to their parents. They also frown or look away if they do not succeed at a task (Stipek et al., 1992). Most 5-year-olds have positive self-esteem (Cvencek et al., 2016).

Self-esteem impacts people's lives in many ways and tends to be relatively stable over a person's lifetime. It influences whether people feel good about themselves or less worthy and insecure and how confident they are when they approach new tasks. It can even affect people's health: People with high self-esteem tend to be healthier than people with low self-esteem (Johnson & Galambos, 2014; Mund et al., 2015; Orth, 2017).

Because high self-esteem has such a positive impact on people's lives, it is important to help children build self-esteem. Strategies include the following:

- letting children make decisions, even if it is just a choice between a red and a green sweater;

- explaining that everybody makes mistakes and that mistakes help a person grow and learn;

- praising children in reasonable ways ("you're the fastest 5-year-old I have ever seen" instead of "you're the fastest girl in the world");

- refraining from comparing siblings, and telling each child what you appreciate about them individually; and

- giving children chores and letting them do some things on their own so they can learn new skills and what it means to be responsible.

> **self-esteem** a person's evaluation of their individual value. It is associated with positive or negative feelings, depending on how people think about themselves.

Developing a Gender Identity

Four-year-old twins Marya and Emily are playing with their dolls at home. They are busy feeding and combing them, making sure their dolls—their "babies"—are all content and happy. Their 5-year-old brother, Simon, is complaining that he is bored and doesn't know what to do. His mother, tired of the fussing, eventually suggests that he join his sisters and play together with them. "But I'm a boy! I'm not playing with dolls!" he cries out in frustration.

© Ronnie Kaufman/Getty Images

■ Early in life, children start to associate some roles more with boys and other roles more with girls.

sex how people are classified into male or female categories based on their sexual anatomy.

gender socially constructed roles and characteristics of people acting and feeling as either a man or woman.

Is this kind of behavior taught, or does it originate in our genes? In the next section, we discuss how children learn to act like boys and girls according to gender norms.

Differences between boys and girls depend on sex and gender

At birth, infants are assigned a **sex** based on their genitals. They soon become aware of their biological sex, although very young children may not understand that their sex is something that does not change, and so you may overhear a 3-year-old boy telling a story that begins, "When I was a girl, . . ." Soon, however, children in most cases become comfortable with their biological sex (Halim et al., 2016), and they declare themselves to be either a boy or a girl, acting in ways they believe that boys and girls should act.

The pattern of roles and behaviors we associate with being a boy or a girl is called **gender**. Some of these behaviors are inborn and universal, like the tendency of young boys to engage in roughhousing and physical play, or the tendency of girls to show nurturing behavior from a young age; these tendencies have been studied and appear across cultures. Other aspects of gender are socially constructed, which means they are conditioned and encouraged by the society in which a child is raised. These socially constructed aspects of gender may vary from culture to culture: A kilt—or anything resembling a skirt—may be an uncommon clothing choice for a North American boy, but it is far from uncommon in Scotland. When children adopt the pattern of roles and behaviors they associate with being a boy or being a girl, they establish their *gender identity*.

In the majority of cases, a child's biological sex and gender identity match: A child born biologically male will identify as a boy, and a child born biologically female will identify as a girl. We use the term *cisgender* to describe children who feel their gender identity matches their biological sex. This chapter focuses mostly on the typical development of cisgender children.

However, a person's sex and gender will not always match: A person born biologically male may feel, dress, and behave in ways conventionally associated with being female and therefore describe their gender as female; likewise, a child born biologically female may feel a much stronger affinity with the male gender. A person's gender identity can also change over time and may incorporate elements of traditional maleness and femaleness; it is for this reason that many people who study sex and gender prefer to view gender as a spectrum of identities. We use the term *transgender* to describe children, as well as adults, who feel that their gender identity—their sense of being male or female—differs from the biological sex they were assigned at birth. Some children may also be *agender*, or gender-free, which means that they identify as neither a boy nor a girl (Shumer et al., 2016), or gender-fluid, which means they move comfortably between traditional notions of male and female genders. Young people who feel a significant difference between their gender identity and their biological sex may experience distress and are at greater risk of developing depression or anxiety (Grant et al., 2010). There is a growing awareness of trans issues among educators, social workers, mental health professionals, and people generally, but because children naturally establish friendships on the basis of "sameness," transgender children who choose to dress and behave according to their gender identity may experience harassment, bullying, or threats (Bradford et al., 2013).

By age 3, boys and girls generally have begun to speak and act differently. Boys use more words commonly associated with their gender, like "car" and "boy." The same goes for girls, who use more words like "doll" and "girl" (Stennes et al., 2005). Boys and girls also tend to play with different toys: Boys often prefer cars and other vehicles and rough-and-tumble play; girls tend to

■ Boys often engage in rough-and-tumble play, whereas girls tend to engage in nurturing behavior more often.

play more with dolls and put themselves more in nurturing roles. They also tend to be somewhat less physically active than boys.

Around the time children start preschool, they also start to prefer playmates of their own gender. In preschools, girls and boys often cluster in separate groups (Telzer et al., 2015). This is called **gender segregation**. Gender segregation is not confined to Western societies; it also can be observed in Eastern cultures like China (Aydt & Corsaro, 2003). When children decide with whom to play, gender is more important than ethnicity: Children more likely will split into two groups of boys and girls, for example, than into groups of African Americans and Asian Americans (Whiting & Edwards, 1988).

As children learn about the roles of men and women, they also acquire gender stereotypes. **Gender stereotypes** are generalized, simplistic views of the roles and behavior that characterize men and women. TABLE 10.1 shows some of the gender stereotypes that persist in American culture (Eagly & Mladinic, 1989; Löckenhoff et al., 2014).

In today's world, stereotypes are present everywhere. In 2012, the website of the Disney store listed 410 toys for boys and 208 toys for girls. Only 91 were listed for both genders (Auster & Mansbach, 2012). In contrast, a 1975 Sears catalog listed less than 2% of its toys for exclusively boys or girls (Sweet, 2014)!

By age 3, children are familiar with many of the gender stereotypes of their culture (Cherney et al., 2006). In early childhood, these stereotypes often can become very rigid so that girls insist, for example, on wearing only dresses and boys avoid playing with anything that seems "girly" to them (Halim et al., 2014). As they get older, children start to understand that stereotypes are not always accurate and that there are individual differences—for example, that

gender segregation separation of the sexes, either voluntarily (for example, in play) or by law/policy.

gender stereotypes generalized and simplistic views of the roles of men and women and what characterizes them.

■ Table 10.1 Gender Stereotypes

Stereotypes describe males and females in very different ways. They can be positive or negative. Are they usually accurate?

	Men	Women
Personality	Aggressive	Shy
	Courageous	Passive
	Determined	Dependent
	Disorderly	Emotional
	Dominant	Submissive
	Self-confident	Soft-hearted
Occupations	Earn more money	Earn less money
	Good at math and jobs like engineering	Good at nurturing jobs like nursing or teaching
	Like "dirty jobs" like mechanics and plumbing	Like "clean" jobs that involve desk work or inside work
	Should be the boss at work	Are in subordinate position at work
Physical appearance	Tall	Small
	Short hair	Long hair
	Wide shoulders	Slim

■ The toys children play with can influence which skills they practice and which professional careers they are interested in.

estrogens a group of sex hormones that promote the development of female body characteristics.

androgens a group of sex hormones that promote the development of male body characteristics (e.g., testosterone).

■ Bruce Reimer was the subject of an experimental—and involuntary—attempt to change a person's sex through socialization and medical intervention. Born biologically male but raised as a girl from age 2, he never felt comfortable with his surgically assigned sex. At age 14 he stopped taking his prescribed treatment of female hormones to reverse the sex conversion. The failed experiment haunted him for the rest of his life, which ended with his suicide at age 38.

men can have long hair and that some women like to repair cars (Halim et al., 2013).

A variety of factors influence children in their gender development. We will explore these influences in the next sections.

Hormones have an impact on sex differences

Soon after conception, hormones start influencing the development of the embryo. Estrogens and androgens are two important groups of hormones that influence sex differences. **Estrogens** are a group of sex hormones that promote the development of female body characteristics. **Androgens** are a group of sex hormones that promote the development of male body characteristics. Both women and men have androgens and estrogens in their bodies but in different quantities: Women have a higher concentration of estrogens, men a higher concentration of androgens.

These hormones lead to physical sex differences in the brain. Men tend to have a larger overall brain volume, although the corpus callosum, which connects the two brain hemispheres, tends to be larger in women (Ruigrok et al., 2014).

Hormones may also influence which toys and activities boys and girls prefer (Berenbaum et al., 2012; Miller & Halpern, 2014). Girls who have a male fraternal twin and were thus exposed to high levels of androgen before birth tend to play more frequently in ways that are typical of boys (Hines et al., 2015).

Psychoanalytic theory provided an early explanation for gender identification

As you may recall from Chapter 2, Sigmund Freud suggested that children develop in a series of distinct stages. From age 3 to age 6, they are in the phallic stage (phallus = penis in Greek), in which they focus on their genitals and masturbation. Freud suggested that in this stage, children develop sexual attraction to their opposite-sex parent. Consequently, the children feel jealous of their same-sex parent: Little boys are attracted to their mothers and thus feel like they are competing with their fathers. Likewise, little girls fall in love with their fathers. The negative feelings toward their same-sex parent obviously create a conflict for little children, who are dependent on both parents. This conflict is called the *Oedipus complex* for boys and the *Electra complex* for girls (the names Oedipus and Electra were taken from characters in Greek mythology). To resolve this conflict, according to Freud, the child starts to identify with the same-sex parent and adopts that parent's characteristics and values (Lindsey, 2015). Most developmentalists do not believe that Freud's theory adequately explains gender development, and there is not much scientific evidence that supports it (Bussey & Bandura, 1999).

Social learning theory suggests children observe and imitate gender roles

Social learning approaches (see also Chapter 2) suggest that children learn gender roles by observation and interaction with others and the media (see also **FIGURE 10.1**).

Children will model and internalize feedback from various sources, including the media, friends, adult caregivers, and especially family (Miller et al., 2006; Prieler et al., 2011). Children often model their same-sex parents, and parents tend to reinforce behavior that they believe is appropriate for their child's gender. This is particularly true for fathers, who tend to be stricter in terms of the gender-appropriate

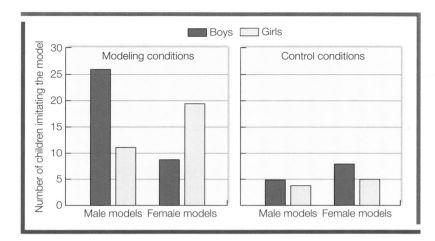

FIGURE 10.1 Bussey and Bandura (1984) had pre-schoolers watch either a cartoon (control condition) or a modeling movie in which male and female models behaved very differently. Afterward, girls were much more likely to imitate the female models, and boys were much more likely to imitate the male models.

After K. Bussey and A. Bandura. 1984. *J Pers Soc Psychol* 47: 1292–1302

behavior they expect of their children. They may admonish their young sons when the sons show distress ("Don't cry like a girl") or discourage girls from rough-and-tumble play (David et al., 2004; Wood et al., 2002).

Children may learn about gender in stages

Lawrence Kohlberg (1966) suggested that children's gender development takes place in three stages between ages 2 and 6. In the first stage (around the age of 2½ years), children develop a **gender identity**: They come to understand they are either a boy or a girl. Being a boy or a girl is then integrated into children's *self-concept* (illustrated by Jason's description of himself above). However, very young children do not yet understand that they cannot change their gender. Sophie, age 3, says: "When I grow up to be a daddy, I'll give my kids lots of chocolate."

In the second stage (age 3–4 years), children develop **gender stability**. They come to understand that typically the gender of a person stays the same over the person's lifetime. Children do not yet understand that a change in appearance does not change the person's gender. A boy may believe, for example, that he would turn into a girl if he wore his sister's dresses.

In the third stage (around age 6), children develop an understanding of **gender constancy**. They realize that a boy stays a boy even if a he has long hair or puts on a princess costume for Halloween. Once children have achieved gender constancy, they start paying particular attention to the behavior of the people

gender identity understanding that one is either a boy or a girl.

gender stability the knowledge that a person's gender remains the same over a lifetime.

gender constancy understanding that a person's gender remains the same even if the person's appearance or behavior changes.

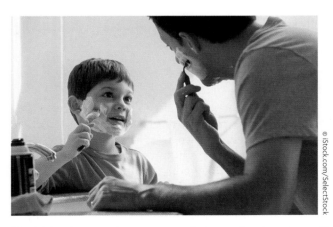

■ Children learn gender-appropriate behaviors by observing and imitating others in real life and in the media.

that share their gender and increasingly act in ways that are consistent with their gender (Halim et al., 2014; Liben et al., 2014).

Research has confirmed that children's gender development indeed goes through the sequence of stages Kohlberg suggested and that children increase their gender-conforming behaviors once they reach an understanding of gender constancy (Martin & Ruble, 2010; Zosuls et al., 2011). However, gender preferences for toys start emerging a lot earlier than does gender constancy. Kohlberg's theory cannot explain how these preferences develop so early (Alexander et al., 2009; Todd et al., 2016).

Gender schemas create the big picture of what it means to be a boy or girl

Gender schema theory was developed as an alternative to Kohlberg's theory of gender development. It suggests that early in life, children construct **gender schemas** that contain all the information they have about their own and the opposite gender (Bem, 1981; Martin & Halverson, 1981) (**FIGURE 10.2**). They learn what men's and women's bodies look like, what activities men and women typically engage in, and what men and women typically behave like. Children collect that information from their own experiences with men and women, from stereotypes ("Girls don't play in the mud!"), and from media like movies and games.

According to gender-schema theory, children start behaving in gender-typical ways as soon as they are aware of their gender and the gender of others (when they are around 2 years of age) (Wong & Hines, 2015a, 2015b). When given a choice to play with an assortment of toys, children as young as 9 months displayed preferences for the toys typical for their gender (Todd et al., 2016). Young children also show a preference for colors that reflect their gender (e.g., pink for girls, blue for boys) (Wong & Hines, 2015a, 2015b).

gender schemas cognitive structures that contain all of the information that children have about their own and the opposite gender.

FIGURE 10.2 Children create gender schemas that contain all the information they collect about what it means to be male or female.

Guiding children in their gender development

As we have seen in the preceding sections, children's toy and activity preferences influence the kinds of skills and abilities they develop (**TABLE 10.2**). In order to assist children to learn a wide range of skills, we can do the following:

- encourage children to play with non-gender-typical toys. For example, boys who play with more gender-neutral toys have better comforting skills than boys who primarily play with cars and trucks (Li & Wong, 2016);
- provide books and games that depict men and women in roles that are contrary to common stereotypes, like male nurses, female engineers, etc.;
- encourage play in mixed-gender groups;
- encourage children to make their own choices when they choose the activities and sports in which to participate;
- encourage boys to express their emotions and be less aggressive as well as to be more empathetic toward others' feelings. Encourage girls to be more ambitious and assertive and to show pride in their interpersonal and caregiving interests and skills; and
- discuss gender stereotypes with children and examine their accuracy (Leaper, 2014).

■ Exposing children to a wide variety of toys, books, and activities helps them develop their own personalities and interests independent of gender stereotypes.

■ **Table 10.2** Theories of Gender Development: Nature and Nurture

THE IMPACT OF NATURE	Major points	Example
Biological approaches: sex hormones	Estrogens and androgens (sex hormones) influence the development of the brain. This influence results in physical differences between male and female brains as well as differences in behavior and thinking processes.	Children show differences in toy preferences before they are even aware of their gender. These preferences as well as other differences may be influenced by hormones.
Evolutionary approaches	Life is a struggle for survival, and only the most successful individuals can pass on their genes to the next generation. Today's gender differences developed because males and females behaving in these gender-typical ways had the best chances to reproduce and raise their offspring successfully.	Females tend to emphasize their physical appearance and to be nurturing and caring because that behavior helps them attract mates and raise their children. Males tend to be aggressive and dominant in order to secure the youngest and healthiest females for mating.

THE IMPACT OF NURTURE		
Psychoanalytic theory	Children go through a series of stages that ultimately lead them to identify with their same-sex parent and thus adopt gender-typical behaviors.	Boys fall in love with their mother, which puts them in direct competition with their father. To resolve this conflict, they later identify with their father and start acting like him. Girls fall in love with their fathers and eventually identify with their mother.
Social learning approaches	Gender roles are learned by observation of others in real life and in the media. Children imitate behavior and get rewarded or punished.	Boys tend to imitate the behavior of men, and girls tend to imitate the behavior of women. Gender-typical behavior is rewarded and thus is likely to be repeated (a girl asking to take ballet lessons may be congratulated on her good choice). Gender-atypical behavior may be admonished and is thus less likely to be repeated (e.g., a boy spending a lot of time in the kitchen may be asked to go outside to play).
Cognitive developmental theory: Kohlberg's stages	Gender development takes place in three stages. First children develop a gender identity, then they develop gender stability, and eventually they achieve gender constancy. At the stage of gender constancy (around age 6), children begin consistently to pay attention to gender-typical behavior and act in gender-typical ways.	Young girls may insist on wearing dresses every day because their understanding of gender is still very rigid and they do not understand that there is significant individual variation in gender behaviors.
Gender schema theory	Early in life, children develop gender schemas that contain information about their own and the opposite gender. As soon as children are aware of their own gender, they strive to behave according to their gender schema.	Children use gender schemas not only to guide their behavior but also to process information. These gender schemas can distort information. For example, when hearing a story in which a girl saws wood, children may later remember that it was a boy who sawed wood (Martin & Halverson, 1983).

Review!

How do children develop an understanding of who they are as a person?

- In early childhood, children start to understand what it means to be boys and girls and increasingly conform to *gender* roles.
- Over the preschool years, children's *self-concept* becomes more realistic and includes increasingly more comparisons with their younger selves and other children.
- At 3 years of age, children mostly think of themselves in terms of their possessions and abilities. As they grow older, they start to compare themselves with others and with themselves at a younger age.

How do children learn what it means to be a boy or girl?

- When children are between 2 and 3 years old, they first understand that they are a boy or a girl and establish a gender identity. By age 3, they begin to act and speak differently.

- Freud suggested that children go through a series of stages that lead them to identify with their same-sex parent and adopt that parent's behaviors.
- Children closely observe how men and women as well as other boys and girls behave and imitate the behavior of these models. Children are more likely to imitate behavior that leads to positive outcomes (as compared with negative outcomes).
- Kohlberg suggested that children go through three stages: *gender identity* (they are a boy or a girl), *gender stability* (they will be a boy or a girl their whole life), and *gender constancy* (no dress or costume will change the fact that they are a boy or girl).
- Children create *gender schemas* that contain all the information they have collected about what it means to be male or female. As soon as they understand they are a boy or girl, most children start acting according to these gender schemas.

Practice!

1. A 3-year-old's self-concept is likely _____ .
   a. rather negative
   b. quite accurate
   c. overly positive
   d. nonexistent

2. The sense of being a boy or girl is expressed in someone's _____ .
   a. gender
   b. sex
   c. gender stereotypes
   d. gender segregation

3. Simplistic and over-generalized views of gender differences are called _____ .
   a. gender segregation
   b. gender development
   c. gender identity
   d. gender stereotypes

4. When learning about gender roles, children find models in _____ .
   a. the media
   b. teachers
   c. siblings
   d. all of the above

5. Children who have developed a gender identity know that _____ .
   a. they will always be a boy or a girl
   b. a boy does not become a girl when he puts on a dress
   c. they are a boy or a girl
   d. boys prefer to play with cars and blocks, whereas girls prefer to play with dolls

Show What You've Learned!

Six-year-old Tina really likes athletic clothes like gym shorts and team-branded T-shirts. She wants to play basketball and has asked her parents to sign her up for lessons. Her mother is hesitant to buy athletic clothing and requests Tina wear more "gender-appropriate" clothing. But Tina doesn't oblige, and most mornings feature an argument about what Tina is wearing. Tina's mom and dad are also trying to convince her to participate in activities they consider more appropriate for a girl, like gymnastics or dance. Do you think Tina will eventually change her behavior and comply with her parents' requests? What advice would you give to Tina's parents?

10.2 Social Life in Early Childhood

- Outline how parents influence the development of their children in Western societies and other cultures.
- List the ways siblings influence the development of a child.
- Demonstrate the impact age-mates and friends have on a child and explain how they differ from relationships with adults.
- Evaluate ways to discipline children in early childhood and assess their impact on the child.

Children learn through interaction with others and through play. Among the different groups that influence their development are their parents and siblings as well as children of the same age they meet on playgrounds and in schools. In this section, we discuss the impact of others on children's development and how children grow through their play.

■ The way parents interact with their children influences what kind of a person their children become.

The Influence of Parents

Over the past decades, there has been a trend toward more single-parent families. In 1960, 88% of children under the age of 18 lived with both parents and 8% lived with single mothers. In 2021, 70% of children lived with both parents; 22% lived with their mother, and 5% with their father (United States Census Bureau, 2021). Many people these days are single parents by choice: They might have chosen to divorce their partner, conceive a child through IVF, or adopt a child without a partner. There are significant differences between different ethnic groups. In 2021, 75% of White children lived with both parents, compared with 43% of Black children and 68% of Hispanic children (United States Census Bureau, 2021). In the next sections, we explore how parents and siblings influence the development of children.

Parents use different parenting styles to interact with their children

Parents interact with their children in very different ways. How they behave strongly influences who their children become. Two variables are especially important in describing parenting styles: (1) how demanding and controlling parents are and (2) how warm and responsive parents are toward their children.

authoritative parenting setting reasonable and consistent limits for children. Using explanations and dialogue rather than punishment. Being warm and accepting toward one's children.

In the early 1970s, researcher Diana Baumrind observed and interviewed 150 families with preschool-age children (Baumrind, 1971, 1980). Based on this study and subsequent ones, researchers often distinguish among four parenting styles described below (see also **TABLE 10.3**).

AUTHORITATIVE PARENTING Parents set limits for their children but explain the reasons for these limits. They encourage verbal exchange about rules and limits. Parents recognize that their children have interests and rights just as adults do. Parents are warm and responsive to their children's opinions and needs. When 5-year-old Nina hits her little brother, her parents might say "Don't hit your brother, Nina. You are hurting him. When you've calmed down, we should sit down and talk about what you can do differently next time when you're annoyed with him."

Children of **authoritative parents** tend to be self-controlled and self-reliant. They are comfortable in social situations and often eager to explore new situations. They tend to have good relationships with adults as well as with their peers and tend to cope well with stress (Hastings et al., 2007; Williams et al., 2009).

AUTHORITARIAN PARENTING Parents set strict and nonnegotiable limits for their children. If the children disobey, they are punished. There is no discussion of the standards and rules parents set for

■ Authoritarian parents have strict expectations for the behavior of their children and punish them if they do not comply.

■ Table 10.3 Summary of Parenting Styles

	DEMANDING/CONTROL			
	High		**Low**	
	Authoritative		**Permissive**	
	Parents	**Children**	**Parents**	**Children**
High	Set limits and explain reasons for limits Encourage communication about limits Warm, responsive	Self-controlled Self-reliant Eager to explore new situations Socially comfortable	Few demands Warm, accepting, Nurturing No punishments	Immature Demanding Have trouble controlling behavior
	Authoritarian		**Neglectful**	
	Parents	**Children**	**Parents**	**Children**
Low	Strict limits No discussion of limits Punish children	Anxious Unhappy Suboptimal communication skills Look to others for guidance	Few limits Unresponsive Cold	Immature Low self-esteem Poor relationships with family Risk of delinquency

(WARMTH/RESPONSIVENESS — row label spanning High and Low)

authoritarian parenting setting strict limits for children and punishing children if they do not obey. Absence of dialogue about rules and limits. Coldness toward children.

their children. Parents are not very warm or responsive toward their children. When Nina is hitting her brother, her parents might say, "Stop hitting your brother, or you'll get a good spanking!" Children of **authoritarian parents** tend to be anxious and unhappy. Their communication skills are not well developed. They tend to avoid social situations and look to others for guidance on how to behave or what to do (Russell et al., 2003).

PERMISSIVE PARENTING Parents have few demands on their children's behavior and are generally accepting, warm, and nurturing. Children essentially can do what they want without having to fear punishment or reprimands. When Nina hits her brother, her parents may not intervene, but rather let the children work out the situation by themselves, believing that this is a good way for children to learn conflict resolution skills.

permissive parenting few, if any, limits for and demands on children. Expect children to learn through experience. Warm toward children.

Children of **permissive parents** tend to be rather immature. They have trouble controlling their behavior and can be quite demanding because their parents set no limits. Because of their self-centered and noncompliant behavior, their relationships with others may be rocky (Linver et al., 2002).

NEGLECTFUL PARENTING Parents set few if any limits and are not very responsive to their children's needs. They do not have a warm relationship with their children and mostly want to be left alone. When Nina hits her brother, her parents may not intervene, reflecting their lack of involvement with their children.

neglectful parenting few, if any, limits for children; little attention paid to children. Not responsive and cold toward children.

Children of **neglectful parents** tend to be immature and to have low self-esteem. They often have poor relationships with family members. As they grow up, they are at risk for becoming delinquent and for having frequent absences from school (Pelaez et al., 2008).

Studies of these parenting styles have been conducted around the world. Many show that in most cultures the authoritative parenting style is associated with the same or better outcomes than other parenting styles (Pezzella et al., 2016; Simons et al., 2013; Uji et al., 2014).

Nevertheless, Baumrind's styles are not applicable to other cultures and parenting situations without reservation. Her subjects were mostly middle-class White Americans. And parents may need to adjust their parenting style to the temperament of their child as well as the situation—for example, potentially dangerous situations need stricter guidance than harmless situations.

In the next section, we will discuss in more detail the influence children and culture can have on parenting.

Children's characteristics and behavior influence the parenting they receive

Parenting is not a one-way street in which parents control and influence their children. On the contrary, children influence their parents with their behavior, personalities, and other characteristics as well.

It may not seem fair, but one factor that influences parents' behavior is the physical attractiveness of their child. Mothers of attractive babies tend to be more affectionate and playful with their child than mothers whose babies are not particularly attractive (Langlois et al., 1995).

Children also influence their caregivers with their temperament and behavior. The way you set limits and reinforce them for one child may not necessarily work for another child. Parents have to adjust the way they treat and discipline their children on a regular basis, depending on the child and situation (Sengsavang & Krettenauer, 2015).

Culture influences parenting styles

Cultural differences in parenting are partly rooted in the different ways that people perceive themselves and their relation to others around them. People in Western cultures tend to have an individualistic orientation, which means they see themselves as essentially separate psychologically from others. They define themselves in terms of their interests, goals, and traits. A European American might describe himself this way: "I am a librarian in our city library. I am rather shy and introverted. I like to read and play the piano." He describes himself in terms of personality, interests, and his profession.

Many societies in Asia, South America, and Africa—making up about three-fourths of the world's cultures—tend to be collectivist (Triandis, 1989; Triandis et al., 1988). Individuals in these cultures see themselves in terms of the groups they belong to and their relationships with other group members. Their group goals are more important than their individual goals. A Chinese person might describe herself this way: "I am a sister and daughter. I am Chinese, and I believe in Confucianism." She describes the different groups she belongs to.

How much cultures are oriented toward individuals or groups influences many other factors as well. TABLE 10.4 shows some of the differences

© Steven Puetzer/Getty Images

■ Children's characteristics like their looks or temperament influence how others react to and treat them.

■ **Table 10.4** The Impact of Individualistic and Collectivist Orientation on Values and Child-rearing

Domain	Orientation	Value	Child-rearing
Decision-making	Individualistic	People should be free to make their own decisions.	Children are given choices and increasingly expected to make their own choices.
	Collectivist	Important decisions are often made by parents or elders.	Children must obey decisions that others have made for them.
Shame/guilt	Individualistic	Felt in case of personal failure	Shaming children is discouraged as a parenting practice and leads to negative outcomes for children (Barber & Xia, 2013).
	Collectivist	Felt if bringing shame to group	Children are taught to meet the family's expectations and "save family's face"; shame-inducing techniques are associated with positive outcomes in children (Takahashi & Takeuchi, 2007).
Interaction	Individualistic	Express opinions freely, ask questions	Children are encouraged to express viewpoints and are potentially included in decisions.
	Collectivist	Questioning elders or people in power is not appropriate.	Expect obedience, do not ask children's opinion on matters.

■ In collectivist cultures, people perceive themselves as being part of a group rather than as an independent individual separate from others.

between individualistic and collectivist cultures and how they translate into different child-rearing approaches.

Even within the United States, ethnic groups differ in terms of the parenting practices and styles they employ. For example, authoritarian parenting is found more commonly among minority ethnic groups (Chao et al., 2002; Deater-Deckard et al., 2011; Pezzella et al., 2016); in European American households, authoritative parenting continues to be regarded, generally, as having the best outcomes for children (Pezzella et al., 2016). It is important to realize that we cannot use a Western model of parenting to draw the conclusion that one parenting style is generally better than any others.

Siblings

More than 80% of American children have at least one sibling. In 2014, around 80% of children lived with at least one sibling. Almost 20% of children live with a half-sibling, step-sibling, or adopted sibling (Knop, 2020).

The birth of a new sibling is a significant and often challenging event for any child. Overall family dynamics change as there is a new family member to take care of. Older children may worry about their place in the family, feel jealous, or behave immaturely to attract the attention of their parents. They might also delight in taking care of the new baby and be eager to help their parents (Underwood & Rosen, 2013)

Sibling interaction is different from interaction with friends. Children between the ages of 2 and 4 have about seven conflicts with their siblings per hour, with most lasting less than a minute (Kramer et al., 1999; Perlman & Ross, 2005). Conflicts with siblings are much more frequent than those with friends (Stauffacher & DeHart, 2005).

Having siblings helps children practice social interactions, helping others, and empathy (Howe et al., 2011; McHale et al., 2012; Whiteman et al., 2007). On the flip side, sibling conflicts teach children how to assert themselves and how to negotiate and handle conflict, which increases their social competence (Kramer, 2014; Updegraff et al., 2002; Whiteman et al., 2011).

But siblings can also teach each other aggressive and antisocial behavior, which can lead children to become bullies, perform less well at school, and to develop addiction problems (Bank et al., 2004; Tucker & Finkelhor, 2015; Whiteman et al., 2014).

only child child who does not have any siblings.

But what about **only children**? Only 3% of adults in the United States believe that the ideal family has only one child (Mancillas, 2010). Yet about

■ Siblings learn by interacting with each other. Do children with no siblings have a disadvantage or advantage over children from larger families?

20% of children do not have siblings, partly because people tend to marry at a later age and are worried about the financial responsibilities of raising a big family.

Research has shown that only children fare better academically and spend more time on homework than those later-born children who have three or more siblings (Chen & Liu, 2014; Falbo, 2012). It is important to make a distinction here between first- and later-born children of larger families, because only the firstborn children had the undivided attention of their parents for a while. In terms of their personality, only children in both the United States and China do not seem to differ much from children with siblings (Chen & Liu, 2014).

Peers and Friendship

When we speak of **peers**, we refer to children who are close in age to each other (also called *age-mates*). Children who have a close, positive relationship with each other are considered friends. Children's understanding of friendship and their interactions with friends and peers change as they get older. Toddlers' interactions are still very limited, and they may spend a significant amount of time observing each other or playing beside each other with hardly any interaction (Bukowski et al., 2011).

Preschoolers have more social interactions with each other. They prefer to play with children they can trust and increasingly engage in elaborate pretend play that depends on mutual understanding, like playing house. Friends give children emotional and social support. Children also come to understand that friendships are mutual (Theobald et al., 2014). Friendships in early childhood become more stable and can last a few months, if not longer—which is a long time for young children (Rubin et al., 2007).

Some children may be shy or prefer to play by themselves. This does not necessarily mean they are loners or rejected by peers; some children just have a vivid imagination and do not need social interaction as much (Coplan et al., 2004).

Children's relationships with peers differ from relationships with adults because peers are the same age. Because they consider themselves equal, they are free to exchange and challenge others' ideas (Kruger & Tomasello, 1986). They learn new skills and practice the skills they already have, like conflict resolution, taking turns, sharing, and supporting each other (Ramani & Brownell, 2014). Children who have good friendships tend to cope better with stress, have

peers children who are close in age to each other.

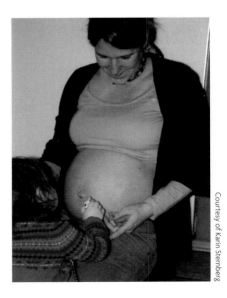

■ The arrival of a new baby gives rise to feelings of both joy and anxiety in older siblings.

■ In preschool or daycare, children find a large number of peers to play with. Are there any differences between sibling interactions and peer interactions?

prosocial behavior any action intended to help others without the expectation of a reward.

greater self-esteem, and show more **prosocial behaviors** (Berndt, 2004; Burk & Laursen, 2005; Holder & Coleman, 2015) (FIGURE 10.3). Rejection can make them feel lonely and depressed (Hymel et al., 2011). Preschools and daycare centers can actively promote positive interactions among their children.

Discipline

Children misbehave; there is no way around it. They test their limits to see how far they can get. What is the best way to react to children's misbehavior? Many discipline methods are based on B. F. Skinner's theory of operant conditioning (see Chapter 2) (Skinner, 1963). According to Skinner, we can influence the likelihood that a child will repeat an action by reinforcing or punishing the behavior. Here is how it works: Four-year-old Ainsely fusses almost every day when she gets home from preschool. Her parents do not like the fussing and can choose to react in the following ways:

FIGURE 10.3 Friends are "kind." Drawing of a 6-year-old girl in response to the question, "What is a friend like to you?"

From M. Theobald et al. 2014. In S. Garvis and D. Pendergast (Eds.), *Health and Wellbeing in Childhood*, 3rd. ed., pp. 235–256. Cambridge University Press, New York; K. Thorpe et al. 2006–08. Compromised or Competent: A longitudinal study of twin children's social competencies, friendships and behavioural adjustment. Australian Research Council. Project ID: DP0666254

- They can punish Ainsely for fussing by not giving her afternoon milk to her (punishment to discourage negative behavior).

- If Ainsely does not fuss, they can profusely praise her or give her a little prize (positive reinforcement to strengthen positive behavior).

- If Ainsely does not fuss, they can release Ainsely from her daily duty to clean up her toys (negative reinforcement to strengthen positive behavior)

All three actions are designed to get Ainsely to behave in a more acceptable way.

Another method to stop undesired behavior is called *extinction*, in which attention-seeking behavior is ignored. Three-year-old Ryder is persistently whining at the supermarket because he wants to get some chocolate. His mother ignores his behavior. She hopes that before long he will stop whining at the supermarket because his whining does not help him get any chocolate.

■ Rewards (positive reinforcements) increase the chance that a child will repeat a behavior.

© iStock.com/jo unruh

Physical discipline remains common among American parents

When people engage in physical punishment, it is also called corporal punishment. **Corporal punishment** is intended to physically hurt a person. In many parts of the world, including North America, corporal punishment is used somewhat frequently to discipline children. In 2014, in the United States, 76% of men and 65% of women aged 18–65 agreed that children sometimes need to be spanked (ChildTrends Databank, 2015). Parents who were spanked as children are more likely, when they become adults, to spank their own children (Gershoff & Grogan-Kaylor, 2016). In 2017, the debate about whether corporal punishment is an acceptable method of disciplining children was engaged anew when NFL star Adrian Peterson was indicted on child-abuse charges because he had hit his 4-year-old son with a switch. He stated that he had been physically punished as well as a child and "believed that the way my parents disciplined me has a great deal to do with the success I have enjoyed as a man" (Wallace, 2017). In 2018, Peterson admitted that he still used physical punishment to discipline his children (Tesfatsion, 2018).

In 19 U.S. states, teachers at public schools are allowed to hit students (Gershoff & Font, 2016). In the 2013–14 school year, more than 160,000 students were physically punished, mostly in Southern states. In many cases, the students are paddled, which means they are struck with a wooden board. Children with disabilities and Black children are around 50% more likely to receive corporal punishment than their classmates, and boys are more likely than girls to receive corporal punishment (Gershoff & Font, 2016). In South America and Europe, spanking is prohibited in a majority of countries (Global Initiative to End All Corporal Punishment of Children, 2022).

Some studies show that spanking has few negative outcomes for children (Ferguson, 2013; Gershoff & Grogan-Kaylor, 2016). Others, however, suggest that spanked children are more aggressive, disobey their parents more, fight more with peers, and have lower cognitive abilities and self-esteem (Alaggia & Vine, 2013; Gershoff, 2013; Kazdin & Benjet, 2003). The American Academy of Pediatrics suggests that children never be physically punished (American Academy of Pediatrics, 2017).

There are several problems with corporal punishment: (1) It teaches children that physically hurting others is acceptable; (2) the line between spanking and physically abusing a child can easily be crossed; (3) it has only a short-term effect on behavior; (4) it does not teach children how to behave better (just that what they

corporal punishment
a punishment that is intended to cause physical pain to a person.

© iStock.com/Hakase

■ In Japanese culture, parents commonly use disciplinary methods that promote their child feeling guilt and shame when the child misbehaves. Unlike in Western countries, doing so does not seem to lead to negative outcomes in Japan.

psychological control discipline that withdraws love from children or makes them feel shame and guilt.

did was not right); and (5) it has a number of negative effects on children's health and behavior.

So how should a child be disciplined to maximize the chances of a positive outcome? TABLE 10.5 gives some suggestions (based on guidelines of the American Academy of Pediatrics) (Committee on Psychosocial Aspects of Child and Family Health, 1998).

Shame and withdrawal of love are examples of psychological control

Some parents try to control their children's behavior by making them feel shame or guilt or by withdrawing their love. When the child misbehaves, they may:

- stop speaking to their child,
- not look at the child anymore,
- be less friendly, or
- tell the child how much they have sacrificed for him.

These tactics are called **psychological control**. Psychological control can be a very powerful discipline method, because children need their parents' love and want to feel accepted and approved.

In Japan, shame and withdrawal of love are used frequently to discipline children and do not seem to have any negative implications for the well-being or future behavior of the child (Rothbaum et al., 2000; Takahashi & Takeuchi, 2007).

In Western societies, however, the same behavior leads to feelings of guilt and anxiety as well as to low self-esteem in children and can have a negative impact on the children's school achievements (Alegre, 2011; Grusec, 2014; Grusec & Davidov, 2015). For this reason, using shame and withdrawal of love is not recommended in the United States as a parenting method. These differences in effectiveness of different parenting methods in different cultures are yet another example of how culture influences the use and effectiveness of disciplinary methods.

■ **Table 10.5** Suggestions on How to Get Positive Results from Discipline

Create a loving, nurturing relationship with the child.
Give children warmth and affection.
Have a positive tone in the house.
Respond to children's needs and wants and reason with them.
Listen to children.
Respond in a consistent way to challenging situations.
Offer explanations.

Increase desired behavior using positive reinforcement.
Praise desired behaviors.
Ignore trivial misbehavior.
Model good behavior.
Give children choices when possible so they can learn how to evaluate choices and realize there are consequences to their behavior.

Decrease undesired behavior by removing reinforcement or using punishment.
Explain what the undesired behavior is and what the consequences are when child misbehaves.
Consequences should be experienced immediately after misbehavior.
Consequences should be related to misbehavior.
React calmly to misbehavior.

Inductive reasoning is used to de-escalate conflict

A method of discipline that is used particularly often by authoritative parents is **inductive reasoning**, where parents speak with the child about the rules they set, explaining what the child did wrong and what she can do better next time (see also **FIGURE 10.4**). While difficult with very young children, even a 2-year-old can understand a simple statement such as "Don't hit your sister—you're hurting her." Induction helps children develop moral reasoning, because the children learn to empathize with others and to consider the consequences of their actions (Grolnick, 2002).

Here is how the mother of 5-year-old Shania is handling misbehavior. Shania is stirring cake batter in the kitchen, but the bowl turns over and ends up on the floor. Shania goes into a tantrum and starts screaming in high pitch. Her mother leads Shania to the living room to calm down. After a few minutes, she sits down with Shania to explain how to better express feelings and deal with frustration than by throwing a tantrum.

In the heat of a conflict, many parents remove their child from a situation in which the child is misbehaving. This method is called **time-out**. In time-outs, children spend a short amount of time (as a general rule, 1 minute per year of life, up to 5 minutes) in a quiet place with no distractions.

More than three-quarters of American parents endorse the use of time-outs. But time-outs are only effective if certain rules are followed when implementing them (Beal, 2017; Riley et al., 2016) (**TABLE 10.6**).

■ In the United States, a majority of parents use time-outs to discipline their children.

time-out a form of discipline in which a misbehaving child is moved to a quiet place with no distractions for a short period (usually 1 minute per year of age).

inductive reasoning reasoning method in which general conclusions are drawn from specific observations.

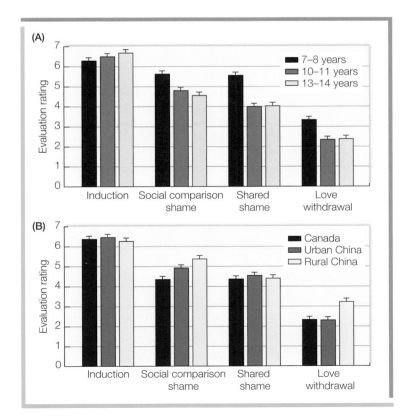

FIGURE 10.4 The older children get, the more they are aware of the benefits of inductive reasoning in parenting. Children in Canada and China prefer it when their parents reason with them instead of inducing shame or withdrawing their love.

After C. C. Helwig et al. 2014. *Child Dev* 85: 1150–1167. © The Society for Research in Child Development

■ Table 10.6 Effective Use of Time-outs

☑ **What to do**	☒ **What not to do**
✓ Make sure time-out immediately follows misbehavior.	✗ Give multiple warnings before putting child into time-out.
✓ Make it short to moderate duration (generally 1 minute per year of life; no more than 5 minutes total).	✗ Talk to child during time-out.
✓ Choose a time-out location that is quiet and does not offer entertainment.	✗ Choose a stimulating, entertaining location for the time-out.
✓ Ensure that parents, and not child, decide when time-out ends.	✗ Give access to entertaining toys during time-out.
✓ Set a timer.	✗ Choose location that lets children see other people during time-out.
✓ Have a strategy for when the child leaves the time-out location before the time-out ends (generally, leading the child back to the location and restarting the timer is best; spanking or physical restraints are not recommended).	

Review!

How do parents influence the development of their children?

■ Parents strongly influence their children's development through the ways they interact with their children. In Western societies, the four most common parenting styles are (1) *authoritative*, (2) *authoritarian*, (3) *permissive*, and (4) *neglectful*. The authoritative style is typically seen as most effective.

■ Parenting practices in other cultures do not always fit neatly into the four parenting styles we observe in the West. Parenting practices that work well in one culture may not work well in other cultures.

■ One factor that leads to cultural differences in parenting is that some cultures are collectivist (individuals see themselves as an integral part of a group), whereas others have an individualistic orientation (individuals see themselves as separate from others; this pattern occurs mostly in Western countries).

■ Children also influence their parents' behavior through their own behavior, temperament, physical attractiveness, and other characteristics.

How do siblings influence the development of a child?

■ Children learn many skills in interaction with their siblings. They act as role models, practice social interactions and conflict resolution, and exhibit *prosocial behavior*. However, they also can introduce their siblings to antisocial behaviors and activities. Academically, only children typically fare better or as well as children from two-child families.

What impact do age-mates and friends have on a child?

■ Being with peers gives children a chance to interact with other children of the same age.

■ With peers, children are more likely to discuss and negotiate ideas.

■ Around the age of 2, we start seeing the first signs of friendship, when children prefer some peers over others as playmates. Friendships intensify as children get older: Children have more interactions with each other and increasingly support and trust each other.

What are common ways to discipline children in early childhood, and what is their impact on the child?

■ The bases of discipline are (1) reinforcement, which rewards positive behavior, and (2) punishment, which punishes negative behavior. Parents also use extinction when they ignore attention-seeking behavior.

■ In the United States, *corporal (physical) punishment* is relatively common as compared with countries in Europe. Researchers do not agree on whether mild spanking has negative effects on children. It certainly does when a child is severely physically punished.

■ Parents also try to discipline children by shaming them and withdrawing their love for a period of time. These techniques are frequently used in Asian cultures and have better outcomes there than in Western culture, where the techniques are generally discouraged.

■ In the United States, reasoning and de-escalation are recommended as some of the most effective means to discipline young children. Using time-outs, children can be removed from a situation that is out of control. Alternative ways to handle conflict situations then can be discussed afterward when the child has calmed down.

Practice!

1. Parenting style tells us something about the way a parent _____ .
   a. dresses their child
   b. interacts with a child
   c. dresses himself or herself
   d. feels about himself or herself

2. In Western societies, the _____ parenting style is considered to be the most effective.
   a. neglectful
   b. authoritarian
   c. authoritative
   d. permissive

3. Peers are children _____ .
   a. aged 0–18 years
   b. of the same age as each other
   c. of the same gender as each other
   d. who are related to each other

4. Societies in which people tend to see themselves as part of different groups and subordinate themselves to the groups' goals have a(n) _____ orientation.
   a. individualistic
   b. eclectic
   c. activist
   d. collectivist

Act It Out!

Let's return for a moment to the scenario we read at the beginning of the chapter. Five-year-old Aldo and 4-year-old Sarina are getting into an argument over the use of a shovel for building their sandcastles. Aldo pulls the shovel away from Sarina, who starts screaming and hitting him in return. Sarina's mother goes to intervene in the dispute. Pick two of the parenting styles presented in this section and role-play the interaction between the two children and Sarina's mother.

What's Your Position?

Can parents make their children get along? We know that lots of siblings fight, from the time they're children well into adulthood. What role can parents play? Write out your opinion, and then go online for more information. Did the material presented online change your position?

Additional Resources Online

- "When siblings won't stop fighting," in Child Mind Institute
- "Handling sibling fights," in RaisingChildren.net
- "Sibling rivalry," in Nemours Kids Health
- "10 tips for dealing with sibling rivalry," from the Cleveland Clinic

10.3 Children's Work: Play

- Identify why and in what ways play is important for young children.

Young children all over the world learn by playing. Consider this example of Tim and Leah (both 5 years old) playing:

Tim: I am the cook. I am making waffles. Do you want some?

Leah: Yes! I LOVE waffles!

Tim: Here is my batter. I am making them now. Do you want butter on top? Or strawberries?

Leah: I want both. I am so hungry.

Tim: Ouch! I hurt myself! The waffle iron is so hot.

Leah: Oh no! Wait! I can get some ice!

While playing with each other, Tim and Leah are practicing a number of skills. They understand how waffles are made and that a waffle iron can be hot. Leah also shows empathy when Tim pretends to get hurt.

In this section, we will learn about two different ways to categorize children's play. Categories can be used to provide an environment and activities that support different kinds of play and skills. They also help us recognize

■ What are the two children in this photo learning?

In practice play, children repeat actions many times. The repeated practice improves their skills.

where children are in their development. Afterward, we discuss an approach called "guided learning" that combines children's play with instruction through adults.

Play and Cognitive Development

Jean Piaget distinguished four different kinds of play that get increasingly difficult in terms of cognitive complexity (DeLisi, 2015):

PRACTICE PLAY   In practice play (also called *functional play*), children repeat behaviors they are learning or have learned. Young preschoolers (ages 2 and 3) engage in a lot of practice play like jumping, running, or throwing balls. The frequency of practice play declines as children enter elementary school age.

SOCIAL PLAY   Preschoolers delight in social play that involves interaction with their peers. Social play increases significantly as children learn to interact and communicate successfully with other children. Children who engage in more social play tend to be more creative, less disruptive, and have better language capabilities than their peers (Fung & Cheng, 2017; Holmes et al., 2015).

CONSTRUCTIVE PLAY   Constructive play builds on activities children perform in practice play. Activities are not performed for their own sake as in practice play, but are used to create something. For example, instead of just cutting paper into little pieces, children may cut out shapes to make a collage. Constructive play also includes activities like building structures with blocks or completing puzzles. Constructive play can be seen frequently not only in preschoolers but also in children of elementary school age.

GAMES   Games are activities that have rules and are fun for the participants. In early childhood, children first start developing an interest in games and are increasingly able to participate in simple games. The importance of games increases through early childhood. During middle childhood, games play a significant role in children's play.

Play and Social Interaction

Mildred Parten (1932) was particularly interested in the extent to which children actually interact with each other when they play. The older children get, the more complex and interactive their play becomes.

Depending on how children interact with others, Parten distinguished six types of play:

1. unoccupied play,

2. solitary play,

3. onlooker play,

4. parallel play,

5. associative play, and

6. cooperative play (see **TABLE 10.7**).

From unoccupied play to cooperative play, play behaviors get increasingly social as children interact more with each other. As children grow up, they tend to engage less in nonsocial ways of play and more in associative and cooperative play; by playing, they gradually learn to interact with each other. Teachers

■ Mildred Parten suggested that there are different kinds of play, depending on the extent to which children interact with each other.

© iStock.com/lisegagne

can encourage social play by providing toys that invite social participation. Interaction between children is more likely when children play with a doll rather than reading a book, for example. Strategies like these can also successfully be used to assist children with developmental challenges (for example, to help integrate children with autistic spectrum disorders into a group of preschool children) (Papacek et al., 2016).

■ **Table 10.7** Types of Social and Nonsocial Play

	Category	Description	Example
Nonsocial play	**Unoccupied play**	• Child does not seem engaged or actively playing. • Random movements • Mostly occurs in children age 0–2	Child sitting in a corner, randomly moving arms or head from time to time.
	Solitary play	• Child plays alone. • Not interested in others surrounding him. • Child learns how to entertain himself. • Mostly occurs in children age 2–3	Child sitting on ground playing with a truck by himself.
More social	**Onlooker play**	• Child observes others playing but does not actively join. • May talk to the observed children or make suggestions, but no participation otherwise	Child watching others play house, sometimes joining in to ask if the baby is sick or when daddy is coming home.
	Parallel play	• Child mimics the play of another child or plays with similar toy. • Children play beside each other but do not interact otherwise. • Mostly occurs in preschool years	Two children sitting beside each other both tending to their dolls.
	Associative play	• Children interact with each other or share toys but do not have a common goal. • Starts to emerge between ages 3 and 4	Children sitting in the sandbox together, both building their own sandcastle, exchanging shovels and buckets and talking to each other as they work.
Social Play	**Cooperative play**	• Children have a common goal in play. • Teamwork • Might have assigned roles or division of labor • Focus on both play task and peers • Develops between ages 4 and 6	Children working together on building one sandcastle, with one child putting sand in buckets and making "bricks," one child getting extra water and adding castle decorations, and one child smoothing the surface between the "bricks."

■ Academic instruction is playing an increasingly large role in the lives of preschoolers and kindergarteners.

Play and Learning

Increasingly, American parents and academic institutions place an emphasis on academic instruction over play. In 2016, only 8 out of the 50 states in the United States required elementary schools to have daily recess (Society of Health and Physical Educators, 2016). Children are spending only half as much time playing outdoors as they used to 20 years ago (Burdette & Whitaker, 2005), and play is increasingly seen as a waste of time (Singer et al., 2006). And yet, play is very important. When our children returned from school in their early elementary years, they played with such intensity until dinnertime that it almost seemed to me that they were trying to catch up on the play that could not happen during the day.

In order to combine children's need and desire to play with today's rigorous curricular expectations, Hirsh-Pasek, Golinkoff, and colleagues suggest an approach called "guided play" (Weisberg et al., 2016; Zosh et al., 2015, 2017). In guided play, an adult coaches children in their play and guides their learning via exploration, which can be very effective (Bonawitz et al., 2011; Sim & Xu, 2015) (see also **FIGURE 10.5**). Division and multiplication can be taught playfully by playing baker and distributing chocolate chips among cookies, for example. Adults can also guide children by asking questions and making comments when the adults observe the children play, essentially providing *scaffolding*. As you may remember, we discussed scaffolding in the context of Vygotsky's theory of development in Chapter 9.

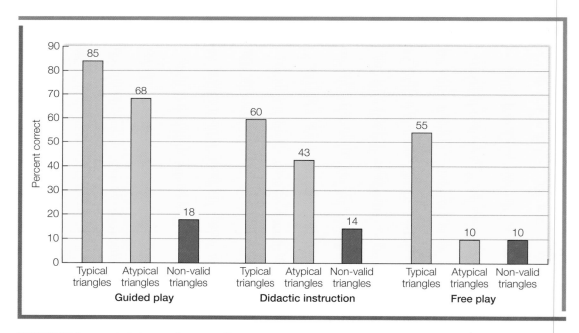

FIGURE 10.5 Guided play can be very effective in teaching children new concepts: Children were presented with bendable wax sticks and with cards that showed typical triangles, atypical triangles, and shapes that were not triangles at all. In the guided play condition, the adult and child explored the shapes together; in the free play condition, children played without instruction; and in the didactic (formal) instruction condition, an adult explored the materials with the child watching. The children in the guided play condition were the most successful at picking out triangles from the shape cards, followed by the children in the formal instruction condition and, last, the children in the free play condition.

After K. R. Fisher et al. 2013. *Child Dev* 84: 1872–1878. © The Society for Research in Child Development

What's It Like...

Helping Children Realize Their Potential

Molly, mom of Fred (4)

These days, more than ever, it is extremely important that children get a head start in their education. A lot of preschools admit children on the basis of tests, and this trend continues. The trend is even more visible in private schools around the country. I believe that Fred will have the best chances for success in life if he can go to the most selective schools that will ultimately increase his chances to be admitted into a selective college. What you get in these colleges is not just a better education, but a network of future professional connections that money can't buy.

To increase Fred's chances of getting admitted into one of the best local private schools, we've hired a tutor since he was 3 years old. Fred does daily worksheets to practice his handwriting, he is familiar with all the common sight words already, and we are working hard on his math skills. We're also practicing with sample tests of all the common private-school admissions tests he might encounter. Yes, he doesn't have as much time to play as other children do, but he's actually working toward his future. Would I rather see him outside more, or would I rather know I did my best to help him get into the best school? For me and my husband, the answer is clear: We'll invest in his future as best as we can. Others may think we are too focused on work, but when Fred gets admitted and their kids don't, they may reconsider.

Ceria, mom of Katelyn (4)

We live in a community where there are lots of expensive private schools. The pressure for children to succeed and to achieve at the highest academic levels is there even for the smallest of children. Babies watch educational TV series, and even toddlers take tests to be admitted to the most prestigious private schools.

I don't want that for my child. I want my child to develop her skills through play and to have a happy childhood she fondly thinks back upon many decades from now. I don't believe in screen time for infants, and I just can't see what the sense is in teaching children skills they're just not ready for. It takes up so much time to teach preschoolers to read and write, and if you wait a bit, they'll pick up on those skills much faster.

Young children, at least my daughter, have an urge to play and to explore the world. I think children can learn much more, and gain knowledge that is much more relevant to them, when they explore the world on their own terms, not terms imposed by parents or society. They'll be better prepared for tomorrow's world when they learn to be independent, solve problems independently, and develop their creativity through free play. Her future will be better if she develops happiness, creativity, and joy in living. I'll do the best I can to keep Katelyn away from the pressure to perform and be a "cookie-cutter" child as long as possible.

Review!

Why is play important for young children, and in which ways is it important?

- Young children learn best through play. Play develops all kinds of skills: social skills (like interacting and negotiating with others), thinking skills (like problem-solving), language skills (when talking to playmates or stuffed animals), and physical skills (when moving around or manipulating toys).
- We can think of play in terms of the thinking skills involved (practice play, social play, constructive play, and games; see Piaget's categorization) or how much children interact with others (unoccupied play, solitary play, onlooker play, parallel play, associate play, and cooperative play; see Parten's categorization).

- Young preschoolers engage a lot in practice play. As they get older, they increasingly play with others (social play) and create things through their play (constructive play). Around the age of 3, children start to interact more with others in play, and between the ages of 4 and 6 they learn to play with others sharing a common goal (cooperative play).
- Current trends in the United States favor academic instruction over play in many preschools and elementary schools. Guided play, in which an adult playfully guides children in their play, is a way of integrating young children's need to play with the need to keep up with an academic curriculum.

Practice!

1. _____ is an example of constructive play.
   a. Hopping on one leg from one side of the room to the other
   b. Making a paper airplane
   c. Sliding down a slide
   d. Throwing a ball back and forth

2. Of the examples below, _____ is the kind of play where children have the most complex social interactions with each other.
   a. onlooker play
   b. associative play
   c. solitary play
   d. parallel play

3. In _____ , children mimic another child's play.
   a. practice play
   b. unoccupied play
   c. parallel play
   d. constructive play

Show What You've Learned!

Your sister Helen has two children: Timo (age 4) and Mirko (age 8). Helen places a strong emphasis on academic education. Every afternoon, Timo has to sit down for 45 minutes to complete worksheets that teach him to write letters, basic reading skills, and some early math. Mirko has to do supplemental academic work as well, in addition to his daily homework from school. You feel that your sister overemphasizes academics. What could you say to her?

10.4 Moral Development

- Explain how children learn positive social behavior.
- Explain how children learn negative social behavior.

Growing up means that children have to learn what is right and what is wrong. Parents and educators try to instill a sense of right and wrong in their children. At the same time, they teach the values and behavior that are not acceptable to them and try to discourage what they see as bad behavior. In the next section, we discuss how different factors influence children's moral development.

empathy ability to understand and experience the feelings of others, imagining oneself in their place.

Positive Social Behavior

Children start behaving prosocially early in life. Even babies sometimes spontaneously share food or toys with others (Markova & Legerstee, 2006). Children between 1 and 2 years of age share, comfort, and help others, or hand others objects they need to complete a task (Liddle et al., 2015; Paulus, 2014; Warneken & Tomasello, 2006). While young children have the capability to act in prosocial ways, they do not always do so. Most of the time, they ignore others' distress (Lamb & Zakhireh, 1997). As they grow older, children increasingly act in prosocial ways. Preschoolers may assist their parents with chores like setting the table or carrying in groceries (Warneken et al., 2006). Children keep becoming more prosocial until they reach a plateau in early adolescence (Luengo Kanacri et al., 2013).

A key component in prosocial behavior is **empathy**—understanding and sharing someone else's emotions. The first signs of empathy may be seen in infants who cry as they witness another child's distress. The infants' reactions may be traced to an inability to distinguish between themselves and other persons. At 1–2 years of age, toddlers begin to distinguish between themselves and others. They can only

© Hello World/Getty Images

■ How does a child learn that lying is not right?

Culture Counts

When Is It Acceptable to Lie?

Have you ever told a "white lie"? Cultures around the world agree that lying is wrong. However, sometimes children and adults may consider lying necessary to benefit themselves or their group.

In one experiment, Fu and colleagues (2007) asked children from China and Canada to evaluate truths and lies using a simple scenario. For example, imagine that Alan is a terrible speller but asks his friend Lily to nominate him to represent their class at the school's spelling bee. Lily has two choices: Either she can either lie and tell the teacher to nominate Alan because he is a good speller (this would make

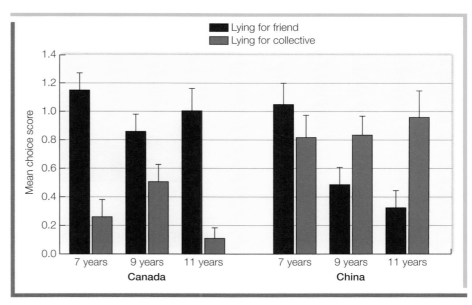

■ Chinese and Canadian children's mean lying-for-friend and lying-for-collective choice scores.

After G. Fu et al. 2007. *Dev Psychol* 43: 278–293

Alan feel good but would hurt the class's chances in the spelling bee), or she can tell the teacher the truth (that Alan is not a good speller), which will hurt Alan but benefit the class. In a number of scenarios, children needed to decide whether to make a decision in favor of a friend or their group. How do you think the children decided?

The figure shows the average number of times children decided lies were acceptable for the benefit of either

their friend or their group. As you can see, Canadian children found it much more acceptable to lie for the benefit of a friend than for the benefit of a group. Chinese children, however, were much more inclined than their Canadian peers to sacrifice their own or a friend's interest for the benefit of the group (the groups did not differ in their ability to determine which statements were lies and which were true).

■ **Question**

Why do you think Canadian and Chinese children evaluate the truth and lies differently? What implications might these findings have in everyday life? Can you draw any conclusions from the discussion earlier in the chapter of individualistic and collectivist cultures?

---

adequately respond to someone's distress once they understand that people may react differently to situations (Damon, 1988; Liddle et al., 2015). Girls tend to be more empathic than boys (Roberts et al., 2014).

Children who help from an early age in their family's household and whose parents explain to them why someone is feeling a particular way tend to show more prosocial behavior (Bremner & Wachs, 2014; Roberts et al., 2014).

Studies with identical and fraternal twins suggest that prosocial behavior is heritable (Israel et al., 2015; Knafo & Plomin, 2006; Knafo et al., 2008). One key to understanding the heritability of prosocial behavior may be hormones. Researchers have identified genes that are associated with people's capacity

■ Children who are involved in their family's household chores typically show more prosocial behavior than their peers who do not help at home. Why?

to feel empathy (one of them is an oxytocin receptor gene—remember that oxytocin prompts bonding in humans) (Davis et al., 1994; Laursen et al., 2014; Melchers et al., 2016).

Antisocial Behavior: Aggression

Negative social behavior, also called *antisocial behavior*, can take many forms. Children may lie, steal, destroy other people's property, or behave noncompliantly. Aggression is one of the most frequent antisocial behaviors in early childhood.

One way we distinguish different kinds of aggression is by intention: An act of **hostile aggression** intends to hurt the victim. When Caden pulls the leg of a classmate and laughs as the classmate is falling down, Caden is engaging in hostile aggression. **Instrumental aggression** is used to achieve a goal—when Tommy wants to play with a car that Carl is playing with and starts hitting Carl to get the car, he is engaging in instrumental aggression. *Relational aggression* is intended to hurt a person's social status or relationships, for example, by excluding a playmate from a game.

hostile aggression a type of aggression that is unplanned and impulsive; in reaction to a perceived insult or threat.

instrumental aggression a type of aggression that aims at helping an individual achieve a purpose.

We can also distinguish different kinds of aggression by their means: *Physical aggression* includes hitting, kicking, striking, and the like. *Verbal aggression* includes actions like taunting, yelling, and name-calling.

Young infants do not act aggressively. Between 1 and 2 years of age, children start to show instrumental aggression, particularly when it comes to competition with peers over the possession of toys (Dunn, 1988; Hay et al., 2011). Due to a lack of language capabilities, very young children mostly engage in physical aggression. They hit, shove, and kick because they cannot speak (Hay et al., 2000; Tremblay et al., 1999). As children learn to speak and express themselves better, they increasingly engage in verbal aggression (Mesman et al., 2009; Miner & Clarke-Stewart, 2008). In early childhood, aggression is mostly instrumental, but as children approach elementary school

■ Using relational aggression, children often exclude others from participation in games and activities.

age, aggressive acts are increasingly of a hostile kind, intending to hurt a peer (Dodge, 1980).

Aggressive children often misinterpret ambiguous interactions in a negative way. Because they believe others are acting hostile toward them, they react with aggression to defend themselves (Lansford et al., 2010; Yaros et al., 2014).

Aggressive behavior is relatively stable throughout life. Children who act aggressively early in their life will likely become aggressive adults (Brame et al., 2001; Tremblay et al., 2004; van Dijk et al., 2017). Boys tend to be more aggressive than girls (Wallinius et al., 2016).

Aggressive children are at higher risk for becoming delinquent or abusing their spouses (Kokko et al., 2014). Children who are particularly aggressive tend to have low IQs, are impulsive, and do not show much empathy for others (Tremblay & LeMarquand, 2001).

Genes play a role in aggression

According to evolutionary theory, life is a struggle for survival (Darwin, 1958). Aggressive males might have been at an advantage because they fought for their resources and access to mates in a particularly successful way. From this perspective, aggression is natural and will inevitably appear in the behavior of young children (Bjorklund & Ellis, 2014; Jonason, 2015). Twins studies suggest that aggression is indeed at least partially genetic, and aggression tends to run in families (Lacourse et al., 2014).

Brain structures may play a role as well. People with a lower volume of the amygdala are more aggressive throughout their lives, from early childhood on (**FIGURE 10.6**). The amygdala helps us interpret the behavior of other people, and an overreactive amygdala may signal that there is danger when in fact there is none (Pardini et al., 2014).

Additionally, the hormone testosterone has been associated with aggressive behavior and rises in competitive situations (Carré et al., 2014). Males, who have a significantly higher level of testosterone than do females, tend to be more aggressive than females.

■ Children who are aggressive at a young age are at higher risk for delinquent behavior as they get older.

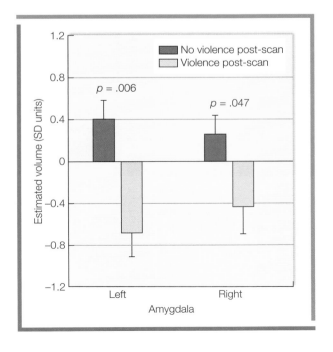

FIGURE 10.6 Differences in volumes of the amygdala between men who did and did not commit violent acts after a brain scan. Men who committed violent acts after the brain scan for the study (lighter bars) had on average lower amygdala volumes than men who did not commit violent acts after the brain scan (darker bars).

After D. A. Pardini et al. 2014. *Biol Psychiatry* 75: 73–80

Aggression may be learned and imitated

Children learn from observing others and are particularly likely to repeat behavior that is rewarded. One of the most famous experiments on how children imitate aggression was conducted by Albert Bandura (Bandura et al., 1963) (**FIGURE 10.7**).

These findings gain even more importance when you consider how much violence children see on television every day and how much antisocial behavior children in crime-ridden neighborhoods witness. We will discuss the effect of media on aggression in more detail below.

Children's television is violent

It may be hard to believe, but children's shows feature more than twice as many violent acts as other shows. Researchers have suggested that children may see around 10,000 violent acts each year (Wilson et al., 2002). Around half of all children ages 4–6 play video games, and around 92% of children ages 7–17 do (Henry H. Kaiser Family Foundation, 2003; Polman et al., 2008). The largest genre of video games played by children is combat games, and almost 90% of the top-selling video games contain some violence.

There are three main concerns about media violence. Viewing violence may lead children to (1) behave more aggressively, (2) increasingly accept violence as a means to solve conflicts in real life and to care less about other people's feelings, and (3) be scared of becoming a victim of violence (Smith & Donnerstein, 1998). Children under age 7 are particularly vulnerable to the effects of televised violence, because they have trouble distinguishing between TV programming and real life (Bushman & Huesmann, 2001).

Children who view violent TV programs tend to be more aggressive physically and verbally toward their peers and are more likely to commit aggressive acts like child and spousal abuse as adults (Buchanan et al., 2002;

From Bandura et al. 1963. J. of Abnormal and Social Psychology 66:1, 3–11. ©1963, American Psychological Association

FIGURE 10.7 Bandura's (1963) famous Bobo doll experiment on the imitation of aggressive behavior. In the experimental conditions, preschool children observed (a) an adult hitting and kicking the Bobo doll in real life, (b) an adult hitting and kicking the Bobo doll in a movie, or (c) a cartoon character hitting and kicking the Bobo doll. In the control condition, children did not witness any aggressive behavior. Afterward, the children were given an opportunity to play with toys, including the Bobo doll. Children who observed an adult hitting and kicking the Bobo doll were likely to imitate that behavior when they got a chance to play with the doll.

From A. Bandura et al. 1963. J Abnorm Psychol 66: 3–11

Huesmann et al., 1984; Krahé & Möller, 2010; Stein & Friedrich, 1972).

In 2000, the American Academy of Pediatrics, American Psychological Association, American Academy of Child & Adolescent Psychiatry, and other institutions explained in a joint statement that "well over 1,000 studies point overwhelmingly to a causal connection between media violence and aggressive behavior in some children" (American Academy of Pediatrics, 2000; Huesmann et al., 1984).

Children's antisocial behavior can be managed

Given that we can frequently see aggressive behavior in children, is there anything we can do to reduce it? Here are some guidelines from the research we reviewed in this chapter:

- **Set firm limits**. Do not tolerate aggressive behavior, and communicate clearly which behaviors are and are not permitted. Consequences should follow immediately if children are aggressive.

- **Model non-aggressive behavior**. Do not spank. Express negative emotions in reasonable, non-aggressive ways so children can observe and learn from acceptable behavior.

- **Teach children to understand their feelings, and help them control their negative emotions**. "You are disappointed because mommy is going out only with your older brother today. It's OK to be sad. Do you want to talk about it, or do you want to go to your quiet space and take a break?"

- **Help children understand that there are different interpretations of social interactions**. "I know you are upset that Sabrina took your fishing boat. Maybe she did not mean to take it from you but thought she could take it because you were not playing with it?"

- **Help children find alternatives to violence for resolving conflicts**. "Instead of hitting, do you think it might work to talk to Gabe and Simon and ask them if they will let you play with them?"

- **Monitor the content of TV shows and video games children watch and play**. Encourage consumption of shows and games that were developed specifically for kids and have an educational purpose, like Sesame Street.

■ Watching violence on TV on a regular basis makes children more aggressive.

Review!

How do children learn to act in ways that help others?

- Prosocial behavior is connected to a person's ability to feel *empathy*, that is, to understand and share someone's emotions.
- In early childhood, children start to understand that different people may not react in the same way to a given situation.

This understanding helps children tailor helping behavior better to the needs of the person they intend to help.

- Genes may affect some behavioral tendencies in people, like how generous they are and how empathic they are. These behaviors in turn translate into more or less prosocial behavior.

How do children learn to act in ways that hurt others?

- Aggressive behavior is one of the most common forms of antisocial behavior.
- In early childhood, physical aggression declines and verbally aggressive behaviors like taunting or teasing increase.
- Children who are aggressive early in life tend to remain aggressive throughout their lives.
- In human history, aggressive behavior may have given people an edge in the struggle to survive and raise offspring. Aggressive tendencies may therefore have been passed on from one generation to the next.

- If children observe others act aggressively or get praised or otherwise rewarded for aggressive behavior, they likely will repeat that behavior.
- Aggressive children tend to interpret social encounters in a more hostile way than less aggressive children. Because they believe people are trying to harm them, they often retaliate quickly, defending themselves in an aggressive way.
- TV shows and video games featuring violence increase aggressive behavior in children. Children in early childhood are particularly vulnerable to these effects, because they have trouble distinguishing between reality and media.

Practice!

1. An action that helps others without the expectation of reward is also called _____ .
   a. empathic behavior
   b. prosocial behavior
   c. sympathetic behavior
   d. egocentric behavior

2. In order to behave prosocially, some researchers suggest we need to be capable of feeling _____ .
   a. empathy
   b. sympathy
   c. love
   d. friendship

3. An example of antisocial behavior is _____ .
   a. sleeping

   b. comforting
   c. stealing
   d. writing

4. When Boris hits Chase because he wants to play with Chase's bike, Boris displays _____ .
   a. relational aggression
   b. hostile aggression
   c. instrumental aggression
   d. verbal aggression

5. Watching violence on TV makes children _____ .
   a. more likely to behave aggressively
   b. less likely to behave aggressively
   c. neither more nor less likely to behave aggressively
   d. more likely to show empathy toward victims of violence

What Would You Do?

Your work requires that you work some afternoons or weekends when your children are home from school. Your children are 5 and 10 years old. A neighbor has agreed to watch your children when you need to work. The children have told you that the neighbor lets them play video games while they're at her place. The games seem to involve shooting and other violence. You are unhappy about them playing these games but cannot afford to lose your babysitter either. What would you do?

See for Yourself!

Go to a place where caregivers are interacting with their children, like a restaurant, a playground, or a supermarket. Watch for children fighting or misbehaving in some way. Can you detect differences in the responses of their caregivers? Are there any responses that are more or less successful? Why?

One year later: Back at the playground

It's 1 year later, and the days are beginning to get longer as the summer turns into fall yet again. Raymo and Sarina are back at the park. But this time, the 5-year-olds are not at the playground. Rather, they're at the baseball diamond playing softball. To Raymo's delight, his father, Ronald, is one of the coaches. Ronald had to complete an online training on treating players and parents with respect, and it has had an impact beyond the diamond. He now interacts differently with his son, paying more attention to Raymo's intentions and emotions when they interact with each other. Sarina is one of the most enthusiastic players on the team. She loves her baseball uniform and wears it whenever she can—at home on weekends, during the week at school, when they're traveling. . . . She also asked her mom to have her hair cut short in order to keep it out of her eyes when she's playing. It may not last, but she is clearly making more forceful choices about her looks and how she spends her time, reflecting her growing sense of self. ■ ▪ ■ ▪

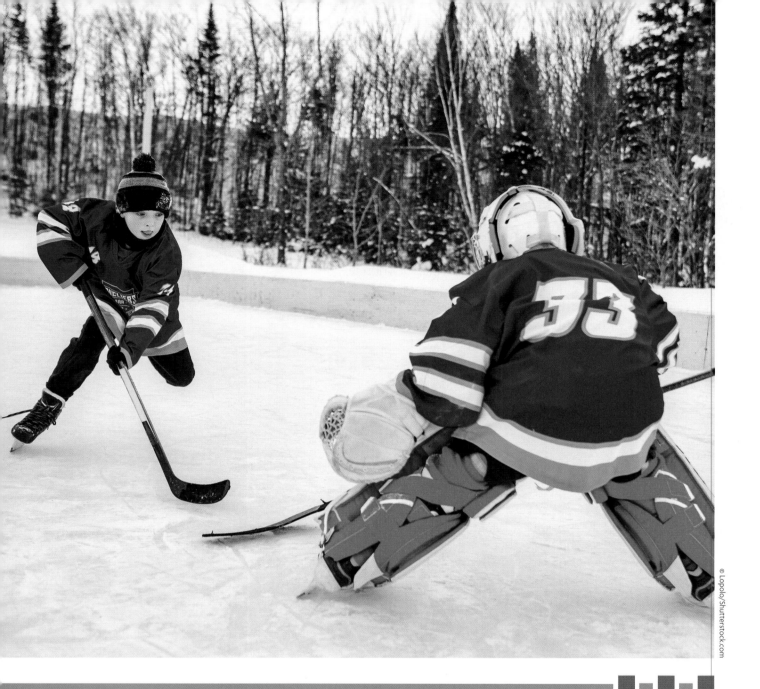

© Lopolo/Shutterstock.com

Overview

Physical Development in Middle Childhood

Children at play

Nine-year-old Melinda is outside playing basketball with her 11-year-old brother, Sean. They have lots of time for outside play these days: Their school has been closed the remainder of the school year due to the arrival and rapid spread of the coronavirus (COVID-19) in the United States. They do schoolwork in the mornings, overseen by their mother, Marian, and when they're not engaged in their studies, they also do some fun projects together and practice their instruments (violin for Melinda, clarinet for Sean).

But mostly the two siblings love playing outside. Sean started playing house league basketball a year ago, but now all games and practices have been cancelled. He was disappointed, thinking he had no one to play with anymore.

Enter his sister, Melinda. Melinda had never shown an interest in basketball, or any ball games for that matter, before. She generally prefers crafting, drawing, or latch hook projects to the rough-and-tumble play that her brother loves.

But Melinda needed a playmate, too. Within just a few months, Melinda has turned into a basketball star. She is fast and has learned to dribble around Sean by pretending to go to one side but then moving to the other. Melinda has also become adept at taking the ball off of Sean when he tries to pass her. She can hold her own in the game against her brother now and has become a serious opponent for her brother.

Melinda has quickly picked up on skills she could not have learned easily a few years ago. She can now run fast and change directions just as quickly; she can estimate distances and coordinate her movements to shoot the ball at the goal successfully. Although growth slows in middle childhood, the gains in motor skills are impressive.

In this chapter, we'll learn how children grow over the period of middle childhood and how their motor skills develop to help them become adept at a wide variety of physical activities. We will also discuss the nutritional needs of growing children and learn about a number of diseases that commonly occur in middle childhood. Last but not least, we will take a closer look at special needs children may have with respect to their education.

■ In middle childhood, children quickly learn new motor skills. Melinda can now hold her own against her older brother Sean in a basketball game.

© iStock.com/NoSystem images

11.1 Brain and Body Growth in Middle Childhood

- Recall how children's bodies change in middle childhood.
- List the changes to the brain during middle childhood.

The photo below shows a class of fourth graders at an elementary school. What do you notice with respect to the children's physical appearance?

There are vast differences in terms of height and weight among the children. In preschoolers, you will see some differences in physical appearance, but they are nowhere near as pronounced as the ones you will find in older children. Children the same age can easily tower over a classmate by a head's height or more. Weight differences become much more distinguished as well.

Around age 10, for example, height differences between the tallest and shortest children can be 10 inches or more; weight differences can be 50 pounds or more between the lightest and heaviest children (Centers for Disease Control and Prevention, 2009).

Height and Weight Changes
Middle childhood is characterized by slow and steady growth

Children's growth in middle childhood slows down considerably compared with infancy and early childhood. Per year, children grow about 2–3 inches and gain around 5–7 pounds. At age 6, children are about 45 inches tall, on average, and will have grown to 56 inches by the time they are 11 years old. In terms of weight, 6-year-olds weigh about 46 pounds on average and will weigh around 80 pounds at age 11. Gender differences are very small, but between 8 and 12 years of age, many girls will be slightly taller and heavier than boys (Centers for Disease Control and Prevention, 2009).

The slow but steady growth of children adds up and ultimately results in dramatic changes. Six-year-olds still look like small children with chubby faces and relatively large heads, but 11-year-olds have a much more adult-like stature with little baby fat remaining. As we have pointed out before, middle childhood is also the time when the individual differences in height and weight we see in adults first become visible in children.

© iStock.com/kali9

■ A group of fourth graders at their elementary school. Note the height and weight differences between the children. The differences are quite apparent and much more pronounced than in younger children.

It is perhaps not surprising, then, that it is in middle childhood that children become more aware of their appearance. Girls may become unduly concerned with their weight, which may lead to them eating less; boys may become more aware of their size, muscles, and strength relative to their peers (Bright Futures, 2020).

Certain factors can affect the rate of growth in middle childhood

The majority of children grow normally; variability in height, weight, and rate of growth depend on genetic makeup and nutrition. Ethnicity also plays a role: Black children tend to grow faster than White, Hispanic, or Asian American children (Komlos & Breitfelder, 2008).

However, there are also a number of growth disorders that can impair children's growth. One of these disorders is *growth hormone deficiency*, where children produce insufficient quantities of growth hormones or, sometimes, none at all. Growth hormone deficiency may have underlying genetic causes or may be caused by a damaged pituitary gland or hypothalamus. The most visible symptom is growth of less than 2 inches per year, but affected children may also look younger or chubby. Onset of puberty may be delayed, but the condition does not lead to any cognitive delays. Children who have been diagnosed with growth hormone deficiency may be treated with regular growth hormone injections (several times a week) over a period of several years (Children's Hospital of Philadelphia, 2020).

While growth hormone treatment is vitally important for children who do not produce enough growth hormones, parents will sometimes request hormone treatment for their short but otherwise healthy children. One reason for such requests is that in Western society being tall is sometimes perceived as better than being short. Parents are concerned their short children (and in particular, boys) might be subjected to taunting or other disadvantages they might not experience if they were taller. Given that all medical treatments can have potential side effects, this practice is questionable. Some studies have shown that growth hormone therapy predisposes children to develop diabetes, cancer, or scoliosis later in life (Collett-Solberg et al., 2019; James, 2009; Nishi & Tanaka, 2017; Yarasheski, 1994).

■ Although children grow at a slower rate in middle childhood, the steady growth adds up. Most 11-year-olds have lost a lot of the childlike features of 6-year-olds and look a lot more like adults.

In middle childhood, children lose the majority of their primary teeth

Starting around the age of 5 or 6 until age 13, children lose their primary teeth, which will be replaced by their permanent teeth. On average, children lose about four teeth per year during this time, but there is considerable variation between children and, from year to year, for each child. It can take up to a year for a new, permanent tooth to erupt through the gum's surface.

One of the most common health problems in children is caries (or tooth decay). About one in five children between the ages of 5 and 11 has an untreated cavity (**FIGURE 11.1**). Cavities can lead not only to pain and infections but also to problems eating, speaking, or learning at school. Public health campaigns and education on the importance of dental hygiene can help address the problem, but these resources may not be equally available in all communities. This may be the reason that children in low-income neighborhoods are more than twice as likely to have cavities as children from households in higher income neighborhoods (Centers for Disease Control and Prevention, 2019b).

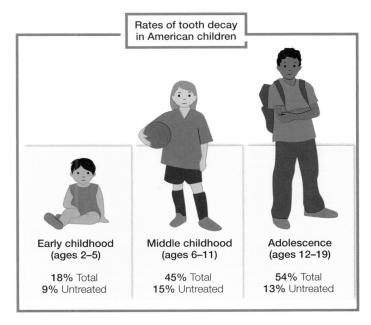

FIGURE 11.1 Total and untreated tooth decay in early childhood, middle childhood, and adolescence.

Data from E. Fleming and J. Afful. 2018. *NCHS Data Brief* 307: 1–8

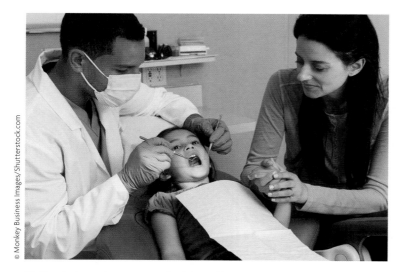

■ Tooth decay is a common health problem in middle childhood. About 20% of children have untreated cavities, which can lead to a variety of health, social, and even academic problems.

The risk of cavities can be decreased by regular tooth brushing with a fluoride toothpaste and visits to the dentist. Dentists can also apply a preventative fluoride varnish on teeth (Dalal et al., 2019). Fluoridated water decreases the risk of cavities as well (McDonagh et al., 2000; Slade et al., 2018; White & Gordon, 2014). Because not all communities fluoridate their water—in 2016, 73% of Americans had access to fluoridated tap water—children may also take a daily fluoride supplement (Centers for Disease Control and Prevention, 2020a).

Brain Growth

As we have seen in previous chapters, the brain experiences its most rapid period of growth early in childhood. However, children's abilities and skills in all domains improve rapidly in middle childhood: Children become physically stronger and more coordinated, they get better at abstract

Culture Counts

Disparities in Access to Safe Drinking Water

Adequate hydration is important for people's cognitive functioning, mood, and overall health. Yet a 2017 study using a nationally representative sample found differences in fluid intake among people of different racial and ethnic groups. According to the study, adults from Black and Hispanic communities had a 40% greater risk than adults of other racial and ethnic communities of inadequate fluid intake.

There were differences in the source of hydration as well. Compared with adults from White communities, adults from Black and Hispanic communities consume more bottled water, which is not fluoridated and thus does not have any dental health benefits; they also drink more sugar-sweetened beverages. The researchers believe that tap water consumption in BIPOC (Black, Indigenous, and people of color) communities may be lower because people in those communities perceive it to be unsafe: They may have poor access to safe drinking water or they may belong to a group that has a history of living in underserved regions with poor access to safe drinking water.

■ Question

What are the consequences for children with inadequate access to safe drinking water? What can be done to help all children get adequately hydrated?

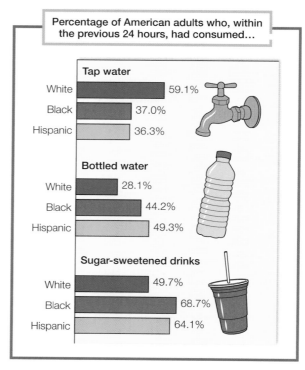

Percentage of American adults who, within the previous 24 hours, had consumed...

Tap water
White 59.1%
Black 37.0%
Hispanic 36.3%

Bottled water
White 28.1%
Black 44.2%
Hispanic 49.3%

Sugar-sweetened drinks
White 49.7%
Black 68.7%
Hispanic 64.1%

■ Percentage of adults who drank any of each beverage type in the previous 24 hours, by race/ethnicity.

Data from C. J. Brooks et al. 2017. *Am J Public Health* 107: 1387–1394

■ The effects of pruning can be observed in children's behavior. When a 6-year-old and a 12-year-old are throwing a ball, the 12-year-old's movements are much more purposeful and targeted compared with those of the 6-year-old, who moves the entire body while throwing.

reasoning, and they learn to control their emotions better. The basis of this progress is a set of changes in the brain.

During middle childhood, neurons continue to myelinate, particularly in the corpus callosum and in the subcortical areas. The increased **myelination** speeds up the transmission of nerve impulses in the brain (see Chapter 5).

At the same time, the gray matter in the brain becomes less dense, which indicates the amount of pruning going on in children's brains (Mah & Ford-Jones, 2012). Pruning means that relevant connections between different neurons are maintained while those that are used less die off. In neuroimaging studies of children working on different tasks, younger children show a pattern of widespread activation in their brain, whereas older children show more regional patterns of activation (Carey et al., 2009).

myelination the process in which axons within the brain become coated in myelin, a fatty substance that allows for faster signal transmission.

Review!

How do children's bodies change in middle childhood?

■ Children's growth slows during middle childhood, but they still gain around 6 pounds in weight and 2–3 inches in height per year. They go from looking like little children at age 6 to resembling young adults at age 12.

■ Significant height and weight differences between children appear for the first time in childhood, and children of the same age may differ in weight by as much as 50 pounds and 10 inches in height. Children also lose most of their primary teeth in middle childhood, at a rate of about four teeth per year.

How does the brain change during middle childhood?

■ While brain growth slows in middle childhood, *myelination* of the brain's neurons continues and helps speed up signal transmission within the brain. Furthermore, unused connections within the brain are pruned.

■ These processes facilitate development in middle childhood in all domains from motor skills to cognitive advances and emotional control.

Practice!

1. In middle childhood, children's growth _____ .
   a. slows down compared with early childhood
   b. speeds up compared with early childhood
   c. continues at about the same rate as in early childhood
   d. comes to a temporary stop before resuming in early adolescence

2. Height and weight among different children of the same age in middle childhood _____ .
   a. do not vary much
   b. vary considerably
   c. are indicators of children's brain development
   d. are more similar than they are in early childhood

3. Normal growth in middle childhood means that children should grow at least _____ .
   a. 1 inch per year
   b. 1.5 inches per year
   c. 2 inches per year
   d. 3.5 inches per year

4. Children's brains continue the process of pruning, which means that _____ .
   a. they establish more and more connections between different neurons
   b. they establish more connections between different brain areas
   c. they grow fatty layers of insulation around neurons so information can be transmitted faster
   d. they reduce the number of connections between neurons

What's Your Position?

Emmett is 9 years old and the shortest kid in his class. A December baby, he was about average size in early childhood, but most children have started to outgrow him ever since he started elementary school. Emmett's parents are very concerned about his height. His father is of average height, but his mother is on the shorter side, and though their pediatrician told them not to worry, they are eager to get Emmett treated with growth hormones so that he does not have to experience the "disadvantages of being short as a grown man," as they phrase it.

Do you think children like Emmett who are small but have not been diagnosed with a growth disorder should be put on growth hormones so they do not have to suffer possible discrimination and other disadvantages as adults? Form a quick opinion and then consult some of the following websites to see if your opinion changes. Debate the issue with a classmate, switching sides partway through so that each of you has a chance to argue for and against hormone treatments to address an unknown cause of shortness.

Additional Resources Online

- "Growth hormone and health policy," from Leona Cuttler & J. B. Silvers, *Journal of Endocrinology and Metabolism*
- "Effect of growth hormone therapy on height in children with idiopathic short stature," from Beth S. Finkelstein et al., *Journal of the American Medical Association*
- "Should growth hormone be used for short stature kids?," from Susan Wisbey-Smith, University of Michigan Health Lab

- "Five things to consider before your kid does growth hormone therapy," from Parents.com
- "When a child is extremely short, should a parent consider growth hormone?," from Sarah Vander Schaff, *The Washington Post*

11.2 Motor Skill Development in Middle Childhood

- Tell the ways motor skills evolve throughout middle childhood.
- Explain the ways playing outside benefits children.
- Identify the opportunities schools provide children to be physically active and name the benefits of such activities.

Middle childhood's slow and steady physical growth is mirrored in the development of children's motor skills. Small changes add up to a substantial refinement in skills, characterized by increased strength, coordination, and balance.

Gross Motor Skills

Remember Melinda, who turned into a successful basketball player during the months-long school break she and her brother had during the COVID-19 pandemic? Sean was lucky his sister was already 9 years old so she could catch up with him quickly in her set of skills.

Children in middle childhood pick up gross motor skills quickly. Their increased muscle mass lets them execute movements with greater force, and they perform movements with better precision and balance (DelGiudice, 2018). Children can learn new skills with relative ease. These skills include biking,

© MarinaKo/Shutterstock.com

■ What gross motor skills are required for a 6-year-old to learn to play a sport like hockey?

■ Many of the skills we use in everyday life require carefully practiced fine motor skills. In middle childhood, children become adept at dressing themselves, tying their shoes, doing delicate craft projects, and eating with a knife and fork or with chopsticks, as shown here.

ice-skating, swimming, or hitting and catching a softball—skills that would have been much harder (if not impossible) to acquire earlier in life. Always practicing and improving their skills, children often love to be physically active and to run, jump, climb, and balance. Not surprisingly, middle childhood is also the time when many children start to become more involved in recreational or competitive sports such as dance, soccer, gymnastics, hockey, or martial arts.

Fine Motor Skills

During the elementary school years, children learn many of the complex everyday tasks that require fine motor skills. By the age of 6 or 7, most children can tie their shoes, and throughout their early school years they continue to refine their handwriting. They learn to fasten buttons and reliably brush their teeth (DelGiudice, 2018). During this period they will also learn how to eat adeptly using both knife and fork. There are few gender differences in motor skills (Jürimäe & Saar, 2003), which is partly due to the fact that there are relatively few physical differences between boys and girls.

Exercise and Physical Play

Physical exercise has many physical, social, and cognitive benefits, for children as well as for adults. Regular exercise improves lung function, strengthens the heart, and has a positive impact on muscle as well as bone health (Bell et al., 2008). But exercise has many benefits beyond physical ones: It improves children's mood and self-esteem and reduces stress (Mah & Ford-Jones, 2012; Mikkelsen et al., 2017). As well, exercising improves executive function (Verburgh et al., 2014), reasoning, and reaction time (Ellemberg & St-Louis-Deschênes, 2010) and has a positive impact on grades in school (Cappelen et al., 2017).

How can exercise have such a positive effect on cognitive performance? Physical activity increases the blood flow in the brain so that the brain areas involved in learning receive more oxygen. Exercise also promotes the release of proteins that increase cognitive performance (Chandler & Tricot, 2015). Exercising is also beneficial for children with special needs. For example, regular exercise improves executive function, attention, and behavior in children with ADHD (attention-deficit/hyperactivity disorder) (Den Heijer et al., 2017).

Although the benefits of regular exercise in children may seem obvious, it is not always a given that children will receive regular opportunities to exercise. Some children do not play outside much or do not get much opportunity to move and exercise at school. What's more, some activities—especially team sports like baseball—involve longer periods of inactivity or low activity and thus provide fewer benefits (Baker et al., 2010). In the following sections, we'll consider the benefits of outside play for children and exercise opportunities at school.

Playing outside has many benefits for children

Some decades ago, streets and neighborhoods were full of children at play after school. They rode their bikes, played ball or catch, skipped, or jumped rope. The neighborhood where I live is full of kids—there are probably kids in at least every second house on our block. But one hardly ever sees those kids play outside.

Many children do not spend nearly enough time playing outside. Children today spend about half as much time playing outside as their parents did (Moss, 2012). One study found that more than one-third of children spend less than 30 minutes playing outside after school (Wen et al., 2009). And yet, just as with exercise, there are numerous benefits that come with outdoor play (**FIGURE 11.2**).

Why are children not playing outdoors as much anymore? One reason is that they are spending more time in front of screens—around 6 hours for 8- to 10-year-olds and 9 hours per day for 11- to 14-year-olds (Centers for Disease Control and Prevention, 2018c). Another reason is that parents increasingly worry about the safety of outdoor play. They feel uneasy thinking about crime, traffic, pollution, and too much sun exposure, as well as diseases transmitted through insect bites and ticks (Kemple et al., 2016). And last but not least, children also spend an increasing amount of time with scheduled activities like planned music lessons, sports, and after-school care.

There are lots of ways to encourage children to play outside. Here are some ideas:

- Make sure the children know it's ok to get dirty.
- Make bird feeders.

Playing outside...

helps children focus their attention and leads to improved self-control (Ridgway et al., 2003)

can reduce ADHD symptoms (Becker et al., 2014; Kemple et al., 2016)

helps children become less inhibited and use more complex language (Frost, 2004; McClintic & Petty, 2015)

reduces children's risk of obesity (Kemple et al., 2016)

increases children's ability to communicate and negotiate with each other and play by rules if they play in groups

improves children's motor skills and general physical fitness and decreases the chances of developing myopia (Little & Wyver, 2008; Rose et al., 2008)

increases children's creativity, emotional well-being, and positive social behavior (Kemple et al., 2016)

FIGURE 11.2 The benefits of outdoor play.

■ When children play outside, they socialize with others, practice both gross and fine motor skills, and exercise. Do you see many children playing outside as you walk around your neighborhood? Where do children spend their time?

- Plant a butterfly garden or an herb garden.
- Provide outdoor play spaces or take them to outdoor places where they can play safely.
- Provide them with materials that encourage outdoor play like chalk, stilts, balls, and jump ropes.
- Craft with outdoor materials or create playthings like cardboard boomerangs that can be used outside.

Schools have decreased the amount of exercise during the school day

Elementary schools provide children the opportunity to move and exercise in two different ways: during recess and during physical education (PE) classes. Although some people dismiss it as unimportant, recess is viewed by the American Academy of Pediatrics as being as important as other school subjects (Murray & Ramstetter, 2013; Rochman, 2012). Recess helps children be more attentive in class, and the unstructured play lets them practice communication with their classmates, cooperation, sharing, and problem-solving (Murray & Ramstetter, 2013).

Unfortunately, recess in many schools is on the decline or even disappearing. Some schools see unstructured play as a liability in the face of rising safety and security concerns. Others, faced with pressure to perform well on the standardized testing that was implemented in the wake of the No Child Left Behind Act, are trading outdoor recess for more time in the classroom.

Many states do not legally mandate the length of recess, so there are significant variations among schools. States like Missouri, Florida, and Rhode Island require 20 minutes of daily recess for elementary schools, whereas Iowa and South Carolina require up to 30 minutes of physical exercise but without specifying whether that time should be spent in unstructured (recess) or structured (gym class) activity (Riser-Kositsky, 2018; Shammas, 2019).

■ Recess and physical education classes at school are the only times when children can get physically active during their long school day. Physical activity helps them focus on their work and gives them an opportunity to practice social skills.

■ Teachers in many classrooms use apps to help children calm down and relax or get some exercise during the school day.

The benefits of physical education are quite similar to those of recess: Children are more physically active and fit, they are better able to focus during their lessons, and their grades tend to improve (Murray & Ramstetter, 2013). Physically active students are also less often absent from school and are much more likely to stay physically active as adults. But not even 4% of K–12 schools in the United States require daily PE lessons.

Schools also use other methods of getting children to move these days, however. Specialized companies offer a large variety of movement and mindfulness videos to get children moving (or settling down) in the classroom.

Review!

How do motor skills change throughout middle childhood?

■ In middle childhood, factors like increased myelination and greater muscle mass help children learn new motor skills quickly. They naturally love to run around and play, and this is the time when many children begin to play sports recreationally or competitively.

■ Children's fine motor skills improve as well, making it easier for them to develop their handwriting and to become more independent by tying their own shoes and fastening their buttons.

How do children benefit from playing outside?

■ The physical activity children tend to get when they are outside improves their lung and heart function, their bone health, and their muscle strength.

■ Outdoor activity also relieves stress and improves children's cognitive function. Because they are often playing with other children outside, they also learn to play by rules as well as to negotiate and communicate with others.

What opportunities do schools provide for children to get physically active, and what are the benefits of such activities?

■ Children are physically active at school mainly during two periods: physical education classes and recess. Both are very important to children's well-being and cognitive as well as social functioning during lessons.

■ Children with opportunities to exercise on a regular basis are better able to concentrate at school and tend to have better grades. They also miss fewer school days.

■ There is no national mandate to regulate the length of recess in the United States. Therefore, the duration of recess varies dramatically from no recess to as much as 45 minutes per day, depending on the school. There are also wide variations with respect to physical education lessons.

■ Schools are trying to bring movement into the classroom by using apps that offer videos with music and rhymes to get kids moving.

Practice!

1. In middle childhood, there are generally _____ .
   a. few gender differences in motor skills
   b. significant gender differences in motor skills, with girls performing a lot better
   c. significant gender differences in motor skills, with boys performing a lot better
   d. few changes in motor skills compared with early childhood

2. Physical exercise positively affects cognitive performance by _____ .
   a. keeping children's weight down
   b. giving parents a break so they're more patient with their children afterward
   c. increasing the blood flow to the brain and promoting the release of specific proteins

3. Children generally play outside _____ .
   a. much more than their parents used to
   b. much less than their parents used to
   c. about as much as their parents used to
   d. despite their parents' best efforts to keep them entertained inside

4. Recess in schools in the United States is _____ .
   a. regulated by a federal mandate
   b. regulated by the individual states
   c. not regulated on a national or state level
   d. regulated by the mayor of each town

Show What You've Learned!

Your two children, aged 5 and 9, attend the local elementary school. You have just learned that the school is thinking of eliminating physical education classes from the schedule and decreasing the duration of recess from two daily 15-minute periods (one in the morning and one in the afternoon) to a single 10-minute period per day. The reasoning behind the proposal is that more time spent on academic instruction will give students a head start in terms of academics that will have a lasting impact for the rest of their school career. Drawing on the information provided in this section, draft a letter or speech to the school council arguing that these changes should not be made.

What's Your Position?

Some researchers (see, for example, Howe et al., 2012) have argued that structured recess, where teachers lead children in playing games that involve physical activity, is more valuable to students than unstructured recess, because most students do not use the opportunity to move during unstructured recess, and this contributes to increased obesity rates.

Do you think that structured recess is better for children than unstructured recess? Write out your opinion and then consult some of the following websites to see if your opinion changes. Debate the issue with a classmate, switching sides partway through so that each of you has a chance to argue for and against structured recess.

Additional Resources Online

- "An evaluation of an unstructured and structured approach to increasing recess physical activity," from T. K. Behrens et al., *Journal of School Health*
- "Systematic review of recess interventions to increase physical activity," from M. J. Ickes, H. Erwin, & A. Beighle, *Journal of Physical Activity & Health*
- "Is structured recess really that bad?," from Joshua Barreiro, *Huffington Post*
- "Increasing physical activity through recess," from Active Living Research

- "Strategies for recess in schools," from the U.S. Department of Health and Human Services
- "The importance of unstructured recess," from Maddie Di Muccio, Troy Media
- "Is unstructured play really that important?," from the *Washington* [IN] *Times Herald*
- "Youth physical activity and enjoyment during semi-structured versus unstructured school recess," from the *Open Journal of Preventive Medicine*

11.3 Nutrition in Middle Childhood

- Relate the reasons why nutrition is so important for growing children.
- Outline some challenges that make providing healthy nutrition more difficult for children in middle childhood.
- Explain the reasons why obesity is a problem for children.
- Identify actions that can be taken to counteract obesity and list their benefits.

Nutrition is always an important factor in determining people's health, but it is of particular importance during childhood. Healthy nutrition promotes children's growth, prevents health problems, and sets the stage for healthy eating habits that may last a lifetime.

Nutritional Needs

Both boys and girls from 4 to 8 years of age need between 1,200 and 1,400 calories a day. From ages 9 to 13, their intake should increase to around 1,400–1,600 calories for girls and 1,600–2,000 calories, on average, for boys (American Academy of Pediatrics, 2016). But not all calories are made equal. It is important for children to eat a healthy diet (FIGURE 11.3). Because children are eager and precise observers, it is easiest for them to develop healthy eating habits if they see their own parents eat a healthy diet and can follow their example.

Healthy eating habits reduce the likelihood of developing a wide range of diseases, including high blood pressure, heart disease, cancer, cavities, and type

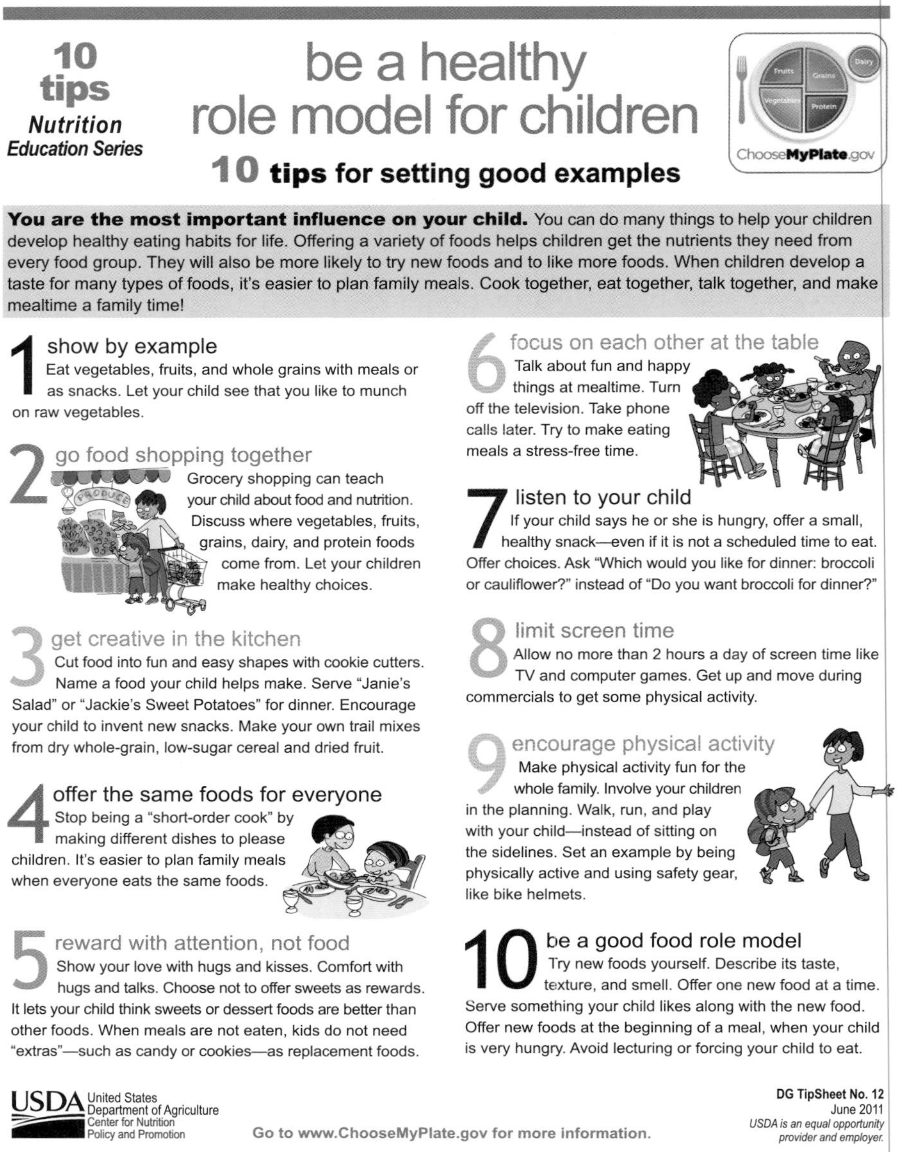

FIGURE 11.3 (A) Healthy nutrition should consist of a variety of fruits and vegetables, whole grains, protein, dairy products, and oils. Parents and adult caregivers play an important role in modeling healthy eating behaviors. (B) The USDA's Healthy Eating Index shows that children in middle childhood have the lowest healthy eating scores. Why do you think that is?

A from U.S. Department of Agriculture. 2011. Be a healthy role model for children: 10 tips for setting good examples. https://naldc.nal.usda.gov; B from U.S. Department of Agriculture. 2015. Healthy eating index. www.fns.usda.gov

10 tips
Nutrition Education Series

be a healthy role model for children

10 tips for setting good examples

You are the most important influence on your child. You can do many things to help your children develop healthy eating habits for life. Offering a variety of foods helps children get the nutrients they need from every food group. They will also be more likely to try new foods and to like more foods. When children develop a taste for many types of foods, it's easier to plan family meals. Cook together, eat together, talk together, and make mealtime a family time!

1 show by example
Eat vegetables, fruits, and whole grains with meals or as snacks. Let your child see that you like to munch on raw vegetables.

2 go food shopping together
Grocery shopping can teach your child about food and nutrition. Discuss where vegetables, fruits, grains, dairy, and protein foods come from. Let your children make healthy choices.

3 get creative in the kitchen
Cut food into fun and easy shapes with cookie cutters. Name a food your child helps make. Serve "Janie's Salad" or "Jackie's Sweet Potatoes" for dinner. Encourage your child to invent new snacks. Make your own trail mixes from dry whole-grain, low-sugar cereal and dried fruit.

4 offer the same foods for everyone
Stop being a "short-order cook" by making different dishes to please children. It's easier to plan family meals when everyone eats the same foods.

5 reward with attention, not food
Show your love with hugs and kisses. Comfort with hugs and talks. Choose not to offer sweets as rewards. It lets your child think sweets or dessert foods are better than other foods. When meals are not eaten, kids do not need "extras"—such as candy or cookies—as replacement foods.

6 focus on each other at the table
Talk about fun and happy things at mealtime. Turn off the television. Take phone calls later. Try to make eating meals a stress-free time.

7 listen to your child
If your child says he or she is hungry, offer a small, healthy snack—even if it is not a scheduled time to eat. Offer choices. Ask "Which would you like for dinner: broccoli or cauliflower?" instead of "Do you want broccoli for dinner?"

8 limit screen time
Allow no more than 2 hours a day of screen time like TV and computer games. Get up and move during commercials to get some physical activity.

9 encourage physical activity
Make physical activity fun for the whole family. Involve your children in the planning. Walk, run, and play with your child—instead of sitting on the sidelines. Set an example by being physically active and using safety gear, like bike helmets.

10 be a good food role model
Try new foods yourself. Describe its taste, texture, and smell. Offer one new food at a time. Serve something your child likes along with the new food. Offer new foods at the beginning of a meal, when your child is very hungry. Avoid lecturing or forcing your child to eat.

USDA United States Department of Agriculture Center for Nutrition Policy and Promotion

Go to www.ChooseMyPlate.gov for more information.

DG TipSheet No. 12
June 2011
USDA is an equal opportunity provider and employer.

2 diabetes (Key et al., 2020; Langin & Viguerie, 2020; Patel & Williams, 2020). Children who eat a healthy breakfast each day are less likely to be absent from school, tend to be in a better mood, and have better memory.

But in middle childhood, children also become more aware of their food choices and the fact that food has an effect on their health and growth. Children can now contribute more actively to meal preparation. It is not that uncommon for them to decide to eat a vegetarian diet (at least for a while). A vegetarian diet itself is not of concern as long as children get enough protein from sources like beans, eggs, and milk (American Academy of Pediatrics, 2016).

While parents are still the strongest influence with respect to children's eating behavior, other influences like friends and the media gain more influence. Children eat increasingly more meals away from their home—at school, friends' houses, or after-school programs (Bright Futures, 2020).

Life in elementary school also brings dietary choices. Children allowed to make their own choices in the cafeteria may establish a rather one-sided diet consisting of bread, potatoes, pizza, ice cream, soda, and candy. It's important for parents to discuss the lunch menu with their children ahead of time so the parents can encourage their children to make healthier choices. Alternatively, parents can pack a healthy lunch at home (American Academy of Pediatrics, 2016).

Obesity

Obesity is a growing problem around the world

Obesity today is a growing problem in many industrialized countries (**FIGURE 11.4**) (Abarca-Gómez et al., 2017). The Centers for Disease Control and Prevention use the **body mass index** (BMI) as a measure to define obesity. The BMI is a measure of body fat that combines a person's height and weight. Any child with a BMI higher than 95% of a reference population of their same-age peers is considered obese (**TABLE 11.1**).

The number of obese children in middle childhood has quadrupled over the past 40 years (Partnership for a Healthier America, 2020). Among American children aged 6–11, over 18% are obese. Children growing up in lower-income households are more likely to be obese (20%) than children growing up in higher-income households (11%). This is likely due at least in part to the fact that fresh vegetables and healthy foods are often much more expensive than highly processed and calorie-rich foods (Centers for Disease Control and Prevention, 2019a). Obesity rates also differ among racial and ethnic groups and are higher among Hispanic (26%) and Black Americans (24%) than among White (16%)

body mass index (BMI) a measure of body fat that is based on a person's height and weight.

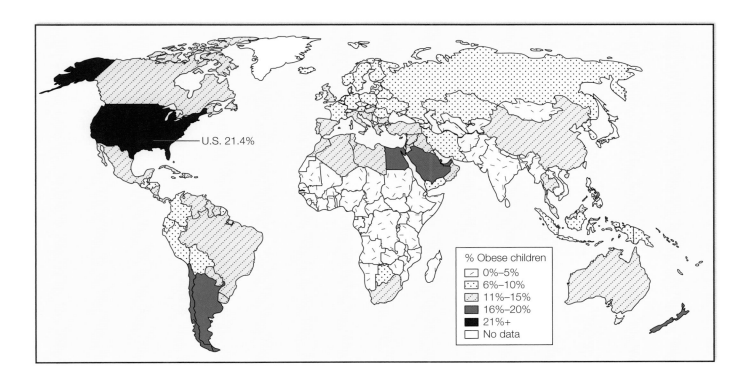

FIGURE 11.4 Obesity rates in children aged 5–19.

Data from World Health Organization. 2017. Global Health Observatory data repository. https://apps.who.int/gho/data

■ **Table 11.1** Weight Status Categories Based on CDC Growth Charts

Underweight	Less than 5th percentile
Normal or healthy weight	5th percentile to less than 85th percentile
Overweight	85th percentile to less than 95th percentile
Obese	95th percentile or greater

Source: Centers for Disease Control and Prevention. 2021. Defining childhood weight status. www.cdc.gov

and Asian Americans (9%) (Centers for Disease Control and Prevention, 2021a). Because it is challenging to lose weight, obese children are 10 times more likely than non-obese children to grow into obese adults and face a lifelong struggle with their weight (Partnership for a Healthier America, 2022).

Obesity affects the physical, cognitive, and socio-emotional development of children

Obesity can adversely affect the healthy development of children in multiple ways. In this section, we will look at how childhood obesity impairs physical, cognitive, and socio-emotional development.

PHYSICAL EFFECTS   Obesity puts children at risk for diabetes, heart disease, and other conditions that can potentially shorten their life span. In fact, for the first time in American history, children today may have a shorter life expectancy than their parents (Biesma & Hanson, 2020; Bjerregaard et al., 2020). Obesity increases children's risk for developing asthma, sleep apnea, and joint problems (Custovic & Martinez, 2020), and healthcare for obese children is, perhaps not surprisingly, three times more expensive than for children of normal weight (Partnership for a Healthier America, 2022).

COGNITIVE EFFECTS   Childhood obesity is a condition with more than just physical implications. Obese children are more likely to miss school or to have to repeat a grade (Partnership for a Healthier America, 2022), and they tend to have deficits in executive function (Hayes et al., 2018). However, the stereotypes associated with being obese may also work against these children: It is a widespread belief, reinforced through television and movies, that overweight people are not as intelligent as others (Davison et al., 2008). When children are aware that they are judged for their weight and assumed to be less intelligent than their slimmer classmates, their working memory is negatively affected (Guardabassi & Tomasetto, 2020).

SOCIO-EMOTIONAL EFFECTS   Finally, obesity in children can impair healthy socio-emotional growth. It puts children at risk for behavior problems and depression (Sagar & Gupta, 2018), and obese children often suffer from low self-esteem and bullying (Koyanagi et al., 2020; Sagar & Gupta, 2018). Obesity often leads to a negative body image, which may lead children to create unhealthy eating habits like dieting, meal skipping, fasting, or using diet pills. These habits put them at elevated risk for developing eating disorders like anorexia or bulimia (Harriger & Thompson, 2012).

A variety of factors lead to obesity

There are a wide variety of factors that lead to obesity, many of which we have already considered in some detail. For instance, we have seen that children today spend a lot of time indoors, and schools are not always able to provide them sufficient opportunities to be physically active (Xu & Xue, 2016). Long periods of screen time lead to long periods of sitting—often while snacking on unhealthy, high-calorie foods. Children are highly susceptible to advertisements for unhealthy foods, which may further influence their choices (American

Culture Counts

Childhood Obesity and Socioeconomic Status

Rates of childhood obesity are correlated with socioeconomic status: Children growing up in lower-income neighborhoods are at greater risk of obesity than children living in higher-income neighborhoods. The graph to the right shows how the rate of childhood obesity in the United States varies by household income level, measured in relation to the federal poverty level (FPL).

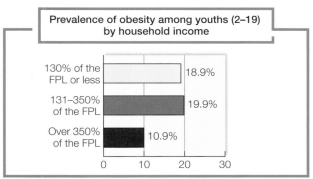

Data from C. L. Ogden et al. 2018. *MMWR Morb Mortal Wkly Rep* 67: 186–189.

■ Question

What are some reasons why children in lower-income households may be at greater risk of obesity than children in higher-income households? In the graph shown here, why might obesity rates go up slightly for children in the middle income category? How could you address these factors in a public-health campaign aimed at reducing obesity rates in children?

Academy of Pediatrics, 2011). An international study found that across all 22 participating countries, there were four times as many television commercials for unhealthy foods and beverages targeted at children than ads for healthier alternatives. Additionally, these ads were broadcast most frequently at peak viewing times for children (Kelly et al., 2019).

Eating behavior is another factor that contributes to obesity. As they get older, children spend increasingly more time at school and at friends' homes. They may not always be presented with healthy choices or may not make healthy choices without assistance. How fast a child's metabolism is (that is, how fast the body transforms food into energy) and how much children sleep each night (Centers for Disease Control and Prevention, 2018b) play a role as well.

Finally, it's important to recognize the role that genetics can play in childhood obesity. Just as some children are predisposed by their genetic makeup to be taller or shorter, a great deal of the variation in childhood weight is a result of genetic factors (Yılmaz & Karadağ, 2020).

■ Obesity in children is caused by a variety of factors like genetics, lack of exercise, and an unhealthy diet. Parents and caregivers play an important role in children's nutrition by modeling healthy eating choices.

Many things can be done to help children keep their weight under control

By now it is clear that children have many disadvantages when they grow up with an unhealthy weight. We cannot change their genes, but there are still a number of things that can be done to help children keep their weight under control. Parents, schools, and the media can all work together to keep the obesity epidemic under control. Here are some things they can do.

Parents can:

- *encourage and model healthy eating habits*: Eat and provide lots of fruits and vegetables as well as whole grains. Restrict eating fast food.
- *keep sugary and calorie-rich snacks out of reach*: Do not buy soda and other sugary drinks; limit the amount of candy and salty snacks children are allowed to eat, and do not store them where they are readily accessible.
- *encourage children to be physically active*: Provide toys for outside play like balls and jump ropes. Take children to playgrounds where they can exercise and run around. Take walks and exercise together.
- *reduce screen time*: Set a daily limit for time spent with television, tablets, smartphones, and computers. Consider using apps that encourage physical activity by leading children to dance, hop, and move.

Outside their home, there is probably no place where children spend as much time as at school. Schools are therefore in a prime position to promote positive health behaviors and attitudes by:

- educating students through nutrition and health behavior lessons;
- offering healthy foods in cafeterias, banning vending machines selling soda and candy, and banning the marketing of unhealthy foods at school;
- supporting the development of safe walking and bike routes to school; and
- offering sufficient recess and physical education time (Harvard School of Public Health, 2020).

© Ellen O'Nan/ASSOCIATED PRESS

■ What are the best ways to guide healthy eating choices in the school environment?

It is questionable whether school food in the United States will improve anytime soon, however. In early 2020, the U.S. Department of Agriculture (which oversees nutritional school programs that feed 30 million students) proposed new rules that allow schools to lower the amount of fruit and vegetables they serve while increasing the amounts of burgers, fries, and pizza (Reiley, 2020; U.S. Department of Agriculture, 2020).

Since children spend so much time watching TV shows punctuated by commercials, there are a number of things the media can do to support healthy development in children (Kaiser Family Foundation, 2004):

- Refrain from broadcasting commercials for unhealthy food choices that are aimed at children or that are broadcast at children's peak viewing times.

- Refrain from promoting unhealthy food with the help of popular movie or TV characters.

- Promote healthy eating habits in movies and TV shows.

- Support the development of healthy body images in children by featuring a variety of body shapes in TV shows and movies.

Review!

Why is nutrition so important for growing children?

■ Nutrition is important not only to ensure proper growth in children but to help prevent future health problems like type 2 diabetes, heart disease, and cancer.

■ A nutritious breakfast helps children focus and perform better in school. Additionally, children who get used to a healthy diet early on are much more likely to keep the habit of healthy eating in adulthood.

What are some challenges that make providing healthy nutrition more difficult for children in middle childhood?

■ As children grow older, they become more proactive and may make the decision to try a vegetarian or vegan diet. However, with proper care a vegetarian diet can provide the necessary nutrients for a growing child.

■ As they get older, children also eat more often outside their own home. School menus do not always offer a variety of healthy choices. Even if they do, without proper guidance children often make unhealthy choices.

■ Socioeconomic factors—including the availability and affordability of healthy food and child recreational programs—can be barriers to helping children attain a healthy lifestyle.

Why is obesity a problem for children?

■ Obesity is a growing problem in many countries around the world. Obese children have an elevated risk for diabetes and heart disease as well as other diseases like asthma and sleep apnea. They tend to fare worse at school than children of average weight and are more likely to be bullied or teased.

■ Comparing their bodies to those of thinner peers or celebrities may cause obese children's self-esteem to suffer. If they develop a negative body image, they run the risk of developing eating disorders.

What are some things that can be done to counteract obesity in children?

■ There are many things that can be done to help children control their weight. First and foremost, parents should model healthy eating habits and encourage these in their children. Sugary and high-calorie snacks should be kept out of reach, and children should be encouraged to be physically active.

■ Since many children spend extensive amounts of their free time in front of screens, limiting their screen time can also help to increase the time they are physically active.

■ Schools can do their part as well by educating students in nutrition and offering healthy foods in the cafeteria. Consumption of soda and candy can be reduced if they are not sold at school. Schools offering recess and physical education classes also encourage physical activity that can help keep weight down.

Practice!

1. Eight-year-olds should consume about _____ calories a day.
   a. 1,200–1,400
   b. 800–1,000
   c. 1,600–1,800
   d. 1,800–2,000

2. Children in _____ households are at greatest risk of obesity.
   a. low-income
   b. middle-income
   c. high-income

3. Body dissatisfaction in obese children may lead to

   _____ .

   a. more social behavior to compensate for their unhappiness
   b. increased focus on academic subjects
   c. eating disorders
   d. severe headaches and migraines

4. Obesity is caused by a lot of factors, including

   _____ .

   a. the rate of a child's metabolism and a child's eating choices
   b. a child's IQ (intelligence quotient)
   c. the number of siblings a child has
   d. the climate where a child grows up

Show What You've Learned!

Seven-year-old Tessa refuses to eat anything but plain pasta and grilled cheese. If she does not get what she wants, she refuses to eat and screams until her parents can't stand it anymore and make her a dinner she likes. As Tessa's parent, how concerned should you be about this situation? Drawing on the information presented in this section, what steps could you take to remedy the situation?

See For Yourself!

The Centers for Disease Control and Prevention recommends a daily diet that balances fruits, grains, vegetables, protein, and dairy while avoiding sodium, saturated fats, and added sugars. You can review their guidelines here: https://www.choosemyplate.gov/.

 The next time you're at a grocery store, look at snacks marketed directly to children. How many of them satisfy the CDC's nutritional guidelines?

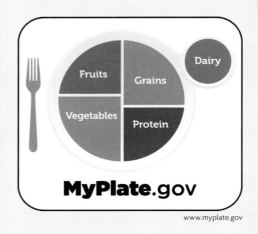

www.myplate.gov

11.4 Health and Safety in Middle Childhood

- Examine why childhood asthma is a chronic condition and its implications for the lives of the affected children.
- Explain what head lice are and how they can be controlled.
- Identify dangers children face online and describe approaches caregivers can take to protect them.
- Demonstrate ways children can be taught to stay safe while online.

Improved healthcare has made middle childhood a period of life that many American children spend in good health. However, at the same time, chronic conditions are steadily on the rise. In this section, we will consider how children's health has changed over the past decades and examine childhood asthma as an example of a chronic health condition. We will discuss head lice, a common nuisance that spares few children in early and middle childhood. We will also discuss how to talk with children about serious threats to their health and safety, like pandemics, terrorist threats, and climate change. And last but not least, we will consider the danger that media and particularly the online world pose to growing children.

The Rise of Chronic Conditions among Children

Over the past few decades, the diseases children suffer and potentially die from have changed significantly. This is a result of two factors. On one hand, healthcare and medical treatments have improved radically. New vaccines have reduced the mortality of children due to viral and bacterial illnesses. Treatments for children with cancer and birth defects like heart defects have vastly improved the odds that affected children may survive (Perrin et al., 2014).

On the other hand, chronic conditions like asthma, obesity, and mental health disorders have steadily increased. Whereas in 1960 fewer than 2% of children were suffering from health conditions that interfered with their daily life, that number had risen to 8% in 2010 (Bethell et al., 2008; Perrin et al., 2014; Van Cleave et al., 2010). In contrast to acute medical conditions, **chronic diseases** are medical conditions that last more than 1 year and require a child to limit daily activities, to seek ongoing medical care, or both.

While it is not entirely clear what has led to the steep rise of chronic conditions in children, several reasons are believed to interact with genetic susceptibility to develop certain diseases:

- Children are exposed to increasingly higher levels of toxins in utero as well as after birth (see also Chapter 3).

- Children spend their time differently than they used to in earlier centuries: They typically eat differently, move less, and spend more time engaged with various media than children did even just a few decades ago.

- Since many people today are more aware of health conditions and schools offer regular health screenings, children whose mental and physical health conditions may have gone undiagnosed years ago are having their conditions recognized (Perrin et al., 2007, 2014).

In the following section, we will have a closer look at one of the chronic health conditions that have been on the rise: childhood asthma.

chronic diseases medical conditions that last more than 1 year and limit daily activities, require ongoing medical care, or both.

Childhood Asthma

Asthma is the most common chronic illness in children, and its growing prevalence among children has health experts perplexed. About 8% of American children have asthma, with boys slightly more affected than girls. Black children (16%) and children of Puerto Rican descent (13%) are affected most often, as are children from households below the poverty line (10%) (Zahran et al., 2018). In 2016, about one-half of all children with asthma had an attack that needed treatment (Centers for Disease Control and Prevention, 2018a).

But treatment options are getting better: The number of school days children missed due to asthma decreased from 4 to 3 between 2003 and 2013. And in 2013, only 5% of children needed to be hospitalized due to an asthma attack—half as many as in 2003 (Zahran et al., 2018).

Signs of asthma are coughing spells as well as less energy at play. Children may also complain of chest tightness and pain, breathe rapidly, or make a whistling sound (called wheezing) when they are breathing. Asthma symptoms may change from one episode to the next and also differ from child to child.

It is during asthma flare-ups that symptoms get worse. While some of the flare-ups develop suddenly, others can take a long time to develop. Asthma attacks can be brought on by exposure to various allergens, including

- pollen, mold, dust, or pets;
- air pollution; and
- tobacco smoke (Chipps et al., 2018).

An asthma attack can also occur when children do not take their asthma medications as prescribed.

It isn't clear what causes asthma. Some of the factors associated with childhood asthma include family history, low birthweight, and persistent exposure to tobacco smoke from a young age. Children are also at a higher risk if they have frequent respiratory infections, are male, and are of African American descent (Noutsios & Floros, 2014).

Researchers also are not yet sure why more children today are developing asthma. One hypothesis is that children are increasingly exposed to a rising number of harmful chemicals in the air. These chemicals are released by a variety of

◼ Children with asthma often use fast-acting medication delivered by an inhaler to open up tightened airways.

consumer products from furniture to detergents and rugs (Population Reference Bureau, 2021). New homes and commercial buildings that are insulated much more efficiently tend to recycle indoor air, trapping any airborne pollutants.

There is no cure for asthma, and the treatment children receive is aimed at preventing flare-ups. This is best done by avoiding triggers: not smoking in the family home and keeping asthmatic children indoors when the pollen count is high. Frequent vacuuming of the family home is discouraged because it can stir up dust particles that asthmatic children may be allergic to (Vicendese et al., 2015). Additionally, children can take two different kinds of medication: fast-acting medication that can be used to open up the tightened airways when necessary and long-term medications that are used to control the asthma and need to be taken every day. About 55% of children with asthma are supposed to take long-term medication, but almost half of them do not do so regularly as prescribed (Centers for Disease Control and Prevention, 2018a).

But even well-managed asthma does not make the symptoms disappear entirely: Children can still have symptoms for about 2 days a week and might take fast-acting medication twice a week (Centers for Disease Control and Prevention, 2018a).

Head Lice

Melinda and Sean are playing outside, and their mom, Marian, is using the rare quiet time to get some work done. Sitting at her desk, she's outlining the work that needs to get done and scratches her head, lost in thought. Upon scratching, she hears the tiniest plop sound of something landing on the paper in front of her. To her dismay, she recognizes it immediately as a head louse. If she has lice, she reasons, she must have gotten them from her children. But the children's school has been teaching online for the past 4 weeks due to the COVID-19 pandemic. Where could they have gotten the lice from?

Unbeknownst to Marian, it often takes a few weeks for parents to discover head lice in their children, particularly when they're not looking for them. By then, of course, there is a good chance that the whole family is hosting these unwelcome visitors.

Head lice are common among preschoolers and elementary school children. The CDC estimates that there are between 6 and 12 million infestations per year in children between the ages of 3 and 12 (Centers for Disease Control and Prevention, 2019f). There are far fewer infestations in African American children, possibly because the lice have more trouble clinging to the shape of their hair (Centers for Disease Control and Prevention, 2019f). Girls are more likely to have head lice than boys—their hair tends to be longer and thus comes more easily into contact with other children's hair, and it is easier for the head lice to hide.

Head lice spread when a child comes into contact with the hair of an infested person. Young children are most frequently affected because they get in close physical contact when playing with each other. Sometimes, lice also spread from hats, hair bands, combs, brushes, or towels that were used by infested persons (Centers for Disease Control and Prevention, 2019e).

Head lice live on the head of a person and suck small amounts of blood from the scalp every few hours. They live for up to 4 weeks and lay up to ten eggs a day. Head lice do not transmit any diseases and are therefore not a health hazard but rather a nuisance that families and schools have to deal with. It can take 4–6 weeks for children to develop the typical itching on their head.

■ Head lice tend to be brownish black and usually hide in a person's hair, so they are hard to spot. They lay their eggs (called nits) close to the scalp where they hatch within a week or so.

The itching comes from an allergic reaction to the louse bites. Children may also be irritable, have trouble sleeping, or develop sores on their head due to scratching their head (Centers for Disease Control and Prevention, 2019d).

It isn't that easy to diagnose head lice, because head lice are small, move quickly, and avoid light. Hair needs to be inspected very closely. Even if there are no live lice you can assume there is an active infestation if there are nits (that is, louse eggs) attached to the hair less than ¼ inch from the root of the hair. Nits can be found most easily by combing the hair with a nit comb, which is a very fine-toothed comb. However, they are easily confused with dandruff, dust, or dirt particles in the hair (Centers for Disease Control and Prevention, 2019c).

Head lice are most commonly treated with over-the-counter or prescription medications. These often consist of a solution or cream that is applied to the hair according to the directions. If head lice are found on one family member, the whole family should be treated to prevent further spread of the lice. The treatment should be followed by thorough nit combing. Many treatments only kill the lice but not the nits, so parents have to continue nit combing and repeat the treatment after around 10 days, when potential leftover nits might have hatched (Centers for Disease Control and Prevention, 2019f). Additionally, linens, pillows, and anything the infested person wore up to 2 days before the treatment should be washed in hot water and dried on a high heat setting in a dryer. Items that cannot be washed should be sealed for 2 weeks in plastic bags—lice cannot survive for 2 weeks away from the human scalp that provides nourishment (Centers for Disease Control and Prevention, 2019g).

Contrary to popular belief, an infestation with head lice is not a sign of poor hygiene. Head lice cannot be gotten rid of by washing hair with regular shampoo, and they are transmitted by head-to-head contact. Yet head lice infestations often come with a certain stigma. For that reason, many schools feel that it is important to handle a case of head lice confidentially. Some schools will do periodic lice checks with a nurse, and if lice are detected in a child, parents may be notified by the school and asked to treat the head lice immediately. Affected children may be asked to refrain from close head-to-head contact with others.

There is no consensus over whether schools should have a no-nit policy for children to be allowed to return to school. Some experts feel such a policy exposes children to unnecessary stigma, whereas others feel it is necessary to keep children lice-free (Devore et al., 2015; National Pediculosis Association,

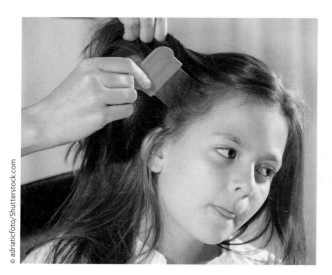

◼ Lice and nits can be removed by combing the hair with a nit comb. Since it is difficult to remove every single nit, most parents choose to treat their children with a medication that is applied to the hair in addition to the nit combing.

2022). Head lice screening programs at school have not been found to be effective, and instead, parents should be educated on screening their children on a regular basis and treating them in case of an infestation (Devore et al., 2015).

Talking to Children About Upsetting Events and Conditions

In the days before Sean and Melinda's school closed—like schools across the nation and around the world—the two kids started asking their parents a lot of questions. Sean and Melinda were old enough to realize that the world was facing a serious crisis. They saw some coverage on TV as well as online and heard lots about the coronavirus at school from friends. But they were not yet in a position to adequately understand the news coverage and develop a thorough understanding of the situation without help. Misinformation and rumors increased the children's anxiety.

The COVID-19 pandemic is an unprecedented event in this country, but the threat it poses to children and the questions it provokes are not unique. Children all over the world are facing threatening and anxiety-provoking situations—think of school shootings, terrorist attacks, or the civil unrest that has caused waves of refugees to make the difficult journey to North America and Europe.

Parents feel the need to talk with their children about the situation they are facing, including possible danger to their family and potential death. But at the same time, parents themselves are confronted with their own anxiety and worries.

For that reason, it is very important that parents, caregivers, and educators approach these conversations in a thoughtful way. Here are some tips on how to approach difficult topics (Center on Media and Child Health, 2020; Centers for Disease Control and Prevention, 2020b; Ehmke, 2020; Grose, 2020):

- *Do not avoid talking about the topic.* Children most likely have already heard about the topic and need factual information. You can help them understand the news and correct possible misinformation by asking what they already know. If you avoid talking about it, children may actually start to worry more.

- *Provide age-appropriate information, using age-appropriate language.* Find out what your children's questions are. Answer those questions sensitively but truthfully, and do not be afraid to admit that there are things that are unknown.

- *Do not transmit your emotions to the child.* If you're extremely worried or anxious, your children will likely pick up on it when you talk to them. Wait until you are feeling calm before starting the conversation with them.

- *Reassure your children.* Give a realistic but reassuring risk assessment. Explain to children that they are not likely to get seriously ill from the coronavirus, nor is it likely they will be involved in a terrorist attack of some kind.

- *Empower your children to look after their own safety.* In the case of a pandemic, explain to children that viruses are spread mostly through touching surfaces and coughing. By adopting proper hygiene techniques like washing their hands often with soap and water for 20 seconds, keeping

▪ As they are growing up, children face a variety of threats and uncertain situations. These may be terrorist attacks, pandemics, or concerns about climate change. These threats need to be addressed in an age-appropriate way to alleviate children's anxiety and address their concerns.

sufficient distance from others, and wearing masks, children can gain some control over this threat by protecting themselves.

- *Provide a routine as best as you can.* Unexpected and threatening events like terrorism and pandemics make life seem very unpredictable, leaving children feeling anxious and insecure. Having a predictable daily routine to follow provides a sense of security. Regular events like family dinners or before-bed reading time are more important than ever to children facing uncertain circumstances.

Media and Children's Health and Safety

As children get older, they spend an increasing amount of time online. At least some of this time is unsupervised, exposing them to dangers many of their parents did not face in this form. Parents may not be aware of these dangers, or they may be ill-prepared to teach their children to stay safe online.

Many children are harassed online

The internet can open many doors for children, and in extraordinary times like the lockdown Sean and Melinda are experiencing due to a pandemic, the internet could be the only way to connect with friends and relatives, as well as teachers and schoolmates. But the internet is also a source of various dangers for children. Often, their parents and teachers are not aware of what the children are going through.

Consider this account from a 13-year-old girl:

> I was sent loads of horrible messages on several social media accounts, sent death threats with people telling me to kill myself. I also received phone calls and text messages attacking me. Furthermore, they were standing outside my house being abusive and saying horrible things to me. Fake accounts were made using my name to be horrible to others and to me. (Ditch the Label, 2017, p. 19)

A survey of more than 170,000 young people in 30 countries showed that every fifth child has been the victim of online bullying (UNICEF, 2019). In the United States, that number is even higher: Around 59% of teens have experienced cyberbullying (Anderson, 2018). There are a variety of ways children can be harassed online. In the survey, the most frequent kind of harassment cited was name-calling, followed by the spread of false rumors (Anderson, 2018b) (FIGURE 11.5).

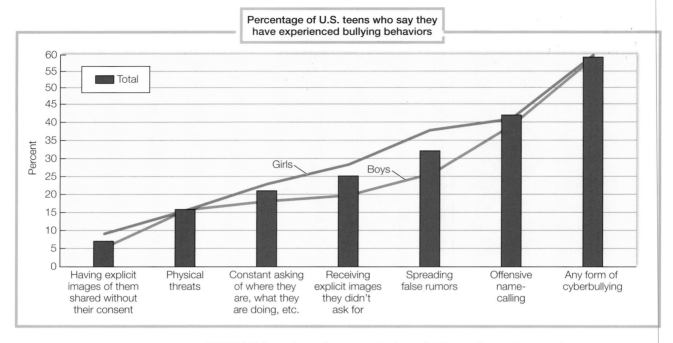

FIGURE 11.5 Cyberbullying can take lots of different forms. The most frequent ones are name-calling, the spreading of false rumors, and being sent unwanted explicit images.

Data from M. Anderson. 2018. A majority of teens have experienced some form of cyberbullying. www.pewresearch.org

While both girls and boys are harassed online, they experience different kinds of harassment: Girls are more likely to be sent unwanted images than boys. Additionally, children from low-income households are more likely to receive physical threats online (Anderson, 2018a).

Children can be harassed on any online platform, but the leading platform for harassment was Instagram (42% of victims were bullied here), followed by Facebook (37%) and Snapchat (31%) (Ditch the Label, 2017). The offenders are most often people the bullied children know: Classmates (62%) and ex-friends (34%) are two of the three largest groups of offenders (the other is peers at school whom the victims don't know, at 37%) (Ditch the Label, 2019).

Bullying has a grave impact on the children who experience it (**FIGURE 11.6**). Forty-five percent of victims feel depressed, 41% feel anxious, 33% have suicidal thoughts, and 26% do some harm to themselves as a consequence of the bullying they've experienced. One out of ten children has tried to commit suicide as a result of being bullied, and almost one-third of the bullied children never told anyone (Ditch the Label, 2019).

Girls are the most frequent victims of online enticement

Digital and online media are also filled with sexual content and requests that are inappropriate for children. In *online enticement*, people contact children with the purpose of ultimately meeting them in person for sexual purposes, having sexual conversations with them online, or getting and trading sexual images. Children can also get blackmailed once others have received (or secretly taken) sexually explicit videos or photos from them.

Any platform can be used for these purposes—social media, messaging apps, and even online games. Children who pretend to be older online than they are and who send explicit photos of themselves to others are at higher risk of becoming victimized (National Center for Missing & Exploited Children, 2022). Most of the victims of online enticement (78%) are girls (National Center for Missing & Exploited Children, 2016).

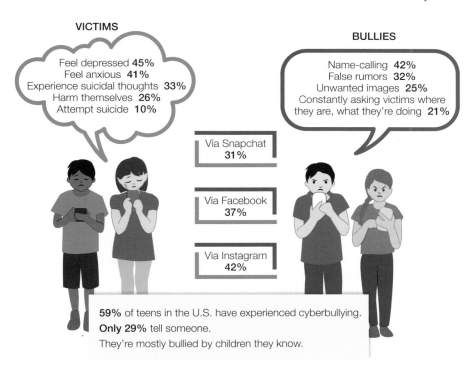

VICTIMS

Feel depressed **45%**
Feel anxious **41%**
Experience suicidal thoughts **33%**
Harm themselves **26%**
Attempt suicide **10%**

BULLIES

Name-calling **42%**
False rumors **32%**
Unwanted images **25%**
Constantly asking victims where
they are, what they're doing **21%**

Via Snapchat
31%

Via Facebook
37%

Via Instagram
42%

59% of teens in the U.S. have experienced cyberbullying.
Only 29% tell someone.
They're mostly bullied by children they know.

FIGURE 11.6 Effects of cyberbullying on young people.

Data from M. Anderson. 2018. A majority of teens have experienced some form of cyberbullying. www.pewresearch.org; Ditch the Label. 2019. The Annual Bullying Survey. www.ditchthelabel.org

In regular online bullying, children are mostly bullied by people they know, but in online enticement almost all children do not know the person they're dealing with in person (National Center for Missing & Exploited Children, 2022).

Children can be taught online safety

Many elementary schools let students use laptop computers and tablets at school. School settings may prevent students from visiting certain web pages or using particular apps, but if they are allowed to bring their school device home, many of these filters may not work. There are a number of things parents and caregivers can do to protect children from online dangers.

A variety of devices and apps are available on the market to help parents limit children's screen time, block or filter children's access to websites and apps, and monitor what they are doing online. But beyond controlling children's behavior, children need to be explicitly taught how to avoid dangers online and what constitutes safe behavior (**TABLE 11.2**).

Making the most of screen time

It's an indisputable fact of life in the twenty-first century that children interact daily with digital and electronic devices. But there are a number of things parents and caregivers can do to maximize the benefits from the time their children spend in front of screens.

RETHINKING SCREEN TIME LIMITS Computers and other digital devices form an

■ Table 11.2 Internet Safety Guidelines for Children

Elementary school age	Middle school age
Children should NOT:	**Children should know how to:**
Publish any personal information like name and address online	Verify the identity of a person they met online
Create online profiles	Identify whether a link is safe
Harass or bully other children online	Identify online scams
Turn on their location services so strangers can see where they are	Identify online bullying and what to do about it
Visit a chat room without permission	Protect their privacy
Visit private chat rooms or meet friends in a private online setting	
Visit new websites without permission	
Respond to offensive messages or posts	
Send or receive images	
Meet online friends in person without their parents	
Share their passwords or use passwords that are easy to guess	

Source: Internet Safety 101. 2020. Safety and Prevention. https://internetsafety101.org/safety

important part of children's lives. Many elementary schools use online programs and games to teach students math facts, math concepts, and spelling, among other things. Testing is done more and more online, even with children who cannot yet type with ten fingers and will thus spend a significant amount of time searching for the right keys on the keyboard. In 2019, our local elementary school was given the choice of whether third- and fourth-grade students were going to take their state math and English tests on paper or on a computer. The COVID-19 pandemic, which forced the closure of many elementary schools in 2020, subsequently hastened the move to greater online learning. Since 2022, every child in fifth grade or higher in our school district gets a loaned laptop they can bring home. Teachers struggle because students challenge each other during instruction to play games on websites that teachers cannot detect with their supervision software. Children at home have an easier time switching from one device to another once their screen time limit has been reached (school and home devices cannot be synced).

With schoolwork, communication with friends and relatives, and playtime all taking place online, experts are starting to rethink screen time limits. Not all screen time is detrimental to children's development once they have outgrown their earliest years: Internet conversations with loved ones and online research are important and should have their place in children's lives, for example. It is mostly TV watching and video games that have been shown to lower school performance (Woodyard, 2019).

Instead of setting a rigid screen time limit, parents can consider setting limits for particular apps and games. Parents can also reflect on their children's daily schedule and whether any desirable or important activities are not getting done because their children are spending too much time with their electronic devices. Time blocks can be set for those desirable activities and screen time allocated to the amount of time that is left (Barton, 2020). Keep in mind, however, that these suggestions do not apply to infants and toddlers, who should have no or only very limited screen time.

ONLINE SCHOOLING NEEDS DIFFER DEPENDING ON AGE   For online schooling, it is helpful to have paper and pencil next to the computer, since writing notes helps to reinforce what children learn. Elementary school students also need help setting up and using their online tools and still need longer amounts of time offline. Middle and high school students, to the contrary, have a strong need to maintain their social connections. For them, efficient learning can often happen through forums and online discussions or collaborations (Barton, 2020).

■ Beginning in the late 1940s, American families would gather around the television to watch programs together, as illustrated in this colorized photo from 1948.

FAMILIES CAN ENJOY SCREEN TIME TOGETHER   When the radio was invented, families spent their evenings together gathered around what must have seemed like a magical device, listening to stories, music, or the news broadcast from afar. Then, in the 1950s, they assembled around their newly acquired TV set to watch the latest shows. Today, every family member spends time alone in front of their own screen. Children often have their own TVs in their bedroom or possess their own tablet or cell phone.

   But families can also integrate some screen time into their lives together. For example, they can watch movies together or even create routines that include a movie and dinner, revolving around special topics like family history or the environment (Family Dinner Project, 2020; Sullivan, 2020).

Review!

Why is childhood asthma a chronic condition, and what are its implications for the lives of affected children?

- Childhood asthma is defined as a *chronic disease* because children are affected by it for years, may need ongoing medical care, and often have to limit their daily activities depending on their condition.

- In the United States, about 8% of children have asthma. They may have coughing spells, trouble breathing, and wheezing when they breathe. Flare-ups can come suddenly and get so bad that the child needs emergency treatment.

- Some children receive medications they have to take daily to manage their asthma. Additionally, there are fast-acting medications that children can take in an emergency. But even well-managed asthma is likely to cause symptoms in children several times a month.

What are head lice, and how can they be controlled?

- Head lice are wingless insects that cause between 6 and 12 million infestations in children aged 3–12 each year. They spread when children get in contact with the hair of an infested person or use an infested person's hat or brush.

- It can take several weeks for itching to develop as a reaction to the head lice sucking blood from the scalp. Head lice are often treated with creams or fluids that are applied to the head and then rinsed. Additionally, nits can be removed from the hair using a special nit comb.

- If one person is affected, it is likely that other persons in the household have lice as well. Thus, all household members should

be treated. Most treatments have to be repeated after 7–10 days so that any lice that have hatched from eggs can be killed.

What are some of the dangers children are exposed to online?

- There are a variety of dangers children are exposed to in an online environment. One of the most prominent ones is cyberbullying.

- Cyberbullying takes different forms, including name-calling, spreading false rumors, and sending unwanted explicit images. Cyberbullying happens on all platforms—gaming platforms, social media, and messaging apps. It can have a grave impact on children's mental health and well-being. Cyberbullies are most often people who know the victim.

- Perpetrators in online enticement are mostly strangers. They contact children online with the purpose of having sexual conversations, trading sexual images, or eventually even meeting offline with the children.

How can we teach children to stay safe online?

- From an early age, children should be supervised when they use online media, and they should be taught age-appropriate ways to keep themselves safe. These include not publishing any personal information about themselves, including their location; not visiting chat rooms or creating online profiles; and not engaging in the harassment of others responding to offensive messages. Children should also refrain from sending or receiving images and be taught how to create and safely use passwords.

- Older children also need to understand how to verify the identity of people they meet online. They also need to be able to find out whether a link is safe and to identify an online scam.

Practice!

1 A chronic health condition is a medical condition that lasts _____ .

   a. more than 3 months and does not require medication to control
   b. more than 1 year and may require ongoing medical care
   c. more than 6 months and may require ongoing medical care
   d. 1 month or longer and requires ongoing medical care

2. Childhood asthma affects about _____ of American children.
   a. 4%
   b. 8%
   c. 12%
   d. 16%

3. Head lice transmit _____ .
   a. a number of serious bacterial infections
   b. viral infections
   c. no serious diseases
   d. parasites that can affect the human nervous system

4. In online enticement, _____ .
   a. children are contacted online in order to sell them consumer goods
   b. children are contacted online in order to sell them illegal drugs
   c. children are contacted online with an ultimate sexual purpose like meeting them online or getting explicit photos
   d. children are contacted online to be recruited into extremist organizations

5. Elementary schoolers _____ .
   a. should be kept from digital devices to keep them safe
   b. should only ever use digital devices in the presence of an adult
   c. should be taught basic online safety rules and behaviors
   d. should be allowed to freely use digital devices and roam the internet so they can learn by doing

Act It Out!

After their online school day, Melinda and Sean are at the playground with their mom, Marian. Javier is there with his daughter Ava, who is a friend and classmate of Melinda's. The two parents chat at a safe physical distance from one another (as they've gotten used to during the COVID-19 pandemic), and after some small talk, Marian leans toward Javier to whisper, "It's a good thing the girls aren't allowed to get too close: I think Melinda may have lice. I'm not sure, though—I've never seen lice before." Javier laughs. "Oh, I can tell you a thing or two about lice—with three daughters, I'm sure we've tried every treatment ever invented!" Drawing on the information presented in this chapter, act out a dialogue between Marian and Javier in which Javier advises Marian on how to treat the potential infestation. As Marian, what are your main concerns and questions? As Javier, what can you say to reassure her?

11.5 Special Needs and Learning

- Define ADHD and explain what effect it has on children's lives.
- Outline the characteristics of the learning disabilities dyslexia, dysgraphia, and dyscalculia and explain how effected students can be supported.
- Explain giftedness and how gifted children can be accommodated in the classroom.

In the United States, every child has the right to an education in a public school. However, not all children have the same needs. Children with disabilities are eligible for accommodations that help them achieve the best learning outcomes.

In the following sections, we will discuss a number of conditions that make it hard for children to learn and succeed at school. We will discuss how their needs can be accommodated in public schools. We will also learn what makes gifted children gifted and what is being done to accommodate their unique needs in the classroom.

Attention-Deficit/Hyperactivity Disorder

Children with attention-deficit/hyperactivity disorder (ADHD) often (1) have trouble paying attention, (2) are restless and have difficulty sitting still, (3) act without thinking first, or (4) show a combination of these patterns. In practice, you might see children overlooking details and making careless mistakes, not listening when someone addresses them, having problems organizing tasks and doing them in the right order, or losing things that are necessary for the completion of their work. Children may also constantly be in motion or talk without end, squirm when they have to be seated, or have trouble waiting their turn in a line (National Institute of Mental Health, 2022a).

© Alona Siniehina/Shutterstock.com

■ Children with ADHD may be aggressive or refuse to comply with requests from their parents and teachers. More than one-half of children diagnosed with ADHD take medication to ease their symptoms. However, some experts are concerned that prescribing medication discourages families from developing problem-solving skills. They also worry that amid the increasing number of children who receive prescriptions, a growing number of children are misdiagnosed.

All children show such behaviors from time to time, but children with an ADHD diagnosis display the behaviors so frequently that they impair their functioning in daily life (Centers for Disease Control and Prevention, 2021c).

Almost 10% of children in the United States have been diagnosed with ADHD. The average age at diagnosis is 7, because formal schooling situations make their symptoms more apparent. Boys are more than twice as likely to be diagnosed as girls (Danielson et al., 2018). Two-thirds of the children also have a second disorder. For example, 50% of the diagnosed children also have a conduct problem, and 30% of them suffer from anxiety (Danielson et al., 2018).

Children with ADHD often struggle with academic work (Rabiner et al., 2000), but many also have behavior problems at school and at home (Daley & Birchwood, 2010; LeFever et al., 2002). They are placed into special education classrooms more often than children without ADHD (Biederman et al., 1996). Children with ADHD also tend to have fewer friends, are more often rejected by peers, and are less socially active than children without ADHD (Aduen et al., 2018; Hoza et al., 2005).

In the first decade of the new millennium, diagnoses of ADHD continued to rise by about 5% each year, from 8% in 2003 to 11% in 2011. However, these rates now seem to have stabilized, if you consider that a 2016 survey found a diagnosis rate of just 10% among children (Danielson et al., 2018; Visser et al., 2014). There is no single test to diagnose ADHD, which can make diagnosis difficult, particularly because other conditions like learning disabilities, depression, or anxiety tend to have similar symptoms (Centers for Disease Control and Prevention, 2020c).

There are a number of causes that may contribute to the development of ADHD. For example, premature birth and low birthweight predispose children to develop ADHD (Škrablin et al., 2008). Prenatal exposure to alcohol and tobacco smoke or environmental toxins like lead increases children's risk as well (Goodlad et al., 2013; Han et al., 2015; Langley et al., 2005). Brain injuries have been connected with ADHD (Ilie et al., 2015), and it also runs in families (Grimm et al., 2020).

There is no cure for ADHD, but there are a number of treatments that can help reduce symptoms. Many children rely on one or a combination of the following:

- *Medication*: Even though it seems counterintuitive, stimulant medications like Ritalin and Adderall help children concentrate, listen, and fidget less. They likely work by increasing quantities of the neurotransmitter dopamine (National Institute of Mental Health, 2022a). Dopamine is commonly thought of as a key ingredient of the brain's reward system, which motivates us to complete tasks. However, a meta-analysis indicates that academic benefits of Ritalin are small to moderate, and there are no data for long-term impact (Kortekaas-Rijlaarsdam et al., 2019). Social functioning does get improved by Ritalin (Carucci et al., 2012). Stimulants such as Ritalin also have a number of side effects like insomnia and decreased appetite (Ahmann et al., 1993) and may slow down children's growth (Zaza et al., 2017). Sixty-two percent of affected children take medication to manage their symptoms (Danielson et al., 2018).

- *Therapy*: Cognitive behavioral therapy can be used to manage symptoms like hyperactivity, inattention, and lack of social skills as well and is often used in addition to medication (Ahmad et al., 2018; Braswell & Bloomquist, 1991; Sprich et al., 2016). About one-half of children diagnosed with ADHD receive behavioral therapy (Danielson et al., 2018).

- *Training and education*: This includes parenting skills training, stress management trainings, and support groups for parents and families to help them cope with the demands and stresses of the condition (National Institute of Mental Health, 2022a).

- *Support at school*: Depending on a child's symptoms, there are a number of accommodations that can be provided by the school. Affected students can sit in the front row, and it may be effective to provide them with checklists for assignments or frequently made mistakes. Children may benefit from getting more time in exams or from getting tasks broken down into smaller steps. Some students may also qualify for an Individualized Education Plan (IEP), which we will discuss further below.

It is not clear whether or not diet has an impact on ADHD symptoms. One study found that children who ate a healthy diet consisting of regular servings of fruit, vegetables, pasta, and rice had a lower incidence of ADHD than children who frequently ate at fast-food restaurants or consumed large amounts of sugar (Ríos-Hernández et al., 2017). Other studies, however, dispute that diets limiting food dyes or sugar have a significant impact on children's symptoms (Millichap & Yee, 2012; Uhlig et al., 1997). Since many diets are hard to follow because they exclude a lot of foods, diet therapy is usually used for children in whom medication does not work or who (or whose parents) do not wish to take medication (Millichap & Yee, 2012).

Learning Disabilities

learning disability any of a group of disorders that impair a person's ability in a specific area, for example, in reading, writing, or mathematics.

Children with **learning disabilities** have trouble understanding or using language (written and/or spoken) or performing mathematical calculations. Learning disabilities exist in very young children, but they are usually only detected and diagnosed once children go to school. A number of well-known and accomplished people have been affected by learning disabilities. General George Patton of the U.S. Army in World War II, comedian Jay Leno, and investor and financial analyst Charles Schwab (founder of the Charles Schwab Corporation) have dyslexia, for example. Two other common learning disorders are dysgraphia and dyscalculia. We will discuss them in more detail in the next section.

Dyslexia

dyslexia a common learning disability that affects a person's ability to spell words and read.

Dyslexia is a common learning disability that affects a person's ability to spell words and read. According to different estimations, between 10 and 20% of the population are affected by dyslexia (Roitsch & Watson, 2019; Siegel, 2006; Yale Center for Dyslexia and Creativity, 2022a). About 80% of people with reading difficulties are affected by dyslexia. Having dyslexia is not a sign of below-average intelligence. Dyslexia can be found among all students—those of average intelligence as well as those of below- and above-average intelligence. Dyslexia tends to be less severe in languages where spelling is consistent with word sounds, like German and Italian. One study found that dyslexia is half as common in Italy as in the United States, where English spelling is considerably at odds with speech sounds (Paulesu et al., 2001).

Here is how Sarah describes her experience with dyslexia:

> I feel like English is my second language even though I don't speak/read anything else. I guess my first language is interpreting pictures and emotions. As an early reader, it took me a long time to branch out away from picture books. I was afraid that without the pictures my comprehension would suffer and that reading would be pointless and boring.
>
> When I read, I generally don't really read the words in their entirety. I see the word more like a picture. I see the first few letters and the last few, and depending on the length of the word and the context, I know what the word is. It is difficult for me when I come across words that I've never read before, even if they are part of my spoken vocabulary (Clark, 2014).

It is not quite clear what causes dyslexia. Between 25 and 65% of children with dyslexia have at least one dyslexic parent, so genetic factors do play a role (Knopik et al., 2017). Many children with dyslexia have trouble identifying speech sounds within words or understanding how letters represent sounds (Shaywitz & Shaywitz, 2013, 2017).

Although dyslexia is most commonly diagnosed in schoolchildren, first signs can appear in preschoolers. For example, they may have trouble learning nursery rhymes, mispronounce familiar words, or have difficulty rhyming easy words like "hen" and "pen." Once they start elementary school, dyslexic children have trouble learning to read and associate letters with sounds. They often cannot even sound out short words like "dog" or "tap." As they progress through school, their gains in reading skills tend to be very slow. They have trouble reading new words and avoid reading out loud. They also encounter some problems in speaking: they may pause a lot, searching for specific words and confusing words that sound alike (Shaywitz, 2020).

There is no cure for dyslexia, though there are a number of interventions that can help children learn to read. Early intervention helps children to develop their reading and writing skills and perform well at school. For example, they may receive exercises that teach them how to blend sounds in order to form words.

Dyslexic students may also be eligible for accommodations at school. For example, they may get extra time on tests or may be allowed to use audio recordings and programs that read out text (Yale Center for Dyslexia and Creativity, 2022b).

Dysgraphia

Dysgraphia is a neurological disorder in which children's writing is distorted or incorrect. For example, their letters may not be adequately spaced or sized, or they may write wrong words or misspell them. They may also have trouble writing with the correct pressure or holding a pencil in a functional way. Children with dysgraphia may have other learning disabilities as well. Some studies have found that more than 50% of children with autism spectrum disorder (ASD) or ADHD are affected by dysgraphia (Mayes et al., 2019).

It is not clear what causes dysgraphia. However, we know that dysgraphia can be acquired later in life when people sustain damage to their parietal lobe (National Institute of Mental Health, 2022b).

Teachers at school will give children with dysgraphia special exercises depending on their challenges. For example, a child may need to be taught how to use punctuation and may be given graphic organizers to help with writing. Occupational therapy can support the development of hand strength and fine motor skills. Pencil grips and similar tools can help children control their writing tools better. Often, children are also given extra time at school when they write tests.

Dyscalculia

dyscalculia an unusual difficulty in math performance, particularly representing and processing numbers despite normal intelligence.

Dyscalculia is also called *specific math disability*. Children with dyscalculia have an unusual difficulty performing in math despite normal intelligence (Shalev & Gross-Tsur, 2001). Preschoolers might have trouble learning how to count and may not understand the meaning of numbers. In elementary school, children with dyscalculia have difficulties learning math facts, using signs like "+" and "−" the right way, or moving on from finger counting to more advanced strategies of mental math. These difficulties make performing math in their later school years challenging as well (Understood, 2020). Between 3 and 7% of children are affected by dyscalculia (Haberstroh & Schulte-Körne, 2019).

Children can be supported in learning math by using visualization tools like blocks and number lines. Older children can benefit from the use of calculators and math apps. Often, they are given extra time for exams that involve numbers and math (Delgado et al., 2019; Monei & Pedro, 2017).

Special Education Services for Children with Learning Disabilities

Before 1975, the services that students with disabilities received from their schools varied significantly from state to state and even from one school district to another. Children with disabilities often were either refused enrollment in public schools or they did not get the services they needed (Griffith, 2015).

In 1975, a law that would eventually be called the Individuals with Disabilities Education Act (IDEA) stipulated that children with one of 13 disabilities specified by IDEA have a right to special education—that is, to free and appropriate education in public schools. These disabilities include not just the learning disabilities discussed above but also conditions like ASD, impairments of hearing or vision, and intellectual disabilities (Butrymowicz & Mader, 2017; U.S. Department of Education, 2006).

The number of children receiving special education services has remained relatively steady at around 14% of all children enrolled in public schools (National Center for Education Statistics, 2022). Learning disabilities make up the biggest group of children receiving special education services (34%) (FIGURE 11.7).

The cost to educate a special education student depends on the specific issues facing the child. Children who require speech therapy because of speech or language impairments may incur significantly fewer expenses than children with ASD, for example. But to give you an idea, in 2019 in California, the per-student cost of public education for a child with one or more disabilities was around $26,000, compared with roughly $9,000 for a student without disabilities (Freedberg, 2019; Kocivar, 2020).

An Individualized Education Program (IEP) can help a child with special requirements achieve the best learning outcomes by setting reasonable learning goals for the child. IEPs also specify the services that are provided by the school district.

The roadmap to an IEP is as follows. Once parents or educators suspect that a child needs special education services, the child needs to be evaluated to determine their eligibility for special education services under IDEA. If they are deemed eligible, an IEP will be written for the child. IEPs also specify the services that are provided by the school district. The child's progress is measured, and the IEP is reviewed at least once a year. Additionally, the child must be reevaluated at least every 3 years.

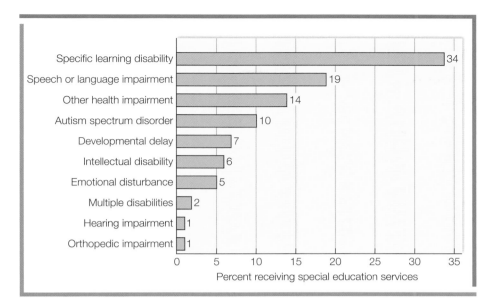

FIGURE 11.7 Children with specific learning disabilities are by far the largest group receiving special education services.

Data from U.S. Department of Education. 2021. Office of Special Education Programs, Individuals with Disabilities Education Act (IDEA) database. https://nces.ed.gov

IDEA also mandates that children be educated in the **least restrictive environment (LRE)**—that is, in a setting that is as similar as possible to that of students with no disabilities. This has led to efforts of *inclusion*, where children who are **neurodiverse** are educated in classrooms with **neurotypical** children as much as possible. For example, in our local school district children with a wide range of neurodiversity including Down syndrome and ASD spend most of their day in regular classrooms. They have an aide by their side who assists the children as needed or might provide exercises that are developmentally appropriate if the students cannot perform at grade level.

Nationwide, the number of students with disabilities included in general classrooms is on the rise: The percentage of students with IEPs who spent the majority of their school day in general classes rose from 47% in 2000 to 63% in 2017 (National Center for Education Statistics, 2019).

least restrictive environment (LRE) the idea that children with disabilities should spend as much time of their school day as possible in a classroom with children who do not receive special education services.

neurodiverse showing atypical patterns of thought or behavior, such as those associated with autism spectrum disorder.

neurotypical having or showing conventional patterns of thought and behavior.

■ In inclusive classrooms, children of all ability levels are taught together. Children who are neurodiverse may have a special tutor or aide by their side to assist them when necessary.

■ ## What's It Like ...

Living with Autism Spectrum Disorder

Marilyn, mother of Joey (12)

My son Joey was diagnosed with autism spectrum disorder (ASD) at the age of 3. ASD looks very different in every person, and some children diagnosed with ASD are only lightly affected. Joey is severely affected: He has significant cognitive challenges and does not speak, and requires care around the clock with no break.

Joey developed normally as a baby until he was around 2 years old. He was very bright—he memorized books and easily recited them back to us—and he talked a lot, more than most children his age. But at the same time, he didn't appear comfortable interacting with others, including us.

During a routine well-child visit, the pediatrician expressed concern because, while Joey was talking a lot, he was not speaking clearly. Joey was referred for a detailed evaluation, which led to some further visits with specialists. But we were confused: Why was he getting so many services just because of his speech? We didn't get clear answers from anyone until he was officially diagnosed with ASD.

I learned from an ASD parents group that you could get someone to come to your house to do ABA (applied behavior analysis) for up to 40 hours per week. It took a lot of negotiation and advocacy, but eventually that service was provided.

Joey was enrolled in an ABA-based program for his first 5 years of school. He wasn't ready to attend a regular school, because he needed to be taught basic behaviors like sitting still and paying attention. ABA was basically life-skills training. After 5 years of ABA we felt he was ready to be integrated into the public school system, so he joined the local elementary school for fifth grade.

It was very important to us that Joey attend the same school as his peers. How would he ever learn to interact with others and become independent if he never got to interact with non-ASD kids his age? None of the adults in Joey's life connect with him the way his peers do: They have been very accepting and supportive, and being at the new school has really helped with his language skills.

Still, the transition to elementary school hasn't been easy. Joey has a team of therapists there to help him, and he has an aide who assists him throughout the school day. But he's not allowed to do many of the things other kids his age do, and that should be part of any child's life. For example, he is not allowed to walk to the school's central bus terminal at the end of the day, not even with his aide. He is also not allowed to carry his laptop or use a locker. I often see people do things for him—not because he can't do them, but because it's easier that way, and they want to be helpful. But we worry that he won't learn the skills to be independent if he's not allowed to do things for himself.

Joey's condition has also very much impacted our family. Our life pretty much revolves around his needs. I cannot work because I always need to be on call in case something goes wrong. At least once a week I get a call and need to go in and get him from school, or he has an appointment during the school day. We are always waiting for the next crisis, so it's very stressful. My husband needs to support me once he gets home in the afternoon and thus has not been able to put in the work hours to advance in his career as he would have liked to. And of course, it's hard to spend as much time with Joey's older brother as we would ideally like to.

Liam (15), brother of Joey

I'm not that much older than Joey, so I don't even remember the time that Joey was not around. Sometimes it's hard having him as a brother. Like, for example, there are some things we can't do because of him. When I have a trumpet recital, I've never had both of my parents attend because Joey just can't sit through the recital. Or it's hard going to the supermarket because he gets agitated if there's a long line at the checkout. Also, what I don't like is when people come up to me and say "Oh, what a great brother you have"—they have no idea how hard it can be at times.

But at the same time, I really like to hang out with Joey. It's fun with him. We have that sofa in the basement that is super soft with lots of pillows, and we love spending time there.

In those moments it doesn't matter to me that he can't really speak. He's my brother, just like anyone else may have a brother or sister.

There's a special lunch club at our school that meets once a week. It's kind of like a counseling group for siblings. We can hang out together during lunch break. I like that a lot. It's nice to connect with other kids who also have siblings with challenges and talk about what it's like. It makes me feel like I'm not alone.

Gifted Education

Gifted students perform, or have the ability to perform, at a higher level than average children the same age. Gifted children are found among all ethnic groups and among households with low or high incomes. However, children from minorities tend to be underrepresented in gifted programs because they are often not tested for giftedness. Schools using universal screenings of all students have a larger number of minority students in their gifted programs (National Association for Gifted Children, 2019).

Some gifted students may also be affected by a learning or physical difference. For example, they may have dyslexia or ADHD. These children are often called *twice exceptional*, referring to both their giftedness and the difference they have. This often creates difficulties in identification of these students because their giftedness may conceal their learning disability, or vice versa (Amran & Majid, 2019). Twice-exceptional children are often in need of interventions for their learning disability as well as for the area of their giftedness.

But how is giftedness defined at all? Traditionally, children with an IQ of around 130 or higher have been designated as gifted. But there is more to giftedness than a high IQ. In Joesph Renzulli's model, gifted children not only have general or specific abilities that are above average compared with other children their age, but they also exhibit high levels of creativity and motivation (Renzulli, 2016). Robert Sternberg argues that gifted children have exceptionally high levels of intelligence, creativity, and wisdom (Sternberg, 2003; Sternberg & Kaufman, 2018).

Most states in the United States have adopted broader definitions of giftedness that include areas like creativity and artistic skills, though the definitions vary from state to state (McClain & Pfeiffer, 2012). In the 2011–12 school year, there were around 3.2 million children in the gifted programs of public schools in the United States (National Association for Gifted Children, 2022).

If gifted children are not sufficiently challenged at school, they may become bored, disruptive in class, and unable achieve to the level of which they are capable (Betts, 2004; Murdock-Smith, 2013). Interventions for gifted children are mostly twofold. Children can receive accelerated instruction in areas in which they excel, which means that they are otherwise instructed at grade level and as such are allowed to remain with their peers.

Alternatively, children can skip one or more grades and are thus placed in groups with older children. Even though fears persist that acceleration may have a negative impact on children's emotional development, research shows that it has academic and, to a smaller extent, also social and emotional benefits (Assouline et al., 2014; Elliott & Resing, 2020; Zeidner, 2017).

Review!

What is ADHD, and what is its effect on children's lives?

- Children with ADHD have trouble paying attention. They are often more restless than other children and struggle with impulse control. These characteristics lead them sometimes to make careless mistakes. They also have trouble finishing even routine tasks, causing them to struggle with their academic work. Many also have behavioral problems at home and at school, which means they often have fewer friends than other children and are less socially active.

■ Almost 10% of children in the United States have been diagnosed with ADHD. While there is no cure for ADHD, children often receive stimulant medication to control their symptoms, sometimes combined with other methods like cognitive behavioral therapy. Children are also often eligible for extra support at school.

Name and explain some learning disabilities and how affected students can be supported.

■ In *dyslexia*, children do not spell and read as well as could be expected given their age and intelligence. Dyslexia is one of the most common learning disabilities.

■ In *dysgraphia*, children's writing is distorted or incorrect, and they may have trouble holding their writing tools in a functional way.

■ Children with *dyscalculia* have difficulty learning their math facts, performing mental math, or using arithmetic signs correctly.

■ Children affected by these and other learning disabilities are eligible for special education services in U.S. public schools. Special education caters to their specific needs and helps them achieve the best learning outcomes. To achieve this, they receive Individualized Education Programs (IEPs) that specify reasonable learning goals and the services that will be provided to the child.

What is giftedness, and how can gifted children be accommodated in the classroom?

■ There is no one definition of giftedness. Beyond merely including children who have an IQ of 130 and higher, states have adopted broader definitions of giftedness that also include creativity and artistic skills, for example.

■ Renzulli argues that gifted children have general or specific abilities above average, as well as high motivation and creativity. Sternberg suggests that giftedness includes components of high levels of intelligence as well as creativity and wisdom.

Practice!

1. Children with attention-deficit/hyperactivity disorder (ADHD) tend to _____ .
   a. sit in class without any movement, showing no sign of participation
   b. think too much before they act
   c. have trouble paying attention
   d. be very popular among their peers

2. _____ % of people in the United States are affected by dyslexia.
   a. Between 5 and 10
   b. Between 10 and 20
   c. Between 20 and 30
   d. Between 30 and 40

3. Children with dyscalculia have difficulty _____ .
   a. concentrating in class
   b. holding their pencil correctly
   c. associating sounds with letter combinations
   d. learning math facts

4. The least restrictive learning environment is a term that means that children with disabilities should _____ .
   a. not be physically punished in school
   b. be taught in a setting that is as similar as possible to that of students with no disabilities
   c. be taught outside the classroom in fresh air as much as possible
   d. be placed in one class together so their lessons can be targeted to their weaknesses

Act It Out!

You are a pediatric nurse at the local pediatrician's office. You are seeing a mother and her 9-year-old son who has recently been diagnosed with ADHD. The mother is exhausted from the difficulties her son is experiencing at school coupled with his behavioral issues at home. These issues seem to be growing worse by the day. Have a conversation with her, and explain what the treatment options and outlook are. Don't forget to mention options to help her cope as a parent.

Children at play—6 months later

The weather has changed, and a hot summer has given way to a cold, wet fall. Melinda and Sean are happily taking advantage of the rare sunshine and are playing outside their house. After a long summer during which they were confined to their house, with no traveling and no summer camps, school started again a few weeks ago. Both children were happy to see their friends again and resume their old routines.

Sean has taken up basketball again, and this time his sister has joined him. Their local basketball club offers co-ed basketball training, and both children enjoy participating together. A year ago, Melinda would have never thought it possible that she would play basketball one day, and even have fun doing it. But their forced home quarantine made both children (as well as their parents) reconsider their likes and dislikes and inspired them to find new ways to enjoy being together. ■ ■

© https://istock.com/Georgijevic

Overview

Cognitive Development in Middle Childhood

Children at school

Nine-year-old Brian has not been enjoying third grade. He always loved going to school, but this year he is really struggling with math. In fact, he dreads the daily math units so much that his entire school days are overshadowed by what he calls his "math-phobia." He particularly struggles with fractions. He complains frequently to his mom, Claudia, that these concepts don't even have any practical meaning to him. "When am I ever going to need to know this!" he will sometimes exclaim in frustration. If it weren't for his "math-phobia," Brian would be doing well. He likes English and social science, and two of his classmates are really good friends.

Claudia's friend Mariella is struggling with a different issue. She and her husband have raised their 11-year-old twins, Sam and Isabella, to be bilingual: From the time they started talking, they have been able to speak both English and Spanish, Mariella's native language. Now that they are older, Mariella has tried to devote a few minutes each day to more formal instruction, teaching them to read and write in Spanish. But the growing amount of homework leaves little time for Mariella's Spanish lessons, and in addition, the twins now often switch to English when Mariella addresses them in Spanish; it's just easier for them to use the language they use at school. Though the novelty of having a second language has worn off for the twins, Mariella feels that being fluent in more than one language is a valuable asset, and she is afraid the twins are losing whatever Spanish skills they have gained.

In middle childhood, children and their parents face new challenges. But the cognitive changes behind Brian's struggle with math and Sam and Isabella's disinterest in their second language are not uncommon. In this chapter, we will learn more about progress in children's thinking as they enter Piaget's concrete operational phase. We will also discuss changes in children's ability to use and analyze language. We will discuss what intelligence is, why it is important, and what influences intelligence, as well as take a closer look at how online schooling and assistive technologies influence children's learning.

12.1 Changes in Children's Thinking

- Tell how Piaget characterizes the thinking of children in middle childhood in the third stage of his theory of cognitive development.
- Explain how attention, memory, and thinking skills evolve in middle childhood.

conservation knowledge that when you change the physical appearance of something, its properties like mass, number, and weight do not necessarily change as well.

reversibility the principle that actions like changing an object's shape or rearranging objects cannot be undone or reversed.

seriation the ability to order objects along a quantitative dimension such as length or weight.

In Chapter 9, we looked at the cognitive changes children undergo in the preoperational stage, the second of Jean Piaget's four stages of cognitive development. Children at that stage do not understand the principles of **conservation** and **reversibility** (see also Chapter 9). Imagine you set out a neat row of eight pennies on a table. Then, in front of an audience of 5- and 6-year-olds, you changed the arrangement of those pennies so that they formed a longer line. Preoperational children would not understand that changing the appearance of an object or set of objects does not necessarily change other characteristics of the set, like the number of pennies making up the line. Learning reversibility—the idea that you can restore the pennies to their original neat row—helps children learn conservation. In this chapter, we will discuss the third stage of Piaget's theory—the concrete operational stage—in which children first develop capabilities to think logically.

Piaget: The Concrete Operational Child

At around the age of 7, children move from the preoperational stage to Piaget's third stage: the concrete operational stage. They will remain in this stage until about age 11. It is during this time that children first start to think logically, which helps them to understand concepts like reversibility and conservation. However, children's logical thinking is limited to "concrete" real-world situations. This is why fractions are so hard for children like Brian to understand: They are abstract and don't make much sense to children of this age, unless they are presented in terms of pizza slices or Lego bricks that children can see and handle.

Children in Piaget's concrete operational stage are now also able to take the perspective of others and consider more than one aspect of a situation—that is, they are able to *decenter*. This ability, together with the understanding of conservation and reversibility, helps children successfully complete a number of tasks they could not complete at a younger age. In the sections that follow, we will learn more about the new abilities that define Piaget's concrete operational stage.

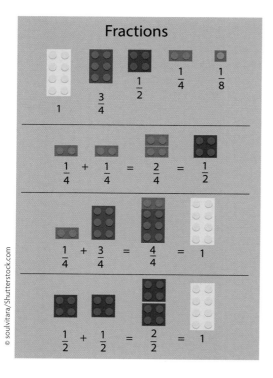

Fractions

- Abstract fractions are often hard to understand for children in the concrete operational stage. It doesn't make sense to them that a fraction with a higher denominator (like $1/12$) represents a smaller amount than a fraction with a lower denominator (like $1/3$). Schools often use examples like pizza and cake slices to help children understand the concept of fractions. But ultimately, children will only truly understand these concepts when they are ready.

Concrete operational children begin to think about the relationships between objects

Concrete operational children are able to understand the concept of *class inclusion* (see also Chapter 9). That is, they understand that objects can belong to more than one group at once. If you show children in this stage an image of brown teddy bears and white teddy bears, they likely will be able to correctly tell you whether there are more teddy bears or white teddy bears. This is because they now understand that white teddy bears form a subgroup of the group "teddy bears." Likewise, they can now understand complex systems like family trees and that a person can be a mother and a daughter at the same time.

Children are increasingly able to sort objects along more than one dimension. Brian can sort his beloved dinosaur collection not only by size, but also by size *and* color (**FIGURE 12.1**). This ability to order objects along a dimension is called **seriation** (**FIGURE 12.2**). Piaget actually tested children's ability to sort objects in a number of ways. For example, Piaget presented children with 49 leaves of different sizes and shades. Thus, they could be ordered in a grid along two different dimensions: lightness and size (Inhelder et al., 1964). Before they reach the concrete operational stage, children are not able to sort according to two different dimensions.

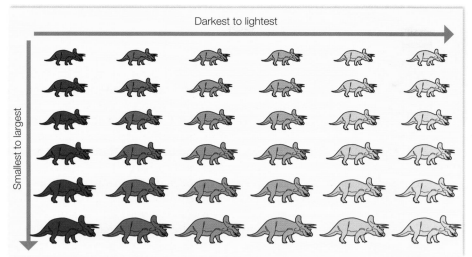

Darkest to lightest

Smallest to largest

FIGURE 12.1 Having reached concrete operational stage, 9-year-old Brian can sort images of dinosaurs in two dimensions, by size and shade.

After S. A. Rathus. 2016. *Childhood and Adolescence: Voyages in Development*, 6th ed. Cengage, Boston

But the relationships among objects also can be used for reasoning. Think about the ages of three different friends, for example. If Sam is older than Brian, and Brian is older than Marcus, then we can conclude that Sam is older than Marcus. Or, in more abstract terms, if A is greater than B, and B is greater than C, then we also know that A is greater than C. This principle is called **transitivity**, and it is acquired during the concrete operational stage.

> **transitivity** the principle that it is possible to infer the relationship between two objects by knowing the relationship each of these objects has with a third object.

Children learn complex numbers and math

The reasoning skills children develop also help them understand mathematical principles better. In the late elementary school years, math facts generally do not have to be memorized anymore, but children start to see relations between the numbers. For example, they now understand that, since 8 + 7 = 15, 15 − 7 must be 8 (*reversibility*). They also understand that 8 is more than 7 (*seriation*) and that all numbers from 400 to 499 are in the 400s (*classification*).

Fractions are typically first taught in third grade, and just like Brian, many children have trouble understanding that ⅓ is more than ⅛ (Gabriel, 2016). Children often benefit from concrete examples or by playing games in which they have to divide objects like cake or bread evenly between a number of children (Empson, 1995; Gabriel et al., 2012).

In the concrete operational stage, children's ability to place numbers on number lines improves as well. When presented with a set of numbers from 1 to 100 to place on a number line, children around age 6 overestimate the distances between lower numbers and underestimate the distances between higher numbers (Siegler & Booth, 2004). For example, they place the numbers 8 and 20 very far apart from each but place the numbers 80 and 92 closer together, even though both number pairs have the same distance from each other. By the time the children are 8 years old, their estimates in placing the numbers on the number line are a lot more accurate.

Children in middle childhood learn math outside the classroom as well. They may instinctively count objects they see on the way to school or on the playground, and parents may turn routine activities into opportunities to practice. ("You've collected eight rocks. How many will you have left if you give me two?") Children from lower socioeconomic status (SES) families tend to have fewer of these math opportunities outside of the classroom, which makes it harder for them to learn new mathematical concepts (Clements & Sarama, 2007). However, it doesn't take much practice to help them develop their number sense. One study showed that just 1 hour of playing a board game in which children rolled dice and moved forward the appropriate number of spaces on

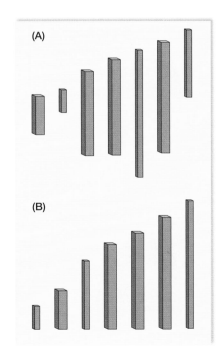

(A)

(B)

FIGURE 12.2 Another example of seriation. When attempting to sort sticks from shortest to tallest, (A) younger children may arrange them so that the top of each stick extends above the previous one regardless of actual size. (B) Children in the concrete operational stage are able to sort the sticks correctly.

■ Abstract concepts are difficult for children in the concrete operational stage to understand. For example, it is not intuitively clear to them that ¼ is more than ⅛. Helping them relate to numbers with concrete objects like fruit enables them to better understand mathematical concepts.

the board made a dramatic difference in the children's ability to place numbers on a number line (Siegler, 2009).

Evaluating Piaget's theory

In Chapters 6 and 9, we discussed some of the limitations to Piaget's theory. For example, Piaget tended to underestimate the abilities of children of a given age. Some researchers believe this is because of the way Piaget framed his tasks: The more familiar children are with a task or with materials, the more likely they are to demonstrate mastery of a skill when using those materials. In the concrete operational stage, children still need concrete objects to enable them to think logically.

Consider this famous study conducted with 12-year-old Brazilian children living on the street. The children were able to perform relatively complex math. For example, if one of their coconuts cost 35 cruzeiros, they were able to compute how much they would have to charge a customer who wanted to buy three coconuts, or five coconuts, or ten. However, when given a paper-and-pencil test of equivalent but purely arithmetical problems taken out of context, the participants solved little more than one-third of the tasks correctly (Nunes et al., 1993). The children were adept at solving practical mathematical

Piaget's Theory in Action

■ Experiencing materials, processes, concepts, and ideas themselves helps children gain a deeper understanding of what they're learning. Building houses and bridges, or scooping play dough "ice cream" with measuring spoons, lets children experience new knowledge firsthand.

There are many ways in which Piaget's theory can inspire us to improve our interactions with, and our teaching of, children. As we have seen in Brian's struggle to learn how to use fractions, children, even in late elementary school and early middle school, benefit greatly from hands-on instruction that relates new information to their lives.

Fractions can be taught in the classroom with the help of models that children can put together and take apart. But it is also important to let children discover how important fractions are in real life. They can cut up a pizza or a pie and figure out which fraction they have eaten, which fraction their siblings will get, and which fraction is left over. They can practice manipulating fractions with dry beans and measuring cups in the kitchen and help cook or bake using the fractions in the recipe.

There are many other ways hands-on learning can be integrated into school lessons or into life at home. Children can create timelines about events and history, or they can conduct experiments at home. Experiments can cover any topic of interest. For example, states of matter can be explored by freezing water in different containers with the goal of creating an ice lantern for an ice hotel. Children can also build 3D models of bridges, skyscrapers, or airplanes.

It is important to ask children at any age open-ended questions to get them thinking about topics creatively and in more depth. Brain teasers, riddles, problem-solving tasks, and logic puzzles also can help children develop their logical thinking.

Children learn through experimentation as well as through trial and error. But just like adults, a number of children are afraid of failure and shy away from some kinds of challenges. For that reason, teachers and parents should continually emphasize that mistakes are a natural part of learning and thus should be welcomed rather than avoided.

problems in their head, but they did not show the same degree of proficiency when performing arithmetic operations on paper because it was unfamiliar to them and not part of their regular experience.

Despite the fact that this and other research has shown that Piaget may have underestimated children's abilities, his theories continue to influence current research. The surprising results of one study show that twenty-first-century children may actually go through Piaget's stages at a later age than they did about 3 decades earlier (**FIGURE 12.3**). When presented with conservation tasks that involved weight and volume, students in 2003 were up to 3 years behind students tested in 1976 (Shayer et al., 2007). These results leave us wondering whether schools today place too much emphasis on pure academics instead of giving children the chance to learn through hands-on experiences.

Vygotsky's Theory in Elementary School

Lev Vygotsky believed that children learn first and foremost through their interactions with others. Depending on the culture in which a child grows up, different skills and abilities will be valued and acquired. Being able to tell apart different plants may be of lesser importance to North American children than it is to children living in rural parts of Africa or tropical regions of the Amazon, where knowledge of local plants may be crucial to their survival.

Vygotsky furthermore created the concept of the *zone of proximal development*. He suggested that children learn most successfully if they have to stretch their abilities and work on a skill that is just beyond their reach but is attainable with some assistance from others (which Vygotsky called *scaffolding*).

Vygotksy recognized that children learn at different paces and in different ways. For that reason, a teacher may engage with a child in *assisted discovery*, in which the teacher guides learning by adjusting the material to the child's zone of proximal development (Alfieri et al., 2011). In Chapter 9, we considered how to identify a child's zone of proximal development and use it to give adequate assistance for learning.

Reciprocal teaching is a method to improve reading comprehension in small-group settings. It consists of four steps:

- *Questioning*: After reading the text for a first time, the teacher starts to ask questions. Students answer, and possibly raise other questions.
- *Summarizing*: Students summarize the text.
- *Clarifying*: The group clarifies any passages or points that someone has not understood.
- *Predicting*: Finally, the students predict what will happen next.

By following these steps, students become increasingly adept at regulating their own reading process, improving their

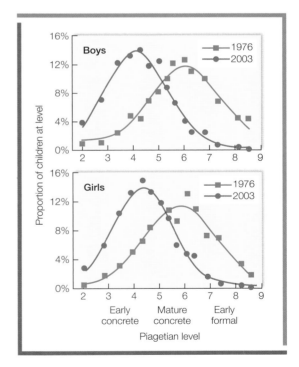

FIGURE 12.3 Comparison of performance for boys and girls on Volume & Heaviness, 1976 and 2003. The performance of children aged 11–12 on the Piagetian Volume & Heaviness test shows that children in 1976 were, on average, at a higher level in terms of Piaget's developmental stages than were children in 2003. Children's development was delayed by 2–3 years compared with 27 years earlier.

After M. Shayer. 2007. *Br J Educ Psychol* 77: 25–41. © The British Psychological Society

comprehension, and assisting others (Spörer et al., 2009). They move through their zone of proximal development and gradually become able to read and understand better, extending their reading proficiency.

Interacting with others by playing educational games can also foster children's learning. In the process of playing, children not only learn new things, but they also learn how to cooperate with others, how to play by rules or potentially to negotiate rules, and how to win and lose (Deater-Deckard et al., 2013; Garzotto, 2007).

Information-Processing Approaches

Isabella is sitting in math class, where her teacher is explaining the concept of decimal numbers. But Isabella's mind is not on ratios. She is thinking about her upcoming playdate with her friend Khalia and how much she is looking forward to showing her friend the new game she just received for her birthday. Later that day, she is stewing over her math homework and wishing she had paid better attention in class that morning.

All of us, regardless of age, experience moments where our attention fails us, but younger children are especially prone to lapses in attention. As we will see in this section, it is in middle childhood that children learn to focus successfully. Later in this section we will consider how children's memory and thinking changes in middle childhood, as well as their ability to reflect on their thinking processes.

Children learn how to ignore distractions

One major element of learning in both children and adults is the ability to pay attention. Young children have a notoriously hard time paying attention to anything for a long stretch of time, and they get distracted very quickly. For example, preschoolers and early elementary school children may have trouble listening to their teacher, and their focus can be pulled away by another child nearby sneezing, by someone cracking a joke, or by something going on outside the classroom window. By second or third grade, children start to be able to focus more on the presentation (or problem) at hand and do not get sidetracked as easily anymore.

selective attention the capacity to focus on just one stimulus at a time while suppressing distractions.

The ability to focus on just one stimulus is called **selective attention**, and it plays an important part in children's academic achievement. After all, students need to pay attention in the classroom or when doing homework in order to master the material (Stevens & Bavelier, 2012). Two areas of the brain that are particularly involved in selective attention are the prefrontal and parietal areas. Researchers suspect that children's increasing ability to focus and block out distractions may have to do with the maturation of these brain areas as children get older (Stevens & Bavelier, 2012).

Fortunately, there are ways in which we can improve our selective attention. Studies have shown that physical activities such as yoga can improve selective attention (Janssen et al., 2014; Ma et al., 2015). Mindfulness activities teach children to attend carefully to the present moment and not to get distracted by other, irrelevant stimuli or events (Tarrasch, 2018).

Children's memory improves

When you speak with children of various ages, you will quickly notice that their memory differs, depending on their age. Take, for example, 9-year-old Brian, who recently visited the zoo with his 3-year-old cousin, Suzi. Brian can remember the day of the week and time they went, and he also remembers a great deal of information about the different animals they saw. To Suzi, it doesn't matter which day of the week it is. She does remember quite well which animals they saw, but her recollection of information is much less detailed than Brian's—she remembers the dirty fur of the polar bears, but not much detail about their arctic habitat or their diet.

One reason for the difference in their memory performance is that Brian has a lot more background knowledge than Suzi. He knows that some animals are predators whereas others are prey for those predators and that some animals are mammals and others are reptiles. His knowledge helps Brian organize what he sees and learns, and the connections he makes to prior knowledge allow him to remember more efficiently what he saw. Brian has several advantages over his cousin Suzi: Not only does his memory have a greater capacity, but he also has at his disposal a variety of strategies he can use if he wants to commit something to memory.

■ In the late elementary school years, children get better at focusing on their classwork, even as distractions are going on around them.

WORKING MEMORY   As we discussed in Chapter 9, *working memory* holds information only for a short time span of a few seconds. The information is then either lost or transferred to long-term memory.

Two-year-olds can hold about two digits in their working memory. By 7 years of age, children already can hold five digits in their working memory—not much less than adults, who can hold an average seven digits (Dempster, 1981). One component that influences working memory is processing speed. Children in early elementary school have a slower processing speed than adults have; without these differences in processing speed, they would have a working memory span quite similar to that of adults (Schneider, 2011).

Working memory is important for, and predicts, children's school performance in several ways (Constantinidis & Klingberg, 2016). Children need working memory to remember instructions, particularly when instructions are more complex and consist of several steps. Children also need their working memory when doing mental math. To solve an addition problem like 346 + 87, they may first add the tens to 346 and then the ones. Before adding the ones, they have to keep in mind the result of 346 + 80; then, they have to remember how many ones to add. If they get lost anywhere in the process, the result of their calculation will not be correct. Likewise, when learning to read, children need to remember the sounds of letters long enough to sound out the entire word.

There are a number of signs that indicate children may have issues with their working memory, including:

- not being able to recall multistep directions,
- having trouble staying on topic in conversations,
- having issues with reading comprehension,
- forgetting what they wanted to say if they don't get a turn to speak right away,

- misplacing items,
- having trouble calculating solutions to math problems with several steps, and
- having memory issues.

Fortunately, there are also a number of strategies children, parents, and teachers can use to help improve children's working memory (**TABLE 12.1**).

USING STRATEGIES TO ENHANCE MEMORY Life is full of things that need to be memorized, and that is particularly true in the lives of students. We already have discussed strategies to improve children's working memory. But there are also specific techniques that help us remember important facts or things we need to do. Sometimes, these techniques are referred to as *mnemonic devices*.

Think about your own life: What do you do in order to prepare for a written exam? You probably have quite a few ways to make sure you're prepared as best as you can be. You may write summaries for yourself of important sections of the text or lecture, you may make lists of points you'd like to remember, or you may repeat some facts to yourself for long enough that you can remember them. These strategies help you achieve your goal.

Researchers distinguish a number of different strategies to enhance memory. One of these is the use of **external memory aids**. These aids involve the use of something in your environment to make you remember. You may make a shopping list to remember the items you need to buy at the supermarket. You probably use a calendar on your phone for important appointments and dates. You may use colorful sticky notes to remind you of tasks you need to complete.

But there are other strategies you can use as well (**TABLE 12.2**). Four of the more common strategies are rehearsal, organization, elaboration, and imagery. In **rehearsal**, you repeat some facts over and over again. This is a useful way to remember phone numbers, for example. In **organization**, you group items into categories that help you retrieve the items from memory. For example, when

external memory aids strategies that use cues from the environment to aid memory.

rehearsal memory strategy: mental repetition of items or information.

organization memory strategy: grouping of items into different categories.

■ **Table 12.1** Strategies to Help Children Improve Working Memory

At Home	At School
Strategies to improve memory	
Teach visualization skills: Children can remember better if they visualize what they need to do or if they rehearse.	Give children checklists that spell out what needs to be done to complete an assignment.
Play games that train children's memory (like "Memory," or finding cities beginning with the letter "A") or that teach them to adhere to rules.	Write down homework assignments.
Let children explain what they learned.	Remind children of due dates.
Teach children to create connections between material to be learned and what they already know.	Teach by interacting with the children.
	Use routines in the classroom.
Strategies to improve daily routines	
Provide checklists for routines, such as how to get ready for school in the morning.	
Provide places to keep important items together, for example, a dedicated space for coat, mittens, boots, and hats, or a place where all school materials are kept.	
Minimize distractions by turning off electronic devices and TV.	

remembering plants in the new school garden, you first can think of plants that are vegetables and then about plants that are fruits. In **elaboration**, you process information in a deeper way. To remember facts about the composer Beethoven and his works, for example, you may think about the symphony you recently heard, the composer's deafness, and some musical concepts you learned in your piano lessons. In **imagery**, you create mental images that help you remember facts or items. To remember the items you were sent to purchase, you may imagine a cheese stick captain sitting in a coconut boat floating on a lake of milk.

elaboration memory strategy: processing of information and embedding it into prior knowledge.

imagery memory strategy: creation of a mental image to aid retrieval of information.

■ **Table 12.2** Memory Strategies

Rehearsal	Age		
Repeating items over and over again	Children below age 7 do not use rehearsal without instruction and may not always benefit from rehearsal even when instructed to rehearse (Lehman, 2015; Miller et al., 2015).		Matteo has to practice math facts many times until he can remember them.
Organization	**Age**		
Grouping items into different categories or by a certain principle	Children start to use organization as an effective strategy at around the age of 11 (Bjorklund et al., 1997).		Miriam groups shopping items into categories like vegetables, fruits, and dairy so she can remember them more easily.
Elaboration	**Age**		
Thinking about information in a deeper way and embedding it into existing knowledge	Elementary school children can benefit from elaboration, but only older children use the strategy spontaneously (Schneider et al., 2004; Willoughby et al., 1999).		Malia can remember more facts about bald eagles than her toddler sister Arun because she knows more about birds of prey and birds in general and has embedded the facts about bald eagles into her existing knowledge.
Imagery	**Age**		
Creating mental images	Children around age 12 can use this strategy successfully; younger children do not benefit as much even when instructed to use this strategy (Willoughby et al., 1999).		Rosa wants to tell her abuelo about her violin lesson and the funny thing that happened during lunch. To remember, she thinks about a banana playing a violin.
External memory aids	**Age**		
Using cues from the environment to remember	Children throughout middle childhood can benefit from this strategy. Independent use increases as children grow older (Izawa, 2014).		Julian keeps sticky notes to remind him of homework assignments.

CULTURAL DIFFERENCES   National and ethnic cultural groups differ dramatically in the way their members perceive the world. In Western cultures, people tend to focus on their personal abilities and skills as well as on objects around them. So, when asked to describe themselves, an American child might say, "I am a good piano player." In Eastern cultures, people often emphasize the context of what they see as well as the groups they belong to (Gutchess & Indeck, 2009). A Chinese child describing themselves might say something like, "I am an older sister to two brothers."

Children's culture influences how they perceive the world: It's like a filter for incoming information about the world around them. If children focus their attention on different things, different things will be processed and transferred into their long-term memory (Gutchess & Indeck, 2009; Ross & Wang, 2010).

Culture also influences the age from which a person can recall their first childhood memory. Of course, there are individual differences, but the general tendency is clear. Maori natives from New Zealand have childhood memories that reach back, on average, to 32 months. The first remembered childhood event for New Zealanders of European background tends to be around 42 months and around 57 months for those of Asian descent. Researchers believe that one factor behind these differences is the elaborative styles of cultures. The Maori culture places great importance on an individual's as well as their family's past (MacDonald et al., 2000; Mullen & Yi, 1995). Parents of European background tend to put more of an emphasis on past events and thus discuss them in more detail with children, inviting children to participate in discussion. Parents of Asian background tend to talk less about past events and ask more closed-ended questions (Wang et al., 2000).

We cannot conclude from these results that people of Asian and European descent have poorer memories than those of Maori New Zealanders. Rather, the results show that for different cultures, different things are important. The significance of past events differs from culture to culture. Children will remember what is important to them, but the culture in which they are raised will play a large role in determining what kinds of events children consider important (Wang et al., 2000).

■ Children's culture influences what and how they remember events from their past. When thinking back to the first event they can remember from their childhood, Asians' memories tend to be from a somewhat later time than those of people of European backgrounds (MacDonald et al., 2000; Mullen & Yi, 1995).

Thinking

All of the processes described above are regulated by the part of the brain known as the central executive (see also Chapter 9). The central executive helps children set goals, create plans for achieving those goals, stay on task when distractions arise, and react in a flexible way when challenges arise (Chang, 2019). A significant improvement in executive functioning happens during the preschool years, but we also can see major improvements during the elementary school years (Gunzenhauser et al., 2017).

Executive function develops throughout childhood and improves as the brain develops and connections between neurons are pruned (Perone et al., 2018; Riggs et al., 2006). Throughout middle childhood, children's behavior reflects changes in executive functioning. In the beginning, children may cram for tests at the last minute, or possibly only at the insistence of their parents. As they get older, they begin to understand the process of planning for tests better and start to prepare earlier. Additionally, children are increasingly able to shut out distractions when studying or to deliberately choose studying over playing video games with a friend, thus keeping their goals in mind as they make decisions (Chevalier & Blaye, 2009). Instead of solely reacting to changes and events in their environment, children begin to predict and foresee challenges that may impede their goal achievement. The children proactively work to remove these challenges (Munakata et al., 2012, 2013).

Children with better executive functioning tend to fare better academically and go on to have better health and more income in adulthood (Moffitt, 2012; Moffitt et al., 2011). Children from more educated families have better inhibitory control—that is, they can inhibit their responses more efficiently—and cognitive flexibility (Gunzenhauser et al., 2017).

Training can improve executive function. The most effective training programs do not focus just on executive function components but rather on addressing the whole child, including social and emotional development as well as physical fitness (Diamond, 2012; Ma et al., 2015). For example, a number of school curricula have been shown to improve children's executive functioning. These curricula do not only train children's executive function but also reduce stress through hands-on activities that engage children in interaction with each other (Diamond et al., 2007; Lillard & Else-Quest, 2006).

Metacognition

There is yet another factor that helps children think and accomplish their goals: It is an awareness and understanding of their own thought processes, also called **metacognition**. It is immensely helpful in everyday life to have an understanding of how your mind works.

You likely realize that if you want to remember a phone number, it's best to write it down somewhere or to repeat it several times in your mind to increase the chances you'll remember it. You are using some of the memory strategies we have discussed above. If you are preparing for an exam, you'll likely make a plan that includes getting an overview of the material, deciding how many days it will take you to learn the material, testing yourself from time to time to see how you're doing, and possibly changing your plan if things don't go as expected. Young children cannot make such an elaborate plan.

Preschoolers have very little knowledge of memory strategies or insight into how their memory works. Even if young children are taught memory strategies they can use to better retain material, they tend to not apply them without prompts. Therefore, elementary school teachers should remind students to use memory strategies. In the preschool or early middle childhood years, children also often do not transfer the use of memory strategies they know to other situations they have not encountered before (Karably & Zabrucky, 2017; Schneider, 1985).

Throughout middle childhood, children start to understand how memory strategies work and how they can best be used (Moore et al., 2018; Schneider, 2008). However, children continue to develop their knowledge about memory past middle childhood and even adolescence. Studies have shown that even young adults are not aware of some potent memory strategies when asked to read and memorize written material (Garner, 1987; Presley & Afflerbach, 1995).

It isn't that young children do not employ any strategies at all. For example, some 4- and 5-year-olds who were asked to remember pictures may name the items they see to help them remember those pictures (Henry, 1996). Likewise, children who were asked to remember toys in one study played much less with

metacognition awareness, understanding, and control of one's own thought processes.

© iStock.com/SeventyFour

■ Being aware of how our mind and memory work helps us to create and use strategies in order to remember important information.

the toys than children who were not asked to remember the toys. Instead, they spent more time in naming and carefully examining the toys (Baker-Ward et al., 1984).

Young children have a deficit in estimating their memory abilities. For example, they have trouble in accurately determining how easy it will be for them to study and memorize materials. In one study, preschoolers were presented with a list of ten items they had to memorize. They were asked to predict how many items they would be able to recall. Most of them optimistically replied they would be able to recall all ten items. However, none of the children actually did recall all ten items (Flavell et al., 1970). Kindergarteners still tend to overestimate their performance significantly, but their estimates improve significantly in the early elementary school years (Karably & Zabrucky, 2017; Lockl & Schneider, 2002).

Information-Processing Approaches in Action

Information-processing approaches cover a broad range of topics, and so they inspire a variety of strategies to help children learn and develop.

As we have seen, having an awareness and understanding of their own mental processes is important for children and can help them accomplish tasks better and more efficiently. You can inspire thinking and insight about metacognitive issues by asking children questions about the way they think (Jacobson, 2020):

- Ask **open-ended questions** to give children the opportunity to think about why they drew a certain conclusion or made a particular decision and what supports that conclusion/decision: "Why did you make that decision?"

- Ask **questions about their own behavior** to help children reflect on why they behave in certain ways: "Why did you hit Mary when she said she didn't want to play with you?" "Why do you think you're having such a hard time finishing your homework?" "What do you think helped you do so well on this test?"

- Ask **questions that center on generating solutions**, so children are better prepared for situations the next time they come up again: "Is there another way you could react when a child doesn't want to play with you?" "Can you use what we learned this morning to help you figure out what to do next?"

- Ask **process-oriented questions** that help children figure out next steps: "What do you need to do to finish building that bridge?" "Can you think of some strategies you've used in the past to prepare for tests where you did well?"

Teaching children to think about their own thinking is important, but it is also a process that takes time. Do not expect to see immediate changes. Oftentimes, children have to be reminded of, and need to practice, skills and strategies many times before they can apply them on their own. Effective teachers not only teach children problem-solving strategies; they also remind the children when to use the strategies and how to choose the best strategy.

Children who have executive functioning issues often have trouble getting organized and staying on track with their tasks. These children can be supported by providing a number of behavior guidelines:

- Schedules or picture schedules: Schedules outline what needs to be done to get ready for school—get dressed, have breakfast, brush hair and teeth, and so on.
- Checklists: Check off any items that need to be packed for school.
- Homework contracts: Spell out when homework needs to be done (at a specific time or after dinner, for example) and which steps need to be followed.
- Behavior contracts: Which kinds of behaviors are expected and which are not acceptable. Knowing expectations helps children control their behavior and can help them work on issues like lying or aggressive behavior. Contracts should give children behavioral alternatives ("instead of hitting your sister, go to your mom and ask her to help resolve the conflict").

Review!

How does Piaget characterize the thinking of children in middle childhood?

- From around 7 to 11 years of age, children are in the third of Piaget's four stages of cognitive development: the concrete operational stage. In this stage, children start to begin to think logically, but their thinking is still constrained to real-word situations. They are now able to understand the principles of class inclusion and to understand that an object can be a member of more than one class at once. They are also able to sort objects according to one or even two criteria at the same time.
- Logical thinking shows up in children's ability to understand *transitivity* and to draw conclusions from the relationships of objects. Children's number sense and understanding of mathematical relationships and operations improves, but children benefit greatly from hands-on experiences with the material they are learning about.

How do attention, memory, and thinking change in middle childhood?

- Throughout middle childhood, children become increasingly able to filter out distractions and focus their attention (*selective attention*). Children's memory also gets better and more reliable. Their working memory at age 7 is almost as good as that of adults.

- Throughout middle childhood, children become increasingly adept at using strategies to help them retain information. However, the process of choosing adequate strategies, applying them without prompting, and actually benefitting from their use is not complete until adulthood. A number of strategies can be used, including notebooks or calendars (*external memory aids*), *rehearsal*, *organization*, *elaboration*, and *imagery*.
- People from different cultures vary in what they recall and how far back their childhood memories reach. These differences reflect the fact that cultures value different kinds of information, and children learn early on to retain those facts that are of importance to them and to those around them.
- Generally, children's thinking as reflected by their executive functioning improves over the course of middle childhood: Children start to plan and take orderly steps when trying to achieve a goal, they can correct their plans if things are not going well, and they can resume their work if they get interrupted. Children also become more aware of their thinking processes (*metacognition*), which allows them to choose adequate strategies and to take proactive action aimed at improving their behavior, thoughts, and actions.

Practice!

1. Children in the concrete operational stage can learn best by _____ .
   a. reading lots of books about the material they learn
   b. writing essays about the material they learn
   c. gaining hands-on experience with the material they learn
   d. playing instructional video games

2. Selective attention helps children _____ .
   a. divide their attention between different tasks
   b. focus on one thing while tuning out distractions

   c. choose which aspects of a situation are important to task completion
   d. complete a task step-by-step

3. Children with working memory issues _____ .
   a. tend to forget their parents' names
   b. have trouble telling colors apart
   c. find it hard to complete tasks with multiple steps
   d. tend to have trouble with toilet training

Act It Out!

Your third grade class has recently started working on time intervals in math: Children need to compute how much time passes from one point of time to another. At pickup one day, you are approached by the mother of 8-year-old Tommy. She feels her son has no concept of time whatsoever. When he is working on his math homework, he shows very little insight into how to compute time intervals. Tommy's mother is concerned that he has a math disability and is in need of special intervention. Act out a conversation between the teacher and Tommy's mother. What advice could you give his mother?

Show What You've Learned!

Ten-year-old Mabel is so forgetful, and it's driving her father crazy! It's always a scramble to get out of the house, and invariably on the trip to school Mabel will announce that she's forgotten her science homework, or that she needs her recorder, or that she thinks she may not have brushed her teeth; some days, they have to return to the house, which makes Mabel late for school and her father late for work. Drawing on the information presented in this chapter, what strategies could you design to make Mabel's mornings less of a scramble?

12.2 Changes in Children's Language

- Identify the ways in which children's language skills advance in middle childhood.
- Outline the various ways and the three cognitive processes important to how children learn to read.

Children in middle childhood generally speak fluently and can express themselves with ease. Nevertheless, language is complex. Using language correctly and with more complexity is an endeavor that will take many years of practice and instruction.

Vocabulary and Grammar

First graders understand and use thousands of words and learn more words every day. All of their interactions—conversations with adults and other children, reading, even consuming digital media—help children increase their vocabulary. The average vocabulary size of a first grader (about 6 years old) is about 14,000 words. It will increase to about 40,000 words by the time they turn 11 (Behrens, 2015).

Children in elementary school are also increasingly able to determine the meanings of new words from the contexts in which the words are used. They also can draw conclusions about word meanings from related words: For example, knowing what "sad" means can help children understand the word "sadness," even if they have never heard that word before (Larsen & Nippold, 2007; Nagy & Scott, 2000).

The development of speech sounds continues into the early years of middle childhood. By the time they enter kindergarten, children can pronounce most words correctly. However, some sounds are more troublesome than others. For example, many children do not correctly pronounce sounds like "th" (as in "the") or "zh" (as in "pleasure") until they are about 7 years old (Sander, 1972).

Children's grammatical understanding and ability to construct increasingly complex grammatical sentences improves as well. Around age 6 or 7, children start to use more conditional sentences that start with the word "if," as in "If Tommy shares his chocolate with me, then I'll let him play with my car later on" (Loban, 1976).

During the elementary school years, use of passive voice increases as well. Sentences like "Mom brought Johnny to the doctor" are more often replaced by "Johnny was brought to the doctor by his mom" (Deen et al., 2018).

Throughout middle childhood, children more frequently use metaphors like "He's got a heart of gold" or "It was raining cats and dogs" (Winner, 2017).

Metaphors can be complicated for children to understand, because the speaker says something that he does not literally mean. As a result, children have to extract the meaning from utterances where people do not actually mean what they say (Lecce et al., 2019).

Around age 9, children also start to use more advanced conjunctions like "although," "unless," and "meanwhile" in sentences like "I won't sit with Tommy anymore unless he gives me back my crayons." However, children frequently will not use these conjunctions until early adolescence (Cain et al., 2005; Loban, 1976). Children also become increasingly adept at understanding *syntax*, that is, the rules that allow us to create well-formed and correct sentences (Chomsky, 1969).

In early childhood, children show the first signs of **metalinguistic awareness**, the ability to reflect on language and its use. They start to understand that the names that are given to objects in their language are arbitrary and can be replaced by other words in another language. In middle childhood, children gain a much deeper understanding of what words are and how language is used. They begin to understand that misunderstandings can arise from a failure in communication. Thus, they are more likely to ask for clarification if they do not understand instructions. They can more easily define words and realize that an object may have more than one label. For example, the words "cat" and "kitty" can both be used to refer to a pet cat (Apperly & Robinson, 2002). Once they understand that words have more than one meaning and can be applied in different contexts, children start to delight in puns and plays on words. One example is, "What do you call an alligator in a vest? An investigator."

Six-year-old Amylha was alarmed and ready to bring her older sister Teeksha to the hospital when Teeksha dramatically announced that her heart had been broken. Amylha believed that Teeksha needed surgical intervention to fix her heart. She did not understand that people using metaphors do not literally mean what they say; it is only in middle childhood that children understand metaphors.

metalinguistic awareness the ability to reflect on language and the way it is used.

Reading

Learning to read opens a new world to children. Suddenly, they are no longer dependent on other people when they need information; they can acquire new information themselves, by reading. Reading also inspires children's creativity and imagination by transporting them into strange, new worlds. It teaches them how to behave and how not to behave: By reading about the consequences of other people's actions, they can learn from their mistakes.

Reading is a skill that comes with practice

Reading is a skill that, unlike speaking, does not come naturally to children and needs to be learned with effort. All neurotypical children learn to speak their native language fluently, but not all of them learn to read fluently in their native language.

Three factors are of particular importance when learning how to read (Hulme & Snowling, 2013):

- *Letter knowledge*: Knowledge of what different letters look like and what sounds they make allows children to sound out words and to make connections between letters and sounds. Children who know more letters at the beginning of first grade tend to be better readers at the end of the school year (Lervåg et al., 2009; Muter et al., 2004).

- *Phonemic awareness*: Phonemic awareness is the understanding that words consist of separate sounds. For example, the word "dog" consists of three different sounds. However, separating the sounds in words is a complex task for preschoolers, and few 5-year-olds can do so correctly. Phonemic awareness predicts later reading ability, however, as does the ability to detect rhymes, which is another aspect of phonemic awareness (Brunswick et al., 2012; Melby-Lervåg et al., 2012).
- *Speed of word processing*: Educators and researchers use rapid automatized-naming (RAN) tasks to assess children's ability to name, as quickly as possible, objects, colors, or symbols shown on a grid. These tasks are an indicator of the time it takes children to process words. A number of studies have shown that RAN scores correlate with children's reading ability (Henry et al., 2018; Kuperman et al., 2016; Li et al., 2011).

Up until third or fourth grade, children need to use most of their cognitive resources for the reading process itself. Therefore, they have few resources left to actually learn facts from reading. The elementary school years are devoted mostly to the teaching of reading itself, whereas in later grades, children are expected to read so fluently that they can acquire a substantial amount of information from the texts they have read.

Children who are good at reading tend to read more readily than children who have trouble reading. Thus, as children get older, the gap between good and bad readers becomes wider. In fact, a study that followed 4,000 students for several years found that children who did not read effortlessly by the end of third grade were four times more likely than good readers to drop out of school (Hernandez, 2011).

There are different approaches to reading instruction

Learning to read in English is hard, and it is harder than learning to read in some other languages, like Dutch or Spanish. On the difficulty of reading English, the Irish playwright George Bernard Shaw is said to have joked that the word "fish" could just as well be spelled "ghoti," provided you pronounce the "gh" as in "laugh," the "o" as in "women," and the "ti" as in "action."

So why is English reading so hard? The reason is that English has *deep orthography*, which means that there is not a direct correspondence between letters and sounds. Dutch, Spanish, German, and Italian, on the contrary, have *shallow orthographies*, where sounds correspond very closely to the letters that represent them (Seymour et al., 2003). For that reason, English-speaking children read only about 34% of words accurately after 1 year of reading instruction, whereas Dutch children read about 95% of words correctly (Seymour et al., 2003).

There are two different approaches to teaching children how to read English, pitting proponents of each approach in a debate sometimes called the "reading wars" (Strauss, 2019). On the one side, there is the **phonics approach**, which teaches children to systematically translate letters into sounds and to put those sounds together to create words. The word "dog," for example, can be divided into three *phonemes*, or distinct units of sound, represented in the International Phonetic Alphabet as /d/, /ɔ/, and /g/. These three sounds are then combined to sound out "dog." The actual meanings of words take a subordinate role in the phonics approach; sounding out words is what is most important (de Graaff et al., 2009). Therefore, more complex reading materials like poems and stories are only used later in the learning process.

The **whole-language approach**, on the other side, emphasizes that words are embedded in a rich context of language that includes speaking, listening, writing, and reading. Reading materials are presented in the form of stories and poems. Students are primarily taught to deduce the meaning of words they cannot read from the context and to recognize whole words by sight. Phonics is used to read words that cannot be guessed, but the use of phonics is not

phonics approach an approach to reading instruction that emphasizes sounding out letters and combining those sounds into words.

whole-language approach an approach to reading instruction that emphasizes the meaning of words and how words are embedded in the context of speaking, listening, reading, and writing.

systematic and does not feature prominently in the approach (Brechtel, 1992; Fukada, 2018).

Which approach to teaching reading should be used in schools? A number of studies and meta-analyses point to the phonics approach as being the more effective of the two approaches (National Reading Panel et al., 2000; Rose, 2006; Willingham, 2015). However, many studies compare the phonics approach to a combination of other methods rather than to just the whole-language approach, so that it is not really possible to conclude that the phonics approach is superior (Bowers, 2020). It therefore may make sense to use a blended approach that emphasizes phonics, particularly in the beginning, and then transitions children to richer reading materials that capture their imagination and develop their reading comprehension and vocabulary (Maddox & Feng, 2013; Stahl & Miller, 2006; Xue & Meisels, 2004).

Using Language in Life

Arguably, one of the most important functions of language is its use in communication with others (an aspect which is called *pragmatics*; see also Chapter 9). Typically, as chidren age, they become more skilled at having conversations with others. Children with autism spectrum disorder (ASD) are an exception to this principle, because their understanding of pragmatics tends to be much less advanced than that of their peers (Conlon et al., 2019). A more advanced understanding of pragmatics also helps children in making friends and makes it easier to participate in a wide variety of social activities (Snow & Douglas, 2017).

During the elementary school years, children also make great strides in their ability to tell stories. They learn that there is a certain structure to stories, including a beginning, middle, and end. They also understand that characters that appear in a story need to be introduced to the listener and that there is usually a conflict arising toward the middle of the story that gets resolved at the end (DelGiudice, 2018). Young children tend to give lots of needless details because they cannot distinguish what is important from what is not. Children in third or fourth grade, on the contrary, are much better at deciding which facts are of actual importance to the story.

However, children in middle childhood still have a deficit in providing sufficient details about information that requires a certain amount of interpretation, such as the emotions, thoughts, and beliefs of a main character. The ability to adequately relay this kind of information does not develop until adolescence (Pasupathi & Wainryb, 2010).

Bilingualism

Sam and Isabella, the 11-year-old twins we met at the beginning of this chapter, are being raised bilingually by their parents in English and Spanish. Their mother, Mariella, immigrated to the United States from Mexico to marry her husband, George, who is from New Jersey. Prior to meeting Mariella, George had only the little bit of Spanish that he learned in school. Together, they visit Mariella's family in Mexico every 2 years, and the twins' ability to speak Spanish is crucial to their communication with grandparents and cousins. And while the children's Spanish improves significantly during those visits, Mariella feels that, overall, their Spanish skills do not make much progress. Much to her chagrin, both children have begun to routinely speak English to their mother, even when she addresses them in Spanish. She is now looking for group activities that involve both languages so the children can keep developing their Spanish skills.

Although many children in the United States grow up speaking only one language, bilingualism (speaking two languages) is the norm in many countries, such as Switzerland, Luxembourg, India, and Singapore. For example, Switzerland has four official languages: German, French, Italian, and Romansh.

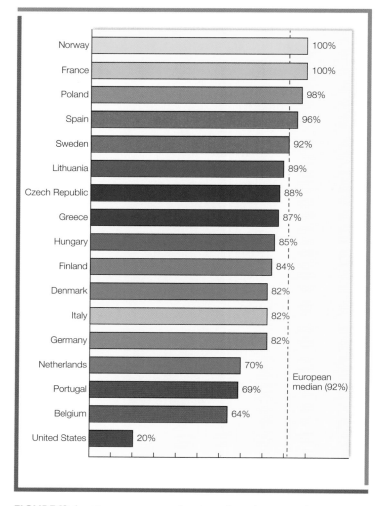

FIGURE 12.4   The percentage of K–12 students learning a foreign language is significantly higher in European countries than it is in the United States. What do you think are some of the consequences?

After Pew Research Center. 2018. Most European students are learning a foreign language in school while Americans lag. www.pewresearch.org

immersion approach   an approach to teaching English to speakers of other languages in which instruction takes place exclusively in English.

dual-language approach   an approach to teaching English to speakers of other languages in which instruction takes place both in English and the native language of the learner.

India has 22 official languages! In some households, children are even trilingual.

The best time to learn languages is early in childhood. Although some parents and educators fear that learning two languages will confuse children and delay their language development, this is not the case. Bilingual children initially tend to have smaller vocabularies in a single language than do their monolingual peers. However, by the age of 6 or 7, the bilingual children typically catch up with their friends (Hoff et al., 2014; Paradis & Jia, 2017). How quickly and to what extent they catch up depends on how much of each language they have the opportunity to hear and speak (Hoff & Core, 2015).

The relationship between age and the learning of a second language is somewhat complex. Grammar and the sounds of a language are best learned at a young age. After the age of 12, children's (or adults') ability to pronounce the sounds and words in a new language like a native speaker decreases significantly. The ability to learn a language's grammar decreases as well. We don't find such a drop with vocabulary—teenagers and adults tend to have no more difficulty learning new words than younger children (Neville, 2006). Children also learn foreign languages differently than do adults. They do not rely as much on rules and memorization as adults do. Rather, they learn by hearing and interacting with others on a frequent basis (Hoff, 2018; Thomas & Johnson, 2008).

Speaking more than one language is usually quite beneficial for children's cognitive development. Bilingual children constantly need to monitor and manage which language they hear and speak. Possibly for this reason, compared with monolingual children, bilingual children often are able to better control their attention. They score better on tests that assess cognitive flexibility, cognitive monitoring, and executive functioning. Better executive functioning, in turn, often translates into higher levels of academic performance. Bilingual children are also more aware of language in general, an awareness that helps them to detect grammatical errors (Kuo et al., 2017; Thomas-Sunesson et al., 2018; Weber et al., 2016). However, keeping up a second language in an environment where just one language is spoken can be quite challenging, as Mariella is experiencing with her efforts to communicate with her children in Spanish.

Foreign-language learning at school is considered much less important in the United States than in many other developed nations. Only 20% of American students learn a foreign language during their school career, and less than 8% of American college students are enrolled in a foreign-language course (Stein-Smith, 2019). Compare those figures with data from nations in the European Union (EU) (**FIGURE 12.4**): In 22 member states of the EU, 60% or more of children start to learn a foreign language in elementary school. And across all 28 EU countries, almost 95% of students study a foreign language in high school (Eurostat, 2019).

Since the United States is a country of immigrants, one controversy is how to best teach English to the children of immigrants. These children are also called *English language learners*, or *ELLs* for short. There are two different options: Children can be taught in English only (**immersion approach**), or they can be taught with a **dual-language approach** that includes instruction in both English

© Eric Sinkins

■ Canada has two official languages: English and French. It means that both languages must be taught in school, government services must be available in both languages, and—sometimes confusingly for international visitors—all commercial packaging must be in both English and French. English-speaking students in some parts of the country are required to learn French beginning in fourth or fifth grade but may begin as early as kindergarten.

and the child's native language. However, comparing those two approaches directly with each other is difficult, because the number of languages in instruction is not the only factor that matters. The quality of instruction, characteristics of teachers and children, and other factors play a role as well. While some argue that the quality of instruction is more important than any one approach, others have argued for the dual-language approach: It is hard for children to understand complex subject matter that is taught in a language the children do not fully understand. Additionally, children learn a new language more easily when their native language can be part of the classroom as well (which ultimately means that there is no stigma attached to their native language) (Garrity et al., 2018; Hakuta, 2020).

Review!

How do children's language skills advance in middle childhood?

■ Throughout middle childhood, children's vocabulary increases significantly to about 40,000 words by the time they are 11 years old. The children get better at guessing a new word's meaning from context or from other related words. Children's understanding of metaphors increases, and the children use increasingly sophisticated grammatical constructions.

■ Children learn how to have more effective conversations by choosing which details are relevant to a particular topic and which are not. However, emotions, thoughts, and beliefs of other people are still somewhat hard to infer.

How do children learn to read?

■ Learning to read is a complex process that does not come naturally to children and needs to be taught at school. Three cognitive processes are of particular importance in learning to read: knowing letters and their sounds, understanding that words consist of a number of different sounds (phonemic awareness), and the ability to process words quickly (rapid automatized naming).

■ There is some disagreement as to whether reading should be taught with an emphasis on decoding letter sounds (the *phonics approach*) or an emphasis on the context of language (the *whole-language approach*). Many experts recommend an approach that blends the teaching of phonics with rich reading materials.

Practice!

1. Children should be able to extract information from the texts they read by _____ .
   a. kindergarten
   b. second grade
   c. fifth grade
   d. tenth grade

2. Knowledge of pragmatics helps children _____ .
   a. learn new words
   b. use language to communicate with others effectively
   c. interpret complex texts
   d. understand grammatical concepts

3. The immersion approach is used to _____ .
   a. teach immigrant children English by teaching in English exclusively
   b. teach young children mental math skills
   c. teach children to write
   d. improve the spelling skills of elementary schoolers

Act It Out!

You recently immigrated to the United States from Mexico with your spouse and two children, aged 8 and 10. You and your spouse are proficient in English, but neither of your children speaks English very well. You intended to keep Spanish as your language of choice at home. To your surprise, your spouse disagrees with you: Your spouse believes that the children need to learn English as quickly as possible. Speaking Spanish at home will slow down their progress at school and put them at risk of falling behind. With a classmate, act out a conversation with your spouse where you discuss your disagreement and try to come to a solution. What concerns is your spouse likely to raise, and how would you address them?

What's Your Position?

We have learned about two different approaches that are used to teach children how to read—the phonics approach and the whole-language approach. Which approach do you favor? Once you have decided, do some research on those two approaches. After your research, has your position changed? Why or why not?

Additional Resources Online

- "Whole language approach: Reading is more than sounding out words and decoding," from Phys.org
- "Whole language approach to reading," from Very Well Family
- "Whole language: What was that all about?" from National Institute for Direct Instruction
- "Learning to read with the whole language approach: The teacher's view," from the Canadian Center of Science and Education
- "At a loss for words: How a flawed approach is teaching millions of kids to be poor readers," from APM Reports
- "Phonics instruction," from Reading Rockets
- "A case for why both sides in the 'reading wars' debate are wrong—and a proposed solution," from *The Washington Post*
- "Whole language instruction vs phonics instruction: Effect on reading fluency and spelling accuracy of first grade students," Presentation at Georgia Educational Research Association Annual Conference

12.3 Intelligence

- Identify and compare Spearman, Carroll, and Gardner's conceptions of intelligence.
- Relate how intelligence is measured and how intelligence tests are used in the United States.

In Western society, intelligence is a concept we seem to encounter just about everywhere. It manifests itself early in life. Even infants show intelligence when they *habituate*, or get used to, novel stimuli. More intelligent infants tend to habituate more quickly than their peers (Bornstein & Colombo, 2012; Bornstein & Sigman, 1986; Bornstein et al., 2017). As early as age 2, some very young applicants to preschools may be expected to take intelligence tests to gain a coveted spot in certain preschools. Or they may need to be tested at school to assist in placements for special education classes, whether classes for children with learning disabilities or children who may be identified as "gifted." Later on, tests like the SAT or ACT (which are very similar to measures of intelligence in what they assess) are used to evaluate applicants for college and university admissions (Sackett et al., 2019).

In this section, we will learn about different theories of intelligence and find out how intelligence is commonly measured. We will also take a closer look at group differences in intelligence and which factors influence children's intelligence.

What Is Intelligence?

Before we can test for and measure intelligence, we need to know what intelligence means. That probably seems simple enough—we know basically what it means to be intelligent—but defining intelligence is no simple exercise. What's more, if you ask experts what intelligence really is, the answer might surprise you: Experts do not really agree on what intelligence is. The twentieth-century experimental psychologist Edwin Boring said, simplistically, that intelligence is what intelligence tests measure (Boring, 1923).

Boring's definition is not very helpful for our purposes. Instead, let us consider the results of two different polls among psychologists conducted over the span of several decades, in 1921 and 1986. Although the polls were separated by 65 years, two themes consistently appeared. The experts agreed that intelligence involves the capacity to learn from experience as well as to adapt to one's environment. A key difference in the results is that later psychologists placed a greater emphasis on the importance of culture than did early psychologists (Sternberg, 2018). We will see in this discussion that culture indeed influences intelligence in various ways. We begin, however, with an overview of theories that describe intelligence in more detail.

Spearman's theory of intelligence

One of the earliest theories of intelligence was proposed by an English psychologist and—importantly—statistician, Charles Spearman (Spearman, 1927). Throughout his career, Spearman applied statistical models to the study of psychology. His theory suggests that there are two prevailing "factors" underlying all of the qualities that make up intelligence. These factors are extracted by analyzing patterns of which tests correlate more or less highly with other tests of intelligence. These factors are

- general intelligence (g), which is measured by all tests of intelligence; and
- specific intellectual abilities (s), each of which is measured by just a single test of intelligence.

To test his theory, Spearman developed a statistical method called factor analysis. Briefly, factor analysis is a way of reducing a large number of related variables down to a smaller number of underlying factors.

Of the two factors that Spearman identified, the one that is of most interest to researchers these days is general intelligence, or g. To many people, it makes sense that there would be one general factor that plays a prominent role in all of a person's cognitive abilities. When we think of a person as being smart (or not so smart), we tend to extend this judgment to the person overall and not just to one area of their thinking. Indeed, many students either excel or don't excel at school in general, even though they may have school subjects in which their performance is particularly good.

The intelligence tests we will discuss, in the section on measuring intelligence, measure g, which correlates modestly to moderately with a whole range of life outcomes (Sackett et al., 2019). Yet some researchers are reluctant to give g such an outsized role in intelligence. Both Robert J. Sternberg and Howard Gardner, in their respective theories of intelligence described below, have questioned just how widely applicable g is to the problems people confront in their daily lives.

Carroll's three-stratum theory involves a taxonomy of factors

Working much later than Spearman, John B. Carroll proposed what he called a three-stratum theory of intelligence (Carroll, 1993). The theory involves a three-level taxonomy of factors that could be used to measure, objectively, individual differences in intelligence. Like Spearman, Carroll recognized general intelligence, g, as the basic factor in intelligence, and he put it at the top of his

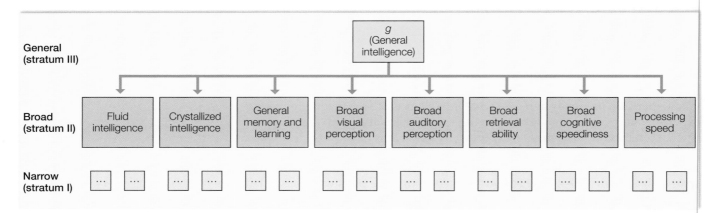

FIGURE 12.5 A model of Carroll's three-stratum theory of intelligence.

After J. B. Carroll. 2012. In D. P. Flanagan and P. L. Harrison (Eds.), Contemporary Intellectual Assessment, pp. 883-890. The Guilford Press, New York; K. S. McGrew. 2009. Intelligence 37: 1–10

three-layer taxonomy. But Carroll placed greater importance on the eight broad cognitive abilities at the middle level of the hierarchy. These abilities are

- fluid intelligence,
- crystallized intelligence,
- cognitive speediness,
- decision speed,
- retrieval fluency,
- memory and learning,
- visual perception, and
- auditory perception.

At the lowest level, or stratum, are specific factors of intelligence that are of little general interest. The combination of factors at all three levels accounts for individual differences in intelligence. The Carroll model is illustrated in **FIGURE 12.5**.

Closely related to three-stratum theory is CHC theory (McGrew, 2005). The first two initials in the acronym refer to Raymond Cattell and his student John Horn, who collaborated on a model of intelligence very similar to the one devised by Carroll (the third letter, and the second "C" in CHC). CHC theory is essentially a synthesis of the Cattell–Horn and Carroll models.

Gardner's theory proposes multiple intelligences

Howard Gardner has argued that there is no one overarching intelligence but rather eight different and distinct multiple intelligences (Gardner, 2011). These intelligences are expressed not in overall achievement but rather in the ability to create things that are valued all over the world or to solve problems in a variety of domains.

Gardner's theory of eight intelligences (**TABLE 12.3**) is based on various kinds of evidence, such as a distinct developmental trajectory, factor-analytic and experimental evidence, and neuropsychological evidence (Gardner, 2000). For example, if brain damage can lead to the impairment of one kind of intelligence but leaves the others intact, this pattern suggested to Gardner a distinct intelligence (Khamo & Johnson, 2019).

People tend to excel in one or multiple areas, but not in all. According to Gardner, the intelligences are independent. The late basketball star Kobe Bryant, for example, would be an example of outstanding bodily kinesthetic intelligence, whereas violinist Hilary Hahn can be considered an example of extremely high musical intelligence.

■ **Table 12.3** Gardner's Eight Intelligences

Intelligence	Definition	Professions using this intelligence
Verbal	Using language to express oneself and to think in words	Lawyer, journalist, playwright, translator
Mathematical	Thinking mathematically	Accountant, analyst, chemist, investment broker
Musical	Composing music or playing an instrument	Conductor, composer, musical performer
Spatial	Solving visual problems and navigating the environment	Photographer, architect, engineer, carpenter, navigator
Naturalist	Knowledge of animals and plants	Botanist, chef, sailor, horticulturalist, ecologist
Bodily kinesthetic	Performing with one's body	Athlete, actor, massage therapist, dancer, gymnast
Intrapersonal	Knowledge of oneself	Actor, comedian, trainer
Interpersonal	Knowledge and understanding of others	Teacher, therapist, manager, salesperson

People often do display a particular strength in one area or perhaps strengths in a few areas. However, some believe what Gardner calls separate intelligences are better characterized as talents (Neisser et al., 1996; Visser et al., 2006). Also, critics question Gardner's criteria for what constitutes an intelligence, because some of his intelligence categories overlap (mathematical and spatial intelligence, for example). The intelligences also do not seem to be fully independent (Visser et al., 2006).

Sternberg's theory of successful intelligence

Robert J. Sternberg has proposed what he calls a *theory of successful intelligence*. What distinguishes this theory of intelligence from others is that that it suggests that intelligence is a slightly different construct for each person (Sternberg, 1997, 2019). Successful intelligence is a person's ability to formulate a set of prosocial life goals and then forge a path that will help them to reach those goals. As people go through life, they need to monitor their goals and their progress in achieving them and set new paths to professional and personal success as their goals change.

According to Sternberg's research (e.g., Sternberg, 2010), four skills are especially relevant to successful intelligence:

- *Creative skills* are used to come up with ideas for one's life that are relatively novel and useful.
- *Analytical skills* are used to determine whether those ideas are good ones.
- *Practical skills* are used to implement the ideas and to persuade others of their value.
- *Wisdom-based skills* are used to help ensure that one's ideas help to serve some kind of common good, not just one's own good.

These skills work together: Successfully intelligent people coordinate the skills in the attainment of their goals. Successfully intelligent people also balance changing themselves to fit their environment (environmental adaptation), changing the environment to fit them (environmental shaping), and finding a new environment when their current environment is not working for them (environmental selection).

Sternberg further has argued that successfully intelligent people are distinguished by their recognition of their strengths and weaknesses and their ability to capitalize on their strengths at the same time that they correct or compensate for their weaknesses. For example, a successfully intelligent person might recognize that although they have not excelled in school, they are exceptionally creative musically, and thus try to find a job in the music industry.

In the latest refinement of his theory, which he calls the *theory of adaptive intelligence* (Sternberg, 2019, 2020, 2021a,b), Sternberg argues that given the perils we face in the world—global climate change, pandemics, bacterial resistance to antibiotics, wars, hatreds, nuclear weapons, air and water pollution, emergence of dictators and would-be dictators—we must adapt an alternative to traditional notions of intelligence to ensure the survival of our species.

Measuring Intelligence

The first intelligence test was created more than 100 years ago by French psychologist Alfred Binet and his collaborator Theodore Simon. Some students in the Paris school system were struggling academically, and the Ministry of Education thought this group would benefit from special instruction. The question was how to identify those children who would qualify for that special instruction. Hence, they asked Alfred Binet to develop a test that assessed children's scholastic abilities. The resulting test, which came to be known as the Binet–Simon scale, was the forerunner of the modern IQ test.

Binet did not devise the concept of an intelligence quotient, or IQ, but his standardized intelligence test helped to usher in the idea. In children, the IQ is derived by comparing a child's actual age with their "mental age," or the mental level at which a child performs. For example, an 8-year-old child who performs mentally at the level of a 10-year-old would have a mental age of 10. The IQ would be the ratio of the mental age to the child's chronological, or physical, age, times 100. So, the formula in this case would be $(10) / (8) \times 100 = 125$. The average IQ is 100, representing a mental age equaling a chronological age (a fraction that will always equal 1) times 100.

Today's IQ scores are adjusted so that the average IQ in the population is always 100. We then can compute what percentage of people in a population have an IQ score above or below the average. For example, roughly two-thirds of people have an IQ of 100 ± 15. Specifically, 68% of the population have IQ scores within the range of 85 to 115 (**FIGURE 12.6**). Just over 95% have an IQ within the range of scores from 70 to 130.

Intelligence tests are usually given to children on a one-on-one basis. An examiner leads the child through the assessment. The interactions between examiner and child are structured so that examiners do not accidentally help one child more than they help another.

FIGURE 12.6 Distribution of IQ scores. The average IQ score in the population is 100, but 68% of people have an IQ score between 85 and 115. Only a bit more than 2% of people have an IQ score higher than 130, and only a bit more than 2% have an IQ lower than 70.

From S. M. Breedlove. 2015. *Principles of Psychology.* Sunderland, MA: Sinauer/Oxford University Press. Based on data in W. C. M. Resing and J. B. Blok. 2002. *Psycholoog* 37: 244–249

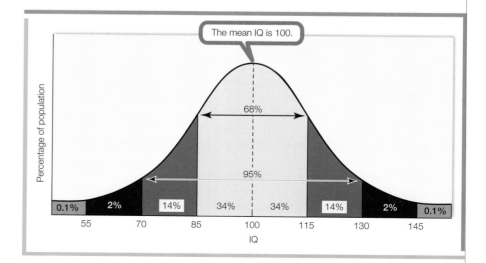

Among the most widely used IQ tests today is the **Stanford–Binet Intelligence Scale**. It was originally developed in 1916 by Lewis Terman, who revised Binet's test to create an American version. Today's version was last revised in 2003 (Roid, 2003). There are different versions of the Stanford–Binet test, depending on the age of the tested person. Children may be asked to identify body parts, recall sentences, or recall bead patterns.

Another popular intelligence test is the **Wechsler Intelligence Scale for Children** (WISC). Designed for children aged 6–17, the WISC is currently in its fifth revision (Wechsler, 2014) **(FIGURE 12.7)**. There are also scales for children aged 2½ to 7 years—the Wechsler Preschool and Primary Scale of Intelligence (WPPSI)—and for adults. The Wechsler scale not only yields an overall

Stanford–Binet Intelligence Scale an intelligence test that is based on Alfred Binet's intelligence assessment, with different problems presented based on the age of the person tested.

Wechsler Intelligence Scale for Children (WISC) an intelligence test for children that gives detailed subscale scores as well as a total score.

For each question, look at the 4 boxes. In the top row the pictures go together in a certain way. In the bottom row there is an empty box. Which of the 4 pictures on the side goes with the picture in the bottom box the same way the 2 pictures in the top row go together?

FIGURE 12.7 Sample questions based on the Wechsler Intelligence Scale for Children.

IQ score but also gives subscores for individual areas like working memory, visual-spatial abilities, and verbal comprehension. Subscores help clinicians determine whether there are some areas in which a child has more problems than others, allowing for decisions on where interventions are most needed.

The second edition of the **Kaufman Assessment Battery for Children** (Kaufman & Kaufman, 2018) is a test for children aged 3–18. Although it can be used for all children, it is particularly useful for assessing children outside of the mainstream, including children with ASD or hearing impairments and children whose first language is not English, who may struggle with tests that are less sensitive to cultural, linguistic, and neurological differences. The Kaufman test permits the examiner to reword a question or give instructions in a different language if the child has trouble understanding the task at hand. Such translation helps give a more nearly accurate picture of the abilities of children who are not neurotypical or whose first language is not English.

Kaufman Assessment Battery for Children an intelligence test for children aged 3–18 in which the examiner can reword tasks or use a different language to maximize children's understanding of the items.

■ What's It Like...

Using Timed Tests: Should They Be the Future of Testing?

Toby, 13 years

I really dislike timed tests. They make me anxious. I need time to think. If I'm always being rushed, I have no time to think. I get more and more nervous, and I hear all the other kids writing. It makes me think I am the only one who doesn't know anything. But it isn't really that I do not know things. I just can't think when I get so anxious.

Instead of adults caring about how much we know or how well we think, they seem to care mostly about how quickly we can get stuff done.

I have always had trouble concentrating on schoolwork. When I start a new task, I just need some time to settle in and get myself focused. When tests are timed, I don't have the time to focus. If I rush in, I just don't do my best work. Once, my teacher saw that I was just sitting there like I was paralyzed. He came over and asked what was going on. I told him I was too nervous to even think clearly about the test. He said I better get my act together because that's what tests are like and I'll have to learn how to perform or I'll never do well on any test.

Why are adults always rushing everything anyway? I keep reading about adults stressing out and even having heart attacks because they're always pushing pushing pushing. We kids don't want to be like them. We want to work, but we also want time to enjoy and learn from life.

Psychometrician (a specialist in testing)

Most standardized tests are timed. There are good reasons for why the tests are timed.

First, tests are timed because it is practical to do so. Imagine students taking a test who had unlimited time. Suppose the large majority finish in 30 minutes. The test publisher then might decide to allow students 30 minutes for the test, realizing that most, although not all, students will finish in the allotted time. But how long will the others take? Some might take 35 minutes, but others might want *much* more time, maybe 1 hour, 2 hours, 3 hours, or possibly more. It just is not practical to allow unlimited time for a standardized test. One cannot practically accommodate the very long periods of time some students might want.

Second, tests are timed because current widely accepted theories of intelligence, such as that of John Carroll (1993), specify speed as an important part of intelligence. Indeed, Carroll's theory has two speed factors, broad cognitive speediness (*gs*), and processing speed (*gt*). This means that there are good reasons for timing tests. Part of being intelligent is being able to think quickly.

Third, test publishers have validated their speeded tests for many years. The publishers know that such tests work—they predict an astonishing variety of criteria with great effectiveness.

There is an overwhelming historical precedent for timing tests. They have worked before and they work today.

Fourth, students who, for one reason or another, need extra time can get it. Psychologists or other licensed professionals can assess students for learning or attentional disabilities, and where appropriate, arrange for those students to receive a special accommodation that allows them to have extra time on the tests—time and a half or even double time. So, if students need more time, they can get it. The existence of learning disabilities does not prevent students from taking standardized tests in a way that is fair for them, if they are given the accommodations they need.

Fifth and finally, if students who do not have disabilities have trouble finishing timed tests on time, then the tests' difficulty alerts the students to a challenge that they may need to correct. They may want to work on speeding themselves up so they can compete with others who work more quickly.

Cultural psychologist

Standardized tests should not be strictly timed. There are good reasons for this.

First, and perhaps most importantly, timing creates a cultural bias. Some cultures, especially some postindustrialized ones such as in the United States, place a heavy emphasis on getting things done quickly. But this view is by no means universal, and in some cultures, the intelligent people are seen as those who do not rush through things but rather think them over deeply and reflectively (Sternberg, 2004). In other words, the very behavior that is viewed as "intelligent" in one culture may be viewed as not so intelligent in another culture.

Second, the problem with strict timing goes beyond culture differences. Most serious problems in life—deciding whom to marry, deciding whether to have children, deciding where to go to college or graduate school, deciding what career to enter—are not problems that should or even can reasonably be solved quickly. Strictly timing tests actually sends the wrong message to test takers in all cultures. Such a practice suggests that speed is more important than reflection and arriving at an optimal decision or solution to a problem.

Third, few psychologists would argue that all tests should be given with no time limits. For example, if you are testing applicants for jobs such as air traffic controller or ship's captain, you need to find people who can make the quick decisions such jobs require. Rather than simply timing all tests, the timing of tests should depend on what is being tested and who is being tested. Time limits should reflect the nature of the type of performance that one is trying to predict.

Fourth and finally, it is true that students with learning disabilities can be given extra time on tests. But doing so risks stigmatizing them. It identifies them as students who need special accommodations. Doing so might make sense if the timing were really important, but it is not, and so there is no reason to identify or potentially stigmatize them.

Group Differences in Intelligence and Cultural Bias

Every test of general intelligence (*g*) measures roughly the same construct, no matter who creates them. However, it has become clear that some groups fare better on these tests than others. Those who have typically done well tend to be of European or Asian descent living in middle-class or upper-middle-class households in urban rather than rural areas (Halpern & Kanaya, 2019). Specifically, the ethnic groups that perform best on intelligence tests in the United States are Asian Americans, followed by White, Hispanic, and then Black populations (Suzuki et al., 2011). Meanwhile, there is a striking correlation between social class and intelligence test results. Children from lower socioeconomic classes score, on average, 10–15 points lower on IQ tests than do children from families with a higher income (Nisbett, 2013; Saklofske et al., 2015).

There may be many reasons that children from higher socioeconomic classes score higher, on average, on tests of intelligence. For example, their parents are

stereotype threat risk of confirming a negative stereotype when engaging in a task about which such a stereotype exists.

more likely to be more educated and thus to have been able to teach the children more scholastic material at home. The parents also may have been able to afford more or better preschool opportunities for their children. There may be more books in the homes of children from higher socioeconomic classes; also, their parents may not have needed to commute as far as parents of children from lower socioeconomic classes and therefore had more time to spend with the children. In addition, paid tutoring services may be available to children in higher-income households.

Children from ethnic minority groups that have traditionally scored poorly on IQ tests face an additional obstacle when taking these tests, a phenomenon that psychologists call **stereotype threat**. This phenomenon occurs when children know that others believe their group performs poorly. Thus, they are anxious that they will confirm the existing stereotype about their group's poor performance (Drace et al., 2020; Spencer et al., 2016), and this ends up negatively affecting their performance.

When considering these trends, keep in mind that these are group averages; individuals of any ethnic or socioeconomic group may perform well above or below their group average. Studies have also shown that Black and Hispanic children's average performance on IQ tests has risen steadily as the economic circumstances of these two groups have improved and as they have gained access to better education (Nisbett et al., 2012).

Nevertheless, these trends have led some researchers to look for reasons behind the differences in intelligence test performance, and specifically into whether mainstream tests misrepresent child intelligence by favoring certain groups over others. What they have found is that cultural issues are inherent in many of the mainstream tests. Consider Figure 12.7 (top). Digital tympanic thermometers can be found in many North American pharmacies and homes. But what if the child taking this test had recently immigrated from a country that relies on alternative methods of gauging temperature and detecting illness? Or what if the child encountering the question in Figure 12.7 (bottom) is from a part of the world where common bat species are diurnal rather than nocturnal? IQ tests do not typically show statistical bias, but a risk is that the criteria against which the tests are validated may have some of the same biases as the tests.

Intelligence tests will always reflect the values and culture of the person developing the test (Sternberg, 2004). A timed test, for example, will place at a disadvantage those children who are not used to working under time pressure because their culture is not as rigidly time-bound as North American culture tends to be. Children from backgrounds in industrialized and knowledge-based economies are likely to be more used to working with geometric abstractions than are children from countries that are less developed industrially. Likewise, children from places that have only two seasons will have trouble reasoning with problems that refer to four seasons; they simply do not have experience with concepts that are common in the lives of people living in the industrialized North.

culture-fair intelligence tests intelligence tests that have been specifically designed with the intention to avoid cultural bias so that they reflect a child's true ability no matter their culture; however, so far none of the tests developed with this intention has succeeded in being truly culture-free.

Raven Progressive Matrices Test an intelligence test created with the intention to be culture-fair, although no test is fully culture-fair; tests nonverbal perceptual and reasoning skills with items based on matrices.

The growing awareness of cultural bias in intelligence testing has led to not-altogether-successful efforts to develop **culture-fair intelligence tests**. Some of these tests, like the **Raven Progressive Matrices Test**, have attempted to be culture-fair through the elimination of verbal items (Raven, 2003) (see **FIGURE 12.8**). However, these efforts have not been entirely successful, as even culture-fair tests tend to favor urban European American children from middle-class households, who are schooled with problems similar to those on the Raven.

Given what we have learned about cultural bias in intelligence testing, it should be no surprise to you that the widespread use of intelligence tests today is hotly debated among experts.

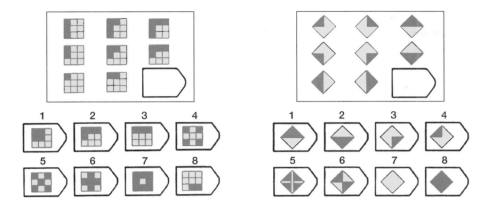

FIGURE 12.8   Items from a culture-fair intelligence test. Intelligence tests created to be culture-fair, such as the Raven Progressive Matrices Test, attempt to decrease or even eliminate cultural bias by presenting children with items that are abstract and do not use language. Do you think the items presented above are equally likely to be solved by children from San Antonio, Texas, and children from a remote village in the rainforest of Papua New Guinea?

After P. A. Carpenter et al. 1990. *Psychol Rev* 97: 404–431. Copyright © 1990 by American Psychological Association. Reproduced with permission

The main use of intelligence tests today is for diagnostic purposes—to understand people's patterns of intellectual strengths and weaknesses—and for identification of gifted children. They are also sometimes used for legal purposes to determine if people charged with certain crimes have the intellectual competence to be held responsible for their actions.

One additional use of intelligence tests has been for identifying people with learning disabilities. Intelligence tests used to be used extensively in the assessment of learning disabilities and, especially, reading disabilities. The idea was that children living with disabilities show substantially higher scores on intelligence tests than on reading tests. But this interpretation of reading disabilities has been questioned. Elliott & Grigorenko (2014) have shown that, in the end, children diagnosed with reading disabilities are, psychologically, no different in their learning needs from children who are simply poor readers. According to this view, intelligence tests simply are not needed in the diagnosis of reading disabilities.

Factors That Influence Children's Intelligence

Let's imagine that we could devise a truly culture-fair intelligence test, allowing us to accurately measure the intelligence of neurodiverse children from a variety of ethnic and socioeconomic backgrounds. *Neurodiverse* children are children who perceive, learn, and think in different ways. Having removed any biases from our testing, we are left with an important question: What factors contribute to children's intelligence?

Experts today agree that children's intelligence is strongly influenced both by genetics and by the environment in which children grow up. This fact is underscored by observations of children like those who were adopted out of Romanian orphanages during the era of Communism when Nicolae Ceaușescu was president. At the time, the care was far from what would have been ideal for the children's development. Let's start with genetics. There is no "intelligence gene" that researchers have discovered. Intelligence is polygenic,

◼ During the COVID-19 pandemic, many schools went from in-person to online learning at home. Many young children struggled to stay focused without the assistance of the parent or caregiver present in the home.

which means it is a trait that is influenced by many different genes (Benyamin et al., 2014). But the influence of the genes increases as people grow older (Plomin & Deary, 2015). When children are very young, environment has a greater influence on intelligence than when the children grow up. A reason environment matters less with age, on average, is that people often eventually find an environmental niche that is compatible with their genetic capabilities.

The more time children spend in Westernized education, the higher their scores on intelligence tests. For example, a review of 39 studies showed that IQ test scores decrease over the course of the extended summer vacation that many North American students enjoy (Cooper et al., 1996). Historical studies show that children whose formal schooling was interrupted or significantly delayed by major life events, such as the Nazi invasion of Holland or the teacher shortage in South Africa, showed decreased IQ scores compared with their peers who received schooling; in fact, the difference was as much as 5 points per year (Ceci & Williams, 1997). We can imagine that future research along these lines will examine the impact that schooling interrupted by COVID-19 restrictions has had on children's intelligence.

While schooling is a key environmental factor in intelligence, the disadvantages that some children experience from their environment begin even before elementary school. Children in lower-income households may have parents working long shifts or multiple jobs just to put food on the table. The parents in these families may not have the same quantity of time as parents in middle- and upper-middle-class households to read with young children and engage them in games and other cognitively stimulating activities. They may lack the means to purchase books, puzzles, and the digital technology that is increasingly used to mediate these kinds of activities.

For this reason, an increasing number of interventions are being implemented that aim at helping families provide more stimulating environments for their children and at providing high-quality childcare for children from low-income and disadvantaged families. For example, the Abecedarian Intervention Program assigned children from low-income families to either an intervention that included full-time, high-quality childcare as well as health and social services, or a control group that received all services except the childcare. By age 3, the children in the intervention group had an average IQ that was 17 points above the average IQ of the children in the control group. Twelve years later, children in the intervention group had retained an advantage of 5 IQ points over the control group and were less likely to drop out of school (Campbell et al., 2019; Ramey, 2018).

Before we leave the topic of intelligence, it may be worth asking if we spend too much time trying to study, define, measure, and improve intelligence scores. Is an IQ score really that important, or is it just something used to give certain children access to special programming, such as gifted education? One reason that intelligence, and particularly *g*, is a much-used concept in today's society is that it correlates clearly with a number of important outcomes. For example, children with higher IQ scores tend to do better later in school; they are more likely to go to college and more likely to have a successful career once they enter the workforce (Brody, 2007; Jencks, 1979). Not only that, but they also have a higher life expectancy, tend to be healthier in middle age, and are less likely to suffer from chronic diseases (Wraw et al., 2015). These correlations make *g* a useful concept in research. However, you need to remember that measures of intelligence and related constructs are used to sort children in many societies, so that the opportunities they eventually are given are influenced in part by their scores on these tests. Better life outcomes may reflect, in part, the additional opportunities children are given who score high on intelligence tests.

Culture Counts

Effects of Socioeconomic Status on Brain Development

As we have seen throughout this book, children's brain development and cognitive functioning depend on a number of factors. One of those factors is *neurotoxins*, or substances that affect brain development. One of the most well-known neurotoxins is lead. When children are exposed to lead, they tend to grow up to have less gray matter as adults (Brubaker et al., 2010; Marshall et al., 2020).

An ongoing longitudinal study is attempting to determine the effects of lead exposure and socioeconomic status (SES) on children's brain development and performance on cognitive tests. One of the results is displayed in the figure shown here. As you can see in the figure, when children live in an environment that doesn't have a high likelihood of exposing them to lead, the effects of SES are clearly visible: The more parents earn, the better children score on cognitive tests. But the study furthermore shows that a family's income can even lessen the impact of lead exposure. You can see that with an increasing risk of lead exposure, low- and middle-income children's cognitive performance drops, whereas there is no drop in the performance of high-income children.

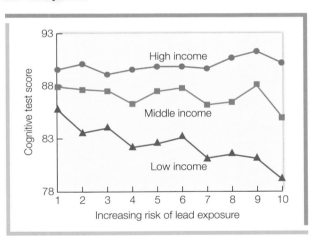

■ Risk of lead exposure and cognition. Overall cognitive function declined most steeply with increasing risk of environmental lead exposure in children of low-income parents. Age, sex, parental education, and race/ethnicity were included as covariates in this analysis.

After A. T. Marshall et al. 2020. *Nat Med* 26: 91–97

■ **Question**

Why do you think high-income children do not experience a drop in cognitive performance even if they have a high risk of being exposed to lead? And what do you think can be done to help children in middle- and lower-income families so their cognitive performance does not decrease when they are exposed to higher lead levels?

Review!

What are some conceptions of intelligence?

■ In 1926, Charles Spearman suggested that intelligence consists of two factors: a general factor (*g*) and specific intellectual abilities. Howard Gardner has suggested that there are actually eight different intelligences. Robert J. Sternberg has suggested that intelligence comprises creative, analytical, practical, and wisdom-based components.

How is intelligence measured, and how are intelligence tests used in the United States?

■ There are a number of intelligence scales for use with children, like the *Stanford–Binet Intelligence Scale* and the *Wechsler*

Intelligence Scale for Children. Several other assessments commonly used in the United States today, like the ACT or the SAT, are close approximations to measures of *g* as well. Culture and intelligence are linked, and some groups (Asians and Whites) tend to do better on them than others (Hispanics and Blacks). The differences may be due in part to the fact that different groups have, on average, different socioeconomic opportunities, which may influence what parents can do for their children.

Practice!

1. Deviation IQ scores are computed and readjusted regularly in such a way that about _____ of the population have an IQ between 85 and 115.
   a. two-thirds
   b. one-half
   c. one-fourth
   d. one-third

2. Stereotype threat in intelligence tests directly affects _____ .
   a. children who get teased regularly for their looks
   b. children who have trouble focusing at school
   c. children belonging to groups that tend to score poorly on IQ tests
   d. children belonging to groups that tend to score above average on IQ tests

3. IQ scores correlate with _____ in later life.
   a. hair color
   b. food preferences
   c. health
   d. height

What's Your Position?

Tests that are closely related to IQ tests, like the SAT, ACT, and GRE, are commonly used in college and university admissions. We know that scores on these tests correlate with a range of outcomes later in life, like income and health. But these tests are also known to systematically put some groups at a disadvantage. Do you think tests approximating IQ should be used in college and university admissions? If not, what are some alternatives that could be used?

Additional Resources Online

■ "We've got intelligence all wrong—and that's endangering our future," from *New Scientist*

■ "Rethinking what we mean by intelligence," from Phi Delta Kappan

■ "Will the new SAT better serve poor students?" from *The Atlantic*

12.4 Assistive Technology for Children with Special Needs

■ Explain how new technologies changed learning for children with special needs.

When we think of media and technology in the context of child development, we tend to think of them—with good reason—as things that need to be limited, or at least used judiciously. But some technologies that have been developed over recent decades have been a blessing, particularly for families with special-needs children. In this section, we'll discover some of the assistive technology that helps children learn and how to support children who do a lot (or all) of their learning online.

Nine-year-old Richard was born with Down syndrome and ASD and does not speak. For most of his life, he has not been able to communicate with his family. His parents did not know any of his wishes and needs; all they could do was guess what was wrong when he showed signs of unhappiness or discomfort. All of this changed when they discovered an iPad app that consists of pictures that Richard can tap. The iPad then says out loud what Richard wants to say. Suddenly, Richard can express his wishes and needs without his parents having to guess anymore (FIGURE 12.9).

There is a whole range of apps and devices that improve the lives of children with chronic diseases, disabilities, and special needs (Lersilp et al., 2018; Morash-Macneil et al., 2018) (TABLE 12.4). Generally speaking, assistive technology is any app or device that helps a child compensate for their specific deficits and improve their capabilities (Behrmann, 1998).

In Chapter 11, we discussed children's right to an appropriate education in the least restrictive environment. There are advantages as well as disadvantages to schooling children with special needs in a mainstream school with their peers or educating them in a school that specializes in special education. Assistive technologies can help integrate more children into regular school classrooms.

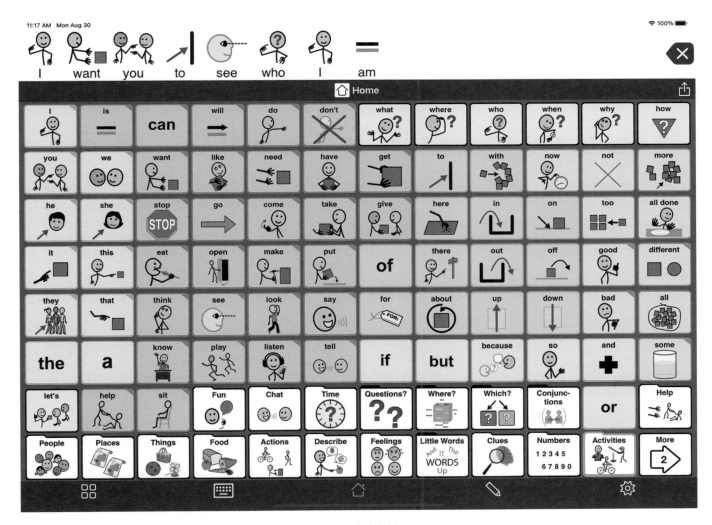

FIGURE 12.9 A screen from the Proloquo2Go app in which nonverbal children can tap pictures to communicate with others. Proloquo2Go® is an AssistiveWare® product. Used with permission.

■ **Table 12.4** Assistive Technology Solutions for Children with Special Needs

Deficit of the affected child	Solutions
Nonverbal (for example, some children affected by Down syndrome or autism spectrum disorder) or speech disabilities	Apps that translate pictures into spoken words for communication purposes
	Speech-to-text software that allows students to speak into a microphone and get an output of text on their computer
Vision-impaired or blind	Screen readers that can read information out loud
	Screen magnifiers
	High-contrast modes
	Audio books
Deaf or hard of hearing	Wireless devices that transmit sounds to hearing aids
	Video apps like FlipGrid that are capable of subtitling
Cognitive disabilities	Memory aids, schedules, task lists, etc., for children who have memory or attention issues
	Spell-checking and grammatical tools as well as read-aloud tools and tools for reading fluency and comprehension for children with dyslexia
	Apps that help with math computations, aligning numbers, and writing math problems down for children with deficits in math
Fine motor issues	Use of touch-screen displays if a keyboard and mouse cannot be used
Chronic diseases	Apps to stay connected with friends and family or participate remotely in school instruction during extended hospital stays
	Apps to organize complex care schedules
	Apps to organize health information to ensure that all doctors have access to it

Source: M. Castelo. 2020. Using Assistive technology to empower students with disabilities. https://edtechmagazine.com

Review!

How have new technologies changed children's learning?

■ New technological developments have led to an increasing number of apps and devices that can help children with special needs compensate for their specific weaknesses. Apps help nonverbal children communicate with others, vision-impaired children can read or let text be read out loud, subtitles can be added to videos for deaf children, and a large number of tools help children organize themselves, write better essays, or do mathematical computations.

Practice!

1. The main purpose of assistive technology is to help children _____ .
   a. make intelligence irrelevant for school performance
   b. of low SES families to improve their school performance
   c. compensate for specific deficits
   d. learn from the comfort of their home

What Would You Do?

Another pandemic has struck the world. For the new school year, your 10-year-old child's school is giving you the choice of attending school physically for 2 days a week and having online lessons for the remaining 3 days or of opting for exclusively virtual learning. What is your choice, and why?

Children at school: 6 months later

Seasons have changed, and the long-awaited summer break has arrived. Brian was able to close out his school year doing better than expected. When his mother, Claudia, says "better than expected," she is mostly referring to his math skills, which took a nose dive during the first half of the school year. She was very concerned and met several times with Brian's teacher. In one of those meetings, the teacher made a comment that saved Brian's year: She mentioned that children of Brian's age are not yet capable of abstract thinking and that he might do better in math if his mother practiced with him at home with hands-on materials like play clocks and pizzas that are sliced into a variety of different pieces to practice fractions. And indeed, manipulating, playing with, and "experiencing" the concepts of time and fractions did wonders for Brian. And to his mother's delight, not only did his grades improve, but so did his self-esteem. ■ ■ ■ ■

Overview

Emotional and Social Development in Middle Childhood

Children at school

Shawna is worried about her 7-year-old son, Jaylen. It's not a big worry; she's not even sure there's something to worry about. He's in second grade and seems to be doing really well academically. A helpful, thoughtful boy, he never gets into trouble and is generally well liked, according to his teachers. And yet, he reports to his mother that he normally plays alone on the monkey bars during recess.

Jaylen's older sister, Tally, who is 10 years old, sometimes sees him on the playground and confirms that Jaylen spends most of his time on his own but doesn't seem too distressed about it. But to Shawna, the thought of her little boy playing all by himself just sounds wrong. He doesn't have any close friends, and he says there isn't really anyone with whom he is interested in being friends. Shawna feels sad for him, but she doesn't want to share her feelings with Jaylen in case it upsets him. After all, maybe he really is fine just as he is.

Tally is the utter opposite of Jaylen. She's very outgoing, and she has many friends. She thinks about her friends almost constantly and often tells her mother what this or that friend is up to. It's such a contrast to Jaylen, who hardly ever talks about the other kids in his class. To Shawna, Tally's experience sounds so much more like a happy childhood! She isn't quite sure if there is something wrong and Jaylen needs help or if it is all in her own mind and she should just let Jaylen be Jaylen.

In this chapter, we will discuss how children's self-concept changes and how their self-esteem develops as they grow older. We will talk about the importance and influence of family as well as the increasing influence of friends and peers. Lastly, we will also have a closer look at which factors make a school good or even great.

13.1 Developing a Sense of Self

■ Explain how children's self-concept and self-esteem change during middle childhood.

Middle childhood is a time of many changes in children's lives. Children start to strive for independence and build up increasingly close friends. Making friends gets easier as children understand more about how others feel and how they might react to displays of feelings from those around them. Children become more aware of who they are, what their strengths and weaknesses are, and how they fare in comparison to their friends and peers. In the following section, we will explore how children develop a more realistic sense of self during middle childhood, how their self-concept relates to their self-esteem, and what caregivers can do to help children develop healthy self-esteem.

Changes in Children's Self-Concept

self-concept people's belief about themselves; it includes characteristics, abilities, attitudes, personality traits, and values.

In middle childhood, children's **self-concept** undergoes some significant changes. As you may remember from our discussion in Chapter 10, our self-concept is the way we see ourselves, including how we see our abilities, attitudes, personality traits, values, and other individual characteristics. When young children describe themselves, they tend to paint a very positive and exaggerated picture. They describe themselves not so much in terms of their psychological traits but rather in terms of their abilities (or the abilities they'd like to have!).

The changes we see in children's self-concept in middle childhood are closely linked to their cognitive development and to changes in their social behavior. Although parents still play a central role in children's lives, the role of peers is increasingly important (Collins & Madsen, 2019).

Consider the self-description of 10-year-old Gianna:

> My name is Gianna and I am 10 years old. I am really good at drawing and I love to spend my time crafting. There are a lot of girls I like at school, but there is one who is my best friend. Her name is Heather and we've been friends since second grade. I think most people like me because I am gentle and I always care about others if they don't feel good. I still can't swim, and I am actually not even sure why because I really try. But I really dislike the cold water. It makes me feel bad to see how all my classmates swim during school lessons and I can't keep up.

Gianna compares herself to her peers and assesses her abilities in a much more realistic way than do younger children (Harter, 2006). She also takes into account psychological traits by emphasizing how much she cares about others. When she speaks about swimming, Gianna does not compare herself favorably with her peers. Often, however, children in middle childhood do the opposite: They employ downward social comparison, which means that they compare themselves to other children who are less competent. These downward comparisons help children to build up and preserve positive self-esteem (Garcia et al., 2020; Gürel et al., 2020).

Children become increasingly likely to describe themselves as a part of groups like their soccer club or school choir (Harter, 2015; Livesley & Bromley, 1973). But their self-concept now goes deeper than plain behavior: They perceive themselves in terms of traits rather than actions (Christner et al., 2020; Harter, 2006, 2015). Am I studious? Smart? Athletic? Kind? Children's self-concept also becomes more realistic. They are better able to distinguish between the abilities and traits they actually have and the ones they would *like* to have (Harter, 2006, 2015).

The period from age 5 to age 12 falls into the fourth of Erik Erikson's eight stages of psychosocial development: *industry (or competence) vs.*

inferiority (Erikson, 1994) (see also Chapter 2). In this stage, children become increasingly independent and develop a large number of abilities and skills. They learn to read and write and gradually take on responsibilities. At the same time, children want their accomplishments to be recognized and valued. Approval by others helps them develop a positive view of themselves.

If, however, they do not feel valued in their accomplishments or feel like they are falling behind their peers, children will develop a sense of inferiority. But there is a simple thing parents can do to help their children develop a strong sense of competence: Parents need to believe in their children and clearly communicate that belief to their children. Studies show that parental beliefs about children's competence are related to their children's beliefs and to children's actual performance (Putnick et al., 2020).

■ As they get older, children increasingly compare themselves with their peers and integrate their assessments into their sense of self.

Self-Esteem

One important aspect of self-concept is **self-esteem**: a person's evaluation of their personal value (see Chapter 10).

One way of viewing self-esteem in children is that it proceeds from their self-concept. After all, the self-concept consists of the beliefs children harbor about their abilities, talents, and so on. Self-esteem is a child's overall sense of self-worth created by pulling all these evaluations together, usually beginning around the age of 8. However, there are not many scientific studies that have confirmed this model (Orth & Robins, 2019).

A newer model suggests that self-esteem is shaped by early experiences with caregivers. This view is rooted in attachment theory, which suggests that children develop a positive view of themselves when they are securely attached to their parents (Bowlby, 1979; Orth & Robins, 2019). Parental warmth and support of children's independence are, indeed, correlated with higher self-esteem (Allen et al., 1994; Brummelman et al., 2015). A longitudinal study that followed children for decades and periodically assessed their self-esteem found that the best predictor of children's self-esteem was the quality of their home environment and parenting quality (Orth, 2018).

Children's self-esteem tends to increase throughout middle childhood and into adolescence. However, there is often a slight drop in self-esteem as children transition from elementary school to middle school (Twenge & Campbell, 2001). Other studies have found that self-esteem may drop throughout middle childhood and adolescence, at which point it increases again throughout adult life (Hyde & Else-Quest, 2012; Robins et al., 2002). Perhaps not surprisingly, higher self-esteem has a number of benefits for children. A study of 13,000 college students found, for example, that higher self-esteem was linked to more happiness (Diener & Diener, 1995; Salavera et al., 2020). Likewise, low self-esteem has been linked to feelings of depression, suicide attempts, and anorexia nervosa (Adamson et al., 2019; Nguyen et al., 2019; Sowislo & Orth, 2013).

Given that it is so essential to children's well-being, how can we help children develop healthy self-esteem? Before we dive into this question, it is important to make a distinction between self-esteem and *narcissism* (Brummelman & Sedikides, 2020; Brummelman et al., 2016). Narcissism is highly inflated self-esteem that can arise when a parent tries to help a child develop self-esteem. Such exaggerated self-esteem, however, is related to

self-esteem a person's evaluation of their individual value. It is associated with positive or negative feelings, depending on how people think about themselves.

anxiety, rage, and depression in children (Thomaes & Brummelman, 2016). So, what parents and caregivers should seek to develop in their children is a healthy, positive self-esteem, rather than narcissism.

Researchers believe that self-esteem is based on three pillars: realism, growth, and robustness (**FIGURE 13.1**).

Self-Esteem and Resilience to Stress

As children grow up and venture out into the world, they are exposed to an increasing number of stressful situations. But with age and growing self-esteem, their ability to cope with stress improves as well. When preschoolers are distressed, their fallback strategy is to seek out their caregivers for support; they do not really use any cognitive strategies to cope with stress. If the parents are not available, they try to escape from the stressful situation or avoid it altogether, if possible (Zimmer-Gembeck & Skinner, 2011).

The most common stressor in middle childhood is interactions with others (Zimmer-Gembeck & Skinner, 2011). Other stressors like the death of a parent or sibling, a natural disaster like an earthquake or tsunami, and terrorism and war are rarer events that can cause emotional **trauma** as well. Trauma is more likely if children:

- have experienced traumatic events before;
- are directly involved in the traumatic events, for example as a victim;
- have a family history of mental illness;
- have insufficient social support from family and friends;
- are older; or
- are subsequently exposed to other long-term stressors like moving or attending a new school (National Institute of Mental Health, 2020; Sun et al., 2017; Tang et al., 2017).

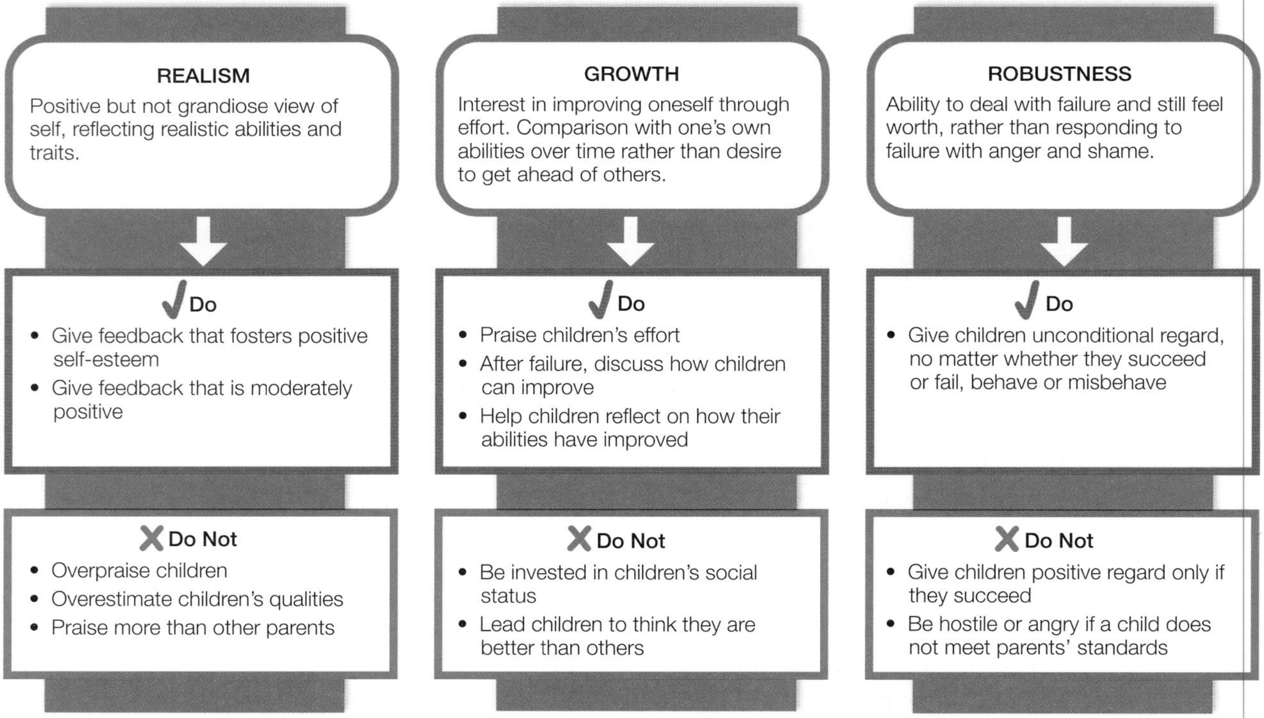

trauma emotional response to negative events that may include long-term reactions such as flashbacks, physical distress, and fluctuating emotions that can result in strained relationships with others.

REALISM
Positive but not grandiose view of self, reflecting realistic abilities and traits.

✓ Do
- Give feedback that fosters positive self-esteem
- Give feedback that is moderately positive

✗ Do Not
- Overpraise children
- Overestimate children's qualities
- Praise more than other parents

GROWTH
Interest in improving oneself through effort. Comparison with one's own abilities over time rather than desire to get ahead of others.

✓ Do
- Praise children's effort
- After failure, discuss how children can improve
- Help children reflect on how their abilities have improved

✗ Do Not
- Be invested in children's social status
- Lead children to think they are better than others

ROBUSTNESS
Ability to deal with failure and still feel worth, rather than responding to failure with anger and shame.

✓ Do
- Give children unconditional regard, no matter whether they succeed or fail, behave or misbehave

✗ Do Not
- Give children positive regard only if they succeed
- Be hostile or angry if a child does not meet parents' standards

FIGURE 13.1 The pillars of self-esteem and how to foster the development of positive self-esteem.

After E. Brummelman and C. Sedikides. 2020. *Child Dev Perspect* 14: 83–89

In response to stress and trauma, children develop a number of coping strategies that help them tailor their reaction to the situation. We particularly see the rise of cognitive coping strategies that include the following:

- *Problem-solving*: Children find a solution to the problem and act in order to resolve it.
- *Information-seeking*: Children read, observe, and talk with others in order to find alternative ways to respond to a situation.
- *Escape*: Children deny that the situation exists, withdraw mentally from the situation, or avoid whatever is causing the stress.
- *Support-seeking*: Children seek contact with and comfort from friends, family members, or other people.
- *Opposition*: Children blame others, have aggressive reactions (Zimmer-Gembeck & Skinner, 2011).

■ A young girl surveys the damage around her family home in Monroe County, Indiana, following a tornado in June 2019. When children experience traumatic events like war, natural disasters, or the death of a loved one, generally, the younger children are, the better they tend to cope with these events.

Naturally, some of these responses are healthier than others. As children grow near adolescence, they more frequently start to use planful actions in order to cope with stressors. They become more adept at distracting themselves, for example by going out or reading a book. They are also more likely to use techniques like positive self-speak ("next time I'll do much better") and to actively try to change their emotions and make themselves feel better. TABLE 13.1 shows how response to stress and trauma changes with age and offers some ways that adult caregivers can support children and help them develop healthy responses to stress and trauma.

■ **Table 13.1** Children's Responses to Traumatic Events and How to Help

Age	Response	How to support children
5 and younger	• Crying and clinging • Tantrums • Irritability • Physical symptoms like stomachache or headache • Increased fearfulness • Return to past behaviors like bed-wetting or thumb-sucking	• Address questions that remain unspoken, like "Will injuries heal, or will victims survive? Is it the child's fault? Can it happen to the child himself? Who will take care of the child now?" • Listen to children if they want to tell their story. • Try to maintain routines as much as possible. • If possible, avoid additional stressors, like a move or school change.
6–11	• School problems • Withdrawal from family and friends • Physical symptoms like stomachache or headache • Loss of interest in activities that they used to enjoy • Inability to concentrate • Nightmares, sleep problems	• Watch out for misunderstandings, like thinking an event was caused by the child. • Give children time to cope • Provide a safe space.
12 and older	• Substance abuse • Nightmares or sleep problems • Disrespectful or destructive behavior • Withdrawal from friends and family • Anger • Physical symptoms like stomachache or headache	

Source: National Institute of Mental Health. 2022. Helping Children and Adolescents Cope with Disasters and Other Traumatic Events: What Parents, Rescue Workers, and the Community Can Do. www.nimh.nih.gov; Johns Hopkins Children's Center. 2020. Helping children cope following trauma. www.hopkinsmedicine.org

Review!

How do children's self-concept and self-esteem change during middle childhood?

- Children's beliefs about themselves—their characteristics, abilities, traits, and values—are called *self-concept*. Self-concept changes in middle childhood along with an increase in cognitive abilities. Children compare themselves more often to their peers and see themselves as parts of different groups. They begin to

perceive themselves in terms of psychological traits, rather than just in terms of their favorite activities.

- Children's evaluation of themselves is called *self-esteem*. Children's self-esteem generally increases through middle childhood, with the exception of the period around the transition to middle school. Supporting children—giving them unconditional positive regard (that is, accepting them as they are)—can help the children develop positive self-esteem.

Practice!

1. As they build their self-concept, children in middle childhood tend to compare themselves mostly _____ .
   a. through comparison with younger peers
   b. through upward social comparison
   c. through downward social comparison
   d. through comparison with older peers

2. The fourth stage of psychosocial development according to Erikson is _____ .
   a. communality vs. inferiority
   b. industry vs. inferiority

   c. self-esteem vs. self-concept
   d. ridicule vs. seriousness

3. Children can be helped in developing positive self-esteem by _____ .
   a. giving them extremely challenging tasks to complete
   b. regularly attending the well-child appointments at the pediatrician
   c. giving them lots of presents
   d. praising children's efforts

Show What You've Learned!

Your 9-year-old daughter, Maura, has always been a happy, confident child, but recently you've begun to worry. There have been a number of occasions on which she felt very down and has said she dislikes herself. As far as you can remember, these

episodes mostly have occurred when she has failed at something. You are worried about her being so hard on herself. What would you do?

13.2 Family Life in Middle Childhood

- Identify the various family structures and explain the influence they have on children.
- Demonstrate how family life influences children.

Middle childhood is a time when parents still have considerable influence on their children's lives, even as children are striving for independence. In fact, the family and interactions within the family have an impact on children's lives in many domains. In this section, we will examine a number of family structures that are commonly found within the United States. We will also consider how the structure of family life and interactions influence the developing child.

Common Family Structures in the United States

Eleven-year-old Josiah returns home from school on a gloomy Friday afternoon and packs a few belongings. In half an hour, his father will come to pick him up so Josiah can spend the weekend with him. Josiah's parents have been divorced for 2 years, following a year-long separation, and throughout that time Josiah has been living with his mother—most of the time. Every other weekend, Josiah stays at his father's place. In the beginning, he loved those weekends, when his father had so much time just for him. But Josiah's father recently got remarried. He now lives with his new wife and her three children. Josiah resents having to share his father with those other children. He also isn't sure how to act toward his stepsiblings and their mother. He wishes he could just stay at his mom's place, play with his friends, and avoid his father's house, where he now feels so awfully uncomfortable.

As Josiah's story illustrates, family life can be complex and hard to navigate for adults as well as children. Nowadays, family structures are more diverse than ever before. In 2019, 70% of children under the age of 18 lived in households with two parents (this number includes adoptive parents or stepparents). In all, 26% of children lived in a household in which only one parent was present. Another 4% lived in a household that was headed by some other relative or nonrelative (Kemp et al., 2019; Stepfamily Foundation, 2020). As **FIGURE 13.2** shows, the number of two-parent families has declined steadily since 1960, while the number of single-parent families has increased. In fact, the ratio of two-parent to one-parent families has changed so much that in 2018, the United States had the world's highest percentage of children raised in single-parent families (see **FIGURE 13.3**).

Culture and income play a role in family size. Family income tends to be higher when more than one adult is part of the family; chores and responsibilities that are divided across more than one adult make everyday life easier as well. Households in more developed nations tend to

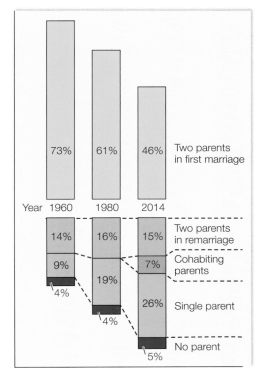

FIGURE 13.2 Living arrangements for children under the age of 18 from 1960 to 2014.

From Pew Research Center. 2015. The American Family Today. www.pewsocialtrends.org

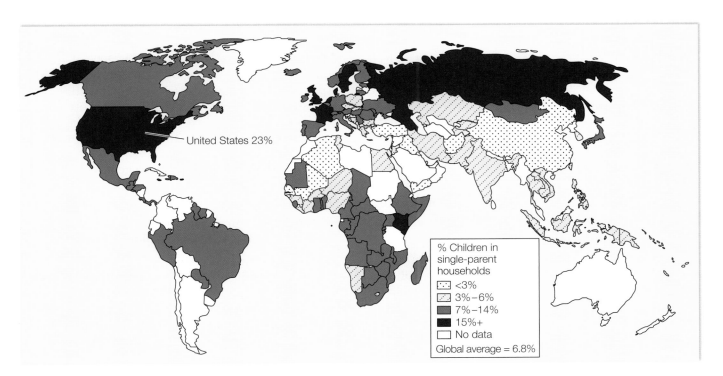

FIGURE 13.3 Percentage of children being raised in single-parent families in select countries of the world.

From Pew Research Center. 2019. U.S. has world's highest rate of children living in single-parent households. www.pewresearch.org

be smaller than in less developed countries for exactly these reasons: People in wealthier countries can afford to live in smaller households on the income of fewer people (Kramer, 2019).

Generally, children living with their two biological parents tend to fare best. Happy couples parent more cooperatively and effectively and can offer their children more financial stability. Children in these happy families are also more likely to have a closer relationship with their father (Amato, 2005). However, since family arrangements and atmosphere within families differ so greatly, it is impossible to draw general conclusions. Children living with two parents who argue viciously on a regular basis may face greater challenges than children whose parents are divorced but share custody of their children and continue to have an amicable relationship. Let's now take a closer look at family life in the United States.

One-fourth of American children live in one-parent households

About 1 in 4 children under the age of 18 live with just one parent. The majority of children in single-parent families live with their mother (21%), while 4% live with their father (Anderson et al., 2022).

Where do these one-parent families come from? A small percentage of one-parent families have experienced the death of a parent. In others, a single mother or father became a parent through sperm donation, surrogacy, or adoption. Most one-parent families have their roots in separation and divorce, however.

In the following section, we will take a closer look at divorce and its effects on children. When children grow up in single-parent households, whether the situation arises as a result of divorce or the death of a parent, there is a risk of financial hardship. But keep in mind that living with just one parent is not necessarily a risk factor if the child is well cared for and lives in a stable environment.

Starting in the 1960s, the divorce rate in the United States increased dramatically. Since the 1980s, it has decreased somewhat, although it remains relatively high compared with other nations (**FIGURE 13.4**). In 2000, there were 4 divorces per 1,000 people in the United States; by 2020, the rate had fallen to 2.3 divorces per 1,000 people (National Center for Health Statistics, 2022). Nevertheless, almost one out of every two marriages ultimately ends in divorce, so that many children are likely to experience the divorce of their parents at some point (American Academy of Child & Adolescent Psychiatry, 2017).

physical custody a custody arrangement that determines which parent(s) a child lives with.

legal custody a custody arrangement that determines the right of a parent to make decisions about a child's upbringing.

sole custody a custody arrangement in which a parent is responsible for all decisions about a child's upbringing (sole legal custody) and/or has a child living exclusively with her (sole physical custody).

joint custody a custody arrangement in which a child spends predetermined periods of time living with each parent and/or the parents share parental responsibilities.

When parents get divorced, they need to decide who gets custody of the child. There are different kinds of custody:

- **Physical custody** determines which parent(s) a child lives with.
- **Legal custody** determines which parent(s) can make decisions about important matters in the child's life, such as schooling, medical care, or religious upbringing.
- **Sole custody** gives one parent alone the right to make decisions for the child or to have the child live with that parent.
- **Joint custody** splits the responsibilities between both parents. In joint physical custody, the child spends a predetermined amount of time with each parent. The time a child spends with each child can be split 50–50, with the child spending equal periods of time with each parent. It can also be divided in unequal ways, such as having a child live most of the time with one parent and spend alternate weekends with the other.

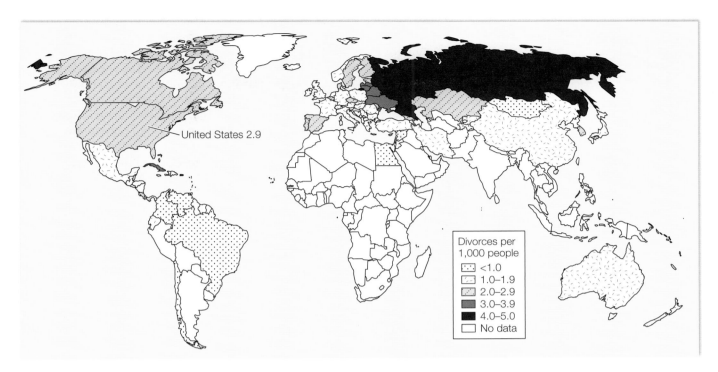

FIGURE 13.4   Divorces per 1,000 people, 2016. Divorce rates differ significantly in countries around the world. The United States is an outlier internationally because the divorce rates there have been consistently high for many decades (although divorce rates have been declining for 4 decades now).

From E. Ortiz-Ospina and M. Roser. 2020. Marriages and divorces. https://ourworldindata.org/CC BY 4.0, based on data from various sources

EFFECTS OF DIVORCE ON CHILDREN   A divorce nearly always has strong effects on both parents and children, but the nature of those effects may be quite different, depending on the circumstances. While divorces can be upsetting, acrimonious, and challenging for parents, they might also bring relief to one or both parents if their relationship has been especially difficult. Children, though, seldom feel relief when they find out their parents are getting divorced. Young children especially cannot begin to understand the complexities of adult relationships, and so a divorce for children is almost always stressful. Only in a minority of cases, where a parent is violent or abusive or where parental conflict dominates daily life, might the divorce come as a relief to children.

Regardless of the circumstances, a divorce affects many aspects of children's lives (Anderson, 2014):

- *Time spent with each parent.* Parents need to adjust to their new life situation and thus may have less time and energy to spend with their children. Single parents are more likely to have to work longer hours, and living with one parent often means seeing the other parent less often.

- *Economic security.* Mothers who have custody of their children typically experience a loss of 25–50% of the income they had before their divorce, and it often takes more than 5 years to get back to their pre-divorce income. A divorce may mean that the family has to move and that children are more likely to grow up in poverty (Edwards, 2014).

- *Emotional security and emotional distress*. After a divorce, children often spend less time with their fathers and as a result their relationship not only with their father but also their paternal grandparents may weaken (Attar-Schwartz & Fuller-Thomson, 2017; Kruk & Hall, 1995). Family traditions and holidays are likely to be celebrated in new and different ways, highlighting what children have lost (Pett et al., 1992). If the custodial parent moves away, children will have to change schools and may lose touch with their friends. Children in single-parent families are at least three times as likely to experience violence in the neighborhood or by a caregiver than children growing up with two biological parents (Bramlett & Radel, 2014). These experiences bring about risks for children's emotional health: A Swedish study of about 1 million children found that children living with one parent were more than twice as likely to attempt suicide, be diagnosed with a psychiatric disorder such as depression, or develop substance abuse problems (Brown et al., 1998; Sands et al., 2017). They are also twice as likely to develop behavioral problems (Auersperg et al., 2019; Kelleher et al., 2000).

- *Sexual behavior and relationships*. Children of divorced parents tend to engage in sexual relations earlier (Jónsson et al., 2000) and are less likely to view marriage as permanent (Jacquet & Surra, 2001). Girls of divorced parents also tend to be less satisfied with their romantic relationships (Jacquet & Surra, 2001).

- *Academic achievement*. Children in one-parent families tend to be more frequently absent from school (Pong et al., 2003), tend to have lower grade point averages, and are more likely to repeat a year in school (Jeynes, 2000). As adults, they often have a lower income than their peers from two-parent families (Anderson, 2014). It is not clear what role income loss plays in the children's lower academic achievements: Some researchers believe income loss plays a great role (Brand et al., 2019), while others believe psychological mechanisms like shock and coping difficulties are to blame (Chen et al., 2019). Since single parents often need to work more to secure the family's income, a lack of quality time with their children may also contribute to lower academic achievement.

- *Physical health*. Children raised by two biological parents were found in one study to be healthier and to use emergency rooms less often than those raised by single parents (Blackwell, 2010; Centers for Disease Control and Prevention, 2012).

Despite the variety of negative effects divorce can have on children, many children do not suffer long-term effects after an initial adjustment period. When parents continue to take their parenting roles seriously, and when they collaborate and allow their children to have a relationship with each parent, children tend to do better after the divorce (Wallerstein & Lewis, 2004).

HELPING CHILDREN COPE WITH DIVORCE Divorce happens; there is no way around it. But there are better and worse ways

■ A divorce requires major adjustments by parents as well as by children. Children are at risk for behavioral, cognitive, and emotional problems when they feel like they have to side with one parent over the other or are being drawn into parental conflicts.

© David Pereiras/Shutterstock.com UN PHOTO 13.4

to handle a separation. There are a number of ways parents can help their children cope with their divorce.

In the very beginning, when parents have to break the news to their children, they often find it very challenging to find the right words. Generally, it is best for both parents to be present when they announce the divorce to their children. It is important for parents to:

- leave their own feelings and animosities out of the discussion;
- adjust the message to the age and maturity level of the children— younger children need fewer details than older children;
- emphasize that the divorce is not the fault of the children or anything they did;
- provide children with information about the changes to come so they can mentally prepare; and
- tell the children both parents still love them and that, while parents can separate, children and parents belong together for life.

Throughout the divorce process and afterward, parents themselves are often very distressed and need to adjust to their new situation. Their distress makes it difficult for them to help their children cope. But parents are not helpless, and they still can help in myriad ways to make their children feel safe. Children need lots of love and reassurance throughout the adjustment period (which can take up to 2 years). They need to know that they are still loved and that things will work out even if circumstances are difficult in the short term. Honesty and generous hugs give children some comfort as well. Children should be encouraged to share their feelings and given the opportunity to articulate what would help them most to cope (Kemp et al., 2019).

Throughout a time of many changes, routines are a subtle way of providing children with security. Parents should not bad-mouth each other, and they should avoid fighting in front of their children. Children should never be in a position where they feel like they have to take sides, mediate conflicts, or choose one parent over the other.

When one parent moves out, children often appreciate being able to see that parent's new home early on. They may even be able to help furnish the new place and bring over some of their own belongings to make it feel more familiar. And perhaps, most of all, parents need to be patient with themselves, each other, and their children so everyone can adjust to the major changes (Nemours Foundation, 2015).

Blended families present challenges and opportunities for children

In 2018, 11% of children lived with their mother and her new partner (United States Census Bureau, 2020a). Stepfamilies are increasingly common in the United States. A stepfamily, or **blended family**, consists of married partners living with one or more children from a previous marriage. Each day, 1,300 new stepfamilies are created in the United States (Stepfamily Foundation, 2020).

blended family a married couple living with at least one child from a previous marriage.

Life in a blended family can be fraught with difficulties for children. They may not know how to behave toward the new stepparent (and possibly, stepsiblings) or may experience loyalty conflicts. At times, the stepparent and biological parent may disagree on parenting issues or offer the child conflicting advice (Jensen & Lippold, 2018). A stepparent may introduce a new culture or traditions to the family dynamic, affecting everything from family meals to holiday observances.

While most stepchildren eventually do adjust to their new family, they are at greater risk for developing a range of problems, compared with children who live with their two biological parents (Ganong et al., 2018). Children from

■ Blended families face unique challenges as two different families come together to create one new, blended family. Will the stepchildren accept the new parent? Will the stepparent be able and willing to treat the new stepchildren like his own? Only time will tell how successful this new family will be.

© kali9/Getty ImagesUN PHOTO 13.5

stepfamilies tend not to perform as well academically as children from biological two-parent families (Jeynes, 2006). They also tend to have more physical and psychological health issues and more trouble with their social relationships (Dunn, 2002).

But stepfamilies also can offer new opportunities for children. When the stepparents combine their incomes, the financial situation usually improves. The development of a good relationship between stepparent and children may take time, but if successful, children experience a reduction in stress, academic problems, and physical and mental health problems (Jensen & Harris, 2017; Jensen et al., 2018; King, 2006).

Children do best when they still have a relationship with their other biological parent and when family dynamics in their new stepfamily are harmonious. The younger children are when the stepfamily is formed, the easier the transition tends to be for them (Pasley & Garneau, 2012).

Children thrive in LGBT families

As of 2017, roughly 4.5% of adults in the United States identified as being lesbian, gay, bisexual, or transgender (LGBT), and around 1 million LGBT people were married (Newport, 2018). About 200,000 children are being raised by same-sex couples, and as many as 3 million children have an LGBT parent (Family Equality Council, 2017). LGBT couples are about four times more likely than heterosexual couples to adopt children (Gates, 2013); they may also conceive children through sperm donors or surrogate mothers, or they may have children from previous heterosexual relationships.

How do children growing up in LGBT families fare? Research shows that children of same-sex couples develop and thrive at a level similar to that of children of different-sex couples (Crowl et al., 2008). For example, children of same-sex couples tend to do as well at school and have the same cognitive and physical abilities as their peers raised by heterosexual parents (Golombok et al., 1997; Wainright et al., 2004). Children with lesbian mothers tend to have more interactions with their mothers than do the children of heterosexual mothers (Golombok et al., 1997). They exhibit the same levels of depression, anxiety, substance abuse, and low self-esteem as their peers from heterosexual families, and they tend to have typical and positive relationships with others (Wainright & Patterson, 2006, 2008; Wainright et al., 2004). Studies also show that children raised by same-sex parents are no more likely to be homosexual themselves or to be gender-nonconforming than children of different-sex couples (Golombok et al., 2003; Pawelski et al., 2006).

Same-sex parents and their children do experience some adversity that heterosexual families do not. Children of same-sex parents are more likely to experience discrimination or social stigma because of their family structure, and they are more likely to be bullied. The extent to which children experience bullying depends on where they grow up. For example, a study that compared children of same-sex couples in the United States and in the Netherlands found that American children were more likely to be bullied and less likely to share information about their parents with others, possibly because same-sex couples are more accepted in the Netherlands than in the United States (Bos et al., 2008).

■ Studies show that children of same-sex couples thrive as much as those who have different-sex parents. However, just like their parents, children are likely to face some rejection and stigma due to their parents' sexual orientation.

Adoption has positive effects on most children

Around 1.5 million American children are adopted, with 140,000 adoptions taking place in the United States each year (Adoption Network, 2020). Children can be adopted through private or public agencies or through a direct agreement between birth parents and adoptive parents. Nowadays, adoptions are more likely to be open adoptions, in which biological and adoptive families stay in touch and remain part of each other's lives in whatever way they choose.

Adoption tends to have generally good benefits for children, particularly when compared with the alternatives of growing up with a family that cannot adequately care for them or of growing up in an orphanage. In terms of cognitive abilities and self-esteem, children in adoptive families tend to do just as well as children who live with their biological parents (Hamilton et al., 2007; Juffer & Van Ijzendoorn, 2007).

Of course, adoptions also pose some unique challenges. First, children need to be integrated into the new family. Obviously, when a new child comes into a family, everybody has to adjust, and that takes time. Adjustment usually goes faster and proceeds with fewer complications the younger the child is (Sharma et al., 1996). Social and emotional adjustment problems are more common in children who have spent a longer time in institutions or who have experienced a number of adversities (Holmgren et al., 2020). Adjustment problems also may occur later, around middle childhood or adolescence, when children become more aware of what it means to be adopted. They face the task of forming an identity that includes the adoption and possible links to both the biological and adoptive families.

Multigenerational families are becoming more common

Multigenerational families are households consisting either of two or more adult generations or of grandparents living together with grandchildren under the age of 25 (Cohn & Passel, 2018). During the recession of 2008–2009, the number of Americans living in multigenerational families rose sharply. As economic conditions improved again, however, the trend toward multigenerational living continued. In 2016, 64 million Americans (20% of the American population) lived in one household with multiple generations (see **FIGURE 13.5**).

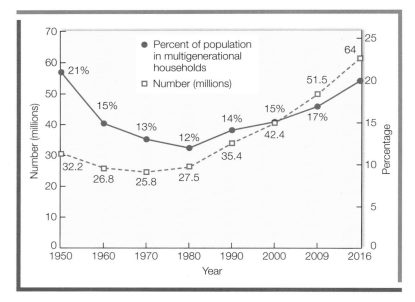

FIGURE 13.5 Multigenerational families in the United States. An increasing number of Americans live with multiple generations in one household. In 2014, for the first time in 130 years, the percentage of young adults aged 18–34 years living with their parents was higher than any other living arrangement.

After D. Cohn and J. S. Passel. 2018. A record 64 million Americans live in multigenerational households. www.pewresearch.org

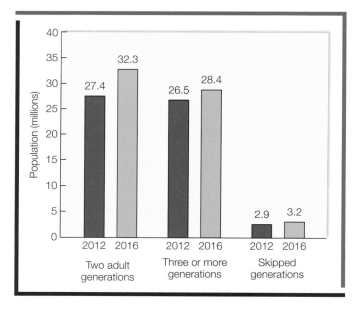

FIGURE 13.6 Compositions of multigenerational households in 2012 and 2016. Within four years, the number of adult children living with their parents has risen significantly (adult children in this study were children 25 years of age and older, so children attending college and living at home are not included in two-adult-generation households) Note: Skipped-generation households include grandparents and grandchildren younger than 25.

After D. Cohn and J. S. Passel. 2018. A record 64 million Americans live in multigenerational households. www.pewresearch.org

Multigenerational households are more common among Asian American and Hispanic American families and less common among White and Black families. The rise of multigenerational families is due to the value of resource-sharing across generations (Park et al., 2019) and to the fact that adults aged 18–34 are now more likely to live with their parents than at any time in the last 130 years (Cohn & Passel, 2018).

Some compositions of multigenerational households are more common than others. The most common configuration is two adult generations living together, followed closely by three or more generations. Only a small fraction of multigenerational families are made up of grandparents and grandchildren living together, with no parent in the household (FIGURE 13.6).

Family Life

Twelve-year-old Stella lives with her two younger brothers and her divorced mother in a small two-bedroom apartment. Life tends to be hectic in her family. Her mother Tanya has to work two jobs in order to afford the rent together with food and clothing bills. Because Tanya works such long hours, Stella takes on the responsibility of looking after her brothers when the three of them aren't in school. It doesn't always work out so well. Stella has trouble coordinating her schedule as well as those of her brothers, so often her mother notices at the last minute that someone is scheduled to be somewhere, and they have to rush out to make the appointment. It's not uncommon for the children to spend mealtimes in front of the TV with something Stella has been able to prepare in the microwave while Tanya is trying to get some housework done.

As Stella's situation illustrates, everyday life does not flow smoothly in many families. Simple things like spending time at dinner together or having a routine for school days can make a big difference. In this section, we examine some aspects of family life that, despite their seeming simplicity, can make a difference to children's lives.

Families that eat together enjoy many short- and long-term benefits

Family meals don't last long—only about 20 minutes on average. And yet, gathering everyone in the household together for a shared meal can be as complicated as it is important (Fiese & Schwartz, 2008). Families with a higher socioeconomic status tend to eat together more frequently than lower socioeconomic status (SES) families (Litterbach et al., 2017). In families like Stella's, parents often have to work more than one job or long hours so that meals together are often out of reach. Media coverage often suggests that American families do not dine together much anymore. However, a recent study found that around 88% of Americans report that they frequently eat dinner with other family members (Ferdman, 2017). That is good news, because there are numerous benefits to parents and children eating their meals together. Cooking and eating meals together without distractions allows families to (Nutrition Education Program, 2020):

■ When a family enjoys frequent meals together, the children have a chance to learn about meal preparation and healthy nutrition. At the same time, children practice social skills and manners at the table, and conversations can help the family connect or highlight issues children may be experiencing in their lives.

- Improve cooking and academic skills: Having fun together in the kitchen lets children develop cooking skills as well as math and reading skills.
- Build relationships: Parents can check in with their children to see how they are doing, give support, and they can all cheer each other on.
- Practice social skills: Conversation skills and manners are honed at the dinner table.
- Consume healthier food, more cheaply: Home-cooked meals are often healthier than fast food picked up when busy families are on the go; they also cost less money.
- Control portion sizes: Fast-food and heat-and-serve meals come in predetermined serving sizes, but when families prepare and eat food together, each person can take an appropriate amount of food first and help themselves to more only if they're still hungry afterward.

Children whose families regularly eat meals together tend to have healthier eating habits. These habits frequently last throughout their lives and can help to prevent future illnesses (Hamilton & Hamilton Wilson, 2009; Kok et al., 2019). Frequent family meals also lower children's risks of becoming overweight and developing eating disorders (Martin-Biggers et al., 2014).

But not all meals are equal. Children whose families often eat fast food and dine in front of the TV do not reap the same benefits as children who cook with their families and have lively exchanges at the dinner table (Martin-Biggers et al., 2014).

Chaos in families often leads to negative outcomes for children

Families differ considerably from each other when you look at the way they are organized and function in daily life. For example, in families with unavoidable household chaos like Stella's, every day is a bit of an adventure. There is no predictable daily schedule governing their fast-paced everyday lives (Marsh et al., 2020). At certain times, everyone is doing their own thing, which means that the TV in one room might be competing with the sound of a video playing in another room, combining to create a significant level of background noise in the small apartment.

Disorganization in households has a number of unfortunate effects on children. For example, children raised in households with higher levels of chaos tend to perform worse at school than children from more organized households.

They also have a higher risk of developing socio-emotional and behavioral problems than children from organized households (Boles et al., 2017; Coldwell et al., 2006; Deater-Deckard et al., 2009; Marsh et al., 2020). One study found that even if investigators take into account IQ and education of parents, parenting behaviors and warmth, stressful events, and housing conditions, household chaos still has a negative effect on children's cognitive abilities (Deater-Deckard et al., 2009). Unfortunately, it is hard to change the way households are run, particularly when parents have to work long hours and have limited financial means.

However, some research indicates that growing up in chaotic and unorganized households can also lead to the development of "hidden talents." Hidden talents are skills that develop from the experience of adversity and that are frequently not noticed by teachers, other professionals, or researchers. These skills include the ability to make decisions under stress or to behave in a very goal-directed way (Ellis et al., 2020).

Parents transfer control to their children

In middle childhood, the interactions of children and parents gradually change. In infancy and early childhood, parents exercise relatively strict control over their children's behavior. In middle childhood, parents begin to share control with their children. This is a stage where children are preparing for adolescence. As teenagers, they will spend much less time with their parents and find themselves frequently in situations where they have to make decisions by themselves. While the transfer of control to children begins around age 6, it isn't until about age 12 that children begin to be truly autonomous in some ways. The process in which parents gradually transfer some control to their children is called **coregulation**.

Coregulation is a process in which both parents and children participate. Parents monitor their children's behavior from a distance, ready to intervene or lend support when things go wrong. They teach children to make decisions about which behaviors are acceptable or unacceptable, how to assess the risk inherent in the actions they may take, and when they need to seek guidance from their parents before acting.

This gradual shift of control from parents to children necessitates that parents be informed about the activities and whereabouts of their children so they can intervene if they deem it necessary (Calkins, 2011). Children spend more time away from their home and at greater distance from their home as they get older. In return for giving that freedom, parents generally expect that their children will let them know where they will be going and when they will be back. A number of parents use smartwatches, dedicated child trackers, and cell phones to get in touch with their children or keep track of their location.

During this phase, we also can observe a shift in the way parents attempt to influence their children's behavior (Kochanska et al., 2008; Maccoby, 1984). They are now more likely to use reasoning, explaining *why* it is dangerous to run into the street without looking. They also discuss moral values with their children, anticipating situations like the taunting of a classmate, so children can decide how to act responsibly without a caregiver present (Colman et al., 2006).

coregulation the process by which parents gradually transfer control to their children.

Working Parents

The afternoon school bus is running late again, as usual. Marietta and Robin are fourth graders who have been friends ever since they met in kindergarten. It is getting toward winter, and the weather is gray and rainy. Robin's stop is first, and her father is waiting for her in their driveway as he always does, rain or shine. Marietta looks out at her friend with a wistful gaze. Her parents both work full time and aren't normally home until 5:30 at the earliest. Marietta will come home to an empty house, and it will be a couple of hours until one of her parents is home.

In 2020, 71% of mothers with children under the age of 18 worked. Of married mothers, 69% worked, whereas 76% of divorced and single mothers worked. Mothers with young children (under 6) worked less often, but the majority (66%) still held a job. Most of the working mothers—80%—were working full time. These numbers are in sharp contrast to the situation a few decades ago, when, in 1975, just 47% of mothers worked (Parcel, 2015).

While the gap between working mothers and working fathers is narrowing, most fathers—and more fathers than mothers—were employed in 2020. Whereas single mothers were more likely than married mothers to be working, the situation was reversed for fathers: 92% of married fathers and 86% of fathers who were divorced or single were working. And 96% of working fathers worked full time (U.S. Bureau of Labor Statistics, 2021).

Parental employment has a variety of effects on children. When parents work, the family tends to have more money. Children whose parents have higher earnings tend to do better at school, particularly in reading. They also show more prosocial behavior and are more likely to attend college (Duncan et al., 2007; Mayer, 2010; Parcel, 2015).

In the United States, there remains a stigma around mothers who choose to work instead of staying at home to care for children. This is evident, anecdotally, in parenting blogs and social media posts that express concern that working mothers put their children's development at risk. However, a meta-analysis of 69 studies examining the issue was unable to substantiate this concern (Friedman, 2018; Lucas-Thompson et al., 2010). Particularly when mothers are single or depend on social assistance programs such as welfare, it benefits the family when they work: As we have discussed throughout this book, there is a positive correlation between healthy child development and total household income. Some studies have also found that child achievement is actually higher and children whine and cling less when mothers work (Parcel & Menaghan, 1994a, 1994b). Likewise, children perceive their mother's employment positively. At the same time, when mothers have more control over their work hours and how they work, and are able to spend some time by themselves, their children tend to have better mental health than if their mothers have little control over their work (Friedman, 2018).

Studies indicate that the hours worked don't play too much of a role in children's well-being as long as parents are responsive to their children's needs when they are home and believe that family should come first (Friedman, 2018; Parcel, 2015). For the majority of parents, balancing work and family is difficult, however.

■ As children grow older, they spend increasingly more time without their parents. The transfer of control from parents to children is a gradual one. In the beginning of middle childhood, parents still exercise much control. With time, they let their children take on more responsibility while supervising from a distance.

■ In parenting blogs and social media posts, it is easy to find evidence of concern that working mothers risk their children's well-being. However, research shows a strong positive correlation between total household income and measures of child well-being, such as success at school. Other studies show that parental employment does not necessarily harm children's development as long as parents value their family and are responsive to their children while at home.

A 2015 survey found that 60% of mothers and 52% of fathers found balancing job and family was somewhat or very difficult. College-educated parents (66%) and White parents (61%) said they found it more difficult to balance work and family than did non-White parents (48%) and those who were not college educated (50%) (Friedman, 2018).

Culture Counts

Individualistic and Collectivist Cultures

Families' culture significantly shapes the environment in which children are raised. Western culture's individualistic style emphasizes that children should become autonomous and self-reliant and that they should watch out for their own interests. Collectivist values, to the contrary, stress that people are dependent on each other and that children also need to attend to the needs of others (Prevoo & Tamis-LeMonda, 2017; Tamis-LeMonda et al., 2008; Yaman et al., 2010). But there is substantial variation even within collectivist and individualistic cultures. For example, Hispanic American and Chinese communities both have roots in collectivism. Hispanic American families expect their children to be well-mannered (bien educado); to adhere to authorities (respecto); to interact with others in a way that avoids, if possible, confrontation (simpatia); and to be warm and respectful in interactions with others (personalismo) (Mogro-Wilson, 2013). Chinese families, to the contrary, trace their roots back to Confucius and expect their children to adhere to social norms (Li), be modest (Qian), control themselves (Yue), and feel shame when they misbehave (Chi) (Luo et al., 2013).

The way parents engage with their children differs as well, depending on their culture. Asian American parents spend more time teaching young children academic concepts such as letters and numbers, whereas White parents engage more frequently in pretend play (Parmar et al., 2008). Italian mothers place more emphasis on touch when they engage with their infants, in contrast to West African mothers, who place more importance on physical movement (Carra et al., 2014).

Race and socioeconomic status often interact with each other, because people belonging to a country's racial majority tend be better off financially and thus to have more resources to invest into activities supporting their children's cognitive, emotional, and physical development than do members of ethnic minority groups (Duncan et al., 2015; Henry et al., 2019). Parents from poorer families are also more often absent when their children are at home because they have to work long or irregular hours (Li et al., 2014). In the United States, systematic discrimination affects even those minority families who earn sufficient income. For example, in the housing market, systematic discrimination against Black, Hispanic, and Native American people has been found. There is some discrimination against Asian Americans as well, but not to the same extent as toward other ethnic minorities (Quillian, Lee, & Honore, 2020).

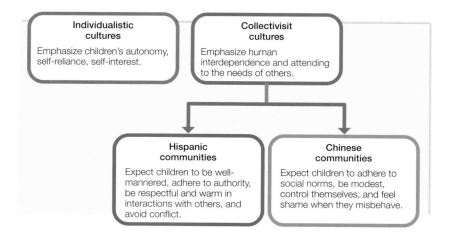

■ Question

What differences might there be between families of different cultural backgrounds when they have to deal with a child who was caught cheating at school or a child who tends to be impolite in interactions with teachers at school?

Review!

What are the effects of family structure on children?

■ Today's families vary widely in their composition. In addition to "traditional" families consisting of opposite-sex married parents with children, one-parent families, stepfamilies, adoptive families, multigenerational families, and LGBT families are increasingly common in the United States.

■ Research suggests that all other things being equal, children in two-parent families fare better than children in one-parent households. This may be because responsibilities can be divided across caregivers, and dual-earning households may have more resources. However, conflict and low household income can create stress in two-parent families. A family environment that is happy and safe will always have the greatest benefits for children's healthy development.

■ Divorce can be stressful for children as well as for parents. That stress can be reduced if the new financial situation of the custodial parent is sound, if the divorced or separated parents get along amicably, and if children are able to spend time with each parent.

■ Blended families bring challenges and opportunities: There are new child–caregiver relationships that need to be navigated, and there are likely to be new family routines and traditions, which may be strange and unfamiliar but also novel and exciting.

■ Studies have shown that children of LGBT couples are as well-adjusted as the children of heterosexual couples.

■ Adopted children tend to do better the younger they are at the time of adoption. They might experience adjustment problems when they are integrated into the new family as well as when they are old enough to come to terms with their adoption.

How does family life influence children?

■ Family life influences children in many different ways. Frequent meals together allow family members to bond as well as to practice healthy eating habits and social skills. Dinnertime conversations may allow parents to learn about problems their children are having that might otherwise go unnoticed.

■ An organized daily life with a regular schedule helps children's development; chaotic and fast-paced households place children at risk for school, socio-emotional, and behavioral problems.

■ In middle childhood, parents increasingly transfer control to their children in a process called *coregulation*. They also start to appeal more to children's moral values and reasoning skills in attempts to influence their children's behavior, particularly while the children are out of the parents' reach.

Practice!

1. In the United States, about _____ children live with one parent.
   a. 1 in 2
   b. 1 in 4
   c. 1 in 10
   d. 1 in 20

2. A parent having joint custody of a child _____ .
   a. provides housing for that child but does not have the right to make legal decisions for the child
   b. makes decisions concerning the child alone, and the child lives with that parent exclusively
   c. makes decisions about the child together with the other parent
   d. can make decisions for the child but does not have any legal visitation rights

3. A blended family is a family where _____ .
   a. two parents with a significant age difference have children together
   b. two partners of different races/ethnicity have children together
   c. two homosexual or transgender persons raise children together
   d. two previously married persons form a new relationship and bring at least one child into the new relationship

Act It Out!

For the past 2 years, you and your spouse haven't been getting along. You were both very young when you married, but your lives and goals since then have become very different. You stayed together as long as you have for the sake of your daughter, Sophie, now 9 years old, but it has become clear to you both that it is time to seek a divorce. On your own or with a classmate as your spouse, act out a conversation with Sophie explaining your decision to get a divorce. Draw on the material presented in this chapter to anticipate the kinds of questions she is likely to have.

What Would You Do?

Your 11-year-old son Myron has always liked to play outside. You generally support his spending lots of time outside. However, recently he has started to disappear for several hours at a time. You don't know where he is, and if you ask him, he just says he's been biking around the neighborhood. He also does not respect the times you set for him to return home and has frequently been an hour or more late. You want to respect his need to become more independent but at the same time feel very

uncomfortable with the current situation. How would you try to resolve this problem?

Additional Resources Online

- "10 Strategies for dealing with a defiant teen," from Middle Earth

- "Effective ways to handle defiant children," from Very Well Family
- "Help for parents of troubled teens," from Help Guide

13.3 Peers and Friends in Middle Childhood

- Evaluate the significance of peer relationships, sociometric status, and friendships in middle childhood.
- List the approaches that can be taken to address bullying.

As we have seen above, the majority of American mothers work at least part-time, and many of them start or return to work while their children are still very young. As a result, children from an early age spend large parts of their weekdays with other children in daycares, preschools, and elementary schools (Pepler & Bierman, 2018). But interacting with others does not always come easily to children, just as it does not come naturally to all adults. There are pronounced differences in sociability (how much children enjoy being in the company of others) and social abilities (the skills we use to interact with others) even between siblings, as we have seen in the beginning of this chapter with Jaylen and Tally. In this section, we will see how children learn to be social by navigating issues of popularity and bullying. We'll explore who children form friendships with and why friendships are important, and we will take a closer look at online dares.

The Importance of Peer Relations

As children progress through elementary school, their social lives become more complex. Their interactions during recess and breaks become longer and more involved, and they collaborate more on schoolwork. They incorporate more rules into their play and distinguish between classmates and friends.

These interactions are important because they differ from the interactions children have with adults. In their peers, children find equals with whom they learn to get along, work out conflicts, and develop problem-solving skills (Rubin et al., 2015). Together, they learn to manage their emotions and help others (Pepler et al., 1998).

But not all children have an easy time getting along with others; some may have no desire for frequent interactions. Jaylen, as we saw at the start of the chapter, tends to play by himself and seems perfectly content to do so. Certainly not every child needs to be at the center of attention. But interacting with others does help children learn many of the social and cognitive skills they will find useful later in life. Children who are aggressive or shy, who lack social skills, or who have difficulties managing their emotions and impulses can find themselves excluded from their peer groups. They are the ones who need social interaction the most in order to hone their skills. But with fewer opportunities to interact with others, they cannot develop their social skills and might even become more reclusive or aggressive (Dishion & Tipsord, 2011).

Popularity

As children begin to interact with each other, a social hierarchy forms based on popularity. Children quickly discover the value of being popular, and throughout their school years many children will actively try to cultivate their popularity (Poorthuis et al., 2019). In order to study children's popularity, researchers have created a measure called *sociometric status*. Children are asked whom they like and dislike among their peers. The resulting sociometric status indicates how liked or disliked children are among their peer group (Cillessen & Bukowski, 2018). Researchers have established a popularity scale based on five different statuses children can have (Cillessen, 2019; Gifford-Smith & Brownell, 2003; Newcomb et al., 1993; van der Wilt et al., 2018):

- *Popular children* are generally well liked. They tend to have excellent social abilities, to have better social problem-solving skills than average children, and to tend to exhibit low levels of aggression.

- *Average children* are, as the term suggests, about average when it comes to how much they are liked by their peers. Children in this category often serve as a baseline comparison group for the other four groups.

- *Controversial children* are well-liked by one group of their peers and disliked by another group. These children tend to be just as sociable as average children. However, they are as aggressive or sometimes even more aggressive than rejected children. They differ from rejected children in that they have better social skills, which make up in part for their increased aggression.

- *Rejected children* are generally disliked. They tend to be less sociable and more aggressive and disruptive than average children.

- *Neglected children* are neither liked nor disliked; they may not be noticed by most of their peers. Compared to average children, they engage in fewer interactions and are more shy or withdrawn.

Being unpopular has negative consequences for children. One study of around 580 Norwegian children aged 6 to 9 found that unpopular children were more likely to get sick than popular children (Ulset et al., 2019). Unpopular children also run a higher risk of becoming delinquent or dropping out of school (Dishion & Tipsord, 2011; Hartup, 1992).

Children who are popular with peers and low in aggression are more likely to have a job high in prestige later in life (Dubow et al., 2014). This finding illustrates how peer relationships influence the development of skills that are important for activities and work decades later.

Parents affect their children's popularity as well through their parenting style, perhaps because children learn at home how to interact with others. Children with authoritarian parents who are very strict and punitive are less popular than children of authoritative parents who are responsive to the children's needs (Deković & Janssens, 1992; Hart et al., 1990).

■ Many children in middle childhood and adolescence strive to be popular. Popular children tend to be ones who have good social and problem-solving skills and who are not aggressive toward their peers.

Friendship

While children interact with many other children on a daily basis, their interactions differ depending on whether they interact with friends or nonfriends (Erdley & Day, 2017). Children tend to seek out friends who are relatively similar to them in terms of age, race, interests, and attitudes (Boivin & Vitaro, 1995; Dishion et al., 1995). Through their frequent interaction, friends tend to become even more similar to each other over time (Giletta et al., 2011).

When children interact with other children they have chosen as friends, they tend to:

- smile, talk, share, and help each other more;
- complete tasks more effectively together;
- use negotiation in conflicts to try to maintain the friendship, rather than using force and power; and
- compete less with each other (Newcomb & Bagwell, 1995).

Friendships in children fulfill a whole range of needs. Friends provide companionship, so that children have someone to spend their time with (Buhrmester & Furman, 1987). Friends help each other in times of need and provide feelings of security, support, and comfort (Furman & Bierman, 1984; Furman & Robbins, 1985). Friends also have a positive impact on a child's self-esteem. Not surprisingly, popular children tend to feel less lonely than do children who get rejected by their peers (Parker & Asher, 1993). Friendship is also strongly associated with positive self-esteem, both in middle childhood and in adolescence (Vandell & Hembree, 1994). One study found that the more and the better friendships children had in elementary school, the higher was the children's self-esteem and the less loneliness they felt as they started middle school—one of the big transitions in middle childhood (Kingery et al., 2011).

A longitudinal study that followed girls from third to sixth grade found that the more friendships the girls had, and the better they felt the quality of those friendships was, the less likely they were to show depressive symptoms (Rudolph et al., 2007). In fact, just having one close friend lowered girls' risk of experiencing depressive symptoms (Brendgen et al., 2013). Likewise, children who rate their friendships as being of lower quality are more at risk for feeling anxious (Kingery et al., 2010).

Unfortunately, friends can also have a range of negative effects on each other. For example, not only do delinquent boys tend to befriend others with the same tendencies, but they also tend to reinforce each other's behavior, which leads to an increase in behavioral problems (Boivin & Vitaro, 1995; Dishion et al., 1996). Elementary school children who befriend others with behavioral problems are more likely to show behavioral problems themselves in the next grade (Patterson et al., 2005). In older children and adolescents, depression has been found to be "contagious": Adolescents who have friends with higher levels of depression tend to experience an increase in their own depressive symptoms (Giletta et al., 2011).

In late elementary school, we can observe the first differences between friendships among boys and girls (Erdley & Day, 2017) (FIGURE 13.7).

While friends are an important part of children's lives, some children have a harder time making or keeping friends. Here are a few things caregivers can do to help their children make friends:

- *Use playdates to practice.* Discuss with children how they can make sure their guests feel comfortable, how to share their belongings, and how to figure out if their friends are having a good time. Discuss afterward what went well and what did not go so well.
- *Practice social skills in role play.* Many interactions will go more smoothly with practice. Practice how to ask other children if you can join them to play, how to assert your rights without being aggressive, and how to take turns.

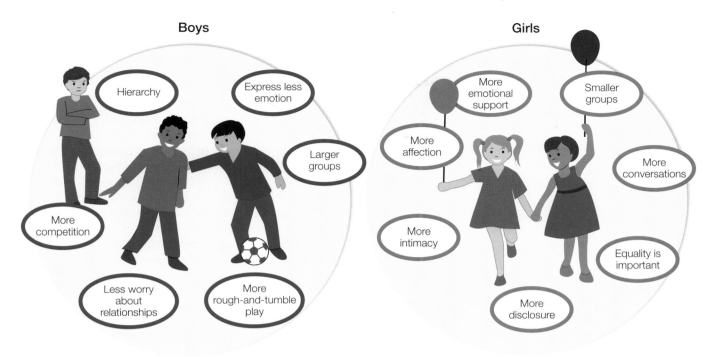

Boys

Hierarchy

Express less emotion

Larger groups

More competition

Less worry about relationships

More rough-and-tumble play

Girls

More emotional support

Smaller groups

More affection

More conversations

More intimacy

Equality is important

More disclosure

FIGURE 13.7 Gender differences in friendship. By late childhood, children mostly have friends of the same gender. Boys' and girls' friendships become increasingly dissimilar.

Data from J. G. Parker and S. R. Asher. 1993. *Dev Psychol* 29: 611; A. J. Rose. 2002. *Child Dev* 73: 1830–1843; A. J. Rose and K. D. Rudolph. 2006. *Psychol Bull* 132: 98; K. D. Rudolph et al. 2007. *Merrill-Palmer Q* 53: 461–488

- *Speak with the teacher.* Children often cannot accurately determine whether they are liked or disliked and what may be going wrong or right in their interactions with others. Teachers often can give valuable insights or even strategically seat a shy child with another one who they think they might become friends with.

- *Help children interpret others' emotions and teach how to express concern for them.* Younger children sometimes have trouble accurately determining how others feel and why. Helping them understand others can make it easier for them to find better ways to react and interact.

Bullying and Aggression among Children

"At first, when they bullied me, it was the silent kind, you know, like they pretended I wasn't even there. And whenever I said something, they behaved like I was an idiot. After a while it got a lot worse. More kids got involved, and one day at lunch I had the whole table kicking me under the table so no teacher could see. When I went to the bathroom, they jumped up over the door and laughed at me. And then, one morning as I arrived at school, a whole gang was waiting for me and surrounded me . . ."

—Janina, age 12

Bullying occurs among humans of all age groups. It happens when one person feels and attempts to demonstrate superiority over another and repeatedly displays unjustified aggression toward the victim. It may be rooted in a perceived power imbalance in social influence, wealth, physical appearance, or even height (U.S. Department of Health and Human Services, 2020). Often the power imbalance does not reflect reality.

bullying repeated unjustified aggression toward a victim based on a perceived power imbalance.

© iStock.com/Highwaystarz-Photography

■ In middle childhood, bullying incidents increase until they peak between ages 11 and 14. Bullying has a number of negative consequences for the victims, including an increased risk of anxiety, depression, and suicidal behavior.

Children tease and harass others early on in life, but during early childhood the victim usually changes and varies depending on the situation. Around age 7, children first start to target a specific person who is then repeatedly bullied. This kind of bullying most frequently occurs between ages 11 and 14 (Smith, 2016). Cyberbullying, that is, bullying using digital devices, peaks somewhat later.

In 2019, about 1 in 5 students between the ages of 12 and 18 experienced bullying in the United States. Most of the bullying at school happened inside the school building, in hallways or classrooms. Only 46% of students who were bullied shared their experience with an adult (U.S. Department of Health and Human Services, 2020).

There are four different kinds of bullying:

- In *physical bullying*, the victim is hit, kicked, tripped, or subjected to other kinds of physical violence.
- In *verbal bullying*, the victim is threatened, teased, made fun of, or called names.
- In *relational bullying*, rumors are spread about the victim, or the victim is excluded from peer social activities (birthday parties, the lunch table, playground games, etc.).
- In *cyberbullying*, the victim is harassed over social media.

Overall, boys are more frequently perpetrators of bullying than girls, but among the victims, both girls and boys are fairly equally represented. Boys tend to engage in more physical bullying. Girls are sometimes found to engage in more relational and cyberbullying, and both boys and girls engage in verbal bullying (Barlett & Coyne, 2014; Smith, 2016).

Why do children bully others? Sometimes, they are trying to increase their status in their peer group. Concerns about popularity are increasing in middle childhood toward adolescence, and some children hope to gain status by dominating other children through bullying (Pepler et al., 1998). Bullies often do well in theory-of-mind tasks: They understand how the victim feels and what actions will most threaten or hurt the victim (Smith, 2016). At the same time, they tend to have less empathy than their peers, are impulsive, and often show high moral disengagement, which makes it easier for them to hurt others without feeling remorse (Gini et al., 2014; Jolliffe & Farrington, 2011).

Being bullied increases children's risk of developing feelings of anxiety and depression (Lereya et al., 2015). Bullied children are also more at risk for self-harming and suicidal behavior (Moore et al., 2017). One study found that repeated bullying in childhood had negative social, economic, and health effects as far out as 4 decades later (Takizawa et al., 2014). These findings illustrate the urgent need for programs that prevent bullying or intervene early when bullying occurs.

There are a number of different approaches that can be taken to prevent bullying and aggression at school. One possibility is to adapt programs at a schoolwide level that teach all children socio-emotional skills. The PATHS (Promoting Alternative Thinking Strategies) Curriculum, for example, has been shown to improve students' social competence and engagement at school while diminishing disruptive behavior (Greenberg & Kusché, 2006; Riggs et al., 2006). School-based programs have also been shown to reduce aggression in students and to promote prosocial behaviors (Espelage et al., 2013; Frey et al.,

2005; Salmivalli & Poskiparta, 2012). A Finnish program was able to reduce the occurrence of bullying by 17% when compared with schools that did not use the program (Kärnä et al., 2011).

A different approach is to provide extra support to children with social difficulties. About 15% of children experience significant problems in interactions with peers (Gresham et al., 2004). These programs typically teach children in small groups, sometimes with added individualized sessions. Children learn how to manage their emotions and impulses. They learn about social skills and practice these skills in small groups. At times, parents are included in the programs as well (Pepler & Bierman, 2018). A review of six meta-analyses involving more than 25,000 children showed that interventions led to improvements in 65% of the children, compared to 35% of children in control groups (Gresham et al., 2004). Programs like Stop Now and Plan find that participating children have fewer behavioral problems and show lower levels of aggression (Burke & Loeber, 2016). Similar programs also exist specifically for bullied children (DeRosier, 2004; DeRosier & Marcus, 2005).

Online Dares: Peer Bonding or a New Form of Bullying?

In middle childhood, children spend increasing amounts of time with their peers in school. They also spend increasing amounts of time with their peers outside of school, and a good portion of that time is spent online. In previous chapters we have seen that online friendships can be important for children, but the internet is also a venue for cyberbullying. Somewhere in between is a new take on a time-honored tradition: the dare.

Dares and challenges are used by children to establish popularity and what sociologists call *in-groups*—social circles with which a person identifies and to which one belongs. In their quest to be accepted by friends and peers—and gain membership to a particular social group—children will sometimes accept dares or challenges that are unreasonable or downright dangerous. Peer pressure and fear of missing out on things that others do are powerful contributing factors.

With the rise of digital media, many risky and dangerous challenges are taking place online, where children often participate without the knowledge of their parents. Here are just a few of the dangerous challenges that have recently made the news:

- *Tide Pod challenge*: Children are dared to bite into laundry detergent pods, take a movie of themselves while doing it, and post the video. The laundry detergent in the pods is toxic and can lead to chemical burns as well as kidney and lung damage.

- *Choking or fainting challenges*: These challenges dare kids to choke each other, hyperventilate, or use other techniques to faint. These procedures can be risky and have led to children dying.

- *Momo challenge*: This turned out to be a fake challenge that nevertheless led to substantial uproar among students as well as school administrators. Allegedly, a scary-looking figure whose image was circulated widely online was encouraging children to hurt themselves. The "fake" challenge was then taken up as a real challenge, and some children were hurt (CBS News, 2019).

- *Hot pepper challenge*: Children are dared to eat extremely hot peppers and film themselves to post the video afterward. Some children needed to be treated in emergency rooms after participating in the challenge.

These examples, current at the time of writing, will likely seem like ancient history as you read this, given the speed at which things change on the internet. You are probably aware of new online dares that have emerged more recently.

■ In the Tide Pod challenge, children are challenged to eat a pod filled with laundry detergent. Laundry detergent is toxic, and some children have been injured from participating in this as well as other challenges.

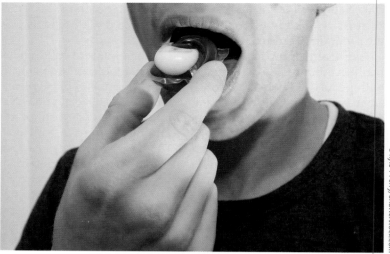

Since children are not constantly supervised, particularly when they spend time on digital devices, it is important that caregivers prepare them for encountering contests like these. Parents can:

- Talk with their children about social media challenges and ask them to check in with a parent before participating.
- Encourage children to think through challenges and their risks before participating in them.
- Discuss peer pressure with their children and how to respond.
- Stay up to date on the latest dares and trends on social media so they can strike up conversations with their children when new issues come up.
- Discuss and model online habits that include assessing risks of participating in challenges and sharing data, photos, and movies online.

Review!

What is the significance of peers and friends for children?

■ As children grow older, they spend increasing amounts of time with their peers at school and in groups pursuing hobbies. Interactions with peers give them the chance to interact with equals, practice solving conflicts, and learn how to help others.

■ Not all children are equally well liked. Researchers conduct studies on popularity by distinguishing five different sociometric statuses:

- popular,
- average,
- controversial,
- rejected, and
- neglected.

■ Children usually choose others as friends who are similar to them in terms of age, race, interests, and attitudes. They collaborate and share with as well as smile more at their friends. Friends provide emotional support, companionship, and help to each other. They also improve each other's self-esteem.

Is there anything that can be done about bullying?

■ There are four different kinds of *bullying*:

- physical,
- verbal,
- relational, and
- cyberbullying.

■ No matter the kind of bullying, bullied children are at increased risk for feeling anxious, depressed, or suicidal. Different approaches can be taken to counter bullying. On a whole-school level, programs can be executed that teach all children socio-emotional skills.

■ For children who have more behavioral problems or who are being bullied, programs that take place in small groups or even at an individual level can help teach them more skills to help them relate positively to their classmates and how to react when interactions do not go well.

Practice!

1. The five different peer statuses researchers distinguish are _____ .
   a. admired, imitated, mistreated, rejected, and neglected
   b. popular, average, controversial, mistreated, and ignored
   c. popular, average, controversial, neglected, and rejected
   d. popular, liked, disliked, hated, and forgotten

2. Children tend to seek friends that _____ .
   a. are older than they are
   b. have similar interests
   c. are younger than they are
   d. have very different interests

3. In 2019, about _____ children was bullied in the United States.
   a. 1 in 200
   b. 1 in 63
   c. 1 in 2
   d. 1 in 5

Act It Out!

Jaylen's mother, Shawna, has booked a meeting with Jaylen's first grade teacher to discuss her concerns about Jaylen's solitary play habits and lack of friends. With a classmate, role-play the conversation between Shawna and Jaylen's teacher. As Shawna, what are your principal concerns? As Jaylen's teacher, draw on the information presented in the chapter to advise Shawna on whether her concerns are valid and, if they are, what she might do about them.

See for Yourself!

The next time you're walking through a park with a playground at a time when a large number of children are there, take note of the group interactions and play behavior. Are most children playing alone or in groups? Does group size depend on age or gender? If you see any conflicts, how do the children resolve them?

What's Your Position?

Most people will agree that bullying is a serious problem, but there are debates on the best way to address bullying in schools. Some argue that schools should devise their own anti-bullying strategies involving education and tailored to their specific circumstances. Others feel that state governments should take a leading role by creating school anti-bullying laws that could, in some cases, require a police response. What's your position? Draft an immediate response to the question, and then read the article at the website below. Did your opinion change after reading the article? How so?

Additional Resource Online

■ "Bullying: Should Congress and state governments pass laws requiring educational institutions to implement anti-bullying measures?" from Facts on File: Issues & Controversies

13.4 Schooling

- Outline various ways to identify a good school.
- Recall the multiple factors that contribute to a child's success in school.

Schooling is arguably one of the most important aspects of children's lives. Children spend a significant amount of their time at school, and the education they receive will influence their lives in many ways. In the following section, we will consider what makes a good school, which school choices parents have in the United States, and which factors influence children's success at school.

What Makes a Good School?

The public elementary school our children attended gets a rating of 7/10 on greatschools.org. Does that sound mediocre? What if I tell you that all three children have made great progress since they started school? Their kindergarten teacher was their self-proclaimed "school mom." The principal stands outside every morning to greet the children and is thus immediately approachable for parents. The children liked to go to school and felt safe there. Does this still sound like a mediocre school, or is it starting to sound more like the kind of school where you'd feel comfortable sending children of your own?

A good school can have a positive influence on a child's well-being, academic success, and future life chances. But if you ask different parents what makes a good school, you are bound to get different answers. The "mediocre" 7/10 rating I mentioned earlier comes from standardized test scores: That provides one picture of school success. The "eye test"—what you see when you walk into the school—provides another. Some parents value athletic amenities and sports programs; others are more interested in specialized learning programs and academic extracurriculars. Let's look at what parents, the government, and researchers consider important for a school's success.

Let's begin with what matters to parents when they choose a school. A study that analyzed the data of around 250,000 high school applicants in New York City through the city's centralized high school–assignment mechanism showed that parents mostly prefer to enroll their children in schools that enroll high-achieving peers. They do not take into account the effectiveness of the school or whether the school is a good academic match for their child. Rather, parents look at the academic success of students in that school. If the students are successful, parents take that as a sign that it's an effective school (Abdulkadiroğlu et al., 2020). Obviously, when children have special needs or interests, parents will take into account whether these needs can be met when choosing a school.

So much for the parents. Researchers have also tried to come up with frameworks that explain what makes for a good school. Here are some of their criteria (Barnes, 2019; Schneider, 2017):

- The principal supports the teachers and encourages the teachers to collaborate and make decisions on their own.
- Teachers believe in their students' ability to succeed.
- Teachers are very familiar with the subjects they are teaching.
- The school frequently communicates with the parents and, as needed, about important issues; it also asks for parents' opinions.
- The school is safe and has plans to deal with bullying and security threats. Students have trust in the school, staff, and one another.
- The school has adequate resources to teach effectively, build a strong curriculum, and offer extracurricular activities.
- Children of all backgrounds learn successfully at the school.

The government, of course, has an interest in seeing schools succeed. In the United States, in 2002 George W. Bush signed into law the No Child Left Behind Act, which increased the federal government's role in the nation's schooling. It placed an emphasis on standardized test scores to evaluate students and schools. Schools were held accountable if their students' learning was found during annual testing to be below standard. In 2010, 38% of schools were failing—a number that rose in subsequent years (Klein, 2015). Then, in 2015, No Child Left Behind was replaced by the Every Student Succeeds Act (ESSA), which returned to the individual states some control over schooling and let states set their own accountability goals in terms of test proficiency, English-language proficiency, and graduation rates (Klein, 2016). Parents became involved in the creation of state plans. ESSA affects all children, including those who receive special-education services.

School Choices

When parents in the United States choose a school for their child, they have a variety of options. Most children attend public schools, but other options include private schools, charter schools, and homeschooling (see **FIGURE 13.8**).

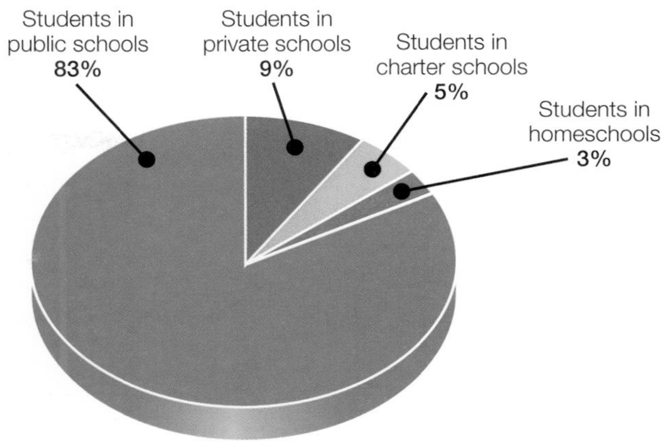

Most children attend public schools

Most school-age children in the United States attend public schools. Public schools in most states are managed within local school districts by school boards consisting primarily or exclusively of community members. The curriculum requirements for public schools and the funding they receive are determined by individual states through a department of education. Often, school boards have some freedom to influence the curriculum or programs as well. Public school costs are covered by local property taxes. Because so many stakeholders are involved, public schools can vary greatly in their curricula as well as courses and activities offered: These will typically depend on where the school is located.

Parents opting to send their children to public school will often not have a choice which school their child will attend: Their child's school is determined by their home address. Public schools sometimes may be underfunded, so that they lack money and other resources to provide services and materials that would be needed to provide students with the best possible education. They may also not be able to offer adequate services for children with special needs (Blad, 2020). For these as well as other reasons, some parents choose other schooling options for their children.

FIGURE 13.8 American students in K–12 schools (2019) by type of school. The vast majority of students in the United States attend public schools. However, depending on other factors like location, interest of the student or specialization of the school, public health crises like the 2020 COVID-19 pandemic, or income of the parents, other options may be an attractive alternative.

Data from M. Riser-Kositsky. 2020. Education statistics: Facts about American schools. www.edweek.org

Private schools are financed by tuition payments and endowments

Private schools typically do not receive funding from the state. Rather, they are financed by tuition payments, endowments, and sponsors. About two-thirds of private schools are sponsored by churches or religious organizations (U.S. Department of Education, 2018). Some provide religious instruction, others do not. Private schools tend to have smaller class sizes than public schools and tend to be smaller in size, in general, than public schools. Private schools often have a student body that is less diverse in terms of ethnicity than public schools (National Center for Education Statistics, 2020a, 2020b).

Charter schools are often specialized

Charter schools are publicly funded but are run independently. Around 3 million students attend charter schools (Riser-Kositsky, 2021). Charter schools are sometimes created around a certain theme, like science, the arts, or environmental issues, and some deliver their entire curriculum online. This specialization makes charter schools an attractive alternative to public school for many families, but if more students are interested in attending the school than the school can accommodate, admission to the charter school is determined by lottery (Prothero, 2018b).

Some critics of charter schools believe that they funnel away money from other public schools while not educating as many ethnically diverse students and students with disabilities (Prothero, 2018a; Samuels, 2018). Because charter schools are privately run, they can also be closed rather suddenly when they are in financial trouble (Prothero, 2018c).

Homeschooling is becoming an increasingly popular alternative

Sometimes, parents choose not to enroll their children in any formal school at all but rather to educate the children at home.

Parents have a variety of reasons for homeschooling. Some may have concerns over the environment and the safety of their public schools (Prothero, 2016). Others may homeschool to impart their religion or culture to their children (Ray, 2015). For other families who move a lot, like military families,

© Rido/Shutterstock.com

■ In the wake of the COVID-19 crisis, a significant number of parents decided to homeschool their children because of health concerns as well as concerns over the viability of online lessons for their children.

homeschooling is an opportunity to give their children more continuity in their education (Sullivan et al., 2019). Some families feel that their special-needs children can best be served at home (Kunzman & Gaither, 2020). Before the COVID-19 pandemic, more than 1.5 million children in the United States were homeschooled (Riser-Kositsky, 2020). In the 2020/2021 school year, the number of homeschooled students increased sharply to 11% due to the pandemic (Eggleston & Fields, 2021). That number is likely to drop at least to some extent again as schools and families adjust to the new situation.

Every state has its own regulations in terms of homeschooling. In New York State, for example, parents must submit an individualized home education plan for each child that lays out the curriculum as well as the resources used. The parents also need to submit reports every quarter and, starting in fourth grade, have their children's achievement tested at least once every 2 years (New York State Department of Education, 2015).

These days, many homeschooling parents also take advantage of the growing number of online courses that are offered through the internet.

There is some debate around homeschools because the regulations vary widely from state to state. Critics argue that, without regular testing of homeschooled children, a quality education cannot be guaranteed. Some parents also may use homeschooling in order to hide the abuse that is taking place at home (Prothero, 2018b). Other critics believe that a big part of schooling is socialization, which does not take place at home to the same extent as if children attended a school with other children outside their family. Homeschool cooperatives take some of those worries away. They consist of local homeschooling families that take excursions together or offer parent-taught classes for all children that belong to the cooperative (Kunzman & Gaither, 2020).

■ What It's Like...

Homeschooling

Kristen, 39 years, mother of Hannah, 8, and Ezekiel, 10

I started homeschooling our children this past fall when it became clear that our elementary school would opt for virtual instruction due to continued issues with COVID-19. I supported their decision, but at the same time, virtual instruction did not work well for us. The switch to homeschooling has been surprisingly pleasant and easy. I needed to submit a home-instruction plan for each of our two children. I also have to submit written progress reports about every 3 months.

We do English and math instruction with regular textbooks. But everything else I am structuring alongside different historical and cultural topics. For example, when discussing Ancient Greece, the children not only learned about history, but also about Greek philosophers; they read maps, explored Pythagoras's theorem, learned about the origins of the Olympic Games, and recreated some simple machines the Greeks invented. I love the freedom to pursue topics of interest to our children in more depth.

Hannah and Ezekiel have learned with much enthusiasm over the past year—so much so that I am considering continuing to homeschool them after the pandemic ends. My main concern is the lack of social interactions in homeschooling. Both children have many friends at the school they used to attend. We have homeschool associations in our town, and we've started to connect with them so the children can participate in group classes through an association next year if we decide to keep homeschooling them.

Homeschooling can be stressful, particularly because I also have a part-time job that I work on from home at night. But the rewards are great, and even if the children go back to their public school next year, I can imagine homeschooling again in the future.

Hannah, 8 years

I love home school. To me, home school is more fun than going to regular school. I enjoy that I can stay home, and we get to decide together with my mom what we will learn next. We do lots of hands-on projects, like building a pyramid with sugar cubes or learning how to use Morse code. I don't so much like the math and writing we're doing. But I guess if I have to do it, I'd rather do it with my mom than with another adult.

I do miss my friends though. At school, my favorite part was recess, when I got to hang out with all my friends. For most of the last year, all we could do is video chats because of COVID-19. That wasn't easy. Some of my friends don't talk much in the video chat, although they talk a lot at school. That makes it hard to talk on the iPad. I also missed my sewing class, but that started up again recently.

I think if I get to visit with my friends at the weekends, then I would like to continue homeschooling with my mom. But I don't think she has decided yet what she's going to do.

Factors That Influence Children's School Performance

Children's school performance depends on a large number of factors, such as the children's parents, their teachers, and factors within the children themselves (FIGURE 13.9).

FIGURE 13.9 Factors influencing school performance.

Teacher influences	
Caring, support, personal involvement	A supportive teacher positively impacts student learning outcomes, motivation, and social and moral development (Ramberg et al., 2019; Velasquez et al., 2013). It is most important for struggling students (Velasquez et al., 2013).
Teacher expectations	Students perform better when their teacher expects them to do well (Ebert & Culyer, 2013).

Student influences	
Self-efficacy: Students' confidence that they can succeed at school	High self-efficacy positively impacts school success (Assouline et al., 2020; Lee & Jonson-Reid, 2016). Children with high self-efficacy are more persistent when encountering challenging tasks (Schunk & Pajares, 2009.)
Gender	Girls tend to perform better at school than do boys (Spinath et al., 2014).
Peer acceptance	Children who feel less accepted by peers tend to perform worse in school (Flook et al., 2005; Walters & Bowen, 1997).

Parent influences	
Socioeconomic status (SES)	Children from families with higher SES tend to do better in school (Sirin, 2005; Yamada et al., 2019).
Parenting practices	When parents are involved with their children's schooling, children tend to perform better and behave better at school (Dotterer & Wehrspann, 2016).

Review!

What is a good school?

- There are many factors that make a school a good school besides the test scores the school's students earn in annual testing. Children need to feel safe at school and need to be able to trust the students and faculty at their school. The school needs to have sufficient resources to provide a quality education and to have a principal who supports teachers.

- Teachers need to believe in their students' ability to succeed and must be intimately familiar with the topics they teach. The school should also involve parents, communicate frequently with the parents, and ask the parents for their opinions on important topics.

Which factors influence children's success at school?

- Parents, teachers, and students themselves all influence whether a given student eventually succeeds at school. When teachers go to bat for their students, support them, and have high expectations for students' success, their students are more likely to succeed.

- Children whose parents have a higher income and whose parents are involved in their schooling tend to do better at school. And students' own traits matter as well: Girls tend to get better grades at school than do boys, and not surprisingly, students who believe in their own ability to succeed are more persistent and successful. Being accepted by their peers also positively influences children's school performance.

Practice!

1. Most children in the United States _____ .
   a. attend public schools
   b. attend charter schools
   c. attend private schools
   d. get homeschooled

2. Children from families with higher SES tend to _____ than children from less well-off families.
   a. do worse at school
   b. be more successful in athletic subjects
   c. do better at school
   d. do neither better nor worse

What's Your Position?

Do you believe that standardized testing (as in statewide mastery tests, for example) is positive or negative in schooling?

Additional Resources Online

- "Do standardized tests improve education in America?" from ProCon.org

- "What are the pros and cons of standardized testing?" from Spark Admissions

- "The pros and cons of standardized testing," from the Whitby School

Children at school 2 years later

Jaylen is now 9 years old. He is still a quiet boy who does not seek to be the center of attention, but at the same time he is well liked by his classmates. Shortly after his seventh birthday, his mother Shawna contacted Jaylen's teacher with her concerns about his social life. Soon thereafter, the school psychologist invited Jaylen to a special lunch group in which a small number of children had lunch together once a week and practiced social skills together. Jaylen liked the group and was part of it for the remainder of second grade. He seemed to be doing well because he was not invited back into the group in third grade. By then, he also reported that he had found a group of children with whom he played kickball during recess. In fourth grade, Jaylen mentioned that he did not have any close friends in his class. After his mother talked to his teacher to find out more, the teacher seated Jaylen with another boy whom she thought Jaylen might get along with. The two boys became fast friends and now love spending time together. ■ ■

Overview

Physical Development in Adolescence

Children at risk

Iris is worried about some behavior changes she has seen in her 17-year-old son, Peter. The changes were subtle at first: His grades started to drop, and he seemed to be hanging out less often with his friends. Then, a year ago, Peter's cousin Kyle died by suicide, bringing despair and chaos into the extended family. Kyle and Peter had been very close, so the situation was particularly traumatic for Peter. After Kyle's death, Peter retreated and isolated himself from the family as well as his friends.

Nowadays, Peter spends a lot of his time at home alone in his room. More often he is out, and his parents have no idea where he is. In the brief moments when she does seem him, Iris finds that Peter seems anxious. At other times, he's slow, almost clumsy in his movements, and she can't help but wonder if he has been doing drugs. Iris and her husband have tried many times to have conversations with Peter about what may be going on, but Peter blocks all of their efforts. Is he just going through a phase, Iris wonders? Does he need space? Or is there something more serious going on that needs her intervention? It doesn't seem so long ago that he was a bright, cheerful child—her pride and joy. Now whenever she thinks about Peter, she feels a knot forming in her stomach.

As we will see in this chapter, adolescence is generally a period of life when young people enjoy good health. Puberty brings physical changes, and different nutritional needs that adult caregivers can support by modeling healthy eating behaviors. We will consider what adolescents can do to stay healthy and which common health threats they encounter. Death is, fortunately, rare among adolescents and tends to result from preventable causes such as drug abuse and suicide, which explains why Peter's parents are so worried about the changes they are observing in their son.

14.1 Brain and Body Growth in Adolescence

■ Define adolescence and puberty and explain the changes that occur during the various stages.

adolescence the transition phase between childhood and adulthood involving significant physical, social, emotional, and cognitive changes.

puberty the stage in which the body changes and becomes sexually mature; marks the beginning of adolescence.

Adolescence is the transitional phase between childhood and adulthood. It is a time of substantial changes in all areas: physical, emotional, cognitive, and social. Adolescence starts with the onset of **puberty**, which is a phase of physical development during which children's bodies become sexually mature and capable of reproduction. Due to the dramatic nature of the changes that children experience during this time, adolescence often brings with it feelings of both anxiety and anticipation for children, as well as for their parents.

Researchers distinguish three phases of adolescence (Allen & Waterman, 2019):

- *Early adolescence* (10–13 years). Early adolescence starts with the beginning of puberty and the physical changes that come along with it (earlier for girls than for boys; we will discuss timing in more detail below). Body changes can result in anxiety as well as curiosity and excitement. Children often feel self-conscious about their bodies and may feel an increased need for privacy. In some children, those bodily changes can lead to a questioning of their gender identity.

- *Middle adolescence* (14–17 years). In middle adolescence, many boys experience a growth spurt, something that many girls have already experienced by this time. Teens become interested in romantic relationships and sexual relations. They strive for more independence from their parents. Adolescents' brains continue to mature, and this will continue throughout the third decade of life.

- *Late adolescence* (18 years and older). Physical development is now complete, and adolescents have a better sense of risks and more impulse control. While they continue to become independent of their family, many adolescents also begin to form adult-like relationships with their parents.

In the following sections, we will explore in more detail the physical changes that come with adolescence and puberty.

Puberty: Physical Changes

Bella's mother is distraught. She recently discovered breast buds and the very beginning of pubic hair growth in her daughter, who just turned 9 years old. Nine years old! Bella is her little girl, childlike in her behavior and very attached to her mother. How could it be possible for Bella to enter puberty when she is still so much a child?

Hormonal changes initiate puberty

hypothalamus a region of the forebrain that controls a number of functions such as body temperature, hunger, thirst, and emotions.

pituitary gland a pea-sized gland at the base of the brain that produces a number of different hormones such as growth hormones, reproductive hormones, and hormones that regulate blood pressure.

Before any physical changes appear, adolescents' bodies have already begun to produce hormones that will eventually bring about maturation. *Hormones* are chemical messengers produced by endocrine glands. They circulate through a person's bloodstream and regulate many different processes, including growth, development, sexual function, and mood (Endocrine Society, 2020).

A number of hormones are of central importance to puberty. The **hypothalamus** in the brain produces *gonadotropin-releasing hormone* (GnRH), which is carried by the bloodstream to the **pituitary gland**. The pituitary gland is a pea-sized gland below the brain that produces many different hormones. In this case, the GnRH stimulates the pituitary gland to make two reproductive hormones: *luteinizing hormone* (LH) and *follicle-stimulating hormone* (FSH). LH and FSH then travel to the gonads, which are a person's reproductive glands (see **FIGURE 14.1**).

Girls' gonads are the ovaries. The ovaries contain the immature eggs that were produced during prenatal development. LH and FSH stimulate the ovaries to produce various estrogens, which are female sex hormones. The estrogen estradiol plays a particularly important role in female puberty by initiating the development of breasts, genitals, and the uterus, as well as the growth of pubic and underarm hair (Wood et al., 2019).

In boys, LH and FSH travel to the male gonads, which are the testes. The testes subsequently begin to produce androgens (male sex hormones), including testosterone, which increases sharply during puberty. Testosterone causes the growth of boys' genitals, muscles, and body hair (Pinyerd & Zipf, 2005; Wood et al., 2019).

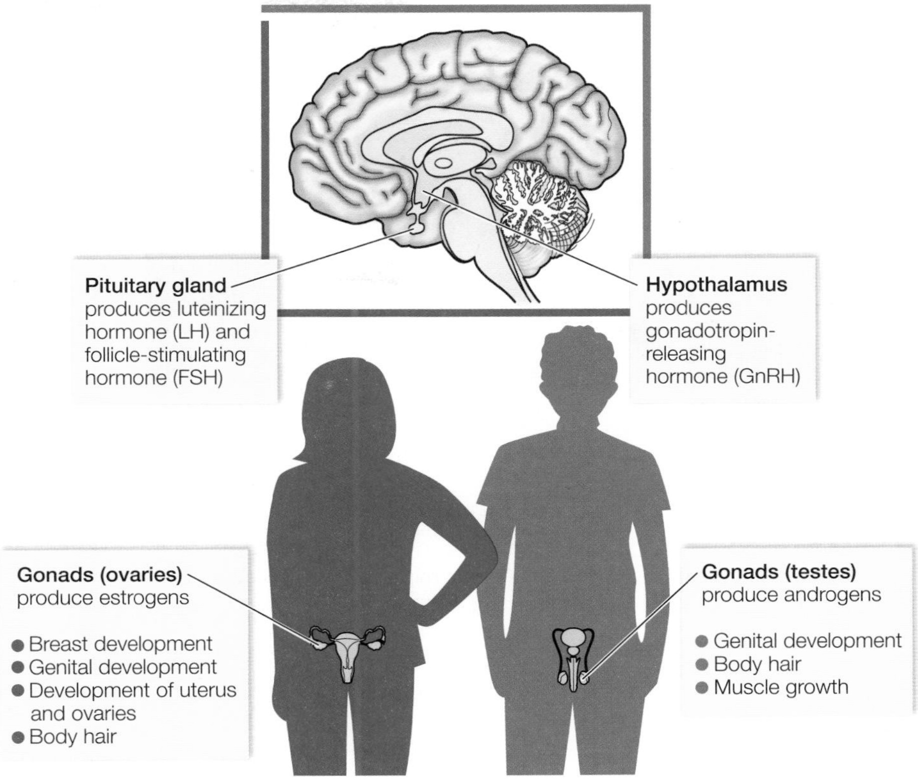

Both sexes have both male and female sex hormones in their bodies. That is, boys produce estradiol and girls produce testosterone. The difference is in the quantities: Boys have much more testosterone than girls do, and girls have a much larger amount of estradiol than boys do (Nottelmann et al., 1984). Even in reduced quantities, these "opposite-sex" hormones have important functions. In women, androgens influence bone growth and sex drive, but also contribute to breast and vaginal health. Estrogens in men play roles in regulating sex drive, the ability to form and keep an erection, and the production of sperm cells (Schulster et al., 2016).

FIGURE 14.1 Puberty hormones.

Physical changes occur during puberty

Now that we know about the hormonal changes that bring about puberty, let's take a closer look at the physical changes that occur in boys and girls and the order in which the changes occur.

In puberty, primary and secondary sex characteristics mature and grow. **Primary sex characteristics** are the inner and outer sex organs that are present at birth. They include the penis, testes, seminal vesicles, and prostate gland in boys. In girls, they are the vagina, uterus, Fallopian tubes, and ovaries. **Secondary sex characteristics** are those that develop during sexual maturation and do not involve the sex organs. They include breast development in girls and facial hair growth as well as broad shoulders in boys. They also include the growth of pubic and underarm hair.

The age at which puberty begins and the age at which adolescents reach adult height and sexual maturity has steadily decreased over the past 150 years in industrialized nations. We use the term **secular trend** to describe a development like this, which continues for many years and does not appear to be cyclical. This particular secular trend is likely due to better health in children as well as better nutrition (Gluckman & Hanson, 2006; Sawyer et al., 2018). In China in recent decades, for example, the average age at which girls have their first period has moved 5 months earlier every 10 years (Song et al., 2014).

primary sex characteristics inner and outer sex organs that are present at birth.

secondary sex characteristics physical signs of sexual maturity that do not involve the sex organs, such as breast development and growth of body hair.

secular trend a trend that remains steady over time and does not undergo cyclical changes; in human development, the observation that over the past 150 years children have entered puberty at increasingly early times.

■ Over the past 150 years, a secular trend has been observed in which children enter puberty increasingly early. What do you think are the implications for the children as well as for those interacting with them?

The age of first menstruation also varies by race, beginning first in African American girls, followed 1–2 months later by Hispanic girls, and 3–5 months after that in White and Asian girls (Biro et al., 2018; Shirazi & Rosinger, 2020).

Puberty marks the onset of adolescence, and as we have seen, it is beginning earlier and earlier in many countries. At the same time, adolescence is also lasting longer. Adolescence was once commonly believed to end around age 19, with young adults taking on "adult" responsibilities—working, moving away from home, starting a family, and so on. These social role transitions are now occurring later, with many young people heading for college, and thus the beginning of adulthood is currently considered to be around age 24 (Sawyer et al., 2018). After college, more young adults are moving back home with their parents again. The COVID-19 pandemic may have accelerated this trend by making employment difficult to find. Families are consequently created later as well: In 1970, the average age at marriage for women in China was 20, and they first gave birth at 21.5 years; in 2019, the average age at marriage had risen to almost 24 years, and the age at first birth was 26 (Raymo et al., 2015). In Europe, many young people today do not marry until their thirties (Kiernan, 2001).

Let us now have a closer look at the physical changes that occur in boys and girls (FIGURE 14.2).

PHYSICAL CHANGES IN BOYS Puberty begins, on average, at around 11 years of age in boys, with the normal age ranging from 9 to 14 years. (The causes of

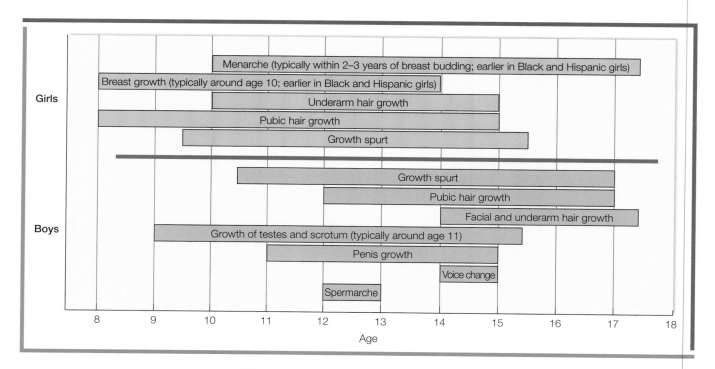

FIGURE 14.2   Pubertal development.

early or late puberty are discussed later in this section.) At the beginning of puberty, the testes become enlarged and the skin of the scrotum thins and reddens. The testicles and scrotum will almost double in size during puberty. Soon after the testes begin to develop, pubic hair begins to grow around the base of the penis. With time, the hair will become coarser, curlier, and darker and will spread out toward the navel and thighs. Around 2 years after the first sprouting of pubic hair, additional hair will begin to grow in other places as well, like the face, legs, arms, and armpits. Chest hair usually develops later. Early in puberty, hormonal changes may result in mild breast growth: Some boys develop a breast bud that can have a diameter of up to 2 inches. This growth obviously worries the affected boys, but the swelling usually subsides within 1–2 years.

The penis grows in length and, later, expands in girth. It will reach adult size sometime between 13 and 18 years of age. Within 1 year of the beginning of testicle growth, boys usually have their first ejaculation, also called **spermarche**. The ejaculate contains sperm, and boys are sexually mature and can father a child as soon as their first ejaculation. Many boys experience "wet dreams," which are involuntary ejaculations that occur while they are sleeping and result in wet bedding. These nighttime ejaculations may or may not be connected with sexual dreams (American Academy of Pediatrics, 2015c).

spermarche a boy's first ejaculation.

Two years after the onset of puberty, boys will typically experience a growth spurt. During the growth spurt, boys grow taller and stronger, with pronounced muscular growth and a broadening of their shoulders. During the growth spurt, the boys' larynx and vocal cords grow larger. These changes result in a deepening of their voices. During the growth period, it sometimes sounds as though the voice "cracks," but the cracking stops when the growth phase has ended (American Academy of Pediatrics, 2015c).

PHYSICAL CHANGES IN GIRLS The first visible signs of puberty in girls include breast budding, in which breasts appear to have small bumps under the nipple. Breast budding tends to start around age 10, but it can appear as early as age 8 or as late as age 13. Bella's mother has nothing to worry about: Her daughter's development is within a completely normal range. As breasts continue to grow, they will first take on a conical shape and later become more rounded. It takes around 3 years for breasts to grow to their full size.

In most girls, pubic hair will begin to grow after the breasts have started to bud. The hair will gradually become coarser and darker. Hair also will begin to grow in the armpits.

Around 6–12 months before their first period, girls' bodies begin to produce more estrogens. As a result, they may experience small amounts of clear or white vaginal discharge. Within 2–3 years of breast budding, girls usually will have their **menarche**, which is their first menstruation. During menstruation, the body sheds the lining of the uterus that builds up every month. The tissue as well as a small amount of blood are discharged through the vagina. The discharges typically occur at regular intervals, which can be as short as 25 days or as long as 35 days.

menarche a girl's first menstrual bleeding.

Girls experience other changes in their bodies as well. Their hips get wider, and they accumulate more fat in their bodies to give them a more adult figure.

Girls' growth spurt usually begins about 1 year after the start of puberty. Growth during puberty is substantial: Children gain about 25% of their total height during puberty. After girls have their first menstruation, their growth starts to slow down, and they usually grow just another 1 or 2 inches afterward. Since girls tend to enter puberty earlier than boys, many of them are taller than their male peers in early adolescence. Later in puberty, boys, on average, will begin to outgrow girls (Allen & Miller, 2019; Wood et al., 2019).

■ Teens who enter puberty earlier tend to start dating and have sexual relations earlier as well. Consequently, such girls are at a higher risk of being pregnant or of having had an abortion by age 18.

When puberty comes early or late

Can you remember how old you were when you entered puberty? How comfortable did you feel anticipating the many changes that lay ahead? Chances are that if the timing of your puberty was about the same as that of your friends, you felt more comfortable than if your puberty was significantly earlier or later than that of your friends.

One of the most important factors in the onset of puberty is inheritance. Between 50 and 80% of the variation in timing of onset can be explained by genetic factors. That is, if you have a parent who entered puberty particularly early or late, you are likely to follow that same pattern (Wood et al., 2019). But early or late onset of puberty can also be a cause for concern, as we shall see next.

precocious puberty the early onset of puberty; before the age of 9 in boys and before the age of 8 in girls.

EARLY MATURATION   When puberty starts before the age of 9 in boys or before the age of 8 in girls, we speak of **precocious puberty**.

The environment plays an important role in the timing of puberty. Children tend to mature earlier when they experience traumatic events or grow up in a harsh, stressful environment (Belsky, 2012; Belsky & Shalev, 2016; Lei et al., 2018). From an evolutionary viewpoint, early puberty in these circumstances is an adaptive response because it prepares the body for difficult future circumstances via early maturation (Ellis et al., 2012).

Likewise, children who are overweight or obese tend to enter puberty earlier than their peers who are of normal weight (Fan et al., 2020). Being of African American or Hispanic descent also increases the chances that a girl will enter puberty earlier.

Early onset of puberty exposes adolescents to a number of health and social risks (see FIGURE 14.3).

■ Late maturation can be stressful for affected children. Knowing that puberty will surely come at some point, why do you think some children feel so distressed?

LATE MATURATION   In both sexes, the start of puberty is distributed over a wide range of ages. If puberty arrives after age 14 in boys or 13 in girls, it is considered late.

Most often, when children experience delayed puberty, the cause is genetic: It is likely that one or both of their parents entered puberty late as well. Children with chronic diseases such as sickle cell disease or inflammatory bowel disease frequently enter puberty late. Girls who have low body fat, often as a result of being athletes or having an eating disorder, tend to enter puberty late as well (American Academy of Pediatrics, 2015a, 2015b). These are just some causes of delayed puberty.

Late puberty can be diagnosed with a physical exam, possibly with some additional blood tests that check hormone levels. Boys with delayed puberty have very low levels of testosterone in their blood. If their late puberty is due to inheritance, nothing more needs to be done but wait. In some cases, physicians may decide to prescribe testosterone injections to stimulate the onset of puberty. In girls, high levels of LH and FSH indicate that the ovaries are not working appropriately and that the body is trying to stimulate the ovaries by producing more LH and FSH. If the late onset of puberty is a result of inherited factors, the best course of action is just to wait or try to gain some weight if the girl doesn't have sufficient body fat. Girls in whom a hormone deficiency has been diagnosed may be given estrogens.

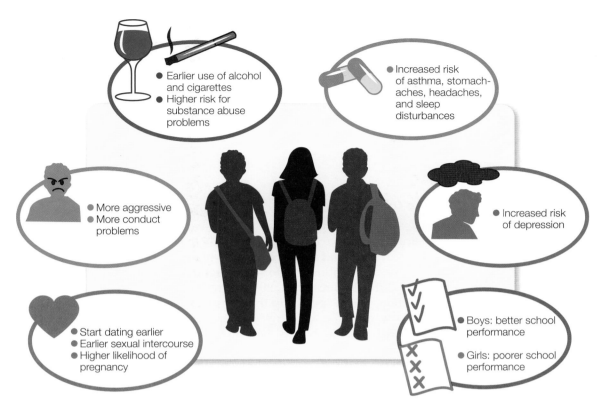

FIGURE 14.3 Risks associated with early onset of puberty. An early onset of puberty is associated with a variety of risks for young people.

Chen et al., 2020; Crocket et al., 1996; Dubas et al., 1991; Ge & Natsuaki, 2009; Hamlat et al., 2020; Lam et al., 2002; Mendle & Ferrero, 2012; Mendle et al., 2007; Najman et al., 2009; Rudolph & Troop-Gordon, 2010; Stice et al., 2001; Udry, 1979.

Often, late maturation is not seen as a factor that exposes children to any particular risks. In fact, late-maturing girls are more likely to excel academically than early-maturing girls (Dubas et al., 1991; Mendle et al., 2007) and tend to have fewer substance abuse problems and less depression (Mendle et al., 2007). However, a review has found that there may be some health risk factors in delayed puberty as well. Late puberty may be associated with an increased risk for heart disease and lower bone mineral density (which increases the risk of breaking bones), as well as reduced height (Zhu & Chan, 2017).

■ Theory in Action

Puberty can be a challenging time for both children and their adult caregivers. Children worry about the changes they are experiencing, about the timing of puberty, and about whether their experiences are normal. Caregivers can help reassure their children in a number of ways:

Give information early

Children should not be surprised by the changes they are experiencing. It is better to bring up physical changes early; as Bella's mother noted, puberty often starts earlier than people expect.

Keep things simple and matter-of-fact

Let adolescents know that these physical changes are part of normal and healthy development. For example, you can say, "Menstruation is when your uterus sheds its lining. It is mixed with blood and looks like it, too."

Focus on the positive and emphasize children's strengths and successes

While children seek to develop their individuality and independence, their behavior may be challenging. Focusing on the positive and their successes may help conversations succeed.

Explain dangers and consequences

Since adolescents are still learning to control their impulses, they need to understand which behaviors are risky and what the consequences are if they engage in such behavior. Set reasonable expectations and make sure children understand what is expected of them.

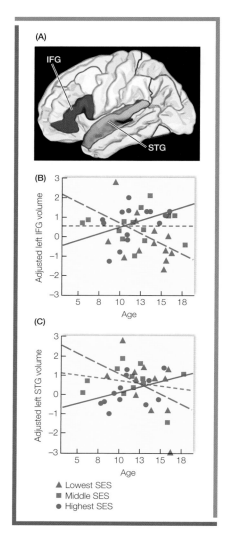

FIGURE 14.4 Some structures of the brain differ in how they physically develop, depending on parental income. In this study, the volumes of the left inferior frontal gyrus and the superior temporal gyrus were tracked over time. As you can see in the two graphs, these structures decrease in volume in children with very low SES, while they increase in children with very high SES. (IFG stands for inferior frontal gyrus, STG for superior temporal gyrus.)

After K. G. Noble et al. 2012. *Dev Sci* 15: 516–527. © John Wiley & Sons Ltd.

Brain Growth

Different structures within the brain mature at different rates, and just as with the physical changes we discussed above, there is a wide variability between individuals. Throughout adolescence, the volume and thickness of the brain's cortex decline and continue to do so throughout early adulthood (Foulkes & Blakemore, 2018; Tamnes et al., 2017). The frontal lobe experiences a surge in myelination, which speeds up the transmission of information within the brain.

Adolescents are able to learn new and complex skills when myelination and the pruning of dendrites create new pathways and strengthen existing pathways in the brain. Brain development does not end with the conclusion of adolescence but continues into early adulthood, at least until the mid-20s (Berman et al., 2009; Simpson, 2021). Factors that influence the brain development of an individual include the stage of puberty they are in, their sex, nutrition and sleep, the environment in which they live, and stress and drug abuse (Arain et al., 2013; Foulkes & Blakemore, 2018).

One factor that is receiving greater attention from researchers today is socioeconomic status (SES) (Farah, 2017; Hackman & Farah, 2009). You can read more about the impact of SES on children's brain development in the Culture Counts box in Chapter 12. Some recent studies have found that the parents' level of education correlates with the physical characteristics of structures in their children's brains. For example, the more educated the parents are, the larger their children's cortical surface as it relates to different functions like spatial skills, reading, language, and executive function. For children from households with a high SES, additional increases in parental income do not make a big difference, but for children from lower-SES families, even a relatively small increase in income makes a big difference in terms of brain development (Noble et al., 2015). SES is also reflected in the volume of some brain structures (see **FIGURE 14.4**). This is a relatively new area of inquiry, and many studies in cognitive neuroscience actually do not take the SES of their participants into account in their data analyses.

Culture and the expectations of teenagers that come with it impact brain growth and activation as well: Are young people expected to become independent and create a new family relatively soon, or are they expected to still depend on their family during their early years of adulthood (Choudhury, 2010)? As you may remember, functional magnetic resonance imaging (fMRI) measures changes in blood oxygen and can thus determine changes in brain activity. In one fMRI study, Hispanic and White adolescents were given a chance to win money. They could win this money either for themselves or for their family. White participants showed increased activity in some brain areas (the dorsal striatum and the ventral tegmental area, to be specific) when they won money *for themselves*, whereas Hispanic adolescents showed comparable activation when they won money *for their families* (Telzer et al., 2010). The researchers believe that this difference in activation may be due to cultural differences: Hispanic culture traditionally places

Physical Development in Adolescence

more value on family and helping one's family than does White culture (a value called *familismo*).

Adolescence is a time in life that comes with some particular and sometimes peculiar behavioral tendencies. For example, adolescents are particularly easily influenced by peers when it comes to taking risks, and although their reasoning skills are near those of adults in their capabilities, adolescents often show poor judgment. Researchers have found that these particularities have some basis in brain development: fMRI studies in decision-making show that adolescents use brain structures associated with emotions (for example, the limbic system) more often than do adults when making decisions. This is particularly the case when the adolescents make actual personal decisions, rather than decisions about hypothetical situations.

Adolescents are also more prone to act impulsively or aggressively, misinterpret social cues, or not think carefully before they act. Their rash decision-making can be explained by a relative immaturity of the prefrontal cortex and the maturity of the amygdala: The amygdala, which controls aggressive behavior and fear reactions and can thus contribute to impulsive behavior, matures early in life. The prefrontal cortex, to the contrary, plays an important role in impulse control and problem-solving, but is also one of the latest brain structures to mature (American Academy of Child & Adolescent Psychiatry, 2016; Casey et al., 2008; Choudhury et al., 2006; Peper et al., 2011; Sales & Irwin, 2009).

Sleep in Adolescence

> The times when I put them to bed are long gone. Nowadays, my boys stay up much longer than I do. . . .
>
> —Rebekkah, mother of three teenage boys

The average teen needs between 8 and 10 hours of sleep per night. However, many teenagers do not get enough sleep (**FIGURE 14.5**).

Getting sufficient sleep is important for a number of reasons. A lack of sleep can harm teens' academic performance (Curcio et al., 2006), but it also can lead to more conflicts with others and increase a teen's risk for developing anxiety or depression (de Zambotti et al., 2018; Perez-Lloret et al., 2013). Sleep-deprived teenagers are also more likely to engage in risky behaviors like drunk driving, texting while driving, and not wearing seat belts (Wheaton et al., 2016).

One factor that makes it hard for teenagers to get enough sleep is often beyond their control: the start time of their school. As children get older, their bodies produce the sleep hormone melatonin later than they used to. Their sleep–wake cycle, also called *circadian rhythm*, shifts to a later time. Thus, their natural drive to go to sleep is shifted to a later time, often toward 11 p.m. Most teens could easily sleep until 8 or 9 a.m., but schools tend to start much earlier (Adolescent Sleep Working Group, 2014; Berger et al., 2019), forcing teens to get up when they haven't yet gotten enough sleep. Additionally, school assignments, hobbies, and adolescents' social lives often make it challenging to get to bed at an early hour. Roughly 89% of teens keep at least one electronic device in their bedroom, making it even harder to fall and stay asleep (National Sleep Foundation, 2014).

In some school districts, there have been discussions about whether to shift school times so that the school day begins later. However, some parents and students have concerns

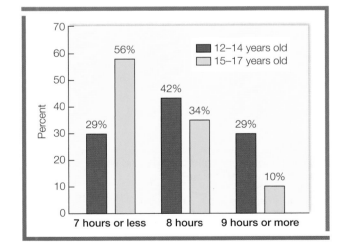

FIGURE 14.5 Percentage of American teenagers who get 7, 8, and 9 hours of sleep per night. The National Sleep Foundation recommends that teenagers get between 8 and 10 hours of sleep per night. However, many teenagers do not even get 8 hours of sleep per night. Why do you think teenagers are not sleeping enough?

Data from National Sleep Foundation. 2014. National Sleep Foundation 2014 poll. www.sleepfoundation.org

Often late for class

Drinks caffeinated beverages to get through the day

Irritable

Difficulty waking in the morning

Extracurricular activities and homework last late into the night

Naps during the week for longer than 45 minutes, sleeps in on weekends for more than 2 hours

FIGURE 14.6 Signs of sleep deprivation in teenagers.

Data from National Sleep Foundation. 2006. Parents of teens: recognize the signs & symptoms of sleep deprivation and sleep problems. www.sleepfoundation.org

that a later start (and thus, end) time would leave less time for extracurricular activities and after-school employment.

Parents who detect signs of sleep deprivation in their adolescents (see **FIGURE 14.6**) can help their children get a good night's sleep. For example, they can set up a schedule with a regular bedtime and encourage a relaxing bedtime ritual that does not involve use of screens and electronic devices. They can also encourage adolescents to avoid caffeinated drinks altogether or at least in the late afternoon and evening.

Review!

What are adolescence and puberty, and what are the changes that occur during that time?

- *Adolescence* is the transitional phase between childhood and adulthood. *Puberty* is a phase of biological growth at the end of which adolescents are sexually mature. While the age at which puberty begins varies widely, in many countries over the past 150 years, puberty has started increasingly earlier (an example of a *secular trend*). Today, puberty often begins in what we consider middle childhood.

- While puberty occurs earlier than it used to, adolescence lasts increasingly longer (sometimes until around the age of 24). This trend is due to the delay with which adolescents take on adult responsibilities and create new families.

- During puberty, both *primary and secondary sex characteristics* develop and mature. In boys, the testicles and scrotum grow and mature, the penis grows, and boys become capable of reproduction as soon as they have had their first ejaculation. Body hair begins to grow, and boys become more muscular and develop wider shoulders.

- In girls, puberty starts with the budding of breasts and is at some point followed by the first menstrual period. Body hair begins to sprout, and girls develop more fat deposits, leading to a feminine figure with wider hips.

- Typically, early puberty is associated with problems like delinquency, earlier start of sexual activities, and a higher likelihood of experiencing depression or anxiety. However, some research suggests that late maturation may also be associated with problems like substance abuse and depression.

■ The brain grows significantly during adolescence. Not all brain structures mature at the same rate, and the brain keeps maturing until far into the third decade of life. The prefrontal cortex (which is involved in logical thinking) matures last, which is one reason why adolescents are often swayed by their emotions rather than their logical thinking when needing to make personal decisions.

Practice!

1. Over the past 150 years, puberty has _____ .
   a. not changed much in terms of age of beginning
   b. been starting increasingly later
   c. been starting increasingly earlier
   d. been taking increasingly long to complete

2. During puberty, the pituitary gland is stimulated to produce _____ .

   a. luteinizing hormone (LH) and follicle-stimulating hormone (FSH)

   b. dopamine and serotonin
   c. gonadotropin-releasing hormone (GnRH)
   d. estrogen and testosterone

3. Menarche refers to _____ .
   a. the onset of the production of sex hormones
   b. a late onset of puberty
   c. an early onset of puberty
   d. a girl's first menstrual bleeding

What's Your Position?

Are you an adult? When do you think adolescence ends and adulthood begins? Consider legal milestones like being legally old enough to drive, to vote, to drink (which varies from state to state), as well as social role transitions, like moving out, going away to college, finding a job, and getting married.

After you have formed your response, compare your answer with that of a classmate. To what extent do you think our perceptions of adolescence are shaped by social expectations that may vary from culture to culture?

14.2 Nutrition in Adolescence

■ Explain the types of eating disorders and their role in adolescents' biological, social, and psychological development.

For any growing child, adequate nutrition is critical to healthy development. Parents and caregivers play a key role in ensuring children eat properly. Diet and nutrition are no less important in adolescence, but during this time, they get complicated by a number of factors, including the fact that adolescents have much more autonomy around what they consume. Body image and social expectations also come into play: As teenagers observe their developing bodies, not all are happy with what they see. A negative body image places adolescents at risk for developing eating disorders. In this section, we review the nutritional needs of adolescents and take a closer look at common eating disorders.

Nutritional Needs

Growth in adolescence is rapid and is rivaled only by the speedy growth of children in infancy. During puberty, adolescents gain about half of their adult body weight. Their bones and muscles grow, and their blood volume increases. Internal organs such as their brain, liver, kidneys, and heart increase in size as well (Corkins et al., 2016).

Compared with children in middle childhood, adolescents have much greater nutritional needs (and appetites!) due to a pubertal growth spurt.

Caloric needs depend on the activity level of a teenager, but generally boys need around 2,600 calories per day and girls need about 2,000 calories per day (U.S. Department of Agriculture and U.S. Department of Health and Human Services, 2020). Many adolescents are so physically active that their increased appetite does not impact their weight. However, young people who do not engage in physical exercise and sports are at a heightened risk for gaining too much weight (Das et al., 2017). In 2018, 1 in 5 youths in the United States between the ages of 12 and 19 were obese (National Center for Health Statistics, 2021).

In addition to needing more calories, adolescents have some very particular nutritional needs (**FIGURE 14.7**). For example, adolescents must take in more amino acids to aid muscle growth. They also have an increased need for vitamin D and calcium to support their growing bones (Das et al., 2017). Unfortunately, surveys have shown that many adolescents do not meet their nutritional needs. In particular, they need more vitamins and minerals than they consume with the food they eat. Girls are more affected by these deficiencies than are boys (Dietary Guidelines Advisory Committee, 2020). The most frequently found deficiency in girls is iron deficiency or even anemia caused by an iron deficiency (Dietary Guidelines Advisory Committee, 2020; Patton et al., 2009).

Factors Affecting Diet and Nutrition

Adolescents tend to have very particular eating habits that may make it difficult for them to meet their nutritional needs. They may miss meals and instead graze and snack their way through the day. They spend more time away from home than do younger children, so they also eat more meals away from home. Having greater autonomy over what they eat means that adolescents may eat less nutritious foods, including fast food and junk food. These unhealthy foods tend to be high in fat, sodium (salt), sugar, and cholesterol (Dietary Guidelines Advisory Committee, 2020; Schneider, 2000; Story et al., 2002), which leads to an increased risk of obesity. Obesity rates have continually risen over the past decades. In the 1980s, 10% of American teenagers were obese, but in 2018, that rate had more than doubled to 21%. There are also stark differences in obesity

Personal factors
● Food likes & dislikes
● Growth
● Attitudes & beliefs

Environmental factors
● Family & friends
● School food
● Restaurants
● Cultural & social norms

Macrosystem factors
● Advertising
● Media coverage
● Food availability

FIGURE 14.7 Eating habits in adolescence are shaped by a range of factors.
Data from J. K. Das et al. 2017. *Ann NY Acad Sci* 1393: 21–33

© GoodStudio/Shutterstock.com

■ As teens spend increasingly more time away from home, they are also more likely to eat junk food. Why do you think many adolescents gravitate toward fast food?

rates between ethnicities: In 2016, 26% of Hispanic children (aged 2–19) and 22% of Black children were obese, compared with 14% of White and 11% of Asian American children (Hales et al., 2017). Income differences predict obesity as well: 19% of children from low- or middle-income groups are obese, compared with 11% from the highest income group (Centers for Disease Control and Prevention, 2019a).

Besides nutrient deficiencies or caloric surpluses, unhealthy food affects adolescents in other ways. They are more likely to feel fatigued and be out of shape. Unhealthy food can even increase aggressive behavior and irritability as well as anxiety and depression (Holubcikova et al., 2015; Lee & Allen, 2021). Many adolescents are preoccupied with their body image, so they also tend to diet more than do younger children if they feel their weight is not close to their cultural ideal (Story & Stang, 2005; Story et al., 2002). This can lead to eating disorders, which we will consider next.

Eating Disorders

When I was 14 years old, I weighed about 124 pounds and was 5'4" tall, so my weight was what you'd consider normal. I thought I was looking all right, although I didn't like my tummy so much. At the time, I was unhappily in love. When I was rejected by the boy I had a crush on, I immediately blamed my looks. I started to eat only foods that didn't have many calories, and I also ate less overall. I had a caloric table with me at all times and made exact calculations throughout the day about what I had already eaten and what I could still afford to eat. But the more weight I lost, the more my parents got upset with me. I ate less and less, and I also felt less and less hungry. I was upset that my parents were working against me. When I reached my 100-pound goal, I just kept going. . . .

—Mariana, 16 years old, in treatment for the eating disorder anorexia nervosa

Just like Mariana, 9% of the American population will at some point in their lives experience an eating disorder (Harvard School of Public Health, 2020). Eating disorders are a group of disorders that cause severe disturbances in people's eating behaviors as well as their thoughts and emotions around food and their weight. In the United States, women make up about two-thirds (20 million) of people with eating disorders, but the remaining one-third—about 10 million people—are male, a figure that comes as a surprise to those who associate eating disorders with women (National Eating Disorders Association, 2020). Eating disorders can be dangerous: They cause more than 10,000 deaths each year (Harvard School of Public Health, 2020).

Although there are a number of different eating disorders (TABLE 14.1), they share common risk factors. These risk factors are biological as well as social and psychological in nature (FIGURE 14.8).

Body image contributes to eating disorders

Many people experiencing eating disorders have one thing in common: They have a negative **body image**. A person's body image is defined by the thoughts and feelings that result from a person's perception of their body.

body image a person's perception of their body along with the feelings and thoughts that result from the perception.

■ Table 14.1 Eating Disorders: A Summary

Prevalence	Physical/psychological symptoms	Red flags in everyday life
Anorexia nervosa 0.9% of women, 0.3% of men (National Institute of Mental Health, 2017)	See signs on the right; additionally: • No menstrual periods • Bone problems due to lack of calcium • Anemia • Wasting of muscles, including heart muscle • Constipation • Low blood pressure • Depression • Fatigue	• Significant weight loss • Tends to be cold; dresses very warmly or in layers to stay warm • Preoccupied with weight and calories • Insists on feeling overweight even if weight is in normal range (or is underweight) • Exercises excessively
Bulimia nervosa 1.21% of men, 2.6% of women (Bagaric et al., 2020)	See signs on the right; additionally: • Sore throat • Puffy face • Tooth decay due to stomach acid • Dehydration due to vomiting • Reflux	• Food containers indicate large amounts of food were eaten • Sudden disappearance of large amounts of food • Regular trips to the bathroom after meals • Bathroom smells like vomiting • Drinking of large amounts of water • Excessive use of mouthwash or chewing gum • Hands are callused from inducing vomiting
Binge eating disorder 0.74% of men 1.85% of women (Bagaric et al., 2020)	See signs on the right.	• Hoards food, often in unusual places • Creates a schedule that allows for binge sessions • Low self-esteem • Disgusted or depressed after bingeing • Sudden disappearance of large food amounts or large number of food boxes/wrappers

Sources: American Psychiatric Association. 2021. What are eating disorders? www.psychiatry.org; M. Bagaric et al. 2020. *Eur Eat Disord Rev* 28: 260–268; National Eating Disorders Association. 2021. Warning signs and symptoms. www.nationaleatingdisorders.org

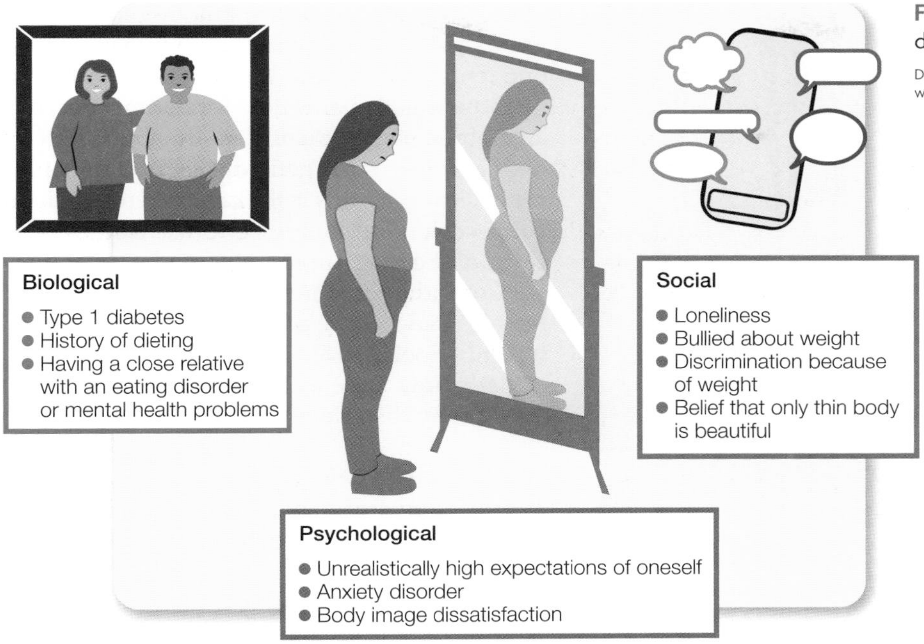

FIGURE 14.8   Risk factors for eating disorders.

Data from National Eating Disorders Association. 2018. Risk factors. www.nationaleatingdisorders.org

As young girls enter puberty, their bodies change significantly over the following years. They typically gain more body fat as they acquire the figure of an adult female. That increase in body fat, however, interacts with a cultural emphasis on slimness in women. As a result, many girls feel somewhat dissatisfied with their body (Voelker et al., 2015). In boys, to the contrary, body image tends to become more positive as they get older. With progressing puberty, they become taller and more muscular, thus moving them closer to the cultural ideal of a tall and strong man. Not surprisingly, early-maturing boys thus tend to be happier with their appearance than late-maturing boys (McCabe & Ricciardelli, 2004). About half of all teenage girls and one-fourth of teenage boys have tried to diet in an attempt to lose weight. Alarmingly, one-third of the girls who try to diet actually have a healthy weight (Paeditrics & Child Health, 2004) and are not in need of a diet at all.

A negative body image can lead adolescents to feel unhappy, anxious, self-conscious, and possibly even ashamed of their body. In an effort to change their body, girls may start dieting. Efforts to lose weight and improve their physical appearance sometimes lead to eating disorders. A negative body image is often one symptom of bulimia nervosa or anorexia nervosa.

It used to be that body-image issues were mainly found in western Europe and North America, where cultural ideals around thinness were promoted in media and popular culture (think of movies and TV shows glamorizing thin female characters). But the spread of these cultural ideals through globalization has affected the body image of girls in other cultures, such as in Asia, where thinness was long believed to be a sign of poverty (Zhang et al., 2018). In India, almost 80% of girls entering college are dissatisfied with their bodies, and 73% of Chinese female college students have dieted over the preceding year (Ganesan et al., 2018; Zhang et al., 2018).

However, there is one group that is significantly less affected by eating disorders than others: Latin American girls as well as Latina girls in the United States.

◼ Western media and culture transmit the idea to adolescent girls that to be beautiful, they have to be thin. How can young girls be helped to accept and like their own body?

anorexia nervosa a potentially life-threatening eating disorder that involves a restriction of the number of calories and types of foods that are eaten.

bulimia nervosa an eating disorder characterized by episodes of extreme overeating followed by self-induced vomiting.

◼ Adolescents who are affected by anorexia nervosa perceive their body as being too fat even when they are severely underweight. Why do you think they are not able to see their bones poking through their skin and their emaciated appearance when they look in the mirror?

Only around 0.1% of Hispanic American girls are diagnosed with anorexia, which is about one-tenth of the rate in the general population; rates among Hispanic girls for bulimia nervosa and binge eating disorders are about half as high as those of the general U.S. population. It is not clear why this is the case, but researchers suspect that Latinas have fewer weight concerns and engage in less dieting because their culture endorses more rounded body shapes in females and is more accepting of a higher body weight (Hoek, 2016).

Let's now have a closer look at three common eating disorders.

Anorexia nervosa

Anorexia nervosa is a potentially life-threatening eating disorder in which people restrict the number of calories and types of food they eat. They do so in order to stay thin or lose weight. They have a distorted body image and perceive themselves to be too heavy even if they are underweight. They exercise excessively even though their bodies have hardly any more fat. They may be preoccupied with calorie tables and the counting of calories they consume and may use laxatives to rid themselves of the food they eat (American Psychiatric Association, 2021). At the same time, they talk about food ceaselessly because they are so consumed with food.

About 0.9% of females and 0.3% of males in the United States will develop anorexia nervosa at some point in their lives (National Institute of Mental Health, 2017). People affected by anorexia are often perfectionists who set very high expectations for themselves. They are unhappy with their looks, and particularly their weight, and often also suffer from anxiety. Being bullied and having few friends increases teenagers' risk of contracting anorexia (National Eating Disorders Association, 2018).

Over time, people with anorexia effectively starve their body and may develop a multitude of physical symptoms as a result. They get brittle hair and nails and develop constipation, low blood pressure, depression, and constant fatigue. Girls stop having menstrual periods. Their muscles, including their heart muscle, weaken due to the starvation (American Psychiatric Association, 2021). In advanced states of the disease, anorexic patients often look utterly thin and as though they consist just of skin and bones.

Of all eating disorders, anorexia is the one most likely to be fatal. About 10% of people with anorexia die within 10 years, most often of starvation (South Carolina Department of Mental Health, 2021). Males have a higher risk of dying from the disease because they are often diagnosed later (Mond et al., 2014).

Bulimia nervosa

Bulimia nervosa is an eating disorder that is characterized by eating binges followed by self-induced vomiting. People affected by bulimia nervosa can be of normal weight, overweight, or somewhat underweight (though not as extremely underweight as those affected by anorexia nervosa). Like anorexic patients, people with bulimia are often obsessed with their physical appearance and weight. About 1.2% of men and 2.6% of women develop bulimia nervosa at some point in their lives (Bagaric et al., 2020). In the United States, the age at which adolescents first develop bulimia is on average 12 years (Hail & Le Grange, 2018).

Teenagers with bulimia often binge eat. During these binge eating episodes, they consume enormous amounts of food, often amounting to thousands of calories. They take no pleasure from these eating binges, however. Instead, they feel out of control and eat very quickly. Binges often last until the person falls asleep, is interrupted by someone, or experiences stomach pain. After binge eating, anxiety of weight gain sets in that leads affected people to "purge," or shed weight, by inducing vomiting, using laxatives, exercising excessively, or going on diets.

The cycle of binge eating and purging may be repeated a few times a week or, in severe cases, several times a day. People with bulimia try to hide their binges, so their friends and family members may not be aware of the condition. In rare cases, bulimia can lead to death due to complications like heart rhythm problems or rupturing of the stomach. Other symptoms of bulimia include tooth decay (because the stomach acid is damaging tooth enamel), chronic sore throat, acid reflux, and dehydration (American Psychiatric Association, 2021).

Frequent trips to the bathroom after meals, consuming large amounts of water, and frequent use of mouthwash can be indicators of bulimia. Often, affected people also have calluses on their hands from making themselves vomit (National Eating Disorders Association, 2021).

Binge eating disorder

People with binge eating disorder binge on large quantities of food and feel out of control during the binge, just like those suffering from bulimia nervosa do. However, people with binge eating disorder do not try to rid themselves of the food after consumption by inducing vomiting or using laxatives. During the binge episodes, they eat much faster than normal and do not stop when they feel full; they may eat when they are not even hungry. After the episode, feelings of guilt and disgust set in.

Excessive eating binges can lead to serious health problems like obesity, heart problems, hypertension, and diabetes (American Psychiatric Association, 2021). About 0.7% of men and 1.8% of women will develop binge eating disorders at some point in their lives (Bagaric et al., 2020).

Treatment of eating disorders

The treatment of eating disorders is complex because it usually requires psychotherapy as well as medical care and nutritional counseling (Zipfel et al., 2015). One part of the treatment is aimed at establishing healthy eating habits. People with anorexia need to regain weight to get to a healthy weight level. That can be difficult because a regular diet can cause serious reactions in people who have starved themselves. For that reason, a nutrition program will be customized to take a step-by-step

■ In binge eating disorder, teenagers are overcome by urges to consume large quantities of food. Why do they gravitate toward unhealthy food, rather than bingeing on fruit and vegetables?

approach to eating more food. If patients are unable to keep food in, they may get high-calorie drinks or nutrition through a nasal tube. Gaining weight is often difficult because patients are not always willing to participate in treatment. Such was the case with Mariana, whom we met at the beginning of this section: She was hospitalized when she fainted during a family outing one day. Only after a first round of intense psychotherapy was she able to overcome her strong aversion to food and to start to participate willingly in the therapy program.

Contrary to anorexic teens, adolescents with bulimia or binge eating disorder may have to lose weight. They need to reestablish healthy eating habits—that is, they need to learn to manage the urge to binge eat and, in the case of bulimia, to break the cycle of binge eating and subsequent purging (Hail & Le Grange, 2018).

Teens will also receive medical care for any health problems they have or that are a result of their eating disorder. Those health problems may include heart problems, dehydration, constipation, or other medical complications. Medications are usually not given to treat the eating disorder itself but may be prescribed to treat physical symptoms or the anxiety or depression that often accompany eating disorders.

Psychotherapy aids patients in developing a healthier body image, changing eating habits, and building self-esteem. Emotions and thoughts play an important role in the development of eating disorders. Understanding how feelings and thinking influence their actions helps adolescents gain control over their behavior. In young people, family therapy is usually the therapy of choice. In family therapy, parents work together with the care team to help their child get better. Parents support their child during mealtimes, help them change their behavior, and assist in the steps to return to everyday life. In the beginning, the parents need to exercise much control over their child's behavior with the goal of returning increasingly more control to the child over time (Lock & Le Grange, 2015). In adults, cognitive behavioral therapy is often the choice for treatment (Hail & Le Grange, 2018).

Treatment is usually lengthy, and adolescents often have to monitor their behavior and nutritional habits for a lifetime so they do not have a relapse. Studies confirm that recovery is difficult: A long-term study following anorexia nervosa patients found that 30% of patients were symptom-free after 10 years and 39% were symptom-free after 20 years (Fichter et al., 2017). A meta-analysis found that after treatment for binge eating disorder, only half of patients did not binge eat anymore (Linardon, 2018). As these numbers clearly show, eating disorders are challenging to treat, and there is not yet a treatment that works for the majority of affected persons.

Helping Adolescents Develop Healthy Eating Habits

As we have seen, adolescents have much more control over what they put—and do not put—into their bodies. However, parents and caregivers can still play an important role in encouraging healthy eating behaviors. Do parents allow their adolescent children to snack on sweets as much as, and whenever, they want? Are teenagers allowed to eat in front of a screen, and do parents expect that their children eat breakfast before school?

In families that set food-related rules for children, teenagers drink fewer sugary drinks, eat more vegetables and fruit, and are more likely to have breakfast before school (see, for example, DeJong et al., 2009; Holubcikova et al., 2016; Verzeletti et al., 2010). Unfortunately, more than 20% of parents do not set any rules regarding nutrition at all. Rule-setting varies with SES: Families with higher income are more likely to set rules for their children's eating behavior than are poorer families. Consequently, children from lower-SES families tend to have poorer eating habits. They skip breakfast more often and eat fewer fruits and vegetables (Holubcikova et al., 2016) (**FIGURE 14.9**).

Besides setting rules, parents can influence their teenagers' diet in other ways as well:

- Expose teens to new foods. Trying out new foods is often fun for teenagers and makes them more aware of the choices they have.

- Ask adolescents for their food preferences and take them into account whenever possible.

- Whatever is in the house gets eaten: If there are particular foods family members should not eat, it's best not to buy them.

- Have snacks readily available. Teenagers often graze throughout the day and pick up whatever is available. It helps to prewash fruit or to dedicate one area in the fridge to healthy snacks.

An active lifestyle plays a role in nutrition as well. Teenagers tend to have healthier eating habits if they participate in organized activities. Active teenagers consume fewer soft drinks and junk food. This is a stable effect, no matter whether teens pursue athletic or nonathletic activities. Perhaps just being away from their screens helps them maintain healthier eating habits; after all, many teenagers consume unhealthy snack food like chocolate and chips in front of the computer and TV (Voráčová et al., 2018).

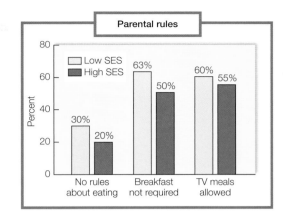

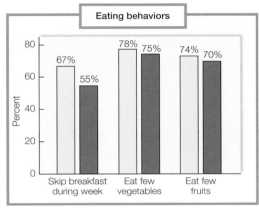

FIGURE 14.9   The impact of SES and parental rules on eating behaviors. More-affluent families set more nutritional rules for their teenagers than families that are less affluent. Perhaps as a result of these rules, teenagers from higher-SES families also have better eating habits than their peers from lower-income families.

Data from J. Holubcikova et al. 2016. *BMC Public Health* 16: 359

■ What's It Like...

Managing Childhood Diabetes

Josh, father of Sophie

Sophie is a very active girl with lots of friends, and she's very involved in a number of social activities in our community. She has been going to the same summer sleepaway camp in a beautiful secluded state park ever since she was 10 years old. This past summer, when we went to pick her up, we were shocked to see that she had lost a lot of weight—almost 30 pounds, as it turned out. We were particularly surprised because she'd always been a healthy girl and had never had any serious health issues before.

At pickup, she seemed fine overall despite her weight loss but complained about a stomachache. Our drive home turned out to be more eventful than planned, however. She threw up in the car and we had to stop for drinks four times, although camp was only an hour away from our house.

The stomachache and nausea got worse overnight, so we went to the emergency room, where they did some blood work. It turned out that Sophie's blood sugar levels were extremely high, and that she needed to be put on insulin immediately. It took three days in the hospital to get her insulin levels back down to a normal level.

From then, everything went very quickly. She was officially diagnosed with diabetes, type 1, which means that her body does not produce insulin to control blood glucose levels. We had to learn a lot of things—how to do finger pricks and measure Sophie's blood sugar levels and how to administer insulin shots (which she now needs several times a day).

We also quickly learned that it's not so easy to calculate the amount of insulin that needs to be administered before a meal, particularly in growing children. There was quite a lot of trial and error involved. Thankfully, Sophie got a device that monitors her glucose levels on a continuous basis and connects to our cell phones, so I got an alert anytime something was off with her levels. That was really helpful, particularly in the beginning, when we still had to figure things out.

At the time, when she got the diagnosis, it was very hard. I was so worried for Sophie, her health, and her future, particularly since I knew that this was something she was going to have to live with for the rest of her life. This was only 2 months ago, but in the meantime, we have already found a new kind of routine, which I found hard to imagine in the beginning. We're still watchful, and always will be, but we've learned that diabetes can be managed successfully and we've come to appreciate the high-tech tools we have at our disposal today that make things so much easier.

Sophie, 13 years

This past summer I got diagnosed with diabetes. It happened very quickly. I didn't realize it at the time, but I actually lost a lot of weight. I was also very thirsty a lot of the time. My mom had a feeling something was up and talked about diabetes, but I kept telling her it wasn't.

Anyway, the weekend I got home from summer camp I needed to go to the emergency room because I really wasn't feeling well and that's where they told me the news. I was calm when they told me because I actually didn't know that much about diabetes. But even later when I learned I was going to have this all my life, I wasn't too upset and didn't get terribly worried.

I did hate the pricks though. It took me quite a while to get used to the needles and the injections, but now I don't care anymore.

It's been hard to get my sugar level stable, so I've been eating a lot of low-carb food. It's not too bad because these days there's lots of low-carb food, like special cereals or protein bars. I also like to eat chicken.

At school, not many things have changed really. When I got my diagnosis, I texted my friends to tell them, and they were all cool with it. I mean, they felt bad for me but that was about it. It wasn't really a big deal. I had been concerned that they'd tell me I can't play sports anymore, but that was not the case. In my free time, I'm as active as I was before my diagnosis.

One thing that has changed at school is that I now need to go to the office at lunchtime so a nurse can help me with my shot. But it doesn't bother me too much, although I actually think I don't need her. I also need to be more mindful of my body now.

Review!

What are eating disorders, and what role do they play in adolescence?

- Nutrition plays an important role in healthy development during adolescence, because bodies grow rapidly during this time. Cultural ideals of how beautiful bodies look strongly influence how young people, and in particular girls, perceive their bodies. Thus, *body image* often plays a crucial role in the development of eating disorders.

- In puberty, girls' bodies gain more body fat, giving them a more female form. Throughout adolescence, their body image often gets more negative. Boys become more muscular as they age and thus get closer to the ideal male body image. For that reason, they generally become more satisfied with their body through-out adolescence.

- Although more girls than boys are affected, a growing number of adolescents as well as adults worldwide suffer from eating disorders. There are three main types of eating disorders: In *anorexia nervosa*, people consume a reduced number of calories to lose weight or stay thin. In *bulimia nervosa*, people engage in binge eating periods and subsequently try to purge the calories they consumed, for example through self-induced vomiting or the use of laxatives. In binge eating disorder, people binge on large quantities of food but do not try to rid themselves of the food afterward, often leading to extreme obesity.

- Eating disorders in adolescents are frequently treated with family therapy, in which the family and particularly parents play a crucial role and work together with the teenager to establish healthy eating patterns and a positive body image. Medical treatment may be necessary for health problems that were caused by the eating disorder. Treatment is lengthy and often not completely successful, however. Decades after treatment, a significant number of patients still have at least some symptoms of an eating disorder.

Practice!

1. In anorexia nervosa, adolescents _____ .
   a. binge eat frequently and then make themselves vomit to rid themselves of the calories yet again
   b. consume very few calories in an attempt to lose weight
   c. binge eat frequently and often gain excessive weight
   d. restrict their food intake to just one type of food, usually carbohydrates like pasta and bread

2. The effects of binge eating disorder frequently include _____ .
   a. sore throat
   b. bone problems due to lack of calcium
   c. excessive weight gain
   d. wasting of muscles

See for Yourself!

Go to a supermarket and examine the aisles. Which foods are offered in the most prominent spots at middle height in shelves or at the checkout? Where are healthy selections located? Is the supermarket of your choice helping shoppers to make healthy choices?

What's Your Position?

What time should school start? Many adolescents are sleep-deprived because they go to bed late and have to wake up early the next morning to get ready for school. In recent years, there have been some initiatives that tried to get high schools to start lessons later. However, these initiatives also have met some virulent resistance from educators, parents, and students.

Write a brief answer to the question *What time should school start?* Then consult some of the websites below. Did they change your opinion? If so, how?

Additional Resources Online

- "Pros and cons of later school start times," by Leigh Ann Morgan
- "Later school start times? Not so fast," in *The Enterprise*

- "How would later school start times affect sleep?" by the Sleep Foundation
- "Teachers overwhelmingly oppose later high school start times in Montgomery," in *The Washington Post*

14.3 Health and Safety in Adolescence

■ Outline the major health risks adolescents face and give reasons why.

Adolescence is one of the healthiest periods of life, and unhealthy habits may not leave noticeable traces until decades later. In a 2018 study in the United States, caregivers rated the health of their 12- to 17-year-olds as very good or excellent in 83% of cases (Centers for Disease Control and Prevention, 2019c). But behaviors during adolescence can undermine adolescents' future health as well as the health of their offspring. Worldwide, around 3,000 adolescents die every day—that amounts to over 1.1 million young people per year! They die mostly from causes that could have been prevented or treated. In this section, we will learn about the lack of exercise we can see in many adolescents. We then take a look at the major causes of death in adolescents, as well as suicide, depression, and drug addiction.

Exercise

An active lifestyle can protect adolescents, just like anyone, from many diseases and future health problems. Yet, many students do not get enough exercise in

■ The majority of middle and high schools do not require students to take physical education classes, even though the value of exercise is widely known, particularly among educators and school personnel. Why do schools not require their students to be physically active?

their daily lives. In fact, only 27% of American high schoolers exercise 60 or more minutes per day (Centers for Disease Control and Prevention, 2017).

Of course, teens may work out in their free time, but not all of them do. For that reason, one important source of physical exercise can be found in schools and the physical education (PE) lessons they offer. However, American schools are falling short of providing adequate PE curricula to enable all youth to exercise daily. At grade level 6, only about one-third of schools require PE classes; in grade 11, only 9% of schools still require PE classes (Centers for Disease Control and Prevention, 2017). These developments come in spite of the fact that students who exercise on a regular basis tend to perform better academically, have fewer behavior problems in the classroom, are more likely to stay active as adults, and do not miss as many school days as their peers who do not engage in physical activities (Kawabata et al., 2021; Kohl & Cook, 2013; Rasberry et al., 2011). Adolescents who do not exercise regularly also have a higher risk of obesity (Kumar et al., 2015; Sagar & Gupta, 2018).

Death among Adolescents

Although adolescence is generally a time of good health for most youngsters, adolescents still do experience major health challenges at times. In many cases, deaths are due to preventable causes. In the following sections, we will examine causes of death in adolescents in more detail.

Causes of death

In 2019, more than 10,000 adolescents aged 15–19 died in the United States. Most of them died of unintentional injuries (35%; this number includes car crashes), suicide (22%), or homicide (18%; see also **FIGURE 14.10**). African American and Native American adolescents have higher death rates than adolescents of other ethnicities (**FIGURE 14.11**).

Suicide

There is another striking difference we see when we examine causes of death in adolescents. In 15- to 19-year-old Blacks, Hispanics, and Asian Americans, the death rate resulting from suicide hovers around 9 out of 100,000 young people. In White adolescents, the suicide death rate climbs to 14 per 100,000. In Native Americans, the suicide rate is drastically higher than in any other group: 33 out of every 100,000. Suicide is the leading cause of death among Native American adolescents and the second or third leading cause of death among adolescents of other ethnicities (Heron, 2019). Males commit suicide more than three times as often as females (Miron et al., 2019).

From 2000 to 2016, the suicide rate in 15- to 24-year-olds increased by 30% (Hedegaard et al., 2018). Researchers are not entirely sure what factors are responsible for the increase in suicides among young people but believe the opioid crisis—the relatively widespread

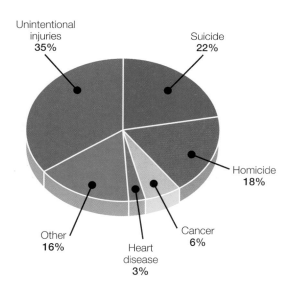

FIGURE 14.10 Causes of death in 10- to 24-year-olds in the United States.

After M. Heron. 2019. Deaths: Leading causes for 2017. National Vital Statistics Reports, Vol. 68, No. 6. National Center for Health Statistics, Hyattsville, MD

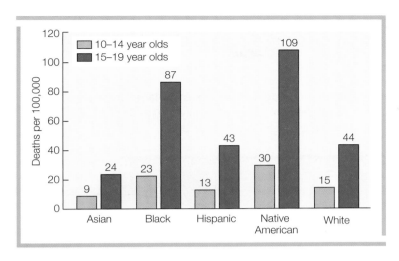

FIGURE 14.11 Death rates vary considerably by ethnicity. Asian Americans have the lowest death rate among adolescents, followed by Hispanic American and White adolescents. Black and Native American adolescents have a much higher death rate than do adolescents of other ethnicities. What might be some reasons that death rates vary by ethnicity?

After M. Heron. 2019. Deaths: Leading causes for 2017. National Vital Statistics Reports, Vol. 68, No. 6. National Center for Health Statistics, Hyattsville, MD

misuse of addictive opioid drugs—may in part be responsible for the rise. Parents today may also be more willing to report their child's death as a suicide because suicide is less stigmatized today than it used to be (Frazee & Morales, 2020). Then came COVID-19, and in 2020 alone, suicide attempts among adolescents increased by 31%, fueled by social isolation, family instability, anxiety, and distress caused by the pandemic. The American Academy of Pediatrics declared the decline in child mental health caused by COVID-19 a national emergency (Yard et al., 2021).

A number of factors increase the risk that adolescents will consider or commit suicide. Teens have a higher risk of committing suicide if they:

- have mental disorders like depression and anxiety or eating disorders (Bridge et al., 2006);
- have a previous history of attempted suicide (Bilsen, 2018);
- have certain personality traits like a lack of impulse control, or have poor problem-solving skills (Apter & Wasserman, 2003; Bilsen, 2018);
- experience family issues like violence, poor communication within the family, or mentally ill family members (Portzky et al., 2005); and/or
- experience stress like difficulties with peers or friends (Amitai & Apter, 2012; Spirito & Esposito-Smythers, 2006).

Although there are no definitive signs that a teen is about to hurt themselves, there are some warning signs. These include, for example:

- Statements like "I wish I was dead";
- Depression and sadness;
- Increasing isolation from friends, family, and activities;
- Changes in eating and sleep habits;
- Dropping grades at school;
- Frequent thinking about death and dying; and
- Complaints about psychosomatic aches like stomachaches and headaches (American Academy of Child & Adolescent Psychiatry, 2018).

It is often hard to predict suicide. Moreover, suicidal teens may try to hide their intentions. However, being aware of changes in teens and taking appropriate action (like talking to a pediatrician or seeking a conversation with the teen) can potentially save lives.

Culture Counts

Suicide: Race and Ethnicity Matter

In the United States, suicide is the third leading cause of death among adolescents (after unintentional injuries and homicides). As the graph to the right shows, there are considerable differences in suicide rates based on race and ethnicity.

In Canada, suicide is the second leading cause of death (Pan-Canadian Health Inequalities Reporting Initiative, 2021). Canadian suicide rates are highest among Indigenous populations: Specifically, the suicide rate among Inuit people in Canada is six times higher than the rate among non-Indigenous Canadians, while the rate of suicide among First Nations people living in Canada is nearly four times as high as the rate in the general population. The reasons are complex, but researchers point to the historical treatment of Indigenous people, including the forced removal of Indigenous children to be placed in state-run residential schools, where physical and sexual abuse was rampant. Marginalization, loss of language and culture, and disruption of family life are factors associated with high rates of suicide.

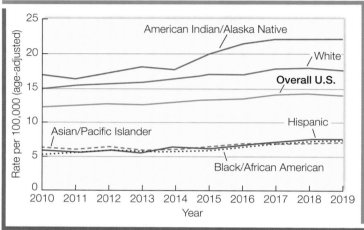

■ Suicide rates by race/ethnicity, U.S. 2010–2019.

After Suicide Prevention Resource Center. 2021. Racial and Ethnic Disparities. www.sprc.org; Centers for Disease Control and Prevention, National Center for Health Statistics. 2021. 1999–2020 Wide Ranging Online Data for Epidemiological Research (WONDER), Multiple Cause of Death files [Data file]. http://wonder.cdc.gov

■ Question

What do you think accounts for the high rate of suicide among Native Americans? Could it be explained, do you think, by some of the factors contributing to high rates of suicide among Indigenous people in Canada?

Sources: Pan-Canadian Health Inequalities Reporting Initiative. 2021. Inequalities in death by suicide in Canada. www.canada.ca; Suicide Prevention Resource Center. (2021). Racial and ethnic disparities. https://sprc.org

Depression

Depression is a mental health disorder that causes persistent sadness. Affected teenagers often lose interest in activities they loved to participate in before. Symptoms of depression may also include changes in weight and eating behavior, difficulties paying attention, and a drop in school grades (American Academy of Pediatrics, 2018). Depression is more often missed in adolescents than in adults because many adolescents have primarily unexplained body aches, anxiety, or irritability; in short, symptoms vary more in teens than in adults (Leaf et al., 1996).

Depression in adolescents is relatively common all around the world. After puberty, depression rates rise sharply, particularly in girls. Roughly 16% of American teenagers have experienced at least one major depressive episode (National Institute of Mental Health, 2021). Youth who are affected by depression have a higher risk of committing suicide; in fact, more than one-half of the teens who have died of suicide experienced depression before their death (Hawton & van Heeringen, 2009). A review of 13 studies found that social media use among teenagers was positively correlated with mental health problems like depression. However, the relationship between social media use and depression is complex. Most likely other factors, like insomnia from social media use, play a role in the development of depression (Keles et al., 2020).

Most depressive episodes subside within 1 year, but more than one-half of affected teens will experience another episode within 5 years (Dunn & Goodyer, 2006). Adolescents have a higher risk of experiencing an episode of depression when someone else in their family suffers from depression or if they experience stressful life events or bullying (Thapar et al., 2012).

There are a number of things parents can do when they suspect their teenager is suffering from depression. They can talk with their child and ask if something is bothering them. It may be worth bringing up the topic of bullying, because bullied teens are at particular risk for developing depression. Parents should contact their pediatrician, who can make recommendations regarding how to proceed. Apart from that, parents can promote healthy behaviors like good nutrition, exercise, and limiting screen time.

Stress-reducing measures can also be helpful. Depressed adolescents are not very resilient to stress, so parents can reduce their teen's stress by temporarily lowering expectations at home and for schoolwork. Parents may offer relaxing activities that their child likes and make themselves available for conversations. Reducing screen time may have an uplifting effect, because screens have been found to worsen the symptoms of depression (Boers et al., 2019).

Parents should look out for signs indicating their teen may be suicidal (see above) and have handy the phone number of a local mental-health crisis service that can be called in case of an emergency (American Academy of Pediatrics, 2018).

Depression is treated somewhat differently in adolescents and children from how it is treated in adults. Psychotherapy is the treatment of choice. Cognitive-behavioral therapy is often used and has been studied widely as a treatment for depression. However, studies also show that psychotherapy is more suitable for milder cases of depression and doesn't deliver consistent results in more severe cases. Adults are often prescribed medication to soothe their symptoms (Thapar et al., 2012), but things are not so easy with adolescents and children. The only group of antidepressants that seems to be effective in children is selective serotonin reuptake inhibitors (SSRIs). However, there is some concern about the safety of SSRI use in youth and children because they can lead to an increase in thoughts of self-harm and suicide attempts. Thus, parents, adolescents, and their treatment team have to carefully weigh benefits and risks of their treatment choices.

■ Depression in teens often has different and more fluctuating symptoms than depression in adults. How can parents and caregivers increase the chances that depression in their teen will be recognized early on?

Drugs

Recreational drug and alcohol use is prevalent among American adolescents, despite the fact that even legal substances—alcohol and, in some states, marijuana—are not legally available for purchase or use by anyone under the age of 21. In this section, we will discuss drug use in adolescents as well as some of the most common drugs.

Some teenagers engage in recreational drug use

Most adolescents do not use drugs, but a minority of them do, sometimes with serious consequences. The most common drugs used by 12th graders in 2019 were alcohol (52%), marijuana (36%), and nicotine (12%) (Centers for Disease Control and Prevention, 2019b).

substance abuse repeated and excessive use of drugs such as alcohol, illegal drugs, or pain medications.

substance dependence addiction to drugs in such a way that users can no longer control their drug use and focus intensely on the use of a substance.

It is important to distinguish between substance abuse and substance dependence. In **substance abuse**, teens excessively use drugs, such as alcohol or pain medications. Not all substance abuse leads to addiction. However, when drugs take over a person's life to the point that they are not able to control their drug use anymore, substance abuse becomes **substance dependence**.

The treatment of substance abuse is challenging. Some teenagers are referred to therapy programs by their parents or their schools, but they do not really wish to stop using drugs. Even if they go through a withdrawal program and do not feel a physical need for the drug anymore, they are still likely to return to the same social environment that led them to start taking drugs in the first place: their friend group or possibly even their own home (Hogue et al., 2018).

Although often not intentionally, drug abuse can be fatal. In 2017, 17 out of every 100,000 adolescents (15–24 years) died of a drug overdose, up from 5 out of 100,000 just 18 years earlier. The majority of drug overdose deaths occur in males, who experience more than twice as many overdose deaths as females. Opioid-related overdose deaths among young people rose sixfold between 1999 and 2017, to 5 deaths per 100,000 youths from heroin and 9.5 deaths per 100,000 youths for other opioids (National Center for Health Statistics, 2019).

Not all teenagers have the same risk of developing a drug addiction. Children and teens who have been abused or suffered a trauma are more at risk. If children were prenatally exposed to drugs or have family members who are addicted to drugs, they also run a greater risk of developing an addiction (Shane et al., 2006). Other factors play a role as well, like whether teens' friends use drugs and to what extent parents monitor their children's behavior (Nash et al., 2005). Children from low-income households and children who live in areas in which crime and drug use are abundant are at higher risk as well (Ali et al., 2011).

Prevention programs through schools have been shown to be effective at reducing smoking and alcohol use in teens. School-based programs that help adolescents improve their social skills have been shown to lower cannabis (marijuana) use. These programs help teens to get along with others and form successful friendships. They also teach them to stand their ground when they disagree with their peers and to critically evaluate "mass opinions" (Das et al., 2016).

MARIJUANA Marijuana comes from the dried flowers and leaves of the cannabis plant. When smoked, vaped, or otherwise consumed, it produces a calming effect on the body. Its best-known compound, THC (delta-9-tetrahydrocannabinol), produces a psychoactive effect, but the plant also yields the non-psychoactive compound CBD, which is often used as an oil. Both compounds have common therapeutic uses.

Marijuana use is legal for recreational purposes in a growing number of states but is restricted to adults 21 years of age and older. Nowhere in the United States is recreational cannabis legal for teenagers (American Academy of Child & Adolescent Psychiatry, 2019).

Marijuana use is more popular than smoking in today's adolescents. In fact, marijuana vaping in 12th graders almost doubled from 2018 to 2019, with more than one-third of 12th graders having used marijuana in the previous year (Centers for Disease Control and Prevention, 2019b; National Institute on Drug Abuse, 2019). At the same time, teens are less likely to perceive marijuana use as risky: In 1992, 80% of teens thought that regular consumption of marijuana was a "great risk"; in 2012, that percentage had decreased to 45% (Gonzalez & Swanson, 2012). Teenagers living in states that have legalized nonmedical use of marijuana in recent years (for example, Colorado or Washington) may be more likely to use marijuana than their peers in states where recreational use of marijuana is not allowed (Bailey et al., 2020).

Marijuana is more potent today than it was in the past. It is grown differently to triple the average amount of THC compared with 30 years ago. As a psychoactive agent, THC changes brain functioning and gives marijuana its special effects. Marijuana is often used in combination with other drugs or alcohol to create more intense effects.

Because it is known to be less addictive than alcohol, marijuana is sometimes believed to have fewer short- and long-term risks. However, THC can lead to problems with attention, memory, and decision-making. In adolescents, whose brains are still developing, there is a risk that these brain changes may become permanent (National Institute on Drug Abuse, 2020b). Additionally, studies have shown that marijuana can affect the cortical thickness in some brain structures. That is, marijuana use changes the development of the brain and may result in tissue loss or changes to the brain structure (Jacobus & Tapert, 2014; Lopez-Larson et al., 2011). Because many teenagers mistakenly believe that marijuana use does not have long-term negative consequences, it is important to have conversations with them early on, and repeatedly so, about the risks of marijuana use.

■ Marijuana is made from the leaves and flowers of the cannabis plant. It can be used for medical purposes, but it is also a popular recreational drug among teenagers.

ALCOHOL Although it is illegal for youth under the age of 21 to drink alcohol in the United States (**FIGURE 14.12**), American adolescents between 12 and 20 years

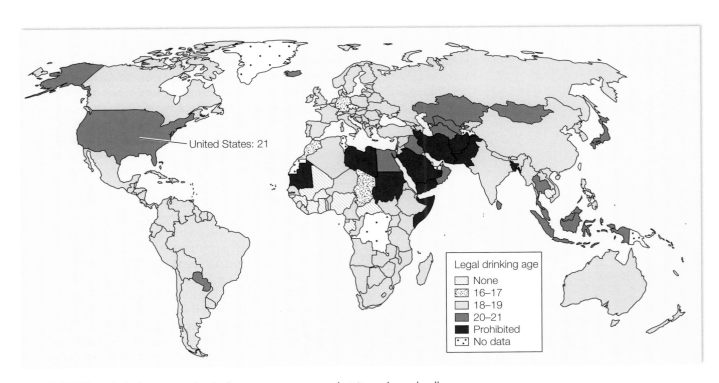

United States: 21

Legend: Legal drinking age
- None
- 16–17
- 18–19
- 20–21
- Prohibited
- No data

FIGURE 14.12 Alcohol use is on the decline among teenagers, but it can have deadly consequences if teens drive after drinking, or if they consume too much alcohol. The legal drinking age in the United States is higher than in many other countries. In Europe, for example, many countries do not have a legal drinking age for private alcohol consumption, and the vast majority allow drinking at age 16 or 18 at the latest. Do you think lowering the legal drinking age in the United States might lower the urge of some youth to drink alcohol?

Data from World Health Organization. 2016. Age limits—Alcohol service/sales by country. https://apps.who.int/gho/data; International Alliance for Responsible Drinking (IARD). 2022. Minimum legal age limits. https://iard.org

binge drinking drinking more than five drinks in a row.

of age drink 11% of the alcohol consumed in the country (Pacific Institute for Research Evaluation, 2005). Most teenagers who consume alcohol do so in a moderate way. Some, however, engage in binge drinking. In **binge drinking**, students drink five or more drinks in a row. More than 3,500 teenagers die each year due to excessive drinking (Das et al., 2016). Binge drinking rates have been declining over the past years; in 2019, 14% of teens admitted to binge drinking. General alcohol use in teenagers is declining as well (National Institute on Drug Abuse, 2019).

Alcohol abuse and binge drinking by adolescents can have many negative consequences. Teens who drink alcohol are more frequently absent from school and get poorer grades. They are more often involved in conflicts and fights, and they participate less often in organized activities. Alcohol consumption puts teens at risk for memory problems and the abuse of other drugs, as well as alcohol addiction in adulthood (U.S. Department of Health and Human Services, 2012). Brain development can be affected as well, and in particular, the development of white matter (McQueeny et al., 2009; Thayer et al., 2020). And of course, drinking adolescents are more likely to be involved in car crashes or other accidents that involve alcohol, including death from alcohol poisoning (Esser et al., 2019; Miller et al., 2007).

NICOTINE Nicotine is a stimulant that is derived from tobacco leaves. It is very addictive in all of its forms, whether smoked, sniffed, inhaled, or chewed. Nicotine stimulates the adrenal glands, which release adrenaline as a response. The adrenaline, in turn, increases heart rate and blood pressure and leads to faster breathing. It isn't so much the nicotine that has negative effects on teenagers' health as other byproducts involved in the consumption of nicotine. Smoking tobacco, for example, can cause cancer, heart and lung problems, and eye problems. Smokeless tobacco products can cause oral cancer as well as heart and gum disease (National Institute on Drug Abuse, 2020a). In addition to containing nicotine, the aerosols in e-cigarettes may harm the lungs. E-cigarette batteries have also caused fires and explosions that have resulted in injuries (U.S. Department of Health and Human Services, 2016).

Smoking cigarettes is not nearly as popular among teens as it once was, but more teens are vaping than ever before. In 2021, 11% of high schoolers used e-cigarettes, with 85% of them using flavored e-cigarettes (Hunt, 2021). Teens vape because they want to experiment (61%), it tastes good (42%), because they want to have a good time with friends (38%), and because it relaxes them (37%) (National Institute on Drug Abuse, 2019).

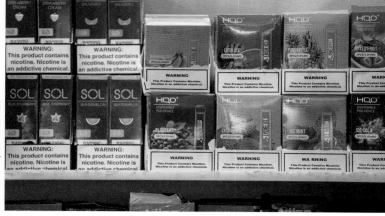

© Marshall Ritzel/Associated Press

■ A large range of flavors are available for vaping. Child-friendly and sweet flavors like mango or cotton candy as well as attractive and colorful packaging appeal to teenagers, encouraging them to give vaping a try. Some of them will develop an addiction that may last a lifetime.

OPIOIDS Opioids are a group of pain relievers that include prescription medications as well as illegal drugs like heroin. Commercially produced opioids are commonly prescribed to treat pain despite their side effects. They can dramatically slow a person's breathing, and in a person who takes too much of an opioid, there is a risk that they could stop breathing. They are also dangerously addictive, causing some people to turn to illegally produced opioids after their prescribed course runs out. Illegal drugs may contain the potent manufactured opioid *fentanyl*, which is so strong that even a very small dose can lead to death.

From 1999 to 2016, the number of children and teens that died due to opioid overdoses nearly tripled (Gaither et al., 2018). Almost

9,000 youth died over that 18-year period, mostly of accidental overdoses; three-fourths of them were boys. The opioid crisis affects mostly White children: 80% of the children who died were White (Gaither et al., 2018).

DRUG USE: WARNING SIGNS AND TREATMENT   Many parents are unaware of just how many teenagers use illegal drugs (National Center on Addiction and Substance Abuse at Columbia University, 2011). Not only can drug use take a toll on adolescents' health, but it also puts them at greater risk for getting involved in criminal behavior, for engaging in risky sexual behaviors, and for developing mental health problems (Ali et al., 2011). For these reasons, early detection of drug use is of great importance.

What are some of the warning signs parents and educators can observe when adolescents engage in the use of illicit drugs? Adolescents often:

- have new friends that parents do not know or approve of;
- withdraw from old friends and family;
- stop engaging in activities they used to do regularly;
- get angry when confronted by parents;
- prefer to spend their time in their room, rather than with their family or siblings;
- ignore curfew rules and make up stories to explain their being late;
- start to skip classes or underperform at school; and/or
- are apathic or aggressive when under the influence of drugs or may have trouble speaking (Baingana et al., 2006; Hawkins et al., 1992; Kuehn, 2011; Montoya & McCann, 2010; Rooney et al., 2012).

Oftentimes, the appearance of the teen's eyes is a good indicator as well: Blood-shot eyes may indicate marijuana use (Baingana et al., 2006; Slutske, 2005); increased pupil size may point to the use of cocaine or amphetamines; and tiny pinpoint pupils may indicate heroin use (Baingana et al., 2006).

Parents and teachers who are familiar with the warning signs and symptoms of drug use are able to intervene faster and improve their children's outcomes. Parents who are concerned about their teen's drug use should first contact their pediatrician, who can refer them to other appropriate practitioners or sources of information. There are many options of inpatient and outpatient treatments, the choice of which will depend on the medical and mental health problems that the teen has. Most teens can be treated as outpatients. However, if adolescents have trouble staying sober or have mental health issues like anxiety or depression, they may benefit from inpatient treatment (American Academy of Pediatrics, 2009).

Health and Social Media Safety

A majority of teens use social media, and the percentage of adolescents who are using social media daily is steadily increasing: It rose from 45% in 2015 to 63% in 2019, with teens using screens an average of 7 hours and 22 minutes per day (Rideout & Robb, 2019). Social media can pose some harm to adolescents, but research has shown there are health benefits as well. In this section we will focus on two issues: how social media influence girls' body image and how social media can be used in order to promote good health behaviors among adolescents.

Social media have an impact on girls' body image

As we have seen in the section above on eating disorders, teens, and in particular, girls, are often self-conscious about their appearance. Unhappiness with their looks can be one factor that may ultimately lead to an eating disorder like anorexia nervosa or bulimia nervosa. Media can contribute to the development of a negative body image. Two theories explain how negative body image develops in girls as they consume media.

The first theory, *sociocultural theory*, suggests that media present girls with beauty ideals of thinness that, for many, are impossible to achieve. When girls fail to become as thin as they aspire to be, they become unhappy with their own body and develop a negative body image (Ata et al., 2007; Cash & Smolak, 2011).

Objectification theory proposes that in Western societies, the female body is like an object that exists to be looked at and evaluated by others (Fredrickson & Roberts, 1997). Throughout their lives, girls consume so much media that they end up perceiving their own body in just that way: as an object whose appearance is appreciated and appraised (Holland & Tiggemann, 2016). Countries like France, Italy, Spain, and Israel have passed laws that prohibit the use of fashion models that are considered "excessively thin" (Sykes, 2017).

Not only are female and male bodies treated differently in the media, but girls also use media differently from boys, which contributes further to their body image issues: Girls, rather than boys, tend to actively use social media to post and share photos, and they are more likely to pay attention to and look at others' photos on social media.

Of course, they are not only passive onlookers. They post images of themselves as well. And when they do so, they tend to choose images that present themselves and their bodies in the best possible light. With today's tools, it is also often not clear whether a photo has been altered. So any young girl using social media is likely to view a lot of images that present idealized versions of her friends' and peers' bodies (Hogue & Mills, 2019; Manago et al., 2008). And indeed, studies show that when girls engage with social media, and particularly when they view images of peers they consider to be more attractive than themselves, their body image turns more negative (Hogue & Mills, 2019; Holland & Tiggemann, 2016).

Social media can be used to promote healthy behaviors

We know that teens spend considerable amounts of time on digital devices engaging actively in social media. We also know that adolescence is a critical development period that sets the stage for future healthy or unhealthy habits. This has led some researchers and health practitioners to wonder whether the power of social media can be harnessed to educate adolescents on important health topics and to influence their health habits and behaviors.

Although studies examining the use of social media for public health efforts in teens are still relatively rare, efforts are being made to find out how to use media in this way. An added advantage of social media is that they reach a broader audience because ethnic minorities such as Hispanics and African Americans use social media apps on their mobile devices more often than Whites (Neiger et al., 2012). African American teens also like different social media platforms compared with their White counterparts (FIGURE 14.13).

There are a large number of platforms that can be used for health promotion: blogs, games, message boards, SMS,

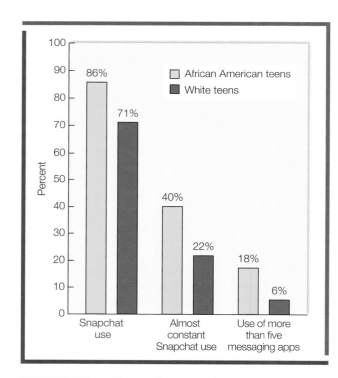

FIGURE 14.13 Difference between African American and White teens in social media use. African American teens tend to use a wider variety of messaging apps and use Snapchat more frequently than White teens.

Data from AP-NORC Center. 2021. Instagram and Snapchat Are Most Popular Social Networks for Teens; Black Teens Are Most Active on Social Media, Messaging Apps. https://apnorc.org

videos, specific social networking sites that allow users to share health information and experiences, widgets, and wikis (Korda & Itani, 2013; Stellefson et al., 2020). These platforms can be used in a variety of ways. They can:

- potentially collect real-time information about exposure to diseases as well as to other health factors like air or water contaminant levels (Schillinger et al., 2020).

- influence attitudes as well as beliefs and behavior and also provide health information. Mostly, when health information is provided, the platforms have focused on a specific disease such as childhood cancer or diabetes (Clerici et al., 2012; Lam et al., 2013; Nordfeldt et al., 2010).

- use social media messages to reduce risky behaviors online (Moreno et al., 2009).

■ Adolescents frequently use social media. Do you think healthcare providers can use social media successfully to educate teens or even to change their behavior?

- be used to engage with adolescents in ways that are not possible in a typical healthcare setting. Portals can offer information about a diversity of health topics in text or video format; they can engage users with games, offer message boards for social networking, and provide the opportunity to request renewals of prescriptions online. However, healthcare providers have found it difficult, in addition to their daily workload, to keep information up-to-date, and log-in procedures tend to be complicated in order to safeguard users' privacy (Nordfeldt et al., 2010).

In order to communicate health messages that are engaging, messages that use inspirational images and focus on a particular product, like a fitness-tracking wearable device such as a Fitbit, seem to be the most successful (Edney et al., 2018). Additionally, Instagram users tend to engage more frequently with health information than users of Twitter (Edney et al., 2018; Guidry et al., 2017). Perhaps this difference in engagement can partly be explained by the fact that Instagram's audience tends to be young and female (Greenwood et al., 2016).

There are some drawbacks to using digital media to communicate health information. First of all, privacy is a key concern when patients engage in a forum. Second, messages on social media need to be monitored because they can spread so quickly and include the danger of infectious messages like those in the case of suicides that spread. Adolescents also tend to seek information mostly from those they know as well as their peers, and healthcare providers do not tend to belong to that group (Moreno et al., 2012; Whitehill et al., 2013; Yonker et al., 2015).

Review!

What are some of the health risks adolescents face?

■ Many adolescents do not exercise sufficiently, a problem that is worsened by the fact that many schools do not require physical education classes for older students. Since adolescents have a tendency to go to bed at a relatively late time, many of them also suffer from sleep deprivation.

- After puberty, depression rates rise significantly, but depression is sometimes not recognized in adolescents because the symptoms are different from those in adults and fluctuate more. Teenagers also may acquire new health problems, such as drug use, which can be fatal. While adolescent alcohol and cigarette use in the United States have been declining, marijuana use, vaping, and opioid misuse have been rising.
- The leading cause of death for adolescents in general in the United States is unintentional injuries, followed by suicide and homicide. However, for Black adolescents (who have a higher death rate in general), the leading cause of death is homicide.
- Almost two-thirds of American teens use social media on a daily basis. Social media use tends to influence teen girls' body image in a negative way. However, social media can also be used to reach adolescents with messages that promote healthy behavior.

Practice!

1. In the United States, the most common cause of death in adolescents is _____ .
   a. unintentional injuries
   b. suicide
   c. homicide
   d. drug overdoses

2. Over the past decades, the number of accidental opioid overdoses in teenagers has _____ .
   a. declined somewhat
   b. declined steeply
   c. increased
   d. stayed the same

What's Your Position?

Should schools conduct random drug tests on students to keep drug abuse problems under control? Write a short answer in response to the question before consulting some of the websites below. Did your opinion change after reading the articles? How?

Additional Resources Online

- "Should schools perform drug tests on students?" in *Public School Review*
- "Random drug testing in U.S. public school districts," in *American Journal of Public Health*
- "The national debate on drug testing in public schools," in *Journal of Adolescent Health*

What's Your Position?

Should the legal drinking age be lowered? Adolescents legally become adults at age 18 in the United States. They can marry and adopt children, serve in the military, gamble, drive cars, and serve on juries. Yet, they are not allowed to drink alcohol.

Write a short answer in response to the question before consulting some of the websites below. Did your opinion change after reading the articles? How?

Additional Resources Online

- "The minimum legal drinking age and public health," in *Journal of Economic Perspectives*
- "A Minimum Legal Drinking Age (MLDA) of 21 saves lives and protects health," in Centers for Disease Control and Prevention
- "Traffic fatality reductions: United States compared with 25 other countries," in *American Journal of Public Health*. The summary focuses on comparing the United States with the Netherlands, where the legal drinking and driving age is 18.

Peter 1 year later

A year has passed since Peter's grades started to drop and he began withdrawing from family and friends. A few weeks ago, Peter approached his mother to come clean and tell her that he needed help. He explained that he had started smoking marijuana occasionally around the age of 15, but that his cannabis use had gotten out of hand after the death of his cousin. While all his family members were trying to cope with his cousin's death, Peter felt increasingly lost and disoriented, unable to deal with his own grief. He realized that marijuana, which he'd started taking just when he was out with friends, helped him cope with his anxiety, and within a relatively short time he was smoking almost around the clock just to get through the day. He started stealing money from his parents to finance his habit. It was at that point that he realized he needed help.

After their conversation, Iris took him to the local addiction therapy center, and Peter started therapy that day. His therapist is helping him to understand when and why he was smoking and how to fight the urge when he gets it again. Since starting his therapy, he has been clean apart from one relapse. He has decided to repeat the school year to get better grades and build better chances for his future. ■ ▪ ■ ▪

© Monkey Business Images/Shutterstock.com

Overview

Cognitive Development in Adolescence

Adolescents on the path to the future

Seventeen-year-old Ray is in his junior year of high school, and like a lot of his peers, he's trying to set the path for his future. But while many of his classmates are excitedly talking about SATs and the letters of recommendation they'll need for their college applications, Ray isn't feeling the same kind of anticipation. He knows his parents expect him to go to college, but he doesn't particularly like school, and the thought of 4 more years of essays, exams, and boring lectures fills him with dread. Why would he sign up for that—especially given the financial costs of college and the debts he'd be paying off for years to come?

Ray's real passion is mechanics. He has always been fascinated by the inner workings of things—clocks and watches, gears and springs, motors and circuits. He'd really like to find a career where he can pursue this passion. But he's not sure where to turn for information and what kind of mechanics he'd really like to get involved in. His parents say that college is an ideal way to explore career options—he could do a degree in engineering or maybe computer science. But Ray just can't bear the thought of 4 more years at school to learn material that doesn't have any practical application in his life. He wants to learn something useful, now.

Ray is not unlike a lot of North American adolescents, whose young minds are still developing even as they're expected to make consequential life decisions that will determine their future trajectory and affect their journey into adulthood. In this chapter we will learn about changes in adolescents' thinking that make planning for the future, as well as ethical reasoning, possible. We will discuss schooling in the United States and which factors increase adolescents' likelihood of succeeding at school or dropping out prematurely. We will also consider the trajectories of teens who go to college and those who don't.

15.1 Changes in Adolescents' Thinking

■ Explain the various ways Piaget characterizes adolescents' thinking in the the fourth stage of cognitive development.

Adolescence is a time of plentiful changes, and these changes are not constrained to the physical realm. Adolescents' thinking develops as well, and their newly gained cognitive skills allow teens to imagine possible futures, lay out detailed plans to achieve their goals, and successfully complete schoolwork that requires abstract thinking. At the same time, adolescents' thinking is still immature, predisposing them to taking risks and indulging in adolescent egocentrism. In this section, we will look closely at the changes that occur in the minds of adolescents.

Piaget: Formal Operational Thinking

Jean Piaget's name will no doubt be familiar to you by now, as we have encountered it in a number of previous chapters. His theory of cognitive development has four stages, and at around 11 or 12 years of age, young people enter the fourth stage. This fourth stage is the **formal operational stage**, in which teens become capable of abstract thought and hypothetical-deductive reasoning.

These changes in their thinking give adolescents a completely different outlook on life. No longer are they limited to thinking about concrete things: Now their imagination can carry their thoughts into the future and to all kinds of unrealized possibilities. The liberation from concrete thought empowers youth to actively think about and plan for their adult lives. Like Ray, teens can now consider what they might like to do for a living, where and how they might like to live, and with whom.

formal operational stage the fourth stage in Piaget's theory of cognitive development, beginning around the age of 11–12, in which the ability to think abstractly develops.

Hypothetical reasoning develops in the formal operational stage

Piaget believed that the ability to think in terms of "what if" questions is at the very core of the formal operational stage. By asking what happens *if,* teens deliberate about situations just like scientists do, adjusting conditions in their mind to predict different outcomes. **Hypothetical-deductive reasoning**, the ability to develop and test hypotheses in order to solve problems, is one of the main characteristics of the formal operational stage.

hypothetical-deductive reasoning the ability, characteristic of Piaget's formal operational stage of cognitive development, to develop and test hypotheses in order to solve problems.

A famous task that Piaget developed to test hypothetical-deductive reasoning is the pendulum experiment (Inhelder & Piaget, 1958). In this experiment, participants are presented with a pendulum and asked to determine which variables affect the speed of the pendulum's swing (**FIGURE 15.1**). Age differences are clearly visible when an experimenter is observing children: Younger children take wild guesses and change chain length and the amount of weight all at once. Youth who are capable of hypothetical-deductive reasoning conduct an experiment in a systematic way: First, they might change the weight of the pendulum, then the height from which the pendulum is released, and finally the chain length. Their systematic approach will lead them to find that only chain length matters.

■ Teens in the formal operational stage are able to imagine themselves in different professions and weigh the pros and cons of their potential choices. Their newly gained thinking abilities help them make better and more informed choices. How do the career aspirations of a teenager differ from those expressed by a 9-year-old?

Adolescents also begin to use symbols in a variety of ways, enabling them to understand subjects like algebra where the symbol x stands in for unknown numbers in

Height at which the
pendulum is released   Length of chain   Weight of the pendulum

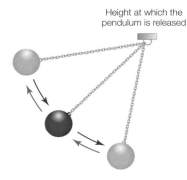  

FIGURE 15.1 In Piaget's pendulum task, participants are asked to determine which of three variable(s) might affect the speed of a swinging pendulum: (1) the height at which the pendulum is released, (2) the length of the chain, and (3) the weight of the pendulum. By systematically adjusting one variable at a time, adolescents can eventually determine that string length is the only variable that influences swing speed.

After C. Tamis-LeMonda. 2022. *Child Development: Context, Culture, and Cascades.* Oxford University Press/Sinauer, Sunderland, MA

equations (Ojose, 2008). Symbolic thinking is also used in language to understand puns, proverbs, and sarcasm as well as metaphors. Children already begin to understand metaphors like "the curtain of night fell upon us" in the concrete-operational stage, but only in the formal operational stage can they fully comprehend the richness and meaning of metaphors. Abstract thinking is required to understand the logic behind the comparison (Billow, 1975; Smith, 1976).

But teens' newly gained ability to think logically also makes parents' lives harder: They become more argumentative. They analyze situations and use reasoning in order to convince others (and, in particular, their parents) of their viewpoints. Fourteen-year-old Matthew argues with his parents that he should be allowed to go out late on a school night because he has completed his homework as well as his chores. This increased argumentativeness, together with teens' striving for independence, can lead to frequent conflicts between adolescent children and their parents.

■ Only in the formal operational stage can youth fully understand metaphors like "a roller coaster of emotions." Teens need to be able to think logically to understand the comparison that is drawn between a roller coaster and life. Can you think of other metaphors that young children cannot understand?

Abstract thinking also enables adolescents to reflect on their own thoughts and thought processes. They can analyze the way they reason and draw conclusions. These metacognitive skills help them find flaws in their own reasoning and revise their conclusions.

Piaget believed that formal operational thought was developed by ages 15–20 (Piaget, 1972; Piaget & Cook, 1952). But research has shown that the age at which teens develop and use formal operational thinking varies widely. Some 15-year-olds may be very adept in formal operational thinking and may use it consistently in many areas of their life. At the same time, some of their peers may just be beginning to develop their abstract-thinking skills.

Evaluation of Piaget's theory

Piaget was undeniably one of the most creative and influential developmental psychologists and influenced psychology and related fields in many ways. His contributions have been documented in previous chapters. However, certain aspects of his theory have come under scrutiny from contemporary researchers. Here, we will concentrate on some criticism of his work that relates to the stage of formal operational reasoning.

One criticism surrounds the timing of the formal operational stage and the fact that it may not be the same for all children. Some cognitive abilities develop earlier than Piaget theorized, and some develop later. For example, studies have shown that children younger than 11 years of age sometimes use abstract thinking (Kuhn, 2009, 2011).

At the same time, some adolescents develop formal operational thinking later than Piaget hypothesized, and some adults do not use formal operational thinking at all (at least not in all domains) (Cohen & Casey, 2017). For example, one study found that only about 30% of eighth graders were capable of formal operational thinking (Strahan, 1983). Even among college students, only between 17 and 67% of students think formal operationally. Thus, even in the best case, around one-third of students do not apply formal operational thinking (Elkind, 1961; Tomlinson-Keasey, 1972). In general, people are more likely to display formal operational thought in their areas of interest or specialty than in other areas.

Culture and schooling make more of a difference in the ability to engage in hypothetical-deductive reasoning than Piaget thought. While not all adolescents in industrialized nations like the United States or in Europe can solve the pendulum task correctly, experiments in Rwanda and Papua New Guinea where formal schooling at the high school level is rare showed that none of the teen participants could solve the task (Gardiner & Kosmitzki, 2008).

Adolescent Egocentrism

Fifteen-year-old Charlotte stands in front of the bathroom mirror, applying her makeup with the utmost care. Once she is done, she treats her hair with meticulous attention, applying a multitude of products until every strand is in exactly the right place. A stray hair somewhere or a rogue pimple can send her into deep desperation. But there are other people who are desperate as well: her 9-year-old brother as well as her parents, who are competing with Charlotte to use the family's only bathroom in the morning. It sometimes seems like a hopeless endeavor. . . .

In previous chapters, we have seen how the worlds of young children revolve around themselves. Adolescents are capable of logical thinking and realize people's viewpoints and knowledge may differ from their own. Yet, egocentrism can frequently be seen in adolescents as well; it just comes in a different flavor.

Adolescents display some behaviors that can seem peculiar to adults, and even their peers. For example, when I was a teenager, some boys at my school dressed in long black leather coats, pretending to be heroes like Neo, the main protagonist from the movie *The Matrix*. They were out on a mission to save the world from all evil, at least in their imagination. And other teenagers, like Charlotte, spend hours in front of a mirror, adjusting their hair and their makeup until they reach "perfection."

Psychologist David Elkind connected these common behaviors with teens' cognitive development through the concept of adolescent

■ Teens often believe that everyone has a watchful eye on them and is very interested in their looks, actions, and troubles. They are embarrassed by things that seem like no big deal to adults. These faulty assumptions can be explained by the imaginary audience and personal fable. Did you ever feel in adolescence like everybody's eyes were on you constantly? Was that a good feeling?

© Prostock-studio/Shutterstock.com

egocentrism (Alberts et al., 2007). Building on Piaget's theory, he suggested two different types of thinking that are inherent to adolescent egocentrism: the *imaginary audience* and the *personal fable* (Elkind, 1967).

Many adolescents feel constantly observed and under scrutiny, as though they are on a stage with an **imaginary audience**. This can make them very self-conscious about their looks and behavior (Alberts et al., 2007; Terán et al., 2020). Charlotte can hardly bear going to school because of the red pimple that blossomed overnight on her nose, and Albert feels that everybody judges him for his perceived lack of beard growth and, thus, masculinity.

Since they feel ever-watched, adolescents develop a **personal fable**: a belief that they are somehow unique and special. Ellen yells at her parents that they'll never understand how she feels. Yasmine's boyfriend broke up with her, and she is convinced that no one has ever had such an excruciatingly broken heart as she does.

But that sense of being special can give rise to a phenomenon that can be dangerous: a sense of invulnerability (**FIGURE 15.2**). For example, adolescents may think that, although smoking may well cause cancer in others, they themselves will not be affected. They likely know that accidents occur when people drive too fast or are intoxicated, but nevertheless believe that accidents won't happen to them. The more teens believe in their specialness and uniqueness, the more they are willing to take risks. Boys tend to feel more invincible than do girls, which explains at least in part why boys tend to take more risks in adolescence than girls do (Alberts et al., 2007; Elkind & Bowen, 1979; Friedl et al., 2020; Tardif & Valls, 2018). But having a strong sense of a personal fable also predisposes adolescents to depression and suicidal tendencies (Aalsma et al., 2006).

Elkind believed that adolescent egocentrism is most intense in early adolescence until around eighth grade and then slowly decreases (Elkind & Bowen, 1979). However, more recent research suggests that adolescent egocentrism is still present in late adolescence and even in emerging adulthood (Schwartz et al., 2008; Soto, 2018).

But adolescents may not always feel invulnerable: One study asked adolescents to estimate their likelihood of dying over both the next year and before they turn 20 years old. Teens estimated their likelihood of an untimely death as much higher than it actually is according to mortality statistics (Fischhoff et al., 2010).

Attention and Memory: Information-Processing Approaches

Let's now take a look at how attention and memory improve during adolescence. An important aspect of memory is working memory. We rely on working memory to retain information for a short time, typically when that information is needed for a task. Working memory is needed for solving math problems, following a recipe, and reading

> **imaginary audience** adolescents' belief that they are constantly watched and scrutinized by others; an aspect of adolescent egocentrism.

> **personal fable** adolescents' belief that they are unique and special as well as invincible; an aspect of adolescent egocentrism.

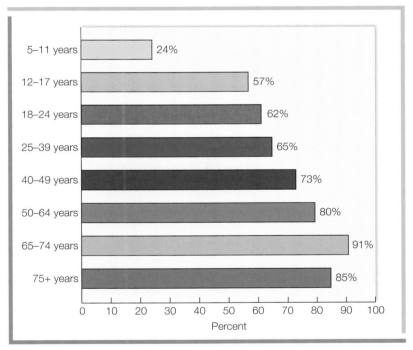

FIGURE 15.2 COVID-19 vaccination rates by age group, U.S. (Feb. 2022). A sense of invulnerability may contribute to the fact that young Americans lag in their vaccination rates behind older adults. The data displayed are from February 2022—a time when the Delta variant had already been circulating for several months, leading to increased hospitalization numbers among younger Americans.

Data from Centers for Disease Control and Prevention. 2022. COVID-19 Vaccination and Case Trends by Age Group, United States. https://data.cdc.gov

comprehension. Working memory improves throughout childhood and adolescence (Simmonds et al., 2017; Ullman et al., 2014). *Visuospatial working memory* (involving visual and spatial information) develops somewhat later than verbal memory (Simmonds et al., 2017). *Memory span* (the number of items or words a person can recall) increases during adolescence as well.

Attention also generally improves during adolescence. As the material taught in school gets more complex, it is important that teens learn to pay attention over a longer period of time. But these days, adolescents often do not have the luxury (or the will) to focus on just one task at a time. Many teens engage in an impressive amount of multitasking, often involving several kinds of media. They may be watching TV while FaceTiming their friends and checking their text messages from time to time (van der Schuur et al., 2018). One study found that about one-fourth of sixth to eighth graders' media time was spent multitasking (Cain et al., 2016).

Most studies that investigate media multitasking examine adults rather than adolescents. In adults, media multitasking is mostly associated with undesirable results—multitasking adults are less able to filter out irrelevant information, do worse on working memory tasks, and become more impulsive (Cain & Mitroff, 2011; Cain et al., 2016; Ophir et al., 2009).

In contrast, one study involving adolescents found that those who engaged in multitasking were better at tuning out distractions (Baumgartner et al., 2014). However, other studies have found that media multitasking leads to poorer performance on achievement tests and lower working memory capacity and reading comprehension, as well as sleep problems (Cain et al., 2016; May & Elder, 2018; van der Schuur et al., 2018).

■ What It's Like...

Having a Child with ADHD

Eric, father of Zoe

Our daughter Zoe was the product of a healthy pregnancy and birth, but we quickly found out she was different from her peers. She had trouble breastfeeding because she was so easily distracted: She was constantly trying to see what was going on around her. We thought it was funny, but it was a sign of things to come. She stopped napping long before any of the other kids in her playgroup. She started talking before them, too—and did she ever talk! She loved story time but could only seem to listen if she was doing something else at the same time, like a puzzle or drawing. It wasn't that she was distracted; more that in order to focus, she had to be paying attention to several things at once.

It wasn't until she was 6 and started school that we realized how very different Zoe was. Her teacher reported that she wouldn't sit still during story circle. She also found creative ways to distract her classmates, leading them on follow-the-leader marches around the classroom, or persuading them all to put on their coats backward. She was extremely social and outgoing, but she sometimes couldn't keep friends for long: She would wear them out with her intensity and her moodiness. She could be extremely joyful one moment, only to fall into tantrums and tears the next. She seemed to have no control over her emotions. In first and second grade, she could breeze through worksheets, but as often as not she'd quit partway through to pursue something more interesting—even as all of her classmates were still working.

When she was 9, her third-grade teacher recommended we have Zoe tested. We really didn't want her stigmatized with any condition that might cause teachers, school administrators, and other students to treat her differently, but we reluctantly agreed. It turned out that she had both ADHD and giftedness. Then came another difficult decision: whether or not to try medication. We weren't worried about academics at that point but about her making friends. Eventually, we gave it a try. We knew that medication would change her personality, and it did: She wasn't as moody. But she also never showed the same excitement or enthusiasm that she did when she was not on the medication. The medication also made her sleep even less, and it curtailed her appetite. When she was 11, we let it be her decision: Zoe thought she should stay on the medication, though she sometimes said she didn't like how it affected her mood. It did help her in high school, but the gifted diagnosis was just as important: She entered a special program where she met a lot of people who seemed to think the same way she did—many of whom, coincidentally, also had ADHD!

Zoe, 17 years

There are a lot of things that I understand now about 9-year-old me that I didn't appreciate at the time. For one thing, having ADHD wasn't always hard. I had a lot of fun—more than most people around me, it seemed. Adults liked me because I was more social than other kids my age. And everyone said I was smart. But as I got older, I started to notice that I was getting in trouble a lot more than others, at home and at school. I know I used to get up in the middle of class to do things—sharpen a pencil, talk to a classmate, get a book from the library rack—but I was still paying attention to the teacher, so I didn't understand what the big deal was. And the things I got up to do seemed *really important* at the time. That's something that people without ADHD don't understand: the way our brains prioritize things. I'd be working on a math worksheet, but it would suddenly occur to me that I had a hair elastic in the pocket of my coat, hanging in a cubby at the back of the classroom, and I'd need to go get that hair elastic *right now*; it felt like the most important thing in the world. I'm still like that now, to be honest.

Things got harder around fourth grade. Expectations of me were becoming greater, and it felt like I was being left behind. It wasn't enough that I understood what we were learning—and I did, easily—but now I had to demonstrate that understanding in a test or an assignment. I struggled to stay focused on assignments and was too slow to finish tests on time. My mentality started to shift from "these assignments are stupid" to "I must be stupid," a mentality that's been hard to kick even now that I'm older. And then there were all the rules: hang up your coat, put your books away, no talking in class. And at home: put away your clothes, clear your dishes from the table, brush your teeth before school. To most people these are easy tasks, like climbing a flight of stairs; to me, these same tasks were like climbing up a downward escalator. I'd forget to clear my dishes, putting clothes away seemed pointless, and I absolutely *hated* the taste of toothpaste. When I finally finished a task and felt really satisfied with myself, I didn't get the positive recognition I was expecting, given the difficulty (to me). It felt like nothing I did was ever good enough.

The biggest thing I got in trouble for was talking in class. Sometimes it was because I was bored by the lesson, or because I wanted to say something before I forgot it, or because I was actually interested in the content and wanted to share my thoughts—right away! It felt like I had so much to say that I couldn't hold it in even if I tried. These infractions usually earned me a time-out in the hallway or a trip to the principal's office or a "stern talking to." People with ADHD, because we tend to feel everything so intensely, take anything that could be perceived as criticism really hard. Looking back, I think that I was sometimes made an example of, because I already had the reputation as the loud kid, or the disruptive kid.

When my parents asked me to go on ADHD medication, it really flattened my moods. Things that once would have got me really excited—or really frustrated—just didn't register the same way. I had mixed feelings about the meds because all of a sudden nothing really made me happy the same way. But I didn't get in trouble as much, and kids said I was less annoying. As I got older, and schoolwork and grades were more important, I appreciated the way the meds kept me focused on what I knew I was supposed to be concentrating on. But things weren't quite as much fun.

Review!

How does Piaget characterize the thinking of adolescents?

- Adolescents are typically in the fourth and last stage of Piaget's theory of cognitive development, the *formal operational stage*, from the age of 11 or 12.

- In this stage, youth become capable of abstract and logical thinking. They are able to consider different actions and their possible consequences, enabling them to make plans for the future. *Hypothetical-deductive reasoning* skills allow teens to test hypotheses and solve problems by changing just one variable and leaving the others constant.

- Research has found that schooling impacts the development of hypothetical-deductive reasoning skills and that in some less industrialized countries, fewer adolescents can solve tasks like Piaget's pendulum task. Abstract-thinking skills help teenagers comprehend metaphors and sarcasm, as well as more complex concepts like those taught in algebra. Much to the dismay of their parents, they are now also in a better position to argue for their own interests.

- Studies have found that, among eighth graders, only about 30% are capable of formal operational thinking. Estimates of formal operational thinking skills even vary widely when college students are concerned—but no estimate found more than two-thirds of college students capable of thinking in formal operational ways.

- The egocentrism that Piaget described in earlier stages is seeing a comeback in terms of adolescent egocentrism, described in detail by David Elkind. Teenagers often feel like they are constantly under observation by an *imaginary audience*. They develop a *personal fable*, believing they are somehow special and unique.

Practice!

1. A person who is capable of hypothetical-deductive reasoning _____ .
   a. has committed to an identity
   b. does not display any signs of egocentrism
   c. can solve problems by developing and testing hypotheses
   d. is likely to be highly popular among his peers.

2. A personal fable _____ .
   a. is a book a teen can most relate to
   b. is a story featuring animals an adolescent identifies with
   c. is the belief all people are intrinsically connected with each other
   d. is the belief that one is special and unique

Act It Out!

Sixteen-year-old Marcie is getting ready to visit the school guidance counselor, rehearsing her talking points in her head. She knows she's a pretty good student who doesn't need to study much to get good grades. Her ability to pick up new knowledge and skills without much effort has also led to a variety of interests, which have started to confuse her: Should she pursue a career in medicine, or in animal conservation? Or how about studying literature, since she loves reading? Or maybe teaching! She doesn't know what to do!

   With a classmate, role-play a conversation between Marcie and the guidance counselor, Mrs. Ramesh. As the guidance counselor, draw on your knowledge of Piaget's formal operational stage and the ability of teens to engage in abstract thought and hypothetical-deductive reasoning.

Show What You've Learned!

Sixteen-year-old Amit is obsessed with taking selfies. No matter where he goes, he pulls out his cell phone and takes a photo of himself, posting it to his social media accounts immediately. Selfie culture has become pervasive, and although people of all ages take selfies, they're particularly popular among young people. Drawing on information presented in this chapter and in the articles below, describe the role that adolescent egocentrism and the imaginary audience play in this trend.

Additional Resources Online

- "But first let me take a selfie': U.S. adolescent girls' selfie activities, self-objectification, imaginary audience beliefs, and appearance concerns," from *Journal of Children and Media*.

- "Selfie posting on social networking sites and female adolescents' self-objectification: The moderating role of imaginary audience ideation," from *Sex Roles*.

15.2 Moral Reasoning

■ Identify and explain Kohlberg's levels of moral reasoning, then outline Carol Gilligan's critique of this approach.

It's the night before Jamaal's 10th grade physics midterm, and he's caught in a moral dilemma: A friend has circulated photos of the exam paper taken by a classmate who was given permission to take the test a day early. Jamaal knows he could benefit from a preview of the exam paper, but even though he'd still need to answer the questions correctly, this feels like cheating, and he's worried he might get caught.

Countless times each day, people have to decide what is right and wrong and what course of action they will take. Children are not born with this ability; it is only in adolescence that they learn to think about moral issues of justice and fairness.

Kohlberg's Theory of Moral Reasoning

Piaget's theory included some ideas about the development of moral reasoning, but it was Lawrence Kohlberg who built upon Piaget's theory and created a comprehensive multistage theory of moral reasoning. Keep in mind that Kohlberg's theory is about moral *reasoning*, or the way people *think* about ethical behavior rather than their *actual* behavior. People do not always act in ways that are consistent with their thinking.

Kohlberg envisioned six stages of moral reasoning

Kohlberg developed his theory by creating a number of scenarios that involved moral dilemmas. He presented these scenarios to his participants and interviewed them extensively to uncover the reasoning behind their judgments.

Here is one of the most famous scenarios that Kohlberg used in his interviews of children and adolescents:

> In Europe, a woman was near death from a very bad disease, a special kind of cancer. There was one drug that the doctors thought might save her. It was a form of radium that a druggist in the same town had recently discovered. The drug was expensive to make, but the druggist was charging ten times what the drug cost him to make. He paid $200 for the radium and charged $2,000 for a small dose of the drug. The sick woman's husband, Heinz, went to everyone he knew to borrow the money, but he could only get together $1,000, which is half of what it cost. He told the druggist that his wife was dying and asked him to sell it cheaper or let him pay later. But the druggist said, "No, I discovered the drug, and I'm going to make money from it." So Heinz got desperate and broke into the man's store to steal the drug for his wife (Kohlberg & Kramer, 1969).

Kohlberg asked his subjects questions about numerous aspects of the scenario, such as whether the druggist had a right to charge what he did, whether Heinz should be punished, and whether it is a husband's duty to steal the drug. After an analysis of the responses, Kohlberg concluded that there are three levels of moral reasoning, each of which has two stages (FIGURE 15.3):

1. *Preconventional level* (children aged 9 and younger). At this level, children's sense of what is right or wrong is based on external standards: the rules that parents and teachers set. These rules are seen as absolute and

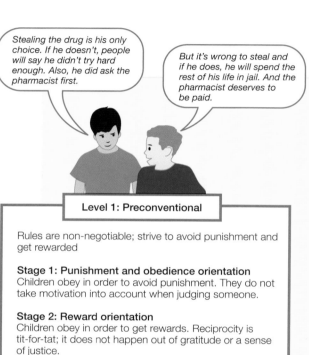

> Stealing the drug is his only choice. If he doesn't, people will say he didn't try hard enough. Also, he did ask the pharmacist first.

> But it's wrong to steal and if he does, he will spend the rest of his life in jail. And the pharmacist deserves to be paid.

Level 1: Preconventional

Rules are non-negotiable; strive to avoid punishment and get rewarded

Stage 1: Punishment and obedience orientation
Children obey in order to avoid punishment. They do not take motivation into account when judging someone.

Stage 2: Reward orientation
Children obey in order to get rewards. Reciprocity is tit-for-tat; it does not happen out of gratitude or a sense of justice.

> I think he should steal the drug because he wants to help his wife. Otherwise, he'll be responsible for her death.

> I understand why he wants to steal the drug, but if he does, everybody will judge him and say he's a criminal. It's still wrong to steal.

Level 2: Conventional

Act according to rules to ensure positive relationships with others

Stage 3: "Good child" orientation
Behavior is judged as good when it pleases or helps others. Children adopt their parents' values to gain approval. For the first time, a person's intention is important.

Stage 4: Law-and-order orientation
Rules need to be followed so that social order can be maintained. Authority and rules need to be respected.

> He should steal the drug because his wife desperately needs help. The laws don't take his situation into account.

> But if everybody started disobeying rules to suit their circumstances, where does it end? You can't put your personal situation above the law.

Level 3: Postconventional

Moral reasoning is independent from societal rules and focuses on abstract principles and values

Stage 5: Social contract orientation
Situations are evaluated in terms of a person's moral values. Laws are needed for a society to work, but sometimes people's needs conflict with laws. This may lead to an update of current laws.

Stage 6: Universal ethical principle orientation
Moral reasoning is based on the concept of justice. Moral decisions incorporate universal principles that may or may not be reflected in society's laws.

FIGURE 15.3 Kohlberg's stages of moral reasoning.

nonnegotiable. Children think in terms of consequences like punishment and reward: They try to avoid punishments and want to be rewarded for their actions. When reasoning about Heinz's problem, children mostly consider which actions would serve Heinz's own interests best.

2. *Conventional level* (older children, adolescents, and most adults). Actions are guided by social expectations and roles. People at this stage have internalized societal rules, and they strive to comply with these rules. However, these standards are still ones that are imposed on them from the outside, rather than from within. The focus at this stage is on doing one's duty and maintaining law and order in society.

3. *Postconventional level* (a small percentage of adults; uncommon in adolescents). Relatively few people ever reach this level. People on this level develop their own moral standards, independent of the standards that authority figures and society set. When faced with a decision, they weigh the options according to their own moral standards, which they will use to reach their decision.

■ In real-life situations, it is often not clear what is the right (and ethical) choice. Consider the case of U.S. Army soldier Bowe Bergdahl. In 2009, he was captured by the Taliban when he walked off his post in Afghanistan. The search for him cost the lives of several soldiers, and he was finally released in 2014 after then-president Barack Obama agreed to a prisoner exchange with some prisoners held in Guantánamo Bay. Do you think it is justified to sacrifice other soldiers' lives to save one of their own? How does your assessment of the situation change when you assume, as some do in Bergdahl's case, that the soldier to be saved deserted the army (that is, he left in a disloyal way)?

The ages at which children reach a particular stage in Kohlberg's theory are widely variable, because cognitive development does not always translate into moral development (Eisenberg & Morris, 2004). Most people do not progress to Level 3.

There have been some promising efforts at teaching students to use ethical reasoning. One study with business students, for example, found that guiding students in thinking about the moral aspects of their work increases their ability to consider potential courses of action when faced with dilemmas (Schmidt et al., 2009). Moral judgment can also be enhanced by providing a supportive and stimulating environment that allows students to freely exchange ideas and challenge each other's viewpoints, particularly those that relate to social systems and values (Chen & Chan, 2020; Parker et al., 2016; Smetana, 2013). Additionally, positive experiences with diversity can help foster the development of integrity and ethics as well as moral reasoning in students (Chen & Chan, 2020; Hurtado et al., 2012).

Evaluation of Kohlberg's theory

Kohlberg's theory provides a reasonable account of the development of children's moral reasoning. Research generally supports the view that children go through a series of stages in their moral development (Boom et al., 2007). But aspects of Kohlberg's theory have been criticized. For example, his research subjects were children and adolescents, but some of the dilemmas he presented would have been unfamiliar to young people—think about the dilemma we discussed above with Heinz and his cancer-stricken wife. In addition, the scenarios are hypothetical, and people facing those scenarios in real life might respond very differently.

Kohlberg believed his stages of moral reasoning were sequential, but research does not always support this assumption. Sometimes, a person might reason at

Level 3 in some scenarios but might use Level 2 reasoning in others. Sometimes people even move backward in their development (Krebs & Denton, 2005; Rest, 1979).

Moral reasoning and behavior may also be less connected than Kohlberg thought. A person's decision to act (or not to act) in a certain way can be influenced by their emotions, their habits, or their belief that someone else will intervene to "do the right thing" (Bee, 1994; Teper et al., 2015). Jamaal knows that cheating on a midterm is morally wrong, but he might decide to go along with his classmates because he risks not getting into college if his physics grade doesn't improve, and so in this instance his motivations outweigh his moral predisposition.

Kohlberg believed that his theory was culturally universal—that is, that people all over the world go through the same stages in the same order in their moral development (Kohlberg & Kramer, 1969). However, research has cast some doubt on this assumption (see CULTURE COUNTS: "MIND NORMS" IN ISLAND CULTURES). A review of 45 studies found evidence of Kohlberg's first two levels in many other cultures, but there are some cultures where no evidence of Level 3 was found (Gibbs et al., 2007; Gray & Graham, 2019).

Finally, Kohlberg did not give much attention to the influence of family in his theory. He believed that the interactions of parents and children were not important in children's moral development. Most researchers today would disagree: They believe that parents do influence their children's moral development with their parenting styles, the way they interact with their children, and the way they discipline the children (Gryczkowski et al., 2018; Narvaez, 2018).

Gilligan's Ethics of Care

One of the most prominent critiques of Kohlberg's theory comes from Carol Gilligan, who suggested that the theory is gender-biased and built on male norms of morality (Murphy & Gilligan, 1980). Research on Kohlberg's model found that both sexes are found most commonly at Level 2—women most commonly rank at Stage 3, whereas men most commonly rank at Stage 4 (Fishkin et al., 1973; Haan et al., 1968; Kohlberg & Kramer, 1969). As you may remember, Stage 3 reasoning is concerned with the desire to meet other's expectations and maintain relationships, whereas Stage 4 reasoning has a law-and-order orientation. Kohlberg had developed his theory based on interviews with boys exclusively, which lent credibility to Gilligan's claim that his theory is gender-biased.

Gilligan suggested that women are not less morally advanced than men but rather emphasize different values in their moral reasoning. Kohlberg, she argued, viewed morality from a *justice perspective.* This perspective is based on the concepts of fairness and justice; it values independence, interpersonal rights, and disconnection from others. These values, Gilligan argued, are specifically connected with the male sex. Women, to the contrary, have more of a *care perspective.* Gilligan suggested that women tend to value intimacy, the care of others, and relationships more than men do. The difference in values leads to women scoring lower on Kohlberg's scale—not because they are less morally mature, but rather because the values they hold are not taken into account by Kohlberg (Gilligan, 1982).

Do Gilligan's claims hold up to research? Although a meta-analysis of 113 studies did find small gender differences in which females favored the care perspective and males favored the justice perspective, the differences were too small to support Gilligan's claim that women predominantly use the care perspective and men predominantly use the justice perspective (Jaffee & Hyde, 2000; see also Maftei & Holman, 2020). It seems more likely that both boys and girls use both perspectives as they deem them appropriate in their reasoning (Blakemore et al., 2009).

Culture Counts

"Mind Norms" in Island Cultures

Some island cultures, such as those on Fiji, Samoa, and Papua New Guinea, have "opacity of mind" norms, which lead members of these cultures to believe that it is impossible to know what someone else is thinking. These norms have an impact on moral reasoning and judgments: People who believe you cannot know what someone else is thinking are unable to take someone's intentions into account when judging their actions.

In a recent experiment, members of two cultural groups from Fiji—Yasawans, who subscribe to the opacity of mind norm, and Indo-Fijians, who do not subscribe to this view—as well as a group of North Americans were presented with scenarios in which a person violated moral norms. For example, one scenario involved a man named Sam, who poured insecticide into a swamp that fed a community well to kill mosquitoes breeding in the swamp, believing the insecticide to be harmless to humans. Sam himself did not use the water from the community well, but many others did. Two different outcomes were described. In the condition with the positive outcome, no one was seriously affected. In the condition with the negative outcome, a neighbor almost died from the insecticide in the community well's water.

The graph shows that when both intention and outcome were positive, Indo-Fijians and North Americans judged the action to be relatively good and worthy of a reward. In contrast, the Yasawans judged the action to be rather neutral and thought, if anything, the actor ought to be punished. When the well-intentioned action resulted in an accident, Yasawans thought the actor was supposed to get punished much more strictly than did Indo-Fijians and North Americans, who took the actor's intentions into account.

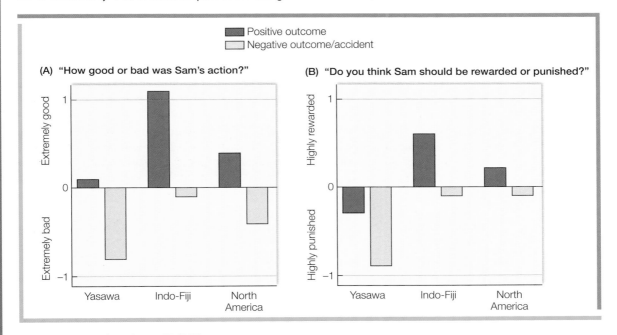

After R. A. McNamara et al. 2019. *Cognition* 182: 95–108

■ Question

How might societies benefit from moral reasoning that does not take an actor's mindset into account, given that a person's mindset can ultimately never truly be determined?

Prosocial Behavior

When we talk of **prosocial behavior**, we refer to voluntary actions that are performed to benefit another person (Eisenberg et al., 2015). Prosocial behavior increases from infancy throughout early adulthood (Carlo et al., 2015).

prosocial behavior voluntary behavior intended to benefit another person.

Improvements in children's physical, cognitive, and social skills are at least partly responsible for the increase in prosocial behavior. Stronger and more mature bodies as well as increasing independence allow adolescents to engage in a greater variety of helpful activities. Cognitive advances help adolescents take other people's perspectives, allowing them to engage in more advanced moral reasoning, which in turn may lead to more prosocial behavior (Eisenberg & Spinrad, 2014; Kohlberg & Kramer, 1969). And a more active social life that centers around friends and intimate relationships may also lead to more prosocial behavior (Carlo et al., 1999; Fabes et al., 1999; Wentzel, 2014). As you know from Chapter 14, girls begin to mature earlier in adolescence than do boys. Consistent with these changes, we also find that increases in prosocial behavior begin earlier in girls than in boys (Hill & Lynch, 1983).

Going shopping for an elderly neighbor, volunteering in an animal shelter or in a church, and helping peers with complex homework are all behaviors that are valuable in and of themselves. But prosocial behavior is also positively linked to adolescents' work values, well-being, and academic success (Johnson et al., 1998; Littman-Ovadia & Steger, 2010; Wentzel, 1993). Additionally, adolescents who habitually behave prosocially are more likely to keep acting this way, thus developing into adults displaying prosocial behavior and high levels of morality (Hardy & Carlo, 2011).

In the United States, as in many other countries, churches, nonprofit organizations, and charities provide essential services to communities throughout the country. These organizations have received record donations of money and time. And yet, the number of Americans who volunteer their time decreased in the years from 2002 to 2015 from almost 29% to 25% (Dietz & Grimm, 2018). Given that many communities have come to depend on volunteer services, some U.S. states have been trying to encourage students to volunteer their time, with mixed results (see CULTURE COUNTS: STUDENT VOLUNTEERING BY STATE).

Culture Counts

Student Volunteering by State

Although 41 U.S. states require a civics course credit for high school graduation, only 11 states have a requirement that students participate in service-learning projects. Maryland is the only state that requires students work a number of hours in community service for graduation (Sparks, 2018). But do requirements like these really make a difference? Among the top 10 states in terms of high school volunteers are some that have service-learning requirements (Maine and Michigan, for example) and others that do not (Kansas and

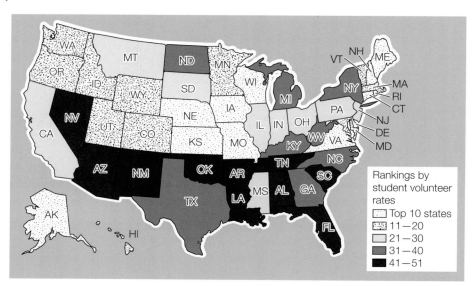

After R. T. Grimm and N. Dietz. 2018. Good Intentions, Gap in Action: The Challenge of Translating Youth's High Interest in Doing Good into Civic Engagement. Research Brief: Do Good Institute, University of Maryland

Culture Counts (Continued)

Nebraska, for example). We can find the same among the lowest-ranking states: Alabama, for example, has a service-learning requirement, and Tennessee does not. And Maryland, the one state that does require volunteering for high school graduation, has a volunteer rate of 33% among high school students—a far cry from the 44% in top-ranking Maine.

■ Question

It seems that state policies do not make that much of a difference in volunteer rates. What do you think could be done to encourage teenagers to volunteer more of their time to charitable causes?

Review!

What stages do children and adolescents go through as they become capable of moral reasoning?

- Lawrence Kohlberg devised the best-known theory of moral reasoning. He developed his theory by presenting research participants with scenarios involving moral dilemmas and by interviewing the participants to learn how they reason about the scenario. Kohlberg found that there are three levels of moral reasoning, each of which has two stages (resulting in six stages overall).
  - The *preconventional level* (Level 1) is the lowest level, most commonly (but not exclusively) found in children under 10. Rules are seen as absolute: They cannot be changed or negotiated. Children want to be rewarded for their actions and to avoid punishment.
  - The *conventional level* (Level 2) is most common in older children, adolescents, and adults. People here are guided by social expectations and rules. These rules are society's rules, however, and not their own.
  - The *postconventional level* (Level 3) is the highest level and reached by relatively few people. People develop their own moral standards that may diverge from society's standards. They aim for their actions to meet their own standards.
- Kohlberg believed that his theory was culturally universal, but Level 3 has not been found in all cultures.

Practice!

1. Carl has trouble doing his math homework. He has asked a classmate to do his homework for him. They agree that Carl will pay him a certain amount of money for each homework assignment. Both children believe this is a fair and morally just agreement: Carl and his friend benefit, and Carl doesn't have a choice but to seek help anyway, since he does not understand what his class does in math. Which of Kohlberg's stages are the two children reasoning at?
   a. Stage 1
   b. Stage 2
   c. Stage 3
   d. Stage 4

2. Stages that are of a sequential nature _____ .
   a. invariably follow each other from the lowest to highest stage
   b. can be passed through in any order
   c. invariably follow each other from the highest to the lowest stage
   d. allow for a child to be simultaneously in more than one stage, even if those stages do not follow each other

3. Prosocial behavior _____ .
   a. ridicules another person
   b. benefits another person
   c. benefits the actor
   d. prevents another person from acting

Show What You've Learned!

You're administering a moral reasoning test to a group of 12-year-olds, based on Kohlberg's framework. Here is one of the scenarios you present:

When 16-year-old Liesl borrowed the family car to visit a friend, she promised to be home by 2:00 to take her grandmother to a scheduled doctor's appointment.

But Liesl loses track of time and doesn't leave her friend's house until 1:45. With only 15 minutes to get home, she knows she'll have to drive above the speed limit to make it on time.

When you ask the group what Liesl should do, one of the 12-year-olds, Oliver, responds: "Liesl has to speed: If she doesn't, her parents will be angry with her and she might not be allowed to use the car anymore."

Based on what you have learned in this chapter, what level and stage of Kohlberg's theory do you think Oliver's reasoning represents? Write a short explanation, and then exchange answers with a classmate to see if you arrived at the same conclusion.

15.3 Adolescents in School

- List the challenges students encounter as they enter middle school.
- Outline the variables that make it more or less likely for students to succeed at school.
- Examine the information provided to determine whether or not virtual schools work.

School makes up a big part of most teenagers' lives. For 5 days a week they may spend 6 hours a day in a classroom—longer if they are involved in after-school clubs. They will do homework on evenings and weekends and meet socially in person or online with school friends.

For many teens, though, school does not always go smoothly—particularly the transitions to middle school and then to high school. Not all students make it all the way to a high school degree: Some drop out of school along the way, usually with negative consequences for their future earning potential. In this section, we will take a closer look at adolescents' school careers.

The Transition to Middle School

In the words of the principal, young Teddy was on the "maintenance plan." After six years in elementary school, he had only a few more hours and he would be finished. Years of work to help him learn to be less disruptive and more focused would be over, at least for the elementary school staff. Teddy worked at the principal's computer for this final day, having exhausted other alternative consequences for misconduct. Just before the final bell, he turned to the principal. His project in hand, the computer shutting down, the rough and tumble Teddy had a tear in his eye.

"I don't want to go to middle school," he said to his principal.

The principal reassured him, "You'll do fine there, Teddy."

"But they won't love me like you do," he said.

With a tear and a hug, the principal replied, "Sure they will, Teddy, but they may love you in a different way." Nevertheless, she thought, "How will he do in middle school?" (Mullins & Irvin, 2000, p. 57)

As Teddy has experienced, the transition to middle school is a difficult time in the lives of many young people. In this section, we'll explore what makes this time so difficult and what can be done to help adolescents adjust well to their new school.

Transitioning to another school brings many challenges

The completion of elementary school is not only a time when children switch schools. It coincides with other changes that make this life period challenging for many young people. Children have recently entered puberty and are still getting used to their changing body. While they were the oldest kids in

■ Experiencing the changes from elementary school to middle school can be difficult for children. Children who had a hard time in elementary school are particularly at risk for adjustment problems. How can schools and parents work together to help their children make a smooth transition?

elementary school, they have entered middle school at the bottom of the pecking order, smaller, weaker, and less mature than the other kids. Additionally, due to COVID-19, many children transitioned to a new school with fewer years of physical school experience, having spent a school year or more engaged in virtual schooling as well as socially distanced learning. They lack crucial experiences and maturity, leading to increased feelings of stress, anxiety, and depression but also to increased disruptive behavior, aggression, and bullying (Pieh et al., 2021; Vestal, 2021).

In many towns, middle schools (generally starting with grade 6) are substantially larger than elementary schools, funneling together the students from several elementary schools. The atmosphere is often less personal and more institutional. Teddy's worries are likely justified: Research has shown that teacher warmth drops in middle school compared with elementary school (Hughes & Cao, 2018).

Middle school students need to be more independent in managing their work load and school day. Academic demands increase dramatically (Hill & Tyson, 2009), while at the same time students are less active in class and like their school less than they liked elementary school (Forster et al., 2020, Wang & Eccles, 2013). Having different classmates for each class creates an opportunity to find new friends, but it can add to students' stress level and the sense of being a very small fish in a very big pond.

With all these changes, it shouldn't be a surprise to learn that many students struggle with the transition. Their self-esteem tends to be lower in the first year of middle school than in their last year of elementary school (Hirsch & Rapkin, 1987). If they do not adjust well, their academic motivation and grades may suffer (Barber & Olsen, 2004; Eccles et al., 1993; Hughes & Cao, 2018). Adjustment difficulties also make it harder for them to feel like they belong to their new school (Anderman, 2003). Teachers can positively influence their students' motivation by actively supporting, listening to, and caring for them (Umarji et al., 2021).

Adults can help smooth the transition to middle school

As challenging as the transition to middle school may be for some children, there are several things caregivers can do to help their children adjust well to their new school. They can:

- Help their student with logistical challenges:
  - Take advantage of a school tour, if one is offered.
  - At the start of the school year, review the child's schedule with the child to make sure she knows where to go for each class. If possible, walk the routes together.
  - Find out how long school breaks are and how long it takes to walk from one classroom to the next.
  - Make sure the child has a watch or cell phone to check the time so he can arrive on time for the next class.
- Prepare students for social challenges:
  - Encourage them to join clubs or participate in extracurricular activities.
  - Model some of the social skills that will help them adjust, like introducing yourself to someone, joining conversations, or negotiating difficult situations.
  - Offer to help arrange social activities.
- Help students help themselves:
  - Teach them to use an agenda to track all assignments.
  - Remind them to take responsibility for themselves by encouraging them to seek extra help, attend lunch hour tutorial sessions, or email a teacher when they have questions. Don't take all struggles away from them, but let them figure things out for themselves.
  - Acknowledge that they're entering a new environment where they may not know as many people, but remind them of the advantages that brings: the opportunity to make new friends, to take up new interests, and even to reinvent themselves through changes in appearance—in clothing, in hairstyle, in makeup—that would have been difficult to adopt in the more intimate setting of their primary school. Remind them, too, that this new environment will be just as unfamiliar and strange to everyone else.
  - Encourage them to get to know their school counselor, who will be a good source of advice on many topics.

Middle and High School Education in the United States

What kind of a school system are new middle schoolers entering, and what is its track record for educating students? We can judge the success of American middle schools by comparing academic results in this country with the results of countries around the world. The standard for international academic comparisons is the Programme for International Student Assessment (PISA), which every 3 years assesses the skills and knowledge of 15-year-olds in member countries of the OECD (Organisation for Economic Co-operation and Development). In 2018, American students scored above the OECD average in reading and science and below average in mathematics. Achievement has been stable since the first decade of the new millennium, with students showing neither significant improvement nor marked decline.

One area where the United States does stand out among OECD countries is the achievement gap between students of high and low socioeconomic status (SES). Students from high-SES families in the United States scored on average 99 points higher in reading than those from low-SES families (for context, the overall average reading score was 505 points). While boys scored higher in math, girls scored higher in reading, and both sexes scored about the same in science. However, girls and boys did not have the same career ambitions: Of the children performing highly in math or science, three times more boys than girls expect to work in engineering or science later on. Immigrants, although often socioeconomically disadvantaged, outperformed American students if socioeconomic differences were taken into account (Schleicher, 2019).

Another significant finding from the PISA is that even low-performing American students have high ambitions. More than 75% of low performers expect to attend and complete college, compared with 48% of low-performing students in other countries. Later in this chapter, we will discuss career choices and chances, and we will see that these ambitions may be related to the fact that, in the United States, a college education is much more important to career success than in many other developed countries. Ambition may also be driven by competition: American students report significantly more competition among their peers than do students in any other country (Schleicher, 2019).

Factors That Influence School Achievement

Many factors combine to influence how well adolescents perform at school. Some of these factors are easier to control than others. In this section, we will look at biological factors that correlate with academic performance, as well as social factors that contribute to success.

Socioeconomic status and race/ethnicity correlate with academic performance

PISA scores and many other studies have shown that gender strongly affects academic performance. In PISA studies, girls on average perform much better than boys in reading, whereas boys tend to do a bit better in math (OECD, 2019). More girls than boys end up going to college in most developed nations of the world (Stoet & Geary, 2020).

There are also strong correlations between race and academic performance. White and Asian American children tend to perform better in school than do Hispanic American or Black students. These academic differences may stem in part from the fact that teachers have higher expectations for Asian American and White students than they have for Black and Hispanic students (Tenenbaum & Ruck, 2007). Minority children are at much higher risk of receiving disciplinary sanctions at school: About 50% of Black boys and 33% of Latino boys are suspended from school at some point in their academic career, compared with just 20% of White boys (Skiba et al., 2002).

In the United States, there is also a close relationship between socioeconomic status (SES) and academic achievement, and this could help to explain racial differences in school performance, given that White households are, on average, more than twelve times as wealthy as Black families and ten times as wealthy as Hispanic families. These ethnic/racial income differences are higher now than they have been for 30 years (Kochhar & Fry, 2014; Quintana & Mahgoub, 2016). The increasing income gap across races/ethnicities has been accompanied by a widening gap in academic achievement, visible in kindergarten (Reardon et al., 2015) or even earlier: At age 4, only half as many Hispanic or Black children can recognize all letters as can White children

■ In the United States, there are persistent racial/ethnic differences in academic performance. What can be done to decrease these differences to give every child the same chance at success in life?

© iStock.com/fstop123

(Aud et al., 2010). These disparities grow throughout children's school career. Academic differences begin to narrow again in high school, but researchers suspect this is due to the fact that minority students drop out altogether at much higher rates than White adolescents (Quintana & Mahgoub, 2016; Reardon et al., 2015).

There are a number of reasons why higher SES may lead to better achievement in adolescents. Families with more financial means may be able to spend more on educational materials, enrichment materials, and tutoring. Parents may have more time to help their children with their homework and may be more engaged in their children's education (Liu et al., 2020; Melby et al., 2008). Schools in lower-income areas usually have fewer resources and less-qualified teachers and need to rely on substitute teachers more often (Duncan et al., 2017). Finally, children from higher-SES families tend to have better executive functioning, which in turn positively influences their school achievement (Lawson & Farah, 2017).

Unfortunately, the number of adolescents growing up in poverty is rising. Between 2000 and 2013, the number of students who are eligible for a free or reduced-price lunch (which is an indicator for poverty) increased in eighth graders from 35% to 52% (Carnoy & Garcia, 2017). This means that increasingly more students in the United States have to deal with the educational and developmental disadvantages that are associated with being from a low-income family.

School performance is affected by the social environment and personal characteristics

Academic performance is also influenced by all those people students spend time with: teachers, peers, and parents. Students learn better when their teachers are motivated, set clear expectations, provide them with feedback, and believe in their students' ability to learn (Kimani et al., 2013; Roehrig et al., 2012). Teachers who are familiar with child development are more effective, because they know what they can and cannot expect from their students. Flexibility and an ability to manage the classroom community help them to further cater to their students' needs and create a setting that promotes learning (Kim & Seo, 2018).

Peers influence adolescents' academic success as well, both favorably and unfavorably. Bullying negatively affects the performance of both bullies and bullied students, and students perform worse at schools where bullying is common (Al-Raqqad et al., 2017; Strøm et al., 2013). Popular students often perform better at school than those who are not popular (Wilson et al., 2011).

As noted earlier, parents play an important role in their children's school success. The more parents are involved, the higher their children's chances to succeed academically (Qu & Pomerantz, 2015). Asian parents tend to be much more involved in their children's schooling than are European American parents (Cheung & Pomerantz, 2012; Pomerantz & Grolnick, 2017; Pomerantz et al., 2012).

A final factor affecting school performance is the child's own drive and determination to succeed—highly motivated teens perform better at school (Amrai et al., 2011). A *growth mindset* (that is, the belief that one can develop one's talents and benefit from adversity) can even protect students from the negative impact of poverty (Claro et al., 2016). Students with a growth mindset see mistakes as learning opportunities and use their mistakes to further develop their abilities. Students with a *fixed mindset*, to the contrary, believe that people are born with certain abilities: They feel that making too many mistakes makes them look bad, and so they may give up rather than risking more errors.

Students acquire their mindsets throughout their lives: Their personal experiences as well as other people's reactions to their work lead them to believe that they can develop and improve their work or that they are defined by their current abilities. Teachers and caregivers can help students with a fixed mindset change their beliefs and understand that everyone can develop their abilities. Self-efficacy (the belief in one's own ability to succeed) and self-regulation (the ability to monitor one's feelings, actions, and thoughts) positively influence scholastic performance as well (Zimmerman & Kitsantas, 2014).

Dropping Out of High School

A significant number of American teenagers never complete their high school education. In this section, we will explore the reasons for dropping out of high school, the consequences, and what can be done to prevent dropouts.

Dropout rates vary by race and sex

The graduation rate in the United States has increased significantly since the mid-twentieth century. High school graduation rates rose from 50% after World War II (1945) to 93% in 2018 (EducationData.org, 2019b). While these numbers sound like an overall success, they still imply that a sizeable number of young people do not receive their high school diploma. Who is dropping out, and why? In 2018, the dropout rate was lowest for Asian American students (less than 2%), followed by White students (4%), Black students (6%), and Hispanic students (8%). More boys than girls drop out of school, and dropout rates vary by state (National Center for Education Statistics, 2020b) (FIGURE 15.4).

Moreover, dropout rates vary by school. About one-half of all students who drop out of school each year come from just 7% of American high schools (National Center for Education Statistics, 2020c). These schools are also called "dropout factories," and many of their students belong to an ethnic/racial minority (Balfanz & Legters, 2004; Sparks, 2017). In the next section, we will explore the reasons why young people drop out of high school even though the costs for their future career and income may be considerable.

Causes of dropouts

A major reason that adolescents drop out of school is poverty (Sarker et al., 2019). Students from low-SES families are more than twice as likely to drop out

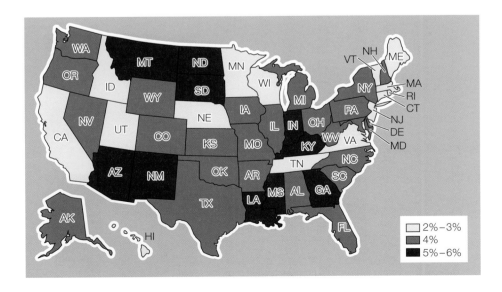

FIGURE 15.4 Adolescents (16–19 years of age) who do not attend school and do not have a high school degree, by state (2019). Why do you think do some states have a higher dropout rate than others? And why has the overall dropout rate decreased so drastically over the past decades?

After Annie E. Casey Foundation. 2019. Teens ages 16 to 19 not in school and not high school graduates in the United States. https://datacenter.kidscount.org

Legend:
- 2%–3%
- 4%
- 5%–6%

of high school as are students from middle-class families and ten times more likely to drop out than students from high-SES families (EducationData.org, 2019b) (see **FIGURE 15.5**).

Students living below the poverty line may go hungry at home, which makes focusing at school very hard, or they may feel they need to work in order to financially support their family (Staff et al., 2020). Students from low-income families are more likely to have parents who are in prison or who are often absent from home; their families move more often, and they have a higher risk of mingling with peers who use drugs and alcohol (Education Data.org, 2019b).

But financial reasons are not the only cause of students dropping out of school. Some students do not get along with their peers or their teachers. They may get bad grades, or they may simply not believe that they're able to complete high school successfully. Adolescents who don't get along with their parents are at higher risk for dropping out as well (Englund et al., 2008).

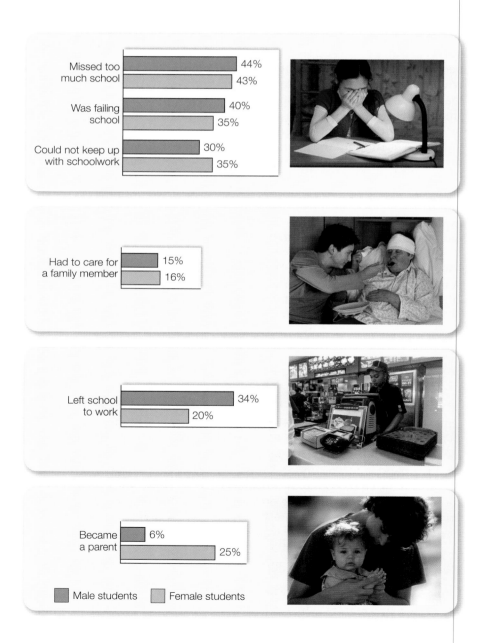

FIGURE 15.5 Some reasons for dropping out of high school.

After EducationData.org. 2019. High school dropout rate. https://educationdata.org

There are consequences of dropping out to both individuals and the state

When adolescents drop out of high school, they put themselves at a big disadvantage. Over a lifetime, people without a high school degree will earn around $200,000 less than high school graduates and almost $1,000,000 less than a person with a college degree (Cheeseman Day & Newburger, 2002). High school dropouts not only earn less money but they are also more likely to slip into poverty, become single parents, or get imprisoned. The consequences of dropping out extend beyond the individual to the state. In 2018, the State of California paid roughly $11,000 to educate each public school student but $65,000 to house an inmate (EducationData.org, 2019b)!

There are strategies to prevent dropouts

It should be clear that the costs of dropping out of high school are high—for the student, the student's family, and society as a whole. And while it is good news that the dropout rate in the United States has fallen sharply in recent decades, there is still plenty of room for improvement.

The Institute of Education Science at the U.S. Department of Education analyzes research and evidence to make recommendations on how to reduce the number of students dropping out of school. Here are their four main recommendations (Rumberger et al., 2017):

- *Monitor students and intervene early, if necessary.* Attendance, course performance, and behavior can be studied to reliably identify struggling students and intervene early. School information sessions for parents and visual reminders like stickers featuring school expectations and recommendations can be helpful as well.

- *Give intensive assistance.* If students are already off track or do not respond to the measures above, scale up the support. Schools can provide a case manager who provides information and support.

- *Create an engaging curriculum.* Classes that are relevant to career pathways or college education are more successful in engaging students. Colleges and local employers can be integrated into these efforts, giving students a window into what their life after high school might look like through tours and internships.

- *If none of the above recommendations work, consider creating small communities within the school.* Large schools can create smaller groups around grades, disciplines, interests, or characteristics of students to help students and teachers connect and build relationships. Small groups also allow teachers to monitor student progress more effectively.

Online Schools

Online schools and classes were already growing in popularity when the COVID-19 outbreak in early 2020 forced many brick-and-mortar schools to move to online teaching. While some schools returned to in-person classes once the pandemic was under control, some schools continue to offer hybrid or fully online course options. Researchers continue to study the effects of the sudden shift to online learning on social and academic development and will probably do so for years to come. Given the scarcity of reliable data on learning during COVID, in this section we will concentrate on those schools that were designed, pre-pandemic, for online education. We will also consider the success of blended schools that offer a mix of in-person and online classes.

Online learning is not right for everyone

There are many reasons why students and parents may find the prospect of an online middle or high school attractive. Some have religious reasons; others feel

■ During the COVID-19 pandemic, many children were taught online while their schools were closed. For both students and teachers, how do the skill sets needed for online versus face-to-face lessons differ?

that their traditional school has an unfavorable learning environment or a poor track record on student safety. High-achieving students may be interested in more challenging, specialized courses sometimes offered online. Students who have been bullied at their school may feel safer learning from home, and students with health issues that require periodic hospitalization as well as those whose families travel frequently may appreciate the opportunity to learn online without the interruptions they would face if they attended classes in person.

However, online education is not right for everyone. Compared with students in traditional schools, online students need to be more independent and able to focus even when their home environment is distracting. They need good reading and typing skills as well as reliable internet access. Lastly, online school is isolating and may be difficult for adolescents who thrive on collaboration and close contact with their peers.

Who attends online school?

A 2019 report found that 2 years before COVID-19 first disrupted classes, almost 300,000 students were enrolled in virtual schools across the United States, while an additional 130,000 students were enrolled in blended schools offering a combination of online and traditional lessons. And enrollment in online courses is growing steadily (Tate, 2019), even in traditional schools (National Center for Education Statistics, 2020a). Of course, online schooling skyrocketed during the COVID-19 pandemic. Particularly higher-income households relied on virtual lessons and online resources in spring 2020. For families with lower incomes, virtual schooling presented challenges because some of them did not have ready access to computers or high-speed internet (McElrath, 2020).

Almost one-half of online schools are charter schools. These schools are typically so big that together they enrolled almost 80% of online students. The ratio of students to teachers in these online schools is not favorable: At 44 students per teacher, it is much higher than the student-to-teacher ratio in traditional schools (16 students per teacher) and higher than the ratio in blended schools (34 students per teacher) (Molnar et al., 2019). The majority of virtual school students are White and from higher-income families (Molnar et al., 2019) (FIGURE 15.6).

White 63%
Hispanic 14%
Black 12%
Asian 2%
Native American 1%
Two or more 5%
Other 3%

FIGURE 15.6 Enrollment in virtual schools by race/ethnicity, U.S. (Molnar et al., 2019). Compared with traditional schools across the United States, virtual schools enroll more White students and fewer minority students. What do you think is the reason for this discrepancy?

Data from A. Molnar. 2019. Virtual Schools in the U.S. 2019. http://nepc.colorado.edu

How does an online school work?

While online education offers students attending remotely some flexibility in where they learn, they rely on routine the same way that traditional schools do, with a daily schedule and breaks throughout the day. Student attendance is tracked in accordance with state laws, and parents must notify the school if a student is unable to attend a class.

Classes may or may not include regular live meetings of students and their teacher. In a live class, students interact with the teacher and their classmates online; they can collaborate in breakout groups and submit assignments online. *Asynchronous learning* involves prerecorded video lectures instead of regular live meetings. In this model, teachers give students a daily plan they can follow at a time of their choosing. Students may still interact with their teacher in live meetings throughout the day or at specific office hours. The graduation requirements are the same for both public in-person and public online schools.

Student success in online schools is lower than in traditional classrooms

Online schools sound appealing to many parents and students, but does the flexibility of online learning produce better academic achievement? A 2012 study found that while 52% of public schools had their students achieve adequate progress each year, this was true for only 27% of virtual schools (Miron & Urschel, 2012). In 2019, the same results were found. And these findings are consistent with most other research on virtual schools. For example, one study in Ohio found that

> students attending online charter schools have substantially weaker growth in both reading and math than the average TPS VCRs [traditional public school virtual control records, which provide the baseline against which online schools are measured]. The gaps translate to 47 fewer days of learning in reading and 136 fewer days of learning in math for online charter students. (Center for Research on Education Outcomes, 2019)

These studies are not anomalies; many others yield similar findings (Fitzpatrick et al., 2020; Freidhoff, 2018; Legislative Division of Post Audit, 2015; National Alliance for Public Charter Schools et al., 2016; Quillen, 2011; Woodworth et al., 2015).

Another way to evaluate the performance of online schools is by looking at performance ratings given out by the state in which they are located. In 2018, 21 states made performance ratings available for virtual schools. Fewer than 49% of virtual schools received acceptable performance ratings. Their graduation rates also lag behind those of traditional schools (Molnar et al., 2019) (see **FIGURE 15.7**).

It is not clear why so many of the virtual schools are failing in their educational purposes; they cannot be explained by teacher or classroom characteristics (Fitzpatrick et al., 2020). Perhaps physical proximity to other students plays more of a role in learning than one would expect, or virtual students spend less time being instructed or on learning in general. There is also little information on the pedagogical practices that online schools employ (Fitzpatrick et al., 2020).

Despite the poor record of virtual and blended schools, the number of such schools continues to grow, enrolling more students every year (Tate, 2019)—trends that are likely to continue in the wake of COVID-19. But schools cannot be improved if the reasons for their failure are not sufficiently known. For that reason, the National Policy Education Center actually recommended that the growth of virtual/blended schools be stopped or at least slowed until reasons for their underperformance have been identified (Molnar et al., 2019).

What should we make of the data on online schools?

While the data on online schools are not promising, remember that averages can be deceptive. Online education might not be right for every student, but many adolescents attend online courses with impressively positive results. **TABLE 15.1** offers some tips to help make the online education experience a successful one (Knorr, 2020; Elgersma, 2020).

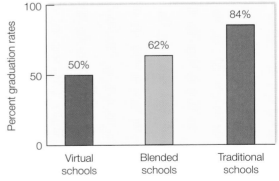

FIGURE 15.7 Graduation rates across school models. Virtual and blended schools have a much lower graduation rate than do traditional schools. What do you think is the reason for the difference in graduation rates?

Data from A. Molnar. 2019. Virtual Schools in the U.S. 2019. http://nepc.colorado.edu

■ Table 15.1 Helping Teens Get the Most from Online Education

Things parents can do	Examples
Set screen time rules	Homework must be completed before meeting friends online.
Give reasons for use of parental controls	Parental controls ensure that children sleep enough and have enough time for homework.
Create screen-free times and zones	Screen-free times help families spend time together and ensure teens completing online education have time for physical activities and exercise.
Check in with children about their social life online	Miscommunications happen easily online. Conversations with children help parents pick up on problems so they can offer help to resolve conflicts.
Set up a space where they learn	Students should have a dedicated space where they keep their materials and can learn without distraction.
Create a routine for them, and make sure it includes breaks	The younger the children, the more routine they need. Young children can use a visual schedule; older children can use a planner, whiteboard, or digital calendar.
Follow a routine similar to that when they go to a physical school	Make sure they shower, get dressed, and eat breakfast before school.
Discuss expectations	When are they expected to learn? When should they not disturb you? What activities are allowed and not allowed during their breaks?
Help them focus	If students have trouble staying focused, stay close and consider setting up verbal cues to get them back to focusing.

So how should parents decide if a virtual school is right for their teen? Here are some questions to consider:

- Is the program accredited by the appropriate accrediting agency? If it is not, you may have difficulty transferring the credits or having them recognized.
- What percentage of students who start the program or school actually finish? Is it most of the students or only a relatively small percentage?
- What percentage of students who start the program finish within the prescribed amount of time?
- Does the institution have adequate additional help for students who need it? Are there additional online resources? Are there staff available to help sort out technical problems?
- Is your child a motivated and independent learner? How willing are they to work as hard as required to fulfill the requirements, even in the absence of the physical presence of professors and other students pushing them to complete the course of instruction?

In other words, be an educated consumer. If you are, you should do fine, with online education or anything else!

Review!

What challenges do students encounter as they enter middle school?

- Students entering middle school are undergoing numerous physical, cognitive, and social changes. Their bodies develop as they enter puberty, and they become increasingly self-conscious. They go from being the oldest kids in elementary school to being at the bottom of the pecking order in middle school.

- Middle school differs from elementary school in many ways: The academic demands are higher, and more independence is expected of students. Middle schools tend to be larger and more nearly anonymous, and teachers tend to be less warm.
- Parents can help students prepare for the changes by bringing them to tour the school in advance, reviewing their schedule with them, encouraging social skills that will help them make new

friends, and encouraging them to become more independent and persist when challenges come their way.

What makes students more or less likely to succeed at school?

- Academic success depends on many factors. Motivation and a growth mindset as well as self-efficacy help students succeed.
- Teachers who are motivated, who communicate clear expectations, and who provide constructive feedback on student work are most likely to support students' learning. Teachers can also create a classroom community that promotes learning by actively and flexibly catering to students' needs.
- Popular students tend to perform better in school; academic performance is lower among students who are bullied and those who bully others.
- Parents play a significant role in student learning as well. Highly educated parents, those with a high income, and parents who are involved in their children's schooling usually have children who perform well at school.
- In the United States, race/ethnicity and socioeconomic status are intertwined in a myriad of ways that also influence academic performance: White and Asian students often perform better at school than do Hispanic or Black students.

Why are high school dropout rates a problem?

- Students who drop out of high school are at risk for many negative consequences. They are more likely to be unemployed or to have a low annual income. They also have a higher risk of ending up in prison.
- In the United States, the high school dropout rate has decreased in recent decades, but students from racial minorities are still much more likely than White students to leave school without a degree.
- Financial issues are frequently cited as a reason for dropping out, with students feeling they need to support their family by getting a job. Other reasons for dropping out include poor academic performance, a lack of belief in one's potential to succeed, and a failure to get along with peers or teachers.
- Early intervention is the best way to prevent dropouts. When students do not attend school regularly, their course performance is insufficient, or they display disruptive or otherwise problematic behavior, schools should intervene early on and offer assistance to both student and parents. A curriculum that is connected with students' lives and interests can be a further incentive for students to finish their high school education.

Do virtual schools work?

- Virtual schools have been growing in popularity for the past 2 decades. They appeal to many families because of the flexibility they offer: High achievers can choose more challenging courses, and students who need to catch up may tailor the curriculum to their needs. Students with chronic diseases or potential long-term hospital stays can continue their schooling from home or the hospital. Bullied students may feel safer in the comfort of their own home. Virtual schools are particularly popular with middle and high school students.
- While some online schools are tremendously successful and offer their students an excellent education, a substantial number of virtual and blended schools do not educate their students as successfully as traditional schools. The reasons for the weak performance of these schools have not yet been identified.

Practice!

1. In the first year of middle school, students _____ .
   a. face fewer social challenges
   b. have self-esteem that is considerably higher than in elementary school
   c. have self-esteem that is often lower than in previous years
   d. tend to connect more with their teachers than they did in elementary school.

2. Compared with other industrialized countries, the United States has _____ .
   a. much more motivated students
   b. a much larger number of secondary schools
   c. much less of an achievement gap between high-income and low-income students
   d. a higher achievement gap between high-income and low-income students

3. Virtual schools are most popular with _____ .
   a. high school students
   b. Hispanic students
   c. Asian American students
   d. low-income students

Show What You've Learned!

Sid plays soccer on the community team you help coach. He recently turned 16 and says it's time to leave school and get a job. His father died when Sid was a toddler, and his mother has been sick for more than a year and doesn't work. The family is struggling financially, and as the eldest of two siblings, Sid feels a responsibility to look after his family. You understand the pressures of his situation but feel that dropping out of high school is a bad decision in the long term. How would you try to persuade Sid to finish high school? Draw on the information presented in this chapter to argue that finishing high school will be better for Sid in the long run despite the challenges he is facing.

What's Your Position?

Should states pause the expansion of virtual schools? As you have seen in the section above, virtual schools face many challenges. Many fail to educate their students in a way comparable to traditional schools. But virtual schools also hold a lot of appeal to students who want greater freedom to design their schedule or curriculum. Because the reasons for their underperformance are not clear, the National Policy Education Center has recommended that states slow or even stop the growth of virtual schools for now. What do you think about this recommendation?

What Would You Do?

It's November, and an infectious new strain of the COVID-19 virus has emerged in your community, causing local schools to adopt measures to reduce class sizes to facilitate physical distancing. Students who are not comfortable attending school in person are being given the option to finish the school year online. Your 16-year-old is in 11th grade, and while you are always concerned about health and safety, you know this year's academic results will be included in college applications. Are you more inclined to have your child attend in person or online? Write out your answer.

15.4 Work and College

- Evaluate the pros and cons of adolescents working while attending high school.
- Relate the options high school graduates have after they have finished school.

Most people find employment at some point in their life. Some teenagers find their first part-time job while they're in school, but the majority of high school students today do not work.

As graduation approaches, young people need to decide what to do after high school. The common options include enrolling in college or entering the labor market, though some teens will take a "gap year" to weigh their options. We will examine these choices below in more detail.

Adolescents at Work

Working adolescents can be roughly divided into two groups: those who work part-time while attending high school and those who have dropped out of school to work. The number of adolescents in both groups is decreasing, and in this section we will take a closer look at the trends.

Who is working, and why?

In 2018, 20% of high school students held part-time jobs compared to 60% in the 1980s. Among the relatively small number of adolescents who did not attend high school, 72% had full- or part-time employment (Bauer et al., 2019; Child Trends Databank, 2020).

There are a few reasons why fewer adolescents are working:

- There are fewer low-skill jobs than there were decades earlier;
- more students are completing course requirements or participate in after-school programs and summer school;
- more teens volunteer their time to satisfy requirements for high school graduation or to spruce up their resumes; and
- more students work as unpaid interns, trading wages for professional experience (DeSilver, 2019).

White students are more frequently employed (22%) than Black and Hispanic (14%) as well as Asian students (11%). Some of these differences may be explained by employment practices, which often favor White youths and adults over those of other races/ethnicities (Child Trends Databank, 2020). Most working teens are in the hospitality and retail sectors (FIGURE 15.8).

Is employment beneficial for adolescents?

Many parents and youth wonder whether adolescents should work while attending high school. Parents of working children hope that their children will learn to be independent and gain new skills (Phillips & Sandstrom, 1990). Teens often find the thought of earning their own money to spend on clothes, entertainment, computer games, or whatever they are interested in quite appealing.

Work can be a helpful learning experience when it leaves enough time for school and homework. In this case, teens can learn skills like time management and taking responsibility and increase their chances of getting future jobs (Horn et al., 2002).

There is some concern that working teens are more likely to develop substance-abuse problems or other problem behaviors, but a review of research has found that this is unlikely. It is not the work itself that is causing undesirable behaviors, but rather that teens who are already prone to problem behaviors gravitate toward working more hours (Staff et al., 2009).

Still, there are a few things parents and teachers can do to improve the odds that teens who wish to work will get on and stay on the right track. They can help teens:

- avoid hazardous workplaces;
- track their work hours (20 hours or less for teens who plan to go to college);
- ensure that work does not compete with other activities important to adolescents' development, like sports and extracurricular activities, friendships, and family time; and
- reflect on how work is connected to their learning at school (Mortimer, 2010).

1,614	Food preparation and service
1,201	Sales and retail
622	Office and administrative support
522	Personal care and service
441	Transportation and material moving
267	Building and grounds cleaning and maintenance
1,561	Other

FIGURE 15.8 Employment of U.S. teens (16–19) in the labor force, summer 2018 (in thousands). A large number of adolescents work in the hospitality or sales sector. While the number of teens working in food services has increased over the past decades, the number of teens working in retail has decreased.

After D. DeSilver. 2019. In the U.S., teen summer jobs aren't what they used to be. www.pewresearch.org

College-Bound Adolescents

Many young Americans plan to go to college or university after they graduate from high school. In fact, among high school graduates in 2019, 62% of males and 70% of females enrolled in college (Bureau of Labor Statistics, 2020). There were substantial ethnic/racial differences with regard to who went to college: Whereas 90% of Asian adolescents went to college, 67% of White adolescents did, as well as 63% of Hispanic adolescents and 51% of Black adolescents. Over the past decades, increasingly more students have been enrolling in college (FIGURE 15.9).

Some high schools partner with community colleges to offer one or two different options to their students interested in furthering their education:

- *Dual credit programs* allow high schoolers to take classes at their high school and receive high school and/or college credits for them.
- *Concurrent enrollment programs* allow high schoolers to attend college classes and get high school and/or college credits for the courses.

■ Working adolescents learn to take responsibility for their actions and acquire a variety of work-related skills. But working obviously also decreases the time they have available for schoolwork. Do you think working is worth the time investment, or are teens better off concentrating on their school career? Why?

FIGURE 15.9 College enrollment rates of recent high school graduates in October of their graduation year, 1995–2016. Since the 1990s, increasingly more high school graduates have been enrolling in college. However, in most years, the number of men enrolling in college is significantly lower than the number of women. Why do you think this is?

After Bureau of Labor Statistics. 2017. TED: The Economics Daily. www.bls.gov

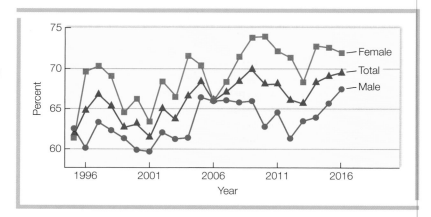

An astounding number of students who go to college never graduate from college. In 2018, only 44% of students enrolled at 4-year colleges graduated after 4 years, and only 62% graduated within 6 years of their enrollment (Digest of Education Statistics, 2020). The more selective the school, the more likely students were to graduate within 6 years: The most selective colleges saw 90% of students graduate within 6 years, whereas colleges with an open-admissions policy had only 34% of students graduate within 6 years (EducationData.org, 2019a; National Center for Education Statistics, 2020d).

The reasons for dropping out of college vary, but financial causes are often at play. Postsecondary education in the United States is very expensive, and if a family's financial situation changes unexpectedly for the worse, it may be impossible for the student to continue to attend college. Sometimes, students find the transition to college difficult: They may struggle with the increased workload, homesickness, loneliness, or mental health issues. But dropping out, even for just one semester, greatly diminishes the chance a student will complete their postsecondary degree; only one-third of students who take a break will finish their degree (EducationData.org, 2019a; Moody, 2019).

Additionally, around 40% of college graduates work in jobs that do not require a college degree, and even more graduates are working in jobs that are not related to what they studied in college (EducationData.org, 2019a). They may not have found jobs in their chosen field, or—like Ray, whom we met in the scenario at the beginning of the chapter—they may have felt pressured by their parents or peers to enter a degree program without a plan for how to apply that degree to a career.

With these facts in mind, parents, caregivers, and guidance counselors should encourage high school–aged adolescents to think carefully about whether college is right for them. Even pausing for a year after high school may help to make sure that a postsecondary education is the right choice.

Adolescents Who Are Not Going to College

In the United States, the job prospects for someone without a college degree are much more limited than they are in many other industrialized nations, where a college degree is not necessary to get a job that pays the kind of salary that leads to independence.

Germany, for example, has a vocational education and training (VET) system that offers entry to a successful career to students without a high school or college degree. Students have the option of getting a school degree after a total of 9, 10, or 12 years of education. The latter degree, with 12 years of education, is equivalent to an American high school degree and qualifies students to attend college (Statista, 2020) (**FIGURE 15.10**).

The majority of German students do not get a high school degree but leave school after 9 or 10 years. They then choose from a variety of professional job choices for which colleges studies are not necessary, like electrical work, plumbing, banking, hairdressing, or sales. Schools work with federal employment agencies to assist students in finding professions that fit their interests and skills.

In Germany's vocational system, non-college-bound school graduates can seek an apprenticeship with a company of their choice that offers vocational training. They spend half their time completing on-the-job training in the company and half their time going to vocational school, where they continue their education with a special focus on the knowledge and skills needed for their profession. They receive salary throughout their apprenticeship, whether they work in the company or attend vocational school. In Germany as well as in the United States, people with a college degree tend to have higher incomes. However, Germans choosing a vocational career still have an income that allows them to have a comfortable living standard (Statista, 2021b).

In the United States, counseling in high schools is geared mostly to students planning to enter college, with little guidance offered to those who do not wish to pursue a college education. Students who are not academically oriented and who would rather learn a vocation still need to complete 12 years of schooling to get a high school degree. Recently, however, the United States has moved to expand industry-recognized apprenticeships. Employers are encouraged to create apprenticeship programs, and young people are encouraged to apply for apprenticeships. Similar to the German system, youth in an apprenticeship hold a paid job with a competitive wage, continue their education with on-the-job training as well as in the classroom, and gain valuable credentials for their future career (Department of Labor, 2021c). The average starting salary is $70,000, and 94% of apprentices continue to work for their employer after they have completed their apprenticeship (Department of Labor, 2021b).

In practice, however, the system is still underdeveloped. As of January 2021, in my hometown of 30,000 people, there were no available apprenticeships offered in town and just two within a radius of 25 miles. In New York City (which has more than 8 million inhabitants), 12 apprenticeships were listed (Department of Labor, 2021a). In comparison, a town of 10,000 in Germany had listed 1,840 apprenticeships within a radius of 20 miles (Ausbildungsmarkt.de, 2021). Thus, it is virtually impossible for U.S. youth to find an apprenticeship in a profession that is of interest to them.

An alternative to apprenticeships is to go to a trade school that offers courses that are highly relevant to the vocation a student chooses. Options are, for example, auto body repair, welding, marine mechanics, carpentry, and nursing. Students are not affiliated with employers, and because the programs are so focused on skills training, many trade school programs can be completed in less than 1 year. Trade-school enrollment increased from almost 10 million students in 1999 to 16 million in 2014 (St-Esprit, 2019).

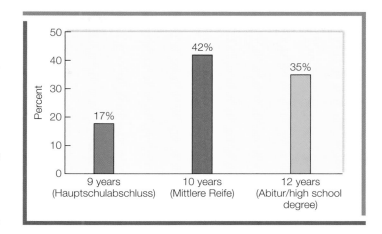

FIGURE 15.10   Percentage of German students who leave school after a total of 9, 10, or 12 years of education, 2020. As you can see, most students do not attain a high school degree, but rather leave school after 10 years to seek vocational training, which enables them to successfully work in a profession of their choice that does not require a college degree.

After Statista. 2021. Anzahl der Schulabsolventen/-abgänger in Deutschland im Abgangsjahr 2019 nach Abschlussart. https://de.statista.com

Culture Counts

Enrollment in Tertiary Education Worldwide

The map below shows the percentage of college- and university-aged people (18–23) enrolled in tertiary education around the world. As you can see, there is wide geographical variation in tertiary school participation, and the United States has one of world's highest rates. Yet nowhere in the world is college education so costly, and nowhere does it leave so many people in debt as in the United States.

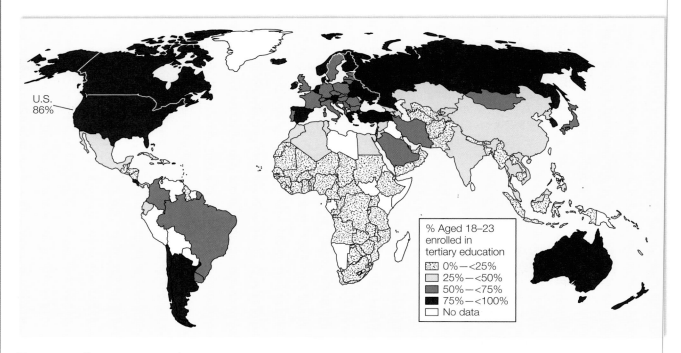

U.S.
86%

% Aged 18–23
enrolled in
tertiary education
▨ 0%—<25%
☐ 25%—<50%
▨ 50%—<75%
■ 75%—<100%
☐ No data

■ Gross enrollment in tertiary education, 2016.

After M. Roser and E. Ortiz-Ospina. 2013. Tertiary Education. https://ourworldindata.org/CC BY 4.0

■ Question

Why do so many young people in the United States choose to pursue a college degree despite the high cost of tertiary school enrollment in the United States?

Review!

Should adolescents work while attending high school?

■ Although the number of working high school students has decreased, employment holds some promises for both students and parents. Students find the prospect of having their own money to spend appealing, and parents hope their children will learn to be responsible and develop a good work ethic.

■ For a positive work experience, families need to ensure that their teen works only as many hours as do not interfere with school performance or other activities vital for their development, like athletics, meeting friends, or spending time with family (20 hours per week is generally the maximum).

■ Teens who do not plan to attend college may be interested in working more hours in order to build their work experience. Teenagers, though, need other experiences to promote social development and help them become well-rounded.

What options do high school graduates have after they have finished school?

■ In the United States, most high school graduates go on to attend college. People with a college degree tend to have a higher annual income than do those without a degree, and they are less at risk for unemployment.

- Although many students enroll in college, more than one-third of them have not graduated after 6 years—mostly for financial, but also for personal or academic, reasons.

- Vocational training and trade school are alternatives for those students who are interested in learning a skilled trade. However, high schools offer little counseling to those students who do not wish to go to college.

Practice!

1. The number of adolescents who are working in high school is decreasing because _____.
   a. families are becoming increasingly wealthier and there is no need for youth to work and earn money
   b. schools generally discourage part-time work
   c. fewer low-skill jobs are available
   d. families are increasingly multigenerational and thus have more financial means when parents' and grandparents' incomes are combined

2. High schoolers tend to work primarily in _____.
   a. food preparation and sales
   b. office support
   c. childcare
   d. house cleaning

3. Trade school is _____.
   a. offering an extended general education in addition to job-related skills training
   b. decreasing in the United States
   c. a popular option for students who have graduated from college
   d. focused on skills training and thus often relatively short in duration

See for Yourself!

As you go about your daily business, keep an eye open for adolescents who work in your community. Can you find many adolescents who are working? What hours are they most frequently working? And in which kinds of businesses do they work?

Are there any differences if you compare your community with neighboring ones that have a different racial/ethnic or socioeconomic profile?

Show What You've Learned!

Sixteen-year-old Marcie, whom we met earlier this chapter, is at her locker between classes when she sees the guidance counselor, Mrs. Ramesh, passing by. "Oh—Mrs. Ramesh! I wanted to tell you my news!" Marcie tells her guidance counselor that she's interviewing for a part-time job at the animal shelter in her neighborhood. "It probably means I'll have to quit the swim team,

but it's a great opportunity for me to make money and gain some experience before college!"

Drawing on the information presented in this chapter, what advice would you give Marcie? Jot down a few points you can share with her in the short time you have before she races off for her next class.

Setting the path for the future: 2 years later

Having graduated from high school, Ray is now into year 2 of an apprenticeship program. After exploring different options with his high school counselor as well as talking to some local contractors he met while doing some construction work the summer after high school, Ray decided that he would like to pursue an apprenticeship as an HVAC (heating, ventilation, and air conditioning) mechanic. This way, he would earn a reasonable salary from the outset, making him financially independent from his parents. His parents were more supportive than he'd expected. Unfortunately, there were not many open positions available locally, so Ray ended up moving away from his hometown to begin his apprenticeship. Ray tremendously enjoys working in his new environment and learning skills on the job. There is also another apprentice with whom Ray has built a friendship. Ray is looking forward to his work every day and hopes that his company will offer him a long-term position once he has completed his apprenticeship.

Overview

Social and Emotional Development in Adolescence

Youth discovering their identity

Summer is drawing to a close, and 14-year-old Doah is looking forward to the start of ninth grade with a mix of excitement and trepidation. This huge change—starting high school—comes after what could be called a summer of discovery for Doah, which began when she asked about her name one night over dinner. Her full name is Shenandoah, but since childhood everybody, including her family, has just called her Doah. She only hears the full name on Day 1 of school, when a teacher takes attendance for the first time; she typically replies, "Just Doah is fine," and that's that. Her father explains that Doah was named after her paternal grandmother, who grew up on lands belonging to the Oneida Indian Nation in Upstate New York.

After dinner, Doah immediately goes online to read about the Oneida. She learns about how they're one of five nations of the Haudenosaunee, how they speak Iroquoian, and how they fought alongside the American colonists in the War of Independence. She also learns that for a period around the turn of the twentieth century, Native American children as young as herself were brought to federally funded boarding schools, where they were forced to learn English and prohibited from speaking their language.

Doah takes after her father, who has always "passed" for White: No one would ever know that either of them had Native American ancestry. "It's just easier," Doah's father explains, given the negative stereotypes some people have about Native Americans. But Doah is proud of this previously undiscovered part of her identity, and she wants to learn the language that Oneida children a century earlier were forced to give up. But she wonders if she really has the courage to let her new teachers and classmates call her by her full name.

Identity development is a critical part of adolescence. Many of the identity traits we take on in adolescence remain well into adulthood, sometimes for life. But issues of identity are as complex as they may be exciting, and as we will see in this chapter, it can take courage to show the world the "real us."

16.1 Creating an Identity

- ■ Outline the theories of adolescent identity formation and describe the role ethnicity and gender play.

As we have seen in the previous two chapters, adolescence is a time of many changes. Physical and cognitive changes come with big life changes: the transition to middle school and then high school, all in preparation for whatever comes after. During this time, adolescents' social lives change, too. Teens gain more independence, and they have more freedom to decide how to spend their free time—and with whom. They go increasingly to their friends for advice instead of their parents, and groups of friends are not constrained to one gender anymore but start to mix. Teens will begin to develop romantic interests in others and may enter into sexual relationships that matter more than their family ties.

With the end of high school nearing, adolescents also have to decide what to do with the rest of their lives. What kind of job will they have, and what kind of person would they like to be? One of the big tasks in adolescent development is the creation of one's own **identity**. An identity is a clear and stable sense of oneself that includes a person's goals, values, and beliefs and that leads to an experience of "wholeness" as a person.

In this section, we will revisit Erik Erikson and his eight stages of psychosocial development. We will also get to know another approach to understanding identity development, from James Marcia, which adds two more dimensions in the quest to explain the way identity develops during adolescence.

> **identity** a clear and stable sense of oneself that includes a person's goals, values, and beliefs.

Erikson's Fifth Stage of Psychosocial Development

Erik Erikson theorized that personality development occurs throughout the entire lifetime of a person and takes place in eight distinct stages. In adolescence, teens go through Erikson's fifth stage of psychosocial development. This stage, which occurs roughly between the ages of 12 and 18, is characterized by a conflict between *identity confusion* and *identity* (Erikson, 1994). Ideally, adolescents will move from the former state to the latter, emerging with a developed sense of self. But creating an identity is not easy and brings up a whole range of issues: What career to pursue? How to dress? What values to prioritize? Whether to have a family? In answering all these questions, adolescents attempt to find their place in society (Côté, 2019).

> **psychosocial moratorium** a period within which adolescents do not have to take on adult responsibilities and therefore can explore different roles and identities.

Obviously, these are hard questions to answer. Many adolescents, particularly in industrialized nations, are lucky to experience a phase called **psychosocial moratorium**, which offers them extra freedom to explore their options. During the psychosocial moratorium, they are still relatively free of adult responsibilities, which gives them a chance to try out different identities, values, and relationships. Teens can explore their sexual orientation, explore values and ideals, or experiment with clothing styles.

Not all adolescents have the luxury of a psychosocial moratorium to explore different roles. Young people in lower-SES families may grow up with social circumstances and expectations that may limit their options. They may feel the need to join the workforce straight out of high school to

■ Sarah and Laila are doing an internship at a local community care center. The internship gives them the chance to explore a possible career path. In industrialized nations, many adolescents experience a psychosocial moratorium that allows them time with few adult responsibilities to figure out who they want to be.

support themselves or their families. Or they may be expected to marry and have children, rather than pursuing a college career or at least having a "pause" after high school to weigh their options (Arnett, 2020; Pastor et al., 2007; Syed & Fish, 2018).

Adolescents who successfully resolve the fifth stage of Erikson's model of psychosocial development emerge with a newfound identity and a sense of who they want to be in life. But not everybody succeeds in finding their identity. Teens who fail to find their own place in society will experience identity confusion. They may withdraw from their friends and family, or they may lose themselves in the opinions and influences of the crowd. Either way, they run a risk of drifting from one job to another or experiencing failing relationships because they do not have a clear goal for their life.

Marcia's Identity Statuses

James Marcia built on Erikson's idea that identity development occurs between the two poles of identity and identity confusion. He suggested that identity development could be better described if two further dimensions were added to the model: *exploration* and *commitment* (Crocetti, 2017). **Exploration** refers to the active exploration of and search for values, goals, and beliefs. **Commitment** involves a stable investment in those goals and values. These two dimensions give rise to four identity statuses that describe if, and how, a person has resolved the identity crisis described by Erikson (**TABLE 16.1**).

Research studies examining adolescents' identity development have found evidence for the four different statuses as Marcia proposes them. The starting point for teens is the *diffused status* (Arnold, 2017; Kroger et al., 2010), and

exploration the active search for an identity involving values, goals, and beliefs in James Marcia's theory of identity development.

commitment a stable investment in one's goals and values in James Marcia's theory of identity development.

■ **Table 16.1** James Marcia's Four Identity Statuses

		EXPLORATION	
		YES	**NO**
COMMITMENT	**YES**	**ACHIEVEMENT** • Has explored different identities • Has made a commitment to an identity based on those prior explorations • Shows self-confidence Since starting high school, Raina has enjoyed her advanced math and science classes, and she's spent a lot of time pondering a career path based on this interest. She has visited several career fairs and attended college and university open houses to explore her options. She eventually narrowed her interest down to astronomy, and so this fall when she starts college, she'll be doing a Bachelor of Science program specializing in astrophysics.	**FORECLOSURE** • Has made a commitment without exploring alternatives • Has based the decision on the opinions of others or pressure from family, teachers, and peers • Has authoritarian parents who give their children little choice or say • Feels comfortable because the decision is made for them Guy's parents both work at a bank; so does his older sister. When Guy was 16, his mother arranged for him to do an internship at the bank where she works. In Guy's family, or so it seems to him, people just are bankers, and that's fine with him. At least he knows what his life is going to be like, unlike many of his friends.
	NO	**MORATORIUM** • Is still exploring different identities • Has made only weak commitments, or no commitment at all • Often feels anxious about the uncertain future Jaime likes kids and thinks that she'd like to devote her life to making a difference in the lives of children. But she doesn't know yet how to do that exactly. She babysits, she has worked at a summer camp, and she occasionally does some filing at her pediatrician's office. Sometimes she thinks about becoming a teacher. She just wishes she knew what to do.	**DIFFUSION** • Is not exploring different identities • Is undecided about identity • Has no interest in search for identity • The least advanced status, often found in early adolescence At 15, Demarcus is a carefree kid who does well at school and loves to play and watch sports. He has no idea what he wants to do when he grows up; he isn't even sure what he'll do after high school. But he is happy with things as they are and figures he has lots of time to figure things out.

Source: E. Crocetti. 2017. *Child Dev Perspect* 11: 145–150.

© Drazen Zigic/Shutterstock.com

■ Girls and boys often differ in the way they assess their strengths. Generally, boys believe they are better in areas like math and athletics, whereas many girls believe their strengths lie in music or language arts. School grades do not reflect boys' and girls' assessments, however. Why do you think boys and girls have a tendency to think they are better in particular areas?

identity development continues beyond adolescence. For example, a study of about 250 Lebanese youth aged 18–21 found that almost one-third of them were in the moratorium status, and the same proportion were in the foreclosure status (Kaddoura & Sarouphim, 2019). A meta-analysis of 124 studies showed that by age 36 only about half of the participants had reached the achievement identity status (Kroger et al., 2010).

An extension of Marcia's model is the newer *dual identity model* (Luyckx, 2013), which suggests that identity development goes through two cycles. The first cycle is a formation phase, in which young people explore their options in depth and eventually commit to the options that seem viable for them. The second cycle comprises an evaluation of these commitments. Young people may continue to explore their choices in depth and talk with others about them. If they are happy with their choices, their commitment to these choices will deepen. However, if any of their choices at some point feel unsatisfactory, they might go back to the first cycle to explore different options in more depth yet again (Luyckx et al., 2008; van Doeselaar et al., 2019; Verschueren et al., 2017).

Boys and girls tend to commit to their identities in different domains at different times. When it comes to teens' political views, for example, boys more often tend to be foreclosed, having formed opinions without thorough consideration of alternatives, whereas girls are more likely in a diffused status, not having considered their standpoint in much detail at all. In terms of family status, girls are more likely than boys to be in moratorium or to have reached achievement status (Archer, 1989; Verschueren et al., 2017). Girls' estimation of their abilities tends to be lower than what their grades indicate, while the opposite is true for boys (Perry & Pauletti, 2011). The imbalance between self-esteem and actual accomplishments means that girls may not explore opportunities because they believe they are not qualified, whereas boys will go after opportunities despite not being as qualified. Girls generally have lower self-esteem than boys, and their self-esteem is more dependent on their relationships and the perceptions of others. For both genders, body image is an important component of self-esteem: If adolescents do not like their body, their self-esteem will suffer (Harter, 2006).

The Influence of Gender and Race on Teens' Identity

ethnic identity a sense of belonging to a particular group of people who share a common culture, nationality, ancestry, language, or religion.

Ethnic identity is one of the factors that help shape individual identity. **Ethnic identity** is a sense of belonging to a particular group defined by a common national or cultural tradition. Adolescents with strong affinity for an ethnic group identify with its customs, beliefs, attitudes, and values. Jewish adolescents in the United States, for example, may find comfort and a sense of identity in celebrating religious holidays such as Hanukkah or Shabbat. They may perceive themselves as different in some ways from teens who belong to other faiths or no faith at all.

Establishing an ethnic identity is not an either/or situation. Often, adolescents identify at least to some extent with the culture of their ethnic group, but also with the culture of the country's majority. Their identity ends up having components of both cultures and is called a **bicultural identity**. And as we saw with Shenandoah at the start of the chapter, choosing to identify with one's ancestral traditions, if they differ from the prevailing traditions of the community, can take some courage.

For members of minority groups, ethnic identity often is much more salient and noticeable than for members of the majority group. Take Jonathan, for example. He spent all his life in the United States until, at age 16, his parents moved to Hong Kong, bringing the family with them. While in the United States, Jonathan spent very little time thinking about what it meant to be an American. But in Hong Kong, things are different. Teens look and dress differently, and he does not speak the Cantonese language of Hong Kong. The Chinese in Hong Kong have customs that seem foreign to him, and he often does not understand their way of doing things. All of a sudden, Jonathan feels very American.

■ Black teens like Jason sometimes feel that they are treated differently than teens of the majority ethnicity. What impact might this experience have on their identity development?

A similar thing often happens to ethnic-minority adolescents within their own country. They may be confronted with their ethnic identity as soon as they leave their home: Their skin may have a different color, they may speak a different language, or they may have different customs or holidays. They may even feel that people treat them differently from the way members of the majority group are treated.

bicultural identity a sense of belonging to two different cultures.

For many White adolescents in the United States, ethnic identity plays much less of a role in their identity development (Charmaraman & Grossman, 2008). They often take their ethnicity for granted in such a way that they feel their race does not play a role in their life at all (Jackson & Heckman, 2002). For that reason, White American youths are much less likely to explore their ethnic identity or to make a commitment to their ethnicity as part of who they are (Hughes et al., 2017).

In early adolescence, teens begin to consider the impact of their ethnic identity

Most adolescents first start thinking about their ethnic identity in early or middle adolescence. If the majority culture and their own culture clash with respect to values, attitudes, way of life, and other factors, adolescents eventually have to make decisions about what and who they want to be.

Often, feelings about their own group become more positive as they explore their identity (French et al., 2006). Toward late adolescence, many teens are ready to commit to an ethnic identity (Pahl & Way, 2006). However, their identity will continue to evolve throughout their life.

A positive ethnic identity is generally beneficial for adolescents. Young people who positively identify with their own ethnic group (or who have a positive bicultural identity) tend to have better mental health and higher self-esteem, because their connection with their group helps them create meaning in life (Bae, 2020; Kiang & Fuligni, 2010; Yip et al., 2010).

A bicultural identity improves integration with youth from the majority group. A study in Germany found that immigrant middle school students who saw themselves as German or at least as partly German (for example, Turkish German) were more likely to have native-born German friends (Jugert et al., 2018).

With permission from Bee Quammie

■ Celebrating Black History Month in February is one way that schools can create a climate where adolescents feel comfortable discussing racial identity.

cultural socialization the way parents teach and communicate their cultural beliefs, customs, values, and behaviors.

Adults can support adolescents' identity development

The search for one's identity can be difficult and stressful. But there are a number of ways adolescents in search of their ethnic identity can be supported by their parents and educators:

- Create a climate at home and in school that makes teens comfortable to talk about and discuss issues related to their ethnicity.

- Give teens opportunities to explore their identity by learning about their ethnic heritage and prominent people from their ethnicity and by attending cultural events.

- Share ethnic customs with children. Teens who experience **cultural socialization**, that is, whose parents teach them their native language, celebrate ethnic customs, and share their ethnic pride, will identify more positively with their ethnic identity than teens whose parents do not share their ethnic customs (Hughes et al., 2006).

Review!

How do adolescents form their identity, and what is the role of their ethnicity and gender?

- Creating an *identity* is a key process in adolescence, but it is not easily accomplished.

- In Erik Erikson's theory of psychosocial development, adolescents are in the fifth stage, in which they either create an identity or remain in a state of identity confusion. If life circumstances and culture permit, teens may take advantage of a *psychosocial moratorium*: This is a period when they do not yet have to take on adult responsibilities and can explore different possibilities for their future life and identity.

- James Marcia built on Erikson's theory by suggesting that adolescent identity formation occurs in stages. In the stage of *identity diffusion*, they are not yet actively exploring possible identities. In *foreclosure*, they accept choices for their future without

exploring alternatives. In *moratorium*, they actively pursue different options without having made a decision yet. In *achievement*, the most advanced status, adolescents have explored different options and have committed to an identity.

- Boys and girls go through the same general process in their identity search, but girls tend to explore and decide on how to create a family earlier than boys do. Girls tend to have lower self-esteem than boys, which impacts their identity formation.

- Adolescents from racial and ethnic minorities face the task of deciding if and how to integrate their culture into their identity. They may form an *ethnic identity*, or possibly a *bicultural identity*, where they feel a sense of belonging to their own ethnic group as well as the majority group. Teens with a positive ethnic or bicultural identity tend to have better mental health and do better in school than those who have a negative ethnic identity.

Practice!

1. In the psychosocial moratorium, _____ .
   a. teenagers commit to an identity
   b. teenagers do not get punished if they violate the law because they are underage
   c. teenagers are relatively free of adult responsibilities and can try out different identities
   d. teenagers develop adult-like critical thinking skills

2. The fifth stage of psychosocial development, according to Erikson, is _____ .
   a. communality vs. inferiority
   b. industry vs. inferiority
   c. self-esteem vs. self-concept
   d. identity vs. identity confusion

3. Teenagers are more likely to develop an ethnic identity if they _____ .
   a. belong to an ethnic minority group
   b. are in the stage of identity diffusion
   c. belong to an ethnic majority group
   d. conform to gender stereotypes

See for Yourself!

Where are you in your own identity development? Many things contribute to our identity, including our political world-view, our religious beliefs, our plans to have (or not have) a family, our hobbies, and the way we view ourselves as different from others, for example. The table below is based on Marcia's view of identity formation. After reading each question, place a checkmark into the box that best describes your own identity status.

	Moratorium	Achievement	Diffusion	Foreclosure
What job or career do you wish to have after finishing college?				
Would you like to marry and/or have children?				
Can you describe what makes your personality unique?				
How well do you know your family history? Does it contribute to how you see yourself?				
Can you describe your political worldview?				
What are your religious beliefs?				
What is your gender?				
What is your sexual orientation?				

16.2 Sexuality

- Explain how sexual orientation develops in teenagers and state when they begin to engage in sexual behaviors.
- Identify the risks of sexual activity in teenagers.

In Chapter 14, we learned about the physical changes that occur throughout adolescence, notably the changes brought about by the onset of puberty. With physical changes comes an increased interest in sexuality and sexual activities. The awakening of adolescent sexuality can be a turbulent time for teens who suddenly experience a range of intense, previously unexperienced emotions.

Sexual Orientation

Teenagers explore their identity in many different areas, such as religion, culture, and race, as well as personal and professional goals. But identity also encompasses sexual aspects (Erikson, 1968). Adolescents' sexual identity involves whether they feel attracted to their own or the opposite sex, or both. But it also encompasses other aspects like teens' sexual activities as well as their interests.

Sexual orientation can change

Adolescents' **sexual orientation** is not quite as fixed as many people believe. A study that followed more than 700 high schoolers for 3 years found that the sexual identity of 19% of the participants changed at least once. For example, they may have identified as bisexual in one year and as gay or straight in

sexual orientation a person's pattern of sexual/romantic attraction to the same gender, opposite gender, or any gender.

■ Teens hold a banner for their school's Gay–Straight Alliance at a Gay Pride Parade. Today, more teenagers identify with a minority sexual orientation, and they often describe their sexuality in very nuanced ways with words that did not even exist until fairly recently. What are some reasons for these changes?

the following year. These changes were more pronounced in girls (26%) than in boys (11%) (Stewart et al., 2019).

Researchers use the term *sexual fluidity* to describe changes in sexual orientation. Research has shown that sexual orientation, like gender identity, can be viewed as a continuum rather than a set of discrete, mutually exclusive categories like *homosexual* and *heterosexual* (Savin-Williams, 2014, 2018). Accordingly, teenagers increasingly describe their sexual orientation in very nuanced ways. One study found that adolescents used more than 100 different words to describe their sexual orientation. Responses included *pansexual* (attraction to people regardless of their sex and gender identity), *monosexual* (attraction to members of one sex only), *sapiosexual* (being attracted to someone's intelligence), *greysexual* (rarely experiencing sexual attraction), *demisexual* (sexual attraction only when one is emotionally connected to a person), and *masexual* (sexual attraction to males) (The Trevor Project, 2019).

Perhaps due to an increasing societal acceptance of various sexual orientations, adolescents increasingly identify with minority sexual orientations. Only 4% of adults identify as homosexual or bisexual compared with 15% of adolescents (Brown, 2017; Gates, 2017; Kann et al., 2018).

Even so, identifying oneself with anything but the majority sexual orientation can be a source of distress: Almost 40% of American LGBT (lesbian, gay, bisexual, and transgender) teens have seriously considered suicide in the previous 12 months. A majority of them feel discriminated against or stated that someone had tried to convince them to change their gender identity or sexual orientation (The Trevor Project, 2019).

Factors that influence the development of sexual orientations

It's Thanksgiving, and brothers Cam and Dru are catching up over a beer before the big meal. "The boys look good," says Cam, nodding in the direction of Dru's two sons, who are chatting on the other side of the room. Sixteen-year-old Alan is having his own reunion with his big brother, Teddy, who's come home from college for the holiday. "Al's looking awful grown up," Cam continues. Then lowering his voice, "Any idea yet if he's got the gay gene like his brother?"

Cam's whispering voice is too loud for Alan not to overhear. He knows it's a tactless question—his uncle has never been discreet—but it keeps coming back to him in the days and weeks after Thanksgiving: *Is* there such a thing as a gay gene?

Psychologists, biologists, and geneticists have contributed greatly to advances in our understanding of human sexuality in recent decades. Yet despite these advances, a great deal of myth and misinformation remains, particularly around what contributes to our sexual orientations.

Genetic factors certainly play a role in shaping sexual preferences. First, identical twins share their sexual orientation more often than fraternal twins do, which is an indicator that genes play a role (Långström et al., 2010; Whitam et al., 1993). Second, researchers have been able to identify a number of specific genes that are correlated with same-sex preferences (Green & Keverne, 2000; Sanders et al., 2015; Wang et al., 2012). However, none of these genes can reliably predict a person's sexuality, so in response to Alan's question, genes are a factor in sexual orientation, but there is no "gay gene."

If genetics does not account entirely for sexual orientation, then what else is at play? Intrauterine factors likely have a role as well. During pregnancy, opposite-sex fraternal twins are exposed to sex hormones of the other sex. Research has found that male fetuses with a female twin are more likely to grow up to develop same-sex preferences than male fetuses with a male twin (Bearman & Brückner, 2002). There may be neurological reasons for different sexual orientations, too: Research has shown that the brain structures of people with same-sex orientations tend to be more similar to people of the opposite sex than is the case with heterosexuals (Cohen-Kettenis et al., 1998; O'Hanlan et al., 2018).

If genetic, biological, and neurological factors all contribute to sexual orientation, does that leave any room for cultural and environmental factors? Studies have shown a positive association between the sexual abuse of children and same-sex sexuality. However, the direction of a causal relationship between maltreatment and same-sex orientation is not clear at this point (Roberts et al., 2013; Xu & Zheng, 2017). Studies investigating the influence of parents' sexual orientation on that of their children have found little evidence that children raised by same-sex parents are more likely to be homosexual themselves than children of different-sex couples (Golombok et al., 2003; LeVay, 2011; O'Hanlan et al., 2018; Pawelski et al., 2006).

Sexual Behavior

American adole-cents are more reluctant to engage in sexual activity than they were even a decade ago. The recent mean age of first intercourse is 17.3 years for girls and 17.0 years for boys (National Center for Health Statistics, 2017), but from 2007 to 2019, the number of high schoolers who had ever had sex decreased significantly (**FIGURES 16.1** and **16.2**). Though the reasons for this development are not entirely clear, teens may be engaging in sexual activities later because they are generally taking longer to enter the phase of adulthood (see also Section 16.5, Emerging Adulthood, below) and are thus delaying a whole range of activities that are associated with adulthood. Additionally, frequent use of media may distract adolescents, leading to less time spent one-on-one and thus less time forging relationships in the real world (Twenge, 2020).

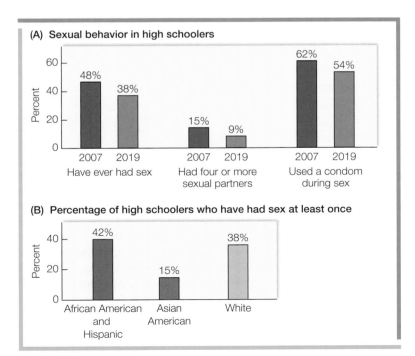

FIGURE 16.1 **(A)** Sexual behavior in high schoolers 2007–2019. Fewer high school students were sexually active in 2019 than were in 2007. When they do engage in sexual intercourse, youth are less frequently using condoms than they did in earlier years. **(B)** Percentage of high schoolers who have had sex at least once, by race/ethnicity. Asian American teens tend to engage in sex later than teens of other races/ethnicities. Why do you think there is such a large difference between Asian Americans and their peers?

Data from Centers for Disease Control and Prevention. 2020. Explore Youth Risk Behavior Survey Questions—United States, 2019. https://yrbs-explorer.services.cdc.gov; L. Kann et al. 2018. *MMWR Surveill Summ* 67: 1–114

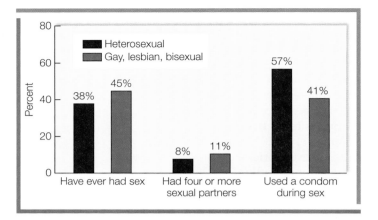

FIGURE 16.2 Sexual behavior in heterosexual and sexual-minority high schoolers. Sexual-minority youth engage in riskier behavior, on average, than do heterosexual youth in all categories. They have sex earlier, have more sexual partners, and use relatively fewer condoms than do their heterosexual peers.

Data from Centers for Disease Control and Prevention. 2020. Explore Youth Risk Behavior Survey Questions—United States, 2019. https://yrbs-explorer.services.cdc.gov; L. Kann et al. 2018. *MMWR Surveill Summ* 67: 1–114

Early sexual activity has risks

Although adolescents today are, on average, delaying their first sexual activity, many parents, along with educators, social workers, and policymakers, are worried about teens having sex at too young an age (Masters et al., 2008). When teenagers become sexually active before age 15, they are more likely to:

- engage in unprotected sex (Heywood et al., 2015; Shrestha et al., 2016);
- become a victim or perpetrator of rape (O'Donnell et al., 2001);
- pay for sex (Shrestha et al., 2016);
- contract sexually transmitted diseases (STDs) (Lee et al., 2015; Shrestha et al., 2016);
- have a higher number of sexual partners, which in turn increases the risk of contracting an STD (Heywood et al., 2015; Shrestha et al., 2016);
- become pregnant (Crosby et al., 2015; Ma et al., 2009);
- experience behavior problems or depression (Spriggs & Halpern, 2008; Udell et al., 2010); or
- end their education after high school (Parkes et al., 2010).

Sex education in schools can help prepare teenagers for sexual encounters and enable them to make more informed choices for themselves. Later in this chapter, we will take a closer look at sex education practices in the United States and around the world.

Why do some adolescents have sex earlier than others?

It is impossible to explain *why* some adolescents have sex before their peers, but researchers have detected some patterns in the demographics of teens who have sex early. Teenagers are more likely to have intercourse at an early age if:

- their parents are less educated;
- they do not live with both of their biological parents;
- they have a poor relationship with their parents;
- they spend more than 2 hours in front of a screen per day; and
- they have behavioral problems or attention-deficit/hyperactivity disorder (Kastbom et al., 2016; Nogueira Avelar et al., 2016; Schofield et al., 2008; Shneyderman & Schwartz, 2013).

Of course, another group of teenagers starts having sex later than their peers. Some of them wait consciously for religious reasons, because they haven't found the right partner, or because they are scared. But when questioned, most teens reply that it just "hasn't happened yet" (Boislard et al., 2016).

An important factor in adolescents' sexual behavior is, not surprisingly, their friends. A meta-analysis of 59 studies including more than 69,000 participants investigated the importance of three factors for teens' sexual activity: peer behavior, peer attitudes, and peer pressure. The researchers found that teens' sexual activity was most strongly influenced by the behavior of their friends, rather than by their friends' attitudes or peer pressure (Van de Bongardt et al., 2015).

A lack of consent can lead to sexual violence

In most American states, the legal age of consent is 16, though there are states where the legal age of consent is 17 or 18 years of age (AgeOfConsent, 2021). Sexual

Culture Counts

Age at First Intercourse by Country

The average age at which young people have sexual intercourse for the first time varies considerably from country to country.

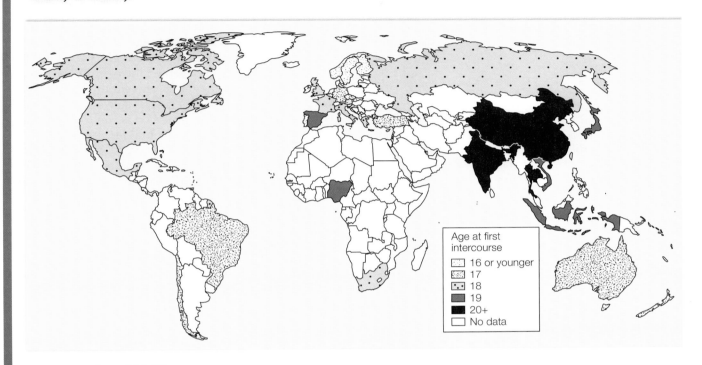

Age at first intercourse
- 16 or younger
- 17
- 18
- 19
- 20+
- No data

Source: Durex Network Research Unit, 2009.

▪ Question

What are some factors that may influence the age at which young people in a country begin to become sexually active?

consent is generally understood to mean **affirmative consent**, which requires the person initiating sexual contact to gain the other party's consent to continue. Affirmative consent must be explicit and voluntary: When a person does not say "no" it doesn't mean they're saying "yes." The concept of affirmative consent might seem straightforward enough, but situations in real life are often messy, and one or both parties may not be sure what it is that they want. Teens may feel pressured or afraid of hurting the other person's feelings (Jacobson, 2021).

A lack of consent can lead to teen dating violence, which includes sexual violence but also comprises physical violence, stalking, and verbal as well as emotional abuse. About 10% of teens aged 12–18 have been affected by teen dating violence, putting them at higher risk of depression, anxiety, and suicidal thoughts, as well as drug abuse (Centers for Disease Control and Prevention, 2021l; Tharp et al., 2017).

Preventing teen dating violence is difficult: A meta-analysis of 38 studies found that current prevention programs are effective at increasing teen's knowledge about dating violence, but they do not decrease the number of teens who get abused (Lee & Wong, 2020).

affirmative consent a person's voluntary and explicit agreement to participate in sexual contact.

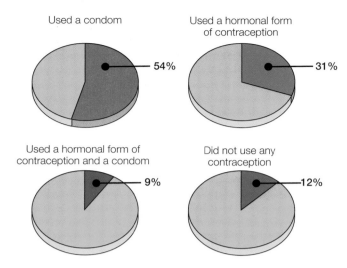

FIGURE 16.3 Contraceptive methods used by high schoolers during their last sexual intercourse (2019). The number of adolescents using condoms is decreasing rather than increasing: In 2003, 63% of high schoolers reported having used a condom during their last sexual intercourse; by 2019, that percentage had fallen to 54%.

Data from Centers for Disease Control and Prevention. 2020. Explore Youth Risk Behavior Survey Questions—United States, 2019. https://yrbs-explorer.services.cdc.gov

Contraception and Teen Pregnancy

For those adolescents who are sexually active, contraception is obviously of utmost importance. There are, at least in theory, a large number of contraceptives available to teenagers. However, for a variety of reasons—including cost, availability, and knowledge of the options—some teens may not have access to efficient contraception.

Different kinds of contraceptives

We can roughly group contraceptive devices and methods into two categories: barrier methods and non-barrier methods (**FIGURE 16.3**). Barrier methods, which work by preventing sperm from reaching the egg, are particularly important, because they help prevent the spread of sexually transmitted diseases (STDs) as well as pregnancy. The most common barrier method is condoms, but other barrier methods, including diaphragms, cervical caps, and contraceptive sponges, are also used. All of these must be used correctly to be effective, and even then they are not 100% reliable. Using a spermicidal cream or foam improves the effectiveness of barrier devices.

Non-barrier methods include hormonal contraceptives, including most notably the birth control pill but also skin patches, implants, and injections, as well as intrauterine devices (IUDs) that prevent the implantation of a fertilized egg. Any of these methods should always be used in combination with a condom to prevent an infection with STDs (American Academy of Pediatrics, 2020).

Teen pregnancies often have far-reaching consequences for mother and child

Although the number of teen pregnancies in the United States has decreased significantly over the past decade, it is still much higher than in many other developed nations (see **FIGURE 16.4**). Black, Hispanic, and Native American

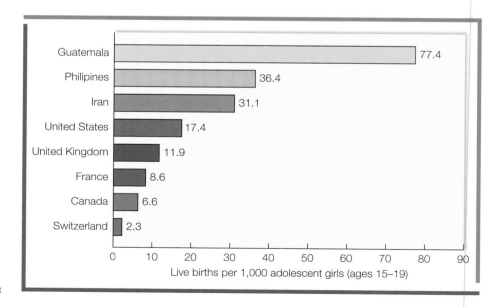

FIGURE 16.4 Live births per 1,000 adolescent girls (ages 15–19), select countries (2018).

Data from UNICEF Data Warehouse. 2021. Indicator: Adolescent birth rate (number of live births to adolescent women per 1,000 adolescent women). https://data.unicef.org

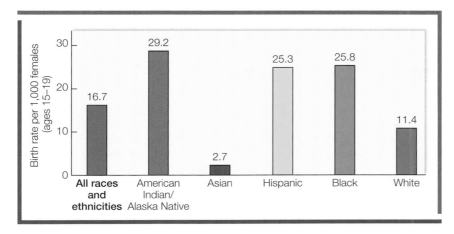

FIGURE 16.5 Birth rates for teenagers in the United States by race/ethnicity. Black, Hispanic, and Native American teens have much higher birth rates than Asian and White teens.

After J. A. Martin et al. 2021. Births: Final data for 2019. www.cdc.gov

girls also have a higher birth rate than White and Asian American girls (see **FIGURE 16.5**).

At some times in human history, it was common for girls to first become pregnant while still in their teens. But today, teen pregnancies are not desirable because

- half of teen mothers do not graduate from high school (Perper & Manlove, 2010),
- teen mothers are more likely to live in poverty and work low-level jobs (Abma & Martinez, 2017),
- teen mothers have a higher risk of pregnancy complications (Kumar et al., 2007), and
- infants born to teen mothers are more likely to be premature or low birthweight and have higher mortality rates (Kumar et al., 2007).

The children of teenage mothers often have negative outcomes in life as well. They tend to do worse in school and are more likely to drop out of high school altogether. They grow up with more health problems and are more likely to become parents in their teens, just like their mothers. They also have a higher risk of being unemployed in early adulthood (Hoffman & Maynard, 2008).

© Antonio Guillem Fernandez/Alamy Stock Photo

■ The number of pregnant teens is relatively high in the United States compared with other industrialized nations. What do you think are some reasons for the high pregnancy rates?

■ What's It Like...

To Experience Teen Pregnancy

Teena, 16 years old

I was 15 years old when I met Paul. He was my first boyfriend. Of course, I knew about birth control and everything. After all, my mom had told me countless times how she had me when she was very young, and that she didn't want the same thing to happen to me. But somehow, I guess we weren't careful enough.

I actually didn't think anything was wrong when I first missed my period, since my periods tend to be a bit irregular. But then I started feeling sick, and when I told my stepsister, who is much older than me and has kids of her own, she took me to the drug store and got me a pregnancy test. And that was that.

My mom didn't say a thing when I told her. She was really quiet, which was kind of scary. My stepdad got angry and called me an idiot (he apologized later). Paul got upset as well. He said he didn't want anything to do with the baby. "It'll ruin our lives," he said; "we're too young for that." He thinks I should have an abortion, but I don't. I mean, my mom was young when she had me. Where would I be if she'd had an abortion?

Last week I had my dating scan, and they said I was 12 weeks and 5 days. I'll never forget that. Afterward, my mom and stepdad sat down with me and talked about what I wanted to do. When I said I wanted to keep the baby, they said they'd support me. I want to finish high school, and I'd like to enroll in our local community college later on if possible. I'll make it work—I'm sure of it—even if Paul isn't involved.

Evita, mother of Teena

I was 17 years old when I had Teena. It was hard back then. I'd dropped out of high school the year before, and I was working part-time and living with my mother. We didn't have much money; we didn't have much food. Thing is, I know that getting pregnant in your teens is like a cycle that can happen to your kids as well, but I just didn't think it was going to happen to Teena because we'd talked about it so much.

When Teena told us she was pregnant, I had flashbacks to what it was like for me, becoming a mom at such a young age. She's determined to keep her baby, and Stephen and I will respect that, but I don't think she has any idea how much her life is going to change.

The good news is that Teena has a good and loving home here. Stephen's strict, but he loves her like I do, and between us, we earn enough for us to have a comfortable life. And I'm determined to make sure things are easier for her than they were for me. I'll take the baby on the days I'm off from work, and my aunt has agreed to step in on the other days, so that Teena can finish high school. I just want her to have a normal life as much as possible, so that her pregnancy doesn't take away her chances at a good future. We will make it work somehow.

Sexually Transmitted Diseases

Sexually transmitted diseases (STDs; also called sexually transmitted infections [STIs]) are infections that are transmitted through oral, vaginal, or anal sexual contact. Across all age groups, cases of STDs are rising in the United States.

People under 25 are particularly susceptible to STDs: They account for about half of the almost 20 million STDs that are diagnosed each year (Centers for Disease Control and Prevention, 2019c).

There are a number of reasons that adolescents are particularly susceptible to STDs:

- They may not have the knowledge necessary to prevent STDs effectively.
- They may not have the money needed to afford condoms and treatment, if necessary.
- Young girls tend to have an increased number of cells on the outside of their uterus that are more susceptible to infections.
- Many STDs do not cause any immediate symptoms (TABLE 16.2), so they can pass on the infection unknowingly (Centers for Disease Control and Prevention, 2020a).
- Teens may hesitate to seek testing because they may lack transportation to treatment facilities, and they may be afraid to seek treatment for confidentiality reasons (Tilson et al., 2004).

HPV, chlamydia, and gonorrhea are the most common STDs

The most common sexually transmitted disease in the United States is human papillomavirus (HPV). In 2014, more than 42% of American adults aged 18–59

■ Table 16.2 Common Sexually Transmitted Diseases

Disease	Prevention	Symptoms	Treatment	Outlook
HPV (Human Papillomavirus) ▶ Viral infection affects 42% of adults aged 18–59	Vaccines are available and recommended for youth 11–12. Condom use recommended	Most people have no symptoms. However, genital warts can develop as well as several kinds of cancer.	There is no treatment for the virus. However, if genital warts or cancer result from the infection those can be treated.	In most cases, HPV goes away without treatment. Untreated HPV can cause genital warts or cancer of the vulva, vagina, penis, anus, or throat.
HIV (Human Immunodeficiency Virus) ▶ Viral infection causes AIDS (acquired immunodeficiency syndrome) and affects 1.2 million people in the United States	Condom use	In some cases, flu-like symptoms 2–4 weeks after infection. However, it can be asymptomatic for a long time. As HIV progresses, it can lead to AIDS, and the patient will develop "opportunistic" infections that attack the compromised immune system.	Cannot be cured but can be controlled with antiretroviral therapy, which prevents HIV from becoming AIDS, and medication reduces the risk of transmission to others.	Delayed treatment will result in harm to immune system, possible infection of others, and a higher risk of developing AIDS, which can lead to death within 3 years.
Chlamydia ▶ Bacterial infection affecting 5% of sexually active young women (total of 539 cases per 100,000 population)	Condom use	Most people have no symptoms. Symptoms include discharge from the vagina/penis and a burning sensation while urinating.	Easily cured with antibiotics	If untreated in females, can lead to chronic pelvic pain and infertility
Gonorrhea ▶ Bacterial infection producing 179 cases per 100,000 population; about half of new cases are among 15- to 24-year-olds	Condom use	Many people do not have symptoms. Symptoms in women include vaginal discharge and bleeding between periods. Symptoms in men include testicular pain and white, green, or yellow discharge from the penis.	Antibiotics can cure the infection but cannot repair physical damage caused by the disease.	If untreated, can cause infertility and serious health problems, including (in women) pelvic inflammatory disease and pelvic pain. Infection can also spread to the blood, which can be life-threatening.
Syphilis ▶ Bacterial infection producing 11 cases per 100,000 population	Condom use	Firm round sores at infection site that last for a few weeks. Later, skin rashes.	Antibiotics	If untreated, the disease can affect organ function and be fatal.
Genital Herpes (HSV-2) ▶ Viral infection affecting 12% of people aged 14–29 (2016)	Condom use to reduce risk of infection. Avoid sexual contact during outbreaks to reduce transmission.	Most people have no symptoms. Symptoms can include blisters on or around genitals or rectum, which can break, leaving painful ulcers that take several weeks to heal; genital pain; and shooting pain or tingling in legs or hips.	There is no cure. Antiviral medication can shorten outbreaks and reduce likelihood of transmission.	Condition can be managed but can cause embarrassment and stigma and thus interfere with intimate relationships.

Sources: Centers for Disease Control and Prevention, www.cdc.gov: Chlamydia—CDC detailed fact sheet (2016); Genital herpes (2017); Syphilis (2017); Genital HPV infection (2019); Gonorrhea (2019); HIV Basics (2020).

were believed to be infected with HPV (McQuillan et al., 2017). In the majority of cases, the infection does not cause any symptoms, so people infected with HPV may pass it on to others unknowingly.

HPV can lead to cervical cancer or genital warts (Doorbar et al., 2012; Saraiya et al., 2015). A vaccine against the virus has been available for more than a decade, and it is recommended for all 12-year-old boys and girls (Petrosky et al., 2015). However, in 2018, only about one-half of all American teenagers had received all recommended doses in the vaccination series (Walker et al., 2019).

Other common sexually transmitted diseases are gonorrhea and chlamydia. Gonorrhea can affect the rectum, genitals, and throat and causes itching, soreness, and discharge. Chlamydia infections usually do not have any symptoms in women, but if left untreated can lead to infertility (Centers for Disease Control and Prevention, 2020c).

■ The United States has a high rate of teen pregnancies compared with other developed countries. Sex education is one way of teaching teens how to prevent STDs and pregnancies. However, many U.S. states do not require that teens be taught about contraceptive methods at school. How can teens be reached and safely as well as effectively educated?

Prevention programs and sex education

The increase in STDs among young people makes prevention efforts extremely important. However, behavior change is never an easy task to accomplish. Two meta-analyses that both looked at samples with a total of around 115,000 participants found that while interventions were successful at increasing condom use and knowledge about STDs, they did not significantly reduce the number of STDs and pregnancies (Mason-Jones et al., 2016; Morales et al., 2018).

Sex education is a critical part of the effort to prevent teen pregnancies and STDs. The Surgeon General's Healthy People 2030 initiative aims for adolescents to receive instruction on delaying sex, birth control methods, and STD prevention (Office of Disease Prevention and Health Promotion, 2021). But the country is falling short of this goal. Fewer adolescents are receiving sex education today than 25 years ago: In 1995, 84% of teens received instruction in birth control methods; in 2019, only 64% received comparable instruction (Lindberg & Kantor, 2021).

Many states in the United States do not have comprehensive requirements for sex education. In 2016, only 33 states required that teens be educated about HIV, and only 18 states required that teens receive information about contraceptive methods. In contrast, 25 states required that abstinence information (that is, that sexual intercourse is delayed until after marriage) be emphasized in sex education. On average, high school courses required only about 6 hours of sex education, and 87% of schools allowed parents to have their children opt out of the instruction (Hall et al., 2016). For comparison, sex education is mandatory in many European countries such as Austria and Germany. Instruction is comprehensive and starts in elementary school (Federal Centre for Health Education, 2018). But ultimately, prevention efforts should focus not only on education but also on providing adolescents access to condoms and healthcare services.

Review!

How does sexual orientation develop, and when do teenagers start to engage in sexual behaviors?

■ *Sexual orientation* is the pattern of a person's sexual, emotional, and romantic attraction

■ Sexual orientation in adolescents is often quite fluid, and they increasingly identify with minority sexual orientations. Among almost one-fifth of adolescents, sexual identity will change at least once.

■ Genes play a role in the development of sexual orientation, as do intrauterine factors. There is no proof that social or environmental factors influence a person's sexual orientation.

■ Young people today are, on average, more reluctant to engage in sexual activity than they used to be even a decade ago. The mean age of first intercourse is 17 years for both boys and

girls. Teens tend to start sexual activities earlier if they come from a poor and less educated household, if they have a poor relationship with their parents, or if they behave antisocially or use drugs.

What are the risks of sexual activity in teenagers?

■ At the same time that adolescents are delaying their first sexual intercourse, they also use fewer precautions when they do. They risk unplanned pregnancy as well as getting infected with sexually transmitted diseases (STDs).

■ Girls who become pregnant as teenagers are at greater risk for dropping out of high school and living in poverty. Their children face those same risks as well and tend to have more health problems than children of older mothers. Compared with other nations, the United States has a relatively higher teen pregnancy rate.

■ Many STDs also do not have symptoms in the short term, although they can have serious long-term health consequences.

Some of the most common STDs in the United States are HPV (human papillomavirus), chlamydia, and genital herpes.

Practice!

1. The number of high schoolers that is sexually active has _____ over recent years.
   a. stayed the same
   b. risen
   c. decreased

2. In the United States, _____ sex education classes.
   a. there is a general mandate that high schools teach
   b. all students must participate in
   c. some states require that abstinence information is featured prominently in
   d. abstinence information is the only contraceptive method featured in

What's Your Position?

The United States has very high teen birth rates compared to many other developed countries. Some people believe this may be partly due to the fact that sex education is legally required in only 29 states and that abstinence is often stressed more than birth control: 37 states require that abstinence be included in the sex education program, whereas only 18 states require that information about birth control be taught. Yet, research has shown that abstinence-only sex education programs do not work. What do you think would be a good approach to sex education?

Additional Resources Online

■ "Texas education officials consider changing state's sex education policy for first time in 23 years," in the *Texas Tribune*

■ "The nuanced push for American sex education," in the *Harvard Political Review*

■ "'Like going back 40 years': dismay as Bolsonaro backs abstinence-only sex ed," in *The Guardian*

■ "Abstinence and abstinence-only education," in *Current Opinion in Obstetrics & Gynecology*

Act It Out!

Dru's doing the laundry, sorting the household's dirty clothes into piles and putting the first load into the washing machine. When he picks up a pair of his son Alan's jeans, a small, square packet slips out of the back pocket. Hmm, he thinks; probably time for a talk . . .

Dru waits till later in the day, when he's got Alan in the car on the drive home from soccer practice. Drawing on the information presented in this chapter, role-play a father–son conversation about sexual health and safety. As Dru, what are the main points you're trying to get across? As Alan, what kinds of questions might you have?

16.3 Relationships

- ■ Evaluate how teenagers' family relationships change throughout adolescence.
- ■ Explain the importance of the various types of peer relations in adolescence.

In adolescence, relationships with peers gain more importance. Friends become an important source of support and advice as well as of companionship. Nevertheless, family relationships have a long-lasting impact on nearly all aspects of a person's life. In this section, we'll examine in more detail adolescents' relationships with their families, peers, and friends.

Parents

Thirteen-year-old Tameka is arguing with her parents. These conflicts have been happening more frequently lately. Tameka feels that she is under constant surveillance from the prying eyes of her mother, whose intrusions into Tameka's life and privacy are not only inappropriate but unwanted and unnecessary. "Where are you going?" she asks every time Tameka leaves the house. "Who are you going out with? Have you finished your homework?" In her mother's world, homework always comes before friends. Tameka feels she doesn't need this level of surveillance; she's perfectly capable of managing things on her own.

Tameka's experiences are not unusual. As children grow into adolescents, they experience changes in attitude, personality, and identity. They will feel increasing need for privacy, autonomy, equality in interactions with their parents and time to spend with friends. These changes will have direct impacts on relationships with their immediate family.

Conflict with parents may temporarily increase

As children grow into adolescents, their desire for independence and "space" can put them at odds with their parents, and the frequency of conflicts increases (Laursen et al., 1998; McGue et al., 2005). Over a short span this is normal: More developed thinking and reasoning skills and a quest for more autonomy lead teens to challenge their parents' authority, which results in more frequent arguments.

Conflicts and negative affect normally decrease in middle adolescence, in both frequency and severity (Kim et al., 2001). Only 14% of teens describe their relationship with their parents as characterized by conflict, and only 25% of parents feel they cannot communicate well with their teens (Child Trends Databank, 2015; Hadiwijaya et al., 2017).

The level of conflict also depends on the relationship children and parents have had throughout their history. Children who have had a good relationship with their parents before adolescence tend to experience fewer relationship problems and conflicts than those who entered adolescence with a history of more troublesome relationships (Laursen et al., 2010; Seiffge-Krenke et al., 2010).

Conflict resolution tends to be more successful when both teens and parents demonstrate *emotional flexibility*, an ability to express a variety of emotions. Rather than getting stuck in negative emotions, emotionally flexible individuals can express their anger and frustration without diminishing their capacity for affection, respect, and empathy (Fogel, 2000; Granic, 2005).

Conflict with parents comes at a cost to adolescents: Teens who have more conflicts tend to have lower self-esteem and more problems at school, experience more sadness and fear, and are more likely to act aggressively or develop substance abuse issues (Dodge et al., 2006; Tucker et al., 2003). These issues, in turn, may lead to more conflict with their parents, resulting in a vicious cycle (Branje, 2018).

The impact of parenting styles and support in adolescence

One cause for increased parent–child conflicts in early adolescence is that children begin to feel that their parents are less supportive of them. As adolescence progresses, they come to feel that their parents are less controlling than they used to be (De Goede et al., 2009).

But actual parenting styles are also of importance. Teens with neglectful or authoritarian

© iStock.com/digitalskillet

■ Over the past months, Warren has had an increasing number of conflicts with his parents who, he feels, are intruding in his life much more than necessary. Is there anything parents and teens can do to reduce the number of their conflicts or to ensure that such conflicts do not get out of hand?

parents report more intense conflicts than do those with permissive parents. The authoritative parenting style tends to produce the best outcomes for teenagers: Teens raised by authoritative parents often have higher self-esteem, are less aggressive, and are more emotionally stable (Perez-Gramaje et al., 2019). They also take more sensible risks, perform better at school, and feel the most bonded with their parents (Bi et al., 2018; Newman et al., 2008; Spera, 2005).

Adolescents still need monitoring

As children grow older and gain more independence, their parents give them increasingly more control. Teens have more freedom to decide when, where, and with whom they spend their time than they did earlier in their lives. However, parents still monitor their children. In fact, three-quarters of parents say that they know their children's friends. Likewise, 90% of 10th graders say that their parents are informed as to where they spend their time after school (Child Trends Databank, 2015). There are socioeconomic differences, however: Only 60% of low-income parents know their children's friends, compared with 84% of parents in higher-income households.

If combined with parental warmth and effective communication, regular monitoring has positive effects like decreased risk taking and substance abuse (Chen et al., 2008; Tobler & Komro, 2010). In ethnic-minority teens, the combination of warmth and monitoring has also been shown to increase academic success (Lowe & Dotterer, 2013).

Culture Counts

Adolescents Raised in Collectivist and Individualistic Families

All adolescents need to develop their independence as they grow older. However, the meaning of independence as well as the timing differ with the family's culture. Earlier in the book we distinguished between *individualistic cultures*, which value personal goals and the interests of the individual, and *collectivist cultures*, which prioritize common values and group goals. Most countries will encompass both cultural types, but individualism is generally seen as the prevailing national culture of countries like the United States, Canada, Britain, and Germany, while collectivism is, broadly speaking, associated with countries of Asia and Central and South America.

Families from individualistic cultures place much more importance on their teens' independence than families from collectivist cultures do. This means that teens from individualistic cultures are both allowed and expected to do things alone earlier than teens from collectivist cultures. For example, White American teens may be allowed to meet up with a friend at the mall at an earlier age than are their Chinese American friends. Teens from collectivist cultures also feel greater obligation toward their family in terms of providing support or being respectful toward their parents (Fuligni et al., 1999).

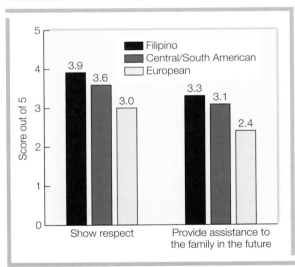

■ **Feelings of respect and obligation of high schoolers toward their families.** Teenagers from different cultures vary in the degree to which they feel obligated toward their family. Teens from collectivist cultures like those in Asia and South America feel a higher degree of obligation than do those from individualistic cultures.

Source: Fuligni et al., 1999

(Continued)

Culture Counts (Continued)

It can be argued that the independence emphasized in Western culture allows adolescents the freedom to explore and achieve a personal identity, but family connectedness is still of tremendous value for teenagers' development. A close connection to family provides teens a sense of identity as well as a support network (Woodman & McArthur, 2018). Adolescents with close, positive family ties tend to have better mental health than do their peers who do not feel connected with their families (Houltberg et al., 2011). Teens with loose family ties are at higher risk for many negative outcomes such as substance abuse, lower self-esteem, and poorer academic achievement (Houltberg et al., 2011; Mueller et al., 2011).

■ Question

Teenagers' interests sometimes collide with those of their parents and families in small and big ways. There may be disagreements on how long a teen can stay out at night, but also over more major issues like which profession to choose. Do you think teenagers with differing cultural backgrounds might handle these conflicts differently? How?

Strategies to successfully navigate challenging times

Although living with teenagers can be stressful and challenging at times, it is also a rewarding time for parents to see their children grow up and gain independence. Conflicts will always be part of family life, but there are a number of things parents and caregivers can do to navigate that difficult time with their maturing adolescents. It is helpful to

- focus on the positive things and concentrate on the relationship they have with their child, rather than just focusing on problems all the time;
- respond flexibly to situations that arise, trying to understand their teens' feelings and motives;
- set limits thoughtfully when they are necessary; and
- realize that everyone makes mistakes, even parents. What matters most is not that parents don't make mistakes, but that they handle their mistakes in a responsible way once they have happened.

© iStock.com/monkeybusinessimages

■ While having siblings comes with its fair share of conflicts, siblings also provide companionship and support throughout turbulent times. If you had a choice, would you rather have siblings or be an only child?

Siblings

Adolescent siblings support each other in ways that adults cannot. More than 40% of adolescents feel that their siblings are a source of companionship and trust (Oliva & Arranz, 2005). Younger siblings often turn to their older siblings for advice (Tucker et al., 2001). Sibling support tends to decrease somewhat during adolescence, perhaps because teens spend increasingly more time with their friends (Kramer et al., 2019). When teens feel supported by their siblings, they tend to have higher self-esteem, a more positive self-concept, and better peer relationships, but they are also more motivated at school (Alfaro & Umaña-Taylor, 2010; Dailey, 2009; Yeh & Lempers, 2004). The effect of sibling support goes beyond adolescence: Young people in emerging adulthood tend to have greater academic achievement when they have felt supported by their siblings during adolescence.

Siblings also provide some protection against adverse life events. One long-term study following children on the Hawaiian island of Kauai found that children who grew up in difficult circumstances involving poverty, divorce, or with mentally ill parents still developed into well-adjusted adults if they had an older sibling who provided support (Werner, 1995).

Sibling conflicts often arise from the difficulties of living within the same household (Campione-Barr & Smetana, 2010; Kramer et al., 2019). But adolescent siblings also engage in relational aggression, and sometimes their actions are intended to hurt their siblings or damage their relationships with peers. This kind of aggression is more often targeted at siblings than at friends (Kramer, 2019; Ostrov et al., 2006; Stauffacher & DeHart, 2005).

Peers

Parents are the most important source of support for young children. But as children grow older, peers become the primary source of support and companionship, and teens will share the intimate details of their life with other teens.

Peer relationships offer a lot of benefits to adolescent growth and development. Through peer friendships, teens learn to accept interpersonal differences and practice prosocial behavior as well as conflict resolution (Bukowski et al., 2011; Shulman et al., 1997). But friendships can also lead to negative behaviors such as substance abuse and delinquency (Albert & Steinberg, 2011).

Interactions with peers happen at different levels. Teens have dyadic friendships with individuals, but they may also belong to *cliques* or even larger groups called *crowds*. We will explore the dynamics inherent in each of these models of peer relationships, beginning with friendships.

Friendships

We have seen in this chapter how friendships help teens figure out their identity and provide companionship and social support (Masten et al., 2012). Almost all teens have at least one close friend, and the majority of them have friends of the opposite gender or belonging to another ethnicity (see **FIGURE 16.6**). After

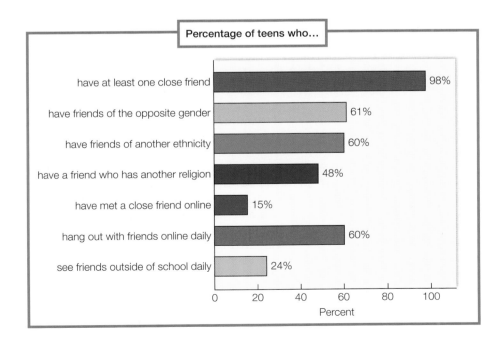

FIGURE 16.6 Friendships are very important to teens, which is also reflected in the fact that almost all teens have at least one close friend. Although teens mostly meet their friends in real life rather than online, they tend to hang out with their friends online more frequently than in person.

Data from M. Anderson and J. Jiang. 2018. Teens, friendships and online groups. www.pewresearch.org

■ Teens from low-income households are more likely not to have a close friend at all (7% vs. 1% from higher-income households), and they are only half as likely as higher-income peers to have more than five close friends.

clique a small group of people connected by a common interest or friendship; they spend time together and do not always allow others to join.

crowd a larger group than a clique; members do not necessarily spend time together; membership is based on reputation or common features.

school, teen friends tend to hang out online more frequently than in person—mostly because they or their friends have too many obligations or are confronted with transportation issues (Anderson & Jiang, 2018).

When it comes to teen friendships, opposites rarely attract. Teens are attracted to peers who resemble themselves in gender, age, ethnicity, attitudes, academic orientation, and hobbies. The less similar friends are to each other, the more likely it is that their friendship will break up at some point (Hartl et al., 2015). Overall, friendships between girls tend to be less stable than friendships between boys (Benenson & Christakos, 2003).

Cliques

Cliques are small groups that consist, on average, of about five or six teens. Like one-to-one friendships, cliques tend to consist of people of the same age, gender, and ethnicity. Clique members are usually connected through friendship or activities they engage in together, like dancing or playing soccer.

Cliques influence teens' behavior in many ways. Members of cliques that behave in positive and helpful ways toward others tend to be less aggressive, anxious, and lonely than members of aggressive cliques (Closson & Watanabe, 2018; Zhao et al., 2016). Likewise, members of cliques that are academically oriented tend to do better at school than those who are members of low-achieving cliques (Chen et al., 2003). When cliques routinely engage in negative behaviors, such as bullying or harassing others, their members are more likely to act in antisocial ways themselves (Ellis & Zarbatany, 2017).

Crowds

In the context of this discussion, the word *crowd* has a very particular meaning, not to be confused with any large gathering of people. **Crowds** are large groups that are socially defined: This means that members of a crowd do not necessarily spend time together, but they are linked together by a shared label or reputation. Membership in a crowd can be based on common features, such as the neighborhood in which teens reside, the music they listen to, or the activities in which they engage. Common types of crowds are jocks (primarily interested in athletics), nerds (introverted and intellectual), populars, loners, and druggies (Crabbe et al., 2019).

As with cliques, identification with a particular crowd can impact teens' behavior. When researchers looked at the substance use of teens and young adults aged 18–34, they found that those who identified as "homebodies" or "religious" were less likely to engage in substance abuse than those belonging to other crowds. "Alternatives" were more likely to use marijuana, whereas "partiers" tended to consume primarily alcohol, tobacco, and e-cigarettes (Moran et al., 2019).

Because certain peer crowds are more likely to engage in risky behavior, public-health campaigns designed to promote a healthier lifestyle among adolescents increasingly target crowds that are otherwise hard to reach. The Fresh Empire campaign, for example, targets the hip-hop peer crowd in an effort to inspire a tobacco-free lifestyle. Their messages are tailored to the values of the hip-hop crowd and interweave social media posts on lifestyle, activities, and social norms with health messages (**FIGURE 16.7**). Additionally, Fresh Empire ambassadors attend local hip-hop events to engage youth one-on-one (Moran et al., 2017). First results indicate the campaign has been positively received by the targeted teens (Guillory et al., 2020).

Conforming to peer pressure has costs and benefits

Tom was hanging out with his friends at the lake. The weather had been cold and gray for a while, so the boys were happy to spend some time outside together again. The lake was frozen, and some of Tom's friends started moving onto the ice. Tom's parents had often talked to him about the dangers of going onto the frozen lake, and he knew he wasn't supposed to go onto the ice. But his friends started taunting and daring him, until finally he decided to join them on the ice. A few minutes later, the ice cracked and one of his friends fell into the freezing cold water. Fortunately, the water level was low and his friend could stand in the water. He eventually got out but he needed to stay in the hospital for a couple days due to severe hypothermia.

Teens like Tom are highly motivated to fit in with their peers. Their relationships are very emotionally involving, and teens tend to experience threats to those relationships as being very serious (Brown & Larson, 2009). Not seldom, their efforts to fit in incur some personal costs—they have to sacrifice fulfillment of some of their own needs and desires to those of the group, submit to a leader rather than being one themselves, and may decide not to assert themselves (Allen et al., 2015; Cohen & Prinstein, 2006). Or they may engage in delinquent activities or take drugs—things that they might not have done if their friends hadn't engaged in that behavior.

Thus, giving in to peer pressure can have some negative effects on teens' behavior and habits. However, efforts to conform ensure close relationships and, as such, also have positive long-term health consequences. Would you have guessed that the quality of relationships at age 13 is predictive of young adults' health at age 25 (Allen et al., 2015)? Although this result may sound surprising, it actually fits in with research in other areas. For example, collectivist culture and behavior (see **CULTURE COUNTS: ADOLESCENTS RAISED IN COLLECTIVIST AND INDIVIDUALISTIC FAMILIES**) have been found to be connected with better health (Talhelm et al., 2014),

FIGURE 16.7 Some teen groups that are hard to reach with regular health messages can be targeted with specific messages that are aimed at their peer crowd and thus have particular appeal to them. Do you know any peer crowds that engage in high-risk behaviors? What features should health campaigns have to appeal to them?

■ At few times in life is the desire to fit in with others as pronounced as during adolescence. The wish to be included in their peer group makes teenagers vulnerable: They may engage in activities they don't truly approve of just to be part of the group. Increasingly, these activities are promoted online as "challenges," where young people are encouraged or dared to record and share videos of their participation in various high-risk stunts. How can teenagers be taught to stand up for themselves even when the perceived cost is high?

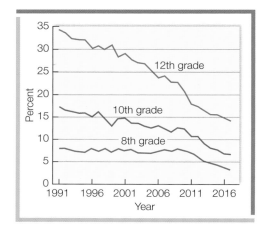

FIGURE 16.8 Percentage of 8th, 10th, and 12th graders who report they date frequently, 1991–2017. While the percentage of teens who date more than once a week among 8th graders has stayed relatively stable, it has declined drastically since 1991 among 12th graders. Why are teens going out so much less frequently than they did just 20 years ago?

After Child Trends Databank. 2018. Dating. www.childtrends.org; data from Monitoring the Future: A Continuing Study of American Youth, 1976–2017. www.monitoringthefuture.org

and even research with primates has shown that the primates experience significant stress when they are separated from their group (Sapolsky, 2004). Although it is not quite clear how relationships and health are connected, youth with good friendships may experience less anxiety and depression, which in turn may lead to better health (Curhan et al., 2014).

Dating

Fourteen-year-old Dalia has a crush on Naveed, a new student who just moved to town and is going to the same school she attends. Dalia's clique of girlfriends has recently grown to include boys, and Naveed has started joining them on their lunch-hour excursions and their after-school trips to the mall. Not so long ago, Dalia would have resented having boys join her peer clique, but being with boys has suddenly taken on a new meaning for her. Although it isn't clear that she will ever form a close relationship with Naveed, his presence in the group and her interest in him give Dalia a chance to practice interacting with members of the opposite sex and forming relationships with them.

Throughout early and middle childhood, children tend to play in same-sex groups. Once they enter adolescence, however, teens start to open up their social circles to members of the opposite sex. Girls enter friendships with boys at an earlier age than boys will make friends with girls, and they may befriend older boys perceived as being more mature (Lam et al., 2014).

As gender relations change, teens think about dating and relationships more frequently, and they discuss these topics with their friends. By age 15, one-half of teens report having had a romantic relationship; among 18-year-olds, 70% have been in a romantic relationship (see also **FIGURE 16.8**). Relationships last longer among older adolescents. In teens under 14, relationships typically last only a few weeks. Among 16-year-olds, relationships tend to last around 6 months, and 18-year-olds often have relationships that last 1 year or longer (Carver et al., 2003).

With age, adolescents become more adept at forming intimate relationships

Intimate relationships are complicated and can be hard to navigate, even for adults. In their quest to become adept at forming and maintaining successful relationships, adolescents go through four stages (Connolly et al., 2014):

■ As teens get older, they are more likely to form friendships with peers of the opposite gender.

1. *Early adolescence (12–14 years).* Teens become increasingly interested in dating and increasingly form groups that consist of members of both sexes. In these groups, teens engage in many activities together, such as going to the movies or attending dances and sports events. More than 80% of teens participate in such activities (Carlson & Rose, 2007).

2. *Middle adolescence (15–17 years).* Activities in mixed-sex groups continue, but teens in the group may now form one-on-one relationships with other group members. These relationships are casual and tend not to last very long. They provide teens with companionship; emotional intimacy is not yet of crucial importance.

3. *Late adolescence (18–20 years).* Increasingly, adolescents search for a partner with a personality compatible with theirs. Relationships last longer, often for 1 year or more (Seiffge-Krenke, 2003). Emotional bonds between the partners become important, and relationships become more exclusive and serious.

4. *Emerging adulthood (21–25 years).* By now, many young adults have acquired the basic skills they need to form long-term relationships with someone else. However, many of them still experience considerable instability in their relationships (Arnett, 2014), often by choice: They delay committing to a partner in order to pursue the career of their choice or to experiment with relationship styles (Dhariwal et al., 2009; Paul et al., 2008).

Breakups are a common experience: The average teen has four relationships in adolescence (Connolly & McIsaac, 2009), so most of them have experienced a split (Connolly et al., 2014). There are few gender differences, but girls tend to experience their relationships as more stable and long-term, whereas boys experience them as more unstable and short-term (Shulman et al., 2009).

Influences on relationship quality

Peer influence increases throughout the teen years, but parents still do have a significant impact on the dating behavior and relationships of their children. In early adolescence, parents play a more direct role by supervising (and possibly even choosing) their children's activities while giving them increasingly more freedom as they get older (Kan et al., 2008). Teens who have a good and close relationship with their parents are likely to also have intimate relationships of good quality (Roisman et al., 2001; Seiffge-Krenke et al., 2001).

Of course, peers play a role in dating as well. In early adolescence, usually the most popular group members open the group to peers of the opposite sex (Franzoi et al., 1994). In these new mixed-sex situations, teens can apply the communication and conflict-resolution skills they have honed with their same-sex peers (Laursen et al., 2001). In late adolescence, teens have generally gained enough self-esteem to defy peer opinions and norms and choose partners that suit their own hopes and needs (Brown, 1999).

Relationships Going Digital

> I can't even tell you how different things are now than they used to be. Sometimes I feel so outdated. When I was young, I hung out with my friends at the mall or in the park. We spent hours together, just chatting, talking about our problems or the guys we had a crush on, or making plans. My daughter is leading a totally different life. Sure, she sees her friends at school, but that's about it. Her free time she mostly spends on her bed glued to screens of various kinds. She says she hangs out with her friends, but I don't know. I feel like she is missing a crucial part of what it means to be a teen.
>
> Cheryl, mom of 15-year-old Sataya

Friendships in the twenty-first century are not only often maintained online; they also increasingly have their beginning in the online world. More than half of teens have met a new friend online, mostly through social media sites like Facebook or Instagram (Lenhart, 2015). Likewise, increasingly more teens search for dating partners online.

Friendships in the virtual realm

Adolescents use digital media to interact with their friends on a regular basis. Almost 90% of teens text their friends at least occasionally, and more than 50%

■ Boys, in particular, like to bond over video games. Is there anything that video games provide to them that interactions in the offline world don't?

of teens do so daily. Instant messaging, email, text messages, video chats, and video games are just some ways adolescents keep in touch. Of particular importance to boys (much more so than girls) are video games: 84% of boys (compared with 59% of girls) play video games with others online (Lenhart, 2015).

Of course, teens also experience challenges using social media. One-half of them have learned about events they were not invited to, and one-fifth have felt worse about their own life after seeing other people's posts. The vast majority of teens believe people share too much about themselves on social media (Lenhart, 2015).

Witnessing the virtual lives of their children, many parents have similar concerns to those of Cheryl. But are teens today indeed lacking the intimacy adolescents of previous offline generations shared with each other? Offline friendships serve a number of functions like self-disclosure, companionship, conflict, and conflict resolution. Can online interactions serve those same functions? It seems the answer is yes. A literature review found that through digital means, conversations can keep going online throughout the day, and teens can take time before they react when distressed if they're not face-to-face with their friend. But of course, rumors also spread a lot faster online than if they are carried face-to-face. Ultimately, the researchers concluded that, particularly since most teens interact with their friends offline as well as online, the digital means of communication add to teens' friendships in unique ways, rather than reducing intimacy (White et al., 2018; Yau & Reich, 2018).

Online dating

Teens are increasingly using dating websites and apps to find partners for both short- and long-term relationships. The number of dating sites has exploded in recent years, and there are platforms designed specifically for teens and catering to every sexual preference. Why are online dating sites so popular? People feel more comfortable sharing information about themselves in an online environment, where they can remain anonymous. Sharing information they might otherwise keep private allows adolescents to meet others with similar interests, preferences, and relationship goals. And because they share more information, and do so more quickly, they create intimacy with others, or the appearance of it, more quickly online than with people they meet offline (O'Sullivan, 2014; Ramirez & Wang, 2008).

Online dating is not without risks. In *cyber dating abuse* (CDA), an individual behaves in an abusive or controlling way online, for example, through arguing, monitoring the partner's activities or location, sending or posting offensive comments or photos, or threatening the partner online (Caridade & Braga, 2020; Draucker & Martsolf, 2010). Studies show that between 5 and 90% of adolescents have been affected by CDA, so at this point it is difficult to draw any conclusions (Brown & Hegarty, 2018; Caridade et al., 2019). In offline dating, around 10% of boys and girls experienced physical violence on a date in 2011 (Centers for Disease Control and Prevention, 2012).

Girls and boys tend to engage in different kinds of aggression: Boys engage more often in direct aggression by threatening their partner or saying offensive things, whereas girls more often engage in indirect acts like monitoring their partner's whereabouts or behavior (Caridade & Braga, 2020; Taylor & Xia, 2018).

Review!

How do teens' relationships with their family change throughout adolescence?

■ One major developmental task of adolescents is to grow increasingly independent of their parents. However, the effort to become more independent and the desire for increased privacy also bring with them increased conflict potential. The number of conflicts with parents rises in the beginning of adolescence but decreases again in mid-adolescence.

■ Most adolescents find they get along with their parents reasonably well, and teens who had good relationships with their parents in the past tend to retain those good relationships throughout adolescence. Parents and teens have to find a balance between parental monitoring and the teens' striving for independence. Generally, regular monitoring has positive effects when parents are warm toward their adolescent and communicate effectively.

■ The time at which parents expect their children to become independent varies depending on the parents' culture. Parents from collectivist cultures usually expect and encourage their children to become independent later than do parents from individualistic cultures.

■ As siblings grow older, the differences in skills between them become smaller and relationships become more egalitarian. Adolescents who have positive and supportive relationships with siblings tend to have better mental health and higher self-esteem and are more motivated at school.

What is the importance of peer relations in adolescence?

■ In adolescence, peers become increasingly more important as a source of support for adolescents. Compared with their relationships with adults, teens have egalitarian relationships with each other, allowing them to practice prosocial behavior and conflict resolution and giving them a source of camaraderie and support.

■ Most teens meet their friends in school, but increasingly they also find friends through online socializing. Due to lack of transportation or busy schedules, a lot of teens can't hang out with each other as much as they would like to, but they stay in touch through digital means like video chats, texting, and social media.

■ *Cliques* are groups of five or six teens that are usually of the same age and gender. Members either are friends with each other or they engage in activities together. *Crowds* are much larger groups of adolescents that are based on factors such as their ethnicity, where they live, or an activity in which they engage. Friends, cliques, and crowds can exert a positive or negative influence on adolescents' behavior.

■ In early adolescence, teens become more interested in dating, but their dating behavior changes as they get older. At first, groups of friends start to open up to the opposite gender, and teens start to date in groups. Successively, relationships become more intimate, longer-lasting, and exclusive. The quality of teens' relationship with their parents is predictive of the quality their intimate relationships have.

Practice!

1. Throughout adolescence, teens strive to become _____ .
   a. more independent of their friends
   b. more connected to their siblings
   c. more independent of their parents
   d. more connected to their teachers

2. Teens raised by _____ parents tend to be more well-adjusted, more emotionally stable, and have higher self-esteem than teens raised by parents with other parenting styles.
   a. authoritative
   b. authoritarian

   c. permissive
   d. uninvolved

3. Teens tend to have intimate relationships of high quality when _____ .
   a. their family lives in a suburban area
   b. their relationship with their parents is good
   c. they are only children
   d. they like to date

See for Yourself!

Go to a mall or another place where adolescents tend to hang out with each other. Take note of the different age groups you see. Are there any differences between younger and older adolescents in terms of group size, activities, gender composition, or other features? Why do you think these differences occur?

Act It Out!

Your younger cousin Beth, who is 17 years old and lives in your neighborhood, has gone through some rather dramatic changes over the past months. Your once polite and sociable cousin suddenly seems rude and rather hostile. She's been hanging out with a group of kids that are known community-wide for small acts of vandalism and doing drugs in the park. You are worried about Beth and want to talk with her. What do you say?

16.4 Juvenile Delinquency

■ Assess why adolescents can exhibit antisocial behavior and the programs meant to prevent it.

On March 1, 2016, a 14-year-old boy walked into a high school at lunchtime in western Ohio and proceeded to the cafeteria. There, he opened fire and injured four students. He then ran out of the school but was soon located by the police and charged with attempted murder.

It wasn't too long ago that there was no such thing as school-shooting drills. Nowadays, these drills are common in schools all over the United States. Students in elementary school up through high school regularly practice lockdowns, barricade windows and doors, and lock themselves in tight bathrooms. Some schools even go as far as simulating unannounced active shooter drills in which masked and armed men burst into classrooms to simulate attacks, leaving children traumatized (Walker, 2020).

juvenile delinquency a variety of actions that break the law and that are committed before a person's 18th birthday.

Of course, school shootings are a rather stark act of violence, and most children do not grow up to be school shooters. **Juvenile delinquency** can take many forms, from vandalism and petty theft to bullying, harassment, and dealing drugs. Adolescents commit more crimes than any other age group: In 2019, 27% of arrests involved youth and young adults up to age 24 (Office of Juvenile Justice and Delinquency Prevention, 2020a).

Criminal psychologists distinguish between early-onset and late-onset antisocial behavior. *Early-onset antisocial behavior* (before age 11) is relatively rare but severe. It has neurological causes, and affected children often have experienced considerable adversity within their family. It continues into adulthood and often leads to negative outcomes like incarceration, sickness, and even early death. *Late-onset antisocial behavior* (at age 11 or older) is often nonviolent. It is relatively common and often situational. Adolescents frequently outgrow it as they become adults (Moffitt, 1993, 2018).

■ The neighborhood in which children grow up influences their development. However, parents often cannot easily relocate to a more affluent or less violent neighborhood for a variety of reasons. What can parents do to help their adolescents to act in consistently prosocial ways if they live in a neighborhood that often provides their children with violent role models?

Causes of Juvenile Delinquency

Youth with antisocial behavior are typically more impulsive than their peers. They have trouble regulating their emotions and do not learn as well from reward and punishment as other teens. Often, they perform poorly at school and come from a low-income family background (Byrd et al., 2014; Waller et al., 2017).

Researchers believe that several brain areas are involved with the development of antisocial behavior. For example, the amygdala and anterior cingulate, which aid in the processing of emotions and threat, may malfunction. Parts of the prefrontal cortex that are involved with reward and inhibition may be involved as well (Blair, 2001; Hyde et al., 2013).

Siblings and peers are a strong influence during adolescence. If they behave in antisocial ways, others are likely to follow their example, even if it is just for fear of being excluded (Huijsmans et al., 2019; Schwartz et al., 2019; Walters, 2019). Likewise, growing up in a neighborhood with high crime rates makes it more likely for adolescents to develop antisocial behavior, as the community provides adolescents with examples of how to misbehave (Rubens et al., 2018).

Preventing Juvenile Delinquency

In the ideal case, prevention of antisocial behavior starts at home. Teens are less likely to become delinquent when parents know where their children spend their time, particularly if the family lives in high-risk neighborhoods (Bendezú et al., 2018; Xiong et al., 2020). Authoritative parenting, in which parents are responsive to their teens' needs while setting high standards, can help encourage teens to not spend time with delinquent companions (Xiong et al., 2020).

It is much more effective to prevent juvenile delinquency than to deal with it later on. Prosocial values are best taught early on, as programs like the Perry Preschool Program show. Participants in this program were followed throughout their lives. The program included the teaching of prosocial values and also provided support to families. When participants were 40 years old, only 28% had been imprisoned, compared with 52% of the control participants (Schweinhart, 2004).

There are many other delinquency-prevention programs in the United States. In its model program guide, the Office of Juvenile Justice and Delinquency Prevention lists 59 effective programs for youth of all ages (Office of Juvenile Justice and Delinquency Prevention, 2020b).

The programs differ considerably. Programs can target individual children and youth, they can be administered to groups in or outside of school, they can target families, or they can be based in communities (Farrington et al., 2017). Community-based programs are particularly effective when community members are involved in the selection of the program—they know the community and its needs best (Evans et al., 2020).

But the most common location for prevention programs to take place is the school. In recent years, social-emotional learning programs are increasingly added to school curricula. These programs do not focus on any one particular skill, but rather on character development as a whole. They include units on communication, goal setting, social interaction, and flexible thinking, for example. Many of these skills directly or indirectly influence delinquency in adolescents. However, more long-term studies are needed to show the effectiveness of these curricula (Evans et al., 2020).

Review!

Why do adolescents act in antisocial ways, and what can be done to prevent antisocial behavior?

■ Teens who act antisocially and harm others, damage property, or break the law in any way are often more impulsive than their peers and have trouble regulating their emotions. Sometimes, teens are influenced in their behavior by siblings, friends, or the neighborhood in which they grow up.

■ It's generally best to prevent delinquency in teens. Parents can teach and model prosocial behavior, use authoritative parenting practices, and request to know where their children are spending their time.

■ There are a number of prevention programs that target individuals, groups, or families, and that are offered at schools or in communities. Often, these programs focus on character development. Their effectiveness differs, but generally the programs work best when they are targeted to the needs of the community where they are offered.

16.5 Emerging Adulthood

■ Define emerging adulthood.

"Becoming an adult" is more of an elusive, sort of abstract concept than I'd thought when I was younger. I just assumed you'd get to a certain age and everything would make sense. Bless my young little heart, I had no idea!

At 28, I can say that sometimes I feel like an adult and a lot of the time, I don't. Being a Millennial and trying to adult is wildly disorienting. I can't figure out if I'm supposed to start a non-profit, get another degree, develop a wildly profitable entrepreneurial venture, or somehow travel the world and make it look effortless online. Mostly it just looks like taking a job that won't ever pay off my student debt in a field that is not the one that I studied. Then, if I hold myself to the traditional ideal of what it means to be an adult, I'm also not nailing it. I am unmarried, and not settled into a long-term, financially stable career.

Maria Eleusiniotis (Beck, 2016)

emerging adulthood the developmental stage between adolescence and adulthood (roughly ages 18–25), characterized by relative freedom from expectations and allowing for exploration of different lifestyles and possibilities.

Becoming adult is not easy. Historically, theorists have believed that adolescence directly gives way to adulthood. But in recent years, developmentalists have suggested another stage of life they called **emerging adulthood**. Throughout emerging adulthood, young adults move toward independence from both family and institutions such as school. Adulthood isn't so much defined by life events such as getting married and moving away from one's parents anymore. Rather, adults are expected to make their own decisions, be financially independent of others, and be responsible for themselves (Arnett, 1998; Scheer et al., 1996).

In industrialized nations, entrance into adulthood has been delayed over the past century. Frequently, careers in the information age require a college education, which adds several years to a person's education. In the United States, college education is also very expensive and often requires the financial assistance of the family, if it is to happen at all (Rifkin, 2011). Youth who are eager to enter the job market right after high school find that there are few work opportunities and that wages are low. Thus, young adults are dependent on their families longer than they used to be (Wood et al., 2018). Many youth use this prolonged period of postponed responsibility to explore different options in terms of career, work, and relationships (Arnett, 2000).

Emerging Adulthood across Cultures

The stage of emerging adulthood differs markedly across cultures. It mostly exists in industrialized nations—few young adults experience this stage in non-industrialized nations such as Ethiopia, Kenya, or Bangladesh. In countries like these, most youth marry around age 20 and soon have children. There are few, if any, educational opportunities that extend beyond the end of their teens. Thus, they have to assume adult responsibilities much earlier than do young adults in developed nations. However, emerging adulthood as a life phase can be increasingly seen in non-industrialized countries such as India, at least among those whose families belong to the middle or upper classes (Arnett, 2020).

Emerging adulthood looks different across various industrialized nations as well. Young adults in Western countries, for example, believe that one of the goals of adulthood is to become financially independent of their parents. Asian young adults, however, feel that adults should be able to financially support their family (Nelson et al., 2004). In collectivist countries, young adults' explorations of career paths and identity may also be more constrained by the wishes of their family, at least compared with individualistic Western cultures (Rosenberger, 2007).

But the end of adolescence does not mean independence and freedom from all the factors, good and bad, that used to influence children's and adolescents' development and well-being. Parents continue to play a crucial role. Having had a positive relationship with one's parents in childhood provides a basis on which good relationships with others later in life can grow as well (Mikulincer & Shaver, 2009). Parental support also leads to higher self-esteem (Ryan & Lynch, 1989). The children of divorced couples may have trouble in forming stable intimate relationships once they are adults themselves, and if parents marry and have children early in life and do not have sufficient financial resources as a result, they may not be able to afford to pay for college for their children (Cherlin et al., 1998; Jacquet & Surra, 2001), thus influencing the future earning potential of their children.

■ Emerging adulthood is a phase of life that not all are afforded the opportunity to experience. Is it a phase of life that you believe ideally all young adults should experience? Or might it be advantageous in some ways to start adulthood earlier in life?

Of particular influence are good relationships with adults who can serve as role models and mentors, guiding young adults in their exploits and planning (Arnett, 2005; Miller et al., 2015). For example, among girls who became pregnant in adolescence and thus are at high risk for living in poverty and not finishing their education, many of those who had positive relationships with adults were able to turn their life around and improve their life circumstances (Phelps et al., 2002).

Unfortunately, the negative life experiences that many children have to endure early on cast a shadow on their future as young adults as well. Growing up in poor circumstances contributes to a poorer quality of life as adults (Aquilino, 1994). People with few financial resources tend to be in worse health than those with more money. Their quality of life is frequently lower as well, simply because they are not able to afford any of those things that make life easier and more convenient and that enhance one's chances to get ahead in life (Kim et al., 2016; Miller et al., 2015; Wadsworth et al., 2016).

Cognitive and Identity Development

The brain continues to mature throughout emerging adulthood. A mature brain as well as the ability for flexible decision-making and for carefully weighing all options helps young adults make sound decisions as they build their adult lives. Emergent adults are increasingly better able to delay gratification and to focus on important information while excluding distractions. Better emotion regulation and problem-solving skills help young adults to solve relationship conflicts in more mature ways.

However, not all young adults have had the opportunity for ideal physical and cognitive development. Adverse childhood conditions may have led to suboptimal development, health problems, and impairments in cognitive development. These young adults are more poorly equipped to face the challenges that life presents them. They are more likely to not finish their education, to engage in impulsive behavior, to become delinquent, or to become addicted to substances (Wood et al., 2018). Not surprisingly, resilience (the ability to adapt and react to stressful life events) is higher among young adults who look toward the future with optimism and have more cognitive resources.

Culture Counts

Median Age at First Marriage

The age at which people first marry decreased considerably from 1890 to the 1950s, only to rise again from then on.

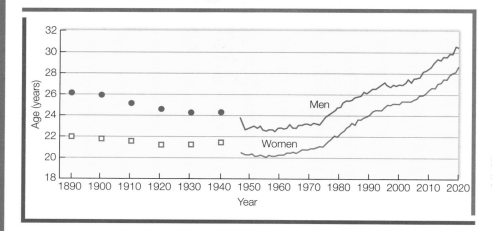

■ **Median age at first marriage, 1890–2020.** *Source*: U.S. Census Bureau, Decennial Censuses, 1890 to 1940 (dots), and Current Population Survey, Annual Social and Economic Supplements, 1947 to 2020 (solid lines). *Note*: Starting in 2019, estimates for marriages now include same-sex married couples.

From U.S. Census Bureau. 2021. Decennial Censuses, 1890 to 1940, and Current Population Survey, Annual Social and Economic Supplements, 1947 to 2021. www.census.gov

■ Question

Why do you think the average age at marriage was lower in the 1950s than in 1890? And why has it started to increase from then on until today? What do you think is the reason that men marry later, on average, than women?

Identity development continues beyond adolescence as well. Young adults continually explore the roles they can take on in society and explore the characteristics that make them unique (Wood et al., 2018).

But development does not stop with the end of emerging adulthood. The whole human life span is marked by change and development, sometimes for the better and sometimes for the worse. Recent research has shown that personality traits keep developing throughout adulthood (Leszko et al., 2016; Reitz & Staudinger, 2017), and some cognitive skills like general knowledge and vocabulary keep improving through people's 60s or 70s (Salthouse, 2016). Improved health and financial stability allow people in older adulthood to live fulfilled and meaningful lives. Ultimately, human life is development from the very beginning to its very end.

Review!

What is emerging adulthood?

- Emerging adulthood is a relatively new stage of life between the ages of 18 and 25 during which young adults are relatively free from adult expectations and can explore different lifestyles and options for work, relationships, and worldviews.

- We mostly find emerging adulthood in developed nations where young adults have the choice to pursue further education and are not required to contribute to their family's income.

- Even beyond adolescence, parents and mentors serve an important role in young adults' lives by guiding and supporting them.

- Development does not stop with the end of adolescence but continues throughout the life span. The brain matures throughout emerging adulthood, and identity as well as personality continue to develop throughout a person's life.

Shenandoah 1 year later

It has been a big year for Shenandoah. During the school year she kept up her research into the history and culture of the Oneida people in New York. Much of this research was done on her own time, online, but she was given permission to work her research into a project for her ninth grade history class, and her work received honorable mention in her class's year-end history fair. She was only too proud to tell anyone who stopped by the display about her Native American ancestry. She even showed off some of her newly learned Oneida language!

The following summer, her father took her to Oneida, New York, where she spent 2 weeks meeting members of the community and learning firsthand about Oneida culture. She even spent time volunteering at the community center, helping run programs for younger kids. It was immensely rewarding. She became close friends with one of the staff there, Leanna. Leanna identifies as "two-spirit," viewing the world through male and female eyes and not belonging exclusively to either gender. It's fascinating for Shenandoah, who had never heard the term before meeting Leeana.

For Shenandoah, the world feels as though it is opening up for her. She has learned so much about herself over the past year and sees new paths to explore all around her. As she reflects on her life during the car trip home with her father, something funny occurs to her: She is now Shenandoah, and nobody calls her just Doah anymore. ■ ▪ ■ ▪

References

Chapter 1

Annie E. Casey Foundation. (2019). Children in poverty by race and ethnicity in the United States. Retrieved from https://datacenter.kidscount.org/data/tables/44-children-in-poverty-by-race-and-ethnicity?loc=1&loct=1#//any/false/any/any/any.

Annie E. Casey Foundation. (2019). Children in poverty (100 percent poverty) in the United States. Retrieved from https://datacenter.kidscount.org/data/tables/43-children-in-poverty-100-percent-poverty#detailed/2/2-53/false/869,11/any/321,322.

Arnett, J. J., & Tanner, J. L. (2016). The emergence of emerging adulthood: The new life stage between adolescence and young adulthood. In *Routledge Handbook of Youth and Young Adulthood* (pp. 50–56). Routledge.

Baker, E. H. (2014). Socioeconomic status, definition. In *The Wiley Blackwell Encyclopedia of Health, Illness, Behavior, and Society*. John Wiley & Sons, Ltd.

Blease, C. (2015). Too many 'friends,' too few 'likes'? Evolutionary psychology and 'Facebook depression.' *Review of General Psychology, 19*(1), 1.

Bradley, R. H., & Corwyn, R. F. (2002). Socioeconomic status and child development. *Annual Review of Psychology, 53*(1), 371–399.

Brittingham, A. & de la Cruz, G. P. (2004). *Ancestry: 2000.* Census 2000 Brief. U.S. Department of Commerce Economics and Statistics Administration, U.S. Census Bureau, Washington, DC.

care.org. (2017). Child poverty. Retrieved from www.care.org/work/poverty/child-poverty.

Centers for Disease Control and Prevention. (2009). Milestone moments. Retrieved from www.cdc.gov/ncbddd/actearly/pdf/parents_pdfs/milestonemomentseng508.pdf.

Chen, Y., & Thomson, D. (2021). Child poverty increased nationally during COVID, especially among Latino and Black children. Retrieved from www.childtrends.org/publications/child-poverty-increased-nationally-during-covid-especially-among-latino-and-black-children.

Child Trends Databank. (2016). Children in poverty. Retrieved from www.childtrends.org/?indicators=children-in-poverty.

Cohn, D. (2016). *It's official: Minority babies are the majority among the nation's infants, but only just.* Retrieved from www.pewresearch.org/fact-tank/2016/06/23/its-official-minority-babies-are-the-majority-among-the-nations-infants-but-only-just/.

Cohn, D., & Caumont, A. (2016). 10 demographic trends that are shaping the U.S. and the world. Retrieved from www.pewresearch.org/fact-tank/2016/03/31/10-demographic-trends-that-are-shaping-the-u-s-and-the-world/.

Common Sense Media. (2013). Zero to eight: Children's media use in America 2013. Retrieved from www.commonsensemedia.org/research/zero-to-eight-childrens-media-use-in-america-2013.

Consumer Insights Microsoft Canada. (2015). Attention spans. Retrieved from https://dl.motamem.org/microsoft-attention-spans-research-report.pdf.

Dahl, G. B., & Lochner, L. (2005). The impact of family income on child achievement: Evidence from the earned income tax credit. Retrieved fromhttps://ideas.repec.org/p/iza/izadps/dp6613.html.

de Leon, L. (2012). *Socializing attention: Directive sequences, participation, and affect in a Mayan family at work.* (Unpublished manuscript). Mexico D. F., Mexico.

Dimock, M. (2019). Defining generations: Where Millennials end and Generation Z begins. *Pew Research Center, 17*(1), 1–7.

Edin, K. J., & Shaefer, H. L. (2015). *$2.00 a day: Living on almost nothing in America*: Houghton Mifflin Harcourt.

Feldman, R. S. (2016). Child Development, 7th Ed. Pearson, New York.

Felt, L., & Robb, M. (2016). Technology addiction: Concern, controversy, and finding a balance. Common Sense Media.

Gates, G. J. (2011). *Family formation and raising children among same-sex couples.* Retrieved from https://williamsinstitute.law.ucla.edu/wp-content/uploads/Gates-Badgett-NCFR-LGBT-Families-December-2011.pdf.

Gibbs, B. G., Shah, P. G., Downey, D. B., & Jarvis, J. A. (2016). The Asian American advantage in math among young children: The complex role of parenting. *Sociological Perspectives*, 0731121416641676.

Hewlett, B. L. (2013). *Listen, here is a story: Ethnographic life narratives from Aka and Ngandu women of the Congo Basin.* Oxford University Press.

Hewlett, B. S., Fouts, H. N., Boyette, A. H., & Hewlett, B. L. (2011). Social learning among Congo Basin hunter–gatherers. *Philosophical Transactions of the Royal Society B: Biological Sciences, 366*(1567), 1168–1178.

Hinduja, S., & Patchin, J. W. (2019). *Summary of Our Cyberbullying Research (2007–2019).* Retrieved from https://cyberbullying.org/2019-cyberbullying-data.

Howard, A. (1970). *Learning to be Rotuman: Enculturation in the South Pacific.* New York: Teachers College Press.

Jacobsen, L. A. (August 18, 2020). Digital and Economic Divides Put U. S. Children at Greater Educational Risk Due to During the COVID-19 Pandemic. Retrieved from https://www.prb.org/resources/economic-and-digital-divide/.

Jones, N. B., Hawkes, K., & O'Connell, J. F. (1996). The global process and local ecology: How should we explain differences between the Hadza and the !Kung. *Cultural diversity among twentieth-century foragers: An african perspective*, 159–187.

Konrath, S. H., O'Brien, E. H., & Hsing, C. (2011). Changes in dispositional empathy in American college students over time: A meta-analysis. *Personality and Social Psychology Review, 15*(2), 180–198.

Lancy, D. F. (2015). *The anthropology of childhood: Cherubs, chattel, changelings*: Cambridge University Press.

Lenhart, A. (2015). Teens, social media & technology overview 2015. *Pew Research Center, 9*.

Marchand, T. (2013). *Minaret building and apprenticeship in Yemen*: Routledge.

Marlowe, F. (2010). *The Hadza: Hunter-gatherers of Tanzania* (Vol. 3): University of California Press.

O'Donnell, K. J., & Meaney, M. J. (2020). Epigenetics, development, and psychopathology. *Annual Review of Clinical Psychology, 16*, 327–350.

Onwuachi-Willig, A. (2016). Race and racial identity are social constructs. Retrieved from www.nytimes.com/roomfordebate/2015/06/16/how-fluid-is-racial-identity/race-and-racial-identity-are-social-constructs.

Oxford University Press. (2018). *Oxford English Dictionary. digital*. Oxford, UK: Oxford University Press.

Pauker, K., Meyers, C., Sanchez, D. T., Gaither, S. E., & Young, D. M. (2018). A review of multiracial malleability: Identity, categorization, and shifting racial attitudes. *Social and Personality Psychology Compass, 12*(6), e12392.

Pew Research Center. (May 29, 2013). Breadwinner Moms. Retrieved from https://www.pewresearch.org/social-trends/2013/05/29/chapter-4-single-mothers/.

Pew Research Center. (May 7, 2015). Childlessness Falls, Family Size Grows Among Highly Educated Women. Retrieved from https://www.pewresearch.org/social-trends/2015/05/07/childlessness-falls-family-size-grows-among-highly-educated-women/.

Pew Research Center. 2015. Modern Immigration Wave Brings 59 Million to U.S., Driving Population Growth and Change Through 2065: Views of Immigration's Impact on U.S. Society Mixed. Washington, DC: September.

Pew Research Center. (May 2020). As Millennials Near 40, They're Approaching Family Life Differently Than Previous Generations. Retrieved from https://www.pewresearch.org/social-trends/2020/05/27/as-millennials-near-40-theyre-approaching-family-life-differently-than-previous-generations/.

Population Reference Bureau. Digital Divide Dashboard: U.S. School-Age Children at Educational Risk Due to COVID-19 Pandemic. Retrieved from https://assets.prb.org/maps/digital-divide-071720.html.

Ratcliffe, C. E., & McKernan, S.-M. (2012). Child poverty and its lasting consequence. Washington, DC: The Urban Institute.

Reichetzeder, C. (2021). Overweight and obesity in pregnancy: Their impact on epigenetics. *European Journal of Clinical Nutrition*, 1–13.

Rideout, V. (2015). *The common sense census: Media use by tweens and teens*. San Francisco, CA: Common Sense Media.

Rideout, V., & Robb, M. B. (2019). *The Common Sense Census: Media use by teens and tweens*. San Francisco, CA: Common Sense Media.

Rogoff, B., Sellers, M. J., Pirrotta, S., Fox, N., & White, S. H. (1975). Age of assignment of roles and responsibilities to children. *Human Development, 18*(5), 353–369.

Rzehak, P., Saffery, R., Reischl, E., Covic, M., Wahl, S., Grote, V., . . . Closa-Monasterolo, R. (2016). Maternal smoking during pregnancy and DNA-methylation in children at age 5.5 years: Epigenome-wide-analysis in the European Childhood Obesity Project (CHOP)-study. *PloS one, 11*(5), e0155554.

Smith, C. J., & Ryckman, K. K. (2015). Epigenetic and developmental influences on the risk of obesity, diabetes, and metabolic syndrome. *Diabetes, metabolic syndrome and obesity: Targets and therapy, 8*, 295.

Sternberg, R. J., Grigorenko, E. L., & Kidd, K. K. (2005). Intelligence, race, and genetics. *American Psychologist, 60*(1), 46.

Tishkoff, S. A., & Kidd, K. K. (2004). Implications of biogeography of human populations for 'race' and medicine. *Nature Genetics, 36*, S21–S27.

U.S. Census Bureau. (2018). American Community Survey. U.S. Census Bureau, Washington, DC.

U.S. Census Bureau. (2021). Poverty Thresholds. Retrieved from www.census.gov/data/tables/time-series/demo/income-poverty/historical-poverty-thresholds.html.

UNICEF Innocenti Research Centre. (2012). *Measuring child poverty*. Retrieved from www.unicef-irc.org/publications/pdf/rc10_eng.pdf.

White House. (2013). Education—Early Learning. Retrieved from https://obamawhitehouse.archives.gov/realitycheck/issues/education/early-childhood.

Whiting, J. W. M. (1941). Becoming a Kwoma: Teaching and learning in a New Guinea tribe. Yale University. Institute of Human Relations.

Yoon, S., Kleinman, M., Mertz, J., & Brannick, M. (2019). Is social network site usage related to depression? A meta-analysis of Facebook–depression relations. *Journal of Affective Disorders, 248*, 65–72.

Chapter 2

Ahern, T. P., Sprague, B. L., Farina, N. H., Tsai, E., Cuke, M., Kontos, D., & Wood, M. E. (2021). Lifestyle, behavioral, and dietary risk factors in relation to mammographic breast density in women at high risk for breast cancer. *Cancer Epidemiology and Prevention Biomarkers, 30*(5), 936–944.

Ainsworth, M. S., & Bowlby, J. (1991). An ethological approach to personality development. *American Psychologist, 46*(4), 333.

Algood, C. L., Harris, C., & Hong, J. S. (2013). Parenting success and challenges for families of children with disabilities: An ecological systems analysis. *Journal of Human Behavior in the Social Environment, 23*(2), 126–136.

Amato, K. R., Mallott, E. K., D'Almeida Maia, P., & Savo Sardaro, M. L. (2021). Predigestion as an evolutionary impetus for human use of fermented food. *Current Anthropology, 62*(S24), S000–S000.

Ariès, P. (1962). *Centuries of childhood: A social history of family life*. New York: Knopf.

Azzopardi, C., Shih, C. S.-Y., Burke, A. M., Kirkland-Burke, M., Moddejonge, J. M., Smith, T. D., & Eliav, J. (2021). Supporting survivors of child sexual abuse during the COVID-19 pandemic: An ecosystems approach to mobilizing trauma-informed telemental healthcare. *Canadian Psychology/Psychologie canadienne* 63(1), 43–55. https://dx.doi.org/10.1037/cap0000298.

Bandura, A. (2011). Social cognitive theory. In P. A. M. V. Lange, A. W. Kruglanski, & E. T. Higgins (Eds.), *Handbook of theories of social psychology* (Vol. 2012, pp. 349–373). Thousand Oaks, CA: Sage.

Bandura, A. (2016). The power of observational learning through social modeling. In R. J. Sternberg, S. T. Fiske, & D. J. Foss (Eds.), *Scientists making a difference: One hundred eminent behavioral and brain scientists talk about their most important contributions* (pp. 235–239). New York: Cambridge University Press.

Bandura, A. (2019). Applying theory for human betterment. *Perspectives on Psychological Science, 14*(1), 12–15.

Boonzaaijer, M., Suir, I., Mollema, J., Nuysink, J., Volman, M., & Jongmans, M. (2021). Factors associated with gross motor development from birth to independent walking: A systematic review of longitudinal research. *Child: Care, Health and Development, 47*(4), 525–561.

Bril, B. (1988). Bain et gymnastique neonatale: Enfants Bambara du Mali (Motion Picture). *France: Centre d'Etude des Processus Cognitifs et du Langage Ecole des Hautes Etudes en Sciences Socieles.*

Bronfenbrenner, U. (1995). Developmental ecology through space and time: A future perspective. In P. Moen, J. G. H. Elder, & K. Luscher (Eds.), *Examining lives in context: Perspectives on the ecology of human development* (Vol. 619, pp. 647). Washington, DC: American Psychological Association.

Bronfenbrenner, U. (2005). *Making human beings human: Bioecological perspectives on human development.* Thousand Oaks, CA: Sage.

Brubaker, J. (2016). Cognitive development theory. *The Wiley Blackwell encyclopedia of family studies.*

Burke, D. (2014). Why isn't everyone an evolutionary psychologist? *Frontiers in Psychology, 5*, 910.

Carraher, T. N., Carraher, D. W., & Schliemann, A. D. (1985). Mathematics in the streets and in schools. *British Journal of Developmental Psychology, 3*(1), 21–29.

Cauda, F., Costa, T., Nani, A., Fava, L., Palermo, S., Bianco, F., . . . Keller, R. (2017). Are schizophrenia, autistic, and obsessive spectrum disorders dissociable on the basis of neuroimaging morphological findings?: A voxel-based meta-analysis. *Autism Research, 10*(6), 1079–1095.

Chang, S. (2021). Supporting expansive learning in preservice bilingual teachers' zone of proximal development of the activity system: An analysis of a four-field model trajectory. *Professional Development in Education, 47*(2–3), 225–242.

Child psychology. (2017). In *Encyclopedia Brittanica Online.*

Conroy-Beam, D., & Buss, D. M. (2018). Why is age so important in human mating? Evolved age preferences and their influences on multiple mating behaviors. *Evolutionary Behavioral Sciences, 13*(2), 127–157.

Darwin, C. (1859). *On the Origin of Species.* John Murray, London.

Erikson, E. H., & Erikson, J. M. (1998). *The life cycle completed (extended version).* WW Norton & Company.

Foreyt, J. P., & Johnston, C. A. (2016). Behavior modification and cognitive therapy. In J. Mechanick & R. Kushner (Eds.), *Lifestyle medicine* (pp. 129–134): Springer.

Fox, A., Palmer, R., & Davies, P. (2002). Do "Shufflebottoms" bottom shuffle? *Archives of Disease in Childhood, 87*(6), 552–554.

Franklin, P., Volk, A. A., & Wong, I. (2018). Are newborns' faces less appealing? *Evolution and Human Behavior, 39*(3), 269–276.

Freud, S. (1917). *Vorlesungen zur Einführung in die Psychoanalyse.* H. Heller.

G. Stanley Hall. (2017). In *Encyclopedia Brittanica Online.*

Gathercole, S. E. (1998). The development of memory. *Journal of Child Psychology and Psychiatry, 39*(1), 3–27.

Giudice, M. D., Gangestad, S. W., & Kaplan, H. S. (2015). Life history theory and evolutionary psychology. In *The handbook of evolutionary psychology* (pp. 1–27). Wiley.

Graziano, P. A., & Hart, K. (2016). Beyond behavior modification: Benefits of social–emotional/self-regulation training for preschoolers with behavior problems. *Journal of School Psychology, 58*, 91–111.

Hulme, J. (2004). Critical evaluation: A student guide. *Psychology Review, 10*(4), 6–8.

Jablonski, N. G., & Chaplin, G. (2010). Human skin pigmentation as an adaptation to UV radiation. *Proceedings of the National Academy of Sciences*, 200914628.

Jablonski, N. G., & Chaplin, G. (2017). The colours of humanity: The evolution of pigmentation in the human lineage. *Phil. Trans. R. Soc. B, 372*(1724), 20160349.

Karasik, L. B., Adolph, K. E., Tamis-LeMonda, C. S., & Bornstein, M. H. (2010). WEIRD walking: Cross-cultural research on motor development. *Behavioral and Brain Sciences, 33*(2–3), 95–96.

Kärtner, J., Crafa, D., Chaudhary, N., & Keller, H. (2016). Reactions to receiving a gift—Maternal scaffolding and cultural learning in Berlin and Delhi. *Child Development, 87*(3), 712–722.

Kholiq, A. (2020). How is Piaget's theory used to test the cognitive readiness of early childhood in school? *Indonesian Journal of Early Childhood Education Studies, 9*(1), 24–28.

Kostogriz, A., & Veresov, N. (2021). The zone of proximal development and diversity. In *Oxford research encyclopedia of education.* Oxford University Press.

Kotlarczyk, M. P., Perera, S., Ferchak, M. A., Nace, D. A., Resnick, N. M., & Greenspan, S. L. (2017). Vitamin D deficiency is associated with functional decline and falls in frail elderly women despite supplementation. *Osteoporosis International, 28*(4), 1347–1353.

Kremer, W. (2014). What medieval Europe did with its teenagers. Retrieved from www.bbc.com/news/magazine-26289459.

Larsen, P. H. H., Bendixen, M., Grøntvedt, T. V., Kessler, A. M., & Kennair, L. E. O. (2021). Investigating the emergence of sex differences in jealousy responses in a large community sample from an evolutionary perspective. *Scientific Reports, 11*(1), 1–9.

Lorenz, K. (2002). *On aggression*: Psychology Press.

Lourenço, O. M. (2015). Piaget's legacy to human development. *World Journal of Behavioral Science, 1*, 53–65.

Lourenço, O. M. (2016). Developmental stages, Piagetian stages in particular: A critical review. *New Ideas in Psychology, 40,* 123–137.

Lucock, M. D., Jones, P. R., Veysey, M., Thota, R., Garg, M., Furst, J., . . . Jablonski, N. G. (2021). Biophysical evidence to support and extend the vitamin D–folate hypothesis as a paradigm for the evolution of human skin pigmentation. *American Journal of Human Biology,* e23667.

Luoto, S., & Varella, M. A. C. (2021). Pandemic leadership: Sex differences and their evolutionary–developmental origins. *Frontiers in Psychology, 12,* 618.

Mahy, C. E., Mohun, H., Müller, U., & Moses, L. J. (2016). The role of subvocal rehearsal in preschool children's prospective memory. *Cognitive Development, 39,* 189–196.

Martin, G., & Pear, J. (2019). *Behavior modification: What it is and how to do it*: Routledge.

Mooney, C. G. (2013). *Theories of childhood: An introduction to Dewey, Montessori, Erikson, Piaget & Vygotsky*: Redleaf Press.

Pereira, V., de Castro-Manglano, P., & Esperon, C. S. (2016). Brain development in attention deficit hyperactivity disorder: A neuroimaging perspective review. *European Psychiatry, 33,* S357.

Pesciarelli, F., Leo, I., & Serafini, L. (2021). Electrophysiological correlates of unconscious processes of race. *Scientific Reports, 11*(1), 1–12.

Puts, D. (2016). Human sexual selection. *Current Opinion in Psychology, 7,* 28–32.

Radhakrishnan, R., Elsaid, N. M., Sadhasivam, S., Reher, T. A., Hines, A. C., Yoder, K. K., . . . Wu, Y.-C. (2021). Resting state functional MRI in infants with prenatal opioid exposure—a pilot study. *Neuroradiology, 63*(4), 585–591.

Rajvanshi, N., Bhakat, R., Saxena, S., Rohilla, J., Basu, S., Nandolia, K. K., . . . Chacham, S. (2021). Magnetic resonance spectroscopy in children with developmental delay: Time to look beyond conventional magnetic resonance imaging (MRI). *Journal of Child Neurology, 36*(6), 440–446.

Riccitelli, G. C., Pagani, E., Meani, A., Valsasina, P., Preziosa, P., Filippi, M., & Rocca, M. A. (2020). Cognitive impairment in benign multiple sclerosis: A multiparametric structural and functional MRI study. *Journal of Neurology, 267*(12), 3508–3517.

Rosenberg, K. R. (2021). The Evolution of human infancy: Why it helps to be helpless. *Annual Review of Anthropology, 50,* 423–440.

Santrock, J. W. (1992). *Child Development: An Introduction,* 5th ed. Wm. C. Brown, Dubuque, IA.

Sternberg, R. J. (2004). Culture and intelligence. *American Psychologist, 59*(5), 325–338.

Sternberg, R. J., & Grigorenko, E. L. (2002). *Dynamic testing: The nature and measurement of learning potential.* Cambridge University Press.

Sternberg, R. J., Nokes, K., Geissler, P. W., Prince, R., Okatcha, F., Bundy, D. A., & Grigorenko, E. L. (2001). The relationship between academic and practical intelligence: A case study in Kenya. *Intelligence, 29,* 401–418.

Storhaugh, C. L., Fosse, S. K., & Fadnes, L. T. (2017). Country, regional, and global estimates for lactose malabsorption in adults: a systematic review and meta-analysis. *The Lancet: Gastroenterology & Hepatology 2*(10), 738–746.

Tang, X., Zhang, H., Zhou, J., Kang, H., Yang, S., Cui, H., & Peng, Y. (2020). Brain development in children with developmental delay using amide proton transfer-weighted imaging and magnetization transfer imaging. *Pediatric Investigation, 4*(4), 250–256.

Tomasello, M., & Gonzalez-Cabrera, I. (2017). The role of ontogeny in the evolution of human cooperation. *Human Nature, 28*(3), 274–288.

Trevathan, W. R., & Rosenberg, K. R. (2016). *Costly and cute: Helpless infants and human evolution*: University of New Mexico Press.

Tuchman, B. W. (1979). *A distant mirror: The calamitous 14th century.* New York: Ballantine Books.

U.S. National Library of Medicine. (2017). What does it mean to have a genetic predispositino to a disease?.

Van de Vliert, E., Welzel, C., Shcherbak, A., Fischer, R., & Alexander, A. C. (2018). Got milk? How freedoms evolved from dairying climates. *Journal of Cross-Cultural Psychology,* 0022022118778336.

Vygotsky, L. S. (1986). *Thought and language* (A. Kozulin, Rev. Ed.). Cambridge, MA: MIT Press.

Watson, J. (1925). *Behaviorism.* New York: Norton.

Watson, J. B., & Rayner, R. (1920). Conditioned emotional reactions. *Journal of Experimental Psychology, 3*(1), 1.

Weber, A. M., Diop, Y., Gillespie, D., Ratsifandrihamanana, L., & Darmstadt, G. L. (2021). Africa is not a museum: The ethics of encouraging new parenting practices in rural communities in low-income and middle-income countries. *BMJ Global Health, 6*(7), e006218.

Willford, J., Smith, C., Kuhn, T., Weber, B., & Richardson, G. (2016). Review of current neuroimaging studies of the effects of prenatal drug exposure: Brain structure and function. In W. M. Meil & C. L Ruby (Eds.), *Recent advances in drug addiction research and clinical applications.* InTech.

Wyer, R. S. (2014). *The automaticity of everyday life: Advances in social cognition* (Vol. 10): Psychology Press.

Chapter 3

Abascal, F., Juan, D., Jungreis, I., Martinez, L., Rigau, M., Rodriguez, J. M., . . . Tress, M. L. (2018). Loose ends: Almost one in five human genes still have unresolved coding status. *Nucleic Acids Research, 46*(14), 7070–7084.

Allen, A. (1998). Nature & nurture. *The Washington Post Magazine.* Retrieved from www.washingtonpost.com/wp-srv/national/longterm/twins/twins1.htm.

American Academy of Pediatrics. (2017). Tests & screenings during pregnancy. Retrieved from www.healthychildren.org/English/ages-stages/prenatal/Pages/Tests-During-Pregnancy.aspx?gclid=Cj0KCQjw3MPNBRDjARIsAOYU6x_JCgGlaNQno8mf94Ef21te45BttYNfET5sYPfl4-YyceXWV99BtbAaAnNNEALw_wcB.

American Cancer Society. (2017). Family cancer syndromes. Retrieved from www.cancer.org/cancer/cancer-causes/genetics/family-cancer-syndromes.html.

American College of Obstetricians and Gynecologists. (2017). Definition of term pregnancy. Retrieved from www

.acog.org/clinical/clinical-guidance/committee-opinion/articles/2013/11/definition-of-term-pregnancy.

American Pregnancy Association. (2015). Weight gain during your pregnancy. Retrieved from americanpregnancy.org/healthy-pregnancy/pregnancy-health-wellness/pregnancy-weight-gain/.

American Pregnancy Association. (2016a). Amniocentesis. Retrieved from americanpregnancy.org/prenatal-testing/amniocentesis/.

American Pregnancy Association. (2016b). Chorionic villus sampling: CVS. Retrieved from americanpregnancy.org/prenatal-testing/chorionic-villus-sampling/.

American Pregnancy Association. (2016c). Triple Screen Test. Retrieved from americanpregnancy.org/prenatal-testing/triple-screen-test/.

American Pregnancy Association. (2017). HIV/AIDS during pregnancy. Retrieved from americanpregnancy.org/healthy-pregnancy/pregnancy-complications/hiv-aids-during-pregnancy/.

American Pregnancy Association. (2021a). Fertility FAQ. Retrieved from americanpregnancy.org/faqs/.

American Pregnancy Association. (2021b). Pregnancy nutrition. Retrieved from americanpregnancy.org/healthy-pregnancy/pregnancy-health-wellness/pregnancy-nutrition/.

American Society for Reproductive Medicine. (2017a). Q02: What causes infertility? Retrieved from www.reproductivefacts.org/faqs/frequently-asked-questions-about-infertility/q02-what-causes-infertilitynew-page/.

American Society for Reproductive Medicine. (2017b). Q05: What is in vitro fertilization? Retrieved from www.reproductive-facts.org/faqs/frequently-asked-questions-about-infertility/q05-what-is-in-vitro-fertilization/.

American Society for Reproductive Medicine. (2021). Q02: What causes infertility? Retrieved from www.reproductive-facts.org/faqs/frequently-asked-questions-about-infertility/q02-what-causes-infertility/.

Ammon Avalos, L., Galindo, C., & Li, D. K. (2012). A systematic review to calculate background miscarriage rates using life table analysis. *Birth Defects Research Part A: Clinical and Molecular Teratology, 94*(6), 417–423.

Anderson, D., Schmid, T. E., & Baumgartner, A. (2014). Male-mediated developmental toxicity. Asian *Journal of Andrology, 16*(1), 81.

Antonson, A. M., Radlowski, E. C., Lawson, M. A., Rytych, J. L., & Johnson, R. W. (2017). Maternal viral infection during pregnancy elicits anti-social behavior in neonatal piglet offspring independent of postnatal microglial cell activation. *Brain, behavior, and immunity, 59*, 300–312.

Arabin, B., & Jahn, M. (2013). Need for interventional studies on the impact of music in the perinatal period: Results of a pilot study on women's preferences and review of the literature. *The Journal of Maternal-Fetal & Neonatal Medicine, 26*(4), 357–362.

Baby Plus. (2017). Give your child a head start. Retrieved from babyplus.com.

Baggini, J. (2015). Do genes determine your entire life? *The Guardian*. Retrieved from www.theguardian.com/science/2015/mar/19/do-your-genes-determine-your-entire-life.

Banderali, G., Martelli, A., Landi, M., Moretti, F., Betti, F., Radaelli, G., . . . Verduci, E. (2015). Short and long term health effects of parental tobacco smoking during pregnancy and lactation: A descriptive review. *Journal of Translational Medicine, 13*(1), 327.

Bao, W., Liu, B., Rong, S., Dai, S. Y., Trasande, L., & Lehmler, H.-J. (2020). Association between bisphenol A exposure and risk of all-cause and cause-specific mortality in US adults. *JAMA Network Open, 3*(8), e2011620–e2011620.

Behnke, M., Smith, V. C., & Abuse, C. o. S. (2013). Prenatal substance abuse: short-and long-term effects on the exposed fetus. *Pediatrics, 131*(3), e1009-e1024.

Benyamin, B., Pourcain, B., Davis, O. S., Davies, G., Hansell, N. K., Brion, M. J., . . . Visscher, P. M. (2014). Childhood intelligence is heritable, highly polygenic and associated with FNBP1L. *Mol Psychiatry, 19*(2), 253–258. doi:10.1038/mp.2012.184.

Berry, R., Buehler, J. W., Strauss, L. T., Hogue, C., & Smith, J. C. (1987). Birth weight-specific infant mortality due to congenital anomalies, 1960 and 1980. *Public Health Reports, 102*(2), 171.

Bianconi, E., Piovesan, A., Facchin, F., Beraudi, A., Casadei, R., Frabetti, F., . . . Piva, F. (2013). An estimation of the number of cells in the human body. *Annals of Human Biology, 40*(6), 463–471.

Bishop, K. S., & Ferguson, L. R. (2015). The interaction between epigenetics, nutrition and the development of cancer. *Nutrients, 7*(2), 922–947.

Bleidorn, W., Kandler, C., & Caspi, A. (2014). The behavioural genetics of personality development in adulthood—Classic, contemporary, and future trends. *European Journal of Personality, 28*(3), 244–255.

Boghossian, N. S., Geraci, M., Lorch, S. A., Phibbs, C. S., Edwards, E. M., & Horbar, J. D. (2019). Racial and ethnic differences over time in outcomes of infants born less than 30 weeks' gestation. *Pediatrics, 144*(3), e20191106.

Bohannon, C. (2014). What you need to know about flame retardants. Retrieved from https://www.scientificamerican.com/article/what-you-need-to-know-about-flame-retardants/.

Bozzone, D. M., & Green, D. S. (2014). *Biology for the Informed Citizen*. Oxford University Press, New York.

Breedlove, S. M. (2015). *Principles of Psychology*. Sinauer/Oxford University Press, Sunderland, MA.

Bricker, L. (2016). Multiple pregnancy: Pathology and epidemiology. In *Fetal Medicine* (p. 297). Cambridge University Press. doi: https://doi.org/10.1017/CBO9781107585843.024.

Bronson, S. L., & Bale, T. L. (2016). The placenta as a mediator of stress effects on neurodevelopmental reprogramming. *Neuropsychopharmacology: official publication of the American College of Neuropsychopharmacology, 41*(1), 207–218.

Brown, G. (2009). NICU noise and the preterm infant. *Neonatal Network, 28*(3), 165–173.

Brown, Q. L., Sarvet, A. L., Shmulewitz, D., Martins, S. S., Wall, M. M., & Hasin, D. S. (2017). Trends in marijuana use among pregnant and nonpregnant reproductive-aged women, 2002–2014. *JAMA, 317*(2), 207–209.

Buckingham-Howes, S., Berger, S. S., Scaletti, L. A., & Black, M. M. (2013). Systematic review of prenatal cocaine exposure and adolescent development. *Pediatrics*, peds. 2012–0945.

Campaign for Safe Cosmetics. (2021). International Laws. Retrieved from www.safecosmetics.org/get-the-facts/regulations/international-laws/.

Carlson, B. M. (2012). Human Embryology and Developmental Biology E-Book: with STUDENT CONSULT Online Access: Elsevier Health Sciences.

Centers for Disease Control and Prevention. (1991). Use of folic acid for prevention of spina bifida and other neural tube defects--1983–1991. *MMWR. Morbidity and Mortality Weekly Report, 40*(30), 513.

Centers for Disease Control and Prevention. (2016). Pregnancy and rubella. Retrieved from www.cdc.gov/rubella/pregnancy.html.

Centers for Disease Control and Prevention. (2019). Racial and ethnic disparities continue in pregnancy-related deaths. Retrieved from www.cdc.gov/media/releases/2019/p0905-racial-ethnic-disparities-pregnancy-deaths.html.

Centers for Disease Control and Prevention. (2020a). CDCs abortion surveillance system FAQs. Retrieved from www.cdc.gov/reproductivehealth/Data_Stats/Abortion.htm.

Centers for Disease Control and Prevention. (2020b). Sickle cell disease. Retrieved from https://www.cdc.gov/ncbddd/sicklecell/data.html.

Centers for Disease Control and Prevention. (2021a). Infertility FAQs. Retrieved from www.cdc.gov/reproductivehealth/infertility/index.htm.

Centers for Disease Control and Prevention. (2021b). Preterm birth. Retrieved from www.cdc.gov/reproductivehealth/maternalinfanthealth/pretermbirth.htm.

Cheroni, C., Caporale, N., & Testa, G. (2020). Autism spectrum disorder at the crossroad between genes and environment: Contributions, convergences, and interactions in ASD developmental pathophysiology. *Molecular Autism, 11*(1), 1–18.

Child Trends Databank. (2021). *Late or no prenatal care.* Retrieved from www.childtrends.org/wp-content/uploads/2015/12/25_Prenatal_Care.pdf.

Cho, E.-S., Kim, S.-J., Kwon, M. S., Cho, H., Kim, E. H., Jun, E. M., & Lee, S. (2016). The effects of kangaroo care in the neonatal intensive care unit on the physiological functions of preterm infants, maternal–infant attachment, and maternal stress. *Journal of Pediatric Nursing, 31*(4), 430–438.

Choi, Y.-H., Terry, M. B., Daly, M. B., MacInnis, R. J., Hopper, J. L., Colonna, S., . . . Kurian, A. W. (2021). Association of risk-reducing salpingo-oophorectomy with breast cancer risk in women With BRCA1 and BRCA2 pathogenic variants. *JAMA Oncology, 7*(4), 585–592.

Cunningham, C., Patton, D., Moore, Z., O'Connor, T., Bux, D., & Nugent, L. (2021). Neonatal kangaroo care—What we know and how we can improve its practice: An evidence review. *Journal of Neonatal Nursing.* https://doi.org/10.1016/j.jnn.2021.10.004.

Cystic Fibrosis Foundation. (2021). About cystic fibrosis. Retrieved from www.cff.org/What-is-CF/About-Cystic-Fibrosis/.

D'Onofrio, B. M., Rickert, M. E., Frans, E., Kuja-Halkola, R., Almqvist, C., Sjölander, A., . . . Lichtenstein, P. (2014). Paternal age at childbearing and offspring psychiatric and academic morbidity. *JAMA Psychiatry, 71*(4), 432–438.

Derauf, C., LaGasse, L. L., Smith, L. M., Grant, P., Shah, R., Arria, A., . . . Grotta, S. D. (2007). Demographic and psychosocial characteristics of mothers using methamphetamine during pregnancy: Preliminary results of the infant development, environment, and lifestyle study (IDEAL). *The American Journal of Drug and Alcohol Abuse, 33*(2), 281–289.

Di Lallo, S. (2014). Prenatal care through the eyes of Canadian Aboriginal women. *Nursing for Women's Health, 18*(1), 38–46.

Dove, F. (2011). What's happened to Thalidomide babies. Retrieved from http://www.bbc.com/news/magazine-15536544.

Dubrova, Y. E., Nesterov, V. N., Krouchinsky, N. G., & Ostapenko, V. A. (1996). Human minisatellite mutation rate after the Chernobyl accident. *Nature, 380*(6576), 683.

Eleonore, N. L. E., Cumber, S. N., Charlotte, E. E., Lucas, E. E., Edgar, M. M. L., Nkfusai, C. N., . . . Fomukong, N. H. (2020). Malaria in patients with sickle cell anaemia: Burden, risk factors and outcome at the Laquintinie Hospital, Cameroon. *BMC Infectious Diseases, 20*(1), 1–8.

Endowment for Human Development. (2017a). Prenatal form and function—The making of an earth suit. Retrieved from www.ehd.org/dev_article_unit1.php.

Endowment for Human Development. (2017b). Prenatal summary. Retrieved from www.ehd.org/prenatal-summary.php.

England, L. J., Bunnell, R. E., Pechacek, T. F., Tong, V. T., & McAfee, T. A. (2015). Nicotine and the developing human: A neglected element in the electronic cigarette debate. *American Journal of Preventive Medicine, 49*(2), 286–293.

Entringer, S., Buss, C., & Wadhwa, P. D. (2015). Prenatal stress, development, health and disease risk: A psychobiological perspective—2015 Curt Richter Award Paper. *Psychoneuroendocrinology, 62*, 366–375.

Environmental Protection Agency. (2021). Endocrine disruption. Retrieved from www.epa.gov/endocrine-disruption/what-endocrine-disruption.

Ezkurdia, I., Juan, D., Rodriguez, J. M., Frankish, A., Diekhans, M., Harrow, J., . . . Tress, M. L. (2014). Multiple evidence strands suggest that there may be as few as 19 000 human protein-coding genes. *Human Molecular Genetics, 23*(22), 5866–5878.

Farren, J., Jalmbrant, M., Ameye, L., Joash, K., Mitchell-Jones, N., Tapp, S., . . . Bourne, T. (2016). Post-traumatic stress, anxiety and depression following miscarriage or ectopic pregnancy: A prospective cohort study. *BMJ Open, 6*(11), e011864.

Fraga, M. F., Ballestar, E., Paz, M. F., Ropero, S., Setien, F., Ballestar, M. L., . . . Esteller, M. (2005). Epigenetic differences arise during the lifetime of monozygotic twins. *Proceedings of the National Academy of Sciences, 102*, 10604–10609.

Ganchimeg, T., Ota, E., Morisaki, N., Laopaiboon, M., Lumbiganon, P., Zhang, J., . . . Tunçalp, Ö. (2014). Pregnancy and childbirth outcomes among adolescent mothers: A World Health Organization multicountry study. *BJOG: An International Journal of Obstetrics & Gynaecology, 121*(s1), 40–48.

Genetic Science Learning Center. (2017). What are DNA and genes? Retrieved from learn.genetics.utah.edu/content/basics/dna.

Glass, H. C., Costarino, A. T., Stayer, S. A., Brett, C., Cladis, F., & Davis, P. J. (2015). Outcomes for extremely premature infants. *Anesthesia and Analgesia, 120*(6), 1337.

Graven, S. N. (2000). Sound and the developing infant in the NICU: Conclusions and recommendations for care. *Journal of Perinatology, 20*(S8), S88.

Gravholt, C. H., Viuff, M. H., Brun, S., Stochholm, K., & Andersen, N. H. (2019). Turner syndrome: Mechanisms and management. *Nature Reviews Endocrinology, 15*(10), 601–614.

Greenwood, D. C., Thatcher, N. J., Ye, J., Garrard, L., Keogh, G., King, L. G., & Cade, J. E. (2014). Caffeine intake during pregnancy and adverse birth outcomes: a systematic review and dose–response meta-analysis. In: Springer.

Gündüz, Ö. D., Eser, A., Çoban, U., & Tekeli, S. (2016). Evaluation of the impact of triple test results on perinatal outcomes. *The Official Publication of Perinatal Medicine Foundation, Turkish Perinatology Society and Turkish Society of Ultrasound in Obstetrics and Gynecology, 24*(1), 26–31.

Gunn, J., Rosales, C., Center, K., Nuñez, A., Gibson, S., Christ, C., & Ehiri, J. (2016). Prenatal exposure to cannabis and maternal and child health outcomes: A systematic review and meta-analysis. *BMJ Open, 6*(4), e009986.

Henry, D., Dormuth, C., Winquist, B., Carney, G., Bugden, S., Teare, G., . . . Platt, R. W. (2016). Occurrence of pregnancy and pregnancy outcomes during isotretinoin therapy. *Canadian Medical Association Journal, 188*(10), 723–730.

Hepper, P. G., Shannon, E. A., & Dornan, J. C. (1997). Sex differences in fetal mouth movements. *The Lancet, 350*(9094), 1820.

Hillis, D. M., Price, M. V., Hill, R. W., Hall, D. W., & Laskowski, M. J. (2019). *Principles of Life*, 3rd ed. Oxford University Press/Sinauer, Sunderland, MA.

Hinterthuer, A. (2008). Just how harmful are bisphenol A plastics? Retrieved from www.scientificamerican.com/article/just-how-harmful-are-bisphenol-a-plastics/.

Holbrook, B. D. (2016). The effects of nicotine on human fetal development. *Birth Defects Research Part C: Embryo Today: Reviews, 108*(2), 181–192.

Huntington's Disease Society of America. (2021). What is Huntington's disease. Retrieved from http://hdsa.org/what-is-hd/.

Ickovics, J. R., Earnshaw, V., Lewis, J. B., Kershaw, T. S., Magriples, U., Stasko, E., . . . Bernstein, P. (2016). Cluster randomized controlled trial of group prenatal care: Perinatal outcomes among adolescents in New York City health centers. *American Journal of Public Health, 106*(2), 359–365.

Jahja, R., Huijbregts, S. C., de Sonneville, L. M., van der Meere, J. J., Legemaat, A. M., Bosch, A. M., . . . Hofstede, F. C. (2017). Cognitive profile and mental health in adult phenylketonuria: A PKU-COBESO study. *Neuropsychology, 31*(4), 437.

Jahn, M., Müller-Mazzotta, J., & Arabin, B. (2016). Music devices for the fetus? An evaluation of pregnancy music belts. *Journal of perinatal medicine, 44*(6), 637–643.

Jirtle, R. L (2009). Epigenome: the program for human health and disease. *Epigenomics 1*, 13–16.

Jordaan, H. V. (1979). Development of the central nervous system in prenatal life. *Obstetrics & Gynecology, 53*(2), 146–150.

Kaempf, J., Morris, M., Steffen, E., Wang, L., & Dunn, M. (2021). Continued improvement in morbidity reduction in extremely premature infants. *Archives of Disease in Childhood-Fetal and Neonatal Edition, 106*(3), 265–270.

Kancherla, V., Wagh, K., Pachón, H., & Oakley Jr, G. P. (2021). A 2019 global update on folic acid-preventable spina bifida and anencephaly. *Birth Defects Research, 113*(1), 77–89.

Kaur, H. (January 16, 2020). No one knew why the kids in 2 Amish families were dying suddenly. Now researchers have some answers. *CNN*. Retrieved from https://www.cnn.com/2020/01/16/health/amish-children-sudden-deaths-mystery-trnd/index.html.

Kenny, L. C., Lavender, T., McNamee, R., O'Neill, S. M., Mills, T., & Khashan, A. S. (2013). Advanced maternal age and adverse pregnancy outcome: Evidence from a large contemporary cohort. *PloS One, 8*(2), e56583.

Khalil, A., Von Dadelszen, P., Draycott, T., Ugwumadu, A., O'Brien, P., & Magee, L. (2020). Change in the incidence of stillbirth and preterm delivery during the COVID-19 pandemic. *JAMA, 324*(7), 705–706.

Krapohl, E., Rimfeld, K., Shakeshaft, N. G., Trzaskowski, M., McMillan, A., Pingault, J.-B., . . . Dale, P. S. (2014). The high heritability of educational achievement reflects many genetically influenced traits, not just intelligence. *Proceedings of the National Academy of Sciences, 111*(42), 15273–15278.

Klein, K. O., Rosenfield, R. L., Santen, R. J., Gawlik, A. M., Backeljauw, P. F., Gravholt, C. H., . . . Mauras, N. (2018). Estrogen Replacement in Turner Syndrome: Literature Review and Practical Considerations. *The Journal of Clinical Endocrinology & Metabolism, 103*(5), 1790–1803.

Lahav, A., & Skoe, E. (2014). An acoustic gap between the NICU and womb: A potential risk for compromised neuroplasticity of the auditory system in preterm infants. *Frontiers in Neuroscience, 8*.

LeVay, S., Baldwin, J., & Baldwin, J. (2021) . *Discovering Human Sexuality*, 5th ed. Oxford University Press/Sinauer, Sunderland, MA.

Levine, H., Jørgensen, N., Martino-Andrade, A., Mendiola, J., Weksler-Derri, D., Mindlis, I., . . . Swan, S. H. (2017). Temporal trends in sperm count: A systematic review and meta-regression analysis. *Human Reproduction Update*, 1–14.

Li, D., Ferber, J., & Odouli, R. (2015). Maternal caffeine intake during pregnancy and risk of obesity in offspring: a prospective cohort study. *International journal of obesity (2005), 39*(4), 658.

López-Teijón, M., García-Faura, Á., & Prats-Galino, A. (2015). Fetal facial expression in response to intravaginal music emission. *Ultrasound, 23*(4), 216–223.

Lullabelly. (2017). Prenatal music belt. Retrieved from www.lullabelly.com.

MacDorman, M., & Gregory, E. (2015). Fetal and perinatal mortality: United States, 2013. *National vital statistics reports: from the Centers for Disease Control and Prevention, National Center for Health Statistics, National Vital Statistics System, 64*(8), 1–24.

MacKinnon, N., Kingsbury, M., Mahedy, L., Evans, J., & Colman, I. (2017). The Association Between Prenatal Stress And Externalizing Symptoms In Childhood: Evidence From The Avon Longitudinal Study Of Parents And Children. *Biological psychiatry*.

Martin, J. A., Hamilton, B. E., Osterman, M. J. K., & Driscoll, A. K. (2019). *Births: Final data for 2018.* Retrieved from https://www.cdc.gov/nchs/data/nvsr/nvsr68/nvsr68_13-508.pdf.

Major, B., Appelbaum, M., Beckman, L., Dutton, M. A., Russo, N. F., & West, C. (2009). Abortion and mental health: Evaluating the evidence. *American Psychologist, 64*(9), 863.

Mbarek, H., Steinberg, S., Nyholt, D. R., Gordon, S. D., Miller, M. B., McRae, A. F., . . . de Geus, E. J. (2016). Identification of common genetic variants influencing spontaneous dizygotic twinning and female fertility. *The American Journal of Human Genetics, 98*(5), 898–908.

Mehler, J., Lambertz, G., Jusczyk, P., & Amiel-Tison, C. (1986). Discrimination of the mother tongue by newborn infants. *Comptes rendus de l'Academie des sciences. Serie III, Sciences de la vie, 303*(15), 637–640.

Moore, K. L. (1974) . *Before We Are Born: Basic Embryology and Birth Defects.* Saunders, Philadelphia.

Moore, K. L., Persaud, T., & Shiota, K. (2000). Color atlas of clinical embryology: Saunders. Stiles, J., & Jernigan, T. L. (2010). The basics of brain development. Neuropsychology review, 20(4), 327–348..

Muscular Dystrophy Association. (2021). Duchenne muscular dystrophy (DMD). Retrieved from Muscular Dystrophy Association..

National Down Syndrome Society. (2017). What is Down syndrome? Retrieved from www.ndss.org/Down-Syndrome/What-Is-Down-Syndrome/.

National Human Genome Research Institute. (2015). Chromosomes. Retrieved from www.genome.gov/26524120/chromosomes-fact-sheet/.

Nepali, K., & Liou, J.-P. (2021). Recent developments in epigenetic cancer therapeutics: Clinical advancement and emerging trends. *Journal of Biomedical Science, 28*(1), 1–58.

Neubauer, K., & Boss, R. D. (2020). Ethical considerations for cardiac surgical interventions in children with trisomy 13 and trisomy 18. Paper presented at the *American Journal of Medical Genetics Part C: Seminars in Medical Genetics.*

Pacheco, C. M., Daley, S. M., Brown, T., Filippi, M., Greiner, K. A., & Daley, C. M. (2013). Moving forward: Breaking the cycle of mistrust between American Indians and researchers. *American Journal of Public Health, 103*(12), 2152–2159.

Papalia, D. E. (2003). *Child Development: A Topical Approach.* McGraw-Hill, New York.

Paulose, T., Speroni, L., Sonnenschein, C., & Soto, A. M. (2015). Estrogens in the wrong place at the wrong time: Fetal BPA exposure and mammary cancer. *Reproductive Toxicology, 54,* 58–65.

Peck, M. S., Porter, A. T., Hayes, B. D., Otieno, D., Hargrove, A. J., Mayhand, C. C., . . . Brown, L. M. (2017). Sex and longevity: Why women live longer than men. *Journal of Student Research, 6*(1), 19–23.

Pesta, B. J., Kirkegaard, E. O., te Nijenhuis, J., Lasker, J., & Fuerst, J. G. (2020). Racial and ethnic group differences in the heritability of intelligence: A systematic review and meta-analysis. *Intelligence, 78,* 101408.

Pinney, S. E., Mesaros, C. A., Snyder, N. W., Busch, C. M., Xiao, R., Aijaz, S., . . . Manson, J. M. (2017). Second trimester amniotic fluid bisphenol A concentration is associated with decreased birth weight in term infants. *Reproductive Toxicology, 67,* 1–9.

Plomin, R., & Deary, I. J. (2015). Genetics and intelligence differences: five special findings. *Molecular psychiatry, 20*(1), 98–108.

Polan, E., & Taylor, D. (2003). *Journey Across the Life Span: Human Development and Health Promotion.* F. A. Davis, Philadelphia.

Prins, G. S., Ye, S.-H., Birch, L., Zhang, X., Cheong, A., Lin, H., . . . Ho, S.-M. (2017). Prostate cancer risk and DNA methylation signatures in aging rats following developmental BPA exposure: A dose–response analysis. *Environmental Health Perspectives, 77007,* 1.

Reigstad, M. M., Larsen, I. K., Myklebust, T. Å., Robsahm, T. E., Oldereid, N. B., Brinton, L. A., & Storeng, R. (2016). Risk of cancer in children conceived by assisted reproductive technology. *Pediatrics, 137*(3), e20152061.

Sandall, J., Soltani, H., Gates, S., Shennan, A., & Devane, D. (2016). Midwife-led continuity models versus other models of care for childbearing women. *The Cochrane Library.*

SART. (2015). Final National Summary Report for 2015. Retrieved from https://www.sartcorsonline.com/rptCSR_PublicMultYear.aspx?reportingYear=2015.

Savage, C. L., Anthony, J., Lee, R., Kappesser, M. L., & Rose, B. (2007). The culture of pregnancy and infant care in African American women: An ethnographic study. *Journal of Transcultural Nursing, 18*(3), 215–223.

Schnieder, K. (1994). *Counseling about cancer: Strategies for genetic counselors.* Boston, MA: Dana-Farber Cancer Institute.

Sedgh, G., Singh, S., Shah, I. H., Åhman, E., Henshaw, S. K., & Bankole, A. (2012). Induced abortion: Incidence and trends worldwide from 1995 to 2008. *Lancet, 379*(9816), 625–632.

Sellers, R., Castillo, J. C., Ten, J., Rodríguez, A., Ortiz, J. A., Sellers, F., . . . Bernabeu, R. (2021). Monozygotic twinning following embryo biopsy at the blastocyst stage. *JBRA Assisted Reproduction, 25*(1), 122.

Shaw, S. D., Harris, J. H., Berger, M. L., Subedi, B., & Kannan, K. (2014). Brominated flame retardants and their replacements in food packaging and household products: uses, human exposure, and health effects. In *Toxicants in Food Packaging and Household Plastics* (pp. 61–93): Springer.

Sicignano, N., Beydoun, H. A., Russell, H., Jones, H., & Oehninger, S. (2010). A descriptive study of asthma in young adults conceived by IVF. *Reproductive biomedicine online, 21*(6), 812–818.

Smith, L. M., Diaz, S., LaGasse, L. L., Wouldes, T., Derauf, C., Newman, E., . . . Strauss, A. (2015). Developmental and behavioral consequences of prenatal methamphetamine exposure: a review of the infant development, environment, and lifestyle (IDEAL) study. *Neurotoxicology and teratology, 51,* 35–44.

Smith, A. M., Mioduszewski, O., Hatchard, T., Byron-Alhassan, A., Fall, C., & Fried, P. A. (2016). Prenatal marijuana exposure impacts executive functioning into young adulthood: An fMRI study. *Neurotoxicology and Teratology, 58,* 53–59.

Stafford, K., Greyner, H., Molina, F., Bucek, A., & Fairweather, D. (2014). Bisphenol A (BPA) exacerbates acute myocarditis in female BALB/c by activating mast cells and the inflammasome (HUM1P. 302). *Journal of Immunology 192* (1 Supplement), 52.2.

Steinberg, J. R., McCulloch, C. E., & Adler, N. E. (2014). Abortion and mental health: findings from the national comorbidity survey-replication. *Obstetrics and gynecology, 123*(2 0 1), 263.

Sternberg, R. J., & Grigorenko, E. L. (2014). *Environmental effects on cognitive abilities*: Psychology Press.

Stiles, J., & Jernigan, T. L. (2010). The basics of brain development. Neuropsychology review, 20(4), 327–348.

Sultana, M., Mahumud, R. A., Ali, N., Ahmed, S., Islam, Z., Khan, J. A., & Sarker, A. R. (2017). The effectiveness of introducing Group Prenatal Care (GPC) in selected health facilities in a district of Bangladesh: Study protocol. *BMC Pregnancy and Childbirth, 17*(1), 48.

Sutcliffe, K., Caird, J., Kavanagh, J., Rees, R., Oliver, K., Dickson, K., . . . Thomas, J. (2012). Comparing midwife-led and doctor-led maternity care: A systematic review of reviews. *Journal of Advanced Nursing, 68*(11), 2376–2386.

Tamis-LeMonda, C. S. (2022) . *Child Development: Context, Culture, and Cascades.* Oxford University Press/Sinauer, Sunderland, MA.

Tomkins, J., Hazel, W., Black, R., Smock, R., & Sear, R. (2020). An age-dependent ovulatory strategy explains the evolution of dizygotic twinning in humans. *Nature Ecology & Evolution, 4*(7), 987–992.

U.S. Department of Health and Human Services. (2021). Trends in foster care & adoption: FY 2010– 2019. Retrieved from https://www.acf.hhs.gov/cb/report/trends-foster-care-adoption.

U.S. National Library of Medicine. (2017). Hemophilia. Retrieved from https://ghr.nlm.nih.gov/condition/hemophilia#inheritance.

U.S. National Library of Medicine. (2021a). What are the risks and limitations of genetic testing? Retrieved from https://ghr.nlm.nih.gov/primer/testing/riskslimitations.

U.S. National Library of Medicine. (2021b). What is genetic discrimination? Retrieved from https://ghr.nlm.nih.gov/primer/testing/discrimination.

U.S. National Library of Medicine. (2022). Hemophilia. Retrieved from https://medlineplus.gov/hemophilia.html.

UNICEF Data. (2021). Only half of women worldwide receive the recommended amount of care during pregnancy. Retrieved from https://data.unicef.org/topic/maternal-health/antenatal-care/#.

van Heeswijk, M., Nijhuis, J. G., & Hollanders, H. M. (1990). Fetal heart rate in early pregnancy. *Early Human Development, 22*(3), 151–156.

van Spronsen, F. J., Blau, N., Harding, C., Burlina, A., Longo, N., & Bosch, A. M. (2021). Phenylketonuria. *Nature Reviews Disease Primers, 7*(1), 1–19.

Vargesson, N., & Stephens, T. (2021). Thalidomide: History, withdrawal, renaissance and safety concerns. *Expert Opinion on Drug Safety, 20*(12), 1455–1457.

Villines, Z. (2018). What are the miscarriage rates by week? *Medical News Today.* Retrieved from www.medicalnewstoday.com/articles/322634.php.

Visser, G., Mulder, E., & Prechtl, H. (1992). Studies on developmental neurology in the human fetus. *Developmental pharmacology and therapeutics, 18*(3–4), 175–183.

Volkow, N. D., Compton, W. M., & Wargo, E. M. (2017). The risks of marijuana use during pregnancy. *JAMA, 317*(2), 129–130.

Vukasović, T., & Bratko, D. (2015). Heritability of personality: A meta-analysis of behavior genetic studies. *Psychological bulletin, 141*(4), 769.

Watson, C. (2020). Stillbirth rate rises dramatically during pandemic. *Nature, 585*(7826), 490–492.

Volkow, N. D., Compton, W. M., & Wargo, E. M. (2017). The risks of marijuana use during pregnancy. *JAMA, 317*(2), 129–130.

White, D., & Rabago-Smith, M. (2011). Genotype–phenotype associations and human eye color. *Journal of human genetics, 56*(1), 5.

Williams, R. A., Mamotte, C. D. S., and Burnett, J. R. (2008). Phenylketonuria: An inborn error of phenylalanine metabolism. *The Clinical Biochemist Reviews, 29*(1), 31–41.

Wojcik, M. H., Schwartz, T. S., Thiele, K. E., Paterson, H., Stadelmaier, R., Mullen, T. E., . . . Gubbels, C. S. (2019). Infant mortality: The contribution of genetic disorders. *Journal of Perinatology, 39*(12), 1611–1619.

World Health Organization. (2017). Genes and human disease. Retrieved from www.who.int/genomics/public/geneticdiseases/en/index2.html.

Zarulli, V., Jones, J. A. B., Oksuzyan, A., Lindahl-Jacobsen, R., Christensen, K., & Vaupel, J. W. (2018). Women live longer than men even during severe famines and epidemics. *Proceedings of the National Academy of Sciences, 115*(4), E832–E840.

Zhu, J. L., Olsen, J., Liew, Z., Li, J., Niclasen, J., & Obel, C. (2014). Parental smoking during pregnancy and ADHD in children: The Danish national birth cohort. *Pediatrics,* peds. 2014–0213.

Chapter 4

Abdollahi, F., Lye, M.-S., Zain, A. M., Ghazali, S. S., & Zarghami, M. (2011). Postnatal depression and its associated factors in women from different cultures. *Iranian Journal of Psychiatry and Behavioral Sciences, 5*(2), 5.

Afand, N., Keshavarz, M., Fatemi, N. S., & Montazeri, A. (2017). Effects of infant massage on state anxiety in mothers of preterm infants prior to hospital discharge. *Journal of Clinical Nursing, 26*(13–14), 1887–1892. doi: 10.1111/jocn.13498.

Agrawal, D., Makhija, B., Arora, M., Haritwal, A., & Gurha, P. (2014). The effect of epidural analgesia on labour, mode of delivery and neonatal outcome in nullipara of India, 2011–2014. *Journal of Clinical and Diagnostic Research, 8*(10), OC03.

Ahearne, C. E., Boylan, G. B., & Murray, D. M. (2016). Short and long term prognosis in perinatal asphyxia: An update. *World Journal of Clinical Pediatrics, 5*(1), 67.

Akcan, E., & Polat, S. (2016). Comparative effect of the smells of amniotic fluid, breast milk, and lavender on newborns' pain during heel lance. *Breastfeeding Medicine, 11*(6), 309–314.

Altenburger, L. E., Schoppe-Sullivan, S. J., & Dush, C. M. K. (2018). Associations between maternal gatekeeping and fathers' parenting quality. *Journal of Child and Family Studies, 27,* 2678–2689.

American Academy of Husband-Coached Childbirth. (2017). The Bradley Method. Retrieved from www.bradleybirth.com/.

American Academy of Husband-Coached Childbirth. (2021). The Bradley Method. Retrieved from www.bradleybirth.com.

American College of Obstetricians and Gynecologists. (2017). Committee opinion: The Apgar score: American College of Obstetricians and Gynecologists.

American College of Obstetricians and Gynecologists. (2017). Committee opinion: Planned home birth. Retrieved from www.acog.org/Clinical-Guidance-and-Publications/Committee-Opinions/Committee-on-Obstetric-Practice/Planned-Home-Birth.

American College of Obstetricians and Gynecologists. (2021). Committee opinion: The Apgar score. In: American College of Obstetricians and Gynecologists.

Anand, K. J., Eriksson, M., Boyle, E. M., Avila-Alvarez, A., Andersen, R. D., Sarafidis, K., . . . Papadouri, T. (2017). Assessment of continuous pain in newborns admitted to NICUs in 18 European countries. *Acta Paediatrica, 106*(8), 1248–1259.

Anding, J. E., Röhrle, B., Grieshop, M., Schücking, B., & Christiansen, H. (2016). Couple comorbidity and correlates of postnatal depressive symptoms in mothers and fathers in the first two weeks following delivery. *Journal of Affective Disorders, 190*, 300–309.

Anisfeld, M. (1996). Only tongue protrusion modeling is matched by neonates. *Developmental Review, 16*(2), 149–161.

Avcin, E., & Kucukoglu, S. (2021). The effect of breastfeeding, kangaroo care, and facilitated tucking positioning in reducing the pain during heel stick in neonates. *Journal of Pediatric Nursing, 61*, 410–416.

Baghirzada, L., Archer, D., Walker, A., & Balki, M. (2021). Anesthesia-related adverse events in obstetric patients: A population-based study in Canada. *Canadian Journal of Anesthesia/Journal canadien d'anesthésie, 69*(1), 72–85.

Baum, N., Weidberg, Z., Osher, Y., & Kohelet, D. (2012). No longer pregnant, not yet a mother: Giving birth prematurely to a very-low-birth-weight baby. *Qualitative Health Research, 22*(5), 595–606.

Beevi, Z., Low, W. Y., & Hassan, J. (2017). The effectiveness of hypnosis intervention for labor: An experimental study. *American Journal of Clinical Hypnosis, 60*(2), 172–191.

Betrán, A. P., Ye, J., Moller, A.-B., Souza, J. P., & Zhang, J. (2021). Trends and projections of caesarean section rates: Global and regional estimates. *BMJ Global Health, 6*(6), e005671.

Biebel, K., & Alikhan, S. (2016). Paternal postpartum depression. *Journal of Parent and Family Mental Health, 1*(1), 1–4.

Bigelow, A. E., & Power, M. (2012). The effect of mother–infant skin-to-skin contact on infants' response to the Still Face Task from newborn to three months of age. *Infant Behavior and Development, 35*(2), 240–251.

Blair, L. M., Porter, K., Leblebicioglu, B., & Christian, L. M. (2015). Poor sleep quality and associated inflammation predict preterm birth: Heightened risk among African Americans. *Sleep, 38*(8), 1259–1267.

Blass, E. M., Ganchrow, J. R., & Steiner, J. E. (1984). Classical conditioning in newborn humans 2–48 hours of age. *Infant Behavior and Development, 7*(2), 223–235.

Blencowe, H., Cousens, S., Oestergaard, M. Z., Chou, D., Moller, A.-B., Narwal, R., . . . Say, L. (2012). National, regional, and worldwide estimates of preterm birth rates in the year 2010 with time trends since 1990 for selected countries: A systematic analysis and implications. *Lancet, 379*(9832), 2162–2172.

Bozzone, D. M., & Green, D. S. (2014). Biology for the Informed Citizen. Oxford University Press: New York.

Bradley, R. (1972). Development of the taste bud and gustatory papillae in human fetuses. In C. C. Thomas (Ed.), *Oral sensation and perception. S* (pp. 137–162). Springfield, IL.

Braveman, P. A., Heck, K., Egerter, S., Marchi, K. S., Dominguez, T. P., Cubbin, C., . . . Curtis, M. (2015). The role of socioeconomic factors in black–white disparities in preterm birth. *American Journal of Public Health, 105*(4), 694–702.

Brazelton Institute. (2013). Understanding the baby's language. Retrieved from www.brazelton-institute.com/intro.html.

Budin, W. C. (2018). Promoting birth advocacy. *Journal of Perinatal Education, 27*(2), 63–65.

Campbell, M., & Jacobs, L. (2021). The effect of parent-administered infant massage on the developmental outcomes of premature infants. *South African Journal of Occupational Therapy, 51*(1), 36–43.

Carlson, E. A., Hostinar, C. E., Mliner, S. B., & Gunnar, M. R. (2014). The emergence of attachment following early social deprivation. *Development and Psychopathology, 26*(2), 479–489.

Carter, E. B., Temming, L. A., Akin, J., Fowler, S., Macones, G. A., Colditz, G. A., & Tuuli, M. G. (2016). Group prenatal care compared with traditional prenatal care: A systematic review and meta-analysis. *Obstetrics & Gynecology, 128*(3), 551.

Centering Healthcare Institute. (2021). Centering pregnancy. Retrieved from https://centeringhealthcare.org/what-we-do/centering-pregnancy.

Centers for Disease Control and Prevention. (2020). Percentage of births born preterm by state. Retrieved from https://www.cdc.gov/nchs/pressroom/sosmap/preterm_births/preterm.htm.

Centers for Disease Control and Prevention. (2021a). Data and statistics about hearing loss in children. Retrieved from www.cdc.gov/ncbddd/hearingloss/data.html.

Centers for Disease Control and Prevention. (2021b). Preterm birth. Retrieved from www.cdc.gov/reproductivehealth/maternalinfanthealth/pretermbirth.htm.

Child Trends Databank. (2016). *Low and very low birthweight infants.* Retrieved from www.childtrends.org/wp-content/uploads/2016/12/57_Low_Birth_Weight.pdf.

Collins J. W., Jr., David, R. J., Handler, A., Wall, S., & Andes, S. (2004). Very low birthweight in African American infants: The role of maternal exposure to interpersonal racial discrimination. *American Journal of Public Health, 94*(12), 2132–2138.

Coulthard, H. (2019). Taste, smell, and touch. In *The encyclopedia of child and adolescent development*, 1–12. Wiley.

Crockett, A. H., Covington-Kolb, S., Zang, L., & Chen, L. (2017). 728: The South Carolina centering pregnancy expansion project: Improving racial disparities in preterm birth. *American Journal of Obstetrics & Gynecology, 216*(1), S424–S425.

Crozer Griffith, J. P. (1906). The baby's growth. *American Motherhood, XXIII.*

DeCasper, A., & Fifer, W. (1980). Of human bonding: Newborns prefer their mothers' voices. *Readings on the development of children*, M. Gauvain and M. Cole (Eds.), Worth Publishers, 208, 1174–1176.

Demers-Mathieu, V., Qu, Y., Underwood, M. A., Borghese, R., & Dallas, D. C. (2018). Premature infants have lower gastric digestion capacity for human milk proteins than term infants. *Journal of Pediatric Gastroenterology and Nutrition, 66*(5), 816–821.

Desor, J., Maller, O., & Andrews, K. (1975). Ingestive responses of human newborns to salty, sour, and bitter stimuli. *Journal of Comparative and Physiological Psychology, 89*(8), 966.

Desor, J., Maller, O., & Turner, R. E. (1973). Taste in acceptance of sugars by human infants. *Journal of Comparative and Physiological Psychology, 84*(3), 496.

Dombrowski, S. C., Gischlar, K. L., Green, L., Noonan, K., & Martin, R. P. (2021). Low birth weight and psychoeducational outcomes: Investigation of an African American birth cohort. *Journal of Psychoeducational Assessment, 39*(3), 346–353.

Downe, S., Finlayson, K., Melvin, C., Spiby, H., Ali, S., Diggle, P., . . . Slade, P. (2015). Self-hypnosis for intrapartum pain management in pregnant nulliparous women: A randomised controlled trial of clinical effectiveness. *BJOG: An International Journal of Obstetrics and Gynaecology, 122*(9), 1226–1234.

Eckstein, A. (1927). Zur Physiologie der Geschmacksempfindung und des Saugreflexes bei Säuglingen. *Zeitschrift für Kinderheilkunde, 45*(1–2), 1–18.

Eker, H. E., Cok, O. Y., Çetinkaya, B., & Aribogan, A. (2017). Oral 30% glucose provides sufficient sedation in newborns during MRI. *Journal of Anesthesia, 31*(2), 206–211.

Eland, J. M., & Anderson, J. E. (1977). The experience of pain in children. In A. K. Jacox (Ed.), *Pain: A sourceook for nurses and other health care professionals* (pp. 453–473). Boston: Little Brown.

Eunice Kennedy Shriver National Institute of Child Health and Human Development. (2017). How many newborns are screened in the United States? Retrieved from www.nichd.nih.gov/health/topics/newborn/conditioninfo/infants-screened.

Evereklian, M., & Posmontier, B. (2017). The Impact of Kangaroo Care on Premature Infant Weight Gain. *Journal of Pediatric Nursing, 34*, e10–e16. doi: 10.1016/j.pedn.2017.02.006.

Fifer, W. P., Byrd, D. L., Kaku, M., Eigsti, I.-M., Isler, J. R., Grose-Fifer, J., . . . Balsam, P. D. (2010). Newborn infants learn during sleep. *Proceedings of the National Academy of Sciences, 107*(22), 10320–10323.

Finlayson, K., Downe, S., Hinder, S., Carr, H., Spiby, H., & Whorwell, P. (2015). Unexpected consequences: Women's experiences of a self-hypnosis intervention to help with pain relief during labour. *BMC Pregnancy and Childbirth, 15*(1), 229.

Font, G., & Testani, E. (2020). Doula programs improve cesarean section rate, breastfeeding initiation, maternal and perinatal outcomes [11P]. *Obstetrics & Gynecology, 135*, 170S.

Forestell, C. A. (2017). Flavor perception and preference development in human infants. *Annals of Nutrition and Metabolism, 70*(Suppl. 3), 17–25.

Frey, H. A., Stout, M. J., Pearson, L. N., Tuuli, M. G., Cahill, A. G., Strauss III, J. F., . . . Macones, G. A. (2016). Genetic variation associated with preterm birth in African-American women. *American Journal of Obstetrics and Gynecology, 215*(2), 235. e231–235. e238.

Glass, H. C., Costarino, A. T., Stayer, S. A., Brett, C., Cladis, F., & Davis, P. J. (2015). Outcomes for extremely premature infants. *Anesthesia and Analgesia, 120*(6), 1337.

Goksan, S., Baxter, L., Moultrie, F., Duff, E., Hathway, G., Hartley, C., . . . Slater, R. (2018). The influence of the descending pain modulatory system on infant pain-related brain activity. *eLife, 7*. doi: 10.7554/eLife.37125.

Ganchrow, J. R., Steiner, J. E., & Daher, M. (1983). Neonatal facial expressions in response to different qualities and intensities of gustatory stimuli. *Infant Behavior and Development, 6*(4), 473–484.

Gruber, K. J., Cupito, S. H., & Dobson, C. F. (2013). Impact of doulas on healthy birth outcomes. *Journal of Perinatal Education, 22*(1), 49.

Haldre, K., Rahu, K., Karro, H., & Rahu, M. (2007). Is a poor pregnancy outcome related to young maternal age? A study of teenagers in Estonia during the period of major socio-economic changes (from 1992 to 2002). *European Journal of Obstetrics & Gynecology and Reproductive Biology, 131*(1), 45–51.

Harper, B. (2014). Birth, bath, and beyond: The science and safety of water immersion during labor and birth. *Journal of Perinatal Education, 23*(3), 124.

Harris, P., & MacFarlane, A. (1974). The growth of the effective visual field from birth to seven weeks. *Journal of Experimental Child Psychology, 18*(2), 340–348.

Hawkins, J. L., Chang, J., Palmer, S. K., Gibbs, C. P., & Callaghan, W. M. (2011). Anesthesia-related maternal mortality in the United States: 1979–2002. *Obstetrics & Gynecology, 117*(1), 69–74.

Hellmich, N. (2013). At 95, Brazelton shares "A life caring for children". Retrieved from www.usatoday.com/story/news/nation/2013/05/01/t-berry-brazelton-memoir/2113683/.

Hoarau, K., Payet, M. L., Zamidio, L., Bonsante, F., & Iacobelli, S. (2021). "Holding–cuddling" and sucrose for pain relief during venepuncture in newborn infants: A randomized, controlled trial (CÂSA). *Frontiers in Pediatrics, 8*, 853.

Holditch-Davis, D., & Shandor Miles, M. (2000). Mothers' stories about their experiences in the neonatal intensive care unit. *Neonatal Network, 19*(3), 13–21.

Horgan, M. J. (2015). Management of the late preterm infant: Not quite ready for prime time. *Pediatric Clinics, 62*(2), 439–451.

Hughes, A. J., Redsell, S. A., & Glazebrook, C. (2016). Motor development interventions for preterm infants: A systematic review and meta-analysis. *Pediatrics*, e20160147.

Iams, J. D. (2003). Prediction and early detection of preterm labor. *Obstetrics & Gynecology, 101*(2), 402–412.

Jacoby, S., Becker, G., Crawford, S., & Wilson, R. D. (2019). Water birth maternal and neonatal outcomes among midwifery clients in Alberta, Canada, from 2014 to 2017: A retrospective study. *Journal of Obstetrics and Gynaecology Canada, 41*(6), 805–812.

Jeong, J., McCoy, D. C., Yousafzai, A. K., Salhi, C., & Fink, G. (2016). Paternal stimulation and early child development in low-and middle-income countries. *Pediatrics*, e20161357.

Jiang, H., Qian, X., Carroli, G., & Garner, P. (2017). Selective versus routine use of episiotomy for vaginal birth. *The Cochrane Library*.

Kajantie, E., & Hovi, P. (2014). Is very preterm birth a risk factor for adult cardiometabolic disease? Paper presented at the Seminars in Fetal and Neonatal Medicine.

Kearns, R. J., Shaw, M., Gromski, P. S., Iliodromiti, S., Lawlor, D. A., & Nelson, S. M. (2021). Association of epidural analgesia in women in labor with neonatal and childhood outcomes in a population cohort. *JAMA Network Open, 4*(10), e2131683–e2131683.

Kim, M., Kang, S.-K., Yee, B., Shim, S.-Y., & Chung, M. (2016). Paternal involvement and early infant neurodevelopment: The mediation role of maternal parenting stress. *BMC Pediatrics, 16*(1), 212.

Klaus, M. H., & Kennell, J. H. (1976). Maternal-infant bonding: The impact of early separation or loss on family development. St. Louis, MO: C.V. Mosby.

Kozhimannil, K. B., Attanasio, L. B., Jou, J., Joarnt, L. K., Johnson, P. J., & Gjerdingen, D. K. (2014). Potential benefits of increased access to doula support during childbirth. *American Journal of Managed Care, 20*(8), e340.

Lamaze International. (2021). Healthy birth practices. Retrieved from www.lamaze.org/childbirth-practices.

Leys, R. (2020). *Newborn imitation: The stakes of a controversy.* Cambridge University Press.

Liszewski, M. C., Stanescu, A. L., Phillips, G. S., & Lee, E. Y. (2017). Respiratory distress in neonates. *Radiologic Clinics, 55*(4), 629–644.

Liu, Y., Wang, Y., Wu, Y., Chen, X., & Bai, J. (2021). Effectiveness of the CenteringPregnancy program on maternal and birth outcomes: A systematic review and meta-analysis. *International Journal of Nursing Studies,* 103981.

Lothian, J. A. (1999). Does lamaze "work"? *Journal of Perinatal Education, 8*(3), x–xii.

MacFarlane, A. (1975). Olfaction in the development of social preferences in the human neonate. In R. Porter & M. O'Connor (Eds.), *Parent–infant interactions* (pp. 103–113). New York: Elsevier.

Mallen-Perez, L., Roé-Justiniano, M., Colomé, N. O., Ferre, A. C., Palacio, M., & Terré-Rull, C. (2017). Use of hydrotherapy during labour: Assessment of pain, use of analgesia and neonatal safety. *Enfermeria Clinica 28*(5), 309–315.

Manning, A. (2017). What it was like being pregnant in 1915. Retrieved from http://publichealthlegacy.americashealthrank ings.org/being-pregnant-in-1915/.

Marin, M., Rapisardi, G., & Tani, F. (2015). Two-day-old new-born infants recognise their mother by her axillary odour. *Acta Paediatrica, 104*(3), 237–240.

Marino, C., & Gervain, J. (2019). The novelty effect as a predictor of language outcome. *Frontiers in Psychology, 10,* 258.

Martin, J. A., Hamilton, B. E., Osterman, M. J., & Driscoll, A. K. (2021). Births: Final data for 2019. *National vital statistics reports: from the Centers for Disease Control and Prevention, National Center for Health Statistics, National Vital Statistics System, 70*(2), 1–51. Retrieved from www.cdc.gov/nchs/data/nvsr/nvsr70/nvsr70-02-508.pdf.

Martin, J. A., Hamilton, B. E., Osterman, M., Driscoll, A. K., & Mathews, T. (2017). Births: Final Data for 2015. *National vital statistics reports:From the Centers for Disease Control and Prevention, National Center for Health Statistics, National Vital Statistics System, 66*(1).

Maurer, D., & Maurer, C. (1988). *The world of the newborn*: Basic Books.

Maxwell, L. G., Fraga, M. V., & Malavolta, C. P. (2019). Assessment of pain in the newborn: An update. *Clinics in Perinatology, 46*(4), 693–707.

Mayer, D. L., & Dobson, V. (1982). Visual acuity development in infants and young children, as assessed by operant preferential looking. *Vision Research, 22*(9), 1141–1151.

McGrath, P. J., & Unruh, A. M. (2000). Social and legal issues. In K. J. S. Anand, P. J. McGrath, & B. J. Stevens (Eds.), *Pain in the neonate.* Elsevier.

Meijssen, D., Wolf, M.-J., van Bakel, H., Koldewijn, K., Kok, J., & van Baar, A. (2011). Maternal attachment representations after very preterm birth and the effect of early intervention. *Infant Behavior and Development, 34*(1), 72–80.

Miles, R., Cowan, F., Glover, V., Stevenson, J., & Modi, N. (2006). A controlled trial of skin-to-skin contact in extremely preterm infants. *Early Human Development, 82*(7), 447–455.

Miller, D. P., Thomas, M. M., Waller, M. R., Nepomnyaschy, L., & Emory, A. D. (2020). Father involvement and socioeconomic disparities in child academic outcomes. *Journal of Marriage and Family, 82*(2), 515–533.

Moshiro, R., Mdoe, P., & Perlman, J. M. (2019). A global view of neonatal asphyxia and resuscitation. *Frontiers in Pediatrics, 7,* 489.

Mott, S. L., Schiller, C. E., Richards, J. G., O'Hara, M. W., & Stuart, S. (2011). Depression and anxiety among postpartum and adoptive mothers. *Archives of Women's Mental Health, 14*(4), 335.

Mughal, S., Azhar, Y., & Siddiqui, W. (2021). Postpartum depression. Retrieved from www.ncbi.nlm.nih.gov/books/NBK519070/.

Murmu, J., Venkatnarayan, K., Thapar, R. K., Shaw, S. C., & Dalal, S. S. (2017). When alternative female Kangaroo care is provided by other immediate postpartum mothers, it reduces postprocedural pain in preterm babies more than swaddling. *Acta Paediatrica, 106*(3), 411–415.

Myrhaug, H. T., Brurberg, K. G., Hov, L., & Markestad, T. (2019). Survival and impairment of extremely premature infants: A meta-analysis. *Pediatrics, 143*(2), e20180933. doi: 10.1542/peds.2018-0933.

National Academies of Sciences & Medicine. (2020). Birth settings in America: Outcomes, quality, access, and choice. doi: 10.17226/25636.

National Institute of Mental Health. (2017). Postpartum depression facts. Retrieved from www.nimh.nih.gov/health/publications/postpartum-depression-facts/index.shtml.

Newman, A. E. (2017). Poor attachment and the socioemotional effects during early childhood. *Electronic Theses, Projects, and Dissertations.* 554. https://scholarworks.lib.csusb.edu/etd/554.

Ohlsson, A., & Shah, P. S. (2016). Paracetamol (acetaminophen) for prevention or treatment of pain in newborns. *The Cochrane Library.*

Oostenbroek, J., Suddendorf, T., Nielsen, M., Redshaw, J., Kennedy-Costantini, S., Davis, J., . . . Slaughter, V. (2016). Comprehensive longitudinal study challenges the existence of neonatal imitation in humans. *Current Biology, 26*(10), 1334–1338.

Østborg, T. B., Romundstad, P. R., & Eggebø, T. M. (2017). Duration of the active phase of labor in spontaneous and induced labors. *Acta Obstetricia et Gynecologica Scandinavica, 96*(1), 120–127.

Osterman, M. J. K. (2020). Recent trends in vaginal birth after cesarean delivery: United States. Retrieved from www.cdc.gov/nchs/products/databriefs/db359.htm.

Pagni, A. M., Kellar, S., & Rood, M. (2017). *Effects of kangaroo care on procedural pain in preterm infants: A systematic review.* (Honors Research Project), University of Akron.

Pappas, A., & Korzeniewski, S. J. (2016). Long-term cognitive outcomes of birth asphyxia and the contribution of identified perinatal asphyxia to cerebral palsy. *Clinics in Perinatology, 43*(3), 559–572.

Peacock, P. J., Zengeya, S. T., Cochrane, L., & Sleath, M. (2018). Neonatal outcomes following delivery in water: Evaluation of safety in a district general hospital. *Cureus, 10*(2), e2208. doi: 10.7759/cureus.2208.

Penfield, C. A., Ibrahim, S. E. H., Nguyen, T., Gornbein, J., & Gregory, K. D. (2016). 797: Prediction of labor duration using individual-level demographic and characteristics. *American Journal of Obstetrics & Gynecology, 214*(1), S415–S416.

Prefumo, F., Ferrazzi, E., Di Tommaso, M., Severi, F. M., Locatelli, A., Chirico, G., . . . Zambolo, C. (2016). Neonatal morbidity after cesarean section before labor at 34+0 to 38+6 weeks: a cohort study. *Journal of Maternal-Fetal & Neonatal Medicine, 29*(8), 1334–1338.

Psouni, E., Agebjörn, J., & Linder, H. (2017). Symptoms of depression in Swedish fathers in the postnatal period and development of a screening tool. *Scandinavian Journal of Psychology, 58*(6), 485–496.

Raby, K. L., & Dozier, M. (2019). Attachment across the lifespan: Insights from adoptive families. *Current Opinion in Psychology, 25*, 81–85.

Ringler, N., Trause, M. A., Klaus, M., & Kennell, J. (1978). The effects of extra postpartum contact and maternal speech patterns on children's IQs, speech, and language comprehension at five. *Child Development, 49*(3), 862–865.

Romero, R., Dey, S. K., & Fisher, S. J. (2014). Preterm labor: One syndrome, many causes. *Science, 345*(6198), 760–765.

Rotstein, M., Stolar, O., Uliel, S., Mandel, D., Mani, A., Dollberg, S., . . . Leitner, Y. (2015). Facial expression in response to smell and taste stimuli in small and appropriate for gestational age newborns. *Journal of Child Neurology, 30*(11), 1466–1471.

Ruhräh, J. (1925). *Pediatrics of the past*. PB Hoeber.

Simon, R. M., Johnson, K. M., & Liddell, J. (2016). Amount, source, and quality of support as predictors of women's birth evaluations. *Birth, 43*(3), 226–232.

Soleimani, F., Zaheri, F., & Abdi, F. (2014). Long-term neurodevelopmental outcomes after preterm birth. *Iranian Red Crescent Medical Journal, 16*(6), e17965.

Spinelli, M., Frigerio, A., Montali, L., Fasolo, M., Spada, M. S., & Mangili, G. (2016). 'I still have difficulties feeling like a mother': The transition to motherhood of preterm infants mothers. *Psychology & Health, 31*(2), 184–204.

Steiner, J. E., Glaser, D., Hawilo, M. E., & Berridge, K. C. (2001). Comparative expression of hedonic impact: Affective reactions to taste by human infants and other primates. *Neuroscience & Biobehavioral Reviews, 25*(1), 53–74.

Still, G. F. (1931). *The history of pediatrics: The progress of the study of diseases of children*. Philadelphia, PA: Saunders.

Sullivan, R. M., Taborsky-Barba, S., Mendoza, R., Itano, A., Leon, M., Cotman, C. W., . . . Lott, I. (1991). Olfactory classical conditioning in neonates. *Pediatrics, 87*(4), 511–518.

Tamis-LeMonda, C. S.. (2022). Child Development: Context, Culture, and Cascades. Oxford University Press/Sinauer: Sunderland, MA.

Tarullo, A. R., Isler, J. R., Condon, C., Violaris, K., Balsam, P. D., & Fifer, W. P. (2016). Neonatal eyelid conditioning during sleep. *Developmental Psychobiology, 58*(7), 875–882.

Tatzer, E., Schubert, M. T., Timischl, W., & Simbruner, G. (1985). Discrimination of taste and preference for sweet in premature babies. *Early Human Development, 12*(1), 23–30.

Taylor, H., Kleine, I., Bewley, S., Loucaides, E., & Sutcliffe, A. (2016). Neonatal outcomes of waterbirth: A systematic review and meta-analysis. *Archives of Disease in Childhood-Fetal and Neonatal Edition, 101*(4), F357–F365.

Temkin, O. (1956). *Soranus' gynecology*: Johns Hopkins Press.

Tully, K. P., Holditch-Davis, D., White-Traut, R. C., David, R., O'shea, T. M., & Geraldo, V. (2016). A test of kangaroo care on preterm infant breastfeeding. *Journal of Obstetric, Gynecologic & Neonatal Nursing, 45*(1), 45–61.

U.S. National Library of Medicine. (2013). Cesarean section—A brief history. Retrieved from www.nlm.nih.gov/exhibition/cesarean/part1.html.

U.S. National Library of Medicine. (2021a). Infant reflexes. Retrieved from https://medlineplus.gov/ency/article/003292.htm.

U.S. National Library of Medicine. (2021b). Pregnancy and birth: Epidurals and painkillers for labor pain relief. Retrieved from www.ncbi.nlm.nih.gov/pubmedhealth/PMH0072751/.

UNICEF. (2021). Undernourishment in the womb can lead to diminished potential and predispose infants to early death. Retrieved from https://data.unicef.org/topic/nutrition/low-birthweight/#.

United Nations Population Fund. (2012). *The state of the world's midwifery 2011: Delivering health, saving lives*. Retrieved from www.who.int/pmnch/media/membernews/2011/2011_sowmr_en.pdf.

Unruh, A. M. (1992). Voices from the past: Ancient views of pain in childhood. *Clinical Journal of Pain, 8*(3), 247–254.

Valenti, J. (2011). Learning to love my baby. Retrieved from www.theguardian.com/lifeandstyle/2011/aug/18/baby-pregnancy-premature-birth.

Ventura, A. K. & Worobey, J. (2013). Early influences on the development of food preferences. *Current Biology, 23*(9), R401–R408.

Villar, J., Ismail, L. C., Victora, C. G., Ohuma, E. O., Bertino, E., Altman, D. G., . . . Jaffer, Y. A. (2014). International standards for newborn weight, length, and head circumference by gestational age and sex: The Newborn Cross-Sectional Study of the INTERGROWTH-21st Project. *Lancet, 384*(9946), 857–868.

Waldenström, U., Cnattingius, S., Vixner, L., & Norman, M. (2017). Advanced maternal age increases the risk of very preterm birth, irrespective of parity: A population-based register study. *BJOG: An International Journal of Obstetrics & Gynaecology, 124*(8), 1235–1244.

Wang, Z., Liu, J., Shuai, H., et al. (2021). Mapping global prevalence of depression among postpartum women. *Translational Psychiatry, 11*(543). doi: https://doi.org/10.1038/s41398-021-01663-6.

Weber, P., Depoorter, A., Hetzel, P., & Lemola, S. (2016). Habituation as parameter for prediction of mental development in healthy preterm infants: An electrophysiological pilot study. *Journal of Child Neurology, 31*(14), 1591–1597.

World Health Organization. (2015). WHO statement on caesarean section rates. Retrieved from www.who.int/reproductive health/publications/maternal_perinatal_health/cs-statement/en/.

World Health Organization. (2021). Preterm birth. Retrieved from www.who.int/mediacentre/factsheets/fs363/en/.

Zimmerman, E., & Rosner, A. (2018). Feeding swallowing difficulties in the first three years of life: A preterm and full-term infant comparison. *Journal of Neonatal Nursing, 24*(6), 331–335.

Chapter 5

Adolph, K. E., Cole, W. G., Komati, M., Garciaguirre, J. S., Badaly, D., Lingeman, J. M., . . . Sotsky, R. B. (2012). How do you learn to walk? Thousands of steps and dozens of falls per day. *Psychological Science, 23*(11), 1387–1394.

American Academy of Pediatrics. (2016a). American Academy of Pediatrics announces new recommendations for children's media use. Retrieved from www.aap.org/en-us/about-the-aap/aap-press-room/pages/american-academy-of-pediatrics-announces-new-recommendations-for-childrens-media-use.aspx.

American Academy of Pediatrics. (2016b). SIDS and other sleep-related infant deaths: Updated 2016 Recommendations for a safe infant sleeping environment. *Pediatrics, 138*(5) e20162938. Retrieved from https://publications.aap.org/pediatrics/article/138/5/e20162938/60309/SIDS-and-Other-Sleep-Related-Infant-Deaths-Updated?autologincheck=redirected.

American Academy of Pediatrics. (2017). Infant food and feeding. Retrieved from www.aap.org/en-us/advocacy-and-policy/aap-health-initiatives/HALF-Implementation-Guide/Age-Specific-Content/Pages/Infant-Food-and-Feeding.aspx.

American Academy of Pediatrics. (2020). Choosing a formula. Retrieved from www.healthychildren.org/English/ages-stages/baby/formula-feeding/Pages/Choosing-an-Infant-Formula.aspx?_ga=2.63351916.292443082.1637526972-1138070981.1637526972&_gl=1*vvkukw*_ga*MTEzODA3MDk4MS4xNjM3NTI2OTcy*_ga_FD9D3XZVQQ*MTYzNzUyNjk3Mi4xLjAuMTYzNzUyNjk3Mi4w.

American Academy of Pediatrics. (2021). Create your family media plan. Retrieved from www.healthychildren.org/English/media/Pages/default.aspx#wizard.

American Optometric Association. (2021). Infant vision: Birth to 24 months. Retrieved from www.aoa.org/healthy-eyes/eye-health-for-life/infant-vision?sso=y.

Babcock, K. R., Page, J. S., Fallon, J. R., & Webb, A. E. (2021). Adult hippocampal neurogenesis in aging and Alzheimer's disease. *Stem Cell Reports, 16*(4), 681–693.

Babic, A., Sasamoto, N., Rosner, B. A., Tworoger, S. S., Jordan, S. J., Risch, H. A., . . . Fortner, R. T. (2020). Association between breastfeeding and ovarian cancer risk. *JAMA Oncology, 6*(6), e200421–e200421.

Ball, H. L., Moya, E., Fairley, L., Westman, J., Oddie, S., & Wright, J. (2012). Infant care practices related to sudden infant death syndrome in South Asian and White British families in the UK. *Paediatric and Perinatal Epidemiology, 26*(1), 3–12.

Barr, R. G. (2012). Preventing abusive head trauma resulting from a failure of normal interaction between infants and their caregivers. *Proceedings of the National Academy of Sciences, 109*(Supplement 2), 17294–17301.

Beck, D., de Lange, A.-M. G., Maximov, I. I., Richard, G., Andreassen, O. A., Nordvik, J. E., & Westlye, L. T. (2021). White matter microstructure across the adult lifespan: A mixed longitudinal and cross-sectional study using advanced diffusion models and brain-age prediction. *Neuroimage, 224*, 117441.

Bick, J., & Nelson, C. A. (2016). Early adverse experiences and the developing brain. *Neuropsychopharmacology, 41*(1), 177–196.

Bombard, J. M., Kortsmit, K., Warner, L., Shapiro-Mendoza, C. K., Cox, S., Kroelinger, C. D. . . . Barfield, W. D. (2018). Vital Signs: Trends and Disparities in Infant Safe Sleep Practices - United States, 2009–2015. *MMWR. Morbidity and mortality weekly report, 67*(1), 39–46.

Boonzaaijer, M., Suir, I., Mollema, J., Nuysink, J., Volman, M., & Jongmans, M. (2021). Factors associated with gross motor development from birth to independent walking: A systematic review of longitudinal research. *Child Care, Health and Development, 47*(4), 525–561.

Bornstein, M. H., Ferdinandsen, K., & Gross, C. G. (1981). Perception of symmetry in infancy. *Developmental Psychology, 17*(1), 82.

Breedlove S. M. (2015). Principles of Psychology. Sunderland, MA: Sinauer/Oxford University Press.

Breedlove, S. M. and Watson, N. V. (2019). *Behavioral Neuroscience*, 9th ed. Sunderland, MA: Sinauer/Oxford University Press.

Burnham, D., & Mattock, K. (2010). Auditory development. In *The Wiley-Blackwell handbook of infant development, Volume 1, Second Edition*, pp. 81–119.

Canadian Association of the Deaf. (2015). Cochlear implants. Retrieved from http://cad.ca/issues-positions/cochlear-implants/.

Carpenter, R., McGarvey, C., Mitchell, E. A., Tappin, D. M., Vennemann, M. M., Smuk, M., & Carpenter, J. R. (2013). Bed sharing when parents do not smoke: is there a risk of SIDS? An individual level analysis of five major case-control studies. *BMJ Open, 3*(5), e002299.

Center on the Developing Child. (2021). Brain architecture. Retrieved from https://developingchild.harvard.edu/science/key-concepts/brain-architecture/.

Centers for Disease Control and Prevention. (2010a). Data table for boys length-for-age and weight-for-age charts. Retrieved from www.cdc.gov/growthcharts/who/boys_length_weight.htm.

Centers for Disease Control and Prevention. (2010b). Data table for girls length-for-age and weight-for-age charts. Retrieved from www.cdc.gov/growthcharts/who/girls_length_weight.htm.

Centers for Disease Control and Prevention. (2017). Breastfeeding: Results: Breastfeeding rates. Retrieved from www.cdc.gov/breastfeeding/data/nis_data/results.html.

Centers for Disease Control and Prevention. (2020). Breastfeeding report card. Retrieved from www.cdc.gov/breastfeeding/data/reportcard.htm.

Centers for Disease Control and Prevention. (2021a). Child health. Retrieved from www.cdc.gov/nchs/fastats/child-health.htm.

Centers for Disease Control and Prevention. (2021b). Infant mortality. Retrieved from www.cdc.gov/reproductivehealth/maternalinfanthealth/infantmortality.htm.

Centers for Disease Control and Prevention. (2021c). Infant mortality rates by state. Retrieved from www.cdc.gov/

nchs/pressroom/sosmap/infant_mortality_rates/infant_mortality.htm.

Centers for Disease Control and Prevention. (2021d). Sudden unexpected infant death and sudden infant death syndrome. Retrieved from www.cdc.gov/sids/data.htm.

Chen, A., Oster, E., & Williams, H. (2016). Why is infant mortality higher in the United States than in Europe? *American Economic Journal. Economic Policy, 8*(2), 89.

Cheung, C. H., Bedford, R., De Urabain, I. R. S., Karmiloff-Smith, A., & Smith, T. J. (2017). Daily touchscreen use in infants and toddlers is associated with reduced sleep and delayed sleep onset. *Scientific Reports, 7*, 46104.

Chiang, K. V., Ruowei, L., Anstey, E. H., & Perrine, C. G. (2021). Racial and ethnic disparities in breastfeeding initiation—United States, 2019. *Morbidity and Mortality Weekly Report, 70*(21), 769–774. Retrieved from www.cdc.gov/mmwr/volumes/70/wr/mm7021a1.htm#T1_down.

Christakis, D. A. (2009). The effects of infant media usage: What do we know and what should we learn? *Acta Paediatrica, 98*(1), 8–16.

Clayton, H. B., Li, R., Perrine, C. G., & Scanlon, K. S. (2013). Prevalence and reasons for introducing infants early to solid foods: Variations by milk feeding type. *Pediatrics, 131*(4), e1108–e1114. doi: 10.1542/peds.2012-2265.

Clerc, O., Fort, M., Schwarzer, G., Krasotkina, A., Vilain, A., Méary, D., . . . Pascalis, O. (2021). Can language modulate perceptual narrowing for faces? Other-race face recognition in infants is modulated by language experience. *International Journal of Behavioral Development*, 01650254211053054.

Common Sense Media. (2020). The Common Sense census: Media use by kids age zero to eight. Retrieved from www.commonsensemedia.org/media-use-by-kids-ages-zero-to-eight-2020-infographic.

Conel, J. L. (1939–1967). *The postnatal development of the human cerebral cortex: Vols. 1–8.* Cambridge, MA: Harvard University Press.

David, P.-J., del Carmen, R.-J. M., María, A. d. l. R. O., & Sandra, M.-M. M. (2016). Evaluation of the effectiveness of cochlear implant according to age of implantation. *Global Advanced Research Journal of Medicine and Medical Sciences, 5*(8), 237–242.

Davis, B. E., Moon, R. Y., Sachs, H. C., & Ottolini, M. C. (1998). Effects of sleep position on infant motor development. *Pediatrics, 102*(5), 1135–1140.

de Faria, O., Pivonkova, H., Varga, B., Timmler, S., Evans, K. A., & Káradóttir, R. T. (2021). Periods of synchronized myelin changes shape brain function and plasticity. *Nature Neuroscience, 24*(11), 1508–1521.

De Paula, M. C. G., Pereira, C. U., & Rabelo, N. N. (2020). Shaken baby syndrome: Literature review in the last 5 years. *Archives of Pediatric Neurosurgery, 2*(2), e392020–e392020.

DeCasper, A. J., & Spence, M. J. (1986). Prenatal maternal speech influences newborns' perception of speech sounds. *Infant Behavior and Development, 9*(2), 133–150.

Dellinger, A., & Gilchrist, J. (2019). Leading causes of fatal and nonfatal unintentional injury for children and teens and the role of lifestyle clinicians. *American Journal of Lifestyle Medicine, 13*(1), 7–21.

Dias, M. S., Smith, K., Mazur, P., Li, V., & Shaffer, M. L. (2005). Preventing abusive head trauma among infants and young children: A hospital-based, parent education program. *Pediatrics, 115*(4), e470–e477.

Duch, H., Fisher, E. M., Ensari, I., & Harrington, A. (2013). Screen time use in children under 3 years old: A systematic review of correlates. *International Journal of Behavioral Nutrition and Physical Activity, 10*(1), 102.

ElShmay, W. M. (2016). The protective effect of longer duration of breastfeeding against pregnancy-associated triple negative breast cancer. *Oncotarget, 7*(33), 53941.

Eunice Kennedy Shriver National Institute of Child Health and Human Development. (2017). Key moments in Safe to Sleep history: 1969–1993. Retrieved from www.nichd.nih.gov/sts/campaign/moments/Pages/1969-1993.aspx.

Fantz, R. L. (1961). The origin of form perception. *Scientific American, 204*(5), 66–73.

FAO, IFAD, UNICEF, WFP and WHO. (2020). The State of Food Security and Nutrition in the World 2020. Transforming food systems for affordable healthy diets. Rome, FAO. Retrieved from https://doi.org/10.4060/ca9692en.

Ge, L., Zhang, H., Wang, Z., Quinn, P. C., Pascalis, O., Kelly, D., . . . Lee, K. (2009). Two faces of the other-race effect: Recognition and categorisation of Caucasian and Chinese faces. *Perception, 38*(8), 1199–1210.

Gesell, A., Thompson, H., & Amatruda, C. S. C. (1934). *Infant behavior: Its genesis and growth.* McGraw-Hill Book Company.

Gibson, E. J., & Walk, R. D. (1960). The "visual cliff." *Scientific American, 202*(4), 64–71.

Gilmore, J. H., Lin, W., Prastawa, M. W., Looney, C. B., Vetsa, Y. S. K., Knickmeyer, R. C., . . . Lieberman, J. A. (2007). Regional gray matter growth, sexual dimorphism, and cerebral asymmetry in the neonatal brain. *Journal of Neuroscience, 27*(6), 1255–1260.

Givrad, S. (2016). Dream theory and science: A review. *Psychoanalytic Inquiry, 36*(3), 199–213.

Götz, M., Nakafuku, M., & Petrik, D. (2016). Neurogenesis in the developing and adult brain—Similarities and key differences. *Cold Spring Harbor Perspectives in Biology, 8*(7), a018853.

Griffey, J. A., & Little, A. C. (2014). Infant's visual preferences for facial traits associated with adult attractiveness judgements: Data from eye-tracking. *Infant Behavior and Development, 37*(3), 268–275.

Gross, R. E. (2020). Functional hemispherectomy in adults: All we have to sphere is sphere itself. *Epilepsy Currents, 20*(3), 144–146.

Heron, M. (2017). *Deaths: Leading causes for 2015.* Retrieved from https://stacks.cdc.gov/view/cdc/50010.

Herzog, J. I., Thome, J., Demirakca, T., Koppe, G., Ende, G., Lis, S., . . . Steil, R. (2020). Influence of severity of type and timing of retrospectively reported childhood maltreatment on female amygdala and hippocampal volume. *Scientific Reports, 10*(1), 1–10.

Hoban, T. F. (2004). Sleep and its disorders in children. *Seminars in Neurology, 24*, 327–340.

Holmes, A. V., Jones, H. G., & Christensen, B. C. (2017). Breastfeeding and cancer prevention. NH Comprehensive Cancer

Collaboration in partnership with Dartmouth-Hitchcock Norris Cotton Cancer Center and its NCI National Outreach Network Community Health Educator Site.

Huang, Y., Xue, X., Spelke, E., Huang, L., Zheng, W., & Peng, K. (2018). The aesthetic preference for symmetry dissociates from early-emerging attention to symmetry. *Scientific Reports, 8*(1), 1–8.

Huh, S. Y., Rifas-Shiman, S. L., Taveras, E. M., Oken, E., & Gillman, M. W. (2011). Timing of solid food introduction and risk of obesity in preschool-aged children. *Pediatrics, 127*(3), e544–e551.

Hunchak, C. (2020). Safe Babies New York: The Upstate New York Shaken Baby Syndrome (SBS) Education Program. In *Casebook of traumatic injury prevention* (pp. 503–517). Springer.

International Monetary Fund. (2018). GDP per capita, current prices. Retrieved from www.imf.org/external/datamapper/NGDPDPC@WEO/OEMDC/ADVEC/WEOWORLD.

Janssen, X., Martin, A., Hughes, A. R., Hill, C. M., Kotronoulas, G., & Hesketh, K. R. (2020). Associations of screen time, sedentary time and physical activity with sleep in under 5s: A systematic review and meta-analysis. *Sleep medicine reviews, 49*, 101226.

Johnson, D. (2014). Will baby crawl? Retrieved from www.nsf.gov/discoveries/disc_summ.jsp?cntn_id=103153.

Johnson, M. H., Dziurawiec, S., Ellis, H., & Morton, J. (1991). Newborns' preferential tracking of face-like stimuli and its subsequent decline. *Cognition, 40*(1), 1–19.

Jusczyk, P. W. (1997). *The discovery of spoken language.* Cambridge, MA: MIT Press.

Kagan, J., & Herschkowitz, N. (2006). *A young mind in a growing brain.* Psychology Press.

Karasik, L. B., Tamis-LeMonda, C. S., Adolph, K. E., & Bornstein, M. H. (2015). Places and postures: A cross-cultural comparison of sitting in 5-month-olds. *Journal of Cross-Cultural Psychology, 46*(8), 1023–1038.

Karasik, L. B., Tamis-LeMonda, C. S., Ossmy, O., & Adolph, K. E. (2018). The ties that bind: Cradling in Tajikistan. *PLOS ONE 13*(10), e0204428.

Kelishadi, R., & Farajian, S. (2014). The protective effects of breastfeeding on chronic non-communicable diseases in adulthood: A review of evidence. *Advanced Biomedical Research, 3*, 3.

Keller, H. (2017). Culture and development: A systematic relationship. *Perspectives on Psychological Science, 12*(5), 833–840.

Kelly, D. J., Liu, S., Lee, K., Quinn, P. C., Pascalis, O., Slater, A. M., & Ge, L. (2009). Development of the other-race effect during infancy: Evidence toward universality? *Journal of Experimental Child Psychology, 104*(1), 105–114.

KidsHealth.org. (2017). Sudden infant death syndrome (SIDS). Retrieved from http://kidshealth.org/en/parents/sids.html.

King, M. D., & Giefer, K. G. (2021). Nearly a third of children who receive SNAP participate in two or more additional programs. Retrieved from www.census.gov/library/stories/2021/06/most-children-receiving-snap-get-at-least-one-other-social-safety-net-benefit.html.

Krasotkina, A., Götz, A., Höhle, B., & Schwarzer, G. (2021). Perceptual narrowing in face-and speech-perception domains in infancy: A longitudinal approach. *Infant Behavior and Development, 64*, 101607.

Kuraguchi, K., Taniguchi, K., Kanari, K., & Itakura, S. (2020). Face preference in infants at six and nine months old: The effects of facial attractiveness and observation experience. *Symmetry, 12*(7), 1082.

Langlois, J. H., Roggman, L. A., Casey, R. J., Ritter, J. M., Rieser-Danner, L. A., & Jenkins, V. Y. (1987). Infant preferences for attractive faces: Rudiments of a stereotype? *Developmental Psychology, 23*(3), 363.

Leat, S. J., Yadav, N. K., & Irving, E. L. (2009). Development of visual acuity and contrast sensitivity in children. *Journal of Optometry, 2*(1), 19–26.

Madrigal, A. C. (2018, May). When did TV watching peak? *The Atlantic.* Retrieved from https://www.theatlantic.com/technology/archive/2018/05/when-did-tv-watching-peak/561464/.

Maurer, D., & Werker, J. F. (2014). Perceptual narrowing during infancy: A comparison of language and faces. *Developmental Psychobiology, 56*(2), 154–178.

McKenzie, I. A., Ohayon, D., Li, H., De Faria, J. P., Emery, B., Tohyama, K., & Richardson, W. D. (2014). Motor skill learning requires active central myelination. *Science, 346*(6207), 318–322.

Mei, J. (1994). The northern Chinese custom of rearing babies in sandbags: Implications for motor and intellectual development. In J. H. A. van Rossum & J. I. Laszlo (Eds.), *Motor development: Aspects of normal and delayed development* (pp. 41–48). Amsterdam: VU Uitgeverij.

Moon, R. Y. (2021). How to keep your sleeping baby safe: AAP policy explained. Retrieved from www.healthychildren.org/English/ages-stages/baby/sleep/Pages/A-Parents-Guide-to-Safe-Sleep.aspx.

Murphy, S. L., Xu, J., Kochanek, K. D., Curtin, S. C., & Arias, E. (2017). *Deaths: Final Data for 2015.* Retrieved from https://stacks.cdc.gov/view/cdc/50011.

Myszkowska-Ryciak, J., Harton, H., Lange, E., Laskowski, W., Wawrzyniak, A., Hamulka, J., & Gajewska, D. (2020). Reduced Screen Time is Associated with Healthy Dietary Behaviors but Not Body Weight Status among Polish Adolescents. Report from the Wise Nutrition—Healthy Generation Project. *Nutrients, 12*(5), 1323.

National Center on Shaken Baby Syndrome. (2017). Learn More. Retrieved from www.dontshake.org/learn-more.

National Institute of Neurological Disorders and Stroke. (2021). Brain basics: Genes at work in the brain. Retrieved from www.ninds.nih.gov/Disorders/Patient-Caregiver-Education/Genes-Work-Brain.

National Institute on Deafness and Other Communication Disorders. (2017). Ear infections in children. Retrieved from www.nidcd.nih.gov/health/ear-infections-children.

National Library of Medicine. (1986). A vulnerable age: Environment, behavior and the spread of diarrhoea. Retrieved from https://pubmed.ncbi.nlm.nih.gov/12315286/.

Nielsen. (2009). Historical daily viewing activity among households & persons 2+. Retrieved from https://www.nielsen.com/wp-content/uploads/sites/3/2019/04/historicalviewing.pdf.

Noble, K. G., Houston, S. M., Kan, E., & Sowell, E. R. (2012). Neural correlates of socioeconomic status in the developing human brain. *Developmental Science, 15*(4), 516–527.

Office of the Surgeon General (US). (2011). The Surgeon General's call to action to support breastfeeding: Rates of breastfeeding. Retrieved from www.ncbi.nlm.nih.gov/books/NBK52681/.

Paruthi, S., Brooks, L. J., D'Ambrosio, C., Hall, W. A., Kotagal, S., Lloyd, R. M. . . . Wise, M. S. (2016). Recommended Amount of Sleep for Pediatric Populations: A Consensus Statement of the American Academy of Sleep Medicine. *Journal of Clinical Sleep Medicine 12*(6), 785–786.

Pattison, K. L., Kraschnewski, J. L., Lehman, E., Savage, J. S., Downs, D. S., Leonard, K. S., . . . Kjerulff, K. H. (2019). Breastfeeding initiation and duration and child health outcomes in the first baby study. *Preventive Medicine, 118*, 1–6.

Przybylski, A. K., & Weinstein, N. (2017). Digital screen time limits and young children's psychological well-being: Evidence From a population-based study. *Child Development, 90*(1), e56–e65.

Quinn, P. C., Lee, K., Pascalis, O., & Tanaka, J. W. (2016). Narrowing in categorical responding to other-race face classes by infants. *Developmental Science, 19*(3), 362–371.

Robertson, J., Simoes-Franklin, C., Ferguson, O., Hussey, A., Costello, P., Walshe, P., . . . Gill, I. (2021). Listening and spoken language outcomes after 5 years of cochlear implant use for children born preterm and at term. *Developmental Medicine & Child Neurology, 64*(4), 481–487.

Safe to Sleep. (2017). Progress in reducing SIDS. Retrieved from https://safetosleep.nichd.nih.gov/activities/SIDS/progress.

Saffran, J. R., Werker, J. F., & Werner, L. A. (2006). The infant's auditory world: Hearing, speech, and the beginnings of language. In D. Kuhn, R. S. Siegler, W. Damon, & R. M. Lerner (Eds.), *Handbook of child psychology: Cognition, perception, and language* (pp. 58–108). John Wiley & Sons Inc.

Sanyaolu, A., Okorie, C., Qi, X., Locke, J., & Rehman, S. (2019). Childhood and Adolescent Obesity in the United States: A Public Health Concern. *Global Pediatric Health, 6*, 2333794X19891305.

Schusse, C. M., Smith, K., & Drees, C. (2017). Outcomes after hemispherectomy in adult patients with intractable epilepsy: Institutional experience and systematic review of the literature. *Journal of Neurosurgery, 128*(3), 1–9.

Shurtleff, H. A., Roberts, E. A., Young, C. C., Barry, D., Warner, M. H., Saneto, R. P., . . . Ellenbogen, R. G. (2021). Pediatric hemispherectomy outcome: Adaptive functioning, intelligence, and memory. *Epilepsy & Behavior, 124*, 108298.

Simonato, I., Janosz, M., Archambault, I., & Pagani, L. S. (2018). Prospective associations between toddler televiewing and subsequent lifestyle habits in adolescence. *Preventive Medicine 110*, 24–30.

Singh, L., Loh, D., & Xiao, N. G. (2017). Bilingual infants demonstrate perceptual flexibility in phoneme discrimination but perceptual constraint in face discrimination. *Frontiers in Psychology, 8*, 1563.

Skaliora, I. (2002). *Experience-dependent plasticity in the developing brain.* Paper presented at the International Congress Series.

Slater, A., Von der Schulenburg, C., Brown, E., Badenoch, M., Butterworth, G., Parsons, S., & Samuels, C. (1998). Newborn infants prefer attractive faces. *Infant Behavior and Development, 21*(2), 345–354.

Smith, L. B. (2006). Movement matters: The contributions of Esther Thelen. *Biological Theory, 1*(1), 87–89.

Spalding, K. L., Bergmann, O., Alkass, K., Bernard, S., Salehpour, M., Huttner, H. B., . . . Buchholz, B. A. (2013). Dynamics of hippocampal neurogenesis in adult humans. *Cell, 153*(6), 1219–1227.

Spelke, E. (1976). Infants' intermodal perception of events. *Cognitive Psychology, 8*(4), 553–560.

Spinelli, J., Collins-Praino, L., Van Den Heuvel, C., & Byard, R. W. (2017). Evolution and significance of the triple risk model in sudden infant death syndrome. *Journal of Paediatrics and Child Health, 53*(2), 112–115.

Stanford Children's Health. (2021a). Failure to thrive. Retrieved from www.stanfordchildrens.org/en/topic/default?id=failure-to-thrive-90-P02297.

Stanford Children's Health. (2021b). Newborn sleep patterns. Retrieved from www.stanfordchildrens.org/en/topic/default?id=newborn-sleep-patterns-90-P02632.

Stiles, J. (2008). *The fundamentals of brain development: Integrating nature and nurture.* Harvard University Press.

Super, C. M. (1976). Environmental effects on motor development: The case of 'African infant precocity'. *Developmental Medicine & Child Neurology, 18*(5), 561–567.

Task Force on Sudden Infant Death Syndrome. (2016). SIDS and other sleep-related infant deaths: Updated 2016 recommendations for a safe infant sleeping environment. *Pediatrics,* e20162938.

Thelen, E. (2005). Dynamic systems theory and the complexity of change. *Psychoanalytic Dialogues, 15*(2), 255–283.

Thompson, A. L., Adair, L. S., & Bentley, M. E. (2013). Maternal characteristics and perception of temperament associated with infant TV exposure. *Pediatrics 131*(2), e390–e397. doi: 10.1542/peds.2012-1224.

Thompson, J. M., Tanabe, K., Moon, R. Y., Mitchell, E. A., McGarvey, C., Tappin, D., . . . Hauck, F. R. (2017). Duration of breastfeeding and risk of SIDS: An individual participant data meta-analysis. *Pediatrics, 140*(5), e20171324.

U.S. Department of Agriculture. (2021). Food security status of U.S. households in 2020. Retrieved from www.ers.usda.gov/topics/food-nutrition-assistance/food-security-in-the-us/key-statistics-graphics.aspx.

U.S. Department of Health and Human Services. (2021). Progress in reducing SIDS. Retrieved from https://safetosleep.nichd.nih.gov/activities/SIDS/progress.

Underwood, M. A. (2013). Human milk for the premature infant. *Pediatric Clinics, 60*(1), 189–207.

Urban Child Institute. (2017). Baby's brain begins now: Conception to age 3. Retrieved from www.urbanchildinstitute.org/why-0-3/baby-and-brain.

Uytun, M. C. (2018). Development period of prefrontal cortex. In A. Starcevic & B. Filipovic (Eds.), *Prefrontal cortex.* IntechOpen.

van Schooneveld, M. M., Braun, K. P., van Rijen, P. C., van Nieuwenhuizen, O., & Jennekens-Schinkel, A. (2016). The spectrum of long-term cognitive and functional outcome after hemispherectomy in childhood. *European Journal of Paediatric Neurology, 20*(3), 376–384.

Villar, J., Ismail, L. C., Victora, C. G., Ohuma, E. O., Bertino, E., Altman, D. G. . . .Kennedy, S. H. (2014). International standards for newborn weight, length, and head circumference by gestational age and sex: the Newborn Cross-Sectional Study of the INTERGROWTH-21st Project. *The Lancet, 384,* 857–868.

Walhof, R. (1996). Blindness—what it means in the mind of a blind child. *Future Reflections, 15*(2), https://nfb.org//sites/default/files/images/nfb/publications/fr/fr15/issue2/f150205.html.

Waidyatillake, N., Dharmage, S., Allen, K., Bowatte, G., Boyle, R., Burgess, J., . . . Lodge, C. (2018). Association between the age of solid food introduction and eczema: A systematic review and a meta-analysis. *Clinical & Experimental Allergy, 48*(8), 1000–1015.

Wallis, L. (2013). Is 25 the new cut-off point for adulthood? Retrieved from www.bbc.com/news/magazine-24173194.

West, B. A., Rudd, R. A., Sauber-Schatz, E. K., & Ballesteros, M. F. (2021). Unintentional injury deaths in children and youth, 2010–2019. *Journal of Safety Research, 78,* 322–330.

Wong, K. (2009). Crawling may be unneccessary for normal child development. *Scientific American.* Retrieved from www.scientificamerican.com/article/crawling-may-be-unnecessary/.

Woolford, S. J.; Sidell, M., Li, X.; Else, V.; Young, D. R.; Resnicow, K.; & Koebnick, C. (2021). Changes in Body Mass Index Among Children and Adolescents During the COVID-19 Pandemic *JAMA, 326*(14), 1434–1436.

World Health Organization. (2020). Newborns: Improving survival and well-being. Retrieved from www.who.int/news-room/fact-sheets/detail/newborns-reducing-mortality.

World Health Organization. (2021a). Malnutrition. Retrieved from www.who.int/mediacentre/factsheets/malnutrition/en/.

World Health Organization. (2021b). Obesity and overweight. Retrieved from www.who.int/news-room/fact-sheets/detail/obesity-and-overweight.

Zero to Three. (2016). Baby brain map. Retrieved from www.zerotothree.org/resources/529-baby-brain-map.

Chapter 6

Afifi, T. O. (2012). The relationship between child maltreatment and Axis I mental disorders: A summary of the published literature from 2006 to 2010. *Open Journal of Psychiatry, 2*(01), 21.

Akers, K. G., Martinez-Canabal, A., Restivo, L., Yiu, A. P., De Cristofaro, A., Hsiang, H.-L. L., . . . Shoji, H. (2014). Hippocampal neurogenesis regulates forgetting during adulthood and infancy. *Science, 344*(6184), 598–602.

Alberini, C. M., & Travaglia, A. (2017). Infantile amnesia: A critical period of learning to learn and remember. *Journal of Neuroscience, 37*(24), 5783–5795.

American Academy of Pediatrics. (2016). American Academy of Pediatrics announces new recommendations for children's media use. Retrieved from www.aap.org/en-us/about-the-aap/aap-press-room/pages/american-academy-of-pediatrics-announces-new-recommendations-for-childrens-media-use.aspx.

American Academy of Pediatrics. (2018). Language delays in toddlers: Information for parents. Retrieved from www.healthychildren.org/English/ages-stages/toddler/Pages/Language-Delay.aspx.

American Academy of Pediatrics. (2021). Language delays in toddlers: Information for parents. Retrieved from www.healthychildren.org/English/ages-stages/toddler/Pages/Language-Delay.aspx.

Arntz, A. (2020). A plea for more attention to mental representations. *Journal of Behavior Therapy and Experimental Psychiatry, 67,* 101510.

Baillargeon, R., & DeVos, J. (1991). Object permanence in young infants: Further evidence. *Child Development, 62*(6), 1227–1246.

Begus, K., Gliga, T., & Southgate, V. (2016). Infants' preferences for native speakers are associated with an expectation of information. *Proceedings of the National Academy of Sciences, 113*(44), 12397–12402.

Belardi, K., Watson, L. R., Faldowski, R. A., Hazlett, H., Crais, E., Baranek, G. T., . . . Oller, D. K. (2017). A retrospective video analysis of canonical babbling and volubility in infants with Fragile X Syndrome at 9–12 months of age. *Journal of autism and developmental disorders, 47*(4), 1193–1206.

Bialystok, E. (2015). Bilingualism and the development of executive function: The role of attention. *Child Development Perspectives, 9*(2), 117–121.

Bloom, L., Lifter, K., & Broughton, J. (1985). The convergence of early cognition and language in the second year of life: Problems in conceptualization and measurement. *Children's single-word speech,* 149–180.

Brubaker, J. (2016). Cognitive Development Theory. *The Wiley Blackwell Encyclopedia of Family Studies.*

Brushe, M. E., Lynch, J., Reilly, S., Melhuish, E., Mittinty, M. N., & Brinkman, S. A. (2021). The education word gap emerges by 18 months: Findings from an Australian prospective study. *BMC pediatrics, 21*(1), 1–9.

Bushnell, I. (2001). Mother's face recognition in newborn infants: Learning and memory. *Infant and Child Development, 10*(1–2), 67–74.

Carroll, R. (2016). Starved, tortured, forgotten: Genie, the feral child who left a mark on researchers. Retrieved from www.theguardian.com/society/2016/jul/14/genie-feral-child-los-angeles-researchers.

Chen, W., & Adler, J. L. (2019). Assessment of Screen Exposure in Young Children, 1997 to 2014. *JAMA Pediatrics.*

Chen, Z., & Siegler, R. S. (2000). II. Overlapping waves theory. *Monographs of the Society for Research in Child Development, 65*(2), 7–11.

Chomsky, N. (1959). A review of BF Skinner's Verbal Behavior. *Language, 35*(1), 26–58.

Chomsky, N. (2014). *Aspects of the Theory of Syntax* (Vol. 11). MIT press.

Chua, H. F., Boland, J. E., & Nisbett, R. E. (2005). Cultural variation in eye movements during scene perception. *Proceedings of the National Academy of Sciences, U.S.A. 102*(35) 12629–12633.

Clemens, L. F., & Kegel, C. A. (2021). Unique contribution of shared book reading on adult-child language interaction. *Journal of child language, 48*(2), 373–386.

Common Sense Media. (2018). *The Common Sense Census: Media use by kids age zero to eight.* Retrieved from https://www.commonsensemedia.org/%20research/the-common-sense-census-media-use-bykids-age-zero-to-eight-2017.

Concannon-Gibney, T. (2021). "Teacher, teacher, can't catch me!": Teaching vocabulary and grammar using nursery rhymes to children for whom English is an additional language. *The Reading Teacher.* doi: 10.1002/trtr.2013.

Cook, A., Spinazzola, J., Ford, J., Lanktree, C., Blaustein, M., Cloitre, M., . . . Liautaud, J. (2017). Complex trauma in children and adolescents. *Psychiatric Annals, 35*(5), 390–398.

Cordon, I. M., Pipe, M.-E., Sayfan, L., Melinder, A., & Goodman, G. S. (2004). Memory for traumatic experiences in early childhood. *Developmental Review, 24*(1), 101–132.

Dale, P. S., Price, T. S., Bishop, D. V., & Plomin, R. (2003). Outcomes of early language delay: I. Predicting persistent and transient language difficulties at 3 and 4 years. *Journal of Speech, Language, and Hearing Research, 46*(3), 544–560.

Davis, B. J., & Evans, M. A. (2021). Children's self-reported strategies in emergent reading of an alphabet book. *Scientific Studies of Reading, 25*(1), 31–46.

De, P., & Chattopadhyay, N. (2019). Effects of malnutrition on child development: Evidence from a backward district of India. *Clinical Epidemiology and Global Health, 7*(3), 439–445.

DeCasper, A., & Fifer, W. (1980). Of human bonding: Newborns prefer their mothers' voices. *Readings on the Development of Children, M. Gauvain and M. Cole, Eds. Worth Publishers, 208,* 1174–1176.

Diamond, A. (1985). Development of the ability to use recall to guide action, as indicated by infants' performance on AB. *Child Development 56*(4), 868–883.

Diamond, A. (1991). Frontal lobe involvement in cognitive changes during the first year of life. In K. R. Gibson & A. C. Petrsen (Eds.), *Brain maturation and cognitive development: Comparative and cross-cultural perspectives,* (pp. 127–180). DeGruyter.

Dore, R. A., Zosh, J. M., Hirsh-Pasek, K., & Golinkoff, R. M. (2018). Plugging into word learning: The role of electronic toys and digital media in language development. In *Cognitive Development in Digital Contexts* (pp. 75–91). Elsevier.

Elkins, J., Briggs, H. E., Miller, K. M., Kim, I., Orellana, R., & Mowbray, O. (2019). Racial/ethnic differences in the impact of adverse childhood experiences on posttraumatic stress disorder in a nationally representative sample of adolescents. *Child and Adolescent Social Work Journal, 36*(5), 449–457.

Ellis, E. M., & Thal, D. J. (2008). Early language delay and risk for language impairment. *Perspectives on Language Learning and Education, 15*(3), 93–100.

Fan, S. P., Liberman, Z., Keysar, B., & Kinzler, K. D. (2015). The exposure advantage: Early exposure to a multilingual environment promotes effective communication. *Psychological Science, 26*(7), 1090–1097.

Fell, J., Ludowig, E., Staresina, B. P., Wagner, T., Kranz, T., Elger, C. E., & Axmacher, N. (2011). Medial temporal theta/alpha power enhancement precedes successful memory encoding: Evidence based on intracranial EEG. *Journal of Neuroscience, 31*(14), 5392–5397.

Fernald, A., & Kuhl, P. (1987). Acoustic determinants of infant preference for motherese speech. *Infant Behavior and Development, 10*(3), 279–293.

Fiske, A., & Holmboe, K. (2019). Neural substrates of early executive function development. *Developmental Review, 52,* 42–62.

Forestier, S., & Oudeyer, P.-Y. (2016). *Overlapping waves in tool use development: A curiosity-driven computational model.* Paper presented at the Development and Learning and Epigenetic Robotics (ICDL-EpiRob), 2016 Joint IEEE International Conference on.

Fromkin, V., Krashen, S., Curtiss, S., Rigler, D., & Rigler, M. (1974). The development of language in genie: A case of language acquisition beyond the "critical period". *Brain and Language, 1*(1), 81–107.

Gaudreau, C., King, Y. A., Dore, R. A., Puttre, H., Nichols, D., Hirsh-Pasek, K., & Golinkoff, R. M. (2020). Preschoolers benefit equally from video chat, pseudo-contingent video, and live book reading: Implications for storytime during the coronavirus pandemic and beyond. *Frontiers in Psychology, 11,* 2158.

Goff, B., Gee, D. G., Telzer, E. H., Humphreys, K. L., Gabard-Durnam, L., Flannery, J., & Tottenham, N. (2013). Reduced nucleus accumbens reactivity and adolescent depression following early-life stress. *Neuroscience, 249,* 129–138.

Goldstein, M. H., King, A. P., & West, M. J. (2003). Social interaction shapes babbling: Testing parallels between birdsong and speech. *Proceedings of the National Academy of Sciences, 100*(13), 8030–8035.

Golinkoff, R. M., Can, D. D., Soderstrom, M., & Hirsh-Pasek, K. (2015). (Baby) talk to me: The social context of infant-directed speech and its effects on early language acquisition. *Current Directions in Psychological Science, 24*(5), 339–344.

Gopnik, A., & Meltzoff, A. N. (2021). Early semantic developments and their relationship to object permanence, means-ends understanding, and categorization. In *Children's language* (pp. 191–212). Psychology Press.

Green, A. H. (1983). Dimension of psychological trauma in abused children. *Journal of the American Academy of Child Psychiatry, 22*(3), 231–237.

Grosjean, F. (2010). *Bilingual: Life and reality.* Harvard University Press.

Gupta, P. M., Perrine, C. G., Mei, Z., & Scanlon, K. S. (2016). Iron, anemia, and iron deficiency anemia among young children in the United States. *Nutrients, 8*(6), 330.

Harper, L. J. (2011). Nursery rhyme knowledge and phonological awareness in preschool children. *Journal of Language and Literacy Education, 7*(1), 65–78.

Hart, B., & Risley, T. R. (1995). *Meaningful differences in the everyday experience of young American children.* Baltimore, MD: Paul H Brookes Publishing.

Hartshorn, K., & Rovee-Collier, C. (1997). Infant learning and long-term memory at 6 months: A confirming analysis. *Developmental Psychobiology: The Journal of the International Society for Developmental Psychobiology, 30*(1), 71–85.

Hartshorne, J. K., Tenenbaum, J. B., & Pinker, S. (2018). A critical period for second language acquisition: Evidence from 2/3 million English speakers. *Cognition, 177,* 263–277.

Hayne, H., & Simcock, G. (2009). Memory development in toddlers. In M. L. Courage & N. Cowan (Eds.), *The development of memory in infancy and childhood* (pp. 43–68). New York: Psychology Press.

Heathcock, J. C., Bhat, A. N., Lobo, M. A., & Galloway, J. C. (2005). The relative kicking frequency of infants born full-term and preterm during learning and short-term and long-term memory periods of the mobile paradigm. *Physical Therapy* 85(1), 8–18.

Heimann, M., Nordqvist, E., Strid, K., Connant Almrot, J., & Tjus, T. (2016). Children with autism respond differently to spontaneous, elicited and deferred imitation. *Journal of Intellectual Disability Research, 60*(5), 491–501.

Hetzel, B. S. (1993). The control of iodine deficiency. *American Journal of Public Health, 83*(4), 494–495.

Hirsh-Pasek, K., Zosh, J. M., Golinkoff, R. M., Gray, J. H., Robb, M. B., & Kaufman, J. (2015). Putting education in "educational" apps: Lessons from the science of learning. *Psychological Science in the Public Interest, 16*(1), 3–34.

Hoff, E. (2003). The specificity of environmental influence: Socioeconomic status affects early vocabulary development via maternal speech. *Child Development, 74*(5), 1368–1378.

Hoff, E. (2006). How social contexts support and shape language development. *Developmental Review, 26*(1), 55–88.

Huttenlocher, J., Haight, W., Bryk, A., Seltzer, M., & Lyons, T. (1991). Early vocabulary growth: Relation to language input and gender. *Developmental Psychology, 27*(2), 236.

Iverson, J. M., & Goldin-Meadow, S. (2005). Gesture paves the way for language development. *Psychological Science, 16*(5), 367–371.

Jáuregui-Lobera, I. (2014). Iron deficiency and cognitive functions. *Neuropsychiatric Disease and Treatment, 10*, 2087.

Johansson, M., Forssman, L., & Bohlin, G. (2014). Individual differences in 10-month-olds' performance on the A-not-B task. *Scandinavian Journal of Psychology, 55*(2), 130–135.

Johnston, J. C., Durieux-Smith, A., & Bloom, K. (2005). Teaching gestural signs to infants to advance child development: A review of the evidence. *First Language, 25*(2), 235–251.

Katerelos, M., Poulin-Dubois, D., and Oshima-Takane, Y. (2011). A cross-linguistic study of word-mapping in 18-to 20-month-old infants. *Infancy 16*, 508–534.

Kids Count Data Center. (2020). Children who speak a language other than English at home in the United States. Retrieved from https://datacenter.kidscount.org/data/map/81-children-who-speak-a-language-other-than-english-at-home?loc=1&loct=2#2/any/true/true/1729/any/397/Orange/.

Kim, S., Mazza, J., Zwanziger, J., & Henry, D. (2014). School and behavioral outcomes among inner city children: Five-year follow-up. *Urban Education, 49*(7), 835–856.

Kinzler, K. D., Dupoux, E., & Spelke, E. S. (2007). The native language of social cognition. *Proceedings of the National Academy of Sciences, 104*(30), 12577–12580.

Kirk, E., Howlett, N., Pine, K. J., & Fletcher, B. C. (2013). To sign or not to sign? The impact of encouraging infants to gesture on infant language and maternal mind-mindedness. *Child Development, 84*(2), 574–590.

Kirkorian, H. L., Pempek, T. A., Murphy, L. A., Schmidt, M. E., & Anderson, D. R. (2009). The impact of background television on parent–child interaction. *Child Development, 80*(5), 1350–1359.

Krasotkina, A., Götz, A., Höhle, B., & Schwarzer, G. (2018). Perceptual narrowing in speech and face recognition: Evidence for intra-individual cross-domain relations. *Frontiers in Psychology, 9*, 1711.

Krasotkina, A., Götz, A., Höhle, B., & Schwarzer, G. (2021). Perceptual narrowing in face-and speech-perception domains in infancy: A longitudinal approach. *Infant Behavior and Development, 64*, 101607.

Kuhl, P. K. (2004). Early language acquisition: Cracking the speech code. *Nature Reviews Neuroscience, 5*(11), 831.

Kuhl, P., & Rivera-Gaxiola, M. (2008). Neural substrates of language acquisition. *Annual Review of Neuroscience, 31*, 511–534.

Kuhl, P. K., Stevens, E., Hayashi, A., Deguchi, T., Kiritani, S., & Iverson, P. (2006). Infants show a facilitation effect for native language phonetic perception between 6 and 12 months. *Developmental Science, 9*(2), F13–F21.

Kuhl, P. K., Tsao, F.-M., & Liu, H.-M. (2003). Foreign-language experience in infancy: Effects of short-term exposure and social interaction on phonetic learning. *Proceedings of the National Academy of Sciences, 100*(15), 9096–9101.

La Greca, A. M., Lai, B. S., Joormann, J., Auslander, B. B., & Short, M. A. (2013). Children's risk and resilience following a natural disaster: Genetic vulnerability, posttraumatic stress, and depression. *Journal of Affective Disorders, 151*(3), 860–867.

Lauricella, A. R., Barr, R., & Calvert, S. L. (2014). Parent–child interactions during traditional and computer storybook reading for children's comprehension: Implications for electronic storybook design. *International Journal of Child-Computer Interaction, 2*(1), 17–25.

Lauricella, A. R., Gola, A. A. H., & Calvert, S. L. (2011). Toddlers' learning from socially meaningful video characters. *Media Psychology, 14*(2), 216–232.

Law, J., Mensah, F., Westrupp, E., & Reilly, S. (2015). Social disadvantage and early language delay. Retrieved from www.mcri.edu.au/sites/default/files/media/documents/cres/cre-cl_policy_brief-1_social_disadvantage_and_early_language_delay.pdf.

Lee, C.-C., Jhang, Y., Relyea, G., Chen, L.-m., & Oller, D. K. (2018). Babbling development as seen in canonical babbling ratios: A naturalistic evaluation of all-day recordings. *Infant Behavior and Development, 50*, 140–153.

Leo, I., Angeli, V., Lunghi, M., Dalla Barba, B., & Simion, F. (2018). Newborns' face recognition: The role of facial movement. *Infancy, 23*(1), 45–60.

Leung, W. (2019). Study links excessive screen time to developmental delays in children. Retrieved from www.theglobeandmail.com/canada/article-excessive-screen-time-could-play-role-in-development-delays-in/.

Lewis, M. P., Simons, G. F., & Fennig, C. D. (2009). *Ethnologue: Languages of the world* (Vol. 16). Dallas, TX: SIL International.

Leyva, D., Reese, E., Laible, D., Schaughency, E., Das, S., & Clifford, A. (2020). Measuring parents' elaborative reminiscing: Differential links of parents' elaboration to children's autobiographical memory and socioemotional skills. *Journal of Cognition and Development, 21*(1), 23–45.

Lieberman, P. (2012). Vocal tract anatomy and the neural bases of talking. *Journal of Phonetics, 40*(4), 608–622.

Lippman, L., Burns, S., & McArthur, E. (1996). *Urban schools: The challenge of location and poverty*. Diane Publishing.

Liu, H.-M., Kuhl, P. K., & Tsao, F. M. (2003). An association between mothers' speech clarity and infants' speech discrimination skills. *Developmental Science, 6*(3), F1–F10.

Liu, H.-M., Tsao, F.-M., & Kuhl, P. K. (2007). Acoustic analysis of lexical tone in Mandarin infant-directed speech. *Developmental Psychology, 43*(4), 912.

Locatelli, C., Onnivello, S., Antonaros, F., Feliciello, A., Filoni, S., Rossi, S., . . . Toffalini, E. (2021). Is the age of developmental milestones a predictor for future development in Down syndrome? *Brain Sciences, 11*(5), 655.

Lowry, L. (2018). Early signs of autism. Retrieved from www .hanen.org/helpful-info/articles/early-signs-of-autism.aspx.

Lynch, M. P., Oller, D. K., Steffens, M. L., & Levine, S. L. (1995). Onset of speech-like vocalizations in infants with Down syndrome. *American Journal on Mental Retardation 100*(1), 68–86.

Macfarlane, A. (1975). Olfaction in the development of social preferences in the human neonate. *Parent-Infant Interaction, 33,* 103–119.

Madigan, S., Browne, D., Racine, N., Mori, C., & Tough, S. (2019). Association between screen time and children's performance on a developmental screening test. *JAMA Pediatrics 173*(3), 244–250.

Madsen, H. B., & Kim, J. H. (2016). Ontogeny of memory: An update on 40 years of work on infantile amnesia. *Behavioural Brain Research, 298,* 4–14.

Mampe, B., Friederici, A. D., Christophe, A., & Wermke, K. (2009). Newborns' cry melody is shaped by their native language. *Current Biology, 19*(23), 1994–1997.

Maurer, D., & Werker, J. F. (2014). Perceptual narrowing during infancy: A comparison of language and faces. *Developmental Psychobiology, 56*(2), 154–178.

McClure, E. R., Chentsova-Dutton, Y. E., Barr, R. F., Holochwost, S. J., & Parrott, W. G. (2015). "Facetime doesn't count": Video chat as an exception to media restrictions for infants and toddlers. *International Journal of Child-Computer Interaction, 6,* 1–6.

McDaniel, B. T., & Radesky, J. S. (2018). Technoference: Parent distraction with technology and associations with child behavior problems. *Child Development, 89*(1), 100–109.

McGillion, M., Herbert, J. S., Pine, J., Vihman, M., DePaolis, R., Keren-Portnoy, T., & Matthews, D. (2017). What paves the way to conventional language? The predictive value of babble, pointing, and socioeconomic status. *Child Development, 88*(1), 156–166.

Meltzoff, A. N., & Kuhl, P. K. (2016). Exploring the infant social brain: What's going on in there? *Zero to Three Journal, 36*(3), 2–9.

Moreno, A., Limousin, F., Dehaene, S., & Pallier, C. (2018). Brain correlates of constituent structure in sign language comprehension. *Neuroimage, 167,* 151–161.

Mulder, H., Van Houdt, C. A., Van der Ham, I., Van der Stigchel, S., & Oudgenoeg-Paz, O. (2020). Attentional flexibility predicts A-not-B task performance in 14-month-old-infants: A head-mounted eye tracking study. *Brain Sciences, 10*(5), 279.

Nencheva, M. L., Piazza, E. A., & Lew-Williams, C. (2021). The moment-to-moment pitch dynamics of child-directed speech shape toddlers' attention and learning. *Developmental Science, 24*(1), e12997.

Nierenberg, C. (2016). Simple trick may improve an infant's attention span. *LiveScience.* Retrieved from www.livescience .com/54594-tips-to-improve-infants-attention-span.html.

Nisbett, R. E., Peng, K., Choi, I., & Norenzayan, A. (2001). Culture and systems of thought: holistic versus analytic cognition. *Psychological Review 108*(2), 291–310.

Oller, D., Levine, S., Cobo-Lewis, A. B., Eilers, R. E., Pearson, B. Z., & Paul, R. (1998). Vocal precursors to linguistic communication: How babbling is connected to meaningful speech. *Exploring the Speech-Language Connection 8,* 1–25.

Orengo-Aguayo, R., Stewart, R. W., de Arellano, M. A., Suárez-Kindy, J. L., & Young, J. (2019). Disaster exposure and mental health among Puerto Rican youths after Hurricane Maria. *JAMA Network Open, 2*(4), e192619–e192619.

Othman, A. (2021). Child developmental delays and disorders: Speech and language delay. *FP Essentials, 510,* 17–21.

Papalia, D. E. (1998). *Human development,* 7th ed. New York: McGraw-Hill.

Papoušek, M. (1994). *Vom ersten Schrei zum ersten Wort: Anfänge der Sprachentwicklung in der vorsprachlichen Kommunikation.* Huber.

Parish-Morris, J., Mahajan, N., Hirsh-Pasek, K., Golinkoff, R. M., & Collins, M. F. (2013). Once upon a time: Parent–child dialogue and storybook reading in the electronic era. *Mind, Brain, and Education, 7*(3), 200–211.

Patten, E., Belardi, K., Baranek, G. T., Watson, L. R., Labban, J. D., & Oller, D. K. (2014). Vocal patterns in infants with autism spectrum disorder: Canonical babbling status and vocalization frequency. *Journal of Autism and Developmental Disorders, 44*(10), 2413–2428.

Peterson, C. (2020). Remembering earliest childhood memories. In *Autobiographical memory development* (pp. 119–135). Routledge.

Petitto, L. A., Holowka, S., Sergio, L. E., Levy, B., & Ostry, D. J. (2004). Baby hands that move to the rhythm of language: Hearing babies acquiring sign languages babble silently on the hands. *Cognition, 93*(1), 43–73.

Pittet, I., Kojovic, N., Franchini, M., & Schaer, M. (2022). Trajectories of imitation skills in preschoolers with autism spectrum disorders. *Journal of Neurodevelopmental Disorders, 14*(1), 2.

Ramsaran, A. I., Schlichting, M. L., & Frankland, P. W. (2019). The ontogeny of memory persistence and specificity. *Developmental Cognitive Neuroscience, 36,* 100591.

Ratner, H. H. (1984). Memory demands and the development of young children's memory. *Child Development 55*(6), 2173–2191.

Reed, J., Hirsh-Pasek, K., & Golinkoff, R. M. (2017). Learning on hold: Cell phones sidetrack parent-child interactions. *Developmental Psychology, 53*(8), 1428.

Renxiu, L. Z. (2020). A brief overview of the discussion on universal grammar with a focus on Chomsky's theory. *European Journal of Language and Literature, 6*(2), 47–49.

Richert, R. A, Robb, M. B., Fender, J. G., & Wartella, E. (2010). Word learning from baby videos. *Archives of Pediatrics and Adolescent Medicine, 164*(5), 432–437.

Ridge, K. E., Weisberg, D. S., Ilgaz, H., Hirsh-Pasek, K. A., & Golinkoff, R. M. (2015). Supermarket speak: Increasing talk among low-socioeconomic status families. *Mind, Brain, and Education, 9*(3), 127–135.

Roberts, S. C., & Eryaman, F. (2017). Mutual olfactory recognition between mother and child. *Human Ethology Bulletin, 32*(1), 42–52.

Romeo, R. R., Leonard, J. A., Robinson, S. T., West, M. R., Mackey, A. P., Rowe, M. L., & Gabrieli, J. D. (2018). Beyond the 30-million-word gap: Children's conversational exposure is associated with language-related brain function. *Psychological Science, 29*(5), 700–710.

Roseberry, S., Hirsh-Pasek, K., & Golinkoff, R. M. (2014). Skype me! Socially contingent interactions help toddlers learn language. *Child Development, 85*(3), 956–970.

Rovee-Collier, C. (1999). The development of infant memory. *Current Directions in Psychological Science, 8*(3), 80–85.

Rovee-Collier, C., & Giles, A. (2010). Why a neuromaturational model of memory fails: Exuberant learning in early infancy. *Behavioural Processes, 83*(2), 197–206.

Sahay, A., Scobie, K. N., Hill, A. S., O'carroll, C. M., Kheirbek, M. A., Burghardt, N. S., . . . Hen, R. (2011). Increasing adult hippocampal neurogenesis is sufficient to improve pattern separation. *Nature, 472*(7344), 466.

Schmitt, S. A., Simpson, A. M., & Friend, M. (2011). A longitudinal assessment of the home literacy environment and early language. *Infant and Child Development, 20*(6), 409–431.

Shields, P. J., & Rovee-Collier, C. (1992). Long-term memory for context-specific category information at six months. *Child Development, 63*(2), 245–259.

Shinskey, J. (2016). *Manipulative features in educational picture books hinder word learning in toddlers.* Paper presented at the Annual meeting of the British Psychological Society, Belfast, UK. www.researchgate.net/profile/Jeanne_Shinskey/publication/312117093_Manipulative_Features_in_Educational_Picture_Books_Hinder_Word_Learning_in_Toddlers/links/586fb9a808ae329d621626a3/Manipulative-Features-in-Educational-Picture-Books-Hinder-Word-Learning-in-Toddlers.pdf.

Singh, L., Loh, D., & Xiao, N. G. (2017). Bilingual infants demonstrate perceptual flexibility in phoneme discrimination but perceptual constraint in face discrimination. *Frontiers in Psychology, 8*, 1563.

Soley, G., & Sebastián-Gallés, N. (2015). Infants prefer tunes previously introduced by speakers of their native language. *Child Development, 86*(6), 1685–1692.

Statista. (2021). Share of U.S. school children who don't speak English at home 1979–2018. Retrieved from www.statista.com/statistics/476804/percentage-of-school-age-children-who-speak-another-language-than-english-at-home-in-the-us/.

Stone, S. S., Teixeira, C. M., DeVito, L. M., Zaslavsky, K., Josselyn, S. A., Lozano, A. M., & Frankland, P. W. (2011). Stimulation of entorhinal cortex promotes adult neurogenesis and facilitates spatial memory. *Journal of Neuroscience, 31*(38), 13469–13484.

Strüber, N., Strüber, D., & Roth, G. (2014). Impact of early adversity on glucocorticoid regulation and later mental disorders. *Neuroscience & Biobehavioral Reviews, 38*, 17–37.

Sturdy, C. B., & Nicoladis, E. (2017). How much of language acquisition does operant conditioning explain? *Frontiers in Psychology, 8*, 1918.

Talbott, M. R., Nelson, C. A., & Tager-Flusberg, H. (2015). Maternal gesture use and language development in infant siblings of children with autism spectrum disorder. *Journal of Autism and Developmental Disorders, 45*(1), 4–14.

Tamis-LeMonda, C. S., & Song, L. (2013). Parent-infant communicative interactions in cultural context. In R. M. Lerner (Ed.), *Handbook of psychology* (Vol. 6, pp. 143–170). New York: Wiley.

Tamis-LeMonda, C. S., Shannon, J. D., Cabrera, N. J., & Lamb, M. E. (2004). Fathers and mothers at play with their 2- and 3-year-olds: Contributions to language and cognitive development. *Child Development, 75*(6), 1806–1820.

Taverna, E. C., Huedo-Medina, T. B., Fein, D. A., & Eigsti, I.-M. (2021). The interaction of fine motor, gesture, and structural language skills: The case of autism spectrum disorder. *Research in Autism Spectrum Disorders, 86*, 101824.

Thomas-Sunesson, D., Hakuta, K., & Bialystok, E. (2018). Degree of bilingualism modifies executive control in Hispanic children in the USA. *International Journal of Bilingual Education and Bilingualism, 21*(2), 197–206.

Thompson, R. A., & Newton, E. K. (2013). Baby altruists? Examining the complexity of prosocial motivation in young children. *Infancy, 18*(1), 120–133.

Thordardottir, E. (2017). Amount trumps timing in bilingual vocabulary acquisition: Effects of input in simultaneous and sequential school-age bilinguals. *International Journal of Bilingualism.* doi: 10.1177/1367006917722418.

Travaglia, A., Bisaz, R., Sweet, E. S., Blitzer, R. D., & Alberini, C. M. (2016). Infantile amnesia reflects a developmental critical period for hippocampal learning. *Nature Neuroscience, 19*(9), 1225.

Tsai, T.-C., Huang, C.-C., & Hsu, K.-S. (2019). Infantile amnesia is related to developmental immaturity of the maintenance mechanisms for long-term potentiation. *Molecular Neurobiology, 56*(2), 907–919.

Vandewater, E. A., Rideout, V. J., Wartella, E. A., Huang, X., Lee, J. H., & Shim, M.-s. (2007). Digital childhood: Electronic media and technology use among infants, toddlers, and preschoolers. *Pediatrics, 119*(5), e1006–e1015.

Wang, Q. (2016). Remembering the self in cultural contexts: A cultural dynamic theory of autobiographical memory. *Memory Studies, 9*(3), 295–304.

Wang, Q., Koh, J. B. K., Song, Q., & Hou, Y. (2015). Knowledge of memory functions in European and Asian American adults and children: The relation to autobiographical memory. *Memory, 23*(1), 25–38.

Waxman, S. R., Fu, X., Ferguson, B., Geraghty, K., Leddon, E., Liang, J., & Zhao, M.-F. (2016). How early is infants' attention to objects and actions shaped by culture? New evidence from 24-month-olds raised in the US and China. *Frontiers in Psychology, 7*, 97.

Wolfe, J. M., Kluender, K. R., Levi, D. M., Bartoshuk, L. M., Herz, R. S., Klatzky, R. L., & Merfeld, D. M. (2021). *Sensation and Perception*, 6th ed. Oxford University Press/Sinauer, Sunderland, MA.

Wooldridge, M. B., & Shapka, J. (2012). Playing with technology: Mother–toddler interaction scores lower during play with electronic toys. *Journal of Applied Developmental Psychology, 33*(5), 211–218.

Yang, C., Crain, S., Berwick, R. C., Chomsky, N., & Bolhuis, J. J. (2017). The growth of language: Universal Grammar, experience, and principles of computation. *Neuroscience & Biobehavioral Reviews, 81*(Pt B), 103–119.

Yow, W. Q., Tan, J. S., & Flynn, S. (2018). Code-switching as a marker of linguistic competence in bilingual children. *Bilingualism: Language and Cognition, 21*(5), 1075–1090.

Yu, C., & Smith, L. B. (2016). The social origins of sustained attention in one-year-old human infants. *Current Biology, 26*(9), 1235–1240.

Zimmerman, F. J., Christakis, D. A., & Meltzoff, A. N. (2007). Associations between media viewing and language development in children under age 2 years. *The Journal of Pediatrics, 151*(4), 364–368.

Zosh, J. M., Lytle, S. R., Golinkoff, R. M., & Hirsh-Pasek, K. (2017). Putting the education back in educational apps: How content and context interact to promote learning. In *Media exposure during infancy and early childhood* (pp. 259–282). Springer.

Zosh, J. M., Verdine, B. N., Filipowicz, A., Golinkoff, R. M., Hirsh-Pasek, K., & Newcombe, N. S. (2015). Talking shape: Parental language with electronic versus traditional shape sorters. *Mind, Brain, and Education, 9*(3), 136–144.

Chapter 7

Aiken, M. (2016). *The cyber effect: A pioneering cyber-psychologist explains how human behavior changes online.* Spiegel & Grau.

Ainsworth, M. D. S., Blehar, M. C., Waters, E., & Wall, S. N. (2015). *Patterns of attachment: A psychological study of the strange situation.* Psychology Press.

Ainsworth, M. S. (1979). Infant–mother attachment. *American Psychologist, 34*(10), 932.

Ainsworth, M. S., & Bowlby, J. (1991). An ethological approach to personality development. *American Psychologist, 46*(4), 333.

American Academy of Pediatrics. (2020). Autism Initiatives. Retrieved from www.aap.org/en-us/advocacy-and-policy/aap-health-initiatives/Pages/autism-initiatives.aspx.

American Academy of Pediatrics. (2021). Vaccines—Autism Toolkit. Pediatric Patient Education.

American Time Use Survey. (2011). American Time Use Survey Leave Module. Retrieved from https://www.atusdata.org/atus/2017_18_leave_module.shtml.

Anderson, C., Law, J. K., Daniels, A., Rice, C., Mandell, D. S., Hagopian, L., & Law, P. A. (2012). Occurrence and family impact of elopement in children with autism spectrum disorders. *Pediatrics, 130*(5), 870–877.

Anisfeld, E. (1982). The onset of social smiling in preterm and full-term infants from two ethnic backgrounds. *Infant Behavior and Development, 5*(2–4), 387–395.

Autism Speaks. (2022). Autism statistics and facts. Retrieved from https://www.autismspeaks.org/autism-statistics-asd Autism Speaks. (2021). Learn the signs of autism. Retrieved from www.autismspeaks.org/signs-autism.

Autism Speaks. (2021). Learn the signs of autism. Retrieved from www.autismspeaks.org/signs-autism.

Balbernie, R. (2013). The importance of secure attachment for infant mental health. *Journal of Health Visiting, 1*(4), 210–217.

Barnes, J., & Melhuish, E. C. (2017). Amount and timing of group-based childcare from birth and cognitive development at 51 months: A UK study. *International Journal of Behavioral Development, 41*(3), 360–370.

Barnett, D., & Vondra, J. I. (1999). Atypical patterns of early attachment: Theory, research, and current directions. *Monographs of the Society for Research in Child Development 64*(3), 1–24.

Bartel, A. P., Kim, S., Nam, J., Rossin-Slater, M., Ruhm, C., & Waldfogel, J. (2019). Racial and ethnic disparities in access to and use of paid family and medical leave: Evidence from four nationally representative datasets." Monthly Labor Review, U.S. Bureau of Labor Statistics, January 2019. Retrieved from https://doi.org/10.21916/mlr.2019.2.

Batha, E. (2018). Factbox: Most children in orphanages are not orphans. Retrieved from www.reuters.com/article/us-slavery-conference-orphanages-factbox/factbox-most-children-in-orphanages-are-not-orphans-idUSKCN1NJ0AG.

BBC. (2017). Adopted Romanian orphans "still suffering in adulthood". Retrieved from www.bbc.com/news/health-39055704.

Bell, R. Q. (2020). Human infant—Effects in the first year. In *Child effects on adults* (pp. 122–148). Routledge.

Berlin, L. J., Martoccio, T. L., & Jones Harden, B. (2018). Improving early head start's impacts on parenting through attachment-based intervention: A randomized controlled trial. *Developmental Psychology, 54*(12), 2316.

Bernier, A., & Meins, E. (2008). A threshold approach to understanding the origins of attachment disorganization. *Developmental Psychology, 44*(4), 969.

Bigelow, A. E., MacLean, K., Proctor, J., Myatt, T., Gillis, R., & Power, M. (2010). Maternal sensitivity throughout infancy: Continuity and relation to attachment security. *Infant Behavior and Development, 33*(1), 50–60.

Bohlin, G., & Hagekull, B. (2009). Socio-emotional development: From infancy to young adulthood. *Scandinavian Journal of Psychology, 50*(6), 592–601.

Borelli, J. L., Crowley, M. J., David, D. H., Sbarra, D. A., Anderson, G. M., & Mayes, L. C. (2010). Attachment and emotion in school-aged children. *Emotion, 10*(4), 475.

Bornstein, M. H., Putnick, D. L., Rigo, P., Esposito, G., Swain, J. E., Suwalsky, J. T., . . . Cote, L. R. (2017). Neurobiology of culturally common maternal responses to infant cry. *Proceedings of the National Academy of Sciences, 114*(45), E9465–E9473.

Bowlby, J. (1979). The Bowlby-Ainsworth attachment theory. *Behavioral and Brain Sciences, 2*(4), 637–638.

Boyer, P., & Bergstrom, B. (2011). Threat-detection in child development: An evolutionary perspective. *Neuroscience & Biobehavioral Reviews, 35*(4), 1034–1041.

Brand, R. J., Escobar, K., & Patrick, A. M. (2020). Coincidence or cascade? The temporal relation between locomotor behaviors and the emergence of stranger anxiety. *Infant Behavior and Development, 58*, 101423.

Braungart-Rieker, J. M., Planalp, E. M., Ekas, N. V., Lickenbrock, D. M., & Zentall, S. R. (2019). Toddler affect with mothers and fathers: The importance of infant attachment. *Attachment & Human Development, 22*(6), 668–686.

Brazelton, T. B. (2018). *The earliest relationship: Parents, infants and the drama of early attachment.* Routledge.

Bretherton, I., Fritz, J., Zahn-Waxler, C., & Ridgeway, D. (1986). Learning to talk about emotions: A functionalist perspective. *Child Development 57*(3), 529–548.

Brooker, R. J., Buss, K. A., Lemery-Chalfant, K., Aksan, N., Davidson, R. J., & Goldsmith, H. H. (2013). The development of stranger fear in infancy and toddlerhood: Normative development, individual differences, antecedents, and outcomes. *Developmental Science, 16*(6), 864–878.

Buescher, A. V., Cidav, Z., Knapp, M., & Mandell, D. S. (2014). Costs of autism spectrum disorders in the United Kingdom and the United States. *JAMA Pediatrics, 168*(8), 721–728.

Bureau of Labor Statistics. (2021). Employee benefits in the United States - March 2021. Retrieved from https://www.bls.gov/news.release/pdf/ebs2.pdf.

Calvert, S. L., & Wilson, B. J. (2010). *The handbook of children, media, and development* (Vol. 10). John Wiley & Sons.

Canadian Encyclopedia. (2020). Residential schools in Canada. Retrieved from https://www.thecanadianencyclopedia.ca/en/article/residential-schools.

Canadian Paediatric Society. (2017). Screen time and young children: Promoting health and development in a digital world. *Paediatrics & Child Health 22*(8), 461–468. Retrieved from https://cps.ca/documents/position/screen-time-and-young-children.

Caspi, A., Roberts, B. W., & Shiner, R. L. (2005). Personality development: Stability and change. *Annual Review of Psychology, 56*, 453–484.

Centers for Disease Control and Prevention. (2019). Autism spectrum disorder. Retrieved from www.cdc.gov/ncbddd/autism/data/index.html.

Chess, S., & Thomas, A. (1977). Temperamental individuality from childhood to adolescence. *Journal of the American Academy of Child Psychiatry, 16*(2), 218–226.

Chohan, M., & Jones, E. A. (2019). Initiating joint attention with a smile: Intervention for children with autism. *Behavioral Development, 24*(1), 29.

Christakis, D. A. (2009). The effects of infant media usage: What do we know and what should we learn? *Acta Paediatrica, 98*(1), 8–16.

Colvert, E., Tick, B., McEwen, F., Stewart, C., Curran, S. R., Woodhouse, E., . . . Garnett, T. (2015). Heritability of autism spectrum disorder in a UK population-based twin sample. *JAMA Psychiatry, 72*(5), 415–423.

Common Sense Media. (2018). *The Common Sense Census: Media use by kids age zero to eight.* Retrieved from https://www.commonsensemedia.org/research/the-common-sense-census-media-use-by-kids-age-zero-to-eight-2017.

Cruz-Vargas, D. J., & Sánchez-Aragón, R. (2021). How do attachment style, optimism, resilience, and self-efficacy impact stress and its control in patients with diabetes? In R. Sánchez-Aragón (Ed.), *Diabetes and couples: Protective and risk factors* (pp. 23–47). Springer.

Davidson, R. J., & Fox, N. A. (1989). Frontal brain asymmetry predicts infants' response to maternal separation. *Journal of Abnormal Psychology, 98*(2), 127.

de Kruijff, I., Veldhuis, M. S., Tromp, E., Vlieger, A. M., Benninga, M. A., & Lambregtse-van den Berg, M. P. (2021). Distress in fathers of babies with infant colic. *Acta Paediatrica 110*(8), 2455–2461.

De Rosnay, M., Cooper, P. J., Tsigaras, N., & Murray, L. (2006). Transmission of social anxiety from mother to infant: An experimental study using a social referencing paradigm. *Behaviour Research and Therapy, 44*(8), 1165–1175.

Department of Labor. (2019). Employment characteristics of families—2018 [Press release]. Retrieved from www.bls.gov/news.release/pdf/famee.pdf.

Donoghue, E. A. (2017). Quality early education and child care from birth to kindergarten. *Pediatrics, 140*(2), e20171488.

Dore, R. A., & Dynia, J. M. (2021). Prevalence and predictors of background television among infants and toddlers from low-income families homes. *Infant Behavior and Development, 64*, 101618.

Drange, N., & Havnes, T. (2019). Early childcare and cognitive development: Evidence from an assignment lottery. *Journal of Labor Economics, 37*(2), 581–620.

Durkin, M. S., Maenner, M. J., Newschaffer, C. J., Lee, L.-C., Cunniff, C. M., Daniels, J. L., . . . Zahorodny, W. (2009). Advanced parental age and the risk of autism spectrum disorder. *Obstetrical & Gynecological Survey, 64*(4), 223–225.

Dyck, M. J., Ferguson, K., & Shochet, I. M. (2001). Do autism spectrum disorders differ from each other and from non-spectrum disorders on emotion recognition tests? *European Child & Adolescent Psychiatry, 10*(2), 105–116.

Eggleston, A., Geangu, E., Tipper, S. P., Cook, R., & Over, H. (2021). Young children learn first impressions of faces through social referencing. *Scientific Reports, 11*(1), 1–8.

Eisenberg, N., & Morris, A. S. (2002). Children's emotion-related regulation. *Advances in Child Development and Behavior, 30*, 189–229.

Emde, R. N., McCartney, R. D., & Harmon, R. J. (1971). Neonatal smiling in REM states, IV: Premature study. *Child Development 42*(5), 1657–1661.

Felfe, C., & Lalive, R. (2018). Does early child care affect children's development? *Journal of Public Economics, 159*, 33–53.

Fernald, A. (1993). Approval and disapproval: Infant responsiveness to vocal affect in familiar and unfamiliar languages. *Child Development, 64*(3), 657–674.

Fidler, A. E., Zack, E., & Barr, R. (2010). Television viewing patterns in 6- to 18-month-olds: The role of caregiver–infant interactional quality. *Infancy, 15*(2), 176–196.

Fiorentino, M. R., & Fasano, A. (2019). The microbiome—Its role in neuroinflammation: The autism spectrum disorder paradigm. In *The Microbiome and the Brain* (pp. 45–62). CRC Press.

Fox, N. A., Henderson, H. A., Perez-Edgar, K., & White, L. K. (2008). The biology of temperament: An integrative approach. In C. A. Nelson & M. Luciana (Eds.), *Handbook of developmental cognitive neuroscience* (pp. 839–853). Boston Review.

Freedman, S. B., Al-Harthy, N., & Thull-Freedman, J. (2009). The crying infant: Diagnostic testing and frequency of serious underlying disease. *Pediatrics, 123*(3), 841–848.

Fuller, B. F. (1991). Acoustic discrimination of three types of infant cries. *Nursing Research 40*(3) 156–160.

Geangu, E., Benga, O., Stahl, D., & Striano, T. (2010). Contagious crying beyond the first days of life. *Infant Behavior and Development, 33*(3), 279–288.

Genyue, F., Heyman, G. D., & Lee, K. (2011). Reasoning about modesty among adolescents and adults in China and the US. *Journal of Adolescence, 34*(4), 599–608.

George, M. R., Cummings, E. M., & Davies, P. T. (2010). Positive aspects of fathering and mothering, and children's attachment in kindergarten. *Early Child Development and Care, 180*(1–2), 107–119.

Gianino, A., & Tronick, E. Z. (1988). The mutual regulation model: The infant's self and interactive regulation and coping and defensive capacities. In T. M. Field, P. M. McCabe, & N. Schneiderman (Eds.), *Stress and coping across development* (pp. 47–68). Lawrence Erlbaum Associates, Inc.

Golding, K. S., Fain, J., Mills, C., Worrall, H., & Frost, A. (2012). *Observing children with attachment difficulties in school: A tool for identifying and supporting emotional and social difficulties in children aged 5–11.* Jessica Kingsley Publishers.

Granqvist, P., Sroufe, L. A., Dozier, M., Hesse, E., Steele, M., van Ijzendoorn, M., . . . Bakermans-Kranenburg, M. (2017). Disorganized attachment in infancy: A review of the phenomenon and its implications for clinicians and policy-makers. *Attachment & Human Development, 19*(6), 534–558.

Greitemeyer, T. (2022). Prosocial modeling: person role models and the media. *Current Opinion in Psychology, 44*, 135–139.

Grey, K. R., Davis, E. P., Sandman, C. A., & Glynn, L. M. (2013). Human milk cortisol is associated with infant temperament. *Psychoneuroendocrinology, 38*(7):1178–1185.

Gunter, B., & Gunter, J. (2019). *Children and television.* Routledge.

Gustafson, G. E., & Green, J. A. (1991). Developmental coordination of cry sounds with visual regard and gestures. *Infant Behavior and Development, 14*(1), 51–57.

Hallmayer, J., Cleveland, S., Torres, A., Phillips, J., Cohen, B., Torigoe, T., . . . Smith, K. (2011). Genetic heritability and shared environmental factors among twin pairs with autism. *Archives of General Psychiatry, 68*(11), 1095–1102.

Hamilton, B. E., Martin, J. A., & Osterman, M. J. K. (2021). Births: Provisional data for 2020. Vital Statistics Rapid Release, 12. National Center for Health Statistics, Hyattsville, MD.

Hansen, S. N., Schendel, D. E., Francis, R. W., Windham, G. C., Bresnahan, M., Levine, S. Z., . . . Bai, D. (2019). Recurrence risk of autism in siblings and cousins: A multinational, population-based study. *Journal of the American Academy of Child & Adolescent Psychiatry, 58*(9), 866–875.

Harker, C. M., Ibañez, L. V., Nguyen, T. P., Messinger, D. S., & Stone, W. L. (2016). The effect of parenting style on social smiling in infants at high and low risk for ASD. *Journal of Autism and Developmental Disorders, 46*(7), 2399–2407.

Harlow, H., & Zimmerman, R. (1959). Affectional responses in the infant monkey, Science *130*, 421–432.

Hart, S. L. (2016). Proximal foundations of jealousy: Expectations of exclusivity in the infant's first year of life. *Emotion Review, 8*(4), 358–366.

Hashemi, S., & Akbari, A. (2017). Explanation of mediating role of life orientation in relationship between attachment styles dimensions and happiness. *Journal of Psychology. 21*(2), 167–183.

Hawes, M. T., Farrell, M. R., Cannone, J. L., Finsaas, M. C., Olino, T. M., & Klein, D. N. (2021). Early childhood temperament predicts intolerance of uncertainty in adolescence. *Journal of Anxiety Disorders, 80*, 102390.

Hazlett, H. C., Gu, H., Munsell, B. C., Kim, S. H., Styner, M., Wolff, J. J., . . . Botteron, K. N. (2017). Early brain development in infants at high risk for autism spectrum disorder. *Nature, 542*(7641), 348–351.

Hill, D., Ameenuddin, N., Chassiakos, Y. L. R., Cross, C., Hutchinson, J., Levine, A., . . . Swanson, W. S. (2016). Media and young minds. *Pediatrics 138*(5), e20162591.

Hoffman, C., Dunn, D. M., & Njoroge, W. F. (2017). Impact of postpartum mental illness upon infant development. *Current Psychiatry Reports, 19*(12), 100.

Holmes, H., Sawer, F., & Clark, M. (2021). Autism spectrum disorders and epilepsy in children: A commentary on the occurrence of autism in epilepsy; how it can present differently and the challenges associated with diagnosis. *Epilepsy & Behavior, 117*, 107813.

Hornik, R., Risenhoover, N., & Gunnar, M. (1987). The effects of maternal positive, neutral, and negative affective communications on infant responses to new toys. *Child Development*, 937–944.

Jain, A., Marshall, J., Buikema, A., Bancroft, T., Kelly, J. P., & Newschaffer, C. J. (2015). Autism occurrence by MMR vaccine status among US children with older siblings with and without autism. *JAMA, 313*(15), 1534–1540.

Joeng, J. R., Turner, S. L., Kim, E. Y., Choi, S. A., Kim, J. K., & Lee, Y. J. (2017). Data for Korean college students' anxious and avoidant attachment, self-compassion, anxiety and depression. *Data in Brief, 13*, 316–319.

Juffer, F., van IJzendoorn, M. H., & Bakermans-Kranenburg, M. J. (2017). Structural neglect in orphanages: Physical growth, cognition, and daily life of young institutionalized children in India. In *Child maltreatment in residential care* (pp. 301–321). Springer.

Kagan, J. (2008). Fear and wariness. In M. M. Haith & J. B. Benson (Eds.), *Encyclopedia of infant and early childhood development*. Oxford, UK: Elsevier.

Karsten, A. E., Foster, T. D., Decker, K. B., & Vallotton, C. (2017). Toddlers take emotion regulation into their own hands with infant signs. *YC Young Children, 72*(1), 38–43.

Kayyal, M. H., & Widen, S. C. (2015). What made Sahar scared?: Imaginary and realistic causes in Palestinian and American children's concept for fear. *Journal of Cognition and Culture, 15*(1–2), 32–44.

Keenan, H. T., Presson, A. P., Clark, A. E., Cox, C. S., & Ewing-Cobbs, L. (2019). Longitudinal developmental outcomes after traumatic brain injury in young children: Are infants more vulnerable than toddlers? *Journal of Neurotrauma, 36*(2), 282–292.

Kim, E., & Koh, E. (2018). Avoidant attachment and smartphone addiction in college students: The mediating effects of anxiety and self-esteem. *Computers in Human Behavior, 84*, 264–271.

Kirkorian, H. L., Pempek, T. A., Murphy, L. A., Schmidt, M. E., & Anderson, D. R. (2009). The impact of background television on parent–child interaction. *Child Development, 80*(5), 1350–1359.

Kirkorian, H. L., Wartella, E. A., & Anderson, D. R. (2008). Media and young children's learning. *The Future of Children* 18(1), 39–61.

Kohlhoff, J., Mahmood, D., Kimonis, E., Hawes, D. J., Morgan, S., Egan, R., Niec, L. N., & Eapen, V. (2020). Callous-Unemotional Traits and Disorganized Attachment: Links with Disruptive Behaviors in Toddlers. *Child Psychiatry and Human Development*, 51(3):399–406.

Komeda, H., Kosaka, H., Fujioka, T., Jung, M., & Okazawa, H. (2019). Do individuals with autism spectrum disorders help other people with autism spectrum disorders? An investigation of empathy and helping motivation in adults with autism spectrum disorder. *Frontiers in Psychiatry, 10,* 376.

Krassner, A. M., Gartstein, M. A., Park, C., Dragan, W. Ł., Lecannelier, F., & Putnam, S. P. (2017). East–west, collectivist-individualist: A cross-cultural examination of temperament in toddlers from Chile, Poland, South Korea, and the US. *European Journal of Developmental Psychology, 14*(4), 449–464.

Kret, M. E., Venneker, D., Evans, B., Samara, I., & Sauter, D. (2021). The ontogeny of human laughter. *Biology Letters, 17*(9), 20210319.

Krug, A., Wöhr, M., Seffer, D., Rippberger, H., Sungur, A. Ö., Dietsche, B., . . . Witt, S. H. (2020). Advanced paternal age as a risk factor for neurodevelopmental disorders: A translational study. *Molecular Autism, 11*(1), 1–19.

Laughlin, L. (2013). *Who's minding the kids? Child care arrangements: Spring 2011.* Current Population Reports, P70-135. U.S. Census Bureau, Washington, DC.

Law, P., & Anderson, C. (2011). IAN research report: Elopement and wandering. Retrieved from https://iancommunity.org/cs/ian_research_reports/ian_research_report_elopement.

Lerner, C. (2018). First feelings: The foundation of healthy development, starting from birth. Retrieved from www.zerotothree.org/resources/294-first-feelings-the-foundation-of-healthy-development-starting-from-birth.

Levendosky, A. A., Bogat, G. A., Huth-Bocks, A. C., Rosenblum, K., & von Eye, A. (2011). The effects of domestic violence on the stability of attachment from infancy to preschool. *Journal of Clinical Child & Adolescent Psychology, 40*(3), 398–410.

Lewis, M. (2011). The self-conscious emotions. In R. E. Tremblay, M. Boivin, & R. DeV. Peters (Eds.), M. Lewis (Topic Ed.), *Encyclopedia on early childhood development.* Retrieved from www.child-encyclopedia.com/emotions/according-experts/self-conscious-emotions.

Lewis, M. (2012). *Children's emotions and moods: Developmental theory and measurement.* Springer Science & Business Media.

Li, T., Horta, M., Mascaro, J. S., Bijanki, K., Arnal, L. H., Adams, M., . . . Rilling, J. K. (2018). Explaining individual variation in paternal brain responses to infant cries. *Physiology & Behavior, 193,* 43–54.

Lincoln, C. R., Russell, B. S., Donohue, E. B., & Racine, L. E. (2017). Mother-child interactions and preschoolers' emotion regulation outcomes: Nurturing autonomous emotion regulation. *Journal of Child and Family Studies, 26*(2), 559–573.

Liu, W., Wu, X., Huang, K., Yan, S., Ma, L., Cao, H., Gan, H. & Tao, F. (2021). Early childhood screen time as a predictor of emotional and behavioral problems in children at 4 years: a birth cohort study in China. *Environmental Health and Preventive Medicine, 26,* 3. https://doi.org/10.1186/s12199-020-00926-w.

Livingston, G., & Thomas, D. (2019). Among 41 countries, only U.S. lacks paid parental leave. Retrieved from www.pewresearch.org/fact-tank/2019/12/16/u-s-lacks-mandated-paid-parental-leave/.

Lorenz, K. (2002). *On aggression.* Psychology Press.

Lurie, Lucy A., Hagen, McKenzie P., McLaughlin, Katie A., Sheridan, Margaret A., Meltzoff, Andrew N., & Rosen, Maya L. (2021). Mechanisms linking socioeconomic status and academic achievement in early childhood: Cognitive stimulation and language. *Cognitive Development, 58,* 101045.

Lyall, K., Song, L., Botteron, K., Croen, L. A., Dager, S. R., Fallin, M. D., . . . Ladd-Acosta, C. (2020). The association between parental age and autism-related outcomes in children at high familial risk for autism. *Autism Research, 13*(6), 998–1010.

Ma, J., Yang, Y., Wan, Y., Shen, C., & Qiu, P. (2021). The influence of childhood adversities on mid to late cognitive function: From the perspective of life course. *PloS ONE, 16*(8), e0256297.

Maenner, M. J., Shaw, K. A., & Baio, J. (2020). Prevalence of autism spectrum disorder among children aged 8 years—autism and developmental disabilities monitoring network, 11 sites, United States, 2016. *MMWR Surveillance Summaries, 69*(4), 1.

Mah, B. L., Van Ijzendoorn, M. H., Out, D., Smith, R., & Bakermans-Kranenburg, M. J. (2017). The effects of intranasal oxytocin administration on sensitive caregiving in mothers with postnatal depression. *Child Psychiatry & Human Development, 48*(2), 308–315.

Martin, K. B., Haltigan, J. D., Ekas, N., Prince, E. B., & Messinger, D. S. (2020). Attachment security differs by later autism spectrum disorder: A prospective study. *Developmental Science, 23*(5), e12953.

Martínez-González, A. E., Cervin, M., & Piqueras, J. A. (2021). Relationships between emotion regulation, social communication and repetitive behaviors in autism spectrum disorder. *Journal of Autism and Developmental Disorders,* 1–9. doi: 10.1007/s10803-021-05340-x.

McDonald, N. M., & Messinger, D. S. (2012). Empathic responding in toddlers at risk for an autism spectrum disorder. *Journal of Autism and Developmental Disorders, 42*(8), 1566–1573.

Mendes, D. M. L. F., Seidl-de-Moura, M. L., & de Oliveira Siqueira, J. (2009). The ontogenesis of smiling and its association with mothers' affective behaviors: A longitudinal study. *Infant Behavior and Development, 32*(4), 445–453.

Messinger, D. S., Cassel, T. D., Acosta, S. I., Ambadar, Z., & Cohn, J. F. (2008). Infant smiling dynamics and perceived positive emotion. *Journal of Nonverbal Behavior, 32*(3), 133.

Mittal, V. K. (2016). *Discriminating the infant cry sounds due to pain vs. discomfort towards assisted clinical diagnosis.* Paper presented at the 7th Workshop on Speech and Language Processing for Assistive Technologies, SLPAT.

Mize, K. D., Pineda, M., Blau, A. K., Marsh, K., & Jones, N. A. (2014). Infant physiological and behavioral responses to a jealousy provoking condition. *Infancy, 19*(3), 338–348.

Moghadam, M., Rezaei, F., Ghaderi, E., & Rostamian, N. (2016). Relationship between attachment styles and happiness in medical students. *Journal of Family Medicine and Primary Care, 5*(3), 593.

Morales, S., Tang, A., Bowers, M. E., Miller, N. V., Buzzell, G. A., Smith, E., . . . Fox, N. A. (2021). Infant temperament prospectively predicts general psychopathology in childhood. *Development and Psychopathology*, 1–10. doi: 10.1017/S0954579420001996.

Moses, L. J., Baldwin, D. A., Rosicky, J. G., & Tidball, G. (2001). Evidence for referential understanding in the emotions domain at twelve and eighteen months. *Child Development, 72*(3), 718–735.

Moullin, S., Waldfogel, J., & Washbrook, E. (2014). *Baby Bonds*. Retrieved from www.suttontrust.com/wp-content/uploads/2019/12/baby-bonds-final-1.pdf.

Naber, F. B., Swinkels, S. H., Buitelaar, J. K., Bakermans-Kranenburg, M. J., Van IJzendoorn, M. H., Dietz, C., . . . Van Engeland, H. (2007). Attachment in toddlers with autism and other developmental disorders. *Journal of Autism and Developmental Disorders, 37*(6), 1123–1138.

Napier, C. (2014). How use of screen media affects the emotional development of infants. *Primary Health Care, 24*(2). **doi:** 10.7748/phc2014.02.24.2.18.e816.

Nathanson, A. I., & Manohar, U. (2012). Attachment, working models of parenting, and expectations for using television in childrearing. *Family Relations, 61*(3), 441–454.

Neumann, A. A., Desmarais, E. E., Iverson, S. L., & Gartstein, M. A. (2020). Ecological contributions to maternal-infant functioning: Differences between rural and urban family contexts. *Journal of Community Psychology 48*(3), 945–959.

NICHD Early Child Care Research Network. (1997). The effects of infant child care on infant-mother attachment security: Results of the NICHD Study of Early Child Care NICHD Early Child Care Research Network. *Child Development, 68*(5), 860–879.

Nigg, J. T. (2017). Annual research review: On the relations among self-regulation, self-control, executive functioning, effortful control, cognitive control, impulsivity, risk-taking, and inhibition for developmental psychopathology. *Journal of Child Psychology and Psychiatry, 58*(4), 361–383.

Odobescu, V. (2015). Half a million kids survived Romania's "slaughterhouses of souls". Now they want justice. Retrieved from www.pri.org/stories/2015-12-28/half-million-kids-survived-romanias-slaughterhouses-souls-now-they-want-justice.

OECD. (2021). Family leave database. Retrieved from https://www.oecd.org/els/family/database.htm.

Okpych, N. J., & Courtney, M. E. (2018). The role of avoidant attachment on college persistence and completion among youth in foster care. *Children and Youth Services Review, 90*, 106–117.

Oksman, E., Rosenström, T., Gluschkoff, K., Saarinen, A., Hintsanen, M., Pulkki-Råback, L., . . . Keltikangas-Järvinen, L. (2019). Associations between early childcare environment and different aspects of adulthood sociability: The 32-year prospective Young Finns Study. *Frontiers in Psychology, 10*, 2060.

O'Toole, K., & Kannass, K. (2021). Background television and distractibility in young children: Does program content matter? *Journal of Applied Developmental Psychology, 75*, 101280.

Poole, K. L., Jetha, M. K., & Schmidt, L. A. (2017). Linking child temperament, physiology, and adult personality: Relations among retrospective behavioral inhibition, salivary cortisol, and shyness. *Personality and Individual Differences, 113*, 68–73.

Posner, M. I., & Rothbart, M. K. (1998). Attention, self-regulation and consciousness. *Philosophical Transactions of the Royal Society of London B: Biological Sciences, 353*(1377), 1915–1927.

Putnam, S. P., Gartstein, M. A., & Rothbart, M. K. (2019). Historical background of the study of temperament and new perspectives on assessment. In R. DelCarmen-Wiggins & A. S. Carter (Eds.), *The Oxford handbook of infant, toddler, and preschool mental health assessment* (pp. 131–156). Oxford University Press.

Repacholi, B. M., Meltzoff, A. N., Toub, T. S., & Ruba, A. L. (2016). Infants' generalizations about other people's emotions: Foundations for trait-like attributions. *Developmental Psychology, 52*(3), 364.

Riem, M. M., Bakermans-Kranenburg, M. J., & van IJzendoorn, M. H. (2016). Intranasal administration of oxytocin modulates behavioral and amygdala responses to infant crying in females with insecure attachment representations. *Attachment & human development, 18*(3), 213–234.

Rilling, J. K., Richey, L., Andari, E., & Hamann, S. (2021). The neural correlates of paternal consoling behavior and frustration in response to infant crying. *Developmental Psychobiology 63*(5), 1370–1383.

Rothbart, M. K. (1989). Temperament in childhood: A framework. In G. A. Kohnstamm, J. E. Bates, & M. K. Rothbart (Eds.), *Temperament in childhood* (pp. 59–73). John Wiley & Sons.

Rothbart, M. K., & Bates, J. E. (2007). Temperament. In N. Eisenberg, W. Damon, & R. M. Lerner (Eds.), *Handbook of child psychology: Social, emotional, and personality development* (pp. 99–166). John Wiley & Sons, Inc..

Rutter, M., Colvert, E., Kreppner, J., Beckett, C., Castle, J., Groothues, C., . . . Sonuga-Barke, E. J. (2007). Early adolescent outcomes for institutionally-deprived and non-deprived adoptees. I: Disinhibited attachment. *Journal of Child Psychology and Psychiatry, 48*(1), 17–30.

Rutter, M., Sonuga-Barke, E. J., Beckett, C., Castle, J., Kreppner, J., Kumsta, R., . . . Gunnar, M. R. (2010). Deprivation-specific psychological patterns: Effects of institutional deprivation. *Monographs of the Society for Research in Child Development 75*, i–253.

Ruvolo, P., Messinger, D., & Movellan, J. (2015). Infants time their smiles to make their moms smile. *PloS ONE, 10*(9), e0136492.

Samian, N. G., Maghooli, K., & Farokhi, F. (2021). Brain volume analysis with T1-MRI data in autism spectrum disorder. *Frontiers in Biomedical Technologies, 8*(1) 37–41.

Schmidt, M. E., Pempek, T. A., Kirkorian, H. L., Lund, A. F., & Anderson, D. R. (2008). The effects of background television on the toy play behavior of very young children. *Child Development, 79*(4), 1137–1151.

Shpancer, N. (2018). Day Care. *Encyclopedia of evolutionary psychological science*. doi: 10.1007/978-3-319-16999-6_2435-1.

Sigman, A. (2012). Time for a view on screen time. *Archives of Disease in Childhood, 97*(11), 935–942.

Slade, A., Holland, M. L., Ordway, M. R., Carlson, E. A., Jeon, S., Close, N., . . . Sadler, L. S. (2020). Minding the Baby®: Enhancing parental reflective functioning and infant attachment in an attachment-based, interdisciplinary home visiting program. *Development and Psychopathology, 32*(1), 123–137.

Soke, G. N., Rosenberg, S. A., Hamman, R. F., Fingerlin, T., Robinson, C., Carpenter, L., . . . Durkin, M. S. (2016). Brief report: Prevalence of self-injurious behaviors among children with autism spectrum disorder—a population-based study. *Journal of Autism and Developmental Disorders, 46*(11), 3607–3614.

Solmeyer, A. R., & Feinberg, M. E. (2011). Mother and father adjustment during early parenthood: The roles of infant temperament and coparenting relationship quality. *Infant Behavior and Development, 34*(4), 504–514.

Sroufe, L. A. (1977). Wariness of strangers and the study of infant development. *Child Development 48*(3), 731–746.

Sroufe, L. A., & Waters, E. (1976). The ontogenesis of smiling and laughter: A perspective on the organization of development in infancy. *Psychological Review, 83*(3), 173.

Stifter, C. A. (2005). Crying behaviour and its impact on psychosocial child development. In: Tremblay RE, Boivin M, Peters RDeV, eds. *Encyclopedia on Early Childhood Development* [online]. https://www.child-encyclopedia.com/crying-behaviour/according-experts/crying-behaviour-and-its-impact-psychosocial-child-development.

Stright, A. D., Gallagher, K. C., & Kelley, K. (2008). Infant temperament moderates relations between maternal parenting in early childhood and children's adjustment in first grade. *Child Development, 79*(1), 186–200.

Suess, G., Bohlen, U., Carlson, E., Spangler, G., & Frumentia Maier, M. (2016). Effectiveness of attachment based STEEP™ intervention in a German high-risk sample. *Attachment & Human Development, 18*(5), 443–460.

Supanitayanon, S., Trairatvorakul, P., & Chonchaiya, W. (2020). Screen media exposure in the first 2 years of life and preschool cognitive development: a longitudinal study. *Pediatric Research, 88*(6), 894–902.

Sylva, K., Stein, A., Leach, P., Barnes, J., Malmberg, L. E., & FCCC-team. (2011). Effects of early child-care on cognition, language, and task-related behaviours at 18 months: An English study. *British Journal of Developmental Psychology, 29*(1), 18–45.

Tajik-Parvinchi, D., Farmus, L., Tablon Modica, P., Cribbie, R. A., & Weiss, J. A. (2021). The role of cognitive control and emotion regulation in predicting mental health problems in children with neurodevelopmental disorders. *Child: Care, Health and Development 47*(5), 608–617.

Taniai, H., Nishiyama, T., Miyachi, T., Imaeda, M., & Sumi, S. (2008). Genetic influences on the broad spectrum of autism: Study of proband-ascertained twins. *American Journal of Medical Genetics Part B: Neuropsychiatric Genetics, 147*(6), 844–849.

TenHouten, W. D. (2017). From primary emotions to the spectrum of affect: An evolutionary neurosociology of the emotions. In *Neuroscience and Social Science* (pp. 141–167). Springer.

Thakkar, R. R., Garrison, M. M., & Christakis, D. A. (2006). A systematic review for the effects of television viewing by infants and preschoolers. *Pediatrics, 118*(5), 2025–2031.

Thompson, R. A. (1991). Emotional regulation and emotional development. *Educational Psychology Review, 3*(4), 269–307.

Trimmer, E., McDonald, S., & Rushby, J. A. (2017). Not knowing what I feel: Emotional empathy in autism spectrum disorders. *Autism, 21*(4), 450–457.

Vandewater, E. A., Rideout, V. J., Wartella, E. A., Huang, X., Lee, J. H., & Shim, M.-s. (2007). Digital childhood: Electronic media and technology use among infants, toddlers, and preschoolers. *Pediatrics, 119*(5), e1006–e1015.

van Londen, W. M., Juffer, F., & van Ijzendoorn, M. H. (2007). Attachment, cognitive, and motor development in adopted children: Short-term outcomes after international adoption. *Journal of Pediatric Psychology, 32*(10), 1249–1258.

Venezia, M., Messinger, D. S., Thorp, D., & Mundy, P. (2004). The development of anticipatory smiling. *Infancy, 6*(3), 397–406.

Vuong, H. E., & Hsiao, E. Y. (2017). Emerging roles for the gut microbiome in autism spectrum disorder. *Biological Psychiatry, 81*(5), 411–423.

Walle, E. A., Reschke, P. J., & Knothe, J. M. (2017). Social referencing: Defining and delineating a basic process of emotion. *Emotion Review, 9*(3), 245–252.

Walsh, E., Blake, Y., Donati, A., Stoop, R., & von Gunten, A. (2019). Early secure attachment as a protective factor against later cognitive decline and dementia. *Frontiers in Aging Neuroscience, 11*, 161.

Wiggins, L. D., DiGuiseppi, C., Schieve, L., Moody, E., Soke, G., Giarelli, E., & Levy, S. (2020). Wandering among preschool children with and without autism spectrum disorder. *Journal of Developmental & Behavioral Pediatrics, 41*(4), 251–257.

World Health Organization. (2021). Autism spectrum disorders. Retrieved from www.who.int/news-room/fact-sheets/detail/autism-spectrum-disorders.

Wright, J. (2017). The real reasons autism rates are up in the US. *Scientific American*. Retrieved from www.scientificamerican.com/article/the-real-reasons-autism-rates-are-up-in-the-u-s/.

Yang, Y., Tian, J., & Yang, B. (2018). Targeting gut microbiome: A novel and potential therapy for autism. *Life Sciences, 194*, 111–119.

Yu, Y., & Zhao, F. (2021). Microbiota-gut-brain axis in ASD. *Journal of Genetics and Genomics 48*(9), 755–762.

Zablotsky, B., Bradshaw, C. P., Anderson, C. M., & Law, P. (2014). Risk factors for bullying among children with autism spectrum disorders. *Autism, 18*(4), 419–427.

Zahn-Waxler, C., Radke-Yarrow, M., Wagner, E., & Chapman, M. (1992). Development of concern for others. *Developmental Psychology, 28*(1), 126.

Zeedyk, S. (2013). Sabre tooth tigers and teddy bears: A brief guide to understanding attachment. Aberdeen, Scotland: Aberdeen City Council.

Zeevenhooven, J., Browne, P. D., L'Hoir, M. P., de Weerth, C., & Benninga, M. A. (2018). Infant colic: Mechanisms and management. *Nature Reviews Gastroenterology & Hepatology, 15*(8), 479–496.

Zerbo, O., Qian, Y., Yoshida, C., Fireman, B. H., Klein, N. P., & Croen, L. A. (2017). Association between influenza infection and vaccination during pregnancy and risk of autism spectrum disorder. *JAMA Pediatrics, 171*(1), e163609–e163609.

Chapter 8

Al-Hashim, A. H., Blaser, S., Raybaud, C., & MacGregor, D. (2016). Corpus callosum abnormalities: Neuroradiological and clinical correlations. *Developmental Medicine & Child Neurology, 58*(5), 475–484.

Aly, M. (2020). Brain dynamics underlying memory for lifetime experiences. *Trends in Cognitive Sciences, 24*(10), 780–781.

American Academy of Pediatrics. (2016). *Guide to toilet training,* 2nd edition. Bantam Books.

American Academy of Pediatrics. (2018). Children and colds. Retrieved from www.healthychildren.org/English/ health-issues/conditions/ear-nose-throat/Pages/Children-and-Colds.aspx.

American Cancer Society. (2021). Childhood cancer. In American Cancer Society (Ed.). Atlanta, GA: American Cancer Society.

Bagateli, L. E., Saeki, E. Y., Fadda, M., Agostoni, C., Marchisio, P., & Milani, G. P. (2021). COVID-19 vaccine hesitancy among parents of children and adolescents living in Brazil. *Vaccines, 9*(10), 1115.

Baird, D. C., Bybel, M., & Kowalski, A. W. (2019). Toilet training: Common questions and answers. *American Family Physician, 100*(8), 468–474.

Birken, C. S., & MacArthur, C. (2004). Socioeconomic status and injury risk in children. *Paediatrics & Child Health, 9*(5), 323.

Blum, M., & Baten, J. (2012). Growing taller, but unequal: Biological well-being in world regions and its determinants, 1810–1989. *Economic History of Developing Regions, 27,* S66–S85.

Borse, N. N., Gilchrist, J., Dellinger, A. M., Rudd, R. A., Ballesteros, M. F., & Sleet, D. A. (2008). *CDC childhood injury report: Patterns of unintentional injuries among 0–19 year olds in the United States, 2000–2006.* Retrieved from https://stacks.cdc.gov/view/cdc/5155.

Boseley, S. (2010). Andrew Wakefield found 'irresponsible' by GMC over MMR vaccine scare. Retrieved from www .theguardian.com/society/2010/jan/28/andrew-wakefield-mmr-vaccine.

Boyse, K., Boujaoude, L., & Laundy, J. (2012). Children with chronic conditions. Retrieved from www.med.umich.edu/ yourchild/topics/chronic.htm.

Bruno, D. (2012). Potty training Chinese style: With a diaper-free child, look for potted plants. Retrieved from www .csmonitor.com/The-Culture/Family/2012/1123/Potty-training-Chinese-style-With-a-diaper-free-child-look-for-potted-plants.

Bryden, M. (2012). *Laterality functional asymmetry in the intact brain.* Elsevier.

Caballero, M. T., Bianchi, A. M., Nuño, A., Ferretti, A. J., Polack, L. M., Remondino, I., . . . Bergel, E. (2019). Mortality associated with acute respiratory infections among children at home. *Journal of Infectious Diseases, 219*(3), 358–364.

Cameron, C. E., Brock, L. L., Murrah, W. M., Bell, L. H., Worzalla, S. L., Grissmer, D., & Morrison, F. J. (2012). Fine motor skills and executive function both contribute to kindergarten achievement. *Child Development, 83*(4), 1229–1244.

Carter, B., Rees, P., Hale, L., Bhattacharjee, D., & Paradkar, M. S. (2016). Association between portable screen-based media device access or use and sleep outcomes: A systematic review and meta-analysis. *JAMA Pediatrics, 170*(12), 1202–1208.

Centers for Disease Control and Prevention. (2016). Parents' guide to childhood immunizations. Retrieved from www.cdc .gov/vaccines/parents/tools/parents-guide/parents-guide-part4.html.

Centers for Disease Control and Prevention. (2017a). Measles cases and outbreaks. Retrieved from www.cdc.gov/measles/ cases-outbreaks.html.

Centers for Disease Control and Prevention. (2017b). Rubella in the U.S. Retrieved from www.cdc.gov/rubella/about/ in-the-us.html.

Centers for Disease Control and Prevention. (2017c). What would happen if we stopped vaccinations? Retrieved from www.cdc.gov/vaccines/vac-gen/whatifstop.htm.

Centers for Disease Control and Prevention. (2021a). Childhood obesity facts. Retrieved from www.cdc.gov/obesity/data/ childhood.html.

Centers for Disease Control and Prevention. (2021b). Drowning prevention. Retrieved from www.cdc.gov/safechild/ drowning/.

Centers for Disease Control and Prevention. (2021c). Immunization schedule. Retrieved from www.cdc.gov/vaccines/ schedules/hcp/imz/child-adolescent.html.

Centers for Disease Control and Prevention. (2021d). Measles cases and outbreaks. Retrieved from www.cdc.gov/measles/ cases-outbreaks.html.

Centers for Disease Control and Prevention. (2021e). Mumps cases and outbreaks. Retrieved from www.cdc.gov/mumps/ outbreaks.html.

Centers for Disease Control and Prevention. (2021f). Smallpox—prevention and treatment. Retrieved from www .cdc.gov/smallpox/prevention-treatment/.

Centers for Disease Control and Prevention. (2021g). Vaccination coverage among young children (0–35 months). Retrieved from www.cdc.gov/vaccines/imz-managers/coverage/ childvaxview/interactive-reports/index.html.

Chen, M., & Chan, E. (2014). *Effects of parenting programs on child abuse prevention: A meta-analytic study.* Paper presented at the ISPCAN International Congress on Child Abuse and Neglect.

Child Welfare Information Gateway. (2021). *Child maltreatment 2019: Summary of key findings.* Retrieved from www.childwelfare .gov/pubPDFs/canstats.pdf.

Children's Hospital of Philadelphia. (2014). *Aluminum in vaccines: What you should know.* Philadelphia, PA: Children's Hospital of Philadelphia.

Children's Hospital of Philadelphia. (2016). Vaccine ingredients—Formaldehyde. Retrieved from www.chop.edu/centers-programs/vaccine-education-center/vaccine-ingredients/ formaldehyde.

Christakis, D., & Zimmerman, F. J. (2006). *The elephant in the living room: Make television work for your kids.* Rodale.

Cleveland Clinic Children's. (2021). Nightmares. Retrieved from http://my.clevelandclinic.org/childrens-hospital/health-info/ diseases-conditions/hic_sleep_in_your_babys_first_year/hic_ nightmares.

Collins, S. C. (2012). Food Allergies in Schools. *Today's Dietitian, 14*(9), 38. Retrieved from www.todaysdietitian.com/ newarchives/090112p38.shtml.

Common Sense Media. (2013). *Zero to eight: Children's media use in America 2013.* Retrieved from www.commonsensemedia.org/ research/zero-to-eight-childrens-media-use-in-america-2013.

Common Sense Media. (2017). Zero to Eight: Children's Media Use in America. Retrieved from https://www.common sensemedia.org/sites/default/files/uploads/research/csm_ zerotoeight_fullreport_release_2.pdf.

Cornejo, R., Martínez, F., Álvarez, V. C., Barraza, C., Cibrian, F. L., Martínez-García, A. I., & Tentori, M. (2021). Serious games for basic learning mechanisms: Reinforcing Mexican children's gross motor skills and attention. *Personal and Ubiquitous Computing, 25*(2), 375–390.

Daro, D., & Cohn-Donnelly, A. (2002). Child abuse prevention. In *APSAC handbook on child maltreatment* (pp. 431–448). Sage Publications Newbury Park, CA.

Davis, M. K., & Gidycz, C. A. (2000). Child sexual abuse prevention programs: A meta-analysis. *Journal of Clinical Child Psychology, 29*(2), 257–265.

Dellinger, A., & Gilchrist, J. (2019). Leading causes of fatal and nonfatal unintentional injury for children and teens and the role of lifestyle clinicians. *American Journal of Lifestyle Medicine, 13*(1), 7–21.

Department of Communities, Child Safety and Disability Services (Queensland Government). (2019). Why does child abuse happen. Retrieved from www.qld.gov.au/community/getting-support-health-social-issue/support-victims-abuse/child-abuse/child-abuse-causes.

Department of Health and Human Services. (2019). *What is child abuse and neglect? Recognizing the signs and symptoms.* Washington, DC: U.S. Department of Health and Human Services, Administration for Children and Families, Children's Bureau.

Dum, R. P., Levinthal, D. J., & Strick, P. L. (2016). Motor, cognitive, and affective areas of the cerebral cortex influence the adrenal medulla. *Proceedings of the National Academy of Sciences, 113*(35), 9922–9927.

Dundas, E. M., Plaut, D. C., & Behrmann, M. (2013). The joint development of hemispheric lateralization for words and faces. *Journal of Experimental Psychology: General, 142*(2), 348.

Faith, M. S., & Hittner, J. B. (2016). Shadows of temperament in child eating patterns: Implications for family and parenting research. *The American Journal of Clinical Nutrition, 103*(4), 961–962.

Fang, K., Mu, M., Liu, K., & He, Y. (2019). Screen time and childhood overweight/obesity: A systematic review and meta-analysis. *Child: Care, Health and Development, 45*(5), 744–753.

Fang, X., Brown, D. S., Florence, C. S., & Mercy, J. A. (2012). The economic burden of child maltreatment in the United States and implications for prevention. *Child Abuse & Neglect, 36*(2), 156–165.

Farrington, C. P., Miller, E., & Taylor, B. (2001). MMR and autism: further evidence against a causal association. *Vaccine, 19*(27):3632–3635.

Fisher, A., McDonald, L., van Jaarsveld, C. H., Llewellyn, C., Fildes, A., Schrempft, S., & Wardle, J. (2014). Sleep and energy intake in early childhood. *International Journal of Obesity, 38*(7), 926–929.

Foerster, M., Henneke, A., Chetty-Mhlanga, S., & Röösli, M. (2019). Impact of adolescents' screen time and nocturnal mobile phone-related awakenings on sleep and general health symptoms: A prospective cohort study. *International Journal of Environmental Research and Public Health, 16*(3), 518.

Food Allergy Research & Education. (2021). Facts and Statistics. Retrieved from www.foodallergy.org/resources/facts-and-statistics.

Forum on Child and Family Statistics. (2021). Chld injury and mortality. Retrieved from www.childstats.gov/americas children/phys7.asp.

Frank, M. G. (2019). Sleep and brain plasticity. In S. K. Jha & V. M. Jha (Eds.), *Sleep, memory and synaptic plasticity* (pp. 107–124). Springer.

Friend, S., Flattum, C., Fulkerson, J., Neumark-Sztainer, D., & Garwick, A. (2014). How does eating family meals during childhood influence parents. *Journal of Nutrition Education and Behavior, 46*(4), S179.

Fryar, C. D., Carroll, M. D., & Ogden, C. L. (2016). Prevalence of overweight and obesity among children and adolescents aged 2–19 years: United States, 1963–1965 through 2013–2014. Retrieved from http://medbox.iiab.me/modules/en-cdc/www.cdc.gov/nchs/data/hestat/obesity_child_13_14/obesity_child_13_14.htm.

Fryar, C. D., Gu, Q., & Ogden, C. L. (2012). Anthropometric reference data for children and adults: United States, 2007–2010. National Center for Health Statistics. *Vital Health Statistics 11*(252). 2012.

Gallagher, J. (2015). Childhood MMR vaccination rates fall. Retrieved from www.bbc.com/news/health-34335509.

Gogtay, N., Nugent, T. F., Herman, D. H., Ordonez, A., Greenstein, D., Hayashi, K. M., . . . Rapoport, J. L. (2006). Dynamic mapping of normal human hippocampal development. *Hippocampus, 16*(8), 664–672.

Gold, J. (2014). *Screen-Smart parenting: How to find balance and benefit in your child's use of social media, apps, and digital devices.* Guilford Publications.

Götz, M., Lemish, D., & Holler, A. (2019). *Fear in front of the screen: Children's fears, nightmares, and thrills from TV.* Rowman & Littlefield.

Gould, F., Clarke, J., Heim, C., Harvey, P. D., Majer, M., & Nemeroff, C. B. (2012). The effects of child abuse and neglect on cognitive functioning in adulthood. *Journal of Psychiatric Research, 46*(4), 500–506.

Hamilton, J. (2015). A man's incomplete brain reveals cerebellum's role in thought and emotion. Retrieved from www.npr.org/sections/health-shots/2015/03/16/392789753/a-man-s-incomplete-brain-reveals-cerebellum-s-role-in-thought-and-emotion.

Hans, J., Lammens, M., Wesseling, P., & Hori, A. (2014). Development and developmental disorders of the human cerebellum. In H. J. ten Donkelaar, M. Lammens, & A. Hori (eds.), *Clinical neuroembryology* (pp. 371–420). Springer.

He, Z., Yang, K., Zhuang, N., & Zeng, Y. (2021). Processing of affective pictures: A study based on functional connectivity network in the cerebral cortex. *Computational Intelligence and Neuroscience, 2021.* doi: 10.1155/2021/5582666.

Healthy Steps. (2021). What is healthy steps? Retrieved from www.healthysteps.org.

Heideman, K., & Poronsky, C. B. (2021). Protocols for managing food allergies in elementary and secondary schools. *Comprehensive Child and Adolescent Nursing*, 1–13. doi: 10.1080/24694193.2021.1883771.

Helm, A. F., & Spencer, R. M. (2019). Television use and its effects on sleep in early childhood. *Sleep Health, 5*(3), 241–247.

Hofman, M. A. (2014). Evolution of the human brain: When bigger is better. *Frontiers in Neuroanatomy, 8*, 15.

Honda, H., Shimizu, Y., & Rutter, M. (2005). No effect of MMR withdrawal on the incidence of autism: a total population study. *Journal of Child Psychology and Psychiatry, 46*(6), 572–579.

Hong, Y. S., & Henly, J. R. (2020). Supplemental nutrition assistance program and school readiness skills. *Children and Youth Services Review, 114*, 105034.

Horváth, K., Myers, K., Foster, R., & Plunkett, K. (2015). Napping facilitates word learning in early lexical development. *Journal of Sleep Research, 24*(5), 503–509.

Jones, B. E. (2003). Arousal systems. *Frontiers in Bioscience, 8*, s438–451.

Kaerts, N., Van Hal, G., Vermandel, A., & Wyndaele, J. J. (2012). Readiness signs used to define the proper moment to start toilet training: A review of the literature. *Neurourology and Urodynamics, 31*(4), 437–440.

Kaerts, N., Vermandel, A., Van Hal, G., & Wyndaele, J. J. (2014). Toilet training in healthy children: Results of a questionnaire study involving parents who make use of day-care at least once a week. *Neurourology and Urodynamics, 33*(3), 316–323.

Kellogg, R. (1969). *Analyzing children's art*. Mayfield Publishing Company.

Kennedy, C., Lordo, R., Sucosky, M. S., Boehm, R., & Brown, M. J. (2016). Evaluating the effectiveness of state specific lead-based paint hazard risk reduction laws in preventing recurring incidences of lead poisoning in children. *International Journal of Hygiene and Environmental Health, 219*(1), 110–117.

Kesson, A. M. (2007). Respiratory virus infections. *Paediatric Respiratory Reviews, 8*(3), 240–248.

Khattak, F. A., Rehman, K., Shahzad, M., Arif, N., Ullah, N., Kibria, Z., . . . ul Haq, Z. (2021). Prevalence of parental refusal rate and its associated factors in routine immunization by using WHO Vaccine Hesitancy tool: A cross sectional study at district Bannu, KP, Pakistan. *International Journal of Infectious Diseases, 104*, 117–124.

Kim, Y. (2021). Group-based parenting education programs and their influence on protective factors for child abuse and neglect. *Journal of Family Trauma, Child Custody & Child Development, 18*, 319–331.

Koçtürk, N., & Yüksel, F. (2019). Characteristics of victims and perpetrators of intrafamilial sexual abuse. *Child Abuse & Neglect, 96*, 104122.

Kurth, S., Achermann, P., Rusterholz, T., & LeBourgeois, M. K. (2013). Development of brain EEG connectivity across early childhood: Does sleep play a role? *Brain Sciences, 3*(4), 1445–1460.

Kushnir, J., & Sadeh, A. (2011). Sleep of preschool children with night-time fears. *Sleep Medicine, 12*(9), 870–874.

Letourneau, E. J., Schaeffer, C. M., Bradshaw, C. P., & Feder, K. A. (2017). Preventing the onset of child sexual abuse by targeting young adolescents with universal prevention programming. *Child Maltreatment, 22*(2), 100–111.

Lewis, K. M., El Rafihi-Ferreira, R., Freitag, G. F., Coffman, M., & Ollendick, T. H. (2021). A 25-year review of nighttime fears in children: Past, present, and future. *Clinical Child and Family Psychology Review, 24*, 391–413.

Liu, Y. H., & Stein, M. T. (2013). Feeding behaviour of infants and young children and its impact on psychosocial and emotional development. In M. S. Faith (Ed.), *Encyclopedia on early childhood development* (2nd ed.).

Liu, Z., Tang, H., Jin, Q., Wang, G., Yang, Z., Chen, H., . . . Owens, J. (2021). Sleep of preschoolers during the coronavirus disease 2019 (COVID-19) outbreak. *Journal of Sleep Research, 30*(1), e13142.

Loomba, N., Beckerson, M. E., Ammons, C. J., Maximo, J. O., & Kana, R. K. (2021). Corpus callosum size and homotopic connectivity in autism spectrum disorder. *Psychiatry Research: Neuroimaging, 313*, 111301.

Luo, Z., Jose, P. E., Huntsinger, C. S., & Pigott, T. D. (2007). Fine motor skills and mathematics achievement in East Asian American and European American kindergartners and first graders. *British Journal of Developmental Psychology, 25*(4), 595–614.

MacDonald, M., Lipscomb, S., McClelland, M. M., Duncan, R., Becker, D., Anderson, K., & Kile, M. (2016). Relations of preschoolers' visual-motor and object manipulation skills with executive function and social behavior. *Research Quarterly for Exercise and Sport, 87*(4), 396–407.

Mayo Clinic. (2020). Children's nutrition: 10 tips for picky eaters. Retrieved from www.mayoclinic.org/healthy-lifestyle/childrens-health/in-depth/childrens-health/art-20044948.

McCord, J. (1983). A forty year perspective on effects of child abuse and neglect. *Child Abuse & Neglect, 7*(3), 265–270.

McPhillips, M., & Jordan-Black, J. A. (2007). The effect of social disadvantage on motor development in young children: A comparative study. *Journal of Child Psychology and Psychiatry, 48*(12), 1214–1222.

Menon, V., & D'Esposito, M. (2022). The role of PFC networks in cognitive control and executive function. *Neuropsychopharmacology, 47*(1), 90–103.

Mitchell, G. L., Farrow, C., Haycraft, E., & Meyer, C. (2013). Parental influences on children's eating behaviour and characteristics of successful parent-focussed interventions. *Appetite, 60*, 85–94.

Mohamed, M. B. H., & O'Brien, B. A. (2022). Defining the relationship between fine motor visual–spatial integration and reading and spelling. *Reading and Writing, 35*, 877–898.

Morrongiello, B. A., Bell, M., Park, K., & Pogrebtsova, K. (2016a). Evaluation of the Safety Detective Program: A classroom-based intervention to increase kindergarten children's understanding of home safety hazards and injury-risk behaviors to avoid. *Prevention Science, 17*(1), 102–111.

Morrongiello, B. A., Hou, S., Bell, M., Walton, K., Filion, A. J., & Haines, J. (2016b). Supervising for Home Safety Program: A randomized controlled trial (RCT) Testing community-based group delivery. *Journal of Pediatric Psychology*, jsw083.

Morrongiello, B. A., McArthur, B. A., & Spence, J. R. (2016c). Understanding gender differences in childhood injuries: Examining longitudinal relations between parental reactions and boys' versus girls' injury-risk behaviors. *Health Psychology, 35*(6), 523.

Morrongiello, B. A., Zdzieborski, D., & Normand, J. (2010). Understanding gender differences in children's risk taking and injury: A comparison of mothers' and fathers' reactions to sons and daughters misbehaving in ways that lead to injury. *Journal of Applied Developmental Psychology, 31*(4), 322–329.

Morrow, E. L., & Duff, M. C. (2020). Sleep supports memory and learning: Implications for clinical practice in speech-language pathology. *American Journal of Speech-Language Pathology, 29*(2), 577–585.

Moser, T., & Reikerås, E. (2016). Motor-life-skills of toddlers—A comparative study of Norwegian and British boys and girls applying the Early Years Movement Skills Checklist. *European Early Childhood Education Research Journal, 24*(1), 115–135.

Murch, S. H., Anthony, A., Casson, D. H., Malik, M., Berelowitz, M., Dhillon, A. P., . . . Walker-Smith, J. A. (2004). Retraction of an interpretation. *Lancet, 363*(9411), 750.

National Library of Medicine. (2021). Normal growth and development. Retrieved from https://medlineplus.gov/ency/article/002456.htm.

National Sleep Foundation. (2004). *Sleep in America*. Retrieved from https://sleepfoundation.org/sites/default/files/FINAL%20SOF%202004.pdf.

National Sleep Foundation. (2015). *2014 Sleep in America Poll*. Retrieved from www.sleepfoundation.org/wp-content/uploads/2018/10/2014-NSF-Sleep-in-America-poll-summary-of-findings-FINAL-Updated-3-26-14-.pdf.

National Sleep Foundation. (2021). Children and Sleep. Retrieved from https://sleepfoundation.org/sleep-topics/children-and-sleep/page/0/2.

Nature Medicine. (2010). A timeline of the Wakefield retraction. *Nature Medicine, 16*(3), 248–248. https://doi.org/10.1038/nm0310-248b.

Pantley, E. (2010). *The no-cry separation anxiety solution: Gentle ways to make good-bye easy from six months to six years*. McGraw Hill Professional.

Paul, L. K., Corsello, C., Kennedy, D. P., & Adolphs, R. (2014). Agenesis of the corpus callosum and autism: A comprehensive comparison. *Brain*, awu070.

Peck, B., & Terry, D. (2021). The kids are alright: Outcome of a safety programme for addressing childhood injury in Australia. *European Journal of Investigation in Health, Psychology and Education, 11*(2), 546–556.

Peterson, C., Florence, C., & Klevens, J. (2018). The economic burden of child maltreatment in the United States, 2015. *Child Abuse & Neglect, 86*, 178–183.

Petrenko, C. L., Friend, A., Garrido, E. F., Taussig, H. N., & Culhane, S. E. (2012). Does subtype matter? Assessing the effects of maltreatment on functioning in preadolescent youth in out-of-home care. *Child Abuse & Neglect, 36*(9), 633–644.

Pica, R. (2008). Why motor skills matter. *Young Children*. Retrieved from www.naeyc.org/files/yc/file/200807/BTJ LearningLeapsBounds.pdf.

Pierce, J. E., & Péron, J. (2020). The basal ganglia and the cerebellum in human emotion. *Social Cognitive and Affective Neuroscience, 15*(5), 599–613.

Prado, E. L., & Dewey, K. G. (2014). Nutrition and brain development in early life. *Nutrition Reviews, 72*(4), 267–284.

Pujol, J., López-Sala, A., Sebastián-Gallés, N., Deus, J., Cardoner, N., Soriano-Mas, C., . . . Sans, A. (2004). Delayed myelination in children with developmental delay detected by volumetric MRI. *Neuroimage, 22*(2), 897–903.

Radesky, J. S., & Christakis, D. A. (2016). Increased screen time: Implications for early childhood development and behavior. *Pediatric Clinics of North America, 63*(5), 827–839.

Reilly, J. J., Armstrong, J., Dorosty, A. R., Emmett, P. M., Ness, A., Rogers, I., . . . Sherriff, A. (2005). Early life risk factors for obesity in childhood: Cohort study. *Bmj, 330*(7504), 1357.

Rimsza, M. E., Schackner, R. A., Bowen, K. A., & Marshall, W. (2002). Can child deaths be prevented? The Arizona child fatality review program experience. *Pediatrics, 110*(1), e11–e11.

Rodríguez-Negro, J., Huertas-Delgado, F. J., & Yanci, J. (2021). Motor skills differences by gender in early elementary education students. *Early Child Development and Care, 191*(2), 281–291.

Rogers, L. J., Zucca, P., & Vallortigara, G. (2004). Advantages of having a lateralized brain. *Proceedings of the Royal Society of London B: Biological Sciences, 271*(Suppl 6), S420–S422.

Rübeling, H., Schwarzer, S., Keller, H., & Lenk, M. (2011). Young Children's nonfigurative drawings of themselves and their families in two different cultures. *Journal of Cognitive Education and Psychology, 10*(1), 63–76.

Satter, E. (1990). The feeding relationship: Problems and interventions. *The Journal of Pediatrics, 117*(2), S181–S189.

Schore, A. N. (2015). *Affect regulation and the origin of the self: The neurobiology of emotional development*. Routledge.

Sdravou, K., Fotoulaki, M., Emmanouilidou-Fotoulaki, E., Andreoulakis, E., Makris, G., Sotiriadou, F., & Printza, A. (2021). Feeding problems in typically developing young children, a population-based study. *Children, 8*(5), 388.

Seah, R., Lystad, R. P., Curtis, K., & Mitchell, R. (2018). Socioeconomic variation in injury hospitalisations in Australian children ≤ 16 years: A 10-year population-based cohort study. *BMC Public Health, 18*(1), 1–9.

Shonkoff, J. P., Garner, A. S., Siegel, B. S., Dobbins, M. I., Earls, M. F., McGuinn, L., . . . Wood, D. L. (2012). The lifelong effects of early childhood adversity and toxic stress. *Pediatrics, 129*(1), e232–e246.

Shqair, A. Q., Pauli, L. A., Costa, V. P. P., Cenci, M., & Goettems, M. L. (2019). Screen time, dietary patterns and intake of potentially cariogenic food in children: A systematic review. *Journal of Dentistry, 86*, 17–26.

Shukla, A., & Jabarkheel, Z. (2019). Sugar-sweetened beverages and screen time: Partners in crime for adolescent obesity. *Journal of Pediatrics, 215*, 285.

Skjåkødegård, H. F., Danielsen, Y. S., Frisk, B., Hystad, S. W., Roelants, M., Pallesen, S., . . . Juliusson, P. B. (2021). Beyond sleep duration: Sleep timing as a risk factor for childhood obesity. *Pediatric Obesity, 16*(1), e12698.

Smith, K. (2007). A switch in handedness changes the brain. Retrieved from www.nature.com/news/2007/070717/full/news070716-4.html.

Son, S.-H., & Meisels, S. J. (2006). The relationship of young children's motor skills to later reading and math achievement. *Merrill-Palmer Quarterly, 52*(4), 755–778.

Spessato, B. C., Gabbard, C., Valentini, N., & Rudisill, M. (2013). Gender differences in Brazilian children's fundamental movement skill performance. *Early Child Development and Care, 183*(7), 916–923.

Spinazzola, J., Hodgdon, H., Liang, L.-J., Ford, J. D., Layne, C. M., Pynoos, R., . . . Kisiel, C. (2014). Unseen wounds: The contribution of psychological maltreatment to child and adolescent mental health and risk outcomes. *Psychological Trauma: Theory, Research, Practice, and Policy, 6*(S1), S18.

Strasburger, V. C. (2011). Children, adolescents, obesity, and the media. *Pediatrics, 128*(1), 201–208.

Stratheam, L., Giannotti, M., Mills, R., Kisely, S., Najman, J., & Abajobir, A. (2020). Long-term cognitive, psychological, and health outcomes associated with child abuse and neglect. *Pediatrics, 146*(4).

Stuss, D. T., & Knight, R. T. (2013). *Principles of frontal lobe function*. Oxford University Press.

Sundnes, A. (2018). Developing a context-sensitive understanding of infant toilet training: Cleanliness regimes adjusted for everyday life considerations. *International Journal of Early Childhood, 50*(3), 279–296.

Suni, E., & Singh, A. (2021). How much sleep do we really need? Retrieved from www.sleepfoundation.org/how-sleep-works/how-much-sleep-do-we-really-need.

Swanson, L. W. (1995). Mapping the human brain: Past, present, and future. *Trends in Neurosciences, 18*(11), 471–474.

Szaflarski, J. P., Rajagopal, A., Altaye, M., Byars, A. W., Jacola, L., Schmithorst, V. J., . . . Holland, S. K. (2012). Left-handedness and language lateralization in children. *Brain Research, 1433*, 85–97.

Taheri, S. (2006). The link between short sleep duration and obesity: We should recommend more sleep to prevent obesity. *Archives of Disease in Childhood, 91*(11), 881–884.

Thompson, D. A., & Christakis, D. A. (2005). The association between television viewing and irregular sleep schedules among children less than 3 years of age. *Pediatrics, 116*(4), 851–856.

Tiemeier, H., Lenroot, R. K., Greenstein, D. K., Tran, L., Pierson, R., & Giedd, J. N. (2010). Cerebellum development during childhood and adolescence: A longitudinal morphometric MRI study. *Neuroimage, 49*(1), 63–70.

Travers, B. G., Tromp, D. P., Adluru, N., Lange, N., Destiche, D., Ennis, C., . . . Fletcher, P. T. (2015). Atypical development of white matter microstructure of the corpus callosum in males with autism: A longitudinal investigation. *Molecular Autism, 6*(1), 1.

Uebergang, L. K., Arnup, S. J., Hiscock, H., Care, E., & Quach, J. (2017). Sleep problems in the first year of elementary school: The role of sleep hygiene, gender and socioeconomic status. *Sleep Health, 3*(3), 142–147.

Uematsu, A., Matsui, M., Tanaka, C., Takahashi, T., Noguchi, K., Suzuki, M., & Nishijo, H. (2012). Developmental trajectories of amygdala and hippocampus from infancy to early adulthood in healthy individuals. *PloS ONE, 7*(10), e46970.

UNICEF. (2016). Immunization saves up to 3 million children each year. Retrieved from www.unicef.org/immunization/.

United States Department of Agriculture. (2021). Back to basics: All about MyPlate food groups. Retrieved from usda.gov/media/blog/2017/09/26/back-basics-all-about-myplate-food-groups.

United States Department of Health & Human Services, Administration for Children and Families, Administration on Children, Youth and Families, Children's Bureau. (2021). Child maltreatment 2019. Retrieved from https://www.acf.hhs.gov/cb/research-data-technology/ statistics-research/child-maltreatment.

Vaughn, A. E., Martin, C. L., & Ward, D. S. (2018). What matters most-what parents model or what parents eat? *Appetite, 126*, 102–107.

Viner, R. M., & Cole, T. J. (2005). Television viewing in early childhood predicts adult body mass index. *Journal of Pediatrics, 147*(4), 429–435.

Vlahovicova, K., Melendez-Torres, G. J., Leijten, P., Knerr, W., & Gardner, F. (2017). Parenting programs for the prevention of child physical abuse recurrence: A systematic review and meta-analysis. *Clinical Child and Family Psychology Review, 20*(3), 351–365.

Wakefield, A. J., Murch, S. H., Anthony, A., Linnell, J., Casson, D., Malik, M., . . . Walker-Smith, J. A. (1998). RETRACTED: Ileal-lymphoid-nodular hyperplasia, non-specific colitis, and pervasive developmental disorder in children. *The Lancet 351*(9103), P637–641.

Wessel, L. (2017). Four vaccine myths and where they came from. Retrieved from www.sciencemag.org/news/2017/04/four-vaccine-myths-and-where-they-came.

World Health Organization. (2021a). Diarrhoea. Retrieved from www.who.int/health-topics/diarrhoea#tab=tab_1.

World Health Organization. (2021b). Immunization coverage. Retrieved from www.who.int/news-room/fact-sheets/detail/immunization-coverage.

Xu, J., Murphy, S. L., Kochanek, K. D., & Arias, E. (2021). *Deaths: Final data for 2019.* Retrieved from www.cdc.gov/nchs/data/nvsr/nvsr70/nvsr70-08-508.pdf.

Yeo, S. S., Chang, P. H., & Jang, S. H. (2013). The ascending reticular activating system from pontine reticular formation to the thalamus in the human brain. *Frontiers in Human Neuroscience, 7*, 416.

Zickert, N., Geuze, R. H., Beking, T., & Groothuis, T. G. (2021). Testing the Darwinian function of lateralization. Does separation of workload between brain hemispheres increase cognitive performance? *Neuropsychologia, 159*, 107884.

Zimmerman, F. J. (2008). Children's media use and sleep problems: Issues and unanswered questions. Research brief. Henry J. Kaiser Family Foundation.

Chapter 9

Ackerman, D. J. (2019). The Montessori preschool landscape in the United States: History, programmatic inputs, availability, and effects. *ETS Research Report Series, 2019*(1), 1–20.

American Academy of Pediatrics. (2018). Children and media tips from the American Academy of Pediatrics. Retrieved from www.aap.org/en-us/about-the-aap/aap-press-room/news-features-and-safety-tips/Pages/Children-and-Media-Tips.aspx.

American Psychological Association. (2016). The effects of poverty, hunger, and homelessness on children and youth. Retrieved from http://www.apa.org/pi/families/poverty.aspx.

Arnold, D. S., & Whitehurst, G. J. (1994). Accelerating language development through picture book reading: A summary of dialogic reading and its effect. *Journal of Educational Psychology, 86*(2), 235–243.

Aro, T., Poikkeus, A.-M., Laakso, M.-L., Tolvanen, A., & Ahonen, T. (2015). Associations between private speech, behavioral self-regulation, and cognitive abilities. *International Journal of Behavioral Development, 39*(6), 508–518. doi:10.1177/0165025414556094.

Asokan, S., Surendran, S., Asokan, S., & Nuvvula, S. (2014). Relevance of Piaget's cognitive principles among 4–7 years old children: A descriptive cross-sectional study. *Journal of Indian Society of Pedodontics and Preventive Dentistry, 32*(4), 292.

Baron-Cohen, S., Leslie, A. M., & Frith, U. (1985). Does the autistic child have a "theory of mind"? *Cognition, 21*(1), 37–46.

Bartsch, K., & Wellman, H. M. (1995). *Children talk about the mind*. Oxford University Press.

Belsky, J. (2006). Early child care and early child development: Major findings of the NICHD Study of Early Child Care. *European Journal of Developmental Psychology, 3*(1), 95–110. doi:10.1080/17405620600557755.

Berko, J. 1958. The child's learning of English morphology. *Word 14*(2–3): 150–177.

Borst, G., Poirel, N., Pineau, A., Cassotti, M., & Houdé, O. (2013). Inhibitory control efficiency in a Piaget-like class-inclusion task in school-age children and adults: A developmental negative priming study. *Developmental Psychology, 49*(7), 1366–1374. doi:10.1037/a0029622.

Brady, K. W., & Goodman, J. C. (2014). The type, but not the amount, of information available influences toddlers' fast mapping and retention of new words. *American Journal of Speech-Language Pathology, 23*(2), 120–133. doi:10.1044/2013_AJSLP-13-0013.

Brown, A. L., & Campione, J. C. (1972). Recognition memory for perceptually similar pictures in preschool children. *Journal of Experimental Psychology, 95*(1), 55–62. doi:10.1037/h0033276.

Bruck, M., & Ceci, S. J. (2013). Expert testimony in a child sex abuse case: Translating memory development research. *Memory, 21*(5), 556–565. doi:10.1080/09658211.2013.769606.

Byun, W., Blair, S. N., & Pate, R. R. (2013). Objectively measured sedentary behavior in preschool children: Comparison between Montessori and traditional preschools. *The International Journal of Behavioral Nutrition and Physical Activity, 10*. doi:10.1186/1479-5868-10-2.

Cabbage, K., Brinkley, S., Gray, S., Alt, M., Cowan, N., Green, S., . . . Hogan, T. P. (2017). Assessing working memory in children: The Comprehensive Assessment Battery for Children—Working Memory (CABC-WM). *Journal of Visualized Experiments, (124)*, e55121. doi: 10.3791/55121.

Castagno-Dysart, D., Matera, B., & Traver, J. (2019). The importance of instructional scaffolding. Retrieved from https://www.teachermagazine.com.au/articles/the-importance-of-instructional-scaffolding.

Ceci, S. J., Gilstrap, L., & Fitneva, S. (2002). Children's testimony. In M. J. Rutter, D. Bishop, D. S. Pine, S. Scott, J. S. Stevenson, E. A. Taylor, A. Thapar (Eds.), *Rutter's child and adolescent psychiatry (pp. 117–127)*. Oxford: Blackwell Science.

Child Trends Databank. (2015). *Reading to young children*. Retrieved from http://www.childtrends.org/wp-content/uploads/2012/11/05_Reading_to_Young_Children.pdf.

Child Welfare Information Gateway. (2021). Child Maltreatment 2019: Summary of Key Findings. Retrieved from https://www.childwelfare.gov/pubpdfs/canstats.pdf.

Children's Bureau, Department of Health and Human Services. (2021). Child Maltreatment 2019: Summary of Key Findings (p. 8). https://www.childwelfare.gov/pubpdfs/canstats.pdf.

Clarke-Stewart, A., & Allhusen, V. D. (2005). *What we know about childcare*. Harvard University Press.

Common Sense Media. (2013). *Media and violence: An analysis of current research*. Retrieved from https://www.commonsensemedia.org/research/media-and-violence-an-analysis-of-current-research#.

Common Sense Media. (2017). Zero to eight: Children's media use in America. Retrieved from www.commonsensemedia.org/sites/default/files/uploads/research/csm_zerotoeight_fullreport_release_2.pdf.

Comstock, G., & Scharrer, E. (2006). Media and Popular Culture. In K. A. Renninger, I. E. Sigel, W. Damon, & R. M. Lerner (Eds.), *Handbook of child psychology, 6th ed.: Vol 4, Child psychology in practice.* (pp. 817–863). Hoboken, NJ, US: John Wiley & Sons Inc.

Coogle, C. G., Parsons, A. W., La Croix, L., & Ottley, J. R. (2020). A comparison of dialogic reading, modeling, and dialogic reading plus modeling. *Infants & Young Children, 33*(2), 119–131.

Cooper, B. R., & Lanza, S. T. (2014). Who benefits most from Head Start? Using latent class moderation to examine differential treatment effects. *Child Development, 85*(6), 2317–2338. doi:10.1111/cdev.12278.

DeLoache, J. S., Chiong, C., Sherman, K., Islam, N., Vanderborght, M., Troseth, G. L., . . . O'Doherty, K. (2010). Do babies learn from baby media? *Psychological Science, 21*(11), 1570–1574. doi:10.1177/0956797610384145.

Deming, D. (2009). Early childhood intervention and life-cycle skill development: Evidence from Head Start. *American Economic Journal: Applied Economics, 1*(3), 111–134.

Diamond, A., & Lee, K. (2011). Interventions shown to aid executive function development in children 4 to 12 years old. *Science, 333*(6045), 959–964. doi:10.1126/science.1204529.

Dilworth-Bart, J. E., Khurshid, A., & Vandell, D. L. (2007). Do maternal stress and home environment mediate the relation between early income-to-need and 54-months attentional abilities? *Infant and Child Development, 16*(5), 525–552. doi:10.1002/icd.528.

Dixson, H. G., Komugabe-Dixson, A. F., Dixson, B. J., & Low, J. (2018). Scaling theory of mind in a small-scale society: A case study from Vanuatu. *Child Development, 89*(6), 2157–2175.

Dodd-Nufrio, A. T. (2011). Reggio Emilia, Maria Montessori, and John Dewey: Dispelling teachers' misconceptions and understanding theoretical foundations. *Early Childhood Education Journal, 39*(4), 235–237. doi:10.1007/s10643-011-0451-3.

Duncan, R. M., & Cheyne, J. A. (2001). Private speech in young adults: Task difficulty, self-regulation, and psychological predication. *Cognitive Development, 16*(4), 889–906.

Emerson, A. M., & Linder, S. M. (2019). A review of research of the Reggio Inspired approach: An integrative re-framing. *Early Years 41*(2), 1–15.

Eun, B. (2019). The zone of proximal development as an overarching concept: A framework for synthesizing Vygotsky's theories. *Educational Philosophy and Theory, 51*(1), 18–30.

Feldman, R. S. (2016). *Child Development,* 7th ed. Pearson, Boston.

Flavell, J. H., Green, F. L., Flavell, E. R., Watson, M. W., & Campione, J. C. (1986). Development of knowledge about the appearance-reality distinction. *Monographs of the Society for Research in Child Development,* i-87.

Francis, J., & Barnett, W. S. (2019). Relating preschool class size to classroom quality and student achievement. *Early Childhood Research Quarterly, 49,* 49–58.

Gardner, H. (2011). *Frames of mind: The theory of multiple intelligences*: Hachette UK.

Gathercole, S. E., & Baddeley, A. D. (2014). *Working memory and language*: Psychology Press.

Gilchrist, A. L., Cowan, N., & Naveh-Benjamin, M. (2009). Investigating the childhood development of working memory using sentences: New evidence for the growth of chunk capacity. *Journal of Experimental Child Psychology, 104*(2), 252–265. doi:10.1016/j.jecp.2009.05.006.

Gleason, T. R., & Hohmann, L. M. (2006). Concepts of real and imaginary friendships in early childhood. *Social Development, 15*(1), 128–144.

Gopnik, A., & Astington, J. W. (1988). Children's understanding of representational change and its relation to the understanding of false belief and the appearance-reality distinction. *Child Development,* 26–37.

Haleakala Waldorf School. (2016). The Waldorf Approach. Retrieved from http://www.waldorfmaui.org/why_waldorf/.

Hardesty, L. (2016). Can technology help teach literacy in poor communities? Retrieved from http://news.mit.edu/2016/literacy-apps-poor-communities-0426.

Hart, B., & Risley, T. R. (1995). *Meaningful differences in the everyday experience of young American children.* Baltimore, MD, US: Paul H Brookes Publishing.

Head Start ECLKC. (2021). Head Start program facts: Fiscal year 2019. Retrieved from https://eclkc.ohs.acf.hhs.gov/about-us/article/head-start-program-facts-fiscal-year-2019.

Heim, S., Benasich, A. A., Wirth, N., & Keil, A. (2015). Tracking the attentional blink profile: A cross-sectional study from childhood to adolescence. *Psychological Research, 79*(1), 19–27. doi:10.1007/s00426-013-0530-8.

Heyman, G. D., & Gelman, S. A. (1999). The use of trait labels in making psychological inferences. *Child Development, 70*(3), 604–619.

Hirsh-Pasek, K., Zosh, J. M., Golinkoff, R. M., Gray, J. H., Robb, M. B., & Kaufman, J. (2015). Putting education in 'educational' apps: Lessons from the science of learning. *Psychological Science in the Public Interest, 16*(1), 3–34. doi:10.1177/1529100615569721.

Hoffmann, J., & Russ, S. (2012). Pretend play, creativity, and emotion regulation in children. *Psychology of Aesthetics, Creativity, and the Arts, 6*(2), 175.

Hong, N., & del Busto, C. T. (2019). Collaboration, scaffolding, and successive approximations: A developmental science approach to training in clinical psychology. *Training and Education in Professional Psychology, 14*(3), 228–234.

Howe, M., Courage, M., & Rooksby, M. (2009). The genesis and development of autobiographical memory. In M. L. Courage, & N. Cowan (Eds.), *The development of memory in infancy and childhood* (2nd ed. ed., pp. 177–196). Psychology Press.

Hughes, M. (1975). Egocentrism in pre-school children. Unpublished PhD dissertation, University of Edinburgh, Edinburgh, Scotland. Retrieved from https://era.ed.ac.uk/handle/1842/22329.

Inagaki, H., Meguro, K., Shimada, M., Ishizaki, J., Okuzumi, H., & Yamadori, A. (2002). Discrepancy between mental rotation and perspective-taking abilities in normal aging assessed by Piaget's three-mountain task. *Journal of Clinical and Experimental Neuropsychology, 24*(1), 18–25.

He, M., Irwin, J. D., Bouck, L. M. S., Tucker, P., & Pollett, G. L. (2005). Screen-Viewing Behaviors Among Preschoolers: Parents' Perceptions. *American Journal of Preventive Medicine, 29*(2), 120–125. doi:10.1016/j.amepre.2005.04.004.

Heim, S., Benasich, A. A., Wirth, N., & Keil, A. (2015). Tracking the attentional blink profile: A cross-sectional study from childhood to adolescence. *Psychological Research, 79*(1), 19–27. doi:10.1007/s00426-013-0530-8.

Huttenlocher, J., Haight, W., Bryk, A., Seltzer, M., & Lyons, T. (1991). Early vocabulary growth: Relation to language input and gender. *Developmental Psychology, 27*(2), 236–248. doi:10.1037/0012-1649.27.2.236.

Jones, G. (2012). Why chunking should be considered as an explanation for developmental change before short-term memory capacity and processing speed. *Frontiers in Psychology, 3,* 167.

Kail, R. V., & Ferrer, E. (2007). Processing speed in childhood and adolescence: Longitudinal models for examining developmental change. *Child Development, 78*(6), 1760–1770. doi:10.1111/j.1467-8624.2007.01088.x.

Kidman, R., Margolis, R., Smith-Greenaway, E., & Verdery, A. M. (2021). Estimates and Projections of COVID-19 and Parental Death in the US. *JAMA Pediatrics.*

Klein, M., Dorsch, C., & Hemmens, C. (2020). Talk to me: An analysis of statutes regulating police interviews of child victims. *Juvenile and Family Court Journal, 71*(2), 5–19.

Klemfuss, J. Z., & Olaguez, A. P. (2020). Individual differences in children's suggestibility: An updated review. *Journal of Child Sexual Abuse, 29*(2), 158–182.

Koball, H., Moore, A., & Hernandez, J. (2021). Basic facts about low-income children. Retrieved from www.nccp.org/wp-content/uploads/2021/03/NCCP_FactSheets_All-Kids_FINAL.pdf.

Kostyrka-Allchorne, K., Cooper, N. R., & Simpson, A. (2017). The relationship between television exposure and children's cognition and behaviour: A systematic review. *Developmental Review, 44,* 19–58.

Kotaman, H. (2020). Impacts of dialogical storybook reading on young children's reading attitudes and vocabulary development. *Reading Improvement, 57*(1), 40–45.

Kundanis, R., & Massaro, D. W. (2004). Televisual Media for Children Are More Interactive. *The American Journal of Psychology, 117*(4), 643–648. doi:10.2307/4149001.

Lamb, M. E., Orbach, Y., Hershkowitz, I., Esplin, P. W., & Horowitz, D. (2007). A structured forensic interview protocol improves the quality and informativeness of investigative interviews with children: A review of research using the NICHD Investigative Interview Protocol. *Child abuse & neglect, 31*(11), 1201–1231.

Leblanc, É., Bernier, A., & Howe, N. (2017). The more the merrier? Sibling composition and early manifestations of theory of mind in toddlers. *Journal of Cognition and Development, 18*(3), 375–391.

Leung, C. H. (2015). Factor structure of PPBS with Chinese preschoolers from low-income families. *Children and Youth Services Review, 53*, 157–165. doi:10.1016/j.childyouth.2015.04.002.

Li, S., Hu, J., Li, C., Wang, Q., He, J., Wang, Y., & Yang, C. (2017). Chunking processing of spatial working memory in autism preschool children. *Acta Psychologica Sinica, 5*, 631–642.

Lillard, A., & Else-Quest, N. (2006). Evaluating montessori education. *Science, 313*(5795), 1893–1894.

Lillard, A. S., & Taggart, J. (2019). Pretend play and fantasy: What if Montessori was right? *Child Development Perspectives, 13*(2), 85–90.

Luby, J., Belden, A., Botteron, K., & et al. (2013). The effects of poverty on childhood brain development: The mediating effect of caregiving and stressful life events. *JAMA Pediatrics, 167*(12), 1135–1142. doi:10.1001/jamapediatrics.2013.3139.

Marcon, R. A. (1999). Positive relationships between parent school involvement and public school inner-city preschoolers' development and academic performance. *School Psychology Review, 28*(3), 395.

Marcus, G. F., Pinker, S., Ullman, M., Hollander, M., Rosen, T. J., Xu, F., & Clahsen, H. (1992). Overregularization in language acquisition. *Monographs of the Society for Research in Child Development, 57*(4), i-182. doi:10.2307/1166115.

Mathis, E. T. B., & Bierman, K. L. (2015). Dimensions of parenting associated with child prekindergarten emotion regulation and attention control in low-income families. *Social Development, 24*(3), 601–620. doi:10.1111/sode.12112.

Mayer, A., & Träuble, B. E. (2013). Synchrony in the onset of mental state understanding across cultures? A study among children in Samoa. *International Journal of Behavioral Development, 37*(1), 21–28.

McAlister, A., & Peterson, C. (2007). A longitudinal study of child siblings and theory of mind development. *Cognitive Development, 22*(2), 258–270.

McClelland, M. M., & Cameron, C. E. (2012). Self-regulation in early childhood: Improving conceptual clarity and developing ecologically valid measures. *Child Development Perspectives, 6*(2), 136–142. doi:10.1111/j.1750-8606.2011.00191.x.

McDonnell, C. G., Valentino, K., Comas, M., & Nuttall, A. K. (2016). Mother–child reminiscing at risk: Maternal attachment, elaboration, and child autobiographical memory specificity. *Journal of Experimental Child Psychology, 143*, 65–84. doi:10.1016/j.jecp.2015.10.012.

Meltzoff, A. N. (2011). Social cognition and the origins of imitation, empathy, and theory of mind. In U. Goswami (Ed.), *The Wiley-Blackwell handbook of childhood cognitive development (2nd ed.).* (pp. 49–75): Wiley-Blackwell.

Merewether, J. (2019). Listening with young children: Enchanted animism of trees, rocks, clouds (and other things). *Pedagogy, Culture & Society, 27*(2), 233–250.

Miller, G. A. (1956). The magical number seven, plus or minus two: some limits on our capacity for processing information. *Psychological review, 63*(2), 81.

Milteer, R. M., Ginsburg, K. R., & Mulligan, D. A. (2012). The importance of play in promoting healthy child development and maintaining strong parent-child bond: Focus on children in poverty. *Pediatrics, 129*(1), e204-e213. doi:10.1542/peds. 2011-2953.

Moffitt, T. E., Arseneault, L., Belsky, D., Dickson, N., Hancox, R. J., Harrington, H., . . . Ross, S. (2011). A gradient of childhood self-control predicts health, wealth, and public safety. *Proceedings of the National Academy of Sciences, 108*(7), 2693–2698.

Moll, H., Khalulyan, A., & Moffett, L. (2017). 2.5-Year-Olds Express Suspense When Others Approach Reality With False Expectations. *Child Development, 88*(1), 114–122.

Montrul, S., & Mason, S. A. (2020). Smaller vocabularies lead to morphological overregularization in heritage language grammars. *Bilingualism: Language and Cognition, 23*(1), 35–36.

Morin, A. (2014). Executive functioning issues: What you're seeing in your preschooler. Retrieved from https://www.understood .org/en/learning-attention-issues/child-learning-disabilities/ executive-functioning-issues/executive-functioning-issues- what-youre-seeing-in-your-preschooler.

Nathanson, A. I., Aladé, F., Sharp, M. L., Rasmussen, E. E., & Christy, K. (2014). The relation between television exposure and executive function among preschoolers. *Developmental Psychology, 50*(5), 1497.National Center for Education Statistics. (2021a). Child care. Retrieved from https://nces.ed.gov/ fastfacts/display.asp?id=4.

National Center for Education Statistics. (2021b). Table 202.25. Retrieved from https://nces.ed.gov/programs/digest/d20/ tables/dt20_202.25.asp.

NICHD Early Child Care Research Network. (1998). Early child care and self-control, compliance, and problem behavior at twenty-four and thirty-six months. *Child Development, 69*(4), 1145–1170. doi:10.2307/1132367.

Office of Head Start. (2019). Head Start services. Retrieved from www.acf.hhs.gov/programs/ohs/about/head-start.

Owens, R. E. (2015). *Language development* (9th ed.). New York: Pearson.

Piaget, J. and B. Inhelder (1967). *A Child's Conception of Space* (F. J. Langdon & J. L. Lunzer, Trans.). New York: Norton (Original French work published 1948).

Piaget, J., & Inhelder, B. (1956). *The child's concept of space*: Routledge & Paul.

Piaget, J., & Inhelder, B. (1969). The psychology of the child. *New York: Basic.*

Pichler, A. S., Powell, M., Sharman, S. J., Westera, N., & Goodman-Delahunty, J. (2019). Discussions about child witness interviews during Australian trials of child sexual abuse. *Police Practice and Research 22*(1), 938–952.

Posner, M. I., Rothbart, M. K., & Sheese, B. E. (2007). Attention genes. *Developmental Science, 10*(1), 24–29.

Puma, M., Bell, S., Cook, R., Heid, C., Shapiro, G., Broene, P., . . . Friedman, J. (2010). Head Start Impact Study. Final Report. *Administration for Children & Families*.

Roth, W.-M. (2020). Zone of proximal development in mathematics education. In S. Lerman (Ed.) *Encyclopedia of mathematics education* (pp. 913–916). Springer.

Saaty, T. L., & Ozdemir, M. S. (2003). Why the magic number seven plus or minus two. *Mathematical and Computer Modelling, 38*(3), 233–244.

Sawyer, J. (2016). In what language do you speak to yourself? A review of private speech and bilingualism. *Early Childhood Research Quarterly, 36*, 489–505.

Schmidt, M. E., Pempek, T. A., Kirkorian, H. L., Lund, A. F., & Anderson, D. R. (2008). The effects of background television on the toy play behavior of very young children. *Child Development, 79*(4), 1137–1151.

Seger, J., & Potts, R. (2017). Construct validity of adults' retrospective memory for childhood TV viewing: Self-reported early exposure to violent TV programs predicts current aggression. *Communication Methods and Measures, 11*(1), 31–48.

Slate, J. R., & Charlesworth, J. R., Jr. (1988). Information processing theory: Classroom applications. Retrieved from https://eric.ed.gov/?id=ED293792.

Slavin, R. E. (2005). *Educational psychology: theory and practice*. Needham Heights, MA: Allyn & Bacon.

Statista. (2021). Number of available apps in the Apple App Store from 2008 to 2021. Retrieved from www.statista.com/statistics/268251/number-of-apps-in-the-itunes-app-store-since-2008/.

Stehlik, T. (2019). The world in 1919: The context for the founding of the first Waldorf School. In *Waldorf Schools and the history of Steiner education* (pp. 1–20). Springer.

Sternberg, R. J., & Grigorenko, E. L. (2002). *Dynamic testing: The nature and measurement of learning potential*: Cambridge University Press.

Stone, V. E., Baron-Cohen, S., & Knight, R. T. (2013). Theory of mind. *Autism Sci Ment Health, 226*.

Tamis-LeMonda, C. S. (2022). *Child Development: Context, Culture, and Cascades*. Oxford University Press/Sinauer, Sunderland, MA.

Taylor, M., Cartwright, B. S., & Carlson, S. M. (1993). A developmental investigation of children's imaginary companions. *Developmental Psychology, 29*(2), 276.

Taylor, M., Shawber, A. B., & Mannering, A. M. (2009). Children's imaginary companions: What is it like to have an invisible friend? In K. D. Markman, W. M. P. Klein, & J. A. Suhr (Eds.), *Handbook of imagination and mental simulation.* (pp. 211–224). New York, NY, US: Psychology Press.

Uchikoshi, Y. (2006). Early Reading in Bilingual Kindergartners: Can Educational Television Help? *Scientific Studies of Reading, 10*(1), 89–120. doi:10.1207/s1532799xssr1001_5.

Vandell, D. L., Belsky, J., Burchinal, M., Steinberg, L., & Vandergrift, N. (2010). Do effects of early child care extend to age 15 years? Results from the NICHD study of early child care and youth development. *Child Development, 81*(3), 737–756. doi:10.1111/j.1467-8624.2010.01431.x.

Vinson, D., & Parker, A. (2019). Vygotsky and sports coaching: Non-linear practice in youth and adult settings. *Curriculum Studies in Health and Physical Education, 10*(1), 91–106.

Warren, A. R., Woodall, C. E., Thomas, M., Nunno, M., Keeney, J. M., Larson, S. M., & Stadfeld, J. A. (1999). Assessing the effectiveness of a training program for interviewing child witnesses. *Applied Developmental Science, 3*(2), 128–135. doi:10.1207/s1532480xads0302_6.

Wellman, H. (2020). *Reading minds: How childhood teaches us to understand people*. Oxford University Press, USA.

Westby, C., & Robinson, L. (2014). A developmental perspective for promoting theory of mind. *Topics in Language Disorders, 34*(4), 362–382. doi:10.1097/TLD.0000000000000035.

Whitebread, D., & O'Sullivan, L. (2020). Pretend play in young children and the emergence of creativity. In *Creativity and the wandering mind* (pp. 205–230). Elsevier.

Wright, J. C., Huston, A. C., Scantlin, R., & Kotler, J. (2001). The Early Window project: Sesame Street prepares children for school.". G" is for growing: Thirty years of research on children and Sesame Street, 97–114.

Zimmerman, F. J., Christakis, D. A., & Meltzoff, A. N. (2007). Associations between media viewing and language development in children under age 2 years. *The Journal of pediatrics, 151*(4), 364–368.

Chapter 10

Alaggia, R., & Vine, C. (2013). *Cruel but not unusual: Violence in Canadian families*. Wilfrid Laurier University Press.

Alegre, A. (2011). Parenting styles and children's emotional intelligence: What do we know? *The Family Journal, 19*(1), 56–62.

Alexander, G. M., Wilcox, T., & Woods, R. (2009). Sex differences in infants' visual interest in toys. *Archives of Sexual Behavior, 38*(3), 427–433.

American Academy of Pediatrics. (2000). Joint statement on the impact of entertainment violence on children. Congressional Public Health Summit.

American Academy of Pediatrics. (2017). Where we stand: Spanking. Retrieved from www.healthychildren.org/English/family-life/family-dynamics/communication-discipline/Pages/Where-We-Stand-Spanking.aspx.

Auster, C. J., & Mansbach, C. S. (2012). The gender marketing of toys: An analysis of color and type of toy on the Disney store website. *Sex Roles, 67*(7–8), 375–388.

Aydt, H., & Corsaro, W. A. (2003). Differences in children's construction of gender across culture: An interpretive approach. *American Behavioral Scientist, 46*(10), 1306–1325.

Bandura, A., Ross, D., & Ross, S. A. (1963). Imitation of film-mediated aggressive models. *Journal of Abnormal and Social Psychology, 66*(1), 3.

Bank, L., Burraston, B., & Snyder, J. (2004). Sibling conflict and ineffective parenting as predictors of adolescent boys' antisocial behavior and peer difficulties: Additive and interactional effects. *Journal of Research on Adolescence, 14*(1), 99–125.

Barber, B. K., & Xia, M. (2013). The centrality of control to parenting and its effects. doi: 10.1037/13948-004.

Baumrind, D. (1971). Current patterns of parental authority. *Developmental Psychology, 4*(1, Ptp2), 1–103.

Baumrind, D. (1980). New directions in socialization research. *American Psychologist, 35*(7), 639–652.

Beal, J. A. (2017). Time-out for young children. *MCN: The American Journal of Maternal/Child Nursing, 42*(1), 57.

Bem, S. L. (1981). Gender schema theory: A cognitive account of sex typing. *Psychological Review, 88*(4), 354.

Berenbaum, S. A., Bryk, K. L. K., & Beltz, A. M. (2012). Early androgen effects on spatial and mechanical abilities: Evidence from congenital adrenal hyperplasia. *Behavioral Neuroscience, 126*(1), 86.

Berndt, T. J. (2004). Children's friendships: Shifts over a half-century in perspectives on their development and their effects. *Merrill-Palmer Quarterly, 50*(3), 206–223.

Bjorklund, D. F., & Ellis, B. J. (2014). Children, childhood, and development in evolutionary perspective. *Developmental Review, 34*(3), 225–264.

Bonawitz, E., Shafto, P., Gweon, H., Goodman, N. D., Spelke, E., & Schulz, L. (2011). The double-edged sword of pedagogy: Instruction limits spontaneous exploration and discovery. *Cognition, 120*(3), 322–330.

Bradford, J., Reisner, S. L., Honnold, J. A., & Xavier, J. (2013). Experiences of transgender-related discrimination and implications for health: Results from the Virginia Transgender Health Initiative Study. American Journal of Public Health, 103(10), 1820–1829. https://doi.org/10.2105/AJPH.2012.300796.

Brame, B., Nagin, D. S., & Tremblay, R. E. (2001). Developmental trajectories of physical aggression from school entry to late adolescence. *Journal of Child Psychology and Psychiatry, 42*(4), 503–512.

Bremner, J. G., & Wachs, T. D. (Eds.). (2014). *The Wiley Blackwell handbook of infant development* (2nd ed.). Chichester, UK: Wiley Blackwell.

Brody, G. (2013). Sibling relationships and their association with parental differential treatment. In E. M. Hetherington, D. Reiss, & R. Plomin (Eds.), *Separate social worlds of siblings: The impact of nonshared environment on development* (pp. 129–142). Routledge.

Buchanan, A. M., Gentile, D. A., Nelson, D. A., Walsh, D. A., & Hensel, J. (2002). *What goes in must come out: Children's media violence consumption at home and aggressive behaviors at school.* Minneapolis, MN: National Institute on Media and the Family.

Bukowski, W. M., Buhrmester, D., & Underwood, M. K. (2011). Peer relations as a developmental context. In M. K. Underwood & L. H. Rosen (Eds.), *Social development: Relationships in infancy, childhood, and adolescence* (pp. 153–179). Guilford Press.

Burdette, H. L., & Whitaker, R. C. (2005). A national study of neighborhood safety, outdoor play, television viewing, and obesity in preschool children. *Pediatrics, 116*(3), 657–662.

Burk, W., & Laursen, B. (2005). Adolescent perceptions of friendship and their associations with individual adjustment. *International Journal of Behavioral Development, 29*(2), 156–164.

Bushman, B. J., & Huesmann, L. R. (2001). Effects of televised violence on aggression. In D. G. Singer, & J. L. Singer (Eds.), *Handbook of children and the media* (pp. 223–254). Thousand Oaks, CA: Sage Publications.

Bussey, K., & Bandura, A. (1984). Influence of gender constancy and social power on sex-linked modeling. *Journal of Personality and Social Psychology, 47*(6), 1292–1302.

Bussey, K., & Bandura, A. (1999). Social cognitive theory of gender development and differentiation. *Psychological Review, 106*(4), 676.

Carré, J. M., Iselin, A.-M. R., Welker, K. M., Hariri, A. R., & Dodge, K. A. (2014). Testosterone reactivity to provocation mediates the effect of early intervention on aggressive behavior. *Psychological Science, 25*(5), 1140–1146.

Chao, R., Tseng, V., & Bornstein, M. H. (2002). Parenting of Asians. In M. H. Bornstein (Ed.), *Handbook of parenting* (pp. 59–93). Lawrence Erlbaum Associates Publishers.

Chen, Z.-y., & Liu, R. X. (2014). Comparing adolescent only children with those who have siblings on academic related outcomes and psychosocial adjustment. *Child Development Research, 2014,* 10. doi: 10.1155/2014/578289.

Cherney, I. D., Harper, H. J., & Winter, J. A. (2006). Nouveaux jouets: Ce que les enfants identifient comme "jouets de garçons" et "jouets de filles". *Enfance, 58*(3), 266–282.

ChildTrends Databank. (2015). Attitudes toward spanking. Retrieved from www.childtrends.org/wp-content/uploads/2012/10/51_Attitudes_Toward_Spanking.pdf.

Committee on Psychosocial Aspects of Child and Family Health. (1998). Guidance for effective discipline. *Pediatrics, 101*(4), 723–728.

Coplan, R. J., Prakash, K., O'neil, K., & Armer, M. (2004). Do you "want" to play? Distinguishing between conflicted shyness and social disinterest in early childhood. *Developmental Psychology, 40*(2), 244.

Cvencek, D., Greenwald, A. G., & Meltzoff, A. N. (2016). Implicit measures for preschool children confirm self-esteem's role in maintaining a balanced identity. *Journal of Experimental Social Psychology, 62,* 50–57.

Damon, W. (1988). *The moral child.* New York: Free Press.

Darwin, C. (1958). *The origin of species by means of natural selection: The descent of man and selection in relation to sex: Or the preservation of favored races in the struggle for life.* Random House.

David, B., Grace, D., & Ryan, M. K. (2004). The gender wars: A self-categorisation theory perspective on the development of gender identity. In M. Bennett & F. Sani (Eds.), *The development of the social self* (pp. 135–157). Psychology Press.

Davis, M. H., Luce, C., & Kraus, S. J. (1994). The heritability of characteristics associated with dispositional empathy. *Journal of Personality, 62*(3), 369–391.

Deater-Deckard, K., Lansford, J. E., Malone, P. S., Alampay, L. P., Sorbring, E., Bacchini, D., . . . Di Giunta, L. (2011). The association between parental warmth and control in thirteen cultural groups. *Journal of Family Psychology, 25*(5), 790.

DeLisi, R. (2015). Piaget's sympathetic but unromantic account of children's play. In J. E. Johnson, S. G. Eberle, T. S. Henricks, & D. Kuschner (Eds.), *The handbook of the study of play* (pp. 227–238). Lanham, MD: Rowman & Littlefield.

Dodge, K. A. (1980). Social cognition and children's aggressive behavior. *Child Development 51*(1), 162–170.

Dunn, J. (1988). *The beginnings of social understanding.* Harvard University Press.

Eagly, A. H., & Mladinic, A. (1989). Gender stereotypes and attitudes toward women and men. *Personality and Social Psychology Bulletin, 15*(4), 543–558.

Falbo, T. (2012). Only children: An updated review. *Journal of Individual Psychology, 68*(1) 38–49.

Ferguson, C. J. (2013). Spanking, corporal punishment and negative long-term outcomes: A meta-analytic review of longitudinal studies. *Clinical Psychology Review, 33*(1), 196–208.

Fisher, K. R., Hirsh-Pasek, K., Newcombe, N., & Golinkoff, R. M. (2013). Taking shape: Supporting preschoolers' acquisition of geometric knowledge through guided play. *Child Development, 84*(6), 1872–1878.

Fu, G., Xu, F., Cameron, C. A., Heyman, G., & Lee, K. (2007). Cross-cultural differences in children's choices, categorizations, and evaluations of truths and lies. *Developmental Psychology, 43*(2), 278.

Fung, W.-k., & Cheng, R. W.-y. (2017). Effect of school pretend play on preschoolers' social competence in peer interactions: Gender as a potential moderator. *Early Childhood Education Journal, 45*(1), 35–42.

Gershoff, E. T. (2013). Spanking and child development: We know enough now to stop hitting our children. *Child Development Perspectives, 7*(3), 133–137.

Gershoff, E. T., & Font, S. A. (2016). Corporal punishment in U.S. public schools: Prevalence, disparities in use, and status in state and federal policies. *Social Policy Report, 30*(1), 1–26.

Gershoff, E. T., & Grogan-Kaylor, A. (2016). Spanking and child outcomes: Old controversies and new meta-analyses. doi: 10.1037/fam0000191.

Global Initiative to End All Corporal Punishment of Children. (2022). Countdown to universal prohibition. Retrieved from https://endcorporalpunishment.org/countdown/.

Grant, J. M., Herman, J., Harrison, J., Keisling, M., Mottet, L., Tanis, J. E. (2010). National Transgender Discrimination Survey Report on Health and Health Care: Findings of a Study by the National Center for Transgender Equality and the National Gay and Lesbian Task Force. United States: National Center for Transgender Equality.

Grolnick, W. S. (2002). *The psychology of parental control: How well-meant parenting backfires.* Psychology Press.

Grusec, J. E. (2014). Parent–child conversations from the perspective of socialization theory. In C. Wainryb & H. E. Recchia (Eds.), *Talking about right and wrong: Parent-child conversations as contexts for moral development* (pp. 334–366). Cambridge University Press.

Grusec, J. E., & Davidov, M. (2015). Analyzing socialization from a domain-specific perspective. In J. E. Grusec & P. D. Hastings (Eds.), *Handbook of socialization: Theory and research* (pp. 158–181). Guilford Press.

Halim, M. L. D., Bryant, D., & Zucker, K. J. (2016). Early gender development in children and links with mental and physical health. In M. R. Korin (Ed.), *Health promotion for children and adolescents* (pp. 191–213). Springer.

Halim, M. L., Ruble, D., Tamis-LeMonda, C., & Shrout, P. E. (2013). Rigidity in gender-typed behaviors in early childhood: A longitudinal study of ethnic minority children. *Child Development, 84*(4), 1269–1284.

Halim, M. L., Ruble, D. N., Tamis-LeMonda, C. S., Zosuls, K. M., Lurye, L. E., & Greulich, F. K. (2014). Pink frilly dresses and the avoidance of all things "girly": Children's appearance rigidity and cognitive theories of gender development. *Developmental Psychology, 50*(4), 1091.

Harter, S. (2015). *The construction of the self: Developmental and sociocultural foundations.* Guilford Publications.

Harter, S., & Pike, R. (1984). The pictorial scale of perceived competence and social acceptance for young children. *Child Development, 55*(6), 1969–1982.

Hastings, P. D., McShane, K. E., Parker, R., & Ladha, F. (2007). Ready to make nice: Parental socialization of young sons' and daughters' prosocial behaviors with peers. *The Journal of Genetic Psychology, 168*(2), 177–200.

Hay, D. F., Castle, J., & Davies, L. (2000). Toddlers' use of force against familiar peers: A precursor of serious aggression? *Child Development, 71*(2), 457–467.

Hay, D. F., Hurst, S. L., Waters, C. S., & Chadwick, A. (2011). Infants' use of force to defend toys: The origins of instrumental aggression. *Infancy, 16*(5), 471–489.

Helwig, C. C., To, S., Wang, Q., Liu, C., & Yang, S. (2014). Judgments and reasoning about parental discipline involving induction and psychological control in China and Canada. *Child Development, 85*(3), 1150–1167.

Henry H. Kaiser Family Foundation. (2003). *Key facts: Children and video games.* Retrieved from https://www.kff.org/wp-content/uploads/2013/04/5959.pdf.

Hines, M., Constantinescu, M., & Spencer, D. (2015). Early androgen exposure and human gender development. *Biology of Sex Differences, 6*(1), 3.

Hoffman, K. L., Kiecolt, K. J., & Edwards, J. N. (2005). Physical violence between siblings a theoretical and empirical analysis. *Journal of Family Issues, 26*(8), 1103–1130.

Holder, M. D., & Coleman, B. (2015). Children's friendships and positive well-being. In M Demir (Ed.), *Friendship and Happiness* (pp. 81–97). Springer.

Holmes, R. M., Romeo, L., Ciraola, S., & Grushko, M. (2015). The relationship between creativity, social play, and children's language abilities. *Early Child Development and Care, 185*(7), 1180–1197.

Howe, N., Ross, H. S., & Recchia, H. (2011). Sibling relations in early and middle childhood. In P. K. Smith & C. H. Hard (Eds.), *The Wiley-Blackwell handbook of childhood social development* (2nd ed., pp. 356–372). Wiley-Blackwell.

Huesmann, L. R., Eron, L. D., Lefkowitz, M. M., & Walder, L. O. (1984). Stability of aggression over time and generations. *Developmental Psychology, 20*(6), 1120.

Hymel, S., Closson, L. M., Caravita, S., & Vaillancourt, T. (2011). Social status among peers: From sociometric attraction to peer acceptance to perceived popularity. In P. K. Smith & C. H. Hard (Eds.), *The Wiley-Blackwell handbook of childhood social development* (2nd ed., pp. 375–392). Wiley-Blackwell.

Israel, S., Hasenfratz, L., & Knafo-Noam, A. (2015). The genetics of morality and prosociality. *Current Opinion in Psychology, 6,* 55–59.

Jensen, A. C., Whiteman, S. D., Fingerman, K. L., & Birditt, K. S. (2013). "Life still isn't fair": Parental differential treatment of young adult siblings. *Journal of Marriage and Family, 75*(2), 438–452.

Johnson, M. D., & Galambos, N. L. (2014). Paths to intimate relationship quality from parent–adolescent relations and mental health. *Journal of Marriage and Family, 76*(1), 145–160. doi:10.1111/jomf.12074.

Jonason, P. K. (2015). An evolutionary perspective on interpersonal violence: Sex differences and personality links. In M. DeLisi & M. G. Vaughn (Eds.), *The Routledge international handbook of biosocial criminology* (pp. 32–45). Routledge.

Kazdin, A. E., & Benjet, C. (2003). Spanking children: Evidence and issues. *Current Directions in Psychological Science, 12*(3), 99–103.

Killoren, S. E., Alfaro, E. C., & Kline, G. (2016). Mexican American emerging adults' relationships with siblings and dimensions of familism values. *Personal Relationships, 23*(2), 234–248.

Kim, J. Y., McHale, S. M., Wayne Osgood, D., & Crouter, A. C. (2006). Longitudinal course and family correlates of sibling relationships from childhood through adolescence. *Child Development, 77*(6), 1746–1761.

Knafo, A., & Plomin, R. (2006). Prosocial behavior from early to middle childhood: Genetic and environmental influences on stability and change. *Developmental Psychology, 42*(5), 771.

Knafo, A., Zahn-Waxler, C., Van Hulle, C., Robinson, J. L., & Rhee, S. H. (2008). The developmental origins of a disposition toward empathy: Genetic and environmental contributions. *Emotion, 8*(6), 737.

Knop, B. (2020). One in six children live with a half sibling under 18. Retrieved from www.census.gov/library/stories/2020/01/more-children-live-with-half-siblings-than-previously-thought.html.

Kohlberg, L. (1966). Cognitive stages and preschool education. *Human Development, 9*(1–2), 5–17.

Kokko, K., Simonton, S., Dubow, E., Lansford, J. E., Olson, S. L., Huesmann, L. R., . . . Dodge, K. A. (2014). Country, sex, and parent occupational status: Moderators of the continuity of aggression from childhood to adulthood. *Aggressive Behavior, 40*(6), 552–567.

Krahé, B., & Möller, I. (2010). Longitudinal effects of media violence on aggression and empathy among German adolescents. *Journal of Applied Developmental Psychology, 31*(5), 401–409.

Kramer, L. (2014). Learning emotional understanding and emotion regulation through sibling interaction. *Early Education and Development, 25*(2), 160–184.

Kramer, L., Perozynski, L. A., & Chung, T. Y. (1999). Parental responses to sibling conflict: The effects of development and parent gender. *Child Development, 70*(6), 1401–1414.

Kruger, A. C., & Tomasello, M. (1986). Transactive discussions with peers and adults. *Developmental Psychology, 22*(5), 681.

Lacourse, E., Boivin, M., Brendgen, M., Petitclerc, A., Girard, A., Vitaro, F., . . . Tremblay, R. (2014). A longitudinal twin study of physical aggression during early childhood: Evidence for a developmentally dynamic genome. *Psychological Medicine, 44*(12), 2617–2627.

Lamb, S., & Zakhireh, B. (1997). Toddlers' attention to the distress of peers in a daycare setting. *Early Education and Development, 8*(2), 105–118.

Langlois, J. H., Ritter, J. M., Casey, R. J., & Sawin, D. B. (1995). Infant attractiveness predicts maternal behaviors and attitudes. *Developmental Psychology, 31*(3), 464.

Lansford, J. E., Malone, P. S., Dodge, K. A., Pettit, G. S., & Bates, J. E. (2010). Developmental cascades of peer rejection, social information processing biases, and aggression during middle childhood. *Development and Psychopathology, 22*(03), 593–602.

Laursen, H. R., Siebner, H. R., Haren, T., Madsen, K., Grønlund, R., Hulme, O., & Henningsson, S. (2014). Variation in the oxytocin receptor gene is associated with behavioral and neural correlates of empathic accuracy. *Frontiers in Behavioral Neuroscience, 8*, 423.

Leaper, C. (2014). Parents' socialization of gender in children. In C. L. Martin (Ed.), *Encyclopedia of early child development*. Center of Excellence for Early Childhood Development and Strategic Knowledge Cluster on Early Child Development.

Li, R. Y. H., & Wong, W. I. (2016). Gender-typed play and social abilities in boys and girls: Are they related? *Sex Roles, 74*(9–10), 399–410.

Liben, L., Bigler, R., Hilliard, L., Gershoff, E., Mistry, R., & Crosby, D. (2014). Gender development: From universality to individuality. In E. T. Gershoff, R. S. Mistry, & D. A. Crosby (Eds.), *Societal contexts of child development: Pathways of influence and implications for practice and policy* (pp. 3–18). Oxford University Press.

Liddle, M. J. E., Bradley, B. S., & Mcgrath, A. (2015). Baby empathy: Infant distress and peer prosocial responses. *Infant Mental Health Journal, 36*(4), 446–458.

Lindsey, L. L. (2015). *Gender roles: A sociological perspective*. Routledge.

Linver, M. R., Brooks-Gunn, J., & Kohen, D. E. (2002). Family processes as pathways from income to young children's development. *Developmental Psychology, 38*(5), 719.

Löckenhoff, C. E., Chan, W., McCrae, R. R., De Fruyt, F., Jussim, L., De Bolle, M., . . . Allik, J. (2014). Gender stereotypes of personality: Universal and accurate? *Journal of Cross-Cultural Psychology, 45*(5), 675–694.

Loeser, M. K., Whiteman, S. D., & McHale, S. M. (2016). Siblings' perceptions of differential treatment, fairness, and jealousy and adolescent adjustment: A moderated indirect effects model. *Journal of Child and Family Studies, 25*(8), 2405–2414.

Luengo Kanacri, B. P., Pastorelli, C., Eisenberg, N., Zuffianò, A., & Caprara, G. V. (2013). The development of prosociality from adolescence to early adulthood: The role of effortful control. *Journal of Personality, 81*(3), 302–312.

Mancillas, A. (2010). Only children. In J. Caspi (Ed.), *Sibling development: Implications for mental health practitioners* (pp. 341–358). New York, NY: Springer.

Markova, G., & Legerstee, M. (2006). Contingency, imitation, and affect sharing: Foundations of infants' social awareness. *Developmental Psychology, 42*(1), 132.

Martin, C. L., & Halverson, C. F., Jr. (1981). A schematic processing model of sex typing and stereotyping in children. *Child Development, 52*(4), 1119–1134.

Martin, C. L., & Halverson, C. F., Jr. (1983). The effects of sex-typing schemas on young children's memory. *Child Development, 54*(3), 563–574.

Martin, C. L., & Ruble, D. N. (2010). Patterns of gender development. *Annual Review of Psychology, 61,* 353–381.

McHale, S. M., Updegraff, K. A., Jackson-Newsom, J., Tucker, C. J., & Crouter, A. C. (2000). When does parents' differential treatment have negative implications for siblings? *Social Development, 9*(2), 149–172.

McHale, S. M., Updegraff, K. A., & Whiteman, S. D. (2012). Sibling relationships and influences in childhood and adolescence. *Journal of Marriage and Family, 74*(5), 913–930.

Melchers, M., Montag, C., Reuter, M., Spinath, F. M., & Hahn, E. (2016). How heritable is empathy? Differential effects of measurement and subcomponents. *Motivation and Emotion, 40*(5), 720–730.

Mesman, J., Stoel, R., Bakermans-Kranenburg, M. J., van IJzendoorn, M. H., Juffer, F., Koot, H. M., & Alink, L. R. (2009). Predicting growth curves of early childhood externalizing problems: Differential susceptibility of children with difficult temperament. *Journal of Abnormal Child Psychology, 37*(5), 625.

Miller, C. F., Trautner, H. M., & Ruble, D. N. (2006). The role of gender stereotypes in children's preferences and behavior. In L. Balter & C. S. Tamis-LeMonda (Eds.), *Child psychology: A handbook of contemporary issues* (pp. 293–323). Psychology Press.

Miller, D. I., & Halpern, D. F. (2014). The new science of cognitive sex differences. *Trends in Cognitive Sciences, 18*(1), 37–45.

Miner, J. L., & Clarke-Stewart, K. A. (2008). Trajectories of externalizing behavior from age 2 to age 9: Relations with gender, temperament, ethnicity, parenting, and rater. *Developmental Psychology, 44*(3), 771.

Mund, M., Finn, C., Hagemeyer, B., Zimmermann, J., & Neyer, F. J. (2015). The dynamics of self-esteem in partner relationships. *European Journal of Personality, 29*(2), 235–249.

Orth, U. (2017). The lifespan development of self-esteem. In J. Specht (Ed.), *Personality development across the lifespan.* Academic Press.

Papacek, A. M., Chai, Z., & Green, K. B. (2016). Play and social interaction strategies for young children with autism spectrum disorder in inclusive preschool settings. *Young Exceptional Children, 19*(3), 3–17.

Pardini, D. A., Raine, A., Erickson, K., & Loeber, R. (2014). Lower amygdala volume in men is associated with childhood aggression, early psychopathic traits, and future violence. *Biological Psychiatry, 75*(1), 73–80.

Parten, M. B. (1932). Social participation among pre-school children. *The Journal of Abnormal and Social Psychology, 27*(3), 243.

Paulus, M. (2014). The emergence of prosocial behavior: Why do infants and toddlers help, comfort, and share? *Child Development Perspectives, 8*(2), 77–81.

Pelaez, M., Field, T., Pickens, J. N., & Hart, S. (2008). Disengaged and authoritarian parenting behavior of depressed mothers with their toddlers. *Infant Behavior and Development, 31*(1), 145–148.

Perlman, M., & Ross, H. S. (2005). If-then contingencies in children's sibling conflicts. *Merrill-Palmer Quarterly, 51*(1), 42–66.

Pezzella, F. S., Thornberry, T. P., & Smith, C. A. (2016). Race socialization and parenting styles: Links to delinquency for African American and White adolescents. *Youth Violence and Juvenile Justice, 14*(4), 448–467.

Polman, H., De Castro, B. O., & van Aken, M. A. (2008). Experimental study of the differential effects of playing versus watching violent video games on children's aggressive behavior. *Aggressive Behavior, 34*(3), 256–264.

Prieler, M., Kohlbacher, F., Hagiwara, S., & Arima, A. (2011). Gender representation of older people in Japanese television advertisements. *Sex Roles, 64*(5–6), 405–415.

Ramani, G. B., & Brownell, C. A. (2014). Preschoolers' cooperative problem solving: Integrating play and problem solving. *Journal of Early Childhood Research, 12*(1), 92–108.

Riley, A. R., Wagner, D. V., Tudor, M. E., Zuckerman, K. E., & Freeman, K. A. (2016). A survey of parents' perceptions and utilization of time-out in comparison to empirical evidence. *Academic Pediatrics, 17*(2), 168–175.

Roberts, W., Strayer, J., & Denham, S. (2014). Empathy, anger, guilt: Emotions and prosocial behaviour. *Canadian Journal of Behavioural Science, 46*(4), 465–474.

Rothbaum, F., Pott, M., Azuma, H., Miyake, K., & Weisz, J. (2000). The development of close relationships in Japan and the United States: Paths of symbiotic harmony and generative tension. *Child Development, 71*(5), 1121–1142.

Rubin, K. H., Bukowski, W. M., & Parker, J. G. (2007). Peer interactions, relationships, and groups. In N. Eisenberg, W. Damon, & R. M. Lerner (Eds.), *Handbook of child psychology: Social, emotional, and personality development* (pp. 571–645). John Wiley & Sons, Inc.

Ruigrok, A. N., Salimi-Khorshidi, G., Lai, M.-C., Baron-Cohen, S., Lombardo, M. V., Tait, R. J., & Suckling, J. (2014). A meta-analysis of sex differences in human brain structure. *Neuroscience & Biobehavioral Reviews, 39,* 34–50.

Russell, A., Hart, C., Robinson, C., & Olsen, S. (2003). Children's sociable and aggressive behaviour with peers: A comparison of the US and Australia, and contributions of temperament and parenting styles. *International Journal of Behavioral Development, 27*(1), 74–86.

Schug, R. A., Geraci, G. G., Holdren, S., Marmolejo, G., McLernon, H. L., & Thompson, S. (2015). Understanding disorders of defiance, aggression, and violence: Oppositional defiant disorder, conduct disorder, and antisocial personality disorder in males. In C. M. Zaroff & R. C. D'Amato (Eds.), *The Neuropsychology of Men* (pp. 111–131). Springer.

Sengsavang, S., & Krettenauer, T. (2015). Children's moral self-concept: The role of aggression and parent–child relationships. *Merrill-Palmer Quarterly, 61*(2), 213–235.

Shin, H., Bjorklund, D. F., & Beck, E. F. (2007). The adaptive nature of children's overestimation in a strategic memory task. *Cognitive Development, 22*(2), 197–212.

Shumer, D. E., Nokoff, N. J., & Spack, N. P. (2016). Advances in the Care of Transgender Children and Adolescents. *Advances in Pediatrics, 63*(1), 79–102. https://doi.org/10.1016/j.yapd.2016.04.018.

Sim, Z. L., & Xu, F. (2015). *Toddlers learn with facilitated play, not free play.* Paper presented at the CogSci.

Simons, L. G., Simons, R. L., & Su, X. (2013). Consequences of corporal punishment among African Americans: The importance of context and outcome. *Journal of Youth and Adolescence, 42*(8), 1273–1285.

Singer, D. G., Golinkoff, R. M., & Hirsh-Pasek, K. (2006). *Play = Learning: How play motivates and enhances children's cognitive and social-emotional growth*. Oxford University Press.

Skinner, B. F. (1963). Operant behavior. *American Psychologist, 18*(8), 503.

Smith, S. L., & Donnerstein, E. (1998). Harmful effects of exposure to media violence: Learning of aggression, emotional desensitization, and fear. In R. G. Geen & E. Donnerstein (Eds.), *Human aggression: Theories, research, and implications for social policy* (pp. 167–202). Academic Press.

Society of Health and Physical Educators. (2016). *Shape of the nation*. Retrieved from www.shapeamerica.org/advocacy/son/2016/upload/Shape-of-the-Nation-2016_web.pdf.

Stauffacher, K., & DeHart, G. B. (2005). Preschoolers' relational aggression with siblings and with friends. *Early Education & Development, 16*(2), 185–206.

Stein, A. H., & Friedrich, L. K. (1972). Television content and young children's behavior. *Television and Social Behavior, 2*, 202–317.

Stennes, L. M., Burch, M. M., Sen, M. G., & Bauer, P. J. (2005). A longitudinal study of gendered vocabulary and communicative action in young children. *Developmental Psychology, 41*(1), 75.

Stipek, D., Recchia, S., McClintic, S., & Lewis, M. (1992). Self-evaluation in young children. *Monographs of the Society for Research in Child Development, 57*(1), 1–98.

Streit, C., Carlo, G., Killoren, S. E., & Alfaro, E. C. (2017). Family members' relationship qualities and prosocial behaviors in us mexican young adults: The roles of familism and ethnic identity resolution. *Journal of Family Issues*, 0192513X16686134.

Sweet, E. (2014). Toys are more divided by gender now than they were 50 years ago. Retrieved from www.theatlantic.com/business/archive/2014/12/toys-are-more-divided-by-gender-now-than-they-were-50-years-ago/383556/.

Takahashi, K., & Takeuchi, K. (2007). Japan. In J. J. Arnett (Ed.), *International encyclopedia of adolescence* (pp. 525–539). New York, NY. Routledge.

Telzer, E. H., Flannery, J., Humphreys, K. L., Goff, B., Gabard-Durman, L., Gee, D. G., & Tottenham, N. (2015). "The cooties effect": Amygdala reactivity to opposite-versus same-sex faces declines from childhood to adolescence. *Journal of Cognitive Neuroscience, 27*(9), 1685–1696.

Tesfatsion, Master (2018, Nov. 21). Adrian Peterson is still the same AP. *Bleacher Report*. Retrieved from https://bleacherreport.com/articles/2807182-adrian-peterson-is-still-the-same-ap?share=other.

Theobald, M., Danby, S., Thompson, C., & Thorpe, K. (2014). Friendships in the early years. In S. Garvis & D. Pendergast (Eds.), *Health and well being in the early years* (pp. 115–132). Cambridge: Cambridge University Press.

Thorpe, K., Danby, S., Hay, D., & Stewart, E. (2006–08). Compromised or Competent: A longitudinal study of twin children's social competencies, friendships and behavioural adjustment. Australian Research Council. Project ID: DP0666254.

Todd, B. K., Barry, J. A., & Thommessen, S. A. (2016). Preferences for 'gender-typed' toys in boys and girls aged 9 to 32 months. *Infant and Child Development, 26*(3). doi: 10.1002/icd.1986.

Tremblay, R. E., & LeMarquand, D. (2001). Individual risk and protective factors. in R. Loeber & D. P. Farrington (Eds.), *Child delinquents: Development, intervention, and service needs* (pp. 137–164). Thousand Oaks, CA: Sage Publications.

Tremblay, R. E., Japel, C., Perusse, D., McDuff, P., Boivin, M., Zoccolillo, M., & Montplaisir, J. (1999). The search for the age of 'onset'of physical aggression: Rousseau and Bandura revisited. *Criminal Behaviour and Mental Health, 9*(1), 8–23.

Tremblay, R. E., Nagin, D. S., Séguin, J. R., Zoccolillo, M., Zelazo, P. D., Boivin, M., . . . Japel, C. (2004). Physical aggression during early childhood: Trajectories and predictors. *Pediatrics, 114*(1), e43–e50.

Triandis, H. C. (1989). The self and social behavior in differing cultural contexts. *Psychological Review, 96*(3), 506.

Triandis, H. C., Bontempo, R., Villareal, M. J., Asai, M., & Lucca, N. (1988). Individualism and collectivism: Cross-cultural perspectives on self-ingroup relationships. *Journal of Personality and Social Psychology, 54*(2), 323.

Trzesniewski, K. H., Kinal, M., & Donnellan, M. (2011). Self-enhancement and self-protection in a developmental context. In M. D. Alicke & C. Sedikides (Eds.), *Handbook of self-enhancement and self-protection* (pp. 341–357). The Guilford Press.

Tucker, C. J., & Finkelhor, D. (2015). The state of interventions for sibling conflict and aggression: A systematic review. *Trauma, Violence, & Abuse, 18*(4), 396–406. doi: 1524838015622438.

Uji, M., Sakamoto, A., Adachi, K., & Kitamura, T. (2014). The impact of authoritative, authoritarian, and permissive parenting styles on children's later mental health in Japan: Focusing on parent and child gender. *Journal of Child and Family Studies, 23*(2), 293–302.

Underwood, M. K., & Rosen, L. H. (2013). *Social development: Relationships in infancy, childhood, and adolescence*. Guilford Publications.

United States Census Bureau. (2021). Historical living arrangements of children. Retrieved from www.census.gov/data/tables/time-series/demo/families/children.html.

Updegraff, K. A., McHale, S. M., & Crouter, A. C. (2002). Adolescents' sibling relationship and friendship experiences: Developmental patterns and relationship linkages. *Social Development, 11*(2), 182–204.

van Dijk, R., Deković, M., Bunte, T. L., Schoemaker, K., Zondervan-Zwijnenburg, M., Espy, K. A., & Matthys, W. (2017). Mother-child interactions and externalizing behavior problems in preschoolers over time: Inhibitory control as a mediator. *Journal of Abnormal Child Psychology, 45*(8), 1503–1517.

Wallace, K. (2017). The cultural, regional and generational roots of spanking. Retrieved from www.cnn.com/2014/09/16/living/spanking-cultural-roots-attitudes-parents/.

Wallinius, M., Delfin, C., Billstedt, E., Nilsson, T., Anckarsäter, H., & Hofvander, B. (2016). Offenders in emerging adulthood: School maladjustment, childhood adversities, and prediction of aggressive antisocial behaviors. *Law and Human Behavior, 40*(5), 551–563. https://doi.org/10.1037/lhb0000202.

Warneken, F., & Tomasello, M. (2006). Altruistic helping in human infants and young chimpanzees. *Science, 311*(5765), 1301–1303.

Warneken, F., Chen, F., & Tomasello, M. (2006). Cooperative activities in young children and chimpanzees. *Child Development, 77*(3), 640–663.

Weisberg, D. S., Hirsh-Pasek, K., Michnick Golinkoff, R., Kittredge, A. K., & Klahr, D. (2016). Guided play: Principles and practices. *Current Directions in Psychological Science, 25*(3), 177–182.

Whiteman, S. D., Jensen, A. C., & Maggs, J. L. (2014). Similarities and differences in adolescent siblings' alcohol-related attitudes, use, and delinquency: Evidence for convergent and divergent influence processes. *Journal of Youth and Adolescence, 43*(5), 687–697.

Whiteman, S. D., McHale, S. M., & Crouter, A. C. (2007). Competing processes of sibling influence: Observational learning and sibling deidentification. *Social Development, 16*(4), 642–661.

Whiteman, S. D., McHale, S. M., & Soli, A. (2011). Theoretical perspectives on sibling relationships. *Journal of Family Theory & Review, 3*(2), 124–139.

Whiting, B., & Edwards, C. P. (1988). A cross-cultural analysis of sex differences in the behavior of children aged 3 through 11. *Journal of Social Psychology, 91*(2), 171–188.

Williams, L. R., Degnan, K. A., Perez-Edgar, K. E., Henderson, H. A., Rubin, K. H., Pine, D. S., . . . Fox, N. A. (2009). Impact of behavioral inhibition and parenting style on internalizing and externalizing problems from early childhood through adolescence. *Journal of Abnormal Child Psychology, 37*(8), 1063–1075.

Wilson, B. J., Smith, S. L., Potter, W. J., Kunkel, D., Linz, D., Colvin, C. M., & Donnerstein, E. (2002). Violence in children's television programming: Assessing the risks. *Journal of Communication, 52*(1), 5–35.

Wong, W. I., & Hines, M. (2015a). Effects of gender color-coding on toddlers' gender-typical toy play. *Archives of Sexual Behavior, 44*(5), 1233–1242.

Wong, W. I., & Hines, M. (2015b). Preferences for pink and blue: The development of color preferences as a distinct gender-typed behavior in toddlers. *Archives of Sexual Behavior, 44*(5), 1243–1254.

Wood, E., Desmarais, S., & Gugula, S. (2002). The impact of parenting experience on gender stereotyped toy play of children. *Sex Roles, 47*(1–2), 39–49.

Yaros, A., Lochman, J. E., Rosenbaum, J., & Jimenez-Camargo, L. A. (2014). Real-time hostile attribution measurement and aggression in children. *Aggressive Behavior, 40*(5), 409–420.

Zosh, J., Hirsh-Pasek, K., & Golinkoff, R. (2015). Guided play. In D. Couchenour & J. K. Chrisman (Eds.), *The SAGE encyclopedia of contemporary early childhood education*. Thousand Oaks, CA: Sage Reference.

Zosh, J. M., Hirsh-Pasek, K., Golinkoff, R. M., & Dore, R. A. (2017). Where learning meets creativity: The promise of guided play. In R. A. Beghetto & B. Sriraman (Eds.), *Creative Contradictions in Education* (pp. 165–180). Springer.

Zosuls, K. M., Miller, C. F., Ruble, D. N., Martin, C. L., & Fabes, R. A. (2011). Gender development research in sex roles: Historical trends and future directions. *Sex Roles, 64*(11–12), 826–842.

Chapter 11

Abarca-Gómez, L., Abdeen, Z. A., Hamid, Z. A., Abu-Rmeileh, N. M., Acosta-Cazares, B., Acuin, C., . . . Aguilar-Salinas, C. A. (2017). Worldwide trends in body-mass index, underweight, overweight, and obesity from 1975 to 2016: A pooled analysis of 2416 population-based measurement studies in 128·9 million children, adolescents, and adults. *Lancet, 390*(10113), 2627–2642.

Aduen, P. A., Day, T. N., Kofler, M. J., Harmon, S. L., Wells, E. L., & Sarver, D. E. (2018). Social problems in ADHD: Is it a skills acquisition or performance problem? *Journal of Psychopathology and Behavioral Assessment, 40*(3), 440–451.

Ahmad, S., Naeem, K., Ali, M., Fatima, S., Asghar, A., Shahid, H., . . . Hussain, S. (2018). Effect of cognitive behavioral therapy in children affected by attention deficit hyperactivity disorder: A meta-analysis. *Trends Journal of Sciences Research, 3*(1), 10–27.

Ahmann, P. A., Waltonen, S. J., Theye, F. W., Olson, K. A., & Van Erem, A. J. (1993). Placebo-controlled evaluation of Ritalin side effects. *Pediatrics, 91*(6), 1101–1106.

American Academy of Pediatrics. (2011). Policy statement—SIDS and other sleep-related deaths: Expansion of recommendations for a safe infant sleep environment. *Pediatrics, 128*(5), 1030–1039.

American Academy of Pediatrics. (2016). Childhood nutrition. Retrieved from www.healthychildren.org/English/healthy-living/nutrition/Pages/Childhood-Nutrition.aspx.

Amran, H. A., & Majid, R. A. (2019). Learning strategies for twice-exceptional students. *International Journal of Special Education, 33*(4), 954–976.

Anderson, M. (2018). A majority of teens have experienced some form of cyberbullying. Retrieved from www.pewresearch.org/internet/2018/09/27/a-majority-of-teens-have-experienced-some-form-of-cyberbullying/.

Assouline, S. G., Marron, M., & Colangelo, N. (2014). Acceleration. In J. A. Plucker & C. M. Callahan (Eds.), *Critical issues and practices in gifted education: What the research says* (2nd ed., pp. 15–28). Waco, TX: Prufrock Press.

Baker, J. S., Buchan, D. S., Malina, R. M., & Thomas, N. E. (2010). Benefits of high intensity anaerobic exercise for adolescents and school children. *British Journal of Sports Medicine*. http://bjsm.bmj.com/content/early/2010/03/08/bjsm.2009.068072.full/reply#bjsports_el_4377.

Barton, A. (2020). Yes, your kids are on screens in these trying times. No, you're not a terrible parent because of coronavirus. Retrieved from www.usatoday.com/story/news/education/2020/03/18/coronavirus-things-to-do-online-school-closings-screen-time/2870490001/.

Becker, D. R., McClelland, M. M., Loprinzi, P., & Trost, S. G. (2014). Physical activity, self-regulation, and early academic achievement in preschool children. *Early Education & Development, 25*(1), 56–70.

Bell, J. F., Wilson, J. S., & Liu, G. C. (2008). Neighborhood greenness and 2-year changes in body mass index of children and youth. *American Journal of Preventive Medicine, 35*(6), 547–553.

Bethell, C. D., Read, D., Blumberg, S. J., & Newacheck, P. W. (2008). What is the prevalence of children with special health care needs? Toward an understanding of variations in findings and methods across three national surveys. *Maternal and Child Health Journal, 12*(1), 1–14.

Betts, G. T. (2004). Profiles of the gifted. *Definitions and Conceptions of Giftedness, 1*, 97.

Biederman, J., Faraone, S., Milberger, S., Guite, J., Mick, E., Chen, L., . . . Moore, P. (1996). Aprospective 4-year follow-up study of attention-deficit hyperactivity and related disorders. *Archives of General Psychiatry, 53*(5), 437–446.

Biesma, R., & Hanson, M. (2020). Childhood obesity. In P. Puri (ed.), *Pediatric surgery: General principles and newborn surgery* (pp. 529–539). Springer.

Bjerregaard, L. G., Adelborg, K., & Baker, J. L. (2020). Change in body mass index from childhood onwards and risk of adult cardiovascular disease. *Trends in Cardiovascular Medicine, 30*(1), 39–45.

Braswell, L., & Bloomquist, M. L. (1991). *Cognitive-behavioral therapy with ADHD children: Child, family, and school interventions.* Guilford Press.

Bright Futures. (2020). Middle childhood. Retrieved from www.brightfutures.org/nutrition/pdf/mc.pdf.

Brooks, C. J., Gortmaker, S. L., Long, M. W., Cradock, A. L., & Kenney, E. L. (2017). Racial/ethnic and socioeconomic disparities in hydration status among US adults and the role of tap water and other beverage intake. *American Journal of Public Health, 107*(9), 1387–1394.

Butrymowicz, S., & Mader, S. (2017). Low academic expectations and poor support for special education students are 'hurting their future'. Retrieved from https://hechingerreport.org/low-academic-expectations-poor-support-special-education-students-hurting-future/.

Cappelen, A. W., Charness, G., Ekström, M., Gneezy, U., & Tungodden, B. (2017). Exercise improves academic performance. *NHH Dept. of Economics Discussion Paper* (08).

Carey, W. B., Crocker, A. C., Elias, E. R., Coleman, W. L., & Feldman, H. M. (2009). *Developmental-behavioral pediatrics e-book.* Elsevier Health Sciences.

Carucci, S., Anchisi, L., Ambu, G., Melis, G., Lecca, L., & Zuddas, A. (2012). Methylphenidate effects on social functioning in children with ADHD. *European Neuropsychopharmacology, 22*, S421–S422. doi: 10.1016/S0924-977X(12)70661-2.

Center on Media and Child Health. (2020). Talking to kids about coronavirus. Retrieved from https://cmch.tv/wp-content/uploads/Talking-to-Kids-About-COVID19-US-Version.pdf.

Centers for Disease Control and Prevention. (2009). CDC growth charts, percentile data files with LMS values. Retrieved from www.cdc.gov/growthcharts/percentile_data_files.htm.

Centers for Disease Control and Prevention. (2018a). Asthma in children. Retrieved from www.cdc.gov/vitalsigns/childhood-asthma/index.html.

Centers for Disease Control and Prevention. (2018b). Obesity. Retrieved from www.cdc.gov/healthyschools/obesity/index.htm.

Centers for Disease Control and Prevention. (2018c). Screen time vs. lean time infographic. Retrieved from www.cdc.gov/nccdphp/dnpao/multimedia/infographics/getmoving.html.

Centers for Disease Control and Prevention. (2019a). Childhood obesity facts. Retrieved from www.cdc.gov/obesity/data/childhood.html.

Centers for Disease Control and Prevention. (2019b). Children's oral health. Retrieved from www.cdc.gov/oralhealth/basics/childrens-oral-health/index.html.

Centers for Disease Control and Prevention. (2019c). Diagnosis—Head lice. Retrieved from www.cdc.gov/parasites/lice/head/diagnosis.html.

Centers for Disease Control and Prevention. (2019d). Disease—Head lice. Retrieved from www.cdc.gov/parasites/lice/head/disease.html.

Centers for Disease Control and Prevention. (2019e). Epidemiology and risk factors. Retrieved from www.cdc.gov/parasites/lice/head/epi.html.

Centers for Disease Control and Prevention. (2019f). Frequently asked questions—headlice. Retrieved from www.cdc.gov/parasites/lice/head/gen_info/faqs.html.

Centers for Disease Control and Prevention. (2019g). Treatment of head lice. Retrieved from www.cdc.gov/parasites/lice/head/treatment.html.

Centers for Disease Control and Prevention. (2020a). Community water fluoridation. Retrieved from www.cdc.gov/fluoridation/basics/index.htm?web=1&wdLOR=c11F5C913-2CE8-6D4B-B9B8-4382019B6FC0.

Centers for Disease Control and Prevention. (2020b). Talking with children about coronavirus. Retrieved from www.cdc.gov/coronavirus/2019-ncov/daily-life-coping/talking-with-children.html.

Centers for Disease Control and Prevention. (2020c). What is ADHD? Retrieved from www.cdc.gov/ncbddd/adhd/facts.html#Causes.

Centers for Disease Control and Prevention. (2021a). Childhood obesity facts. Retrieved from www.cdc.gov/obesity/data/childhood.html.

Centers for Disease Control and Prevention. (2021b). Defining childhood weight status. Retrieved from www.cdc.gov/obesity/childhood/defining.html#:~:text=Obesity%20is%20defined%20as%20a,as%20BMI%2Dfor%2Dage.

Centers for Disease Control and Prevention. (2021c). Symptoms and diagnosis of ADHD. Retrieved from www.cdc.gov/ncbddd/adhd/diagnosis.html.

Chandler, P., & Tricot, A. (2015). Mind your body: The essential role of body movements in children's learning. *Educational Psychology Review, 27*, 365–370.

Children's Hospital of Philadelphia. (2020). Growth hormone deficiency. Retrieved from www.chop.edu/conditions-diseases/growth-hormone-deficiency.

Chipps, B. E., Haselkorn, T., Rosén, K., Mink, D. R., Trzaskoma, B. L., & Luskin, A. T. (2018). Asthma exacerbations and triggers in children in TENOR: Impact on quality of life. *Journal of Allergy and Clinical Immunology: In Practice, 6*(1), 169–176. e162.

Clark, D. (2014). Growing up with dyslexia: Additional insight for teachers, parents and students. Retrieved from www.readinghorizons.com/blog/growing-up-with-dyslexia-additional-insight-for-teachers-parents-and-students.

Collett-Solberg, P. F., Jorge, A. A., Boguszewski, M. C., Miller, B. S., Choong, C. S. Y., Cohen, P., . . . Saenger, P. (2019). Growth hormone therapy in children; research and practice–a review. *Growth Hormone & IGF Research, 44,* 20–32.

Custovic, A., & Martinez, F. D. (2020). The epidemiology of severe childhood asthma. In E. Forno & S. Saglani (Eds.), *Severe asthma in children and adolescents* (pp. 3–18). Springer.

Dalal, M., Clark, M., & Quiñonez, R. B. (2019). Pediatric oral health: Fluoride use recommendations. *Contemporary Pediatrics, 36*(2).

Daley, D., & Birchwood, J. (2010). ADHD and academic performance: Why does ADHD impact on academic performance and what can be done to support ADHD children in the classroom? *Child: Care, Health and Development, 36*(4), 455–464.

Danielson, M. L., Bitsko, R. H., Ghandour, R. M., Holbrook, J. R., Kogan, M. D., & Blumberg, S. J. (2018). Prevalence of parent-reported ADHD diagnosis and associated treatment among US children and adolescents, 2016. *Journal of Clinical Child & Adolescent Psychology, 47*(2), 199–212.

Davison, K. K., Schmalz, D. L., Young, L. M., & Birch, L. L. (2008). Overweight girls who internalize fat stereotypes report low psychosocial well-being. *Obesity, 16*(S2), S30–S38.

Delgado, M. A. C., Delgado, R. I. Z., Palma, R. P., & Moya, M. E. (2019). Dyscalculia and pedagogical intervention. *International Research Journal of Management, IT and Social Sciences, 6*(5), 95–100.

DelGiudice, M. (2018). Middle childhood: An evolutionary-developmental synthesis. In N. Halfon, C. Forrest, R. Lerner, & E. Faustman, E. (Eds.), *Handbook of life course health development* (pp. 95–107). Springer, Cham.

Den Heijer, A. E., Groen, Y., Tucha, L., Fuermaier, A. B., Koerts, J., Lange, K. W., . . . Tucha, O. (2017). Sweat it out? The effects of physical exercise on cognition and behavior in children and adults with ADHD: A systematic literature review. *Journal of Neural Transmission, 124*(1), 3–26.

Devore, C. D., Schutze, G. E., Health, Council on School Health and Committee on Infectious Disease (2015). Head lice. *Pediatrics, 135*(5), e1355–e1365.

Ditch the Label. (2017). *The annual bullying survey 2017.* Retrieved from www.ditchthelabel.org/wp-content/uploads/2017/07/The-Annual-Bullying-Survey-2017-1.pdf.

Ditch the Label. (2019). *The annual bullying survey 2019.* Retrieved from www.ditchthelabel.org/wp-content/uploads/2019/11/The-Annual-Bullying-Survey-2019-1.pdf.

Ehmke, R. (2020). Talking to kids about the coronavirus crisis. Retrieved from https://childmind.org/article/talking-to-kids-about-the-coronavirus/.

Ellemberg, D., & St-Louis-Deschênes, M. (2010). The effect of acute physical exercise on cognitive function during development. *Psychology of Sport and Exercise, 11*(2), 122–126.

Elliott, J. G., & Resing, W. C. (2020). Can intelligence be increased in those at the extremes? In R. J. Sternberg (Ed.), *Human intelligence.* New York, NY: Cambridge University Press.

Family Dinner Project. (2020). Dinner and a movie. Retrieved from https://thefamilydinnerproject.org/?s=dinner+and+a+movie.

Fleming, E., & Afful, J. (2018). Prevalence of total and untreated dental caries among youth: United States, 2015–2016. NCHS Data Brief 307, 1–8.

Freedberg, L. (2019). California spending over $13 billion annually on special education. Retrieved from https://edsource.org/2019/california-spending-over-13-billion-annually-on-special-education/619542.

Frost, J. L. (2004). How adults enhance or mess up children's play. *Archives of Pediatrics & Adolescent Medicine, 158*(1), 16.

Goodlad, J. K., Marcus, D. K., & Fulton, J. J. (2013). Lead and attention-deficit/hyperactivity disorder (ADHD) symptoms: A meta-analysis. *Clinical Psychology Review, 33*(3), 417–425.

Griffith, M. (2015). *A look at funding for students with disabilities.* Retrieved from Denver, CO: www.ecs.org/clearinghouse/01/17/72/11772.pdf.

Grimm, O., Kranz, T. M., & Reif, A. (2020). Genetics of ADHD: What should the clinician know? *Current Psychiatry Reports, 22*(4), 1–8.

Grose, J. (2020). How to talk to kids about coronavirus. Retrieved from www.nytimes.com/2020/03/17/parenting/coronavirus-kids-talk.html.

Guardabassi, V., & Tomasetto, C. (2020). Weight status or weight stigma? Obesity stereotypes—Not excess weight—Reduce working memory in school-aged children. *Journal of Experimental Child Psychology, 189,* 104706.

Haberstroh, S., & Schulte-Körne, G. (2019). The diagnosis and treatment of dyscalculia. *Deutsches* Ärzteblatt International, 116(7), 107.

Han, J.-Y., Kwon, H.-J., Ha, M., Paik, K.-C., Lim, M.-H., Lee, S. G., . . . Kim, E.-J. (2015). The effects of prenatal exposure to alcohol and environmental tobacco smoke on risk for ADHD: A large population-based study. *Psychiatry Research, 225*(1–2), 164–168.

Harriger, J. A., & Thompson, J. K. (2012). Psychological consequences of obesity: Weight bias and body image in overweight and obese youth. *International Review of Psychiatry, 24*(3), 247–253.

Harvard School of Public Health. (2020). School obesity prevention recommendations: Complete list. Retrieved from www.hsph.harvard.edu/obesity-prevention-source/obesity-prevention/schools/school-obesity-prevention-recommendations-read-and-print/.

Hayes, J. F., Eichen, D. M., Barch, D. M., & Wilfley, D. E. (2018). Executive function in childhood obesity: Promising intervention strategies to optimize treatment outcomes. *Appetite, 124,* 10–23.

Howe, C., Freedson, P., Alhassan, S., Feldman, H., & Osganian, S. (2012). A recess intervention to promote moderate-to-vigorous physical activity. *Pediatric Obesity, 7*(1), 82–88.

Hoza, B., Mrug, S., Gerdes, A. C., Hinshaw, S. P., Bukowski, W. M., Gold, J. A., . . . Arnold, L. E. (2005). What aspects of peer relationships are impaired in children with attention-deficit/hyperactivity disorder? *Journal of Consulting and Clinical Psychology, 73*(3), 411.

Ilie, G., Vingilis, E. R., Mann, R. E., Hamilton, H., Toplak, M., Adlaf, E. M., . . . Asbridge, M. (2015). The association between traumatic brain injury and ADHD in a Canadian adult sample. *Journal of Psychiatric Research, 69,* 174–179.

Internet Safety 101. (2020). Saftey and prevention. Retrieved from https://internetsafety101.org/safety.

James, S. D. (2009). Growth hormones on rise in healthy kids. Retrieved from https://abcnews.go.com/Health/growth-hormones-healthy-kids-increase/story?id=8571628.

Jürimäe, T., & Saar, M. (2003). Self-perceived and actual indicators of motor abilities in children and adolescents. *Perceptual and Motor Skills, 97*(3), 862–866.

Kaiser Family Foundation. (2004). The role of media in childhood obesity. Retrieved from www.kff.org/wp-content/uploads/2013/01/the-role-of-media-in-childhood-obesity.pdf.

Kelly, B., Vandevijvere, S., Ng, S., Adams, J., Allemandi, L., Bahena-Espina, L., . . . Carmona-Garcés, I. C. (2019). Global benchmarking of children's exposure to television advertising of unhealthy foods and beverages across 22 countries. *Obesity Reviews, 20*, 116–128.

Kemple, K. M., Oh, J., Kenney, E., & Smith-Bonahue, T. (2016). The power of outdoor play and play in natural environments. *Childhood Education, 92*(6), 446–454.

Key, T. J., Bradbury, K. E., Perez-Cornago, A., Sinha, R., Tsilidis, K. K., & Tsugane, S. (2020). Diet, nutrition, and cancer risk: What do we know and what is the way forward? *BMJ, 368*. doi: 10.1136/bmj.m511.

Knopik, V. S., Neiderhiser, J. M., DeFries, J. C., & Plomin, R. (2017). *Behavioral genetics*. New York, NY: Worth.

Kocivar, C. (2020). Special education costs flood school budgets. Retrieved from https://ed100.org/blog/special-education-costs-flood-school-budgets.

Komlos, J., & Breitfelder, A. (2008). Differences in the physical growth of US-born black and white children and adolescents ages 2–19, born 1942–2002. *Annals of Human Biology, 35*(1), 11–21.

Kortekaas-Rijlaarsdam, A. F., Luman, M., Sonuga-Barke, E., & Oosterlaan, J. (2019). Does methylphenidate improve academic performance? a systematic review and meta-analysis. *European Child & Adolescent Psychiatry, 28*(2), 155–164.

Koyanagi, A., Veronese, N., Vancampfort, D., Stickley, A., Jackson, S. E., Oh, H., . . . Smith, L. (2020). Association of bullying victimization with overweight and obesity among adolescents from 41 low-and middle-income countries. *Pediatric Obesity, 15*(1), e12571.

Langin, D., & Viguerie, N. (2020). Nutrients and Gene Expression in Type 2 Diabetes. In R. DE Caterina, J. A. Martinez, & M. Kohlmeier (Eds.), *Principles of Nutrigenetics and Nutrigenomics* (pp. 441–445). Elsevier.

Langley, K., Rice, F., van den Bree, M. B., & Thapar, A. (2005). Maternal smoking during pregnancy as an environmental risk factor for attention deficit hyperactivity disorder behaviour. A review. *Minerva Pediatrica, 57*(6), 359.

LeFever, G. B., Villers, M. S., Morrow, A. L., & Vaughn, E. S. III, (2002). Parental perceptions of adverse educational outcomes among children diagnosed and treated for ADHD: A call for improved school/provider collaboration. *Psychology in the Schools, 39*(1), 63–71.

Little, H., & Wyver, S. (2008). Outdoor play: Does avoiding the risks reduce the benefits? *Australasian Journal of Early Childhood, 33*(2), 33–40.

Mah, V. K., & Ford-Jones, E. L. (2012). Spotlight on middle childhood: Rejuvenating the 'forgotten years'. *Paediatrics & Child Health, 17*(2), 81–83.

Mayes, S. D., Breaux, R. P., Calhoun, S. L., & Frye, S. S. (2019). High prevalence of dysgraphia in elementary through high school students with ADHD and autism. *Journal of Attention Disorders, 23*(8), 787–796.

McClain, M.-C., & Pfeiffer, S. (2012). Identification of gifted students in the United States today: A look at state definitions, policies, and practices. *Journal of Applied School Psychology, 28*(1), 59–88.

McClintic, S., & Petty, K. (2015). Exploring early childhood teachers' beliefs and practices about preschool outdoor play: A qualitative study. *Journal of Early Childhood Teacher Education, 36*(1), 24–43.

McDonagh, M. S., Whiting, P. F., Wilson, P. M., Sutton, A. J., Chestnutt, I., Cooper, J., . . . Kleijnen, J. (2000). Systematic review of water fluoridation. *BMJ, 321*(7265), 855–859.

Mikkelsen, K., Stojanovska, L., Polenakovic, M., Bosevski, M., & Apostolopoulos, V. (2017). Exercise and mental health. *Maturitas, 106*, 48–56.

Millichap, J. G., & Yee, M. M. (2012). The diet factor in attention-deficit/hyperactivity disorder. *Pediatrics, 129*(2), 330–337.

Monei, T., & Pedro, A. (2017). A systematic review of interventions for children presenting with dyscalculia in primary schools. *Educational Psychology in Practice, 33*(3), 277–293.

Moss, S. M. (2012). *Natural childhood*. National Trust London.

Murdock-Smith, J. (2013). Understanding the social and emotional needs of gifted children. *Rivier Academic Journal, 9*(2), 1.

Murray, R., & Ramstetter, C. (2013). The crucial role of recess in school. *Pediatrics, 131*(1), 183–188.

National Association for Gifted Children. (2019). *A definition of giftedness that guides best practice*. Retrieved from www.nagc.org/sites/default/files/Position%20Statement/Definition%20of%20Giftedness%20%282019%29.pdf.

National Association for Gifted Children. (2022). Gifted education in the US. Retrieved from www.nagc.org/resources-publications/resources/gifted-education-us.

National Center for Education Statistics. (2019). Children and youth with disabilities. Retrieved from https://nces.ed.gov/programs/coe/indicator_cgg.asp.

National Center for Education Statistics. (2022). Children and youth with disabilities. Retrieved from https://nces.ed.gov/programs/coe/indicator_cgg.asp.

National Center for Missing & Exploited Children. (2016). Sextortion factsheet. Retrieved from https://www.missingkids.org/content/dam/missingkids/pdfs/ncmec-analysis/sextortion factsheet.pdf.

National Center for Missing & Exploited Children. (2022). Online enticement. Retrieved from www.missingkids.org/theissues/onlineenticement.

National Institute of Mental Health. (2022a). Attention-deficit/hyperactivity disorder (ADHD): The basics. Retrieved from www.nimh.nih.gov/health/publications/attention-deficit-hyperactivity-disorder-adhd-the-basics/index.shtml.

National Institute of Mental Health. (2022b). Dysgraphia information page. Retrieved from www.ninds.nih.gov/Disorders/All-Disorders/Dysgraphia-Information-page.

National Pediculosis Association. (2022). The No Nit Policy. Retrieved from www.headlice.org/comb/what-are-head-lice-and-nits/no-nit-policy/.

Nishi, Y., & Tanaka, T. (2017). Growth hormone treatment and adverse events. *Pediatric Endocrinology Reviews: PER, 14*(Suppl 1), 235.

Noutsios, G. T., & Floros, J. (2014). Childhood asthma: Causes, risks, and protective factors; a role of innate immunity. *Swiss Medical Weekly, 144*(5152).

Office of Disease Prevention and Health Promotion. (2022). Social determinants of health. Retrieved from www.healthypeople .gov/2020/topics-objectives/topic/social-determinants-of-health.

Ogden, C. L., Carroll, M. D., Fakhouri, T. H., Hales, C. M., Fryar, C. D., Li, X., & Freedman, D. S. (2018). Prevalence of obesity among youths by household income and education level of head of household—United States 2011–2014. *Morbidity and Mortality Weekly Report, 67*(6), 186–189.

Partnership for a Healthier America. (2020). Facts about childhood obesity. Retrieved from www.ahealthieramerica.org/articles/facts-about-childhood-obesity-102.

Partnership for a Healthier America. (2022). Facts about childhood obesity. Retrieved from www.ahealthieramerica.org/articles/facts-about-childhood-obesity-102.

Patel, H. N., & Williams, K. A. (2020). Plant-based nutrition. In J. Uribarri & J. A. Vassalotti (Eds.), *Nutrition, fitness, and mindfulness* (pp. 33–44). Springer.

Paulesu, E., Démonet, J.-F., Fazio, F., McCrory, E., Chanoine, V., Brunswick, N., . . . Frith, C. D. (2001). Dyslexia: Cultural diversity and biological unity. *Science, 291*(5511), 2165–2167.

Perrin, J. M., Anderson, L. E., & Van Cleave, J. (2014). The rise in chronic conditions among infants, children, and youth can be met with continued health system innovations. *Health Affairs, 33*(12), 2099–2105.

Perrin, J. M., Bloom, S. R., & Gortmaker, S. L. (2007). The increase of childhood chronic conditions in the United States. *JAMA, 297*(24), 2755–2759.

Population Reference Bureau. (2021). Childhood asthma: A growing American epidemic. Retrieved from www.prb.org/childhoodasthmaagrowingamericanepidemic/.

Rabiner, D., & Coie, J. D. (2000). Early attention problems and children's reading achievement: A longitudinal investigation. The Conduct Problems Prevention Research Group. *Journal of the American Academy of Child & Adolescent Psychiatry, 39*(7), 859–867.

Reiley, L. (2020). More pizza, fewer vegetables: Trump adiministration further undercuts Obama school-lunch rules. Retrieved from www.washingtonpost.com/business/2020/01/17/usda-proposes-changing-school-menus-allow-more-fries-pizza-fewer-vegetables-fruits-reversing-michelle-obama-effort/.

Renzulli, J. S. (2016). *The three-ring conception of giftedness: A developmental model for promoting creative productivity*. Prufrock Press.

Ridgway, A., Northup, J., Pellegrin, A., LaRue, R., & Hightsoe, A. (2003). Effects of recess on the classroom behavior of children with and without attention-deficit hyperactivity disorder. *School Psychology Quarterly, 18*(3), 253.

Ríos-Hernández, A., Alda, J. A., Farran-Codina, A., Ferreira-García, E., & Izquierdo-Pulido, M. (2017). The Mediterranean diet and ADHD in children and adolescents. *Pediatrics, 139*(2), e20162027.

Riser-Kositsky, M. (2018). 7 things to know about school recess. Retrieved from www.edweek.org/ew/issues/school-recess/index.html.

Rochman, B. (2012). Yay for recess: Pediatricians say it's as important as math and reading. Retrieved from https://healthland.time.com/2012/12/31/yay-for-recess-pediatricians-say-its-as-important-as-math-or-reading/.

Roitsch, J., & Watson, S. (2019). An overview of dyslexia: Definition, characteristics, assessment, identification, and intervention. *Science, 7*(4), 81–86.

Rose, K. A., Morgan, I. G., Ip, J., Kifley, A., Huynh, S., Smith, W., & Mitchell, P. (2008). Outdoor activity reduces the prevalence of myopia in children. *Ophthalmology, 115*(8), 1279–1285.

Sagar, R., & Gupta, T. (2018). Psychological aspects of obesity in children and adolescents. *Indian Journal of Pediatrics, 85*(7), 554–559.

Shalev, R. S., & Gross-Tsur, V. (2001). Developmental dyscalculia. *Pediatric Neurology, 24*(5), 337–342.

Shammas, B. (2019). Time to play: More state laws require recess. Retrieved from www.edutopia.org/article/time-play-more-state-laws-require-recess.

Shaywitz, S. (2020). *Overcoming dyslexia*. New York, NY: Knopf.

Shaywitz, S. E., & Shaywitz, B. A. (2013). Psychopathology of dyslexia and reading disorders. In A. S. Davis (Ed.), *Psychopathology of childhood and adolescence: A neuropsychological approach* (pp. 109–126). Springer Publishing Company.

Shaywitz, S. E., & Shaywitz, B. A. (2017). Dyslexia. In R. G. Schwartz (Ed.), *Handbook of child language disorders* (pp. 130–148). Psychology Press.

Siegel, L. S. (2006). Perspectives on dyslexia. *Paediatrics & Child Health, 11*(9), 581–587.

Škrablin, S., Maurac, I., Banović, V., & Bošnjak-Nadj, K. (2008). Perinatal factors associated with the neurologic impairment of children born preterm. *International Journal of Gynecology & Obstetrics, 102*(1), 12–18.

Slade, G., Grider, W., Maas, W., & Sanders, A. (2018). Water fluoridation and dental caries in US children and adolescents. *Journal of Dental Research, 97*(10), 1122–1128.

Sprich, S. E., Safren, S. A., Finkelstein, D., Remmert, J. E., & Hammerness, P. (2016). A randomized controlled trial of cognitive behavioral therapy for ADHD in medication-treated adolescents. *Journal of Child Psychology and Psychiatry, 57*(11), 1218–1226.

Sternberg, R. J. (2003). WICS as a model of giftedness. *High Ability Studies, 14*(2), 109–137.

Sternberg, R. J., & Kaufman, S. B. (2018). Theories and conceptions of giftedness. In S. I. Pfeiffer (Ed.), *Handbook of giftedness in children* (pp. 29–47). Springer.

Sullivan, J. F. (2020). Could families bond around the TV, like they used to? Retrieved from www.bostonglobe.com/2020/03/27/arts/could-families-bond-around-tv-like-they-used/.

U.S. Department of Agriculture. (2011). Be a healthy role model for children: 10 tips for setting good examples. Retrieved from https://naldc.nal.usda.gov/catalog/1333665.

U.S. Department of Agriculture. (2015). Healthy eating index. Retrieved from https://www.fns.usda.gov/hei-scores-americans.

U.S. Department of Agriculture. (2020). USDA announces school and summer meals reform. Retrieved from www.usda.gov/media/press-releases/2020/01/17/usda-announces-school-and-summer-meals-reforms.

U.S. Department of Education. (2006). Individualized Education Programs–Special Education Research Retrieved from www2.ed.gov/programs/specediep/index.html.

U.S. Department of Education. (2021). Office of Special Education Programs, Individuals with Disabilities Education Act (IDEA) database. Retrieved from https://nces.ed.gov/programs/coe/indicator/cgg.

Uhlig, T., Merkenschlager, A., Brandmaier, R., & Egger, J. (1997). Topographic mapping of brain electrical activity in children with food-induced attention deficit hyperkinetic disorder. *European Journal of Pediatrics, 156*(7), 557–561.

Understood. (2020). Signs of dyscalculia at different ages. Retrieved from www.understood.org/en/learning-thinking-differences/signs-symptoms/could-your-child-have/signs-of-dyscalculia-in-children.

UNICEF. (2019). UNICEF poll: More than a third of young people in 30 countries report being a victim of online bullying. Retrieved from www.unicef.org/press-releases/unicef-poll-more-third-young-people-30-countries-report-being-victim-online-bullying.

Van Cleave, J., Gortmaker, S. L., & Perrin, J. M. (2010). Dynamics of obesity and chronic health conditions among children and youth. *JAMA, 303*(7), 623–630.

Verburgh, L., Königs, M., Scherder, E. J., & Oosterlaan, J. (2014). Physical exercise and executive functions in preadolescent children, adolescents and young adults: A meta-analysis. *British Journal of Sports Medicine, 48*(12), 973–979.

Vicendese, D., Dharmage, S. C., Tang, M. L., Olenko, A., Allen, K. J., Abramson, M. J., & Erbas, B. (2015). Bedroom air quality and vacuuming frequency are associated with repeat child asthma hospital admissions. *Journal of Asthma, 52*(7), 727–731.

Visser, S. N., Danielson, M. L., Bitsko, R. H., Holbrook, J. R., Kogan, M. D., Ghandour, R. M., . . . Blumberg, S. J. (2014). Trends in the parent-report of health care provider-diagnosed and medicated attention-deficit/hyperactivity disorder: United States, 2003–2011. *Journal of the American Academy of Child & Adolescent Psychiatry, 53*(1), 34–46. e32.

Wen, L. M., Kite, J., Merom, D., & Rissel, C. (2009). Time spent playing outdoors after school and its relationship with independent mobility: A cross-sectional survey of children aged 10–12 years in Sydney, Australia. *International Journal of Behavioral Nutrition and Physical Activity, 6*(1), 15.

White, B. A., & Gordon, S. M. (2014). Preventing dental caries through community water fluoridation. *North Carolina Medical Journal, 75*(6), 430–431.

Woodyard, C. (2019). Attention, parents: You may be doing screen time limits all wrong. Retrieved from www.usatoday.com/story/news/education/2019/10/06/screen-time-kids-limit-how-much-tv-video-games-phone/3781282002/.

World Health Organization. (2017). Global Health Observatory data repository. Retrieved from https://apps.who.int/gho/data/view.main.BMIPLUS2C05-19v?lang=en.

Xu, S., & Xue, Y. (2016). Pediatric obesity: Causes, symptoms, prevention and treatment. *Experimental and Therapeutic Medicine, 11*(1), 15–20.

Yale Center for Dyslexia and Creativity. (2022a). Dyslexia FAQ. Retrieved from http://dyslexia.yale.edu/dyslexia/dyslexia-faq/.

Yale Center for Dyslexia and Creativity. (2022b). Time & tools. Retrieved from http://dyslexia.yale.edu/resources/accommodations/time-and-tools/.

Yarasheski, K. E. (1994). Growth hormone effects on metabolism, body composition, muscle mass, and strength. *Exercise and Sport Sciences Reviews, 22*, 285–312.

Yılmaz, B., & Karadağ, M. G. (2020). The current review of adolescent obesity: The role of genetic factors. *Journal of Pediatric Endocrinology and Metabolism, 34*(2), 151–162.

Zahran, H. S., Bailey, C. M., Damon, S. A., Garbe, P. L., & Breysse, P. N. (2018). Vital signs: Asthma in children—United States, 2001–2016. *Morbidity and Mortality Weekly Report, 67*(5), 149–155. Retrieved from www.cdc.gov/mmwr/volumes/67/wr/mm6705e1.htm#T1_down.

Zaza, A., Abrego, K., Gabra, M., & Champsi, A. (2017). More focus, less growth? Exploring the association between growth deficits and ADHD medication. Retrieved from https://ruor.uottawa.ca/bitstream/10393/37080/1/More-Focus-Less-Growth-2017.pdf.

Zeidner, M. (2017). Tentative guidelines for the development of an ability-based emotional intelligence intervention program for gifted students. *High Ability Studies, 28*(1), 29–41.

Chapter 12

Alfieri, L., Brooks, P. J., Aldrich, N. J., & Tenenbaum, H. R. (2011). Does discovery-based instruction enhance learning? *Journal of Educational Psychology, 103*(1), 1.

Apperly, I. A., & Robinson, E. J. (2002). Five-year-olds' handling of reference and description in the domains of language and mental representation. *Journal of Experimental Child Psychology, 83*(1), 53–75.

Baker-Ward, L., Ornstein, P. A., & Holden, D. J. (1984). The expression of memorization in early childhood. *Journal of Experimental Child Psychology, 37*(3), 555–575.

Behrens, H. (2015). Grammatical categories. In E. L. Bavin & L. R. Naigles (Eds.), *The Cambridge handbook of child language.* New York: Cambridge University Press.

Behrmann, M. (1998). Assistive technology for young children in special education: It makes a difference. Retrieved from www.edutopia.org/assistive-technology-young-children-special-education.

Benyamin, B., Pourcain, B., Davis, O. S., Davies, G., Hansell, N. K., Brion, M. J., . . . Visscher, P. M. (2014). Childhood intelligence is heritable, highly polygenic and associated with FNBP1L. *Molecular Psychiatry, 19*(2), 253–258. doi: 10.1038/mp.2012.184.

Bjorklund, D. F., Miller, P. H., Coyle, T. R., & Slawinski, J. L. (1997). Instructing children to use memory strategies: Evidence of utilization deficiencies in memory training studies. *Developmental Review, 17*(4), 411–441.

Boring, E. (1923). Intelligence as the tests test it. *New Republic, 35*(7).

Bornstein, M. H., Putnick, D. L., Rigo, P., Esposito, G., Swain, J. E., Suwalsky, J. T., . . . Cote, L. R. (2017). Neurobiology of culturally common maternal responses to infant cry. Proceedings of the National Academy of Sciences, 114(45), E9465-E9473.

Bornstein, M. H., & Colombo, J. (2012). Infant cognitive functioning and mental development. In S. M. Pauen (Ed.), *Early childhood development and later outcome* (pp. 118–147). Cambridge University Press.

Bornstein, M. H., & Sigman, M. D. (1986). Continuity in mental development from infancy. *Child Development*, 251–274.

Bowers, J. S. (2020). Reconsidering the evidence that systematic phonics is more effective than alternative methods of reading instruction. *Educational Psychology Review, 32*(3), 681–705.

Brechtel, M. (1992). *Bringing the whole together: An integrated, whole language approach for the multilingual classroom.* ERIC.

Breedlove, S. M. 2015. *Principles of psychology.* Sinauer/Oxford University Press, Sunderland, MA.

Brody, N. (2007). Does education influence intelligence? In R. D. Roberts, L. Stankov, & P. C. Kyllonen (Eds.), *Extending intelligence: Enhancement and new constructs* (pp. 363–370). New York: Erlbaum.

Brubaker, C. J., Dietrich, K. N., Lanphear, B. P., & Cecil, K. M. (2010). The influence of age of lead exposure on adult gray matter volume. *Neurotoxicology, 31*(3), 259–266.

Brunswick, N., Martin, G. N., & Rippon, G. (2012). Early cognitive profiles of emergent readers: A longitudinal study. *Journal of Experimental Child Psychology, 111*(2), 268–285.

Cain, K., Patson, N., & Andrews, L. (2005). Age- and ability-related differences in young readers' use of conjunctions. *Journal of Child Language, 32*(4), 877–892.

Campbell, F. A., Pan, Y., & Burchinal, M. (2019). Sustaining gains from early childhood intervention: The Abecedarian program. In A. J. Reynolds & J. A. Temple (Eds.), *Sustaining early childhood learning gains: Program, school, and family influences* (pp. 268–286). doi: 10.1017/9781108349352.013.

Carpenter, P. A., Just, M. A., and Shell, P. 1990. What one intelligence test measures: A theoretical account of the processing in the Raven progressive matrices test. *Psychological Review, 97*(3), 404–431.

Carroll, J. B. (1993). *Human cognitive abilities: A survey of factor-analytic studies.* Cambridge University Press.

Castelo, M. (2020). Using assistive technology to empower students with disabilities. Retrieved from https://edtechmagazine.com/k12/article/2020/03/using-assistive-technology-empower-students-disabilities-perfcon.

Ceci, S. J., & Williams, W. M. (1997). Schooling, intelligence, and income. *American Psychologist, 52*(10), 1051.

Chang, I. (2019). Influences of executive function, language comprehension, and fluency on reading comprehension. *Journal of Early Childhood Research*, 1476718X19875768.

Chevalier, N., & Blaye, A. (2009). Setting goals to switch between tasks: Effect of cue transparency on children's cognitive flexibility. *Developmental Psychology, 45*(3), 782.

Chomsky, C. (1969). *The acquisition of syntax in children from 5 to 10.* Cambridge, MA: MIT Press.

Clements, D. H., & Sarama, J. (2007). Effects of a preschool mathematics curriculum: Summative research on the Building Blocks project. *Journal for Research in Mathematics Education, 38*(2), 136–163.

Conlon, O., Volden, J., Smith, I. M., Duku, E., Zwaigenbaum, L., Waddell, C., . . . Bennett, T. (2019). Gender differences in pragmatic communication in school-aged children with autism spectrum disorder (ASD). *Journal of Autism and Developmental Disorders, 49*(5), 1937–1948.

Constantinidis, C., & Klingberg, T. (2016). The neuroscience of working memory capacity and training. *Nature Reviews Neuroscience, 17*(7), 438.

Cooper, H., Nye, B., Charlton, K., Lindsay, J., & Greathouse, S. (1996). The effects of summer vacation on achievement test scores: A narrative and meta-analytic review. *Review of Educational Research, 66*(3), 227–268.

de Graaff, S., Bosman, A. M., Hasselman, F., & Verhoeven, L. (2009). Benefits of systematic phonics instruction. *Scientific Studies of Reading, 13*(4), 318–333.

Deater-Deckard, K., Chang, M., & Evans, M. E. (2013). Engagement states and learning from educational games. *New Directions for Child and Adolescent Development, 2013*(139), 21–30.

Deen, K., Bondoc, I., Camp, A., Estioca, S., Hwang, H., Shin, G.-H., . . . Zhong, J. (2018). Repetition brings success: Revealing knowledge of the passive voice. Paper presented at the Proceedings of the 42nd Annual Boston University Conference on Language Development.

DelGiudice, M. (2018). Middle childhood: An evolutionary-developmental synthesis. In N. Halfon, C. B. Forrest, R. M. Lerner, & E. M. Faustman (Eds.), *Handbook of life course health development* (pp. 95–107). Springer, Cham.

Dempster, F. N. (1981). Memory span: Sources of individual and developmental differences. *Psychological Bulletin, 89*(1), 63.

Diamond, A. (2012). Activities and programs that improve children's executive functions. *Current Directions in Psychological Science, 21*(5), 335–341.

Diamond, A., Barnett, W. S., Thomas, J., & Munro, S. (2007). Preschool program improves cognitive control. *Science, 318*(5855), 1387–1388.

Drace, S., Korlat, S., & Đokić, R. (2020). When stereotype threat makes me more or less intelligent: The informative role of emotions in effort mobilization and task performance. *British Journal of Social Psychology, 59*(1), 137–156.

Elliott, J. G., & Grigorenko, E. L. (2014). *The dyslexia debate*: Cambridge University Press.

Empson, S. B. (1995). Using sharing situations to help children learn fractions. *Teaching Children Mathematics, 2*(2), 110–115.

Eurostat. (2019). Foreign language learning statistics. Retrieved from https://ec.europa.eu/eurostat/statistics-explained/index.php/Foreign_language_learning_statistics#Upper_secondary_education.

Flavell, J. H., Friedrichs, A. G., & Hoyt, J. D. (1970). Developmental changes in memorization processes. *Cognitive Psychology, 1*(4), 324–340.

Fukada, Y. (2018). Whole language approach. In J. I. Liontas (Ed.), *The TESOL Encyclopedia of English Language Teaching*, 1–7.

Gabriel, F. (2016). Understanding magnitudes to understand fractions. *Australian Primary Mathematics Classroom, 21*(2), 36.

Gabriel, F., Coché, F., Szucs, D., Carette, V., Rey, B., & Content, A. (2012). Developing children's understanding of fractions: An intervention study. *Mind, Brain, and Education, 6*(3), 137–146.

Gardner, H. (2000). A case against spiritual intelligence. *International Journal for the Psychology of Religion, 10*(1), 27–34.

Gardner, H. (2011). *Frames of mind: The theory of multiple intelligences.* Hachette Uk.

Garner, R. (1987). Strategies for reading and studying expository text. *Educational Psychologist, 22*(3–4), 299–312.

Garrity, S., Aquino-Sterling, C. R., Van Liew, C., & Day, A. (2018). Beliefs about bilingualism, bilingual education, and dual language development of early childhood preservice teachers raised in a Prop 227 environment. *International Journal of Bilingual Education and Bilingualism, 21*(2), 179–196.

Garzotto, F. (2007). Was Vygotsky right? Evaluating learning effects of social interaction in children internet games. Paper presented at the IFIP Conference on Human-Computer Interaction.

Gunzenhauser, C., Saalbach, H., & Von Suchodoletz, A. (2017). Boys have caught up, family influences still continue: Influences on executive functioning and behavioral self-regulation in elementary students in Germany. *PsyCh Journal, 6*(1), 29–42.

Gutchess, A. H., & Indeck, A. (2009). Cultural influences on memory. *Progress in Brain Research, 178*, 137–150.

Hakuta, K. (2020). A policy history of leadership dilemmas in English learner education. *Leadership and Policy in Schools, 19*(1), 6–9.

Halpern, D. F., & Kanaya, T. (2019). Group Differences in Intelligence. In R. J. Sternberg (Ed.), *Human intelligence: An introduction* (pp. 349–380). New York: Cambridge University Press.

Henry, L. A. (1996). The relationships between memory performance, use of simple memory strategies and metamemory in young children. *International Journal of Behavioral Development, 19*(1), 177–200.

Henry, R., Van Dyke, J. A., & Kuperman, V. (2018). Oculomotor planning in RAN and reading: A strong test of the visual scanning hypothesis. *Reading and Writing, 31*(7), 1619–1643.

Hernandez, D. J. (2011). Double jeopardy: How third-grade reading skills and poverty influence high school graduation. New York, NY: Annie E. Casey Foundation.

Hoff, E. (2018). Bilingual development in children of immigrant families. *Child Development Perspectives, 12*(2), 80–86.

Hoff, E., & Core, C. (2015). What clinicians need to know about bilingual development. Paper presented at the Seminars in Speech and Language.

Hoff, E., Rumiche, R., Burridge, A., Ribot, K. M., & Welsh, S. N. (2014). Expressive vocabulary development in children from bilingual and monolingual homes: A longitudinal study from two to four years. *Early Childhood Research Quarterly, 29*(4), 433–444.

Hulme, C., & Snowling, M. J. (2013). Learning to read: What we know and what we need to understand better. *Child Development Perspectives, 7*(1), 1–5.

Inhelder, B., Piaget, J., & Papert, D. (1964). *The early growth of logic in the child: Classification and seriation.* Routledge.

Izawa, C. (2014). *Cognitive psychology applied: A symposium at the 22nd International Congress of Applied Psychology.* Psychology Press.

Jacobson, R. (2020). Metacognition: How thinking about thinking can help kids. Retrieved from https://childmind.org/article/how-metacognition-can-help-kids/.

Janssen, M., Chinapaw, M., Rauh, S., Toussaint, H., Van Mechelen, W., & Verhagen, E. (2014). A short physical activity break from cognitive tasks increases selective attention in primary school children aged 10–11. *Mental Health and Physical Activity, 7*(3), 129–134.

Jencks, C. (1979). *Who gets ahead? The determinants of economic success in America.* Basic Books.

Karably, K., & Zabrucky, K. M. (2017). Children's metamemory: A review of the literature and implications for the classroom. *International Electronic Journal of Elementary Education, 2*(1), 32–52.

Kaufman, A. S., & Kaufman, N. L. (2018). *Kaufman Assessment Battery for Children - Second Edition Normative Update.* Circle Pines, MN: Pearson (AGS)..

Khamo, A., & Johnson, A. (2019). Literature review of multiple intelligences. Paper presented at the Global Learn.

Kuo, L.-J., Ramirez, G., de Marin, S., Kim, T.-J., & Unal-Gezer, M. (2017). Bilingualism and morphological awareness: A study with children from general education and Spanish-English dual language programs. *Educational Psychology, 37*(2), 94–111.

Kuperman, V., Van Dyke, J. A., & Henry, R. (2016). Eye-movement control in RAN and reading. *Scientific Studies of Reading, 20*(2), 173–188.

Larsen, J. A., & Nippold, M. A. (2007). Morphological analysis in school-age children: Dynamic assessment of a word learning strategy. *Language, Speech, and Hearing Services in Schools, 38*(3), 201–212.

Lecce, S., Ronchi, L., Del Sette, P., Bischetti, L., & Bambini, V. (2019). Interpreting physical and mental metaphors: Is Theory of Mind associated with pragmatics in middle childhood? *Journal of Child Language, 46*(2), 393–407.

Lehmann, M. (2015). Rehearsal development as development of iterative recall processes. *Frontiers in Psychology, 6*, 308.

Lersilp, S., Putthinoi, S., & Lersilp, T. (2018). Facilitators and barriers of assistive technology and learning environment for children with special needs. *Occupational Therapy International, 2018*, 1–9.

Lervåg, A., Bråten, I., & Hulme, C. (2009). The cognitive and linguistic foundations of early reading development: A Norwegian latent variable longitudinal study. *Developmental Psychology, 45*(3), 764.

Li, M., Kirby, J., & Georgiou, G. K. (2011). Rapid naming speed components and reading comprehension in bilingual children. *Journal of Research in Reading, 34*(1), 6–22.

Lillard, A., & Else-Quest, N. (2006). Evaluating montessori education. *Science, 313*(5795), 1893–1894.

Loban, W. (1976). Language development: Kindergarten through grade twelve. NCTE Committee on Research Report No. 18.

Lockl, K., & Schneider, W. (2002). Developmental trends in children's feeling-of-knowing judgements. *International Journal of Behavioral Development, 26*(4), 327–333.

Ma, J. K., Le Mare, L., & Gurd, B. J. (2015). Four minutes of in-class high-intensity interval activity improves selective attention in 9- to 11-year olds. *Applied Physiology, Nutrition, and Metabolism, 40*(3), 238–244.

MacDonald, S., Uesiliana, K., & Hayne, H. (2000). Cross-cultural and gender differences in childhood amnesia. *Memory, 8*(6), 365–376.

Maddox, K., & Feng, J. (2013). Whole language instruction vs. phonics instruction. *ERIC Institute of Education Sciences*, 2–28.

Marshall, A. T., Betts, S., Kan, E. C., McConnell, R., Lanphear, B. P., & Sowell, E. R. (2020). Association of lead-exposure risk and family income with childhood brain outcomes. *Nature Medicine, 26*(1), 91–97.

McGrew, K. S. (2005). The Cattell-Horn-Carroll theory of cognitive abilities: Past, present, and future. In D. P. Flanagan & P. L. Harrison (Eds.), *Contemporary intellectual assessment: Theories, tests, issues* (pp. 136–181). Guilford Press.

Melby-Lervåg, M., Lyster, S.-A. H., & Hulme, C. (2012). Phonological skills and their role in learning to read: A meta-analytic review. *Psychological Bulletin, 138*(2), 322.

Miller, S., McCulloch, S., & Jarrold, C. (2015). The development of memory maintenance strategies: Training cumulative rehearsal and interactive imagery in children aged between 5 and 9. *Frontiers in Psychology, 6*, 524.

Moffitt, T. E. (2012). Childhood self-control predicts adult health, wealth, and crime. Paper presented at the Symposium on Symptom Improvement in Well-Being.

Moffitt, T. E., Arseneault, L., Belsky, D., Dickson, N., Hancox, R. J., Harrington, H., . . . Ross, S. (2011). A gradient of childhood self-control predicts health, wealth, and public safety. *Proceedings of the National Academy of Sciences, 108*(7), 2693–2698.

Moore, K. N., Lampinen, J. M., Gallo, D. A., Adams, E. J., & Bridges, A. J. (2018). Children's use of memory editing strategies to reject source misinformation. *Child Development, 89*(1), 219–234.

Morash-Macneil, V., Johnson, F., & Ryan, J. B. (2018). A systematic review of assistive technology for individuals with intellectual disability in the workplace. *Journal of Special Education Technology, 33*(1), 15–26.

Mullen, M. K., & Yi, S. (1995). The cultural context of talk about the past: Implications for the development of autobiographical memory. *Cognitive Development, 10*(3), 407–419.

Munakata, Y., Michaelson, L., Barker, J., & Chevalier, N. (2013). Executive functioning during infancy and childhood. In R. E. Tremblay, M. Boivin, & R. DeV. Peters, (Eds.), J. B. Morton (Topic Ed.), *Encyclopedia on Early Childhood Development.* Retrieved from https://www.child-encyclopedia.com/executive-functions/according-experts/executive-functioning-during-infancy-and-childhood.

Munakata, Y., Snyder, H. R., & Chatham, C. H. (2012). Developing cognitive control: Three key transitions. *Current Directions in Psychological Science, 21*(2), 71–77.

Muter, V., Hulme, C., Snowling, M. J., & Stevenson, J. (2004). Phonemes, rimes, vocabulary, and grammatical skills as foundations of early reading development: Evidence from a longitudinal study. *Developmental Psychology, 40*(5), 665.

Nagy, W., & Scott, J. (2000). Vocabulary processes. In M. L. Kamil, P. B. Mosenthal, P. D. Pearson, & R. Barr (Eds.), *Handbook of reading research,* Vol. 3 (pp. 269–284). Lawrence Erlbaum Associates Publishers.

National Reading Panel (U.S.), National Institute of Child Health and Human Development (U.S.) (2000). *Report of the National Reading Panel: Teaching children to read: An evidence-based assessment of the scientific research literature on reading and its implications for reading instruction: Reports of the subgroups.* Washington, D.C.: National Institute of Child Health and Human Development, National Institutes of Health.

Neisser, U., Boodoo, G., Bouchard, T. J., Jr., Boykin, A. W., Brody, N., Ceci, S. J., . . . Sternberg, R. J. (1996). Intelligence: Knowns and unknowns. *American Psychologist, 51*(2), 77.

Neville, H. J. (2006). Different profiles of plasticity within human cognition. In Y. Munakata & M. H. Johnson (Eds.), *Attention and performance XXI: Processes of change in brain and cognitive development* (pp. 287–314). Oxford University Press.

Nisbett, R. E. (2013). Schooling makes you smarter: What teachers need to know about IQ. *American Educator, 37*(1), 10.

Nisbett, R. E., Aronson, J., Blair, C., Dickens, W., Flynn, J., Halpern, D. F., & Turkheimer, E. (2012). Intelligence: New findings and theoretical developments. *American Psychologist, 67*(2), 130.

Nunes, T., Carraher, T. N., Schliemann, A. D., & Carraher, D. W. (1993). *Street mathematics and school mathematics.* Cambridge University Press.

Paradis, J., & Jia, R. (2017). Bilingual children's long-term outcomes in English as a second language: Language environment factors shape individual differences in catching up with monolinguals. *Developmental Science, 20*(1).

Pasupathi, M., & Wainryb, C. (2010). On telling the whole story: Facts and interpretations in autobiographical memory narratives from childhood through midadolescence. *Developmental Psychology, 46*(3), 735.

Perone, S., Almy, B., & Zelazo, P. D. (2018). Toward an understanding of the neural basis of executive function development. In R. Gibb & B. Kolb (Eds.), *The neurobiology of brain and behavioral development* (pp. 291–314). Elsevier.

Pew Research Center. (2018). Most European students are learning a foreign language in school while Americans lag. Retrieved from www.pewresearch.org/fact-tank/2018/08/06/most-european-students-are-learning-a-foreign-language-in-school-while-americans-lag/.

Plomin, R., & Deary, I. J. (2015). Genetics and intelligence differences: Five special findings. *Molecular Psychiatry, 20*(1), 98–108.

Presley, M., & Afflerbach, P. (1995). Verbal protocols of reading: The nature of constructively reading. New Jersey: Lawrence Eribaum.

Ramey, C. T. (2018). The Abecedarian approach to social, educational, and health disparities. *Clinical Child and Family Psychology Review, 21*(4), 527–544.

Raven, J. C. (2003). *Raven's Standard Progressive Matrices* Bloomington, MN: Pearson.

Resing, W. C. M. & Blok, J. B. 2002. De classificatie van intelligentiescores: Voorstel voor een eenduidig systeem [Towards a uniform classification system for intelligence test scores]. *Psycholoog, 37*(5), 244–249.

Riggs, N. R., Jahromi, L. B., Razza, R. P., Dillworth-Bart, J. E., & Mueller, U. (2006). Executive function and the promotion of social–emotional competence. *Journal of Applied Developmental Psychology, 27*(4), 300–309.

Roid, G. (2003). *Stanford-Binet Intelligence Scales,* 5th Edition. Torrance, CA: WPS.

Rose, J. (2006). *Independent review of the teaching of early reading.* Retrieved from https://dera.ioe.ac.uk/5551/2/report.pdf.

Ross, M., & Wang, Q. (2010). Why we remember and what we remember: Culture and autobiographical memory. *Perspectives on Psychological Science, 5*(4), 401–409.

Sackett, P. R., Shewach, O. R., & Dahlke, J. A. (2019). The predictive value of general intelligence. In R. J. Sternberg (Ed.), *Human intelligence: An introduction* (pp. 381–414). Cambridge University Press.

Saklofske, D. H., Van de Vijver, F. J., Oakland, T., Mpofu, E., & Suzuki, L. A. (2015). Intelligence and culture: History and assessment. In S. Goldstein, D. Princiotta, & J. A. Naglieri (Eds.), *Handbook of intelligence* (pp. 341–365). Springer.

Sander, E. K. (1972). When are speech sounds learned? *Journal of Speech and Hearing Disorders, 37*(1), 55–63.

Scarr, S., & Weinberg, R. A. (1976). IQ test performance of Black children adopted by White families. *American Psychologist, 31*(10), 726.

Schneider, W. (1985). Developmental trends in the metamemory-memory behavior relationship: An integrative review. In Forrest-Pressley DL, GE Mac Kinnon, T. Gray Waller (Eds.), *Metacognition, cognition and human performance. Vol 1. Theoretical perspectives.* Orlando: Academic Press.

Schneider, W. (2008). The development of metacognitive knowledge in children and adolescents: Major trends and implications for education. *Mind, Brain, and Education, 2*(3), 114–121.

Schneider, W. (2011). Memory development in childhood. In U. Goswami (Ed.), *The Wiley-Blackwell handbook of childhood cognitive development* (pp. 347–376). Wiley Blackwell.

Schneider, W., Kron, V., Hünnerkopf, M., & Krajewski, K. (2004). The development of young children's memory strategies: First findings from the Würzburg Longitudinal Memory Study. *Journal of Experimental Child Psychology, 88*(2), 193–209.

Seymour, P. H., Aro, M., & Erskine, J. M. (2003). Foundation literacy acquisition in European orthographies. *British Journal of Psychology, 94*(2), 143–174.

Shayer, M., Ginsburg, D., & Coe, R. (2007). Thirty years on—a large anti-Flynn effect? The Piagetian test Volume & Heaviness norms 1975–2003. *British Journal of Educational Psychology, 77*(1), 25–41.

Siegler, R. S. (2009). Improving the numerical understanding of children from low-income families. *Child Development Perspectives, 3*(2), 118–124.

Siegler, R. S., & Booth, J. L. (2004). Development of numerical estimation in young children. *Child Development, 75*(2), 428–444.

Snow, P., & Douglas, J. (2017). Psychosocial aspects of pragmatic disorders. In Cummings, L. (Ed.), *Research in clinical pragmatics* (pp. 617–649). Springer.

Spearman, C. (1927). *The abilities of man: Their nature and measurement.* New York: Macmillan.

Spencer, S. J., Logel, C., & Davies, P. G. (2016). Stereotype threat. *Annual Review of Psychology, 67*, 415–437.

Spörer, N., Brunstein, J. C., & Kieschke, U. (2009). Improving students' reading comprehension skills: Effects of strategy instruction and reciprocal teaching. *Learning and Instruction, 19*(3), 272–286.

Stahl, S. A., & Miller, P. D. (2006). Whole language and language experience approaches for beginning reading: A quantitative research synthesis. Paper presented at the National Reading Conference, US; An earlier version of this article was presented at the aforementioned conference.

Stein-Smith, K. (2019). Foreign language classes becoming more scarce. Retrieved from www.amacad.org/news/foreign-language-classes-becoming-more-scarce.

Sternberg, R. J. (1997). *Successful intelligence.* New York: Plume.

Sternberg, R. J. (2004). Culture and intelligence. *American Psychologist, 59*(5), 325–338.

Sternberg, R. J. (2018). Theories of intelligence. In S. I. Pfeiffer, E. Shaunessy-Dedrick, & M. Foley-Nicpon (Eds.), *APA handbook of giftedness and talent* (pp. 145–161). American Psychological Association.

Sternberg, R. J. (2019). A theory of adaptive intelligence and its relation to general intelligence. *Journal of Intelligence, 7*(4), 23.

Sternberg, R. J. (2020). 28 The augmented theory of successful intelligence. In R. J. Sternberg (Ed.), *Cambridge handbook of intelligence* (2nd ed., Vol. 2, pp. 679–708). New York: Cambridge University Press.

Sternberg, R. J. (2021a). Adaptive intelligence: Intelligence is not a personal trait but rather a person × task × situation interaction. *Journal of Intelligence, 9*, 58, doi: 10.3390/jintelligence 9040058.

Sternberg, R. J. (2021b). *Adaptive intelligence: Surviving and thriving in a world of uncertainty.* New York: Cambridge University Press.

Stevens, C., & Bavelier, D. (2012). The role of selective attention on academic foundations: A cognitive neuroscience perspective. *Developmental Cognitive Neuroscience, 2*, S30–S48.

Strauss, V. (2019). A case for why both sides in the "reading wars" debate are wrong—and a proposed solution. Retrieved from www.washingtonpost.com/education/2019/03/27/case-why-both-sides-reading-wars-debate-are-wrong-proposed-solution/.

Suzuki, L. A., Short, E. L., & Lee, C. S. (2011). Racial and ethnic group differences in intelligence in the United States: Multicultural perspectives. In R. J. Sternberg & S. B. Kaufman (Eds.), *The Cambridge handbook of intelligence* (pp. 273–292). Cambridge University Press.

Tarrasch, R. (2018). The effects of mindfulness practice on attentional functions among primary school children. *Journal of Child and Family Studies, 27*(8), 2632–2642.

Thomas, M. S., & Johnson, M. H. (2008). New advances in understanding sensitive periods in brain development. *Current Directions in Psychological Science, 17*(1), 1–5.

Thomas-Sunesson, D., Hakuta, K., & Bialystok, E. (2018). Degree of bilingualism modifies executive control in Hispanic children in the USA. *International Journal of Bilingual Education and Bilingualism, 21*(2), 197–206.

Visser, B. A., Ashton, M. C., & Vernon, P. A. (2006). g and the measurement of Multiple Intelligences: A response to Gardner. *Intelligence, 34*(5), 507–510.

Wang, Q., Leichtman, M. D., & Davies, K. I. (2000). Sharing memories and telling stories: American and Chinese mothers and their 3-year-olds. *Memory, 8*(3), 159–177.

Weber, R. C., Johnson, A., Riccio, C. A., & Liew, J. (2016). Balanced bilingualism and executive functioning in children. *Bilingualism: Language and Cognition, 19*(2), 425–431.

Wechsler, D. (2014). *Wechsler Intelligence Scale for Children.* Bloomington, MN: Pearson.

Willingham, D. T. (2015). *Raising kids who read: What parents and teachers can do.* John Wiley & Sons.

Willoughby, T., Porter, L., Belsito, L., & Yearsley, T. (1999). Use of elaboration strategies by students in grades two, four, and six. *Elementary School Journal, 99*(3), 221–231.

Winner, E. (2017). *Developmental perspectives on metaphor: A special issue of metaphor and symbolic activity.* Psychology Press.

Wraw, C., Deary, I. J., Gale, C. R., & Der, G. (2015). Intelligence in youth and health at age 50. *Intelligence, 53*, 23–32.

Xue, Y., & Meisels, S. J. (2004). Early literacy instruction and learning in kindergarten: Evidence from the early childhood longitudinal study—kindergarten class of 1998–1999. *American Educational Research Journal, 41*(1), 191–229.

Chapter 13

Abdulkadiroğlu, A., Pathak, P. A., Schellenberg, J., & Walters, C. R. (2020). Do parents value school effectiveness? *American Economic Review, 110*(5), 1502–1539.

Adamson, J., Ozenc, C., Baillie, C., & Tchanturia, K. (2019). Self-esteem group: Useful intervention for inpatients with anorexia nervosa? *Brain Sciences, 9*(1), 12.

Adoption Network. (2020). U.S. adoption statistics. Retrieved from https://adoptionnetwork.com/adoption-statistics.

Adoption Network. (2022). U.S. Adoption Statistics. Retrieved from https://adoptionnetwork.com/adoption-statistics.

Allen, J. P., Hauser, S. T., Bell, K. L., & O'Connor, T. G. (1994). Longitudinal assessment of autonomy and relatedness in adolescent-family interactions as predictors of adolescent ego development and self-esteem. *Child Development, 65*(1), 179–194.

Amato, P. R. (2005). The impact of family formation change on the cognitive, social, and emotional well-being of the next generation. *Future of Children, 15*(2), 75–96.

American Academy of Child & Adolescent Psychiatry. (2017). Children and divorce. Retrieved from www.aacap.org/AACAP/Families_and_Youth/Facts_for_Families/FFF-Guide/Children-and-Divorce-001.aspx.

Anderson, J. (2014). The impact of family structure on the health of children: Effects of divorce. *Linacre Quarterly, 81*(4), 378–387.

Anderson, L. R., Hemez, P. F., & Kreider, R. M. (2022). *Living arrangements of children: 2019.* Retrieved from www.census.gov/content/dam/Census/library/publications/2022/demo/p70-174.pdf.

Attar-Schwartz, S., & Fuller-Thomson, E. (2017). Adolescents' closeness to paternal grandmothers in the face of parents' divorce. *Children and Youth Services Review, 77*, 118–126.

Auersperg, F., Vlasak, T., Ponocny, I., & Barth, A. (2019). Long-term effects of parental divorce on mental health—A meta-analysis. *Journal of Psychiatric Research, 119*, 107–115.

Barlett, C., & Coyne, S. M. (2014). A meta-analysis of sex differences in cyber-bullying behavior: The moderating role of age. *Aggressive Behavior, 40*(5), 474–488.

Barnes, S. S. (2019). Here are 8 things that make a good school. Retrieved from https://educationpost.org/here-are-8-things-that-make-a-good-school/.

Blackwell, D. L. (2010). Family structure and children's health in the United States; findings from the National Health Interview Survey, 2001–2007. *Vital and Health Statistics, 10*(246), 1–166.

Blad, E. (2020). Why the Feds still fall short on special education funding. Retrieved from www.edweek.org/ew/articles/2020/01/15/why-the-feds-still-fall-short-on.html.

Boivin, M., & Vitaro, F. (1995). The impact of peer relationships on aggression in childhood: Inhibition through coercion or promotion through peer support. In J. McCord (Ed.), *Coercion and punishment in long-term perspectives* (pp. 183–197). Cambridge University Press.

Boles, R. E., Halbower, A. C., Daniels, S., Gunnarsdottir, T., Whitesell, N., & Johnson, S. L. (2017). Family chaos and child functioning in relation to sleep problems among children at risk for obesity. *Behavioral Sleep Medicine, 15*(2), 114–128.

Bos, H. M., Gartrell, N. K., Van Balen, F., Peyser, H., & Sandfort, T. G. (2008). Children in planned lesbian families: A cross-cultural comparison between the United States and the Netherlands. *American Journal of Orthopsychiatry, 78*(2), 211–219.

Bowlby, J. (1979). The Bowlby-Ainsworth attachment theory. *Behavioral and Brain Sciences, 2*(4), 637–638.

Bramlett, M. D., & Radel, L. (2014). Adverse family experiences among children in nonparental care, 2011–2012. *National Health Statistics Reports, 74*, 1–8.

Brand, J. E., Moore, R., Song, X., & Xie, Y. (2019). Why does parental divorce lower children's educational attainment? A causal mediation analysis. *Sociological Science, 6*, 264–292.

Brendgen, M., Vitaro, F., Bukowski, W. M., Dionne, G., Tremblay, R. E., & Boivin, M. (2013). Can friends protect genetically vulnerable children from depression? *Development and Psychopathology, 25*(2), 277–289.

Brown, J., Cohen, P., Johnson, J. G., & Salzinger, S. (1998). A longitudinal analysis of risk factors for child maltreatment: Findings of a 17-year prospective study of officially recorded and self-reported child abuse and neglect. *Child Abuse & Neglect, 22*(11), 1065–1078.

Brummelman, E., & Sedikides, C. (2020). Raising children with high self-esteem (but not narcissism). *Child Development Perspectives, 14*(2), 83–89.

Brummelman, E., Thomaes, S., & Sedikides, C. (2016). Separating narcissism from self-esteem. *Current Directions in Psychological Science, 25*(1), 8–13.

Brummelman, E., Thomaes, S., Nelemans, S. A., De Castro, B. O., Overbeek, G., & Bushman, B. J. (2015). Origins of narcissism in children. *Proceedings of the National Academy of Sciences, 112*(12), 3659–3662.

Buhrmester, D., & Furman, W. (1987). The development of companionship and intimacy. *Child Development*, 1101–1113.

Burke, J. D., & Loeber, R. (2016). Mechanisms of behavioral and affective treatment outcomes in a cognitive behavioral intervention for boys. *Journal of Abnormal Child Psychology, 44*(1), 179–189.

Calkins, S. D. (2011). Caregiving as coregulation: Psychobiological processes and child functioning. In A. Booth, S. M. McHale, & N. S. Landale (Eds.), *Biosocial foundations of family processes* (pp. 49–59). Springer.

Carra, C., Lavelli, M., & Keller, H. (2014). Differences in practices of body stimulation during the first 3 months:

Ethnotheories and behaviors of Italian mothers and West African immigrant mothers. *Infant Behavior and Development, 37*(1), 5–15.

CBS News. (2019). "Momo challenge" nearly deadly for family, California mother says. Retrieved from https://www.cbsnews.com/news/momo-challenge-nearly-deadly-for-family-california-mother-says/.

Centers for Disease Control and Prevention. (2012). National Health Interview Survey. Retrieved from www.cdc.gov/nchs/nhis/nhis_2012_data_release.htm.

Chen, Y.-C., Fan, E., & Liu, J.-T. (2019). *Understanding the mechanisms of parental divorce effects on child's higher education* (0898–2937). Retrieved from https://www.nber.org/papers/w25886.

Christner, N., Pletti, C., & Paulus, M. (2020). Emotion understanding and the moral self-concept as motivators of prosocial behavior in middle childhood. *Cognitive Development, 55*, 100893.

Cillessen, A. H. (2019). Sociometric status types. In S. Hupp & J. Jewell (Eds.), *The encyclopedia of child and adolescent development*. https://doi.org/10.1002/9781119171492.wecad271.

Cillessen, A. H., & Bukowski, W. M. (2018). Sociometric perspectives. In W. M. Bukowski, B. Laursen, & K. H. Rubin (Eds.), *Handbook of peer interactions, relationships, and groups* (pp. 64–83). The Guilford Press.

Cohn, D., & Passel, J. S. (2018). A record 64 million Americans live in multigenerational households. Retrieved from www.pewresearch.org/fact-tank/2018/04/05/a-record-64-million-americans-live-in-multigenerational-households/.

Coldwell, J., Pike, A., & Dunn, J. (2006). Household chaos—links with parenting and child behaviour. *Journal of Child Psychology and Psychiatry, 47*(11), 1116–1122.

Collins, W. A., & Madsen, S. D. (2019). Parenting during middle childhood. In M. H. Bornstein (Ed.), *Handbook of parenting* (Vol. 1) (pp. 73–101). Taylor & Francis.

Colman, R. A., Hardy, S. A., Albert, M., Raffaelli, M., & Crockett, L. (2006). Early predictors of self-regulation in middle childhood. *Infant and Child Development, 15*(4), 421–437.

Crowl, A., Ahn, S., & Baker, J. (2008). A meta-analysis of developmental outcomes for children of same-sex and heterosexual parents. *Journal of GLBT Family Studies, 4*(3), 385–407.

Deater-Deckard, K., Mullineaux, P. Y., Beekman, C., Petrill, S. A., Schatschneider, C., & Thompson, L. A. (2009). Conduct problems, IQ, and household chaos: A longitudinal multi-informant study. *Journal of Child Psychology and Psychiatry, 50*(10), 1301–1308.

Deković, M., & Janssens, J. M. (1992). Parents' child-rearing style and child's sociometric status. *Developmental Psychology, 28*(5), 925.

DeRosier, M. E. (2004). Building relationships and combating bullying: Effectiveness of a school-based social skills group intervention. *Journal of Clinical Child and Adolescent Psychology, 33*(1), 196–201.

DeRosier, M. E., & Marcus, S. R. (2005). Building friendships and combating bullying: Effectiveness of SS GRIN at one-year follow-up. *Journal of Clinical Child and Adolescent Psychology, 34*(1), 140–150.

Diener, E., & Diener, C. (1995). The wealth of nations revisited: Income and quality of life. *Social Indicators Research, 36*(3), 275–286.

Dishion, T. J., & Tipsord, J. M. (2011). Peer contagion in child and adolescent social and emotional development. *Annual Review of Psychology, 62*, 189–214.

Dishion, T. J., Andrews, D. W., & Crosby, L. (1995). Antisocial boys and their friends in early adolescence: Relationship characteristics, quality, and interactional process. *Child Development, 66*(1), 139–151.

Dishion, T. J., Spracklen, K. M., Andrews, D. W., & Patterson, G. R. (1996). Deviancy training in male adolescent friendships. *Behavior Therapy, 27*(3), 373–390.

Dubow, E. F., Huesmann, L. R., Boxer, P., & Smith, C. (2014). Childhood predictors and age 48 outcomes of self-reports and official records of offending. *Criminal Behaviour and Mental Health, 24*(4), 291–304.

Dumas, J. E., Nissley, J., Nordstrom, A., Smith, E. P., Prinz, R. J., & Levine, D. W. (2005). Home chaos: Sociodemographic, parenting, interactional, and child correlates. *Journal of Clinical Child and Adolescent Psychology, 34*(1), 93–104.

Duncan, G. J., Huston, A. C., & Weisner, T. S. (2007). *Higher ground: New hope for the working poor and their children.* Russell Sage Foundation.

Duncan, G. J., Magnuson, K., & Votruba-Drzal, E. (2015). Children and socioeconomic status. In M. H. Bornstein, T. Leventhal, & R. M. Lerner (Eds.), *Handbook of child psychology and developmental science: Ecological settings and processes* (pp. 534–573). John Wiley & Sons, Inc.

Dunn, J. (2002). The adjustment of children in stepfamilies: Lessons from community studies. *Child and Adolescent Mental Health, 7*(4), 154–161.

Edwards, A. (2014). Dynamics of economic well-being: Poverty 2009–2011 (Household Economic Studies, P70-137). *Washington, DC: US Government Printing Office.* Retrieved from www.census.gov/prod/2014pubs/p70-137.pdf.

Eggleston, C., & Fields, J. (2021). Census Bureau's Household Pulse Survey Shows Significant Increase in Homeschooling Rates in Fall 2020. Retrieved from https://www.census.gov/library/stories/2021/03/homeschooling-on-the-rise-during-covid-19-pandemic.html.

Ellis, B. J., Abrams, L. S., Masten, A. S., Sternberg, R. J., Tottenham, N., & Frankenhuis, W. E. (2020). Hidden talents in harsh environments. *Development and Psychopathology, 1*, 19.

Erdley, C. A., & Day, H. J. (2017). Friendship in childhood and adolescence. In A. Moyer & M. Hojjat (Eds.), *The psychology of friendship* (pp. 3–19). New York: Oxford University Press.

Erikson, E. H. (1994). *Identity and the life cycle.* WW Norton & Company.

Espelage, D. L., Low, S., Polanin, J. R., & Brown, E. C. (2013). The impact of a middle school program to reduce aggression, victimization, and sexual violence. *Journal of Adolescent Health, 53*(2), 180–186.

Family Equality Council. (2017). LGBTQ family fact sheet. Retrieved from www2.census.gov/cac/nac/meetings/2017-11/LGBTQ-families-factsheet.pdf.

Ferdman, R. A. (2017). The death of the American family dinner has been greatly exaggerated. Retrieved from www.washingtonpost.com/news/wonk/wp/2014/12/17/the-death-of-the-american-family-dinner-has-been-greatly-exaggerated/.

Fiese, B. H., & Schwartz, M. (2008). Reclaiming the family table: Mealtimes and child health and wellbeing. *Social Policy Report, 22*(4), 1–20.

Frey, K. S., Nolen, S. B., Edstrom, L. V. S., & Hirschstein, M. K. (2005). Effects of a school-based social–emotional competence program: Linking children's goals, attributions, and behavior. *Journal of Applied Developmental Psychology, 26*(2), 171–200.

Friedman, S. D. (2018). How our careers affect our children. Retrieved from https://hbr.org/2018/11/how-our-careers-affect-our-children.

Furman, W., & Bierman, K. L. (1984). Children's conceptions of friendship: A multimethod study of developmental changes. *Developmental Psychology, 20*(5), 925.

Furman, W., & Robbins, P. (1985). What's the point? Issues in the selection of treatment objectives. In B. H. Schneider, K. H. Rubin, & J. E. Ledingham (Eds.), *Children's peer relations: Issues in assessment and intervention* (pp. 41–54). Springer.

Ganong, L., Coleman, M., Chapman, A., & Jamison, T. (2018). Stepchildren claiming stepparents. *Journal of Family Issues, 39*(6), 1712–1736.

Garcia, S. M., Reese, Z. A., & Tor, A. (2020). Social comparison before, during, and after the competition. In J. Suls, R. L. Collins, & L. Wheeler (Eds.), *Social comparison, judgment, and behavior* (pp. 105–142). Oxford University Press.

Gates, G. J. (2013). LGBT parenting in the United States. Retrieved from https://williamsinstitute.law.ucla.edu/publications/lgbt-parenting-us/.

Gates, G. J. (2015). Marriage and family: LGBT individuals and same-sex couples. *Future of Children 25*(2), 67–87.

Gifford-Smith, M. E., & Brownell, C. A. (2003). Childhood peer relationships: Social acceptance, friendships, and peer networks. *Journal of School Psychology, 41*(4), 235–284.

Giletta, M., Scholte, R. H., Burk, W. J., Engels, R. C., Larsen, J. K., Prinstein, M. J., & Ciairano, S. (2011). Similarity in depressive symptoms in adolescents' friendship dyads: Selection or socialization? *Developmental Psychology, 47*(6), 1804.

Gini, G., Pozzoli, T., & Hymel, S. (2014). Moral disengagement among children and youth: A meta-analytic review of links to aggressive behavior. *Aggressive Behavior, 40*(1), 56–68.

Golombok, S., Perry, B., Burston, A., Murray, C., Mooney-Somers, J., Stevens, M., & Golding, J. (2003). Children with lesbian parents: A community study. *Developmental Psychology, 39*(1), 20.

Golombok, S., Tasker, F., & Murray, C. (1997). Children raised in fatherless families from infancy: Family relationships and the socioemotional development of children of lesbian and single heterosexual mothers. *Journal of Child Psychology and Psychiatry, 38*(7), 783–791.

Greenberg, M. T., & Kusché, C. A. (2006). Building social and emotional competence: The PATHS curriculum. In S. R. Jimerson & M. Furlong (Eds.), *Handbook of school violence and school safety: From research to practice* (pp. 395–412). Lawrence Erlbaum Associates Publishers.

Gresham, F. M., Cook, C. R., Crews, S. D., & Kern, L. (2004). Social skills training for children and youth with emotional and behavioral disorders: Validity considerations and future directions. *Behavioral Disorders, 30*(1), 32–46.

Gürel, Ç., Brummelman, E., Sedikides, C., & Overbeek, G. (2020). Better than my past self: Temporal comparison raises children's pride without triggering superiority goals. *Journal of Experimental Psychology: General, 149*(8), 1554–1566.

Hamilton, L., Cheng, S., & Powell, B. (2007). Adoptive parents, adaptive parents: Evaluating the importance of biological ties for parental investment. *American Sociological Review, 72*(1), 95–116.

Hamilton, S. K., & Hamilton Wilson, J. (2009). Family mealtimes: Worth the effort? *ICAN: Infant, Child, & Adolescent Nutrition, 1*(6), 346–350.

Hart, C. H., Ladd, G. W., & Burleson, B. R. (1990). Children's expectations of the outcomes of social strategies: Relations with sociometric status and maternal disciplinary styles. *Child Development, 61*(1), 127–137.

Harter, S. (2006). Developmental and individual difference perspectives on self-esteem. In D. K. Mroczek & T. D. Little (Eds.), *Handbook of personality development* (pp. 311–334). Lawrence Erlbaum.

Harter, S. (2015). *The construction of the self: Developmental and sociocultural foundations.* Guilford Publications.

Hartup, W. W. (1992). Peer relations in early and middle childhood. In V. B. Van Hasselt & M. Hersen (Eds.), *Handbook of social development* (pp. 257–281). Springer.

Henry, D. A., Votruba-Drzal, E., & Miller, P. (2019). Child development at the intersection of race and SES: An overview. *Advances in Child Development and Behavior, 57*, 1–25.

Holmgren, E., Raaska, H., Elovainio, M., & Lapinleimu, H. (2020). Behavioral and emotional adjustment in adoptees. In G. M. Wrobel, E. Helder, & E. Marr (Eds.), *The Routledge handbook of adoption* (pp. 353–366). Routledge.

Hyde, J. S., & Else-Quest, N. (2012). *Half the human experience* (Vol. 1): Nelson Education.

Jacquet, S. E., & Surra, C. A. (2001). Parental divorce and premarital couples: Commitment and other relationship characteristics. *Journal of Marriage and Family, 63*(3), 627–638.

Jensen, T. M., & Harris, K. M. (2017). Stepfamily relationship quality and stepchildren's depression in adolescence and adulthood. *Emerging Adulthood, 5*(3), 191–203.

Jensen, T. M., & Lippold, M. A. (2018). Patterns of stepfamily relationship quality and adolescents' short-term and long-term adjustment. *Journal of Family Psychology, 32*(8), 1130.

Jensen, T. M., Lippold, M. A., Mills-Koonce, R., & Fosco, G. M. (2018). Stepfamily relationship quality and children's internalizing and externalizing problems. *Family Process, 57*(2), 477–495.

Jeynes, W. H. (2000). The effects of several of the most common family structures on the academic achievement of eighth graders. *Marriage & Family Review, 30*(1–2), 73–97.

Jeynes, W. H. (2006). The impact of parental remarriage on children: A meta-analysis. *Marriage & Family Review, 40*(4), 75–102.

Johns Hopkins Children's Center. (2020). Helping children cope following trauma. Retrieved from www.hopkinsmedicine

.org/johns-hopkins-childrens-center/what-we-treat/specialties/ palliative-care/grief-bereavement/sibling-young-children-support/helping-children-cope-following-trauma.html.

Johns Hopkins Children's Center. (2022). Helping children cope following trauma. Retrieved from www.hopkinsmedicine .org/johns-hopkins-childrens-center/what-we-treat/specialties/ palliative-care/grief-bereavement/sibling-young-children-support/helping-children-cope-following-trauma.html.

Jolliffe, D., & Farrington, D. P. (2011). Is low empathy related to bullying after controlling for individual and social background variables? *Journal of Adolescence, 34*(1), 59–71.

Jónsson, F., H, Njarðvik, U., Ólafsdóttir, G., & Grétarsson, S. (2000). Parental divorce: Long-term effects on mental health, family relations and adult sexual behavior. *Scandinavian Journal of Psychology, 41*(2), 101–105.

Juffer, F., & Van Ijzendoorn, M. H. (2007). Adoptees do not lack self-esteem: A meta-analysis of studies on self-esteem of transracial, international, and domestic adoptees. *Psychological Bulletin, 133*(6), 1067.

Kärnä, A., Voeten, M., Little, T. D., Poskiparta, E., Kaljonen, A., & Salmivalli, C. (2011). A large-scale evaluation of the KiVa antibullying program: Grades 4–6. *Child Development, 82*(1), 311–330.

Kelleher, K. J., McInerny, T. K., Gardner, W. P., Childs, G. E., & Wasserman, R. C. (2000). Increasing identification of psychosocial problems: 1979–1996. *Pediatrics, 105*(6), 1313–1321.

Kemp, G., Smith, M., & Segal, J. (2019). Children and divorce. Retrieved from www.helpguide.org/articles/ parenting-family/children-and-divorce.htm.

King, V. (2006). The antecedents and consequences of adolescents' relationships with stepfathers and nonresident fathers. *Journal of Marriage and Family, 68*(4), 910–928.

Kingery, J. N., Erdley, C. A., & Marshall, K. C. (2011). Peer acceptance and friendship as predictors of early adolescents' adjustment across the middle school transition. *Merrill-Palmer Quarterly, 57*(3), 215–243.

Kingery, J. N., Erdley, C. A., Marshall, K. C., Whitaker, K. G., & Reuter, T. R. (2010). Peer experiences of anxious and socially withdrawn youth: An integrative review of the developmental and clinical literature. *Clinical Child and Family Psychology Review, 13*(1), 91–128.

Klein, A. (2015). No Child Left Behind: An overview. Retrieved from www.edweek.org/ew/section/multimedia/no-child-left-behind-overview-definition-summary.html?s_kwcid=AL!6416!3! 262985296925!b!!g!!&cmp=cpc-goog-ew-dynamic+ads& ccid=dynamic+ads&ccag=nclb+summary+dynamic& cckw=&cccv=dynamic+ad&gclid=EAIaIQobChMI0PG_3_ yT6wIVB77ACh2INAniEAAYASAAEgKWePD_BwE.

Klein, A. (2016). The Every Student Succeeds Act: An ESSA overview. *Education Week.* Retrieved from www.edweek.org/ ew/issues/every-student-succeeds-act/index.html.

Kochanska, G., Aksan, N., Prisco, T. R., & Adams, E. E. (2008). Mother–child and father–child mutually responsive orientation in the first 2 years and children's outcomes at preschool age: Mechanisms of influence. *Child Development, 79*(1), 30–44.

Kok, C. M., Torquati, J., & de Guzman, M. (2019). The family mealtime study: Parent socialization and context during family meals. *Journal of Extension, 57*(3), n3.

Kramer, S. (2019). U.S. has world's highest rate of children living in single-parent households. Retrieved from www .pewresearch.org/fact-tank/2019/12/12/u-s-children-more-likely-than-children-in-other-countries-to-live-with-just-one-parent/.

Kruk, E., & Hall, B. L. (1995). The disengagement of paternal grandparents subsequent to divorce. *Journal of Divorce & Remarriage, 23*(1–2), 131–148.

Kunzman, R., & Gaither, M. (2020). Homeschooling: An updated comprehensive survey of the research. *Other Education, 9*(1), 253–336.

Lereya, S. T., Copeland, W. E., Costello, E. J., & Wolke, D. (2015). Adult mental health consequences of peer bullying and maltreatment in childhood: Two cohorts in two countries. *The Lancet Psychiatry, 2*(6), 524–531.

Li, J., Johnson, S. E., Han, W.-J., Andrews, S., Kendall, G., Strazdins, L., & Dockery, A. (2014). Parents' nonstandard work schedules and child well-being: A critical review of the literature. *Journal of Primary Prevention, 35*(1), 53–73.

Litterbach, E.-K., Campbell, K. J., & Spence, A. C. (2017). Family meals with young children: An online study of family mealtime characteristics, among Australian families with children aged six months to six years. *BMC Public Health, 17*(1), 111.

Livesley, W. J., & Bromley, D. B. (1973). *Person perception in childhood and adolescence.* John Wiley & Sons.

Lucas-Thompson, R. G., Goldberg, W. A., & Prause, J. (2010). Maternal work early in the lives of children and its distal associations with achievement and behavior problems: A meta-analysis. *Psychological Bulletin, 136*(6), 915.

Luo, R., Tamis-LeMonda, C. S., & Song, L. (2013). Chinese parents' goals and practices in early childhood. *Early Childhood Research Quarterly, 28*(4), 843–857.

Maccoby, E. E. (1984). Middle childhood in the context of the family. In W. A. Collins (Ed.), *Development during middle childhood: The years from six to twelve* (pp. 184–239). National Academies Press.

Marsh, S., Dobson, R., & Maddison, R. (2020). The relationship between household chaos and child, parent, and family outcomes: A systematic scoping review. *BMC Public Health, 20,* 1–27.

Martin-Biggers, J., Spaccarotella, K., Berhaupt-Glickstein, A., Hongu, N., Worobey, J., & Byrd-Bredbenner, C. (2014). Come and get it! A discussion of family mealtime literature and factors affecting obesity risk. *Advances in Nutrition, 5*(3), 235–247.

Mayer, S. E. (2010). Revisiting an old question: How much does parental income affect child outcomes? *Focus, 27*(2), 21–26.

Mogro-Wilson, C. (2013). Parenting in Puerto Rican families. *Families in Society, 94*(4), 235–241.

Moore, S. E., Norman, R. E., Suetani, S., Thomas, H. J., Sly, P. D., & Scott, J. G. (2017). Consequences of bullying victimization in childhood and adolescence: A systematic review and meta-analysis. *World Journal of Psychiatry, 7*(1), 60.

National Center for Education Statistics. (2020a). Percentage distribution of private school teachers by stayer, mover, and leaver status for selected teacher and school characteristics in the base year: 1994–95, 2000–01, 2004–05, and 2008–09. Retrieved from https://nces.ed.gov/surveys/sass/tables/ tfs0809_022_cf2n.asp.

National Center for Education Statistics. (2020b). Percentage distribution of publich school teachers by stayer, mover, and leaver status. Retrieved from https://nces.ed.gov/surveys/sass/tables/tfs0809_021_cf1n.asp.

National Institute of Mental Health. (2020). Helping children and adolescents cope with disasters and other traumatic events: What parents, rescue workers, and the community can do. Retrieved from www.nimh.nih.gov/health/publications/helping-children-and-adolescents-cope-with-disasters-and-other-traumatic-events/index.shtml.

National Institute of Mental Health. (2022). Helping children and adolescents cope with disasters and other traumatic events: What parents, rescue workers, and the community can do. Retrieved from www.nimh.nih.gov/health/publications/helping-children-and-adolescents-cope-with-disasters-and-other-traumatic-events/index.shtml.

Nemours Foundation. (2015). Helping your child through a divorce. Retrieved from https://kidshealth.org/en/parents/help-child-divorce.html.

New York State Department of Education. (2015). 100.10 Home Instruction. Retrieved from www.p12.nysed.gov/part100/pages/100_10.html.

Newcomb, A. F., & Bagwell, C. L. (1995). Children's friendship relations: A meta-analytic review. *Psychological Bulletin, 117*(2), 306.

Newcomb, A. F., Bukowski, W. M., & Pattee, L. (1993). Children's peer relations: A meta-analytic review of popular, rejected, neglected, controversial, and average sociometric status. *Psychological Bulletin, 113*(1), 99.

Newport, F. (2018). In U.S., Estimate of LGBT Population Rises to 4.5%. Retrieved from https://news.gallup.com/poll/234863/estimate-lgbt-population-rises.aspx.

Nguyen, D. T., Wright, E. P., Dedding, C., Pham, T. T., & Bunders, J. (2019). Low self-esteem and its association with anxiety, depression, and suicidal ideation in Vietnamese secondary school students: A cross-sectional study. *Frontiers in Psychiatry, 10*, 698.

Nutrition Education Program, Purdue University. (2020). Benefits of family mealtime. Retrieved from https://www.eatgathergo.org/gather/benefits-of-family-mealtime/.

Orth, U. (2018). The family environment in early childhood has a long-term effect on self-esteem: A longitudinal study from birth to age 27 years. *Journal of Personality and Social Psychology, 114*(4), 637.

Orth, U., & Robins, R. W. (2019). Development of self-esteem across the lifespan. In D. P. McAdams, R. L. Shiner, & J. L. Tackett (Eds.), *Handbook of Personality Development* (pp. 328–344). Guilford Press.

Ortiz-Ospina, E., & Roser, M. (2020). Marriages and divorces. Retrieved from https://ourworldindata.org/marriages-and-divorces.

Parcel, T. L. (2015). Parental employment in the United States. In C.L. Shehan (Ed.), *Encyclopedia of Family Studies*. https://doi.org/10.1002/9781119085621.wbefs103.

Parcel, T. L., & Menaghan, E. G. (1994). Early parental work, family social capital, and early childhood outcomes. *American Journal of Sociology, 99*(4), 972–1009.

Parcel, T. L., & Menaghan, E. G. (1994). *Parents' jobs and children's lives*. Transaction Publishers.

Park, S. S., Wiemers, E. E., & Seltzer, J. A. (2019). The family safety net of Black and White multigenerational families. *Population and Development Review, 45*(2), 351–378.

Parker, J. G., & Asher, S. R. (1993). Friendship and friendship quality in middle childhood: Links with peer group acceptance and feelings of loneliness and social dissatisfaction. *Developmental Psychology, 29*(4), 611.

Parmar, P., Harkness, S., & Super, C. M. (2008). Teacher or playmate? Asian immigrant and Euro-American parents' participation in their young children's daily activities. *Social Behavior and Personality: An International Journal, 36*(2), 163–176.

Pasley, K., & Garneau, C. (2012). Remarriage and stepfamily life. In F. Walsh (Ed.), *Normal family processes: Growing diversity and complexity* (pp. 149–171). The Guilford Press.

Patterson, G., Stoolmiller, M., & Johnson, K. (2005). Deviancy training and association with deviant peers in young children: Occurrence and contribution to early-onset conduct problems. *Development and Psychopathology, 17*, 397–413.

Pawelski, J. G., Perrin, E. C., Foy, J. M., Allen, C. E., Crawford, J. E., Del Monte, M., . . . Springer, S. (2006). The effects of marriage, civil union, and domestic partnership laws on the health and well-being of children. *Pediatrics, 118*(1), 349–364.

Pepler, D. J., & Bierman, K. L. (2018). *With a little help from my friends: The importance of peer relationships for social-emotional development.* Retrieved from https://www.rwjf.org/en/library/research/2018/11/with-a-little-help-from-my-friends--the-importance-of-peer-relationships-for-social-emotional-development.html.

Pepler, D. J., Craig, W. M., & Roberts, W. L. (1998). Observations of aggressive and nonaggressive children on the school playground. *Merrill-Palmer Quarterly, 44*(1), 55–76.

Pett, M. A., Lang, N., & Gander, A. (1992). Late-life divorce: Its impact on family rituals. *Journal of Family Issues, 13*(4), 526–552.

Pew Research Center. (2015). The American family today. Retrieved from www.pewsocialtrends.org/2015/12/17/1-the-american-family-today/.

Pew Research Center. (2019). U.S. has world's highest rate of children living in single-parent households. Retrieved from www.pewresearch.org/fact-tank/2019/12/12/u-s-children-more-likely-than-children-in-other-countries-to-live-with-just-one-parent/.

Pong, S. l., Dronkers, J., & Hampden-Thompson, G. (2003). Family policies and children's school achievement in single-versus two-parent families. *Journal of Marriage and Family, 65*(3), 681–699.

Poorthuis, A. M., Slagt, M., van Aken, M. A., Denissen, J. J., & Thomaes, S. (2019). Narcissism and popularity among peers: A cross-transition longitudinal study. *Self and Identity, 20*(2), 1–15.

Prevoo, M. J., & Tamis-LeMonda, C. S. (2017). Parenting and globalization in western countries: Explaining differences in parent–child interactions. *Current Opinion in Psychology, 15*, 33–39.

Prothero, A. (2016). Why most parents home school: Safety, drugs, and peer pressure, study finds. Retrieved from http://blogs.edweek.org/edweek/charterschoice/2016/11/why_most_parents_home_school_report.html.

Prothero, A. (2018a). Diversity in charter schools: Another look at the data and the debate. Retrieved from https://blogs.edweek.org/edweek/charterschoice/2017/12/diversity_in_charter_schools_another_look_at_the_data_and_the_debate.html.

Prothero, A. (2018b). Homeschooling: Requirements, research, and who does it. Retrieved from www.edweek.org/ew/issues/home-schooling/index.html.

Prothero, A. (2018c). What are charter schools? Retrieved from www.edweek.org/ew/issues/charter-schools/.

Putnick, D. L., Hahn, C. S., Hendricks, C., Suwalsky, J. T., & Bornstein, M. H. (2020). Child, mother, father, and teacher beliefs about child academic competence: Predicting math and reading performance in European American adolescents. *Journal of Research on Adolescence, 30*, 298–314.

Ray, B. (2015). African American homeschool parents' motivations for homeschooling and their Black children's academic achievement. *Journal of School Choice, 9*(1), 71–96.

Riggs, N. R., Greenberg, M. T., Kusché, C. A., & Pentz, M. A. (2006). The mediational role of neurocognition in the behavioral outcomes of a social-emotional prevention program in elementary school students: Effects of the PATHS curriculum. *Prevention Science, 7*(1), 91–102.

Riser-Kositsky, M. (2020). Education statistics: Facts about American schools. Retrieved from www.edweek.org/ew/issues/education-statistics/index.html.

Riser-Kositsky, M. (2021). Education statistics: Facts about American schools. Retrieved from https://www.edweek.org/ew/issues/education-statistics/index.html.

Robins, R. W., Trzesniewski, K. H., Tracy, J. L., Gosling, S. D., & Potter, J. (2002). Global self-esteem across the life span. *Psychology and aging, 17*(3), 423.

Rose, A. J. (2002). Co-rumination in the friendships of girls and boys. *Child Development, 73*(6), 1830–1843.

Rose, A. J., & Rudolph, K. D. (2006). A review of sex differences in peer relationship processes: Potential trade-offs for the emotional and behavioral development of girls and boys. *Psychological Bulletin, 132*(1), 98.

Rubin, K. H., Bukowski, W. M., & Bowker, J. C. (2015). Children in peer groups. In M. H. Bornstein, T. Leventhal, & R. M. Lerner (Eds.), *Handbook of child psychology and developmental science* (pp. 175–222). John Wiley & Sons, Inc.

Rudolph, K. D., Ladd, G., & Dinella, L. (2007). Gender differences in the interpersonal consequences of early-onset depressive symptoms. *Merrill-Palmer Quarterly, 53*(3), 461–488.

Salavera, C., Usán, P., & Teruel, P. (2020). The mediating role of positive and negative affects in the relationship between self-esteem and happiness. *Psychology Research and Behavior Management, 13*, 355.

Salmivalli, C., & Poskiparta, E. (2012). KiVa antibullying program: Overview of evaluation studies based on a randomized controlled trial and national rollout in Finland. *International Journal of Conflict and Violence (IJCV), 6*(2), 293–301.

Samuels, C. (2018). Special education enrollment on upwards trend in charter schools. Retrieved from https://blogs.edweek.org/edweek/speced/2018/02/special_education_enrollment_up_in_charter_schools.html.

Sands, A., Thompson, E. J., & Gaysina, D. (2017). Long-term influences of parental divorce on offspring affective disorders: A systematic review and meta-analysis. *Journal of Affective Disorders, 218*, 105–114.

Schneider, J. (2017). *Beyond test scores: A new way of measuring school quality.* Cambridge, MA: Harvard University Press.

Sharma, A. R., McGue, M. K., & Benson, P. L. (1996). The emotional and behavioral adjustment of United States adopted adolescents: Part I. An overview. *Children and Youth Services Review, 18*(1–2), 83–100.

Smith, P. K. (2016). Bullying: Definition, types, causes, consequences and intervention. *Social and Personality Psychology Compass, 10*(9), 519–532.

Sowislo, J. F., & Orth, U. (2013). Does low self-esteem predict depression and anxiety? A meta-analysis of longitudinal studies. *Psychological Bulletin, 139*(1), 213.

Stepfamily Foundation. (2020). Stepfamily statistics. Retrieved from www.stepfamily.org/stepfamily-statistics.html.

Sullivan, R. M., Cozza, S. J., & Dougherty, J. G. (2019). Children of military families. *Child and Adolescent Psychiatric Clinics, 28*(3), 337–348.

Sun, M., Xue, Z., Zhang, W., Guo, R., Hu, A., Li, Y., . . . Chen, X. (2017). Psychotic-like experiences, trauma and related risk factors among "left-behind" children in China. *Schizophrenia Research, 181*, 43–48.

Takizawa, R., Maughan, B., & Arseneault, L. (2014). Adult health outcomes of childhood bullying victimization: Evidence from a five-decade longitudinal British birth cohort. *American Journal of Psychiatry, 171*(7), 777–784.

Tamis-LeMonda, C. S., Way, N., Hughes, D., Yoshikawa, H., Kalman, R. K., & Niwa, E. Y. (2008). Parents' goals for children: The dynamic coexistence of individualism and collectivism in cultures and individuals. *Social Development, 17*(1), 183–209.

Tang, B., Deng, Q., Glik, D., Dong, J., & Zhang, L. (2017). A meta-analysis of risk factors for post-traumatic stress disorder (PTSD) in adults and children after earthquakes. *International Journal of Environmental Research and Public Health, 14*(12), 1537.

Thomaes, S., & Brummelman, E. (2016). Narcissism. In D. Cicchetti (Ed.), *Developmental psychopathology: Maladaptation and psychopathology* (pp. 679–725). John Wiley & Sons, Inc.

Twenge, J. M., & Campbell, W. K. (2001). Age and birth cohort differences in self-esteem: A cross-temporal meta-analysis. *Personality and Social Psychology Review, 5*(4), 321–344.

U.S. Bureau of Labor Statistics. (2021). Employment characteristics of families summary. Retrieved from www.bls.gov/news.release/famee.nr0.htm.

U.S. Department of Education. (2018). Characteristics of private schools in the United States: Results from the 2015–2016 private school universe survey. Retrieved from https://nces.ed.gov/pubs2017/2017073.pdf.

U.S. Department of Health and Human Services. (2020). Facts about bullying. Retrieved from www.stopbullying.gov/resources/facts.

Ulset, V. S., Czajkowski, N. O., Kraft, B., Kraft, P., Wikenius, E., Kleppestø, T. H., & Bekkhus, M. (2019). Are unpopular children more likely to get sick? Longitudinal links between popularity and infectious diseases in early childhood. *PloS One, 14*(9), e0222222.

United States Census Bureau. (2020a). Families and households. Retrieved from www.census.gov/topics/families/families-and-households.html.

United States Census Bureau. (2020b). U.S. marriage and divorce rates by state. Retrieved from www.census.gov/library/visualizations/interactive/marriage-divorce-rates-by-state.html.

van der Wilt, F., van der Veen, C., van Kruistum, C., & van Oers, B. (2018). Popular, rejected, neglected, controversial, or average: Do young children of different sociometric groups differ in their level of oral communicative competence? *Social Development, 27*(4), 793–807.

Vandell, D. L., & Hembree, S. E. (1994). Peer social status and friendship: Independent contributors to children's social and academic adjustment. *Merrill-Palmer Quarterly, 40*(4), 461–477.

Wainright, J. L., & Patterson, C. J. (2006). Delinquency, victimization, and substance use among adolescents with female same-sex parents. *Journal of Family Psychology, 20*(3), 526.

Wainright, J. L., & Patterson, C. J. (2008). Peer relations among adolescents with female same-sex parents. *Developmental Psychology, 44*(1), 117.

Wainright, J. L., Russell, S. T., & Patterson, C. J. (2004). Psychosocial adjustment, school outcomes, and romantic relationships of adolescents with same-sex parents. *Child Development, 75*(6), 1886–1898.

Wallerstein, J. S., & Lewis, J. M. (2004). The unexpected legacy of divorce: Report of a 25-year study. *Psychoanalytic Psychology, 21*(3), 353.

Yaman, A., Mesman, J., van IJzendoorn, M. H., Bakermans-Kranenburg, M. J., & Linting, M. (2010). Parenting in an individualistic culture with a collectivistic cultural background: The case of Turkish immigrant families with toddlers in the Netherlands. *Journal of Child and Family Studies, 19*(5), 617–628.

Zimmer-Gembeck, M. J., & Skinner, E. A. (2011). The development of coping across childhood and adolescence: An integrative review and critique of research. *International Journal of Behavioral Development, 35*(1), 1–17.

Chapter 14

Adolescent Sleep Working Group. (2014). School start times for adolescents. *Pediatrics, 134*(3), 642–649.

Ali, S., Mouton, C. P., Jabeen, S., Ofoemezie, E. K., Bailey, R. K., Shahid, M., & Zeng, Q. (2011). Early detection of illicit drug use in teenagers. *Innovations in Clinical Neuroscience, 8*(12), 24.

Allen, B., & Miller, C. F. (2019). Physical development in girls: What to expect during puberty. Retrieved from www.healthychildren.org/English/ages-stages/gradeschool/puberty/Pages/Physical-Development-Girls-What-to-Expect.aspx.

Allen, B., & Waterman, H. (2019). Stages of adolescence. Retrieved from www.healthychildren.org/English/ages-stages/teen/Pages/Stages-of-Adolescence.aspx.

American Academy of Child & Adolescent Psychiatry. (2016). Teen brain: Behavior, Problem solving, and decision making. Retrieved from www.aacap.org/AACAP/Families_and_Youth/Facts_for_Families/FFF-Guide/The-Teen-Brain-Behavior-Problem-Solving-and-Decision-Making-095.aspx.

American Academy of Child & Adolescent Psychiatry. (2018). Suicide in children and teens. Retrieved from www.aacap.org/AACAP/Families_and_Youth/Facts_for_Families/FFF-Guide/Teen-Suicide-010.aspx.

American Academy of Child & Adolescent Psychiatry. (2019). Marijuana and teens. Retrieved from www.aacap.org/AACAP/Families_and_Youth/Facts_for_Families/FFF-Guide/Marijuana-and-Teens-106.aspx.

American Academy of Pediatrics. (2009). When teens use drugs: Taking action. Retrieved from www.healthychildren.org/English/ages-stages/teen/substance-abuse/Pages/When-Teens-Use-Drugs-Taking-Action.aspx.

American Academy of Pediatrics. (2015a). Delayed puberty in boys. Retrieved from www.healthychildren.org/English/ages-stages/gradeschool/puberty/Pages/Delayed-Puberty.aspx.

American Academy of Pediatrics. (2015b). Delayed puberty in girls. Retrieved from www.healthychildren.org/English/ages-stages/gradeschool/puberty/Pages/Delayed-Puberty-in-Girls-Information-for-Parents.aspx.

American Academy of Pediatrics. (2015c). Physical development in boys: What to expect. Retrieved from www.healthychildren.org/English/ages-stages/gradeschool/puberty/Pages/Physical-Development-Boys-What-to-Expect.aspx.

American Academy of Pediatrics. (2018). Adolescent depression: What parents can do to help. Retrieved from www.healthychildren.org/English/health-issues/conditions/emotional-problems/Pages/Childhood-Depression-What-Parents-Can-Do-To-Help.aspx.

American Psychiatric Association. (2021). What are eating disorders. Retrieved from www.psychiatry.org/patients-families/eating-disorders/what-are-eating-disorders.

Amitai, M., & Apter, A. (2012). Social aspects of suicidal behavior and prevention in early life: A review. *International Journal of Environmental Research and Public Health, 9*(3), 985–994.

AP-NORC Center. (2021). Instagram and Snapchat are Most Popular Social Networks for Teens; Black Teens are Most Active on Social Media, Messaging Apps. Retrieved from https://apnorc.org/projects/instagram-and-snapchat-are-most-popular-social-networks-for-teens-black-teens-are-most-active-on-social-media-messaging-apps/.

Apter, A., & Wasserman, D. (2003). Adolescent attempted suicide. In R. A. King & A. Apter (Eds.), *Suicide in children and adolescents* (pp. 63–86). Cambridge University Press.

Arain, M., Haque, M., Johal, L., Mathur, P., Nel, W., Rais, A., . . . Sharma, S. (2013). Maturation of the adolescent brain. *Neuropsychiatric Disease and Treatment, 9*, 449.

Ata, R. N., Ludden, A. B., & Lally, M. M. (2007). The effects of gender and family, friend, and media influences on eating behaviors and body image during adolescence. *Journal of Youth and Adolescence, 36*(8), 1024–1037.

Bagaric, M., Touyz, S., Heriseanu, A., Conti, J., & Hay, P. (2020). Are bulimia nervosa and binge eating disorder increasing? Results of a population-based study of lifetime prevalence and lifetime prevalence by age in South Australia. *European Eating Disorders Review, 28*(3), 260–268.

Bailey, J. A., Epstein, M., Roscoe, J. N., Oesterle, S., Kosterman, R., & Hill, K. G. (2020). Marijuana legalization and youth marijuana, alcohol, and cigarette use and norms. *American Journal of Preventive Medicine, 59*(3), 309–316.

Baingana, F. K., Alem, A., & Jenkins, R. (2006). Mental health and the abuse of alcohol and controlled substances. In D. T. Jamison, R. G. Feachem, M. W. Makgoba, E. R. Bos, F. K. Baingana, K. J Hofman, & K. O. Rogo (Eds.), *Disease and mortality in Sub-Sahara Africa*, 2nd ed. (pp. 329–350). Washington (DC): The International Bank for Reconstruction and Development/The World Bank.

Belsky, J. (2012). The development of human reproductive strategies: Progress and prospects. *Current Directions in Psychological Science, 21*(5), 310–316.

Belsky, J., & Shalev, I. (2016). Contextual adversity, telomere erosion, pubertal development, and health: Two models of accelerated aging, or one? *Development and Psychopathology, 28*(4), 1367–1383.

Berger, A. T., Widome, R., & Troxel, W. M. (2019). Delayed school start times and adolescent health. In M. A. Grandner (Ed.), *Sleep and health* (pp. 447–454). Elsevier.

Berman, S. M., Brown, K., Dittus, P., Ferdon, C. D., Gavin, L. E., Harrier, S., . . . Markowitz, L. (2009). Sexual and reproductive health of persons aged 10–24 years—United States, 2002–2007. Surveillance Summaries. *Morbidity and Mortality Weekly Report 58*(No. SS-6).

Bilsen, J. (2018). Suicide and youth: Risk factors. *Frontiers in Psychiatry, 9*, 540.

Biro, F. M., Pajak, A., Wolff, M. S., Pinney, S. M., Windham, G. C., Galvez, M. P., . . . Teitelbaum, S. L. (2018). Age of menarche in a longitudinal U.S. cohort. *Journal of Pediatric and Adolescent Gynecology, 31*(4), 339–345.

Boers, E., Afzali, M. H., Newton, N., & Conrod, P. (2019). Association of screen time and depression in adolescence. *JAMA Pediatrics, 173*(9), 853–859.

Bridge, J. A., Goldstein, T. R., & Brent, D. A. (2006). Adolescent suicide and suicidal behavior. *Journal of Child Psychology and Psychiatry, 47*(3–4), 372–394.

Casey, B. J., Getz, S., & Galvan, A. (2008). The adolescent brain. *Developmental Review, 28*(1), 62–77.

Cash, T. F., & Smolak, L. (2011). *Body image: A handbook of science, practice, and prevention.* Guilford Press.

Centers for Disease Control and Prevention. (2017). Strengthen physical education in schools. Retrieved from https://www .cdc.gov/healthyschools/physicalactivity/pdf/pe_data_brief_ cdc_logo_final_191106.pdf.

Centers for Disease Control and Prevention. (2019a). Childhood obesity facts. Retrieved from www.cdc.gov/obesity/data/ childhood.html.

Centers for Disease Control and Prevention. (2019b). Heatlh Survey: Table 20. Use of selected substances in the past month among persons aged 12 years and over, by age, sex, race, and Hispanic origin: United States, selected years 2002–2017. Retrieved from www.cdc.gov/nchs/data/hus/2018/020.pdf.

Centers for Disease Control and Prevention. (2019c). Summary health statistics: National Health Interview Survey, 2018.

Retrieved from https://ftp.cdc.gov/pub/Health_Statistics/ NCHS/NHIS/SHS/2018_SHS_Table_C-5.pdf.

Centers for Disease Control and Prevention, National Center for Health Statistics. (2021). 1999–2020 Wide Ranging Online Data for Epidemiological Research (WONDER), Multiple Cause of Death files [Data file]. Retrieved from http://wonder. cdc.gov/ucd-icd10.html.

Chen, Y. C., Fan, H. Y., Yang, C., & Lee, Y. L. (2020). Early pubertal maturation and risk of childhood asthma: A mendelian randomization and longitudinal study. *Allergy, 75*(4), 892–900.

Choudhury, S. (2010). Culturing the adolescent brain: What can neuroscience learn from anthropology? *Social Cognitive and Affective Neuroscience, 5*(2–3), 159–167.

Choudhury, S., Blakemore, S.-J., & Charman, T. (2006). Social cognitive development during adolescence. *Social Cognitive and Affective Neuroscience, 1*(3), 165–174.

Clerici, C. A., Veneroni, L., Bisogno, G., Trapuzzano, A., & Ferrari, A. (2012). Videos on rhabdomyosarcoma on YouTube: An example of the availability of information on pediatric tumors on the web. *Journal of Pediatric Hematology/Oncology, 34*(8), e329–e331.

Corkins, M. R., Daniels, S. R., de Ferranti, S. D., Golden, N. H., Kim, J. H., Magge, S. N., & Schwarzenberg, S. J. (2016). Nutrition in children and adolescents. *Medical Clinics, 100*(6), 1217–1235.

Crockett, L. J., Bingham, C. R., Chopak, J. S., & Vicary, J. R. (1996). Timing of first sexual intercourse: The role of social control, social learning, and problem behavior. *Journal of Youth and Adolescence, 25*(1), 89–111.

Curcio, G., Ferrara, M., & De Gennaro, L. (2006). Sleep loss, learning capacity and academic performance. *Sleep Medicine Reviews, 10*(5), 323–337.

Das, J. K., Salam, R. A., Arshad, A., Finkelstein, Y., & Bhutta, Z. A. (2016). Interventions for adolescent substance abuse: An overview of systematic reviews. *Journal of Adolescent Health, 59*(4), S61–S75.

Das, J. K., Salam, R. A., Thornburg, K. L., Prentice, A. M., Campisi, S., Lassi, Z. S., . . . Bhutta, Z. A. (2017). Nutrition in adolescents: Physiology, metabolism, and nutritional needs. *Annals of the New York Academy of Sciences, 1393*(1), 21–33.

de Zambotti, M., Goldstone, A., Colrain, I. M., & Baker, F. C. (2018). Insomnia disorder in adolescence: Diagnosis, impact, and treatment. *Sleep Medicine Reviews, 39*, 12–24.

DeJong, C. S., van Lenthe, F. J., van der Horst, K., & Oenema, A. (2009). Environmental and cognitive correlates of adolescent breakfast consumption. *Preventive Medicine, 48*(4), 372–377.

Dietary Guidelines Advisory Committee. (2020). *Scientific report of the 2020 Dietary Guidelines Advisory Committee: Advisory report to the Secretary of Agriculture and the Secretary of Health and Human Services.* Retrieved from Washington, DC: www.dietaryguidelines.gov/sites/default/files/2020-07/ ScientificReport_of_the_2020DietaryGuidelinesAdvisory Committee_first-print.pdf.

Dubas, J. S., Graber, J. A., & Petersen, A. C. (1991). The effects of pubertal development on achievement during adolescence. *American Journal of Education, 99*(4), 444–460.

Dunn, V., & Goodyer, I. M. (2006). Longitudinal investigation into childhood- and adolescence-onset depression: Psychiatric outcome in early adulthood. *The British Journal of Psychiatry, 188*(3), 216–222.

Edney, S., Bogomolova, S., Ryan, J., Olds, T., Sanders, I., & Maher, C. (2018). Creating engaging health promotion campaigns on social media: Observations and lessons from Fitbit and Garmin. *Journal of Medical Internet Research, 20*(12), e10911.

Ellis, B. J., Del Giudice, M., Dishion, T. J., Figueredo, A. J., Gray, P., Griskevicius, V., . . . Volk, A. A. (2012). The evolutionary basis of risky adolescent behavior: Implications for science, policy, and practice. *Developmental Psychology, 48*(3), 598.

Endocrine Society. (2020). Your health and hormones. Retrieved from www.hormone.org/your-health-and-hormones.

Esser, M. B., Guy Jr, G. P., Zhang, K., & Brewer, R. D. (2019). Binge drinking and prescription opioid misuse in the U.S., 2012–2014. *American Journal of Preventive Medicine, 57*(2), 197–208.

Fan, H.-Y., Lee, Y. L., Hsieh, R.-H., Yang, C., & Chen, Y.-C. (2020). Body mass index growth trajectories, early pubertal maturation, and short stature. *Pediatric Research, 88*(1), 117–124.

Farah, M. J. (2017). The neuroscience of socioeconomic status: Correlates, causes, and consequences. *Neuron, 96*(1), 56–71.

Fichter, M. M., Quadflieg, N., Crosby, R. D., & Koch, S. (2017). Long-term outcome of anorexia nervosa: Results from a large clinical longitudinal study. *International Journal of Eating Disorders, 50*(9), 1018–1030.

Foulkes, L., & Blakemore, S.-J. (2018). Studying individual differences in human adolescent brain development. *Nature Neuroscience, 21*(3), 315–323.

Frazee, G., & Morales, P. G. (2020). Suicide among teens and young adults reaches highest level since 2000. Retrieved from www.pbs.org/newshour/nation/suicide-among-teens-and-young-adults-reaches-highest-level-since-2000.

Fredrickson, B. L., & Roberts, T. A. (1997). Objectification theory: Toward understanding women's lived experiences and mental health risks. *Psychology of Women Quarterly, 21*(2), 173–206.

Gaither, J. R., Shabanova, V., & Leventhal, J. M. (2018). U.S. national trends in pediatric deaths from prescription and illicit opioids, 1999–2016. *JAMA Network Open, 1*(8), e186558–e186558.

Ganesan, S., Ravishankar, S., & Ramalingam, S. (2018). Are body image issues affecting our adolescents? A cross-sectional study among college going adolescent girls. *Indian Journal of Community Medicine: Official Publication of Indian Association of Preventive & Social Medicine, 43*(Suppl 1), S42.

Ge, X., & Natsuaki, M. N. (2009). In search of explanations for early pubertal timing effects on developmental psychopathology. *Current Directions in Psychological Science, 18*(6), 327–331.

Gluckman, P., & Hanson, M. (2006). Changing times: The evolution of puberty. *Molecular and Cellular Endocrinology, 254*, 26–31.

Gonzalez, R., & Swanson, J. M. (2012). Long-term effects of adolescent-onset and persistent use of cannabis. *Proceedings of the National Academy of Sciences, 109*(40), 15970–15971.

Greenwood, S., Perrin, A., & Duggan, M. (2016). Social media update 2016. *Pew Research Center, 11*(2), 1–18.

Guidry, J. P., Jin, Y., Orr, C. A., Messner, M., & Meganck, S. (2017). Ebola on Instagram and Twitter: How health organizations address the health crisis in their social media engagement. *Public Relations Review, 43*(3), 477–486.

Hackman, D. A., & Farah, M. J. (2009). Socioeconomic status and the developing brain. *Trends in Cognitive Sciences, 13*(2), 65–73.

Hail, L., & Le Grange, D. (2018). Bulimia nervosa in adolescents: Prevalence and treatment challenges. *Adolescent Health, Medicine and Therapeutics, 9*, 11.

Hales, C. M., Carroll, M. D., Fryar, C. D., & Ogden, C. L. (2017). *Prevalence of obesity among adults and youth: United States, 2015–2016.* NCHS data brief, no 288. Hyattsville, MD: National Center for Health Statistics. 2017.

Hamlat, E. J., McCormick, K. C., Young, J. F., & Hankin, B. L. (2020). Early pubertal timing predicts onset and recurrence of depressive episodes in boys and girls. *Journal of Child Psychology and Psychiatry, 61*(11), 1266–1274.

Harvard School of Public Health. (2020). Report: Economic costs of eating disorders. Retrieved from www.hsph.harvard.edu/striped/report-economic-costs-of-eating-disorders/.

Hawkins, J. D., Catalano, R. F., & Miller, J. Y. (1992). Risk and protective factors for alcohol and other drug problems in adolescence and early adulthood: Implications for substance abuse prevention. *Psychological Bulletin, 112*(1), 64.

Hawton, K., & van Heeringen, K. (2009). Suicide. Retrieved from https://pubmed.ncbi.nlm.nih.gov/19376453/.

Hedegaard, H., Curtin, S. C., & Warner, M. (2018). *Suicide rates in the United States continue to increase.* NCHS Data Brief, 309, 1–8.

Heron, M. (2019). Deaths: Leading causes for 2017. National Vital Statistics Reports, Vol. 68, No. 6. National Center for Health Statistics, Hyattsville, MD.

Hoek, H. W. (2016). Review of the worldwide epidemiology of eating disorders. *Current Opinion in Psychiatry, 29*(6), 336–339.

Hogue, A., Henderson, C. E., Becker, S. J., & Knight, D. K. (2018). Evidence base on outpatient behavioral treatments for adolescent substance use, 2014–2017: Outcomes, treatment delivery, and promising horizons. *Journal of Clinical Child & Adolescent Psychology, 47*(4), 499–526.

Hogue, J. V., & Mills, J. S. (2019). The effects of active social media engagement with peers on body image in young women. *Body Image, 28*, 1–5.

Holland, G., & Tiggemann, M. (2016). A systematic review of the impact of the use of social networking sites on body image and disordered eating outcomes. *Body Image, 17*, 100–110.

Holubcikova, J., Kolarcik, P., Geckova, A. M., Reijneveld, S. A., & van Dijk, J. P. (2015). The mediating effect of daily nervousness and irritability on the relationship between soft drink consumption and aggressive behaviour among adolescents. *International Journal of Public Health, 60*(6), 699–706.

Holubcikova, J., Kolarcik, P., Geckova, A. M., van Dijk, J. P., & Reijneveld, S. A. (2016). Lack of parental rule-setting on eating is associated with a wide range of adolescent unhealthy eating behaviour both for boys and girls. *BMC Public Health, 16*(1), 359.

Hunt, A. (2021). Youth e-cigarette use remains serious public health concern amid COVID-19 pandemic. Retrieved from www.cdc.gov/media/releases/2021/p0930-e-cigarette.html.

International Alliance for Responsible Drinking (IARD). (2022). Minimum legal age limits. Retrieved from https://iard.org/science-resources/detail/Minimum-Legal-Age-Limits.

Jacobus, J., & F Tapert, S. (2014). Effects of cannabis on the adolescent brain. *Current Pharmaceutical Design, 20*(13), 2186–2193.

Kawabata, M., Lee, K., Choo, H. C., & Burns, S. F. (2021). Breakfast and exercise improve academic and cognitive performance in adolescents. *Nutrients, 13*(4), 1278.

Keles, B., McCrae, N., & Grealish, A. (2020). A systematic review: the influence of social media on depression, anxiety and psychological distress in adolescents. *International Journal of Adolescence and Youth, 25*(1), 79–93.

Kiernan, K. (2001). The rise of cohabitation and childbearing outside marriage in Western Europe. *International Journal of Law, Policy and the Family, 15*(1), 1–21.

Kohl, H. W., III, & Cook, H. D. (2013). *Educating the student body: Taking physical activity and physical education to school.* National Academies Press.

Korda, H., & Itani, Z. (2013). Harnessing social media for health promotion and behavior change. *Health Promotion Practice, 14*(1), 15–23.

Kuehn, B. M. (2011). Teen marijuana use on the rise. *JAMA, 305*(3), 242–242.

Kumar, B., Robinson, R., & Till, S. (2015). Physical activity and health in adolescence. *Clinical Medicine, 15*(3), 267.

Lam, C. G., Roter, D. L., & Cohen, K. J. (2013). Survey of quality, readability, and social reach of websites on osteosarcoma in adolescents. *Patient Education and Counseling, 90*(1), 82–87.

Lam, T., Shi, H., Ho, L., Stewart, S. M., & Fan, S. (2002). Timing of pubertal maturation and heterosexual behavior among Hong Kong Chinese adolescents. *Archives of Sexual Behavior, 31*(4), 359–366.

Leaf, P. J., Alegria, M., Cohen, P., Goodman, S. H., Horwitz, S. M., Hoven, C. W., . . . Regier, D. A. (1996). Mental health service use in the community and schools: Results from the four-community MECA study. *Journal of the American Academy of Child & Adolescent Psychiatry, 35*(7), 889–897.

Lee, J., & Allen, J. (2021). Gender differences in healthy and unhealthy food consumption and its relationship with depression in young adulthood. *Community Mental Health Journal, 57*(5), 898–909.

Lei, M.-K., Beach, S. R., & Simons, R. L. (2018). Childhood trauma, pubertal timing, and cardiovascular risk in adulthood. *Health Psychology, 37*(7), 613.

Linardon, J. (2018). Rates of abstinence following psychological or behavioral treatments for binge-eating disorder: Meta-analysis. *International Journal of Eating Disorders, 51*(8), 785–797.

Lock, J., & Le Grange, D. (2015). *Treatment manual for anorexia nervosa: A family-based approach.* Guilford Publications.

Lopez-Larson, M. P., Bogorodzki, P., Rogowska, J., McGlade, E., King, J. B., Terry, J., & Yurgelun-Todd, D. (2011). Altered prefrontal and insular cortical thickness in adolescent marijuana users. *Behavioural Brain Research, 220*(1), 164–172.

Manago, A. M., Graham, M. B., Greenfield, P. M., & Salimkhan, G. (2008). Self-presentation and gender on MySpace. *Journal of Applied Developmental Psychology, 29*(6), 446–458.

McCabe, M., & Ricciardelli, L. (2004). A longitudinal study of pubertal timing and extreme body change behaviors among adolescent boys and girls. *Adolescence, 39*(153), 145–166.

McQueeny, T., Schweinsburg, B. C., Schweinsburg, A. D., Jacobus, J., Bava, S., Frank, L. R., & Tapert, S. F. (2009). Altered white matter integrity in adolescent binge drinkers. *Alcoholism: Clinical and Experimental Research, 33*(7), 1278–1285.

Mendle, J., & Ferrero, J. (2012). Detrimental psychological outcomes associated with pubertal timing in adolescent boys. *Developmental Review, 32*(1), 49–66.

Mendle, J., Turkheimer, E., & Emery, R. E. (2007). Detrimental psychological outcomes associated with early pubertal timing in adolescent girls. *Developmental Review, 27*(2), 151–171.

Miller, J. W., Naimi, T. S., Brewer, R. D., & Jones, S. E. (2007). Binge drinking and associated health risk behaviors among high school students. *Pediatrics, 119*(1), 76–85.

Miron, O., Yu, K.-H., Wilf-Miron, R., & Kohane, I. S. (2019). Suicide rates among adolescents and young adults in the United States, 2000–2017. *JAMA, 321*(23), 2362–2364.

Mond, J., Mitchison, D., & Hay, P. (2014). Eating disordered behavior in men: Prevalence, impairment in quality of life, and implications for prevention and health promotion. In L. Cohn & R. Lemberg (Eds.), *Current findings on males with eating disorders* (pp. 195–215). Philadelphia, PA: Routledge.

Montoya, I. D., & McCann, D. J. (2010). Drugs of abuse: Management of intoxication and antidotes. In A. Luch (Ed.), *Molecular, Clinical and Environmental Toxicology* (pp. 519–541). Springer.

Moreno, M. A., Grant, A., Kacvinsky, L., Egan, K. G., & Fleming, M. F. (2012). College students' alcohol displays on Facebook: Intervention considerations. *Journal of American College Health, 60*(5), 388–394.

Moreno, M. A., VanderStoep, A., Parks, M. R., Zimmerman, F. J., Kurth, A., & Christakis, D. A. (2009). Reducing at-risk adolescents' display of risk behavior on a social networking web site: A randomized controlled pilot intervention trial. *Archives of Pediatrics & Adolescent Medicine, 163*(1), 35–41.

Najman, J. M., Hayatbakhsh, M. R., McGee, T. R., Bor, W., O'Callaghan, M. J., & Williams, G. M. (2009). The impact of puberty on aggression/delinquency: Adolescence to young adulthood. *Australian & New Zealand Journal of Criminology, 42*(3), 369–386.

Nash, S. G., McQueen, A., & Bray, J. H. (2005). Pathways to adolescent alcohol use: Family environment, peer influence, and parental expectations. *Journal of Adolescent Health, 37*(1), 19–28.

National Center for Health Statistics. (2019). Drug overdose death rates, 1999–2017. Retrieved from https://www.cdc.gov/nchs/products/databriefs/db329.htm.

National Center for Health Statistics. (2021). Adolescent health. Retrieved from www.cdc.gov/nchs/fastats/adolescent-health.htm.

National Center on Addiction and Substance Abuse at Columbia University. (2011). National survey of American attitudes on substance abuse: Teens and parents. Retrieved from www.casacolumbia.org/templates/publications_reports.aspx.

National Eating Disorders Association. (2018). Risk factors. Retrieved from www.nationaleatingdisorders.org/risk-factors.

National Eating Disorders Association. (2020). What are eating disorders. Retrieved from www.nationaleatingdisorders.org/what-are-eating-disorders.

National Eating Disorders Association. (2021). Warning signs and symptoms. Retrieved from www.nationaleatingdisorders.org/warning-signs-and-symptoms.

National Institute of Mental Health. (2017). Eating disorders. Retrieved from www.nimh.nih.gov/health/statistics/eating-disorders.shtml.

National Institute of Mental Health. (2021). Major depression. Retrieved from www.nimh.nih.gov/health/statistics/major-depression.

National Institute on Drug Abuse. (2019). Monitoring the Future 2019 survey results: Overall findings. Retrieved from www.drugabuse.gov/sites/default/files/nida_mtfinfographic2019_fullgraphic.pdf.

National Institute on Drug Abuse. (2020a). Mind matters—The body's response to nicotine, tobacco, and vaping. Retrieved from https://teens.drugabuse.gov/sites/default/files/NIDA_MindMatters_Nicotine_2020_508.pdf.

National Institute on Drug Abuse. (2020b). The real risks of marijuana. Retrieved from http://headsup.scholastic.com/sites/default/files/NIDA_YR18_INS1_downloadall_508.pdf.

National Sleep Foundation. (2006). Parents of teens: Recognize the signs & symptoms of sleep deprivation and sleep problems. Retrieved from www.sleepfoundation.org/wp-content/uploads/2018/10/teensigns.pdf?x99977.

National Sleep Foundation. (2014). National Sleep Foundation 2014 poll. Retrieved from www.sleepfoundation.org/wp-content/uploads/2018/10/2014-NSF-Sleep-in-America-poll-summary-of-findings-FINAL-Updated-3-26-14-.pdf?x99977.

Neiger, B. L., Thackeray, R., Van Wagenen, S. A., Hanson, C. L., West, J. H., Barnes, M. D., & Fagen, M. C. (2012). Use of social media in health promotion: Purposes, key performance indicators, and evaluation metrics. *Health Promotion Practice, 13*(2), 159–164.

Noble, K. G., Houston, S. M., Brito, N. H., Bartsch, H., Kan, E., Kuperman, J. M., . . . Libiger, O. (2015). Family income, parental education and brain structure in children and adolescents. *Nature Neuroscience, 18*(5), 773–778.

Noble, K. G., Houston, S. M., Kan, E., & Sowell, E. R. (2012). Neural correlates of socioeconomic status in the developing human brain. *Developmental Science, 15*(4), 516–527.

Nordfeldt, S., Hanberger, L., & Berterö, C. (2010). Patient and parent views on a Web 2.0 diabetes portal—The management tool, the generator, and the gatekeeper: Qualitative study. *Journal of Medical Internet Research, 12*(2), e17.

Nottelmann, E. D., Susman, E. J., Blue, J. H., Dorn, L. D., & Inoff, G. E. (1984). Gonadal and adrenal hormone correlates of selfconcept in early adolescence. *Pediatric Research, 18*(4), 98–98.

Pacific Institute for Research Evaluation. (2005). *Drinking in America: Myths, realities, and prevention policy.* Calverton, MD: Pacific Institute for Resarch and Evaluation.

Paeditrics & Child Health. (2004). Dieting: Information for teens. *Paeditrics & Child Health, 9*(7), 495–496. Retrieved from www.ncbi.nlm.nih.gov/pmc/articles/PMC2720872/.

Pan-Canadian Health Inequalities Reporting Initiative. 2021. Inequalities in death by suicide in Canada. Retrieved from https://www.canada.ca/content/dam/phac-aspc/documents/services/publications/science-research/phac-suicide-en.pdf.

Patton, G. C., Coffey, C., Sawyer, S. M., Viner, R. M., Haller, D. M., Bose, K., . . . Mathers, C. D. (2009). Global patterns of mortality in young people: A systematic analysis of population health data. *Lancet, 374*(9693), 881–892.

Peper, J. S., van den Heuvel, M. P., Mandl, R. C., Pol, H. E. H., & van Honk, J. (2011). Sex steroids and connectivity in the human brain: A review of neuroimaging studies. *Psychoneuroendocrinology, 36*(8), 1101–1113.

Perez-Lloret, S., Videla, A. J., Richaudeau, A., Vigo, D., Rossi, M., Cardinali, D. P., & Perez-Chada, D. (2013). A multi-step pathway connecting short sleep duration to daytime somnolence, reduced attention, and poor academic performance: An exploratory cross-sectional study in teenagers. *Journal of Clinical Sleep Medicine, 9*(5), 469–473.

Pinyerd, B., & Zipf, W. B. (2005). Puberty—Timing is everything! *Journal of Pediatric Nursing, 20*(2), 75–82.

Portzky, G., Audenaert, K., & van Heeringen, K. (2005). Suicide among adolescents. *Social Psychiatry and Psychiatric Epidemiology, 40*(11), 922–930.

Rasberry, C. N., Lee, S. M., Robin, L., Laris, B., Russell, L. A., Coyle, K. K., & Nihiser, A. J. (2011). The association between school-based physical activity, including physical education, and academic performance: A systematic review of the literature. *Preventive Medicine, 52*, S10–S20.

Raymo, J. M., Park, H., Xie, Y., & Yeung, W.-j. J. (2015). Marriage and family in East Asia: Continuity and change. *Annual Review of Sociology, 41*, 471–492.

Rideout, V., & Robb, M. (2019). The Common Sense census: Media use by tweens and teens. Retrieved from www.commonsensemedia.org/sites/default/files/uploads/research/2019-census-8-to-18-full-report-updated.pdf.

Rooney, M., Chronis-Tuscano, A., & Yoon, Y. (2012). Substance use in college students with ADHD. *Journal of Attention Disorders, 16*(3), 221–234.

Rudolph, K. D., & Troop-Gordon, W. (2010). Personal-accentuation and contextual-amplification models of pubertal timing: Predicting youth depression. *Development and Psychopathology, 22*(2), 433.

Sagar, R., & Gupta, T. (2018). Psychological aspects of obesity in children and adolescents. *Indian Journal of Pediatrics, 85*(7), 554–559.

Sales, J. M., & Irwin Jr, C. E. (2009). Theories of adolescent risk taking: The biopsychosocial model. In R. J. DiClemente, J. S. Santelli, R. A. Crosby (Eds.), *Adolescent health: Understanding and preventing risk behaviors* (pp. 31–50). John Wiley & Sons.

Sawyer, S. M., Azzopardi, P. S., Wickremarathne, D., & Patton, G. C. (2018). The age of adolescence. *Lancet Child & Adolescent Health, 2*(3), 223–228.

Schillinger, D., Chittamuru, D., & Ramírez, A. S. (2020). From "infodemics" to health promotion: A novel framework for the role of social media in public health. *American Journal of Public Health, 110*(9), 1393–1396.

Schneider, D. (2000). International trends in adolescent nutrition. *Social Science & Medicine, 51*(6), 955–967.

Schulster, M., Bernie, A. M., & Ramasamy, R. (2016). The role of estradiol in male reproductive function. *Asian Journal of Andrology, 18*(3), 435.

Shane, P., Diamond, G. S., Lynn Mensinger, J., Shera, D., & Wintersteen, M. B. (2006). Impact of victimization on substance abuse treatment outcomes for adolescents in outpatient and residential substance abuse treatment. *American Journal on Addictions, 15,* s34–s42.

Shirazi, T. N., & Rosinger, A. Y. (2020). Reproductive Health disparities in the U.S.A: Self-reported race/ethnicity predicts age of menarche and live birth ratios, but not infertility. *Journal of Racial and Ethnic Health Disparities, 8*(1), 33–46.

Simpson, R. (2021). Brain changes—Young adult development project. Retrieved from https://hr.mit.edu/static/worklife/youngadult/brain.html.

Slutske, W. S. (2005). Alcohol use disorders among U.S. college students and their non–college-attending peers. *Archives of General Psychiatry, 62*(3), 321–327.

Song, Y., Ma, J., Wang, H.-J., Wang, Z., Hu, P., Zhang, B., & Agardh, A. (2014). Trends of age at menarche and association with body mass index in Chinese school-aged girls, 1985–2010. *Journal of pe\diatrics, 165*(6), 1172–1177. e1171.

South Carolina Department of Mental Health. (2021). Eating disorder statistics. Retrieved from www.state.sc.us/dmh/anorexia/statistics.htm.

Spirito, A., & Esposito-Smythers, C. (2006). Attempted and completed suicide in adolescence. *Annual Review of Clinical Psychology, 2,* 237–266.

Stellefson, M., Paige, S. R., Chaney, B. H., & Chaney, J. D. (2020). Evolving role of social media in health promotion: Updated responsibilities for health education specialists. *International journal of environmental research and public health, 17*(4), 1153.

Stice, E., Presnell, K., & Bearman, S. K. (2001). Relation of early menarche to depression, eating disorders, substance abuse, and comorbid psychopathology among adolescent girls. *Developmental Psychology, 37*(5), 608.

Story, M., & Stang, J. (2005). Understanding adolescent eating behaviors. *Guidelines for Adolescent Nutrition Services,* 9–19.

Story, M., Neumark-Sztainer, D., & French, S. (2002). Individual and environmental influences on adolescent eating behaviors. *Journal of the American Dietetic Association, 102*(3), S40–S51.

Suicide Prevention Resource Center. (2021). Racial and ethnic disparities. Retrieved from https://sprc.org/scope/racial-ethnic-disparities.

Sykes, S. (2017). Six countries taking steps to tackle super-skinny models Retrieved from www.euronews.com/2017/09/06/counties-fighting-underweight-modelling.

Tamnes, C. K., Herting, M. M., Goddings, A.-L., Meuwese, R., Blakemore, S.-J., Dahl, R. E., . . . Crone, E. A. (2017). Development of the cerebral cortex across adolescence: A multisample study of inter-related longitudinal changes in cortical volume, surface area, and thickness. *Journal of Neuroscience, 37*(12), 3402–3412.

Telzer, E. H., Masten, C. L., Berkman, E. T., Lieberman, M. D., & Fuligni, A. J. (2010). Gaining while giving: An fMRI study of the rewards of family assistance among White and Latino youth. *Social Neuroscience, 5*(5–6), 508–518.

Thapar, A., Collishaw, S., Pine, D. S., & Thapar, A. K. (2012). Depression in adolescence. *Lancet, 379*(9820), 1056–1067.

Thayer, R. E., Hansen, N. S., Prashad, S., Karoly, H. C., Filbey, F. M., Bryan, A. D., & Ewing, S. W. F. (2020). Recent tobacco use has widespread associations with adolescent white matter microstructure. *Addictive Behaviors, 101,* 106152.

U.S. Department of Agriculture and U.S. Department of Health and Human Services. (2020). *Dietary guidelines for Americans 2020–2025.* Retrieved from www.dietaryguidelines.gov/sites/default/files/2020-12/Dietary_Guidelines_for_Americans_2020–2025.pdf.

U.S. Department of Health and Human Services. (2012). *Report to Congress on the prevention and reduction of underage drinking.* Retrieved from https://www.stopalcoholabuse.gov/media/ReportToCongress/2012/report_main/report_to_congress_2012.pdf.

U.S. Department of Health and Human Services. (2016). E-cigarette use among youth and young adults. Retrieved from www.cdc.gov/tobacco/data_statistics/sgr/e-cigarettes/pdfs/2016_sgr_entire_report_508.pdf.

Udry, J. R. (1979). Age at menarche, at first intercourse, and at first pregnancy. *Journal of Biosocial Science, 11*(4), 433–441.

Verzeletti, C., Maes, L., Santinello, M., Baldassari, D., & Vereecken, C. A. (2010). Food-related family lifestyle associated with fruit and vegetable consumption among young adolescents in Belgium Flanders and the Veneto Region of Italy. *Appetite, 54*(2), 394–397.

Voelker, D. K., Reel, J. J., & Greenleaf, C. (2015). Weight status and body image perceptions in adolescents: Current perspectives. *Adolescent Health, Medicine and Therapeutics, 6,* 149.

Voráčová, J., Badura, P., Hamrik, Z., Holubčíková, J., & Sigmund, E. (2018). Unhealthy eating habits and participation in organized leisure-time activities in Czech adolescents. *European Journal of Pediatrics, 177*(10), 1505–1513.

Wheaton, A. G., Olsen, E. O. M., Miller, G. F., & Croft, J. B. (2016). Sleep duration and injury-related risk behaviors among high school students—United States, 2007–2013. *Morbidity and Mortality Weekly Report, 65*(13), 337–341.

Whitehill, J. M., Brockman, L. N., & Moreno, M. A. (2013). "Just talk to me": Communicating with college students about depression disclosures on Facebook. *Journal of Adolescent Health, 52*(1), 122–127.

Wood, C. L., Lane, L. C., & Cheetham, T. (2019). Puberty: Normal physiology (brief overview). *Best Practice & Research Clinical Endocrinology & Metabolism, 33*(3), 101265.

World Health Organization. (2016). Age limits - Alcohol service/sales by country. Retrieved from https://apps.who.int/gho/data/node.main.A1144.

Yard, E., & et al. (2021). *Emergency Department Visits for Suspected Suicide Attempts Among Persons Aged 12–25 Years Before and During the COVID-19 Pandemic — United States, January 2019–May 2021.* Retrieved from https://www.cdc.gov/mmwr/volumes/70/wr/mm7024e1.htm#suggestedcitation.

Yonker, L. M., Zan, S., Scirica, C. V., Jethwani, K., & Kinane, T. B. (2015). "Friending" teens: Systematic review of social media in adolescent and young adult health care. *Journal of Medical Internet Research, 17*(1), e4.

Zhang, L., Qian, H., & Fu, H. (2018). To be thin but not healthy—The body-image dilemma may affect health among female university students in China. *PloS one, 13*(10), e0205282.

Zhu, J., & Chan, Y.-M. (2017). Adult consequences of self-limited delayed puberty. *Pediatrics, 139*(6).

Zipfel, S., Giel, K. E., Bulik, C. M., Hay, P., & Schmidt, U. (2015). Anorexia nervosa: Aetiology, assessment, and treatment. *Lancet Psychiatry, 2*(12), 1099–1111.

Chapter 15

Aalsma, M. C., Lapsley, D. K., & Flannery, D. J. (2006). Personal fables, narcissism, and adolescent adjustment. *Psychology in the Schools, 43*(4), 481–491.

Alberts, A., Elkind, D., & Ginsberg, S. (2007). The personal fable and risk-taking in early adolescence. *Journal of Youth and Adolescence, 36*(1), 71–76.

Al-Raqqad, H. K., Al-Bourini, E. S., Al Talahin, F. M., & Aranki, R. M. E. (2017). The impact of school bullying on students' academic achievement from teachers point of view. *International Education Studies, 10*(6), 44–50.

Amrai, K., Motlagh, S. E., Zalani, H. A., & Parhon, H. (2011). The relationship between academic motivation and academic achievement students. *Procedia-Social and Behavioral Sciences, 15*, 399–402.

Anderman, L. H. (2003). Academic and social perceptions as predictors of change in middle school students' sense of school belonging. *Journal of Experimental Education, 72*(1), 5–22.

Annie E. Casey Foundation. (2019). Teens ages 16 to 19 not in school and not high school graduates in the United States. Retrieved from https://datacenter.kidscount.org/data/map/73-teens-ages-16-to-19-not-in-school-and-not-high-school-graduates?loc=1&loct=2#2/any/false/false/1729/any/381/Orange/.

Aud, S., Fox, M. A., & KewalRamani, A. (2010). Status and trends in the education of racial and ethnic groups.

Ausbildungsmarkt.de. (2021). Ausbildungsstellen Weingarten. Retrieved from www.ausbildungsmarkt.de/suche.html?q=&l=76356&r=30.

Balfanz, R., & Legters, N. (2004). Locating the dropout crisis. Retrieved from https://files.eric.ed.gov/fulltext/ED484525.pdf.

Barber, B. K., & Olsen, J. A. (2004). Assessing the transitions to middle and high school. *Journal of Adolescent Research, 19*(1), 3–30.

Bauer, L., Liu, P., Moss, E., Nunn, R., & Shambaugh, J. (2019). All school and no work becoming the norm for American teens. Retrieved from www.brookings.edu/blog/up-front/2019/07/02/all-school-and-no-work-becoming-the-norm-for-american-teens/.

Baumgartner, S. E., Weeda, W. D., van der Heijden, L. L., & Huizinga, M. (2014). The relationship between media multitasking and executive function in early adolescents. *Journal of Early Adolescence, 34*(8), 1120–1144.

Bee, H. L. (1994). *Lifespan development.* HarperCollins College Publishers.

Billow, R. M. (1975). A cognitive developmental study of metaphor comprehension. *Developmental Psychology, 11*(4), 415.

Blakemore, J. E. O., Berenbaum, S. A., & Liben, L. S. (2009). *Gender development.* Psychology Press.

Boom, J., Wouters, H., & Keller, M. (2007). A cross-cultural validation of stage development: A Rasch re-analysis of longitudinal socio-moral reasoning data. *Cognitive Development, 22*(2), 213–229.

Bureau of Labor Statistics. (2017). TED: The Economics Daily. Retrieved from https://www.bls.gov/opub/ted/2017/69-point-7-percent-of-2016-high-school-graduates-enrolled-in-college-in-october-2016.htm.

Bureau of Labor Statistics. (2020). *College enrollment and work activity of recent high school and college graduates—2019.* Retrieved from www.the74million.org.

Cain, M. S., & Mitroff, S. R. (2011). Distractor filtering in media multitaskers. *Perception, 40*(10), 1183–1192.

Cain, M. S., Leonard, J. A., Gabrieli, J. D., & Finn, A. S. (2016). Media multitasking in adolescence. *Psychonomic Bulletin & Review, 23*(6), 1932–1941.

Carlo, G., Fabes, R. A., Laible, D., & Kupanoff, K. (1999). Early adolescence and prosocial/moral behavior II: The role of social and contextual influences. *Journal of Early Adolescence, 19*(2), 133–147.

Carlo, G., Padilla-Walker, L. M., & Nielson, M. G. (2015). Longitudinal bidirectional relations between adolescents' sympathy and prosocial behavior. *Developmental Psychology, 51*(12), 1771.

Carnoy, M., & Garcia, E. (2017). Five key trends in U.S. student performance: Progress by Blacks and Hispanics, the takeoff of Asians, the stall of non-English speakers, the persistence of socioeconomic gaps, and the damaging effect of highly segregated schools. *Economic Policy Institute.*

Center for Research on Education Outcomes. (2019). Charter school performance in Ohio 2019. Retrieved from http://edex.s3-us-west-2.amazonaws.com/publication/pdfs/OH_state_report_2019_FINAL.pdf.

Centers for Disease Control and Prevention. (2022). COVID-19 vaccination and case trends by age group, United States. Retrieved from https://data.cdc.gov/Vaccinations/COVID-19-Vaccination-and-Case-Trends-by-Age-Group-/gxj9-t96f.

Cheeseman Day, J., & Newburger, E. C. (2002). The big payoff: Educational attainment and synthetic estimates of work-life earnings. Retrieved from www.census.gov/prod/2002pubs/p23-210.pdf.

Chen, W.-L., & Chan, Y.-W. (2020). Can higher education increase students' moral reasoning? The role of student engagement in the U.S. *Journal of Moral Education, 51*(2), 169–185.

Cheung, C. S.-S., & Pomerantz, E. M. (2012). Why does parents' involvement enhance children's achievement? The role of parent-oriented motivation. *Journal of Educational Psychology, 104*(3), 820.

Child Trends Databank. (2020). Key facts about youth employment. Retrieved from www.childtrends.org/indicators/youth-employment.

Claro, S., Paunesku, D., & Dweck, C. S. (2016). Growth mindset tempers the effects of poverty on academic achievement. *Proceedings of the National Academy of Sciences, 113*(31), 8664–8668.

Cohen, A. O., & Casey, B. (2017). The neurobiology of adolescent self-control. In T. Egner (Ed.), *The Wiley handbook of cognitive control* (pp. 457–475). Wiley Blackwell.

Department of Labor. (2021a). Apprenticeship jobs search. Retrieved from www.apprenticeship.gov/finder/listings?occupation=&location=14850.

Department of Labor. (2021b). Industry-recognized apprenticeship programs. Retrieved from www.apprenticeship.gov/?utm_source=dol_gov_agencies_eta_apprenticeship&utm_medium=text&utm_campaign=apprenticeship_homepage.

Department of Labor. (2021c). Jumpstart your career through apprenticeship. Retrieved from www.apprenticeship.gov/career-seekers.

DeSilver, D. (2019). In the U.S., teen summer jobs aren't what they used to be. Pew Research Center, June, 27. Retrieved from www.pewresearch.org/fact-tank/2019/06/27/teen-summer-jobs-in-us/.

Dietz, N., & Grimm, T. J. J. (2018). Where are America's volunteers. Retrieved from https://dogood.umd.edu/research-impact/publications/where-are-americas-volunteers.

Digest of Education Statistics. (2020). Table 326.10. Graduation rate from first institution attended for first-time, full-time bachelor's degree-seeking students at 4-year postsecondary institutions, by race/ethnicity, time to completion, sex, control of institution, and percentage of applications accepted: Selected cohort entry years, 1996 through 2012. Retrieved from https://nces.ed.gov/programs/digest/d19/tables/dt19_326.10.asp.

Duncan, G. J., Magnuson, K., & Votruba-Drzal, E. (2017). Moving beyond correlations in assessing the consequences of poverty. *Annual Review of Psychology, 68*, 413–434.

EducationData.org. (2019a). College dropout rates. Retrieved from https://educationdata.org/college-dropout-rates#when-college-completion-may-not-matter.

EducationData.org. (2019b). High school dropout rate. Retrieved from https://educationdata.org/high-school-dropout-rate.

Eisenberg, N., & Morris, S. (2004). Moral cognitions and prosocial responding in adolescence. In R. M. Lerner and L. Stinberg (Eds.), *Handbook of adolescent psychology* (2nd ed.) (pp. 155–188). Hoboken, New Jersey: John Wiley & Sons, Inc.

Eisenberg, N., & Spinrad, T. L. (2014). Multidimensionality of prosocial behavior: Rethinking the conceptualization and development of prosocial behavior. In L. M. Padilla-Walker & G. Carlo (Eds.), *Prosocial development: A multidimensional approach* (pp. 17–39). Oxford University Press.

Eisenberg, N., Spinrad, T., & Knafo-Noam, A. (2015). Prosocial development In M. E. Lamb and R. M. Lerner (Eds.), *Handbook of child psychology and developmental science, Vol. 3: Socioemotional processes*. Hoboken, New Jersey: Wiley.

Elgersma, C. (2020). Help parents and caregivers keep kids focused, interested, and balanced while learning from home. Retrieved from https://www.commonsense.org/education/articles/parent-tips-and-tricks-for-distance-learning.

Elkind, D. (1961). Quantity conceptions in junior and senior high school students. *Child Development, 32*, 551–560.

Elkind, D. (1967). Egocentrism in adolescence. *Child Development, 38*(4), 1025–1034.

Elkind, D., & Bowen, R. (1979). Imaginary audience behavior in children and adolescents. *Developmental Psychology, 15*(1), 38.

Englund, M. M., Egeland, B., & Collins, W. A. (2008). Exceptions to high school dropout predictions in a low-income sample: Do adults make a difference? *Journal of Social Issues, 64*(1), 77–94.

Fabes, R. A., Carlo, G., Kupanoff, K., & Laible, D. (1999). Early adolescence and prosocial/moral behavior I: The role of individual processes. *Journal of Early Adolescence, 19*(1), 5–16.

Fischhoff, B., de Bruin, W. B., Parker, A. M., Millstein, S. G., & Halpern-Felsher, B. L. (2010). Adolescents' perceived risk of dying. *Journal of Adolescent Health, 46*(3), 265–269.

Fishkin, J., Keniston, K., & McKinnon, C. (1973). Moral reasoning and political ideology. *Journal of Personality and Social Psychology, 27*(1), 109.

Fitzpatrick, B. R., Berends, M., Ferrare, J. J., & Waddington, R. J. (2020). Virtual illusion: Comparing student achievement and teacher and classroom characteristics in online and brick-and-mortar charter schools. *Educational Researcher, 49*(3), 161–175.

Freidhoff, J. R. (2018). *Michigan's K-12 virtual learning effectiveness report 2016–17*. Lansing, MI: Michigan Virtual University. Retrieved from https://mvlri.org/research/effectiveness-report/.

Friedl, A., Pondorfer, A., & Schmidt, U. (2020). Gender differences in social risk taking. *Journal of Economic Psychology, 77*, 102182.

Gardiner, H. W., & Kosmitzki, C. (2008). *Lives across cultures* (4th ed.). Pearson.

Gibbs, J. C., Basinger, K. S., Grime, R. L., & Snarey, J. R. (2007). Moral judgment development across cultures: Revisiting Kohlberg's universality claims. *Developmental Review, 27*(4), 443–500.

Gilligan, C. (1982). *In a different voice: Psychological theory and women's development*. Harvard University Press.

Gray, K., & Graham, J. (2019). *Atlas of moral psychology*. Guilford Publications.

Grimm, R. T., Jr., & Dietz, N. (2018). Good intentions, gap in action: The challenge of translating youth's high interest in doing good into civic engagement. Research brief. Do Good Institute, University of Maryland.

Gryczkowski, M., Jordan, S. S., & Mercer, S. H. (2018). Moderators of the relations between mothers' and fathers' parenting practices and children's prosocial behavior. *Child Psychiatry & Human Development, 49*(3), 409–419.

Haan, N., Smith, M. B., & Block, J. (1968). Moral reasoning of young adults: Political-social behavior, family background, and personality correlates. *Journal of Personality and Social Psychology, 10*(3), 183.

Hardy, S. A., & Carlo, G. (2011). Moral identity: What is it, how does it develop, and is it linked to moral action? *Child Development Perspectives, 5*(3), 212–218.

Hill, J. P., & Lynch, M. E. (1983). The intensification of gender-related role expectations during early adolescence. In J. Brooks-Gunn and A. C. Petersen (Eds.), *Girls at puberty* (pp. 201–228). Springer.

Hill, N. E., & Tyson, D. F. (2009). Parental involvement in middle school: A meta-analytic assessment of the strategies that promote achievement. *Developmental Psychology, 45*(3), 740.

Hirsch, B. J., & Rapkin, B. D. (1987). The transition to junior high school: A longitudinal study of self-esteem, psychological symptomatology, school life, and social support. *Child Development, 58*(5), 1235–1243.

Horn, L., Peter, K., & Rooney, K. (2002). Profile of undergraduates in U.S. postsecondary institutions: 1999–2000. Statistical analysis report. National Postsecondary Student Aid Study.

Hughes, J. N., & Cao, Q. (2018). Trajectories of teacher-student warmth and conflict at the transition to middle school: Effects on academic engagement and achievement. *Journal of School Psychology, 67*, 148–162.

Hurtado, S., Mayhew, M. J., & Engberg, M. E. (2012). Diversity courses and students' moral reasoning: A model of predispositions and change. *Journal of Moral Education, 41*(2), 201–224.

Inhelder, B., & Piaget, J. (1958). The oscillation of a pendulum and the operations of exclusion. In B. Inhelder, J. Piaget & A. Parsons, S. Milgram (Trans.), *The growth of logical thinking: From childhood to adolescence* (pp. 67–79). Basic Books.

Jaffee, S., & Hyde, J. S. (2000). Gender differences in moral orientation: A meta-analysis. *Psychological Bulletin, 126*(5), 703.

Johnson, M. K., Beebe, T., Mortimer, J. T., & Snyder, M. (1998). Volunteerism in adolescence: A process perspective. *Journal of Research on Adolescence, 8*(3), 309–332.

Kim, K. R., & Seo, E. H. (2018). The relationship between teacher efficacy and students' academic achievement: A meta-analysis. *Social Behavior and Personality: An International Journal, 46*(4), 529–540.

Kimani, G. N., Kara, A. M., & Njagi, L. W. (2013). Teacher factors influencing students' academic achievement in secondary schools in Nyandarua County, Kenya. *International Journal of Education and Research, 1*, 1–14.

Knorr, C. (2020). Tips and Scripts for Managing Screen Time When School Is Online. Retrieved from https://www.commonsensemedia.org/blog/tips-and-scripts-for-managing-screen-time-when-school-is-online-0?j=7932191&sfmc_sub=167911793&l=2048712_HTML&u=151350850&mid=6409703&jb=98&utm_source=media_nl_20200812&utm_medium=email.

Kochhar, R., & Fry, R. (2014). Wealth inequality has widened along racial, ethnic lines since end of Great Recession. *Pew Research Center, 12*(104), 121–145.

Kohlberg, L., & Kramer, R. (1969). Continuities and discontinuities in childhood and adult moral development. *Human Development, 12*(2), 93–120.

Krebs, D. L., & Denton, K. (2005). Toward a more pragmatic approach to morality: A critical evaluation of Kohlberg's model. *Psychological Review, 112*(3), 629.

Kuhn, D. (2009). Do students need to be taught how to reason? *Educational Research Review, 4*(1), 1–6.

Kuhn, D. (2011). What is scientific thinking and how does it develop? In U. Goswami (Ed.), *Blackwell handbook of childhood cognitive development* (pp. 371–393). Blackwell Publishing.

Lawson, G. M., & Farah, M. J. (2017). Executive function as a mediator between SES and academic achievement throughout childhood. *International Journal of Behavioral Development, 41*(1), 94–104.

Legislative Division of Post Audit. (2015). Performance audit report—K-12 education: Reviewing virtual schools costs and student performance. Retrieved from www.ksde.org/Portals/0/TLA/Graduation%20and%20School%20Choice/Virtual/Final%20LPA%20Report%20on%20Virtual%20Schools%202015.pdf.

Littman-Ovadia, H., & Steger, M. (2010). Character strengths and well-being among volunteers and employees: Toward an integrative model. *Journal of Positive Psychology, 5*(6), 419–430.

Liu, J., Peng, P., & Luo, L. (2020). The relation between family socioeconomic status and academic achievement in China: A meta-analysis. *Educational Psychology Review, 32*(1), 49–76.

Maftei, A., & Holman, A. (2020). Representation of morality in children: A qualitative approach. *Journal of Moral Education, 49*(2), 194–208.

May, K. E., & Elder, A. D. (2018). Efficient, helpful, or distracting? A literature review of media multitasking in relation to academic performance. *International Journal of Educational Technology in Higher Education, 15*(1), 13.

McElrath, K. (2020). Nearly 93% of households with school-age children report some form of distance learning during COVID-19. Retrieved from www.census.gov/library/stories/2020/08/schooling-during-the-covid-19-pandemic.html.

McNamara, R. A., Willard, A. K., Norenzayan, A., & Henrich, J. (2019). Weighing outcome vs. intent across societies: How cultural models of mind shape moral reasoning. *Cognition, 182*, 95–108.

Melby, J. N., Conger, R. D., Fang, S.-A., Wickrama, K., & Conger, K. J. (2008). Adolescent family experiences and educational attainment during early adulthood. *Developmental Psychology, 44*(6), 1519.

Miron, G., & Urschel, J. L. (2012). Understanding and improving full-time virtual schools: A study of student characteristics, school finance, and school performance in schools operated by K12 Inc.[with Appendices]. National Education Policy Center.

Molnar, A., Miron, G., Elgeberi, N., Barbour, M. K., Huerta, L., Shafer, S. R., & Rice, J. K. (2019). Virtual schools in the U.S. 2019. Retrieved from http://nepc.colorado.edu/publication/virtual-schools-annual-2019.

Moody, J. (2019). How to avoid dropping out of college. Retrieved from www.usnews.com/education/best-colleges/articles/2019-03-20/dropping-out-of-college-why-students-do-so-and-how-to-avoid-it.

Mortimer, J. T. (2010). The benefits and risks of adolescent employment. *Prevention Researcher, 17*(2), 8.

Mullins, E. R., & Irvin, J. L. (2000). Transition into middle school. *Middle School Journal, 31*(3), 57–60.

Murphy, J. M., & Gilligan, C. (1980). Moral development in late adolescence and adulthood: A critique and reconstruction of Kohlberg's theory. *Human Development, 23*(2), 77–104.

Narvaez, D. (2019). Moral development and moral values: Evolutionary and neurobiological influences. In D. P. McAdams, R. L. Shiner, & J. L. Tackett (Eds.), Handbook of personality development (pp. 345–363). The Guilford Press.

National Alliance for Public Charter Schools, 50-State Campaign for Achievement Now, & National Association of Charter School Authorizers. (2016). A call to action to improve the quality of full-time virtual charter public schools. Retrieved from https://www.publiccharters.org/publications/call-action-improve-quality-full-time-virtual-charter-public-schools.

National Center for Education Statistics. (2020a). Distance learning. Retrieved from https://nces.ed.gov/fastfacts/display.asp?id=79.

National Center for Education Statistics. (2020b). Dropout rates. Retrieved from https://nces.ed.gov/fastfacts/display.asp?id=16.

National Center for Education Statistics. (2020c). Educational institutions. Retrieved from https://nces.ed.gov/fastfacts/display.asp?id=84.

National Center for Education Statistics. (2020d). Graduation rates. Retrieved from https://nces.ed.gov/fastfacts/display.asp?id=40.

OECD. (2019). PISA 2018 results: Where all students can suceed (Vol. II). OECD.

Ojose, B. (2008). Applying Piaget's theory of cognitive development to mathematics instruction. *Mathematics Educator, 18*(1), 26–30.

Ophir, E., Nass, C., & Wagner, A. D. (2009). Cognitive control in media multitaskers. *Proceedings of the National Academy of Sciences, 106*(37), 15583–15587.

Parker III, E. T., Barnhardt, C. L., Pascarella, E. T., & McCowin, J. A. (2016). The impact of diversity courses on college students' moral development. *Journal of College Student Development, 57*(4), 395–410.

Phillips, S., & Sandstrom, K. L. (1990). Parental attitudes toward youth work. *Youth & Society, 22*(2), 160–183.

Piaget, J. (1972). Intellectual evolution from adolescence to adulthood. *Human Development, 15*(1), 1–12.

Piaget, J., & Cook, M. (1952). *The origins of intelligence in children* (Vol. 8). New York: International Universities Press.

Pieh, C., Dale, R., Plener, P. L., Humer, E., & Probst, T. (2021). Stress levels in high-school students after a semester of home-schooling. *European Child & Adolescent Psychiatry*, 1–3. https://doi.org/10.1007.

Pomerantz, E. M., & Grolnick, W. S. (2017). The role of parenting in children's motivation and competence: What underlies facilitative parenting? In A. J. Elliot, C. S. Dweck, & D. S. Yeager (Eds.), *Handbook of competence and motivation: Theory and application* (pp. 566–585). The Guilford Press.

Pomerantz, E. M., Kim, E. M., & Cheung, C. S.-S. (2012). Parents' involvement in children's learning. In K. R. Harris, S. Graham, T. Urdan, S. Graham, J. M. Royer, & M. Zeidner (Eds.), *APA educational psychology handbook, Vol. 2. Individual differences and cultural and contextual factors* (pp. 417–440). American Psychological Association.

Qu, Y., & Pomerantz, E. M. (2015). Divergent school trajectories in early adolescence in the United States and China: An examination of underlying mechanisms. *Journal of Youth and Adolescence, 44*(11), 2095–2109.

Quillen, I. (2011). Virtual ed. faces sharp criticism. *Education Week, 31*(13), 1–22.

Quintana, S. M., & Mahgoub, L. (2016). Ethnic and racial disparities in education: Psychology's role in understanding and reducing disparities. *Theory Into Practice, 55*(2), 94–103.

Reardon, S. F., Robinson-Cimpian, J. P., & Weathers, E. S. (2015). Patterns and trends in racial/ethnic and socioeconomic academic achievement gaps. In H. F. Ladd & M. E. Goertz (Eds.), *Handbook of research in education finance and policy* (pp. 497–516). New York: Routledge.

Rest, J. (1979). *Development in judging moral issues.* Minneapolis, MN: University of Minnesota Press.

Roehrig, A. D., Turner, J. E., Arrastia, M. C., Christesen, E., McElhaney, S., & Jakiel, L. M. (2012). Effective teachers and teaching: Characteristics and practices related to positive student outcomes. In K. R. Harris, S. Graham, T. Urdan, S. Graham, J. M. Royer, & M. Zeidner (Eds.), *APA educational psychology handbook, Vol 2: Individual differences and cultural and contextual factors.* (pp. 501–527). American Psychological Association.

Roser, M. and Ortiz-Ospina, E. (2013). Tertiary education. *OurWorldInData.org.* Retrieved from https://ourworldindata.org/tertiary-education.

Rumberger, R., Addis, H., Allensworth, E., Balfanz, R., Bruch, J., Dillon, E., . . . Tuttle, C. (2017). Preventing dropout in secondary schools (NCEE 2017-4028). Retrieved from https://ies.ed.gov/ncee/wwc/Docs/PracticeGuide/wwc_dropout_092617.pdf.

Sarker, M. N. I., Wu, M., & Hossin, M. A. (2019). Economic effect of school dropout in Bangladesh. *International Journal of Information and Education Technology, 9*(2), 136–142.

Schleicher, A. (2019). PISA 2018: Insights and interpretations. Retrieved from https://www.oecd.org/pisa/PISA%202018%20Insights%20and%20Interpretations%20FINAL%20PDF.pdf.

Schmidt, C. D., McAdams, C. R., & Foster, V. (2009). Promoting the moral reasoning of undergraduate business students through a deliberate psychological education-based classroom intervention. *Journal of Moral Education, 38*(3), 315–334.

Schwartz, P. D., Maynard, A. M., & Uzelac, S. M. (2008). Adolescent egocentrism: A contemporary view. *Adolescence, 43*(171), 441–448.

Simmonds, D. J., Hallquist, M. N., & Luna, B. (2017). Protracted development of executive and mnemonic brain systems underlying working memory in adolescence: A longitudinal fMRI study. *Neuroimage, 157*, 695–704.

Skiba, R. J., Michael, R. S., Nardo, A. C., & Peterson, R. L. (2002). The color of discipline: Sources of racial and gender disproportionality in school punishment. *Urban Review, 34*(4), 317–342.

Dunn, J. (2014). Moral development in early childhood and social interaction in the family. In M. Killen & J. G. Smetana (Eds.), *Handbook of moral development* (pp. 135–159). Psychology Press.

Smith, J. (1976). Children's comprehension of metaphor: A Piagetian interpretation. *Language and Speech, 19*(3), 236–243.

Soto, P. J. (2018). *Investigating the extent to which adolescent egocentrism may carry over into adulthood: An exploratory study.* Northcentral University,.

Sparks, S. D. (2017). Study points to fewer 'dropout factory' schools. *Education Week.* Retrieved from https://www.edweek.org/teaching-learning/study-points-to-fewer-dropout-factory-schools/2010/11.

Staff, J., Messersmith, E. E., & Schulenberg, J. E. (2009). Adolescents and the world of work. In R. M. Lerner & L. Steinberg (Eds.), *Handbook of adolescent psychology: Contextual influences on adolescent development* (pp. 270–313). John Wiley & Sons, Inc..

Staff, J., Yetter, A. M., Cundiff, K., Ramirez, N., Vuolo, M., & Mortimer, J. T. (2020). Is adolescent employment still a risk factor for high school dropout? *Journal of Research on Adolescence, 30*(2), 406–422.

Statista. (2020). Anzahl der Schulabsolventen/-abgänger in Deutschland im Abgangsjahr 2019 nach Abschlussart. Retrieved from https://de.statista.com/statistik/daten/studie/235973/umfrage/schulabsolventen-abgaenger-in-deutschland-nach-abschlussart/.

Statista. (2021). Anzahl der Schulabsolventen/-abgänger in Deutschland im Abgangsjahr 2019 nach Abschlussart. Retrieved from https://de.statista.com/statistik/daten/studie/235973/umfrage/schulabsolventen-abgaenger-in-deutschland-nach-abschlussart/.

Statista. (2021). Höhe der durchschnittlichen Lebensverdienste in Deutschland nach Bildungsabschluss. Retrieved from https://de.statista.com/statistik/daten/studie/288922/umfrage/durchschnittliche-lebensverdienste-in-deutschland-nach-bildungsabschluss/.

St-Esprit, M. (2019). The stigma of choosing trade school over college. Retrieved from www.theatlantic.com/education/archive/2019/03/choosing-trade-school-over-college/584275/.

Stoet, G., & Geary, D. C. (2020). Gender differences in the pathways to higher education. *Proceedings of the National Academy of Sciences, 117*(25), 14073–14076.

Strahan, D. (1983). The emergence of formal operations in adolescence. *Transcendence, 11*, 7–14.

Strøm, I. F., Thoresen, S., Wentzel-Larsen, T., & Dyb, G. (2013). Violence, bullying and academic achievement: A study of 15-year-old adolescents and their school environment. *Child Abuse & Neglect, 37*(4), 243–251.

Tamis-LeMonda, C. (2022). Child Development: Context, Culture, and Cascades. Oxford University Press/Sinauer, Sunderland, MA.

Tardif, E., & Valls, M. (2018). Personal fables and rational thinking in adolescence. *Psychoeducational Assessment, Intervention and Rehabilitation, 1*, 25–30.

Tate, E. (2019). Despite poor performance, virtual school enrollment continues to grow. Retrieved from www.edsurge.com/news/2019-05-28-despite-poor-performance-virtual-school-enrollment-continues-to-grow.

Tenenbaum, H. R., & Ruck, M. D. (2007). Are teachers' expectations different for racial minority than for European American students? A meta-analysis. *Journal of Educational Psychology, 99*(2), 253.

Teper, R., Zhong, C. B., & Inzlicht, M. (2015). How emotions shape moral behavior: Some answers (and questions) for the field of moral psychology. *Social and Personality Psychology Compass, 9*(1), 1–14.

Terán, L., Yan, K., & Aubrey, J. S. (2020). "But first let me take a selfie": US adolescent girls' selfie activities, self-objectification, imaginary audience beliefs, and appearance concerns. *Journal of Children and Media, 14*(3), 343–360.

Tomlinson-Keasey, C. (1972). Formal operations in females from eleven to fifty-four years of age. *Developmental Psychology, 6*(2), 364.

Ullman, H., Almeida, R., & Klingberg, T. (2014). Structural maturation and brain activity predict future working memory capacity during childhood development. *Journal of Neuroscience, 34*(5), 1592–1598.

van der Schuur, W. A., Baumgartner, S. E., Sumter, S. R., & Valkenburg, P. M. (2018). Media multitasking and sleep problems: A longitudinal study among adolescents. *Computers in Human Behavior, 81*, 316–324.

Vestal, C. (2021). COVID harmed kids' mental health—And schools are feeling it. Retrieved from www.pewtrusts.org/en/research-and-analysis/blogs/stateline/2021/11/08/covid-harmed-kids-mental-health-and-schools-are-feeling-it.

Wentzel, K. R. (1993). Motivation and achievement in early adolescence: The role of multiple classroom goals. *Journal of Early Adolescence, 13*(1), 4–20.

Wentzel, K. R. (2014). Prosocial behavior and peer relations in adolescence. In L. M. Padilla-Walker & G. Carlo (Eds.), *Prosocial development: A multidimensional approach* (pp. 178–200). Oxford University Press.

Wilson, T., Karimpour, R., & Rodkin, P. C. (2011). African American and European American students' peer groups during early adolescence: Structure, status, and academic achievement. *Journal of Early Adolescence, 31*(1), 74–98.

Woodworth, J. L., Raymond, M. E., Chirbas, K., Gonzales, M., Negassi, Y., Snow, W., & Van Dongle, C. (2015). Online charter school study. Retrieved from https://credo.stanford.edu/pdfs/OnlineCharterStudyFinal2015.pdf.

Zimmerman, B. J., & Kitsantas, A. (2014). Comparing students' self-discipline and self-regulation measures and their prediction of academic achievement. *Contemporary Educational Psychology, 39*(2), 145–155.

Chapter 16

Abma, J. C., & Martinez, G. M. (2017). Sexual activity and contraceptive use among teenagers in the United States, 2011–2015. *National Health Statistics Reports, 104*, 1–23. Retrieved from www.cdc.gov/nchs/data/nhsr/nhsr104.pdf.

AgeOfConsent.net. (2021). United States Age of Consent Map. Retrieved from https://www.ageofconsent.net/states.

Albert, D., & Steinberg, L. (2011). Peer influences on adolescent risk behavior. In M. T. Bardo, D. H. Fishbein, & R. Milich (Eds.), *Inhibitory control and drug abuse prevention* (pp. 211–226). Springer.

Alfaro, E. C., & Umaña-Taylor, A. J. (2010). Latino adolescents' academic motivation: The role of siblings. *Hispanic Journal of Behavioral Sciences, 32*(4), 549–570.

Allen, J. P., Uchino, B. N., & Hafen, C. A. (2015). Running with the pack: Teen peer-relationship qualities as predictors of adult physical health. *Psychological Science, 26*(10), 1574–1583.

American Academy of Pediatrics. (2020). Contraception explained: Options for teens & adolescents. Retrieved from www.healthychildren.org/English/ages-stages/teen/dating-sex/Pages/Birth-Control-for-Sexually-Active-Teens.aspx.

Anderson, M., & Jiang, J. (2018). Teens, friendships and online groups. Retrieved from www.pewresearch.org/internet/2018/11/28/teens-friendships-and-online-groups/.

Aquilino, W. S. (1994). Impact of childhood family disruption on young adults' relationships with parents. *Journal of Marriage and the Family, 56*(2), 295–313.

Archer, S. L. (1989). Gender differences in identity development: Issues of process, domain and timing. *Journal of Adolescence, 12*(2), 117–138.

Arnett, J. J. (1998). Learning to stand alone: The contemporary American transition to adulthood in cultural and historical context. *Human Development, 41*(5–6), 295–315.

Arnett, J. J. (2000). Emerging adulthood: A theory of development from the late teens through the twenties. *American Psychologist, 55*(5), 469.

Arnett, J. J. (2005). The developmental context of substance use in emerging adulthood. *Journal of Drug Issues, 35*(2), 235–254.

Arnett, J. J. (2014). *Emerging adulthood: The winding road from the late teens through the twenties*. Oxford University Press.

Arnett, J. J. (2020). Emerging adulthood. Retrieved from https://nobaproject.com/modules/emerging-adulthood.

Arnold, M. E. (2017). Supporting adolescent exploration and commitment: Identity formation, thriving, and positive youth development. *Journal of Youth Development, 12*(4), 1–15.

Bae, S. M. (2020). The relationship between bicultural identity, acculturative stress, and psychological well-being in multicultural adolescents: Verification using multivariate latent growth modelling. *Stress and Health, 36*(1), 51–58.

Bearman, P. S., & Brückner, H. (2002). Opposite-sex twins and adolescent same-sex attraction. *American Journal of Sociology, 107*(5), 1179–1205.

Beck, J. (2016). When are you really an adult? Retrieved from www.theatlantic.com/health/archive/2016/01/when-are-you-really-an-adult/422487/.

Bendezú, J. J., Pinderhughes, E. E., Hurley, S. M., McMahon, R. J., & Racz, S. J. (2018). Longitudinal relations among parental monitoring strategies, knowledge, and adolescent delinquency in a racially diverse at-risk sample. *Journal of Clinical Child & Adolescent Psychology, 47*(sup1), S21–S34.

Benenson, J. F., & Christakos, A. (2003). The greater fragility of females' versus males' closest same-sex friendships. *Child Development, 74*(4), 1123–1129.

Bi, X., Yang, Y., Li, H., Wang, M., Zhang, W., & Deater-Deckard, K. (2018). Parenting styles and parent–adolescent relationships: The mediating roles of behavioral autonomy and parental authority. *Frontiers in Psychology, 9*, 2187.

Blair, R. J. R. (2001). Neurocognitive models of aggression, the antisocial personality disorders, and psychopathy. *Journal of Neurology, Neurosurgery & Psychiatry, 71*(6), 727–731.

Boislard, M.-A., Van de Bongardt, D., & Blais, M. (2016). Sexuality (and lack thereof) in adolescence and early adulthood: A review of the literature. *Behavioral Sciences, 6*(1), 8.

Branje, S. (2018). Development of parent–adolescent relationships: Conflict interactions as a mechanism of change. *Child Development Perspectives, 12*(3), 171–176.

Brown, A. (2017). 5 key findings about LGBT Americans. Retrieved from www.pewresearch.org/fact-tank/2017/06/13/5-key-findings-about-lgbt-americans/.

Brown, B. B. (1999). " You're going out with who?": Peer group influences on adolescent romantic relationships. In W. Furman, B. B. Brown, & C. Feiring (Eds.), *The development of romantic relationships in adolescence* (pp. 291–329). Cambridge University Press.

Brown, B. B., & Larson, J. (2009). Peer relationships in adolescence. In R. M. Lerner & L. Steinberg (Eds.), *Handbook of adolescent psychology: Contextual influences on adolescent development* (pp. 74–103). John Wiley & Sons, Inc.

Brown, C., & Hegarty, K. (2018). Digital dating abuse measures: A critical review. *Aggression and Violent Behavior, 40*, 44–59.

Bukowski, W. M., Buhrmester, D., & Underwood, M. K. (2011). Peer relations as a developmental context. In M. K. Underwood & L. H. Rosen (Eds.), *Social development: Relationships in infancy, childhood, and adolescence* (pp. 153–179). Guilford Press.

Byrd, A. L., Loeber, R., & Pardini, D. A. (2014). Antisocial behavior, psychopathic features and abnormalities in reward and punishment processing in youth. *Clinical Child and Family Psychology Review, 17*(2), 125–156.

Campione-Barr, N., & Smetana, J. G. (2010). "Who said you could wear my sweater?" Adolescent siblings' conflicts and associations with relationship quality. *Child Development, 81*(2), 464–471.

Caridade, S., & Braga, T. (2020). Youth cyber dating abuse: A meta-analysis of risk and protective factors. *Cyberpsychology: Journal of Psychosocial Research on Cyberspace, 14*(3), Article 2. https://doi.org/10.5817/CP2020-3-2.

Caridade, S., Braga, T., & Borrajo, E. (2019). Cyber dating abuse (CDA): Evidence from a systematic review. *Aggression and Violent Behavior, 48*, 152–168.

Carlson, W., & Rose, A. J. (2007). The role of reciprocity in romantic relationships in middle childhood and early adolescence. *Merrill-Palmer Quarterly, 53*(2), 262–290.

Carver, K., Joyner, K., & Udry, J. R. (2003). National estimates of adolescent romantic relationships. In P. Florsheim (Ed.), *Adolescent romantic relations and sexual behavior: Theory, research, and practical implications* (pp. 23–56). Lawrence Erlbaum Associates Publishers.

Centers for Disease Control and Prevention. (2012). Youth risk behavior surveillance—United States, 2011. *Morbidity and Mortality Weekly Report, 61*(4), 1–166.

Centers for Disease Control and Prevention. (2016). Chlamydia—CDC detailed fact sheet. Retrieved from www.cdc.gov/std/chlamydia/stdfact-chlamydia-detailed.htm.

Centers for Disease Control and Prevention. (2017a). Genital herpes. Retrieved from www.cdc.gov/std/herpes/stdfact-herpes-detailed.htm.

Centers for Disease Control and Prevention. (2017b). Syphilis. Retrieved from www.cdc.gov/std/syphilis/stdfact-syphilis-detailed.htm.

Centers for Disease Control and Prevention. (2019a). Genital HPV infection. Retrieved from www.cdc.gov/std/hpv/stdfact-hpv.htm.

Centers for Disease Control and Prevention. (2019b). Gonorrhea. Retrieved from https://www.cdc.gov/std/gonorrhea/default.htm.

Centers for Disease Control and Prevention. (2019c). The State of STDs in the United States. Retrieved from www.cdc.gov/std/stats18/national-2018.pdf.

Centers for Disease Control and Prevention. (2020a). Explore youth risk behavior survey questions—United States, 2019. Retrieved from https://yrbs-explorer.services.cdc.gov/#/.

Centers for Disease Control and Prevention. (2020b). HIV Basics. Retrieved from www.cdc.gov/hiv/basics/index.html.

Centers for Disease Control and Prevention. (2020c). NCHHSTP AtlasPlus. Retrieved from www.cdc.gov/nchhstp/atlas/index.htm.

Charmaraman, L., & Grossman, J. (2008). *Relationship between racial/ethnic composition of school and centrality of race/ethnicity to adolescent identity.* Paper presented at the Poster Presented at the Annual Meeting of the American Educational Research Association. New York, NY.

Chen, M.-J., Grube, J. W., Nygaard, P., & Miller, B. A. (2008). Identifying social mechanisms for the prevention of adolescent drinking and driving. *Accident Analysis & Prevention, 40*(2), 576–585.

Chen, X., Chang, L., & He, Y. (2003). The peer group as a context: Mediating and moderating effects on relations between academic achievement and social functioning in Chinese children. *Child Development, 74*(3), 710–727.

Cherlin, A. J., Chase-Lansdale, P. L., & McRae, C. (1998). Effects of parental divorce on mental health throughout the life course. *American Sociological Review, 63*(2), 239–249.

Child Trends Databank. (2015). *The family environment and adolescent well-being*. Retrieved from www.childtrends.org/publications/the-family-environment-and-adolescent-well-being-2.

Closson, L. M., & Watanabe, L. (2018). Popularity in the peer group and victimization within friendship cliques during early adolescence. *Journal of Early Adolescence, 38*(3), 327–351.

Cohen, G. L., & Prinstein, M. J. (2006). Peer contagion of aggression and health risk behavior among adolescent males: An experimental investigation of effects on public conduct and private attitudes. *Child Development, 77*(4), 967–983.

Cohen-Kettenis, P. T., Van Goozen, S. H., Doorn, C. D., & Gooren, L. J. (1998). Cognitive ability and cerebral lateralisation in transsexuals. *Psychoneuroendocrinology, 23*(6), 631–641.

Connolly, J. A., & McIsaac, C. (2009). Romantic relationships in adolescence. In R. M. Lerner & L. Steinberg (Eds.), *Handbook of adolescent psychology: Contextual influences on adolescent development* (pp. 104–151). John Wiley & Sons, Inc.

Connolly, J., McIsaac, C., Shulman, S., Wincentak, K., Joly, L., Heifetz, M., & Bravo, V. (2014). Development of romantic relationships in adolescence and emerging adulthood: Implications for community mental health. *Canadian Journal of Community Mental Health, 33*(1), 7–19.

Côté, J. E. (2019). Eriksonian Theory. *The encyclopedia of child and adolescent development*, 1–10. https://doi.org/10.1002/9781119171492.wecad307.

Crabbe, R., Pivnick, L. K., Bates, J., Gordon, R. A., & Crosnoe, R. (2019). Contemporary college students' reflections on their high school peer crowds. *Journal of Adolescent Research, 34*(5), 563–596.

Crocetti, E. (2017). Identity formation in adolescence: The dynamic of forming and consolidating identity commitments. *Child Development Perspectives, 11*(2), 145–150.

Crosby, R., Geter, A., Ricks, J., Jones, J., & Salazar, L. F. (2015). Developmental investigation of age at sexual debut and subsequent sexual risk behaviours: A study of high-risk young black males. *Sexual Health, 12*(5), 390–396.

Curhan, K. B., Sims, T., Markus, H. R., Kitayama, S., Karasawa, M., Kawakami, N., . . . Ryff, C. D. (2014). Just how bad negative affect is for your health depends on culture. *Psychological Science, 25*(12), 2277–2280.

Dailey, R. M. (2009). Confirmation from family members: Parent and sibling contributions to adolescent psychosocial adjustment. *Western Journal of Communication, 73*(3), 273–299.

De Goede, I. H., Branje, S. J., & Meeus, W. H. (2009). Developmental changes in adolescents' perceptions of relationships with their parents. *Journal of Youth and Adolescence, 38*(1), 75–88.

Dhariwal, A., Connolly, J., Paciello, M., & Caprara, G. V. (2009). Adolescent peer relationships and emerging adult romantic styles: A longitudinal study of youth in an Italian community. *Journal of Adolescent Research, 24*(5), 579–600.

Dodge, K. A., Malone, P. S., Lansford, J. E., Miller-Johnson, S., Pettit, G. S., & Bates, J. E. (2006). Toward a dynamic developmental model of the role of parents and peers in early onset substance use. In A. Clarke-Stewart & J. Dunn (Eds.), *Families count: Effects on child and adolescent development* (pp. 104–131). Cambridge University Press.

Doorbar, J., Quint, W., Banks, L., Bravo, I. G., Stoler, M., Broker, T. R., & Stanley, M. A. (2012). The biology and life-cycle of human papillomaviruses. *Vaccine, 30*, F55–F70.

Draucker, C. B., & Martsolf, D. S. (2010). The role of electronic communication technology in adolescent dating violence. *Journal of Child and Adolescent Psychiatric Nursing, 23*(3), 133–142.

Durex Network Research Unit. (2009). Face of global sex report. Retrieved from http://www.durexnetwork.org/en-GB/research.

Ellis, W. E., & Zarbatany, L. (2017). Understanding processes of peer clique influence in late childhood and early adolescence. *Child Development Perspectives, 11*(4), 227–232.

Erikson, E. H. (1968). *Identity: Youth and crisis*. WW Norton & Company.

Erikson, E. H. (1994). *Identity and the life cycle*. WW Norton & Company.

Evans, C. B., Stalker, K. C., & Brown, M. E. (2020). A systematic review of crime/violence and substance use prevention programs. *Aggression and Violent Behavior*, 101513.

Farrington, D. P., Gaffney, H., Lösel, F., & Ttofi, M. M. (2017). Systematic reviews of the effectiveness of developmental prevention programs in reducing delinquency, aggression, and bullying. *Aggression and Violent Behavior, 33*, 91–106.

Federal Centre for Health Education. (2018). Sexuality education in Europe and Central Asia. Retrieved from www.ippfen.org/sites/ippfen/files/2018-05/Comprehensive%20Country%20Report%20on%20CSE%20in%20Europe%20and%20Central%20Asia_0.pdf.

Fogel, A. (2000). Systems, attachment, and relationships. *Human Development, 43*(6), 314–320.

Franzoi, S. L., Davis, M. H., & Vasquez-Suson, K. A. (1994). Two social worlds: Social correlates and stability of adolescent status groups. *Journal of Personality and Social Psychology, 67*(3), 462.

French, S. E., Seidman, E., Allen, L., & Aber, J. L. (2006). The development of ethnic identity during adolescence. *Developmental Psychology, 42*(1), 1.

Fuligni, A. J., Tseng, V., & Lam, M. (1999). Attitudes toward family obligations among American adolescents with Asian, Latin American, and European backgrounds. *Child Development, 70*(4), 1030–1044.

Gates, G. J. (2017). In US, more adults identifying as LGBT. *Gallup News*. Retrieved from https://news.gallup.com/poll/201731/lgbt-identification-rises.aspx.

Golombok, S., Perry, B., Burston, A., Murray, C., Mooney-Somers, J., Stevens, M., & Golding, J. (2003). Children with lesbian parents: a community study. *Developmental Psychology, 39*(1), 20.

Granic, I. (2005). Timing is everything: Developmental psychopathology from a dynamic systems perspective. *Developmental Review, 25*(3–4), 386–407.

Green, R., & Keverne, E. B. (2000). The disparate maternal aunt–uncle ratio in male transsexuals: An explanation invoking genomic imprinting. *Journal of Theoretical Biology, 202*(1), 55–63.

Guillory, J., Henes, A., Farrelly, M. C., Fiacco, L., Alam, I., Curry, L., . . . Delahanty, J. (2020). Awareness of and receptivity to the fresh empire tobacco public education campaign among hip hop youth. *Journal of Adolescent Health, 66*(3), 301–307.

Hadiwijaya, H., Klimstra, T. A., Vermunt, J. K., Branje, S. J., & Meeus, W. H. (2017). On the development of harmony, turbulence, and independence in parent–adolescent relationships: A five-wave longitudinal study. *Journal of Youth and Adolescence, 46*(8), 1772–1788.

Hall, K. S., Sales, J. M., Komro, K. A., & Santelli, J. (2016). The state of sex education in the United States. *The Journal of Adolescent Health: Official Publication of the Society for Adolescent Medicine, 58*(6), 595.

Harris Interactive. (2006). The Durex Sexual Wellbeing Global Survey, 2006. SSL International plc, Cambridge. Retrieved from http://www.durex.com/en-US/SexualWellbeingSurvey.

Harter, S. (2006). The Self. In U. W. Damon & R. Lerner (Eds.) *Handbook of child development* (Vol 3). New Jersey: Wiley and Sons, Inc.

Hartl, A. C., Laursen, B., & Cillessen, A. H. (2015). A survival analysis of adolescent friendships: The downside of dissimilarity. *Psychological Science, 26*(8), 1304–1315.

Heywood, W., Patrick, K., Smith, A. M., & Pitts, M. K. (2015). Associations between early first sexual intercourse and later sexual and reproductive outcomes: A systematic review of population-based data. *Archives of Sexual Behavior, 44*(3), 531–569.

Hoffman, S. D., & Maynard, R. A. (2008). *Kids having kids: Economic costs & social consequences of teen pregnancy.* The Urban Insitute.

Houltberg, B. J., Henry, C. S., Merten, M. J., & Robinson, L. C. (2011). Adolescents' perceptions of family connectedness, intrinsic religiosity, and depressed mood. *Journal of Child and Family Studies, 20*(1), 111–119.

Hughes, D. L., Del Toro, J., & Way, N. (2017). Interrelations among dimensions of ethnic-racial identity during adolescence. *Developmental Psychology, 53*(11), 2139.

Hughes, D., Rodriguez, J., Smith, E. P., Johnson, D. J., Stevenson, H. C., & Spicer, P. (2006). Parents' ethnic-racial socialization practices: A review of research and directions for future study. *Developmental Psychology, 42*(5), 747.

Huijsmans, T., Eichelsheim, V. I., Weerman, F., Branje, S. J., & Meeus, W. (2019). The role of siblings in adolescent delinquency next to parents, school, and peers: Do gender and age matter? *Journal of Developmental and Life-Course Criminology, 5*(2), 220–242.

Hyde, L. W., Shaw, D. S., & Hariri, A. R. (2013). Understanding youth antisocial behavior using neuroscience through a developmental psychopathology lens: Review, integration, and directions for research. *Developmental Review, 33*(3), 168–223.

Jackson, R. L., & Heckman, S. M. (2002). Perceptions of white identity and white liability: An analysis of white student responses to a college campus racial hate crime. *Journal of Communication, 52*(2), 434–450.

Jacobson, R. (2021). How to Talk to Kids About Sex and Consent. Retrieved from https://childmind.org/article/how-talk-kids-sex-consent-boundaries/.

Jacquet, S. E., & Surra, C. A. (2001). Parental divorce and premarital couples: Commitment and other relationship characteristics. *Journal of Marriage and Family, 63*(3), 627–638.

Jugert, P., Leszczensky, L., & Pink, S. (2018). The effects of ethnic minority adolescents' ethnic self-identification on friendship selection. *Journal of Research on Adolescence, 28*(2), 379–395.

Kaddoura, N., & Sarouphim, K. M. (2019). Identity development among Lebanese youth: An investigation of Marcia's paradigm. *Heliyon, 5*(11), e02851.

Kan, M. L., McHale, S. M., & Crouter, A. C. (2008). Parental involvement in adolescent romantic relationships: Patterns and correlates. *Journal of Youth and Adolescence, 37*(2), 168–179.

Kann, L., McManus, T., Harris, W. A., Shanklin, S. L., Flint, K. H., Queen, B., . . . Thornton, J. (2018). Youth risk behavior surveillance—United States, 2017. *MMWR Surveillance Summaries, 67*(8), 1.

Kastbom, Å. A., Sydsjö, G., Bladh, M., Priebe, G., & Svedin, C. G. (2016). Differences in sexual behavior, health, and history of child abuse among school students who had and had not engaged in sexual activity by the age of 18 years: A cross-sectional study. *Adolescent Health, Medicine and Therapeutics, 7*, 1.

Kiang, L., & Fuligni, A. J. (2010). Meaning in life as a mediator of ethnic identity and adjustment among adolescents from Latin, Asian, and European American backgrounds. *Journal of Youth and Adolescence, 39*(11), 1253–1264.

Kim, K. J., Conger, R. D., Lorenz, F. O., & Elder Jr, G. H. (2001). Parent–adolescent reciprocity in negative affect and its relation to early adult social development. *Developmental Psychology, 37*(6), 775.

Kim, P., Neuendorf, C., Bianco, H., & Evans, G. W. (2016). Exposure to childhood poverty and mental health symptomatology in adolescence: A role of coping strategies. *Stress and Health, 32*(5), 494–502.

Kramer, L., Conger, K. J., Rogers, C. R., & Ravindran, N. (2019). Siblings. In B. H. Fiese, M. Celano, K. Deater-Deckard, E. N. Jouriles, & M. A. Whisman (Eds.), *APA handbook of contemporary family psychology: Foundations, methods, and contemporary issues across the lifespan* (pp. 521–538). American Psychological Association.

Kramer, S. (2019). U.S. has world's highest rate of children living in single-parent households. Retrieved from www.pewresearch.org/fact-tank/2019/12/12/u-s-children-more-likely-than-children-in-other-countries-to-live-with-just-one-parent/.

Kroger, J., Martinussen, M., & Marcia, J. E. (2010). Identity status change during adolescence and young adulthood: A meta-analysis. *Journal of Adolescence, 33*(5), 683–698.

Kumar, A., Singh, T., Basu, S., Pandey, S., & Bhargava, V. (2007). Outcome of teenage pregnancy. *The Indian Journal of Pediatrics, 74*(10), 927–931.

Lam, C. B., McHale, S. M., & Crouter, A. C. (2014). Time with peers from middle childhood to late adolescence: Developmental course and adjustment correlates. *Child Development, 85*(4), 1677–1693.

Långström, N., Rahman, Q., Carlström, E., & Lichtenstein, P. (2010). Genetic and environmental effects on same-sex sexual behavior: A population study of twins in Sweden. *Archives of Sexual Behavior, 39*(1), 75–80.

Laursen, B., Coy, K. C., & Collins, W. A. (1998). Reconsidering changes in parent-child conflict across adolescence: A meta-analysis. *Child Development, 69*(3), 817–832.

Laursen, B., DeLay, D., & Adams, R. E. (2010). Trajectories of perceived support in mother–adolescent relationships: The poor (quality) get poorer. *Developmental Psychology, 46*(6), 1792.

Laursen, B., Finkelstein, B. D., & Betts, N. T. (2001). A developmental meta-analysis of peer conflict resolution. *Developmental Review, 21*(4), 423–449.

Lee, S. Y., Lee, H. J., Kim, T. K., Lee, S. G., & Park, E. C. (2015). Sexually transmitted infections and first sexual intercourse age in adolescents: The Nationwide Retrospective Cross-Sectional Study. *The Journal of Sexual Medicine, 12*(12), 2313–2323.

Lee, C., & Wong, J. S. (2020). Examining the effects of teen dating violence prevention programs: a systematic review and meta-analysis. *Journal of Experimental Criminology,* 1–40.

Lenhart, A. (2015). Teens, technology and friendships. Retrieved from www.pewresearch.org/internet/2015/08/06/teens-technology-and-friendships/.

Leszko, M., Elleman, L. G., Bastarache, E. D., Graham, E. K., & Mroczek, D. K. (2016). Future directions in the study of personality in adulthood and older age. *Gerontology, 62*(2), 210–215.

LeVay, S. (2011). From mice to men: Biological factors in the development of sexuality. *Frontiers in Neuroendocrinology, 2*(32), 110–113.

Lindberg, L. D., & Kantor, L. M. (2021). Adolescents' receipt of sex education in a nationally representative sample, 2011–2019. *Journal of Adolescent Health, 70*(2):290–297.

Lowe, K., & Dotterer, A. M. (2013). Parental monitoring, parental warmth, and minority youths' academic outcomes: Exploring the integrative model of parenting. *Journal of Youth and Adolescence, 42*(9), 1413–1425.

Luyckx, K., Schwartz, S. J., Berzonsky, M. D., Soenens, B., Vansteenkiste, M., Smits, I., & Goossens, L. (2008). Capturing ruminative exploration: Extending the four-dimensional model of identity formation in late adolescence. *Journal of Research in Personality, 42*(1), 58–82.

Luyckx, K., Klimstra, T. A., Duriez, B., Petegem, S. V., Beyers, W., Teppers, E., & Goossens, L. (2013). Personal identity processes and self-esteem: Temporal sequences in high school and college students. *Journal of Research in Personality, 47*(2), 159–170. https://doi.org/10.1016/j.jrp.2012.10.005.

Ma, Q., Ono-Kihara, M., Cong, L., Xu, G., Pan, X., Zamani, S., . . . Kihara, M. (2009). Early initiation of sexual activity: A risk factor for sexually transmitted diseases, HIV infection, and unwanted pregnancy among university students in China. *BMC Public Health, 9*(1), 111.

Martin, J. A., Hamilton, B. E., Osterman, M. J. K., & Driscoll, A. K. (2021). Births: Final data for 2019. Retrieved from www.cdc.gov/teenpregnancy/about/index.htm.

Mason-Jones, A. J., Sinclair, D., Mathews, C., Kagee, A., Hillman, A., & Lombard, C. (2016). School-based interventions for preventing HIV, sexually transmitted infections, and pregnancy in adolescents. *Cochrane Database of Systematic Reviews, 11*(11), CD006417.

Masten, C. L., Telzer, E. H., Fuligni, A. J., Lieberman, M. D., & Eisenberger, N. I. (2012). Time spent with friends in adolescence relates to less neural sensitivity to later peer rejection. *Social Cognitive and Affective Neuroscience, 7*(1), 106–114.

Masters, N. T., Beadnell, B. A., Morrison, D. M., Hoppe, M. J., & Gillmore, M. R. (2008). The opposite of sex? Adolescents' thoughts about abstinence and sex, and their sexual behavior. *Perspectives on Sexual and Reproductive Health, 40*(2), 87–93.

McGue, M., Elkins, I., Walden, B., & Iacono, W. G. (2005). Perceptions of the parent-adolescent relationship: A longitudinal investigation. *Developmental Psychology, 41*(6), 971.

McQuillan, G. M., Kruszon-Moran, D., Markowitz, L. E., Unger, E. R., & Paulose-Ram, R. (2017). *Prevalence of HPV in adults aged 18–69: United States, 2011–2014. NCHS data brief, 280,* 1–8.

Mikulincer, M., & Shaver, P. R. (2009). An attachment and behavioral systems perspective on social support. *Journal of Social and Personal Relationships, 26*(1), 7–19.

Miller, G. E., Yu, T., Chen, E., & Brody, G. H. (2015). Self-control forecasts better psychosocial outcomes but faster epigenetic aging in low-SES youth. *Proceedings of the National Academy of Sciences, 112*(33), 10325–10330.

Moffitt, T. E. (1993). Adolescence-limited and life-course-persistent antisocial behavior: A developmental taxonomy. *Psychological Review, 100*(4), 674.

Moffitt, T. E. (2018). Male antisocial behaviour in adolescence and beyond. *Nature Human Behaviour, 2*(3), 177–186.

Morales, A., Espada, J. P., Orgilés, M., Escribano, S., Johnson, B. T., & Lightfoot, M. (2018). Interventions to reduce risk for sexually transmitted infections in adolescents: A meta-analysis of trials, 2008–2016. *PloS One, 13*(6), e0199421.

Moran, M. B., Villanti, A. C., Johnson, A., & Rath, J. (2019). Patterns of alcohol, tobacco, and substance use among young adult peer crowds. *American Journal of Preventive Medicine, 56*(6), e185–e193.

Moran, M. B., Walker, M. W., Alexander, T. N., Jordan, J. W., & Wagner, D. E. (2017). Why peer crowds matter: Incorporating youth subcultures and values in health education campaigns. *American Journal of Public Health, 107*(3), 389–395.

Mueller, C. E., Bridges, S. K., & Goddard, M. S. (2011). Sleep and parent-family connectedness: Links, relationships and implications for adolescent depression1. *Journal of Family Studies, 17*(1), 9–23.

National Center for Health Statistics. (2017). Key statistics from the National Survey of Family Growth—S Listing. Retrieved from www.cdc.gov/nchs/nsfg/key_statistics/s.htm.

Nelson, L., Badger, S., & Wu, B. (2004). The influence of culture in emerging adulthood: Perspectives of Chinese college students. *International Journal of Behavioral Development, 28*(1), 26–36.

Newman, K., Harrison, L., Dashiff, C., & Davies, S. (2008). Relationships between parenting styles and risk behaviors in adolescent health: An integrative literature review. *Revista Latino-Americana de Enfermagem, 16*(1), 142–150.

Nogueira Avelar e Silva, R., Wijtzes, A., van de Bongardt, D., van de Looij-Jansen, P., Bannink, R., & Raat, H. (2016). Early sexual intercourse: Prospective associations with adolescents physical activity and screen time. *PloS One, 11*(8), e0158648.

O'Donnell, L., O'Donnell, C. R., & Stueve, A. (2001). Early sexual initiation and subsequent sex-related risks among urban minority youth: The reach for health study. *Family Planning Perspectives*, 268–275.

Office of Disease Prevention and Health Promotion. (2021). Healthy People 2030 framework. Retrieved from www .healthypeople.gov/2020/About-Healthy-People/Development-Healthy-People-2030/Framework.

Office of Juvenile Justice and Delinquency Prevention. (2020a). Age profile of arrests by offense, 2019. Retrieved from www.ojjdp.gov/ojstatbb/crime/ucr.asp?table_in=1&selYrs=2019&rdoGroups=1&rdoData=rp.

Office of Juvenile Justice and Delinquency Prevention. (2020b). Delinquency prevention. Retrieved from www.ojjdp.gov/mpg/Topic/Details/79.

O'Hanlan, K. A., Gordon, J. C., & Sullivan, M. W. (2018). Biological origins of sexual orientation and gender identity: Impact on health. *Gynecologic Oncology, 149*(1), 33–42.

Oliva, A., & Arranz, E. (2005). Sibling relationships during adolescence. *European Journal of Developmental Psychology, 2*(3), 253–270.

Ostrov, J. M., Crick, N. R., & Stauffacher, K. (2006). Relational aggression in sibling and peer relationships during early childhood. *Journal of Applied Developmental Psychology, 27*(3), 241–253.

O'Sullivan, L. F. (2014). Linking online sexual activities to health outcomes among teens. *New Directions for Child and Adolescent Development, 2014*(144), 37–51.

Pahl, K., & Way, N. (2006). Longitudinal trajectories of ethnic identity among urban Black and Latino adolescents. *Child Development, 77*(5), 1403–1415.

Parkes, A., Wight, D., Henderson, M., & West, P. (2010). Does early sexual debut reduce teenagers' participation in tertiary education? Evidence from the SHARE longitudinal study. *Journal of Adolescence, 33*(5), 741–754.

Pastor, J., McCormick, J., Fine, M., Andolsen, R. C., Friedman, N. C., Richardson, N. C., . . . Tavarez, M. C. (2007). Makin' homes: An urban girl thing. In B. J. R. Leadbeater & N. Way (Eds.), *Urban girls revisited: Building strengths* (pp. 75–96). New York University Press.

Paul, E. L., Wenzel, A., & Harvey, J. (2008). Hookups: A facilitator or a barrier to relationship initiation and intimacy development? In S. Sprecher, A. Wenzel, & J. Harvey (Eds.), *Handbook of relationship initiation* (pp. 375–390). Psychology Press.

Pawelski, J. G., Perrin, E. C., Foy, J. M., Allen, C. E., Crawford, J. E., Del Monte, M., . . . Springer, S. (2006). The effects of marriage, civil union, and domestic partnership laws on the health and well-being of children. *Pediatrics, 118*(1), 349–364.

Perez-Gramaje, A. F., Garcia, O. F., Reyes, M., Serra, E., & Garcia, F. (2019). Parenting styles and aggressive adolescents: Relationships with self-esteem and personal maladjustment. *European Journal of Psychology Applied to Legal Context, 12*(1), 1–10.

Perper, K., & Manlove, J. (2010). Diploma attainment among teen mothers.Retrieved from https://www.childtrends.org/publications/diploma-attainment-among-teen-mothers.

Perry, D. G., & Pauletti, R. E. (2011). Gender and adolescent development. *Journal of Research on Adolescence, 21*(1), 61–74.

Petrosky, E., Bocchini Jr, J. A., Hariri, S., Chesson, H., Curtis, C. R., Saraiya, M., . . . Markowitz, L. E. (2015). Use of 9-valent human papillomavirus (HPV) vaccine: Updated HPV vaccination recommendations of the advisory committee on immunization practices. *MMWR. Morbidity and Mortality Weekly Report, 64*(11), 300.

Phelps, E., Furstenberg Jr, F. F., & Colby, A. (2002). *Looking at lives: American longitudinal studies of the twentieth century*. Russell Sage Foundation.

Ramirez, A., & Wang, Z. (2008). When online meets offline: An expectancy violations theory perspective on modality switching. *Journal of Communication, 58*(1), 20–39.

Reitz, A. K., & Staudinger, U. M. (2017). Getting older, getting better? Toward understanding positive personality development across adulthood. In J. Specht (Ed.), *Personality development across the lifespan* (pp. 219–241). Elsevier.

Rifkin, J. (2011). *The third industrial revolution; How lateral power is transforming energy the economiy and the world*. New York: St Martin's Press.

Roberts, A. L., Glymour, M. M., & Koenen, K. C. (2013). Does maltreatment in childhood affect sexual orientation in adulthood? *Archives of Sexual Behavior, 42*(2), 161–171.

Roisman, G. I., Madsen, S. D., Hennighausen, K. H., Sroufe, L. A., & Andrew Collins, W. (2001). The coherence of dyadic behavior across parent–child and romantic relationships as mediated by the internalized representation of experience. *Attachment & Human Development, 3*(2), 156–172.

Rosenberger, N. (2007). Rethinking emerging adulthood in Japan: Perspectives from long-term single women. *Child Development Perspectives, 1*(2), 92–95.

Rubens, S. L., Gudiño, O. G., Michel, J., Fite, P. J., & Johnson-Motoyama, M. (2018). Neighborhood and cultural stressors associated with delinquency in Latino adolescents. *Journal of Community Psychology, 46*(1), 95–106.

Ryan, R. M., & Lynch, J. H. (1989). Emotional autonomy versus detachment: Revisiting the vicissitudes of adolescence and young adulthood. *Child Development, 60*(2), 340–356.

Salthouse, T. A. (2016). Continuity of cognitive change across adulthood. *Psychonomic Bulletin & Review, 23*(3), 932–939.

Sanders, A. R., Martin, E. R., Beecham, G. W., Guo, S., Dawood, K., Rieger, G., . . . Kolundzija, A. B. (2015). Genome-wide scan demonstrates significant linkage for male sexual orientation. *Psychological Medicine, 45*(7), 1379–1388.

Sapolsky, R. M. (2004). *Why zebras don't get ulcers*. New York, NY: St. Martins Press.

Saraiya, M., Unger, E. R., Thompson, T. D., Lynch, C. F., Hernandez, B. Y., Lyu, C. W., . . . Hopenhayn, C. (2015). US assessment of HPV types in cancers: Implications for current and 9-valent HPV vaccines. *JNCI: Journal of the National Cancer Institute, 107*(6), djv086.

Savin-Williams, R. C. (2014). An exploratory study of the categorical versus spectrum nature of sexual orientation. *Journal of Sex Research, 51*(4), 446–453.

Savin-Williams, R. C. (2018). An exploratory study of exclusively heterosexual, primarily heterosexual, and mostly heterosexual young men. *Sexualities, 21*(1–2), 16–29.

Scheer, S. D., Unger, D. G., & Brown, M. B. (1996). Adolescents becoming adults: Attributes for adulthood. *Adolescence, 31*(121), 127–132.

Schofield, H.-L. T., Bierman, K. L., Heinrichs, B., Nix, R. L., & Group, C. P. P. R. (2008). Predicting early sexual activity with behavior problems exhibited at school entry and in early adolescence. *Journal of Abnormal Child Psychology, 36*(8), 1175–1188.

Schwartz, J. A., Solomon, S. J., & Valgardson, B. A. (2019). Socialization, selection, or both? The role of gene–environment interplay in the association between exposure to antisocial peers and delinquency. *Journal of Quantitative Criminology, 35*(1), 1–26.

Schweinhart, L. J. (2004). *The High/Scope Perry Preschool study through age 40: Summary, conclusions, and frequently asked questions*. High/Scope Educational Research Foundation.

Seiffge-Krenke, I. (2003). Testing theories of romantic development from adolescence to young adulthood: Evidence of a developmental sequence. *International Journal of Behavioral Development, 27*(6), 519–531.

Seiffge-Krenke, I., Overbeek, G., & Vermulst, A. (2010). Parent–child relationship trajectories during adolescence: Longitudinal associations with romantic outcomes in emerging adulthood. *Journal of Adolescence, 33*(1), 159–171.

Seiffge-Krenke, I., Shulman, S., & Kiessinger, N. (2001). Adolescent precursors of romantic relationships in young adulthood. *Journal of Social and Personal Relationships, 18*(3), 327–346.

Shneyderman, Y., & Schwartz, S. J. (2013). Contextual and intrapersonal predictors of adolescent risky sexual behavior and outcomes. *Health Education & Behavior, 40*(4), 400–414.

Shrestha, R., Karki, P., & Copenhaver, M. (2016). Early sexual debut: A risk factor for STIs/HIV acquisition among a nationally representative sample of adults in Nepal. *Journal of Community Health, 41*(1), 70–77.

Shulman, S., Laursen, B., Kalman, Z., & Karpovsky, S. (1997). Adolescent intimacy revisited. *Journal of Youth and Adolescence, 26*(5), 597–617.

Shulman, S., Walsh, S. D., Weisman, O., & Schelyer, M. (2009). Romantic contexts, sexual behavior, and depressive symptoms among adolescent males and females. *Sex Roles, 61*(11–12), 850–863.

Spera, C. (2005). A review of the relationship among parenting practices, parenting styles, and adolescent school achievement. *Educational Psychology Review, 17*(2), 125–146.

Spriggs, A. L., & Halpern, C. T. (2008). Sexual debut timing and depressive symptoms in emerging adulthood. *Journal of Youth and Adolescence, 37*(9), 1085–1096.

Stauffacher, K., & DeHart, G. B. (2005). Preschoolers' relational aggression with siblings and with friends. *Early Education & Development, 16*(2), 185–206.

Stewart, J., Spivey, L. A., Widman, L., Choukas-Bradley, S., & Prinstein, M. J. (2019). Developmental patterns of sexual identity, romantic attraction, and sexual behavior among adolescents over three years. *Journal of Adolescence, 77*, 90–97.

Syed, M., & Fish, J. (2018). Revisiting Erik Erikson's legacy on culture, race, and ethnicity. *Identity, 18*(4), 274–283.

Talhelm, T., Zhang, X., Oishi, S., Shimin, C., Duan, D., Lan, X., & Kitayama, S. (2014). Large-scale psychological differences within China explained by rice versus wheat agriculture. *Science, 344*(6184), 603–608.

Taylor, S., & Xia, Y. (2018). Cyber partner abuse: A systematic review. *Violence and Victims, 33*(6), 983–1011.

Tharp, A. T., McNaughton Reyes, H. L., Foshee, V., Swahn, M. H., Hall, J. E., & Logan, J. (2017). Examining the prevalence and predictors of injury from adolescent dating violence. *Journal of aggression, maltreatment & trauma, 26*(5), 445–461.

The Trevor Project. (2019). National survey on LGBTQ youth mental health. Retrieved from www.thetrevorproject.org/survey-2019/?section=Youth-Support-Preferences.

Tilson, E. C., Sanchez, V., Ford, C. L., Smurzynski, M., Leone, P. A., Fox, K. K., . . . Miller, W. C. (2004). Barriers to asymptomatic screening and other STD services for adolescents and young adults: Focus group discussions. *BMC Public Health, 4*(1), 21.

Tobler, A. L., & Komro, K. A. (2010). Trajectories or parental monitoring and communication and effects on drug use among urban young adolescents. *Journal of Adolescent Health, 46*(6), 560–568.

Tucker, C. J., McHale, S. M., & Crouter, A. C. (2001). Conditions of sibling support in adolescence. *Journal of Family Psychology, 15*(2), 254.

Tucker, C. J., McHale, S. M., & Crouter, A. C. (2003). Dimensions of mothers' and fathers' differential treatment of siblings: Links with adolescents' sex-typed personal qualities. *Family Relations, 52*(1), 82–89.

Twenge, J. M. (2020). Possible reasons US adults are not having sex as much as they used to. *JAMA network open, 3*(6), e203889-e203889.

Udell, W., Sandfort, T., Reitz, E., Bos, H., & Dekovic, M. (2010). The relationship between early sexual debut and psychosocial outcomes: A longitudinal study of Dutch adolescents. *Archives of Sexual Behavior, 39*(5), 1133–1145.

UNICEF Data Warehouse. (2021). Indicator: Adolescent birth rate (number of live births to adolescent women per 1,000 adolescent women). Retrieved from https://data.unicef.org/resources/data_explorer/unicef_f/?ag=UNICEF&df=GLOBAL_DATAFLOW&ver=1.0&dq=.MNCH_ABR..&startPeriod=2015&endPeriod=2021.

U.S. Census Bureau. (2021). Decennial Censuses, 1890 to 1940, and Current Population Survey, Annual Social and Economic Supplements, 1947 to 2021. Retrieved from www.census.gov/content/dam/Census/library/visualizations/time-series/demo/families-and-households/ms-2.pdf.

Van de Bongardt, D., Reitz, E., Sandfort, T., & Deković, M. (2015). A meta-analysis of the relations between three types of peer norms and adolescent sexual behavior. *Personality and Social Psychology Review, 19*(3), 203–234.

van Doeselaar, L., McLean, K. C., Meeus, W., Denissen, J. J., & Klimstra, T. A. (2019). Adolescents' identity formation: Linking the narrative and the dual-cycle approach. *Journal of Youth and Adolescence, 49*(4), 1–18.

Verschueren, M., Rassart, J., Claes, L., Moons, P., & Luyckx, K. (2017). Identity statuses throughout adolescence and emerging adulthood: A large-scale study into gender, age, and contextual differences. *Psychologica Belgica, 57*(1), 32.

Wadsworth, M. E., Evans, G. W., Grant, K., Carter, J. S., & Duffy, S. (2016). Poverty and the development of psychopathology. In D. Cicchetti (Ed.), *Developmental psychopathology: Risk, resilience, and intervention* (pp. 136–179). John Wiley & Sons, Inc.

Walker, R. (2020). Ban traumatic 'shooter drills' in US schools, urge teachers. Retrieved from www.theguardian.com/us-news/2020/feb/29/teachers-call-for-ban-on-shooter-drills-in-us-schools.

Walker, T. Y., Elam-Evans, L. D., Yankey, D., Markowitz, L. E., Williams, C. L., Fredua, B., . . . Stokley, S. (2019). National, regional, state, and selected local area vaccination coverage among adolescents aged 13–17 years—United States, 2018. *Morbidity and Mortality Weekly Report, 68*(33), 718.

Waller, R., Dotterer, H. L., Murray, L., Maxwell, A. M., & Hyde, L. W. (2017). White-matter tract abnormalities and antisocial behavior: A systematic review of diffusion tensor imaging studies across development. *NeuroImage: Clinical, 14,* 201–215.

Walters, G. D. (2019). Tracing the delinquency acquisition sequence from older siblings, to friends, to self: A mediation analysis. *Journal of Adolescence, 75,* 113–122.

Wang, B., Zhou, S., Hong, F., Wang, J., Liu, X., Cai, Y., . . . Ma, X. (2012). Association analysis between the tag SNP for sonic hedgehog rs9333613 polymorphism and male sexual orientation. *Journal of Andrology, 33*(5), 951–954.

Werner, E. E. (1995). Resilience in development. *Current Directions in Psychological Science, 4*(3), 81–84.

Whitam, F. L., Diamond, M., & Martin, J. (1993). Homosexual orientation in twins: A report on 61 pairs and three triplet sets. *Archives of Sexual Behavior, 22*(3), 187–206.

White, A. E., Weinstein, E., & Selman, R. L. (2018). Adolescent friendship challenges in a digital context: Are new technologies game changers, amplifiers, or just a new medium? *Convergence, 24*(3), 269–288.

Wood, D., Crapnell, T., Lau, L., Bennett, A., Lotstein, D., Ferris, M., & Kuo, A. (2018). Emerging adulthood as a critical stage in the life course. In *Handbook of life course health development* (pp. 123–143). Springer, Cham.

Woodman, E., & McArthur, M. (2018). Young people's experiences of family connectedness: Supporting social work practice with families and young people. *British Journal of Social Work, 48*(3), 693–713.

Xiong, R., Li, S. D., & Xia, Y. (2020). A longitudinal study of authoritative parenting, juvenile delinquency and crime victimization among Chinese adolescents. *International Journal of Environmental Research and Public Health, 17*(4), 1405.

Xu, Y., & Zheng, Y. (2017). Does sexual orientation precede childhood sexual abuse? Childhood gender nonconformity as a risk factor and instrumental variable analysis. *Sexual Abuse, 29*(8), 786–802.

Yau, J. C., & Reich, S. M. (2018). Are the qualities of adolescents' offline friendships present in digital interactions? *Adolescent Research Review, 3*(3), 339–355.

Yeh, H.-C., & Lempers, J. D. (2004). Perceived sibling relationships and adolescent development. *Journal of Youth and Adolescence, 33*(2), 133–147.

Yip, T., Seaton, E. K., & Sellers, R. M. (2010). Interracial and intraracial contact, school-level diversity, and change in racial identity status among African American adolescents. *Child Development, 81*(5), 1431–1444.

Zhao, S., Chen, X., Ellis, W., & Zarbatany, L. (2016). Affiliation with socially withdrawn groups and children's social and psychological adjustment. *Journal of Abnormal Child Psychology, 44*(7), 1279–1290.

Glossary

accommodation modification of existing schemata because new information or experiences do not fit the existing schemata.

adaptation in Piaget's theory, a reaction to new experiences and information. It consists of two alternative processes: assimilation and accommodation.

adolescence transition phase between childhood and adulthood involving significant physical, social, emotional, and cognitive changes.

affirmative consent a person's voluntary and explicit agreement to participate in sexual contact.

allele one of several alternative forms of a gene.

ambivalent/resistant attachment attachment pattern where infants protest loudly when the caregiver leaves but show a mix of approach and avoidance behaviors at the caregiver's return.

amniotic fluid protective fluid that surrounds the fetus in the amniotic sac.

amniotic sac fluid-filled pouch made of membranes that protects the fetus as it grows in the womb.

androgens a group of sex hormones that promote the development of male body characteristics (e.g., testosterone).

anesthetics medications administered to produce insensitivity to pain.

animism tendency to believe that inanimate things have a consciousness and are alive

anorexia nervosa a potentially life-threatening eating disorder that involves a restriction of the number of calories and types of foods that are eaten.

Apgar scale a measure of a newborn's physical condition based on its appearance, pulse, grimace, activity, and respiration.

artificial insemination sperm is transferred to the women's uterus during ovulation.

assimilation the process by which new information is incorporated into existing thinking and schemata.

attachment an affectional bond between two persons that is expressed in behaviors like proximity seeking or distress upon separation.

authoritarian parenting setting strict limits for children and punishing children if they do not obey. Absence of dialogue about rules and limits. Coldness toward children.

authoritative parenting setting reasonable and consistent limits for children. Using explanations and dialogue rather than punishment. Being warm and accepting toward one's children.

autobiographical memories the memories you have of your own life.

autosome any of the 44 chromosomes that do not determine a person's sex.

avoidant attachment attachment pattern where infants do not interact much with the caregiver and show little reaction to the caregiver's leaving or return.

babbling a child's repetitious production of speech-like syllables, first appearing between 6 and 8 months of age.

bicultural identity a sense of belonging to two different cultures.

binge drinking drinking more than five drinks in a row.

birth asphyxia a condition characterized by a lack of oxygen supply to the body and brain.

blended family a married couple living with at least one child from a previous marriage.

body image a person's perception of their body along with the feelings and thoughts that result from the perception.

body mass index (BMI) a measure of body fat that is based on a person's height and weight.

bonding the development of a close attachment between an infant and its parents.

brain stem a set of structures that regulate basic but vital body functions like breathing, heart rate and blood pressure.

Braxton Hicks contractions intermittent weak contractions of the uterus during pregnancy; also called "practice contractions".

Brazelton Neonatal Behavioral Assessment Scale (NBAS) a neurobehavioral test that assesses newborns' behaviors and neurological status.

breech position the position a baby is in when it enters the birth canal feet-first or buttocks-first rather than head-first.

bulimia nervosa an eating disorder characterized by episodes of extreme overeating followed by self-induced vomiting.

bullying repeated unjustified aggression toward a victim based on a perceived power imbalance.

central executive the part of the brain that controls information processing and attention within working memory.

centration focusing on only on aspect of a situation and while ignoring other aspects

cerebellum the part of the brain that coordinates movements, balance, and posture.

cerebral cortex the furrowed outer surface the cerebrum, composed mostly of gray matter, and involved in complex brain functions like thinking and reasoning.

cerebral palsy a neurological disorder that affects body movements and muscle coordination.

cerebrum the largest part of the brain, divided into two hemispheres and responsible for complex cognitive processes.

cesarean section (or c-section) a surgical intervention in which an incision is made in the mother's abdominal wall and uterus in order to remove the baby.

child abuse any intentional actions that harm a child physically or psychologically.

child-directed speech high-pitched style of speech in which adults speak with infants, drawing out vowels to highlight differences between speech sounds.

child maltreatment mistreatement or abuse of a child, including physical abuse, sexual abuse, psychological maltreatment, and neglect.

child neglect a failure to provide a child with essentials like food, housing, medical care, and education to such an extent that the child's health and well-being are endangered.

chromosome a threadlike structure found in the nucleus of most living cells, containing the genetic information of an organism.

chronic diseases medical conditions that last more than one year and limit daily activities, require ongoing medical care, or both.

classical conditioning the learning process that occurs when a neutral stimulus (which originally did not provoke a response) comes to elicit a response as a result of being paired repeatedly with an unconditioned stimulus.

class inclusion a child's ability to understand that objects can to more than one group at once.

clique a small group of people connected by a common interest or friendship; they spend time together and do not always allow others to join.

cochlea the part of the inner ear that receives sound vibrations and converts these into nerve impulses that are sent to the brain.

cognitive approaches theories of child development that explain human behavior in terms of a combination of mental processes like thinking, reasoning, and perception.

cohort a group of people who were born around the same time and share some significant experiences.

commitment a stable investment in one's goals and values in James Marcia's theory of identity development.

conservation the principle that when you change the physical appearance of something, its properties like mass, number, or weight do not necessarily change as well.

continuous development development in which changes are gradual and build on each other.

coregulation the process by which parents gradually transfer control to their children.

corporal punishment actions that physically hurt a person.

corpus callosum a thick bundle of neuronal fibers connecting the right and the left hemisphere.

crowd a group larger than a clique; members do not necessarily spend time together, and membership is based on reputation or common features.

cultural socialization the way parents teach and communicate their cultural beliefs, customs, values, and behaviors.

culture the beliefs, customs, arts and values of a society or group of people.

culture-fair intelligence tests intelligence tests that have been specifically designed with the intention to avoid cultural bias so that they reflect a child's true ability no matter its culture; however, so far none of the tests developed with this intention has succeeded in being truly culture-free.

cystic fibrosis a recessive genetic disorder in which lungs and pancreas are clogged by mucus.

deferred imitation the performance of an observed action after a significant delay.

dendrites branchlike structures that receive information from other neurons and transmit it to the cell body.

dilation an increase in size of the cervical opening during the birth process.

discontinuous development development that happens in stages, with each stage bringing about behavior and abilities that differ qualitatively from the behavior and abilities in other stages.

disorganized (or disoriented) attachment an attachment pattern in which infants seem confused and show contradictory behaviors when the caregiver returns.

dizygotic twins twins who develop from two zygotes and share 50% of their genome, like regular siblings who are born at different times.

DNA deoxyribonucleic acid; a molecule that carries hereditary material in humans and most other organisms.

dominant trait a heritable trait that is expressed in offspring even when the gene for that trait is inherited from only one parent.

doula a professional without formal medical training who provides physical and emotional support during pregnancy, labor, and birth.

Down syndrome a congenital chromosomal disorder arising from an additional (third) copy of chromosome 21.

dual-language approach an approach to teaching English in which instruction takes place both in English and the native language of the learner.

Duchenne muscular dystrophy a recessive X-linked genetic disorder in which muscles grow progressively weaker, usually affecting boys.

dynamic systems theory a theory by Esther Thelen that proposes that motor development is the result of interaction between different systems and the environment.

dyscalculia an unusual difficulty in math performance, particularly representing and processing numbers despite normal intelligence.

dyslexia a common learning disability which affects a person's ability to spell words and read.

ecological systems theory a theory by Urie Bronfenbrenner that development is shaped by the interactions of a child with five different environmental systems.

egocentrism a young child's inability to view things from a viewpoint other than their own.

elaboration a memory strategy that involves processing information and embedding it into prior knowledge.

embryonic stage the second stage of prenatal development (lasting from the third through the eighth week), during which all major organs are formed.

emerging adulthood a developmental stage between adolescence and adulthood (roughly age 18–25), characterized by relative freedom from expectations and allowing for exploration of different lifestyles and possibilities.

emotion a state of feeling that usually arises from interaction with people or objects, and that leads to physiological and behavioral changes.

encoding the process of preparing information so it can be stored in and retrieved from long term memory.

epigenetic modification a process that activates or deactivates genes by tightly or loosely winding up DNA.

epigenetics the study of the bidirectional relationship between the environment and the expression of genes (that is, the phenotype).

episiotomy an incision in the muscular tissue between vagina and anus, following childbirth.

equilibrium a state of mental balance, in which children can explain new experiences and ideas with their existing knowledge; achieved through the processes of assimilation and accommodation.

estrogens a group of sex hormones that promote the development of female body characteristics.

ethnic group a group of people who share a common culture, nationality, ancestry, language, or religion.

ethnic identity a sense of belonging to a particular group of people who share a common culture, nationality, ancestry, language, or religion.

ethology the study of animal (including human) behavior and how it is influenced by genetics and evolution.

exploration the active search for an identity, involving values, goals, and beliefs in James Marcia's theory of identity development.

external memory aids strategies that use cues from the environment to aid memory.

failure to thrive a condition in which children's weight and height gain is slowed abnormally.

fast mapping the process in which children learn the meaning of new words after having heard them just once or twice in a conversation.

fetus an unborn human child from the start of the ninth week of pregnancy until birth.

fine motor skills motor skills that involve movements of smaller muscles and small movements like those of hands and fingers.

formal operational stage the fourth stage in Piaget's theory of cognitive development, beginning around the age of 11–12, in which the ability to think abstractly develops.

fragile X syndrome a chromosomal disorder affecting males and females in which a gene located on the X chromosome and responsible for producing a particular protein is turned off.

gatekeeping the tendency for parents (most often mothers) to engage in activities that control others' access to or interaction with the child.

gender socially constructed roles and characteristics associated with male or female.

gender constancy (or stability) understanding that a person's gender remains the same even if the person's appearance or behavior changes.

gender identity an individual's sense of their own gender.

gender segregation the separation of services, programs, activities, interests, etc., by sex, either voluntarily (for example, in play) or by law/policy.

gender stereotypes generalized and simplistic views of the roles of men and women, and what characterizes them.

gene a segment of a DNA strand in a chromosome, which carries genetic information.

generation a group of people of roughly the same age, with shared historical experiences; a generation often spans a time range of more than a decade.

genome the entirety of an organism's genes.

genotype the genetic makeup of a person.

germinal stage the first stage of prenatal development (lasting for 2 weeks from conception), in which the zygote starts to divide and attaches to the uterine wall.

gestation the time between conception and birth, in which an unborn child develops in the mother's womb.

goodness of fit the degree of match between a child's temperament and the environmental constraints.

gross motor skills motor skills that are involved when we move large body parts like arms and legs.

habituation a form of learning in which the response to a stimulus decreases when that stimulus is presented repeatedly.

hemophilia a recessive X-linked disorder in which blood does not clot properly.

herd immunity indirect protection from infectious diseases for non-immunized individuals, resulting from vaccinations of a large part of the population.

heritability extent to which genetic differences contribute to individual differences in traits; expressed as numerical value ranging from 0 (genes do not contribute to individual differences in traits) to 1.0 (genes account for the entirety of individual differences in a trait).

heterozygous having two different alleles of a gene for a particular trait.

hippocampus each of two structures of the limbic system (there is one in each hemisphere) that are central to emotion regulation, memory formation, and learning.

HIV (human immunodeficiency virus) an incurable but treatable infection that weakens the human immune system.

holophrase a word that expresses an entire sentence or thought.

homozygous having identical alleles of a gene for a particular trait on both chromosomes.

Huntington's disease a fatal dominant genetic disorder in which nerve cells in the brain die; onset is most often in middle age.

hypothalamus a region of the forebrain that controls a number of functions like body temperature, hunger, thirst, and emotions.

hypothesis a testable prediction about the relationship between at least two variables.

hypothetical-deductive reasoning the ability, characteristic of Piaget's formal operational stage of cognitive development, to develop and test hypotheses in order to solve problems.

identity a clear and stable sense of oneself that includes a person's goals, values, and beliefs.

imagery a memory strategy that involves creating mental images to aid retrieval of information.

imaginary audience an adolescents' belief that they are constantly watched and scrutinized by others; an aspect of adolescent egocentrism.

immersion approach an approach to teaching English in which instruction takes place exclusively in English.

immunization the process of becoming protected against a disease.

in vitro fertilization (IVF) the process in which ova and sperm are combined in a laboratory; three to five days later, one or several embryos are transferred to the woman's uterus.

incubator an apparatus consisting of a bed enclosed in a clear plastic shield, in which air temperature and oxygen content can be controlled.

irreversibility the inability to understand that changing an object's shape or rearranging objects is a reversible action.

joint custody a child custody arrangement in which a child spends predetermined periods of time living with each parent.

juvenile delinquency actions that break the law and that are committed before a person's 18th birthday.

karyotype a complete set of 46 chromosomes.

Kaufman Assessment Battery for Children intelligence test for children aged 3–18 in which the examiner can reword tasks or use a different language to maximize children's understanding of the items.

Klinefelter syndrome a chromosomal disorder in which a male has an extra copy of the X chromosome.

Kwashiorkor a syndrome resulting from insufficient protein intake that results in developmental delays and changes of hair and skin color and texture.

language acquisition device (LAD) a hypothetical brain mechanism that helps humans to speak and understand language.

lateralized (of the brain) divided into hemispheres or halves that control separate activities or functions; (of a function) controlled by one part of the brain.

learning disability any of a group of disorders that impair a person's ability in a specific area, for example, in reading, writing, or mathematics.

least restrictive environment (LRE) the idea that children with disabilities should spend as much time of their school day as possible in a classroom with children who do not receive special education services.

legal custody a child custody arrangement that determines the right of a parent to make decisions about a child's upbringing.

limbic system a set of structures that are involved in emotion regulation as well as forming memories.

long-term memory the ability to store information over long periods of time with nearly unlimited capacity.

marasmus a syndrome resulting from chronic undernutrition and lack of protein that results in diarrhea, dizziness and rapid weight loss.

menarche a girl's first menstrual bleeding.

metacognition awareness, understanding, and control of one's own thought processes.

metalinguistic awareness the ability to reflect on language and the way it is used.

midwife a healthcare worker, usually a registered nurse, with specialized training to assist a woman during pregnancy and natural childbirth.

milestone a significant accomplishment in physical, cognitive, or socio-emotional skills that is typical of children at a certain age.

modeling (or observational learning) a form of learning that occurs through observation of others.

monozygotic (MZ) twins twins who develop from one zygote and who have the same genome.

myelin a fatty substance that covers axons and allows for faster signal transmission.

naming explosion rapid word learning, starting on average at about 18 months of age. Also called vocabulary spurt.

natural childbirth a birth process with minimal medical intervention, usually emphasizing breathing strategies and relaxation techniques to manage pain and discomfort.

negative reinforcement an event that strengthens behavior by removing an unpleasant stimulus from a situation following a positive behavior.

neglectful parenting a parenting style that involves few, if any, limits for children; little attention is paid to the child, and the parent is cold and not responsive toward the child.

neuron a cell of the nervous system that can receive and send nerve impulses in the form of electrical signals.

neurotransmitters chemical substances that transmit neural impulses from one neuron to another.

nightmares vivid and realistic dreams that are disturbing and anxiety-provoking.

nighttime fears fears that appear at night.

object permanence the understanding that objects and people continue to exist when they are out of sight.

obstetrician a physician trained in the branch of medicine and surgery concerned with pregnancy, labor, and childbirth.

operant conditioning a form of learning in which the consequences of an activity—positive or negative—determine the likelihood that the individual will continue to engage in the activity.

operations organized, flexible, and reversible mental thinking processes like sorting objects according to size or recognizing relations between objects and drawing conclusions.

organization a memory strategy in which items are grouped into different categories.

other-race effect the phenomenon that people are better at recognizing faces of their own race than faces of other races.

overregularization the application of regular grammatical patterns to irregular words.

ovum (*plural* ova) a mature female reproductive cell (egg) that can develop into an embryo after fertilization by a male sperm cell.

peers children who are close in age to each other.

perceptual narrowing a process by which infants become increasingly attuned to the sensory stimuli of their environment, at the cost of becoming less efficient at processing stimuli that are foreign to their environment (see, for example, the other-race effect).

permissive parenting a parenting style in which few, if any, limits and demands are placed on the child; parents may be warm toward the child, but the child is expected to learn through experience rather than teaching.

personal fable an adolescent's belief that they are unique and special as well as invincible; an aspect of adolescent egocentrism.

phenotype the actual characteristics of a person that are the result of the interaction between genes and environment.

phonics approach an approach to reading instruction that emphasizes sounding out letters and combining those sounds into words.

physical custody a child custody arrangement that determines which parent(s) a child lives with.

pincer grasp a grasp using the thumb and index or middle finger of the same hand to pick up small objects.

pituitary gland a pea-sized gland at the base of the brain that produces a number of different hormones like growth hormones, reproductive hormones, and hormones that regulate blood pressure.

placenta a temporary organ that sustains the life of the fetus during pregnancy by delivering nutrients and oxygen from mother while eliminating waste products.

plasticity the ability of the brain to change and reorganize itself.

polygenic trait a trait that is controlled by two or more genes.

positive reinforcement an event that strengthens behavior by providing a positive consequence when a particular behavior is performed.

postpartum depression depression that affects a parent after their chid is born; it is characterized by feelings of sadness, exhaustion, anxiety, and guilt.

pragmatics the knowledge needed to use language effectively for communication with others.

precocious puberty early onset of puberty; before the age of 9 in boys and before the age of 8 in girls.

preoperational stage the second stage in Piaget's theory of cognitive development, in which children cannot yet use logic and reasoning skills.

preterm birth childbirth that occurs before the completion of the 37th week of pregnancy.

primary circular reaction an action that first occurred by chance and now is repeated by the infant to reproduce a pleasant sensation; it centers on the child's body.

primary emotions emotions that develop early in life and that can be observed in both humans and animals.

primary sex characteristics the inner and outer sex organs that are present at birth.

private speech speech directed to oneself in order to understand something or guide one's behavior.

prosocial behavior any voluntary action intended to help others without the expectation of a reward.

psychoanalytic theory Freud's theory that human behavior and personality are rooted in unconscious thoughts, drives, and desires.

psychological control a form of discipline that involves withdrawing love from a child or making them feel shame and guilt.

psychosocial moratorium a period in which adolescents do not have to take on adult responsibilities and therefore explore different roles and identities.

psychosocial theory Erikson's theory of development through eight stages, each one marked by an identity crisis that must be resolved before the person can continue to the next stage.

puberty a development stage in which the body changes and becomes sexually mature, marking the beginning of adolescence.

punishment an unpleasant consequence of a behavior that diminishes the chance that the behavior will occur again.

Raven Progressive Matrices Test an intelligence test created with the intention to be culture-fair, although no test is fully culture-fair; tests nonverbal perceptual and reasoning skills with items based on matrices.

recall the ability to produce information from memory.

recessive trait a heritable trait that is expressed in offspring only when the gene for the trait has been inherited from both parents.

recognition the ability to identify something seen before.

reflexes automatic und unlearned responses to a stimulus.

rehearsal a memory strategy that involves the mental repetition of items or information.

reinforcement an event that increases the probability that a behavior will be repeated.

REM sleep a phase of sleep that is associated with rapid eye movements, body movements, and dreaming (in adults).

reticular formation the part of the brain that regulates consciousness and attention.

retrieval the process of accessing information from memory storage.

reversibility the principle that changing an object's shape or rearranging objects is an action that can be undone or reversed.

scaffold a temporary aid used to assist children in the acquisition of new skills.

schemata (*singular* schema) patterns of action or thought that organize our knowledge about the world and influence the way we think and behave.

scientific theory   a set of ideas designed to explain a phenomenon and make predictions about it.

script   a sequence of expected behaviors in a particular situation.

secondary circular reaction   a repetitive action that produces an effect involving other people or objects.

secondary sex characteristics   physical signs of sexual maturity that do not involve the sex organs, including breast development and growth of body hair.

secular trend   a trend that remains steady over time and does not undergo cyclical changes; in human development, the observation that over the past 150 years children have entered puberty at increasingly early times.

secure attachment   an attachment pattern where infants use the mother as a safe base for exploration; show some distress when the caregiver leaves and seek the caregiver's comfort upon return.

selective attention   the capacity of focusing on just one stimulus at a time while suppressing distractions.

self-concept   an individual's beliefs about themselves, including characteristics, abilities, attitudes, personality traits, and values.

self-conscious emotions   emotions that depend on a sense of self and include jealousy, empathy, embarrassment, shame and guilt.

self-esteem   a person's evaluation of their individual value; it is associated with positive or negative feelings, depending on how people think about themselves.

sensitive period   the period when a child is particularly receptive to particular kinds of stimuli in the environment, aiding in the acquisition of new skills like language.

sensorimotor stage   the first stage in Piaget's theory of cognitive development, in which children learn primarily through their senses and motor activity.

separation anxiety   an infant's expression of distress when being separated from a caregiver.

seriation   the ability to order objects along a quantitative dimension such as length or weight.

sex   how people are classified as male or female based on their sexual anatomy.

sex chromosome   each of a pair of chromosomes that determine a person's sex. Females have two X chromosomes; males have one X chromosome and one Y chromosome.

sexual orientation   a person's pattern of sexual/romantic attraction to the same gender, opposite gender, or any gender.

shaping   in operant conditioning, the process of reinforcing successively closer approximations of a target behavior.

sickle-cell anemia   a blood disorder in which red blood cells are misshapen, which leads to clogged blood vessels and impaired oxygen transport throughout the body.

social referencing   a smile elicited by the sight of another human; appears around 6 weeks of age.

social smile   a smile elicited by the sight of another human; appears around 6 weeks of age.

social speech   speech that is used in order to communicate with another person.

socioeconomic status   an indicator of the social standing and financial resources of a person, based on income, education, and occupation.

sole custody   a child custody arrangement in which a parent is responsible for all decisions about a child's upbringing (sole legal custody) and/or has a child living exclusively with them (sole physical custody).

spermarche   a boy's first ejaculation.

Stanford–Binet Intelligence Scales   an intelligence test based on Alfred Binet's intelligence assessment, with different problems presented based on the age of the person tested.

stereotype threat   the risk of confirming a negative stereotype when engaging in a task about which such a stereotype exists.

storing   the ability to place new information into memory for later retrieval.

stranger anxiety   fear or wariness evoked by the presence of strangers, typically appearing around 9 months of age.

substance abuse   repeated and excessive use of drugs such as alcohol, illegal drugs, or pain medications.

substance dependence   addiction to drugs in such a way that users cannot control their drug use anymore and focus intensely on the use of a substance.

sudden infant death syndrome   the sudden and unexpected death during sleep of an infant younger than 1 year.

symbolic thought   a type of thinking that uses symbols (words, numbers, or internal images) to represent objects, events, or people who are not present.

synapse   a gap through which neurotransmitters transmit a signal from the axon terminal of one neuron to the dendrite of another neuron.

telegraphic speech   an early, efficient form of speech that uses only the most important words to convey meaning.

temperament   the characteristic way people respond to different situations, reflected in behavior and display of emotions.

teratogen   a substance that can interfere with the healthy development of the fetus.

tertiary circular reaction   actions that are aimed at exploration of the environment and involve changes of schemata to fit new situations.

transitivity   the principle that it is possible to infer the relationship between two objects by knowing the relationship each of these objects has with a third object.

trauma   an emotional response to negative events that may include long-term reactions like flashbacks, physical distress, and fluctuating emotions that can result in strained relationships with others.

triple X syndrome   a chromosomal disorder in females resulting from an extra copy of the X chromosome.

Turner syndrome   a chromosomal disorder in females resulting from the lack of a part or all of an X chromosome.

universal grammar   in Chomsky's theory of language acquisition, the structure that all human languages share.

vaccines   substances prepared from weakened or dead germs that help the immune system to fight a disease more effectively.

vernix   a white, oily substance that protects the fetus's skin in the womb.

viability   the gestational age at which half of all infants born will survive.

Wechsler Intelligence Scale for Children   an intelligence test for children that gives detailed subscale scores as well as a total score.

whole-language approach   an approach to reading instruction that emphasizes the meaning of words and how words are embedded in the context of speaking, listening, reading, and writing.

working memory   the store of information we are currently processing; it is typically very limited in capacity.

zone of proximal development   the range of tasks a child cannot yet do alone but can do with assistance.

Name Index

Page numbers followed by *b, f,* and *t* refer to boxes, figures, and tables, respectively.

Ainsworth, Mary, 221, 222
Apgar, Virginia, 108
Arnett, Jeffrey, 6

Bandura, Albert, 46–47, 319*f*, 342, 342*f*
Bates, John E., 218
Baumrind, Diana, 323, 324
Binet, Alfred, 408
Boring, Edwin, 405
Bowlby, John, 62, 221
Brazelton, T. Berry, 125
Bronfenbrenner, Urie, 56–58
Bussey, Kay, 319*f*

Carroll, John B., 405–6
Cattell, Raymond, 406
Chess, Alexander, 217
Chomsky, Noam, 192, 193
Crozer Griffith, J. P., 125

Darwin, Charles, 35, 59

Elkind, David, 492, 493
Erikson, Erik, 42–43, 42*t*, 422–23, 524–25

Fu, G. and colleagues, 339*b*
Freud, Sigmund, 22, 23, 41–42, 42*t*, 318

Gardner, Howard, 294, 405–7, 407*t*
Gilligan, Carol, 500
Graham, Bob, 224

Hall, G. Stanley, 36
Harlow, Harry, 221
Hart, B., 187
Horn, John, 406
Hunt, Patricia, 89

Kohlberg, Lawrence, 319–20, 497–500

Lancy, David, 9
Lewis, M., 204
Locke, John, 35
Lorenz, Konrad, 61–62, 130, 220–21

Malaguzzi, Loris, 304
Marcia, James, 525–26, 526*t*
Moll, Henrike, 291–92
Montessori, Maria, 303

Parten, Mildred, 334
Pavlov, Ivan, 44, 127

Peterson, Adrian, 329
Piaget, Jean, 22, 48–49, 50*t*, 54, 54*t*, 174–79, 274–80, 274*f*, 304, 334, 386–89, 490–92, 497

Renzulli, Joseph, 381
Risley, T. R., 187
Rothbart, M. K., 218
Rousseau, Jean-Jacques, 35

Siegler, Robert, 178
Simon, Theodore, 408
Skinner, B. F., 45, 46, 191, 328
Spearman, Charles, 405
Steiner, Rudolf, 304
Sternberg, Robert J., 55*b*, 381, 405, 407–8

Terman, Lewis, 409
Thelen, Esther, 152
Thomas, Stella, 217

Vygotsky, Lev, 54–55, 54*t*, 280–83, 304, 336, 388–90

Wakefield, Andrew, 261
Watson, John B., 43–44, 46

Subject Index

Page numbers followed by *b, f,* and *t* refer to boxes, figures, and tables, respectively.